Behavioral Law and Economics

Behavioral Law and Economics

Eyal Zamir
Doron Teichman

OXFORD
UNIVERSITY PRESS

OXFORD
UNIVERSITY PRESS

Oxford University Press is a department of the University of Oxford. It furthers the University's objective of excellence in research, scholarship, and education by publishing worldwide. Oxford is a registered trademark of Oxford University Press in the UK and certain other countries.

Published in the United States of America by Oxford University Press
198 Madison Avenue, New York, NY 10016, United States of America.

Library of Congress Cataloging-in-Publication Data

Names: Zamir, Eyal, author. | Teichman, Doron, author.
Title: Behavioral law and economics / Eyal Zamir, Doron Teichman.
Description: New York : Oxford University Press, 2018. | Includes bibliographical references and index.
Identifiers: LCCN 2017057744 | ISBN 9780190901349 (hardback) |
ISBN 9780190901356 (pbk.)
Subjects: LCSH: Law and economics—Psychological aspects. | Economics—Psychological aspects. |
Human behavior models—Economic aspects.
Classification: LCC K487.E3 Z359 2018 | DDC 340/.19—dc23
LC record available at https://lccn.loc.gov/2017057744

Note to Readers

This publication is designed to provide accurate and authoritative information in regard to the subject matter covered. It is based upon sources believed to be accurate and reliable and is intended to be current as of the time it was written. It is sold with the understanding that the publisher is not engaged in rendering legal, accounting, or other professional services. If legal advice or other expert assistance is required, the services of a competent professional person should be sought. Also, to confirm that the information has not been affected or changed by recent developments, traditional legal research techniques should be used, including checking primary sources where appropriate.

(Based on the Declaration of Principles jointly adopted by a Committee of the American Bar Association and a Committee of Publishers and Associations.)

To my parents, Yona and Meir Teichman
D.T.

To Daphna, Abigail, and Yaara
E.Z.

Contents

Preface

Notwithstanding the great impact behavioral law and economics has had on legal theory and policymaking in the past two decades, to date no comprehensive textbook or treatise has been written on the subject. This is the first textbook-treatise aimed at providing readers with a general overview of the field—including its economic and behavioral background, methodology, normative and policy implications, and applications in various legal fields.

Our collaboration in this sphere began when, a few years ago, we were asked to co-edit *The Oxford Handbook of Behavioral Economics and the Law* (2014)—the first handbook in this area, whose chapters were written by some of the leading figures in the field. While we were very proud of the Handbook, we felt that there was still a need for a unified treatment of the field, for novices and experts alike. We hope that this book will introduce the fascinating world of behavioral legal studies to broader audiences, and trigger further research by jurists, psychologists, economists, and others.

Each draft chapter of the book was initially written by one of us (with some sections occasionally written by the other co-author), but the outcome is a product of a truly collaborative effort and joint deliberation.*

Some parts of the book draw on our previous publications, including the chapters on "Loss Aversion," "The Hindsight Bias," and "Judicial Decision-Making," included in the above-mentioned handbook.

We are very grateful to many colleagues with whom we had fruitful exchanges throughout the years—in particular, to Ilana Ritov and Yuval Feldman, our long-time research partners. Special thanks are also due to Ilan Benshalom, Barak Medina, and Anne-Lise

* The initial versions of Chapters 1–6, 8, 11, 13, 14, part of 15, and 16 were mostly written by Eyal Zamir. The initial versions of Chapters 7, 9, 10, 12, and part of 15 were mostly written by Doron Teichman.

Sibony, who insightfully commented on chapters of the book, and to Shmuel Baron, Inbal Elbaz, Yuval Farkash, Elisha Harlev, Carl Nathan Johnson, Ben Levko, Tal Mendelson, Tal Nisim, Elad Spiegelman, and Roi Yair, who provided excellent research assistance. Generous financial support was received from the I-CORE Program of the Planning and Budgeting Committee and the Israel Science Foundation (Grant No. 1821/12).

Introduction

For several decades, one of the leading perspectives in legal theory—perhaps *the* leading perspective—has been the economic analysis of law. The theory of human behavior underlying standard economic analysis of law—like economic analysis in general—has been the rational choice theory. According to this theory, people always strive to enhance their own well-being, by choosing the available option that maximizes their expected utility. In the past few decades, hand in hand with comparable developments in economics, economic analysis of law has been challenged by a growing body of experimental and empirical studies that attest to prevalent and systematic deviations from the assumptions of economic rationality. These studies contested the assumption of thin, cognitive rationality by showing that people's preferences often do not comply with the formal requirements of dominance, transitivity, invariance, etc. These studies also called into question the assumption of thick, motivational rationality, by highlighting the role of motivations such as fairness, envy, and altruism in people's behavior. From a slightly different angle, experimental and empirical studies have shown that most people's moral judgments do not fall in line with the consequentialist underpinnings of welfare economics—the normative branch of economic analysis—but are much more aligned with deontological morality.

While these insights were initially perceived as antithetical to standard economic and legal-economic analysis, over time they have been largely integrated into mainstream economic analysis, including economic analysis of law. Moreover, the impact of behavioral insights has long since transcended purely *economic* analysis of law: in recent years, the behavioral movement has become one of the most influential developments in legal scholarship in general. Much as economic reasoning became a standard form of legal analysis in the 1980s and 1990s (at least in some parts of the world), behavioral analysis has become a standard form of interdisciplinary analysis. It is also gradually influencing legislative, administrative, and judicial policymaking throughout the world.

Behavioral Law and Economics. Eyal Zamir and Doron Teichman.

In recent years, the growing impact of behavioral law and economics has been accompanied by the emergence of empirical and experimental legal studies. This new paradigm has transformed the nature and scope of the research conducted by behavioral-legal scholars. Rather than just draw on the results of empirical studies conducted by non-jurists, a growing number of researchers have engaged in experimental and empirical studies of their own, designed specifically to answer distinctively legal questions. Thanks to these developments, the integration of economics, psychology, and law is breaking exciting new ground in legal theory, social sciences, and governmental policymaking.

Consuming behavioral-economic scholarship—let alone producing it—requires familiarity with three different disciplines. Unfortunately, there are practically no textbooks on behavioral economics, and very few on judgment and decision-making—the primary body of psychological studies informing behavioral legal analysis. While this state of affairs has heightened the need for a textbook-treatise on behavioral law and economics, it has also made our task particularly challenging.

The book comprises sixteen chapters, organized in five parts. Part I lays the groundwork for the ensuing discussion: Chapter 1 introduces the basic tenets of positive and normative economics; Chapter 2 then reviews the psychological findings that form the basis of behavioral law and economics. While focusing on studies of judgment and decision-making, Chapter 2 also draws on research in social and moral psychology, experimental game theory, and experimental philosophy. It describes in some detail numerous documented heuristics and biases, as well as issues that cut across the various phenomena—such as the effect of expertise on decision-making, group decision-making, individual and cultural differences, and debiasing.

Part II consists of three chapters that provide an overview of behavioral law and economics, and discuss some general themes. These include an overview of the field, its history, methodology, and the challenges it faces (Chapter 3); a general discussion of the normative and policy implications of behavioral insights (Chapter 4); and an analysis of the intriguing correspondence between cognitive psychology, morality, and law (Chapter 5).

The remaining three parts provide a critical survey of existing contributions of behavioral studies to various legal fields. Starting with private and commercial law, Part III offers five chapters (6–10) on property law (including intellectual property, and the property rules versus liability rules debate), contract law, consumer contracts, tort law, and commercial law (including corporate, securities, and antitrust law), respectively. Part IV is devoted to public law—starting with a discussion of administrative, constitutional, and international law (Chapter 11), through criminal law and enforcement (Chapter 12), and concluding with tax law (Chapter 13). Finally, Part V discusses the legal process—namely, litigants' behavior, judicial decision-making, and the law of evidence (Chapters 14, 15, and 16, respectively).

While offering a broad overview of behavioral law and economics, this book does not exhaust all contributions of behavioral insights to legal scholarship. In particular, we felt that in some areas, existing behavioral scholarship—as important and influential as it might be—does not yet lend itself to systematic synthesis (although it may well do so in the future). Thus, for example, the book does not include chapters on labor and employment law[1] or on family law[2] (although, some of the topics that would have been discussed under these headings are discussed elsewhere in the book).

1. With few exceptions, the behavioral analysis of labor and employment law focuses on two issues: insufficient saving for old age, and employment discrimination. *See* Deborah M. Weiss, *Paternalistic Pension Policy: Psychological Evidence and Economic Theory*, 58 U. CHI. L. REV. 1275 (1991); Linda Hamilton Krieger, *The Content of Our Categories: A Cognitive Bias Approach to Discrimination and Equal Employment Opportunity*, 47 STAN. L. REV. 1161 (1995); Samuel Issacharoff, *Contracting for Employment: The Limited Return of the Common Law*, 74 TEX. L. REV 1783 (1996); Cass R. Sunstein, *Human Behavior and the Law of Work*, 87 VA. L. REV. 205 (2001); Cass R. Sunstein, *Switching the Default Rule*, 77 N.Y.U. L. REV. 106 (2002); Samuel R. Bagenstos, *The Structural Turn and the Limits of Antidiscrimination Law*, 94 CALIF. L. REV. 1 (2006); Linda Hamilton Krieger & Susan T. Fiske, *Behavioral Realism in Employment Discrimination Law: Implicit Bias and Disparate Treatment*, 94 CALIF. L. REV. 997 (2006); Christine Jolls & Cass R. Sunstein, *The Law of Implicit Bias*, 94 CALIF. L. REV. 969 (2006); Christine Jolls, *Behavioral Economics Analysis of Employment Law*, *in* THE BEHAVIORAL FOUNDATIONS OF PUBLIC POLICY 264 (Eldar Shafir ed., 2013).

2. Examples of the relatively scarce behavioral research in family law include: Brian Bix, *Bargaining in the Shadow of Love: The Enforcement of Premarital Agreements and How We Think about Marriage*, 40 WM. & MARY L. REV. 145, 193–200 (1998); Daphna Lewinsohn-Zamir, *In Defense of Redistribution through Private Law*, 91 MINN. L. REV. 326, 385–89 (2006); Sean Hannon Williams, *Postnuptial Agreements*, 2007 WIS. L. REV. 827; Tess Wilkinson-Ryan & Deborah Small, *Negotiating Divorce: Gender and the Behavioral Economics of Divorce Bargaining*, 26 LAW & INEQ. 109 (2008); Sean Hannon Williams, *Sticky Expectations: Responses to Persistent Over-Optimism in Marriage, Employment Contracts, and Credit Card Use*, 84 NOTRE DAME L. REV. 733 (2009).

PART ONE

Economic and Psychological Background

1

Economic Analysis of Law: An Overview

A. Introduction

Behavioral insights can, and should, inform the law and legal theory, irrespective of one's approach to law. Since the law strives to influence human behavior, it must heed empirical findings about human motivation, decision-making, and moral judgments. The association of behavioral studies with *economic analysis of law*—rather than with *legal analysis* in general—is partly a product of a particular historical development, rather than an analytical truth. Historically, much of the judgment-and-decision-making research that forms the core of behavioral analysis of law has been conducted in the light of, and in response to, the postulates of traditional economic analysis.[1] While behavioral insights have met with considerable resistance from economic orthodoxy, they have gradually been incorporated into mainstream economic analysis to form the new field of *behavioral economics* (BE). Two factors have contributed to the equally rapid (if not rapider) emergence of *behavioral law and economics* (BLE). One is that jurists, including lawyer-economists, are particularly interested in applied, rather than basic, social science. They are more interested than non-lawyer economists in the real world, as opposed to the world of abstract models.[2] Second, unlike other social scientists, lawyer-economists are not content with the understanding of human behavior. They regularly engage in normative and policy analysis—namely, in advising policymakers how to use the coercive power of the law to shape human behavior. To that end, they should, and often do, take a more pluralistic perspective.

To be sure, writing this book about behavioral law and economics, rather than on behavioral law, has not been primarily driven by historical developments. Rather, it reflects our appreciation of the great contribution of economic methodology to legal thinking in virtually every field of law. Economic analysis compels one to consider the interrelationships

1. *See infra* pp. 19–21, 25, 27.

2. Guido Calabresi, The Future of Law and Economics 17–21 (2016).

Behavioral Law and Economics. Eyal Zamir and Doron Teichman.

between goals, means, incentives, and outcomes, in a systematic and rigorous fashion. And while behavioral insights are vital to any interpretative or normative theory of law, it remains true that they are particularly important as qualifiers and modifiers of standard economic analysis of law, which assumes that people are rational maximizers of their utility and which is founded on a particular normative outlook.

Thus, to lay the groundwork for the ensuing discussion, this chapter offers a bird's-eye view of economic analysis of law.[3] Section B describes the main features of economic analysis in general, with a focus on positive economics, and Section C describes the tenets of the normative branch of economic analysis.

B. Positive Economics

In the past few decades, the most influential interdisciplinary school of thought in legal theory and practice in the United States—and, increasingly, in other parts of the world—has been the economic analysis of law. Economics is the study of human behavior in a world where resources are scarce in relation to human desires.[4] Standard economic analysis strives to explain, predict, and assess human behavior and its outcomes under well-defined assumptions—in particular, the assumption that people rationally strive to maximize the fulfillment of their preferences. Although initially focusing on material goods and explicit markets, contemporary economic analyses deal with all spheres of life and all mechanisms of allocation, including governmental command and intra-family relationships. In addition to directly analyzing the effect of *legal norms* on human behavior, economic analysis of law strives to understand *human behavior* in virtually any context that is of interest to jurists, from littering to litigation—thus leaving very few issues outside its purview.

Economic analysis is conventionally classified as either *positive* or *normative*. Positive economics seeks to describe, explain, and predict human behavior and its social consequences. It does not deal with how people *should* behave, or what legal norms *should* be adopted, etc. Rather, it asks questions, such as "How would lack of information on the part of buyers affect the quality of goods in an otherwise competitive market?" or "How would the imposition of a pre-contractual disclosure duty influence the production of different types of information ex ante?" Most economists engage primarily in positive analysis—or, at least, so they believe.[5] However, some economic analyses—and most economic analyses of law—are distinctively normative. They prescribe how people ought to behave, what policies the state should pursue, and so forth. They ask questions such as: "Under what circumstances, if any, would the imposition of a pre-contractual disclosure

3. For excellent book-long introductions to the field, see RICHARD A. POSNER, ECONOMIC ANALYSIS OF LAW (9th ed. 2014); ROBERT COOTER & THOMAS ULEN, LAW & ECONOMICS (6th ed. 2012).

4. *See* GARY S. BECKER, THE ECONOMIC APPROACH TO HUMAN BEHAVIOR 3–14 (1976); POSNER, *supra* note 3, at 3.

5. For the claim that even purportedly positive economic analysis, including its underlying theory of human rationality, are not free of normative assumptions, see DANIEL M. HAUSMAN, MICHAEL S. MCPHERSON & DEBRA SATZ, ECONOMIC ANALYSIS, MORAL PHILOSOPHY, AND PUBLIC POLICY 39–91 (3d ed. 2017); Eyal Zamir, *Tastes, Values, and the Future of Law and Economics*, JERUSALEM REV. LEGAL STUD. (forthcoming 2018, *available at*: https://ssrn.com/abstract=2887951).

duty increase aggregate social utility?" The normative branch of economics—also known as *welfare economics*—is a moral theory. Positive and normative economic analyses of law use similar methodologies, which the present section describes. The following section outlines the tenets of welfare economics.

With the exception of economic analysis of public law, which draws on *public choice theory*,[6] most economic analyses of law primarily use the tools of *microeconomics*, and to some extent those of *game theory*.[7] Microeconomics deals with the behavior of individuals and small groups, including firms and families, given a scarcity of resources. Scarce resources include means of production, money, and time. Game theory deals with people's decisions when the outcomes of those decisions are affected by the decisions made by other people—and vice versa.

Economic analysis, like the natural sciences, uses models to explain and predict behavior and outcomes. Typically, models are very different from reality, and much simpler. An economic model does not aim to depict reality precisely, but rather strives to explain and analyze reality by focusing on a small number of variables, and assuming away the complexity of the real world. The more parsimonious a model is—that is, the smaller the number of variables it takes into account and the larger the range of social phenomena it explains—the better. The creators of economic models are obviously aware of the fact that models do not capture the full complexity of reality—otherwise, they would not be models. Models are fruitful when they are sufficiently akin to reality to provide insights about the latter, but also when they draw our attention to the differences between model and reality. For example, the *Coase theorem* posits that in a perfectly competitive market, where there are no limitations on the transfer of legal entitlements, and transaction costs are nil, an efficient allocation of entitlements ensues, regardless of their initial allocation by law.[8] Of course, there are hardly any markets where transaction costs are actually zero. Nevertheless, the Coase theorem is crucially important, for two reasons. First, many environments sufficiently resemble the Coasian world of zero transaction costs to make the theorem's predictions valuable. Second, the Coase theorem highlights the importance of studying transaction costs: when and why they are high, how social outcomes might be affected by increasing or decreasing transaction costs, and so forth.

A distinctive feature of standard economic analysis is the assumption that economic players are *rational maximizers*. Let us begin with the notion of *maximization*, and then proceed to *rationality*. Individuals are conventionally assumed to maximize their utility, and firms—their profits. When several (or many) maximizers interact with one another, a pattern of interactions—an equilibrium—may ensue (which may be more or less stable, i.e., less or more sensitive to external events). Indeed, repeated interactions between rational maximizers often create an equilibrium, be it in games, markets, or the political arena.

6. *See infra* pp. 395–96.

7. For overviews, see, e.g., N. Gregory Mankiw, Principles of Microeconomics (7th ed. 2015); Walter Nicholson & Christopher M. Snyder, Microeconomic Theory: Basic Principles and Extensions (12th ed. 2017); Drew Fudenberg & Jean Tirole, Game Theory (1991).

8. Ronald Coase, *The Problem of Social Cost*, 3 J.L. & Econ. 1 (1960).

An equilibrium is not the product of the economic players' deliberate attempt to produce one, but rather the spontaneous outcome of each player striving to maximize the realization of its own interests. Maximizing behavior and ensuing equilibria may be formulized mathematically, thus equipping economics with powerful analytical tools. Luckily for most jurists, economic insights can usually be understood, at least in general terms, without the formal math.

As previously noted, standard economic analysis assumes not only that economic players strive to maximize their utility or profits, but also that they do so rationally. In this regard, it is assumed that people know what they want, and that they are able to rank different combinations of goods and services, including leisure, according to the utility they derive from each one. Thus, for example, the utility for someone who prefers one more hour of leisure over the goods she could buy with the income from an additional hour of paid work is greater if she does not spend that hour on paid work. There are various possible definitions of economic rationality, some more demanding than others. At a minimum, economic rationality assumes that people's sets of preferences meet basic requirements, such as *completeness, transitivity, dominance*, and *invariance*. *Completeness* means that for any two combinations of goods or services, the economic agent either prefers A to B, B to A, or is indifferent between the two. While this requirement may seem trivial, in fact it is not, because it assumes that any two things can be compared—including, for example, the health of one's mother and different sums of money.[9] *Transitivity* means that if one prefers combination A to B, and B to C, she necessarily prefers A to C (and if she prefers A to B and is indifferent between B and C, she necessarily prefers A to C, etcetera). *Dominance* means that if one prefers combination A over B under some circumstances or in certain respects, and there are no circumstances or respects in which she prefers B to A, then she necessarily prefers A to B. *Invariance* means that the ranking of combinations A and B is independent of how they are described. Another standard simplifying assumption of economic models is that people's preferences are exogenously given and do not change over time. Economic models also conventionally assume that people take into account all relevant, available information; disregard irrelevant information; make accurate use of the rules of probability and logical inferences; and so forth. Rational people thus react to incentives so as to maximize the satisfaction of their desires. In fact, some models are founded on fairly demanding assumptions about the rationality of people and firms.

Once again, it should be emphasized that economists are aware that people's preferences are not unchangeable (as the existence of the advertising industry suggests), and that they do not invariably make decisions as rational maximizers of their utility or profits (as evident from divorce rates). However, they do tend to believe that people's deviations from these assumptions are sufficiently small and randomly distributed to make the assumptions fruitful, and that replacing them with assumptions that are more realistic is not worth the cost in added complexity. Economic models need not even assume that people deliberately strive to maximize their utility. If a model that assumes that people behave *as if* they were

9. *See generally* INCOMMENSURABILITY, INCOMPARABILITY, AND PRACTICAL REASON (Ruth Change ed., 1997).

rational maximizers produces testable predictions that turn out to be more accurate than the predictions of competing, reasonably parsimonious models, then the model is useful whether or not its assumptions precisely capture reality.[10]

In theory, economic analysis takes people's preferences as given. It does not deal with the question of how preferences are created, nor does it judge their content. However, economic models generally assume not only *thin*, or *cognitive* rationality, as described above, but also *thick*, or *motivational* rationality. They assume that every economic player cares exclusively about its own welfare (or profits, in the case of a firm), to the exclusion of true altruism (or envy), and commitment to other values, such as fairness, promise-keeping, and truth-telling.[11]

To exemplify these general observations, consider two of the classic models in microeconomics and game theory: a *perfectly competitive market* and the *prisoner's dilemma*. In a perfectly competitive market—plausibly the most famous economic model—there are many sellers and buyers; all of them are rational maximizers, both cognitively and motivationally; everyone has full information; transaction costs are low; people's behavior and transactions have no externalities (i.e., effects whose costs or benefits are not fully internalized by the actor); and there are no restraints of trade. In such a market, no actor can dictate the price of any product or service. Rather, the rules of supply and demand (the *invisible hand* of the market) determine the quantity, quality, and prices of all goods. The market mechanism incentivizes sellers to produce goods and services that would best fit buyers' preferences, inasmuch as the latter are willing to pay for their satisfaction. If a single seller raises its prices, buyers will opt for other sellers, and if the costs of producing a certain product increase, resulting in a price increase, buyers may opt for substitutes that better satisfy their desires. Market transactions facilitate specialization, which is key to increasing the quantity and quality of goods and services, and to reducing the costs of their production. In a perfectly competitive market, resources gravitate toward their most valuable uses, thus maximizing aggregate human welfare, as measured by the satisfaction of preferences that are backed by an ability to pay.

The perfectly competitive market is a hugely useful model—even though it rarely exists in reality. For one thing, many markets are sufficiently competitive to render any governmental regulation counterproductive. For another, the model calls attention to the various impediments to the functioning of a competitive market, that is, to *market failures*. These include restraints of trade, information problems, externalities, public goods, etc. Much of economic analysis is dedicated to studying market failures, and how to remedy them.

The *prisoner's dilemma* is a stylized model of the interaction between two (cognitively and motivationally) rational maximizers who possess full information about the environment in which they function, but who cannot communicate with one another and cannot commit themselves to any course of action. Imagine that two individuals are arrested and

10. Milton Friedman, *The Methodology of Positive Economics*, *in* Essays in Positive Economics 3 (1953).

11. For a classic critique of this feature of economic analysis, see Amartya K. Sen, *Rational Fools: A Critique of the Behavioral Foundations of Economic Theory*, 6 Phil. & Pub. Aff. 317 (1977). For a recent critique, see Calabresi, *supra* note 2. *See also infra* pp. 94–110.

questioned on suspicion of committing a grave crime and a lesser offense. They cannot communicate with one another, and neither of them knows how the other behaves. It is, however, common knowledge that the police has sufficient evidence to convict both of them for the lesser offense, but not enough evidence to produce a conviction for the grave crime—unless one or both of them confess to committing it and incriminate the other. It is also known that the punishment for the lesser offense is two years in prison, and for the grave crime—ten years. If, however, only one of them confesses and incriminates the other suspect, the confessor would be rewarded by a reduced sentence of one year. If both confess and incriminate each other, they are both convicted for the grave crime, but rewarded for their cooperation with the police (while betraying each other) by having their sentence reduced to six years.

Under these assumptions, each suspect knows that if the other keeps silent, he can reduce his own sentence from two years to one year in prison by confessing and incriminating the other. Each suspect also knows that if the other does confess and incriminate him, it is better for him to confess and incriminate the other as well, thereby reducing his own sentence from ten to six years. Hence, the dominant strategy of both suspects is to confess and incriminate the other, whatever the other does. Put differently, there is no dilemma in the prisoner's dilemma—only a single dominant strategy.

In real life, there are very few situations where two people whose decisions affect each other cannot communicate at all, they do not care about the welfare of others, and there are no commitment devices (formal or informal) to foster cooperation. Nevertheless, the prisoner's dilemma is a powerful model, because it provides insight into a broad array of human behaviors. To give one example: Why do people often litter? One possible answer is that people generally prefer a clean environment, but they also know that whether or not the environment remains clean is not just a function of their own behavior. People might rank the different possibilities as follows: (1) Everybody else keeps the environment clean and only I litter (in which case the environment is still essentially clean, and I do not have to carry my litter to the nearest garbage can); (2) Everybody, including me, keeps the environment clean; (3) Everybody litters; and (4) Only I refrain from littering (in which case both the environment is littered and I bear the costs of not littering). The unhappy outcome is that, although everyone prefers everyone to keep the environment clean (the second-best option), everyone litters (the third-best option). People's greed (the desire to attain their first-ranked option) and fear (of ending up in the fourth) lead to an equilibrium of no-cooperation—even though everyone would have been better off cooperating. While the assumptions of the stylized prisoner's dilemma are seldom realistic, we can see how a very simple model—whose predictions should, of course, be tested empirically and compared to those of other models—can provide insight into fundamental questions, such as why a society needs central legal enforcement.

These are but some of the fundamental characteristics of economic analysis of law. Additional characteristics, such as the meaning and role of preferences in economic analysis, will be further elucidated in the next section. Many more aspects and applications of the economic perspective, on different levels of specificity, will be discussed throughout the book.

C. Normative Economics

Having described the basic features of economic analysis in general, this section discusses welfare economics—the normative branch of economics. While welfare economics is by no means monolithic, it is useful to describe its basic tenets as a background for the discussion of the challenges posed by behavioral findings.

In its basic form, welfare economics is a *consequentialist* moral theory.[12] This means that, contrary to *deontological* theories, it maintains that the only factor that ultimately counts in evaluating the morality of an act or a rule is its consequences. For instance, according to welfare economics, there is nothing immoral per se in actively or deliberately harming another person (including killing her), as long as such harming produces desirable outcomes. If, all things considered, a certain conduct that involves harming someone, breaking a promise, or lying produces better outcomes than a conduct that does not involve such harm, promise-breaking, or lying, then the former should be pursued. Of course, consequentialists—including welfare economists—may try to avoid such troubling conclusions. They may, for example, emphasize the long-term and indirect adverse effects of breaking promises, or argue that given the risk of erroneous calculations, it may be preferable to impose a rather strict prohibition on harming other people. Critics of consequentialism respond that while these and comparable arguments may overcome some of the most abhorrent implications of consequentialism, they do not provide a complete answer to the critique leveled against it.[13]

As a consequentialist theory, welfare economics not only places no constraints on promoting good outcomes, but also does not recognize options (or prerogatives) not to promote good outcomes. Thus, if donating one's money to charity promotes better outcomes than spending it, then donation is mandatory, rather than merely praiseworthy or optional. Apparently, to promote good outcomes the well-to-do should donate most of their fortune. Consequentialism is therefore faulted not only for allowing too much (due to the absence of moral constraints), but for being overly demanding, as well (due to the absence of moral options). Again, consequentialists offer some responses to this critique, including the fear that requiring productive people to donate most of their earnings would diminish the incentive to be productive in the first place, thus adversely affecting society at large.[14]

While the persuasiveness of these responses is debatable, it should be noted that the charge of over-demandingness is considerably less troubling for welfare economics than for other consequentialist theories. As explained in Section B, standard economic analysis makes the simplifying assumption that people are rational maximizers of their own welfare and argues that under relatively broad circumstances—notably, wherever there is a competitive market—human welfare is enhanced when every individual is pursuing his or her own interests. Even when there is no competitive market, standard economic analyses rarely if ever conclude that people should forsake their own interests for the sake of the common

12. *See generally* Hausman, McPherson & Satz, *supra* note 5, at 107–25; Eyal Zamir & Barak Medina, Law, Economics, and Morality 11–40 (2010). *See also infra* pp. 94–97.

13. Shelly Kagan, Normative Ethics 59–69 (1998); Zamir & Medina, *supra* note 11, at 18–40.

14. On this feature of consequentialism, see generally Shelly Kagan, The Limits of Morality (1989).

good. Instead, economists look for ways to overcome market failures and align the private interest with the social one.

Welfare economics not only limits the scope of morally relevant factors to consequences, but also restricts the scope of relevant consequences to human welfare.[15] This excludes the intrinsic value of the welfare of nonhuman creatures, the natural environment, and such notions as culpability, fairness, and desert. Welfare economics considers the welfare of nonhumans and notions such as fairness and desert only instrumentally: they are worth promoting to the extent that they are conducive to human welfare. Thus, for example, damage to ecosystems should be avoided to the extent that such damage reduces human welfare. Similarly, treating people unfairly is wrong to the extent that it creates undesirable incentives for their future conduct, or reduces the welfare of people who resent such treatment—and these costs outweigh the benefits of the unfair treatment. Critics of welfarism believe that ecosystems and fairness are intrinsically important, rather than merely means to promoting human welfare.

Another characteristic of welfare economics is that it takes into account the welfare of all human beings and attributes equal weight to the welfare of every person. Thus, unlike ethical egoism, for example, welfare economics requires consideration of people's welfare in an impersonal fashion, with no priority to one's own welfare—or that of one's family or community—over the welfare of the rest of humanity. Again, people's partiality may be justified to the extent that it ultimately promotes overall social welfare.

Like any moral theory that takes human welfare into account (that is, like all moral theories), welfare economics must address the question of what constitutes human welfare. Schematically, there are three conceivable criteria: subjective happiness or pleasure, satisfaction of preferences, and objective goods.[16] Focusing on theories that attribute equal weight to every individual's well-being and seek to maximize the total well-being in society, these criteria correspond to the following normative theories. According to psychological hedonism, the first of the three criteria, people seek to enhance their own happiness and to minimize their pain. Thus, ethical hedonism argues that morally we should maximize total human pleasure. The second criterion, preferences theory, maintains that people's well-being is enhanced to the extent that their preferences and desires are fulfilled (even when they prefer things other than their own pleasure). In this context, the pertinent preferences are either those that one actually has (*actual preferences theory*) or those that one would have if one calmly and rationally considered the issue, taking into account all the relevant information, free of any external pressure or prejudice (*ideal preferences theory*). Finally, according to objective goods theories, well-being consists of having certain things that are intrinsically good, regardless of their contribution to one's happiness, or one's personal preferences. The list of objective goods might include things such as good health, freedom, self-respect, knowledge, meaningful social relationships, and happiness.[17]

15. Louis Kaplow & Steven Shavell, Fairness versus Welfare (2002).

16. *See generally* Derek Parfit, Reasons and Persons 493–502 (1984); Kagan, *supra* note 12, at 25–41 (1998).

17. Daphna Lewinsohn-Zamir, *The Objectivity of Well-Being and the Objectives of Property Law*, 78 N.Y.U. L. Rev. 1669 (2003).

Economic analysis is commonly presumed to rest on an actual preferences theory.[18] However, since standard economic analysis assumes that people are rational maximizers, it is arguably closer to an ideal preferences theory, or at least its normative implications are tantamount to those of a theory of rational/ideal preferences. Insofar as welfare economics rests on actual preferences, this may exacerbate the perils of its consequentialist nature. The effect of the absence of constraints on maximizing human welfare coupled with an actual-preferences theory of human welfare implies that fulfilling racist or chauvinist preferences contributes to social welfare, and may even justify abhorrent actions, as long as the utility to those who favor such actions is greater than the disutility to those who object to them. Moving from actual to rational preferences might mitigate this danger, but not avoid it altogether.

More directly relevant to the theme of this book, the normative claim that people's welfare is enhanced to the extent that their desires are fulfilled is susceptible to the critique that people sometimes desire things that do not enhance their objective—or even subjective—well-being. The fulfillment of uninformed, ill-conceived, bigoted, overly modest, self-sacrificing, irrational, or psychologically biased preferences may be a poor measure of human welfare (of course, other measures of well-being have their faults, as well).

Since welfare economics takes everyone's welfare into account and attributes equal weight to the welfare of all individuals, and since very often a given conduct, rule, or anything else may enhance the welfare of some while diminishing the welfare of others, welfare economics appears to require interpersonal comparisons of welfare (or utility). Nevertheless, modern welfare economics searches for ways to avoid such direct comparisons. One such way, associated with the *Pareto principle*, avoids interpersonal comparisons altogether. Instead of directly trying to measure well-being or welfare, it only describes the order in which any individual ranks different alternatives. According to the Pareto principle, state A is socially preferable (or *Pareto superior*) to state B if at least one person prefers A to B and everyone else either prefers A to B as well, or is indifferent between the two. A given state A is a *Pareto optimum* if there is no other possible state that is socially preferable to A in that sense. This principle underpins the two fundamental theorems of welfare economics. The first theorem states that under certain conditions, any competitive equilibrium satisfies the conditions for a Pareto optimum. The second theorem states that under other specific conditions, any Pareto optimum can be obtained as a competitive equilibrium after the agents' initial endowments have been modified by suitable lump-sum transfers.[19]

However, analyzing actual policy questions exclusively through the prism of the Pareto criterion and the two theorems of welfare economics leaves economists handicapped. In practically every given state there are some people who are worse off than in another state, and thus hardly any policy is Pareto superior to any other.[20] This weakness has spawned two

18. Hausman, McPherson & Satz, *supra* note 5, at 127–30.

19. *See, e.g.*, Allan M. Feldman & Roberto Serrano, Welfare Economics and Social Choice Theory 51–75 (2006).

20. Guido Calabresi, *The Pointlessness of Pareto: Carrying Coase Further*, 100 Yale L.J. 1211 (1991); Michael B. Dorff, *Why Welfare Depends on Fairness: A Reply to Kaplow and Shavell*, 75 S. Cal. L. Rev. 847, 858–59 (2002).

different schools of thought. The more traditional approach uses a social welfare function (SWF) (also known as a Bergson-Samuelson welfare function) that represents changes of welfare of all members of society.[21] Although in principle any variable related to society's well-being might be included in the SWF, economists have focused on SWFs in which the variables in the welfare function are utility indices of each individual. The SWF thus assigns a value to every possible distribution of individual utilities in society. Depending on its form, the SWF embodies different normative judgments about distribution. For example, a SWF that puts greater emphasis on the welfare of individuals who are the least well-off may promote more egalitarian policies than one that places equal weight on each person's welfare.

The aim was that cardinal, interpersonally comparable utility functions would not be needed for SWF. However, it follows from Arrow's Impossibility Theorem that SWF must be based on cardinal, rather than ordinal, utility functions, and interpersonal comparability is required.[22] The alternative to this approach is the one identified with the Compensation Principle—also known as *Kaldor-Hicks* or Potential Pareto. It is an attempt to go beyond the Pareto principle, while stopping short of utilitarianism, by measuring welfare in monetary terms rather than by happiness. This principle asserts that a given state A is socially preferable to state B if those who prefer A stand to gain more, in monetary terms, from being in A rather than B, than those who prefer B stand to lose. Thus, a social change that does not meet the Pareto criterion should still be carried out if the gainers from the change can compensate the losers and still remain better off.[23] In accordance with the assumption that people's preferences are complete, it is assumed that every person can compare any entitlement to a sum of money. Preferences are therefore measured by people's willingness to pay (WTP) for their satisfaction.[24] This is the basis of the procedure known as *Cost-Benefit Analysis* (CBA), which assumes that each person's WTP is an adequate representation of the difference in his or her utility arising from the change from the status quo and a given alternative state.[25] Like utilitarianism, the Kaldor-Hicks criterion and CBA thus ordinarily assess the desirability of any act, rule, policy, or project according to its effect on the total welfare of all people. Since economic analysis of law is policy-oriented, it usually uses the Kaldor-Hicks criterion.

21. Abram Bergson, *A Reformulation of Certain Aspects of Welfare Economics*, 52 Q. J. ECON. 314 (1938); PAUL A. SAMUELSON, FOUNDATIONS OF ECONOMIC ANALYSIS (1947).

22. According to Arrow's theorem, when there are three or more options to choose from, it is impossible to formulate a social preference ordering that satisfies a certain set of reasonable criteria, such as transitivity, independence of irrelevant alternatives, and non-dictatorship. *See* KENNETH J. ARROW, SOCIAL CHOICE AND INDIVIDUAL VALUES (1951, rev. ed. 1963).

23. *See, e.g.*, RICHARD A. POSNER, FRONTIERS OF LEGAL THEORY 95–141 (2001).

24. Cass R. Sunstein, *Lives, Life-Years, and Willingness to Pay*, 104 COLUM. L. REV. 205 (2004); Elizabeth Hoffman & Matthew L. Spitzer, *Willingness to Pay vs. Willingness to Accept: Legal and Economic Implications*, 71 WASH. U. L.Q. 59 (1993).

25. *See* ANTHONY E. BOARDMAN ET AL., COST-BENEFIT ANALYSIS: CONCEPTS AND PRACTICE (1996).

One distinctive advantage of the use of WTP as a measure of human well-being in economic analysis is that it facilitates mathematical economic models and formalizes normative issues. However, measuring welfare in monetary terms raises several concerns. To begin with, the assumption that everything a person might desire is commensurable with money is controversial.[26] Even if the principled objection of incommensurability is rejected, the WTP criterion has been criticized for systematically favoring the rich. This is because the amount of money one is willing to pay for a given entitlement is a function of one's wealth.[27] This problem may be mitigated by shifting from WTP to WTA (willingness to accept)—that is, the minimum amount of money one would accept to forgo a given entitlement if one already had it.[28] This response is, however, incomplete. A person who is desperately poor is likely to be willing to forgo a given entitlement for less money than a wealthy person—notwithstanding the greater happiness or satisfaction that she would derive from the entitlement. WTA is also much more susceptible to manipulations, as it ordinarily relies on people's statements rather than their actual behavior.[29]

The regressive effect of monetizing preferences through WTP is linked to a fundamental critique of the Kaldor-Hicks criterion, namely its disregard for distributive concerns.[30] In its basic form, Kaldor-Hicks efficiency only measures total welfare, with no intrinsic value attributed to its distribution among people. The Kaldor-Hicks criterion may favor the redistribution of *resources* as a means of maximizing aggregate social welfare in light of the rule of decreasing marginal utility, namely the descriptive observation that people ordinarily derive less utility from any additional resource (be it another car or another dollar), compared to the previous one.[31] However, this is merely a means of maximizing total welfare, and does not refer to the distribution of welfare as such. Many economic analyses attempt to address this deficiency of CBA by taking into account distributive concerns and incorporating them into predictive and normative economic models.

A final distinction within normative ethics worth mentioning here is between idealized and realistic theories. When formulating the norms that people should follow, a moral theory might rely on different assumptions about the environment in which the rules operate. A moral theory may assume idealized conditions, in which everyone accepts, understands, and obeys the rules. In contrast, a realistic theory searches for the best set of rules, given that some people will not understand, accept, or obey the rules.[32] While some

26. *See generally* Incommensurability, Incomparability, and Practical Reason, *supra* note 9.

27. *See, e.g.*, Ronald W. Dworkin, *Is Wealth a Value?*, 9 J. Legal Stud. 191 (1980); Donald Hubin, *The Moral Justification of Benefit/Cost Analysis*, 10 Econ. & Phil. 169 (1994).

28. Hoffman & Spitzer, *supra* note 24, at 85–87.

29. Daniel Kahneman, Jack Knetsch & Richard Thaler, *Experimental Tests of the Endowment Effect and the Coase Theorem*, 98 J. Pol. Econ. 1325, 1336 (1990) (suggesting that individuals habitually misstate WTA as greater than WTP because in many contexts they are rewarded for doing so).

30. *See, e.g.*, Amartya Sen, *The Discipline of Cost-Benefit Analysis*, 29 J. Legal Stud. 931, 945–48 (2000).

31. R. Layard & A.A. Walters, *Income Distribution*, *in* Cost-Benefit Analysis 179, 192–97 (Richard Layard & Stephen Glaister eds., 2d ed. 1994).

32. Kagan, *supra* note 12, at 227–28.

(but not all) abstract economic models assume idealized conditions of compliance, when it comes to economic analysis of law and to legal policymaking, a realistic theory of human behavior and human compliance with rules is called for. This is why behavioral insights are of particular interest to lawyer-economists, and to legal policymaking more generally.

D. Conclusion

It is impossible to give a full account of positive and normative analysis of law in a short chapter; hence readers who are not familiar with this literature are advised to turn to more comprehensive introductions. Once one becomes familiar with the numerous applications of economic analysis to legal issues, two observations, or conclusions, emerge. One is that the factual assumptions underlying standard economic analysis are unrealistic, and the moral judgments underlying normative economics are often counterintuitive and questionable. The second is that, despite its unrealistic assumptions and problematic normative tenets, economic analysis is an immensely fruitful perspective on legal issues. Among other things, the economic perspective has sharpened the distinction between descriptive and normative legal analyses, highlighted the importance of viewing rules and rulings from both ex post and ex ante standpoints (that is, drawing attention to their incentive effects), and provocatively called into question any number of established truths. While the rest of this book in no way tries to discard economic analysis, it does strive to improve it, and to improve legal analysis more generally, by incorporating insights from behavioral research.

2

Behavioral Studies

A. An Overview

1. History, Methodology, and Interdisciplinary Impact

While it has antecedent intellectual roots, the psychological research of human *judgment and decision-making* (JDM) has mainly evolved since the 1950s—in part in response to the *expected utility theory* put forward by John von Newman and Oskar Morgenstern.[1] While economists have tended to view expected utility as both a normative and a descriptive model of human preferences and choices (and many of them still do), psychologists from early on have focused on experimentally questioning the descriptive validity of expected utility theory.[2]

As we shall see below, both the reference to expected utility theory as a normative benchmark (implying that deviations from it are "biases"), and the extensive resort to laboratory experiments, have been the subject of some controversy. Nevertheless, the bulk of JDM studies, including those that have had a particular impact on legal research and policymaking, share these characteristics. Thousands of studies have identified a long list of biases—such as the availability heuristic, self-serving biases in recalling information, and bounded willpower—in performing tasks.

Throughout the years, JDM studies have gradually expanded in scope and methodology, blurring the borders between them and other spheres of psychology, including studies of emotions, learning, and memory. In particular, there is considerable overlap

1. John von Neumann & Oskar Morgenstern, Theory of Games and Economic Behavior (2d ed. 1947).

2. On the intellectual roots of JDM research and its development, see William M. Goldstein & Robin M. Hogarth, Research on Judgment and Decision Making: Currents, Connections, and Controversies 3–65 (1997); Ulrike Hahn & Adam J.L. Harris, *What Does It Mean to Be Biased: Motivated Reasoning and Rationality*, 61 Psychol. Learning & Motivation 42 (2014); Gideon Keren & George Wu, *A Bird's-Eye View of the History of Judgment and Decision Making*, *in* 1 The Wiley Blackwell Handbook of Judgment and Decision Making 1 (Gideon Keren & George Wu eds., 2015).

Behavioral Law and Economics. Eyal Zamir and Doron Teichman.

between JDM and social psychology, the study of the influence of other people's (actual and imagined) presence on people's thoughts, feelings, and behavior.[3] Notable progress in JDM studies is also due to methodological innovations. In addition to laboratory experiments—which are still the most prevalent methodology—JDM studies employ field experiments and analyze the results of natural experiments that shed light on human judgments and choices. A rapidly growing body of neuropsychological studies based on functional magnetic resonance imaging (fMRI) and similar techniques is opening up new frontiers in understanding the neural underpinnings of cognitive processes.[4]

Finally, in addition to the links and overlap between JDM and other spheres of psychological research, there is an ongoing dialogue between JDM research and other disciplines dealing with human behavior, such as economics,[5] finance,[6] political science,[7] and law.[8] These dialogues have been extended following the introduction of experimental methodologies into economic, legal, and even philosophical studies.[9] The important contribution of psychological studies to economics was recognized in 2002, when Daniel Kahneman won the Nobel Prize in economics. The powerful impact of those studies on legal analysis is reflected throughout this book.

As previously noted, the borderlines between JDM and other spheres of psychological research, and between the psychological and other perspectives on human decision-making, are blurred. However, as our focus is not on JDM and the law, but rather on behavioral law and economics, drawing these borderlines is not important for our purposes. Instead, we shall discuss the main findings that are relevant to behavioral law and economics, regardless of whether or not they belong to JDM *stricto sensu*. Thus, in addition to deviations from the assumptions of cognitive, or "thin" economic rationality—that is, the formal elements pertaining to the structure of people's preferences (such as transitivity)

3. On the connections between JDM and social psychology, see Thomas D. Gilovich & Dale W. Griffin, *Judgment and Decision Making, in* 1 HANDBOOK OF SOCIAL PSYCHOLOGY 542 (Susan T. Fiske, Daniel T. Gilbert & Gardner Lindzey eds., 5th ed. 2010).

4. *See, e.g.,* Alan G. Sanfey & Mirre Stallen, *Neurosciences Contribution to Judgment and Decision Making: Opportunities and Limitations, in* WILEY BLACKWELL HANDBOOK, *supra* note 2, at 268; HANDBOOK OF NEUROSCIENCE FOR THE BEHAVIORAL SCIENCES (Gary G. Berntson & John T. Cacioppo eds., 2009).

5. *See, e.g.,* ADVANCES IN BEHAVIORAL ECONOMICS (Colin F. Camerer, George Loewenstein & Matthew Rabin eds., 2003); Nicholas C. Barberis, *Thirty Years of Prospect Theory in Economics: A Review and Assessment,* 27 J. ECON. PERSP. 173 (2013).

6. *See, e.g.,* Nicholas C. Barberis & Richard H. Thaler, *A Survey of Behavioral Finance, in* 1B HANDBOOK OF THE ECONOMICS OF FINANCE 1053 (George M. Constantinides, René M. Stulz & Milton Harris eds., 2003); HANDBOOK OF BEHAVIORAL FINANCE (Brian Bruce ed., 2010).

7. *See, e.g.,* THE OXFORD HANDBOOK OF POLITICAL PSYCHOLOGY (Leonie Huddy, David O. Sears & Jack S. Levy eds., 2013). For an application of JDM insights to political philosophy, see, e.g., JAMIE TERENCE KELLEY, FRAMING DEMOCRACY: A BEHAVIORAL APPROACH TO DEMOCRATIC THEORY (2012).

8. *See, e.g.,* BEHAVIORAL LAW AND ECONOMICS (Cass R. Sunstein ed., 2000); THE OXFORD HANDBOOK OF BEHAVIORAL ECONOMICS AND THE LAW (Eyal Zamir & Doron Teichman eds., 2014).

9. THE HANDBOOK OF EXPERIMENTAL ECONOMICS RESULTS (Charles R. Plott & Vernon L. Smith eds., 2008); Christoph Engel, *Behavioral Law and Economics: Empirical Methods, in* THE OXFORD HANDBOOK OF BEHAVIORAL ECONOMICS AND THE LAW, *supra* note 8, at 125; EXPERIMENTAL PHILOSOPHY (Joshua Knobe & Shaun Nichols eds.) Vols. 1 (2008) & 2 (2014).

and people's strategy of decision-making—we are interested in systematic deviations from motivational, or "thick" rationality, namely the assumption that people only seek to maximize their own utility.[10] Numerous studies, by psychologists and experimental economists alike, have shown that maximizing one's utility is not the only motivation that drives people: people also care about the welfare of other people, act out of envy or altruism, and show commitment to values of reciprocity and fairness.[11] More recently, much attention has been given to people's moral judgments, as well as to automatic psychological processes that lead ordinary people to violate moral and social norms.[12]

Before turning to specific psychological phenomena, this overview discusses a few general themes, including dual-process theories, theories of heuristics and biases, and the challenges posed to JDM by the approach known as *Fast-and-Frugal Heuristics.*

2. Dual-Process Theories

Dual-process theories posit that there is more than one way in which people perceive information, process it, and make decisions.[13] Originally coined by Keith Stanovich and Richard West, and subsequently adopted by Kahneman, the terms *System 1* and *System 2* have gained great popularity in describing human judgment and decision-making.[14]

System 1 operates automatically and quickly, with little or no effort, and with no sense of voluntary control. It is commonly described as spontaneous, intuitive, associative, context-dependent, and holistic. It uses mental shortcuts, or *heuristics,* that people learn through personal experience, or even on innate ones. In contrast, System 2 involves effortful mental activity. It is conscious, deliberative, and analytic—and thus also slow and exacting. It employs rules that are explicitly learned. System 1 thinking is used in most of our daily tasks—such as identifying familiar faces and recognizing other people's strong emotional reactions, driving a car (when the road is relatively empty), understanding simple sentences, and answering trivial math questions. Examples of tasks involving System 2 thinking include answering complex math questions, finding an address in an unfamiliar neighborhood, and writing this paragraph.

Some accounts of dual-process thinking link it to the role played by emotions in decision-making, maintaining that emotional reactions influence decision-making through System 1.[15] This claim is part of a large body of research about the impact of emotions on

10. On cognitive and motivational rationality, see *supra* pp. 8–12.

11. *See infra* pp. 101–10.

12. *See infra* pp. 94–97 and 72–76, respectively.

13. *See generally* Dual-Process Theories in Social Psychology (Shelly Chaiken & Yaacov Trope eds., 1999).

14. Keith E. Stanovich & Richard F. West, *Individual Differences in Reasoning: Implications for the Rationality Debate?,* 23 Behav. & Brain Sci. 645 (2000); Daniel Kahneman, Thinking, Fast and Slow (2011). *See also* Daniel Kahneman & Shane Frederick, *Representativeness Revisited: Attribute Substitution in Intuitive Judgment, in* Heuristics and Biases: The Psychology of Intuitive Judgment 49 (Thomas Gilovich, Dale Griffin & Daniel Kahneman eds., 2002); Jonathan St. B.T. Evans, *Dual-Processing Accounts of Reasoning, Judgment, and Social Cognition,* 59 Ann. Rev. Psychol. 255 (2008).

15. *See, e.g.,* Seymour Epstein, *Integration of the Cognitive and the Psychodynamic Unconscious,* 49 Am. Psychologist 709 (1994).

judgment (including moral judgment) and decision-making.[16] There is also some evidence that separate regions of the brain are involved in the different types of cognitive processes.[17] Relatedly, there are hypotheses about the evolution of the two systems in humans and animals—essentially, that System 2 is uniquely, or characteristically, human.[18]

The use of System 1 heuristics and shortcuts is inevitable, given the endless stimuli that we are constantly exposed to, and the huge number of decisions we make every day. System 1 is usually very effective. However, it also results in systematic and predictable deviations from the axioms of rational decision-making, which are known as *cognitive biases*.

In general, the speedy and autonomous nature of System 1 processes makes it dominant a priori—that is, it controls behavior by default, unless analytical reasoning intervenes.[19] While System 2 may intervene when System 1 leads to suboptimal results, people usually stick to their intuitive System 1 choices, and use System 2 chiefly to provide justifications for those choices.[20] In this respect, Stanovich has proposed distinguishing between the *reflective* and the *algorithmic* components of System 2. The so-called *reflective mind* determines whether System 1 is interrupted and suppressed by System 2; and when it is, the *algorithmic mind* processes the information and makes the deliberative and analytic judgment or decision. Unless the higher-level, reflective mind intervenes *and* the algorithmic mind comes up with a more rational, accurate, and consistent judgment/decision than the one provided by System 1, the cognitive biases of System 1 prevail.[21] Obviously, these constructs are simplified accounts of what may well be much more complex processes in reality.[22]

People vary in their disposition to use an analytic, rather than intuitive, mode of thinking. One test that is often employed to measure people's disposition in this regard is the *cognitive reflection test* (CRT). The CRT includes questions such as: "A bat and a ball

16. *See, e.g.*, ANTONIO R. DAMASIO, DESCARTES' ERROR: EMOTION, REASON, AND THE HUMAN BRAIN (1994); Jonathan Haidt, *The Emotional Dog and Its Rational Tail: A Social Intuitionist Approach to Moral Judgment*, 108 PSYCHOL. REV. 814 (2001). For recent overviews, see Dacher Keltner & E.J. Horberg, *Emotion-Cognition Interactions*, *in* APA HANDBOOK OF PERSONALITY AND SOCIAL PSYCHOLOGY, VOL. 1: ATTITUDES AND SOCIAL COGNITION 623, 637–52 (Mario Mikulincer et al. eds., 2015); Jennifer S. Lerner et al., *Emotions and Decision Making*, 66 ANN. REV. PSYCHOL. 799 (2015). *See also infra* pp. 44–45, 100.

17. *See, e.g.*, Vinod Goel & Raymond J. Dolan, *Explaining Modulation of Reasoning by Belief*, 87 COGNITION B11 (2003); Matthew D. Lieberman, *Social Cognitive Neuroscience: A Review of Core Processes*, 58 ANN. REV. PSYCHOL. 259 (2007).

18. Evans, *supra* note 14, at 259–61; Jonathan St. B.T. Evans, *Two Minds Rationality*, 20 THINKING & REASONING 129, 131–32 (2014) (discussing humans' "old" and "new" minds).

19. Jonathan St. B.T. Evans, *The Heuristic-Analytic Theory of Reasoning: Extension and Evaluation*, 13 PSYCHONOMIC BULL. & REV. 378 (2006); KEITH E. STANOVICH, RATIONALITY AND THE REFLECTIVE MIND 19–22 (2011).

20. Valerie Thompson, *Dual-Process Theories: A Metacognitive Perspective*, *in* IN TWO MINDS: DUAL PROCESSES AND BEYOND 171 (Jonathan St. B.T. Evans & Keith Frankish eds., 2009). *See also* Emmanuel Trouche et al., *The Selective Laziness of Reasoning*, 40 COGNITIVE SCI. 2122 (2016).

21. STANOVICH, *supra* note 19. For a shorter exposition, see Keith E. Stanovich, *On the Distinction between Rationality and Intelligence: Implications for Understanding Individual Differences in Reasoning*, *in* THE OXFORD HANDBOOK OF THINKING AND REASONING 343 (Keith J. Holyoak & Robert G. Morrison, Jr. eds., 2012).

22. Thus, both systems are often involved in a single decision, and there may be a continuum, rather than a dichotomy, between the automatic and deliberative modes of thinking. *See* Magda Osman, *An Evaluation of Dual-Process Theories of Reasoning*, 11 PSYCHONOMIC BULL. & REV. 988 (2004).

cost $1.10. The bat costs $1.00 more than the ball. How much does the ball cost?" The first answer that comes to mind is 10 cents, but a moment's reflection shows that the right answer is 5 cents. People who give the former answer display a lesser disposition for cognitive reflection than those who give the latter.[23] Originally comprising only three questions, the CRT has subsequently been expanded by adding more questions.[24] Another test of the tendency to engage in effortful cognitive endeavors is the *need for cognition scale* (NCS), which comprises a relatively long list of self-characterization statements, such as: "I find satisfaction in deliberating hard and for long hours." Subjects indicate the extent to which each statement characterizes them, and are assessed based on the aggregation of their replies.[25]

Whether a person uses one system or the other in any particular context is not only a matter of personal disposition, but a function of training and experience as well. Tasks that initially require conscious effort—such as speaking a foreign language or driving a car—may become automatic and effortless over time. The use of one system or the other also depends on the cognitive resources available to the decision-maker at the time of making the decision. Thus, when people make extensive use of their controlled deliberation resources, the resulting resource depletion may result in more intuitive, System 1 decision-making in a subsequent, unrelated task.[26]

Notwithstanding the shortcomings of System 1's heuristics, it should be noted that sometimes System 1 produces more accurate decisions than System 2, and people often consciously use simple heuristics (rather than exacting, analytical thought-processes) in their judgments and decision-making.[27] The bright and dark sides of heuristics are further discussed below.[28]

3. Theories of Heuristics and Biases

Several theories have been proposed to explain how the heuristics used by System 1 operate, and why they result in systematic errors. One such model is *attribute substitution.* It posits that many heuristics "share a common process . . . in which difficult judgments are made by substituting conceptually or semantically related assessments that are simpler and more readily accessible."[29] For example, when a person is asked which of two events is more

23. Shane Frederick, *Cognitive Reflection and Decision Making,* 19 J. Econ. Persp. 25 (2005).

24. Maggie E. Toplak, Richard F. West & Keith E. Stanovich, *Assessing Miserly Information Processing: An Expansion of the Cognitive Reflection Test,* 20 Thinking & Reasoning 147 (2014).

25. John T. Cacioppo & Richard E. Petty, *The Need for Cognition,* 42 J. Personality & Soc. Psychol. 116 (1982); John T. Cacioppo, Richard E. Petty & Chuan Feng Kao, *The Efficient Assessment of Need for Cognition,* 48 J. Personality Assessment 306 (1984).

26. *See, e.g.,* Anastasiya Pocheptsova et al., *Deciding without Resources: Resource Depletion and Choice in Context,* 46 J. Marketing Res. 344 (2009).

27. Gerd Gigerenzer & Daniel G. Goldstein, *Reasoning the Fast and Frugal Way: Models of Bounded Rationality,* 103 Psychol. Rev. 650 (1996); Kahneman & Fredrick, *supra* note 14, at 59–60. *See also* Better than Conscious? Decision Making, the Human Mind, and Implications for Institutions (Christoph Engel & Wolf Singer eds., 2008).

28. *See infra* pp. 25–26.

29. Daniel Kahneman & Shane Frederick, *A Model of Heuristic Judgment, in* The Cambridge Handbook of Thinking and Reasoning 267, 287 (Keith J. Holyoak & Robert G. Morrison eds., 2005).

probable, she might substitute it with the simpler question: "Instances of which event come more readily to mind?" (the *availability heuristic*).[30] Similarly, when asked about the probability that something belongs to a certain category, one might substitute for the question a simpler one: "How similar is it to a typical member of that category?" (the *representativeness heuristic*).[31] Thus, in one study students were asked how happy they were with their lives in general, and how many dates they had had in the previous month. When the two questions were asked in that order, there was almost no correlation between the answers; but when the dating question was asked first, there was a high correlation between the two—presumably because the answer to the dating question became the heuristic attribute in answering the global happiness question.[32]

According to a more elaborate model, attribute substitution is but one of five *effort-reduction* mechanisms—the other four being (1) examining fewer cues, (2) simplifying the weighting principles for cues, (3) integrating less information, and (4) examining fewer alternatives.[33] According to this model, the five mechanisms can be used separately, or in combination with each other.

Another mechanism (overlapping some of the aforementioned ones) that may account for certain heuristics is the *isolation effect*—namely ignoring anything that is not within one's immediate field of consciousness. The isolation effect may explain, for example, why people who are normally risk-averse continue to gamble with money they have just won, or why thrifty people spend lottery gains on luxury items. In both cases, they are isolating the present decision from the overall picture.[34] Relatedly, Kahneman proposed the acronym WYSIATI (for *What You See Is All There Is*) to describe System 1's tendency to jump to conclusions based on the immediately available information, while neglecting all other information.[35]

The last explanation to be mentioned here is *overgeneralization*. People may follow useful judgment- and choice-rules even when the rationale of those rules do not, or no longer, apply—thus making systematic mistakes. For example, an overgeneralization of the useful heuristic *Do not waste* may lead to *escalation of commitment*—that is, the inability to disregard *sunk costs* and to make decisions regarding the investment of additional resources based on the future costs and benefits of that investment only.[36] Similarly, people who have

30. *See also infra* pp. 34–36.

31. *See infra* pp. 28–30.

32. Fritz Strack, Leonard L. Martin & Norbert Schwarz, *Priming and Communication: The Social Determinants of Information Use in Judgments of Life Satisfaction,* 18 EUR. J. SOC. PSYCHOL. 429 (1988); Kahneman & Frederick, *supra* note 29, at 269.

33. Anuj K. Shah & Daniel M. Oppenheimer, *Heuristics Made Easy: An Effort-Reduction Framework,* 134 PSYCHOL. BULL. 207 (2008).

34. Jonathan Baron, *Heuristics and Biases, in* THE OXFORD HANDBOOK OF BEHAVIORAL ECONOMICS AND THE LAW, *supra* note 8, at 3, 17–18.

35. KAHNEMAN, *supra* note 14, at 85–88.

36. Baron, *supra* note 34, at 15–17. On sunk costs and escalation of commitment, see *infra* pp. 56–57.

learned to trust the power of their own and other people's vision more than their or other people's power of deduction tend to give more weight to direct evidence, such as eyewitness testimony, than to inferences from circumstantial evidence. They may do so even when the circumstantial evidence is as conclusive as direct evidence, or more so.[37]

4. Cognitive Biases versus Fast-and-Frugal Heuristics

Much of JDM research, particularly the early studies that had a strong impact on economics and legal theory, has developed through the documentation of specific errors of judgment in laboratory experiments, taking economic rationality as the normative benchmark—and only then looking for their causes, if at all. Experimentally studying a system's failures can provide valuable insight about its successful functioning.[38] However, several important critiques have been leveled against this type of research, notably by Gerd Gigerenzer and his colleagues, who advocate the *fast-and-frugal* approach as an alternative to the *heuristics-and-biases* research program, associated with Daniel Kahneman and Amos Tversky.[39]

One critique is that the heuristics-and-biases program is lacking in ecological validity, due to the differences between laboratory experiments and real-life decision-making. Specifically, it has been argued that at least some of the laboratory experiments highlighting people's cognitive biases involve abstract tasks that are quite different from the tasks that people face in their daily life. For example, in one of the famous demonstrations of the *confirmation bias*,[40] participants were presented with four cards, two with letters and two with numbers. They were told that each card had a letter on one side and a number on the other, and were asked to indicate which cards they would *need* to turn over in order to find out whether the following rule is true: if a card has a vowel on one side, then it has an even number on the other side. Most participants incorrectly suggested turning over cards that would *confirm* the rule, when in fact the correct answer is to choose the combination that could potentially *falsify* it. However, when the same task was presented in a real-life, social context, rather than in abstract terms, participants were found to do much better.[41]

37. Eyal Zamir, Ilana Ritov & Doron Teichman, *Seeing Is Believing: The Anti-Inference Bias*, 89 Ind. L.J. 195 (2014).

38. Amos Tversky & Daniel Kahneman, *Extensional versus Intuitive Reasoning: The Conjunction Fallacy in Probability Judgment*, 90 Psychol. Rev. 293, 313 (1983).

39. *See, e.g.*, Gerd Gigerenzer, Peter Todd & the ABC Research Group, Simple Heuristics That Make Us Smart (1999).

40. Peter C. Wason, *Reasoning*, *in* 1 New Horizons in Psychology 135, 145–46 (Brian M. Foss ed., 1966). On the confirmation bias, see *infra* pp. 58–61.

41. Gerd Gigerenzer & Klaus Hug, *Domain-Specific Reasoning: Social Contracts, Cheating and Perspective Change*, 42 Cognition 127 (1992). In the same vein, it was found that people's probability inferences are more accurate when probabilities are presented in frequency formats (e.g., 1 in 20) than in percentages (e.g., 5 percent). *See, e.g.*, Gerd Gigerenzer & Ulrich Hoffrage, *How to Improve Bayesian Reasoning without Instruction: Frequency Formats*, 102 Psychol. Rev. 684 (1995). Note, however, that nowadays, probabilities are more often presented in real life in percentage than in frequency formats.

Another critique of the heuristics-and-biases school is that it tends to paint a bleak picture of human decision-making being systematically irrational and fallible (and then, possibly, look for debiasing techniques), when in fact people do remarkably well under most ordinary circumstances. Unlike the well-defined conditions of laboratory experiments, in real life people have partial information about an uncertain world. Rather than maximizing their utility according to rational choice theory, what they need—and actually use—are effective and frugal decision algorithms that function well under real-life circumstances.[42] In fact, simple heuristics, based on limited information, may do better than complex decision rules that incorporate more information. For example, it was found that German students who were asked to judge which of two U.S. cities was larger, and who used the heuristic that the more familiar city is larger, did better than U.S. students who had more information about those cities (and vice versa).[43] Such heuristics may be consciously adopted.[44]

Finally, researchers of the fast-and-frugal-heuristics school also tend to emphasize the adaptive advantages of heuristics that developed when humans were mostly hunter-gatherers, and to criticize heuristics-and-biases research for producing a long list of biases with little understanding of the underlying psychological processes.[45]

Delving into these controversies is beyond the scope of the present discussion. While some of the critiques of the heuristics-and-biases school are well taken, others seem less and less compelling as heuristics-and-biases scholars formulate broader theories of the cognitive processes underlying biases (some of which were described in the previous subsection), and pay more heed to the ecological validity of their findings. Generally speaking, the differences between the two schools appear to be much smaller than scholars of the fast-and-frugal school tend to portray. As Ulrike Hahn and Adam Harris have succinctly pointed out, whether one should emphasize the "adaptive rationality" of using effective heuristics, or the predictable and systematic errors produced by those heuristics, is like asking whether a glass is half empty or half full.[46] Moreover, some of the issues, such as that of the evolutionary roots of heuristics, are hardly resolvable by scientific means, and at any rate do not necessarily bear upon the use of behavioral insights by jurists and legal policymakers (which is the focus of this book). Moreover, legal policymakers understandably tend to focus on people's judgment and decision-making, rather than on their underlying psychological processes.

42. This claim echoes Herbert Simon's claim that due to their limitations, people often act as "satisficers"—rather than maximizers—of their utility, and sensibly so. *See, e.g.*, Herbert A. Simon, Administrative Behavior: A Study of Decision-Making Processes in Administrative Organization (1947; 4th ed. 1997); Herbert Simon, *A Behavioral Model of Rational Choice*, 69 Q.J. Econ. (1955).

43. *See, e.g.*, Daniel G. Goldstein & Gerd Gigerenzer, *Models of Ecological Rationality: The Recognition Heuristic*, 109 Psychol. Rev. 75 (2002).

44. Gerd Gigerenzer & Wolfgang Gaissmaier, *Heuristic Decision Making*, 62 Ann. Rev. Psychol. 451, 455 (2011).

45. For a comprehensive analysis of the debate between the heuristics-and-biases and the fast-and-frugal-heuristics schools, see Mark Kelman, The Heuristics Debate 19–116 (2011). For concise descriptions, see, e.g., Hahn & Harris, *supra* note 2, at 49–53; Jonathan Baron, *supra* note 34, at 11–14.

46. Hahn & Harris, *supra* note 2, at 50.

5. Typology of Phenomena and Structure of the Chapter

One of the critiques commonly leveled against behavioral studies is that they produce a long list of heuristics and biases, rather than a simple, unifying model of judgment and decision-making of the sort provided by rational choice theory.[47] Inasmuch as this is due to the focus on deviations from economic rationality, especially in earlier JDM studies,[48] perhaps doing away with this benchmark—as advocated by the fast-and-frugal school—would bring about greater clarity and coherence.[49] Ultimately, however, there is an inevitable trade-off between descriptive validity and simplicity. Human psychology is too complex to be captured by a simple theory. As Kahneman has put it, "life is more complex for behavioral economists than for true believers in human rationality."[50] As long as one does not treat the behavioral outlook as a substitute for economic and other perspectives on legal and policy issues, but rather as a complementary and corrective measure, the absence of a unifying theory and our limited understanding of the underlying psychological processes of decision-making are less of an issue.[51]

Such modesty notwithstanding, some classification of heuristics and biases is essential, if only for expositional purposes. A notable proposal of such a classification has been put forward by Jonathan Baron.[52] Baron classifies the myriad heuristics and biases into three major categories. The first category is of biases of attention. It comprises three subcategories: (1) availability, attention to here and now, easy, and compatible information; (2) heuristics based on imperfect correlations (such as the hindsight bias and omission bias); and (3) focus on a single attribute to the exclusion of others. The second category involves biases that stem from the effects of goals and desires on perceptions and information processing (such as wishful thinking). The last category concerns the relationship between quantitative attributes and their perception, including diminishing sensitivity to changes in gains, losses, and probabilities.

As Baron readily concedes, his classification is suggestive rather than definitive. The complex interrelations between the various phenomena make any attempt at classification rather challenging. Fortunately for us, we do not need to offer such a classification. This chapter does not purport to provide a systematic survey of all behavioral findings,[53] or even of those that might be relevant to behavioral law and economics. Rather, it focuses

47. *See, e.g.*, Jonathan Baron, Thinking and Deciding 54 (4th ed. 2008).

48. Another possible cause is the diversity of disciplines to which researchers in the field belong, including psychology, economics, marketing, finance, and law. *See* Gilovich & Griffin, *supra* note 3, at 542.

49. Joachim I. Krueger & David C. Funder, *Towards a Balanced Social Psychology: Causes, Consequences, and Cures for the Problem-Seeking Approach to Social Behavior and Cognition*, 27 Behav. & Brain Sci. 313 (2004) (the article is followed by thirty-five critical comments and the authors' reaction. *See id.* at 328–67); Elke U. Weber & Eric J. Johnson, *Mindful Judgment and Decision Making*, 60 Ann. Rev. Psychol. 53 (2009).

50. Kahneman, *supra* note 14, at 412.

51. *See also infra* pp. 152–54.

52. Baron, *supra* note 47, at 54–58.

53. For comprehensive reviews and analyses of JDM, see Baron, *supra* note 47; Wiley Blackwell Handbook, *supra* note 2.

on phenomena whose understanding is necessary for the ensuing analyses. Additional phenomena, which are uniquely relevant to specific legal issues (or whose broader significance has not yet been realized), will be discussed apropos of those issues.

This goal shapes the structure of the remainder of this chapter. Given our perspective of behavioral law and economics, we distinguish between deviations from thin, *cognitive* rationality (Sections B–E), and deviations from thick, *motivational* rationality, including studies of moral judgments (Section G).

Within the former category, the chapter first discusses probability assessments and related issues (Section B), and then preferences and decisions. The latter category is divided into phenomena related to *prospect theory*—arguably the most influential theory in behavioral economics (Section C), phenomena associated with motivated reasoning and egocentrism (Section D), and those related to reference-dependence and order effects (Section E).

Section F discusses bounded willpower and procrastination. These phenomena do not fit squarely into either the cognitive or motivational rationality constructs—although they are closely connected to both.

While economic analysis *normatively* prioritizes the maximization of overall human welfare over other values, it *descriptively* assumes that people are rational maximizers of their own welfare. Section G describes studies that show that most people neither share this normative outlook nor conform to the descriptive assumption.

Finally, Section H discusses several issues that cut across the phenomena described in the previous sections. These are: individual differences in judgment and decision-making; the significance of professional training, experience, and expertise; deciding for others; group decision-making; cultural differences; and debiasing.

B. Probability Assessments and Related Issues

Many of the early groundbreaking studies in JDM have dealt with frequency and probability assessments, statistical inferences, and perceptions of risk and uncertainty. This section surveys the main findings in this sphere.

1. Conjunction and Disjunction Fallacies

One of the most famous (and controversial) characters in JDM is Linda. As described in a classic experiment conducted by Tversky and Kahneman, "Linda is 31 years old, single, outspoken and very bright. She majored in philosophy. As a student, she was deeply concerned with issues of discrimination and social justice, and also participated in anti-nuclear demonstrations."[54] In one version of the experiment, subjects were asked which of the following alternatives is more probable: "Linda is a bank teller," or "Linda is a bank teller and is active in the feminist movement." According to the conjunction rule, the probability of a conjunction, P(A&B), cannot exceed the probabilities of its constituents, P(A) and P(B), because the former is included in each of the latter. Nevertheless, in what Tversky and

54. Amos Tversky & Daniel Kahneman, *Extension versus Intuitive Reasoning: The Conjunction Fallacy in Probability Judgment*, 90 PSYCHOL. REV. 293, 297 (1983).

Kahneman dubbed a "flagrant violation of the conjunction rule," 85 percent of respondents indicated that it was more probable that Linda was a bank teller and an active feminist than a bank teller.[55] Additional experiments demonstrated that this logical error occurs in other experimental designs and in other areas (such as predicting the outcomes of sport contests). It is committed, to varying degrees, by students who have studied advanced courses in statistics and decision theory, and by experts making assessments within their area of expertise. It occurs even when financial incentives are given to give the right answer, and despite people's ability to understand the conjunction fallacy.[56]

Tversky and Kahneman sought to explain the conjunction fallacy, as well as other biases in probability assessments and related issues, by means of the *representativeness heuristic*. People who resort to this heuristic assess the probability of an uncertain event by "the degree to which it is: (*i*) similar in essential properties to its parent population; and (*ii*) reflects the salient features of the process by which it is generated."[57] In the present context, Linda seems to have the characteristics of a feminist activist, rather than those of a bank teller. Hence, her description as a bank teller and a feminist activist sounds more representative—and hence more probable—than her description as a bank teller, despite the fact that the probability of her being both things cannot logically exceed the probability of her being just a bank teller.

The causes, generality, and very existence of the conjunction fallacy have been questioned, especially by members of the *fast-and-frugal* school of JDM.[58] It has been argued that what looks like a conjunction fallacy is actually a product of the multiplicity of meanings of the terms "probable" (which may refer to mathematical frequency, but also to intensity of belief, and more),"[59] and "and" (which in probability theory refers to an intersection, but in natural language may refer to an intersection or to a union of events, as in the expression "Dear friends and colleagues").[60] Without going into details, we note that while the conjunction fallacy is diminished when subjects are instructed to estimate frequencies rather than probability, such instructions do not eliminate the fallacy. Neither is the conjunction fallacy caused by misunderstanding of the meaning of the word "and." However, some experimental designs, which draw subjects' attention to the conjunction rule, do eliminate the fallacy.[61]

55. *Id.* at 299.

56. *Id.* at 297–309; Rodrigo Moro, *On the Nature of the Conjunction Fallacy*, 171 Synthese 1 (2009) (analyzing dozens of studies of the conjunction fallacy).

57. Daniel Kahneman & Amos Tversky, *Subjective Probability: A Judgment of Representativeness*, 3 Cognitive Psychol. 430, 431 (1972).

58. On the Fast-and-Frugal school, see *supra* pp. 25–26.

59. *See, e.g.*, Ralph Hertwig & Gerd Gigerenzer, *The "Conjunction Fallacy" Revisited: How Intelligent Inferences Look Like Reasoning Errors*, 12 J. Behav. Decision Making 275 (1999).

60. Barbara Mellers, Ralph Hertwig & Daniel Kahneman, *Do Frequency Representations Eliminate Conjunction Effects? An Exercise in Adversarial Collaboration*, 12 Psychol. Sci. 269 (2001).

61. *Id.* at 271–273; Daniel Kahneman & Amos Tversky, *On the Reality of Cognitive Illusions: A Reply to Gigerenzer's Critique*, 103 Psychol. Rev. 582 (1996); Moro, *supra* note 56.

Further support for the existence of the representativeness heuristic comes from studies of the *disjunction fallacy*. According to the disjunction rule, the probability of A-or-B cannot be smaller than the probability of A or the probability of B. For example, the probability that a woman, who smoked over a packet of cigarettes a day for many years, died of cancer, cannot be smaller than the probability that she died of lung cancer. Using this and comparable examples, Maya Bar-Hillel and Efrat Neter conducted carefully designed experiments in which subjects were asked to rank the outcomes by their willingness to bet on each one and by their probability. Since the examples were chosen such that the narrower category was somewhat more representative than the broader one (as in the lung cancer example), most subjects violated the disjunction rule in both their willingness to bet on them and in assessing their probability.[62] Across ten different descriptions and the two questions, 64 percent of the answers violated the disjunction rule.

2. Base-Rate Neglect

Base-rate neglect refers to estimations of likelihood. It is the tendency to ignore the frequency with which an event occurs, and focus instead on individuating information—rather than integrate the two. More specific information is deemed to be more relevant; hence it dominates less specific information,[63] and more vivid and concrete data makes greater impact on inferences than dull and abstract data.[64] The following famous example from one of Kahneman and Tversky's experiments[65] demonstrates the phenomenon: Jack is a forty-five-year-old man. He is married with four children. He is generally conservative, careful, and ambitious. He shows no interest in political and social issues, and spends most of his free time on his many hobbies, which include home carpentry, sailing, and mathematical puzzles. Subjects in one condition in this study were told that Jack was randomly drawn from a pool of people consisting of seventy engineers and thirty lawyers, while subjects in the other group were told that the pool was composed of thirty engineers and seventy lawyers. When asked to estimate what Jack does for a living, subjects paid very little attention to the base rate, and based their assessment almost exclusively on the individuating information.

Along with studies that replicated this result, the robustness, generality, and ecological validity of the base-rate neglect have been questioned over the years. An analysis of many experimental and empirical studies demonstrated that people do not routinely ignore base rates.[66] It has been suggested that "a base rate has its greatest impact in tasks that (1) are structured in ways that sensitize decision makers to the base rate, (2) are conceptualized by the

62. Maya Bar-Hillel & Efrat Neter, *How Alike Is It versus How Likely Is It: A Disjunction Fallacy in Probability Judgments*, 65 J. PERSONALITY & SOC. PSYCHOL. 1119 (1993).

63. Maya Bar-Hillel, *The Base-Rate Fallacy in Probability Judgments*, 44 ACTA PSYCHOLOGICA 211 (1980).

64. RICHARD NISBETT & LEE ROSS, HUMAN INFERENCE: STRATEGIES AND SHORTCOMINGS OF SOCIAL JUDGMENT 147–50 (1980).

65. Daniel Kahneman & Amos Tversky, *On the Psychology of Prediction*, 80 PSYCHOL. REV. 237 (1973).

66. Jonathan J. Koehler, *The Base Rate Fallacy Reconsidered: Descriptive, Normative, and Methodological Challenges*, 19 BEHAV. & BRAIN SCI. 1 (1996).

decision maker in relative frequentist terms, (3) contain cues to base rate diagnosticity, and (4) invoke heuristics that focus attention on the base rate."[67] Thus, when subjects are asked to make a series of assessments, they pay more attention to information that varies from one task to another, than to information that is common to all tasks. Consequently, subjects pay more attention to the base rate when it is manipulated within subject than when it is manipulated between subjects (as in Kahneman and Tversky's study).[68] Similarly, expressing a problem in frequentist terms, rather than as the probability of a single event, elicits correct Bayesian reasoning in the great majority of subjects.[69] However, in most real-world contexts, people face only one set of values at a time, and probabilities are often presented in percentages.

Another limitation of some studies of base-rate neglect stems from the questionable assumption that people's subjective probability assessments equal the stated base rate. People's assessment of the prior probability may be affected by other (relevant or irrelevant) information, besides the information provided by the experimenter. In such cases, what appears to be a base-rate neglect may actually result from a different subjective assessment of the base rate.[70] In general, people's attention to base rates sensibly depends on the diagnosticity and reliability of the individuating information: the less stereotypical the individuating information is, the more weight is given to the base rate.[71] It has also been demonstrated that people neglect base rates to a lesser extent in tasks involving concrete, familiar situations (such as reviewing job applications) than in abstract, unfamiliar ones.[72]

Along with the complex picture regarding the extent to which people ignore base rates, there is also disagreement over the extent to which people *should* consider base rates when making probability assessments. The relative weight given to the base rate, in relation to the individuating information, varies from one case to another. To use the lawyer-engineer example, if it is given that Jack had studied law, then although it is possible that he works as an engineer, it would be sensible to give exceedingly low weight to the fact that lawyers constitute only 30 percent of the entire pool. Unfortunately, there is no easy answer to the question of what weight should be given to the base rate under different circumstances, if at all.[73]

67. *Id.* at 5.

68. *See, e.g.*, Baruch Fischhoff, Paul Slovic & Sarah Lichtenstein, *Subjective Sensitivity Analysis*, 23 Org. Behav. & Hum. Performance 339 (1979).

69. Leda Cosmides & John Tooby, *Are Humans Good Intuitive Statisticians After All? Rethinking Some Conclusions from the Literature on Judgment under Uncertainty*, 58 Cognition 1 (1996).

70. Kohler, *supra* note 66, at 12–13. In real life, including in the legal arena, objective data about the base rate is often unavailable. This means that even decision-makers who pay attention to the base rate may come to wrong conclusions if their subjective assessment of the base rate is inaccurate. *See* Michael J. Saks & Michael Risinger, *The Presumption of Guilt, Admissibility Rulings, and Erroneous Convictions*, 2003 Mich. St. DCL L. Rev. 1051.

71. Kahneman & Tversky, *supra* note 65; Zvi Ginossar & Yaacov Trope, *The Effects of Base Rates and Individuating Information on Judgments about Another Person*, 16 J. Experimental Soc. Psychol. 228 (1980).

72. Lívia Markóczy & Jeffrey Goldberg, *Women and Taxis and Dangerous Judgments: Content Sensitive Use of Base-Rate Information*, 19 Managerial & Decision Econ. 481 (1998).

73. *See generally* L. Jonathan Cohen, *Can Human Irrationality Be Experimentally Demonstrated?*, 4 Behav. & Brain Sci. 317, 328–30 (1981); Koehler, *supra* note 66, at 11–12. *See also infra* pp. 579–80.

3. Inverse Fallacy

Closely connected to base-rate neglect is the phenomenon known as confusion of the inverse, or the *inverse fallacy*. Given two events, A and B, people tend to assume—contrary to the Bayes theorem—that the probability of A given B is about the same as the probability of B given A.[74] Assume, for example, that a certain medical condition is found in 1 of every 100 people, and that according to a test for diagnosing this condition, which is 90 percent accurate, a person has this condition. Given the base rate, the likelihood that the person actually has the condition is about 8 percent. There is about a 92 percent likelihood that the results of the test are false positive.[75] People who estimate that the likelihood of the person having the condition is around 90 percent are not only neglecting the base rate—they are also mistakenly assuming that the probability of the person having the condition, given the positive test results, roughly equals the probability that the results are positive, given that the person has the condition.[76] Studies have shown that not only laypeople, but also experts, such as physicians, fall prey to this fallacy.[77]

4. Insensitivity to Sample Size and Related Phenomena

According to the law of large numbers, the larger the sample, the closer its mean is to the mean of the population as a whole. However, people tend to overestimate the extent to which small samples represent the population from which they are drawn.[78] This tendency may lead to various erroneous inferences.

One typical error refers to the assessment of whether a certain sequence of events is random. The *law of small numbers* (a phrase coined by Tversky and Kahneman)[79] leads people to believe that apparently patterned sequences are not random even when they may well be.[80] For example, people tend to believe that in a family of six children, the sequence BBBGGG is less likely than the sequence GBBGBG (plausibly because the latter appears to be more representative of a random sequence), when in fact they are equally likely.[81] A famous real-world example is the "hot hand" in basketball. Players, coaches, and fans tend

74. Scott Plous, The Psychology of Judgment and Decisionmaking 131–34 (1993); Gaëlle Villejoubert & David R. Mandel, *The Inverse Fallacy: An Account of Deviations from Bayes's Theorem and the Additivity Principle,* 30 Memory & Cognition 171 (2002).

75. Jeffrey J. Rachlinski, *Heuristics and Biases in the Courts: Ignorance or Adaptation?,* 79 Or. L. Rev. 61, 82–85 (2000).

76. Villejoubert & Mandel, *supra* note 74.

77. *See* Ward Casscells, Arno Schoenberger & Thomas B Graboys, *Interpretation by Physicians of Clinical Laboratory Results,* 299 New Eng. J. Med. 999 (1978); David M. Eddy, *Probabilistic Reasoning in Clinical Medicine: Problems and Opportunities, in* Judgment under Uncertainty: Heuristics and Biases 249 (Daniel Kahneman, Paul Slovic & Amos Tversky eds., 1982). *See also infra* p. 581.

78. Amos Tversky & Daniel Kahneman, *Belief in the Law of Small Numbers,* 76 Psychol. Bull. 105 (1971).

79. *Id.*

80. Maya Bar-Hillel & Willem A. Wagenaar, *The Perception of Randomness,* 12 Advances Applied Mathematics 428 (1991).

81. Kahneman & Tversky, *supra* note 57, at 432.

to believe that a player's chance of hitting a shot are greater following a previous hit or a few consecutive hits, than following a miss or a few misses. Consequently, players may take more difficult shots after successful attempts, and fellow players are often instructed to pass the ball to the player who has just made several shots. In fact, however, while some players are obviously better shooters than others, a large-scale analysis of the performance of professional and nonprofessional players found no evidence for a positive correlation between the outcomes of successive shots of the same player.[82] Similarly, there is some evidence that investors put too much weight on the track record of fund managers, causing them to take suboptimal investment decisions based on a relatively short successful or unsuccessful performance streak, albeit the picture in this sphere is far from clear.[83]

Another erroneous inference is known as *the gambler's fallacy*. When events are known or presumed to be random, as in fair coin tosses, people tend to believe that if something happened more (less) frequently than expected during a given period, it will happen less (more) frequently in the next period, as though there were some kind of corrective mechanism.[84] Intriguingly, in experiments conducted by Eric Gold and Gordon Hester, while subjects exhibited the gambler's fallacy, its incidence was significantly reduced when the coin was switched before the next toss, or was allowed "to rest" a while before it.[85] The gambler's fallacy has been documented in people's actual behavior outside the laboratory, as well.[86]

Yet another ramification of insensitivity to sample size is neglect of the fact that considerable deviations from the mean of the entire population are much more likely in small samples than in large ones. This neglect often leads people to look for—and find—alternative explanations for atypical results in small samples. For example, following the finding that small schools are disproportionally represented in the top echelon of successful schools, huge sums of money have been invested in the United States in establishing such schools and splitting large schools into smaller ones. However, it appears that small schools are disproportionally represented not only at the high end of the spectrum, but at the low end as well, simply because there is greater variability among small schools than among large ones.[87]

A failure to account for natural fluctuations in the data may also lead to false causal inferences. Due to the phenomenon known as *regression to the mean*, large deviations from

82. Thomas Gilovich, Robert Vallone & Amos Tversky, *The Hot Hand in Basketball: On the Misperception of Random Sequences*, 17 Cognitive Psychol. 295 (1985).

83. *See, e.g.*, Mark M. Carhart, *On Persistence in Mutual Fund Performance*, 52 J. Fin. 57 (1997); Guillermo Baquero, On Hedge Fund Performance, Capital Flows and Investor Psychology 89–126 (2006).

84. Tversky & Kahneman, *supra* note 78; Bar-Hillel & Wagenaar, *supra* note 80.

85. Eric Gold. & Gordon Hester, *The Gambler's Fallacy and the Coin's Memory*, *in* Rationality and Social Responsibility: Essays in Honor of Robyn Mason Dawes 21 (Joachim I. Krueger ed., 2008).

86. *See, e.g.*, Charles Clotfelter & Phil Cook, *The "Gambler's Fallacy" in Lottery Play*, 39 Mgmt. Sci. 1521 (1993).

87. Howard Wainer & Harris L. Zwerling, *Evidence That Smaller Schools Do Not Improve Student Achievement*, 88 Phi Delta Kappan 300 (2006).

the mean are relatively rare, and they are usually followed by outcomes that are closer to the mean. To use one of Kahneman's examples,[88] imagine that trainees are praised following exceptionally good performances, and scolded following exceptionally bad ones. Since exceptional performances are, by their very nature, exceptional, they are likely to be followed by more ordinary ones. Trainers may thus incorrectly conclude that reproach is effective and praise is counterproductive.

5. Certainty Effect

According to expected utility theory, a certain increase or decrease in the probability of a given risk or prospect should have the same effect on people's utility, regardless of the baseline probability. However, as Maurice Allais pointed out in the early 1950s,[89] and as Kahneman and Tversky demonstrated in the late 1970s,[90] this premise is descriptively incorrect: people give greater weight to outcomes that are considered certain relative to outcomes that are only probable. Thus, most people are willing to pay much more to increase the probability of winning a moderate gain from 90 percent to 100 percent than they would to increase the probability from 40 percent to 50 percent. In the same vein, they would be willing to pay more to reduce the probability of a given risk from 5 percent to 0 percent than they would to reduce it from, say, 48 percent to 43 percent. Put differently, people display *diminishing sensitivity* to changes in probability as they move further away from the two boundaries: certainty and impossibility.[91] The more emotionally salient the relevant outcomes (such as an electric shock versus a monetary loss, or meeting and kissing one's favorite movie star versus a monetary gain), the more pronounced the certainty effect.[92] Various real-world behaviors have been associated with the certainty effect.[93]

6. Availability

Some of the heuristics and biases described above concern people's inferences from known probabilities. But how do people estimate probabilities in the first place? Drawing on substantial experimental findings, Tversky and Kahneman argued that people often determine the likelihood of events and the frequency of occurrences according to the ease of recalling

88. KAHNEMAN, *supra* note 14, at 175–76.

89. Maurice Allais, *Le comportement de l'homme rationnel devant le risque: Critique des postulats et axiomes de l'école Américaine,* 21 ECONOMETRICA 503 (1953).

90. Daniel Kahneman & Amos Tversky, *Prospect Theory: An Analysis of Decision under Risk,* 47 ECONOMETRICA 263, 265–67, 280–84 (1979).

91. Amos Tversky & Daniel Kahneman, *Advances in Prospect Theory: Cumulative Representation of Uncertainty,* 5 J. RISK & UNCERTAINTY 297, 303 (1992).

92. Yuval Rottenstreich & Christopher K. Hsee, *Money, Kisses, and Electric Shocks: On the Affective Psychology of Risk,* 12 PSYCHOL. SCI. 185 (2001).

93. Sean Hannon Williams, *Probability Errors: Overoptimism, Ambiguity Aversion, and the Certainty Effect, in* THE OXFORD HANDBOOK OF BEHAVIORAL ECONOMICS AND THE LAW, *supra* note 8, at 335, 348–49.

similar events or occurrences.[94] They dubbed this heuristic the *availability effect*.[95] For example, one may assess the frequency of divorce in society by recalling instances of divorce among one's acquaintances. As Tversky and Kahneman noted, availability is a useful clue for estimating frequency or probability, because there is usually a good correlation between the prevalence of occurrences and the ease of recalling them. Alas, since availability is influenced by additional factors besides frequency, reliance on this heuristic leads to predictable mistakes.[96]

The exact mechanism behind the availability effect—people's subjective experience of the ease or difficulty of recalling items, or their actual ability to recall those items within the allotted time—is unclear. While Tversky and Kahneman believed that it is the former, subsequent studies have indicated that at least sometimes it is the latter, and that the two may lead to different outcomes.[97] Since the availability heuristic is based on a recall of specific instances, people are more inclined to use it when they are primed to think at a more concrete and less abstract level.[98]

Among the factors affecting the availability of events or other items, one may mention their familiarity, vividness, and recency. In a classic experiment, subjects listened to a list of names, and were then asked to indicate whether the list contained more men or more women. The lists used in the experiment contained nineteen names of very famous figures of one gender, and twenty names of less famous figures of the other gender. Most subjects erroneously believed that the lists contained more people of the gender represented by more famous people, as those names were easier to recall.[99]

In another experiment, subjects who were given descriptions of symptoms of a disease that were easier to imagine assessed the likelihood that they would contract that disease higher than did subjects who had been given less easily imaginable descriptions of symptoms—especially when they were asked to actually imagine experiencing those symptoms. In fact, subjects who were asked to imagine difficult-to-imagine symptoms gave lower estimates of the likelihood of contracting the disease than subjects who received

94. Amos Tversky & Daniel Kahneman, *Availability: A Heuristic for Judging Frequency and Probability*, 4 Cognitive Psychol. 207 (1973) [hereinafter Tversky & Kahneman, *Availability*]. *See also* Amos Tversky & Daniel Kahneman, *Judgment under Uncertainty: Heuristics and Biases*, 185 Sci. 1124, 1127–28 (1974) [hereinafter Tversky & Kahneman, *Heuristics and Biases*].

95. In addition to availability in the sense of the ease of retrieving information from memory, Tversky and Kahneman discussed also *availability of construction*, namely the ease of generating examples of items that meet a certain criterion, such as words starting with the letter "K" versus words in which the third letter is "K." They showed that availability in that sense also affects judgments of frequency. Tversky & Kahneman, *Availability*, *supra* note 94, at 211–20.

96. Tversky & Kahneman, *Heuristics and Biases*, *supra* note 94, at 1127.

97. For an overview, see Norbert Schwartz & Leigh Ann Vaughn, *The Availability Heuristic Revisited: Ease of Recall and Content of Recall as Distinct Sources of Information*, *in* Heuristics and Biases, *supra* note 14, at 103.

98. João N. Braga, Mário B. Ferreira & Steven J. Sherman, *The Effects of Construal Level on Heuristic Reasoning: The Case of Representativeness and Availability*, 2 Decision 216 (2015). *See also* Cheryl Wakslak & Yaacov Trope, *The Effect of Construal Level on Subjective Probability Estimates*, 20 Psychol. Sci. 52 (2010).

99. Tversky & Kahneman, *Availability*, *supra* note 94, at 220–21.

the same descriptions, without any instruction to try and imagine them.[100] More vivid events are often more accessible also because they produce a greater emotional reaction. The availability effect is therefore sometimes connected to the *affect heuristic*—the automatic, negative or positive, affective response to stimuli that steers people's judgments and decision-making.[101]

It follows, then, that actually seeing an event, such as a car accident, has a greater impact on the estimated likelihood of car accidents than merely reading about the accident in a newspaper. However, an extensive and vivid media coverage of events may also significantly affect people's assessments of frequency (and severity). In this context, Timur Kuran and Cass Sunstein have called attention to the perils of *availability cascades*—namely, "a self-reinforcing process of collective belief formation, by which an expressed perception triggers a chain reaction that gives the perception [of] increasing plausibility through its rising availability in public discourse."[102] Thus, "availability entrepreneurs" may manipulate the content of public discourse in order to advance their agendas. The resulting mass pressure is likely to result in questionable regulation of particular risks, and a problematic increase in punishment of certain offenses.[103]

Of course, availability is not the only factor affecting assessments of likelihood,[104] and once subjects realize the perils of this heuristic, they can overcome its biasing effect to some extent.[105] Concomitantly, availability affects people's judgment and decision-making in other ways besides its impact on likelihood assessments. For example, it has been found that individual investors are considerably more likely to invest in attention-attracting stocks—"stocks in the news, stocks experiencing high abnormal trading volume, and stocks with extreme one-day returns"—simply because they do not even consider investing in most other stocks.[106]

100. Steven J. Sherman et al., *Imagining Can Heighten or Lower the Perceived Likelihood of Contracting a Disease: The Mediating Effect of Ease of Imagery,* 11 Personality & Soc. Psychol. Bull. 118 (1985).

101. Carmen Keller, Michael Siegrist & Heinz Gutscher, *The Role of the Affect and Availability Heuristics in Risk Communication,* 26 Risk Analysis 631 (2006). On the affect heuristic, see generally Paul Slovic et al., *The Affect Heuristic, in* Heuristics and Biases, *supra* note 14, at 397.

102. Timur Kuran & Cass R. Sunstein, *Availability Cascades and Risk Regulation,* 51 Stan. L. Rev. 683 (1999). For a specific example, see Russell Eisenman, *Belief That Drug Usage in the United States Is Increasing when It Is Really Decreasing: An Example of the Availability Heuristic,* 31 Bull. Psychonomic Soc'y 249 (1993).

103. Availability cascades may even bring about *moral panic*, namely the disproportionate public reaction to perceived threats to moral values, coupled with widespread anxiety and strong hostility toward the people involved in the threatening activities. *See* Erich Goode & Nachman Ben-Yehuda, Moral Panics: The Social Construction of Deviance (2nd ed. 2009).

104. Tilmann Betsch & Devika Pohl, *Tversky and Kahneman's Availability Approach to Frequency Judgment: A Critical Analysis, in* Etc. Frequency Processing and Cognition 109 (Peter Sedlmeier & Tilmann Betsch eds., 2002).

105. Diederik A. Stapel, Stephen D. Reicher & Russell Spears, *Contextual Determinants of Strategic Choice: Some Moderators of the Availability Choice,* 52 Eur. J. Soc. Psychol. 141 (1995).

106. Brad M. Barber & Terrance Odean, *All That Glitters: The Effect of Attention and News on the Buying Behavior of Individual and Institutional Investors,* 21 Rev. Fin. Stud. 785 (2008).

7. Subadditivity

In a seminal study, Baruch Fischhoff, Paul Slovic, and Sarah Lichtenstein presented subjects—both laypersons and experienced mechanics—with a list of possible causes for a car's failure to start, and asked them to assess the frequency of each cause.[107] In addition to several specific causes, the list included a residual category of "all other problems." They found that the subjects largely disregarded causes that were not explicitly mentioned. For example, when the list contained six specific causes and the residual category, the estimated frequency of each possible cause was considerably smaller than when the list contained only three of the specified causes in the unpruned list, and the residual category. The assessed likelihood of "all other problems" in the pruned list was much lower than the sum of frequencies of the removed causes plus the residual category in the unpruned list. In addition, they found that the assessed frequency of any given cause was higher once its constituent components were presented separately.

Both these phenomena may be explained by the availability heuristic: causes that had not been mentioned were less likely to come to the subjects' mind; hence they overestimated the frequency of the causes that had been brought to their attention. The former phenomenon also reflects what Kahneman has dubbed *what you see is all there is* (WYSIATI).[108] The second phenomenon, which was further examined in subsequent studies, is known as *subadditivity*.[109]

Subadditivity—the tendency to judge the probability of an event as smaller than the sum of probabilities of mutually exclusive and collectively exhaustive sub-events—is particularly troubling when the sum of the probabilities of the sub-events exceeds 1 (100 percent). In one study, subjects were asked to estimate the percentage of U.S. married couples with a given number of children—the number being the last digit of each subject's telephone number, that is, 0 through 9.[110] The sum of the means assigned by each group was 1.99, and the sum of the medians was 1.8. The sum of the mean probabilities for 0, 1, 2, and 3 children was 1.45.

Several studies have shown that subadditivity does not characterize complementary binary events, such as when subjects are asked to estimate either the percentage of U.S. married couples with "less than 3 children," or with "3 or more children."[111] Possibly,

107. Baruch Fischhoff, Paul Slovic & Sarah Lichtenstein, *Fault Trees: Sensitivity of Estimated Failure Probabilities to Problem Representation*, 4 J. EXPERIMENTAL PSYCHOL.: HUM. PERCEPTION & PERFORMANCE 330 (1978).

108. *See supra* p. 24.

109. Amos Tversky & Derek J. Koehler, *Support Theory: A Nonextensional Representation of Subjective Probability*, 101 PSYCHOL. REV. 547 (1994). Subadditivity in probability judgments is possibly one manifestation of a broader phenomenon whereby an increase in the number of assessed categories results in higher assessment of their value, attractiveness, and so forth. *See* Ian Bateman et al., *Does Part-Whole Bias Exist? An Experimental Investigation*, 107 ECON. J. 322 (1997); Avishalom Tor & Dotan Oliar, *Incentives to Create under a "Lifetime-Plus-Years" Copyright Duration: Lessons from a Behavioral Economic Analysis of* Eldred v. Ashcroft, 36 LOY. L.A. L. REV. 437, 463–76 (2002) (surveying the literature).

110. Tversky & Koehler, *supra* note 109, at 553.

111. *Id.* at 555, 557.

this is because in binary complementarity, people estimate the probability of an event relative to its complement. However, some studies report subadditivity in binary events as well,[112] and there is also evidence of *superadditivity* (sum of probabilities of complementary events smaller than 1) in such assessments under particular conditions.[113]

8. Hindsight Bias

At times, people are asked to assess the ex-ante probability of events in hindsight. In such instances, the available information—the fact that the outcome did in fact occur—could cause people to mis-assess the probability of the event taking place. More specifically, people may overestimate the initial probability of an event once they are aware that the event has occurred.

This *hindsight bias* (and its close relative, the "I knew it all along" bias) is one of the first phenomena to be systematically documented in the JDM literature. The initial contribution to the study of this bias was presented by Baruch Fischhoff.[114] In a classic study, Fischhoff asked his subjects to read a detailed description of the historical background leading to the nineteenth-century British-Gurka war, and then estimate the likelihood of four different potential outcomes of the event. Unbeknownst to the participants, they were randomly assigned to either a foresight or a hindsight condition. Participants in the foresight group were given no outcome information. Participants in the hindsight groups were informed that one of the potential outcomes was the "true" outcome of the event. The results of the experiment showed that subjects were unable to ignore outcome information. Once they were told that a certain outcome occurred, they tended to view it as significantly more likely to have happened.

The basic finding of Fischhoff's experiment has been replicated in dozens of studies.[115] These studies employed both the between-subject design described above, and a within-subject design focusing on peoples' assessment of the probability of an event before and after it occurred.[116] In addition, researchers have examined the effect of numerous variables such as subjects' level of expertise and age on the size of the bias.[117] Applied studies have

112. Lorraine Chen Idson et al., *The Relation between Probability and Evidence Judgment: An Extension of Support Theory*, 22 J. Risk & Uncertainty 227 (2001).

113. *Id.*; Laura Macchi, Daniel Osherson & David H. Krantz, *A Note on Superadditive Probability Judgment*, 106 Psychol. Rev. 210 (1999).

114. Baruch Fischhoff, *Hindsight ≠ Foresight: The Effect of Outcome Knowledge on Judgment under Uncertainty*, 1 J. Experimental Psychol.: Hum. Perception & Performance 288 (1975).

115. For reviews and meta-analyses, see Scott A. Hawkins & Reid Hastie, *Hindsight: Biased Judgments of Past Events after the Outcomes are Known*, 107 Psychol. Bull. 311 (1990); Jay J.J. Christensen-Szalanski & Cynthia Fobian Willham, *The Hindsight Bias: A Meta-analysis*, 48 Org. Behav. & Hum. Decision Processes 147 (1991); Rebecca L. Guilbault et al., *A Meta-Analysis of Research on Hindsight Bias*, 26 Basic & App. Soc. Psychol. 103 (2004); Neal J. Roese & Kathleen D. Vohs, *Hindsight Bias*, 7 Persp. Psychol. Sci. 411 (2012).

116. *See e.g.*, Baruch Fischhoff & Ruth Beyth, *"I Knew It Would Happen" Remembered Probabilities of Once-Future Things*, 13 Org. Behav. & Hum. Performance 1 (1975).

117. *See* Dustin P. Calvillo & Abraham M. Rutchick, *Domain Knowledge and Hindsight Bias among Poker Players*, 27 J. Behav. Decision Making 259 (2014); Daniel M. Bernstein et al., *Hindsight Bias from 3 to 95 Years of Age*, 37 J. Experimental Psychol.: Learning, Memory & Cognition 378 (2011).

documented the existence of the hindsight bias in specific areas such as auditing, medicine, and the law.[118] As one review concluded, "results from many experiments converge on the conclusion that outcome feedback sharply inhibits thinking about alternatives to the reported outcome."[119]

While the existence of the hindsight bias is undisputed, researchers have highlighted distinct underlying processes that might explain it. One group of explanations focuses on the cognitive aspects of the bias.[120] According to this perspective, people search their memories for old beliefs that are confirmed by the outcome information. Another cluster of explanations focuses on motivational aspects of the bias.[121] Since people want to perceive themselves in a favorable light, and the ability to predict events precisely is praiseworthy, they tend to overstate their ability to do so.

The hindsight bias exhibits strong resilience in the face of different debiasing efforts, such as adding incentives for accuracy, and drawing participants' attention to it.[122] The general picture emerging from a meta-analysis of this point is that "manipulations to reduce hindsight bias did not result in significantly smaller effect sizes . . . than studies in which no manipulations to increase or reduce hindsight bias were included."[123] Nonetheless, one debiasing technique that has proven relatively effective is the *consider-the-opposite* strategy—namely, encouraging people to actively think about counterfactual scenarios that do not involve the outcome that had materialized. As further described below, Hal Arkes and his colleagues have demonstrated the effectiveness of the strategy in the context of evaluating medical decisions.[124]

9. Ambiguity Aversion

Thus far we have examined how people estimate probabilities and how they draw inferences from known probabilities. We now turn to yet another dimension of people's attitude to risk and uncertainty. The distinction between risk (or *measurable uncertainty*)—a situation in which outcomes are not certain, but the probabilities of the possible outcomes are known—and uncertainty (or *unmeasurable uncertainty*)—a situation in which not only the outcomes, but also their probabilities, are unknown—was introduced by Frank

118. *See e.g.*, John C. Anderson, D. Jordan Lowe, Philip M.J. Reckers, *Evaluation of Auditor Decisions; Hindsight Bias Effects and the Expectation Gap*, 14 J. Econ. Psychol. 711 (1993) (auditing); Hal R. Arkes et al., *Eliminating the Hindsight Bias*, 73 J. App. Psychol. 305 (1988) (medicine); Kim A. Kamin & Jeffrey J. Rachlinski, *Ex Post ≠ Ex Ante: Determining Liability in Hindsight*, 19 Law & Hum. Behav. 89 (1995) (law).

119. Hawkins & Hastie, *supra* note 115, at 316.

120. *See* Roese & Vohs, *supra* note 115, at 413–15.

121. *See id.* at 415–16.

122. *See, e.g.*, Baruch Fischhoff, *Perceived Informativeness of Facts*, 3 J. Experimental Psychol.: Hum. Perception & Performance 349, 354–6 (1977) (debiasing instructions); Wolfgang Hell et al., *Hindsight Bias: An Interaction of Automatic and Motivational Factors?*, 16 Memory & Cognition 533 (1988) (financial incentives).

123. Guilbault et al., *supra* note 115, at 111.

124. *See* Arkes et al., *supra* note 118; *infra* pp. 135–36.

Knight in 1921.[125] Forty years later, Daniel Ellsberg demonstrated people's aversion to uncertainty—commonly dubbed the *ambiguity aversion*—through two famous thought experiments demonstrating what is now known as the *Ellsberg paradox*.[126]

Imagine there are two urns, each containing red and black balls, from which a single ball is drawn at random. It is known that in one of them there are exactly 50 red balls and 50 black ones—while the other also contains 100 balls, but at an unknown ratio of red and black balls. If you draw a red ball, you win a prize. Which urn would you prefer to draw from? Most people prefer to draw a ball from the first urn—the one with the known probabilities. Arguably, people express this preference out of suspicion that the person in charge of the game has placed a small number of red balls (or perhaps none at all) in the second urn, to minimize or avoid having to award the prize. Interestingly, however, most people persist in preferring to draw from the urn with the known probabilities, even if, immediately after making their first choice, they are offered a similar prize if they draw a *black* ball from one of the two urns. Thus, it cannot be said that people prefer the first urn because they suspect that there are fewer red—or black—balls in the other urn.

Ambiguity may have various sources. It may, for example, result from missing information about the credibility of one's sources of information, or from a narrow evidentiary basis for determining the distribution of possible outcomes. There is some evidence that people's ambiguity aversion depends on its source. Specifically, it has been shown that insurance professionals charged a higher "ambiguity premium" when ambiguity resulted from disagreement among experts about the probability of certain risks, than from other sources (thus supporting a *conflict aversion* hypothesis).[127] Ambiguity may also come in varying degrees. Thus, rather than choosing between an urn with 50 red balls and 50 black ones, and an urn in which there may be any number of red balls from 0 to 100, the number of red balls in the latter urn may be somewhere between 20 and 80, or between 40 and 60, etc. More generally, one may lack information about the distribution of possible outcomes, but know the exact distribution of conceivable distributions of the outcomes—or may lack information even about the distribution of possible distributions.[128]

Numerous experimental studies have confirmed that people tend to be ambiguity-averse, and are willing to pay considerable sums of money to avoid ambiguity. Increasing the range of probabilities increases ambiguity aversion. Some studies have found that ambiguity aversion is weaker, or even eliminated or reversed, with regard to losses. Indeed, there is some evidence of a fourfold pattern of ambiguity attitudes, with ambiguity aversion for high-likelihood and ambiguity seeking for low-likelihood gain events, and the opposite

125. FRANK H. KNIGHT, RISK, UNCERTAINTY AND PROFIT (1921).

126. Daniel Ellsberg, *Risk, Ambiguity, and the Savage Axioms*. 75 Q.J. ECON. 643 (1961).

127. Laure Cabantous, *Ambiguity Aversion in the Field of Insurance: Insurers Attitude to Imprecise and Conflicting Probability Estimates*, 62 THEORY & DECISION 219 (2007). On source-dependence in ambiguity aversion, see also Stefan T. Trautmann & Gijs van de Kuilen, *Ambiguity Attitudes*, *in* WILEY BLACKWELL HANDBOOK, *supra* note 2, at 89, 94–96, 106–07.

128. Colin Camerer & Martin Weber, *Recent Developments in Modeling Preferences: Uncertainty and Ambiguity*, 5 J. RISK & UNCERTAINTY 325, 330–32 (1992).

pattern for losses. Some studies found slightly weaker ambiguity aversion for small payoffs than for large ones. Conflicting results have been obtained in studies of the correlation between individuals' risk aversion and their attitude to ambiguity.[129] It was found that observation by peers increases ambiguity aversion, but that group decision-making—especially when groups consist of both ambiguity-neutral members and members who are either ambiguity-averse or ambiguity-seeking—increases ambiguity neutrality.[130] The above findings were generally, albeit not invariably, replicated in studies of particular activities, outside of the laboratory, such as buying and selling insurance, and marketing.[131]

While risk aversion is conventionally explained by the diminishing marginal utility of resources, there is no obvious explanation for ambiguity aversion. One explanation views ambiguity aversion as an overgeneralization of the rule that it is preferable to avoid decisions where there is insufficient information—especially when this information is known to exist or may become available in the future.[132] A complementary explanation, offered by Chip Heath and Amos Tversky, draws on the finding that people are less ambiguity-averse the more they feel knowledgeable about the relevant issue.[133] According to this explanation, people consider not only the expected payoffs of a bet, but also the credit or blame associated with the outcome. Since they value the expected credit for a successful decision within their area of expertise—while believing that a failure might be attributed to chance—they are less reluctant to make decisions in ambiguous environments within their area of expertise.[134]

Ambiguity aversion poses a challenge to expected utility theory (as well as to Leonard Savage's *subjective expected utility theory*)[135] as a descriptive theory of human decision-making, because in the real world, but for games of chance, the exact probabilities of uncertain events are rarely known with much precision. It does not follow, however, that ambiguity aversion is irrational.[136] For example, when a decision-maker faces more than one possible distribution of probabilities, she may use the *maximin choice rule*, and choose the option that maximizes the minimum expected utility over those distributions. In Ellsberg's urn example discussed above, the decision-maker would thus opt for the first

129. For a review of these and additional experimental findings, see *id.* at 332–41; Trautmann & van de Kuilen, *supra* note 127, at 104–06.

130. Trautmann & van de Kuilen, *supra* note 127, at 102–03.

131. Camerer & Weber, *supra* note 128, at 353–60; Trautmann & van de Kuilen, *supra* note 127, at 107–09.

132. Deborah Frisch & Jonathan Baron, *Ambiguity and Rationality*, 1 J. Behav. Decision Making 149 (1988).

133. Chip Heath & Amos Tversky, *Preference and Belief: Ambiguity and Competence in Choice under Uncertainty*, 4 J. Risk & Uncertainty 5 (1991).

134. Indirect support for this conjecture may be found in a subsequent study that showed that ambiguity aversion is present when people face a choice between risky and ambiguous bets, or when they compare themselves with more knowledgeable individuals, but not when such comparisons are unavailable. *See* Craig R. Fox & Amos Tversky, *Ambiguity Aversion and Comparative Ignorance*, 110 Q.J. Econ. 585 (1995).

135. Leonard J. Savage, The Foundations of Statistics (1954).

136. *Cf.* Frisch & Baron, *supra* note 132.

urn, because it guarantees a 50 percent probability of winning, whereas in the other urn the probability may be much higher (up to 100 percent), but also much lower (including 0 percent).[137] Various other suggestions have been made to formally model ambiguity aversion—some of which fit the available data on this phenomenon more than others.[138] The finding that ambiguity aversion is largely immune to debiasing by explanations[139] lends support for the view that it is not akin to an arithmetic or logical error. Be that as it may, a descriptive theory of human decision-making should take this phenomenon into account.

C. Prospect Theory and Related Issues

In 1979, Kahneman and Tversky proposed *prospect theory* as a descriptive theory of people's decisions under risk.[140] Almost forty years later, it is still the most ambitious and influential behavioral theory. This section describes prospect theory in general (Subsection 1), as well as key elements of it whose significance extends beyond prospect theory: the role of emotions (Subsection 2), reference-dependence (Subsection 3), and framing effects (Subsection 4). The section then describes several phenomena that have been associated with elements of prospect theory: *status quo and omission biases*, the *endowment effect*, and *sunk costs and escalation of commitment* (Subsections 5, 6, and 7, respectively).

1. General

Prospect theory consists of several elements, all of which deviate from the tenets of expected utility theory. Most important, prospect theory posits that people ordinarily perceive outcomes as gains and losses, rather than as final states of wealth or welfare. Gains and losses are defined in relation to some reference point. The value function is normally concave for gains (implying risk aversion) and convex for losses (reflecting risk-seeking). Thus, most people would prefer to receive $100 than take part in a gamble in which they are equally likely to receive either $200 or nothing. However, most people would prefer participating in a gamble in which they are equally likely to lose $200 or nothing, over paying a sum of $100 with certainty. To put it in another way, the concavity of the value function in the domain of gains and its convexity in the domain of losses reflect *diminishing sensitivity*: the further away a certain gain or a loss is from the reference point, the smaller its effect on one's utility.[141]

137. Itzhak Gilboa & David Schmeidler, *Maxmin Expected Utility with Non-unique Prior,* 18 J. MATHEMATICAL ECON. 141 (1989).

138. Camerer & Weber, *supra* note 128, at 341–53.

139. *See, e.g.*, Paul Slovic & Amos Tversky, *Who Accepts Savage's Axiom*? 19 BEHAV. SCI. 368 (1974).

140. Kahneman & Tversky, *supra* note 90.

141. Tversky & Kahneman, *supra* note 91, at 303. For a review of the literature on risk attitude under prospect theory, see Craig R. Fox, Carsten Erner & Daniel J. Walters, *Decision under Risk: From the Field to the Laboratory and Back, in* WILEY BLACKWELL HANDBOOK, *supra* note 2, at 41. *See also infra* pp. 85–86.

According to prospect theory, not only does the attitude to risk-taking differ between the domain of gains and the domain of losses, but the value function is also generally steeper for losses than for gains. This means that the disutility generated by a loss is greater than the utility produced by a similar gain. Since losses loom larger than gains, people are generally loss-averse. The subjective value function therefore has a "kink" at the reference point. Tversky and Kahneman estimated that monetary losses loom larger than gains by a factor of 2.25.[142] A meta-analysis of forty-five studies of the related phenomenon of endowment effect (discussed below) found that the median ratio between people's willingness to pay (WTP) for an item they don't yet have and their willingness to accept (WTA) to part with a similar item is 1:2.6 (mean 1:7.17).[143] A subsequent meta-analysis of 164 experiments of the endowment effect found that the median ratio between WTP and WTA is 1:2.9 (with very substantial variation).[144]

Prospect theory also posits that people's risk aversion in the domain of gains, and risk-seeking in the domain of losses, are reversed for low-probability gains and losses.[145] Were it not for this reversal, prospect theory would be incompatible with the fact that many people buy insurance against low-probability risks, and lottery tickets. Finally, prospect theory postulates that the subjective weighing of probabilities systematically deviates from the objective probabilities, exhibiting the certainty effect discussed above.[146] The key elements of prospect theory—what Kahneman hailed as "the core idea of prospect theory"—are, however, reference-dependence (the notion that "the value function is kinked at the reference point") and loss aversion.[147]

Prospect theory has proven useful in explaining various real-world phenomena, such as the so-called *equity premium puzzle*,[148] the prevalence of contingent-fee arrangements among plaintiffs and its rarity among defendants,[149] and more.[150] To use the first example, the demand for Treasury bills and other bonds, whose long-term returns are much smaller than that of stocks, is incompatible with standard notions of risk aversion. However, it is perfectly compatible with the notion of loss aversion, assuming investors evaluate their

142. *Id.* at 311.

143. John K. Horowitz & Kenneth E. McConnell, *A Review of WTA/WTP Studies,* 44 J. Envtl. Econ. & Mgmt. 426 (2002). On the endowment effect, see *infra* pp. 50–56.

144. Serdar Sayman & Ayşe Öncüler, *Effects of Study Design Characteristics on the WTA-WTP Disparity: A Meta Analytical Framework,* 26 J. Econ. Psychol. 289, 300, 302 (2005).

145. Tversky & Kahneman, *supra* note 91, at 306; Chris Guthrie, *Framing Frivolous Litigation: A Psychological Theory,* 67 U. Chi. L. Rev. 163 (2000).

146. *See supra* p. 34.

147. Daniel Kahneman, *Maps of Bounded Rationality: Psychology for Behavioral Economists,* 93 Am. Econ. Rev. 1449, 1457 (2003).

148. Shlomo Benartzi & Richard H. Thaler, *Myopic Loss Aversion and the Equity Premium Puzzle,* 110 Q.J. Econ. 73 (1995).

149. *See infra* pp. 510–12.

150. Colin F. Camerer, *Prospect Theory in the Wild: Evidence from the Field, in* Choices, Values, and Frames 288 (Daniel Kahneman & Amos Tversky eds., 2000); Stefano DellaVigna, *Psychology and Economics: Evidence from the Field,* 47 J. Econ. Literature 315, 324–36 (2009); Barberis, *supra* note 5.

portfolios on an annual basis and are willing to forgo considerable expected gains to avoid even a small risk of loss.

Prospect theory has been the subject of considerable criticism. Some studies have challenged the experimental findings underlying the theory, and others have questioned the generality of the notions of reference-dependence and loss aversion. Other studies have offered alternative explanations for the main features of prospect theory.[151] However, the overall picture emerging from hundreds of studies is clear: people's preferences, choices, and judgments do generally depend on the perceived reference point, and exhibit loss aversion and diminishing sensitivity to marginal gains and losses. In what follows, we focus on loss aversion, which carries the broadest implications for legal analysis.[152]

2. Loss Aversion and Emotions

Many studies have pointed to the existence of a *negativity bias*—namely the phenomenon whereby negative experiences have a greater impact on individuals than positive ones.[153] For example, negative social interactions affect people's well-being to a greater extent than positive ones.[154] Studies of physiological arousal—as measured by autonomic activation indicators, such as pupil dilation and increased heart rate—similarly demonstrated that negative events or outcomes yield greater arousal than positive ones.[155]

Gains and losses are closely connected to emotions of pleasure and pain.[156] In fact, neurological studies using fMRI have demonstrated that decision-making in general, and decisions characterized by loss aversion in particular, involve regions in the brain, such as the amygdala, which are known to be associated with emotions.[157] Similarly, it has been

151. For overviews of critiques, replies, and alternative theories, see Fox, Erner & Walters, *supra* note 141, at 59–67; EYAL ZAMIR, LAW, PSYCHOLOGY, AND MORALITY 11–13 (2015).

152. *See also infra* pp. 187–97. For further refinements of prospect theory's claims about people's attitude to risk and uncertainty, and competing accounts of these issues, see, e.g., Tversky & Kahneman, *supra* note 91; Amos Tversky & Craig R. Fox, *Weighing Risk and Uncertainty,* 102 PSYCHOL. REV. 269 (1995); Michael H. Birnbaum & Alfredo Chavez, *Tests of Theories of Decision Making: Violations of Branch Independence and Distribution Independence,* 71 ORG. BEHAV. & HUM. DECISION PROCESSES 161 (1997); Charles A. Holt & Susan K. Laury, *Risk Aversion and Incentive Effects,* 92 AM. ECON. REV. 1644 (2002); BARON, *supra* note 47, at 271–74. On the neural basis of these phenomena, see, e.g., Joshua A. Weller et al., *Neural Correlates of Adaptive Decision Making for Risky Gains and Losses,* 18 PSYCHOL. SCI. 958 (2007). Finally, on the evolutionary roots and neural basis of loss aversion and related phenomena, see ZAMIR, *supra* note 151, at 42–46.

153. *See, e.g.,* Roy F. Baumeister et al., *Bad Is Stronger than Good,* 5 REV. GENERAL PSYCHOL. 323 (2001); Paul Rozin & Edward B. Royzman, *Negativity Bias, Negativity Dominance, and Contagion,* 5 PERSONALITY & SOC. PSYCHOL. REV. 296 (2001).

154. Karen S. Rook, *The Negative Side of Social Interaction: Impact on Psychological Well-Being,* 46 J. PERSONALITY & SOC. PSYCHOL. 1097 (1984).

155. *See, e.g.,* Guy Hochman & Eldad Yechiam, *Loss Aversion in the Eye and in the Heart: The Autonomic Nervous System's Responses to Losses,* 24 J. BEHAV. DECISION MAKING 140 (2011).

156. Kahneman & Tversky, *supra* note 90, at 279.

157. *See, e.g.,* Peter Sokol-Hessner et al., *Emotion Regulation Reduces Loss Aversion and Decreases Amygdala Responses to Losses,* 8 SOC. COGNITIVE & AFFECTIVE NEUROSCI. 341 (2013).

found that amygdala damage eliminates monetary loss aversion,[158] and that deficient ability to process emotional information is correlated with reduced loss aversion in both risky and riskless decisions.[159]

3. Reference-Dependence

Prospect theory posits that the benchmark with reference to which people perceive outcomes as gains or losses depends on how they frame the scenario or the choice facing them. Ordinarily, people take the status quo as the reference point, and view changes from this point as either gains or losses. It has been plausibly argued, however, that this assumption pertains only, or primarily, when people expect the status quo to be maintained. When expectations differ from the status quo, using those expectations as the reference point may yield better explanations and predictions of people's behavior.[160] People's perception of the reference point is also influenced by the status of other people. For example, when an employee receives a smaller salary raise than everyone else in a workplace, she may view it as a loss—even though it has improved her position in absolute terms.[161]

A person's reference point may change in dynamic situations. Most research suggests that people quickly adjust their reference point after making gains (in relation to their initial position), but are much more reluctant to do so after incurring losses.[162] In the long run, people's subjective feeling adapts even to extreme changes, such as winning large sums of money in a lottery, or losing a limb in an accident.[163] A considerable body of research has studied situations where there is more than one plausible reference point. Basically, in such cases, people appear not to compare outcomes with a single reference point that is a weighted composite of the competing ones. In some cases there is a single dominant reference point; in others, people learn that it is possible to view the same outcome as either a gain or a loss, and their decisions may be affected by the relative strength of each framing.[164]

158. Benedetto De Martino, Colin F. Camerer & Ralph Adolphs, *Amygdala Damage Eliminates Monetary Loss Aversion*, 107 Proced. Nat'l Acad. Sci. USA 3788 (2010).

159. Peter A. Bibby & Eamonn Ferguson, *The Ability to Process Emotional Information Predicts Loss Aversion*, 51 Personality & Individual Differences 263 (2011).

160. *See, e.g.*, Botond Köszegi & Matthew Rabin, *Reference-Dependent Risk Attitude*, 97 Am. Econ. Rev. 1047 (2007); Johannes Abeler et al., *Reference Points and Effort Provision*, 101 Am. Econ. Rev. 470 (2011).

161. Daniel Kahneman & Amos Tversky, *Choices, Values, and Frames*, 39 Am. Psychologist 341, 349 (1984).

162. *See, e.g.*, Hal R. Arkes et al., *Reference Point Adaptation: Tests in the Domain of Security Trading*, 105 Org. Behav. & Hum. Decision Processes 67 (2008); Daniel Kahneman, Jack L. Knetsch & Richard H. Thaler, *Experimental Tests of the Endowment Effect and the Coase Theorem*, 98 J. Pol. Econ. 1325 (1990).

163. Philip Brickman, Dan Coates & Ronnie Janoff-Bulman, *Lottery Winners and Accident Victims: Is Happiness Relative?*, 36 J. Personality & Soc. Psychol. 917 (1978); Jason Riis et al., *Ignorance of Hedonic Adaptation to Hemodialysis: A Study Using Ecological Momentary Assessment*, 134 J. Experimental Psychol.: General 3 (2005). *See also infra* pp. 343–48.

164. *See generally* Zamir, *supra* 151, at 9–10.

People sometimes consciously create a reference point by setting a goal for themselves. Perceiving one's goal as the reference point is instrumental to achieving it. Once a goal is set, it divides outcomes into regions of success and failure. Since outcomes that are worse than the reference point yield a greater hedonic impact, the mere adoption of a goal provides a stronger motivation to attain it.[165] Prospect theory provides an explanation for another well-documented finding of the psychological goal literature: the fact that people make a greater effort to achieve a goal the closer they are to doing so. This phenomenon is compatible with the convexity of the value function for losses.[166]

Reference-dependence is not unique to judgments and decision-making in risky and riskless environments. This phenomenon and related issues are further discussed below.[167]

4. Framing Effects

A key notion associated with prospect theory, but whose potential implications go far beyond this theory, is framing of decisions, or the *framing effect*. In their seminal study that introduced this effect, Tversky and Kahneman presented subjects with one of two problems.[168] Problem 1 read as follows:

> Imagine that the U.S. is preparing for the outbreak of an unusual Asian disease, which is expected to kill 600 people. Two alternative programs to combat the disease have been proposed. Assume that the exact scientific estimate of the consequences of the programs are as follows:
>
> If Program A is adopted, 200 people will be saved.
>
> If Program B is adopted, there is 1/3 probability that 600 people will be saved and 2/3 probability that no people will be saved.
>
> Which of the two programs would you favor?

In Problem 2, the outcomes of the alternative programs were described as follows:

> If Program C is adopted, 400 people will die.
>
> If Program D is adopted, there is 1/3 probability that nobody will die and 2/3 probability that 600 people will die.
>
> Which of the two programs would you favor?

165. Chip Heath, Richard P. Larrick & George Wu, *Goals as Reference Points*, 38 COGNITIVE PSYCHOL. 79 (1999); Russell Korobkin, *Aspirations and Settlement*, 88 CORNELL L. REV. 1, 44–48 (2002); Abeler et al., *supra* note 160.

166. Excessively high rewards may, however, produce the opposite effect. *See* Heath, Larrick & Wu, *supra* note 165, at 89–93; Vikram S. Chib et al., *Neural Mechanisms Underlying Paradoxical Performance for Monetary Incentives Are Driven by Loss Aversion*, 74 NEURON 582 (2012).

167. *See infra* pp. 76–86.

168. Amos Tversky & Daniel Kahneman, *The Framing of Decisions and the Psychology of Choice*, 211 SCI. 453, 453 (1981).

Evidently, the only difference between the two problems was that in Problem 1 the outcomes were framed as possible gains (survival), while in Problem 2 as possible losses (death). Consistent with prospect theory, 72 percent of the respondents in Problem 1 opted for the less risky Program (A), while in Problem 2, 78 percent favored the riskier Program (D).

The Asian disease problem is but one among several paradigms in the vast literature on framing effects.[169] It exemplifies what Irwin Levin and his coauthors have labeled *risky choice framing*—namely, the effect of different descriptions of the same outcomes on people's risk attitude.[170] Another type of framing effect is *goal framing*.[171] While in risky choice framing, different frames may induce opposite choices, in goal framing the various frames are all aimed at promoting a single behavior or end result. To that end, people's attention is drawn either to the expected benefits of the pertinent behavior/result (a positive framing) or to the expected costs that it would avoid (a negative framing). For example, to promote breast self-examination, women may be presented with information highlighting the positive consequences of conducting the examination, or the negative consequences of not conducting it. Consistent with loss aversion, some studies have demonstrated that negative framings are more effective than positive ones; but other studies found no such effect.[172]

Finally, the simplest paradigm is *attribute framing*. Unlike the previous two, it does not involve a choice between two options, or even an attempt to induce a single behavior, but simply an assessment of the quality or desirability of an object.[173] For example, in one study, subjects rated ground beef as better tasting and less greasy when it was labeled "75% lean" than when it was labeled "25% fat."[174]

In a meta-analysis of 136 published studies from which 230 effect sizes were calculated, Anton Kühberger has found that the framing effect does exist, but its magnitude is small to moderate.[175] As he concludes, "[d]iverse operational, methodical and task-specific features

169. For various typologies of these paradigms, see Anton Kühberger, *The Influence of Framing on Risky Decisions: A Meta-analysis*, 75 Org. Behav. & Hum. Decision Processes 23 (1998); Irwin P. Levin, Sandra L. Schneider & Gary J. Gaeth, *All Frames Are Not Created Equal: A Typology and Critical Analysis of Framing Effects*, 76 Org. Behav. & Hum. Decision Processes 149 (1998).

170. Levin, Schneider & Gaeth, *supra* note 169, at 152–58.

171. *Id.* at 167–78.

172. Beth E. Meyerowitz & Shelly Chaiken, *The Effect of Message Framing on Breast Self-Examination Attitudes, Intentions, and Behavior*, 52 J. Personality & Soc. Psychol. 500 (1987) (finding an effect); Karen M. Lalor & B. Jo Hailey, *The Effects of Message Framing and Feelings of Susceptibility to Breast Cancer on Reported Frequency of Breast Self-Examination*, 10 Int'l Q. Community Health Educ. 183 (1990) (failing to replicate Meyerowitz and Chaiken's results). For a literature review, see Levin, Schneider & Gaeth, *supra* note 169, at 167–78; Kühberger, *supra* note 169, at 32–33, 37–38 (concluding, on the basis of meta-analysis of thirteen studies using the *message compliance design*— the equivalent of *goal framing*—that this design does not generally produce a framing effect).

173. Levin, Schneider & Gaeth, *supra* note 169, at 158–67.

174. Irwin P. Levin & Gary J. Gaeth, *How Consumers Are Affected by the Framing of Attribute Information Before and After Consuming the Product*, 15 J. Consumer Res. 374 (1988).

175. Kühberger, *supra* note 169, at 35–36, 42.

make the body of data heterogeneous to a degree that makes it impossible to speak of 'the framing effect.' Framing appears in different clothes, some effective in producing an effect and some ineffective."[176] Other reviews of the literature have reached similar conclusions.[177]

The picture does not become clearer when turning from the laboratory to the real world. Some studies—particularly those dealing with default arrangements in specific contexts—point to robust framing effects.[178] The prevalent use of various kinds of framing techniques in marketing similarly indicates that marketers believe in the effectiveness of these techniques.[179] At the same time, some studies have found no framing effects in the real world;[180] and it is difficult to assess the robustness and generality of the effect outside of the laboratory, since in the laboratory decisions are often made in isolation from social contact and context.[181] It appears that "[m]any simple choice problems are so well-structured—experimentally or naturally—that the reference point is for all practical purposes determined by the situation."[182]

Having discussed the main features of prospect theory in general, we now turn to three more specific phenomena that have been associated with it: the status quo and omission biases, the endowment effect, and sunk costs (also known as escalation of commitment).

5. Status Quo and Omission Biases

The *status quo bias* refers to the phenomenon that, other things being equal, people tend to stick to the state of affairs they perceive as the status quo rather than opting for an alternative one.[183] Usually, changing the status quo requires an action, while maintaining the status quo involves a mere omission. Hence, the tendency to keep the status quo and the tendency to prefer omission to commission (commonly dubbed the *omission bias*) are confounded. However, there is experimental evidence that these biases also exist separately, and that their effects are additive.[184] When the two biases pull in opposite directions—as when inaction is expected to result in a change, while maintaining the status quo requires

176. *Id.*

177. Lewis Petrinovich & Patricia O'Neill, *Influence of Wording and Framing Effects on Moral Intuitions,* 17 Ethology & Sociobiology 145, 162–64 (1996); Levin, Schneider & Gaeth, *supra* note 169, at 153, 174.

178. *See infra* pp. 179–82, 249–52, 427–28.

179. *See infra* pp. 286–87, 292–96.

180. *See, e.g.*, Laura A. Siminoff & John H. Fetting, *Effects of Outcome Framing on Treatment Decisions in the Real World: Impact of Framing on Adjuvant Breast Cancer Decisions,* 9 Med. Decision Making 262 (1989); Annette M. O'Connor, Ross A. Penne & Robert E. Dales, *Framing Effects on Expectations, Decisions, and Side Effects Experienced: The Case of Influenza Immunization,* 49 J. Clinical Epidemiology 1271 (1996) (describing the results of a field experiment).

181. James N. Druckman, *Using Credible Advice to Overcome Framing Effects,* 17 J.L. Econ. & Org. 62 (2001).

182. Jack S. Levy, *Applications of Prospect Theory to Political Science,* 135 Synthese 215, 218 (2003).

183. William Samuelson & Richard Zeckhouser, *Status Quo Bias in Decision Making,* 1 J. Risk & Uncertainty 7 (1988); Daniel Kahneman, Jack L. Knetsch & Richard H. Thaler, *The Endowment Effect, Loss Aversion, and Status Quo Bias,* 5 J. Econ. Persp. 193, 197–99 (1991).

184. Maurice Schweitzer, *Disentangling Status Quo and Omission Effects: An Experimental Analysis,* 58 Org. Behav. & Hum. Decision Processes 457 (1994).

an action—there is evidence that subjects prefer inaction.[185] Putting aside such exceptional cases, we shall mostly discuss the status quo and omission biases together.

To illustrate, in one experiment, William Samuelson and Richard Zeckhouser asked subjects to imagine that they had inherited a large sum of money and had to choose between several investment options. In the neutral version, all options were presented on an equal footing. In the status quo version, subjects were asked to imagine that they had inherited a portfolio of cash and securities and had to decide whether to retain this portfolio or switch to an alternative one. No matter which option was presented as the status quo, the probability that it would be chosen increased significantly compared with the alternative options and with the probability that it would be chosen in the neutral version. The more options included in the choice set, the stronger was the relative bias in favor of the status quo.[186] The status quo/omission bias has been experimentally demonstrated in other hypothetical choice tasks, and with different types of subjects.

Several natural experiments have also provided strong empirical support for the status quo/omission bias. For example, the rate of employee participation in a retirement savings plan at a large U.S. corporation was studied before and after a change in the default.[187] Before the change, employees were required to affirmatively elect participation. After the change, new employees were automatically enrolled in the plan unless they opted out of it. The change of default resulted in a dramatic increase in retirement plan participation. Comparable data exists in relation to postmortem organ donations. Within the European Union, in some countries people are organ donors unless they register not to be, whereas in others no one is an organ donor without registering to be one. The donation rate in most presumed-consent countries is close to 100 percent, while in the explicit-consent countries it ranges from 4 percent to 27 percent.[188] Experimental studies have indicated that this difference is most plausibly a product of the status quo/omission bias.[189]

A common explanation for the status quo/omission bias is loss aversion.[190] When departing from the status quo involves both advantages and disadvantages, people are inclined to avoid such a departure, because the disadvantages likely loom larger than the advantages. For the same reason, when there is uncertainty about whether departing from the status quo would result in gains or losses, people are inclined to avoid such a departure.

185. Ilana Ritov & Jonathan Baron, *Status-Quo and Omission Biases*, 5 J. RISK & UNCERTAINTY 49 (1992).

186. Samuelson & Zeckhouser, *supra* note 183, at 12–21. For an empirical support of this phenomenon, see Alexander Kempf & Stefan Ruenzi, *Status Quo Bias and the Number of Alternatives: An Empirical Illustration from the Mutual Fund Industry*, 7 J. BEHAV. FIN. 204 (2006).

187. Brigitte Madrian & Dennis Shea, *The Power of Suggestion: Inertia in 401(k) Participation and Savings Behavior*, 66 Q.J. ECON. 1149 (2001). *See also infra* p. 180.

188. Eric J. Johnson & Daniel Goldstein, *Do Defaults Save Lives?*, 302 SCI. 1338 (2003).

189. *Id.*; Shai Davidai, Thomas Gilovich & Lee D. Ross, *The Meaning of Default Options for Potential Organ Donors*, 109 PROC. NAT'L ACAD. SCI. USA 15201 (2012). *See also infra* pp. 180–81.

190. *See, e.g.*, Kahneman, Knetsch & Thaler, *supra* note 183, at 197–99; Jonathan Baron & Ilana Ritov, *Reference Points and Omission Bias*, 59 ORG. BEHAV. & HUM. DECISION PROCESSES 475, 479–80 (1994); Avital Moshinsky & Maya Bar-Hillel, *Status Quo Label Bias*, 28 SOC. COGNITION 191 (2010).

However, loss aversion is not the only explanation for the tendency to maintain the status quo and to prefer inaction to action. To begin with, when people have no clear preference between the status quo and an alternative option, and departing from the status quo entails transaction or decision costs, doing nothing (hence keeping the status quo) seems sensible. However—unless the choice is between near-identical options—this explanation is problematic when decision and transaction costs are trivial. The incompleteness of this explanation has been further demonstrated by carefully designed experiments, in which subjects were not asked to choose between policies but merely to rate them (thus avoiding decision costs). The results showed that merely labeling a policy as the status quo enhanced its likeability by providing a biased viewpoint from which its relative pros and cons were evaluated.[191]

The very fact that a certain state of the world already exists may cause people to favor it: "what is, is good."[192] People tend to rationalize and legitimize the existing state of affairs.[193] However, these explanations were directly ruled out in the context of rating competing policies, where subjects rated the policies described as the status quo more highly than alternative ones, even though they did not believe that the very fact that a policy is in force attests to its merit.[194]

People are also viewed as bearing a greater moral responsibility for harmful outcomes they actively brought about than for those they brought about passively.[195] Inaction thus entails less responsibility taking. Consequently, people will sometimes prefer harmful omissions to less harmful commissions.[196]

6. Endowment Effect

(a) Significance and Scope

The *endowment effect* (also known as the *WTA-WTP disparity*) is the phenomenon whereby individuals tend to place a higher value on objects and entitlements they already have, compared with objects and entitlements they do not.[197] The maximum amount people are

191. Moshinsky & Bar-Hillel, *supra* note 190.

192. Craig R.M. McKenzie, Michael J. Liersch, & Stacey R. Finkelstein, *Recommendations Implicit in Policy Defaults,* 17 Psychol. Sci. 414 (2006).

193. Scott Eidelman & Christian S. Crandall, *Bias in Favor of the Status Quo,* 6 Soc. & Personality Psychol. Compass 270, 272 (2012). *See also infra* p. 106.

194. Moshinsky & Bar-Hillel, *supra* note 190, at 199–203.

195. Mark Spranca, Elisa Minsk & Jonathan Baron, *Omission and Commission in Judgment and Choice*, 27 J. Experimental Soc. Psychol. 76 (1991); Johanna H. Kordes-de Vaal, *Intention and the Omission Bias: Omissions Perceived as Nondecisions*, 93 Acta Psychologica 161 (1996); Peter DeScioli, John Christner & Robert Kurzban, *The Omission Strategy*, 22 Psychol. Sci. 442 (2011).

196. Ilana Ritov & Jonathan Baron, *Reluctance to Vaccinate: Omission Bias and Ambiguity,* 3 J. Behav. Decision Making 263 (1990).

197. Richard H. Thaler, *Toward a Positive Theory of Consumer Choice,* 1 J. Econ. Behav. & Org. 39 (1980); Kahneman, Knetsch & Thaler, *supra* note 162; Russell Korobkin, *Wrestling with the Endowment Effect, or How to Do Law and Economics without the Coase Theorem, in* The Oxford Handbook of Behavioral Economics and the Law, *supra* note 8, at 300.

willing to pay (WTP) for a certain good or entitlement they do not yet have is often lower than the minimal amount they would be willing to accept (WTA) for relinquishing it if they already owned it. This WTA-WTP disparity runs counter to a fundamental independence assumption of standard economic theory, namely that "the value of an entitlement to an individual is independent of the relationship between the individual and the entitlement in the current state of the world."[198] Hence, it contradicts the notion that in a world of zero transaction costs and no limitations on trade, the initial allocation of legal entitlements would not determine their final allocation.[199] Unsurprisingly, the endowment effect has been one of the most extensively studied phenomena in behavioral and experimental economics.

Evidence of the gap between the maximal amount of money people are willing to pay for an entitlement and the minimal sum they are willing to accept to give up a similar entitlement was offered as early as the 1960s and 1970s.[200] However, only in 1980 was the notion of the endowment effect and its association with loss aversion put forward by Richard Thaler.[201] Since then, the endowment effect has been confirmed in numerous experimental studies. These studies have usually taken one of two forms. In one form, subjects were asked how much money they would be willing to pay for a certain item or an entitlement, and how much they would require to part with a similar item or entitlement, thus establishing the WTA-WTP disparity.[202] In the other form, subjects were given various items and the opportunity to trade them for other items. These experiments found a trading anomaly in the form of a reluctance to trade a received item for an alternative one, whatever the received item was.[203]

Closely related to the status quo and omission biases, the endowment effect has been found to apply not only to tangible goods, but to intangible entitlements as well—such as working hours,[204] exposure to health risks,[205] and contractual rights under default rules.[206]

198. Russell Korobkin, *The Endowment Effect and Legal Analysis*, 97 Nw. U. L. Rev. 1227, 1228 (2003).

199. *See supra* p. 9; *infra* pp. 232–34.

200. *See, e.g.*, C.H. Coombs, T.G. Bezembinder & F.M. Goode, *Testing Expectation Theories of Decision Making without Measuring Utility or Subjective Probability*, 4 J. Math. Psychol. 72 (1967); Judd Hammack & Gardner M. Brown Jr., Waterfowl and Wetlands: Toward Bio-Economic Analysis 26–27 (1974).

201. Thaler, *supra* note 197.

202. *See, e.g.*, Jack L. Knetsch & J.A. Sinden, *Willingness to Pay and Compensation Demanded: Experimental Evidence of an Unexpected Disparity in Measures of Value*, 99 Q.J. Econ. 507 (1984); Kahneman, Knetsch & Thaler, supra note 162.

203. *See, e.g.*, Jack L. Knetsch, *The Endowment Effect and Evidence of Nonreversible Indifference Curves*, 79 Am. Econ. Rev. 1277 (1989). Jack L. Knetsch, *Preferences and Nonreversibility of Indifference Curves*, 17 J. Econ. Behav. & Org. 131 (1992).

204. Guido Ortona & Francesco Scacciati, *New Experiments on the Endowment Effect*, 13 J. Econ. Psychol. 277 (1992); Vera Hoorens, Nicole Remmers & Kamieke Van de Reit, *Time Is an Amazingly Variable Amount of Money: Endowment and Ownership Effects in the Subjective Value of Working Time*, 20 J. Econ. Psychol. 383 (1999).

205. W. Kip Viscusi, Wesley A. Magat & Joel Huber, *An Investigation of the Rationality of Consumer Valuations of Multiple Health Risks*, 18 Rand J. Econ. 465, 469, 477–78 (1987).

206. Russell Korobkin, *The Status Quo Bias and Contract Default Rules*, 83 Cornell L. Rev. 608 (1998).

Various factors determine the existence and scope of the endowment effect. Thus, the reluctance to trade decreases dramatically when the two items are identical and owners are offered a minor incentive to trade.[207] As the similarity between the items increases, the reluctance to trade decreases.[208] The more difficult it is for people to compare the endowment item and the proposed alternative, the greater the reluctance to trade.[209]

Money does not create an endowment effect.[210] More generally, there is no endowment effect when goods are held for exchange (such as commercial stock), rather than for use.[211] However, the endowment effect does apply to financial instruments or bargaining chips whose value is uncertain.[212]

Another factor bearing on the strength of the endowment effect is the source of the object. Thus, subjects who believed that they received an object as a prize for their performance on a classroom exercise displayed a stronger endowment effect than those who believed that they obtained the object by chance.[213] Similarly, a stronger endowment effect was found with regard to objects received as gifts from a close friend.[214] Finally, creators of artistic goods (paintings) showed a particularly strong endowment effect regarding their creations.[215]

There is some evidence that trading experience reduces or even eliminates the endowment effect.[216] However, it appears that experience does not eliminate the WTA-WTP disparity with regard to non-market items that are difficult to compare.[217] Plausibly, then, the elimination of the endowment effect stems not from trading experience, but from the

207. Maya Bar-Hillel & Efrat Neter, *Why Are People Reluctant to Exchange Lottery Tickets?*, 70 J. PERSONALITY & SOC. PSYCHOL. 17, 22–24 (1996). When items are identical and there is no incentive to trade, no trade is expected. *See* David Gal, *A Psychological Law of Inertia and the Illusion of Loss Aversion,* 1 JUDGMENT & DECISION MAKING 23, 26–27 (2006).

208. Gretchen B. Chapman, *Similarity and Reluctance to Trade,* 11 J. BEHAV. DECISION MAKING 47 (1998).

209. Eric van Dijk & Daan van Knippenberg, *Trading Wine: On the Endowment Effect, Loss Aversion, and the Comparability of Consumer Goods,* 19 J. ECON. PSYCHOL. 485 (1998); Jason F. Shogren et al., *Resolving Differences in Willingness to Pay and Willingness to Accept,* 84 AM. ECON. REV. 255 (1994).

210. Nathan Novemsky & Daniel Kahneman, *The Boundaries of Loss Aversion,* 32 J. MARKETING RES. 119 (2005).

211. Kahneman, Knetsch & Thaler, *supra* note 162; Amos Tversky & Daniel Kahneman, *Loss Aversion in Riskless Choice: A Reference-Dependent Model,* 106 Q.J. ECON. 1039, 1055 (1991); Novemsky & Kahneman, *supra* note 210, at 124–25.

212. Samuelson & Zeckhouser, *supra* note 183, at 12–22 (investment portfolios); van Dijk & van Knippenberg, *supra* note 209 (bargaining chips). *Cf.* Bar-Hillel & Neter, *supra* note 207 (lottery tickets).

213. George Loewenstein & Samuel Issacharoff, *Source Dependence in the Valuation of Objects,* 7 J. BEHAV. DECISION MAKING 157 (1994).

214. Therese Jefferson & Ross Taplin, *An Investigation of the Endowment Effect Using a Factorial Design,* 32 J. ECON. PSYCHOL. 899 (2011).

215. Christopher Buccafusco & Christopher Jon Sprigman, *The Creativity Effect,* 78 U. CHI. L. REV. 31 (2011). *See also infra* pp. 226–27.

216. John List, *Does Market Experience Eliminate Market Anomalies?,* 41 Q.J. ECON. 46 (2003); John A. List, *Does Market Experience Eliminate Market Anomalies? The Case of Exogenous Market Experience,* 101(3) AM. ECON. REV. PAPERS & PROC. 313 (2011).

217. *See* Shogren et al., *supra* note 209.

fact that traders are holding goods for exchange—where, as previously indicated, the effect does not apply.

(b) Causes and Explanations

While the existence of the endowment effect is rarely denied,[218] the causes and explanations for the WTA-WTP disparity are hotly debated.[219] One primary explanation is loss aversion. "[R]emoving a good from the endowment creates a loss while adding the same good (to an endowment without it) generates a gain."[220] Since money is valued for its exchange value, it does not create an endowment effect; hence the seller's perceived loss due to parting with the object is not paralleled by the buyer's loss due to parting with her money.

Another explanation for the endowment effect draws on the notion that owning an object creates an association between the item and one's self. When owning an object becomes part of one's self-definition, a self-serving bias (i.e., people's desire to see themselves in a favorable light)[221] likely results in an increased valuation of the object—the so-called *mere ownership effect*.[222] This hypothesis has been corroborated by experiments in which the WTP of buyers who happened to own an item identical to the one they were offered was equivalent to the sellers' WTA.[223] It also falls in line with findings that there is no endowment effect in relation to money and other goods held for exchange, and that the endowment effect is stronger for goods received as a reward for a successful performance.

218. *But see* Charles R. Plott & Kathryn Zeiler, *The Willingness to Pay—Willingness to Accept Gap, the "Endowment Effect," Subject Misconceptions, and Experimental Procedures for Eliciting Valuations*, 95 Am. Econ. Rev. 530 (2005) [hereinafter Plott & Zeiler, *The WTP-WTA Gap*]; Charles R. Plott & Kathryn Zeiler, *Exchange Asymmetries Incorrectly Interpreted as Evidence of Endowment Effect Theory and Prospect Theory?*, 97 Am. Econ. Rev. 1449 (2007) [hereinafter Plott & Zeiler, *Exchange Asymmetries*]; Gregory Klass & Kathryn Zeiler, *Against Endowment Theory: Experimental Economics and Legal Scholarship*, 61 UCLA L. Rev. 2 (2013). Note that a WTA-WTP disparity may exist even if, contrary to both expected utility theory and prospect theory, the WTA and WTP are hardly correlated within subjects. *See* Jonathan Chapman et al., *Willingness-to-Pay and Willingness-to-Accept Are Probably Less Correlated than You Think* (working paper, 2017, *available at*: https://ssrn.com/abstract=2988958).

219. For overviews, see Thomas C. Brown & Robin Gregory, *Why the WTA-WTP Disparity Matters?*, 28 Ecological Econ. 323, 326–29 (1999); Korobkin, *supra* note 197, at 304–18; Carey K. Morewedge & Colleen E. Giblin, *Explanations of the Endowment Effect: An Integrative Review*, 19 Trends Cognitive Sci. 339 (2015); Kathryn Zeiler, *What Explains Observed Reluctance to Trade? A Comprehensive Literature Review*, *in* Research Handbook on Behavioral Law and Economics (Kathryn Zeiler & Joshua Teitelbaum eds., 2018, *available at*: https://ssrn.com/abstract=2862021).

220. Thaler, *supra* note 197, at 44. *See also* Tversky & Kahneman, *supra* note 211; Michal A. Strahilevitz & George Loewenstein, *The Effect of Ownership History on the Valuation of Objects*, 25 J. Consumer Res. 276 (1998); Brown & Gregory, *supra* note 219, at 327.

221. *See infra* pp. 58–76.

222. K.J. Beggan, *On the Social Nature of Nonsocial Perception: The Mere Ownership Effect*, 62 J. Personality & Soc. Psychol. 229 (1992) (*but see* Michael J. Barone, Terence A. Shimp & David E. Sprott, *Mere Ownership Revisited: A Robust Effect?*, 6 J. Consumer Psychol. 257 (1997)). On *psychological ownership* and the endowment effect, see *infra* pp. 203–04, 209–13. For a theory of the endowment effect as self-enhancement in response to a threat—combining elements of ownership and loss aversion—see Promothesh Chatterjee, Caglar Irmak & Randall L. Rose, *The Endowment Effect as Self-Enhancement in Response to Threat*, 40 J. Consumer Res. 460 (2013).

223. Carey K. Morewedge et al., *Bad Riddance or Good Rubbish? Ownership and Not Loss Aversion Causes the Endowment Effect*, 45 J. Experimental Soc. Psychol. 947 (2009).

It is, however, difficult to see how this explanation can apply, for instance, to people's reluctance to trade lottery tickets or bargaining chips whose value is uncertain.

Yet another psychological explanation rests on biased information uptake and processing: owning an object increases the accessibility of, and attention to, information that supports keeping the object, whereas a decision whether to acquire an object increases the accessibility of, and attention to, information that supports keeping one's money or receiving money rather than the object.[224] Like the self-definition explanation, this explanation hardly applies to lottery tickets, but perhaps people's reluctance to trade lottery tickets is not a manifestation of the endowment effect, but rather of expected regret.[225]

Others have argued that standard economic theory can explain at least some manifestations of the WTA-WTP disparity without resorting to psychological phenomena. According to one such explanation—based on the decreasing marginal utility of wealth—the very fact that a person does not have a certain asset makes her poorer. She therefore values each dollar more than the endowed person does, and thus her WTP is smaller than the owner's WTA. However, this explanation is irrelevant to most manifestations of the endowment effect. It is neither relevant to objects that constitute a minuscule portion of people's wealth, nor to experiments in which potential buyers receive a sum of money equivalent to the value of the object given to potential sellers.

Another attempt to square the endowment effect with standard economic theory is the argument that the effect results from an inappropriate application of the normal bargaining strategy of "Buy low, sell high." However, this argument does not account for the findings of experiments where subjects choose between keeping an object and trading it for another object without stating their WTA or WTP values. It is also difficult to accept when experiments are designed so that the subject's dominant strategy is to reveal their true WTP and WTA.[226]

Yet another economic explanation relies on the income and substitution effects. In the absence of substitutes for an entitlement or a good, WTA may be infinite, whereas WTP will always be capped by one's income, thus resulting in a large WTA-WTP disparity. The more an entitlement or an object is perceived as being unique, the greater the expected WTA.[227] However, while this explanation applies to unique and valuable goods, it can hardly explain the endowment effect with regard to ordinary, inexpensive goods such as coffee mugs, and even less so the trading anomaly over lottery tickets, which are perfect substitutes.[228]

224. Nathaniel J.S. Ashby, Stephan Dickert & Andreas Glöckner, *Focusing on What You Own: Biased Information Uptake due to Ownership*, 7 JUDGMENT & DECISION MAKING 254 (2012); Morewedge & Giblin, *supra* note 219.

225. On *cost of regret*, see *infra* pp. 505–07.

226. Andrea Isoni, Graham Loomes & Robert Sugden, *The Willingness to Pay—Willingness to Accept Gap, the "Endowment Effect," Subject Misconceptions, and Experimental Procedures for Eliciting Valuations: Comment*, 101 AM. ECON. REV. 991 (2011).

227. W. Michael Hanemann, *Willingness to Pay and Willingness to Accept: How Much Can They Differ?*, 81 AM. ECON. REV. 635 (1991).

228. Brown & Gregory, *supra* note 219, at 326.

Additional possible causes of trading anomalies include owners' attachment to goods;[229] individuals' disinclination to sell common items (which they usually only buy);[230] the herd effect (when subjects publicly signal their willingness/unwillingness to trade by raising/not raising their hand);[231] transaction and decision costs; lack of information about the value of goods,[232] and their market price;[233] subjects' misinterpretation of their receipt of an item from the experimenter as an indication of its high value or the desirability of keeping it;[234] and misconceptions about the elicitation-of-value procedure.[235]

While all these factors may indeed contribute to the WTA-WTP disparity, the overall picture emerging from dozens of studies is that none of them—either individually or in any combination—fully explains the disparity. Thus, for example, while valuation likely increases with the duration of ownership, some experiments have found "an instant endowment effect."[236] The WTA-WTP disparity was found even when decision and transaction costs were practically the same for trading and not trading.[237] Likewise, while the herd effect may explain extreme reluctance to trade when subjects were asked to express their willingness to trade by raising their hand, it cannot account for the reluctance they exhibited when asked to mark their choice on a form.[238] Similarly, the endowment effect has been found even when experiments were conducted in a manner that eliminated any possible inference from the fact that subjects received one object rather than the other.[239] The same is true for measures taken to eliminate misconceptions of the elicitation-of-value procedure.[240]

When controlling for such variables, it appears that the main explanation for the absence of an endowment effect in some experimental designs (which were designed to question its very existence), is that these designs considerably weakened the perception

229. Strahilevitz & Loewenstein, *supra* note 220; Korobkin, *supra* note 198, at 1251–52 (critically discussing this argument). *See also infra* pp. 203–04, 209–13.

230. Russell Korobkin, *Policymaking and the Offer/Asking Price Gap: Toward a Theory of Efficient Entitlement Allocation,* 46 Stan. L. Rev. 663, 693–96 (1994).

231. Plott & Zeiler, *Exchange Asymmetries, supra* note 218, at 1461.

232. Plott & Zeiler, *Exchange Asymmetries, supra* note 218, at 1463.

233. Ray Weaver & Shane Frederick, *A Reference Price Theory of the Endowment Effect,* 49 J. Marketing Res. 696 (2012); Itamar Simonson & Aimee Drolet, *Anchoring Effects on Consumers' Willingness to Pay and Willingness to Accept,* 31 J. Consumer Res. 681 (2004).

234. Plott & Zeiler, *Exchange Asymmetries, supra* note 218, at 1463.

235. Plott & Zeiler, *The WTP-WTA Gap, supra* note 218.

236. Kaheman, Knetsch & Thaler, *supra* note 197, at 1342.

237. Brown & Gregory, *supra* note 219, at 326.

238. The latter procedure was used, for example, by Kentsch and Wong: Jack L. Kentsch & Wei-Kang Wong, *The Endowment Effect and the Reference State: Evidence and Manipulations,* 71 J. Econ. Behav. & Org. 407 (2009).

239. Knetsch & Wong, *id.* at 410–11.

240. Isoni, Loomes & Sugden, *supra* note 226.

of reference states.[241] There is no endowment effect without a sense of endowment. These designs were also very different from the conditions outside the laboratory, where the reference state is usually quite clear and the endowment effect is equally apparent.[242] Ultimately, loss aversion remains one of the central explanations for the endowment effect.

7. Sunk Costs and Escalation of Commitment

Expected utility theory posits that when choosing between different courses of action, only future costs and benefits should be taken into account. Unrecoverable, incurred costs that would not affect future costs or benefits should not affect decisions, as the past cannot be changed. For instance, a ticket holder should decide whether to go to a concert according to the expected net benefit of doing so, irrespective of how much she has paid for the ticket, if at all. However, numerous laboratory and field experiments, as well as empirical studies, have shown that very often, people do not disregard such *sunk costs* in their decisions. Rather, they tend to persist in endeavors the more resources, time, or efforts they have already invested in them. Thus, in a randomized field experiment, people who paid more for theater season tickets attended more plays than those who paid less.[243] Similarly, after having purchased two differently priced items, and forced to choose only one of them to consume, most people choose to consume the more expensive item, even if they might otherwise have preferred the other one, or had no particular preference.[244] In the same vein, entrepreneurs keep investing in failed projects,[245] and countries persist in fighting hopeless wars.[246] Such *escalation of commitment* characterizes decisions made by laypeople and professional decision-makers alike.[247]

Various determinants—economic, organizational, social, and psychological—influence escalation of commitment.[248] If we focus on psychological determinants, two primary explanations have been offered for the escalation-of-commitment phenomenon: self-justification, and avoidance of sure losses. According to the first explanation,

241. Knetsch & Wong, *supra* note 238; Weining Koh & Wei-Kang Wong, *The Endowment Effect and the Willingness to Accept-Willingness to Pay Gap: Subject Misconceptions or Reference Dependence?* (working paper, 2011), *available at:* http://courses.nus.edu.sg/course/ecswong/research/WTA-WTP.pdf).

242. Knetsch & Wong, *supra* note 238, at 412–13.

243. Hal R. Arkes & Catherine Blumer, *The Psychology of Sunk Costs,* 35 Org. Behav. & Hum. Decision Processes 124, 127–29 (1985).

244. *Id.* at 126–27.

245. Anne M. McCarthy, F. David Schoorman & Arnold C. Cooper, *Reinvestment Decisions by Entrepreneurs: Rational Decision-Making or Escalation of Commitment?,* 8 J. Bus. Venturing 9 (1993).

246. Robert Jervis, *Political Implications of Loss Aversion,* 13 Pol. Psychol. 187 (1992); Levy, *supra* note 182, at 227 (2003).

247. *See, e.g.,* McCarthy, Schoorman & Cooper, *supra* note 245; Barry M. Staw & Ha Hoang, *Sunk Costs in the NBA: Why Draft Order Affects Playing Time and Survival in Professional Basketball,* 40 Admin. Sci. Q. 474 (1995).

248. Barry M. Staw & Jerry Ross, *Understanding Behavior in Escalation Situations,* 246 Sci. 216 (1989); Gillian Ku, *Learning to De-escalate: The Effects of Regret in Escalation of Commitment,* 105 Org. Behav. & Hum. Decision Processes 221, 222–23 (2008).

people are unwilling to admit to themselves and to others that their initial decision has proven wrong and wasteful.[249] Self-justification is related to the *confirmation bias*, that is, the tendency to gather and process information in a manner that conforms to one's prior commitments.[250] According to the other explanation, escalation of commitment stems from people's aversion to sure losses. To avoid sure losses, people tend to keep investing in failing projects even if the prospects of turning them into successful (or break-even) ones are slim.[251] In one of the early escalation experiments, Barry Staw found that participants allocated significantly more research and development money to failing corporate divisions than to successful ones.[252] In accordance with prospect theory, sure losses are overvalued (the certainty effect), and people are risk-seeking in the domain of losses.[253]

The two explanations are not mutually exclusive, and they both play important roles. While escalation of commitment is stronger when the decision-maker is responsible for the initial investment, it is also evident when the initial decision was made by someone else.[254] Sunk costs affect people's decisions even when they do not feel responsible for a wrong decision, as in the case of choosing which of two products to consume, when one costs more than the other. It has also been suggested that the two explanations are interrelated: people who are in greater need for self-justification are less likely to adjust their reference point after the failure of the initial investment, and are therefore more susceptible to escalation of commitment.[255]

Interestingly, the different attitude to losses and gains possibly explains not only deviations from expected utility theory by overinvesting in failed projects, but also by underinvesting in projects whose costs exceed their initial mental budget—the so-called *de-escalation of commitment*. When people set a mental budget to control their resource expenditures, they may stop investing in an endeavor when additional expenditures would exceed this budget, even if the expected benefit from such an investment is larger than the incremental cost.[256]

249. Barry M. Staw, *Knee-Deep in the Big Muddy: A Study of Escalating Commitment to a Chosen Course of Action*, 16 Org. Behav. & Hum. Decision Processes 27 (1976); Joel Brockner, *The Escalation of Commitment to a Failing Course of Action: Toward Theoretical Progress*, 17 Acad. Mgmt. Rev. 39 (1992).

250. *See infra* pp. 59–61.

251. Richard H. Thaler & Eric J. Johnson, *Gambling with the House Money and Trying to Break Even: The Effects of Prior Outcomes on Risky Choice*, 36 Mgmt. Sci. 643 (1990).

252. Staw, *supra* note 249.

253. Thaler, *supra* note 197, at 48–49; Arkes & Blumer, *supra* note 243, at 130–32; Glen Whyte, *Escalating Commitment to a Course of Action: A Reinterpretation*, 11 Acad. Mgmt. Rev. 311 (1986).

254. Staw, *supra* note 249; Whyte, *supra* note 253.

255. Whyte, *supra* note 253, at 316.

256. Chip Heath, *Escalation and De-escalation of Commitment in Response to Sunk Costs: The Role of Budgeting in Mental Accounting*, 62 Org. Behav. & Hum. Decision Processes 38 (1995).

D. Egocentrism and Motivated Reasoning

1. General

Several interrelated biases revolve around the role of motivation—especially self-serving motivation—in people's perceptions, judgments, and choices. Beginning with Leon Festinger's influential theory of *cognitive dissonance* in the 1950s,[257] and continuing with Peter Wason's seminal studies of the *confirmation bias* in the 1960s,[258] a very large body of research has dealt with these phenomena.[259] However, while it was stated that the confirmation bias "has probably attracted the most enduring interest of all cognitive biases,"[260] it was also noted that "the proof of this bias remains elusive"[261] (and it may be the case that the former statement reflects the self-serving bias of those who study the confirmation bias). This section highlights the main findings (and controversies) regarding motivated reasoning and confirmation bias, as well as several related phenomena, such as *overoptimism, naïve realism,* and *illusion of control.* It also discusses studies of *behavioral ethics,* which predicate unethical behavior on self-serving biases.

2. Motivated Reasoning and Confirmation Bias

While people are sometimes motivated to arrive at an accurate conclusion, whatever that may be, at times they aim to reach a particular, directional conclusion—often the one that best serves their interests. When people truly strive to reach an accurate conclusion, they use the most appropriate strategy to attain that goal. In contrast, directional goals prompt people to use strategies that are likely to yield the desired conclusion. Interestingly, directional processing of information can be as detailed and thorough as accuracy-motivated processing. Information processing can be thorough and biased at the same time.[262] Motivated reasoning is evident in both pre-decisional acquisition and processing of information, and in post-hoc justification of one's decisions.[263] While people may knowingly and purposively acquire and process information in a way that confirms their prior views, expectations, and decisions, our focus is on the less conscious and mostly automatic processes—namely,

257. LEON FESTINGER, A THEORY OF COGNITIVE DISSONANCE (1957).

258. Peter C. Wason, *On the Failure to Eliminate Hypotheses in a Conceptual Task,* 12 Q.J. EXPERIMENTAL PSYCHOL. 129 (1960) [hereinafter Wason, *Failure*]; Peter C. Wason, *Reasoning about a Rule,* 20 Q.J. EXPERIMENTAL PSYCHOL. 273 (1968).

259. For overviews of different parts of this body of research, see Ziva Kunda, *The Case for Motivated Reasoning,* 108 PSYCHOL. BULL. 480 (1990); Raymond S. Nickerson, *Confirmation Bias: A Ubiquitous Phenomenon in Many Guises,* 2 REV. GENERAL PSYCHOL. 175 (1998); Hahn & Harris, *supra* note 2; BARON, *supra* note 47, at 199–227; Symposium, *Motivated Beliefs,* 30 J. ECON. PERSP. 133–212 (2016).

260. Hahn & Harris, *supra* note 2, at 44.

261. Steven E. Clark & Gary L. Wells, *On the Diagnosticity of Multiple-Witness Identifications,* 23 LAW & HUM. BEHAV. 406 (2008).

262. Kunda, *supra* note 259.

263. *Id.*; Lisa L. Shu, Francesca Gino & Max H. Bazerman, *Dishonest Deed, Clear Conscience: When Cheating Leads to Moral Disengagement and Motivated Forgetting,* 37 PERSONALITY & SOC. PSYCHOL. BULL. 330 (2011).

on System 1 thinking, which is then backed up by System 2 reasoning.[264] This interplay between System 1 and System 2 may explain why motivated decision-makers tend to bias their judgments only to the extent necessary to corroborate their judgment, subject to a reasonableness constraint.[265]

One key manifestation of motivated reasoning is the *confirmation bias*. Confirmation bias (also known as the *myside bias*) denotes the tendency to seek and process information in ways that are partial to one's interests, beliefs, and expectations.[266] In an early study, Wason presented participants with triplets of numbers (e.g., 2-4-6), and asked them to infer the rule used to generate them (e.g., numbers increasing by 2, or increasing even numbers). The participants then tested their hypothesis by suggesting other triplets and being told whether they were consistent with the rule. To test their hypothesis, participants should have logically suggested triplets that *did not* conform with the hypothesis. In fact, they tended to suggest triplets that conformed with it.[267] It has been found that people learn from experience to use better strategies for testing their hypotheses, but that time pressure exacerbates the bias.[268] The tendency to look for confirmatory evidence may be stronger in some laboratory experiments involving abstract and unfamiliar tasks than in familiar, daily ones, but it characterizes the latter as well.[269]

People not only look for confirmatory evidence, they also tend to ignore disproving evidence, or at least give it less weight, and to interpret the available evidence in ways that confirm their prior attitudes. People see in the data what they are looking for, or expect to see.[270] When people are presented with arguments that are incompatible with their existing beliefs, they automatically scrutinize them longer, subject them to more critical analyses, and consequently judge them to be weaker than arguments compatible with their own beliefs.[271]

Biased search, interpretation, and recollection may account for *belief perseverance* (irrationally sticking to beliefs notwithstanding falsifying evidence),[272] the *primacy effect*

264. On dual-system theories of judgment and decision-making, see *supra* pp. 21–23.

265. Lindsley G. Boiney, Jane Kennedy & Pete Nye, *Instrumental Bias in Motivated Reasoning: More When More Is Needed*, 72 Org. Behav. & Hum. Decision Proc. 1 (1997).

266. For an overview, see Nickerson, *supra* note 259.

267. Wason, *Failure, supra* note 258. On numerous other experimental studies of the confirmation bias in information gathering, see Nickerson, *supra* note 259, at 177–80, 184–87.

268. Anna Coenen, Bob Rehder & Todd M. Gureckis, *Strategies to Intervene on Causal Systems Are Adaptively Selected*, 79 Cognitive Psychol. 102 (2015).

269. *See generally* Andrew J. Wistrich & Jeffrey J. Rachlinski, *How Lawyers' Intuitions Prolong Litigation*, 86 S. Cal. L. Rev. 571, 594–96 (2013).

270. For an overview of studies, see Nickerson, *supra* note 259, at 180–84.

271. Kari Edwards & Edward E. Smith, *A Disconfirmation Bias in the Evaluation of Arguments*, 71 J. Personality & Soc. Psychol. 5 (1996).

272. *See, e.g.*, Lee Ross, Mark R. Lepper & Michael Hubbard, *Perseverance in Self-Perception and Social Perception: Biased Attributional Processes in the Debriefing Paradigm*, 32 J. Personality & Soc. Psychol. 880 (1975).

(attributing greater weight to the first piece of evidence, compared with subsequent ones),[273] and *attitude polarization* (increased disagreement between people who are exposed to the same additional information).[274]

The confirmation bias is stronger for emotionally charged issues and for deep-seated beliefs.[275] It also correlates with some personal traits. For example, it was found that people vary in terms of their *defensive confidence,* namely their belief in their ability to successfully defend their attitudes against counterarguments. Ironically, it was found that people with greater defensive confidence are less prone to the confirmation bias, because they are more willing to consider antithetical evidence, which sometimes lead them to change their minds (whereas people with low defensive confidence tend to disregard disconfirming information).[276] Very little correlation has been found between the tendency to gather and interpret information in a way that would confirm people's prior beliefs and attitudes, and their intelligence.[277] A specific measure of individual-level cognitive openness—the antonym of close-mindedness and susceptibility to the confirmation bias—has been developed recently.[278]

As is often the case in JDM research, it is one thing to characterize the confirmation bias, and another to assess the extent to which it deviates from a normative model of decision-making. Skepticism toward evidence and arguments that are contradictory to one's established beliefs is often prudent and rational. Constant questioning of one's own attitudes is mentally stressful, and practically impossible given our limited cognitive resources. More troubling, Baron has found that college students tended to assess sets of arguments, ostensibly made by other students, as better when the arguments all pointed in one direction than when both sides were presented—even when the final conclusion was contrary to the assessors' position.[279] The confirmation bias may therefore be generally adaptive, yet detrimental in predictable ways.[280]

The tendency to gather and process information in a confirmatory manner has been invoked to explain various real-life phenomena, from mystical beliefs and witch-hunting, to policymaking, judicial reasoning, and the slow development of medical and scientific knowledge throughout history.[281] In fact, many of the controversies in the social (and

273. *See infra* pp. 82–83.

274. *See, e.g.*, Charles G. Lord, Lee Ross & Mark R. Lepper, *Biased Assimilation and Attitude Polarization: The Effects of Prior Theories on Subsequently Considered Evidence,* 37 J. Personality & Soc. Psychol. 2098 (1979).

275. *See, e.g.*, Edwards & Smith, *supra* note 271.

276. Dolores Albarracín & Amy L. Mitchell, *The Role of Defensive Confidence in Preference for Proattitudinal Information: How Believing That One Is Strong Can Sometimes Be a Defensive Weakness,* 30 Personality & Soc. Psychol. Bull. 1565 (2004).

277. Keith E. Stanovich, Richard F. West & Maggie E. Toplak, *Myside Bias, Rational Thinking, and Intelligence,* 22 Current Directions Psychol. Sci. 259 (2013).

278. Erika Price et al., *Open-Minded Cognition,* 41 Personality & Soc. Psychol. Bull. 1488 (2015).

279. Jonathan Baron, *Myside Bias in Thinking about Abortion,* 1 Thinking & Reasoning 221 (1995).

280. Nickerson, *supra* note 259, at 205–10.

281. Nickerson, *supra* note 259, at 189–97.

other) sciences, including those between economists committed to rational choice theory and behavioral economists, may be rooted in each camp's confirmation bias (and there is no reason to assume that the authors of this book are immune to it, either). Plausibly, what makes scientific knowledge more reliable than other forms of knowledge is not each scientist's open-minded attempts to falsify her own findings, but rather the insistence of science as an institution on falsifiability and the strong motivation of scientists to falsify *other scientists'* theories.[282]

3. Overoptimism and the Better-than-Average Effect

The term *overoptimism* has been used to describe various psychological phenomena.[283] Here we use it to denote instances where people overestimate the prospects of positive or desirable things, or underestimate the prospects of negative or undesirable ones. We therefore exclude from the present discussion optimism as a personality trait, as well as the framing of situations or events as either positive or negative (whether the glass is half empty or half full, so to speak). The present discussion includes the *better-than-average effect,* but leaves out *overconfidence,* which will be discussed separately.[284]

Overoptimism requires a comparison between one's estimations and an external benchmark. Depending on the circumstances, various benchmarks may be deemed relevant, including actual future outcomes (in the case of predictions), probability value based on the general base rate (e.g., in the case of one's probability of divorce), and social comparison (i.e., estimates made by other people).[285]

Overoptimism has been found in various experimental settings. In an early study, subjects were each given a pack of cards, told that it contained marked cards in a certain ratio (e.g., 7 out of 10) and then asked whether or not they expect to draw a marked card. Half of the subjects were told that they would gain a point if they drew a marked card (the *desirable condition*), and the other half that they would lose a point if they drew a marked card (the *undesirable condition*). Other subjects participated in the *neutral condition*—where no points were gained or lost when a marked card was drawn. All subjects were informed of the outcomes of their draws only at the end of the entire procedure. It was found that the stated expectations were highest in the desirable condition and lowest in the undesirable condition, with the neutral condition in-between.[286] Similar results were obtained in studies in which the desirable outcomes (from the participants' perspective) were not manipulated experimentally, but preexisted—as in predictions about

282. Nickerson, *supra* note 259, at 194–97, 206–08.

283. For a thoughtful taxonomy of phenomena related to overoptimism, see Paul D. Windschitl & Jillian O'Rourke Stuart, *Optimism Biases: Types and Causes, in* 2 Wiley Blackwell Handbook, *supra* note 2, at 431, 432–36.

284. *See infra* pp. 64–66.

285. Wihdschitl & Stuart, *supra* note 283, at 433–44.

286. Francis W. Irwin, *Stated Expectations as Functions of Probability and Desirability of Outcomes,* 21 J. Personality 329 (1953).

one's future health or professional success, election outcomes, or the results of football games.[287] In one survey, conducted in the United States, people who had just married, or were about to get married, were asked about the divorce rate in the United States and the likelihood that they personally would divorce. While the median response to the first question was 50 percent, which was the correct answer, the median answer to the second question was 0 percent.[288]

Many studies have shown that people evaluate themselves more favorably than they evaluate their peers. In one study, about half of the subjects believed that they were among the safest 20 or 30 percent of the drivers, and about 80 percent believed themselves to be safer than the median driver.[289] In another study, subjects who scored in the bottom quartile on tests of various intellectual skills believed that they did better than the average participant.[290] The magnitude of this *better-than-average effect* has been found to be greater for controllable traits than for uncontrollable ones,[291] and for ambiguously defined than for specific ones.[292] The magnitude of the effect also depends on the level of abstraction of the comparison target. People are less biased when they compare themselves with an individuated target—especially someone with whom they have personal contact—than with a non-individuated target, such as the average student.[293]

It has been demonstrated that people update their estimates once they receive information indicating that their initial estimate was overly *pessimistic*, much more so than following information showing that the initial estimate was overly *optimistic*. Such selective updating (resulting from reduced coding of negative information in the brain) allows people to maintain their overoptimism despite the presence of disconfirming evidence.[294]

287. Neil D. Weinstein, *Unrealistic Optimism about Future Life Events*, 39 J. PERSONALITY & SOC. PSYCHOL. 806 (1980); Zlatan Krizan, Jeffrey C. Miller & Omesh Johar, *Wishful Thinking in the 2008 U.S. Presidential Election*, 21 PSYCHOL. SCI. 140 (2010); Cade Massey, Joseph P. Simmons & David A. Armor, *Hope over Experience: Desirability and the Persistence of Optimism*, 22 PSYCHOL. SCI. 274 (2011).

288. Lynn A. Baker & Robert E. Emery, *When Every Relationship Is above Average: Perceptions and Expectations of Divorce at the Time of Marriage*, 17 LAW & HUM. BEHAV. 439, 443 (1993).

289. Ola Svenson, *Are We All Less Risky and More Skillful than Our Fellow Drivers?*, 47 ACTAPSYCHOLOGICA 143 (1981).

290. Justin Kruger & David Dunning, *Unskilled and Unaware of It: How Difficulties in Recognizing One's Own Incompetence Lead to Inflated Self-Assessments*, 77 J. PERSONALITY & SOC. PSYCHOL. 1121 (1999).

291. Mark D. Alicke, *Global Self-Evaluation as Determined by the Desirability and Controllability of Trait Adjectives*, 49 J. PERSONALITY & SOC. PSYCHOL. 1621 (1985).

292. David Dunning, Judith A. Meyerowitz & Amy D. Holzberg, *Ambiguity and Self-Evaluation: The Role of Idiosyncratic Trait Definitions in Self-Serving Assessments of Ability*, 57 J. PERSONALITY & SOC. PSYCHOL. 1082 (1989).

293. Mark D. Alicke et al., *Personal Contact, Individuation, and the Above-Average Effect*, 68 J. PERSONALITY & SOC. PSYCHOL. 804 (1995). On these and other variables, see also Peter R. Harris, Dale W. Griffin & Sandra Murray, *Testing the Limits of Optimistic Bias: Event and Person Moderators in a Multilevel Framework*, 95 J. PERSONALITY & SOC. PSYCHOL. 1225 (2008).

294. Tali Sharot, *The Optimism Bias*, 21 CURRENT BIOLOGY R941, R942–44 (2011).

Relatedly, people tend to attribute positive events to their own internal and stable character, and negative events to external, unstable causes. They make more internal attributions for success than for failure.[295]

Another manifestation of a self-serving bias—on the borderline between overoptimism and overconfidence, which is particularly germane to legal contexts—refers to people's assessment of their ability to provide justification through arguments. People tend to overestimate this ability, especially when they are emotionally invested in the issue in question.[296]

It is important to note that overoptimism and the better-than-average effect do not necessarily stem from *motivated reasoning* or *wishful thinking*. Some of the effects described above appear to be byproducts of other, non-motivated cognitive biases. According to the egocentric-thinking account, when comparing themselves to others, people focus on the likelihood that they would experience an event, rather than on the likelihood that the comparison target would. This theory accounts for the finding that sometimes people give higher comparative estimates when the absolute frequency of a negative events is high, but lower comparative estimates, and even overly pessimistic ones, when the frequency is low (whereas wishful thinking would predict overoptimism in both cases).[297] It has similarly been shown that when predicting the results of football games, subjects assign higher probability of winning to a team not only when they are promised a money reward if that team wins, but also when a team is made more salient by other means, without the promise of any reward.[298] Overoptimism may also be associated with the so-called *projection bias*, namely people's tendency to underestimate the extent to which their tastes and preferences might change in the future.[299] Projection bias leads to overoptimism when, for example, people underappreciate the effects of the gradual increase in their standard of living on their consumption preferences—which may in turn lead to insufficient saving. Some instances of overoptimism may also be perfectly rational given people's limited information about others.[300] However, motivation-based overoptimism—that is, overoptimism originating in people's desire to be more skillful (in absolute terms and in comparison with others), to

295. Amy H. Mezulis et al., *Is There a Universal Positivity Bias in Attributions? A Meta-analytic Review of Individual, Developmental, and Cultural Differences in the Self-Serving Attributional Bias,* 130 Psychol. Bull. 711 (2004). On attribution theories, see also *infra* pp. 68–69.

296. Matthew Fisher & Frank C. Keil, *The Illusion of Argument Justification,* 143 J. Experimental Psychol.: General 425 (2014).

297. Justin Kruger & Jeremy Burrus, *Egocentrism and Focalism in Unrealistic Optimism (and Pessimism),* 40 J. Experimental Soc. Psychol. 332 (2004); John R. Chambers, Paul D. Windschitl & Jerry Suls, *Egocentrism, Event Frequency, and Comparative Optimism: When What Happens Frequently Is "More Likely to Happen to Me,"* 29 Personality & Soc. Psychol. Bull. 1343 (2003).

298. Maya Bar-Hillel, David V. Budesku & Moti Amar, *Predicting World Cup Results: Do Goals Seem More Likely When They Pay off?,* 15 Psychonomic Bull. & Rev. 278 (2008).

299. George Loewenstein, Ted O'Donoghue & Matthew Rabin, *Projection Bias in Predicting Future Utility,* 118 Q.J. Econ. 1209 (2003).

300. Adam J. L. Harris & Ulrike Hahn, *Unrealistic Optimism about Future Life Events: A Cautionary Note,* 118 Psychol. Rev. 135 (2011); Wihdschitl & Stuart, *supra* note 283, at 438.

have positive experiences, win competitions, and attain higher social status by appearing more optimistic—does exist.[301]

Presumably, accurate beliefs about reality are key to optimal decision-making. However, the prevalence of overoptimism suggests that it may actually be adaptive. Indeed, a meta-analysis of the available empirical evidence attests to a small overall *depressive realism* effect: depressed individuals are less prone to overoptimism than non-depressed ones.[302] Optimism also contributes to one's physical health. Since expecting positive outcomes reduces stress and anxiety, and facilitates health-promoting activities, optimists tend to live longer and be healthier. Overoptimism may lead people to work harder, which in turn may facilitate greater achievements. Better-than-average perceptions of one's spouse and children are also very prevalent and highly adaptive.[303]

That said, overoptimism has adverse and even dangerous effects, as well. Overly optimistic people are more likely to procrastinate when required to perform an unpleasant task.[304] They may refrain from taking necessary precautions, neglect periodic medical examinations, and fail to watch their diet. Similarly, unrealistic optimism about one's future income may lead to excessive borrowing;[305] entrepreneurial wishful thinking may lead to excessive entry into competitive markets;[306] and overoptimism about litigation outcomes may hinder mutually-beneficial compromises.[307]

4. Overconfidence

The term "overconfidence" has been used to denote several phenomena, including the better-than-average effect discussed above.[308] In this section we focus mainly on the degree of confidence that people express about the accuracy of their assessments and judgments (also known as *overprecision* or *miscalibration*).

A common method of examining people's confidence is to ask them to answer a list of questions, and then state their degree of confidence in the correctness of their answers to each question. For example, a participant may indicate that she is 10, 20 . . . or 100 percent

301. Wihdschitl & Stuart, *supra* note 283, at 437–40.

302. Michael T. Moore & David M. Fresco, *Depressive Realism: A Meta-analytic Review*, 32 Clinical Psychol. Rev. 496 (2012).

303. *See generally* Ryan T. McKay & Daniel C. Dennett, *The Evolution of Misbelief*, 32 Behav. & Brain Sci. 493, 505–07 (2009); Sharot, *supra* note 294, at R944–45.

304. Harold Sigall, Arie Kruglanski & Jack Fyock, *Wishful Thinking and Procrastination*, 15 J. Soc. Behav. & Personality 283 (2000). On procrastination, see also *infra* pp. 87–88.

305. *See also infra* pp. 298–99.

306. Colin Camerer & Dan Lovallo, *Overconfidence and Excess Entry: An Experimental Approach*, 89 Am. Econ. Rev. 306 (1999). *See also infra* pp. 385–86.

307. Linda Babcock & George Loewenstein, *Explaining Bargaining Impasse: The Role of Self-Serving Biases*, 11 J. Econ. Persp. 109 (1997). *See also infra* pp. 497–500.

308. Don A. Moore & Paul J. Healy, *The Trouble with Overconfidence*, 115 Psychol. Rev. 502 (2008); Don A. Moore, Elizabeth R. Tenney & Uriel Haran, *Overprecision in Judgment*, *in* Wiley Blackwell Handbook, *supra* note 2, at 182, 183–84. *See also supra* pp. 61–64.

confident in the correctness of any answer. For each level of confidence (say, all the answers that the participant was 70 percent confident about), the percentage of correct answers is then compared with the stated confidence. Such experiments have traditionally used general knowledge questions, word-spelling tasks, and the like.[309] Typically, a considerable gap is found between the percentage of questions participants had answered correctly and their stated degree of confidence (which is higher). Another widely used method for examining confidence utilizes the *confidence interval paradigm*: asking people to make an assessment or prediction within a given interval of confidence, say 90 percent (so that there is only a 10 percent chance that the assessment is wrong), or to estimate the percentile at which they are confident in their estimation.[310] Again, it has been found that the correct figure lies outside the stated interval much more often than subjects expect it to be. Several explanations have been offered for overconfidence, but none appears to be general or conclusive.[311]

Overconfidence has been found to be most pronounced when tasks are very difficult, and to diminish with the ease of the task—possibly due to people's limited ability to assess the difficulty of various tasks. The finding that overconfidence considerably diminishes with easier tasks raises concerns about the external validity and generalizability of the laboratory findings, since in the natural environment people are arguably better at assessing the difficulty of common tasks.[312] Furthermore, the difference between hard and easy tasks raises doubts as to whether revealed overconfidence is at all related to a self-serving bias, as the latter should presumably characterize both hard and easy tasks.[313]

However, overconfidence has also been found in experiments that appear to be less vulnerable to these critiques, such as one in which subjects were asked to identify contradictions in a text.[314] In another experiment, subjects who were provided with a simple decision rule tended to use their own judgment rather than to follow the rule—which led them to do worse. Such overconfidence was even more pronounced among subjects who had (or thought they had) a relevant expertise. Consequently, they not only did worse than they would have done had they followed the decision rule, but even worse than the nonexperts.[315]

309. For overviews, see Sarah Lichtenstein, Baruch Fischhoff & Lawrence D. Phillips, *Calibration of Probabilities: The State of the Art to 1980, in* Judgment under Uncertainty, *supra* note 77, at 306; Nickerson, *supra* note 259, at 188–89; Ulrich Hoffrage, *Overconfidence, in* Cognitive Illusions: A Handbook on Fallacies and Biases in Thinking, Judgement and Memory 235 (Rüdiger Pohl ed., 2004).

310. *See* Marc Alpert and Howard Raiffa, *A Progress Report on the Training of Probability Assessors, in* Judgment under Uncertainty, *supra* note 77, at 295.

311. Moore, Tenney & Haran, *supra* note 308, at 190–93.

312. Peter Juslin, *The Overconfidence Phenomenon as a Consequence of Informal Experimenter-Guided Selection of Almanac Items,* 57 Org. Behav. & Hum. Decision Processes 226 (1994).

313. Gerd Gigerenzer, Ulrich Hoffrage & Heinz Kleinbölting, *Probabilistic Mental Models: A Brunswikian Theory of Confidence,* 98 Psychol. Rev. 506 (1991).

314. Arthur M. Glenberg, Alex Cherry Wilkinson & William Epstein, *The Illusion of Knowing: Failure in the Self-Assessment of Comprehension,* 10 Memory & Cognition 597 (1982).

315. Hal R. Arkes, Robyn M. Dawes & Caryn Christensen, *Factors Influencing the Use of a Decision Rule in a Probabilistic Task,* 37 Org. Behav. & Hum. Decision Processes 93 (1986).

There is conflicting evidence about the effect of professional training and expertise on people's confidence. On the one hand, the assessments by meteorologists of the correctness of their own weather forecasts were found to be fairly accurate—plausibly thanks to the constant feedback they receive.[316] On the other hand, other professionals—such as physicians, lawyers, and scientists—were found to be overconfident.[317] Overconfidence may affect the choice between discretionary, holistic decision-making and the use of evidence-based guidelines that integrate data based on statistical meta-analyses. Much of the detrimental underuse of such guidelines is attributed to professionals' overconfidence.[318]

Encouraging people to consider more information and possible alternatives reduces overconfidence. Providing people with feedback has not, however, produced clear-cut results.[319]

In general, overconfidence may have beneficial side effects in social interactions, such as negotiation, persuasion, and medical treatment (where a physician's overconfidence in the expected success of a treatment may enhance the prospect of success, thanks to the placebo effect).[320] Hence, it may have evolutionary adaptive advantages. However, such incidental benefits are likely to exacerbate this bias, and overconfidence may well lead people astray—for example, in litigation and settlement decisions.[321]

5. Naïve Realism and False-Consensus Effect

People perceive and interpret reality differently. In one famous study, undergraduate students from two universities watched a film of a rough football game that actually took place between their universities' teams. The students were asked to mark any rule violation by each team, and whether those violations were "mild" or "flagrant." Judging from their answers, one might think that the students saw different games, although for each student the version that he or she saw was very real.[322] For example, Stanford students saw twice

316. Allan H. Murphy & Robert L. Winkler, *Can Weather Forecasters Formulate Reliable Probability Forecasts of Precipitation and Temperature?*, 2 Nat'l Weather Dig. 2 (1977).

317. Nickerson, *supra* note 259, at 189; Moore, Tenney & Haran, *supra* note 308, at 187–88, 189; Jane Goodman-Delahunty et al., *Insightful or Wishful: Lawyers' Ability to Predict Case Outcomes,* 16 Psychol. Pub. Pol'y & L. 133 (2010); Craig R.M. McKenzie, Michael J. Liersch & Ilan Yaniv, *Overconfidence in Interval Estimates: What Does Expertise Buy You?,* 107 Org. Behavior & Hum. Decision Processes 179 (2008); Itzhak Ben-David, John R. Graham & Campbell R. Harvey, *Managerial Miscalibration,* 128 Q.J. Econ. 1547 (2013). *See also* Deborah J. Miller, Elliot S. Spengler & Paul M. Spengler, *A Meta-analysis of Confidence and Judgment Accuracy in Clinical Decision Making,* 62 J. Counseling Psychol. 553 (2015) (a meta-analysis revealing a small but statistically significant correlation between counseling psychologists' confidence and the accuracy of their judgments); *infra* pp. 513–14.

318. *See, e.g.*, Eta S. Berner & Mark L. Graber, *Overconfidence as a Cause of Diagnostic Error in Medicine,* 121 Am. J. Med. S2 (2008).

319. On these and other debiasing techniques, see Moore, Tenney & Haran, *supra* note 308, at 195–97.

320. Hoffrage, *supra* note 309, at 250.

321. *See infra* pp. 499–500, 513–14.

322. Albert H. Hastorf & Hadley Cantril, *They Saw a Game: A Case Study,* 49 J. Abnormal & Soc. Psychol. 129 (1954).

as many infractions made by the Dartmouth team as the Dartmouth students saw, and while almost nine-tenths of the Stanford students thought that the Dartmouth team had instigated the rough play, a majority of Dartmouth students believed that both teams were to blame.[323]

This football experiment demonstrates one aspect of *naïve realism*—namely, the human tendency to believe that we see the world around us objectively, while people who disagree with us must be uninformed or biased.[324] People assume that they see reality "as it is," and that their beliefs and attitudes emanate from an unbiased comprehension of the evidence available to them. It follows that other rational people who have access to the same information and process it in open-minded fashion should reach the same conclusions. It further follows that if other people do not share their conclusions, it must be because the former are un- or misinformed, because they are irrational or otherwise unable to consider the data, or because they are biased by self-interest, ideology, or some other distorting influence.[325]

Naïve realism underpins the *false-consensus effect*—people's tendency to overestimate the extent to which their beliefs and opinions are shared by others.[326] People also believe that whereas their own beliefs are not indicative of their personal dispositions, conflicting attitudes do reflect the personality of their proponents.[327] The more a situation or a choice is open to conflicting interpretations, the greater the false-consensus effect—which points to the role played by people's subjective interpretation in producing this effect.[328]

A corollary of naïve realism is that people readily recognize this bias, and a host of other biases, in *other* people's perceptions and judgments, but they often have a blind spot regarding their own naïve realism (and other biases).[329] Even when people are aware of their own biases, they tend to believe that they are more capable than others of assessing the magnitude and effect of those biases.[330]

323. An experiment in which subjects of opposing ideological inclinations were asked to describe a political demonstration yielded similar results. *See* Dan M. Kahan et al., *"They Saw a Protest": Cognitive Illiberalism and the Speech-Conduct Distinction,* 64 Stan. L. Rev. 851 (2012).

324. Lee Ross & Andrew Ward, *Naive Realism in Everyday Life: Implications for Social Conflict and Misunderstanding, in* Values and Knowledge 103 (Edward S. Reed, Elliot Turiel & Terrance Brown eds., 1996).

325. *Id.* at 110–11.

326. Thomas Gilovich, *Differential Construal and the False Consensus Effect,* 59 J. Personality & Soc. Psychol. 623 (1990).

327. Lee Ross, David Greene & Pamela House, *The "False Consensus Effect": An Egocentric Bias in Social Perception and Attribution Processes,* 13 J. Experimental Soc. Psychol. 279 (1977).

328. Gilovich, *supra* note 326.

329. Emily Pronin, Daniel Y. Lin & Lee Ross, *The Bias Blind Spot: Perceptions of Bias in Self versus Others,* 28 Personality & Soc. Psychol. Bull. 369 (2002).

330. Emily Pronin, Tom Gilovich & Lee Ross, *Objectivity in the Eye of the Beholder: Divergent Perceptions of Bias in Self versus Others,* 111 Psychol. Rev. 781 (2004).

Naïve realism is related to the formation and maintenance of in-group and out-group identities. It thus makes the resolution of social, ethnic, and political conflicts extremely difficult.[331]

6. Fundamental Attribution Error

Understanding why other people behave as they do is as essential in daily life as it is in professional decision-making by educators, managers, and judges. *Attribution theories* seek to explain this process. They usually distinguish between internal causes of behavior, such as personal traits and dispositions, and external or situational ones, such as social norms and obedience to instructions. In a classic experiment, Edward Jones and Victor Harris asked participants to assess the true attitude of a person who had written an essay that was either supportive or critical of Castro's regime. Participants were also told either that the author had written the essay voluntarily, or had been instructed to do so by an authority figure. While subjects took the issue of choice into account, one striking finding was that even in the no-choice condition, they tended to believe that the essay reflected the writer's true attitude.[332] Subsequently dubbed the *fundamental attribution error*[333]—also known as the *correspondence bias*—the tendency to attribute other people's behavior to their personal attitudes and motivations, rather than to environmental influences and constraints, has been documented in numerous studies.[334] However, like virtually all phenomena discussed in this chapter, the fundamental attribution error, and the very distinction between dispositional and external causes of behavior, have been the subject of some controversy.[335]

One explanation for the fundamental attribution error is observers' lack of awareness of situational constraints. To judge the extent to which a given behavior is a product of inner inclinations or external forces, one must be aware of the latter. Sometimes, however, external forces, such as audience pressure or parental threats, are simply invisible to the onlooker, and the onlooker fails to grasp their true impact on the person in question, for example due to naïve realism.[336] Another explanation is unrealistic expectations of

331. In a seminal study, pro-Israeli and pro-Arab subjects watched the same media reports of the massacre conducted by Falangist gunmen on the Sabra and Chatilla refugee camps. Both groups overwhelmingly saw the media coverage as slanted in favor of the other side and both recalled more negative references to their side. *See* Robert P. Vallone, Lee Ross & Mark R. Lepper, *The Hostile Media Phenomenon: Biased Perception and Perceptions of Media Bias in Coverage of the Beirut Massacre,* 49 J. PERSONALITY & SOC. PSYCHOL. 577 (1985).

332. Edward E. Jones & Victor A. Harris, *The Attribution of Attitudes,* 3 J. EXPERIMENTAL SOC. PSYCHOL. 1 (1967).

333. Lee Ross, *The Intuitive Psychologist and His Shortcomings: Distortions in the Attribution Process,* 10 ADVANCES EXPERIMENTAL SOC. PSYCHOL. 173, 184–87 (1977).

334. For an overview, see Daniel T. Gilbert & Patrick S. Malone, *The Correspondence Bias,* 117 PSYCHOL. BULL. 21 (1995). For a discussion of the fundamental attribution error within the broader context of cognitive social psychology, see LEE ROSS & RICHARD E. NISBETT, THE PERSON AND THE SITUATION: PERSPECTIVES OF SOCIAL PSYCHOLOGY (1991).

335. John Sabini, Michael Siepmann & Julia Stein, *The Really Fundamental Attribution Error in Social Psychological Research,* 12 PSYCHOL. INQUIRY 1 (2001).

336. *Id.* at 25–27.

behavior—expectations that do not give due weight to people's conformity, that is, to their tendency to adapt their behavior to match group norms.[337] Other explanations have been offered as well.[338]

The fundamental attribution error is affected by various variables. People are more prone to commit it when they have fewer cognitive resources at their disposal to assess the causes of the observed behavior (for example, when they perform an additional cognitive task at the same time).[339] It thus appears that correcting the initial perception of people's behavior by considering external circumstances is a more demanding, deliberative process. Studies have also shown that negative moods decrease, and positive moods increase, the fundamental attribution error.[340] Finally, there appear to be cultural differences regarding the inclination to attribute behavior to personal dispositions. Specifically, some studies have shown that East Asians tend to recognize the causal power of situations more than Westerners.[341]

7. Planning Fallacy

Overly optimistic predictions regarding the time (and costs) involved in completing projects have been repeatedly noted, for example, in the construction and the software engineering industries. This phenomenon, known as the *planning fallacy*,[342] is equally prevalent in daily life. Thus, having published several books with a leading publishing house, one of us has noticed that whenever he submitted a book manuscript by the deadline set out in the publication agreement, it took several months before the production process actually got underway. It occurred to him that the publisher had learned from experience that authors rarely submit manuscripts on time, and adjust their work plans accordingly. Realizing this, in his next publication agreement, the author set an unrealistically early submission date.

Kahneman and Tversky have argued that a sound prediction should rest on two types of information: information about the particular case under consideration (the so-called

337. *Id.* at 27–28. For famous demonstrations of people's conformity, see Solomon E. Asch, *Effects of Group Pressure upon the Modification and Distortion of Judgments, in* GROUPS, LEADERSHIP AND MEN; RESEARCH IN HUMAN RELATIONS 177 (Harold Guetzkow ed., 1951); Stanley Milgram, *Behavioral Study of Obedience,* 67 J. ABNORMAL & SOC. PSYCHOL. 371 (1963). For an overview, see Donelson R. Forsyth, *Social Influence and Group Behavior, in* HANDBOOK OF PSYCHOLOGY, Vol. 5: PERSONALITY AND SOCIAL PSYCHOLOGY 305–328 (Irving B. Weiner, Howard A. Tennen & Jerry M. Suls eds., 2d ed. 2012).

338. Gilbert & Malone, *supra* note 334, at 28–32; Darren Lagdridge & Trevor Butt, *The Fundamental Attribution Error: A Phenomenological Critique,* 43 BRITISH J. SOC. PSYCHOL. 357 (2004).

339. Daniel T. Gilbert, Brett W. Pelham & Douglas S. Krull, *On Cognitive Busyness: When Person Perceivers Meet Persons Perceived,* 54 J. PERSONALITY & SOC. PSYCHOL. 733 (1988).

340. Joseph P. Forgas, *On Being Happy and Mistaken: Mood Effects on the Fundamental Attribution Error,* 75 J. PERSONALITY & SOC. PSYCHOL. 318 (1998).

341. Ara Norenzayan & Richard E. Nissbet, *Culture and Causal Cognition,* 9 CURRENT DIRECTIONS PSYCHOL. SCI. 132 (2000). *But see* Douglas S. Krull et al., *The Fundamental Attribution Error: Correspondence Bias in Individualist and Collectivist Cultures,* 25 PERSONALITY & SOC. PSYCHOL. BULL. 1208 (1999).

342. For overviews, see Roger Buehler, Dale Griffin & Michael Ross, *Inside the Planning Fallacy: The Causes and Consequences of Optimistic Time Predictions, in* HEURISTICS AND BIASES, *supra* note 97, at 250; Roger Buehler, Dale Griffin & Johanna Peetz, *The Planning Fallacy: Cognitive, Motivational, and Social Origins,* 42 ADVANCES EXPERIMENTAL SOCIAL PSYCHOLOGY 1 (2010).

singular information) and information about similar cases, based on past experience, when available (*distributional information*). They attributed the planning fallacy to excessive focus on the singular information, compared with the distributional one,[343] as the latter cautions against overoptimism. Further experimental studies have shown that the comparative neglect of past experience is due to several factors.[344] First, the very engagement in a planning activity elicits concentration on the future rather than on the past. It follows that providing incentives for early task completion exacerbates the planning fallacy, since it reinforces the focus on detailed future plans, at the expense of relevant past experiences.[345] Similarly, since a sense of power and control induces goal-directed attention (and disregard of other information), it similarly aggravates the planning fallacy.[346] A second reason for neglecting past experience is that, as in the case of *base-rate neglect* in probability assessments,[347] people tend to focus on specific, rather than general, information—that is, on the case at hand, rather than past experience. Third, when judging their previous behavior, people tend to attribute success to their own abilities and efforts—and failures to external, supervening events, which may not seem relevant to the current project.[348] Unsurprisingly, when subjects are led to recall past experiences and relate them to the task at hand, they make much more realistic predictions.[349] It has also been found that while people are overly optimistic about the completion time of their own projects, external observers may be overly pessimistic.[350] Finally, overoptimism about task completion is also linked to the desire to be seen in a positive light by others. Thus, in one experiment, people exhibited the planning fallacy when they made predictions verbally to a familiar experimenter, but not when making them anonymously.[351]

Forecasting an early completion may incentivize people to meet their goals by increasing their effort and persistence, and by inducing consistency motivations.[352] It may

343. Daniel Kahneman & Amos Tversky, *Intuitive Prediction: Biases and Corrective Procedures, in* JUDGMENT UNDER UNCERTAINTY, *supra* note 77, at 414. *See also* David Lagnado & Steven Sloman, *Inside and Outside Probability Judgement, in* BLACKWELL HANDBOOK OF JUDGMENT AND DECISION MAKING 155 (Derek Koehler & Nigel Harvey eds., 2004) (reviewing this phenomenon in the context of probability judgment).

344. Roger Buehler, Dale Griffin & Michael Ross, *Exploring the "Planning Fallacy": Why People Underestimate Their Task Completion Times,* 67 J. PERSONALITY & SOC. PSYCHOL. 366 (1994).

345. Roger Buehler, Dale Griffin & Heather MacDonald, *The Role of Motivated Reasoning in Optimistic Time Predictions,* 23 PERSONALITY & SOC. PSYCHOL. BULL. 238 (1997). *See also* Buehler, Griffin & Peetz, *supra* note 342, at 27–31.

346. Mario Weick & Ana Guinote, *How Long Will It Take? Power Biases Time Predictions,* 46 J. EXPERIMENTAL SOC. PSYCHOL. 595 (2010).

347. *See supra* pp. 30–31.

348. On the fundamental attribution error, see *supra* pp. 68–69.

349. Buehler, Griffin & Ross, *supra* note 344, at 374–77. On other debiasing techniques, see Buehler, Griffin & Ross, *supra* note 342, at 268–70; Buehler, Griffin & Peetz, *supra* note 342, at 53–55.

350. *Id.* at 377–79.

351. Stephanie P. Pezzo, Mark V. Pezzo & Eric R. Stone, *The Social Implications of Planning,* 42 J. EXPERIMENTAL SOC. PSYCHOL. 221 (2006).

352. Buehler, Griffin & Peetz, *supra* note 342, at 48.

thus be evolutionary adaptive—at least on some occasions. There are, however, grounds to believe that there is a difference in this regard between tasks that can be completed in a single, continuous session (and are therefore less susceptible to interruptions), and those that cannot: overly optimistic predictions foster early completion of the former, but not the latter.[353]

Besides the automatic and largely unconscious mechanisms that produce the planning fallacy, underestimating the time and costs of future projects may have strategic advantages. For example, once an organization has embarked on a project, it is most likely to keep investing in it (possibly due to the *sunk costs effect*), even if it turns out that the predicted costs and completion time were overly optimistic. Hence, when decision-makers must choose between competing projects, those who advocate a particular project may strategically underestimate its costs and completion time. Consequently, it may be difficult to disentangle automatic and deliberative causes of the present phenomenon.

8. Illusion of Control

People's tendency to attribute their successes to themselves, and their failures to external factors,[354] is apparently inapplicable to circumstances in which outcomes depend on sheer chance. Nevertheless, it has long been shown experimentally that skill-related factors—such as competition, choice, contemplating successful strategies, active involvement, and familiarity—lead people to believe that they have control over objectively chance-determined events.[355] For instance, observers tend to assume, implicitly, that a person who rolls dice himself has greater control over the outcome then when someone else rolls the dice for him.[356] In fact, it has been observed that dice players behave as if they were controlling the outcome of the toss: they threw the dice softly when they needed low numbers, and hard for high numbers.[357]

A meta-analysis of dozens of studies has shown that the illusion of control manifests itself across various tasks and circumstances.[358] The illusion's effect was found to be larger with regard to participants' belief in their ability to *predict* outcomes than in relation to their ability to *control* them. It has also been shown that the magnitude of the effect is significantly greater in experiments that employ an indirect, qualitative measure of the effect (for example, whether participants are willing to trade a lottery ticket) than in those using an indirect, quantitative measure (such as the number of trials in which participants feel

353. *Id.* at 46–53.

354. *See supra* pp. 68–69.

355. Ellen J. Langer, *The Illusion of Control*, 32 J. PERSONALITY & SOC. PSYCHOL. 311 (1975).

356. John H. Fleming & John M. Darley, *Perceiving Choice and Constraint: The Effects of Contextual and Behavioral Cues on Attitude Attribution*, 56 J. PERSONALITY & SOC. PSYCHOL. 27 (1989).

357. James N. Henslin, *Craps and Magic*, 73 AM. J. SOC. 316 (1967).

358. Paul K. Presson & Victor A. Benassi, *Illusion of Control: A Meta-analytic Review*, 11 J. SOC. BEHAV. & PERSONALITY 493 (1996).

confident about the outcome) or direct assessments (such as when participants are asked how much control they feel they had over the outcome).[359]

A common denominator of the studies described thus far is that they have focused on situations where people have very little or no control over outcomes, but nevertheless believe that they do have such control. A more recent study revealed a complementary—and in a sense, opposite—phenomenon: when people have a great deal of control, they tend to underestimate it.[360]

9. Behavioral Ethics

Egocentrism and motivated reasoning are crucial to understanding people's ethical behavior—especially the mechanisms that allow ordinary people to violate ethical norms while preserving their self-image as moral people. This topic—commonly known as *behavioral ethics*—has attracted considerable attention in recent years.[361]

Behavioral ethics draws heavily on the notion of *dual reasoning* (System 1 and System 2),[362] and argues that self-interested behavior is largely automatic. While JDM research focuses on how people's heuristics and biases often *hinder* the advancement of their interests and goals, behavioral-ethics studies show how automatic processes *facilitate* the promotion of people's interests and goals. However, unlike standard economic analysis, which posits that people deliberately maximize their own utility, behavioral ethics focuses on the effect of self-interest on people's automatic cognitive processes.

Motivation—in particular, the motivation to advance one's self-interest—affects reasoning through the cognitive processes by which people form impressions, determine their beliefs, assess evidence, and make decisions.[363] Motivated, self-serving reasoning affects not only the decision process, but also ex-post recollection. Lisa Shu and her colleagues have demonstrated that people misremember both what they have done and what they were told to do, when it allows them to believe that they have acted ethically.[364] In their experiments, participants who were given an opportunity to cheat tended to forget the contents of an honor code they had previously read, far more than participants who were not given such an opportunity.

359. *Id.*

360. Francesca Gino, Zachariah Sharek & Don A. Moore, *Keeping the Illusion of Control under Control: Ceilings, Floors, and Imperfect Calibration*, 114 ORG. BEHAVIOR & HUM. DECISION PROCESSES 104 (2011).

361. For an overview of behavioral ethics, see Yuval Feldman, *Behavioral Ethics Meets Behavioral Law and Economics*, *in* THE OXFORD HANDBOOK OF BEHAVIORAL ECONOMICS AND THE LAW, *supra* note 8, at 213. *See also* Jennifer J. Kish-Gephart, David A. Harrison & Linda Klebe Treviño, *Bad Apples, Bad Cases, and Bad Evidence about Sources of Unethical Decisions at Work*, 95 J. APPLIED PSYCHOL. 1 (2010); Max H. Bazerman & Francesca Gino, *Behavioral Ethics: Toward a Deeper Understanding of Moral Judgment and Dishonesty*, 8 ANN. REV. L. & SOC. SCI. 85 (2012). *See also infra* pp. 455–61.

362. *See supra* pp. 21–23.

363. *See supra* pp. 58–61.

364. Shu, Gino & Bazerman, *supra* note 263.

Considerable evidence supports the claim that self-interest affects ethical behavior through System 1. Self-interest is "automatic, viscerally compelling, and often unconscious," whereas compliance with professional obligations is "a more thoughtful process."[365] The automatic nature of self-interest makes it difficult for people to be aware of it; hence they are unlikely to counteract its impact on their reasoning. Thus, in some experiments, subjects were first asked to make estimates on behalf of one party (e.g., a prospective buyer or seller), and then incentivized to make as objective estimates as possible. Not only did the affiliation with one party bias the subjects' original estimates, but this bias carried over to the subsequent estimate, despite the monetary incentive for accuracy. It appears that subjects actually believed their biased assessments.[366] The notion that unethical behavior is automatic (and is sometimes curtailed by self-control) is supported by the finding that time pressure increases self-serving unethical behavior, whereas ample time reduces such behavior (provided that people are unable to come up with justifications for their deeds).[367] Finally, a recent study showed that when subjects were experimentally manipulated into an intuitive/automatic mindset, they tended to act in a more self-interested manner than when they were manipulated into an analytical/deliberative mindset.[368]

While the majority view in the literature emphasizes the role of System 1 in unethical behavior, the picture is more nuanced: System 1 thinking does not always lead to selfish behavior, and people do sometimes deliberately and consciously violate moral and social norms.[369] In circumstances of explicit social exchange (such as prisoner's dilemma and public goods games), cooperation and reciprocity, rather than self-interested defection, appear to be the automatic response.[370]

A common theme of behavioral-ethics studies—closely related to the notion that unethical behavior is often automatic rather than calculated—is that ordinary, "good people" sometimes do "bad things."[371] People tend to display *moral hypocrisy*: they are motivated

365. Don A. Moore & George Loewenstein, *Self-Interest, Automaticity, and the Psychology of Conflict of Interest,* 17 Soc. Just. Res. 189, 189 (2004). *See also* Nicholas Epley & Eugene M. Caruso, *Egocentric Ethics,* 17 Soc. Just. Res. 171 (2004); Brent L. Hughes & Jamil Zaki, *The Neuroscience of Motivated Cognition,* 19 Trends Cognitive Sci. 62 (2015).

366. Don A. Moore, Lloyd Tanlu & Max H. Bazerman, *Conflict of Interest and the Intrusion of Bias,* 5 Judgment & Decision Making 37 (2010).

367. Shaul Shalvi, Ori Eldar & Yoella Bereby-Meyer, *Honesty Requires Time (and Lack of Justifications),* 23 Psychol. Sci. 23:1264 (2012).

368. Yuval Feldman & Eliran Halali. *Can We Regulate "Good" People in Subtle Conflicts of Interest Situations* (working paper, 2015), *available at*: http://ssrn.com/abstract=2536575.

369. Feldman, *supra* note 361, at 219–20; Yoella Bereby-Meyer & Shaul Shalvi, *Deliberate Honesty,* 6 Current Opinion Psychol. 195 (2015); Hughes & Zaki, *supra* note 365.

370. David G. Rand, Joshua D. Greene & Martin A. Nowak, *Spontaneous Giving and Calculated Greed,* 489 Nature 427 (2012); Eliran Halali, Yoella Bereby-Meyer & Nachshon Meiran, *Between Rationality and Reciprocity: The Social Bright Side of Self-Control Failure,* 143 J. Experimental Psychol.: General 745 (2014).

371. David M. Bersoff, *Why Good People Sometimes Do Bad Things: Motivated Reasoning and Unethical Behavior,* 25 Personality & Soc. Psychol. Bull. 28 (1999); Max H. Bazerman, George Loewenstein & Don A. Moore, *Why Good Accountants Do Bad Audits,* 80 Harv. Bus. Rev. 96 (2002); Nina Mazar, On Amir & Dan Ariely, *The Dishonesty of Honest People: A Theory of Self-Concept Maintenance,* 45 J. Marketing Res. 633 (2008).

"to appear moral in one's own and other's eyes while, if possible, avoiding the cost of actually being moral."[372] However, while rational choice theory might predict total disregard of ethical norms, in reality people tend to infringe ethical norms only to the extent that allows them to maintain their self-image as honest people.[373] As Nina Mazar and her colleagues have put it, "people behave dishonestly enough to profit but honestly enough to delude themselves of their own integrity. A little bit of dishonesty gives a taste of profit without spoiling a positive self-view."[374]

A telling demonstration of this observation is found in an experiment conducted by David Bersoff, in which all subjects were "mistakenly" overpaid for their participation.[375] The conspicuousness of the unethicality of not correcting this mistake was varied between subjects, as was the identity of the victim of this behavior (an overseas firm that had financed the experiment, or the experimenter himself), and the extent to which subjects were indirectly induced to deliberate on ethical issues. The more difficult it was made for subjects to ignore the unethicality of keeping the overpayment for themselves, the more they tended to correct the overpayment (the same was true when the victim of cheating was a specific person, the experimenter, rather than a faceless, big foreign firm).[376] By the same token, when people are faced with a self-benefitting choice that might potentially harm someone else, they prefer not to know whether such harm would ensue, so as to make that choice in good conscience.[377] Other studies similarly support the claim that people tend to cheat only to the extent that they can maintain their self-image as honest people.[378]

Ann Tenbrunsel and David Messick have argued that people use several devices to avoid recognizing the unethicality of their behavior.[379] These include the use of euphemisms (e.g., "creative accounting"), *ethical numbing* when a morally dubious behavior is repeated,[380] and putting the blame on others (either an entire group of people, or one's superiors). In fact, under certain circumstances, these and comparable mechanisms of *moral disengagement*

372. C. Daniel Batson et al., *Moral Hypocrisy: Appearing Moral to Oneself without Being So*, 77 J. PERSONALITY & SOC. PSYCHOL. 525 (1999).

373. Bazerman & Gino, *supra* note 361, at 93.

374. Mazar, Amir & Ariely, *supra* note 371, at 633.

375. Bersoff, *supra* note 371.

376. Other experiments have similarly demonstrated that increasing the saliency of dishonesty reduces cheating. *See* Francesca Gino, Shahar Ayal & Dan Ariely, *Contagion and Differentiation in Unethical Behavior: The Effect of One Bad Apple on the Barrel*, 20 PSYCHOL. SCI. 393 (2009).

377. Jason Dana, Roberto A. Weber & Jason Xi Kuang, *Exploiting Moral Wiggle Room: Experiments Demonstrating an Illusory Preference for Fairness*, 33 ECON. THEORY 67 (2007).

378. Mazar, Amir & Ariely, *supra* note 371; Shaul Shalvi et al., *Justified Ethicality: Observing Desired Counterfactuals Modifies Ethical Perceptions and Behavior*, 115 ORG. BEHAV. & HUM. DECISION PROCESSES 181 (2011).

379. Ann E. Tenbrunsel & David M. Messick, *Ethical Fading: The Role of Self-Deception in Unethical Behavior*, 17 SOC. JUST. RES. 223 (2004).

380. When ethical degradation occurs gradually rather than abruptly, it is also less likely to be noticed by others, including those whose role is to monitor the behavior of the actors. *See* Francesca Gino & Max H. Bazerman, *When Misconduct Goes Unnoticed: The Acceptability of Gradual Erosion in Others' Unethical Behavior*, 45 J. EXPERIMENTAL PSYCHOL. 708 (2009).

can lead not only to lying and cheating, but to the perpetration of large-scale atrocities as well.[381] Other mechanisms of moral disengagement include *moral justification,* namely rationalizing immoral behavior as serving an important purpose; *advantageous comparison,* that is contrasting the behavior in question with an even more reprehensible conduct; and *distortion of consequences,* especially minimizing the seriousness of the adverse effects of one's behavior.[382] Unethical behavior is also deemed more justified when it benefits not only the actor but others as well—and thereby perceived as altruistic.[383]

Although studies have shown that people care about fairness,[384] it appears that concerns about fairness do not necessarily curb unethical behavior, because fairness is a highly malleable concept. Thus, studies conducted in the context of bargaining have shown that people make self-serving judgments of fairness, and that this bias increases with the complexity of the situation.[385] As previously noted, people can also bypass the fairness issue by avoiding information about the effect of their behavior on others.[386]

So far, we have described situational factors that affect people's ethical behavior, and the mechanisms that facilitate unethical behavior by ordinary people. To fully understand unethical behavior, however, two further dimensions should be taken into account: individual characteristics—including personality traits and demographic variables—and the social and organizational environment.

A meta-analysis of dozens of studies has found that cognitive moral development and the inclination to attribute life's events to one's own conduct (as opposed to external causes, such as fate or powerful others) were both inversely related to unethical behavior. A relativistic moral worldview and Machiavellianism (the inclination to promote one's interests even if it entails harming or deceiving other people) were both positively related to unethical behavior.[387] Based on Albert Bandura's list of mechanisms of moral disengagement,[388] Celia Moore and her colleagues developed a single measure of people's propensity to morally disengage, based on subjects' answers to eight questions, and demonstrated its usefulness in predicting several types of unethical organizational behavior.[389]

381. Albert Bandura, *Moral Disengagement in the Perpetration of Inhumanities,* 3 Personality & Soc. Psychol. Rev. 193 (1999).

382. *Id.*; Celia Moore et al., *Why Employees Do Bad Things: Moral Disengagement and Unethical Organizational Behavior,* 65 Personnel Psychol. 1 (2012). *See also* Shahar Ayal & Francesca Gino, *Honest Rationales for Dishonest Behavior, in* The Social Psychology of Morality: Exploring the Causes of Good and Evil 149 (Mario Mikulincer & Phillip R. Shaver eds., 2012).

383. Francesca Gino, Shahar Ayal & Dan Ariely, *Self-Serving Altruism? The Lure of Unethical Actions That Benefit Others,* 93 J. Econ. Behav. & Org. 285 (2013).

384. *See infra* pp. 102–04.

385. Leigh Thompson & George Loewenstein, *Egocentric Interpretations of Fairness and Interpersonal Conflict,* 51 Org. Behav. & Hum. Decision Processes 176 (1992).

386. *See supra* note 377 and accompanying text.

387. Kish-Gephart, Harrison & Treviño, *supra* note 361, at 2–4, 12 (2010).

388. Bandura, *supra* note 381.

389. Moore et al., *supra* note 382.

Turning to demographic variables, the meta-analysis mentioned above found a weak correlation between gender and the inclination to behave unethically (men are more inclined to behave unethically than women), and between age and unethicality (younger people tend to act more unethically). No correlation was found between level of education and unethicality.[390]

The third dimension explored by behavioral ethics, along with situational factors and individual characteristics, is that of social norms (including organizational culture, when relevant). Psychologists have long studied the *conformity effect*.[391] People's tendency to adapt their behavior to match group norms is manifested in unethical behavior, as in other contexts. Thus, for example, Francesca Gino and her colleagues examined experimentally how an example of unethical behavior by a confederate affects the behavior of other participants.[392] They found that such an example increased unethical behavior when the confederate was perceived as an in-group member, but decreased when he was considered an out-group member.[393] The closer people feel to someone who has set an example of unethical behavior, the less harshly they judge that behavior, and the more likely they are to engage in such behavior themselves.[394] More generally, it has been demonstrated that cooperation significantly increases unethical behavior.[395]

E. Reference-Dependence and Order Effects

1. General

A common feature of human perception and processing of information, judgment (including self-assessment) and decision-making, prevailing moral convictions, and bounded ethicality, is relativity, or reference-dependence. People's perceptions, judgments, and choices are strongly affected by context, and are typically comparative in nature, rather than context-independent or reflecting absolute measures.[396] This is true of basic perceptions of temperature, brightness, and size.[397] It is similarly true of gauging outcomes as either gains or losses relative to some reference point, and the related tendencies to attribute greater weight to losses than to gains, and to display risk aversion in the domain of gains and

390. Kish-Gephart, Harrison & Treviño, *supra* note 361, at 4–5, 12.

391. *See supra* note 337 and accompanying text.

392. Gino, Ayal & Ariely, *supra* note 376.

393. *Id. See also* Ayal & Gino, *supra* note 382.

394. Francesca Gino & Adam D. Galinsky, *Vicarious Dishonesty: When Psychological Closeness Creates Distance from One's Moral Compass*, 119 ORG. BEHAV. & HUM. DECISION PROCESSES 15 (2012).

395. Ori Weisel & Shaul Shalvi, *The Collaborative Roots of Corruption*, 112 PROC. NAT'L ACAD. SCI. USA 10651 (2015).

396. Thomas Mussweiler, *Comparison Processes in Social Judgment: Mechanisms and Consequences*, 110 PSYCHOL. REV. 472 (2003); Kahneman, *supra* note 147, at 1454–55.

397. *See, e.g.*, Robert Shapley & R. Clay Reid, *Contrast and Assimilation in the Perception of Brightness*, 82 PROC. NAT'L ACAD. SCI. USA 5983 (1985); Edward H. Adelson, *Perceptual Organization and the Judgment of Brightness*, 262 SCI. 2042 (1993).

risk-seeking in the domain of losses.[398] By the same token, people show a greater tendency to violate moral and social norms to avoid losses than to attain extra gains.[399] Evaluations of fairness and justice are similarly comparative in nature.[400] Finally, according to prevailing moral convictions, reference-dependence is essential to determining the morality of actions that involve harming and benefitting people, since the distinctions between benefitting and not-harming and between harming and not-benefitting presuppose a reference point.[401]

Rather than try to systematically review the numerous manifestations of reference-dependence, this section focuses on several aspects of judgment and decision-making, namely the *contrast and assimilation effects*, *order* (*primacy* and *recency*) *effects*, the *compromise effect*, *anchoring*, and *diminishing sensitivity*.

2. Contrast and Assimilation Effects

Is it preferable to be a big fish in a small pond, or a small fish in a big pond? This and similar proverbs reflect the familiar observation that assessments, including self-assessments, are largely comparative. However, it turns out that comparisons may lead in different directions. Very often, they result in a *contrast effect*, whereby people overestimate the differences between the target and the reference. For example, in one experiment, some subjects were asked to name politicians who had been involved in a political scandal, while other subjects were not. When subsequently asked to assess the trustworthiness of specific politicians who were not involved in the said scandal, subjects in the first group judged those politicians as more trustworthy than did subjects in the second group. Evidently, the accessibility of the first names set a particularly low benchmark for the subjects in the first group, against which other politicians appeared to be more trustworthy.[402] In another study, subjects who implicitly judged themselves against a well-groomed, highly skilled, and self-confident person tended to show decreased self-esteem, whereas subjects who implicitly compared themselves with an untidy, incompetent, and helpless person showed enhanced self-esteem.[403]

However, comparisons may also result in an *assimilation effect*, whereby people overestimate the similarities between the target and the reference. Thus, in the politicians' trustworthiness experiment, while specific politicians were judged more trustworthy following the increased accessibility of examples of corrupt ones, politicians in general were perceived as less trustworthy.[404] In a similar fashion, while exposure to archetypal examples of

398. *See supra* pp. 42–57.

399. *See* Zamir, *supra* note 151, at 31–33; *infra* pp. 458–59.

400. *See infra* p. 104.

401. *See infra* pp. 94–101, 187–88, 194–95.

402. Norbert Schwarz & Herbert Bless, *Scandals and the Public's Trust in Politicians: Assimilation and Contrast Effects*, 18 Personality & Soc. Psychol. Bull. 574 (1992).

403. Stan Morse & Kenneth J. Gergen, *Social Comparison, Self-Consistency, and the Concept of Self*, 16 J. Personality & Soc. Psychol. 148 (1970).

404. Schwartz & Bless, *supra* note 402.

extremely hostile figures (such as Dracula or Adolf Hitler), or *extremely* friendly ones (such as Santa Claus or Shirley Temple) produced a contrast effect in the subjects' assessments of the hostility of an ambiguously described individual, exposure to exemplars of *moderately* hostile or friendly figures yielded an assimilation effect.[405]

Whether a comparison results in a contrast or an assimilation effect thus depends on various factors, such as the extremity of the reference (the initial assessment is more likely to indicate similarity for moderate than for extreme references),[406] and whether self-assessment is made in comparison with an in-group or an out-group member (similarity testing is more likely when the reference and the target belong to the same category, and vice versa).[407] It has been suggested that whether a comparison triggers a contrast or an assimilation effect depends on the process of comparison. Whereas similarity testing—leading to assimilation—makes accessible information that suggests similarity, dissimilarity testing (which leads to the contrast effect) makes accessible information that points to dissimilarity.[408]

Even an apparently insignificant variable—such as whether participants believed that they were born on the same day as the reference—affected the self-evaluation of physical attractiveness by low-self-esteem subjects.[409] Those subjects exhibited a contrast effect when assessing their own attractiveness after viewing photos of attractive or unattractive same-sex others, whose birthdays did not match. However, after viewing photos of people whose birthday matched theirs, they assessed themselves as more attractive after viewing photos of attractive people than after viewing photos of unattractive ones.

Contrast and assimilation effects presuppose a comparison of the target with a given benchmark, yet the pertinent benchmark is often not "given," but rather constructed or selected from among several conceivable ones. Accordingly, much of the research on contrast and assimilation effects—as well as other reference-dependence effects—has dealt with the construction of the pertinent benchmark. It has been suggested that the standard against which events are judged is often constructed post hoc through counterfactual thinking, rather than existing in advance.[410]

Numerous studies of contrast and assimilation have shown that these effects can be influenced by *priming*.[411] Priming is a process in which exposure to one stimulus—be it sensory information (such as a visual image) or a concept—unconsciously influences the

405. Paul M. Herr, *Consequences of Priming: Judgment and Behavior,* 51 J. PERSONALITY & SOC. PSYCHOL. 1106 (1986).

406. *Id.*

407. Marilynn B. Brewer & Joseph G. Weber, *Self-Evaluation Effects of Interpersonal versus Intergroup Social Comparison,* 66 J. PERSONALITY & SOC. PSYCHOL. 268 (1994).

408. Mussweiler, *supra* note 396. *See also* Norbert Schwarz & Herbert Bless, *Assimilation and Contrast Effects in Attitude Measurement: An Inclusion/Exclusion Model,* 19 ADVANCES CONSUMER RES. 72 (1992).

409. Jonathon D. Brown et al., *When Gulliver Travels: Social Context, Psychological Closeness, and Self-Appraisals,* 62 J. PERSONALITY & SOC. PSYCHOL. 717, 722–25 (1992).

410. Daniel Kahneman & Dale T. Miller, *Norm Theory: Comparing Reality to Its Alternatives,* 93 PSYCHOL. REV. 136 (1986).

411. *See, e.g.,* Herr, *supra* note 405; E. Tory Higgins & C. Miguel Brendl, *Accessibility and Applicability: Some Activation Rules Influencing Judgment,* 31 J. EXPERIMENTAL SOC. PSYCHOL. 218 (1995); Nira Liberman, Jens Förster

subsequent response to the same stimulus and related ones.[412] For example, people who are exposed to the word "bird" later recognize this word and the word "sparrow" faster than people who are exposed to the word "building."[413] Similarly, when subjects are first exposed to positive words (such as "adventurous" or "self-confident") or negative ones (such as "reckless" or "conceited"), and subsequently asked a seemingly unrelated question such as to describe a person who engages in a series of ambiguous activities (such as considering going skydiving), those who were exposed to the positive words tended to describe the person more positively than those exposed to the negative ones.[414] The common theory is that information is encoded in cognitive units, which form an interconnected network in our brain. The retrieval of information from memory is performed by spreading activation throughout the network. Priming increases the level of activation and consequently the accessibility of certain information, thereby increasing the rate and probability of recalling the primed information and of recognizing related images and concepts. Priming can influence various cognitive processes, including the construction or selection of a benchmark with which a target is compared.[415]

3. Anchoring and Adjustment

A specific example of salient information that influences people's decisions can be found in the context of *anchoring*. Anchoring alludes to peoples' tendency to estimate values in relation to certain focal values, or "anchors," that they are drawn to focus on while making their decisions.[416] As a large body of work has demonstrated, anchors can unduly influence peoples' choices. More specifically, anchors might draw decision-makers toward them, thus causing decision-makers to systematically misestimate target values.

In the typical anchoring study, subjects are asked to estimate the value of a target quantity after being exposed to a certain numeric figure that serves as the anchor. In one of their early studies, Tversky and Kahneman demonstrated how such irrelevant anchors might alter peoples' evaluations.[417] The participants in this study were asked to estimate the percentage of African countries in the United Nations. Before giving their estimates, however, the participants observed a spin of a "wheel of fortune" that was rigged to stop at either 10 or 65 and were asked whether the percentage of African countries in the United Nations

& E. Tory Higgins, *Completed vs. Interrupted Priming: Reduced Accessibility from Post-Fulfillment Inhibition*, 43 J. Experimental Soc. Psychol. 258 (2007).

412. *See generally* Jens Förster & Nira Liberman, *Knowledge Activation*, *in* Social Psychology: Handbook of Basic Principles 201 (Arie W. Kruglansky & E. Tory Higgins eds., 2d ed. 2007).

413. David E. Meyer & Roger W. Schvaneveldt, *Facilitation in Recognizing Pairs of Words: Evidence of a Dependence between Retrieval Operations*, 90 J. Experimental Psychol. 227 (1971).

414. E. Tory Higgins, William S. Rholes & Carl R. Jones, *Category Accessibility and Impression Formation*, 13 J. Experimental Soc. Psychol. 141 (1977).

415. John R. Anderson, *A Spreading Activation Theory of Memory*, 22 J. Verbal Learning & Verbal Behav. 261 (1983); Förster & Liberman, *supra* note 412.

416. *See, e.g.*, Kahneman, *supra* note 14, at 119–20.

417. Tversky & Kahneman, *supra* note 94, at 1128.

was higher or lower than the figure that came up on the wheel. This initial meaningless spin greatly influenced peoples' decisions. Whereas participants who were exposed to a wheel outcome of 10 estimated the number of African countries to be 25 percent of UN member states, those who were exposed to a wheel outcome of 65 estimated them to be 45 percent.

Numerous studies have replicated this result and demonstrated the key role that anchors play in our decisions. Typical studies examine whether, and how, anchors affect the assessment of factual questions—such as the length of the Mississippi River,[418] the height and width of the Brandenburg Gate,[419] the number of countries in the United Nations,[420] and the year that Einstein first visited the United States.[421] At some level, these findings are unsurprising: when people are asked to estimate values that they are completely ignorant about, they may grasp at any available piece of information.[422]

More recent findings on anchoring, however, have demonstrated that the phenomenon is not limited to the narrow category of estimating obscure facts. For instance, Dan Ariely and his colleagues conducted a study in which they demonstrated that anchors can influence peoples' willingness to pay for goods, such as a rare bottle of wine.[423] Subjects who were exposed to a high anchor were willing to pay more than subjects who were exposed to a low anchor. In another study, Robyn LeBoeuf and Eldar Shafir demonstrated that anchoring influences how people assess physical stimuli, such as length, weight, and sound.[424] In one of their experiments, participants first listened to a music clip at a volume level of 35 (the participants could not see the numeric representations of volume throughout this experiment). They then listened to the clip again, and were asked to adjust the volume to replicate the volume level that they had previously heard. While half of the subjects started this process from a level of 1 and were required to adjust the volume upward (i.e., from a low anchor), the other half started the process from a level of 70 and were required to adjust the volume downward (i.e., from a high anchor). The results showed that even in this non-numeric, purely physical setting, anchoring affected peoples' choices: the participants in the low-anchor group chose a volume level that was significantly lower than those in the high-anchor group.

A key aspect of anchoring studies is that they usually build on an *uninformative* anchor. As noted above, in their original anchoring experiment, Tversky and Kahneman used

418. Daniel M. Oppenheimer, Robyn A. LeBoeuf & Noel T. Brewer, *Anchors Aweigh: A Demonstration of Cross-Modality Anchoring and Magnitude Priming*, 106 COGNITION 13, 16–17 (2008).

419. Fritz Strack & Thomas Mussweiler, *Explaining the Enigmatic Anchoring Effect: Mechanisms of Selective Accessibility*, 73 J. PERSONALITY & SOC. PSYCHOL. 437, 439–40 (1997).

420. Timothy D. Wilson et al., *A New Look at Anchoring Effects: Basic Anchoring and Its Antecedents,* 125.4 J. EXPERIMENTAL PSYCHOL. 387, 390–92 (1996).

421. Strack & Mussweiler, *supra* note 419, at 442–43.

422. KAHNEMAN, *supra* note14, at 125.

423. Dan Ariely, George Loewenstein & Drazen Prelec, *"Coherent Arbitrariness": Stable Demand Curves without Stable Preferences*, 118 Q.J. ECON. 73 (2006).

424. Robyn A. LeBoeuf & Eldar Shafir, *The Long and Short of It: Physical Anchoring Effects*, 19 J. BEHAV. DECISION MAKING 393 (2006).

a wheel of fortune to generate the anchor.[425] Later studies used other tools, such as the result of a die toss and subjects' social security number.[426] It is this nature of anchors that enables us to interpret the phenomenon as a *bias*—there is no reason that your valuation of a rare bottle of wine should be influenced by the last two digits of your social security number.[427]

The JDM literature has identified several potential mechanisms that might drive anchoring. The first focuses on the process of adjustment.[428] According to this line of thought, the anchor serves as the starting point for the analysis, and people slowly adjust their estimates from the anchor toward their final estimate. However, this adjustment process tends to end prematurely, and as a result, final estimates are biased in the direction of the anchor. A second theory focuses on the suggestive process triggered by the anchor.[429] It asserts that anchoring is an automatic process that occurs subconsciously. The anchor focuses our attention on a certain potential answer to the question that we face, and causes us to retrieve from our memory information that is consistent with the anchor as a plausible solution. Finally, more recent findings suggest that the anchor may distort peoples' sense of scale.[430] According to this interpretation, numerical anchors do not affect one's representation or beliefs about the target stimulus, but rather alter the response scale by which judgments are rendered.

Given the strong foundations of the anchoring effect, countering the influence of anchors on decision-makers is quite difficult. Adding incentives to the decision-making environment in the form of payments for accurate answers has been showed to be ineffective.[431] Similarly, instructions highlighting the effect of anchors did not yield a significant reduction of their effect.[432] Even expertise in the relevant area does not seem to matter much. For example, Gregory Northcraft and Margaret Neale conducted a controlled experiment in which experts (real estate brokers) and nonexperts (students) were asked to evaluate the value of property.[433]

425. Tversky & Kahneman, *supra* note 94, at 1128.

426. *See* Birte Englich, Thomas Mussweiler & Fritz Strack, *Playing Dice with Criminal Sentences: The Influence of Irrelevant Anchors on Experts' Judicial Decision Making*, 32 Personality Soc. Psychol. Bull. 188, 194–95 (2006) (die toss); Ariely, Loewenstein & Prelec, *supra* note 423, at 75–77 (last two digits of participants' social security number).

427. *See* Ariely, Loewenstein & Prelec, *supra* note 423, at 75–77.

428. For a more detailed review of the theory and the studies supporting it, see Kahneman, *supra* note14, at 120–22. For a critical review of the theory, see Gretchen B. Chapman & Eric J. Johnson, *Incorporating the Irrelevant, in* Heuristics and Biases, *supra* note 14, at 120, 127–30.

429. For a more detailed review of the theory and the studies supporting it, see Kahneman, *supra* note14, at 122–23; Chapman & Johnson, *supra* note 428, at 130–33.

430. *See* Shane W. Frederick & Daniel Mochon, A *Scale Distortion Theory of Anchoring*, 141 J. Experimental Psychol. 124 (2012).

431. *See* Timothy D. Wilson et al., *A New Look at Anchoring Effects: Basic Anchoring and Its Antecedents*, 125 J. Experimental Psychol. 387, 395–97 (1996).

432. *Id.* at 397–98.

433. Gregory B. Northcraf & Margaret A. Neale, *Experts, Amateurs, and Real Estate: An Anchoring-and-Adjustment Perspective on Property Pricing Decisions*, 39 Org. Behav. & Hum. Decision Processes 84, 87–94 (1987).

The subjects were randomly assigned to either a high or a low asking price, which served as the anchor in the experiment. The results showed that both the experts and the nonexperts were significantly influenced by the list price: a higher list price elicited higher valuations, and vice versa. Interestingly, while the unprofessional subjects conceded that they were influenced by the anchor, the experts presumed that they were immune to its effect.[434] Employing the consider-the-opposite strategy did, however, mitigate (albeit not eliminate) the effect of anchors.[435] That is, asking people to actively think of arguments in favor of a low value when facing a high anchor (and vice versa) reduces the effect of the anchor on their final decision.

4. Order Effects: Primacy and Recency

Gathering and integrating information is usually a sequential process. Presumably, unless the order in which information is received is meaningful in itself, the order should not affect one's final judgment or choice. Often, however, human judgment and decision-making do not follow this logic. In a classic study, Solomon Asch presented subjects with a list of personal characteristics, and asked them to describe a person who possessed those characteristics. One group of subjects heard the following list: intelligent, industrious, impulsive, critical, stubborn, and envious. The other group heard the same list in reverse order: envious, stubborn, critical, impulsive, industrious, and intelligent. The ensuing descriptions differed considerably. The subjects hearing the list that began with positive qualities described an able person, whose shortcomings do not overshadow his merits. In contrast, subjects who heard the reverse list described a person whose abilities are hampered by his serious difficulties. Moreover, whereas in the first group most subjects tended to interpret the ambiguous characteristics (being impulsive and critical) in a positive fashion, subjects in the second group tended to portray them negatively.[436] Order effects have been documented in various contexts, including attitude and other surveys,[437] persuasion in conversational communication,[438] legal decision-making,[439] auditing,[440] and moral judgment.[441]

434. *Id.* at 95.

435. Thomas Mussweiler, Fritz Strack & Tim Pfeiffer, *Overcoming the Inevitable Anchoring Effect: Considering the Opposite Compensates for Selective Accessibility*, 26 Personality & Soc. Psychol. Bull. 1142 (2000). On this debiasing technique, see *infra* pp. 135–36.

436. Solomon E. Asch, *Forming Impressions of Personality*, 43 J. Abnormal & Soc. Psychol. 258, 270–72 (1946).

437. For a collection of studies on this subject, see Context Effects in Social and Psychological Research 5–218 (Norbert Schwartz & Seymour Sudman eds., 1992).

438. Eric R. Igou & Herbert Bless, *Conversational Expectations as a Basis for Order Effects in Persuasion,* 26 J. Language & Soc. Psychol. 260 (2007).

439. Adrian Furnham, *The Robustness of the Recency Effect: Studies Using Legal Evidence,* 113 J. General Psychol. 351 (1986); José H. Kerstholt & Janet L. Jackson, *Judicial Decision Making: Order of Evidence Presentation and Availability of Background Information,* 12 Applied Cognitive Psychol. 445 (1998). *See also infra* pp. 532–33.

440. Alison Hubbard Ashton & Robert H. Ashton, *Sequential Belief Revision in Auditing,* 63 Accounting Rev. 623 (1988); Richard M. Tubbs, William F. Messier, Jr. & W. Robert Knechel, *Recency Effects in the Auditor's Belief-Revision Process,* 65 Accounting Rev. 452 (1990).

441. Eric Schwitzgebel & Fiery Cushman, *Expertise in Moral Reasoning? Order Effects on Moral Judgment in Professional Philosophers and Non-philosophers,* 27 Mind & Language 135 (2012). Order effects are also manifested when people memorize a list of items. They tend to remember better items at the beginning and at the end of the list, rather than in the middle.

Asch's experiment demonstrated a *primacy effect*—namely, the greater influence of earlier information on the final judgment—which falls into line with the *confirmation bias*.[442] However, some studies have demonstrated a *recency effect*, that is, a greater impact of the later information on the final judgment.[443] As in the case of the contrast and assimilation effects discussed above, there is no simple rule to determine which of the two effects, if at all, characterizes judgment and decision-making under any circumstances. The most notable model, proposed by Robin Hogarth and Hillel Einhorn, and reinforced by subsequent studies, is the *belief-adjustment model*.[444] The model describes an anchoring-and-adjustment process in which various factors, including the complexity of the stimuli, the amount of information items, and whether the information is processed step by step or at the end of the sequence, produce different order effects.[445]

Order effects depend, among other things, on people's expectations about the order in which the pieces of information are presented to them. In persuasive communications, people usually expect the most important arguments to be presented first. Accordingly, when experimenters made clear to participants that the arguments were presented in a random order, no reliable order effect was found. As hypothesized, this result was mediated by the perceived importance of the arguments.[446] This observation does not, however, pertain to other contexts in which an order effect has been identified.

Order effects have shown to be eliminated or mitigated when people are accountable for their judgment,[447] when experts have control over the order in which they review the evidence within their sphere of expertise,[448] and when auditors, who worked in groups of three, believed there was a high risk of fraudulent financial reporting.[449]

5. Compromise and Attraction Effects

Rational choice theory assumes that the relative ranking of two options is context-independent—namely, that the ranking of these options is not influenced by the availability of other options. For example, a customer in a restaurant should not change her ranking

442. *See supra* pp. 58–61.

443. *See, e.g.*, Ashton & Ashton, *supra* note 440; Tubbs, Messier & Knechel, *supra* note 440.

444. Robin M. Hogarth & Hillel J. Einhorn, *Order Effects in Belief Updating: The Belief-Adjustment Model*, 24 Cognitive Psychol. 1 (1992). On subsequent studies, see, e.g., Jane Kennedy, *Debiasing Audit Judgment with Accountability: A Framework and Experimental Results*, 31 J. Accounting Res. 231, 235–36 (1993).

445. On order effects, see also Baron, *supra* note 47, at 205–08.

446. Igou & Bless, *supra* note 438.

447. Kennedy, *supra* note 444. *See also infra* pp. 132–34.

448. Andrew D. Cuccia & Gary A. McGill, *The Role of Decision Strategies in Understanding Professionals' Susceptibility to Judgment Biases*, 38 J. Accounting Res. 419 (2000).

449. Philip M.J. Reckers & Joseph J. Schultz, Jr., *The Effects of Fraud Signals, Evidence Order, and Group-Assisted Counsel on Independent Auditor Judgment*, 5 Behav. Res. Accounting 124 (1993).

of the steak and chicken options simply because a fish is added to the menu. However, empirical findings, primarily from the area of consumer behavior, have demonstrated that decisions often display *compromise* or *attraction effects*.

The compromise effect denotes peoples' tendency to choose intermediate rather than extreme options. For example, when consumers were asked to choose between a mid-range and a low-end camera, 50 percent of them chose each type. When, however, they were asked to choose among those two cameras and an additional high-end camera, 72 percent chose the mid-range option.[450] Outside the market sphere, the compromise effect may explain decision-making in the political sphere (a choice between different policies)[451] and in adjudication (e.g., a choice between different offenses for which a defendant may be convicted).[452]

The attraction effect refers to instances in which adding an inferior option (a decoy) to a choice set increases the choice share of the superior option it most closely resembles.[453] For example, when subjects were asked to choose between a roll of paper towels and a box of facial tissues, more subjects chose the paper towels when the third option was a roll of clearly inferior paper towels, than when the third option was a box of clearly inferior facial tissues. In another experiment, subjects in one condition were asked whether they would like to trade $6 for an elegant pen or keep the money. In the other condition, subjects could trade the $6 for the same elegant pen or for a lesser, unattractive pen, or keep the money. More subjects opted for the elegant pen in the three-option condition than in the two-option one (almost none opted for the lesser pen).[454]

The compromise effect is relevant to choices involving a trade-off between different attributes, such as product quality and price (when the comparison is one-dimensional, people naturally prefer the superior option). Although it violates the assumption that people's preferences are context-independent, the strategy of choosing the intermediate option (e.g., the product whose quality and price are both intermediate), appears to be perfectly rational when information problems and uncertainty (e.g., regarding the relative importance of various attributes) render the making of an optimal choice prohibitively costly—as they

450. Itamar Simonson & Amos Tversky, *Choice in Context: Tradeoff Contrast and Extremeness Aversion,* 29 J. Marketing Res. 281 (1992).

451. Kaisa Herne, *Decoy Alternatives in Policy Choices: Asymmetric Domination and Compromise Effects,* 13 Eur. J. Pol. Econ. 575 (1997).

452. Mark Kelman, Yuval Rottenstreich & Amos Tversky, *Context-Dependence in Legal Decision Making,* 25 J. Legal Stud. 287 (1996); *infra* pp. 532–34.

453. Joel Huber, John W. Payne & Christopher Puto, *Adding Asymmetrically Dominated Alternatives: Violations of Regularity and the Similarity Hypothesis,* 9 J. Consumer Res. 90 (1982).

454. Simonson & Tversky, *supra* note 450, at 287. *But see* Shane Frederick, Leonard Lee & Ernest Baskin, *The Limits of Attraction,* 51 J. Consumer Res. 487, 498 (2014) (failing to replicate the pen experiment). Related phenomena refer to the effect of elimination of an option from a choice-set (in marketing and other spheres). *See* William Hedgcock, Akshay R. Rao & Haipeng Chen, *Could Ralph Nader's Entrance and Exit Have Helped Al Gore? The Impact of Decoy Dynamics on Consumer Choice,* 46 J. Marketing Res. 330 (2009).

often do.[455] Hence, unlike other heuristics, the compromise effect may well be a product of a deliberative process, leading to a choice that is perceived as (among other things) less likely to be criticized by others.[456] Indeed, it has been found that cognitive resources depletion (due to engagement in a previous exacting task), which commonly enhances the use of System 1's heuristics, decreases the compromise effect,[457] as do time constraints.[458]

Moreover, assuming that quality and prices correlate, rational consumers who cannot meaningfully calculate the quality-price trade-off, but who consider themselves as having moderate needs and tastes, may rationally opt for a compromise choice.[459]

While the tendency to choose an intermediate option may be a rational means of dealing with information problems, it may also, along with the attraction effect, be manipulated by marketers and other persuaders. Thus, a firm may introduce an oversized product, or one of extremely high or extremely low quality, even if it expects very low demand for it, to boost the demand for its other products.[460] Concomitantly, policymakers can nudge consumers to decrease their consumption of soft drinks, for example, by requiring sellers to offer small-size drinks along with the large and very large ones.[461]

6. Diminishing Sensitivity

Reference-dependence underlies yet another psychological phenomenon in perception, judgment, and decision-making—namely *diminishing sensitivity*: the further a change is from the reference point, the smaller its impact. Two contexts in which diminishing sensitivity has been noted already are prospect theory's value function and probability weighting.[462] The *reflection effect*—the decreasing marginal effect of both gains and losses, resulting in risk aversion in the domain of gains and risk-seeking in the domain of losses—signifies a diminishing sensitivity to outcomes the further away they are from the reference

455. Itamar Simonson, *Choice Based on Reasons: The Case of Attraction and Compromise Effects*, 16 J. Consumer Res. 158 (1989). *See also* Nathan Novemsky et al., *Preference Fluency in Choice*, 44 J. Marketing Res. 347 (2007) (finding an increasing tendency to opt for the compromise option when the choice task is experienced as more difficult).

456. Simonson, *supra* note 455, at 161–62, 167–68.

457. Pocheptsova et al., *supra* note 26, at 346–47, 349–51.

458. Ravi Dhar, Stephen M. Nowlis & Steven J. Sherman, *Trying Hard or Hardly Trying: An Analysis of Context Effects in Choice*, 9 J. Consumer Psychol. 189 (2000). The evidence regarding the effect of time constraints on the attraction effect is mixed. *See* Lisa D. Ordóñez, Lehman Benson III & Andrea Pittarello, *Time-Pressure Perception and Decision Making*, *in* 2 Wiley Blackwell Handbook, *supra* note 2, at 519, 531.

459. Birger Wernerfelt, *A Rational Reconstruction of the Compromise Effect: Using Market Data to Infer Utilities*, 21 J. Consumer Res. 627 (1995); Emir Kamenica, *Contextual Inference in Markets: On the Informational Content of Product Lines*, 98 Am. Econ. Rev. 2127 (2008).

460. Kamenica, *supra* note 459; Kathryn M. Sharpe, Richard Staelin & Joel Huber, *Using Extremeness Aversion to Fight Obesity: Policy Implications of Context Dependent Demand*, 35 J. Consumer Res. 406 (2008). *See also infra* pp. 294–95.

461. Sharpe, Staelin & Huber, *supra* note 460. On nudging, see also *infra* pp. 177–85.

462. *See supra* pp. 42–44 and 34, respectively.

point. As for probabilities, the greater impact of moving from impossibility to low probability and from certainty to high probability, compared with similar changes in intermediate probabilities, signifies a diminishing sensitivity to changes in probability the further away they are from the two boundaries.

More specifically, diminishing sensitivity explains why adding a new feature to a product with relatively inferior existing features increases the demand for the product more than adding the same feature to a product with relatively superior quality.[463] It also explains why—contrary to standard economic analysis—a consumer may drive across town to buy a product for $30 rather than $40 (thus saving $10), but would not make a similar effort to buy one for $2,970 instead of $2,990 (thereby saving $20).[464] By the same token, offering gifts is a more effective marketing technique than small price reductions: since a gift is valued separately, receiving it is compared with not having it, rather than as a tiny decrease of a large loss.[465] Another finding compatible with diminishing sensitivity is the fact that people tend to make a greater effort to achieve a goal the closer they are to accomplishing it. For example, it was found that members of a reward program, who were entitled to a free cup of coffee after purchasing ten cups, increased the frequency of buying coffee the closer they were to earning the free cup.[466]

Diminishing sensitivity refers also to spatial distances. It has been invoked to explain why consumers prefer a shopping tour consisting, for example, of three journeys of Home–Store 1–Store 2–Home in which the distances are 40–10–40 miles, over a tour in which the distances are 30–30–30, although the total travel distance is the same.[467]

Finally, diminishing sensitivity is akin to the notion of *psychic numbing*.[468] While people recognize that every human life is of equal value, the effort they are willing to exert to save human lives (or otherwise help other people) diminishes as the number of endangered victims increases. Thus, for example, people would be willing to make greater effort to save the lives of nine out of ten endangered people, than to save the lives of ten out of ten thousand.

463. Stephen M. Nowlis & Itamar Simonson, *The Effect of New Product Features on Brand Choice,* 33 J. Marketing Res. 36 (1996).

464. Thaler, *supra* note 197, at 50–51 (1980); Kahneman & Tversky, *supra* note 161, at 347. Similar results were obtained in survey experiments pertaining to saving time (rather than money), in riskless—but not in risky—decision problems. *See* France Leclerc, Bernd H. Schmitt & Laurette Dubé, *Waiting Time and Decision Making: Is Time Like Money?,* 22 J. Consumer Res. 110 (1995).

465. Joseph C. Nunes & C. Whan Park, *Incommensurate Resources: Not Just More of the Same,* 40 J. Marketing Res. 26 (2003); Peter Jarnebrant, Olivier Toubia & Eric Johnson, *The Silver Lining Effect: Formal Analysis and Experiments,* 55 Mgmt. Sci. 1832 (2009).

466. Ran Kivetz, Oleg Urminsky & Yuhuang Zheng, *The Goal-Gradient Hypothesis Resurrected: Purchase Acceleration, Illusionary Goal Progress, and Customer Retention,* 43 J. Marketing Res. 39 (2006).

467. Charles M. Brooks, Patrick J. Kaufmann & Donald R. Lichtenstein, *Travel Configuration on Consumer Trip-Chained Store Choice Source,* 31 J. Consumer Res. 241 (2004); M. Brooks, Patrick J. Kaufmann & Donald R. Lichtenstein, *Trip Chaining Behavior in Multi-destination Shopping Trips: A Field Experiment and Laboratory Replication,* 84 J. Retailing 29 (2008). In the same vein, diminishing sensitivity with regard to temporal distances is associated with myopia. *See infra* pp. 88–93.

468. *See, e.g.,* Paul Slovic, *"If I Look at the Mass I Will Never Act": Psychic Numbing and Genocide,* 2 Judgment & Decision Making 79 (2007).

F. Procrastination, Myopia, and Bounded Willpower

Commentators sometimes classify the entire realm of deviations from economic rationality into three categories: *bounded rationality* (deviations from thin, cognitive rationality), *bounded self-interest* (deviations from thick, motivational rationality), and *bounded willpower* (behaving in a manner that people "know to be in conflict with their own long-term interests").[469] While the third category is not nearly as large or discrete as the first two, we nevertheless discuss it separately, because it does not fit in easily with the other categories. This section discusses first procrastination, then myopia and bounded willpower.

1. Procrastination

Unlike an intentional avoidance of a task or a decision, procrastination involves a voluntary delay of the beginning or completion of a task, or of making a decision, despite the procrastinator's realization that the delay adversely affects his or her interests and may even result in harmful nonperformance or no decision.[470] As Amos Tversky and Eldar Shafir have put it: "Many things never get done not because someone has chosen not to do them, but because the person has chosen not to do them *now*."[471] Procrastination appears to be a very common phenomenon, resulting in poor performance and considerable monetary and other losses to procrastinators, as well as self-resentment.[472] Procrastination may also negatively affect others besides the procrastinator, as in the case of delaying contributions to public causes.

People vary in their tendency to procrastinate. Some studies have demonstrated that this tendency is consistent across time and context, which means that it can be thought of as a personality trait. Of the *big-five* personality dimensions,[473] procrastination is closely correlated with *conscientiousness* and its constituents. Thus, the tendency to procrastinate is negatively correlated with *organization* (planning and structuring one's endeavors), and *achievement-motivation*, and positively correlated with *distractibility* (failure to manage distracting cues), and the *intention–action gap* (the degree to which people do not follow up on their plans).[474] It has also been shown that more overly optimistic people are more prone to procrastinate when they face an unpleasant task.[475]

469. Christine Jolls, Cass R. Sunstein & Richard Thaler, *A Behavioral Approach to Law and Economics,* 50 Stan. L. Rev. 1471, 1476–79 (1998).

470. Piers Steel, *The Nature of Procrastination: A Meta-analytic and Theoretical Review of Quintessential Self-Regulatory Failure,* 133 Psychol. Bull. 65, 66 (2007).

471. Amos Tversky & Eldar Shafir, *Choice under Conflict: The Dynamics of Deferred Decision,* 3 Psychol. Sci. 358, 361 (1992).

472. Steel, *supra* note 470, at 65, 80.

473. According to a prevailing notion in personality psychology, there are five basic dimensions of personality: extraversion, agreeableness, openness, conscientiousness, and neuroticism. *See generally* John M. Digman, *Personality Structure: Emergence of the Five-Factor Model,* 41 Ann. Rev. Psychol. 417 (1990); Lewis R. Goldberg, *An Alternative "Description of Personality": The Big-Five Factor Structure,* 59 J. Personality & Soc. Psychol. 1216 (1990).

474. For a meta-analysis, see Steel, *supra* note 470, at 67, 70, 78–79.

475. Sigall, Kruglanski & Fyock, *supra* note 304. On overoptimism, see *supra* pp. 61–64.

Procrastination depends on the characteristics of the task at hand. The further away the task's expected rewards or punishments, the greater the tendency to procrastinate,[476] which arguably reflects people's hyperbolic discount rate of future costs and benefits, discussed below.[477] Similarly, the more boring or unpleasant a task or a decision is, the more likely it is to be postponed.[478]

Given the prevalence and harmfulness of procrastination, considerable attention has been given to means of overcoming it, including self- and externally-imposed deadlines, and mandated decision-making. As for deadlines, in one study a paid task was completed by 60 percent of the participants who were given a five-day deadline, by 42 percent of those given a three-week deadline, and by only 25 percent of those receiving no deadline.[479] Deadlines may, however, induce people to do things that are arguably less desirable, such as appealing exam grades and court judgments.[480] A few studies have compared the efficacy of self- versus externally-imposed deadlines, with mixed results: while some found that self-imposed deadlines are more effective at ensuring performance,[481] others showed that externally imposed deadlines are more effective.[482] Another antidote to procrastination (and the omission bias) is compelling people to make decisions. For example, people who apply for a driver's license may be required to indicate whether they consent to donate their organs posthumously, and new employees may be required to decide whether to enroll in a pension plan.[483]

2. Myopia and Bounded Willpower

A large body of experimental and theoretical research in economics and psychology has studied people's choices involving costs and benefits occurring at different times—particularly the tendency to discount future costs and benefits compared with immediate ones.[484] This research on *intertemporal preferences* has largely emerged in response to normative economic models, and has been advanced by both behavioral economists and

476. *Id.* at 68, 75.

477. *See infra* pp. 88–93.

478. For a review of studies supporting this claim, see Steel, *supra* note 470, at 75, 78.

479. Tversky & Shafir, *supra* note 471, at 361.

480. Eyal Zamir, Daphna Lewinsohn-Zamir & Ilana Ritov, *It's Now or Never! Using Deadlines as Nudges*, 42 Law & Soc. Inquiry 769 (2017).

481. M. Susan Roberts & George B. Semb, *Analysis of the Number of Student-Set Deadlines in a Personalized Psychology Course*, 17 Teaching Psychol.170 (1990).

482. Dan Ariely & Klaus Wertenbroch, *Procrastination, Deadlines, and Performance: Self-Control by Precommitment*, 13 Psychol. Sci. 219 (2002).

483. Gabriel D. Carroll et al., *Optimal Defaults and Active Decisions*, 124 Q.J. Econ. 1639 (2009). *See also* Punam Anand Keller et al., *Enhanced Active Choice: A New Method to Motivate Behavior Change*, 21 J. Consumer Psychol. 376 (2011) (describing randomized laboratory and field studies showing that mandated active choice increases the willingness to vaccinate).

484. *See generally* Shane Frederick, George Loewenstein & Ted O'Donoghue, *Time Discounting and Time Preference: A Critical Review*, 40 J. Econ. Literature 351 (2002); Oleg Urminsky & Gal Zauberman, *The*

psychologists. Consequently, much of the literature tends to discuss intertemporal choices in isolation, rather than as one aspect of the broader issues of self-regulation and self-control.[485] A detailed discussion of self-control failures—associated, inter alia, with issues of crime and violence—is beyond the scope of the present discussion.[486] However, from psychological and legal policy perspectives, the issues of myopia and self-control are hardly distinguishable in contexts such as spending versus saving, consumption of unhealthy food, and smoking. Hence this subsection discusses both intertemporal choices and closely related issues of self-control.

The standard economic model for intertemporal choices, proposed in 1937 by Paul Samuelson, has long assumed that people discount future costs and benefits at a constant *discount rate*.[487] Indeed, in many contexts, discounting of future costs and benefits is perfectly sensible. Receiving a sum of money earlier may enable a person to earn interest on that sum, repay an interest-bearing debt, or otherwise invest the money profitably. However, people discount future outcomes even when this logic does not apply, such as with regard to health conditions and the saving of human lives (e.g., in choosing between saving the lives of ten people tomorrow versus saving the lives of eleven other people a year from now). Moreover, people's subjective discount rate is often much higher than any available interest rate. Most important, it appears that people's discount rate is generally not constant but rather *hyperbolic*—that is, it declines as time increases.[488] For example, many people would prefer to receive ten dollars today than twelve dollars in two weeks' time—yet would rather receive twelve dollars in a year and two weeks' time, than ten dollars in a year from now. A hyperbolic discount rate implies that people have time-inconsistent preferences, depending on when they make the choice.

Intertemporal preferences pertain to a wide range of outcomes and circumstances, and are very often confounded with other factors. For example, the decreasing marginal utility of resources implies that the temporal discount rate of a person who prefers to receive $100,000 immediately over receiving $200,000 in a year's time is considerably lower than 100 percent, because typically, the expected utility derived from $200,000 is significantly lower than twice the utility from $100,000. By the same token, in real life, the further away outcomes are, the greater their uncertainty, which in turn likely decreases their expected

Psychology of Intertemporal Preferences, in Wiley Blackwell Handbook, *supra* note 2, at 141. *See also* Time and Decision: Economic and Psychological Perspectives on Intertemporal Choice (George Loewenstein, Daniel Read & Roy Baumeister eds., 2003).

485. Urminsky & Zauberman, *supra* note 484, at 157.

486. *See, e.g.*, Michael R. Gottfredson & Travis Hirschi, A General Theory of Crime (1990); Travis C. Pratt & Francis T. Cullen, *The Empirical Status of Gottfredson and Hirschi's General Theory of Crime: A Meta-analysis*, 38 Criminology 931 (2000).

487. Paul A. Samuelson, *A Note on Measurement of Utility*, 4 Rev. Econ. Stud. 155 (1937).

488. R.H. Strotz, *Myopia and Inconsistency in Dynamic Utility Maximization*, 23 Rev. Econ. Stud. 165 (1955–1956); George Ainslie, *Specious Reward: A Behavioral Theory of Impulsiveness and Impulse Control*, 82 Psychol. Bull. 463 (1975); David Laibson, *Golden Eggs and Hyperbolic Discounting*, 112 Q.J. Econ. 443 (1997).

value. For example, the utility from a given amount of money in the future depends on one's financial condition at that time: it would be lower if one somehow became considerably richer in the interim—and higher if one became considerably poorer. Indeed, the future utility might even be nil if one passes away before the designated future time. Even if these and comparable factors could somehow be separated, it is highly unlikely that any individual would have a single (constant or hyperbolic) discount rate for different objects, time spans, and outcome magnitudes. In fact, the notion of a single discount rate is not borne out by the available evidence.[489]

In addition to time-inconsistency, studies have revealed that gains are discounted at a higher rate than losses.[490] In fact, a substantial proportion of subjects prefer to incur a loss immediately rather than to put it off.[491] Intertemporal choices are also vulnerable to framing effects: people are willing to pay considerably less to expedite the receipt of a given good from T_2 to T_1 than they demand in return for delaying its receipt from T_1 to T_2.[492] Finally, contrary to the logic of discounting future costs and benefits, people prefer improving sequences of good outcomes (such as gradually increasing wages) to declining ones,[493] and decreasing sequences of bad outcomes (such as physical discomfort).[494] Some of these characteristics, including the diminishing sensitivity to temporally remote outcomes, reference-dependence, and the gain-loss asymmetry, are analogous to prospect theory's value function.[495]

Myopic behavior interacts with other biases in the perception and processing of information, as well. For example, when people set saving or dietary goals, they perceive goal-consistent behaviors (such as saving a certain amount of money) as contributing more to attaining the goal than they perceive goal-inconsistent behaviors (such as spending the exact same amount) as obstructing it. The more people expect to meet their goal, the greater this so-called *progress bias*.[496]

Excessive discount rates are related to issues of impulsiveness and self-control. The famous *marshmallow experiments*, conducted by Walter Mischel and his colleagues in the 1960s and 1970s, examined four-year-old children's ability to forgo immediate gratification

489. Uri Benzion, Amnon Rapoport & Joseph Yagil, *Discount Rates Inferred from Decisions: An Experimental Study*, 35 MGMT. SCI. 270 (1989); Frederick, Loewenstein & O'Donoghue, *supra* note 484, at 390–93; Urminsky & Zauberman, *supra* note 484, at 147–52.

490. *See, e.g.*, Richard Thaler, *Some Empirical Evidence on Dynamic Inconsistency*, 8 ECON. LETTERS 201 (1981).

491. Frederick, Loewenstein & O'Donoghue, *supra* note 484, at 363.

492. George F. Loewenstein, *Frames of Mind in Intertemporal Choice*, 34 MGMT. SCI. 200 (1988).

493. *See, e.g.*, George Loewenstein & Nachum Sicherman, *Do Workers Prefer Increasing Wage Profiles?*, 9 J. LABOR ECON. 67 (1991).

494. Gretchen B. Chapman, *Preferences for Improving and Declining Sequences of Health Outcomes*, 13 J. BEHAV. DECISION MAKING 203 (2000).

495. George Loewenstein & Drazen Prelec, *Anomalies in Intertemporal Choice: Evidence and an Interpretation*, 107 Q.J. ECON. 573 (1992). On prospect theory, see *supra* pp. 42–57.

496. Margaret C. Campbell & Caleb Warren, *The Progress Bias in Goal Pursuit: When One Step Forward Seems Larger than One Step Back*, 41 J. CONSUMER RES. 1316 (2015).

in order to get a larger, delayed reward, and the strategies they used to achieve this goal.[497] Interestingly, follow-up studies have shown that children who displayed greater self-control in those experiments tended to be more cognitively and academically competent and to cope better with frustration and stress in adolescence,[498] and to do better in interpersonal relationships as adults.[499] Another study found correlation between high discount rates and (self-reported) earlier age of first sexual activity and recent relationship infidelity, smoking, and higher body mass index.[500]

The context-dependence of discount rates, their vulnerability to framing effects, the aforementioned progress bias, and the close link between myopia and self-control—all cast doubt on the very notion that people's myopic behavior can be adequately captured by a utility-discounting function. Accordingly, several alternative accounts of people's intertemporal choices have been proposed. One such account is analogous to dual-process theories of decision-making. George Loewenstein has pointed out that when people act against their own long-term interests, they are often aware that this is the case, but experience a feeling of being "out of control."[501] Often, such behavior arises from impulse or sudden emotion, such as hunger or craving. The immediate, powerful effect of these visceral factors crowds out other goals. Furthermore, people tend to underestimate their own susceptibility, and the susceptibility of others, to these factors. Experimental support for this account was provided by a study in which subjects who performed a cognitively demanding task, thus using much of their deliberative resources elsewhere, tended to choose a less healthy food.[502]

Relatedly, according to the *construal level theory*, the mental representation of chronologically remote outcomes is more abstract than of chronologically close ones.[503] Accordingly, it has been hypothesized that people's smaller WTP for expediting the receipt of a given good, compared with their WTA for delaying its receipt, has to do with the initial construal of receiving it as abstract (in the former framing) or concrete (in the

497. For an overview, see Walter Mischel, Yuichi Shoda & Monica L. Rodriguez, *Delay of Gratification in Children,* 244 Sci. 933 (1989).

498. Yuichi Shoda, Walter Mischel & Philip K. Peake, *Predicting Adolescent Cognitive and Self-Regulatory Competencies from Preschool Delay of Gratification: Identifying Diagnostic Conditions,* 26 Developmental Psychol. 978 (1990).

499. Ozlem Ayduk et al., *Regulating the Interpersonal Self: Strategic Self-Regulation for Coping with Rejection Sensitivity,* 79 J. Personality & Soc. Psychol. 776 (2000).

500. Stian Reimers et al., *Associations between a One-Shot Delay Discounting Measure and Age, Income, Education and Real-World Impulsive Behavior,* 47 Personality & Individual Differences 973 (2009).

501. George Loewenstein, *Out of Control: Visceral Influences on Behavior,* 65 Org. Behav. & Hum. Decision Processes 272 (1996). *Cf.* Richard H. Thaler & H.M. Shefrin, *An Economic Theory of Self-Control,* 89 J. Pol. Econ. 392 (1981).

502. Baba Shiv & Alexander Fedorikhin, *Heart and Mind in Conflict: The Interplay of Affect and Cognition in Consumer Decision Making,* 26 J. Consumer Res. 278 (1999).

503. *See, e.g.,* Yaacov Trope & Nira Liberman, *Construal-Level Theory of Psychological Distance,* 117 Psychol. Rev. 440 (2010); Kentaro Fujita, Yaacov Trope & Nira Liberman, *On the Psychology of Near and Far, in* Wiley Blackwell Handbook, *supra* note 2, at 404.

latter). Indeed, it has been found that asking subjects to concretely visualize the moment of receiving the good and using it—thus removing this difference between the two framings—eliminated the WTA-WTP difference.[504]

It has also been suggested that intertemporal choices may be the product of simple heuristics (rather than settled intertemporal utility functions), taking into account the absolute differences and relative percentage differences of the attributes of the outcomes in the relevant choice set.[505] Additional psychological determinants that impinge on intertemporal choices are the degree to which people feel connected to their future selves,[506] inattentiveness to the future ramifications of present behavior,[507] and people's perception of future time durations.[508]

Unlike some erroneous logical inferences, and similarly to phenomena such as loss aversion, the very existence of a high discount rate is not "irrational" per se.[509] However, hyperbolic discount rates imply that choices are not time-consistent. They are also associated with impulsiveness, myopia, and deficient self-control. While it is possible to incorporate such phenomena, and the measures people take to overcome them, into economic analysis by stretching the notion of "information costs" or by modeling individuals as consisting of "multiple selves,"[510] such extensions are no substitute for empirical study of these phenomena, their personal and social costs, and the possible ways of dealing with them.

Myopia and failures of self-control have particularly large, adverse effects in the contexts of dieting,[511] smoking,[512] drug addiction,[513] saving for retirement,[514] and consumer behavior.[515] These issues have several common features. First, people's failure to

504. Selin A. Malkoc & Gal Zauberman, *Deferring versus Expediting Consumption: The Effect of Outcome Concreteness on Sensitivity to Time Horizon*, 43 J. Marketing Res. 618 (2006).

505. Ariel Rubinstein, *"Economics and Psychology"? The Case of Hyperbolic Discounting*, 44 Int'l Econ. Rev. 1207 (2003); Keith M. Marzilli Ericson et al., *Money Earlier or Later? Simple Heuristics Explain Intertemporal Choices Better than Delay Discounting Does*, 26 Psychol. Sci. 826 (2015).

506. Daniel M. Bartels & Oleg Urminsky, *On Intertemporal Selfishness: The Perceived Instability of Identity Underlies Impatient Consumption*, 38 J. Consumer Res. 182 (2011).

507. *See generally* Urminsky & Zauberman, *supra* note 484, at 155–57, 158–59 (discussing opportunity costs consideration and the order of reflection on reasons and events stored in memory).

508. *See generally id.* at 160–61.

509. Frederick, Loewenstein & O'Donoghue, *supra* note 484, at 364–65.

510. *See, e.g.*, Thaler & Shefrin, *supra* note 501; Richard A. Posner, *Rational Choice, Behavioral Economics, and the Law*, 50 Stan. L. Rev. 1551, 1555–57 (1998).

511. Robert L. Scharff, *Obesity and Hyperbolic Discounting: Evidence and Implications*, 32 J. Consumer Pol'y 3 (2009); Shinsuke Ikedaa, Myong-Il Kang & Fumio Ohtake, *Hyperbolic Discounting, the Sign Effect, and the Body Mass Index*, 29 J. Health Econ. 268 (2010).

512. Warren K. Bickel, Amy L. Odum & Gregory J. Madden, *Impulsivity and Cigarette Smoking: Delay Discounting in Current, Never, and Ex-smokers*, 146 Psychopharmacology 447 (1999).

513. Warren K. Bickel & Lisa A. Marsch, *Toward a Behavioral Economic Understanding of Drug Dependence: Delay Discounting Processes*, 96 Addiction 73 (2001).

514. *See infra* pp. 180, 184, 379–80.

515. Stefano DellaVigna & Ulrike Malmendier, *Contract Design and Self-Control: Theory and Evidence*, 119 Q.J. Econ. 353 (2004); Klaus Wertenbroch, *Self-Rationing: Self-Control in Consumer Choice*, *in* Time and Decision, *supra* note 484, at 491. On firms' exploitation of consumer biases, see generally *infra* pp. 281–324.

behave in accordance with their long-term interests results in major harms to themselves and significant social ills, such as obesity and insufficient savings for old age. Second, firms often take positive steps to induce myopic behavior for their own benefit—such as promoting the consumption of unhealthy food through aggressive advertisement, encouraging smoking, and convincing people to borrow for present consumption instead of saving for old age. Third, people sometimes use precommitment, self-paternalistic devices to curtail their impulsive decision-making. Keeping away from tempting food products and cigarettes, and depositing money in saving accounts with no option for early withdrawal, are two examples. Fourth, the market sometimes offers mechanisms that help people overcome their myopia (such as saving plans), and new proposals for such mechanisms are constantly being put forward and examined.[516] Notable examples are changing the default from employees' nonparticipation to participation in retirement saving plans,[517] and employees' precommitment to increasing the percentage of their salary saved for retirement whenever they get a salary raise.[518] Finally, governments throughout the world take measures to deal with the social problems associated with failures of self-control. These measures range from very mild, psychologically inspired *nudges*—such as requiring producers to inform consumers about products' risks in a more salient and vivid manner—to compulsory measures, such as outlawing particularly unhealthy food products, and criminalizing the sale of tobacco products and alcohol to minors.[519]

G. Moral Judgment and Human Motivation

1. General

Philosophers debate the question of how important it is for a moral theory to align with prevalent, deeply held moral intuitions. Some hold that a moral theory that does not fit with at least some intuitions is unacceptable, while others give very little weight to this criterion. Many philosophers take intermediate positions (the fact that people sometimes have different intuitions, or that the same individual may have conflicting intuitions about a particular question, further complicates the issue). One need not resolve this question to acknowledge that psychological studies of moral intuitions are interesting in their own right, and are important for policymaking. People's moral judgments are important whenever one aims to understand, predict, or influence people's behavior, because moral judgments influence behavior. Contrary to the assumption of rational choice theory, there is much

516. *See, e.g.*, IAN AYRES, CARROTS AND STICKS: UNLOCK THE POWER OF INCENTIVES TO GET THINGS DONE (2010).

517. Brigitte Madrian & Dennis Shea, *The Power of Suggestion: Inertia in 401(k) Participation and Savings Behavior*, 66 Q.J. ECON. 1149 (2001).

518. Richard H. Thaler & Shlomo Benartzi, *Save More Tomorrow™: Using Behavioral Economics to Increase Employee Saving*, 112 J. POL. ECON. S164 (2004). *See also infra* p. 180.

519. *See infra* pp. 162–85.

evidence that people are not driven exclusively by self-interest, but also by moral norms and prosocial motivations.

Prevailing moral intuitions are also important for the law. If the validity of legal norms depends on their morality (as some theories of law contend), and if the validity of moral theories depends (at least to some extent) on their compatibility with moral intuitions, then moral intuitions are essential to the law. Moreover, even if one denies that the law's validity hinges on its morality, or that compatibility with moral intuitions is vital to a moral theory, the compatibility of legal norms with prevailing moral intuitions is important for purely instrumental reasons: people are more likely to follow legal norms that they perceive as just and desirable than norms that they perceive as unjust.[520] The compatibility of legal norms with prevailing moral intuitions may also be mandated by democratic principles.

In the following subsections we briefly discuss several aspects of people's moral judgment and motivation.[521] We begin with the distinction between *consequentialist* and *deontological* morality. While normative economics rests on consequentialist morality, many studies have shown that most people predominantly reason, and conduct themselves, as moderate deontologists. We then turn to more specific aspects of people's perceptions of justice, with particular focus on notions of substantive and procedural fairness, and the belief in a just world. Next, we discuss another aspect of human behavior that appears to be at odds with the postulates of standard economic analysis—namely, people's prosocial and altruistic behavior. Finally, we touch upon the relationships between moral judgments and the distinction between intuitive and deliberative judgment and decision-making.

2. Deontology versus Consequentialism

(a) Normative Ethics

Welfare economics is a consequentialist moral theory. It holds that the only factor that ultimately determines the ethicality of acts, omissions, or anything else is their consequences, and mandates that people should always promote the best outcomes. It recognizes no deontological constraints on promoting the good, or options to prioritize other goals.[522] In contrast, while deontological moral theories acknowledge the importance of promoting good outcomes, they deny that promoting them is the only morally decisive factor.[523] Deontological theories prioritize such values as autonomy, basic liberties, truth-telling, fair play, and promise-keeping over the promotion of good outcomes. They include *constraints* on attaining the best outcomes. At the same time, deontological morality admits of *options*: in many circumstances, an agent may legitimately give precedence to her own interests or the interests of her loved ones or members of her community over the

520. *See infra* pp. 436–43. For a descriptive and normative account of the compatibility between legal norms and prevailing moral convictions, see generally Zamir, *supra* note 151, at 193–95.

521. Another important aspect of human ethicality, namely the mechanisms allowing ordinary people to violate ethical norms, are discussed under the heading of behavioral ethics (*supra* pp. 72–76; *infra* pp. 455–61), and additional issues will be discussed throughout the book apropos of specific legal issues.

522. *See generally supra* pp. 13–14.

523. John Rawls, A Theory of Justice 26 (rev. ed. 1999).

enhancement of the overall good. Thus, the affluent need not donate most of their money to alleviate the suffering of the underprivileged. They may legitimately spend their money on "luxuries" such as going to the movies and reading fiction, even if giving that money to the poor would enhance net human welfare.[524] Deontological theories thus recognize agent-relative constraints (on promoting the good) and agent-relative options (of not promoting the good).[525]

The central deontological constraint is against harming other people. It usually includes restrictions on violating rights such as the rights to life and bodily integrity, human dignity, and freedom of speech. It also includes special obligations created by promises, and restrictions on lying and betrayal.[526] There is additionally a "deontological requirement of fairness, of evenhandedness or equality in one's treatment of people."[527]

The notion of agent-relativity implies that there is a difference between the duty to refrain from violating a constraint and the duty not to bring about, or to prevent, other violations—even where such violations are the expected outcome of avoiding the current one. Otherwise, the prohibition of killing one person to save two others would preclude both killing that person and not killing him (thereby allowing the death of the other two). Deontology therefore must resort to a distinction between actively violating a constraint and not preventing the violation of constraints by others—or some such distinction.[528] In the context of the constraint against harming people, deontology thus distinguishes between *actively harming* a person and *not aiding* her (often referred to as the *doing/allowing distinction*).[529] While doing harm is at least presumably immoral, allowing harm is not ordinarily regarded as such. At the very least, the constraint against active harming is much stricter than the duty to come to the aid of others.

Another distinction deontologists often draw is between *intending* harm and merely *foreseeing* it. Intending harm is immoral even if the harm is merely allowed, while foreseeing harm is not necessarily immoral.[530] The constraint against intending harm forbids not only harming a person as an end, but also as a *means* to attaining another goal. Thus, killing someone to inherit her money is an intended harm, even if the killer would have preferred

524. *See generally* Shelly Kagan, Normative Ethics 161–70 (1998).

525. Compared to other consequentialist theories, the over-demandingness objection is less applicable to economic analysis, because it assumes that under a relatively broad range of circumstances, the best way to maximize overall welfare is by each person rationally pursuing his or her own interests. Economic analysis rarely, if ever, suggests that people should strive to maximize overall utility.

526. *See* Kagan, *supra* note 524, at 84–94, 106–52; Christopher McMahon, *The Paradox of Deontology*, 20 Phil. & Pub. Aff. 350, 354–68 (1991); Stephen Darwall, *Introduction, in* Deontology 1 (Stephen Darwall ed., 2003).

527. Thomas Nagel, The View from Nowhere 176 (1986). On deontological notions of fairness, see also Frances M. Kamm, Morality, Mortality, Vol. I: Death and Whom to Save from It 76 (1993); Iwao Hirose, *Aggregation and Numbers,* 16 Utilitas 62 (2004).

528. David Enoch, *Intending, Foreseeing, and the State,* 13 Legal Theory 69, 97–99 (2007).

529. A useful collection of studies of the doing/allowing distinction is Killing and Letting Die (Bonnie Steinbock & Alastair Norcross eds., 2d ed. 1994).

530. *See* Shelly Kagan, The Limits of Morality 128–82 (1989); Nagel, *supra* note 527, at 179–80.

that there were other ways of obtaining the money. Using a person as a means violates the requirement to respect people as ends.

These distinctions are often discussed in reference to the *trolley problem*.[531] Suppose that an uncontrolled trolley is hurtling down a track. Directly in its path are five people, who cannot escape and will be killed by it unless it is diverted. An agent can flip a switch that would divert the trolley to another track, where it would kill a single individual. Should the agent flip that switch? Alternatively, suppose that the only way the agent can save the five people is by flipping a switch that would cause another individual to fall off a footbridge onto the track, thereby blocking the trolley and killing that individual. Should the agent cause the fall of the other individual? While some deontologists would object to flipping the switch in both cases, others may find diverting the trolley morally permissible, or perhaps even imperative, while causing the fall of the individual morally forbidden. While both killings are active, they ground the difference in the distinction between killing as a mere side effect (in the diversion scenario) and killing as a means (in the footbridge scenario).

Deontological moral theories are either absolutist or moderate.[532] While *absolutist* deontology maintains that constraints must not be violated for any amount of good outcomes, *moderate* deontology holds that constraints have *thresholds*: a constraint may be overridden for the sake of furthering good outcomes, or avoiding bad ones if sufficient good or bad is at stake. For example, even the constraint against actively/intentionally killing an innocent person may be justifiably infringed if it is the only way to save the lives of thousands of others.[533] The thresholds that have to be met to justify the infringement of other constraints, such as those against lying or breaking one's promise, are much lower. Correspondingly, deontological options need not be absolute: when enough good or bad outcomes are at stake, there is no longer an option not to further the good or avoid the bad. In determining the amount of good/bad outcomes that may justify infringement of a constraint, a moderate deontologist may reasonably take into account both the doing/allowing and the intending/foreseeing distinctions. Thus, the threshold that has to be met to justify harming someone when the harm is intended is plausibly much higher than when it is a mere side effect.

Moderate deontology not only forbids the infringement of moral constraints unless a sufficiently large net benefit is produced by such an infringement, but also excludes or gives lesser weight to certain costs and benefits when determining whether the net benefit meets a given threshold. For example, deontology may hold that certain values take lexical priority over others (e.g., human lives versus pecuniary losses); that small benefits (such as eliminating headaches) should not be taken into account at all when more serious values (such as human lives) are at stake; that chronologically distant benefits and costs

531. *See, e.g.*, Philippa Foot, *The Problem of Abortion and the Doctrine of the Double Effect*, *in* Virtues and Vices and Other Essays in Moral Philosophy 19, 23 (1978); Judith Jarvis Thomson, *The Trolley Problem*, 94 Yale L.J. 1395 (1985); Alison McIntyre, *Doing Away with Double Effect*, 111 Ethics 219 (2001).

532. *See generally* Eyal Zamir & Barak Medina, Law, Economics, and Morality 41–56, 79–104 (2010).

533. *See, e.g.*, Judith Jarvis Thomson, *Some Ruminations on Rights*, *in* Rights, Restitution, and Risk 49 (William Parent ed., 1986); Samantha Brennan, *Thresholds for Rights*, 33 Southern J. Phil. 143 (1995); Kagan, *supra* note 524, at 78–80.

should be hugely discounted; and that eliminating bad outcomes takes precedence over promoting good ones.[534] Lastly, deontological morality may distinguish between harming (saving) an unidentified person and an identified one. Whereas from a consequentialist viewpoint harming (or saving) an unknown individual is identical to harming (or saving) an identified one, deontology may distinguish between the two, and find the latter more objectionable (or justifiable).[535]

(b) Behavioral Studies

While ethicists hotly debate which normative theory is correct, they have long recognized that of the three families of theories—consequentialism, absolutist deontology, and moderate deontology—the third is most consistent with *commonsense morality,* or prevailing moral convictions.[536]

Both absolutist deontology and simple consequentialism are often counterintuitive. For example, the absolutist judgment that one must never actively or intentionally lie—even if, by doing so, one might save the life of an innocent person—sounds rather strange to most people. At the same time, most people find the consequentialist judgment that it is morally obligatory to kill 100 innocent people as a means to saving the lives of 101 others (or to save the lives of 100 others and prevent a minor injury to one more) equally abhorrent. In fact, both consequentialists and absolutist deontologists go to great lengths to try and square their respective theories with prevailing moral convictions. For example, absolutist deontologists may draw a fine line between lying and failing to tell the truth, to avoid the untenable results of an absolute prohibition on lying. At the same time, consequentialists may shift from act- to rule-consequentialism—which, in the main, is a way of providing a consequentialist foundation to commonsense morality.[537]

Numerous experimental studies have indeed demonstrated that most people's moral judgments are neither consequentialist nor absolutist deontological. One line of research has studied the related notions of *protected values* and *taboo trade-offs,* which deal with values that resist trade-offs with other values (especially economic ones).[538] Contrary to consequentialism, it has been found that many people initially opine that such values should

534. *See generally* Zamir & Medina, *supra* note 532, at 86–93.

535. *See, e.g.,* Charles Fried, *The Value of Life,* 82 Harv. L. Rev. 1415 (1969); Mark Kelman, *Saving Lives, Saving from Death, Saving from Dying: Reflection on "Over-Valuing" Identifiable Victims,* 11 Yale J. Health Pol'y. L. & Ethics 51 (2011).

536. *See, e.g.,* Samuel Scheffler, *Introduction, in* Consequentialism and Its Critics 1, 9 (Samuel Scheffler ed. 1988); Samantha Brennan, *Thresholds for Rights,* 33 Southern J. Phil. 143, 145 (1995); Kagan, *supra* note 530, at 1–5.

537. On this and other attempts "to consequentialize" deontology, see, e.g., Zamir & Medina, *supra* note 532, at 21–40 (2010); Douglas W. Portmore, Commonsense Consequentialism: Wherein Morality Meets Rationality (2011); Tom Dougherty, *Agent-Neutral Deontology,* 163 Phil. Stud. 527 (2013).

538. *See, e.g.,* Jonathan Baron & Mark Spranca, *Protected Values,* 70 Org. Behav. & Hum. Decision Processes 1 (1997); Ilana Ritov & Jonathan Baron, *Protected Values and Omission Bias,* 79 Org. Behav. & Hum. Decision Processes 79 (1999). For an overview, see Daniel M. Bartels et al., *Moral Judgment and Decision Making, in* Wiley Blackwell Handbook, *supra* note 2, at 478, 483–87.

never be violated (for example, that doctors should never remove dying patients' organs without their consent). However, contrary to absolutist deontology, when asked to think of counterexamples, many of those espousing protected values qualify this statement.[539] Moreover, politicians making policy decisions often face unavoidable trade-offs that involve protected values.[540] Policymakers who must decide whether to invest in public health programs, highway safety, saving an endangered species, or simply balancing the budget cannot escape the need to put such goals in a single policy metric. Yet, when doing so they must be careful, since treating a protected value like any other commensurable good is tantamount to "political suicide."[541] Consequently, the public discourse surrounding protected values tends to resort to rhetorical obfuscation.[542] By labeling a policy choice as "moral" or "just," rather than as "efficient" or "cost-justified" people can overlook their transgression with regard to the protected value.[543]

It has also been shown that, contrary to consequentialism, people are viewed—and view themselves—as bearing a greater moral responsibility for harmful outcomes that they actively bring about, as opposed to those that they passively allow to happen.[544] These studies have also demonstrated that for most people, the prohibition of actively causing death has thresholds, such that infringing actions are permissible if they are the only way to prevent sufficiently larger number of deaths.[545]

In recent years, many studies have examined people's reactions to various versions of the trolley problem and comparable moral dilemmas. For example, most subjects judge harmful actions to be morally worse than harmful omissions, and intended harm as worse than foreseen harm.[546] Most subjects believe that harming a person in order to save others (intended harm) is unacceptable, while harming a person as a side effect

539. Jonathan Baron & Sara Leshner, *How Serious Are Expressions of Protected Values?*, 6 J. EXPERIMENTAL PSYCHOL.: APPLIED 183 (2000).

540. *See* Daniel M. Bartels & Douglas L. Medin, *Are Morally Motivated Decision Makers Insensitive to the Consequences of Their Choices?*, 18 PSYCHOL. SCI. 24, 24 (2007).

541. Baron & Spranca, *supra* note 538, at 14.

542. Michael R. Waldmann, Jonas Nagel & Alex Wiegmann, *Moral Judgments*, *in* THE OXFORD HANDBOOK OF THINKING AND REASONING, *supra* note 21, at 364, 383. *See also* GUIDO CALABRESI & PHILIP BOBBIT, TRAGIC CHOICES (1978); GUIDO CALABRESI, THE FUTURE OF LAW AND ECONOMICS (2016).

543. For an experimental demonstration of this point, see Philip E. Tetlock, *Coping with Trade-Offs: Psychological Constraints and Political Implications*, *in* ELEMENTS OF REASON: COGNITION, CHOICE, AND THE BOUNDS OF RATIONALITY 239, 254–55 (S. Lupia et al. eds., 2000).

544. *See, e.g.*, Ilana Ritov & Jonathan Baron, *Reluctance to Vaccinate: Omission Bias and Ambiguity*, 3 J. BEHAV. DECISION MAKING 263 (1990); Mark Spranca, Elisa Minsk & Jonathan Baron, *Omission and Commission in Judgment and Choice*, 27 J. EXPERIMENTAL SOC. PSYCHOL. 76 (1991); Peter DeScioli, John Christner & Robert Kurzban, *The Omission Strategy*, 22 PSYCHOL. SCI. 442 (2011). On the *omission bias*, see also *supra* pp. 48–50.

545. Ritov & Baron, *supra* note 544; Ritov & Baron, *supra* note 538.

546. Fiery Cushman, Liane Young & Marc Hauser, *The Role of Conscious Reasoning and Intuition in Moral Judgment: Testing Three Principles of Harm*, 17 PSYCHOL. SCI. 1082, 1086 (2006).

of saving others (foreseen harm) is permissible—although many subjects are unable to provide an adequate explanation for this distinction.[547] Subjects also tend to judge harm involving physical contact as morally worse than harm without contact.[548] Contrary to the agent-neutrality mandated by simple consequentialism, and in line with deontological agent-relativity, it was found that people judge both intended and foreseen killing in a bid to save oneself and others as more acceptable than killing to save only others.[549] In the same spirit, sacrificing a stranger to save several people is deemed more acceptable than sacrificing a relative.[550]

It has also been demonstrated that, contrary to absolutist deontology, people justify the active killing of one person as a means to saving a vast number of other people.[551] A divergence between absolutist deontology and prevailing moral judgments has also been found in experimental designs in which subjects thought that killing the person in the standard footbridge scenario was permissible.[552]

In summary, while people's moral judgments vary—some are consequentialist, some are absolutist deontological, and some are moderate deontological (and the judgments of the same person may vary from one context to another)—most moral judgments appear to be more in line with moderate deontology than with either consequentialism or absolutist deontology. People tend to believe that maximizing good outcomes is subject to moral constraints—including the constraint against actively or intentionally harming other people—but that these constraints may be overridden if good or bad outcomes of sufficient magnitude are at stake. It should also be noted that large-scale experiments and surveys have revealed a remarkable uniformity in people's reactions to various versions of the trolley problem and comparable moral dilemmas.[553] An analysis of the moral judgments of thousands of people, from around the world, has shown that while variables such as gender,

547. JOHN MIKHAIL, ELEMENTS OF MORAL COGNITION 77–85, 319–60 (2011). For comparable findings, see Marc Hauser et al., *A Dissociation between Moral Judgments and Justifications,* 22 MIND & LANGUAGE 1 (2007); Cushman, Young & Hauser, *supra* note 546.

548. Cushman, Young & Hauser, *supra* note 546.

549. Adam B. Moore, Brian A. Clark & Michael J. Kane, *Who Shalt Not Kill? Individual Differences in Working Memory Capacity, Executive Control, and Moral Judgment,* 19 PSYCHOL. SCI. 549 (2008).

550. Lewis Petrinovich, Patricia O'Neill & Matthew Jorgensen, *An Empirical Study of Moral Intuitions: Toward an Evolutionary Ethics,* 64 J. PERSONALITY & SOC. PSYCHOL. 467 (1993).

551. Shaun Nichols & Ron Mallon, *Moral Dilemmas and Moral Rules,* 100 COGNITION 530 (2006).

552. *See, e.g.,* Daniel M. Bartels, *Principled Moral Sentiment and the Flexibility of Moral Judgment and Decision Making,* 108 COGNITION 381 (2008). *See also* Tage S. Rai & Keith J. Holyoak, *Moral Principles or Consumer Preferences? Alternative Framings of the Trolley Problem,* 34 COGNITIVE SCI. 311 (2010). While this study focused on other aspects of choices in the trolley problem, in all the reported experiments, under all conditions, people's judgments were consistent with moderate deontology. Only a small minority of subjects expressed judgments that conformed to either consequentialism or absolutist deontology.

553. MARC D. HAUSER, MORAL MINDS: HOW NATURE DESIGNED OUR UNIVERSAL SENSE OF RIGHT AND WRONG 111–31 (2006).

education, political involvement, and religiosity yielded statistically significant effects, these were nevertheless extremely small, and inconsistent.[554]

It has been argued, based in part on neurological studies, that deontological judgments are more associated with emotions, and consequentialist judgments with deliberative thinking.[555] Patients with focal bilateral damage to a brain region involved in the normal generation of emotions produced "an abnormally 'utilitarian' pattern" of judgments in trolley-like dilemmas (in other classes of moral dilemmas, the judgments of patients with similar brain damage were normal).[556] Correspondingly, people with a propensity for an intuitive mode of decision-making were found to give more weight to deontological constraints than those with a tendency for deliberative thinking.[557]

However, Shaun Nichols and Ron Mallon have demonstrated that people's judgments reflected the deontological distinction between intending harm and merely foreseeing it, even in scenarios involving no bodily harm to anyone, thus casting doubt on the claims that deontological constraints are primarily driven by emotions.[558] Similarly, coping with moral dilemmas while performing a cognitively demanding task—a manipulation reducing people's resort to System-2 reasoning—did not affect subjects' sensitivity to the conflicting moral arguments.[559]

Furthermore, studies of trolley-type dilemmas have arguably confounded deontological versus consequentialist judgments and intuitive versus counterintuitive judgments. Accordingly, it has been found that counterintuitive moral judgments—be they consequentialist or deontological—were associated with greater difficulty and activated parts of the brain involved in emotional conflicts.[560] In general, in recent years there is a growing consensus that moral judgments are reached by multiple systems at once—both affective and cognitive—and involve both emotions and principles, intuition and deliberation.[561]

554. Konika Banerjee, Bryce Huebner & Marc D. Hauser, *Intuitive Moral Judgments Are Robust across Demographic Variation in Gender, Education, Politics, and Religion: A Large-Scale Web-Based Study*, 10 J. COGNITION & CULTURE 253 (2010).

555. *See, e.g.*, Joshua D. Greene et al., *fMRI Investigation of Emotional Engagement in Moral Judgment*, 293 SCI. 2105 (2001); Joshua D. Greene et al., *The Neural Bases of Cognitive Conflict and Control in Moral Judgment*, 44 NEURON 389 (2004). For an overview, see Bartels et al., *supra* note 538, at 488–90.

556. Michael Koenigs et al., *Damage to the Prefrontal Cortex Increases Utilitarian Moral Judgments*, 446 NATURE 908 (2007). *See also* Guy Kahane & Nicholas Shackel, *Do Abnormal Responses Show Utilitarian Bias?*, 452 NATURE E5 (2008); Michael Koenigs et al., *Reply*, 452 NATURE E5 (2008).

557. Bartels, *supra* note 552.

558. Nichols & Mallon, *supra* note 551. *See also* Charles Millar et al., *It's Personal: The Effect of Personal Value on Utilitarian Moral Judgments*, 11 JUDGMENT & DECISION MAKING 326 (2016).

559. Michał Białek & Wim De Neys, *Dual Processes and Moral Conflict: Evidence for Deontological Reasoners' Intuitive Utilitarian Sensitivity*, 12 JUDGMENT & DECISION MAKING 148 (2017).

560. Guy Kahane et al., *The Neural Basis of Intuitive and Counterintuitive Moral Judgment*, 7 SOC. COGNITIVE & AFFECTIVE NEUROSCI. 393 (2012).

561. *Id.*; Cushman, *supra* note 546; Fiery Cushman, Liane Young & Joshua D. Greene, *Multi-system Moral Psychology*, *in* JOHN M. DORIS AND THE MORAL PSYCHOLOGY RESEARCH GROUP, THE MORAL PSYCHOLOGY HANDBOOK 47 (2010); Jesse J. Prinz & Shaun Nichols, *Moral Emotions*, *in* THE MORAL PSYCHOLOGY HANDBOOK, *id.*

Besides the greater support for moderate deontology than for either consequentialism or absolutist deontology, more specific psychological phenomena are compatible with (moderate) deontology as well. For example, in recent years several experimental studies have established the *identifiability effect*—namely, people's tendency to react more generously or more punitively toward identified individuals than toward unidentified ones.[562]

To be sure, neither the prevalence of deontological moral convictions, nor the (moot) argument that consequentialist reasoning is more deliberative, prove that either type of moral theories is philosophically superior to the other.[563] But even if prevailing moral convictions are wrong, since compatibility of legal norms with prevailing moral judgments is important for principled and instrumental reasons, policymakers should take these findings into account.[564]

3. Fairness and Social Justice

(a) General

Following Aristotle, philosophers and jurists commonly distinguish between two primary forms of justice: corrective and distributive. Corrective justice deals with the duty to remedy wrongful losses that one person inflicts on another in voluntary (e.g., contractual) or involuntary (e.g., tortious) interactions. It is attained by depriving the gainer of her ill-gotten gains and remedying the loser's losses. Distributive justice deals with the allocation of benefits and burdens among members of society. It requires that each person receives the allocated benefits or burdens in proportion to the pertinent criterion (such as merit, need, or excellence).

Since the 1960s, social psychologists have extensively studied people's judgments of justice and fairness in various contexts. The social psychology literature does not usually distinguish between corrective and distributive justice—often using the latter term to include the former as well. Social psychologists contrast "distributive justice" with *procedural justice*—the fairness of the procedures by which allocation decisions are made. Some social psychology studies have also investigated retributive justice—namely, the psychological processes relating to punishing people who violate social, legal, or moral norms. This

at 111; Fiery Cushman et al., *Judgment before Principle: Engagement of the Frontoparietal Control Network*, *in* 7 SOC. COGNITIVE & AFFECTIVE NEUROSCI. 888 (2012); Daniel M. Bartels, *Principled Moral Sentiment and the Flexibility of Moral Judgment and Decision Making*, 108 COGNITION 381 (2008); Jana Schaich Borg et al., *Consequences, Action, and Intention as Factors in Moral Judgments: An fMRI Investigation*, 18 J. COGNITIVE NEUROSCI. 803 (2006).

562. For an overview, see Daphna Lewinsohn-Zamir, Ilana Ritov & Tehila Kogut, *Law and Identifiability*, 92 IND. L. REV. 505, 509–19 (2017).

563. For conflicting arguments in these debates, see, e.g., Cass R. Sunstein, *Moral Heuristics*, 28 BEHAV. & BRAIN SCI. 531 (2005) (the article is followed by twenty-four commentaries and the author's response; *see* 28 BEHAV. & BRAIN SCI. 542–70 (2005)); Joshua D. Greene, *The Secret Joke of Kant's Soul*, *in* MORAL PSYCHOLOGY, VOL. 3: THE NEUROSCIENCE OF MORALITY: EMOTION, BRAIN DISORDERS, AND DEVELOPMENT 35 (W. Sinnot-Armstrong ed., 2008); S. Matthew Liao, *A Defense of Intuitions*, 140 PHIL. STUD. 247 (2008); F.M. Kamm, *Neuroscience and Moral Reasoning: A Note on Recent Research*, 37 PHIL. & PUB. AFF. 330 (2009); Waldmann, Nagel & Wiegmann, *supra* note 542, at 373–74; Bartels et al., *supra* note 538, at 495–96.

564. *See also* ZAMIR, *supra* note 151, at 193–95.

subsection discusses substantive ("distributive") fairness and procedural fairness, as well as a phenomenon that is relevant to all forms of fairness judgments: the *belief in a just world*. Retributive justice is alluded to elsewhere in the book.[565]

(b) Substantive Fairness

The most influential theory in the social-psychological study of substantive fairness has been *equity theory*. It posits that people perceive that they are treated fairly when the ratio between their received outcomes (for example, their salary) and their input (e.g., the effort, talent, and commitment they put into their work) is equal to the ratio between the received outcomes and the inputs of other people.[566] A key element of equity theory is that people are distressed not only when they are treated less favorably than they feel they deserve, but also—albeit to a lesser extent—when they are treated more favorably. When people are treated unfairly and less favorably than others, both fairness and self-interest are violated, which in turn leads to greater resentment.

When people feel that they are treated unfairly, they might restore equity in several ways, including by increasing or decreasing their contributions, by changing their assessment of their own input or output or those of others, or by quitting the relationship entirely. Perceived unfairness may also lead to unethical behavior, such as stealing from one's employer.[567] People may object to unfairness not only in their own relationships, but also in relationships between others.

Thus, contrary to rational choice theory, psychological studies reveal that people care about fairness even when it is at odds with, or unrelated to, their self-interest. Indeed, a meta-analysis of dozens of studies has shown that outcome fairness has a stronger effect on variables such as organizational commitment than outcome favorability.[568]

The claim that fairness serves as a constraint on profit maximization has also been established by experimental game theory. Two pertinent games are *Ultimatum* and *Dictator*. Ultimatum is a game in which one person (the proposer) is asked to divide a sum of money between herself and another person. The other person (the responder) may either accept the proposed division (in which case the division is implemented), or reject it (in which case both players receive nothing). Dictator is a game where one party unilaterally decides how to divide a sum of money between herself and another person. Rational choice theory predicts that in an Ultimatum game the proposer will offer the responder the smallest unit

565. *See infra* p. 436.

566. *See, e.g.*, J. Stacy Adams, *Inequality in Social Exchange*, *in* 2 ADVANCES IN EXPERIMENTAL SOCIAL PSYCHOLOGY 267 (1965); Elaine Walster, Ellen Berscheid & G. William Walster, *New Directions in Equity Research*, 25 J. PERSONALITY & SOC. PSYCHOL. 151 (1973). For overviews, see Linda J. Skitka & Daniel C. Wisneski, *Justice Theory and Research: A Social Functionalist Perspective*, *in* HANDBOOK OF PSYCHOLOGY, *supra* note 337, at 406, 407–10; John T. Jost & Aaron C. Kay, *Social Justice: History, Theory, and Research*, *in* 2 HANDBOOK OF SOCIAL PSYCHOLOGY, *supra* note 3, at 1122, 1130–33.

567. Jerald Greenber, *Stealing in the Name of Justice: Informational and Interpersonal Moderators of Theft Reactions to Underpayment Inequity*, 54 ORG. BEHAV. & HUM. DECISION PROCESSES 81 (1993).

568. Linda J. Skitka, Jennifer Winquist & Susan Hutchinson, *Are Outcome Fairness and Outcome Favorability Distinguishable Psychological Constructs? A Meta-analytic Review*, 16 SOC. JUST. RES. 309 (2003).

of money used in the game and the responder will accept this offer; and that in a Dictator game the dictator will appropriate the entire sum. However, numerous experiments have established that in Ultimatum games most proposers offer responders a generous share of the pie (40 percent on average) and that responders reject very low offers.[569] These results were obtained even under conditions of complete anonymity, thus indicating that it is not only the fear of retaliation that induces people to behave fairly. Responders' rejections of clearly disproportionate divisions in the Ultimatum game indicate that people are willing to bear some costs to punish others for what they perceive as an unfair division of resources.[570] Even in the Dictator game, while a substantial minority (36 percent) keep all the money for themselves, most people share a substantial fraction of their endowment (28 percent on average) with the passive participant.[571]

The concern among commercial enterprises about fairness—be it for its own sake or as a means of maintaining positive reputation—may explain otherwise puzzling market behaviors, such as the failure of firms to immediately raise prices when excess demand is not accompanied by increase in suppliers' costs (contrary to standard economic models).[572] The fairness constraint may also explain the rarity of very high contingency fee rates in the market for legal services, even when such rates would be mutually beneficial.[573]

Equity theory has greatly advanced our understanding of exchange relationships, that is, relationships in which people give something and get something in return. However, it neither satisfactorily explains fairness judgments in other contexts (such as allocation of civil and political rights), nor does it provide a complete explanation of people's judgments of fairness in exchange relationships. Studies have shown that while equity is the primary determinant of fairness in exchange relationships, in the context of minimizing suffering, and in intimate relationships such as within a family or among close friends, needs are an important factor, as well.[574] Equal division is preferred over an equitable one in contexts that emphasize cooperation and partnership.[575] Interestingly, where both equity (the outputs/

569. *See, e.g.*, Hessel Oosterbeek, Randolph Sloof & Gijs van De Kuilen, *Cultural Differences in Ultimatum Game Experiments: Evidence from a Meta-analysis*, 7 Experimental Econ. 171 (2004).

570. For a general survey and analysis of the experimental data, see Colin F. Camerer, Behavioral Game Theory—Experiments in Strategic Interaction 43–117 (2003).

571. Christoph Engel, *Dictator Games: A Meta Study*, 14 Experimental Econ. 583 (2011). *See also infra* pp. 106–10.

572. Daniel Kahneman, Jack L. Knetsch & Richard Thaler, *Fairness as a Constraint on Profit Seeking: Entitlements in the Market*, 76 Am. Econ. Rev. 728 (1986).

573. Eyal Zamir & Ilana Ritov, *Notions of Fairness and Contingent Fees*, 74 Law & Contemp. Probs. 1 (2010); *infra* pp. 510–12.

574. Gerald S. Leventhal, *Fairness in Social Relationships*, *in* Contemporary Topics in Social Psychology 211 (John W. Thibaut, Janet T. Spence & Robert C. Carson eds., 1976); Melvin J. Lerner, Dale T. Miller & J.G. Holmes, *Deserving and the Emergence of Forms of Justice*, *in* 9 Advances in Experimental Social Psychology 133, 152–60 (1976); Helmut Lamm & Thomas Schwinger, *Norms concerning Distributive Justice: Are Needs Taken into Consideration in Allocation Decisions?*, 43 Soc. Psychol. Q. 425 (1980).

575. *See, e.g.*, Melvin J. Lerner, *The Justice Motive: Some Hypotheses as to Its Origins and Forms*, 45 J. Personality 1, 24–28 (1977).

inputs ratio) and equality (similar outcomes for all) are plausible criteria, men tend to prioritize equity, while women are more inclined toward equality.[576]

A common denominator of people's judgment of fairness is the key role played by social comparison. Whether one adopts equity, equality, need, or any other distribution criterion, its implementation requires comparisons with others: what others have received (in the case of equality), the ratio between other people's contributions and outcomes (in the case of equity), other people's neediness (in the case of need), and so forth. It follows that people may perceive the same output as more or less fair, depending on which reference group they compare themselves (or others) with.[577] Various psychological factors determine which competing reference point prevails.[578] People may also draw a comparison between their current output/input ratio and their previous one, which may lead to a different judgment than a comparison with other people. Judgments of fairness thus depend on a variety of factors, including personal traits and heuristics (such as availability) that determine the perceived reference group.

Additional limitations of equity theory stem from the fact that both contributions and outputs are often multidimensional and do not lend themselves to easy quantification and summation. For example, some workers may be more hard-working but less productive or less innovative than others. Similarly, workers' outputs comprise not only their salaries but also non-monetary benefits, respect, and so forth. Judgments of fairness are particularly challenging when an outcome comprises several elements and people differ in their assessment of the comparative worth of those elements.[579] Finally, it has been demonstrated that people may have an independent motivation "to do the right thing." Hence, when they choose between two prosocial courses of action (e.g., one that minimizes inequality and one that maximizes overall welfare), they are more likely to choose the one that is labeled the moral choice, whatever it is.[580]

(c) Procedural Fairness

One important challenge to equity theory (and to other theories focusing on the fairness of outcomes) has been posed by studies that demonstrate that people care about the fairness of the processes by which decisions about allocation of benefits and burdens are

576. *See, e.g.*, Brenda Major & Jeffrey B. Adams, *Role of Gender, Interpersonal Orientation, and Self-Presentation in Distributive-Justice Behavior*, 45 J. PERSONALITY & SOC. PSYCHOL. 598 (1983).

577. For a brief survey of the pertinence of reference points in judgments of fairness, see Zamir & Ritov, *supra* note 573, at 7–11. On reference-dependence, see generally *supra* pp. 76–86.

578. *See, e.g.*, Carol T. Kulik & Maureen L. Ambrose, *Personal and Situational Determinants of Referent Choice*, 17 ACAD. MGMT. REV. 212 (1992); Lisa D. Ordóñez, Terry Connolly & Richard Coughlan, *Multiple Reference Points in Satisfaction and Fairness Assessment*, 13 J. BEHAV. DECISION MAKING 329 (2000).

579. *See, e.g.*, Menachem Yaari & Maya Bar-Hillel, *On Dividing Justly*, 1 SOC. CHOICE & WELFARE 1 (1984).

580. Valerio Capraro & David G. Rand, *Do The Right Thing: Preferences for Moral Behavior, Rather than Equity or Efficiency Per Se, Drive Human Prosociality* (working paper, Nov. 2017), *available at*: https://ssrn.com/abstract=2965067).

made, sometimes no less than about the outcomes of those decisions.[581] Both laboratory experiments and field studies have demonstrated that people are more willing to accept unfavorable outcomes when they are the product of a fair process—particularly if it allowed them to express their concerns. People care about procedural fairness both in resource allocation and in dispute resolution contexts.[582] Similarly, they value procedural fairness in their encounters with public authorities, such as the police.[583] While this phenomenon was initially explained by people's desire for power and process control,[584] subsequent studies have highlighted the importance of dignity and respect within social groups, and the maintenance of ongoing relationships.[585] People care about procedural justice both because they believe that a fair procedure—particularly a fair opportunity to voice their concerns before a decision is made—is more likely to produce a favorable allocation, and because they care about procedural fairness per se.[586] Procedural fairness may also serve as a heuristic for the fairness of outcomes, when the latter is difficult to assess.[587]

People may reasonably disagree as to the fairness of particular procedures. As in the context of substantive fairness, here too, social comparisons—that is, comparing the procedures applied in one's own case with those applied in others' cases—play an important role in people's judgments of fairness.[588]

While the importance of perceived procedural fairness can hardly be denied, the precise relationships between different aspects of procedural fairness, the relative importance of procedural versus substantive fairness, and the complex, context-dependent interactions between these (and other) aspects of fairness, are the subject of ongoing debates.[589] Research in the field of policing, for example, indicates that certain measures are perceived negatively even when conducted with strict adherence to the dictates of procedural justice.[590]

581. *See generally* Jost & Kay, *supra* note 566, at 410–14; Skitka & Wisneski, *supra* note 566, at 1140–42; Robert J. MacCoun, *Voice, Control, and Belonging: The Double-Edged Sword of Procedural Fairness*, 1 ANN. REV. L. & SOC. SCI. 171 (2005) (including implications for the law).

582. *See, e.g.*, Robert Folger et al., *Effects of "Voice" and Peer Opinions on Responses to Inequity*, 45 J. PERSONALITY & SOC. PSYCHOL. 268 (1979) (resource allocation); Robert Folger et al., *Elaborating Procedural Fairness: Justice Becomes Both Simpler and More Complex*, 22 PERSONALITY & SOC. PSYCHOL. BULL. 435 (1996) (dispute resolution).

583. *See, e.g.*, Tom T. Tyler & Robert Folger, *Distributional and Procedural Aspects of Satisfaction with Citizen-Police Encounters*, 1 BASIC & APPLIED SOC. PSYCHOL. 281 (1980).

584. JOHN THIBAUT & LAURENS WALKER, PROCEDURAL JUSTICE: A PSYCHOLOGICAL ANALYSIS (1975).

585. E. ALLAN LIND & TOM R. TYLER, THE SOCIAL PSYCHOLOGY OF PROCEDURAL FAIRNESS 230–41 (1988).

586. Debra L. Shapiro & Jeanne M. Brett, *What Is the Role of Control in Organizational Justice?*, *in* HANDBOOK OF ORGANIZATIONAL RESEARCH 155 (Jerald Greenberg & Jason A. Colquitt eds., 2005).

587. Kees van den Bos et al., *How Do I Judge My Outcome when I Do Not Know the Outcome of Others? The Psychology of the Fair Process Effect*, 72 J. PERSONALITY & SOC. PSYCHOL. 1034 (1997).

588. Ilse V. Grienberger, Christel G. Rutte & Ad F.M. van Knippenberg, *Influence of Social Comparisons of Outcomes and Procedures on Fairness Judgments*, 82 J. APPLIED PSYCHOL. 913 (1997).

589. *See generally* Skitka & Wisneski, *supra* note 566, at 412, 413–14, 418–20.

590. *See* Jacinta M. Gau, *Consent Searches as a Threat to Procedural Justice and Police Legitimacy: An Analysis of Consent Requests During Traffic Stops*, 24 CRIM. JUS. POL'Y REV. 759 (2013); Tal Jonathan-Zamir, Badi Hasisi & Yoram Margalioth, *Is It the* What *or the* How? *The Roles of High-Policing Tactics and Procedural Justice in Predicting Perceptions of Hostile Treatment: The Case of Security Checks at Ben-Gurion Airport, Israel*, 50 LAW & SOC'Y REV. 608 (2016).

Apparently, politeness coupled with a genuine willingness to listen cannot negate the adverse effects of a highly intrusive police search.

(d) Belief in a Just World

The last phenomenon to be mentioned in the present context—belief in a just world[591]—operates at a different level than the notions of substantive and procedural fairness discussed above. People have a need to believe that they live in a just world, that they and others deserve their fate. They believe that efforts and good deeds are reciprocated. Such belief encourages people to commit to the pursuit of long-term goals, and helps them cope with their own misfortunes. In these respects, it seems to be personally and socially beneficial. However, the belief in a just world may hinder attempts to advance necessary social changes, since both the privileged and the underprivileged may approve of the status quo.[592]

People experience distress and threat when they observe, or come to know about, people who suffer undeserved misfortune, and use various means to avoid such distress. Helping or compensating the victim is one possibility;[593] dissociation from the victim is another.[594] The most studied—and most troubling—device is to blame or derogate the victim. People who are otherwise unable to restore justice, tend to devalue and denigrate those who are victims of various crimes, the impoverished, and those who are sick with cancer and other diseases.[595]

4. Prosocial Behavior and Altruism

(a) Helping Others

Contrary to rational choice theory, people often do not act egoistically, but rather for the benefit of others and for society at large. The term *prosocial behavior* is used in social psychology to cover a wide range of phenomena, including coming to the aid of people in emergency situations, contributing money to charity, volunteering in communities, voting, and participating in social movements. The term *altruism* denotes a possible motivation for action, namely the desire to benefit other people. The two notions often overlap, but there can be prosocial behavior that is not altruistically motivated, and altruism does not necessarily translate into action.[596]

591. For overviews, see Melvin J. Lerner & Dale T. Miller, *Just World Research and the Attribution Process: Looking Back and Ahead,* 85 PSYCHOL. BULL. 1030 (1978); Adrian Furnham, *Belief in a Just World: Research Progress over the Past Decade,* 34 PERSONALITY & INDIVIDUAL DIFFERENCES 795 (2003); Jost & Kay, supra note 566, at 1136–38.

592. Gary Blasi & John T. Jost, *System Justification Theory and Research: Implications for Law, Legal Advocacy, and Social Justice,* 94 CAL. L. REV. 1119 (2006).

593. Melvin J. Lerner & Carolyn H. Simmons, *Observer's Reaction to the "Innocent Victim": Compassion or Rejection?,* 4 J. PERSONALITY & SOC. PSYCHOL. 203 (1966).

594. Carolyn L. Hafer, *Do Innocent Victims Threaten the Belief in a Just World? Evidence from a Modified Stroop Task,* 79 J. PERSONALITY & SOC. PSYCHOL. 165 (2000).

595. Carolyn L. Hafer & Laurent Bègue, *Experimental Research on Just-World Theory: Problems, Developments, and Future Challenges,* 131 PSYCHOL. BULL. 128 (2005).

596. C. Daniel Batson & Adam A. Powell, *Altruism and Prosocial Behavior, in* HANDBOOK OF PSYCHOLOGY, Vol. 5: PERSONALITY AND SOCIAL PSYCHOLOGY 463, 463 (Theodore Millon & Melvin J. Lerner eds., 2003).

While most early studies focused on interpersonal helping, more recent research has been extended to planned and continuous activities by groups of people.[597] Furthermore, a comprehensive concept of prosocial behavior includes not only unilateral benefitting, but also reciprocal relationships of cooperation between equally situated individuals or groups—a topic extensively studied by experimental economists.[598]

A basic question in the study of individual and collective prosocial behavior is what determines whether a person will act in a prosocial manner. With regard to the paradigmatic situation of a bystander who may or may not intervene in an emergency situation, numerous studies have highlighted the importance of situational determinants, with particular emphasis on the presence of other people at the scene. In addition to the *bystander effect*—the phenomenon that an individual's likelihood of coming to the aid of another person decreases when other passive bystanders are present, due to a subjective diffusion of responsibility—several other factors have been found to affect this likelihood. Inter alia, people are more likely to intervene when the other person's need is more vivid, more severe, and less ambiguous; when the other person is a friend rather than a stranger; when the costs of helping are low; and in rural areas (compared with urban locations). Finally, it has been found that a larger number of bystanders may increase, rather than decrease, the likelihood of intervention when intervening by oneself is dangerous and assistance of others reduces that danger.[599]

Contrary to the established effect of such situational variables, early studies did not find clear correlations between the tendency to intervene in a bystander situation and specific personal traits, such as religiosity, self-esteem, or social responsibility. However, subsequent studies have found that aggregate measures of prosocial orientation, and certain interactions between situational and dispositional variables, do provide good predictors of people's likelihood to come to the aid of others.[600] Prosocial behavior is positively correlated with the likelihood of experiencing affective and cognitive empathy and feeling responsibility for the welfare of others, as well as with belief in one's self-efficacy. Of the big-five personality dimensions,[601] the inclination to act in a prosocial manner is primarily correlated with *agreeableness*—namely, the inclination to maintain positive relations with others, and to

597. *See generally* Mark Snyder & Allen M. Omoto, *Volunteerism: Social Issues Perspectives and Social Policy Implications,* 2 Soc. Issues & Pol'y Rev. 1 (2008).

598. Mark Snyder & Patrick C. Dwyer, *Altruism and Prosocial Behavior, in* Handbook of Psychology, *supra* note 337, at 467, 467. For a lucid overview of behavioral-economics studies of cooperation, see Simon Gächter, *Human Prosocial Motivation and the Maintenance of Social Order, in* The Oxford Handbook of Behavioral Economics and the Law, *supra* note 8, at 28.

599. For overviews and meta-analyses, see Bibb Latané & Steve Nida, *Ten Years of Research on Group Size and Helping,* 89 Psychol. Bull. 308 (1981); John F. Dovidio et al., The Social Psychology of Prosocial Behavior 65–105 (2006); Peter Fischer et al., *The Bystander-Effect: A Meta-analytic Review on Bystander Intervention in Dangerous and Non-dangerous Emergencies,* 137 Psychol. Bull. 517 (2011).

600. *See, e.g.,* Louis A. Penner et al., *Measuring the Prosocial Personality, in* 10 Advances in Personality Assessment 147 (James N. Butcher & Charles D. Spielberger eds., 1995).

601. *See supra* note 473.

act altruistically and cooperatively.[602] Such traits, along with self-transcendence values (e.g., a recognition of the equal worth of all humans), and self-efficacy beliefs, significantly account for prosocial behavior.[603] Prosocial orientation is predictive of involvement in sustained prosocial behavior in both ordinary life (such as volunteering), and extreme conditions (such as rescuing Jews in Nazi Europe).[604] Prosocial behavior is negatively correlated with experiencing self-oriented discomfort when another person is in extreme distress.[605]

The inclination to help others is affected by one's mood. Pleasant moods, whether induced or naturally occurring, increase helpfulness. People are more inclined to help others after successfully completing a task, when thinking happy thoughts, or even when experiencing sunny weather.[606] The effect of negative moods on prosocial behavior is considerably more complex. Feelings of guilt generally induce prosocial behavior.[607] However, the effect of sadness is inconsistent: while it may increase helping, more often than not it decreases prosocial behavior, or has no effect. A major explanation for the negative effect of sorrow on the inclination to help others is that sorrow leads to preoccupation with oneself and reduced concern for others.[608]

Not only does feeling good increase the likelihood of doing good, doing good usually results in feeling good. For this reason, it has been argued that seemingly altruistic behaviors are actually motivated by the egoistic desire to improve one's mood and relieve negative feelings,[609] or as a way to reduce the unpleasant, emphatic arousal generated by witnessing the suffering of other people.[610] However, other studies, controlling for subjects' expectation of improving their mood by helping others or providing alternative ways to attain that goal, have shown that prosocial behavior may also be motivated by empathy and altruism, rather than self-benefit.[611] Notwithstanding these findings, studies have shown that people

602. William G. Graziano & Nancy Eisenberg, *Agreeableness: A Dimension of Personality, in* HANDBOOK OF PERSONALITY PSYCHOLOGY 795 (Robert Hogan, John Johnson & Stephen Briggs eds., 1997).

603. *See, e.g.,* Gian Vittorio Caprara, Guido Alessandri & Nancy Eisenberg, *Prosociality: The Contribution of Traits, Values, and Self-Efficacy Beliefs,* 102 J. PERSONALITY & SOC. PSYCHOL. 1289 (2012).

604. *See, e.g.,* SAMUEL P. OLINER & PEARL M. OLINER, THE ALTRUISTIC PERSONALITY: RESCUERS OF JEWS IN NAZI EUROPE (1988); Penner et al., *supra* note 600; Caprara, Alessandri & Eisenberg, *supra* note 603.

605. Penner et al., *supra* note 600, at 153–56.

606. Peter Salovey & David L. Rosenhan, *Mood States and Prosocial Behavior, in* HANDBOOK OF SOCIAL PSYCHOPHYSIOLOGY 371, 372–74 (Hugh Wagner & Antony Mansfield eds., 1989); Snyder & Dwyer, *supra* note 598, at 472.

607. Salovey & Rosenhan, *supra* note 606, at 373–78.

608. For a review of the conflicting evidence, see *id.* at 378–79.

609. *See, e.g.,* Robert B. Cialdini et al., *Empathy-Based Helping: Is It Selflessly or Selfishly Motivated?,* 52 J. PERSONALITY & SOC. PSYCHOL. 749 (1987).

610. JANE ALLYN PILIAVIN ET AL., EMERGENCY INTERVENTION (1981); DOVIDIO ET AL., *supra* note 599, at 126–31 (2006).

611. *See, e.g.,* David A. Schroeder et al., *Empathic Concern and Helping Behavior: Egoism or Altruism?,* 24 J. EXPERIMENTAL SOC. PSYCHOL. 333 (1988); C. Daniel Batson et al., *Negative-State Relief and the Empathy-Altruism Hypothesis,* 56 J. PERSONALITY & SOC. PSYCHOL. 922 (1989); C. DANIEL BATSON, THE ALTRUISM QUESTION: TOWARD A SOCIAL-PSYCHOLOGICAL ANSWER (1991). For an overview of the debate, see DOVIDIO ET AL., *supra* note 599, at 118–43.

engage in volunteer work for a multitude of motives, including a sense of commitment and idealism, a desire to meet new people, and an enhancement of one's self-esteem.[612]

Another perspective on prosocial behavior underscores the role of social learning: people observe the behavior of others and emulate it.[613] People tend to comply with social norms, such as the norm of reciprocity: the felt obligation to repay past favors by helping those who have helped us, and not helping those who have not.[614] As one might expect, however, by following this norm people tend to make self-centered assessments, such that givers focus on the costs they incur, and recipients on the benefit they derive from what they receive.[615] Equally unsurprising, salespersons, fundraisers, and contributors to political campaigns, among others, regularly take advantage of the entrenched norm of reciprocation.[616]

(b) Cooperation

While helping is unidirectional, much prosocial behavior takes the form of bidirectional cooperation within, and even between, groups. In comparison to unilateral helping, cooperation characterizes interdependent relationships between similarly situated people, and often involves repeated interactions.[617] Cooperation is necessary to overcome *social dilemmas*—that is, situations in which selfish behavior is rational, but when everybody behaves selfishly, everybody is worse off, compared to the situation in which everybody cooperates.[618] The well-known *prisoner's dilemma* game is a simple model of such a situation in a two-person scenario. The *tragedy of the commons* and *public goods* describe social dilemmas in multi-person scenarios.[619] Since social dilemmas are commonly invoked by legal economists as a justification for various legal rules and institutions, behavioral studies of such dilemmas are particularly important for behavioral law and economics.

In keeping with rational choice theory, the prisoner's dilemma, tragedy of the commons, and the problem of public goods assume that all people seek to maximize their own utility.

612. *See generally* Snyder & Dwyer, *supra* note 598, at 472–73.

613. *See generally* DOVIDIO ET AL., *supra* note 599, at 106–18, 199–210; Batson & Powell, *supra* note 596, at 465–66.

614. ROBERT B. CIALDINI, INFLUENCE: SCIENCE AND PRACTICE 18–50 (5th ed. 2009); DOVIDIO ET AL., *supra* note 599, at 49–51, 111–13.

615. Yan Zhang & Nicholas Epley, *Self-Centered Social Exchange: Differential Use of Costs versus Benefits in Prosocial Reciprocity*, 97 J. PERSONALITY & SOC. PSYCHOL. 796 (2009).

616. CIALDINI, *supra* note 614, at 22–49.

617. DOVIDIO ET AL., *supra* note 599, at 270.

618. *See generally* PAUL A.M. VAN LANGE ET AL., SOCIAL DILEMMAS: THE PSYCHOLOGY OF HUMAN COOPERATION (2014).

619. *Tragedy of the commons* denotes a situation in which a resource is open for use by many individuals, and overusing it results in its destruction, such as a pasture used for grazing. Since each user reaps the benefit of his or her use, but the costs are born collectively, in the absence of coordination, self-interested behavior is expected to harm everybody. A *public good* is a good that is *non-excludable*, that is, people cannot be effectively excluded from using it, and *non-rivalrous*, that is, its use by one person does not reduce its availability to others. For example, national security is a public good. Since people can free-ride on other's investment in producing public goods, according to standard economic theory no individual would contribute to their production, to the detriment of all.

However, social psychologists have found that people's motivations vary. According to a common, basic classification, people's *social-value orientation* (SVO) is either individualistic, prosocial, or competitive. Individualists seek to maximize their lot regardless of the outcomes for others; prosocials prefer an equal distribution of resources and seek to maximize aggregate resources; and competitors seek to maximize their relative advantage over others.[620] A meta-analysis of forty-seven studies using *decomposed games* found that 50 percent of people were classified as prosocials, 24 percent as individualists, and 13 percent as competitors—the remaining 13 percent displaying no consistent SOV.[621] Another meta-analysis of eighty-two studies revealed that overall, prosocials cooperated in social dilemmas more than individualists, and individualists cooperated more than competitors.[622]

A huge body of research in experimental game theory has established that, rather than behaving as rational maximizers of their own utility, most people behave as reciprocators: they treat others as others treat them, and are willing to punish free-riders, even at some cost to themselves. This research also provides insight into the motivations underlying reciprocity—including inequality aversion, consideration of other people's intentions in addition to their actions, and concern for overall social welfare (when it conflicts with inequality aversion). The research also highlights the importance of a threat of punishment in stabilizing cooperation over repeated interactions.[623]

To fully comprehend people's cooperation, one must consider the dynamics of in-group and out-group relations, including the formation and effect of social identity. Delving into these issues would, however, exceed the scope of the present discussion.[624]

H. Cross-Phenomenal Factors

This section examines several issues that cut across various cognitive phenomena: individual differences, the effect of expertise and experience on judgment and decision-making, the possible differences between self-regarding decisions and decisions made on behalf of others, group decision-making, cultural differences, and possible reactions to the adverse effects of suboptimal decision-making. While some of these issues have been discussed sporadically above, this section discusses them from a broader and more methodical perspective.

620. On this and more elaborate typologies, see, e.g., Paul A.M. Van Lange, *The Pursuit of Joint Outcomes and Equality in Outcomes: An Integrative Model of Social Value Orientation,* 77 J. PERSONALITY & SOC. PSYCHOL. 337 (1999); Wing Tung Au & Jessica Y.Y. Kwong, *Measurements and Effects of Social-Value Orientation in Social Dilemmas: A Review, in* CONTEMPORARY PSYCHOLOGICAL RESEARCH ON SOCIAL DILEMMAS 71 (Ramzi Suleiman et al. eds., 2004).

621. Au & Kwong, *supra* note 620, at 72–74. In a decomposed game, a subject is instructed to allocate a certain pie between self and another (imaginary) person, and the total payoff the subject is expected to receive is the sum of the "self" allocation she chose plus the "other" allocation chosen by the other (imaginary) person.

622. Daniel Balliet, Craig Parks & Jeff Joireman, *Social Value Orientation and Cooperation: A Meta-analysis,* 12 GROUP PROCESSES & INTERGROUP REL. 533 (2009).

623. For an overview, see Gächter, *supra* note 598.

624. For a brief overview, see Snyder & Dwyer, *supra* note 598, at 479–81.

1. Individual Differences

Judgments and decisions depend on three types of factors: task features, environmental conditions, and personal characteristics. While the first two have been extensively studied from early on, considerably less attention has been given to the third. In this respect, JDM research lags behind other areas of psychological research.[625] In recent years, considerable evidence has emerged about individual differences in judgment and decision-making, but there is still much room for systematization and theorization in this field.[626]

People differ in their judgments and decisions, including in terms of their inclination to use various heuristics, their vulnerability to cognitive biases, and their moral beliefs. This is evident in daily life, and has been manifested in thousands of experimental studies. Such individual differences do not imply that there are no predictable and systematic patterns of human judgment, motivation, and decision-making. As the numerous studies surveyed throughout this book have established, such patterns do exist. The variability between individuals in this respect nevertheless poses a challenge to policymakers, because it means that any single measure may have varying effects on different people: it may be beneficial for many, unnecessary for some, and even harmful for others. We will return to this point in Chapter 4.[627] Here we only give a glimpse into studies that have sought to identify correlations between well-known heuristics and biases—and between intelligence, thinking dispositions, personality traits, and demographic variables, as well as between different heuristics and biases.[628] These correlations provide some insight into the causes of the various phenomena, and into human reasoning in general.[629]

Keith Stanovich and Richard West have found a negative correlation between subjects' scores on cognitive ability tests and their proneness to errors in probability assessments and syllogistic reasoning.[630] Less obviously, they found weak, but statistically significant, correlation between low scores in cognitive ability tests and proneness to the hindsight bias and overconfidence. No such correlation was found, however, with the false-consensus effect.[631] Likewise, no correlation was found between cognitive ability and people's susceptibility to the conjunction

625. Susan Mohammed & Alexander Schwall, *Individual Differences and Decision Making: What We Know and Where We Go from Here,* 24 Int'l Rev. Indus. & Org. Psychol. 249, 249–54 (2009). On the intellectual roots of this deficiency in JDM research and in behavioral economics, see Jeffrey J. Rachlinski, *Cognitive Errors, Individual Differences, and Paternalism,* 73 U. Chi. L. Rev. 207, 209–10 (2006).

626. Kirstin C. Appelt et al., *The Decision Making Individual Differences Inventory and Guidelines for the Study of Individual Differences in Judgment and Decision-Making Research,* 6 Judgment & Decision Making 252 (2011).

627. *See infra* pp. 170–71, 177–85.

628. For additional studies of individual differences and their correlates, see *supra* pp. 75–76, 87, 107–08.

629. Stanovich, *supra* note 19; Stanovich, *supra* note 21.

630. Keith E. Stanovich & Richard F. West, *Individual Differences in Rational Thought,* 127 J. Experimental Psychol.: General 161, 161–64 (1998).

631. *Id.* at 175–78. On the false-consensus effect, see *supra* pp. 66–68.

fallacy, base-rate neglect, certainty effect, framing effects, omission bias, sunk-costs, confirmation bias, anchoring, and other known cognitive biases.[632]

The relative independence of cognitive biases and cognitive ability is likely related to the attribution of many heuristics and biases to intuitive, System 1 thinking. According to a model put forward by Keith Stanovich, System 2 comprises two elements: *reflective* and *algorithmic*.[633] The reflective mind determines whether System 1 thinking would be suppressed by algorithmic, System 2 thinking. While there is some correlation between the cognitive abilities measured by intelligence tests and people's algorithmic abilities that are the focus of much JDM research, there is weaker correlation between one's cognitive and algorithmic abilities and one's tendency to engage in deliberative thinking. Numerous studies have demonstrated that measures of intelligence display only moderate to weak correlations with thinking dispositions (such as active open-minded thinking and need for cognition), and almost no correlations with others (such as conscientiousness, curiosity, and diligence).[634] Hence, high cognitive ability does not necessarily translate into less susceptibility to cognitive biases.

This is not to say that a greater tendency to engage in deliberative thinking necessarily translates into lower susceptibility to cognitive biases. Here, too, the picture is not very clear. Several studies have examined the correlation between people's score on the *need for cognition scale* (NCS)—a common test for the tendency to engage in effortful cognitive endeavors[635]—and framing effects. While the results are mixed, most studies found no such correlation.[636] Similarly, Shane Frederick examined correlations between people's score in the *cognitive reflection test* (CRT)—another measure of the inclination to use an analytic mode of thinking[637]—and several phenomena in judgment and decision-making.[638] He found that people who are low on CRT (that is, inclined to more intuitive thinking) had higher discount rates. No correlation was found between CRT scores and self-perceived tendency to procrastinate.[639] Subjects high on cognitive reflection were less risk-averse for gains and more risk-averse for losses, compared with subjects with low CRT scores. Thus, unlike the latter, the former did not display prospect theory's reflection effect.[640] Curiously, CRT scores were more tightly linked with time preferences for

632. Keith E. Stanovich & Richard F. West, *On the Relative Independence of Thinking Biases and Cognitive Ability*, 94 J. Personality & Soc. Psychol. 672 (2008). On these biases, see generally *supra* pp. 28–29, 30–31, 34, 46–48, 48–50, 56–57, 58–61, and 79–82, respectively.

633. *See supra* p. 22.

634. Stanovich, *supra* note 21, at 354.

635. *See supra* note 25 and accompanying text.

636. *See, e.g.*, Irwin P. Levin et al., *A New Look at Framing Effects: Distribution of Effect Sizes, Individual Differences, and Independence of Types of Effects*, 88 Org. Behav. & Hum. Decision Processes 411, 427 (2002); Mohammed & Schwall, *supra* note 625, at 255–59, 280.

637. *See supra* pp. 22–23.

638. Shane Frederick, *Cognitive Reflection and Decision Making*, 19 J. Econ. Persp. 25 (2005).

639. *Id.* at 28–32.

640. *Id.* at 32–33. On the reflection effect, see *supra* pp. 42, 85–86.

women than for men, but were more tightly linked with risk preferences for men than for women.[641]

Notwithstanding the considerable progress that has been made in recent years, it appears that we still lack a comprehensive, satisfactory theory of the relationships between cognitive abilities, thinking dispositions, and susceptibility to cognitive biases. The only thing that can be said with some confidence at this point is that there are no strong correlations between susceptibility to cognitive bias and either cognitive ability or thinking dispositions.

Turning to another line of research, some studies have looked into the relationship between personality traits—especially the big-five personality dimensions[642]—and decision-making. For example, one study found that high scores on *openness to experience*—a trait consisting of active imagination, aesthetic sensitivity, attentiveness to inner feelings, preference for variety, and intellectual curiosity—were associated with greater risk-taking in the domain of gains. High scores on *neuroticism*—characterized by anxiety, fear, moodiness, worry, envy, frustration, jealousy, and loneliness—were associated with less risk-taking in the domain of gains, and more risk-taking in the domain of losses.[643] Another study found that two facets of *conscientiousness*—striving for achievement and dutifulness—were correlated with *escalation of commitment*, but in opposite directions: whereas subjects who scored highly in achievement striving were more susceptible to this bias, those who scored highly in dutifulness were less so.[644]

Quite many studies have examined correlations between decision-making and demographic variables. Thus, for example, one large-scale study found that the *myopic discount rate* (measured by the subject's choice between a smaller, hypothetical reward sooner and a larger one later) was weakly but significantly higher for respondents who were younger, less educated, and of lower incomes (although the causal relationship with the latter two variables is unclear).[645] A meta-analysis of 150 studies found that women are generally more risk-averse than men, although the gender difference varies from one context to another.[646] It was also found that there are significant differences in the magnitude of the gender gap across age levels—although this, too, varied from one context to another. Generally, the

641. *Id.* at 37–38.

642. *See supra* note 473.

643. Marco Lauriola & Irwin P. Levin, *Personality Traits and Risky Decision-Making in a Controlled Experimental Task: An Exploratory Study*, 31 PERSONALITY & INDIVIDUAL DIFFERENCES 215 (2001). For additional findings regarding personality traits and risk attitude, see Marvin Zuckerman & D. Michael Kuhlman, *Personality and Risk-Taking: Common Biosocial Factors*, 68 J. PERSONALITY 999 (2000); Marco Lauriola et al., *Individual Differences in Risky Decision Making: A Meta-analysis of Sensation Seeking and Impulsivity with the Balloon Analogue Risk Task*, 27 J. BEHAV. DECISION MAKING 20 (2014).

644. Henry Moon, *The Two Faces of Conscientiousness: Duty and Achievement Striving in Escalation of Commitment Dilemmas*, 86 J. APPLIED PSYCHOL. 533 (2001). On escalation of commitment, see *supra* pp. 56–57.

645. Reimers et al., *supra* note 500. For a critical review of comparable findings, see Urminsky & Zauberman, *supra* note 484, at 147–48.

646. James P. Byrnes, David C. Miller & William D. Schafer, *Gender Differences in Risk Taking: A Meta-analysis*, 125 PSYCHOL. BULL. 367 (1999). *See also* Fox, Erner & Walters, *supra* note 141, at 75.

evidence shows that women exhibit greater loss aversion than men,[647] that older people tend to be more loss-averse than younger ones,[648] and that higher education reduces (but does not eliminate) loss aversion.[649] While some decision-making skills (such as applying decision rules) were found to diminish with old age—arguably due to decline in cognitive ability—others (such as consistency in risk perception) did not, and still others (such as resistance to overconfidence) were found to improve, arguably thanks to greater experience.[650]

Finally, another line of research has examined the correlations between different aspects of decision-making—particularly in relation to tasks where there is a normatively accurate (or consistent) decision. In general, these studies found statistically significant, positive correlations between the subjects' resistance to different biases, but that these correlations were mostly weak.[651] Some correlation has also been found between subjects' aggregate score in batteries of decision tasks and their socioeconomic status—although, once again, correlation does not imply causality.[652]

2. Expertise

Expertise is the possession of domain-specific knowledge that is acquired through experience or training and that leads to sustainable superior performance in domain-related tasks.[653] Experts not only possess more information than laypersons; they also organize information into higher-level schemas that allow them to quickly perceive and recall domain-relevant information, recognize situations, and rapidly and accurately respond to them—without considering all of the available data or all conceivable options.[654] As such, expertise effectively converts System 2 thinking (which may be crucial at the initial stages of acquiring the expertise) into heuristic-based, System 1 thinking.

While the findings are somewhat ambiguous, it appears that judgments can reflect true expertise if they are reached within a decision-making environment that: (1) is regular and predictable, and (2) offers people an opportunity to learn the relevant patterns.[655] If the

647. Ulrich Schmidt & Stefan Traub, *An Experimental Test of Loss Aversion*, 25. J. RISK & UNCERTAINTY 233 (2002); Peter Brooks & Horst Zank, *Loss Averse Behavior*, 31 J. RISK & UNCERTAINTY 301 (2005); Adam S. Booij & Gijs van de Kuilen, *A Parameter-Free Analysis of the Utility of Money for the General Population under Prospect Theory*, 30 J. ECON. PSYCHOL. 651 (2009).

648. Daniel Klapper, Christine Ebling & Jarg Temme, *Another Look at Loss Aversion in Brand Choice Data: Can We Characterize the Loss Averse Consumer?*, 22 INT'L J. RES. MARKETING 239 (2005).

649. Booij & van de Kuilen, *supra* note 647.

650. Wändi Bruine de Bruin, Andrew M. Parker & Baruch Fischhoff, *Explaining Adult Age Differences in Decision-Making Competence*, 25 J. BEHAV. DECISION MAKING 352 (2012).

651. *See, e.g.*, Wändi Bruine de Bruin, Andrew M. Parker & Baruch Fischhoff, *Individual Differences in Adult Decisionmaking Competence*, 92 J. PERSONALITY & SOC. PSYCHOL. 938 (2007).

652. *Id.*

653. Richard P. Larrick & Daniel C. Feiler, *Expertise in Decision Making*, *in* 2 WILEY BLACKWELL HANDBOOK, *supra* note 2, at 696, 697.

654. *Id.* at 698–702.

655. Daniel Kahneman & Gary Klein, *Conditions for Intuitive Expertise: A Failure to Disagree*, 64 AM. PSYCHOLOGIST 515 (2009).

outcomes of decisions are uncontrollable or unpredictable, the very notion of expert decision-making does not apply. But even if the first condition is met, often the second is not, since people do not get clear feedback whether they have made the right decision. One reason for the absence of feedback is that the outcomes of the forgone course of action may never become known, thus precluding meaningful comparison. For example, a manager may know how well the employees she has hired are doing, but she will never know how well those she has not hired would have done. Such asymmetric feedback likely distorts learning: a manager who rejects prospective recruits who do not meet an ill-conceived criterion may never find out that this is the case. Another reason for insufficient feedback is that the outcomes of one's decision may be multidimensional, and hence not conducive to a clear assessment. Finally, in complex environments, the outcomes of a specific decision may only become known long after it is made, and the causal link between a decision and a certain outcome may be difficult to identify.

The common tendency to appeal to experts in all spheres of life reflects their obvious advantages. Experts produce more and better products and services, at a lower cost. For decision-making purposes, the use of experience- and training-based heuristics by experts is as crucial as the use of heuristics by laypersons in daily life. Moreover, experts often use strategies that replace or complement intuitive or "holistic" judgments with structured decision processes that employ linear models, multi-attribute utility analysis, and computer-based decision support systems.[656] Such processes and systems can dramatically improve experts' accuracy and consistency.

This is not to say that experts are immune to cognitive errors. Experts are particularly prone to two types of biases: schematic thinking and overconfidence. While the use of schemas is a hallmark of expertise, it may also lead to inattention to relevant information and to false recall of schema-relevant information.[657] More importantly, the benefits of fast-and-frugal expert heuristics often come at a price of loss of flexibility, adaptation, and creativity.[658] Such rigidity is particularly costly when tasks involve atypical characteristics or when circumstances change.

With regard to overconfidence, studies have shown that professionals are typically overly optimistic about the correctness of their judgments and decision-making.[659] One adverse effect of such overconfidence is their underuse of decision aids that might improve decision-making.[660] That said, the self-assessed correctness of some professionals, such as weather forecasters, was found to be well calibrated, plausibly thanks to the constant feedback they receive.[661]

656. *See infra* pp. 128–29.

657. Larrick & Feiler, *supra* note 653, at 711.

658. Erik Dane, *Reconsidering the Trade-Off between Expertise and Flexibility: A Cognitive Entrenchment Perspective*, 35 Acad. Mgmt. Rev. 579 (2010).

659. *See supra* note 317 and accompanying text.

660. *See* Berner & Graber, *supra* note 318.

661. Murphy & Winkler, *supra* note 316; *see also* Fergus Bolger & George Wright, *Assessing the Quality of Expert Judgment: Issues and Analysis*, 11 Decision Support Sys. 1, 14 (1994).

Beyond experts' "occupational hazards" of schematic thinking and overconfidence, numerous behavioral studies have examined whether, and to what extent, expertise affects people's susceptibility to various other cognitive biases. While the reported results are mixed, it is fair to say that experts are not generally immune to biases. For example, one of Tversky and Kahneman's demonstrations of *the law of small numbers* was the erroneous answers given by participants at a meeting of the Mathematical Psychology Group of the American Psychology Association—people who are presumably experts in probability estimates.[662] Similarly, the moral judgments of trained philosophers were as susceptible to *order effects* as those of laypersons.[663] However, another study showed that the order effect was mitigated when tax professionals had control over the order in which they review the evidence within their sphere of expertise (but not outside it).[664]

Physicians have been found to be just as susceptible as laypeople to *framing effects* when choosing between alternative therapies—displaying risk aversion when outcomes were framed as gains, and risk-seeking when the same outcomes were framed as losses.[665] In the same vein, Chicago Board of Trade traders were far more likely to take risks in the afternoon after morning losses than after morning gains.[666]

One empirical study found that professional investors exhibit a *disposition effect*—the tendency to sell stocks and other assets that appreciated in value sooner than those whose prices have declined—a phenomenon commonly associated with loss aversion and the anchoring effect.[667] In contrast, a subsequent empirical study of the same phenomenon found that sophistication and trading experience eliminate the reluctance to realize losses—but do not entirely eliminate the propensity to realize gains.[668] Other empirical studies of the behavior of professional investors found diminished—albeit not eliminated—aversion to losses.[669] Other studies have demonstrated loss aversion and closely related phenomena among economics professors and lawyers.[670]

662. Tversky & Kahneman, *supra* note 78. On the law of small numbers, see *supra* pp. 32–33.

663. Schwitzgebel & Cushman, *supra* note 441. On order effects, see *supra* pp. 82–83.

664. Cuccia & McGill, *supra* note 448.

665. Barbara J. McNeil et al., *On the Elicitation of Preferences for Alternative Therapies,* 306 New England J. Med. 1259 (1982). Similar results were obtained with professional investment managers and financial planners. *See* Robert A. Olsen, *Prospect Theory as an Explanation of Risky Choice by Professional Investors: Some Evidence,* 6 Rev. Fin. Econ. 225, 228–29 (1997); Michael J. Roszkowski & Glenn E. Snelbecker, *Effects of "Framing" on Measures of Risk Tolerance: Financial Planners Are Not Immune,* 19 J. Behav. Econ. 237 (1990).

666. Joshua D. Coval & Tyler Shumway, *Do Behavioral Biases Affect Prices?,* 60 J. Fin. 1 (2005).

667. Zur Shapira & Itzhak Venezia, *Patterns of Behavior of Professionally Managed and Independent Investors,* 25 J. Banking & Fin. 1573 (2001).

668. Lei Feng & Mark S. Seasholes, *Do Investor Sophistication and Trading Experience Eliminate Behavioral Biases in Financial Markets?,* 9 Rev. Fin. 305 (2005).

669. *See, e.g.,* Gregory Gurevich, Doron Kliger & Ori Levy, *Decision-Making under Uncertainty—A Field Study of Cumulative Prospect Theory,* 33 J. Banking & Fin. 1221 (2009).

670. Ofer H. Azar, *Do People Think about Absolute or Relative Price Differences When Choosing between Substitute Goods?,* 32 J. Econ. Psychol. 450 (2011); Eyal Zamir & Ilana Ritov, *Revisiting the Debate over Attorneys' Contingent Fees: A Behavioral Analysis,* 39 J. Legal Stud. 245, 255–59 (2010).

Finally, the greater inclination to behave unethically to avoid losses than to obtain gains has been found in the behavior of both laypeople and professionals.[671] Apropos of unethical behavior, in one experiment employees of a large bank behaved less honestly when their professional identity as bank employees was rendered salient—thus pointing to a causal connection between the two.[672]

In summary, it would be absurd to deny the superiority of experts over laypersons in making decisions in any number of spheres—from aircraft engineering to language editing. At the same time, experts are human beings, and as such are not immune to cognitive biases. Depending on the particular bias, context, and decision environment, experts sometimes overcome common biases, but on other occasions are equally, or even more, susceptible to them.

3. Deciding for Others

People often make decisions for others, or advise others how to decide. Parents decide for their children, policymakers set rules for the entire population, lawyers represent clients, and physicians answer patients' questions such as: "What would you do if you were me?" As the latter two examples demonstrate, the self/other distinction sometimes coincides with the distinction between lay and professional decision-making—however, since professionals also decide for themselves and laypersons decide for others, the two situations merit separate discussion.[673]

Deciding for others raises two basic issues: motivational and cognitive. According to rational choice theory, people ultimately care only about their own interests. Hence, whenever a person advises others or decides on their behalf, there is an *agency problem*—that is, a concern that the agent would advance his or her own interests rather than those of the principal. The other issue is whether, and how, the heuristics and biases characterizing personal decisions affect decisions regarding others as well. The former issue is discussed elsewhere in the book;[674] here we focus on the latter.

While research on this topic is still comparatively young, there is some evidence that making decisions on behalf of others can mitigate cognitive biases. Thus, in one study, participants were asked to imagine themselves either as a patient who must decide whether to undergo a certain medical treatment, as a parent faced with the same decision with regard to his or her child, or as a physician making recommendations to a patient (or establishing a general policy) about the treatment. The treatment is expected to eliminate a 10 percent risk of dying from a certain fatal disease, but carries a 5 percent risk of death from its own side effects.

671. *See* Kaye J. Newberry, Philip M.J. Reckers & Robert W. Wyndelts, *An Examination of Tax Practitioner Decisions: The Role of Preparer Sanctions and Framing Effects Associated with Client Condition*, 14 J. Econ. Psychol. 439 (1993).

672. Alain Cohn, Ernst Fehr & Michel André Maréchal, *Business Culture and Dishonesty in the Banking System*, 516 Nature 86 (2014).

673. On professional decision-making, see *supra* pp. 114–17.

674. *See infra* pp. 360–61, 393–99, 509–19.

It was found that changing the participants' perspective changed their decision. Significantly more respondents opted for the treatment when making the decision for (or recommending the treatment to) other people, compared with deciding for themselves—thus overcoming the well-known omission bias.[675] Likewise, it was found that when deciding for others, people overcome the status quo bias.[676]

In the same vein, although the findings are not unequivocal, it appears that when making decisions for others or advising others how to decide, people exhibit significantly less loss aversion than when they decide for themselves.[677] Similarly, a series of survey and real-money exchange experiments have shown that when advisors evaluate entitlements on behalf of third parties, the WTA-WTP disparity is far smaller than when they act on their own behalf.[678]

In one study, physicians were asked to choose between two treatments for a fatal illness: one with higher prospects of survival but with a risk of unpleasant side effects (such as colostomy and chronic diarrhea), and the other with a lower survival rate but no risk of such effects. The physicians were significantly more inclined to choose the treatment with a lower survival rate for themselves than for others.[679] Possibly, this is because they are better able to imagine their patients successfully adapting to a significant disability, and can imagine the attendant suffering only with regard to themselves.[680] At any rate, this study demonstrates that it is not always clear which of the two decisions—the self- or other-regarding—is normatively superior.

It is sometimes difficult to determine whether self/other differences are due to variations in decision-making processes. For example, the fact that physicians recommend

675. Brian J. Zikmund-Fisher et al. *A Matter of Perspective—Choosing for Others Differs from Choosing for Yourself in Making Treatment Decisions,* 21 J. Gen. Internal Med., 618 (2006). *See also* Peter A. Ubel, Andrea M. Angott & Brian J. Zikmund-Fisher, *Physicians Recommend Different Treatments for Patients than They Would Choose for Themselves,* 117 JAMA Internal Med. 630 (2011) (the influenza scenario).

676. Jingyi Lu & Xiaofei Xie, *To Change or Not to Change: A Matter of Decision Maker's Role,* 124 Org. Behav. & Hum. Decision Processes 47 (2014). On the status-quo and omission biases, see generally *supra* pp. 48–50.

677. Evan Polman, *Self–Other Decision Making and Loss Aversion,* 119 Org. Behav. & Hum. Decision Processes 141 (2012); Flavia Mengarelli et al., *Economic Decisions for Others: An Exception to Loss Aversion Law,* 9 PLoS One e85042 (2014). *See also* Jingyi Lu et al., *Missing the Best Opportunity; Who Can Seize the Next One? Agents Show Less Inaction Inertia than Personal Decision Makers,* 54 J. Econ. Psychol. 100 (2016) (finding that in deciding for others, people are less vulnerable to the *inaction inertia*—the phenomenon, associated with loss aversion, "whereby missing a superior opportunity decreases the likelihood of acting on a subsequent opportunity in the same domain"). On loss aversion, see generally *supra* pp. 42–57.

678. James D. Marshall, Jack L. Knetsch, & J.A. Sinden, *Agents' Evaluations and the Disparity in Measures of Economic Loss,* 7 J. Econ. Behav. & Org. 115 (1986); Jennifer Arlen & Stephan Tontrup, *Does the Endowment Effect Justify Legal Intervention? The Debiasing Effect of Institutions,* 44 J. Legal Stud. 143 (2015). *But see* Russell Korobkin, *The Status Quo Bias and Contract Default Rules,* 83 Cornell L. Rev. 608, 633–47 (1998) (finding an endowment effect for entitlements under default contract rules when subjects—first-year law students—were asked to imagine themselves advising a client about a transaction). On the endowment effect, see generally *supra* pp. 50–56.

679. Ubel, Angott & Zikmund-Fisher, *supra* note 675.

680. Eric Shaban, Roshni Guerry & Timothy E. Quill, *Reconciling Physician Bias and Recommendations,* 117 JAMA Internal Med. 634 (2011). An alternative explanation is that physicians are overoptimistic regarding themselves more than regarding others—hence they underweight the risk of death to a greater extent when deciding for themselves.

routine medical examinations to their patients, but fail to undergo them themselves,[681] may be due to the physicians' procrastination and failure of self-control, rather than to self/other differences in decision-making. Similarly, the finding that psychiatrists prefer less invasive and less effective treatment for themselves than for their patients may be justified on the grounds that psychiatrists view themselves as more capable of taking action if the conservative treatment has been found to fail.[682]

True differences in self-versus-other decision-making may have various explanations. One hypothesis is that cognitive biases are often a product of System 1 thinking; System 1 thinking is considerably more influenced by emotions than System 2; and people are presumably more dispassionate when they make decisions for others than for themselves.[683] However, some experimental results appear to contradict this claim.[684] Relatedly, there is support for the notion that when people decide for others, they pay more attention to abstract considerations (such as an object's desirability), whereas when deciding for themselves, they focus more on concrete considerations (such as the difficulties involved in attaining the object).[685] According to *construal level theory*, this difference lies in the fact that there is greater psychological distance when deciding for others, and the greater the psychological distance, the more abstract people's thinking tends to be.[686]

It has also been argued that, in self-regarding choices, people tend to give relatively equal weights to different considerations, whereas in other-regarding decisions they tend to focus on the most important consideration(s) and attribute lesser weight to secondary ones.[687] One may, however, doubt the generality of this explanation, as many decisions are not multidimensional. As the study of self/other differences in decision-making proliferates, other accounts and additional mediating factors are constantly being offered.[688]

681. Pavel Atanasov et al., *Comparing Physicians Personal Prevention Practices and Their Recommendations to Patients,* 37 J. Healthcare Quality 189 (2015). On procrastination and self-control, see generally *supra* pp. 87–93.

682. Rosmarie Mendel et al., *'What Would You Do If You Were Me, Doctor?': Randomised Trial of Psychiatrists' Personal v. Professional Perspectives on Treatment Recommendations,* 197 Brit. J. Psychiatry 441 (2010).

683. Mengarelli et al., *supra* note 677, at 4.

684. Zikmund-Fisher et al., *supra* note 675, at 621. The authors found the highest emotional engagement when respondents were asked to decide as parents, next highest when deciding as a physician, and lowest when deciding for themselves—whereas, as described in the text above, the omission bias was greatest when people decided for themselves.

685. Jingyi Lu, Xiaofei Xie & Jingzhe Xu, *Desirability or Feasibility: Self–Other Decision-Making Differences,* 39 Personality & Soc. Psychol. Bull. 144 (2013).

686. *See generally* Trope & Liberman, *supra* note 503; Fujita, Trope & Liberman, *supra* note 503. *See also* Rachel Barkan, Shai Danziger & Yaniv Shani, *Do as I Say, Not as I Do: Choice–Advice Differences in Decisions to Learn Information,* 125 J. Econ. Behav. & Org. 57 (2016).

687. Laura Kray & Richard Gonzalez, *Differential Weighting in Choice versus Advice: I'll Do This, You Do That,* 12 J. Behav. Decision Making 207 (1999); Zikmund-Fisher et al., *supra* note 675.

688. *See, e.g.,* Polman, *supra* note 677; Evan Polman & Kathleen D. Vohs, *Decision Fatigue, Choosing for Others, and Self-Construal,* 7 Soc. Psychol. & Personality Sci. 471 (2016).

In addition to the self/other distinction, there may be a difference between *deciding* for others and *advising* others how to decide. It was found that when people advise others, they tend to conduct a more balanced information search than when they decide for others.[689] A follow-up experiment revealed that the *confirmation bias* characterizing self- and other-regarding decisions (but less so advice-giving), is eliminated in decisions concerning others when the decision-maker is not expected to communicate with the other person. Thus, the need to justify a decision (to oneself or to another person) appears to trigger the confirmation bias, and in the absence of this need—either because one is not making the decision but merely giving advice, or because one is not expected to communicate with the other person—the bias is reduced.[690]

4. Group Decision-Making and Advice-Taking

Many decisions are made by groups rather than by individuals. Examples include elections, decisions by boards of directors, and jury verdicts. Group decision-making varies immensely in terms of group characteristics (size, composition, internal hierarchy, relative expertise of members, etc.),[691] decision procedures (e.g., the extent of information sharing and discussion prior to decision and the required majority),[692] and the object of decision (e.g., whether the decision directly affects members' interests, and if so, whether it refers to common goods or to private ones—and, if the latter, whether the group decision applies to all goods).[693] Group decision-making is of great interest to various disciplines, including political science, public administration, social psychology, economic analysis, and law. This subsection focuses on decisions by small groups of people who interact with one another, from a JDM perspective.[694] It also briefly discusses an intermediate phenomenon of *advice-taking*, which lies between individual and group decision-making.

Group decision-making may be warranted for non-instrumental reasons, such as fairness and democratic values. It may also be preferred when groups are expected to outperform individuals. It has been demonstrated that on some task-dimensions, such as information retrieval, groups perform better than an average individual; in some tasks (e.g., finding out a pattern by induction) they perform as well as the best of an equivalent

689. Eva Jonas, Stefan Schulz-Hardt & Dieter Frey, *Giving Advice or Making Decisions in Someone Else's Place: The Influence of Impression, Defense, and Accuracy Motivation on the Search for New Information*, 31 Persp. Soc. Psychol. Bull. 977 (2005).

690. These observations refer to advice giving. On advice taking, see *infra* pp. 123–24.

691. *See, e.g.*, Christoph Engel, *The Behaviour of Corporate Actors: How Much Can We Learn from the Experimental Literature?*, 6 J. Institutional Econ. 445 (2010).

692. *See, e.g.*, Steven R. Elliot & Michael McKee, *Collective Risk Decision in the Presence of Many Risks*, 48 Kyklos 541 (1995).

693. *Id.*

694. On simple aggregation of judgments or preferences and aggregation with minimal information exchange, see generally R. Scott Tindale & Katherina Kluwe, *Decision Making in Groups and Organizations*, *in* 2 Wiley Blackwell Handbook, *supra* note 2, at 849, 851–54. On group decision-making in specific legal contexts, see *infra* pp. 365–66, 369, 372, 394, 416, 424, 559–61.

number of individuals; and in other tasks, such as letters-to-numbers problems (i.e., problems in which digits are coded as letters, and solvers are asked to identify the digit coded by each letter), they perform better than the best individual.[695] However, along with such advantages, the characteristics of group information sharing, deliberation, and decision-making may also lead groups astray and result in suboptimal outcomes.[696]

Indeed, while many studies have examined the effect of group decision-making, no consistent conclusions have emerged. In some instances, the transition from individual to group decision-making mitigates divergences from expected utility theory—on other occasions it has no effect, and in still others it increases them.[697] The disparate effects of group deliberation are not surprising given the great diversity of groups, their decision procedures, and goals. We shall focus on the impact of group decision-making on deviations from thin, cognitive rationality. One should mention, however, that group deliberation has been found to affect motivation as well. Specifically, studies of mixed-motives games, such as the prisoner's dilemma, reveal that, compared with individuals, groups tend to behave *less* cooperatively vis-à-vis other groups and individuals.[698]

One factor affecting the success of group decision-making is the nature of the task at hand—in particular, its position on the spectrum between *intellective* and *judgmental* tasks.[699] According to this typology, in intellective tasks there is a demonstrably correct answer within the relevant conceptual framework. In contrast, in judgmental tasks there is no generally accepted, demonstrably correct answer, as they involve contestable normative, aesthetic, or comparable aspects. For example, solving a mathematical or logical problem is typically very close to the intellective end of the spectrum, while choosing the best candidate for a job or determining the punitive damages in a lawsuit reside in the judgmental region. When the correct answer is easily demonstrable, and the group member or members who are able to find the answer have sufficient incentives to correct other members' errors, groups are likely to come up with the correct answer. They are likely to do as well as the most competent member in the group. However, for the reasons discussed below, when it comes to judgmental tasks, group deliberation may actually exacerbate individual biases.[700]

A key reason for preferring group decision-making to individual decision-making is the possibility of tapping into a broader expertise and integrating more information. One challenge

695. PATRICK R. LAUGHLIN, GROUP PROBLEM SOLVING 22–44, 57–108 (2011).

696. *See, e.g.*, GROUP CREATIVITY: INNOVATION THROUGH COLLABORATION (Paul B. Paulus & Bernard A. Nijstad eds., 2003); Norbert L. Kerr & R. Scott Tindale, *Group-Based Forecasting: A Social Psychological Analysis*, 27 INT'L J. FORECASTING 14 (2011).

697. Norbert L. Kerr, Robert J. MacCoun & Geoffrey P. Kramer, *Bias in Judgment: Comparing Individuals and Groups*, 103 PSYCHOL. REV. 687 (1996).

698. Tindale & Kluwe, *supra* note 694, at 864–65.

699. LAUGHLIN, *supra* note 695, at 5–6.

700. Patrick R. Laughlin & Alan L. Ellis, *Demonstrability and Social Combination Processes on Mathematical Intellective Tasks*, 22 J. EXPERIMENTAL SOC. PSYCHOL. 177 (1986).

facing any group is therefore to make optimal use of its members' knowledge, and to assimilate as much of the available information as sensibly possible. However, a robust finding of many studies is the so-called *common knowledge effect*:[701] information that is initially shared by all group members is much more likely to be brought up in deliberation and affect the final decision than unshared information—which compromises decisions' quality. The extent to which this unfortunate result ensues depends on several factors. One is the way group members perceive the process. There is evidence that groups whose members perceive the process as a negotiation between conflicting views in which each member seeks to prevail, rather than as a concerted attempt to reach an optimal decision, are likely to share less information and process it less thoroughly. Another factor is the discussion process itself: by its nature, shared information is more likely to be brought up, and repeatedly so, so it is likely to have a greater impact. Finally, the fact that certain information is shared by several or all members makes it sound more valid, and members are more likely to rely on it because it tends to evoke reassuring reactions from other members. Setting a common goal of reaching optimal outcomes (rather than an adversarial, negotiation-like process), and encouraging members to share information and to reserve judgment until all information is shared, may thus improve group decision-making.[702]

Another well-studied phenomenon is *group polarization*, which characterizes group *judgmental* tasks. This occurs when an initial tendency of individual group members in one direction is enhanced following group discussion. The two primary explanations for this phenomenon are *social comparison* and *informational influences*. According to the former, people strive to perceive themselves, and to be perceived by others, in a favorable light. Thus, when observing a general tendency in the group, they tend to adopt a position in the same direction, only more extreme. According to the latter explanation, when group members are initially inclined in one direction, the number and persuasiveness of arguments articulated in that direction during deliberation are greater than in the opposite direction, thus strengthening the initial tendency.[703]

Turning to specific phenomena in judgment and decision-making, unlike the bat-and-ball and similar questions, where the common error is easily demonstrable,[704] many cognitive phenomena, such as loss aversion, cannot be characterized as erroneous or irrational per se. Hence they are not expected to disappear following group deliberation. Interestingly, even the *conjunction fallacy* and *base-rate neglect* do not necessarily disappear (and at times

701. *See, e.g.*, Garold Stasser & William Titus, *Pooling of Unshared Information in Group Decision Making: Biased Information Sampling during Discussion*, 48 J. PERSONALITY & SOC. PSYCHOL. 1467 (1985); Daniel Gigone & Reid Hastie, *The Common Knowledge Effect: Information Sharing and Group Judgment*, 65 J. PERSONALITY & SOC. PSYCHOL. 959 (1993).

702. Felix C. Brodbeck et al., *Group Decision Making under Conditions of Distributed Knowledge: The Information Asymmetries Model*, 32 ACAD. MGMT. J. 459 (2007); Tindale & Kluwe, *supra* note 694, at 859–62, 864–66.

703. David. J. Myers & Helmut Lamm, *The Group Polarization Phenomenon*, 83 PSYCHOL. BULL.602 (1976); Daniel J. Isenberg, *Group Polarization: A Critical Review and Meta-analysis*, 50 J. PERSONALITY & SOC. PSYCHOL. 1141 (1986); Cass R. Sunstein, *Deliberative Trouble? Why Groups Go to the Extreme*, 110 YALE L.J. 71 (2000).

704. *See supra* pp. 22–23.

are even exacerbated) when moving from individual to group decision-making—which indicates that they are not easily demonstrable errors.[705]

Some experimental studies of the effect of loss aversion and related phenomena have dealt specifically with group decision-making. These studies demonstrate that the tendencies to be risk-averse in the realm of gains, and risk-seeking in the realm of losses, do not disappear, but rather increase, when decisions are made by groups.[706] When various group members frame the choice problem differently, the choice usually follows that of the majority.[707] Group polarization has been found in experiments studying the effect of team deliberation on individuals' endowment effect and status quo bias, as well. For instance, the gap between subjects' willingness to sell a legal entitlement and their willingness to buy it—reflecting an endowment effect and a status quo bias—has been found to widen after deliberation in small groups of two to four members.[708] While it is possible for group deliberation to reduce loss aversion, the available data indicates that it may actually magnify it. Support for this hypothesis was also found in a study of escalation of commitment in individual and group decision-making.[709]

Finally, studies of overoptimism in predicting the completion time of projects—the so-called *planning fallacy*—have shown that this bias is also exacerbated following group consultation.[710] This is because group discussion increases members' focus on factors that lead to positive forecasts.

Having discussed individual decision-making (throughout this chapter) and group decision-making (in this subsection), it should be noted that great many decision processes do not fit neatly into either of these two models. Specifically, many decisions are made by a single person after consulting with others.[711] People seek advice to improve their decisions and

705. R. Scott Tindale, *Decision Errors Made by Individuals and Groups, in* INDIVIDUAL AND GROUP DECISION MAKING: CURRENT ISSUES 109 (N. John Castellan, Jr., ed., 1993). On the conjunction fallacy and base-rate neglect, see generally *supra* pp. 28–31.

706. Timothy W. McGuire, Sara Kiesler & Jane Siegel, *Group and Computer-Mediated Discussion Effects in Risk Decision Making*, 52 J. PERSONALITY & SOC. PSYCHOL. 917 (1987); Paul W. Paese, Mary Bieser & Mark E. Tubbs, *Framing Effects and Choice Shifts in Group Decision Making*, 56 ORG. BEHAV. & HUM. DECISION PROCESSES 149 (1993); Whyte, *supra* note 253.

707. Tatsuya Kameda & James H. Davis, *The Function of the Reference Point in Individual and Group Risk Decision Making*, 46 ORG. BEHAV. & HUM. DECISION PROCESSES 55 (1990); R. Scott Tindale, Susan Sheffey & Leslie A. Scott, *Framing and Group Decision-Making: Do Cognitive Changes Parallel Preference Changes?*, 55 ORG. BEHAV. & HUM. DECISION PROCESSES 470 (1993). Tindale and his coauthors found that the group's decision is usually in line with the majority's framing, without necessarily changing the minority's framing.

708. Jeremy A. Blumenthal, *Group Deliberation and the Endowment Effect: An Experimental Study*, 50 HOUS. L. REV. 41 (2012); Amira Galin, *Endowment Effect in Negotiations: Group versus Individual Decision-Making*, 75 THEORY & DECISION 389 (2013).

709. Glen Whyte, *Escalating Commitment in Individual and Group Decision Making: A Prospect Theory Approach*, 54 ORG. BEHAV. & HUM. DECISION PROCESSES 430 (1993). *See also* Max Bazerman, Toni Giuliano & Alan Appelman, *Escalation of Commitment in Individual and Group Decision Making*, 33 ORG. BEHAV. & HUM. PERFORMANCE 141 (1984).

710. Buehler, Griffin & Peetz, *supra* note 342, at 42–46. On the planning fallacy, see generally *supra* pp. 69–71.

711. *See generally* Silvia Bonaccio & Reeshad S. Dalal, *Advice Taking and Decision Making: An Integrative Literature Review and Implications for the Organizational Sciences*, 101 ORG. BEHAV. & HUM. DECISION PROCESSES 127 (2006). On advice *giving*, see *supra* p. 120.

to share accountability, especially in organizational settings.[712] In fact, most studies show that using advice does improve decisions.[713]

However, the central finding of JDM studies with regard to advice-taking is *egocentric advice discounting*: decision-makers systematically place greater weight on their own opinion relative to that of their advisors, and consequently make less accurate decisions than they would have made had they followed the received advice more closely.[714] As might be expected, the more knowledgeable decision-makers are, and the greater the discrepancy between their own judgment and the advice they receive, the greater their tendency to discount the advice. While some advice discounting may be due to the fact that decision-makers have better access to their own reasons than to those of their advisors,[715] or caused by insufficient adjustment of the decision-makers' initial estimation,[716] the main cause of advice discounting appears to be egocentrism.[717]

Possibly due to the sunk-costs effect, decision-makers tend to give more weight to advice that they have paid for than to that which they have received for free.[718] Decision-makers also tend to use the *confidence heuristic*—assuming (often unwittingly) that the more confident the advisor is, the greater his or her expertise or accuracy.[719] Clearly, then, advice-taking is no panacea.

5. Cultural Differences

While in the past JDM scholars have tended to assume that the phenomena they study are universal,[720] recent years have seen a growing recognition of cross-cultural differences in judgment and decision-making.[721] Nevertheless, this field of study is still underdeveloped,

712. Nigel Harvey & Ilan Fischer, *Taking Advice: Accepting Help, Improving Judgment, and Sharing Responsibility*, 70 Org. Behav. & Hum. Decision Processes 117 (1997); Ilan Yaniv, *Receiving Other People's Advice: Influence and Benefit*, 93 Behav. & Hum. Decision Processes 1 (2004).

713. Bonaccio & Dalal, *supra* note 711, at 133–34.

714. *See, e.g.*, Yaniv, *supra* note 712; Bonaccio & Dalal, *supra* note 711, at 129–32.

715. Yaniv, *supra* note 712.

716. On this possibility, see Harvey & Fischer, *supra* note 712, at 130. On anchoring and adjustment, see generally *supra* pp. 79–82.

717. *See, e.g.*, Nigel Harvey & Clare Harries, *Effects of Judges' Forecasting on Their Later Combination of Forecasts for the Same Outcomes*, 20 Int'l J. Forecasting 391 (2004); Joachim I. Krueger, *Return of the Ego—Self-Referent Information as a Filter for Social Prediction: Comment on Karniol (2003)*, 110 Psychol. Rev. 585 (2003). On egocentrism, see generally *supra* pp. 58–76.

718. Francesca Gino, *Do We Listen to Advice Just Because We Paid for It? The Impact of Advice Cost on Its Use*, 107 Org. Behav. & Hum. Decision Processes 234 (2008). On sunk costs, see generally *supra* pp. 56–57.

719. Paul C. Price & Eric R. Stone, *Intuitive Evaluation of Likelihood Judgment Producers: Evidence for a Confidence Heuristic*, 17 J. Behav. Decision Making 39 (2004); Bonaccio & Dalal, *supra* note 711, at 132–33. *See also infra* p. 572.

720. Incheol Choi, Jong An Choi & Ara Norenzayan, *Culture and Decisions*, *in* Blackwell Handbook of Judgment and Decision Making, *supra* note 343, at 504.

721. *See generally* Krishna Savani et al., *Culture and Judgment and Decision Making*, *in* Wiley Blackwell Handbook, *supra* note 2, at 456. On cross-cultural differences in experimental game theory, see, e.g., Oosterbeek, Sloof & van De Kuilen, *supra* note 569.

and there is much more to be learned about the interplay between culture and decision-making. Understanding cultural differences is especially important for policymakers, as policies based on unwarranted generalizations may prove counterproductive.

Cross-cultural studies—many of which focus on East-Asian versus Western societies—have found significant differences in terms of people's collectivist versus individualist orientation,[722] interdependent versus independent self-construals,[723] and holistic versus analytical cognitive styles.[724] These differences sometimes affect people's judgment and decision-making.

Thus, while both Americans and Chinese believe that Chinese are more risk-averse than Americans, experiments have shown that in the sphere of financial investments the opposite is true.[725] At the same time, Chinese are more risk-averse in the medical and academic spheres. It appears that Chinese and Americans do not differ in their inherent risk attitude, but rather in the perceived riskiness of decisions in each domain. In collectivist societies, such as China, people expect to receive financial support from their extended family when they are in need. Accordingly, they are less risk-averse in the financial sphere—but not in others.

Cross-cultural differences have also been found with regard to intertemporal preferences—in particular, the tendency to excessively discount future gains and losses.[726] Besides macro-level differences in saving rates between different nations, micro-level differences were found between people from different societies and different ethnic origins. Tellingly, subjects' intertemporal preferences can be manipulated by priming techniques.[727] In one study, Singaporean students were exposed to either Western or Singaporean cultural symbols, and then asked how much they would be willing to pay for an expedited, one-day delivery of a book, instead of the standard five-day delivery. As hypothesized, exposure to Western symbols resulted in greater impatience.[728] In another study, the ethnic identity of American students was primed by getting them to fill out a background questionnaire about the languages spoken at home and the number of generations their families have lived in the United States. The participants were then asked to choose whether they would

722. *See, e.g.*, Harry C. Triandis, *The Self and Social Behavior in Differing Cultural Contexts*, 96 Psychol. Rev. 506 (1989).

723. Hazel R. Markus & Shinobu Kitayama, *Culture and the Self: Implications for Cognition, Emotion, and Motivation*, 98 Psychol. Rev. 224 (1991).

724. Richard E. Nisbett, The Geography of Thought: How Asians and Westerners Think Differently . . . and Why (2003).

725. Elke U. Weber & Christopher Hsee, *Cross-Cultural Differences in Risk Perception, But Cross-Cultural Similarities in Attitudes towards Perceived Risk*, 44 Mgmt. Sci. 1205 (1998); Christopher Hsee & Elke U. Weber, *Cross-National Differences in Risk Preference and Lay Predictions*, 12 J. Behav. Decision Making 165 (1999).

726. *See generally supra* pp. 88–93.

727. On priming techniques, see *supra* pp. 78–79.

728. Haipeng (Allan) Chen, Sharon Ng & Akshay R. Rao, *Cultural Differences in Consumer Impatience*, 42 J. Marketing Res. 291 (2005).

prefer to receive a certain amount of money earlier, or a larger amount at a later date. It was found that, after the priming of their ethnic identity, participants of Asian descent were more likely to opt for the larger amounts at a later date.[729]

Unsurprisingly, cultural differences have been found with regard to phenomena associated with egocentrism—including overoptimism, overconfidence, and the tendency to attribute other people's behavior to their personal attitudes, rather than to environmental influences (the fundamental attribution error).[730] For example, in one study, Canadian participants showed significantly greater unrealistic optimism than their Japanese counterparts.[731] In fact, a meta-analysis of ninety-one studies has revealed that within cultures, Westerners showed a clear tendency to think positively about themselves, while East Asians did not, with Asian Americans falling in-between.[732] Relatedly, it was found that the endowment effect among East Asians was less pronounced than among Westerners.[733] It was demonstrated experimentally that this difference may be influenced by the degree to which independence and self-enhancement (versus interdependence and self-criticism) are culturally valued. Cultural differences were apparent when self-object associations were made salient, but disappeared when such associations were minimized.[734]

Interestingly, several studies have shown that Chinese, Malaysian, and Indonesian participants—but not Japanese or Singaporeans—exhibited *greater* overconfidence than Westerners.[735] It turned out that this result was mediated by the subjects' ability to generate conflicting arguments regarding their answers—which suggests that it may have to do with the degree to which their respective education systems nurture critical thinking (which tends to reduce overconfidence).[736]

729. Daniel J. Benjamin, James J. Choi & A. Joshua Strickland, *Social Identity and Preferences*, 100 AM. ECON. REV. 1913 (2010).

730. On these phenomena, see pp. 61–64, 64–66, and 68–69, respectively.

731. Steven J. Heine & Darrin R. Lehman, *Cultural Variation in Unrealistic Optimism: Does the West Feel More Vulnerable than the East?*, 68 J. PERSONALITY & SOC. PSYCHOL. 595 (1995). *See also* Savani et al., *supra* note 721, at 468–69.

732. Steven J. Heine & Takeshi Hamamura, *In Search of East Asian Self-Enhancement*, 11 PERSONALITY & SOC. PSYCHOL. REV. 4 (2007). *See also* Amy H. Mezulis et al., *Is There a Universal Positivity Bias in Attributions? A Meta-analytic Review of Individual, Developmental, and Cultural Differences in the Self-Serving Attributional Bias*, 130 PSYCHOL. BULL. 711, 714–15, 729–32 (2004).

733. William W. Maddux et al., *For Whom Is Parting with Possessions More Painful? Cultural Differences in the Endowment Effect*, 21 J. ASS'N PSYCHOL. SCI. 1910 (2010). On the endowment effect, see *supra* pp. 50–56.

734. Two other studies have found cross-cultural differences with regard to phenomena associated with prospect theory, namely reference point adaptation and the escalation of commitment (on these phenomena, see *supra* pp. XX and XX, respectively). *See* Hal R. Arkes et al., *A Cross-Cultural Study of Reference Point Adaptation: Evidence from China, Korea and the US*, 112 ORG. BEHAV. & HUM. DECISION PROCESSES 99 (2010); David J. Sharp & Stephen B. Salter, *Project Escalation and Sunk Costs: A Test of the International Generalizability of Agency and Prospect Theories*, 28 J. INT'L BUS. STUD. 101 (1997).

735. For a review of these studies, see J. Frank Yates, *Culture and Probability Judgment*, 4 SOC. & PERSONALITY PSYCHOL. COMPASS 174 (2010).

736. Savani et al., *supra* note 721, at 467–68.

Finally, cross-cultural studies, including studies using priming techniques, have demonstrated that Asians are considerably less prone to make the fundamental attribution error: they are considerably less likely to attribute other people's behavior to their personal dispositions as opposed to situational factors.[737]

6. Debiasing

(a) Preliminary Comments

This subsection discusses techniques of improving judgment and decision-making in response to cognitive biases. To be sure, cognitive biases are not the only source of suboptimal decisions. For example, illiteracy and innumeracy are two major causes of poor decision-making, but they should be handled primarily by education, not by debiasing. Similarly, many suboptimal decisions are the product of misinformation. Inasmuch as providing people with accurate information overcomes information problems, there may be no need to change their JDM processes (although in practice, the borderline between cognitive biases and information problems is often blurred, and behavioral insights may contribute greatly to the design of disclosure duties).[738]

Debiasing should also be differentiated from *insulation*.[739] Rather than trying to alter the cognitive processes leading to self-injurious or socially undesirable behaviors, some conducts are prohibited altogether, and some decisions are deemed ineffective. For example, the duty to wear seat belts while driving and the imposition of speed limits basically replace drivers' decision-making with mandatory rules backed by legal sanctions. Such rules may play an educational role and alter people's preferences and judgments, but in the main they change behavior not by improving people's reasoning, but by increasing the costs associated with harmful conducts.[740]

Furthermore, debiasing *stricto sensu* should be distinguished from measures whose primary goal is not to change people's judgments and decisions, but to replace them with those of other people. To the extent that professionals are better decision-makers than laypeople, and that when people make decisions for others they do a better job than when they do so for themselves, and that groups outperform individuals, entrusting decisions to professionals, agents, or groups may overcome cognitive biases. Of course, inasmuch as professionals, agents, and groups fall prey to their own biases, alternative or additional measures may be called for.[741]

Having delineated the concept of debiasing, it is important to note that debiasing assumes that something is wrong with the way that people reason otherwise. Indeed, phenomena such as the inverse fallacy and the gamblers' fallacy lead to demonstrably erroneous decisions. However, other deviations from economic rationality or from consequentialist

737. For a brief overview, see *id.* at 463–65.

738. *See infra* pp. 171–77, 314–18.

739. Daniel Pi, Francesco Parisi & Barbara Luppi, *Biasing, Debiasing, and the Law, in* THE OXFORD HANDBOOK OF BEHAVIORAL ECONOMICS AND THE LAW, *supra* note 8, at 143, 149–52.

740. *See also infra* p. 185.

741. *See supra* pp. 114–17, 117–20, and 120–24, respectively.

morality, such as loss aversion and deontological morality, are arguably very sensible. Other things being equal, the more a judgment or a decision is patently wrong, the stronger the case for trying to correct it. When it comes to sensible judgments and decisions, not only is there no reason to debias them, but attempts to change them are also generally doomed to fail, since people often adhere to them even after careful deliberation. This means that debiasing—especially when initiated by the government—inevitably involves normative questions.[742]

Before we examine specific debiasing techniques, one last comment is in order. In principle, people can adopt their own debiasing strategies. However, debiasing often requires an external intervention. This is because, due to self-serving biases and blind spots, people are commonly unaware of their cognitive biases.[743] External interventions may be initiated by friends and family, implemented in organizations, or carried out by governmental authorities. Such interventions raise a host of normative and pragmatic concerns, which exceed the scope of the present discussion.[744] Here we focus on behavioral studies of debiasing, and the normative and policy issues of debiasing *by the law* will be discussed in Chapter 4.

Debiasing strategies may generally be classified as technological, motivational, or cognitive.[745] Each of these three categories is discussed below.

(b) Technological Strategies

A straightforward "means of debiasing judgment is to take [judgment] out of the equation altogether, or rather, to replace it with an equation."[746] A famous example is the transformation of the market for professional baseball players in the United States following the adoption of evidence-based, rigorous statistical methods instead of the traditional methods, based on scouting, experience, and expert judgment.[747] In general, technological debiasing strategies replace or complement intuitive or "holistic" judgments by structured decision processes involving linear models, multi-attribute utility analysis, computer-based decision-support systems, and the like.[748]

Thus, using statistical analysis software instead of relying on one's intuitive assessments of probability would most likely improve one's performance. Similarly, a checklist is a very simple—and often very effective—tool for overcoming forgetfulness, especially when decision tasks are complex and decision-makers may be tired or stressed. Using checklists

742. *See also infra* pp. 157–86.

743. *See* Richard P. Larrick, *Debiasing*, *in* BLACKWELL HANDBOOK OF JUDGMENT AND DECISION MAKING, *supra* note 343, at 316, 318.

744. On policy and pragmatic issues associated with the adoption of debiasing techniques, see generally Larrick, *supra* note 743, at 331–34; Jack B. Soll, Katherine L. Milkman & John W. Payne, *A User's Guide to Debiasing*, *in* 2 WILEY BLACKWELL HANDBOOK, *supra* note 2, at 924, 940–44.

745. Larrick, *supra* note 743.

746. Soll, Milkman & Payne, *supra* note 744, at 933.

747. MICHAEL LEWIS, MONEYBALL: THE ART OF WINNING AN UNFAIR GAME (2003).

748. Larrick, *supra* note 743, at 327–34.

assures that all considerations are taken into account, and all relevant tests or actions are carried out.[749]

Linear models are a more sophisticated tool. Based on statistical analysis of the correlations between various attributes (e.g., publications record and teaching experience), and their values (e.g., number of publications), linear models provide a combined score for each alternative (e.g., each candidate for a given academic position), based on the weighted value of each attribute. It has long been demonstrated that decision-making based on empirically established relationships between data and a given dependent variable (in our example, success as an academic) is superior to discretionary, holistic decision-making, which may reflect any number of cognitive biases.[750] More intriguingly, even linear models in which the weights of the attribute values cannot be based on reliable empirical data (and are therefore based on experts' intuition, or even set to be equal) are superior to holistic judgments. At the very least, such models guarantee that all attributes are considered, and that the resulting conclusions are consistent.[751]

Using technological techniques to avoid irrational, intuitive decisions is not necessarily rational, however. The benefits of such techniques should always be weighed against their costs. If, for example, the adverse effects of a cognitive bias are rare or trivial, resorting to technological techniques may be unwarranted.[752] However, there is evidence that even professionals underutilize cost-effective decision-support systems. Two explanations for this regrettable phenomenon are overconfidence,[753] and the concern that professionals who use such systems are viewed by others as less competent.[754] In the absence of clear feedback on the quality of their decisions, professionals who have a blind spot regarding their fallibilities may never learn the importance of using decision aids.

(c) Motivational Strategies: Incentives and Accountability

Motivational techniques focus on increasing the motivation to perform well. This may be done by providing *incentives* to overcome decision errors, and by asking people to provide other people with reasons for their decisions (*accountability*).

In light of the central role that incentives play in standard economic analysis (and as a corollary, the different conventions concerning the use of incentives in experimental economics and experimental psychology), the controversy over the effectiveness of incentives

749. Soll, Milkman & Payne, *supra* note 744, at 941.

750. *See, e.g.*, Robyn M. Dawes, David Faust & Paul E. Meehl, *Clinical versus Actuarial Judgment*, 243 Sci. 1668 (1989).

751. Robyn M. Dawes, *The Robust Beauty of Improper Linear Models in Decision Making*, 34 Am. Psychologist 571 (1979); Larrick, *supra* note 743, at 327–28.

752. *Cf.* Nisbett & Ross, *supra* note 64, at 276–80.

753. *See supra* note 318 and accompanying text.

754. Hal R. Arkes, Victoria A. Shaffer & Mitchell A. Medow, *Patients Derogate Physicians Who Use a Computer-Assisted Diagnostic Aid*, 27 Med. Decision Making 189 (2007).

in eliminating cognitive biases is hardly surprising.[755] As a matter of fact, incentives have been proven useful in overcoming issues of procrastination and bounded willpower—cases where people know what they want to achieve, but fail to exercise the self-control necessary to achieving it. Thus, some studies have demonstrated that large financial incentives, in the range of hundreds of dollars, were effective in inducing obese people to lose weight,[756] helping smokers to quit smoking,[757] and forming a habit of gym exercise.[758] The evidence, however, is far from conclusive.[759] Incentives may be provided externally, but people can also create incentives for themselves through various commitment devices.[760]

Beyond issues of bounded willpower, incentives are useful when more effort produces better results, as when the quality of a decision depends on the time and energy one puts into acquiring and systematically processing information.[761] Indeed, based on a review of seventy-four studies, Colin Camerer and Robin Hogarth have concluded that incentives improve recalling remembered items, resolving easy problems, making certain predictions, and the like.[762]

Incentives are considerably less effective, or even counterproductive, when cognitive biases are not primarily due to insufficient effort.[763] Thus, for example, neither framing effects nor the hindsight bias have been eliminated when experiments involved real payoffs.[764] Evidence regarding the effect of incentives on the anchoring effect is mixed.[765] Incentives to

755. *See, e.g.*, Gregory Mitchell, *Why Law and Economics' Perfect Rationality Should Not Be Traded for Behavioral Law and Economics' Equal Incompetence*, 91 Geo. L.J. 67, 114–19 (2002); Eldar Shafir & Robyn A. LeBoeuf, *Rationality*, 53 Ann. Rev. Psychol. 491, 501–02 (2002).

756. Kevin G. Volpp et al., *Financial Incentive-Based Approaches for Weight Loss: A Randomized Trial*, 300 J. Am. Med. Ass'n. 2631 (2008).

757. Kevin G. Volpp et al., *A Randomized, Controlled Trial of Financial Incentives for Smoking Cessation*, 360 New England J. Med. 699 (2009).

758. Gary Charness & Uri Gneezy, *Incentives to Exercise*, 77 Econometrica 909 (2009); Dan Acland & Matthew R. Levy, *Naivité, Projection Bias, and Habit Formation in Gym Attendance*, 61 Mgmt. Sci. 146 (2015).

759. *See, e.g.*, Kevin G. Volpp et al., *A Randomized Controlled Trial of Financial Incentives for Smoking Cessation*, 15 Cancer Epidemiology, Biomarkers & Prevention 12 (2006) (finding that incentives increased quit rates after seventy-five days, but not after six months); Mitesh S. Patel et al., *Premium-Based Financial Incentives Did Not Promote Workplace Weight Loss in a 2013–15 Study*, 35 Health Aff. 71 (2016).

760. *See generally* Ayres, *supra* note 516.

761. *See, e.g.*, Dan A. Stone & David A. Ziebart, *A Model of Financial Incentive Effects in Decision Making*, 61 Org. Behav. & Hum. Decision Processes 250 (1995).

762. Colin F. Camerer & Robin M. Hogarth, *The Effects of Financial Incentives in Experiments: A Review and Capital-Labor-Production Framework*, 19 J. Risk & Uncertainty 7, 19–21 (1999).

763. Amos Tversky & Daniel Kahneman, *Rational Choice and the Framing of Decisions*, 59 J. Bus. S251, S274 (1986); Camerer & Hogarth, *supra* note 762, at 21–23.

764. Tversky & Kahneman, *supra* note 168, at 455 (a similar pattern of the framing effect was found with and without real payoffs); Wolfgang Hell et al., *Hindsight Bias: An Interaction of Automatic and Motivational Factors?*, 16 Memory & Cognition 533 (1988) (real payoffs did not have a statistically significant effect on the hindsight bias per se, but did interact with other variables manipulated in the experiment).

765. *See, e.g.*, Gretchen B. Chapman & Eric J. Johnson, *Incorporating the Irrelevant: Anchors in Judgments of Belief and Value*, *in* Heuristics and Biases, *supra* note 14, at 120; Nicholas Epley & Thomas Gilovich, *When Effortful Thinking Influences Judgmental Anchoring: Differential Effects of Forewarning and Incentives on Self-Generated and Externally Provided Anchors*, 18 J. Behav. Decision Making 199 (2005).

give the right answer do not eliminate overconfidence.[766] Greater effort may result in greater confidence in one's judgments, even if it does not actually improve accuracy.[767] In one study, incentives strengthened preference reversals;[768] in another, incentivized subjects were less likely to follow a reliable decision rule, and more likely to change their decision strategy after incorrect judgments—resulting in worse performance than non-incentivized subjects.[769] Given the complex relationships between the various factors affecting judgment and decision-making, where motivation is but one factor, the varying effects of incentives should not be surprising.

Even when incentives have a beneficial effect, calibrating the optimal incentive may not be an easy task: when the external incentive is too small, its negative effect as a result of crowding out intrinsic motivation may surpass its positive effect;[770] and when it is too big, it may result in over-motivation and lesser performance.[771] In line with the former observation, incentives have also been found to reduce cooperation when they adversely affect trust, and reduce prosocial behavior when they transform a social framing into a monetary one.[772] The same is true of ethical behavior, where implementing mild measures of detecting and sanctioning improper behavior may result in a reframing of the situation as involving risky costs (probability of detection and sanction levels) and benefits (from unethical behavior) to the actor, instead of an ethical dilemma.[773]

Finally, behavioral insights can help design effective incentives. Roland Fryer and his colleagues conducted a randomized field experiment to test the effect of financial incentives for teachers on their students' achievements. While teachers in the control group were promised a considerable monetary award for a certain target increase in students' performance, teachers in the treatment group were paid the same award in advance and asked to return the money if their students had not improved to the same degree. Reframing the failure to attain the desirable increase in students' performance as a loss, rather than as an unobtained gain, had a dramatic effect. While no significant improvement was found in

766. Baruch Fischhoff, Paul Slovic & Sarah Lichtenstein, *Knowing with Certainty: The Appropriateness of Extreme Confidence,* 3 4 J. Experimental Psychol.: Hum. Perception & Performance 552 (1977).

767. Paul W. Paese & Janet A. Sniezek, *Influences on the Appropriateness of Confidence in Judgment: Practice, Effort, Information, and Decision-Making,* 48 Org. Behav. & Hum. Decision Processes 100 (1991).

768. David Grether & Charles Plott, *Economic Theory of Choice and the Preference Reversal Phenomenon,* 69 Am. Econ. Rev. 623, 632 (1979).

769. Arkes, Dawes & Christensen, *supra* note 315.

770. Uri Gneezy, Stephan Meier & Pedro Rey-Biel, *When and Why Incentives (Don't) Work to Modify Behavior,* 25 J. Econ. Persp. 191, 192–94 (2011).

771. Dan Ariely et al., *Large Stakes and Big Mistakes,* 76 Rev. Econ. Stud. 451 (2009).

772. Gneezy, Meier & Rey-Biel, *supra* note 770, at 199–201.

773. Ann E. Tenbrunsel & David M. Messick, *Sanctioning Systems, Decision Frames, and Cooperation,* 44 Admin. Sci. Q. 684 (1999).

the control group, the improvement in the treatment group was equivalent to increasing teacher quality by more than one standard deviation.[774]

Similarly to incentives, accountability—the need to justify one's decisions to others—has mixed effects on people's judgments and choices.[775] At the outset, it should be noted that accountability is much more than just a debiasing technique: since the costs of formal means of assuring people's compliance with social norms are usually prohibitive, internalized accountability is a powerful form of social control.[776] Hence, accountability not only strengthens the motivation to make the right decision; it may alter "the right decision," as well. Inasmuch as social approval affects one's well-being, factoring such approval into one's decision may turn an otherwise improper decision into a proper one, and vice versa.[777] For example, it was found that accountability *amplifies* the effect of the status quo and omission biases in choices that involve a risk of imposing losses on identifiable constituencies.[778] Arguably, this is a perfectly rational consideration from the decision-maker's perspective.

To understand the effect of accountability on people's judgment and decision-making, several distinctions must be drawn. One concerns timing: when a person is asked to justify a decision she has already made, accountability cannot affect the decision. However, accountability is consequential when a person makes an initial decision and then faces additional ones. Since people dislike admitting that their initial decision was wrong, accountability may enhance the confirmation bias and exacerbate the escalation of commitment.[779] This is not the case with accountability for an initial decision.

Another relevant distinction is between *outcome accountability* and *process accountability*. While accountability for the quality of outcomes tends to produce greater escalation of commitment, accountability for the procedure in which a decision is made tends to reduce escalation of commitment, increase consistency in applying a judgment strategy, and encourage the consideration of more information in a more analytical

774. Roland G. Fryer, Jr. et al, *Enhancing the Efficacy of Teacher Incentives through Loss Aversion: A Field Experiment* (working paper, July 2012, *available at* http://www.nber.org/papers/w18237). *See also* Tanjim Hossain & John A. List, *The Behavioralist Visits the Factory: Increased Productivity Using Simple Framing Manipulations*, 58 Mgmt. Sci. 2151 (2012); Fuhai Hong, Tanjim Hossain & John A. List, *Framing Manipulations in Contests: A Natural Field Experiment*, 118 J. Econ. Behav. & Org. 372 (2015).

775. For a thorough review, see Jennifer S. Lerner & Philip E. Tetlock, *Accounting for the Effects of Accountability*, 125 Psychol. Bull. 255 (1999).

776. Jennifer S. Lerner & Philip E. Tetlock, *Bridging Individual, Interpersonal, and Institutional Approaches to Judgment and Choice: The Impact of Accountability on Cognitive Bias*, *in* Emerging Perspectives on Judgment and Decision Research 431, 433–34 (Sandra L. Schneider & James Shanteau eds., 2003).

777. Lerner & Tetlock, *supra* note 775, at 269–70.

778. Philip E. Tetlock & Richard Boettger, *Accountability Amplifies the Status Quo Effect when Change Creates Victims*, 7 J. Behav. Decision Making 1 (1994).

779. Lerner & Tetlock, *supra* note 775, at 257–58. On the confirmation bias and escalation of commitment, see *supra* pp. 58–61 and 56–57, respectively.

manner.[780] Possibly, the adverse effects of outcome accountability are due to decision stress and narrowing of attention.

Finally, one should distinguish between instances where the views of the person(s) that the decision-maker is accountable to are known, and those where they are not. Due to the conformity effect, when the audience's views are known, accountability is likely to induce people to shift their judgments and decisions closer to those of the audience.[781] This may result in a biased judgment or decision. Whether accountability transforms the way people think, or merely affects what they *say* they think—in this and other cases—may differ from one setting to another (and the very distinction between the two is sometimes unclear).[782] In contrast, accountability to an audience whose views are unknown is much more likely to result in a thorough consideration of more information and conflicting arguments, so as to prepare the decision-maker for possible objections—a process that helps overcome cognitive biases.[783]

Having reviewed the research on these and other factors, Jennifer Lerner and Philip Tetlock concluded: "Self-critical and effortful thinking is most likely to be activated when decision makers learn prior to forming any opinions that they will be accountable to an audience (a) whose views are unknown, (b) who is interested in accuracy, (c) who is interested in processes rather than specific outcomes, (d) who is reasonably well informed, and (e) who has a legitimate reason for inquiring into the reasons behind participants' judgments."[784]

However, even when all these conditions are met, the beneficial effect of accountability is not guaranteed. Accountability is particularly beneficial when erroneous judgments and decisions are the product of lack of effort. To come up with a defensible decision, accountable people are more likely to thoroughly and self-critically consider more information and conflicting arguments. Accordingly, accountability has been found to reduce the order effect and anchoring effect, and to increase the calibration between the accuracy of the decision-maker's decisions and his or her confidence.[785] In contrast, when a person lacks the intellectual tools or knowledge necessary to overcome cognitive errors, more effort is unlikely to improve one's judgments. Indeed, accountability had no effect on base-rate neglect or insensitivity to sample size.[786]

780. Itamar Simonson & Barry M. Staw, *Deescalation Strategies: A Comparison of Techniques for Reducing Commitment to Losing Courses of Action*, 77 J. Applied Psychol. 419 (1992); Karen Siegel-Jacobs & J. Frank Yates, *Effects of Procedural and Outcome Accountability on Judgment Quality*, 65 Org. Behav. & Hum. Decision Processes 1 (1996). These characteristics are not universal, however. *See* Bart de Langhe, Stijn M.J. van Osselaer & Berend Wierenga, *The Effects of Process and Outcome Accountability on Judgment Process and Performance*, 115 Org. Behav. & Hum. Decision Processes 238 (2011).

781. On the conformity effect, see *supra* note 337 and accompanying text.

782. Lerner & Tetlock, *supra* note 775, at 266–69.

783. *Id.* at 256–57.

784. *Id.* at 259.

785. *Id.* at 263.

786. Itamar Simonson & Peter Nye, *The Effect of Accountability on Susceptibility to Decision Errors*, 51 Org. Behav. & Hum. Decision Processes 416, 435–37 (1992). On these biases, see *supra* pp. 30–31 and 32–34, respectively.

Moreover, sometimes accountability makes things worse. This is expected to be the case when the easier-to-justify decision is the normatively inferior one. There is some evidence that accountability amplifies the compromise and attraction effects because choices reflecting these biases are easier to justify.[787] For similar reasons, an effort to take into account all available information, induced by accountability, may result in worse decisions when the additional information is non-diagnostic, and preferably should have been ignored.[788]

In summary, while incentives and accountability sometimes help overcoming cognitive biases, they are certainly no panacea. Depending on the circumstances, they may fail to improve judgments and choices, and even make things worse.

(d) Cognitive Strategies

Having discussed technological debiasing techniques (which may be too costly for everyday decision-making) and motivational ones (which are often ineffective), we turn to cognitive techniques. Cognitive strategies for debiasing aim to help people overcome their cognitive biases, or to modify the decision environment so that people's ordinary cognitive processes would bring about better judgments and decisions. Thus, a distinction may be drawn between *direct* and *indirect* debiasing techniques. While the former aim to help people make more rational (or at least more consistent) decisions, the latter strive to counteract the effect of some biases by triggering other biases.[789] Examples of direct debiasing techniques include drawing the decision-maker's attention to the existence of the bias, asking people to think about alternative possibilities or perspectives, and training in probabilistic reasoning. Examples of indirect debiasing include the setting of a beneficial default, for example, for participation in a pension saving plan (thus using the omission bias to counteract people's myopia and bounded willpower), and rearranging the food display in a cafeteria to encourage the consumption of healthy food. Whereas direct debiasing invokes System 2 thinking to correct System 1's biases, indirect debiasing utilizes System 1's biases to counteract other biases. Therefore, indirect debiasing does not require that the decision-maker would be cognizant of his or her bias. In fact, it may be more effective when the decision-maker is unaware of the cognitive processes involved. Indirect-debiasing measures are closely connected to the notions of *nudges* and *libertarian paternalism*; hence they are discussed in Chapter 4.[790] Here we review some of the findings on direct debiasing techniques.

787. Lerner & Tetlock, *supra* note 775, at 264. It should be noted, however, that the findings that accountability amplifies the compromise and attraction effects (Simonson, *supra* note 455) have been qualified in subsequent studies (Itamar Simonson & Stephen M. Nowlis, *The Role of Explanations and Need for Uniqueness in Consumer Decision Making: Unconventional Choices Based on Reasons,* 27 J. CONSUMER RES. 49 (2000)).

788. Lerner & Tetlock, *supra* note 775, at 264–65.

789. Barbara E. Kahn, Mary Frances Luce & Stephen M. Nowlis, *Debiasing Insights from Process Tests,* 33 J. CONSUMER RES. 131 (2006); ZAMIR, *supra* note 151, at 39, 220.

790. *See infra* pp. 177–85.

The most straightforward reaction to cognitive biases is to draw decision-makers' attention to their existence. However, the evidence regarding the success of such alerting is mixed. For example, drawing subjects' attention to the "I knew it all along" effect,[791] and asking them to do their best to overcome it, failed to achieve this result.[792] Other studies on the effectiveness of warnings to undo the *hindsight bias* produced mixed results.[793] Warning subjects that their assessments were too close to a given anchor (e.g., within ±10 percent or within ±20 percent of it) similarly failed to debias the *anchoring and adjustment effect.*[794] In contrast, warnings successfully debiased a *framing effect* when subjects' level of involvement in the decision was high, and very strong warnings debiased this effect even when subjects' involvement was low.[795]

Another technique, which has proven more effective than simple warnings, is asking people to consider evidence or arguments that might lead to a different conclusion (*consider the opposite*), or to generate additional alternatives to choose from.[796] Since many biases are the outcome of System 1, associative thinking, rather than a systematic consideration of arguments and possibilities, this simple technique induces people to employ a more analytical mode of thinking. For example, in one study, neuropsychologists were presented with an ambiguous case history, and asked to estimate the probability of three possible diagnoses. In the hindsight conditions, subjects were informed that one diagnosis was correct, and asked what probability they would have assigned to each diagnosis if they were making the original diagnosis. Some of the subjects, in both the foresight and hindsight conditions, were first asked to list one reason why each of the possible diagnoses might be correct. Answering this question reduced the percentage of subjects exhibiting the hindsight bias from 58 percent to 41 percent.[797] A more recent study concerned the discrepancy between the economic imperative to consider any possible purchase vis-à-vis alternative uses of one's money (its *opportunity costs*), and WYSIATI—the tendency to base one's decision on immediately available information to the exclusion of all other information. It was found that, in a choice between an expensive and a cheaper product, merely adding a reminder of the possibility of using the price-difference for another purpose (e.g., "leaving you with $X dollars

791. This effect denotes people's tendency, when provided with the correct answers to questions, to misremember how much they knew those answers, as well as to overstate how much they would have known them, in response to a hypothetical question. *See also supra* pp. 38–39.

792. Baruch Fischhoff, *Perceived Informativeness of Facts,* 3 J. Experimental Psychol.: Hum. Perception & Performance 349 (1977).

793. *See* Kamin & Rachlinskil, *supra* note 118 (failed debiasing); Merrie Jo Stallardl & Debra L. Worthington, *Reducing the Hindsight Bias Utilizing Attorney Closing Arguments,* 22 Law & Hum. Behav. 671 (1998) (effective debiasing).

794. Joey F. George, Kevin Duffy & Manju Ahuja, *Countering the Anchoring and Adjustment Bias with Decision Support Systems,* 29 Decision Support Sys. 195 (2000). On anchoring, see generally *supra* pp. 79–82.

795. Fei-Fei Cheng & Chin-Shan Wu, *Debiasing the Framing Effect: The Effect of Warning and Involvement,* 49 Decision Support Sys. 328 (2010). On framing effects, see *supra* pp. 46–48.

796. *See* Charles G. Lord, Mark R. Lepper & Elizabeth Preston, *Considering the Opposite: A Corrective Strategy for Social Judgment,* 47 J. Personality & Soc. Psychol. 1231 (1984).

797. Arkes et al., *supra* note 118.

to spend on something else") considerably increased the incidence of selecting the cheaper product.[798] Consider-the-opposite strategy has also been found effective in reducing the anchoring effect,[799] overconfidence,[800] self-serving biases,[801] and more.[802] However, these techniques are not always effective[803]—and even when they are, they usually only reduce cognitive biases, and not eliminate them.

Another debiasing technique that rests on inducing people to consider more information and additional perspectives is to ask them to make the same judgment or estimation twice—possibly with a time delay between the two assessments, or by using different thinking modes—and then average the responses.[804]

An additional set of debiasing techniques is founded on training people to use adequate decision rules (instead of intuitive heuristics).[805] For instance, people's probabilistic assessments may be improved by studying statistics,[806] and cost-benefit analysis may be improved by studying economics.[807] However, there is conflicting evidence about the extent to which learning to use the relevant rules in one domain extends to other domains, as well as the extent to which such training has a lasting effect on people's judgment and decision-making.[808] People may not pause to use the rules they know—especially when their intuitive judgments are strong. In any event, very few people actually get such training.

A potentially fruitful approach is to design a debiasing device based on the variables that mediate cognitive biases.[809] Thus, the finding that people make better judgments when thinking in terms of frequency rather than probability (e.g., "1 in 20," rather than "5 percent"), has led to a training program in which subjects were taught to make probabilistic inferences by

798. Shane Frederick et al., *Opportunity Cost Neglect*, 36 J. CONSUMER RES. 553 (2009).

799. Thomas Mussweiler, Fritz Strack & Tim Pfeiffer, *Overcoming the Inevitable Anchoring Effect: Considering the Opposite Compensates for Selective Accessibility*, 26 PERSONALITY & SOC. PSYCHOL. BULL. 1142 (2000).

800. Asher Koriat, Sarah Lichtenstein & Baruch Fischhoff, *Reasons for Confidence*, 6 J. EXPERIMENTAL PSYCHOL.: HUM. LEARNING & MEMORY 107 (1980); Moore, Tenney & Haran, *supra* note 308, at 195.

801. Linda Babcock, George Loewenstein & Samuel Issacharoff, *Creating Convergence: Debiasing Biased Litigants*, 22 LAW & SOC. INQUIRY 913 (1997).

802. Edward R. Hirt & Keith D. Markman, *Multiple Explanation: A Consider-an-Alternative Strategy for Debiasing Judgments*, 69 J. PERSONALITY & SOC. PSYCHOL. 1069 (1995).

803. Buehler, Griffin & Peetz, *supra* note 342, at 269.

804. Soll, Milkman & Payne, *supra* note 744, at 932–33.

805. RULES OF REASONING (Richard E. Nisbett ed., 1993); Larrick, *supra* note 743, at 324–25.

806. Geoffrey T. Fong, David H. Krantz & Richard E. Nisbett, *The Effects of Statistical Training on Thinking about Everyday Problems*, 18 COGNITIVE PSYCHOL. 253 (1986).

807. Richard P. Larrick, James N. Morgan & Richard E. Nisbett, *Teaching the Use of Cost-Benefit Reasoning in Everyday Life*, 1 PSYCHOL. SCI. 362 (1990).

808. *See, e.g.*, Geoffrey T. Fong & Richard E. Nisbett, *Immediate and Delayed Transfer of Training Effects in Statistical Reasoning*, 120 J. EXPERIMENTAL PSYCHOL.: GENERAL 34 (1991) (finding that after two weeks there was a significant decline in performance in the untrained domain, though performance was still better than for untrained subjects). *See generally* RULES OF REASONING, *supra* note 805; Soll, Milkman & Payne, *supra* note 744, at 930–31; Rachlinski, *supra* note 625, at 219–21.

809. Larrick, *supra* note 743, at 325.

constructing frequency representations.[810] It was found that teaching people to represent information in that way was more effective than teaching them Bayesian rules. While both types of training produced substantial short-term improvement, training in frequency representations was more effective in the short run and considerably more effective in the long run.

In general, debiasing techniques are likely to be more effective when there is an easily demonstrable "right answer" than when decisions depend on attitudes to risks, losses, discount rates of future outcomes, and the like. Accordingly, while the findings are far from conclusive, there is some support for the claim that framing effects can be more easily debiased than, for example, the sunk-costs effect. It has been demonstrated experimentally that framing effects can be eliminated by giving appropriate warnings,[811] by asking people to list the advantages and disadvantages of each option and the rationale for their decision,[812] and by instructions to specifically analyze each piece of evidence.[813] In contrast, attempts at debiasing the sunk-costs effect produced mixed results. While there is evidence that studying economics—including being exposed to the notion of sunk costs—does not affect the sunk-costs effect,[814] it was found that economics professors are less vulnerable to this effect than professors of other disciplines.[815] Instructing subjects to outline the pros and cons of each option prior to reaching a decision did not affect escalation of commitment.[816]

In sum, the vast literature on debiasing provides no clear, general conclusion. Some debiasing techniques are more effective than others, efficacy varies from one context to another, and some strategies are actually counterproductive. Moreover, just as it has been argued that some of the biases identified in laboratory experiments may disappear in real-life contexts, it may well be that debiasing measures that have been proven effective in the laboratory would not be as effective in the real world, if at all.[817] Some of the abovementioned

810. Peter Sedlmeier & Gerd Gigerenzer, *Teaching Bayesian Reasoning in Less than Two Hours*, 130 J. Experimental Psychol.: General 380 (2001).

811. Cheng & Wu, *supra* note 795.

812. Sammy Almashat et al., *Framing Effect Debiasing in Medical Decision Making*, 71 Patient Educ. & Counseling 102 (2008).

813. Craig Emby & David Finley, *Debiasing Framing Effects in Auditors' Internal Control Judgments and Testing Decisions*, 14(2) Contemp. Accounting Res. 55 (1997).

814. Arkes & Blumer, *supra* note 243, at 136. Similarly, no statistically significant difference was found between the WTP-WTA gap of economics students and students of other fields, regarding Christmas presents. *See* Thomas K. Bauer & Christoph M. Schmidt, *WTP vs. WTA: Christmas Presents and the Endowment Effect, in* 232 Jahrbücher für Nationalökonomie und Statistik 4 (2012).

815. Richard P. Larrick, Richard E. Nisbett & James N. Morgan, *Who Uses the Normative Rules of Choice? Implications for the Normative Status of Microeconomic Theory*, 56 Org. Behav. & Hum. Decision Processes 331 (1993).

816. Itamar Simonson & Barry M. Staw, *Deescalation Strategies: A Comparison of Techniques for Reducing Commitment to Losing Courses of Action*, 77 J. Applied Psychol. 419 (1992); Itamar Simonson & Peter Nye, *The Effect of Accountability on Susceptibility to Decision Errors*, 51 Org. Behav. & Hum. Decision Processes 416 (1992).

817. *See, e.g.*, Ward Farnsworth, *The Legal Regulation of Self-Serving Bias*, 37 U.C. Davis L. Rev. 567, 581–83 (2003) (questioning the external validity of the findings of Babcock, Loewenstein & Issacharoff, *supra* note 801).

techniques may be used by individuals, some could be employed by organizations, and some could be implemented by the government. Implementing those techniques (and all the more so, *indirect* debiasing techniques and nudges) by the government raises a host of normative and policy questions that will be discussed in Chapter 4.[818]

I. Concluding Remarks

This chapter offered a bird's-eye view of the psychological studies informing the behavioral-economic analyses of law. It focused on JDM research, but integrated the findings of other areas in psychology and touched upon other disciplines, such as experimental economics.

The numerous references to specific studies, meta-analyses, and reviews of the psychological literature, provided throughout the chapter, should enable the interested reader to get a fuller and more nuanced picture of the pertinent issues. Since the psychological research is constantly developing, to get an up-to-date glance at current research, one would have to read the very recent studies, possibly by looking at studies that cite the articles and books cited in this chapter.

While there are still many unknowns in people's motivation, judgment, and decision-making, so much is known that it would seem pointless to ignore this huge body of knowledge and stick to unrealistic, abstract models of human behavior. Against this backdrop, Part II will provide a general synopsis of behavioral law and economics, and the ensuing parts will discuss specific legal fields.

818. *See infra* pp. 177–85.

PART TWO

Behavioral Law and Economics: A Synopsis

3

An Overview of Behavioral Law and Economics

A. Introduction

Part I laid the groundwork for this book by introducing economic analysis and the behavioral findings underpinning behavioral law and economics (BLE). Before we move on to analyzing the contribution of BLE to positive and normative analyses of specific legal fields, Part II discusses general aspects of BLE, starting with an overview of the field in this chapter.

This chapter is divided into three sections—on the history of BLE, its methodologies, and the challenges it faces, respectively. To minimize the overlap with other chapters, this chapter does not delve into the psychological and economic roots of BLE, its normative implications, or its contributions to specific legal issues.

B. History

Since the late 1970s, economic analysis has emerged as the most prominent cross-disciplinary approach to law and legal theory.[1] Following standard economic analysis, and in keeping with *rational choice theory*, economic analysis of law has traditionally assumed that people are rational maximizers of their utility. Ever since the 1980s, this assumption has been challenged by behavioral insights, relying on research into judgment and decision-making.[2] Despite considerable resistance from economic orthodoxy, by the early 2000s behavioral economics (BE) became largely

1. *See generally* Richard A. Posner, Economic Analysis of Law (9th ed. 2014); *supra* pp. 7–18.

2. Many consider Richard Thaler's seminal article *Toward a Positive Theory of Consumer Choice* (1 J. Econ. Behav. & Org. 39 (1980)) to be the first notable contribution to modern behavioral economics. Herbert Simon's earlier work on *bounded rationality* is an important precursor to the modern developments. *See, e.g.*, Herbert A. Simon, *A Behavioral Model of Rational Choice*, 69 Q.J. Econ. 99 (1955); Herbert A. Simon, Models of Man (1957).

mainstream.[3] Along with the introduction of behavioral insights into economics, these insights were incorporated into economic analysis of law, as well. Thus, just as economist Richard Thaler was quick to point out the significance of *prospect theory*[4] for market behavior, jurist Mark Kelman quickly highlighted its significance for the Coase theorem, a basic tenet of law and economics.[5]

In the 1980s, a number of pioneering studies explored the ramifications of behavioral studies for economic analysis of law, and for law and legal policymaking more generally. Notable early contributions include Michael Saks and Robert Kidd's study of the implications of intuitive reasoning for evidence law,[6] John Coffee's discussion of corporate punishment,[7] James Cox and Harry Munsinger's examination of the behavior of independent directors,[8] Howard Latin's analysis of tort law,[9] and Thomas H. Jackson's critique of the "fresh start" policy in bankruptcy law.[10] Along with the steady increase of applications of behavioral insights to legal analysis, some scholars have taken a broader look at the heuristics-and-biases literature and its implications for legal policymaking. These include Cass Sunstein's examination of the interplay between the law and people's preferences;[11] Ward Edwards and Detlof von Winterfeldt's overview of behavioral studies and their significance for the law (which served as a lead article for a 1986 symposium on *Legal Implications of Human Error*);[12] and Robert Ellickson's call to further integrate psychological and sociological insights into economic analysis of law.[13]

3. *See generally* ADVANCES IN BEHAVIORAL ECONOMICS (Colin F. Camerer, George Loewenstein & Matthew Rabin eds., 2003).

4. Daniel Kahneman & Amos Tversky, *Prospect Theory: An Analysis of Decision under Risk,* 47 ECONOMETRICA 263 (1979). *See also supra* pp. 42–57.

5. Thaler, *supra* note 2; Mark Kelman, *Consumption Theory, Production Theory, and Ideology in the Coase Theorem,* 52 S. CAL. L. REV. 669 (1979). Remarkably, both Thaler and Kelman relied on Kahneman and Tversky's article even before it was published—years before the emergence of the World Wide Web.

6. Michael J. Saks & Robert F. Kidd, *Human Information Processing and Adjudication: Trial by Heuristics,* 15 LAW & SOC'Y REV. 123 (1980). *See also infra* pp. 578, 585.

7. John C. Coffee, Jr., *"No Soul to Damn: No Body to Kick": An Unscandalized Inquiry into the Problem of Corporate Punishment,* 79 MICH. L. REV. 386 (1981).

8. James D. Cox & Harry L. Munsinger, *Bias in the Boardroom: Psychological Foundations and Legal Implications of Corporate Cohesion,* 48 LAW & CONTEMP. PROBS. 83 (1985).

9. Howard A. Latin, *Problem-Solving Behavior and Theories of Tort Liability*, 73 CAL. L. REV. 677 (1985).

10. Thomas H. Jackson, *The Fresh-Start Policy in Bankruptcy Law,* 98 HARV. L. REV. 1393 (1985).

11. Cass R. Sunstein, *Legal Interference with Private Preferences,* 53 U. CHI. L. REV. 1129 (1986).

12. Ward Edwards & Detlof von Winterfeldt, *Cognitive Illusions and Their Implications for the Law,* 59 S. CAL. L. REV. 225 (1986).

13. Robert C. Ellickson, *Bringing Culture and Human Frailty to Rational Actors: A Critique of Classical Law and Economics,* 65 CHI.-KENT L. REV. 23 (1989). *See also* Thomas S. Ulen, *Cognitive Imperfections and the Economic Analysis of Law,* 12 HAMLINE L. REV. 385 (1989); Hal R. Arkes, *Principles of Judgment/Decisionmaking Research Pertinent to Legal Proceedings,* 7 BEHAV. SCI. & L. 429 (1989).

The 1990s saw further growth in the scope and sophistication of behavioral legal studies,[14] as did the 2000s and 2010s. Two influential articles—which raised the visibility of, and general interest in, BLE—were Christin Jolls, Cass Sunstein, and Richard Thaler's programmatic article of 1998, and Russell Korobkin and Thomas Ulen's article of 2000.[15] Both these articles are the most cited legal articles in their respective years of publication.[16] In fact, according to a citation count from 2012, the Jolls, Sunstein, and Thaler article is the most cited legal article published between 1990 and 2009 (including articles published up to seven years before it).[17]

As further elaborated in the next section, in recent years BLE has been boosted by the emergence of empirical legal research. While BLE scholars initially used to rely mostly on empirical data produced by psychologists and behavioral economists, today many of them conduct their own empirical studies, designed to answer distinctly *legal* questions.

Although the reaction of legal economists to BLE was initially somewhat skeptical and even hostile (much like economists' reaction to BE),[18] over time, in keeping with the old adage "If you can't beat them, join them," BLE has become part of mainstream law and economics.[19] Leading venues of legal-economic scholarship, such as the *Journal of Legal Studies*, feature many behavioral studies, and the annual meetings of the American and European Law and Economics Associations include many presentations on behavioral research. Accordingly, in 2011, Russell Korobkin declared "victory in the battle for the methodological soul of the law and economics discipline."[20] Moreover, just as economic analysis has gradually become part and parcel of academic legal discourse—first in the United States, then in other legal systems (including Canada, Israel, and the Netherlands)—so has BLE. Even scholars who are not particularly interested in economic or behavioral

14. For a systematic survey of the literature up to 1998, see Donald C. Langevoort, *Behavioral Theories of Judgment and Decision Making in Legal Scholarship: A Literature Review*, 51 Vand. L. Rev. 1499 (1998).

15. Christine Jolls, Cass R. Sunstein & Richard Thaler, *A Behavioral Approach to Law and Economics*, 50 Stan. L. Rev. 1471 (1998); Russell B. Korobin & Thomas S. Ulen, *Law and Behavioral Science: Removing the Rationality Assumption from Law and Economics*, 88 Cal. L. Rev. 1051 (2000).

16. Fred R. Shapiro & Michelle Pearse, *The Most-Cited Law Review Articles of All Time*, 110 Mich. L. Rev. 1483 (2012).

17. *Id.* at 1507.

18. *See, e.g.*, Robert E. Scott, *Error and Rationality in Individual Decision-Making: An Essay on the Relationship between Cognitive Illusions and the Management of Choices*, 59 S. Cal. L. Rev. 329 (1986); Richard A. Posner, *Rational Choice, Behavioral Economics and the Law*, 50 Stan. L. Rev. 1551 (1998).

19. Sixteen years after the publication of Richard Posner's harsh critique of BLE (Posner, *supra* note 18), he acknowledged in the preface to the latest edition of his book that the book is "more hospitable to criticisms of the 'rational choice' approach to law—criticisms that have persuaded me among other things to supplement that approach with insights from psychology." Posner, *supra* note 1, at xxii. To be sure, some lawyer-economists have remained as skeptical about BLE as they have ever been. *See, e.g.*, Alan Schwartz, *Regulating for Rationality*, 67 Stan. L. Rev. 1373 (2015). On the critiques of BLE, see *infra* pp. 150–56.

20. Russell Korobkin, *What Comes after Victory for Behavioral Law and Economics*, 2011 U. Ill. L. Rev. 1653, 1656.

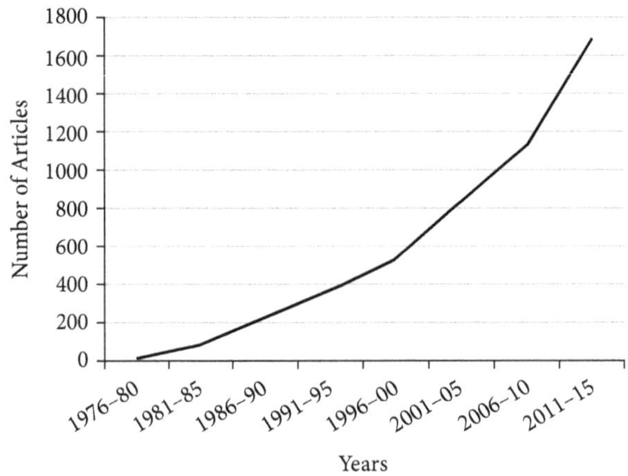

FIGURE 3.1 Legal Articles Citing Kahneman.

analysis of law show considerable interest in behavioral findings and their implications for the law.[21]

To gain a rough estimate of the growing interest of academic jurists in BLE, one may look at the number of references to the work of Daniel Kahneman—one of the pillars of BE—in legal scholarship. According to the Law Journal Library of HeinOnLine (containing more than 2,400 law and law-related periodicals), twenty articles mentioned Kahneman in the years 1976–1980. Thirty-five years later, in the 2011–2015 period, he was mentioned 1,685 times.[22] The exponential increase in references to Kahneman's work is depicted in Figure 3.1. Other signs of the growth and maturation of BLE include the publication of several anthologies of articles in the 2000s,[23] and more recently a handbook[24] and several monographs.[25] Possibly due to the challenge posed by the complex, multidisciplinary nature of the field, the present book is a first attempt at consolidating BLE in the form of a textbook-treatise.

The rising academic interest in BE and BLE has eventually made its way into the world of governmental policymaking. In addition to the consideration of behavioral insights by ordinary legislative bodies and executive agencies, a growing number of countries and

21. *See, e.g.*, Melvin Aron Eisenberg, *The Limits of Cognition and the Limits of Contract*, 47 Stan. L. Rev. 211 (1995); Russell Covey, Reconsidering the Relationship between Cognitive Psychology and Plea Bargaining, 91 Marq. L. Rev. 213 (2007).

22. http://heinonline.org/HOL/Index?collection=journals (last visited Aug. 1, 2017).

23. Behavioral Law and Economics (Cass R. Sunstein ed., 2000); The Law and Economics of Irrational Behavior (Francesco Parisi & Vernon Smith eds., 2005); Behavioral Law and Economics (Jeffrey Rachlinski ed., 2009).

24. The Oxford Handbook of Behavioral Economics and the Law (Eyal Zamir & Doron Teichman eds., 2014).

25. *See, e.g.*, Oren Bar-Gill, Seduction by Contract: Law, Economics, and Psychology in Consumer Markets 2 (2012); Eyal Zamir, Law, Psychology, and Morality: The Role of Loss Aversion (2015).

supranational institutions have established (or are in the process of establishing) special units whose primary role is to initiate and advance evidence-based, behaviorally-informed policies.[26]

C. Methodology

As early as the 1920s and 1930s, the American legal realists advocated introducing social-science research methods into legal theory and policymaking.[27] However, it took several decades before the interdisciplinary revolution actually occurred in legal scholarship—first in the United States, and gradually in other parts of the globe. As noted, of the various cross-disciplinary movements, the most influential one, since the 1970s, has been the economic analysis of law.[28]

Why has economics had greater impact on legal analysis than other disciplines, such as sociology or psychology? One answer points to a notable similarity between economics and traditional legal analysis: both enable scholars to "embrace science without undertaking empirical investigation."[29] Jurists accustomed to theoretical analysis felt particularly comfortable using an abstract theory of human behavior that does not require one to engage in messy empirical inquiries, or to directly interact with the people whose behavior is studied (as would, for example, sociology and criminology).

However, while this characterization of economic analysis may have been correct in the early 1990s, it is no longer accurate. In the past few decades, empirical studies have taken center stage in economics, including in highly theoretical spheres, such as game theory. Moreover, the most dramatic development in legal scholarship at the beginning of the twenty-first century appears to be the emergence of the *empirical legal studies* (ELS) movement.[30] Thus, while during the 1972–2002 period, 38.5 percent of the articles published

26. For reviews, see The Behavioral Foundations of Public Policy (Eldar Shafir ed., 2013); Raj Chetty, *Behavioral Economics and Public Policy: A Pragmatic Perspective*, 105 Am. Econ. Rev. 1 (2015). *See also infra* pp. 177–79.

27. *See, e.g.*, Karl N. Llewellyn, *A Realistic Jurisprudence—The Next Step*, 30 Colum. L. Rev. 431, 444 (1930); Roscoe Pound, *The Call for a Realist Jurisprudence*, 44 Harv. L. Rev. 697, 703 (1931). Comparable calls have been made in Europe. *See, e.g.*, Guido Tedeschi, *Su lo Studio dell'applicazione del Diritto civile*, 7 Ann. dir. Comparato Studi Legisl. 89 (1933) (It.)

28. It is sometimes useful to distinguish between *interdisciplinary* and *cross-disciplinary* research. Cross-disciplinarity (or, as it is sometimes called, *weak* interdisciplinarity) denotes the use of insights, concepts, perspectives, and research methodologies of one discipline to enrich and improve the research in another discipline. Interdisciplinarity (or *strong* interdisciplinarity) denotes the synthesis and integration of two (or more) disciplines to create a new body of knowledge (such as criminology or biochemistry). *See, e.g.*, Arabella Lyon, *Interdisciplinarity: Giving Up Territory*, 54 College English 681 (1992). According to this distinction, most interdisciplinary legal studies—including BLE—are actually cross-disciplinary, although economic analysis of law may be the closest to constituting a distinctive body of knowledge.

29. Mark Cooney, *Why Is Economic Analysis So Appealing to Law Professors?*, 45 Stan. L. Rev. 2211, 2229 (1993) (reviewing Robert C. Ellickson, Order without Law: How Neighbors Settle Disputes (1991)).

30. *See generally* Jeffrey J. Rachlinski, *Evidence-Based Law*, 96 Cornell L. Rev. 901 (2011); *Symposium: Empirical and Experimental Methods in Law*, 2002 U. Ill. L. Rev. 791–1176; Jonah B. Gelbach & Jonathan Klick, *Empirical*

in the *Journal of Legal Studies*, the leading peer-reviewed journal in law and economics, were empirical,[31] in 2015–2016 the percentage rose to 61.8 percent (thirty-four out of fifty-five). This trend increasingly affects BLE.[32] One may therefore divide BLE scholarship into two genres, which partially correspond to two periods: *theoretical studies*, which apply empirical findings produced by psychologists and economists to legal issues; and (mostly more recent) *empirical studies*, which produce new data specifically tailored to shed light on legal issues.[33]

As reflected throughout this book, most of the behavioral findings underpinning BLE are the product of basic research conducted by researchers in other disciplines—mostly psychologists and behavioral and experimental economists. This picture is unlikely to change in the future. In this regard, BLE is no different from other cross-disciplinary approaches to law, such as law and literature, or law and philosophy. Jurists could not, and need not, (re)produce the vast, sophisticated knowledge originated in other disciplines. However, drawing on behavioral findings in making legal arguments is subject to the perils facing any cross-disciplinary approach. In the present context, jurists should take into account the inconclusiveness and context-dependence of many psychological findings, note individual differences in people's susceptibility to cognitive biases, and recognize possible gaps between laboratory and real-life decision-making.[34] Most important, they should be cautious when drawing normative conclusions and policy recommendations from empirical data.[35] However, behavioral ELS can overcome, or at least mitigate, some of these concerns.

Empirical legal research "involves the systematic collection of information ('data') and its analysis according to some generally accepted method."[36] Most of the researchers associated with the ELS movement engage in *quantitative* studies: they analyze the data using statistical, mathematical, or computational techniques. But empirical studies in law also include, and have long included, *qualitative* methods, such as in-depth interviews aiming at understanding people's motives and attitudes.

Focusing on quantitative research, ELS may be divided into three categories: observational, lab-experimental, and field-experimental studies—the last category comprising

Law and Economics, *in* The Oxford Handbook of Law and Economics 29 (Francesco Parisi ed., 2017). *See also* The Oxford Handbook of Empirical Legal Research (Peter Cane & Herbert M. Kritzer eds., 2010); Robert M. Lawless, Jennifer K. Robbennolt & Thomas S. Ulen, Empirical Methods in Law (2010).

31. William M. Landes, *The Empirical Side of Law and Economics*, 70 U. Chi. L. Rev. 167, 170 (2003).

32. On ELS and BLE, see generally Avishalom Tor, *The Methodology of the Behavioral Analysis of Law*, 4 Din U'Dvarim (Haifa L. Rev.) 237, 272–91 (2008); Christoph Engel, *Behavioral Law and Economics: Empirical Methods*, *in* The Oxford Handbook of Behavioral Economics and the Law, *supra* note 24, at 125.

33. Tor, *supra* note 32, at 272–91; Daphna Lewinsohn-Zamir, *Behavioral Law and Economics of Property Law: Achievements and Challenges*, *in* The Oxford Handbook of Behavioral Economics and the Law, *supra* note 24, at 377, 378–79.

34. Tor, *supra* note 32, at 274–81; *infra* pp. 150–56.

35. *See also* Jeffery J. Rachlinski, *The Uncertain Psychological Case for Paternalism*, 97 Nw. U. L. Rev. 1165 (2003); *infra* pp. 157–86.

36. Peter Cane & Hebert M. Kritzer, *Introduction*, *in* The Oxford Handbook of Empirical Legal Research, *supra* note 30, at 1, 4.

randomized field experiments and natural experiments. Observational studies analyze data of real-world phenomena, such as litigants' decisions concerning settlements or plea bargains. Due to the high costs of collecting and coding information, more often than not such studies rely on preexisting databases. Using statistical tools, they look for *correlations* (or *associations*) between factors—for example, between characteristics of procedural and substantive legal rules and litigants' inclination to settle lawsuits. The primary advantage of observational studies is that they look at the real world, so their *external validity* is typically high. The primary limitation of these studies is that it is very difficult to identify causal relationships between factors, since behavior in the real world is simultaneously influenced by numerous factors, many of which are hard to identify or quantify.[37] For example, when comparing people's behavior in two different time periods, or in two jurisdictions, which differ in their legal regimes, the differences in the legal regime may be conflated with any number of other differences between the two periods or jurisdictions. When two variables are correlated, it is often unclear which one causes the other, or if there is a third variable causing them both. This limitation makes the drawing of policy recommendations from observational studies—a major goal of ELS—very challenging.[38] While observational ELS are prevalent in areas such as financial markets and higher courts' decisions on constitutional matters, they are not as commonly used to study the impact of psychological variables on people's judgments and decisions. For this reason, we will not elaborate on their difficulties or the possible ways to mitigate such difficulties.[39] We would only note that, while the methodological conventions in the social sciences focus on preventing unreliable evidence of the kind of false positives, depending on the issue at hand, legal policymakers might be as, or even more, concerned about false negatives—which may require adaptations when conducting empirical legal studies, interpreting empirical findings, and drawing normative conclusions from them.[40]

Lab experiments meet the challenge of identifying causal connections by creating an artificial decision-making environment, in which the experimenter controls the relevant variables. Experimental studies typically involve random allocation of participants to two (or more) conditions, which are identical in every respect except the variable(s) whose impact on judgments or decisions is being tested.[41] The random allocation of a sufficiently large number of participants to each condition (and compliance with additional requirements)

37. Gelbach & Klick, *supra* note 30.

38. Jeffrey J. Rachlinski, *Does Empirical Legal Studies Shed More Heat than Light? The Case of Civil Damage Awards*, 29 Ratio Juris 556 (2016).

39. *See generally* Richard Blundell & Monica Costa Dias, *Alternative Approaches to Evaluation in Empirical Microeconomics*, 44 J. Human Resources 565 (2009).

40. Christoph Engel, *Empirical Methods for the Law*, J. Institutional & Theoretical Econ. (forthcoming 2018) (working paper, May 2017, *available at*: https://ssrn.com/abstract=2966095).

41. The experimental design may be *between-subjects* (whereby participants are subjected to different treatments), or *within-subjects* (whereby the same participants make judgments or decisions under different conditions). An experiment might involve both between- and within-subjects elements.

guarantees, with some degree of confidence, that differences in judgments or decisions are not due to differences between the participants, but rather between the conditions.

Behavioral experiments often use vignettes—that is, participants are presented with hypothetical scenarios and asked how they would behave, how they expect others to behave in such circumstances, or how they assess such behavior. Another type of experiment—more commonly used by experimental economists—involves an interactive game between participants in a highly stylized, context-free environment, where the participants' actual payoffs depend on their performance.[42]

Much like observational studies, experimental studies pose a host of methodological challenges, and their results may be open to different interpretations. Besides, two major limitations of lab experiments concern the external validity and generalizability of their findings. External validity refers to the degree to which findings generated in a laboratory setting hold true for the real world, and generalizability concerns the scope of contexts that the findings are applicable to. Some trade-off between external and internal validity is inevitable. By their very nature, laboratory experiments abstract away the richness and complexity of real life, so it is difficult to rule out the possibility that people behave differently in the real world, or that they behave differently in different contexts (which they surely do). Attempts to mitigate these challenges include conducting experiments with subjects who possess relevant training and experience—for example, judges, retired judges, lawyers, or senior law students, when the object of research is judicial decision-making—and providing monetary incentives for success when studying market behavior.

In the absence of established conventions for ELS, researchers usually follow the conventions of other disciplines, such as psychology or economics. Since BLE is primarily inspired by psychological research, most scholars engaging in behavioral ELS follow the conventions of experimental psychology. Unlike experimental economists, they do not necessarily provide subjects with performance-based monetary incentives, do not ordinarily use repeated experimental trials that allow participants to learn the task, and sometimes deceive participants. Based on meta-analyses of the limited impact of monetary incentives, such incentives are usually used when they can be expected to affect decision-making.[43] Such incentives are irrelevant, for example, when studying moral judgments of other people's behavior, and are ineffective when greater effort does not improve people's decisions. As for repetition, many real-world decisions are not made repeatedly; hence asking participants to make a single decision does not detract from the external validity of the results, and may actually enhance it. Deception allows hypotheses to be examined that might otherwise be impossible to test. The prevalent use of vignettes, which describe real-life decision tasks, allows behavioral ELS to be much more realistic than economic lab experiments—thereby making them more directly relevant to actual legal questions.

42. On the differences between experimental psychology and experimental economics, see Ralph Hertwig & Andreas Ortmann, *Experimental Practices in Economics: A Methodological Challenge for Psychologists?*, 24 Behav. & Brain Sci. 383 (2001); Engel, *supra* note 32, at 134–36.

43. *See supra* pp. 129–34.

Importantly, in the past decade or so, considerable internal and external critique has been voiced regarding the limited replicability of experimental results in the social sciences, including experimental psychology.[44] Various steps have been taken in recent years to meet this challenge in other disciplines—such as requiring researchers to make their raw data publicly available to the research community, and systematically examining the replicability of published findings. The concerns raised in other disciplines regarding the quality of empirical studies are at least as relevant to law, if only because virtually all editors of student law reviews lack the necessary expertise to assess the methodological soundness of behavioral experiments, and U.S. student law reviews do not ordinarily make use of expert reviews.[45] One should hope that the ELS community will take the necessary measures to ensure the quality of experimental legal studies.[46]

Regardless of whether the quality of ELS will improve in the future, much like in relying on basic behavioral research, the unavoidable and avoidable limitations of laboratory experiments call for caution in identifying psychological phenomena, in making assumptions about their generality, and especially in drawing policy conclusions from them. In both scholarly writing and legal policymaking, it is much safer to rely on findings that are corroborated by many experiments, in various settings, and conducted by diverse researchers (and on their meta-analysis), than on a single or very few experiments. Another recommendation is to combine lab experiments with other types of empirical research, including quantitative and qualitative observational studies, as well as field experiments, to which we now turn.

As previously noted, the major difficulty with observational studies lies in inferring causal connections from correlations, and the primary limitation of lab experiments concerns their external validity. In an attempt to combine the advantages of both types of research and to avoid their limitations, scholars are increasingly using field experiments. These studies use external changes in a natural decision-making environment to document how those changes affect people's behavior. In *randomized field experiments*, the experimenter initiates an artificial intervention in reality, such that people are randomly allocated to different treatments—much as in laboratory experiments.[47] Such interventions usually require close cooperation with the organization where the experiment is conducted, which is not always possible. Another type of field experiments are *natural experiments*, which

44. *See, e.g.*, Open Letter from Daniel Kahneman, Nature (Sept. 26, 2012, *available at:* http://www.nature.com/polopoly_fs/7.6716.1349271308!/suppinfoFile/Kahneman%20Letter.pdf); Kathryn Zeiler, *The Future of Empirical Legal Scholarship: Where Might We Go from Here?*, 66 J. Legal Educ. 78, 81–84 (2016); Open Science Collaboration, *Estimating the Reproducibility of Psychological Science*, 349 Sci. aac4716-1 (2015).

45. Zeiler, *supra* note 44. Indeed, an initial attempt to replicate the findings of three behavioral empirical legal studies yielded mixed results. *See* Kristin Firth, David A. Hoffman & Tess Wilkinson-Ryan, *Law and Psychology Grows Up, Goes Online, and Replicates* (working paper, Aug. 2017, *available at:* http://ssrn.com/abstract=3020401).

46. A first step in that direction is the inaugural Empirical Legal Studies Replication Conference, scheduled to take place in Clermont, California, in April 2018.

47. *See, e.g.*, Barak Ariel, *Deterrence and Moral Persuasion Effects on Corporate Tax Compliance: Findings from a Randomized Controlled Trial*, 50 Criminology 27 (2012); Eyal Zamir, Daphna Lewinsohn-Zamir & Ilana Ritov, *It's Now or Never! Using Deadlines as Nudges*, 42 Law & Soc. Inquiry 769, 780–84 (2017).

build upon a single, exogenous change in the decision-making environment, and which compare decisions and outcomes under the various conditions.[48] While potentially superior to both observational and laboratory experiments, field experiments can raise comparable difficulties. For example, the findings of a natural experiment might be called into question if it transpires that what was believed to be a random allocation was not actually random.[49]

Given the limited number of behavioral empirical legal studies, the findings of such studies should be combined with those of basic research conducted by behavioral researchers in other disciplines.[50] If possible, the findings of laboratory experiments should be complemented with observational and field experiments, including qualitative empirical studies.[51] Finally, jurists should be very cautious when moving from descriptive to normative arguments—since even a good grasp of reality rarely, if ever, yields direct normative or policy conclusions.

Ultimately, legal policymakers—including legislators, judges, and other public officials—are often compelled to make decisions based on imperfect, or even slim, scientific empirical data. We maintain that, even in such cases, it is almost always preferable to take into account imperfect empirical data than to ignore it altogether and to stick to assumptions of rational choice theory, as some scholars suggest.[52]

D. Challenges

As noted, in the past decades behavioral insights have had a great impact on economic analysis of law and on legal analysis in general, much as they have had on other disciplines.[53] However, like any cross-disciplinary endeavor, BLE faces considerable challenges.[54]

48. *See, e.g.*, David S. Abrams & Albert H. Yoon, *The Luck of the Draw: Using Random Case Assignment to Investigate Attorney Ability*, 74 U. Chi. L. Rev. 1145 (2007); Zamir, Lewinsohn-Zamir & Ritov, *supra* note 47, at 784–87.

49. *See, e.g.*, Keren Weinshall-Margel & John Shapard, *Overlooked Factors in the Analysis of Parole Decisions*, 108 Proc. Nat'l Acad. Sci. USA E833 (2011) (criticizing Shai Danziger, Jonathan Levav & Liora Avniam-Pesso, *Extraneous Factors in Judicial Decisions*, 108 Proc. Nat'l Acad. Sci. USA 6889 (2011)).

50. *See also* Tor, *supra* note 32, at 290–91.

51. For such combinations within a single publication, see, e.g., Eric J. Johnson et al., *Framing, Probability Distortions, and Insurance Decisions*, 7 J. Risk & Uncertainty 35, 46–48 (1993); Zamir, Lewinsohn-Zamir & Ritov, *supra* note 47. On these studies, see *infra* pp. 250–51 and 183, respectively.

52. *See, e.g.*, Schwartz, *supra* note 18.

53. *See supra* pp. 19–21, 141–45.

54. *See generally* Gregory Mitchell, *Alternative Behavioral Law and Economics*, *in* The Oxford Handbook of Behavioral Economics and the Law, *supra* note 24, at 167; Thomas S. Ulen, *The Importance of Behavioral Law*, *in* The Oxford Handbook of Behavioral Economics and the Law, *supra* note 24, at 93, 110–20.

Even before crossing disciplinary lines, the psychological studies that form the basis of BLE are not free of critique. This includes concerns about the external (or ecological) validity of laboratory, vignette-based experiments,[55] and the overly bleak portrayal of human decision-making as systematically irrational.[56] Fortunately, a growing body of observational and field-experimental studies gradually mitigates the former concern,[57] and a more nuanced description of the relationships between models of rationality and actual decision-making addresses the latter.[58]

Another difficulty is that, notwithstanding the immense progress made in behavioral studies, there are still serious gaps in what we know about human judgment and decision-making—notably with regard to differences between cultures, and between individuals within any given culture.[59] Indeed, trading the blanket assumption of people's economic rationality with a sweeping assumption that people's judgments and decisions invariably and similarly deviate from economic rationality is unacceptable, as it runs counter to the empirical data about individual and cultural differences.[60] Fortunately, the allegation that BLE is generally guilty of this "sin" is overstated.[61] Nonetheless, recognizing people's cognitive and behavioral heterogeneity poses great challenges for both empirical studies and legal policymaking.[62]

To be sure, there are considerable gaps in what we know about people's judgments and choices, and these gaps are especially large in newer areas of study, such as behavioral ethics.[63] However, new studies are filling these gaps and gradually advancing our knowledge. Experimental and observational *legal* studies do so with regard to issues that are of interest to the law. In general, social and cognitive psychology, and other sub-disciplines underpinning BLE (such as experimental economics and experimental philosophy), are dynamic fields whose common wisdom is continuously evolving. Whereas opponents of BE and BLE tend to overstate these difficulties, proponents must not underestimate them. Rather, we should all be aware of the sound empirical basis of some behavioral phenomena, in and outside the laboratory, as well as of the incompleteness and tentative nature of other

55. *See, e.g.*, Gregory Mitchell, *Taking Behavioralism Too Seriously?: The Unwarranted Pessimism of the New Behavioral Analysis of Law*, 43 Wm. & Mary L. Rev. 1907 (2002); *supra* p. 25.

56. *See supra* p. 26.

57. *See, e.g.*, Colin F. Camerer, *Prospect Theory in the Wild: Evidence from the Field*, *in* Choices, Values, and Frames 288 (Daniel Kahneman & Amos Tversky eds., 2000); Stefano DellaVigna, *Psychology and Economics: Evidence from the Field*, 47 J. Econ. Lit. 315 (2009).

58. *See* Jonathan Baron, *Heuristics and Biases*, *in* The Oxford Handbook of Behavioral Economics and the Law, *supra* note 24, at 3, 12–14.

59. *See supra* pp. 124–27 and 111–14, respectively.

60. Gregory Mitchell, *Why Law and Economics' Perfect Rationality Should Not Be Traded for Behavioral Law and Economics' Equal Incompetence*, 91 Geo. L.J. 67 (2003). *See also* Jeffrey J. Rachlinski, *Heuristics, Biases, and Philosophy*, 43 Tulsa L. Rev. 865, 870–75 (2008).

61. Robert A. Prentice, *Chicago Man, K-T Man, and the Future of Behavioral Law and Economics*, 56 Vanderbilt L. Rev. 1663, 1722–65 (2003).

62. Korobkin, *supra* note 20, at 1668–73.

63. *See supra* pp. 72–76; *infra* pp. 455–61.

findings—and proceed accordingly. Regrettably, however, a host of cognitive phenomena, such as motivated reasoning and the confirmation bias, might distort scholars' assessment of the achievements and limitations of behavioral studies in either direction (and mere awareness of the existence of biases does not necessarily neutralize them).[64]

Once behavioral insights are integrated into economic analysis, including economic analysis of law, the challenges facing behavioral studies per se are complemented by those created by such integration. Crossing disciplinary borders is often tricky, since academic disciplines differ in their tacit assumptions, paradigms, vocabulary, and even ideological inclinations.[65] In the present context, this problem is exacerbated if one uses behavioral insights to enrich economic analysis of law (rather than legal analysis per se), since there are considerable differences between law, economics, and psychology. Given the high costs of gaining true expertise in more than one discipline, interdisciplinary work thus runs the risk of misunderstandings and superficiality. Rather than reflecting "a nuanced view of the social science literature," legal academics might "rely on the sound bite version of social science studies and fail[ed] to return to the original sources."[66] Obviously, cross-disciplinarity is no license for superficiality. Just as scholars are expected to be mindful of the nuances and complexity of their own discipline when referring to its state-of-the-art research, so, too, they should do when drawing on the dynamic research of other disciplines.

One unique aspect of the integration of behavioral insights with traditional economic analysis (including economic analysis of law) concerns the gulf between the simplicity, generality, and elegance of rational choice theory, and the complexity, context-dependence, and messiness of empirical behavioral studies that do not lend themselves to a simple, unified theory.[67] Indeed, while the deviations of people's choices from the models of rational choice theory are not erratic but rather systematic and predictable, they do vary from one person to another, and across contexts and cultures. In fact, one of the insights of behavioral studies is that people's judgments and decisions are context-dependent. There are complex interactions between various heuristics and biases, the social and organizational environment, and demographic variables. Arguably, these intricacies render the construction of models unmanageable, or at least overly costly.

One response to this critique is to turn it on its head: "psychological theories of intuitive thinking cannot match the elegance and precision of formal normative models of belief and choice, but this is just another way of saying that rational models are psychologically

64. *See supra* pp. 58–61, 134–35.

65. To use a trivial but telling example, the term "paradigm" used in the text has very different meanings in behavioral sciences (where it denotes an experimental setup defined by certain standards) and in other disciplines, including law (where it denotes a set of thought patterns, including theories, research methods, common assumptions, and conventions regarding what constitutes a legitimate contribution to the field).

66. Max Minzner, *Detecting Lies Using Demeanor, Bias, and Context*, 29 Cardozo L. Rev. 2557, 2558 (2008) (alluding to studies of the value of demeanor evidence; *see also infra* pp. 572–74).

67. *See, e.g.*, Posner, *supra* note 18, at 1552, 1558–61 (characterizing BE as "antitheoretical"); Ulen, *supra* note 54, at 111–12.

unrealistic."[68] Another response is to point out that considerable progress has already been made in theorizing about human judgment and decision-making. This includes the development of dual-process theories of judgment and decision-making, as well as theories of how the heuristics used by System 1 operate.[69]

Moreover, when moving from the world of abstract models to the real world—and legal policymaking *is* about the real world—sticking to unrealistic assumptions is not a viable option. As Kahneman has put it, "life is more complex for behavioral economists than for true believers in human rationality."[70] Without denying the trade-off between theoretical elegance and real-world complexity, jurists and legal policymakers may sensibly strike a balance that places more weight on the latter, compared to, say, mathematical economists or non-experimental game-theoreticians.

That said, a word of caution with respect to the theoretical strand of BLE scholarship is in order. The complexity of BE can potentially provide a great degree of freedom, thus allowing legal scholars to promote policies by adding the allure of science to their claims. While one scholar might stress the *salience* of a given phenomenon and argue that people overestimate its occurrence, another might argue that people are *overly optimistic*, and consequently underestimate the probability of the same phenomenon.[71] Note that this difference of opinion cannot be resolved by fine-tuning the model, as the two assumptions might lead to opposite policy prescriptions.[72] In the long run, the growth of empirical BLE is expected to constrain legal scholars' ability to freely make conjectures based on BE arguments. Hopefully, the shifting of publications to emerging peer-reviewed avenues will further restrict scholars in the field.

A final, noteworthy observation on the lack-of-a-unified-theory critique is that BE, BLE, and non-economic behavioral analyses of law all ordinarily employ behavioral insights as correctives for economic and other perspectives on legal and policy issues, rather than as substitutes for them—thus removing much of the sting from the critique. Even prominent proponents of BE and BLE do not call for abandoning the tools of traditional economic analysis, but rather for enriching and improving them by adopting more accurate assumptions about human behavior.[73] Similarly, even harsh critics of BE

68. Daniel Kahneman, *Maps of Bounded Rationality: Psychology for Behavioral Economists*, 93 Am. Econ. Rev. 1449, 1449 (2003). *See also* Richard H. Thaler, The Winner's Curse: Paradoxes and Anomalies of Economic Life 198 (1992) ("Would you rather be elegant and precisely wrong, or messy and vaguely right?").

69. *See supra* pp. 21–25.

70. Daniel Kahneman, Thinking, Fast and Slow 412 (2011).

71. *Compare* Jolls, Sunstein & Thaler, *supra* note 15, at 1525 (discussing people's estimation of the probability of tort liability and noting that "in a case in which the threat of being found liable is highly salient, individuals may tend to *overestimate* the likelihood of being sanctioned"), *with* Christine Jolls, *Behavioral Economic Analysis of Redistributive Legal Rules*, 51 Vand. L. Rev. 1653, 1663 (1998) (examining the same question while emphasizing excessive optimism and concluding that "[i]t is difficult to come up with examples of events giving rise to individual liability the probability of which is likely to be overestimated rather than (as suggested above) underestimated.")

72. Doron Teichman, *The Optimism Bias of the Behavioral Analysis of Criminal Law*, 2011 U. Ill. L. Rev 1697, 1704.

73. *See, e.g.*, Daniel Kahneman, *A Psychological Perspective on Economics*, 93 Am. Econ. Rev. 162, 165–66 (2003); Jolls, Sunstein & Thaler, *supra* note 15, at 1474, 1545.

do not object to a careful use of behavioral insights as correctives and complements to standard economic analysis.[74] Scholars and policymakers alike should concede the limitations of our understanding of human behavior, and proceed cautiously with these limitations in mind. Abstract economic models that assume perfect rationality successfully clarify important aspects of law-related issues, and prompt a rethinking of old truths. However, in addition to models that assume economic rationality, it is useful to construct models that relax this assumption, and actual policymaking cannot rest on unrealistic assumptions.

As is often the case in scholarly debates, opponents of BE and BLE not only question the validity of the behavioral claims, but concomitantly maintain that traditional economics has long accommodated them. Thus, it is argued that much of what BE (or some version of it) treats as deviations from rationality are merely special preferences that some people have, and are therefore perfectly compatible with conventional economic analysis. For example, a person who chooses surface transportation due to his or her fear of flying may be described as irrational—given that surface transportation is actually more dangerous—but conventional economics may treat this simply as a given preference.[75] While this defense is often sensible, it also runs the risk of rendering the notion of preferences tautological: if any choice a person makes is, by definition, a reflection of his or her idiosyncratic preferences, then predictions become virtually irrefutable.[76] By the same token, overexpansion of the notion of *information problems,* to cover instances of imprudent decisions that people make even when they possess all the necessary information, hardly contributes to clarity of thought.

More importantly, neither the we-knew-it-all-along argument, nor the claim that behavioral insights can be integrated into conventional models, threaten the behavioral project. If economists knew that people are not rational maximizers of their utility even prior to the emergence of behavioral economics (which to some extent they surely did)—so be it; and as long as behavioral insights are integrated into economic models to capture human behavior more accurately, the choice of modeling techniques is mainly a matter of methodological convenience.[77] To take another example, it has been suggested that issues of myopia and bounded willpower (and even addictive behavior) need not be seen as incompatible with rational choice theory, but rather can be accommodated within the rational choice framework by treating people as comprising different selves.[78] Again, as long

74. *See, e.g.,* David K. Levine, Is Behavioral Economics Doomed? The Ordinary versus the Extraordinary (2012).

75. Posner, *supra* note 18, at 1554. Similarly, while voting may be regarded as irrational given the infinitesimal chance that one's vote may affect election outcomes, it may also be taken as a given preference (*id.* at 1554–55).

76. Korobin & Ulen, *supra* note 15 at 1061–62.

77. On the prospect of incorporating behavioral insights into economic modeling, see Chetty, *supra* note 26.

78. Matthew Rabin, *Psychology and Economics,* 36 J. Econ. Literature 11, 39–40 (1998); Posner, *supra* note 18, at 1555–57. On myopia and bounded willpower, see generally *supra* pp. 88–93.

as economic analysis does not close its eyes to these documented phenomena, such analysis is compatible with BE and BLE.

Much of the critique leveled at the behavioral turn in economics and economic analysis of law—its overreliance on lab experiments, lack of a unified theory, incompleteness, complexity, etc.—is driven by the objection to the potential normative implications of BE and BLE. As elaborated in the next chapter, behavioral findings are often relied upon to advocate greater governmental interventions both in and outside the market (whether to protect people from exploitation by others, or from their own fallibility), and the use of behaviorally informed regulation (so-called *nudges*).[79] In fact, some of the methodical and methodological debates surrounding BE and BLE appear to be a thin disguise for normative and ideological controversies. To promote clarity of thought, we recommend distinguishing empirical and methodological issues from normative ones (while bearing in mind their important interrelationships). Indeed, no normative conclusion necessarily follows on from empirical findings—and sometimes behavioral insights lend support to both sides of normative and policy debates.[80] Proponents of BLE should be careful not to jump from behavioral findings to normative conclusions, and opponents of the alleged normative conclusions of behavioral findings should not close their eyes to empirical findings. The normative issues are discussed in Chapter 4.

On the bright side, integrating insights from economics, psychology, and law can help in decoupling methodology from ideology. The conceptual and methodological divides between different cross-disciplinary approaches to law often go hand in hand with ideological inclinations: scholars who share a particular cross-disciplinary perspective also tend to share the same normative worldview. Specifically, economic analysis of law is often associated with the right-wing economic philosophy of the "Chicago School."[81] Using behavioral studies to question the assumptions of rational choice theory can therefore prompt a re-examination of ideological inclinations—first and foremost, the "syllogistic relationship between the goal of welfare maximization and a bias against regulation."[82]

At the end of the day, the integration of behavioral insights into legal and legal-economic analyses faces real challenges. While none of these challenges is insurmountable, they do call for caution and sophistication when producing more and better empirical data, interpreting the data, or drawing on it in legal analyses. As demonstrated in Parts III through V of this book, while BLE has already made substantial impact on many legal

79. *See infra* pp. 162–85.

80. *See, e.g., infra* pp. 226–27, 230–34.

81. Gary Minda, *The Jurisprudential Movements of the 1980s*, 50 Ohio St. L.J. 599, 602 (1989).

82. Korobkin, *supra* note 20, at 1658. *See also infra* pp. 158–61. Alternatively, economists committed to libertarian values may react to the behavioral findings by reformulating the basis of normative economic analysis, putting less weight on welfare and more on autonomy. *See* Péter Cserne, *Behavioural Law and Economics as Litmus Test*, 7 Œconomia—Hist., Methodology, Phil. 305 (2017).

fields, the extent of this impact varies considerably from one field to another, and in some fields most of the work has yet to be done. Another necessary extension is to apply behavioral insights to non-U.S. legal norms and institutions, since much of the current literature is overly U.S.-centered.

E. Conclusion

Behavioral studies have had a great impact on economics, economic analysis of law, and legal theory—and this impact is constantly growing. A welcome development in legal research in recent years has been the emergence of empirical research in law, which has further bolstered BLE. As is often the case with cross-disciplinary endeavors—especially those that seek to integrate insights from three disciplines—BLE faces many challenges. But none of these challenges is insurmountable, and the enormous contributions that BLE has already made to legal theory and policymaking demonstrate that the effort is worthwhile.

4

Normative Implications

A. Introduction

The previous chapters introduced the economic background and psychological foundations of behavioral law and economics, as well as an overview of this cross-disciplinary perspective. The present chapter discusses the normative implications of the psychological findings. When we turn from the descriptive to the normative, the complexity of the psychological phenomena is compounded by the wide range of current normative theories. Accordingly, instead of trying to cover all interactions between cognitive psychology, normative theories, and the law, this chapter focuses on fundamental issues that cut across different fields. Normative implications of specific cognitive phenomena will be examined in the chapters devoted to particular legal fields.

Our discussion does not assume that one can directly derive "ought" from "is."[1] Rather, the claim is that the psychological findings can contribute to legal policymaking in at least three ways. First, human psychology is relevant to the construction of any normative theory. Basic elements of any normative theory—including its underlying conception of human well-being and its focal point, such as acts or rules—are grounded in assumptions about human psychology. Second, once a normative theory is formulated, legal policymakers who aim at a particular goal—be it the promotion of economic equality or deterrence of antisocial behavior—face pragmatic choices between different means to achieving that goal. Positive theories of human psychology may prove essential to making these choices.[2] Finally, legal policymakers should take into account the heuristics and biases of those implementing the law, such as judges, juries, and administrators. Ideally, policymakers should be aware of their own heuristics and biases, and try to cope with them—as should scholars who evaluate the law and legal institutions.

1. *See generally* Adrian Vermeule, *Connecting Positive and Normative Legal Theory*, 10 U. Pa. J. Const. L. 387 (2008).

2. *Id.* at 390–91.

Section B first outlines the contribution of happiness studies and heuristics-and-biases research to theories of human welfare. It then examines the impact of the latter research on the choice of a normative theory's focal point (acts, rules, etc.). Section C focuses on the normative significance of the prevailing moral judgments, which have been systematically studied by moral psychologists. It argues that the law should take these judgments into account, both for principled reasons (democratic values) and for instrumental ones (assuring the law's acceptability and effectiveness). Section D turns from ethics and legal theory to more pragmatic issues of legal policymaking. It first discusses two major implications of behavioral studies for setting the goals of legal norms: preventing the exploitation of people's cognitive biases by other people and protecting people from their own fallibility. Turning from goals to means, Section D then goes on to highlight the contribution of behavioral studies to the design of disclosure duties and behaviorally informed regulation.

B. Behavioral Findings and Normative Theories

Normative legal analysis draws on normative ethics. Although the landscape of normative ethics theories is complex, there is one factor that virtually all normative theories view as important in judging the morality of any act, rule, or anything else: its outcomes.[3] Moreover, although normative theories differ over the scope of outcomes that they deem relevant, there is one type of outcomes that all theories take into account—namely the impact of an act, a rule, or anything else on human welfare. As explained in Chapter 1, welfare economics views human welfare as the only factor that ultimately determines the morality of any act or rule.[4]

While all normative theories acknowledge the importance of human welfare, they adopt different conceptions of it. Schematically, there are three major categories of theories of human welfare: (1) hedonistic, mental-state theories; (2) preference-based theories; and (3) objective-list theories.[5] According to mental-state theories, human welfare is determined by the presence of pleasure and the absence of pain. Preference-based theories maintain that people's welfare is enhanced to the extent that their desires are fulfilled. According to actual-preferences theories, one's welfare is enhanced to the extent that one's actual preferences are satisfied. Ideal-preference theories, in contrast, hold that a person's welfare is enhanced to the extent that her ideal preferences are fulfilled. Ideal preferences are those she would have were she to calmly and rationally consider any issue, taking into account all relevant information, ignoring irrelevant information, and so forth. Finally, objective-list theories posit that human welfare consists of having certain things, such as good health, autonomy, and accomplishment. While the objective list plausibly includes freedom (thus valuing people's

3. *See, e.g.*, John Rawls, A Theory of Justice 26 (rev. ed. 1999) ("deontological theories are defined as non-teleological ones, not as views that characterize the rightness of institutions and acts independently from their consequences. All ethical doctrines worth our attention take consequences into account in judging rightness.").

4. *See supra* pp. 13–14.

5. *See supra* pp. 14–15.

ability to fulfill their desires) and happiness (thus appreciating positive mental states), neither preference satisfaction nor mental states serve as the ultimate measure of human welfare under objective theories.

The choice of a theory of human welfare carries significant implications for legal policymaking. Due to the prominence of standard economic analysis in legal theory in recent decades, much of the legal analysis has implicitly or explicitly assumed that human welfare consists of the satisfaction of (actual) preferences. However, other theories of human welfare may be substantively superior, and may provide better explanations and justifications for existing or proposed legal norms. For example, adherence to an actual-preferences theory of well-being presumably militates against legal paternalism—whereas hedonistic, ideal-preferences, and objective-list theories are more receptive to the paternalistic policies that pervade the law.[6] Less obviously, when it comes to redistributive legal policies, actual-preferences theories are likely to endorse redistribution of money—which recipients can spend as they wish—whereas objective-list and ideal-preferences theories are more likely to endorse redistribution in kind, that is, giving people things that will enhance their well-being objectively defined, such as decent dwellings and respect.[7]

One contribution of psychological studies to these debates comes from research on subjective feelings. Some studies have demonstrated that people maintain a relatively stable level of happiness despite (some types of) major positive or negative events (so-called *hedonic adaptation*).[8] Other studies have shown that people judge an experience based largely on how it was at its peak and at its end (the *peak-end effect*), rather than on the aggregate of every moment of the experience—thus pointing to a gap between people's actual experience and how they assess it in retrospect.[9] Mental-state theories of well-being are likely to emphasize the actual experience, which serves as the ultimate measure of well-being. In contrast, preference-satisfaction theories might give more weight to people's ex-ante expectation about a given experience, and their ex-post assessment of it, as these expectation or assessment are likely to shape their preferences. In any event, since people usually prefer positive mental states over negative ones, and since positive mental states (and the avoidance of negative ones) are also part of any plausible objective list, happiness studies are relevant to all normative theories.

In the legal sphere, the findings of these studies are especially relevant whenever the law seeks to compensate people for their suffering, or to punish wrongdoers (for purposes of deterrence or desert), etc.[10] However, whereas under mental-state theories these findings

6. Eyal Zamir, *The Efficiency of Paternalism*, 84 Va. L. Rev. 229, 237–40 (1998).

7. *See* Daphna Lewinsohn-Zamir, *The Objectivity of Well-Being and the Objectives of Property Law*, 78 N.Y.U. L. Rev. 1669 (2003); *infra* pp. 488–89.

8. *See generally infra* pp. 343–48, 451–54.

9. *See infra* pp. 453–54.

10. *See generally* John Bronsteen, Christopher Buccafusco & Jonathan S. Masur, Happiness and the Law (2015). *See also infra* pp. 343–48, 451–54, 504.

are decisive, they count for much less under preference-based or objective-list theories of human welfare.

Another contribution to the debate over human welfare comes from studies of judgment and decision-making that attest to the systematic errors that people make when perceiving and processing information, forming judgments, and making choices. Regardless of whether such errors are regrettable imperfections or ecologically adaptive traits, their existence is a major argument against treating the fulfillment of people's actual preferences as the ultimate measure of human welfare.[11] It is not only external observers who often judge people's choices as self-harming—sometimes those people themselves realize, ex post, that their predictions about the impact of certain choices on their well-being had been wrong. To be sure, there may be compelling arguments against depriving people of the freedom to make their own decisions, even if those decisions are unlikely to promote their welfare, ideally or objectively defined. However, such arguments are very different from the assertion that fulfilling people's actual desires ipso facto enhances their welfare. In fact, even ardent advocates of a preference-based, welfarist normative theory, such as Louis Kaplow and Steven Shavell, concede that "if individuals do not understand how situations affect their well-being," the authors' analysis "may be applied to individuals' actual well-being—what they would prefer if they correctly understood how they would be affected—rather than to individuals' well-being as reflected in their mistaken preferences."[12]

Another context in which behavioral studies might inform normative theories is the choice of the appropriate focal point of analysis: actions, rules, motivations, virtues, etc.[13] Thus, for example, act-consequentialism posits that agents should always strive to produce the best outcomes. In contrast, rule-consequentialism holds that agents should abide by the set of rules the compliance with which would produce the best outcomes, even if, on occasion, following the rules would result in suboptimal outcomes.[14] Once again, we cannot delve here into the philosophical debate about focal points. However, it is worth noting that a key argument for preferring rules over acts as the relevant focal point is rooted in the concern that people are prone to making errors when judging the desirability of each and every option available to them. Requiring people to follow simpler, general rules may produce better overall outcomes.[15]

11. *See, e.g.*, JAMES GRIFFIN, WELL-BEING: ITS MEANING, MEASUREMENT AND MORAL IMPORTANCE 10 (1986); Lewinsohn-Zamir, *supra* note 7, at 1677–80; Zamir, *supra* note 6, at 238, 267–71; Péter Cserne, *Behavioural Law and Economics as Litmus Test*, 7 ŒCONOMIA—HIST., METHODOLOGY, PHIL. 305 (2017).

12. LOUIS KAPLOW & STEVEN SHAVELL, FAIRNESS VERSUS WELFARE 23 (2002). *See also id.* at 410–13; Lewinsohn-Zamir, *supra* note 7, at 1690–700.

13. *See generally* MORALITY, RULES, AND CONSEQUENCES: A CRITICAL READER (Brad Hooker et al. eds., 2000); Shelly Kagan, *The Structure of Normative Ethics*, 6 PHIL. PERSP. 223, 236–42 (1992); SHELLY KAGAN, NORMATIVE ETHICS 204–39 (1998).

14. *See generally* Brad Hooker, *Rule Consequentialism*, *in* STANFORD ENCYCLOPEDIA OF PHILOSOPHY (2003, updated 2015), *available at*: http://plato.stanford.edu/entries/consequentialism-rule.

15. Those simpler rules (such as "Do not kill") may well correspond with commonsense (that is, moderate deontological) morality. Thus, even if one does not accept that promoting good outcomes should be subject to moral constraints, one may nevertheless support the imposition of such constraints instrumentally, to guard against

To use an example from the legal sphere: if all people were perfect decision-makers, we might adopt the rule that drivers must not cross at a red light—unless, all things considered, the total benefits of such crossing outweigh the costs. However, realizing that drivers are prone to misjudging the speed and distance of other objects, to miscalculate probabilities due to the availability and other heuristics, and to process information in a self-serving manner (to mention just a few of the relevant psychological phenomena), adopting an absolute prohibition on crossing a red light seems preferable. Although such prohibition sometimes results in a waste of time and additional air pollution, these costs are worth bearing given the risks of entrusting drivers with the task of conducting a cost-benefit analysis whenever they approach a road junction.

C. Prevailing Moral Judgments and the Law

In the past few decades, and especially in recent years, a host of experimental studies have examined people's judgments in various moral dilemmas. As detailed in Chapter 2, many of these studies have used various versions of the trolley problem to elicit people's judgments about the permissibility of actively or intentionally harming some people to save others.[16] Experimental studies have also examined people's normative judgments of various legal issues, such as whether the severity of criminal sanctions should depend on the probability of detection and apprehension;[17] the effect of defendants' engagement in cost-benefit analysis of safety measures on the award of punitive damages;[18] the significance of social roles and personal relationships in determining the morality of pre-contractual active deception and non-disclosure;[19] the moral dimension of breach of contract under varying circumstances, including the breacher's motivation;[20] the fairness of contingent fee arrangements between lawyers and their clients;[21] and the imposition of civil and criminal liability based on naked statistical evidence, or circumstantial evidence more generally.[22]

human fallibility in conducting complex cost-benefit analyses. *See also* Eyal Zamir & Barak Medina, Law, Economics, and Morality 24–27 (2010). On consequentialism and deontology, see generally *supra* pp. 13, 94–97; *infra* pp. 194–95.

16. *See supra* pp. 97–101.

17. *See, e.g.*, Kevin M. Carlsmith et al., *Why Do We Punish? Deterrence and Just Deserts as Motives for Punishment*, 83 J. Personality & Soc. Psychol. 284 (2002); *infra* pp. 436–37.

18. *See, e.g.*, W. Kip Viscusi, *Corporate Risk Analysis: A Reckless Act?*, 52 Stan. L. Rev. 547 (2000); *infra* pp. 555–56.

19. Jonathan Haidt & Jonathan Baron, *Social Roles and the Moral Judgement of Acts and Omissions*, 26 Eur. J. Soc. Psychol. 201 (1996).

20. Tess Wilkinson-Ryan & Jonathan Baron, *Moral Judgment and Moral Heuristics in Breach of Contract*, 6 J. Empirical Legal Stud. 405 (2009); *infra* pp. 272–73.

21. Eyal Zamir & Ilana Ritov, *Notions of Fairness and Contingent Fees*, 74 Law & Contemp. Probs. 1 (2011); *infra* p. 512.

22. *See, e.g.*, Gary L. Wells, *Naked Statistical Evidence of Liability: Is Subjective Probability Enough?*, 62 J. Personality & Soc. Psychol. 739 (1992); Eyal Zamir, Ilana Ritov & Doron Teichman, *Seeing Is Believing: The Anti-Inference Bias*, 89 Ind. L.J. 195 (2014); *infra* pp. 576–79, 582–85.

The finding that a majority, or even a great majority, of respondents—whether laypersons or experts—hold certain normative judgments does not establish that those judgments are sound. Nonetheless, such judgments carry normative implications for the law.

In a democracy, where popular will is the source of political power and legitimacy, the law should generally correlate with prevailing moral convictions. As Harold Berman has pointed out: "Just as the English common law was supposed to reflect the common sense of the English people, so the German *jus commune* was supposed to reflect the common consciousness of the German nation as it developed."[23] Such correlation is essential according to natural law theories, which maintain that law is intimately connected with morality, and that an immoral law is not valid.[24] It is also consistent with legal positivism. While rejecting the notion that the validity of law depends on its merits, legal positivists do not deny the connection between law and morality. Thus, for example, H.L.A. Hart readily conceded that "[t]he law of every modern state shows at a thousand points the influence of both the accepted social morality and wider moral ideals."[25]

Legal policymakers should take prevailing normative judgments into account not only for principled reasons, but for pragmatic ones, as well. A significant body of work has demonstrated the importance of the perceived fairness of the criminal justice system for its effectiveness.[26] More recently, scholars have extended this argument to suggest that perceived fairness might play a key role in fostering cooperation in civil contexts, as well.[27] To achieve legitimacy and compliance, legal rules should be consistent with prevailing moral intuitions.

D. Behaviorally Informed Lawmaking

1. General

This section turns from ethics and legal theory to legal policymaking. It discusses two basic questions: what goals the law should seek to achieve, and what means it should use to achieve its goals. Rather than trying to provide comprehensive answers to these momentous questions, we will only highlight the key contributions of behavioral insights to these issues.

23. Harold J. Berman, *Toward an Integrative Jurisprudence: Politics, Morality, History*, 76 Cal. L. Rev. 779, 791 (1988). *See also* Robert A. Prentice & Jonathan J. Koehler, *A Normality Bias in Legal Decision Making*, 88 Cornell L. Rev. 583, 592. (2003).

24. *See, e.g.*, David O. Brink, *Legal Positivism and Natural Law Reconsidered*, 68 Monist 364, 365 (1985).

25. H.L.A. Hart, The Concept of Law 203–04 (2d ed. 1994). *See also* John Gardner, *Legal Positivism: 5½ Myths*, 46 Am. J. Juris. 199, 222–23 (2001); Neil MacCormick, *Natural Law and the Separation of Law and Morals*, *in* Natural Law Theory: Contemporary Essays 105, 107 (Robert P. George ed., 1992).

26. *See, e.g.*, Paul H. Robinson & John M. Darley, *The Utility of Desert*, 91 Nw. U. L. Rev. 453, 454 (1997); *infra* pp. 436–43.

27. Yuval Feldman & Doron Teichman, *Are All Contractual Obligations Created Equal?*, 100 Geo. L.J. 5, 36 (2011) (noting the connection between perceived fairness and contractual compliance). This argument is tied to the vast literature on the influence of procedural justice on behavior at the workplace. For a review see Jason A. *Colquitt, Justice at the Millennium: A Meta-analytic Review of 25 Years of Organizational Justice Research*, 86 J. App. Psychol. 425 (2001).

Behavioral insights are relevant to legal policymaking in two primary ways. First, inasmuch as cognitive biases hinder people from achieving their goals, the law can try to help people to overcome such biases, or to negate their effect. At the very least, it should seek to minimize the exploitation of such biases by others. Second, whatever the reason for people's suboptimal conduct—be it traditional market failures, behavioral market failures, or anything else—psychological insights can inform the law on how to improve people's choices and behavior. The following subsections take up these two issues in turn. A third way in which cognitive psychology may contribute to legal policymaking is by exposing how legal decision-makers' own heuristics and biases affect lawmaking. We will touch upon this issue here, and examine it more fully in the chapters on public law and judicial decision-making.[28]

2. Ends

(a) Introduction

In a perfectly competitive market, perfectly rational people enhance their own well-being, and the rules of supply and demand ensure that overall social utility is maximized when people pursue their own interests. In such an environment, the legal system might be content with merely defining and protecting property rights, and enforcing freely made transactions. In the real world, however, public goods are often supplied by non-market mechanisms; market failures such as monopolies, externalities, and information problems obstruct the maximization of overall social welfare; and bounded rationality hinders the enhancement of people's own welfare. In addition to maximizing overall social welfare and (more controversially) protecting people from their own fallibility, the law may also strive to promote or protect various other values—ranging from human dignity, equality, and fairness, to the preservation of ecosystems and nonhuman species.

While behavioral insights are potentially relevant to any legal issue, there are two contexts where they appear to be particularly important in setting the law's goals: preventing the exploitation of people's cognitive biases by others, and protecting people from their own fallibility.[29]

(b) Preventing Exploitation

Knowingly or unknowingly, we all sometimes exploit other people's cognitive biases to achieve our goals: we present the option that we want others to choose as the default, or describe it as a compromise between two extreme options; we mention dramatic events to persuade people to take certain precautions, and so forth. Usually, the stakes in such cases are not high enough to justify legal intervention, or even seriously consider it. However, when repeat players systematically manipulate people's biases—as in the case of dubious

28. *See infra* pp. 393–405, 409–31, and 525–65, respectively.

29. Unless one defines paternalism very narrowly, there is considerable overlap between anti-exploitative and paternalistic legal norms, as often one's cognitive limitations are exploited by others. For our purpose, however, it is not necessary to delineate the exact border between the two types of norms.

marketing techniques used by firms—regulation may be warranted on efficiency, fairness, or distributive grounds.

Marketers take advantage of customers' heuristics and biases in innumerable ways, including odd pricing (for example, $99.99); framing prices as involving discounts (e.g., for paying in cash) rather than surcharges (e.g., for buying on credit); giving customers gifts (which are framed separately) instead of small price reductions; artificially limiting the availability of products to make them appear more attractive; postponing the provision of negative information (such as one-sided contract terms) to the very end of the contracting process, to exploit consumers' escalation of commitment; drawing up long-term contracts (for instance, for gym membership) that capitalize on people's overoptimism and myopia; employing automatic renewal arrangements that exploit people's omission bias; and using exceedingly complex pricing formulas that customers fail to understand.[30]

To be sure, not all marketing (or other) techniques that take advantage of people's heuristics and biases merit legal regulation. For example, framing of prices as involving discounts rather than surcharges does not seem to warrant legal intervention (or at least not obviously so). To use a more specific example, there is evidence that contingent-fee arrangements—under which the attorney's fee is contingent upon the success of the claim, calculated as a percentage of the amount recovered, and paid on recovery—result in considerably higher average fees than fixed or hourly fees.[31] Inasmuch as it can be shown that clients pay higher fees under contingent-fee arrangements due to asymmetric information or other market failures, there may be grounds for regulating such contracts. However, there is evidence that one major reason for clients' willingness to pay higher expected fees under such arrangements is that contingent fees protect clients from the risk of losing their claim and still having to pay the fee. Unlike fixed or hourly fees, contingent fees turn a mixed gamble—in which clients may either gain or lose—into a pure positive one, in which they may either gain or break even, which is a very attractive feature to loss-averse clients.[32] The fact that attorneys charge higher expected fees by catering to clients' loss aversion (a phenomenon that is not irrational per se)[33] does not appear to be illegitimate advantage-taking. Hence, it does not necessitate regulation.

Drawing the lines between legitimate and illegitimate advantage-takings, and between illegitimate advantage-takings that merit regulation and those that do not, requires close attention to the circumstances of the particular context and the relevant liberty, efficiency, redistribution, fairness, and institutional considerations. Instead of tackling such a daunting undertaking here, let us give a couple of examples of arguably sensible, behaviorally-based

30. On these and other techniques, see *infra* pp. 281–306.

31. *See, e.g.*, Herbert M. Kritzer, *Seven Dogged Myths concerning Contingency Fees*, 80 Wash. U. L.Q. 739, 761–72 (2002).

32. Eyal Zamir & Ilana Ritov, *Revisiting the Debate over Attorneys' Contingent Fees: A Behavioral Analysis*, 39 J. Legal Stud. 245 (2010); *infra* pp. 510–12.

33. Eyal Zamir, Law, Psychology, and Morality: The Role of Loss Aversion 205–07 (2015).

regulation.[34] One example is from the EU Directive on Unfair Commercial Practices, which characterizes as unfair and misleading the practice of misstating that a product will only be available for a very limited time, in order to elicit an immediate decision and deprive consumers of sufficient opportunity or time to make an informed choice.[35] This rule aims to prevent unfair exploitation of people's loss aversion and stressful decision-making. The other example is a 2014 amendment to the Israeli Consumer Protection Law, 1981, which provides customers with an inalienable right to unilaterally cancel gym memberships.[36] This rule aims to prevent the exploitation of people who exhibit overoptimism about their expected gym attendance, and then fail to meet their expectations due to lack of self-discipline.[37]

While the design of anti-exploitation rules requires careful examination of the social reality and pertinent policy considerations in each particular context, this much is clear: once it is understood that deviations from perfect rationality are prevalent and systematic, considerably more regulation against exploitation of such deviations is called for, than under the assumption that all people are rational maximizers.

(c) Legal Paternalism

Paternalism is an intervention in a person's freedom aimed at furthering his or her own good. Paternalistic interventions are prevalent in both private and public life, including the law. Examples of legal paternalism include restrictions on the legal capacity of minors and the mentally disabled; the compelled use of various safety measures while driving or working in high-risk environments; banning of the use of certain drugs; forbidding of swimming in the absence of a lifeguard; the exclusion of victim consent as a defense in certain criminal offenses; the inalienability of certain basic liberties; compulsory social security, pension arrangements, and health insurance; compulsory elementary education; "sin taxes" on tobacco and other unhealthy products; helping the poor by providing them with food stamps rather than cash; cooling-off periods in door-to-door sales; and the limited enforceability of forfeiture clauses and liquidated damages.

Notwithstanding its prevalence, legal paternalism is hotly debated.[38] The central justification for paternalism is welfarist: the paternalistic intervention aims to promote the well-being of the person whose freedom is being curtailed. The chief objection to paternalism is that it infringes upon people's autonomy and freedom. This conflict between

34. For additional examples, see *infra* pp. 246–47, 252, 256–58, 262, 273–78, 281–324, 330–36, 351–54, 370–83, 408–09, 490–92.

35. Item 7 of Annex I of Directive 2005/29/EC of 11 May 2005 concerning Unfair Business-to-Consumer Commercial Practices in the Internal Market. *See also infra* pp. 289–90.

36. Consumer Protection Law, 1981, Section 13A1 & Fourth Supplement (Amendment no. 37).

37. *See, e.g.*, Jean-Denis Garona, Alix Massea & Pierre-Carl Michauda, *Health Club Attendance, Expectations and Self-Control*, 119 J. Econ. Behav. & Org. 364 (2015).

38. It is impossible to analyze, or even mention, the full panoply of arguments made in this debate. For recent book-long discussions, including extensive bibliography, see Ricardo Rebonato, Taking Liberties: A Critical Examination of Libertarian Paternalism (2012); Sarah Conly, Against Autonomy: Justifying Coercive Paternalism (2013); Cass R. Sunstein, Why Nudge? The Politics of Libertarian Paternalism (2014).

welfare and self-determination echoes the fundamental conflict between consequentialism and deontology. While deontology prioritizes liberty and autonomy over promotion of the good, consequentialism values freedom only as a component of well-being (or as a means of attaining it). Hence, one might think that deontologists would reject paternalism, while consequentialists would embrace it. In reality, however, numerous attempts have been made to justify paternalism according to deontological theories, whereas many consequentialists—including, so it seems, most economists—strongly object to it.

The consequentialist position regarding paternalism depends on its underlying theory of human welfare. Limiting people's choices may cause displeasure and frustration, and run the risk that the precluded options might actually be superior to those left open to the agent. Nevertheless, if one adopts a mental-state, an objective-list, or an ideal-preferences theory of human well-being, it may well be that limiting a person's options would make her happier in the long run, enhance her objectively defined well-being, and comport with her ideal preferences.[39]

It is more difficult to square paternalism with a consequentialist theory whose underlying theory of well-being is the fulfillment of *actual* preferences. Apparently, if a person's well-being is enhanced to the extent that her actual desires are fulfilled—as standard economic analysis appears to assume—frustrating those desires can never enhance a person's well-being. This conclusion, however, may be unwarranted.[40] First, people have preferences not only regarding different bundles of goods, but also about their own preferences. For example, a person may regularly eat junk food, and at the same time wish that his eating preferences were different.[41] In a typical case of dissonance between first- and second-order preferences, the first-order preferences are conceived by the person as self-injurious. In such cases, fulfilling the second-order preferences by frustrating first-order ones may be efficient.

A second reason why legal paternalism is not incompatible with actual-preferences theory of well-being is that people's preferences are influenced by legal norms. Interventions in people's choices and behavior often result in an adaptation of their preferences to conform with the rules. These people may, in hindsight, be grateful for the initial paternalistic treatment. Thus, to the extent that this is true, there may be no consequentialist reason to give greater weight to ex-ante actual preferences than to ex-post ones.

Finally, even if people's actual preferences are unaffected by legal norms, they do change over time. For example, people may regret their past decisions about pension savings. According to an actual-preferences theory of well-being, the well-being of a person is enhanced to the extent that her actual desires are satisfied over the course of her lifetime. Hence, what matters is not only current desires, but future ones, as well. People are not very good at precisely predicting their future desires (and even if they were, their current preferences need not correspond to the overall balance of their lifetime desires).

39. Zamir, *supra* note 6, at 237–40.

40. *Id.* at 240–46.

41. On procrastination, myopia, and bounded willpower, see *supra* pp. 87–93.

The divergence between present actual preferences and overall balance of lifetime actual preferences leaves room for paternalistic intervention, for example, by compelling people to save for retirement.

For all these reasons, paternalism is not incompatible with a consequentialist theory that is based on an actual-preferences theory of well-being. Under such a theory, the costs and benefits of paternalistic interventions should be carefully considered in any given context. Moreover, it is not at all clear that standard economic analysis itself is founded on an unalloyed actual-preferences theory. Economic analysis assumes that people are rational, and makes policy recommendations accordingly. The more demanding the definition of rationality in a given theory, the closer it comes to an ideal-preferences theory—which, as previously noted, can endorse legal paternalism whenever a person's actual preferences deviate from his or her ideal ones. Being a consequentialist normative theory, welfare economics does not, therefore, rule out paternalism. In fact, welfare economics presumably warrants paternalism whenever the latter's benefits exceed its costs, however slightly.[42]

Apparently, principled anti-paternalism is more compatible with deontological morality, under which maximizing human well-being is subject to constraints—including a constraint against interfering with people's autonomy or freedom. Specifically, there are three possible deontological positions toward paternalism. A deontologist may (1) rule out paternalism under any circumstances; (2) endorse seemingly paternalistic measures whenever it can be shown that they do not, in fact, infringe a deontological constraint; or (3) justify paternalism whenever there is sufficient good (or bad) at stake to override the constraint.

The first position, which reflects absolutist deontology,[43] is internally coherent but leads to extreme, counterintuitive conclusions, which are at odds with prevailing moral judgments that legitimize a great deal of paternalism in both private and public spheres. The second position—justifying certain instances of paternalism on the grounds that, contrary to appearances, they do not infringe deontological constraints—is common in the philosophical literature. Several types of arguments are made in this regard. The primary one is that very often, what appears to be a curtailment of a person's freedom is in fact not so, because the frustrated choice was not actually free (due to ignorance, intoxication, etc.), while the apparent curtailment actually falls in line with the person's tacit, prior, anticipated, subsequent, or hypothetical consent.[44] The third position (which does not preclude the second) reflects *threshold deontology*. It maintains that there is a moral constraint against curtailing people's freedom, but that this constraint may be justifiably infringed if enough net benefit is anticipated as a result. Eyal Zamir and Barak Medina have advocated this last position.[45]

42. Zamir, *supra* note 6, at 246–52; *see also* ZAMIR & MEDINA, *supra* note 15, at 318–32.

43. On the distinction between absolutist and moderate deontology, see KAGAN, *supra* note 13, at 78–84; *supra* pp. 96–97.

44. *See, e.g.*, 3 JOEL FEINBERG, THE MORAL LIMITS OF THE CRIMINAL LAW: HARM TO SELF 12–16, 98–343 (1986); DONALD VANDEVEER, PATERNALISTIC INTERVENTION: THE MORAL BOUNDS OF BENEVOLENCE 45–94 (1986); Donald H. Regan, *Paternalism, Freedom, Identity, and Commitment*, *in* PATERNALISM 113 (Rolf Sartorius, ed., 1983); Dan W. Brock, *Paternalism and Autonomy*, 98 ETHICS 550 (1988).

45. ZAMIR & MEDINA, *supra* note 15, at 335–47.

When considering whether deviations from expected utility theory justify legal paternalism, both welfarist and deontological theories point to the importance of the distinction between thin, cognitive rationality, and thick, motivational rationality.[46] Examples of deviations from cognitive rationality include miscalculating the true costs of a transaction due to its complexity, misjudging probabilities (due to the availability heuristic), and underestimating future costs (due to shortsightedness). Deviations from motivational rationality include non-selfish motivations resulting from altruism and commitment to certain ideals, but also from envy or vengeance. In extreme cases, to save other people's lives or achieve other goals, people might risk their life and limb with their eyes wide open.

From a welfarist perspective, curtailing self-harming choices that are due to deviations from thin rationality is more acceptable, because it usually causes less displeasure and frustration on the part of the person whose liberty is curtailed. From a deontological perspective, interference due to the agent's cognitive errors does not necessarily infringe upon his or her autonomy—or at least less significantly so. It helps people accomplish their own goals, irrespective of their biases and cognitive errors. Conversely, precluding choices based on the agent's "motivational irrationality" is a far more blatant assault on people's autonomy, as it pertains to ends, rather than just means. That said, the very distinction between ends and means (or, for that matter, between cognitive and motivational rationality) is sometimes hazy.[47]

Clearly, the most important contribution of behavioral studies to the issue of legal paternalism lies in the recognition that even in the absence of information problems or other external obstacles to making rational choices, people sometimes fail to maximize their own utility due to various cognitive limitations and biases. The deviations from the suppositions of expected utility theory are not random, but systematic and predictable. These findings certainly do not give policymakers carte blanche to paternalistically curtail people's freedom. Careful examination of the factual circumstances and normative considerations must be made in each given context before people's freedom is restricted for their own good. Behavioral research nevertheless largely refutes the epistemological argument against paternalism—namely that individuals always know best what would make their lives better (or that the risk of mistake on the part of policymakers is so great as to rule out any paternalistic regulation).[48]

In recent years, some anti-paternalists have questioned the validity of empirical studies that substantiate the prevalence of bounded rationality, on the grounds that seemingly mistaken judgments are not in fact mistakes, or that they would disappear with monetary incentives, or that the market would drive out poor judgment.[49] However, these claims

46. *See generally supra* pp. 9–12.

47. Sunstein, *supra* note 38, at 61–71.

48. This argument has famously been made by Mill. *See* John Stuart Mill, On Liberty (1859), reprinted in On Liberty and Other Essays 14, 84–85, 92–93 (Oxford Univ. Press, 1991). For critical responses, see, e.g., Richard J. Arneson, *Mill versus Paternalism*, 90 Ethics 470 (1980); Conly, *supra* note 38.

49. *See, e.g.*, Richard A. Posner, *Rational Choice, Behavioral Economics, and the Law*, 50 Stan. L. Rev. 1551 (1998); Gregory Mitchell, *Why Law and Economics' Perfect Rationality Should Not Be Traded for Behavioral Law and*

run counter to the findings of thousands of empirical and experimental studies, and it is unclear how further motivation or stronger incentives "work the magic" of eliminating deeply rooted cognitive biases.[50] Incentives are helpful when cognitive biases are due primarily to insufficient effort, but considerably less effective—or even counterproductive—in other cases.[51] Other anti-paternalist arguments stress the long-term and indirect adverse effects of paternalism on people's motivation to act deliberately, and on the "development of effective decision-making skills and strategies."[52] However, these arguments ignore the fact that paternalistic interventions can actually promote learning.[53] By having a certain entitlement, people learn to appreciate its true worth and develop a stronger preference for it. Moreover, some decisions are made very infrequently, so in those cases learning through trial and error would be very costly and ineffective.[54] Even decisions that are made on a regular basis, such as signing standard-form contracts, may not yield meaningful feedback about their prudence inasmuch as they entail low-probability risks, which rarely materialize.[55] Other decisions (such as whether to use a seat belt or to take out a mortgage loan) may have devastating consequences, and the outcomes of other decisions (such as how much to save for retirement) only materialize after a very long time. In all such cases, learning from one's mistakes may come too late.

Impediments to learning also include people's overconfidence; the reluctance to admit that one has made a mistake; the tendency to attribute one's success to one's own decisions, and one's failures to external events; and the fact that it is often impossible to know with great certainty what would have happened had one made a different choice.[56] Indeed, numerous studies have shown that cognitive biases are common even among seasoned professionals.[57] Furthermore, it has been shown that learning leads to decidedly greater risk aversion in the domain of gains than in the domain of losses[58]—and yet the latter is the area typically targeted by legal paternalism.

Economics' Equal Incompetence, 91 Geo. L.J. 67 (2002); Steven Winter, A Clearing in the Forest: Law, Life, and Mind 92–96 (2001).

50. Jeffery J. Rachlinski, *The Uncertain Psychological Case for Paternalism*, 97 Nw. U. L. Rev. 1165, 1167–8 (2003).

51. *See supra* pp. 129–34.

52. Jonathan Klick & Gregory Mitchell, *Government Regulation of Irrationality: Moral and Cognitive Hazards*, 90 Minn. L. Rev. 1620, 1626 (2006). For similar arguments, see Mill, *supra* note 48, at 62–82.

53. On various ways in which paternalistic interventions facilitate learning that is unlikely to occur otherwise, see Colin F. Camerer, *Wanting, Liking, and Learning: Neuroscience and Paternalism*, 73 U. Chi. L. Rev. 87, 96–97, 99–102, 104–06 (2006).

54. Rachlinski, *supra* note 50, at 1223.

55. *See also supra* pp. 114–15.

56. On these phenomena, see generally *supra* pp. 64–66, 58–61, and 114–15, respectively.

57. *See generally supra* pp. 114–17.

58. James G. March, *Learning to Be Risk Averse*, 103 Psychol. Rev. 309 (1996).

Another line of anti-paternalist argument stresses the risks of errors and abuse—especially when paternalism is practiced by state officials.[59] These arguments are overstated.[60] When setting paternalistic rules aimed at protecting people from their short-sightedness, computation limitations, overoptimism, etc., policymakers can rely on professional, technical, and statistical data that is often unavailable to individuals. While it is true that professional expertise is no panacea for cognitive biases,[61] policymakers weigh the options in a more detached and calmer manner, based on objective, general statistics—whereas individuals are often called upon to make decisions hastily, or while in the grip of emotions. Similarly, policymakers are less susceptible to self-serving biases that adversely affect people's decisions about themselves. The various inputs to the legislative, administrative, and judicial processes, coupled with the decision-makers' cumulative experience, are likely to result in a sensible assessment of the relevant factors.

These claims are supported by the *construal-level theory of psychological distance*.[62] According to this theory—which has been borne out by numerous studies—decisions relating to oneself, to the here and now, or to actual events, differ from those that one makes about other people, or about events that are chronologically or spatially remote, or hypothetical. Greater psychological distance gives rise to more abstract thinking, and the prioritization of more fundamental goals. It enhances planning for the future, learning from the past, and considering alternatives. Since policymakers are likely to approach issues on a higher construal level, their decisions are more likely to fall in line with people's more basic and long-term objectives.

As for the risk of abuse, in the current public discourse in Western democracies, policymakers rarely conceal their ulterior motives behind paternalistic rhetoric, because paternalism has negative connotations. There is a greater risk of abuse in allowing policymakers to rely on justifications such as unequal bargaining power or market failure.

An important challenge facing paternalistic lawmaking—and indeed, any lawmaking that is founded on people's susceptibility to heuristics and biases, and to some extent any lawmaking—is people's heterogeneity.[63] People vary in how they use heuristics and display cognitive biases, and not enough is known about these individual differences.[64] This means

59. *See, e.g.*, Edward L. Glaeser, *Paternalism and Psychology*, 73. U. Chi. L. Rev. 133 (2006); Niclas Berggren, *Time for Behavioral Political Economy? An Analysis of Articles in Behavioral Economics*, 25 Rev. Austrian Econ. 199 (2012); W. Kip Viscusi & Ted Gayer, *Behavioral Public Choice: The Behavioral Paradox of Government Policy*, 28 Harv. J. L. & Pub. Pol'y 973 (2015).

60. *See* Jeremy A. Blumenthal, *Expert Paternalism*, 64 Fla. L. Rev. 721, 732–56 (2012).

61. *See supra* pp. 114–17. *See also infra* pp. 396–99.

62. *See, e.g.*, Yaacov Trope & Nira Liberman, *Construal-Level Theory of Psychological Distance*, 117 Psychol. Rev. 440 (2010); Kentaro Fujita, Yaacov Trope & Nira Liberman, *On the Psychology of Near and Far*, *in* 1 The Wiley Blackwell Handbook of Judgment and Decision Making 404 (Gideon Keren & George Wu eds., 2015).

63. Jeffrey J. Rachlinski, *Cognitive Errors, Individual Differences, and Paternalism*, 73 U. Chi. L. Rev. 207 (2006). *See also* Robert A. Prentice, *Chicago Man, K-T Man, and the Future of Behavioral Law and Economics*, 56 Vanderbilt L. Rev. 1663, 1722–44 (2003).

64. *See generally supra* pp. 111–14.

that the very need for paternalistic intervention and its actual effect differ from one person to another.[65] As pointed out in the next subsection, some forms of behaviorally informed regulation—so-called *asymmetric* or *libertarian* paternalism—arguably meet this challenge. At any rate, this is a valid concern that must be taken into account when considering the pros and cons of legal paternalism in any given context.

3. Means

(a) Introduction

The range of means used by the law to achieve its goals, whatever they might be, is huge. It imposes disclosure duties, sets formal requirements, lays down default and mandatory rules, and provides for cooling-off periods for certain transactions. The law invalidates certain contract clauses, and denies people's capacity to perform certain acts. It uses both preventive and ex-post measures, including criminal, civil, and administrative sanctions. It awards remedies of all sorts: monetary and non-monetary, privately or publicly enforced, etc. In this section, we focus on the contribution of behavioral studies to the design of disclosure duties and nudges.[66] These are by no means the only contexts where behavioral insights can contribute to the design of legal and other tools for affecting people's behavior. For example, behavioral insights may be used to enhance the efficacy of monetary and non-monetary incentives,[67] and to shape or change people's preferences.[68] The behavioral aspects of various legal means will be studied in the ensuing chapters, as well.[69]

(b) Disclosure Duties

Information problems—in particular, asymmetric information in bargaining—are a well-known and well-studied type of market failure. Standard economic analysis has grappled with this issue from early on,[70] and the legal-economic literature on the subject is rich.[71] Disclosure duties, and prohibitions of deception even more so, may also be based on deontological grounds.[72]

65. For a critical examination of this argument, see Conly, *supra* note 38, at 63–66.

66. The term "nudge" is sometimes used liberally to include also behaviorally informed improvements to disclosure duties. We distinguish between the two types of measures, but as far as we can see, nothing really hinges on this terminological choice.

67. Brigitte C. Madrian, *Applying Insights from Behavioral Economics to Policy Design*, 6 Ann. Rev. Econ. 663, 679–81 (2014).

68. Daphna Lewinsohn-Zamir, *The Importance of Being Ernst: Two Notions of Internalization*, 65 U. Toronto L.J. 37 (2015).

69. *See, e.g., infra* pp. 290–92 (on cooling-off periods in consumer transactions).

70. *See* George A. Akerlof, *The Market for "Lemons": Quality Uncertainty and the Market Mechanism*, 84 Q.J. Econ. 488 (1970).

71. For overviews, see Steven Shavell, Foundations of Economic Analysis of Law 331–35 (2004); Zamir & Medina, *supra* note 15, at 269–74.

72. For an overview, see Zamir & Medina, *supra* note 15, at 274–77. For an economic analysis subject to deontological constraints of disclosure duties in contractual relations, see *id.* at 277–91.

Behavioral insights are key to disclosure duties. First, behavioral insights may be used to improve disclosure duties by identifying which information should be disclosed, and highlighting how it should be disclosed. Second, behavioral studies have pointed to the limited effectiveness (some would say futility) of disclosure duties in certain contexts. Rather than trying to improve disclosure techniques, these findings may call for other, more effective regulatory means.[73] We take up these two issues in turn.

The traditional analysis of disclosure duties focused on private information held by one party.[74] In the paradigmatic case, a seller holds superior information about the quality of the goods she is selling. To the extent that this information is negative (that is, price-reducing), the seller has a strong incentive not to divulge it. Competitive forces might mitigate this effect, through a dynamic process in which suppliers with high-quality products reveal their private information voluntarily to secure a higher price, resulting in silence being equated with low quality.[75] Nonetheless, behavioral analysis suggests that the effectiveness of such market mechanisms may be limited. The cognitive assumption underlying such models is that people are attuned to the *lack* of information, and can draw the proper inferences from it. Given the subtle and non-salient nature of missing information, however, individuals often fail to reach the proper conclusions in such settings (especially when dealing with parties who swamp them with additional irrelevant information, through advertising and similar tools).[76]

Behavioral analysis further suggests that the scope of disclosure should be greater than the one prescribed by traditional economic analysis. Given people's susceptibility to cognitive biases, disclosures ought to encompass dimensions of decisions related to people's inability to make optimal choices, and not merely their inability to distinguish between high- and low-quality products.[77] For example, disclosure should aim to target self-control problems by highlighting the long-term consequences of a given choice. To this end, disclosures are needed even with respect to the price of the product, when the price is multidimensional, or includes deferred costs. Additionally, behavioral studies suggest that the informational advantage that suppliers have might relate not only to the nature of their product, but also to the predicted future behavior of the individuals they are dealing with.[78]

73. Inasmuch as the ineffectiveness of disclosure stems from exploitation of people's cognitive limitations and biases, the present discussion is linked to the issue of exploitation, *supra* pp. 163–65.

74. *See* Akerlof, *supra* note 70.

75. *See* Sanford J. Grossman, *The Informational Role of Warranties and Private Disclosure about Product Quality*, 24 J.L. & ECON 461 (1981).

76. Lyle A. Brenner, Derek J. Koehler & Amos Tversky, *On the Evaluation of One-Sided Evidence*, 9 J. BEHAV. DECISION MAKING 59 (1996). *See also supra* p. 24; *infra* pp. 284–85.

77. *See* George Loewenstein, Cass R. Sunstein & Russell Golman, *Disclosure: Psychology Changes Everything*, 6 ANN. REV. ECON. 391, 394 (2014).

78. Oren Bar-Gill & Oliver Board, *Product Use Information and the Limits of Voluntary Disclosure*, 14 AM. L. & ECON. REV. 235 (2014).

A significant body of behavioral work has been devoted to examining the proper means of promoting the broad disclosure agenda just described.[79] Reviewing this entire body of work is beyond the scope of this chapter, but its key message is simplification. Given people's limited ability to grasp large quantities of complex information, disclosures should be timely, brief, salient, and graphic (where possible). On the other hand, disclosures should not include lengthy wording in complex language (such as legalese), or be presented in a way that draws attention away from them (e.g., through the use of small print). Numerous controlled field experiments have shown that the simplification of disclosures brought about significant changes in behavior in areas such as the use of tax credits and saving for retirement.[80]

Thus far, we have referred to disclosure toward the end-users of the information. A second strand of disclosure pertains to sophisticated players.[81] These players might be market intermediators who can optimize choices for end-users, or competitors who wish to highlight their relative advantage. Disclosures aimed at such players need not be simple, or brief. Rather, they should be comprehensive and standardized, to facilitate a competitive process that enlists market forces to help boundedly rational actors make better choices.

However, while behavioral analysis has been used both to justify disclosure and to guide its use, it has also revealed the limitations and potential harm of disclosure. For one, while proponents of disclosure advocate simplification, the truth of the matter is that reality is often complex, and cannot be disclosed in a simple manner. There is no way one can collapse a complex financial instrument into a simple comprehensible disclosure, or explain the potential risks associated with a drug in an accessible manner. This difficulty is exacerbated by individual differences between disclosees, which might require incorporating information that is relevant to some, but not to others.[82]

Even assuming that clear and simple disclosures can be designed, the effectiveness of these disclosures might be hampered by a more basic problem—the so-called *no-reading problem*.[83] The lack of reading on the part of disclosees might stem from information

79. *See, e.g.*, Cass Sunstein, *Nudges.Gov: Behaviorally Informed Regulation*, *in* The Oxford Handbook of Behavioral Economics and the Law 719, 727–33 (Eyal Zamir & Doron Teichman eds., 2014); Oren Bar-Gill, Seduction by Contract 32–46 (2012); Richard Craswell, *Taking Information Seriously: Misrepresentation and Nondisclosure in Contract Law and Elsewhere*, 92 Va. L. Rev. 565, 581–93 (2006); Loewenstein, Sunstein & Golman, *supra* note 77, at 405–11.

80. *See* Saurabh Bhargava & Day Manoli, *Why Are Benefits Left on the Table? Assessing the Role of Information, Complexity, and Stigma on Take-Up with an IRS Field Experiment*, *in* 40 Advances in Consumer Research 298 (Zeynep Gürhan-Canli, Cele Otnes & Rui (Juliet) Zhu eds., 2012); Robert L. Clark, Jennifer A. Maki & Melinda Sandler Morrill, *Can Simple Informational Nudges Increase Employee Participation in a 401(k) Plan?*, 80 S. Econ. J. 677 (2014).

81. *See* Bar-Gill, *supra* note 79, at 5, 40–41, 43, 244–45.

82. To some degree this problem can be ameliorated with the use of disclosures that are based on personalized information. Such disclosures, however, raise an array of practical problems. *See* Loewenstein, Sunstein & Golman, *supra* note 77 at 409–10. For an analysis of how this goal can be achieved by harnessing the vast amount of personal data collected, see Ariel Porat & Lior Jacob Strahilevitz, *Personalized Default Rules and Disclosure with Big Data*, 112 Mich. L. Rev. 1417, 1470–76 (2014).

83. *Cf.* Ian Ayres & Alan Schwartz, *The No-Reading Problem in Consumer Contract Law*, 66 Stan. L. Rev. 545 (2014).

overload, as people are constantly exposed to endless disclosures. When any acquisition of a new product, a meal at a restaurant, a visit to a website, and a medical treatment entails a lengthy disclosure—the outcome is that none of these disclosures are read. Moreover, even if, within the ocean of disclosures, a given disclosure is read (because it is simple and salient), this does not assure that it will have a lasting effect on behavior. As Todd Rogers and Erin Frey note, "an individual's behavioral response to the first instance of a stimulus tends to be more pronounced than his or her behavioral response to the *n*th repetition of that same stimulus."[84] Thus, the effect of well-designed disclosures might erode over time, unless special effort is put into constantly altering the disclosure in a bid to stave off habituation.[85]

In addition, even if we were to assume (unrealistically) that disclosees are willing to read all disclosures that they are exposed to, illiteracy and innumeracy often stand in their way. In reality, many people lack the basic skills that would enable them to make use of the disclosed information.[86] While the readers of this book undoubtedly know how many times a coin comes up heads if flipped 1,000 times, can calculate what 1 percent of 1,000 is, and can convert a ratio such as 1:1,000 into a percentage, a significant portion of the population cannot.[87] More specifically, one study found that 30 percent of people with above-average literacy "had 0 correct answers, 28% had 1 correct answer, 26% had 2 correct answers, and 16% had 3 correct answers."[88]

Finally, while disclosure advocates emphasize that disclosures must be "timely,"[89] in reality disclosures are often presented to decision-makers at a late stage. This may be for strategic reasons (for example, when a website intentionally defers the disclosure of information to the last stage of the transaction), or for practical ones (as in the case of mortgage disclosures, that are dealt with at closing as part of a large complex transaction). When disclosures appear late, people are unlikely to change their choices in light of the new information, due to the *confirmation bias* (the tendency to seek and process information in a way that validates one's prior beliefs and expectations),[90] and the *sunk-costs effect* (the tendency to continue with a project once one has made an initial investment of time, effort, or money in it).[91] Both these attributes of human decision-making suggest that if people invest significant time, effort, or money prior to disclosure—as they often do—and develop an inclination toward a certain choice, they tend to stick with their initial choice, despite the

84. Todd Roger & Erin Frey, *Changing Behavior beyond the Here and Now*, *in* Wiley Blackwell Handbook, *supra* note 62, at 725, 734.

85. *Id.* at 734–36.

86. *See* Omri Ben-Shahar & Carl Schneider, More than You Wanted to Know: The Failure of Mandated Disclosure 79–93 (2014).

87. *See* Lisa M. Schwartz et al., *The Role of Numeracy in Understanding the Benefit of Screening Mammography*, 127 Annals Internal Med. 966, 969 (1997).

88. *Id.* For similar findings with a more educated pool of subjects, see Isaac M. Lipkus et al., *General Performance on a Numeracy Scale among Highly Educated Samples*, 21 Med. Decision Making 37, 39 (2001).

89. Cass Sunstein, *Empirically Informed Regulation*, 78 U. Chi. L. Rev. 1349, 1369 (2011).

90. *See supra* pp. 58–61.

91. *See supra* pp. 56–57.

disclosure. Under such circumstances, people tend to disregard or downplay the relevance and import of information that militates against their prior choice.

By now, a large body of research has demonstrated the limited effect of disclosure on behavior.[92] Studies have shown that the vast majority of the population does not read many of the disclosures it is bombarded with,[93] and even when disclosures are read, they are often misunderstood.[94] For example, many consumers (apparently even those enrolled in a real-estate transaction class in law school) cannot distinguish between adjustable-rate and fixed-rate loans.[95] One study conducted in Illinois found that an overwhelming majority of borrowers who took out an adjustable-rate loan thought that they had taken out a fixed-rate loan.[96]

A further body of work has demonstrated the limited effect of disclosures on actual behavior. In the area of calorie labeling in restaurants, for example, most studies have found little to no effect due to disclosure.[97] A review of this body of work concluded that "overall the best designed studies (real world studies, with a comparison group) show that calorie labels do not have the desired effect in reducing total calories ordered at the population level."[98] This is not an isolated result, as similar ineffectiveness of disclosures was observed in contexts such as credit card borrowing and energy cost labeling.[99]

Although the evidence seems to suggest that disclosure is of limited value, it remains a highly popular policy tool in both academic and political circles.[100] This popularity appears to stem from the belief that disclosure is a cheap policy tool, that at the very least is harmless.

92. For a review of the findings, see BEN-SHAHAR & SCHNEIDER, *supra* note 86, at 33–54.

93. *See* Yannis Bakos, Florencia Marotta-Wurgler & David R. Trossen, *Does Anyone Read the Fine Print? Consumer Attention to Standard Form Contracts*, 43 J. LEGAL STUD. 1 (2014).

94. *See* Jeff Sovern et al., *"Whimsy Little Contracts" with Unexpected Consequences: An Empirical Analysis of Consumer Understanding of Arbitration Agreements*, 75 MD. L. REV. 1 (2015); Kirsten Martin, *Privacy Notices as Tabula Rasa: An Empirical Investigation into How Complying with a Privacy Notice Is Related to Meeting Privacy Expectations Online*, 34 J. PUB. POL'Y & MARKETING 210 (2015).

95. *See* Debra Pogrund Stark & Jessica M. Choplin, *A Cognitive and Social Psychological Analysis of Disclosure Laws and Call for Mortgage Counseling to Prevent Predatory Lending*, 16 PSYCHOL. PUB. POL. & L. 85, 101 (2010).

96. *See* Ill. Dep't Fin. and Prof'l Regulation, *Findings from the HB 4050 Predatory Lending Database Pilot Program* 1, 3–4 (2007), *available at:* http://nlihc.org/library/sirr/IL-2007.

97. *See, e.g.*, Lisa J. Harnack et al., *Effects of Calorie Labeling and Value Size Pricing on Fast Food Meal Choices: Results from an Experimental Trial*, 5 INT'L. J. BEHAV. NUTRITION & PHYSICAL ACTIVITY 63 (2008); Maya K. Vadiveloo, L. Beth Dixon & Brian Elbel, *Consumer Purchasing Patterns in Response to Calorie Labeling Legislation in New York City*, 8 INT'L. J. BEHAV. NUTRITION & PHYSICAL ACTIVITY 51 (2011). *But see* Bryan Bollinger, Philip Leslie & Alan Sorensen, *Calorie Posting in Chain Restaurants*, 3 AM. ECON. J. ECON. POL'Y 91 (2011).

98. Kamila M. Kiszko, *The Influence of Calorie Labeling on Food Orders and Consumption: A Review of the Literature*, 39 J. COMMUNITY HEALTH 1248 (2014).

99. Enrique Seira, Alan Elizondo & Eduardo Laguna-Muggenburg, *Are Information Disclosures Effective? Evidence from the Credit Card Market*, 9 AM. ECON. J.: ECON. POL'Y 277 (2017); James Carroll, Eleanor Denny & Seán Lyons, *The Effects of Energy Cost Labelling on Appliance Purchasing Decisions: Trial Results from Ireland*, 39 J. CONSUMER POL'Y 23 (2016).

100. *See* Cass R. Sunstein, *Informational Regulation and Informational Standing: Akins and Beyond*, 147 U. PA. L. REV. 613, 618–33 (1999).

After all, who could oppose something such as added transparency? Furthermore, since disclosure continues to leave the ultimate decisions in the hands of disclosees, it sidesteps the difficult issues associated with more intrusive regulation that limits individual choice. This view of disclosure, however, overlooks the pitfalls associated with such policies.

Even within the realm of traditional economic analysis, the view of disclosure as costless is unfounded.[101] While disclosure policies might entail limited budgetary costs to the government, they involve significant costs to disclosers and disclosees. On the disclosing side, assembling and publishing the information required by the different mandates often involves substantial costs—such as employing lawyers, compliance officers, and the like. Similarly, disclosees are required to invest time and cognitive effort to navigate their choices within the web of disclosures they are subjected to. One study estimated that the value of the time that American households would need to put annually into reading the privacy policies of the websites they visit is $781 billion (an entirely unwarranted concern, however, since no one actually reads these notices).[102]

Aside from these obvious costs, behavioral research has uncovered perverse effects that disclosure can have on the conduct of disclosers and disclosees. In the case of disclosers, experimental studies have shown that the introduction of disclosure may crowd out the disclosers' inner motivation to behave fairly in situations of conflict of interest—inasmuch as they might feel that, given their transparency, they are entitled to further their own interests.[103] In these studies, participants functioned either as estimators or as advisors. The advisors' incentives were determined randomly to be either aligned with the estimators' or not—and when incentives were not aligned, this conflict was either disclosed, or not. The key finding from this body of work is that when the conflict was disclosed, advisors offered more biased advice to the estimators. Furthermore, estimators did not account for this effect, and as a result disclosure resulted in increased payoffs to advisors, and a decline in the payoffs to estimators.

Moreover, while behavioral studies show that disclosure of conflict of interest brings about the intended effect of reducing the trust that disclosees place in the advice they receive, it also creates pressure on disclosees to accept the biased advice.[104] This pressure, in turn, causes disclosees in controlled experiments to comply with advice that they know is biased, and diminishes their payoffs. It stands to reason, therefore, that in real-world settings involving personal relationships (such as doctor-patient settings) the pressure generated by

101. Omri Ben-Shahar & Carl E. Schneider, *The Futility of Cost Benefit Analysis in Financial Disclosure Regulation*, 43 J. Legal Stud. S253 (2014).

102. Alecia M. McDonald & Lorrie Faith Cranor, *Cost of Reading Privacy Policies*, 4 I/S: J. Law & Pol'y Info. Soc. 540, 562 (2008).

103. *See* Daylian M. Cain, George Loewenstein & Don A. Moore, *The Dirt on Coming Clean: Perverse Effects of Disclosing Conflicts of Interest*, 34 J. Legal Stud. 1 (2005); Daylian M. Cain, George Loewenstein & Don A. Moore, *When Sunlight Fails to Disinfect: Understanding the Perverse Effects of Disclosing Conflicts of Interest*, 37 J. Consumer Res. 836 (2011).

104. Sunita Sah, George Loewenstein & Daylian M. Cain, *The Burden of Disclosure: Increased Compliance with Distrusted Advice*, 104 J. Personality & Soc. Psychol. 289 (2013).

disclosures will have an even greater influence on the choices made by disclosees. This effect might be mitigated through secondary disclosure that requires parties to disclose their legal obligation to disclose,[105] though, the concerns relating to disclosure hold for this secondary obligation as well.

Perhaps the most troubling aspect of disclosure policies is their influence on the politics of regulation, and the choice presented between disclosure and other forms of governmental intervention.[106] Regulatory reform often occurs in the wake of a significant event that highlights the need for some type of legal intervention (the 2008 financial meltdown is a notable case in point). Given their low budgetary cost and high popularity, disclosure policies can function as a quick fix for any pressing problem arising within the public discourse. This allows politicians to reap political gains for apparently dealing with a pressing need, without delving into the complex world of intrusive regulation (such as removing dangerous products from the market, or imposing licensing requirements on certain professions), which is bound to raise fierce political opposition from interest groups. The result is a regulatory substitution effect in which popular but ineffective disclosure drives out alternative modes of regulation that are less popular, but direly needed.

To be sure, we do not argue that disclosure should be abandoned as a regulatory tool. Smart disclosures are a viable policy tool that can help part of the population in certain settings. In addition, it has been suggested that disclosures may improve the behavior of disclosers who assume (however erroneously) that disclosures influence the choices made by disclosees.[107] That said, the current degree of reliance on disclosure, especially in the United States, cannot be justified. Even under the most optimistic assumptions, disclosure policies do not offer an effective solution to many of the regulatory problems they are meant to address. Furthermore, the heavy reliance on disclosures undermines the entire regulatory regime. As disclosures become more prevalent and encompass every aspect of our lives, their value is diminished, since they become no more than background noise for decision-makers.[108] In this regard, the greatest challenge facing regulators is to find ways to significantly *curtail* the current scope of mandated disclosure, rather than discover new areas in which it can be implemented.

(c) Nudges and Shoves

In recent years, many references to behavioral law and economics in the public and legal discourse have revolved around the legitimacy and effectiveness of *nudges*—"low-cost,

105. Ahmed E. Taha & John V. Petrocelli, *Disclosures about Disclosures: Can Conflict of Interest Warnings Be Made More Effective?*, 12 J. Empirical L. Stud. 236 (2015).

106. *See* Doron Teichman, *Too Little, Too Much, Not Just Right: Behavioral Analysis and the Desirable Regulation of Consumer Contracts*, 9 Jerusalem Rev. Legal Stud. 52, 58–60 (2014); Ben-Shahar & Schneider, *supra* note 86, at 170–74.

107. *See* Loewenstein, Sunstein & Golman, *supra* note 77 at 403–04. While we acknowledge this possibility, we are somewhat skeptical of its long-term viability as sophisticated disclosers are likely to learn over time that disclosure has a limited effect on choices.

108. *See* Ben-Shahar & Schneider, *supra* note 86.

choice-preserving, behaviorally informed approaches to regulatory problems."[109] It is important to note at the outset that this discussion occasionally conflates two related but separate issues: legal paternalism and behaviorally informed regulation. These two issues are related inasmuch as behaviorally informed regulation minimizes the curtailment of people's freedom—thereby making paternalistic policies less intrusive and more acceptable. The two issues are nevertheless distinct, because people's cognitive limitations may well justify hard forms of paternalism (for example, the imposition of criminal sanctions for failing to wear seat belts), and nudges can be used to encourage prosocial—as opposed to self-benefitting—conduct, such as encouraging posthumous organ donation by setting presumed consent as the default, or informing people about their neighbors' socially desirable practices. The latter use of nudges has nothing to do with paternalism. Accordingly, paternalism was addressed in Subsection D.2.(c) above, and behaviorally informed regulation is discussed here.

Relatedly, while there is considerable overlap between *nudging* and *debiasing*, they are distinct from one another.[110] On the one hand, the term "debiasing" conventionally includes strategies that people might employ by themselves, such as postponing a decision when one is distracted or agitated, or using decision-support systems rather than making an intuitive decision, whereas nudging connotes external (often governmental) intervention. On the other hand, nudging includes behaviorally informed interventions in perfectly rational decisions (typically to advance the social good), and may cover the use of behavioral insights to improve disclosure duties by making information more accessible or vivid, whereas debiasing usually does not cover those cases.

Nudge advocates claim that behaviorally-informed regulation can induce self-benefitting and socially desirable behaviors, as well as discourage self-injurious and socially undesirable conducts, with little infringement of autonomy.[111] Legal policymakers on both sides of the Atlantic have embraced behavioral insights.[112] Thus, in 2009 Professor Cass Sunstein was appointed Administrator of the White House Office of Information and Regulatory Affairs (OIRA)—also known as the "Regulation Czar." Under Sunstein's leadership, OIRA has adopted many initiatives that may be described as nudges.[113] Often, the incorporation of behavioral insights into the design of legislative and regulatory policies

109. Sunstein, *supra* note 79, at 719.

110. On debiasing, see *supra* pp. 127–38.

111. *See generally* Cass R. Sunstein & Richard H. Thaler, *Libertarian Paternalism Is Not an Oxymoron*, 70 U. Chi. L. Rev. 1159 (2003) [hereinafter Sunstein & Thaler, *Libertarian Paternalism*]; Colin F. Camerer et al., *Regulation for Conservatives: Behavioral Economics and the Case for "Asymmetric Paternalism,"* 151 U. Pa. L. Rev. 1211 (2003); Richard H. Thaler & Cass R. Sunstein, Nudge: Improving Decisions about Health, Wealth, and Happiness (rev. ed. 2009) [hereinafter Thaler & Sunstein, Nudge].

112. *See, e.g.*, Rebonato, *supra* note 38, at 1 ("With little exaggeration one can say that [libertarian paternalism] has taken the political and cultural landscape by storm"); Robert Baldwin, *From Regulation to Behaviour Change: Giving Nudge the Third Degree*, 77 Mod. L. Rev. 831, 831 (2014). For reviews, see The Behavioral Foundations of Public Policy (Eldar Shafir ed., 2013); Raj Chetty, *Behavioral Economics and Public Policy: A Pragmatic Perspective*, 105 Am. Econ. Rev. 1 (2015); David Halpern & Michael Sanders, *Nudging by Government: Progress, Impact, and Lessons Learned*, 2 Behav. Sci. & Pol'y 53 (2016).

113. Sunstein, *supra* note 109.

(including, but not limited to, the design of disclosures) has been done by ordinary government agencies.[114] In addition, governments and supranational organizations have established (or are in the process of establishing) special units whose primary role is to advance evidence-based, behaviorally-informed policies. Thus, in the United Kingdom, the Behavioural Insights Team (BIT or Nudge Unit), founded in 2010, actively pursues these goals.[115] Comparable initiatives are taking root in other countries and in international organizations, such as the World Bank and the European Commission.[116] Behaviorally-informed regulators have been using such measures as prompting people to do the right thing by making it the default arrangement, forcing people to decide, and providing them with information about other people's behavior. We will describe some of these measures, their advantages and limitations.[117]

The Default Effect. Standard economic analysis perceives default rules as a means of enhancing efficiency, by reducing transaction costs and inducing information sharing. Default rules that reflect the prevailing preferences of the people to whom they apply save those people the costs of actively adopting those arrangements. Concomitantly, when people opt out of the default, they convey information to uninformed parties.[118] For example, a default that states that a supplier is liable for certain product defects unless it explicitly and conspicuously exempts itself from such liability conveys valuable information to the customer because opting out clarifies the scope of the supplier's liability. While this analysis is illuminating, it has long been realized that it does not fully account for the observed "stickiness" of default rules. If the direct costs of negotiating a contract, or of registering one's decision to opt out of the default rule regarding postmortem organ donation, were the only hurdle involved, we should have witnessed far more opt-outs than occur in reality.[119]

114. *See, e.g.*, Michael S. Barr, Sendhil Mullainathan & Eldar Shafir, *Behaviorally Informed Regulation*, *in* THE BEHAVIORAL FOUNDATIONS OF PUBLIC POLICY, *supra* note 112, at 440, 447–57 (describing the influence of BE on financial regulation).

115. Baldwin, *supra* note 112, at 831–34. On BIT's goals, activities, and publications, see its official website at http://www.behaviouralinsights.co.uk. For a critical review of the applications of behavioral economics to policymaking, primarily in the United States and Britain, see Peter D. Lunn, *Behavioural Economics and Policymaking: Learning from the Early Adopters*, 43 ECON. & SOC. REV. 423 (2012).

116. *See, e.g.*, EUROPEAN COMMISSION—JOINT RESEARCH CENTRE, APPLYING BEHAVIOURAL SCIENCES TO EU POLICY-MAKING (2013); NUDGE AND THE LAW: A EUROPEAN PERSPECTIVE (Alberto Alemanno & Anne-Lise Sibony eds., 2015); Halpern & Sanders, *supra* note 112. *See also* NUDGING—POSSIBILITIES, LIMITATIONS AND APPLICATIONS IN EUROPEAN LAW AND ECONOMICS (Klaus Mathis & Avishalom Tor eds., 2016).

117. The following list is not exhaustive. For theoretical and empirical studies of additional measures, which may be employed by public and private entities, see, e.g., THALER & SUNSTEIN, NUDGE, *supra* note 111; Anne N. Thorndike et al., *A 2-Phase Labeling and Choice Architecture Intervention to Improve Healthy Food and Beverage Choices*, 102 AM. J. PUB. HEALTH 527 (2012).

118. Ian Ayres & Robert Gertner, *Filling Gaps in Incomplete Contracts: An Economic Theory of Default Rules*, 99 YALE L.J. 87 (1989).

119. *See, e.g.*, Karen Eggleston, Eric A. Posner & Richard Zeckhauser, *The Design and Interpretation of Contracts: Why Complexity Matters*, 95 NW. U. L. REV. 91, 107–08 (2000).

A primary explanation for default-rules stickiness, or the *default effect*, lies in the *omission bias*—people's tendency to avoid active choices between options that involve both advantages and disadvantages, prospects and risks.[120] It has been shown that default rules set a reference point from which people are often reluctant to deviate, thereby directing behavior in desirable ways. For instance, due to shortsightedness and hyperbolic discounting, people often do not save enough for retirement.[121] One study examined the rate of employee participation in a retirement savings plan at a large U.S. corporation, before and after a change in the default. Before the change, employees were required to affirmatively choose to participate; after the change, new employees were automatically enrolled in the plan unless they opted out of it. The change of default resulted in a dramatic increase in retirement plan participation.[122] Importantly, the effect was largest among the groups with the lowest participation rate under the previous arrangement: blacks and Hispanics, the young, and low-paid workers.[123] In the same vein, Richard Thaler and Shlomo Benartzi proposed a savings plan whereby employees commit in advance to allocating a portion of their future salary increases to a retirement plan, which they can opt out of at any time.[124] This proposal harnesses the status quo bias (and overcomes loss aversion, as it does not involve reduction in present consumption) to overcome people's myopia and bounded willpower.

As mentioned in Chapter 2, a powerful default effect has been demonstrated in relation to postmortem organ donations, as well. In some countries of the European Union, people are considered organ donors unless they register not to be, while in others no one is an organ donor unless he or she has registered to be one. The donation rate in most presumed-consent countries is close to 100 percent, while in the explicit-consent countries it ranges from 4 percent to 27 percent.[125] Experimental studies have indicated that this difference is most plausibly a product of the omission bias.[126] As the cost of registering one's choice in those experiments was negligible, the effort needed to opt out of the default

120. *See supra* pp. 48–50. The stickiness of default rules has also been associated with people's *ambiguity aversion* (*see generally supra* pp. 39–42. *See* Omri Ben-Shahar & John A.E. Pottow, *On the Stickiness of Default Rules*, 33 FLA. ST. UL REV. 651, 665–66 (2005). Yet another explanation lies in the expressive effect of default rules: the very setting of a default by a legal policymaker may be perceived as endorsing and recommending that arrangement—thereby shaping people's preferences. *See* Eyal Zamir, *The Inverted Hierarchy of Contract Interpretation and Supplementation*, 97 COLUM. L. REV. 1710, 1758–59 (1997); N. Craig Smith, Daniel G. Goldstein & Eric J. Johnson, *Choice without Awareness: Ethical and Policy Implications of Defaults*, 32 J. PUB. POL'Y & MARKETING 159, 161 (2013).

121. HERSH SHEFRIN, BEYOND GREED AND FEAR: UNDERSTANDING BEHAVIORAL FINANCE AND THE PSYCHOLOGY OF INVESTING 139–56 (2002).

122. Brigitte Madrian & Dennis Shea, *The Power of Suggestion: Inertia in 401(k) Participation and Savings Behavior*, 66 Q. J. ECON. 1149 (2001).

123. *Id.* at 1161.

124. Richard H. Thaler & Shlomo Benartzi, *Save More Tomorrow™: Using Behavioral Economics to Increase Employee Saving*, 112 J. POL. ECON. S164, S170–S179 (2004).

125. Eric J. Johnson & Daniel G. Goldstein, *Do Defaults Save Lives?*, 302 SCI. 1338 (2003). *See also supra* p. 49.

126. Shai Davidai, Thomas Gilovich & Lee D. Ross, *The Meaning of Default Options for Potential Organ Donors*, 109 PROC. NAT'L ACAD. SCI. USA 15201 (2012).

cannot account for the dramatic differences in people's choices under the two default rules; and since participants were randomly assigned to one of the conditions, neither can their prior preferences account for it.

The default effect appears to be particularly strong in the organ-donation context, because decisions in this regard require one to face one's own mortality—an issue that most people prefer not to think about. The same phenomenon may explain why many people refrain from writing a will, thus leaving in place the default rules governing the division of their estate.[127] While trying to be in line with people's common preferences, the intestacy rule also reflects policymakers' perceptions of socially desirable norms.[128]

Default rules may also contribute to environmental protection. For example, it is possible to have electricity customers signed up by default to participate in a renewable energy development fund.[129] More generally, Cass Sunstein and Lucia Reisch have advocated the use of defaults to steer consumer choices toward environmental-friendly products and services.[130]

In setting default rules, the legal policymaker should arguably take distributive concerns into account. Among other things, the costs of opting out of a default may vary from one person to another, depending on their level of sophistication and socioeconomic status. To minimize the total costs of such opting out, and/or to attain desirable redistributive outcomes, it might make sense to set the default so that the costs of opting out would be borne by those who are better able to bear these costs.

In fact, behavioral studies show that default arrangements may have an even more direct distributive effect due to the *endowment effect*.[131] If people who have a certain entitlement by default value it more highly than people who have to purchase it, the very allocation of the entitlement benefits those people. In one experimental study, students took part in a simulation of bargaining between a union and an employer. It was found that when the default rule favored one party (be it the employer or the union), that party did significantly better than when the default rule favored the other party.[132] Interestingly, even contractual default rules—which arguably do not endow people with any entitlement unless they find a partner willing to contract with them without deviating from the default—create a default effect.[133]

127. Adam J. Hirsch, *Default Rules in Inheritance Law: A Problem in Search of Its Context*, 73 FORDHAM L. REV. 1031, 1047–50 (2004).

128. *Id.* at 1042–58.

129. Adrian Kuenzler & Douglas A. Kyser, *Environmental Law, in* THE OXFORD HANDBOOK OF BEHAVIORAL ECONOMICS AND THE LAW, *supra* note 109, at 748, 757.

130. Cass R. Sunstein & Lucia A. Reisch, *Automatically Green: Behavioral Economics and Environmental Protection*, 38 HARV. ENVTL. L. REV. 127 (2014).

131. On the endowment effect, see *supra* pp. 50–56.

132. Stewart Schwab, *A Coasean Experiment on Contract Presumptions*, 17 J. LEGAL STUD. 237 (1988). For a fuller description of the study, see *infra* p. 250.

133. Zamir, *supra* note 120, at 1782–84 (1997); Russell Korobkin, *The Status Quo Bias and Contract Default Rules*, 83 CORNELL L. REV. 608 (1998); *infra* pp. 247–52.

Like any rule, default rules face a major challenge whenever, due to people's heterogeneity, different arrangements better suit different people. Thus, for example, automatically enrolling employees in a retirement savings plan very likely benefits the employees who would otherwise fail to save. However, it adversely affects other employees who, absent the default, might have saved at a higher rate than the default, but fail to do so due to the omission bias once the default is in place.[134] The very fact that an arrangement is set as a default, rather than as a mandatory rule, arguably decreases the attention it receives from policymakers.[135] One possible way to address this challenge, at least to some extent, is to use personalized default rules.[136] Following existing marketing practices, it has been suggested that people's particular needs and preferences could be identified through data mining, and that default rules could then be tailored accordingly. Such proposals raise various concerns whose discussion exceeds the scope of our analysis. Another possibility is to supplement the default rule with mechanisms that encourage those who are better off opting out of the rule, to do so.

Because most people are unlikely to opt out of a self- or socially-beneficial default arrangement due to their omission bias, adopting such well-crafted arrangements is expected to benefit people and society. At the same time, since people are allowed to opt out of the default, default rules hardly curtail their freedom and autonomy. For this reason, even when paternalistically motivated, the use of default rules has been described as asymmetric, or even libertarian, paternalism.[137] Nevertheless, the use of defaults as a regulatory means—particularly when aimed at helping people to advance their own interests—has been subject to much criticism—a point to which we will return below.

Forced Choices. Another human weakness that may adversely affect individuals and society at large is *procrastination*—the detrimental postponement of performance or decision that one intends to pursue, which may result in delay or even nonperformance, or no decision.[138] One method of helping people to overcome their omission bias and tendency to procrastinate is to compel them to make decisions.[139] For example, people who apply for a driver's license may be required to indicate whether they consent to donate their organs posthumously. A natural experiment revealed that requiring new employees to make an active decision about enrollment in a pension plan, without changing the default, increased enrollment

134. Madrian, *supra* note 67, at 668–69; Ryan Bubb & Richard H. Pildes, *How Behavioral Economics Trims Its Sails and Why*, 127 Harv. L. Rev. 1593, 1616–25 (2014).

135. Bubb & Pildes, *supra* note 134, at 1616–25.

136. Cass R. Sunstein, *Deciding by Default*, 162 U. Pa. L. Rev. 1, 48–56 (2013); Smith, Goldstein & Johnson, *supra* note 120, at 166–68; Porat & Strahilevitz, *supra* note 82, at 1433–53.

137. Colin F. Camerer et al., *Regulation for Conservatives: Behavioral Economics and the Case for "Asymmetric Paternalism"*, 151 U. Pa. L. Rev. 1211 (2003). Sunstein & Thaler, *Libertarian Paternalism*, *supra* note 111; Thaler & Sunstein, Nudge, *supra* note 111, at 4–6, 85–89.

138. *See supra* pp. 87–88.

139. Gabriel D. Carroll et al., *Optimal Defaults and Active Decisions*, 124 Q.J. Econ. 1639 (2009).

by twenty-eight percentage points.[140] Randomized laboratory and field studies have also shown an increased rate of willingness to vaccinate when an active choice is required.[141]

Compelled decisions are particularly appropriate whenever there is considerable heterogeneity among people, and the legal policymaker lacks information about the optimal choice for each individual under any circumstances. It may also have a side benefit of prompting those who make the decision to learn more about the issue. Arguably, compelled decisions are less intrusive than default rules, because the policymaker does not impose its own conception of the right decision—not even as the default. However, critics of this approach point out that there are certain choices that people strongly prefer not to make—for example, due to their unpleasantness, or for fear of regret. Forcing people to make such decisions may thus adversely affect their welfare and autonomy.[142] Compelled decisions are neither an appropriate solution when the decision task is too complex or too costly for laypersons.

Deadlines. Another technique—which is used extensively in marketing,[143] but rarely as a nudging technique, as yet—is the setting of deadlines for people's decisions and actions. For example, to induce employees to join a pension plan, a deadline might be set for joining the plan, or for joining it under particularly favorable conditions. Unlike the manipulation of a default, setting a deadline does not supplant the agent's decision with someone else's: the individual is not automatically entered into a given default position that the policymaker has deemed desirable, such as saving for retirement. Unlike compelled decision-making, a deadline allows individuals to avoid making any active choice. There is some experimental evidence for the potential effectiveness of deadlines as a means of inducing self-benefitting and socially desirable behavior, as well as for the effectiveness of removing deadlines to discourage less desirable behavior.[144]

Social Norms. Yet another technique is to trigger people's conformity, that is, the inclination to adapt one's behavior to that of others. Survey and field experiments have shown that people's behavior is unconsciously but strongly influenced by what they believe other people are doing—more so than by other factors, such as people's opinion about the desirability of a given behavior.[145] It follows that providing people with information about other people's behavior is likely to be more effective than trying to persuade them that such behavior is desirable.

140. *Id.* at 1643–58.

141. Punam Anand Keller et al., *Enhanced Active Choice: A New Method to Motivate Behavior Change*, 21 J. CONSUMER PSYCHOL. 376 (2011).

142. Cass R. Sunstein, *Choosing Not to Choose*, 64 DUKE L.J. 1 (2014).

143. *See, e.g.*, Praveen Aggarwal & Rajiv Vaidyanathan, *Use It or Lose It: Purchase Acceleration Effects of Time-Limited Promotions*, 2 J. CONSUMER BEHAV. 393 (2003).

144. Eyal Zamir, Daphna Lewinsohn-Zamir & Ilana Ritov, *It's Now or Never! Using Deadlines as Nudges*, 42 LAW & SOC. INQUIRY 769 (2017).

145. *See, e.g.*, Jessica M. Nolan et al., *Normative Social Influence Is Underdetected*, 34 PERSONALITY & SOC. PSYCHOL. BULL. 913 (2008); Noah Goldstein, Robert B. Cialdini & Vladas Griskevicius, *A Room with a Viewpoint: Using Social Norms to Motivate Environmental Conservation in Hotels*, 35 J. CONSUMER RES. 472 (2008).

However, such campaigns may also backfire, on occasion. People who discover that they have been outperforming others—for example, when their energy consumption has been particularly low—may downshift their conduct to fit the norm. This boomerang effect may be eliminated or mitigated by accompanying the descriptive information about other people's behavior with social approval or disapproval.[146] Thus, two large-scale, randomized field experiments have demonstrated that household electricity consumption may be reduced by providing people with emoticons on their energy consumption compared to the consumption of their neighbors.[147]

A different boomerang effect was found in a field experiment that studied the effect of information about the retirement savings of one's peers. The default in that case was non-enrollment in a pension plan. As expected, people who were already enrolled in such plans increased their savings when told that their peers were saving more than them. However, the same information *decreased* the savings put aside by participants who were not enrolled in a pension plan and whose income was relatively low, because they were discouraged by the reminder of their low economic status.[148]

Critique. Despite their innocuous nature, nudges—particularly the use of self-benefitting default rules—have been subject to considerable criticism from two opposite directions. Specifically, it has been claimed that these techniques work best "in the dark," and therefore manipulate people's cognitive limitations. Arguably, exploitation of imperfections in human judgment and decision-making—such as the omission bias—undermines people's control over their choices, and is therefore more threatening to their autonomy than overt coercion.[149] One possible response to this objection is that the use of nudges can be, and often is, transparent. Another response is that mundane choices are often made without conscious deliberation, and trying to force people to deliberate on them would likely be futile. In such cases, some choice architecture is inevitable, and there appears to be no good reason not to adopt the architecture that is more likely to produce self-beneficial choices.[150]

Ultimately, nudges that aim to help people make self-benefitting decisions are indeed paternalistic to some extent. There is probably not much point in trying to persuade extreme libertarians to embrace nudges. However, since extreme anti-paternalism—based on

146. P. Wesley Schultz et al., *The Constructive, Destructive, and Reconstructive Power of Social Norms*, 18 Psychol. Sci. 429 (2007).

147. Ian Ayres, Sophie Raseman & Alice Shih, *Evidence from Two Large Field Experiments That Peer Comparison Feedback Can Reduce Residential Energy Usage*, 29 J.L. Econ. & Org. 992 (2013).

148. John Beshears et al., *The Effect of Providing Peer Information on Retirement Savings Decisions*, 70 J. Fin. 1161 (2015).

149. *See, e.g.*, Luc Bovens, *The Ethics of Nudge*, *in* Preference Change: Approaches from Philosophy, Economics and Psychology 207, 216–17 (Till Grüne-Yanoff & Sven Ove Hansson eds., 2009); Daniel M. Hausman & Brynn Welch, *Debate: To Nudge or Not to Nudge*, 18 J. Pol. Phil. 123, 128–32 (2010); Evan Selinger & Kyle Whyte, *Is There a Right Way to Nudge? The Practice and Ethics of Choice Architecture*, 5 Soc. Compass 923, 928–30 (2011); Till Grüne-Yanoff, *Old Wine in New Casks: Libertarian Paternalism Still Violates Liberal Principles*, 38 Soc. Choice & Welfare 635 (2012).

150. Sunstein, *supra* note 38, at 144–51.

either deontological or consequentialist grounds—is unpersuasive (and strikingly incompatible with the existing rules in practically all legal systems),[151] policymakers should not, in our view, be deterred from using those technique. Some support for this conclusion may be found in public surveys that found that people do approve of governmental use of nudges.[152] However, this approval varies across different types of nudges and different societies; and in any event, public surveys do not resolve normative questions.

A more compelling critique has been made from the opposite direction. In order to make their suggestions more palatable politically (especially in the U.S. discourse), proponents of libertarian paternalism have often disregarded the behavioral findings that call for much stricter limitations on people's choices—thus failing to pursue the full implications of the behavioral findings.[153] Thus, for example, default rules are largely ineffective in transactional contexts whenever motivated suppliers set out to shift consumers out of the default.[154] More generally, private firms and interest groups may well outdo the government in the use of psychological insights to their advantage and counteracting nudges, because they are subject to fewer institutional constraints, can change tactics more quickly, and may be more skilled in using powerful tools of visual imagery and the like.[155] By the same token, there is no point in forcing individuals to make decisions (or nudging them to decide, by setting a deadline for making a decision) when they lack the necessary expertise or information to make a rational and informed decision, and the costs of obtaining such expertise or information are prohibitive. Similarly, when mistaken decisions are likely to have devastating consequences—such as being killed in a motorcycle crash for not wearing a helmet, or having people living in extreme poverty because they have not saved for old age—the only sensible legal reaction may be to preclude such decisions altogether.

E. Conclusion

The foregoing analysis highlighted some of the normative implications—or more precisely, the controversies surrounding the normative implications—of behavioral findings for the law. These implications range from the formulation of general moral-legal theories, to the nitty-gritty of designing specific rules that improve people's judgment and

151. *See supra* pp. 165–71.

152. *See, e.g.*, William Hagman et al., *Public Views on Policies Involving Nudges*, 6 Rev. Phil. & Psychol. 439 (2015); Janice Y. Jung & Barbara A. Mellers, *American Attitudes toward Nudges*, 11 Judgment & Decision Making 62 (2016); Lucia A. Reisch & Cass R. Sunstein, *Do Europeans Like Nudges?*, 11 Judgment & Decision Making 310 (2016); Cass R. Sunstein, *Do People Like Nudges?*, Admin. L. Rev. (forthcoming 2018, *available at*: https://ssrn.com/abstract=2604084).

153. Bubb & Pildes, *supra* note 135. *See also supra* pp. 165–71, 171–77.

154. Lauren E. Willis, *When Nudges Fail: Slippery Defaults*, 80 U. Chi. L. Rev. 1155 (2013).

155. Stephanie Stern, *Outpsyched: The Battle of Expertise in Psychology-Informed Law*, 57 Jurimetrics 45 (2016).

decision-making—for their own good and for that of the public. Rather than resolving the various issues, or even thoroughly canvassing them, the above analysis was designed to serve as a background for the examination of specific issues in the ensuing chapters. If there is one general lesson to be learned from the behavioral findings, it is that legal policymaking can no longer be content with the assumptions of economic rationality underlying abstract economic models. Unfortunately, however, even this modest conclusion is not shared by everyone.

5

Behavioral Insights and Basic Features of the Law

A. Introduction

The prevailing moral judgments described in Chapter 2—that achieving good outcomes is subject to moral constraints; that people bear greater responsibility for outcomes that they actively bring about (as opposed to allowing them to happen), and for outcomes that they intend to happen (as opposed to merely foreseeing them); as well as common notions of substantive and procedural fairness[1]—are all reflected in the law. Indeed, the correlation between prevailing moral convictions (often called "commonsense morality") and the law has long been pointed out by legal theoreticians, and is shared by virtually all major philosophical theories of law, from natural law to legal positivism.[2]

Thus, for example, criminal liability is more often imposed for harm caused by commission than by omission.[3] Content-based restrictions of free speech are scrutinized far more strictly than content-neutral restrictions on the time and place of expression, aimed at preventing excessive noise in a residential neighborhood or traffic congestion—thus reflecting the intending/foreseeing distinction.[4] Juries' aversion to consequentialist reasoning is evident in their tendency to increase punitive damages when firms engage in cost-benefit analysis of their safety measures.[5] Notions of procedural fairness are reflected, for example, in the requirement, under administrative law, to hold hearings in which those who may

1. *See supra* pp. 93–106.

2. *See* Eyal Zamir, Law, Psychology, and Morality: The Role of Loss Aversion 193–95 (2015).

3. *See, e.g.*, Wayne R. LaFave, Criminal Law § 6-2, at 329–41 (5th ed. 2010); Jacobo Dopico Gómez-Aller, *Criminal Omissions: A European Perspective*, 11 New Crim. L. Rev. 419 (2008).

4. *See infra* pp. 411, 413–14.

5. *See supra* p. 161; *infra* pp. 350, 554–56.

Behavioral Law and Economics. Eyal Zamir and Doron Teichman.

be adversely affected by a certain decision can voice their concerns.[6] In these and many other contexts, behavioral studies of moral judgments can shed light on the legal doctrine—including cases where the doctrine may seem puzzling from a purely consequentialist or economic perspective.

We return to this observation in Section D below, but most of this chapter focuses on another, less obvious compatibility between the law and certain fundamental features of people's psychology—specifically, *reference-dependence* and *loss aversion*.[7]

Reference-independence is a basic feature of positive and normative economic analysis. People are assumed to be rational maximizers of their own utility. Among all available options, they choose the one that would maximize their expected utility, as measured in absolute terms. Losses are equivalent to forgone gains, and gains are equal to avoided losses. Normatively speaking, people should maximize aggregate social welfare where, once again, forgone gains are considered equivalent to losses, and avoided losses are treated like gains.

In reality, however, a basic characteristic of human perceptions, preferences, judgments, and choices is reference-dependence. People judge temperature, brightness, and size in relative terms. They do not perceive outcomes as final states of wealth or welfare, but rather as gains or losses relative to some reference point. People usually prefer to avoid a loss over making a gain, thus exhibiting loss aversion. They judge harming other people as more reprehensible than not benefitting them.[8]

Reference-dependence and loss aversion are key to a better understanding of human behavior in contexts that are of interest to the law, such as consumer behavior.[9] These notions are also crucial to understanding how the law shapes people's behavior, particularly by setting default arrangements—thereby framing people's choices.[10] This chapter focuses on yet another link between loss aversion and the law: it argues that reference-dependence and loss aversion can explain—and possibly justify—basic features of the law itself.[11] Section B shows how these psychological notions permeate the law and illuminate fundamental characteristics of the legal system. Section C then considers an evolutionary explanation for the congruency between loss aversion and the law. In view of certain limitations of this evolutionary hypothesis, Section D puts forward another explanation, based on the correspondence between loss aversion, the prevailing moral judgments, and the law. Finally, Section E argues that reference-dependence and loss aversion not only explain basic features of the law, but can justify them as well.

6. *See, e.g.*, Vicki Lens, *Seeking Justice: Citizens' Use of Fair Hearings to Correct Errors in Public Welfare Bureaucracies*, 19 J. Pub. Admin. Res. & Theory 817 (2009); Paul Craig, Administrative Law 339–84 (7th ed. 2012).

7. *See supra* pp. 42–57.

8. *See generally supra* pp. 42–57, 76–86, 94–101.

9. *See infra* pp. 281–306.

10. *See supra* pp. 179–82; *infra* pp. 247–52.

11. The chapter draws on Zamir, *supra* note 2, at 119–99, 212–15 (2015).

B. Law, Reference-Dependence, and Loss Aversion

This section uses two primary examples—the different roles that tort law and the law of unjust enrichment fulfill in all legal systems, and the greater protection afforded to civil and political human rights compared to social and economic human rights—to demonstrate the congruence between loss aversion and the law. Additional illustrations will be briefly mentioned.

1. Private Law: Tort versus Unjust Enrichment

A common feature of virtually all legal systems is the marked contrast between the centrality of the law of tort and the relative marginality of the law of restitution and unjust enrichment.[12] Interactions in which one person suffers injury or loss due to another person's conduct result far more frequently in legal entitlements and remedies than interactions where one person receives a considerable benefit from someone else's conduct.[13] Relatedly, when the same interaction results in both injury to one party and a benefit to the other, the injured party's remedial rights are usually based on his or her losses, rather than on the other party's gain.[14]

However positive and negative externalities are defined, from an economic perspective the actor should internalize both types of externalities to induce efficient behavior.[15] In fact, however, the law of tort requires injurers to pay for their negative externalities far more often than the law of unjust enrichment entitles benefactors to recapture the benefits that they conferred upon others. Various explanations have been put forward for this puzzling discrepancy. Economic explanations focus on factors such as the alleged differences between involuntary injuries and benefits with respect to the feasibility of bargaining between the parties,[16] and the expected results of providing veto power to the people affected by the (injurious or beneficial) activity in question.[17] Other explanations refer to the valuation difficulties courts would face if a broad right for restitution of benefits were recognized.[18]

Without necessarily rejecting these explanations, reference-dependence and loss aversion appear to provide a particularly strong explanation for the discrepancy. If losses loom larger than gains, and if the parties' positions prior to the infliction of the loss or the bestowing of the benefit is the natural reference point, then a person who has suffered

12. Wendy J. Gordon, *Of Harms and Benefits: Torts, Restitution, and Intellectual Property,* 21 J. LEGAL STUD. 449, 450 (1992); Richard A. Epstein, *The Ubiquity of the Benefit Principle,* 67 S. CAL. L. REV. 1369, 1369–71 (1994); Brice Dickson, *Unjust Enrichment Claims: A Comparative Overview,* 54 CAMBRIDGE L.J. 100 (1995).

13. Saul Levmore, *Explaining Restitution,* 71 VA. L. REV. 65, 71 (1985).

14. Ofer Grosskopf, *Protection of Competition Rules via the Law of Restitution*, 79 TEX. L. REV. 1981, 1994–95 (2001).

15. *See also* Lisa Grow Sun & Brigham Daniels, *Mirrored Externalities,* 90 NOTRE DAME L. REV. 135 (2013).

16. Levmore, *supra* note 13, at 79–82.

17. Ariel Porat, *Private Production of Public Goods: Liability for Unrequested Benefits,* 108 MICH. L. REV. 189 (2009).

18. Levmore, *supra* note 13, at 69–72; Gordon, *supra* note 12, at 456–57.

a loss is much more likely to seek redress from the injurer than one whose behavior has yielded an unsolicited benefit to someone else. In the former instance, the redress is viewed as a remedy for a loss, whereas in the latter it is more likely to be seen as an attempt to obtain a gain. From the viewpoint of a disinterested arbiter, such as a judge or a legislator, compensating the injured person for her strongly-felt loss is seen as much more pressing than entitling the provider of the unsolicited benefit to recover for the less-strongly-felt unattained benefit.[19]

2. Human Rights: Civil and Political versus Social and Economic

Human rights are fundamental rights to which all human beings are entitled qua human beings.[20] Within this broad category, a basic distinction is drawn between civil and political rights (CPR), and social and economic rights (SER). CPR include rights and liberties such as the rights to life, bodily integrity, freedom of speech and religion, and the right to participate in the political process. SER include the right to an adequate standard of living, including adequate nutrition, clothing, and housing. They also include the rights to medical services and education, the right to work, and the right to property.

In many jurisdictions, the scope of constitutional protection afforded to SER is far narrower than that given to CPR—if it exists at all.[21] Various explanations have been offered for this differentiation. It is most commonly associated with the distinction between negative and positive rights. CPR are perceived as merely requiring the state to refrain from certain acts, whereas SER are thought to impose positive duties on it, and entail substantial public expenditure.[22] Deontological morality prioritizes the prohibition on actively or intentionally harming other people over the duty to promote human welfare.[23] Contrary to this argument, however, protecting CPR often requires positive steps and considerable costs.[24] For example, to guarantee freedom of assembly, the police may have to allocate large resources to protecting demonstrators from attack by their opponents.

Institutionally, effective protection of human rights usually entails judicial review of legislation and administrative actions. While courts arguably possess the professional competence and enjoy the legitimacy necessary to identify and prevent CPR violations, they

19. On loss aversion and other aspects of unjust enrichment law, see ZAMIR, *supra* note 2, at 124–25.

20. JACK DONNELLY, UNIVERSAL HUMAN RIGHTS IN THEORY AND PRACTICE 7–21 (2d ed. 2003).

21. Cass R. Sunstein, *Why Does the American Constitution Lack Social and Economic Guarantees?*, *in* AMERICAN EXCEPTIONALISM AND HUMAN RIGHTS 90 (Michael Ignatieff ed., 2005); Stephen Gardbaum, *The Myth and the Reality of American Constitutional Exceptionalism*, 107 MICH. L. REV. 391, 446–53 (2008) (analyzing U.S. law from a broad comparative perspective); Ruth Gavison, *On the Relationships between Civil and Political Rights, and Social and Economic Rights*, *in* THE GLOBALIZATION OF HUMAN RIGHTS 23 (Jean-Marc Coicaud et al. eds., 2003).

22. MAURICE W. CRANSTON, WHAT ARE HUMAN RIGHTS? (1973); Frank B. Cross, *The Error of Positive Rights*, 48 UCLA L. REV. 857 (2001).

23. *Cf.* EYAL ZAMIR & BARAK MEDINA, LAW, ECONOMICS, AND MORALITY 41–48, 57–78 (2010).

24. STEPHEN HOLMES & CASS R. SUNSTEIN, THE COST OF RIGHTS: WHY LIBERTY DEPENDS ON TAXES (1999); Gavison, *supra* note 21, at 33–35; Gardbaum, *supra* note 21, at 444–46, 453–61.

lack the macroeconomic data, skills, and legitimacy needed to define the scope of SER and to enforce them.[25] In response, it is argued that judicial enforceability is not a precondition for the recognition of human rights, and that delineating the scope of human rights inescapably entails value judgments and impinges on the allocation of public resources, whether it pertains to CPR or to SER.[26]

One powerful alternative or complementary explanation—though not necessarily a justification—for the lesser protection of SER is based on the distinction between losses and gains. Both when the state refrains from silencing people or taking their land, and when it takes positive measures to protect free speech against suppression by other people or to protect private property from intruders, it is preventing a loss or harm to the speaker or landowner. Conversely, freedom of speech does not necessarily require the government to provide therapy for people with speech impediments, or to facilitate access to communications media. In the sphere of SER, the provision of housing or health services is far more likely to be perceived as granting people a benefit they did not have, and thus as belonging to the domain of gains.

This conjecture is consistent with cases in which legal systems that do not generally protect social rights, nevertheless impose certain positive duties on the government. Thus, in *Goldberg v. Kelly* the Supreme Court of the United States ruled that due process forbids the *termination* of welfare benefits without a fair hearing.[27] In a similar vein, the notion of a reference point may also help explaining why it is that, while the Constitution does not mandate the provision of economic benefits, once such benefits are provided to some segments of society, they must be extended without discrimination to similarly situated people.[28] The fact that certain benefits are granted to some people likely changes the reference point for people in similar situations, such that those who do not receive them experience this as a loss.

3. Additional Examples

The congruency of law and loss aversion is manifested in a host of additional spheres, of which we will mention but a few. One is remedies for breach of contract. While the law readily compensates an injured party for its losses (in the form of either expectation or reliance damages), it does not ordinarily entitle her to the gains the breaching party made from the breach (the so-called *disgorgement remedy*).[29] Another sphere is affirmative action. Although affirmative plans are highly controversial, there appears to be a general consensus that, even if they are justifiable in hiring procedures (which are commonly perceived as involving a gain), they can hardly ever be justified in dismissals (which are perceived as

25. Cross, *supra* note 22.

26. Gavison, *supra* note 21.

27. Goldberg v. Kelly, 397 U.S. 254 (1970).

28. David Currie, *Positive and Negative Constitutional Rights*, 53 U. Chi. L. Rev. 864, 881–82 (1986).

29. Zamir, *supra* note 2, at 125–33.

inflicting a loss).[30] If we turn from private law and civil rights to criminal law, an action that the actor believes to be necessary to avoid harm or evil may be deemed justifiable under certain circumstances, but no such justification would extend to an action believed to be necessary to produce a benefit or good.[31] Under international and domestic refugee law, asylum seekers who are physically present within a country enjoy various substantive and procedural rights. It is much more controversial, however, whether and to what extent countries may legitimately prevent asylum seekers from ever reaching their territory. Expelling physically present people is likely perceived as inflicting a loss, while denying a visa and other pre-entry devices is seen as not providing a benefit.[32]

Having presented a few examples of the compatibility between loss aversion and the law, the following sections propose two possible explanations for this compatibility.

C. Evolutionary Theories

Legal economists have long argued that, by and large, the common law is efficient. One of the explanations for this observation has been evolutionary. Starting with the seminal articles of Paul Rubin and George Priest,[33] an extensive body of literature has examined the hypothesis that even if judges do not care about efficiency, the self-serving behavior of litigants can produce a process in which inefficient rules are gradually extinguished, while efficient ones survive.[34] Although all versions of this hypothesis have been sharply criticized, this body of literature contains valuable insights that may shed light on the correspondence between loss aversion and basic features of the law. One such insight is that the direction that the law's evolution takes is established not only by the reasoned decisions of the courts, but by the behavior of the litigants as well.[35] Another insight is that the existence of a dispute is a precondition for the evolution of judge-made law, efficient or not.[36] No judge-made rule could evolve in the absence of a legal dispute.

The economic literature assumes that whenever there is a legal dispute, the parties decide whether to litigate or settle out of court based on the expected costs and benefits of

30. *See infra* pp. 419–22.

31. Zamir, *supra* note 2, at 137–39.

32. Zamir, *supra* note 2, at 149–53; *infra* pp. 429–30. For other examples, see Zamir, *supra* note 2, at 133–37 (takings versus givings in constitutional property law), 139–40 ("bad Samaritan laws" in criminal law), 153–57 (tax exemptions and tax withholdings), 157–61 (burden of proof in civil litigation), and 162–65 (preliminary injunctions). *See also infra* pp. 213–15, 472–74, 593–95.

33. Paul H. Rubin, *Why Is the Common Law Efficient?* 6 J. Legal Stud. 51 (1977); George L. Priest, *The Common Law Process and the Selection of Efficient Rules*, 6 J. Legal Stud. 65 (1977).

34. *See generally* Paul H. Rubin, *Micro and Macro Legal Efficiency: Supply and Demand*, 13 Sup. Ct. Econ. Rev. 19 (2005); Francesco Parisi, *The Efficiency of the Common Law Hypothesis*, *in* 2 The Encyclopedia of Public Choice 195–98 (Charles K. Rowley & Friedrich Schneider eds., 2004).

35. Priest, *supra* note 33; John C. Goodman, *An Economic Theory of the Evolution of the Common Law*, 7 J. Legal Stud. 393 (1978).

36. Jeffrey Evans Stake, *Status and Incentive Aspects of Judicial Decisions*, 79 Geo. L.J. 1447, 1492 (1991).

each alternative. If, however, people perceive losses as much more painful than unobtained gains, then potential plaintiffs would be much less inclined to sue for unobtained gains than for losses. Since unobtained gains are less likely to result in a disutility large enough to justify legal action (which typically entails high costs—direct and indirect, pecuniary and non-pecuniary), considerably fewer disputes are expected to arise from unobtained gains. Since legal norms develop out of disputes, it stands to reason that the law of unjust enrichment and disgorgement remedies—to name but two examples—would be considerably less developed than the law of torts and reliance or expectation remedies. While this hypothesis focuses on judge-made law evolving as a result of the behavior of plaintiffs who are "one-shot" players, it remains substantially true for plaintiffs who are repeat players (but nevertheless loss averse), with regard to the "supply-side" of precedents (i.e., competition between courts), and for statutory law (which is also affected by the demand for legal norms).[37]

The evolutionary theory can be faulted on several counts. First, even if losers are more likely to file suits than no-gainers, one should expect significant differences in the incidence of lawsuits only with regard to relatively small gains. Hence, while the evolutionary theory may explain why legal norms surrounding losses evolve more quickly than norms concerning unobtained gains, it does not necessarily account for the dramatic asymmetries observed in Section B. Nonetheless, if the analogy between legal and biological evolution is valid, and given that the resources of litigants, lobbyists, and legal policymakers are limited, it is to be expected that the greater resources devoted to developing doctrines aimed at protecting people from losses would result in "crowding out" doctrines surrounding unobtained gains. Also, although norms pertaining to losses are more developed than those dealing with unattained gains, the latter do exist.

The evolutionary theory may also be criticized on the grounds that from the plaintiff's perspective, legal relief may always be perceived as belonging to the domain of gains.[38] It nevertheless remains true that people who have incurred a loss are more strongly motivated to seek legal redress than those who have failed to obtain a gain.

These and other criticisms call for caution and modesty. The evolutionary theory about the compatibility between law and loss aversion does not purport to explain the intricacies of any particular legal field, but rather to account for general, basic features of the law. It is also modest in the sense that it is not offered as the exclusive or even the primary explanation for this compatibility. It is only meant to be supplementary to an explanation focusing on the mindset of legal policymakers, to which we now turn.

37. Zamir, *supra* note 2, at 173–74. *See also* Caroline Freund & Çağlar Özden, *Trade Policy and Loss Aversion*, 98 Am. Econ. Rev. 1675 (2008).

38. *See infra* pp. 503–04.

D. Cognitive Psychology, Commonsense Morality, and the Law

While the evolutionary hypothesis is plausible, a more robust explanation for the correspondence between the law and psychological notions of reference-dependence and loss aversion may be found in an intermediate factor: the prevailing moral convictions. This explanation posits that, by and large, the law conforms to prevailing moral convictions, and since the latter are closely linked to notions of reference points and loss aversion, these notions shape the law as well.

As explained in Chapter 2,[39] prevailing moral convictions are deontological. People believe that enhancing good outcomes is desirable, but also that this should be subject to moral constraints. These constraints include prohibitions against intentionally or actively harming other people. It is immoral, for example, to kill one person and harvest her organs to save the lives of three other people, even though the benefit of such an act (saving three people) outweighs the cost (killing one person).

Deontological morality distinguishes between harming a person and not benefiting her. Were promoting the good as compelling as eliminating the bad, the doing/allowing and the intending/foreseeing distinctions, which are essential for the deontological moral constraint against harming people (or at least either of the two is), would have collapsed. According to these distinctions, while it is forbidden to intentionally/actively harm people, there is a far less compelling prohibition on merely foreseeing harm to someone, or allowing it to happen. The prohibition against killing one person for the sake of saving the lives of three other people necessarily implies that intentionally/actively killing the one is worse than merely foreseeing or allowing the death of the other three people to occur. Otherwise, there would be a prohibition against both killing the one and not killing her (thus foreseeing/allowing the death of the three).

Now, whenever an agent abides by the prohibition against intentionally/actively doing harm (e.g., refrains from killing one person), she simultaneously avoids *intending/doing harm* to the one and avoids *intending/doing good* to the three. The distinctions between intending and merely foreseeing, and between doing and merely allowing, thus inevitably entail distinctions between intending good and intending bad, and between doing good and doing bad. Promoting the good is less morally compelling than eliminating the bad.[40]

The moral distinction between promoting the good and eliminating the bad corresponds straightforwardly with the psychological notions of reference points and loss aversion. Losses, unhappiness, disutility, and harm loom larger than gains, happiness, utility,

39. *Supra* pp. 94–101.

40. On this distinction, see Shelly Kagan, The Limits of Morality 121–25 (1989) (a critique); Frances M. Kamm, *Non-consequentialism, the Person as an End-in-Itself, and the Significance of Status,* 21 Phil. & Pub. Aff. 354, 381–82 (1992) (a defense).

and benefit.[41] Indeed, most psychological studies have focused on people's perceptions and choices concerning gains and losses to themselves, whereas morality primarily centers on the effects of one's conduct on other people. However, as several studies have demonstrated, loss aversion characterizes not only people's perceptions and choices regarding their own health, wealth, or welfare, but also regarding the effects of one's decisions on the health, wealth, or welfare of others.[42] Therefore, even if one sets aside the evolutionary explanations based on plaintiffs' behavior, the prevailing moral intuitions of legal policymakers—legislators, judges, and administrators—can account for the marked correlation between psychology and law, as described in Section B.

In addition to the close correspondence between psychology and morality, this thesis assumes a correlation between morality and law. There is indeed a broad consensus across different theories of law that such a correlation does exist.[43] In fact, the basic features of the law discussed in Section B correspond to the distinction between doing bad (inflicting a loss) and doing good (conferring a gain), presupposed by the deontological doing/allowing and intending/foreseeing distinctions.

E. A Normative Perspective

The congruence between law and loss aversion as described in Section B has a normative aspect as well. Loss aversion not only explains fundamental features of the law and particular legal norms, but arguably may justify those features as well.

All normative theories take outcomes into account, either as the sole factor that ultimately determines the morality of an act, rule, or anything else (consequentialism), or as one of several such factors (deontology). Furthermore, all normative theories agree that the effect of any act, rule, or anything else on human welfare is morally important. All else being equal, the law should strive to maximize human welfare. Now, if losses adversely affect human welfare to a greater extent than unobtained gains, it stands to reason that the law should put greater efforts into deterring the infliction of losses (and remedying losses that have been incurred) than into incentivizing the conferring of benefits (and rectifying the non-attainment of gains).[44]

This normative conclusion may raise two objections. First, it may be argued that reference-dependence and loss aversion are inherently irrational, and therefore that the law should not take them into account. This objection is, however, unsound. Even under a

41. One may also observe a correspondence between the moral doing/allowing distinction (which is closely connected to the doing good/doing bad distinction) and the psychological omission bias (which is linked to the status quo bias and loss aversion). On the link between omission bias and loss aversion, see *supra* pp. 48–50.

42. *See, e.g.*, Ilana Ritov & Jonathan Baron, *Reluctance to Vaccinate: Omission Bias and Ambiguity*, 3 J. BEHAV. DECISION MAKING 263 (1990); Fredrick E. Vars, *Attitudes toward Affirmative Action: Paradox or Paradigm?*, *in* RACE VERSUS CLASS: THE NEW AFFIRMATIVE ACTION DEBATE 73 (Carol M. Swain ed., 1996); Avital Moshinsky & Maya Bar-Hillel, *Loss Aversion and Status Quo Label Bias*, 28 SOC. COGNITION 191 (2010).

43. ZAMIR, *supra* note 2, at 193–95. *See also supra* pp. 161–62.

44. *See*, in greater detail, ZAMIR, *supra* note 2, at 212–15.

narrow definition of rationality as maximization of one's own utility, reference-dependence and loss aversion are not irrational in and of themselves. Nothing in expected utility theory necessitates a reference-independent utility function. Just as a utility function may reflect risk aversion, risk neutrality, or risk-seeking, it may reflect either reference-independence or reference-dependence.[45]

The other objection to the normative claim is that it assumes that reference points are relatively stable. If legal norms can change the reference point, then rather than treating losses and unobtained gains differently, the law could simply reframe people's perceptions. Without getting into details,[46] a meta-analysis of hundreds of experimental studies has found that while the framing effect does exist, its size is only small to moderate.[47] Outside the laboratory, while some studies—especially those dealing with default rules in specific contexts—point to robust framing effects,[48] others have found no such effects.[49] It is therefore difficult to assess the robustness and generality of the effect in the real world. Perceived reference points are determined by a confluence of psychological, social, and legal factors, and the role of the law should not be overstated. It is unlikely, for example, that legal norms would be able to reframe government appropriations of private property, or people's suffering from road accidents, as "forgone gains" of the property owners or accident victims, respectively. It is similarly unlikely that the law could reframe an unjust-enrichment claim of a person whose behavior benefitted another person without involving any costs to herself, as a claim belonging to the realm of losses.[50]

Indeed, inasmuch as the law can reframe people's reference points to negate the dissimilar effect of gains and losses on their welfare, taking such measures might serve as an alternative to the basic features of the law as set out in Section B. However, since the malleability of reference points by legal norms is context-dependent and fairly limited, loss aversion does seem to provide at least a prima facie justifications for those features.

45. Ariel Rubinstein, Lecture Notes in Microeconomic Theory 107–11 (2006); Christine Jolls & Cass R. Sunstein, *Debiasing through Law,* 35 J. Legal Stud. 199, 220 (2006) (discussing the endowment effect); Zamir, *supra* note 2, at 205–07.

46. *See generally supra* pp. 46–48.

47. Anton Kühberger, *The Influence of Framing on Risky Decisions: A Meta-analysis,* 75 Org. Behav. & Hum. Decision Processes 23, 35–36, 42 (1998). Other reviews of the framing-effect literature have reached similar conclusions. *See, e.g.,* Irwin P. Levin, Sandra L. Schneider & Gary J. Gaeth, *All Frames Are Not Created Equal: A Typology and Critical Analysis of Framing Effects,* 76 Org. Behav. & Hum. Decision Processes 149, 153, 174 (1998). *See also* Zamir, *supra* note 2, at 207–12.

48. *See supra* pp. 179–82.

49. *See, e.g.,* Laura A. Siminoff & John H. Fetting, *Effects of Outcome Framing on Treatment Decisions in the Real World: Impact of Framing on Adjuvant Breast Cancer Decisions,* 9 Med. Decision Making 262 (1989); Annette M. O'Connor, Ross A. Penne & Robert E. Dales, *Framing Effects on Expectations, Decisions, and Side Effects Experienced: The Case of Influenza Immunization,* 49 J. Clinical Epidemiology 1271 (1996).

50. On the failed attempt to reframe tax exemptions as expenditures, see *infra* pp. 472–74.

F. Conclusion

This chapter highlighted the correspondence between the law and basic elements of human psychology, including prevailing moral judgments, reference-dependence, and loss aversion. It argued that this correspondence is not coincidental. Specifically, the correlation between loss aversion and the law may be the product of the evolution of judicial and statutory law, given the stronger motivation of plaintiffs (and interest groups) to seek redress for losses than for unobtained gains. In the main, however, the law reflects the mindset of legal policymakers, whose moral intuitions conform to commonsense morality. Commonsense morality is deontological: it distinguishes between acts and omissions, intended and merely foreseen outcomes, harms and benefits—and so, too, does the law.

This chapter concludes Part II of this book, which provided an overview of behavioral law and economics—its past, present, and prospects; its normative implications; and its ability to explain basic features of the law. The remaining Parts will discuss the contribution of behavioral studies to specific legal spheres, beginning with private and commercial law.

PART THREE

Private and Commercial Law

6

Property Law

A. Introduction

Property rights are a basic social and legal institution in any society. They have been justified by both deontological and consequentialist normative theories. From a rights-based perspective, private property has been associated with people's rights to their own person and the products of their labor, with the need to fulfill one's autonomy and develop one's personality, with people's right to subsistence, and the like.[1] From an economic perspective, property rights are essential to incentivizing people to invest in tangible and intangible assets and to facilitating the efficient allocation of resources through market transactions.[2]

While contractual rights and obligations are generally the product of voluntary agreements between promisees and promisors and do not directly affect other people, the holders of property rights are protected vis-à-vis the entire world—or, more precisely, vis-à-vis an unidentified set of people, including non-consenting ones. Property law determines how property rights are created, transferred, and extinguished; resolves conflicts between competing claims to assets; and shapes the relationships between people who have contemporaneous rights in the same object, whether similar (as in the case of joint ownership), or dissimilar (as in the case of landlord and tenant).

In addition to governing the relationships between individuals and private entities, property law also deals with the protection of property rights from governmental takings. *Constitutional property law* deals with the power of governmental authorities to take private property for public purposes (e.g., to build roads or schools) and to regulate the use of private property (e.g., by limiting buildings' height)—as well as the authorities' duty to compensate owners for such physical or regulatory takings.

Broadly conceived, property law pertains not only to tangible—movable and immovable—assets, but also to people's rights to intellectual creations. *Intellectual property*

1. Jeremy Waldron, The Right to Private Property (1988); Margaret J. Radin, *Property and Personhood*, 34 Stan. L. Rev. 957 (1982).

2. Steven Shavell, Foundations of Economic Analysis of Law 9–23 (2004).

law grants qualified monopoly rights to inventors, authors, and creators of artistic works and commercial names and images. It rewards people and organizations for their talents and efforts, and incentivizes them to create.

Of course, there are fundamental differences between private and constitutional property law (the latter encompasses the taking of *contractual* rights, as well), and between the law of tangible assets and that of intellectual property. Grouping these three large topics together in one chapter is not meant to downplay these differences; it merely reflects the fact that existing behavioral research does not warrant separate chapters for each one.

For similar reasons, this chapter discusses a fourth issue that transcends the conventional boundaries of property law (as it applies, for example, to contract law, as well)—namely, the choice between *property rules* and *liability rules*. The former denote the protection of legal entitlements through injunctions—meaning that one cannot appropriate an entitlement without first securing its owner's voluntary consent; the latter pertains to protection through monetary relief, thus enabling a forced transfer subject to judicially determined compensation.

Generally speaking, the behavioral research in the field of property law is "in the early stage of testing or applying basic insights and theories, and currently covers rather limited or sporadic issues."[3] Nonetheless, as this chapter demonstrates, behavioral insights—whether based on general studies of judgment and decision-making, or on specifically designed, empirical legal studies—have already made a valuable contribution to the analysis of property law.[4] This chapter critically examines this contribution in four sections—namely: ownership and possession, constitutional property law, intellectual property, and the distinction between property and liability rules.

B. Ownership and Possession

This section discusses the contribution of behavioral studies to the understanding, assessment, and implementation of the most basic building blocks of property law: ownership and possession. It first briefly describes the notion of *psychological ownership*, then reviews psychological studies of how people determine ownership of given items. It then proceeds to juxtapose two notions of ownership that have attracted considerable scholarly attention—property as a "thing" versus property as a "bundle of sticks"—and concludes by examining the implications of the *endowment effect* for norms governing ownership and possession, including doctrines such as adverse possession and self-help. To avoid repetition, some ramifications of the notions of psychological ownership and the endowment

3. Daphna Lewinsohn-Zamir, *Behavioral Law and Economics of Property Law: Achievements and Challenges, in* THE OXFORD HANDBOOK OF BEHAVIORAL ECONOMICS AND THE LAW 377, 377 (Eyal Zamir & Doron Teichman eds., 2014). *See also* Jeremy A. Blumenthal, *Property Law: A Cognitive Turn,* 17 PSYCHONOMIC BULL. & REV. 186 (2010).

4. For critical overviews of behavioral analyses of property law, see Lewinsohn-Zamir, *supra* note 3; Jeremy A. Blumenthal, *"To Be Human:" A Psychological Perspective on Property Law,* 83 TUL. L. REV. 609 (2009).

effect are discussed elsewhere in this chapter, apropos of more specific issues, such as the law of governmental takings, and intellectual property.[5]

1. Psychological Ownership

Legal systems have struggled for thousands of years with the concepts of property, ownership, and possession. However, the psychological and social attitudes of owning objects and respecting other people's ownership surely preceded the law as we know it. Studies of territorial animals reveal that defenders of a territory almost invariably defeat intruders of the same species who try to take over the territory.[6] From the perspective of evolutionary game theory, this phenomenon can be explained as a stable solution to a coordination problem—one that is superior to the alternative strategies of always-fleeing, or always-fighting.[7] The notion of ownership is also shared by toddlers, who resist attempts by others to take "their" toy.[8] Social scientists, including anthropologists and psychologists, have long studied *psychological ownership*—its meaning, genesis, functions, and the conditions under which it emerges.[9]

The attitude of ownership is essential for human efficacy, self-identity, and having a place. To satisfy their needs and attain their goals, people must interact with the environment and gain control over some elements of it. Such control is essential for the feeling of personal efficacy and competence. In addition to their instrumental role, possessions also serve as symbolic expressions. They constitute part of one's extended self or self-identity. Self-identity is developed, in part, by reflection on how we are viewed by others—which, in turn, is partly determined by our possessions. Some possessions also contribute to the sense of continuity of the self, as they connect us to our past and serve as repositories of memories. Finally, much like other animals, humans are territorial. They need to possess a certain space, a fixed point of reference, a home. Our home provides us with physical and psychic security.[10] Accordingly, people invest considerable effort and resources in acquiring, personalizing, and protecting their homes.

Psychological ownership typically emerges through (1) controlling an object, (2) coming to know it intimately, and/or (3) investing oneself in it. In general, the greater one's control over an object, and the more exclusive the control is, the stronger one's sense

5. *See infra* pp. 213–17, 226–27.

6. *See* John Alcock, Animal Behavior: An Evolutionary Approach 146–52 (10th ed. 2013) (discussing various theoretical and experimentally-tested explanations for this phenomenon); Jack W. Bradbury & Sandra L. Vehrencamp, Principles of Animal Communication 711–30 (1998) (using game theory models to examine various explanations for this phenomenon).

7. Hanna Kokko, Andrés López-Sepulcre & Lesley J. Morrell, *From Hawks and Doves to Self-Consistent Games of Territorial Behavior*, 167 Am. Naturalist 901 (2006).

8. *See, e.g.*, Federico Rossano, Hannes Rakoczy & Michael Tomasello, *Young Children's Understanding of Violations of Property Rights*, 121 Cognition 219 (2011).

9. The following summary draws heavily on the comprehensive survey and integration of this large body of literature, in Jon L. Pierce, Tatiana Kostova & Kurt T. Dirks, *The State of Psychological Ownership: Integrating and Extending a Century of Research*, 7 Rev. Gen. Psychol. 84 (2003). *See also* Helga Dittmar, The Social Psychology of Material Possessions: To Have Is to Be (1992).

10. *See also infra* pp. 219–22.

of psychological ownership toward the object. Typically, control manifests itself in using an object and excluding others from it. The longer and closer one's interaction with the object—possessing, using, or altering it—the more one becomes familiar with it, and the more likely one is to perceive it as an extension of oneself. Finally, in addition to the control of, and familiarity with, an object, psychological ownership is enhanced to the extent that one has invested oneself in the object. The clearest form of investment is the actual creation of an object: irrespective of legal ownership, creators of objects tend to view their creations as theirs, and so do others. The more personal, unique, and effortful a creation is, the greater this attitude is likely to be. However, investments may take other forms as well. The more time, effort, and expertise one puts into selecting, bargaining over, and purchasing an object, the more one feels invested in it. The same may be true of an object won in a competition or as a recognition of one's achievements.

As this brief overview of a very large body of literature makes clear, legal ownership is neither a necessary nor a sufficient condition for the existence of psychological ownership, and vice versa. Nevertheless, inasmuch as the law strives to influence people's conduct, it cannot ignore the prevailing psychological and social aspects of property, ownership, and possession.

2. Determining Ownership

The widespread recognition of, and respect for, ownership—shared, in some form or another, by animals, young children, and adults alike—raises the question of who owns what. While the law need not mirror prevailing intuitions in this regard, these intuitions are of interest to legal policymakers, because inconsistency between the law and prevailing convictions may be troubling for both principled, democratic reasons and instrumental ones. Psychologists have studied these convictions extensively, both with children and with adults. The psychological studies centered on three modes of acquiring ownership: first possession, creation, and transfer. First possession draws on the *occupation theory* of property, which states that a person who finds and takes possession of an ownerless object should be regarded as its owner, and as such, entitled to possess, use, and transfer it to others. The second mode of ownership acquisition—creation—draws on the *labor theory* of property, attributed to John Locke. It maintains that since individuals own their own person, they are entitled to the fruits of their labor. Both theories view property rights as natural rights, which the state should honor and protect.[11]

An early observational study of toddlers (12–24 months old) and preschoolers (40–48 months old) found that in the younger group, the inclination of object-holders to resist other children's attempts to take the object from them was best predicted by the relative sizes of the children involved. In contrast, in the older group this inclination was best predicted by information about who had previously possessed the object.[12] These findings

11. *See generally* Jeremy Waldron, *Property and Ownership*, *in* STANFORD ENCYCLOPEDIA OF PHILOSOPHY (2004), *available at*: https://plato.stanford.edu/entries/property.

12. Roger Bakeman & John R. Brownlee, *Social Rules Governing Object Conflicts in Toddlers and Preschoolers*, *in* PEER RELATIONS 99 (Kenneth H. Rubin & Hildy S. Ross eds., 1982).

suggest that a "prior possession rule"—consistent with the occupation theory of property—develops at an early age. Subsequent experimental studies have confirmed that people in general follow this rule, even when it runs counter to gender stereotypes: while respondents believed that girls like teddy bears more than boys, and that boys like a ball more than girls, they judged ownership not according to such likes, but according to first possession.[13] The first possessor was judged to be the owner even if another child had played with the toy for a longer period.[14]

As actual disputes have long demonstrated, things get more complex when two or more people are involved in acquiring possession over an unowned object (as in the case of hunters who simultaneously pursue an animal, and one of them kills or wounds it, while the other gets physical possession over it), or when someone finds a lost object on another person's premises.[15] Studies of people's judgments in such cases—using vignettes based on real court cases—have shown that these judgments resemble court decisions, in the sense that they do not follow a simple rule, but rather appear to be affected by subtle differences between scenarios. And just as courts' rulings on those issues are sometimes inconsistent, laypersons may differ in their judgments, even with respect to the same case.[16] Regrettably, these studies do not significantly advance our understanding of the pertinent issues, nor do they tell us much about how the next case may come out.

A second set of studies have examined the impact of creative work on perceived ownership. In one study, subjects were asked to resolve a conflict between two boys over a tree branch found on the ground. The branch was either naturally shaped like an airplane, or had been carved into that shape by the first boy, who either played or did not play with it for a while, before putting it down. The second boy then found the branch and played with it, when the first one returned and demanded it. Respondents believed that the first boy had a stronger claim on the branch when he had carved it.[17] The first boy's claim was considered stronger when he left the branch with the intention of returning to it later, than when he had no intention of playing with it again.[18]

13. Ori Friedman, *First Possession: An Assumption Guiding Inferences about Who Owns What*, 15 Psychonomic Bull. & Rev. 290, 291-92 (2008). *See also* Ori Friedman & Keren R. Neary, *Determining Who Owns What: Do Children Infer Ownership from First Possession?*, 107 Cognition 829 (2008).

14. Friedman, *supra* note 13, at 292-93.

15. *See, e.g.*, Christopher Serkin, The Law of Property 27–54 (2d ed. 2016); Joseph William Singer, Property 820-29 (5th ed. 2017); Carol M. Rose, *Possession as the Source of Property*, 52 U. Chi. L. Rev. 73 (1985).

16. *See* Peter DeScioli & Rachel Karpoff, *People's Judgments about Classic Property Law Cases*, 26 Hum. Nature 184 (2015); Peter DeScioli, Rachel Karpoff & Julian De Freitas, *Ownership Dilemmas: The Case of Finders versus Landowners*, 41 Cognitive Sci. 502 (2017); Ori Friedman, *Necessary for Possession: How People Reason about the Acquisition of Ownership*, 36 Personality & Soc. Psychol. Bull. 1161 (2010); Friedman, *supra* note 13, at 293-94.

17. James K. Beggan & Ellen M. Brown, *Association as a Psychological Justification of Ownership*, 128 J. Psychol. 365, 369-73 (1993).

18. *Id.* at 373-76. Another study found that children tend to believe, much more than adults, that by creatively changing the form of someone else's object, with the latter's consent, one becomes its owner. *See* Patricia Kanngiesser, Nathalia Gjersoe & Bruce M. Hood, *The Effect of Creative Labor on Property-Ownership Transfer by Preschool Children and Adults*, 21 Psychol. Sci. 1236 (2010).

Another study described a dispute between a person who owned a block of wood (that he had found in a vacant lot) and one who borrowed the block and carved it into a beautiful statue. A clear majority of children and adults alike opined that the prior possessor was the owner of the statue. However, when asked how to divide the proceeds of a sale of the statue to an art dealer (for $100), most subjects thought that the creator, rather than the owner, should receive more than half of the proceeds.[19]

A third study examined people's judgments of ownership when one person took another person's materials and turned them into an artwork (the vignette did not specify whether this was done with the owner's consent). Respondents were more inclined to see the creator as the owner of the object when the materials were inexpensive, when the creator put more effort into the creation, and when it increased the value of the materials.[20] The results of another set of experiments suggest that people tend to regard someone who creates an object from unowned materials as its owner even without any physical contact with it (e.g., by throwing a rock at a can, to create an ashtray), or when creation involved no real effort, or when the new creation was worth less than the materials from which it was made.[21]

In addition to first possession and creation, the third mode of ownership—and the most common these days—is a transfer from a previous owner. One study has found that, while children up to the age of four often struggle to distinguish between voluntary transfer and stealing, by the age of five they do distinguish between the effects of legitimate and illegitimate transfers.[22] In general, it appears that people's intuitions about transfer of ownership of corporeal objects are in line with the legal norms, and that these intuitions develop during childhood.[23]

The factors affecting people's judgment of ownership according to the studies described above are largely in line with the criteria used by the law.[24] However, most studies in this field have neither drawn on the legal literature nor have been conducted with an eye to enrich legal theory. Factors that appear to be important from a legal standpoint—such as whether someone who transforms someone else's object mistakenly thought that it was hers,

19. Jay Hook, *Judgments about the Right to Property from Preschool to Adulthood*, 17 Law & Hum. Behav. 135, 143-44 (1993).

20. Patricia Kanngiesser & Bruce Hood, *Not by Labor Alone: Considerations for Value Influence Use of the Labor Rule in Ownership Transfers*, 38 Cognitive Sci. 353 (2014).

21. Merrick Levene, Christina Starmans & Ori Friedman, *Creation in Judgments about the Establishment of Ownership*, 60 J. Experimental Soc. Psychol. 103 (2015).

22. Peter R. Blake & Paul L. Harris, *Children's Understanding of Ownership Transfers*, 24 Cognitive Dev. 133 (2009).

23. *See, e.g.*, Sunae Kim & Charles W. Kalish, *Children's Ascriptions of Property Rights with Changes of Ownership*, 24 Cognitive Dev. 322 (2009).

24. *See, e.g.*, Serkin, *supra* note 15, at 34-41 (discussing acquisition by creation and accession); Singer, *supra* note 15, at 820–32 (discussing acquisition of wild animals and through finding and gifts); Lars Van Vilet, *Transfer of Property Inter Vivos*, *in* Comparative Property Law: Global Perspectives 150 (Michele Graziadei & Lionel Smith eds., 2017) (providing a comparative overview of transfer of property).

or whether the original owner consented to its taking—were not even mentioned in some experiments. Apparently, the fruitful dialogue that exists between jurists and psychologists in other contexts is only beginning to emerge in the area of property law.

That said, the findings about people's prevailing judgments about property rights are of considerable interest to legal theory and policymaking. Such perceptions and beliefs do not decide normative questions, but are worth taking into account nonetheless. One should therefore hope that future research in this area will more directly address jurists' concerns.

3. Framing Ownership

Legal systems differ in how they define property rights. A systematic survey of these definitions lies beyond the scope of the present discussion. There is, however, much interest in two conceptions of property—or, more precisely, of ownership—that have attracted considerable scholarly attention, especially among American jurists: the *thing* versus the *bundle of sticks* conceptions. Schematically, the former focuses on the relationship between a person and a given object. It tends to view ownership as an absolute control over that thing, and unlimited power to exclude others from it. The *bundle-of-sticks* approach portrays ownership as a set of relationships between people. Ownership includes, inter alia, the rights to possess, use, exclude others from the use of, transfer, and destroy the object in question—and may imply certain obligations toward others.[25] The *property-as-thing* approach is conventionally described as the lay understanding of ownership, while the *bundle-of-sticks* paradigm is thought to be the sophisticated, analytically superior understanding.[26] As further discussed below, the two concepts are also thought to have normative implications.[27] The bundle-of-sticks approach is seen as more consistent with legal limitations on owners' rights (e.g., pursuant to land use regulation), and hence with the owners' social responsibilities. In contrast, according to the *thing* approach, any restriction of owners' exclusive rights is likely to be perceived as an encroachment on private property.

From a behavioral perspective, the *bundle-of-sticks* conception of property is a product of System 2, deliberative and analytical thinking, while the *thing* approach appears to reflect a more spontaneous and intuitive thinking. Nonetheless, Jonathan Nash and Stephanie Stern have argued that people's framing of property rights can be relatively easily manipulated, and that no legal training is necessary to reframe property as a bundle of rights.[28] Specifically, they conducted experiments in which incoming law students were

25. *See generally* J. E. Penner, *The "Bundle of Rights" Picture of Property*, 43 UCLA L. REV. 711 (1996); Jonathan Remy Nash, *Packaging Property: The Effects of Paradigmatic Framing of Property Rights*, 83 TULANE L. REV. 691, 694–707 (2009).

26. *See also* BRUCE A. ACKERMAN, PRIVATE PROPERTY AND THE CONSTITUTION (1977). Whichever concept of ownership is adopted, one may try to identify the rights or "sticks" that are essential to the category of "ownership"—namely, the elements without which one is no longer the owner of a thing. To do so, it may be useful to draw on the rich psychological research on schemata, prototypes, and mental representations. *See* Blumenthal, *supra* note 3, at 187.

27. *See infra* pp. 215–17.

28. Nash, *supra* note 25; Jonathan Remy Nash & Stephanie Stern, *Property Frames*, 87 WASH. U. L. REV. 449 (2010).

informed that the law school is considering the adoption of a new laptop policy, whereby all students are to use the same type of laptops. In the *discrete-asset* conditions, subjects received a "Laptop Purchase Notification" whereby they would be required "to purchase a laptop computer."[29] In the *bundle-of-rights* conditions, subjects received a "Laptop Usage Purchase Notification," stating that they would be required "to purchase the right to use a laptop computer" or "to purchase rights to a laptop computer."[30] As hypothesized, the bundle-of-rights formulation was found to reduce the subjects' expectations about the strength of their property rights, making them more receptive to subsequent right restrictions, such as requiring prior permission to upload large files and obliging them to allow others to use their laptop from time to time.[31]

However, as Daphna Lewinsohn-Zamir aptly points out, there is reason to doubt that these experiments actually captured two framings of the same thing.[32] Plausibly, subjects in the bundle-of-rights conditions did not get a sense of being the owners of a laptop, because they had merely purchased a set of rights to it, rather than "a laptop." This perception was possibly reinforced by the fact that the laptops (or rights to them) were purchased from the law school (or from the campus computer store, pursuant to the law school's policy), and not independently from a third party—thus possibly rendering the situation one of "limited giving" rather than "taking." The finding that students in the bundle-of-rights conditions were willing to pay considerably less for the set of rights to the computer than the students in the discrete-asset conditions were willing to pay for the laptop strengthens this concern.[33] Finally, as the authors concede, it is unclear whether the experimentally-induced, bundle-of-rights framing would not have disappeared in real life after prolonged, actual possession and use of the laptop.[34]

Anecdotally, both of us regularly use our research budget to purchase laptop computers. While we are aware that "our" computers are formally the university's property, we do resent the (newly enforced) requirement to hand in the old computer once we purchase a new one. To cite another example, on a much larger scale, most lands in Israel belong to the state, and individuals ordinarily receive only long-term leases for their residential or commercial property (typically for a term of forty-nine years, with the option to renew for a similar period thereafter). Nonetheless, most "tenants" see themselves as the owners of their property, and market prices hardly differentiate between ownership and such long-term leases.

29. Nash, *supra* note 25, at 712; Nash & Stern, *supra* note 28, at 467.

30. Nash, *supra* note 25, at 712–13; Nash & Stern, *supra* note 28, at 467.

31. Nash, *supra* note 25, at 715–20; Nash & Stern, *supra* note 28, at 470–78. In a 2x2 factorial design, the two studies crossed the *discrete-asset / bundle-of-rights* manipulation with a *forewarning / no-forewarning* manipulation, whereby the former included a description of the ways in which the students' use of the computer would be limited by the law school. Forewarning subjects about future restrictions had a similar effect to the bundle-of-rights manipulation, and the combination of the two produced the greatest reduction in the subjects' expectations with regard to their property rights.

32. Lewinsohn-Zamir, *supra* note 3, at 381–82.

33. Nash & Stern, *supra* note 28, at 478–79.

34. *Id.* at 491–92.

Cognizant of this prevailing perception, and knowing that requiring "tenants" to vacate the land at the end of the lease would result in an immense public outcry, the Israeli government is gradually equating the rights of tenants to those of owners, and even transfers full ownership to long-term tenants.[35] Inasmuch as the Israeli experience is generalizable, it indicates that even when people are granted only an incomplete bundle of rights in property, they nonetheless tend to perceive it as a discrete asset, and legal policymakers cannot be oblivious to this reality. In this context, the law may be said to have adapted itself to psychological ownership. Of course, this does not mean that private and commercial landowners would necessarily treat their long-term tenants in the same manner as the Israeli government does. The psychological ownership of tenants is but one of several factors determining their own behavior and the behavior of landowners.

4. Ownership, Possession, and the Endowment Effect

One of the typical components of ownership in tangible assets (and by extension, in intangible ones) is possession. Possession consists of a physical element of control over an asset (*corpus*), and a mental one of intention to control (*animus*). Very often, the owner of a movable or an immovable property is also its possessor, but sometimes—as in the cases of landlord and tenant, bailor and bailee, and pledgor and pledgee—ownership and possession diverge. Possession may serve as evidence of ownership, and it is often presumed, in the absence of evidence to the contrary, that the possessor of an asset is also its owner.[36] The law of property protects possession by lawful possessors—and occasionally by unlawful ones, as well—against other people.[37]

To date, the behavioral phenomenon that appears to be most relevant to the understanding and assessing of the legal treatment of ownership and possession is the *endowment effect*: the tendency to place a higher value on objects and entitlements that one already has, compared with objects and entitlements that one does not.[38] However, the great majority of psychological studies of the endowment effect have not differentiated between ownership and possession. The endowment effect has predominantly been demonstrated in situations where people were given both ownership and possession of the items in question—or neither of the two. This is hardly surprising. Inasmuch as the heuristics used by System-1 thinking—including the related phenomena of loss aversion and the endowment effect—are evolutionarily adaptive; they must have evolved long before the comparatively recent development (in biological evolutionary terms) of the legal distinction between ownership

35. Lewinsohn-Zamir, *supra* note 3, at 387–88.

36. As described in pp. 204–07, children and adults alike tend to infer ownership from first possession. It has also been found that children infer ownership from a person's exercise of control over the use of an object by others. *See* Keren R. Neary, Ori Friedman & Corinna L. Burnstein, *Preschoolers Infer Ownership from "Control of Permission,"* 45 Dev. Psychol. 873 (2009).

37. On the legal concept of possession, see generally Yaëll Emerich, *Possession*, *in* Comparative Property Law, *supra* note 24, at 171.

38. *See generally supra* pp. 50–56.

and possession.[39] For this reason, psychologists and behavioral economists with no particular interest in legal issues sensibly use the vague concept of "endowment," without differentiating between ownership and possession.[40] However, this makes the drawing of lessons from psychological research and applying them to property law rather difficult.[41]

Nevertheless, some insights can be gleaned from psychological studies of the endowment effect. First, the endowment effect has been shown to exist not only with regard to tangible goods, but to intangible entitlements as well—such as working hours, hunting rights, academic chores, exposure to health risks, and contractual rights under default rules.[42] It stands to reason, therefore, that it applies to proprietary (and even contractual) rights that do not include physical possession. As studies of reference-dependence have shown, even expectations about future outcomes can serve as a reference point for people when perceiving changes as gains or losses.[43]

Second, a few studies have specifically examined the effect of ownership and possession on the endowment effect. In one study by Jack Knetsch and Wei-Kang Wong, participants were assigned to one of three treatments—two of which are particularly germane to the present issue.[44] In one treatment, participants were told that they earned a mug or a pen for taking part in the experiment, that they own it, and that they would be able to collect and take it with them at the end of the experiment. They were also given an opportunity to examine the object, but had to return it to the experimenter before completing the questionnaire. At the end of the experiment, they were asked to indicate whether they would like to trade the object they had earned (the mug or the pen) for the other one. In another treatment, participants were in possession of the object throughout the experiment, but explicitly told that they did not own it yet, but rather would earn it if they complete the questionnaire. At the end of the experiment, they examined the alternative object and could choose between earning and keeping the one they initially received, or give up earning it and earn the other object instead. In the first condition—ownership without possession—50 percent of those who initially owned mugs opted to keep them, and only 31 percent of those who owned pens exchanged them for a mug. In the second condition—possession without ownership—67 percent of the mug holders opted to keep them, and only 14 percent of the pen holders exchanged them for mugs.

39. On the evolutionary roots and neural basis of loss aversion and related phenomena, see EYAL ZAMIR, LAW, PSYCHOLOGY, AND MORALITY 42–46 (2015).

40. The same is true of other social scientists, who tend to use the notions of *feelings of ownership* and *feelings of possession* interchangeably. *See, e.g.*, Pierce, Kostova & Dirks, *supra* note 9, at 85 n.1.

41. Daphna Lewinsohn-Zamir, *What Behavioral Studies Can Teach Jurists about Possession and Vice Versa*, *in* LAW AND ECONOMICS OF POSSESSION 128, 136–38 (Yun-chien Chang ed., 2015).

42. *See* Lewinsohn-Zamir, *supra* note 41, at 131–33; *supra* p. 51; *infra* pp. 247–52.

43. *See supra* p. 45.

44. Jack L. Knetsch & Wei-Kang Wong, *The Endowment Effect and the Reference State: Evidence and Manipulations*, 71 J. ECON. BEHAV. & ORG. 407 (2009). The following description refers to reported treatments 2 and 3.

These results suggest that possession and ownership can each separately produce an endowment effect, and that the effect produced by possession is stronger. However, the latter inference is inconclusive, because the primary purpose of the study was not to compare ownership with possession, so other, slight differences between the two conditions might have come into play. Another study demonstrated that ownership produces an endowment effect, and that the opportunity to touch an object increased its valuation in the eyes of both owners (sellers) and non-owners (buyers).[45] It has also been found that extending the length of time during which subjects could examine an object from ten to thirty seconds increased their willingness to pay for it.[46]

Most relevant to the ownership/possession distinction, Jochen Reb and Terry Connolly directly compared the effects of ownership and possession on the endowment effect.[47] Drawing on theories of psychological ownership,[48] they hypothesized that possession would induce a stronger endowment effect than mere ownership. Their two experiments differed in terms of the object used (a chocolate bar versus a university coffee mug) and in other minor respects, but shared a similar 2 (ownership versus no-ownership) x 2 (possession versus no-possession) between-subjects factorial design. Thus, in the mug experiment, participants were told either that they own the mug, or not; and while all of them were shown a sample mug, they were either given the mug, or not. Shortly afterward, their valuations of the mug were elicited. In both the chocolate and mug experiments, the endowment effect was replicated in the sense that participants in the ownership-plus-possession condition valued the object considerably (and statistically significantly) more than those in the no-ownership-no-possession condition. However, upon examination of the two independent variables, it was found that whereas possession had produced a significant endowment effect, ownership had not.

It is impossible to infer from these results that ownership without possession does not produce an endowment effect—in fact, other studies have shown otherwise.[49] The results do suggest, however, that in itself, legal ownership is insufficient to produce the endowment effect: psychological ownership is necessary to shift the reference point.[50] Other studies have similarly shown that psychological ownership underpins the endowment effect.[51]

45. Joann Peck & Suzanne B. Shu, *The Effect of Mere Touch on Perceived Ownership,* 36 J. CONSUMER RES. 434 (2009).

46. James R. Wolf, Hal R. Arkes & Waleed A. Muhanna, *The Power of Touch: An Examination of the Effect of Duration of Physical Contact on the Valuation of Objects,* 3 JUDGMENT & DECISION MAKING 476 (2008).

47. Jochen Reb & Terry Connolly, *Possession, Feelings of Ownership and the Endowment Effect,* 2 JUDGMENT & DECISION MAKING 107 (2007).

48. *See supra* pp. 203–04.

49. Knetsch & Wong, *supra* note 44.

50. In fact, Reb and Connolly presented their subjects with questions designed to elicit their feelings of ownership, and found that the rating of those feelings—which were enhanced by possessing the object—had fully mediated their monetary valuations (*id.* at 110, 112). However, this finding should be interpreted with caution because, inter alia, subjects answered the subjective feelings questions only after providing their monetary valuations, so the former may have been influenced by the latter (*id.* at 112).

51. *See, e.g.,* Suzanne B. Shu & Koann Peck, *Psychological Ownership and Affective Reaction: Emotional Attachment Process Variables and the Endowment Effect,* 21 J. CONSUMER PSYCHOL. 439 (2011).

The finding that mere possession tends to yield a stronger endowment effect than mere ownership is hardly surprising, given what we know about psychological ownership: the more control one has over an object and the more one is familiar with it, the stronger the psychological ownership. While legal ownership may well create an endowment effect, as long as it is abstract in nature and does not involve actual control and familiarity with the object, a weaker sense of endowment is expected.

One must be cautious in drawing normative conclusions from behavioral insights, especially when the empirical basis of those insights is limited. Nonetheless, it appears that the abovementioned findings may contribute to our understanding and assessment of property law. One doctrine in point is *adverse possession*. Under this doctrine, one may acquire title to land (or at least immunity from eviction suit by its rightful owner), if one has been in possession of the land for the statutory period of limitation and one's possession has been actual, open and notorious, exclusive, continuous, adverse to the owner's interest (that is, not by virtue of the owner's right, or with the latter's permission)—and, by some accounts, also with good faith belief on the part of the possessor that she is entitled to the property.[52] The doctrine of adverse possession runs counter to the basic justifications of private property. It has nevertheless been justified on several interrelated grounds, including the evidentiary difficulty of proving stale claims; enhancing the marketability of property; incentivizing owners to make productive use of their land, or at least to assert their rights in a timely fashion (and their fault for not doing so); and protecting the possessor's reliance on her long-standing possession and her consequent attachment to it.[53]

Behaviorally minded scholars have complemented these traditional rationales by pointing to the change of reference point induced by a long-term adverse possession.[54] Plausibly, the longer and the more open and exclusive the adverse possession, the weaker the true owner's psychological ownership. At some point, the latter is more likely to perceive reinstatement of his or her title and possession as a gain, rather than as an averted loss. At the same time (and plausibly much more quickly, given people's tendency to update their reference points upward much more rapidly than downward),[55] the adverse possessor's psychological ownership is gradually strengthened, even in the absence of a legal title. The more extensive and exclusive the possessor's use of the land, and the more she invests in the land in the belief that it is hers, the more her reference point is likely to shift, such that she would view eviction from the land as a loss, rather than as a forgone gain. The requirement that the possession be adverse is also consistent with this explanation, since both the

52. *See generally* Thomas W. Merrill, *Property Rules, Liability Rules, and Adverse Possession*, 79 NW. U. L. REV. 1122 (1985) (analyzing U.S. law).

53. *Id.* at 1126–37.

54. Robert C. Ellickson, *Bringing Culture and Human Frailty to Rational Actors: A Critique of Classical Law and Economics*, 65 CHI.-KENT L. REV. 23, 38–39 (1989); David Cohen & Jack L. Knetsch, *Judicial Choice and Disparities between Measures of Economic Values*, 30 OSGOODE HALL L.J. 737, 751–52 (1992); Jeffrey Evans Stake, *The Uneasy Case for Adverse Possession*, 89 GEO. L.J. 2419, 2459–71 (2001).

55. *See supra* p. 45.

owner's and the possessor's reference points are less likely to shift if the possessor holds the property with the owner's consent.

To be sure, the posited reference-points shift and ensuing psychological ownership and endowment effect do not provide a conclusive normative, or even explanatory, account of the law. As always, there are other, competing considerations (in particular, in the present context, the general justifications for protecting the property rights of the true owner), and as is often the case, more direct empirical research could further illuminate the behavioral argument.[56]

Insights concerning psychological ownership are relevant to other property-law doctrines, such as self-help. The doctrine of self-help allows rightful possessors (but not non-possessing owners) to use reasonable force to avert attempted invasion of their land, or to evict very recent invaders.[57] The doctrine has traditionally been justified as sanctioning the spontaneous and instinctive reaction of a property holder against dispossession.[58] Given this rationale and the factors giving rise to psychological ownership, it has been suggested that the self-help doctrine be extended to cover unlawful possessors, as well—at least in relation to subsequent intruders.[59]

C. Constitutional Property Law

In addition to consensual transactions in property and the protection of property against other people's intrusions, property law lato sensu is also about the protection of private property vis-à-vis the government. Governmental actions—including the taking of property for public purposes and restricting the development and use of private property by its owner—directly and indirectly affect people's proprietary rights. This section discusses four basic issues in constitutional property law that behavioral studies have shed light upon: the disparate treatment of governmental takings and "givings," the distinction between physical and nonphysical taking, scope and mode of compensation, and the special treatment of homes.

1. Takings versus Givings

Throughout the world, legal systems prohibit the taking of private property for public use without just compensation—yet they do not limit government's power to *confer* property upon private individuals or entities, nor do they require that recipients be charged for such benefits. The prevailing notion is that governmental conferring of special benefits (even if they are disproportionate) is not objectionable or problematic in the same way that

56. Lewinsohn-Zamir, *supra* note 41, at 137–38.

57. *See, e.g.*, RESTATEMENT (SECOND) OF TORTS §§ 77–99 (AM. LAW INST. 1965).

58. OLIVER WENDELL HOLMES, THE COMMON LAW 143–44 (American Bar Association ed. 2009) (1881).

59. Lewinsohn-Zamir, *supra* note 41, at 141. On similar grounds, Lewinsohn-Zamir proposes to ban contractual waivers of tenants' right to judicial eviction proceedings, and to afford tenants, especially long-term ones, some of the rights and protection currently available to owners (*id.* at 141–42).

takings are.[60] As a matter of fact, various mechanisms are used to charge private recipients of property rights and regulatory benefits (such as expansion of building rights by zoning ordinances) for such givings.[61] However, in virtually all legal systems the safeguards against unjustified or uncompensated takings are more robust than the safeguards against unjustified or uncharged-for givings; the judicial scrutiny of takings is stricter than that of givings; and the takings scholarship is far more elaborate than the one concerning governmental givings.[62]

This asymmetry appears to be neither efficient nor fair. From an efficiency standpoint, the government should internalize both the costs and benefits of its activities, so as to avoid the inefficiencies associated with negative and positive externalities.[63] From a fairness perspective, it is unfair for a few people to be enriched at the expense of the general public—just as it is unfair for a few people to bear the public burden.[64] Accordingly, Abraham Bell and Gideon Parchomovsky have powerfully argued that this disparate legal and scholarly treatment of governmental takings and givings should be abandoned.[65] Other studies have similarly criticized the takings/givings distinction, and have called for the implementation of a system of charges for governmental givings.[66]

Several explanations (if not justifications), have been offered for the existing distinction. The most obvious one is that "losers cry for compensation while winners never cry for taxation."[67] However, there is typically no difference between takings and givings in terms of the number of people who stand to lose or gain from any governmental action, or the magnitude of such losses or gains. In both instances, the impact of governmental actions may be concentrated or dispersed, large or small.[68] Thus, one might expect that those who do not receive the benefits would call for subjecting winners to taxation or charges of some other sort. Moreover, charging givings may be an effective and fair means for raising revenue for the government's activities. Indeed, when benefit recipients are few,

60. *See, e.g.*, Thomas W. Merrill & Henry E. Smith, *The Morality of Property*, 48 WM. & MARY L. REV. 1849, 1884 & n.151 (2007).

61. For a comprehensive comparative survey of such mechanisms, see WINDFALLS FOR WIPEOUTS: LAND VALUE CAPTURE AND COMPENSATION 311–488 (Donald G. Hagman & Dean J. Misczynski eds., 1978).

62. Louis Kaplow, *An Economic Analysis of Legal Transitions*, 99 HARV. L. REV. 509, 554 (1986); Abraham Bell & Gideon Parchomovsky, *Givings*, 111 YALE L.J. 547, 549 (2001).

63. Bell & Parchomovsky, *supra* note 62, at 580–84.

64. *Id.* at 554.

65. *Id.* A symmetric economic analysis of governmental takings and givings in the broadest sense of these terms was offered earlier by Louis Kaplow. *See, e.g.*, Kaplow, *supra* note 62. While Bell and Parchomovsky conclude that givings should be charged just as takings are compensated, Kaplow claims that the government should neither compensate nor charge, in either instance.

66. *See, e.g.*, Lindsay Warren Bowen, Jr., Note, *Givings and the Next Copyright Deferment*, 77 FORDHAM L. REV. 809 (2008); Daniel D. Barnhizer, *Givings Recapture: Funding Public Acquisition of Private Property Interests on the Coasts*, 27 HARV. ENVTL. L. REV. 295 (2003).

67. Kaplow, *supra* note 62, at 555.

68. Lee Anne Fennell, *Taking Eminent Domain Apart*, 2004 MICH. ST. L. REV. 957, 967–71.

the many non-recipients may encounter difficulties in organizing to stake their claim for charging recipients. However, this collective-action problem does not explain why legal policymakers, including the framers of constitutions, treat takings and givings so differently, nor does it necessarily explain why the government does not effectively charge recipients of benefits, at least when the latter are not its allies.

A more compelling explanation (and partial justification) for the takings/givings distinction may be provided by the phenomenon of loss aversion.[69] Assuming that people normally view the status quo as the pertinent benchmark, when the government takes their property or otherwise adversely affects its value, such taking is painful and causes considerable resentment. Conversely, when the government benefits other people, it is more likely to be perceived as an unobtained gain, rather than as a loss, or to be disregarded altogether. Hence, it is considerably less painful and less cause for resentment.

As in other contexts, the distinction is not hermetic. If everyone but me gets something, I may view everyone else's position as the reference point—and experience my not-receiving it as a loss. The smaller the number of other people who get a given benefit, and the greater the distance and dissimilarity between the agent and the recipients, the less such a shift of reference point is expected. In the less likely (albeit still logically possible) event that the thing that is taken had previously been given by the government, the taking may be seen as belonging to the domain of (forgone) gains.[70] Interestingly, the issue of the relevant baseline is a recurring theme in takings and givings debates.[71] Nonetheless, the salience of the status quo as the natural reference point appears to provide the best explanation for the takings/givings asymmetry.

Of course, an explanation is not necessarily a justification. Although the dissimilar impact of takings and givings on people's welfare provides a pro tanto justification for the current distinction,[72] other considerations call for a stricter regulation and scrutiny of governmental givings.

2. Physical versus Nonphysical Taking

Planning and building laws regulate the use of land and restrict its development. They do so to enhance the welfare, health, and security of communities, and to facilitate the provision of various public goods. Changes in zoning ordinances can dramatically decrease or increase a land's value. While the physical taking of a parcel of land or part thereof is generally conditioned upon the payment of adequate compensation, legal systems markedly differ about the scope of the right to compensation for nonphysical takings (such as the elimination or reduction of development rights), and for *indirect* injuries due to zoning

69. *See generally supra* pp. 42–57.

70. This possibility is less likely, because studies show that people quickly update their reference points after gains (but not after losses). *See supra* p. 45.

71. *See, e.g.*, Bell & Parchomovsky, *supra* note 62, at 552, 612–14; Cass R. Sunstein, *Lochner's Legacy*, 87 Colum. L. Rev. 873 (1987); Richard E. Levy, *Escaping* Lochner's *Shadow: Toward a Coherent Jurisprudence of Economic Rights*, 73 N.C. L. Rev. 329, 390–442 (1995).

72. *See also supra* pp. 195–96.

ordinances that apply to other parcels in the vicinity. From a comparative viewpoint, legal systems run the gamut from those that grant no compensation whatsoever for regulatory takings (except in extreme cases), to those that do grant such compensation in a wide range of cases.[73] Thus, in many jurisdictions, an economic loss due to direct or indirect regulatory injuries to land is not compensable even if it entails a loss similar to, or even greater than, a physical taking. Interestingly, there is no clear correlation between the existence and wording of the constitutional protection of private property and the scope of the right to compensation for regulatory takings in various countries.[74]

Is the distinction between physical and nonphysical takings justifiable? Some efficiency arguments against compensation—such as the concern about overinvestment in land (i.e., owners' disregard of the risks of appropriation, if full compensation is guaranteed),[75] and the alleged superiority of private insurance against takings[76]—are rather dubious;[77] and at any rate, do not warrant a distinction between physical and regulatory takings.[78] Another argument against compensation for regulatory taking is that it would eliminate the redistributive effect of such actions. This argument is not very compelling either: unlike taxes and subsidies, the losses inflicted by planning ordinances are usually incidental to the planning considerations underlying the land-use designations of particular plots—resulting in arbitrary and unjust distributive results if no compensation is awarded.[79] Other considerations might, however, weigh against full (or any) compensation for some direct and indirect regulatory takings. These include the magnitude of the loss of the land's value; the distribution of the public burden borne by landowners; the costs of administering the compensation system; the non-monetary benefits accruing to landowners; and the nonrecognition of some injuries on moral grounds.[80]

This is a very skeletal description of a lively debate that has gone on for decades, primarily in the United States. Can a behavioral perspective enrich the debate? Some scholars have argued that behavioral insights do provide some justification, or at least an explanation, for the current distinction between physical and nonphysical takings—and perhaps even show the way to improvements in this regard.

73. *See generally* TAKINGS INTERNATIONAL: A COMPARATIVE PERSPECTIVE ON LAND USE REGULATIONS AND COMPENSATION RIGHTS (Rachelle Alterman ed., 2010) [hereinafter TAKINGS INTERNATIONAL].

74. Rachelle Alterman, *Comparative Analysis: A Platform for Cross-National Learning*, *in* TAKINGS INTERNATIONAL, *id.* at 21, 23–35. *See also* GREGORY S. ALEXANDER, THE GLOBAL DEBATE OVER CONSTITUTIONAL PROPERTY: LESSONS FOR AMERICAN TAKINGS JURISPRUDENCE 24–30 (2006).

75. *See, e.g.*, Kaplow, *supra* note 62, at 529–31.

76. *Id.* at 537–41.

77. In part, because they do not give sufficient weight to the fear of governmental authorities' *fiscal illusion* in the absence of a duty to pay compensation. *See, e.g.*, Lawrence Blume & Daniel L. Rubinfeld, *Compensation for Takings: An Economic Analysis*, 72 CAL. L. REV 569, 620–22 (1984).

78. Daphna Lewinsohn-Zamir, *Compensation for Injuries to Land Caused by Planning Authorities: Towards a Comprehensive Theory*, 46 U. TORONTO L.J. 47, 61–69 (1996).

79. *Id.* at 53–60. In fact, a no-compensation rule may leave weaker parties, who lack the lobbying power to influence government decisions, worse off.

80. *Id.* at 76–113.

One, relatively modest, claim, is that landowners usually take the status quo as the reference point, so they are likely to perceive a physical taking as a loss. Conversely, the loss of unrealized development rights is more likely to be perceived as an unobtained gain—even if the resulting drop in the land's market value is larger than in the case of a physical taking.[81] Once a landowner is granted a building permit or actually starts building, however, her reference point likely changes; hence she is entitled to compensation for what is no longer an unobtained gain, but rather a loss.[82]

However, even if loss aversion can explain the intuitive appeal of the physical/nonphysical distinction, it hardly justifies a denial of compensation for nonphysical takings, which may well be very substantial.[83] Moreover, it is not self-evident that landowners do not perceive reductions in their development rights as losses, especially if those rights were reflected in the purchase price they had paid for the land.[84]

Another, potentially more far-reaching, contribution of the behavioral perspective to the debate regarding compensation for nonphysical takings draws on the distinction between framing property as a "thing" or as a bundle of rights, and the alleged possibility of reframing people's perceptions in this regard.[85] It has been argued that the bundle-of-rights perspective renders regulatory limitations on land use more legitimate and acceptable, and that inducing such framing may therefore serve to reduce the hostility to such regulation—for example, in the context of protection of endangered species.[86] However, even if we set aside the question of whether such reframing by legal means or otherwise is feasible,[87] it is unclear how the choice between these two frames can affect the compensation debate. On the one hand, greater legitimization of regulatory restrictions on land use might reduce the demand for compensation for such restrictions—thus indirectly reinforcing the physical/nonphysical takings distinction. On the other hand, it has been repeatedly pointed out that the tendency to deny compensation for regulatory takings stems not from a bundle-of-rights understanding of property, but rather from the adoption of the lay understanding of property as a thing: it follows from such understanding that as long as a landowner is not deprived of her ownership and possession, there is no real "taking" of her property.[88] Highlighting the bundle-of-sticks conception of property may therefore actually intensify the demand for compensation, when even a single "stick" is taken from the owner's bundle.[89]

81. Ellickson, *supra* note 54, at 37–38; Christopher Serkin, *Existing Uses and the Limits of Land Use Regulations*, 84 N.Y.U. L. Rev. 1222, 1267–70 (2009).

82. Ellickson, *supra* note 54, at 38.

83. Serkin, *supra* note 81, at 1267–70.

84. Lewinsohn-Zamir, *supra* note 3, at 384–85.

85. *See supra* pp. 207–09.

86. Nash, *supra* note 25, at 724–26; Nash & Stern, *supra* note 28, at 451–55, 457–59, 462–65, 492–94. *See also* Joseph William Singer, Entitlement: The Paradoxes of Property (2010).

87. *See supra* pp. 207–09. *See also supra* pp. 46–48, 196.

88. *See, e.g.*, Ackerman, *supra* note 26, at 113–67.

89. Nash, *supra* note 25, at 726; Lewinsohn-Zamir, *supra* note 3, at 380–82.

3. Scope and Mode of Compensation

One major question in takings law is how to calculate the monetary compensation for taking. Both efficiency and fairness considerations generally call for full compensation in accordance with the subjective valuation of the property by its owner, but since it is (almost) impossible to reliably determine this value, the common measure is the property's fair market price.[90] In other contexts, such as remedies for breach of contract, this consideration militates against the protection of entitlements through liability rules (damages), and for enforcing them through property rules (specific performance).[91] This does not appear to be a viable solution for governmental takings, if only because the typical market failures—chiefly the holdout and assembly problems—are likely to hinder voluntary transactions.[92] The next subsection discusses this issue in the context of homes. Here we discuss regular ("fungible") property.

While the possible difference between market value and subjective value has long been recognized by standard economic analysis (in fact, it is part and parcel of the competitive market model), it has recently been argued that the involuntary nature of governmental takings poses further difficulty. Experimental findings suggest that being paid the full market value of a property when it is expropriated by the government is perceived as a far worse outcome than being paid full market value in a voluntary transaction.[93] Significantly, this dissimilar assessment of the outcome occurred when the property was described as an undeveloped parcel of land (rather than a unique or personal property), the owner was described as a real estate company (rather than an individual), and it was specifically noted that the parcel's value to the company matched its market value.[94] Moreover, these results were replicated in an experiment conducted with experienced businesspeople, rather than laypersons.[95] These preliminary findings imply that compensating landowners for the taking of their property according to its market value is systematically under-compensatory, even when the owners' subjective valuation is no higher than its market value, and when it is not unique or personal.

Behavioral studies shed light on the mode of compensation, as well. As in other legal spheres, such as tort and contract law, the default means of compensation for governmental takings is monetary. However, this is not the only conceivable mode: landowners

90. *See, e.g.*, Abraham Bell & Gideon Parchomovsky, *Taking Compensation Private*, 59 STAN. L. REV. 871 (2007).

91. *See, e.g.*, Anthony T. Kronman, *Specific Performance*, 45 U. CHI. L. REV. 351 (1978).

92. When a project (such as a new road or a large shopping center) requires the assembly of the lands of many owners, each owner effectively holds monopoly power, because without her consent the entire project cannot be realized. The rational strategy under such circumstances is to hold out in an attempt to capture the largest possible proportion of the project's surplus—which may scuttle the project entirely, especially if landowners overestimate that surplus. *See, e.g.*, Lloyd Cohen, *Holdouts and Free Riders*, 20 J. LEGAL. STUD. 351 (1991); Thomas J. Miceli & C.F. Sirmans, *The Holdout Problem, Urban Sprawl, and Eminent Domain*, 16 J. HOUSING ECON. 309 (2007).

93. Daphna Lewinsohn-Zamir, *Taking Outcomes Seriously*, 2012 UTAH L. REV. 861, 869–72, 876.

94. *Id.* at 876.

95. *Id.* at 879–84.

are sometimes compensated by enhancing their development rights with regard to the rest of the parcel (or to another parcel they own), or by receiving substitute land (primarily when takings are part of a land-readjustment process). Although such in-kind compensation is not always feasible, experimental findings show that when it is, it is more likely to provide effective compensation to landowners for the harm caused by a physical or regulatory taking.[96] People's documented preference for in-kind compensation plausibly echoes the prevailing sentiment that positive and negative reciprocation should be carried out with resources of the same kind.[97]

4. Homes versus Other Property

A place to live in is a basic physical and psychological human need.[98] A home provides people with shelter and security; promotes freedom, intimacy, and privacy; and facilitates family life. Indeed, psychological studies have indicated that homes (but not other residences) are associated with the "qualities of continuity, privacy, self-expression and personal identity, social relationships, warmth, and a suitable physical structure."[99] Accordingly, the right to adequate housing is regarded as a basic human right.[100] Homeownership is both a major investment (very often, the household's largest investment), and a major consumption item.[101] Usually, people are emotionally attached to their homes. On a spectrum from fungible and replaceable assets to non-fungible and unique ones, the home epitomizes the personal, non-fungible end of the spectrum.

96. Daphna Lewinsohn-Zamir, *Can't Buy Me Love: Monetary versus In-Kind Remedies,* 2013 U. ILL. L. REV. 151, 157–77 (experimental results), 186–88 (normative implications for the law of takings).

97. *See* Uriel G. Foa, *Interpersonal and Economic Resources,* 171 SCI. 345 (1971); Edna B. Foa et al., *Response Generalization in Aggression,* 25 HUM. REL. 337 (1972). *See also infra* pp. 469–70.

98. Some of the behavioral insights and normative arguments discussed in this subsection are potentially relevant to the broader issue of fungible versus non-fungible assets, and for the legal treatment of homes in other legal fields. On these broader issues, see Lewinsohn-Zamir, *supra* note 3, at 382–87.

99. Sandy G. Smith, *The Essential Qualities of a Home,* 14 J. ENVTL. PSYCHOL. 31, 31 (1994). *See also* Karin Zingmark, Astrid Norberg, & Per-Olof Sandman, *The Experience of Being at Home throughout the Life Span; Investigation of Persons Aged from 2 to 102,* 41 INT'L J. AGING & HUM. DEV. 47 (1995).

100. *See, e.g.,* Art. 11(1) of the International Covenant on Economic, Social and Cultural Rights, adopted by G.A. Res. 2200A (XXI) (Dec. 16, 1966).

101. Various studies have argued that the real-estate investment decisions made by households (particularly the decision to buy a home) are often not the product of a rational cost-benefit analysis, but rather of systematic cognitive biases, including overoptimism, irrational probability assessments, the herd effect, regret avoidance, mental accounting, loss aversion, and a failure to accurately understand the impact of inflation. *See generally* Diego Salzman & Remco C.J. Zwinkels, *Behavioral Real Estate,* 25 J. REAL ESTATE LITERATURE 77, 83–88 (2017). However, in assessing the rationality of home owning, one must consider not only its financial aspects, but its consumption ones, as well. Empirical studies have documented a host of non-financial benefits accruing from owning one's home. For a critical survey of these studies, see Robert D. Dietz & Donald R. Haurin, *The Social and Private Micro-level Consequences of Homeownership,* 54 J. URBAN ECON. 401 (2003). *See also* Luis Diaz-Serrano, *Disentangling the Housing Satisfaction Puzzle: Does Homeownership Really Matter?,* J. ECON. PSYCHOL. 745 (2009); N. Edward Coulson & Herman Li, *Measuring the External Benefits of Homeownership,* 77 J. URBAN ECON. 57 (2013). In any event, the 2007–2009 subprime mortgage crisis does indicate that decisions to purchase a home are not necessarily rational or informed, to say the least.

Accordingly, the home enjoys special status in various legal contexts, including search-and-seizure law, landlord-and-tenant law (which, in some systems, distinguishes between residential and commercial leases), and debtor-creditor relationships.[102] Similarly, it has been argued that homes should be afforded special protection against governmental taking. For example, Margaret Radin—the proponent of the influential *personhood theory* of property—has argued that given the key role that homes play in facilitating the development of people's personality, governmental taking thereof should either be totally banned, or at least be subject to considerably more stringent limitations.[103]

The special protection of homeownership and its underlying psychological justifications have been challenged, however. Stephanie Stern has argued that the case for residential protectionism had been overstated. Social and interpersonal relationships, rather than homeownership, are key to human flourishing and psychological thriving. Residential dislocation does not ordinarily harm people's mental health, as dislocated people usually acclimatize to their new environment.[104] Accordingly, she has advocated limiting the scope of legal protection to homes.[105] Others have argued that the special protection afforded to homes has a regressive effect, as it overly protects the owners of expensive homes.[106] In any event, it is generally accepted that an outright ban on the taking of homes would be overly drastic. A less radical measure—one that has actually been adopted in some legal systems and recommended in others—is to set the compensation for the taking of homes at a higher level than their market value.[107]

In line with the personhood theory and its psychological underpinnings (and with conventional economic analysis, which posits that a person who does not initiate the sale of her property likely values it above its market value), an experimental study by Janice Nadler and Shari Diamond has shown that even under threat of compulsory taking at market price, a large majority (80.7 percent) of respondents were unwilling to settle for the market value of their home—as evidenced by their refusal to accept any offer whatsoever (9.4 percent of the participants), or by their demand for higher compensation. Of those who were willing to move in return for monetary compensation, the average demand was approximately

102. *See, e.g.*, D. Benjamin Barros, *Home as a Legal Concept*, 46 SANTA CLARA L. REV. 255 (2006); Stephanie M. Stern, *Residential Protectionism and the Legal Mythology of Home*, 107 MICH. L. REV. 1093, 1100–05 (2009).

103. Radin, *supra* note 1, at 988–91, 1005–1006. *See also* Margaret Jane Radin, *The Liberal Conception of Property: Cross Currents in the Jurisprudence of Takings*, 88 COLUM. L. REV. 1667 (1988).

104. Stern, *supra* note 102, at 1109–20. *See also* D. Benjamin Barros, *Legal Questions for the Psychology of Home*, 83 TUL. L. REV. 645, 654–59 (2009).

105. Stern, *supra* note 102, at 1139–44. *See also* Stephanie M. Stern, *Reassessing the Citizen Virtues of Homeownership*, 111 COLUM. L. REV. 890 (2011).

106. Lewinsohn-Zamir, *supra* note 3, at 382; Daphna Lewinsohn-Zamir, *The Objectivity of Well-Being and the Objects of Property Law*, 78 N.Y.L. L. REV. 1669, 1721, 1725–30 (2003). For further critique of the conservative nature of Radin's analysis, see Stephen J. Schnably, *Property and Pragmatism: A Critique of Radin's Theory of Property and Personhood*, 45 STAN. L. REV. 347 (1993).

107. *See, e.g.*, MICH. CONST. art. X, § 2 (125 percent of fair market value); IND. CODE § 32-24-4.5-8(2) (2006) (150 percent of fair market value); John Fee, *Eminent Domain and the Sanctity of Home*, 81 NOTRE DAME L. REV. 783, 803–17 (2006).

30 percent above market price (an average of $61,942 for a property worth $200,000).[108] The refusal rate and the additional compensation demanded were much higher among respondents whose home had been owned by the family for a century than among those who had owned it for only two years.[109] Unsurprisingly, people judged the taking of a home to build a children's hospital somewhat more acceptable than for a shopping mall. Less obviously, when the public purpose of the taking was not indicated, its acceptability resembled that of the taking for the mall.[110]

Nadler and Diamond interpreted their findings to mean that in judging the perceived justice of a taking, the "subjective attachment to property looms far larger" than the purpose of the taking.[111] However, this interpretation is hardly warranted, since the relative impact of the two variables may have stemmed from the specific variables used in that study. Indeed, a subsequent study by Logan Strother, using both survey and experimental methods, found that people strongly oppose takings, and that they resent takings for "economic development" or commercial use (a mall), much more than for a "vital public purpose" or a road.[112] In the experimental study, respondents' attitudes were strongly influenced by the purpose of the taking—a road or a mall—but not by the type of property (a family home or a vacant lot). These results were obtained irrespective of whether the subjects were asked to imagine themselves as the property owner, or as an external observer. However, as with the previous study, it is impossible to draw general conclusions from Strother's study about the comparative impact of the property's type and the taking's purpose, as these results may have been driven by the relative strength of the two manipulations. Thus, it stands to reason that both personal attachment to the property and the purpose of taking impinge on people's attitudes. People's attitudes to takings are likely influenced by various other factors, including the fact that, while the future beneficiaries of the taking are as yet anonymous and unidentified, those who bear the burden are identified.[113]

108. Janice Nadler & Shari Seidman Diamond, *Eminent Domain and the Psychology of Property Rights: Proposed Use, Subjective Attachment, and Taker Identity*, 5 J. Empirical Legal Stud. 713, 731 (2008). *See also* Cherie Metcalf, *Property Law Culture: Public Law, Private Preferences and the Psychology of Expropriation*, 39(2) Queen's L.J. 685 (2014) (essentially replicating Nadler and Shari's results in an experiment conducted with Canadian students). The two studies were prompted by the controversial decision of the U.S. Supreme Court in *Kelo v. City of New London*, 545 U.S. 469 (2005), that upheld the taking of a residential neighborhood for the purpose of private redevelopment, and the ensuing public outcry. *See also* Ilya Somin, The Grasping Hand: *Kelo v. City of New London* and the Limits of Eminent Domain (2015); Janice Nadler, Shari Seidman Diamond & Mathew M. Patton, *Government Takings of Private Property*, *in* Public Opinion and Constitutional Controversy (Nathaniel Persily, Jack Citrin & Patrick J. Egan eds., 2008).

109. Nadler & Diamond, *supra* note 108, at 731–34.

110. *Id.* at 731–37.

111. *Id.* at 713.

112. Logan Strother, *Beyond* Kelo: *An Experimental Study of Public Opposition to Eminent Domain*, 4 J. Law & Courts 339 (2016).

113. On the identifiability effect and its relevance to legal issues, see generally Daphna Lewinsohn-Zamir, Ilana Ritov & Tehila Kogut, *Law and Identifiability*, 92 Ind. L.J. 505 (2017).

Thus far, we have focused on homes (comparing them, in Strother's study, to a vacant lot). But inasmuch as the justification for granting special protection to homes lies in their special role in the development of people's personality and in people's special attachment to them, these characteristics may also apply to commercial property, such as a family business. It is, therefore, unclear that only homes deserve special protection.[114] Ultimately, while considerable progress has been made in recent years, more behavioral studies are needed to confirm or refute the intuitive distinction between homes and other property[115]—and the same is true of other aspects of governmental takings.

D. Intellectual Property

1. General

Information—including inventions, literary and other forms of art, and trademarks—is typically a public good. It is non-rivalrous (can be used simultaneously by more than one person), and non-excludable (it is difficult to exclude its use by others. The basic economic justification for intellectual property (IP) law, therefore, is that without such laws, market forces would not provide adequate incentives for the production of information, since people who invest in creating it would be unable to reap the fruits of their investment due to free-riding by others. More specifically, IP law incentivizes people to create and invent, to share information that they would otherwise try to keep secret, and to turn ideas into marketable products. The main challenge from this perspective is how to strike a balance between the positive incentive effects of IP law, and the concerns of holdup costs and potential monopoly harms. Other justifications for IP law are non-instrumental: artists and inventors deserve to have rights to their creations because they created them, because their creations are manifestations of their personality, and because it is unfair for people to reap the fruits of other people's talent and efforts—regardless of whether the creators would have engaged in such creative activities in the absence of external incentives.[116]

Interestingly, there appears to be a divergence between the prevailing perceptions held by IP practitioners and theoreticians with regard to IP law and its aims, and those of the public at large—with the latter focusing on the prevention of plagiarism.[117] While the very existence of such a divergence does not carry normative conclusions, it may have normative implications, and it can explain important phenomena, such as widespread infringements of IP rights (such as copying part of a book or downloading music from the internet in the belief that this is permissible, since one is not passing it off as one's own work). In fact,

114. Mary L. Clark, *Reconstructing the World Trade Center: An Argument for the Applicability of Personhood Theory to Commercial Property Ownership and Use*, 109 PENN ST. L. REV. 815 (2005); Lewinsohn-Zamir, *supra* note 3, at 383–84.

115. Barros, *supra* note 104.

116. *See generally* William Fisher, *Theories of Intellectual Property*, *in* NEW ESSAYS IN THE LEGAL AND POLITICAL THEORY OF PROPERTY 168 (Stephen R. Munzer ed., 2001).

117. Gregory N. Mandel, Anne A. Fast & Kristina R. Olson, *Intellectual Property Law's Plagiarism Fallacy*, 2015 BYU L. REV. 913.

the divergence between IP law and social norms has attracted considerable attention.[118] In addition to the commonly perceived justifications for IP law, possible explanations for the pervasiveness of IP infringements include the intangibility of IP, which leads to the perception of infringement as a victimless crime;[119] the notion of the internet as a free domain;[120] and the perception of copyright law as nothing more than protection of greedy record labels.[121] One possible reaction to the disparity between IP law and social norms is to adapt the law to those norms.[122] Whatever the merits of such a proposal, it is unlikely to be accepted in the foreseeable future, for obvious political economy reasons. Other alternatives include stricter enforcement of the law and reshaping people's attitudes to IP law. However, such initiatives appear to have failed,[123] and experimental studies of possible techniques for changing people's beliefs in this regard have not yielded firm conclusions.[124]

Insights about human motivation and behavior are relevant to IP law whatever its basis might be, but are particularly important for instrumental theories that justify IP law on the grounds of its impact on human behavior—the currently predominant theories, at least in the United States. The introduction of behavioral insights into IP law and policy has been rather slow, but of late there has been increased interest in this approach.[125] As in other spheres, scholars have begun by borrowing insights from existing behavioral studies,[126] then moving on to conducting specifically tailored experiments.[127] Notably, in addition to judgment and decision-making, IP scholars have drawn on psychological studies of

118. *See, e.g.*, Christopher Jensen, *The More Things Change, the More They Stay the Same: Copyright, Digital Technology, and Social Norms*, 56 Stan. L. Rev. 531 (2003); Steven Lysonski & Srinivas Durvasula, *Digital Piracy of MP3s: Consumer and Ethical Predispositions*, 25 J. Consumer Marketing 167 (2008); Yuval Feldman & Janice Nadler, *The Law and Norms of File Sharing*, 47 San Diego L. Rev. 577 (2006); Yuval Feldman, *The Behavioral Foundations of Trade Secrets: Tangibility, Authorship and Legality*, 3 J. Empirical Legal Stud. 197 (2006).

119. *See, e.g.*, Jensen, *supra* note 118, at 540.

120. Feldman & Nadler, *supra* note 118, at 585.

121. *Id.* at 587–88.

122. *See, e.g.*, Mark F. Schultz, *Reconciling Social Norms and Copyright Law: Strategies for Persuading People to Pay for Recorded Music*, 17 J. Intell. Prop. L. 59, 59–70 (2009).

123. *See, e.g.*, Lee Edwards et al., *Framing the Consumer: Copyright Regulation and the Public*, 19 Convergence: J. Res. New Media Tech. 9 (2013).

124. *See, e.g.*, Anne A. Fast, Kristina R. Olson & Gregory N. Mandel, *Experimental Investigations on the Basis for Intellectual Property Rights*, 40 Law & Hum. Behav. 458 (2016).

125. *See, e.g.*, Stephanie P. Bair, *The Psychology of Patent Protection*, 48 Conn. L. Rev. 297 (2015); Stefan Bechtold, Christopher Buccafusco & Christopher J. Sprigman, *Innovation Heuristics: Experiments on Sequential Creativity in Intellectual Property*, 91 Indiana L.J. 1251 (2016).

126. *See, e.g.*, Dennis D. Crouch, *The Patent Lottery: Exploiting Behavioral Economics for the Common Good*, 16 Geo. Mason L. Rev. 141 (2008).

127. *See, e.g.*, Christopher Buccafusco & Christopher Sprigman, *Valuing Intellectual Property: An Experiment*, 96 Cornell L. Rev. 1 (2010) [hereinafter Buccafusco & Sprigman, *Valuing IP*]; Christopher Buccafusco & Christopher Jon Sprigman, *The Creativity Effect*, 78 U. Chi. L. Rev. 31 (2011) [hereinafter Buccafusco & Sprigman, *Creativity*]; Bechtold, Buccafusco & Sprigman, *supra* note 125.

creativity and collaboration.[128] This trend is associated with a broader skepticism toward the very desirability, in terms of cost-benefit analysis, of much of current IP law.[129]

One thread in the literature emphasizes the complexity of motives for engaging in creative activities and sharing information—which may be internal and external, monetary and reputational—as well as the inherent value of engaging in such activities, regardless of whether they result in valuable products or not. It is argued that, given the nuanced relationships between internal and external motivations and the huge uncertainty as to which creations would become profitable, copyright and other IP law may not only fail to create adequate incentives, but may even have a chilling effect.[130] At the very least, the complexity of human motivations, the role of social norms, and the possible differences between individuals and large organizations in this regard cast doubt on the external validity of simple economic models that focus on monetary rewards.[131] Thus, it has been experimentally demonstrated that creators highly value the attribution of their work to them, and are even willing to forgo significant payments in return for such attribution.[132] However, as in other contexts, the creators' valuation of attribution has been found to be strongly influenced by the default legal regime.[133] Since legal systems differ in their recognition of the right of attribution, this finding potentially carries practical implications.

2. The Innovation Lottery

More specific behavioral insights have been brought to bear upon IP law as well. Thus, embarking on inventive efforts has been analogized to playing the lottery. While there are many dissimilarities between the two, an attempt to come up with a new, patentable invention that would enrich the inventor—especially when the latter is an individual or a small firm—resembles a lottery in the sense that the reward for success may be very high, but the probability of success is often extremely low.[134] Many research-and-development initiatives do not yield patentable innovations—and even if they do, most patents are

128. *See, e.g.*, Jeanne C. Fromer, *A Psychology of Intellectual Property*, 104 Nw. U. L. Rev. 1441 (2010); Gregory N. Mandel, *To Promote the Creative Process: Intellectual Property Law and the Psychology of Creativity*, 86 Notre Dame L. Rev. 1999 (2011).

129. *See, e.g.*, Adam B. Jaffe & Josh Lerner, Innovation and Its Discontents: How Our Broken Patent System Is Endangering Innovation and Progress, and What to Do about It (2004); Dan L. Burk, *Law and Economics of Intellectual Property: In Search of First Principles*, 8 Ann. Rev. L. & Soc. Sci. 397 (2012); Mark A. Lemley, *Faith-Based Intellectual Property*, 62 UCLA L. Rev. 1328 (2015).

130. *See, e.g.*, Rebecca Tushnet, *Economies of Desire: Fair Use and Marketplace Assumptions*, 51 Wm. & Mary L. Rev. 513 (2009); Mandel, *supra* note 128; Eric E. Johnson, *Intellectual Property and the Incentive Fallacy*, 39 Fla. St. U. L. Rev. 623 (2012).

131. Bair, *supra* note 125, at 312–37. *Cf.* Christopher Buccafusco et al., *Experimental Tests of Intellectual Property Laws' Creativity Thresholds*, 93 Tex. L. Rev. 1921 (2014).

132. Christopher Jon Sprigman, Christopher Buccafusco & Zachary Burns, *What's a Name Worth?: Experimental Tests of the Value of Attribution in Intellectual Property*, 93 B.U. L. Rev. 1389 (2013).

133. *Id.* at 1417–24. On the default effect of legal norms, see generally *supra* pp. 179–82.

134. Crouch, *supra* note 126.

practically worthless, as they are never licensed, enforced, or otherwise commercialized.[135] Perfectly rational agents would weigh the expected costs of innovation against the expected benefits of a successful patent—that is, the probability of success multiplied by the expected reward—possibly while taking into account their own risk aversion. However, an imperfectly rational agent is likely to be affected by several heuristics and biases. According to prospect theory, while people are ordinarily risk-averse in the domain of gains, they tend to be risk-seeking when it comes to low-probability gains.[136] Moreover, media reports and word of mouth may give exaggerated exposure of successful innovation initiatives, making them appear somewhat more probable than they really are, due to the availability heuristic.[137] Finally, overoptimism, illusion of control, and other self-serving biases may lead people to overestimate the prospect of success.[138] The upshot of all these phenomena may well be that people invest in research-and-development projects and subsequently in patent commercialization more than they rationally should.

It does not follow, however, that inventors and other creators engage in such activities more than is *socially* desirable, as there may be positive externalities to research, creative activity, and commercialization attempts, even if they do not yield net profits to the creator. To the extent that this is true, not only should the law not try to counteract the aforementioned biases and heuristics—it may actually capitalize on them.[139] Specifically, while some modifications of patent law may make it more likely for an inventor to secure a profitable patent, others (such as stricter enforcement of patent rights) may make such patents more valuable. If policymakers wish to encourage risk-seeking inventors to engage in research and development that yield positive externalities, they should arguably opt for the latter course of action, rather than the former—as do lottery organizers.[140] Obviously, other considerations, such as the existence of intrinsic motivations for innovation, may weigh against this argument.

Another context where it has been argued that the law can—and does—take advantage of people's biases is in establishing the duration of copyright protection based on the creator's lifetime plus a certain number of years. Overoptimistic authors who are susceptible to the *better-than-average* effect are likely to overestimate their longevity, and hence the protection period.[141] Moreover, the very description of the protection period as comprising

135. F.M. Scherer, *The Innovation Lottery: The Empirical Case for Copyright and Patents*, *in* Expanding the Boundaries of Intellectual Property: Innovation Policy for the Knowledge Society 3 (Rochelle Cooper Dreyfuss, Diane L. Zimmerman & Harry First eds., 2001).

136. *See supra* p. 43.

137. *See supra* pp. 34–36.

138. *See supra* pp. 58–72; *infra* pp. 385–86.

139. Ofer M. Tur-Sinai, *The Endowment Effect in IP Transactions: The Case against Debiasing*, 18 Mich. Telecomm. & Tech. L. Rev. 117, 153–56 (2011).

140. Crouch, *supra* note 126.

141. Avishalom Tor & Dotan Oliar, *Incentives to Create under a "Lifetime-Plus-Years" Copyright Duration: Lessons from a Behavioral Economic Analysis of* Eldred v. Ashcroft, 36 Loy. L.A. L. Rev. 437, 459–62 (2002). On overoptimism and the better-than-average effect, see generally *supra* pp. 61–64.

two elements—the author's lifetime plus the additional period—may lead authors to perceive it as longer than a fixed period of a similar expected length, due to the *subadditivity or part-whole bias.*[142] However, given what we know about people's myopia and the hyperbolic discount rate of chronologically remote (costs and) benefits,[143] one may question the practical effect of these rules.

3. Endowment and Creativity Effects

Standard economic analysis of IP law assumes that once IP rights are conferred, voluntary market transactions facilitate their allocation to those who can make the most out of them, thereby maximizing aggregate social utility. However, just as the endowment effect allegedly hinders efficient transactions in corporeal goods,[144] it may hinder such transactions in IP rights. In fact, there is evidence that, when it comes to personal creations, such as paintings, the combination of emotional attachment and self-serving biases (including overoptimism) produces a "creativity effect" that is considerably stronger than the ordinary endowment effect.

This is clearly illustrated in an experiment conducted by Christopher Buccafusco and Christopher Sprigman, in which the object of a possible trade was a painting's chance of winning a $100 prize in a contest between ten paintings. The participants consisted of three groups: Painters, Owners, and Buyers. Painters were art students who created those paintings. They were asked to state the lowest price they would be willing to accept (WTA) in return for their winning chance. Owners were law students who were randomly assigned to one of the paintings and asked to indicate their WTA for the same winning chance. Finally, Buyers were law students who were randomly assigned to one of the paintings and asked to indicate the highest price they would be willing to pay (WTP) for the same winning chance.

The Buyers' mean WTP was $17.88; the Owners' mean WTA was $40.67; and the Painters' mean WTA was $74.53.[145] Thus, while all three groups exhibited considerable overoptimism or risk-seeking (since the mean value of the winning chance across the ten paintings was only $10), the Owners' WTA ($40.67) was more than double that of the Buyers' WTP ($17.88), and the Painters' WTA ($74.53) was more than four times higher.[146]

Buccafusco and Sprigman have argued that their findings indicate that the endowment effect extends to non-rivalrous goods: as is generally the case with IP rights, in their

142. *Id.* at 462–81. On subadditivity and the part-whole bias, see generally *supra* pp. 37–38.

143. *See supra* pp. 88–93.

144. *See infra* pp. 232–34.

145. Buccafusco & Sprigman, *Creativity, supra* note 127, at 39–40.

146. That said, another set of experiments conducted by the same researchers found no statistically significant difference between creators' and owners' WTA—both of which were significantly higher than the buyers' WTP (Buccafusco & Sprigman, *Valuing IP, supra* note 127). Possibly, this was due to the fact that in the latter experiments the motivation for creation (writing a short poem) was purely external, and the effort involved was fairly insignificant (*id.* at 29).

experiments the creators kept the physical object (painting), as well as the IP rights (in the painting or the poem).[147] On the normative level, since the endowment effect—and even more so, the creativity effect—hinder otherwise efficient transactions, Buccafusco and Sprigman have suggested several reforms of IP law, including a move from property rules to liability rules,[148] expansion of the fair use doctrine,[149] and vesting IP rights in entities other than the creators.[150]

However, both the interpretation of the results and their policy implications have been subject to considerable critique. As for the alleged endowment effect in non-rivalrous goods, Ofer Tur-Sinai has rightly pointed out that the object of trade in Buccafusco and Sprigman's experiments was not, in fact, non-rivalrous. The object was the chance to win a specific monetary prize for the work, which was as rivalrous as the chance to win any amount of money.[151] As for the policy implications, even if Buccafusco and Sprigman's findings capture a real characteristic of IP rights—which we believe they do—it does not follow that the endowment effect in general, or the creativity effect in particular, are inherently irrational or inefficient.[152] As previously noted, it is also unclear that the creators' overoptimism, risk-seeking, or emotional attachment to their creations are *socially* undesirable (even if overoptimism and risk-seeking are detrimental to the creator). More empirical data and additional normative consideration are essential to resolving this large question, as well as the specific policy recommendations advocated by Buccafusco and Sprigman.[153]

4. Sequential Innovations

Thus far, the analysis has unrealistically ignored the fact that creativity and inventions almost invariably draw on previous ideas. In reality, the role of IP law is to incentivize both initial creators and subsequent ones. A perfectly rational creator would therefore decide whether to rely on existing IP, by paying for the right to use it, or innovate around it, according to the expected costs and benefits of each alternative.[154]

Experimental findings suggest, however, that people often do not make this decision—which may be quite complex given the risks and uncertainties involved—based on rational

147. *Id.* at 4, 17–21, 26–27, 30; Buccafusco & Sprigman, *Creativity, supra* note 127, at 32, 35, 37.

148. Buccafusco & Sprigman, *Valuing IP, supra* note 127, at 33–35; Buccafusco & Sprigman, *Creativity, supra* note 127, at 51–52. *See also infra* pp. 229–34.

149. Buccafusco & Sprigman, *Valuing IP, supra* note 127, at 42–44. According to the *fair use* doctrine, a limited use of copyrighted material for purposes such as criticism, teaching, or research is permissible; and a major justification for the doctrine is that the transaction costs of acquiring a license for such use would be prohibitive.

150. Buccafusco & Sprigman, *Creativity, supra* note 127, at 48–50.

151. Tur-Sinai, *supra* note 139, at 128–31. Tur-Sinai further argues that other factors, including the fact that IP owners usually only license the use of their rights, are likely to mitigate the endowment and creativity effects in the real world of IP (*id.* at 132–37).

152. *Id.* at 137–56. *See also* ZAMIR, *supra* note 39, at 205–07.

153. *Id.* at 156–68.

154. For the sake of the present discussion, we are excluding the possibility of illegal use of protected IP without its owner's consent, which a rational maximizer should presumably consider as well.

cost-benefit analysis, but rather use a simple heuristic, namely their subjective assessment of the difficulty of innovating.[155] This heuristic systematically induces people to pay for using existing IP when innovating is preferable (when they overestimate the difficulty of innovation, regardless of its high expected reward)—or conversely (and more commonly) to try to innovate when drawing on existing IP would be optimal (when they underestimate the difficulty of innovation). The resulting equilibrium may well be suboptimal, especially when overly-optimistic subsequent innovators interact with initial creators whose asking prices reflect the creativity effect we noted earlier.[156]

5. Hindsight Bias

Behavioral insights shed light not only on the decisions made by inventors and creators, but also on those of patent examiners and courts that implement IP law. A key case in point is the requirement of *non-obviousness* in patent law. To obtain a patent, an invention must be non-obvious. Obvious scientific and technological advancements are routinely made without patent protection. They do not warrant the social costs of patent monopoly. The difficulty posed by this doctrine is that patent examiners and courts are called upon to determine ex post whether an invention had been obvious ex ante. Alas, numerous experimental studies of judicial and other decision-making have demonstrated that such determination is affected by a *hindsight bias*: people are mostly unable to disregard ex-post outcome information.[157] They tend to view what actually happened as having been foreseeable or even inevitable; and debiasing attempts are largely unsuccessful in this context. While the hindsight bias often pertains to judgments of probability, in the present context the question is qualitative. Under U.S. law the question is whether "the differences between the claimed invention and the prior art are such that the claimed invention as a whole would have been obvious before the effective filing date of the claimed invention to a person having ordinary skill in the [pertinent art]."[158] Experimental studies with laypersons revealed a dramatic hindsight bias. In two vignettes, the fraction of participants who judged an invention to be obvious in foresight was 24 percent and 23 percent, respectively, while in the hindsight condition it was 71 percent and 54 percent, respectively.[159] Informing participants of the hindsight bias, warning them about it, and instructing them not to use hindsight in judging the obviousness of the invention had no statistically significant effect on their answers.[160]

155. Bechtold, Buccafusco & Sprigman, *supra* note 125. *See also* Christopher Buccafusco, Stefan Bechtold & Christopher Jon Sprigman, *Innovate or Borrow?: A Model for Regulating Sequential Innovation* (working paper, 2017, *available at*: https://ssrn.com/abstract=2902937).

156. Bechtold, Buccafusco & Sprigman, *supra* note 125, at 1291–96. *See also* Julia Brüggemann et al., *Intellectual Property Rights Hinder Sequential Innovation. Experimental Evidence,* 45 RES. POL'Y 2054 (2016).

157. *See generally supra* pp. 38–39; *infra* pp. 535–36.

158. 35 U.S.C. § 103 (2011).

159. Gregory N. Mandel, *Patently Non-obvious: Empirical Demonstration That the Hindsight Bias Renders Patent Decisions Irrational,* 67 OHIO ST. L.J. 1391, 1409 (2006).

160. *Id.* at 1410.

Possibly, the only viable way to minimize the bias—which may be feasible in the patent approval stage and in jury trials, but apparently not in trials heard by a judge—is to bifurcate the decision process, such that the issue of non-obviousness is decided without the decision-maker being exposed to the invention.[161]

E. Protecting Property Rights: Property Rules versus Liability Rules

Much of the theoretical discussion about private law remedies, particularly from an economic perspective, has been shaped in recent decades by Guido Calabresi and Douglas Melamed's distinction between *property rules* and *liability rules*, as presented in their seminal 1972 article.[162] According to this distinction, a legal entitlement may be protected by a property rule (namely, by an injunctive remedy, whereby a court orders a person to perform or refrain from performing a certain act), or by a *liability rule* (whereby someone who has infringed upon someone else's rights is ordered to compensate the latter for the infringement). According to Calabresi and Melamed, the key difference between the two regimes is that, under a property rule, anyone "who wishes to remove the entitlement from its holder must buy it from him in a voluntary transaction in which the value of the entitlement is agreed upon by the seller;" whereas under a liability rule, anyone "may destroy the initial entitlement if he is willing to pay an objectively determined value [i.e., determined by some organ of the state] for it."[163]

Much like economic analysis in general, this distinction abstracts away the peculiarities of different legal fields—property, tort, contract, etc. Moreover, in keeping with the consequentialist underpinnings of welfare economics, it sidesteps the normative issue of the legitimacy of the infringement: compensating a car owner for the destruction of her car by someone else's reckless driving and compensating a landowner for the taking of her property by governmental authorities to satisfy vital public needs are both instances of "liability rules." The distinction has become a cornerstone of economic analysis of law, and has spawned an outpouring of ever more sophisticated and abstract scholarship.[164]

This section discusses the contribution of behavioral insights to this scholarship—but does so with a grain of salt. While many of the analyses constituting this body of literature are ingenious and thought-provoking, they are often detached from the complex normative and pragmatic considerations that shape the law and practice of remedy rules in any legal

161. *Id.* at 1447–50; Gregory Mandel, *Patently Non-Obvious II: Experimental Study on the Hindsight Issue before the Supreme Court in* KSR v. Teleflex, 9 YALE J.L. & TECH. 1 (2007).

162. Guido Calabresi & Douglas Melamed, *Property Rules, Liability Rules, and Inalienability: One View of the Cathedral,* 85 HARV. L. REV. 1089 (1972).

163. *Id.* at 1092.

164. *See, e.g.,* Ian Ayres & Eric Talley, *Solomonic Bargaining: Dividing a Legal Entitlement to Facilitate Coasean Trade,* 104 YALE L.J. 1027 (1995); Symposium: *Property Rules, Liability Rules, and Inalienability: A Twenty-Five Year Retrospective,* 106 YALE L.J. 2081 (1997); Lee Anne Fennel, *Revealing Options,* 118 HARV. L. REV. 1399 (2005); Richard R.W. Brooks, *The Efficient Performance Hypothesis,* 116 YALE L.J. 568 (2006); IAN AYRES, OPTIONAL LAW: THE STRUCTURE OF LEGAL ENTITLEMENTS (2010).

field.[165] To make the discussion somewhat more concrete, we focus here on remedies for the protection of property rights, leaving the examination of contract- and tort-law remedies to their respective chapters.[166]

Calabresi and Melamed have offered a simple criterion for the choice between property and liability rules, namely transaction costs. Property rules should be adopted when transaction costs are low, and the parties can bargain with one another. In contrast, when transaction costs are prohibitive, liability rules should be employed. When it comes to property rights, such as one's title to land or a chattel, this criterion implies that they should ordinarily be enforced by a property rule (whereas tort remedies for injury inflicted by a stranger should usually be designed as liability rules, and the picture in the contractual sphere is rather complex).

However, Ian Ayres and Eric Talley, among others, have challenged this accepted wisdom, arguing that even when transaction costs are low, liability rules may be superior to property rules.[167] The crux of the argument is that the choice between property rules and liability rules is not necessarily a choice between bargaining and litigation. Rather, bargaining is likely to take place under both property and liability rules, and liability rules may actually induce successful bargaining in situations where property rules might not. This would be the case in "thin" markets, where unilateral or bilateral monopoly (due, for example, to the uniqueness of the object) and information problems regarding the parties' true valuations of the object may lead to negotiation impasse. The fact that the court may err in determining the owner's valuation does not necessarily render a property rule superior in this regard. Liability rules, so the argument goes, facilitate one of two transactions: the non-owner buying the object from its owner, or the owner "bribing" the non-owner not to unilaterally appropriate the object. The fact that the owner is the payee under one possible transaction, and the payer under the other (and vice versa for the non-owner), arguably forces the parties to reveal their true valuations.

Behavioral findings provide additional arguments for both sides of the debate. In keeping with rational choice theory, the assertion that liability rules are more conducive to successful bargaining than property rules assumes that when people bargain in the shadow of a property rule in a thin market, each party would try to capture the entire surplus of the transaction, thus possibly leading to a bargaining failure. However, as Lewinsohn-Zamir has pointed out, this assumption is overly simplistic.[168] It does not fall in line with

165. Let us mention but two, apparently mundane considerations, which may have a greater impact on legal reality than many of the considerations discussed in the property-versus-liability-rules scholarship. First, an injunctive order is much more attractive in a legal system that is capable of issuing and enforcing such an order in a matter of weeks or months, than in a system where it takes several years. Second, an order to perform an act is much less appropriate than monetary relief when performance requires close cooperation between people who have come to loathe and distrust each other.

166. *See infra* pp. 262–73, 341–48.

167. Ayres & Tally, *supra* note 164; *see also* Louis Kaplow & Steven Shavell, *Property Rules versus Liability Rules: An Economic Analysis,* 109 HARV. L. REV. 713, 717–18, 732–37 (1996).

168. Daphna Lewinsohn-Zamir, *The Choice between Property Rules and Liability Rules Revisited: Critical Observations from Behavioral Studies,* 80 TEXAS L. REV. 219 (2001).

the findings of many studies in experimental game theory that show that fairness concerns serve as a constraint on profit maximization.[169] Studies of the *ultimatum* game[170] have repeatedly demonstrated that even under conditions of complete anonymity, most proposers offer responders a generous share of the pie (40 percent on average), and that responders reject very low offers.[171] Negotiating the transfer of a property right resembles an ultimatum game, in which the buyer is the proposer and the owner/seller is the responder—without whose consent no deal is struck. Potential buyers know that low offers would not be accepted even if they improve the seller's position compared to no bargain—hence they tend to make fair offers. Ultimatum studies have shown that even one-period games between complete strangers who interact anonymously usually yield an agreement to split the pie fairly between the parties. Such success is all the more likely in real-life negotiations between a property owner and a potential buyer, who can discuss and resolve their disagreements and are likely to be influenced by reputational, social, and moral considerations. Moreover, experimental studies of bargaining show that sellers tend to be risk-averse (plausibly, because they take the status quo as their reference point, and consider the possible profits from trade as belonging to the realm of gains).[172] Inasmuch as this is the case, risk-averse sellers are unlikely to hold out in an attempt to appropriate the lion's share of the transaction's surplus, especially if they are unsure what the buyer's reservation price is.[173]

A voluntary transfer of an asset may well be mutually beneficial under a *liability rule* as well, because it saves both parties the costs of litigation. However, it has been argued that the prospects of successful bargaining under this regime are actually slimmer.[174] Experimental studies of the *dictator* game[175] show that a substantial minority (36 percent) keep all the money for themselves, yet most people share a substantial fraction of their endowment (28 percent on average) with the passive participant.[176] The difference between the outcomes of the ultimatum and dictator games indicates that people are not exclusively motivated by considerations of fairness (if this were so, there would be no difference between the two games' outcomes). Evidently, proposers in the ultimatum game offer a greater

169. *See supra* pp. 102–03.

170. *Ultimatum* is a game in which one player (the proposer) is asked to divide a sum of money between herself and the other player. The other player (the responder) may either accept the proposed allocation (in which case, it is implemented), or reject it (in which case neither player receives anything).

171. *See, e.g.*, Hessel Oosterbeek, Randolph Sloof & Gijs van De Kuilen, *Cultural Differences in Ultimatum Game Experiments: Evidence from a Meta-analysis*, 7 Experimental Econ. 171 (2004); *supra* pp. 102–03.

172. Margaret A. Neale & Max H. Bazerman, Cognition and Rationality in Negotiation 156–57 (1991).

173. Lewinsohn-Zamir, *supra* note 168, at 235–39. One counterargument may be that bargaining may fail due to the buyer's comparatively greater willingness to take risks. However, this concern is mitigated by the fairness constraint.

174. Lewinsohn-Zamir, *supra* note 168, at 239–50.

175. *Dictator* is a game where one party unilaterally decides how to divide a sum of money between herself and another person.

176. Christoph Engel, *Dictator Games: A Meta Study*, 14 Experimental Econ. 583 (2011).

share of the pie to responders because they predict that otherwise no deal would be struck. Now, the primary difference between negotiating under a property rule and a liability rule is that only under the latter does the proposer know that even if her offer is rejected, she can unilaterally take the responder's asset without his or her consent. Consequently, potential buyers are likely to make lower offers under a liability rule, which may in turn lead to fewer transactions.

Even if an owner accepts an offer to sell her asset under the threat of a forced taking, it is far from clear that such a transaction is mutually beneficial. The standard measure of compensation under liability rules is market value. Knowing that she is unlikely to be awarded more than that in compensation, the owner might agree to part with her asset for such an amount, but the transaction may well leave her worse off. This would be the case if her subjective valuation of the asset is *higher* than its market value, which is often the case with non-fungible, unique property, or a property that is held for its use-value (as opposed to its exchange-value).[177] Moreover, as nicely demonstrated in one survey study, laypersons and experienced businesspeople alike strongly resent the possibility of getting a monetary remedy instead of an in-kind entitlement—even when the entitlement is to a fungible, easily replaceable asset whose market value is easily ascertainable, and which is held for commercial purposes.[178]

So far, we have described some of the behavioral insights that point to the superiority of property rules over liability rules. However, behavioral insights have served to support the opposite position, as well. Specifically, it has been argued that fewer mutually beneficial transactions are likely to ensue under property rules due to the endowment effect. According to the Coase theorem—a postulate of standard economic analysis—in a world of zero transaction costs and no restrictions on trade, an efficient allocation of entitlements would ensue irrespective of their initial allocation.[179] However, if the very allocation of an entitlement produces an endowment effect, entitlements might remain in the hands of those to which they have been initially allotted.[180] Arguably, protecting entitlements through liability rules, rather than property rules, weakens psychological ownership and the endowment effect, thus facilitating more efficient transactions.[181]

Jeffrey Rachlinski and Forest Jourdan have provided experimental support for this claim.[182] They used two vignettes concerning environmental entitlements, of which, for the sake of brevity, we will describe only one. Subjects were asked to imagine that they were

177. *See also supra* pp. 218–22.

178. Lewinsohn-Zamir, *supra* note 96.

179. Ronald H. Coase, *The Problem of Social Cost*, 3 J.L. & ECON. 1 (1960).

180. Mark Kelman, *Consumption Theory, Production Theory, and Ideology in the Coase Theorem*, 52 S. CAL. L. REV. 669 (1979); Jeffrey J. Rachlinski & Forest Jourden, *Remedies and the Psychology of Ownership*, 51 VAND. L. REV. 1541, 1553–56 (1998).

181. *See, e.g.*, Ian Ayres, *Protecting Property with Puts*, 32 VAL. U. L. REV. 793, 809–13 (1998); Buccafusco & Sprigman, *Valuing IP*, *supra* note 127, at 33–35; Buccafusco & Sprigman, *Creativity*, *supra* note 127, at 51–52.

182. Rachlinski & Jourden, *supra* note 180, at 1559–74.

directors of an environmental preservation trust that had purchased a wetland in order to protect nesting and migratory birds. However, the birds were severely disturbed by a nearby heliport that a commercial company had started to operate. In the three versions of the *Sell* conditions, subjects were asked to rate their willingness to concede the trust's right to prevent the helicopter company's operations, in return for a sum of money that would allow the trust to purchase an island elsewhere, where it could protect seals. In the *Injunctive* condition, subjects were told that by law, the trust could get a court order requiring the helicopter company to cease operations. In the *High Damages* condition, subjects were told that the trust could get a judgment for monetary damages that would be so high as to effectively cause the company to cease operations. In the *Low Damages* condition, the expected damages were so low that the company would probably be willing to absorb them as a cost of doing business, and continue operations. In the three *Buy* conditions, the trust had no rights against the helicopter company, but the latter offered to sell the trust its right to operate at its current location, and move its operations elsewhere. If such a sale took place, the trust's rights would be enforceable by one of the three remedies described above, depending on the condition. To purchase these rights, the trust would have to use funds earmarked for the purchase of the seals island. In all six conditions, subjects were asked to indicate their inclination to sell/buy the entitlement on a five-point scale ranging from definitely buy/sell the rights to definitely not buy/sell them. The magnitude of the endowment effect was measured by comparing the willingness of buyers to buy and the willingness of sellers to sell.

As expected, across the two experiments, only in the *Injunction* conditions was there a significant difference between the subjects' inclination to sell the entitlement and their inclination to buy it. Surprisingly, however, the absence of an endowment effect in the High Damages conditions across the two vignettes (which were described as effectively tantamount to an injunction) stemmed from the fact that in one vignette *there was* such an effect (albeit smaller), and in the other there was a *reverse* (small) endowment effect.[183]

While these findings are interesting and important, one may question their generalizability, as they were obtained through vignettes dealing with environmental entitlements, rather than typical property rights in movable or immovable property,[184] and involved choosing between two competing, worthwhile uses of funds.[185] Other studies have shown a clear endowment effect with regard to entitlements that are ordinarily protected by liability rules, such as exposure to health risks.[186] In light of the limitations of their study—including the possible confounding of the type of remedy and its certainty—Rachlinski and Jourden

183. *Id.* at 1566–69.

184. Russell B. Korobkin, *The Endowment Effect and Legal Analysis*, 97 NW. U. L. REV. 1227, 1284–85 (2003) (explaining that "the results might have been driven by what the choice of remedies says about society's commitment to the environment rather than by any differences in feelings of ownership that the choice creates").

185. Lewinsohn-Zamir, *supra* note 3, at 392–93; Lewinsohn-Zamir, *supra* note 168, 254 n.121.

186. *See, e.g.*, W. Kip Viscusi, Wesley A. Magat & Joel Huber, *An Investigation of the Rationality of Consumer Valuations of Multiple Health Risks*, 18 RAND J. ECON. 465 (1987).

recommended that a similar experiment be conducted with actual commodities, such as a mug or a pen, as has regularly been done in other endowment effect studies.[187] Regrettably, we are not aware of any such study that might replicate, refute, or refine their findings.[188]

Setting the issues of the generalizability and external validity of Rachlinski and Jourden's results to one side, and assuming that injunctive remedies do produce a stronger endowment effect than standard monetary ones, this finding hardly establishes a case for the major reform involved in denying property rights the protection afforded by property rules. Encouraging transactions in entitlements (including by reducing the endowment effect) is but one goal of remedy rules. From both economic and natural-rights perspectives, private property serves additional goals, such as incentivizing people to invest efficiently in tangible and intangible assets and furthering individuals' need to effectuate their autonomy and to develop their personality.[189] Protecting property rights by liability rules might undermine the very notion of private property as conceived by laypeople and jurists alike, render it less efficient (due, for example, to concerns about under-compensation for injuries to property rights), and undercut its moral basis.[190] Protecting property rights with property rules may also be warranted as a means of saving on information costs, deterring opportunism by potential takers, and discouraging owners from engaging in wasteful self-help.[191]

F. Conclusion

This chapter reviewed the key contributions of behavioral studies to the economic and non-economic analysis of property law.[192] Three general observations emerge from the overview.

187. Rachlinski & Jourden, *supra* note 180, at 1573.

188. The study that comes closest is Oren Bar-Gill & Christoph Engel, *How to Protect Entitlements: An Experiment* (working paper, April 2017, *available at:* https://ssrn.com/abstract=2949851). However, while comparing various remedy rules (damages ranging from zero to above the taker's valuation of the entitlement, and a property rule) on owners' willingness to pay potential takers for not taking their entitlement, and on takers willingness to accept such a payment, the experimental design in this study basically ruled out the emergence of an endowment effect (because the object of entitlement was a token representing an entitlement to a specified sum of money). Instead, it focused on the impact of various judgments of fairness on the magnitude of those WTP and WTA.

189. Note that, contrary to first appearances, dilution of owners' remedies for the taking of their entitlements does not necessarily serve takers' interests, as they, too, might become the victims of such taking by others in the future. *Cf.* Barak Medina, *Augmenting the Value of Ownership by Protecting It only Partially: The "Market-Overt" Rule Revisited,* 19 J.L. ECON. & ORG. 343 (2003).

190. Merrill & Smith, *supra* note 60; Lewinsohn-Zamir, *supra* note 3, at 392, 394.

191. Henry E. Smith, *Property and Property Rules,* 79 N.Y.U. L. REV. 1719 (2004).

192. This review is not meant to be exhaustive. Other contributions to the behavioral analysis of property law include Lee Anne Fennell, *Death, Taxes, and Cognition,* 81 N.C. L. REV. 567, 581–93 (2003) (explaining why people are reluctant to avoid estate tax by inter vivos transfer of their property by reference to phenomena such as overoptimism, procrastination, loss aversion and regret avoidance, and mental accounting); Daphna Lewinsohn-Zamir, *More Is Not Better than Less: An Exploration in Property Law,* 92 MINN. L. REV. 634, 661–65, 681–87 (2008) (pointing to regret avoidance as an explanation for why the law sometimes does not limit owners' freedom to actively destroy their property—and yet incentivizes them not to neglect using it); Stephanie Stern, *Encouraging Conservation of Private Lands: A Behavioral Analysis of Financial Incentives,* 48 ARIZ. L. REV. 541

First, behavioral studies provide invaluable insights into the understanding of property and property law. Two obvious examples are the doubt cast by the endowment effect on the Coase theorem, and the implications of the possible divergence between legal and psychological ownership.[193]

Second, compared with other legal fields, such as evidence and consumer protection (and even contract and tax law), the behavioral study of property law is still at a relatively early stage of its development. The empirical data regarding basic issues (such as the effect of remedy rules on the endowment effect, or the personhood-enhancing nature of commercial property) are still scarce. Other issues have not been studied empirically at all in the legal context, so scholars still rely on general behavioral findings, whose manifestations are often context-dependent. While considerable work has been done on the quintessentially personal property—that is, the home—less attention has been given to non-personal property, including commercial real property and movables.[194] There is considerable room for future behavioral research of specific property-law concepts and doctrines (such as the conflict between an original owner and a good-faith purchaser, landlord and tenant law, security interests in property, and easements)—not to mention the vast domain of intellectual property.[195]

One fruitful direction in which considerable progress has been made in recent years, but where there is still scope for more work, is the study of the common perceptions of property rights and rules. We mentioned studies of how people determine ownership, frame ownership, judge the morality of a governmental taking, and perceive IP law,[196] but very little is known about the compatibility of current property law with prevailing perceptions and judgments on any number of other issues (which may vary from one society to another). Studies of this sort have been fruitfully conducted, for example, in the fields of taxation and contract law.[197] Inasmuch as there are notable discrepancies between the law and the prevailing normative judgments, this should be a cause of concern on both democratic and pragmatic grounds.[198] In that case, one might wish to consider whether the law should

(2006) (discussing the concern that financial incentives for environmental conservation of private lands might backfire due to the crowding-out effect, and offering behaviorally-informed recommendations to design financial incentives to enhance their effectiveness and reduce their adverse effects); Daphna Lewinsohn-Zamir, *Do the Right Thing: Indirect Remedies in Private Law*, 94 B.U. L. REV. 55, 81–85 (2014) (pointing to the advantages of "indirect remedies," such as inducing the payment of a debt through a possessory lien, based, in part, on the notion of cognitive dissonance).

193. *See supra* p. 232 (the Coase theorem) and 211–13 (psychological ownership).

194. Lewinsohn-Zamir, *supra* note 3, at 378–79.

195. These observations are shared by Blumenthal (*supra* note 4) and Barros (*supra* note 104), among others.

196. *See supra* pp. 204–07, 207–09, 219–22, and 222–23, respectively.

197. *See, e.g., infra* pp. 241–43, 245, 253–55, 272–73, 465–66, 468–70.

198. *See supra* pp. 161–62.

be reformed so that it more closely follows the prevailing convictions—or alternatively, try to change public perceptions.[199]

The third observation emerging from the above discussion is that, as in other legal fields, even when the behavioral findings are clear, one must be extremely cautious in drawing normative conclusions from these findings. The normative landscape is usually too complex to allow for such direct conclusions.

199. Blumenthal, *supra* note 4, at 623–25.

7

Contract Law

A. Introduction

Economic analysis has emerged from thinking about markets. In a competitive market, voluntary transactions allow people to exchange goods and services, such that each party receives something she values more than what she parts with. Voluntary transactions thus facilitate division of labor and specialization, which are key to increasing the quality and quantity of production, and hence to advancing human welfare. Presumably, therefore, voluntary transactions that are carried out through contracts are both Kaldor-Hicks and Pareto efficient. Contract law strives to facilitate voluntary transactions, reduce their costs, and overcome various obstacles to efficient contract formation and performance.

Unsurprisingly, contract law is an area in which scholars who use an economic framework have long since felt particularly comfortable in applying their insights. Basing contract law on people's actual preferences seems natural, given the consensual nature of the contractual relationship. If one accepts that fulfilling the goals of the contracting parties is a primary objective of contract law, then a theory of contract should address those goals and the ways in which legal regulation might help the parties achieve them. Furthermore, even if one wishes to promote other goals through contract law—such as fairness of exchange or redistribution of power and wealth[1]—the ability of contracting parties to contract around provisions that are geared toward these goals should be incorporated into the analysis.[2] Thus, even people who adopt non-instrumentalist conceptions of contracts and contract law (such as a liberal, promise-based conception) should take positive economic analysis of contract law into account.[3]

1. On fairness of exchange, see generally Eyal Zamir, *The Inverted Hierarchy of Contract Interpretation and Supplementation*, 97 Colum. L. Rev. 1710, 1778–82 (1997). On redistribution through contract law, see, e.g., *id.* at 1782–84; Anthony T. Kronman, *Contract Law and Distributive Justice*, 89 Yale L.J. 472 (1980).

2. *See* Richard Craswell, *Passing on the Costs of Legal Rules: Efficiency and Distribution in Buyer-Seller Relationships*, 43 Stan. L. Rev. 361 (1991); Louis Kaplow & Steven Shavell, Fairness versus Welfare 213–15 (2002).

3. As Charles Fried indeed does in the second edition of his influential book of 1981. *See* Charles Fried, Contract as Promise: A Theory of Contractual Obligation 133–61 (2d ed. 2015).

Behavioral Law and Economics. Eyal Zamir and Doron Teichman.

Generally speaking, the economic analysis of contract law focuses on the goal of maximizing the contractual surplus, while presuming people's preferences are compatible with the tenets of rational choice theory.[4] This normative and positive combination has brought law and economics scholars to adopt a laissez-faire attitude toward contract law.[5] The default position within this analysis is that contract law should avoid placing restrictions on the freedom of the contracting parties to design contractual provisions that best fit their needs. Only when market failures, such as imperfect information or negative externalities, are present, might legal intervention be justified.[6] In actuality, however, contract-law doctrines reflect competing values, and some legal economists have expressed doubts about the ability of economic analysis to explain existing law, or to come up with workable suggestions about the optimal design of contract doctrine.[7]

This chapter does not explore the entire terrain of contract law and theory, but rather focuses on the contribution of behavioral insights and recent empirical (including experimental) findings to our understanding of some key issues.[8] It begins by setting out a behavioral theory of contracts that underlines the role of factors such as promise-keeping and trust, and examines how these are affected by the mode of contracting used—namely, individually negotiated versus standard-form contracts. The chapter then explores concrete areas of contract law through a behavioral prism. Specifically, it will survey areas such as pre-contractual negotiations, with special emphasis on the role of default rules and other reference points (Section C); contract formation (Section D); interpretation and supplementation (Section E); performance (Section F); and remedies for breach of contract, including agreed-upon remedies (Sections G and H). As the analysis demonstrates, once the assumptions of thick and thin rationality are relaxed, some of the key conclusions of economic analysis of contract law are called into question (and, as always, the behavioral insights should be of interest to those who do not share the methodological and normative outlook of standard economic analysis, as well).

A few preliminary comments should be made at the outset regarding the scope of this chapter. First, the chapter will only briefly draw from the vast body of literature on behavioral contract theory.[9] The literature on behavioral contract theory has focused mostly on contracting, rather than contract law, and has highlighted the implications of behavioral findings for issues of contract design. Accordingly, this body of work has illuminated issues

4. *See, e.g.*, Eric A. Posner, *Economic Analysis of Contract Law after Three Decades: Success or Failure?*, 112 YALE L.J. 829, 832–34 (2003).

5. *Id.* at 842.

6. *See, e.g.*, Alan Schwartz & Robert E. Scott, *Contract Theory and the Limits of Contract Law*, 113 YALE L.J. 541, 609–10 (2003); STEVEN SHAVELL, FOUNDATIONS OF ECONOMIC ANALYSIS OF LAW 320–22 (2004).

7. Posner, *supra* note 4.

8. For other contributions to the field, see Melvin A. Eisenberg, *Behavioral Economics and Contract Law*, *in* THE OXFORD HANDBOOK OF BEHAVIORAL ECONOMICS AND THE LAW 438 (Eyal Zamir & Doron Teichman eds., 2014); Ann-Sophie Vandenberghe, *Behavioral Approaches to Contract Law*, *in* CONTRACT LAW AND ECONOMICS 401 (Gerrit De Geest ed., 2011).

9. For a review, see Botond Kőszegi, *Behavioral Contract Theory*, 52 J. ECON. LITERATURE 1075 (2014).

such as the desirable level of contract enforcement,[10] incomplete contracts compared with control through detailed provisions,[11] compensation schemes dealing with moral hazards,[12] and the optimal design of auctions.[13]

Second, behavioral economics has made an immense contribution to our understanding of consumer contracts, and the proper legal response to them. Given the scope of this topic and its importance, the whole of the next chapter is devoted to it. Certain issues, which are of particular relevance to consumer contracts, will be discussed there, although they are relevant to non-consumer contracts, as well. For example, it has been demonstrated that practically no one reads standard-form contracts, whether consumer or commercial.[14] In the same vein, studies have shown that neither experience nor professional training necessarily eliminates, or even reduces, various cognitive biases[15]—thus calling for consideration of their implications for both professional and lay contracting parties. Nonetheless, to avoid repetition, the present chapter does not systematically discuss standard-form contracts, disclosure duties, or regulation of the content of the contract—issues that will be taken up in the next chapter. Since much of the analysis offered in the next chapter applies mutatis mutandis to non-consumer contracts, readers are advised to read both chapters in tandem, lest they get a distorted picture of (the behavioral analysis of) contract law.

B. Trust, Promise, and Contract

1. General

At the core of the economic analysis of contract law lies the conception that contracts are a tool that helps parties achieve mutually beneficial cooperation in a bid to further their welfare, and that contract law should help them achieve that goal.[16] The law-and-economics literature often equates contracting parties with players in a trust (or agency) game.[17] Such a game involves a strategic interaction between two players regarding an efficient investment. In the classic trust game, Player 1 is endowed with an asset (e.g., $10) and needs to decide whether to transfer control of the asset or part of it to Player 2. If Player 1 chooses not to transfer the asset, the game ends with the asset in Player 1's hands. If Player 1 decides to transfer the asset or part of it to Player 2, then the value of the transferred asset is

10. *See* Iris Bohnet, Bruno S. Frey & Steffen Huck, *More Order with Less Law: On Contract Enforcement, Trust, and Crowding*, 95 Am. Pol. Sci. Rev. 131 (2001).

11. *See* Armin Falk & Michael Kosfeld, *The Hidden Costs of Control*, 96 Am. Econ. Rev. 1611, 1614 (2006).

12. *See, e.g.*, Fabian Herweg, Daniel Muller & Philipp Weinschenk, *Binary Payment Schemes: Moral Hazard and Loss Aversion*, 100 Am. Econ. Rev. 2451 (2010).

13. *See, e.g.*, Emel Filiz-Ozbay & Erkut Y. Ozbay, *Auctions with Anticipated Regret: Theory and Experiment*, 97 Am. Econ. Rev. 1407 (2007).

14. *See* Yannis Bakos, Florencia Marotta-Wurgler & David R. Trossen, *Does Anyone Read the Fine Print? Consumer Attention to Standard Form Contracts*, 43 J. Legal Stud. 1 (2014); *infra* pp. 301–04.

15. *See supra* pp. 114–17.

16. *See* Kaplow & Shavell, *supra* note 2, at 155.

17. *See* Robert Cooter & Thomas Ulen, Law and Economics 283–86 (6th ed. 2012).

automatically multiplied by a given factor (e.g., with a multiplier of 3, Player 2 gets $30). At this point, Player 2 is free to decide whether to give back to Player 1 part or all of the larger asset that he now controls.

While the efficient outcome of a trust game is cooperation (i.e., Player 1 transferring her full entitlement to Player 2), game theory suggests that the players in this game will be driven to a non-cooperative equilibrium. If Player 2 is entrusted with the asset, he is expected to keep all of it to himself. Knowing this in advance, Player 1 is expected to transfer nothing to Player 2 in the first place. In terms of the preceding example, rather than reaching a total asset of $30, the parties end up with the original $10. In a world in which legally enforceable contracts are available, however, the parties can overcome this problem. By precommitting to sharing the fruits of cooperation, Player 2 can induce Player 1 to transfer the asset to him, and both parties can reap the benefits of trust.

However, experimental studies have shown that the behavior of people in a trust game deviates significantly from the predictions of rational choice theory. In a classic early study—which included a setup identical to that described above—Joyce Berg, John Dickhaut, and Kevin McCabe documented both trust (in the form of positive contributions made by Player 1) and trustworthiness (in the form of reciprocal payments made by Player 2).[18] The vast majority of first movers in their study chose to transfer at least some money to the other party, and a third of those who chose to make the transfer ended up with more money than they initially had. This result has since been replicated in dozens of studies, and while the variance within these studies is significant, the general picture of trust without contracts is consistent.[19]

Furthermore, the paradigm of trust games has been used to demonstrate how promises that are not legally enforceable can influence cooperation. Gary Charness and Martin Dufwenberg allowed participants in a trust game to communicate in writing prior to making their choices.[20] They then measured how communications influenced players' expectations from the game and measured the level of cooperation. The results show that an unenforceable promise made by Player 2—in game-theory terms, *cheap talk*—brought about a significant increase in cooperation rates. When communication was absent, both parties cooperated in only 20 percent of the pairs, while the introduction of a single anonymous written message from Player 2 to Player 1 increased this figure to 50 percent. Charness and Dufwenberg argue that this result stems from the expectations that a promise creates, and the fact that frustrating those expectations will generate guilt, which people want to avoid.

Note, however, that this experimental design cannot rule out an alternative explanation that focuses on the intrinsic power of a promise as the driving force for heightened cooperation when the parties can communicate. This later hypothesis was pitted against the expectation hypothesis by Christoph Vanberg in a study that presented a nuanced version

18. Joyce Berg, John Dickhaut & Kevin McCabe, *Trust, Reciprocity, and Social History*, 10 GAMES & ECON. BEHAV. 122, 130–32 (1995).

19. *See* Noel D. Johnson & Alexandra A. Mislin, *Trust Games: A Meta-analysis*, 32 J. ECON. PSYCHOL. 865 (2011).

20. Gary Charness & Martin Dufwenberg, *Promise and Partnership*, 74 ECONOMETRICA 1579 (2006).

of the dictator game.[21] In this study, subjects could communicate prior to a draw that determined their role in the dictator game. Most subjects used the communication option to indicate that, if they became dictator, they would choose the surplus maximizing strategy that is beneficial for both parties, rather than the option that maximizes their own individual payoff.[22] Importantly, however, after the roles of the players had been determined, half the couples were switched and rematched. This switch was known to dictators, but not to the other player. Dictators who were matched with new partners could view their new partner's communications with the latter's original partner prior to the switch.

This somewhat elaborate design enabled the researcher to randomly manipulate whether the dictator faced a party to whom she had made a promise (i.e., dictators in the no-switch condition), while holding the expectations of the counterparty constant. The results showed that cooperation rates in the switch condition were significantly lower than in the group in which subjects were not switched. While 73 percent of the dictators who made a promise in the latter group fulfilled it, only 54 percent of the dictators who made a promise in the former group did. This difference was not driven by how dictators' perceived their counterparties' expectations, as there were no differences between the groups in this regard. Thus, one can conclude from this experiment that promises, per se, influence behavior.[23] Note that both the expectation-based and the promise-based accounts are consistent with the theory of guilt aversion: people may experience guilt because they frustrated another person's expectations, or because they breached the norm of promise-keeping per se.

While the behavioral-economic literature on promise-keeping and trust has focused on abstract games, the legal literature on the topic has attempted to contextualize the issue in the realm of contracts. It demonstrates that people do not view their contractual obligations in purely instrumental terms—rather, contractual choices are made within a rich decision-making environment, which is not exclusively driven by self-interest. Although connecting the dots between all of the behavioral findings in this area is a complicated task, the overall picture emerging from the findings is that "contracts are promises to perform, and breaching a contract is morally wrong in the same way that breaking a promise is morally wrong."[24]

21. Christoph Vanberg, *Why Do People Keep Their Promises: An Experimental Test of Two Explanations*, 76 Econometrica 1467 (2008). On the dictator game, see *supra* pp. 102–03.

22. Unlike the standard dictator game, in this version the dictator could choose between two options: for the dictator to receive 14 euros and the recipient to receive nothing, or for the dictator to receive 10 euros, and the recipient to receive either 12 euros with probability 5/6 and nothing with probability 1/6. Recall that the communication is made before one knows whether one will be the dictator or the recipient.

23. *Id.* at 1476.

24. Tess Wilkinson-Ryan, *Legal Promise and Psychological Contract*, 47 Wake Forest L. Rev. 843, 845 (2012). Interestingly, in one study U.S. subjects judged opportunistic breaches of contract by individuals more harshly than by corporations. While breach by an individual was viewed as a moral transgression, the same behavior by an organization was seen more as a legitimate business decision. It was also found that using a "promise" terminology may eliminate this discrepancy. *See* Uriel Haran, *A Person-Organization Discontinuity in Contract Perception: Why Corporations Can Get away with Breaking Contracts but Individuals Cannot,* 59 Mgmt. Sci. 2837 (2013). More studies are necessary to establish the generality and external validity of these findings, as well as to examine the possibility of cross-cultural differences in this regard.

Vanberg's version of the dictator game described above somewhat resembles a contractual assignment. In this setting, one of the original contracting parties transfers the rights and obligations created by the contract to a third party. While such an assignment does not change the fundamental incentive structure set out in the contract, research suggests that it does alter people's behavior.[25] Specifically, promisors view a breach as less morally reprehensible when they commit it toward an assignee rather than toward the original promisee—and indeed can be induced to breach for less money in that circumstance. Much like Vanberg's results—which suggest that the moral obligation to perform a promise is tied to the relationship between the promisor and promisee—these results suggest that the moral obligations associated with a contract are linked to the relationship between the contracting parties.

At a more general level, researchers have shown that breach decisions are not exclusively governed by the expected price tag that the legal system attaches to nonperformance.[26] To explore this point, in one study subjects were asked to consider their behavior when faced with a breach dilemma involving quality of performance. Participants were then informed that their legal liability was uncertain—but the source of uncertainty was randomly assigned (while holding the expected cost of breach constant). In the "enforcement uncertainty" group, subjects learned that poor performance clearly constituted a breach, but that enforcement was uncertain, due to detection problems. Conversely, in the "legal uncertainty" group, subjects were told that enforcement is certain, but that poor performance might be deemed legal. The results showed that despite the identical payoff structures, the source of uncertainty influenced people's decisions: specifically, people exhibit a greater willingness to breach when there was legal uncertainty about the content of their obligation, as opposed to enforcement uncertainty. When the source of uncertainty stems from enforcement problems, people are faced with the norm of promise-keeping and are relatively reluctant to renege. However, when the issue is legal uncertainty about the content of the contract, people may attempt to rationalize selfish choices as a legitimate interpretive decision, rather than as a willful breach of promise. These findings are consistent with the insights of behavioral ethics more generally.[27]

The body of work documenting norms of trust and promise-keeping does not negate the economic justification for contracts. While such norms help facilitate cooperation between people, they do not always allow people to reap the full potential payoff of cooperation. In the absence of an enforcement device, some people rationally violate such norms, and others cooperate only partially, for fear of non-cooperation by the other party. While Berg, Dickhaut, and McCabe's classic study of the trust game documented a significant degree of irrational cooperation, the average total return in the experiment was only $15.48—about half of what the parties could have achieved.[28] The findings about trust,

25. Tess Wilkinson-Ryan, *Transferring Trust: Reciprocity Norms and Assignment of Contract*, 9 J. EMPIRICAL LEGAL STUD. 511, 529–31 (2012).

26. Yuval Feldman & Doron Teichman, *Are All Contractual Obligations Created Equal?*, 100 GEO. L.J. 5 (2011).

27. *See supra* pp. 73–75.

28. *See* Berg, Dickhaut & McCabe, *supra* note 18 at 130.

promise-keeping, and cooperation do suggest, however, that the psychology of contracts is more complicated than wealth maximization. Even without legally binding obligations and reputational concerns, parties are often bound by moral obligations to avoid breaking promises and to reciprocate cooperative behavior. As the rest of this chapter shows, this insight can illuminate several doctrines within contract law.

2. Standard-Form Contracts

Do the norms of trust and promise-keeping equally apply to all contracts? Specifically, are there differences in this regard between individually negotiated and standard-form contracts? Since the lion's share of written contracts these days are unilaterally drafted by one party, this question is of great importance.[29]

Theories of human behavior suggest that people may be less committed to standard-form contracts than to negotiated ones, and that, in the standard-form scenario, their performance decisions will tend to favor their self-interest. First, standard-form contracts routinely involve asymmetric information with regard to their content, since customers practically never read them.[30] The fact that customers are not aware of the content of a given contract may lead them to discount their obligations under the contract. They may, for example, convince themselves, through a process of motivated reasoning, that breaching the contract does not violate the prohibition against breaking promises, as they never truly agreed to the relevant provisions of the contract.[31]

Second, the procedure of signing a standard-form contract may be perceived by some as unfair. Standard-form contracts are usually offered on a take-it-or-leave-it basis. Unlike a negotiated contract, they allow for no input from the customer (aside from assent). The literature on procedural fairness shows that compliance is enhanced when people feel that the process allows for their voice to be heard.[32] Therefore, the unilateral nature of the formation of a standard-form contract might reduce the sense of procedural fairness, thus diminishing people's inclination to respect the allocation of risks stipulated in the contract.

A further psychological mechanism that is likely to support greater adherence to negotiated contract terms is the phenomenon of *cognitive dissonance*. When contracting is the result of free choice and deliberation, it can lead to a deeper commitment to the contract's terms, since people adjust their attitudes to suit their contractual choices. In contrast, because in standard-form contracts people do not exercise choice regarding the contract terms, a dissonance is less likely to be created.

Finally, standard-form contracts are often perceived as reflecting an imbalanced division of power that has even been described as "authoritarian."[33] The drafter is conventionally

29. Other aspects of standard-form contracts will be discussed in the next chapter. *See infra* pp. 301–04.

30. *See* Bakos, Marotta-Wurgler & Trossen, *supra* note 14; *infra* pp. 301–02.

31. On motivated reasoning, see generally *supra* pp. 58–61.

32. On procedural fairness, see generally *supra* pp. 104–06.

33. Friedrich Kessler, *Contracts of Adhesion—Some Thoughts about Freedom of Contract*, 43 COLUM. L. REV. 629, 640 (1943).

viewed as powerful and sophisticated, whereas the other party is seen as weak and vulnerable.[34] As a result, customers may be more inclined to behave selfishly in the context of standard-form contracts, in the belief that it is a means of transferring wealth from the powerful to the powerless.

In the study of people's attitudes toward enforcement uncertainty and contractual uncertainty mentioned above, researchers found an interaction between how a contract was formed and people's moral judgments of breach:[35] when the uncertainty stemmed exclusively from enforcement problems, there was virtually no difference between subjects' judgments of breach of a standard-form contract versus a negotiated one. However, when the source of uncertainty stemmed from the language of the contract, people viewed a breach of the standard-form contract by the non-drafting party as significantly less immoral than a breach of the negotiated contract. This confirms the readiness of people to adopt more self-serving interpretations when it comes to standard-form contracts.

This finding is consistent with the results of a later study that documented people's actual behavior.[36] Subjects in this study agreed to complete an online survey in exchange for a free DVD. In the Conventional Boilerplate condition, subjects simply clicked "I Agree" to a standard-form contract. In the Marginal Choice and Choice Plus Notice conditions, subjects were instructed to choose between two terms that would "become part of the contract between [them] and the researchers conducting this survey." In Marginal Choice, these two terms were insignificant. In the Choice-Plus-Notice condition, one of the two terms included an undertaking to complete the survey in its entirety and to answer all questions carefully, honestly, and completely to the best of the subject's ability, in return for the right to choose the DVD that they would receive (the small minority of subjects who chose the alternative term in this condition were dropped from the study).[37]

Unbeknownst to participants at the time of contracting, the survey they were asked to complete consisted of 480 questions, and was deliberately designed to be difficult to answer quickly (e.g., there was a four-second delay between each question). While the vast majority of subjects abandoned the survey without completing it,[38] the rate at which they did so depended on their mode of assent. As expected, participants in the Choice-Plus-Notice condition answered significantly more questions before quitting, compared with those in

34. *See, e.g.*, Warren Mueller, *Residential Tenants and Their Leases: An Empirical Study*, 69 MICH. L. REV. 247, 247 (1970). Relatedly, social psychology research has identified a phenomenon dubbed the *Robin Hood effect*—the inclination to transfer wealth from the rich to the poor—which is driven by both envy of the affluent and empathy toward the disadvantaged. *See, e.g.*, Francesca Gino & Lamar Pierce, *Robin Hood under the Hood: Wealth-Based Discrimination in Illicit Customer Help*, 21 ORG. SCI. 1176 (2010).

35. Feldman & Teichman, *supra* note 26, at 29–30.

36. *See* Zev Eigen, *When and Why Individuals Obey Contracts: Experimental Evidence of Consent, Compliance, Promise, and Performance*, 41 J. LEGAL STUD. 67 (2012).

37. In a fourth, control condition, subjects were taken directly to the survey. The experiment also examined the effectiveness of different requests to continue performing the task, but this variable lies beyond the scope of the present discussion.

38. Approximately 3 percent of the subjects completed the entire survey without trying to exit. Apparently, some people *really* want a free DVD.

the Conventional-Boilerplate condition. It remains to be seen, however, to what extent this result was driven by the choice or the notice element of the experimental treatment (there was no statistically significant difference between the Conventional-Boilerplate and Marginal-Choice conditions).

On the other hand, several experimental and observational studies suggest that standard-form contracts continue to enjoy the allure of contracts, and as a result people tend to presume that they are legally and morally obligated to the text of the boilerplate—a text that they have never read.[39] Apparently, many contracting parties follow a formalist heuristic, according to which those who do not read the contract do so at their own peril. Sophisticated drafters aware of this heuristic include in their contracts harsh, and at times even unenforceable provisions, knowing that their mere inclusion in the contract will cause some parties to adhere to them ex post.

In addition to their contribution to explaining the observed behavior of contracting parties, the findings about people's attitudes about standard-form contracts may shed light on contract doctrine. One example would be the *contra proferetem* rule, discussed below.[40]

C. Pre-contractual Negotiations

1. General

A large body of behavioral research has studied negotiations, with particular emphasis on the psychological causes of bargaining impasse. It has found that a host of heuristics and biases may hinder mutually beneficial agreements, or lead to suboptimal ones. These include self-serving biases that make negotiators inclined to reject offers as unfair;[41] framing effects (inducing those who frame the negotiations as pertaining to gains to exhibit risk aversion, and those who frame them as pertaining to losses to be risk-seeking);[42] anchoring and adjustment (rendering the first offer, or listing price, overly impactful);[43] the fixed-pie error (causing parties who erroneously assume that negotiations are a zero-sum game to miss desirable, multidimensional and integrative solutions);[44] the availability effect (leading

39. *See, e.g.*, Meirav Furth-Matzkin, *On the Unexpected Use of Unenforceable Contract Terms: Evidence from the Residential Rental Market*, 9 J. LEGAL ANALYSIS 1 (2017); Tess Wilkinson-Ryan, *The Perverse Consequences of Disclosing Standard Terms*, 103 CORNELL L. REV. 117 (2017).

40. *See infra* p. 58.

41. *See, e.g.*, Linda Babcock & George Loewenstein, *Explaining Bargaining Impasse: The Role of Self-Serving Biases*, 11 J. ECON. PERSP. 109 (1997). On self-serving biases, see generally *supra* pp. 58–76.

42. *See, e.g.*, Margaret A. Neale & Max H. Bazerman, *The Effects of Framing and Negotiator Overconfidence on Bargaining Behaviors and Outcomes*, 28 ACAD. MGMT. J. 34 (1985). On framing effects, see generally *supra* pp. 46–48.

43. *See, e.g.*, Gregory B. Northcraft & Margaret A. Neale, *Experts, Amateurs, and Real Estate: An Anchoring-and-Adjustment Perspective on Property Pricing Decisions*, 39 ORG. BEHAV. & HUM. DECISION PROCESSES 84 (1987). On anchoring, see generally *supra* pp. 79–82.

44. *See, e.g.*, Max H. Bazerman & Margaret A. Neale, *Heuristics in Negotiation: Limitations to Effective Dispute Resolution*, *in* NEGOTIATING IN ORGANIZATIONS 51, 62–63 (Max H. Bazerman & Roy J. Lewicki eds., 1983).

negotiators to weigh some events as more probable than others, and vice versa);[45] and reactive devaluation (devaluing a proposal made by one's counterparty, as opposed to a neutral party, or ally).[46]

Somewhat surprisingly, these findings appear to have had a greater impact on the analysis of litigants' settlement negotiations[47] than on contract law in general. One plausible explanation for this gap is that, compared with civil law systems, U.S. contract law—which has served as the doctrinal background for much of the behavioral legal analysis—pays relatively little attention to the pre-contractual process, especially when negotiations do not come to fruition.

If we put aside the doctrinal issues, litigation is certainly not the only sphere in which behavioral insights may enrich the analysis of bargaining and negotiation. While existing behavioral legal analysis of pre-contractual decision-making has focused on consumer decision-making and its manipulation by marketers (and is therefore discussed in the next chapter),[48] there is also considerable room for analyzing the pre-contractual process in non-consumer transactions—and initial steps in this direction have already been taken.

Thus, while rational maximizers who contemplate a bargain presumably consider all aspects of all available options, boundedly rational people may suffer from information overload.[49] They are unable to process large amounts of information, especially if the transaction is complex, so they use simplifying decision strategies (which, given the constraints of their cognitive ability, may well be the rational thing to do). One such strategy, first described by Amos Tversky and subsequently supported empirically, is the *elimination-by-aspect* method.[50] When using this method, each option is viewed as a set of aspects. The decision-maker first applies a single criterion (such as a maximum price when buying a truck, or a certain location when looking for an apartment to rent), and eliminates all options that do not meet this criterion. Of the remaining options, the decision-maker then eliminates those that do not meet another criterion, and so forth. While considerably less

45. *See, e.g.*, Margaret A. Neale, *The Effects of Negotiation, Arbitration and Cost Salience on Bargainer Behavior: The Role of the Arbitrator and Constituency on Negotiator Judgment*, 34 ORG. BEHAV. & HUM. DECISION PROCESSES 97 (1984). On availability, see generally *supra* pp. 34–36.

46. *See, e.g.*, Constance Stillinger et al., The Reactive Devaluation Barrier to Conflict Resolution (unpublished manuscript, 1990, described in Lee Ross & Constance Stillinger, *Barriers to Conflict Resolution*, 7 NEGOTIATION J. 389, 394 (1991)).

47. *See infra* pp. 497–505.

48. *See infra* pp. 283–304.

49. *See infra* p. 285.

50. *See* Amos Tversky, *Elimination by Aspect: A Theory of Choice*, 79 PSYCHOL. REV. 281 (1972); Peter S. Fader & Leigh McAlister, *An Elimination by Aspects Model of Consumer Response to Promotion Calibrated on UPC Scanner Data*, 27 J. MARKETING RES. 322 (1990). Elimination by aspect is not the only heuristic used by customers. For a review of other simplifying decision techniques, see John R. Hauser, Min Ding & Steven P. Gaskin, *Non-compensatory (and Compensatory) Models of Consideration-Set Decisions*, *in* 2009 SAWTOOTH SOFTWARE CONFERENCE PROCEEDINGS 207 (2009). For a theory of consumer choice that integrates *elimination by aspect* and other models of non-compensatory decision processes (that is, processes that do not trade off the costs and benefits of all options), see James R. Bettman, Mary Frances Luce & John W. Payne, *Constructive Consumer Choice Processes*, 25 J. CONSUMER RES. 187 (1998).

exacting, such a process may lead to suboptimal choices—and in any event it markedly differs from the decision process envisioned by rational choice theory, which assumes that all options are considered in their entirety, and all their aspects are commensurable. For instance, given the choice between several trucks, if the price of truck X exceeds the limit the buyer has set for herself, she may not consider it at all, even if in fact it is the option that maximizes her utility thanks to its superior safety and lower fuel consumption. Inasmuch as elimination-by-aspect better captures the realities of contracting decision-making, a party may shape the other party's choices by influencing the order in which the latter considers the various aspects. In the above example, if the seller convinces the buyer that the price could be negotiated later on, the buyer might end up buying truck X at a higher price than her initial limit.[51] Escalation of commitment may strengthen this tendency.[52]

As we shall see below, the clear boundary between pre-contractual and contractual stages, as envisioned by classical contract law, does not necessarily reflect the gradual development of commitment between the parties before and after the formal moment of contracting—and when people do perceive the two stages differently, they often misidentify the moment at which a contract has been formed.[53] These phenomena further support the view that contract law and behavioral studies should pay more attention to the pre-contractual process.[54]

2. The Role of Default Rules and Other Reference Points

One aspect of contract negotiation that has attracted considerable attention is the role of default rules and other reference points, such as general trade usages, and course of dealing between the same parties. While rational choice theory assumes that people's preferences, judgments, and choices are reference-independent, behavioral research has demonstrated that they are all very much reference-dependent.[55] This phenomenon is of particular interest to legal policymakers, because the law can potentially alter the relevant reference points.[56]

51. Elimination by aspect may be particularly impactful in standard-form, consumer contracts. *See* Russell Korobkin, *Bounded Rationality, Standard Form Contracts, and Unconscionability*, 70 U. Chi. L. Rev. 1203, 1222–25 (2003); *infra* pp. 287, 303.

52. *See infra* pp. 287, 290, 304, 316. On escalation of commitment in general, see *supra* pp. 56–57.

53. *See infra* pp. 254–55.

54. For initial steps in this direction, see, e.g., Tess Wilkinson-Ryan & David A. Hoffman, *Breach Is for Suckers*, 63 Vand. L. Rev. 1003, 1039–41 (2010) [hereinafter Wilkinson-Ryan & Hoffman, *Breach*] (arguing that some of the confusion surrounding the doctrine of promissory estoppel stems from a mismatch between the legal doctrine and people's perceptions); David A. Hoffman & Tess Wilkinson-Ryan, *The Psychology of Contract Precautions*, 80 U. Chi. L. Rev. 395, 429–30 (2013) [hereinafter Hoffman & Wilkinson-Ryan, *Precautions*] (arguing that the greater precautions people take during pre-contractual negotiations, compared with the performance stage, may justify a smaller role for legal norms at that stage).

55. *See generally supra* pp. 42–57, 76–86.

56. Note that although we are discussing the role of default rules and other reference points in the context of pre-contractual negotiation, they are just as pertinent to the formation, interpretation, supplementation, and performance of contracts. In fact, the notion of default rules is relevant to any aspect of contract law that is governed by such rules, including remedy rules.

Unlike the Coasian world of zero transaction costs and fully specified contracts, in the real world contracts are invariably incomplete. The parties' express terms are routinely supplemented by implied terms and understandings based on their previous transactions, general trade usages, and legal default rules. Default rules often evolve through court judgments (which may then be codified in legislation), reflecting common usages and prevailing notions of reasonableness and fairness. In the absence of explicit or implicit agreement between the parties, even major issues—such as time and place of performance, quality of the sales object, and even price[57]—may be determined by default rules.

While effectuating the intentions and expectations of the contracting parties is by no means the only goal of default rules,[58] it is surely a primary, perhaps *the* primary, purpose in many contexts.[59] There is typically a two-way process, whereby prevailing social and commercial norms shape—and are shaped by—the law. For example, the gradual shift from *caveat emptor* (let the buyer beware), to *caveat venditor* (let the seller beware) in many Western countries in the past century or so, has taken place in both the legal and the social-commercial spheres, with each process reinforcing the other. The notion that legal rules have a significant expressive or educational impact on people's preferences and judgments is controversial,[60] and is surely more powerful in some contexts than in others.[61] However, inasmuch as legal default rules are consistent with people's common expectations—because the law followed those expectations, or shaped them, or both—most people, most of the time, can be expected not to opt out of legal default rules.[62]

In recent decades, a large body of law-and-economics literature has examined the role of contract default rules. Default rules are said to enhance efficiency by reducing transaction costs and inducing information sharing. Default rules that reflect the prevailing preferences of contracting parties save them the need to consider the various contingencies that might affect the performance of the contract, to negotiate the arrangements that would govern those contingencies, and to formulate the agreed terms.[63]

Parties whose preferences differ from the default are free to negotiate an alternative arrangement that more accurately reflects their particular needs and preferences. While opting out of the default involves costs, these costs are worth bearing to fulfill the needs involved, and to convey crucial information. Thus, for example, when a promisee expects to

57. *See, e.g.*, U.C.C. §§ 2-308, 2-314(2)(b), and 2-305 (AM. LAW INST. & UNIF. LAW COMM'N, 2002), respectively.

58. On various goals that may be served by default rules, see Zamir, *supra* note 1, at 1768–802.

59. *See, e.g.*, Randy E. Barnett, *The Sound of Silence: Default Rules and Contractual Consent*, 78 VA. L. REV. 821, 880 (1992); Jody S. Kraus, *The Correspondence of Contract and Promise*, 109 COLUM. L. REV. 1603, 1631–34 (2009).

60. *See, e.g.*, Cass R. Sunstein, *On the Expressive Function of Law*, 144 U. PA. L. REV. 2021 (1996); Matthew D. Adler, *Expressive Theories of Law: A Skeptical Overview*, 148 U. PA. L. REV. 1363 (2000); Elizabeth S. Anderson & Richard H. Pildes, *Expressive Theories of Law: A General Restatement*, 148 U. PA. L. REV. 1503 (2000).

61. *See, e.g.*, Adam J. Hirsch, *Default Rules in Inheritance Law: A Problem in Search of Its Context*, 73, FORDHAM L. REV. 1031, 1053–58 (2004) (disputing the expressive effect of inheritance law).

62. Zamir, *supra* note 1, at 1753–55.

63. *See, e.g.*, COOTER & ULEN, *supra* note 17, at 292–94. Trade usages, used by courts to fill gaps in contracts, serve the same function.

suffer an exceptionally high loss as a result of a promisor's breach, she may contract around the default rules of contract damages and insist on a high liquidated damages clause. The promisor would likely demand a higher price in return, but both parties are expected to benefit from the clause. The high liquidated damages alerts the promisor to the expected costs of her breach, thereby creating a more appropriate incentive for performance—for which the promisee, in turn, should be willing to pay an extra price. It follows that in circumstances where there is a prevailing and acute information asymmetry, a *penalty default rule* that induces most parties to contract around the default—thereby sharing important information—may be more efficient than one that simply echoes the revealed preferences of most parties, given the information problem.[64]

While this economic analysis is illuminating, it fails to fully account for what has come to be known as the "stickiness" of default rules. If the direct costs of bargaining a contract were the only hurdle involved, we should have witnessed far more opt-outs than occur in reality.[65] The stickiness of default rules may be partly explained by the existence of various indirect costs of opting out. A detailed and prolonged negotiation over unlikely eventualities may adversely affect the spirit of trust and cooperation necessary for the success of contractual endeavors.[66] The very proposal by one party to opt out of the default, even if it is in the other party's favor, may raise suspicions about the proposer's character and motives.[67] Indeed, concern about such adverse inferences may cause the more informed party to refrain from proposing contract terms that may be mutually beneficial,[68] thus leaving the default rule in place. The information-revelation effect of contracting around a default rule may also discourage such contracting when people do not wish to share information.[69]

Not all these explanations for the reluctance to contract around default rules (and trade usages) are equally convincing.[70] In any event, an important element of the story appears to be that default rules typically set a reference point. They trigger people's status quo and

64. Ian Ayres & Robert Gertner, *Filling Gaps in Incomplete Contracts: An Economic Theory of Default Rules*, 99 Yale L.J. 87 (1989).

65. *See, e.g.*, Karen Eggleston, Eric A. Posner & Richard Zeckhauser, *The Design and Interpretation of Contracts: Why Complexity Matters*, 95 Nw. U. L. Rev. 91, 107–08 (2000).

66. Stewart Macaulay, *Non-contractual Relations in Business: A Preliminary Study*, 28 Am. Soc. Rev. 55, 64 (1963); Zamir, *supra* note 1, at 1756–57; Lisa Bernstein, *Social Norms and Default Rules Analysis*, 3 S. Cal. Interdisc. L.J. 59, 70–72 (1993).

67. Omri Ben-Shahar & John A. E. Pottow, *On the Stickiness of Default Rules*, 33 Fla. St. U. L. Rev. 651 (2006); Zamir, *supra* note 1, at 1757. *See also infra* p. 502.

68. Kathryn E. Spier, *Incomplete Contracts and Signaling*, 23 Rand J. Econ. 432 (1992).

69. Jason Scott Johnston, *Strategic Bargaining and the Economic Theory of Contract Default Rules*, 100 Yale L.J. 615 (1990). *See also* Ian Ayres & Robert Gertner, *Strategic Contractual Inefficiency and the Optimal Choice of Legal Rules*, 101 Yale L.J. 729 (1992).

70. For critiques of the abovementioned and other economic explanations of the stickiness of default rules, see, e.g., Russell Korobkin, *The Status Quo Bias and Contract Default Rules*, 83 Cornell L. Rev. 608, 613–25 (1998) [hereinafter Korobkin, *Status Quo Bias*]; Russell Korobkin, *Inertia and Preference in Contract Negotiation: The Psychological Power of Default Rules and Form Terms*, 51 Vand. L. Rev. 1583, 1592–603 (1998).

omission biases (associated with the cost of regret), and may create an endowment effect.[71] Admittedly, when it comes to contract default rules, it is not obvious that they should produce those effects. The title to an asset, or the right for one's organs not to be harvested posthumously for donation, exists as long as one does not give it away. In contrast, a buyer does not have the right to goods of merchantable quality, or the right not to pay damages for losses that he could not have reasonably foreseen at the time of contracting, unless he finds a seller who agrees to contract with him without deviating from these default rules. Arguably, the consent to contract around a default rule (or a trade usage) does not deprive a party of an entitlement he already has; hence one should not expect default rules (or trade usages) to create an endowment effect.[72]

However, the question as to whether contractual default rules create an endowment effect is not analytical or logical, but psychological.[73] People do not negotiate in a legal, social, or economic vacuum, but rather against the backdrop of prevailing legal and social norms. In fact, several studies have shown that contract default rules do create an endowment effect. Thus, Stewart Schwab's study featured a simulation of bargaining between a union and an employer.[74] Participants in the experiment negotiated a labor contract along three dimensions: salary, paid vacation, and the transfer of work to a non-union plant. The two first dimensions were negotiated with no default in the background, and the final point was negotiated with a randomly determined default rule: a right for the employer to transfer work, or a right for the union to prevent such a transfer. With regard to each of the three issues, participants received predetermined specifications of the value of various bargaining outcomes for the party they represented, and were instructed to try to achieve the best overall outcome for that party. It was found that, while the default rule had no effect on whether the most efficient agreement was achieved, it did affect the distribution of the contractual surplus: when the default rule favored one party (be it the employer or the union), that party did significantly better than when the default rule favored the other party. This was true whether the default rule was efficient or inefficient—that is, whether or not it allocated the entitlement to the party who valued it more highly.

Other studies have demonstrated that the default rule affects not only the distribution of contract surplus, but also the agreed allocation of the relevant entitlement. Thus, Eric Johnson and his colleagues asked participants to imagine that they had just moved to a new state, and had to choose between two standard insurance policies: one offering a right to sue for any auto-related injury, and a cheaper one that placed restrictions on the right to sue. The policy that was presented as the default was varied between the subjects. While 53 percent of the subjects who were told that the more expensive policy was the default opted for

71. On these interrelated phenomena, see *supra* pp. 48–56. On the default effect, see also *supra* pp. 179–82.

72. Craswell, *supra* note 2, at 387–90; Robert A. Hillman, *The Limits of Behavioral Decision Theory in Legal Analysis: The Case of Liquidated Damages*, 85 CORNELL L. REV. 717, 730 (2000).

73. Zamir, *supra* note 1, at 1760–62; David Millon, *Default Rules, Wealth Distribution, and Corporate Law Reform: Employment at Will versus Job Security*, 146 U. PA. L. REV. 975, 1011 (1998).

74. Stewart Schwab, *A Coasean Experiment on Contract Presumptions*, 17 J. LEGAL STUD. 237 (1988).

that policy, only 23 percent opted for it when they were told that the limited coverage was the default. Moreover, in response to an additional question, subjects in the full-coverage default condition indicated that they were willing to pay an average of 32 percent more for full coverage, while those in the limited-coverage default condition were only willing to pay an average of 8 percent for the broader coverage.[75] A comparison of the policy choices of car owners in New Jersey and Pennsylvania—where the default coverage is different—corroborated these experimental findings.[76] Similar experimental support for the default effect of contractual default rules has been provided by Russell Korobkin. Korobkin asked law students to assume the role of attorneys who are advising a client about three different contract terms, and found that they valued entitlements more highly when they were provided under the default rule.[77] Likewise, Cass Sunstein explored the willingness of law students to buy or sell two weeks of vacation time as part of their negotiations for an employment contract with a law firm.[78] He found that students "endowed" with two additional weeks of vacation by the default rule demanded significantly more money to forgo this right than the non-endowed students were willing to pay in order to gain it.

The power of the default has also been documented in the context of arm's-length transactions in which the parties actively negotiated the terms of the deal. Real-estate contracts in Israel are a case in point.[79] In view of the hyperinflation during the 1970s and early 1980s, the Israeli real-estate market moved to a U.S. dollar-denominated pricing system. At the time, this move was perfectly rational, as it offered a convenient index that preserved the fundamental financial values of the deal. However, by the late 1990s, when hyperinflation had subsided and Israel's deregulation of its foreign currency market had severed the link between local inflation and the price of the U.S. dollar, the inclusion of this term in real-estate contracts became increasingly unwarranted. As a result, indexing real-estate contracts to the U.S. dollar introduced tremendous volatility into these high-stakes contracts. In fact, to cover this risk, both buyer and seller would often purchase costly put and call dollar options upon entering a real-estate contract. Yet, despite the inefficiency associated with dollar indexing, and the fact that parties actively negotiated the price provision in their contracts, it took the market a further decade to settle on a new norm based on the local currency. This occurred only after the United States entered a severe recession in 2008, which brought about a dramatic and unprecedented decline in the value of the U.S. dollar. Only then—when any feeling of entitlement to index the price to the dollar had dissolved—did buyers and sellers feel they could safely opt for the efficient term.

75. Eric J. Johnson et al., *Framing, Probability Distortions, and Insurance Decisions*, 7 J. Risk & Uncertainty 35, 46–48 (1993).

76. *Id.* at 48.

77. Korobkin, *Status Quo Bias, supra* note 70, at 633–47.

78. *See* Cass R. Sunstein, *Switching the Default Rule*, 77 N.Y.U. L. Rev. 106, 113–14 (2002).

79. Doron Teichman, *Old Habits Are Hard to Change: A Case Study of Israeli Real Estate Contracts*, 44 Law & Soc'y Rev. 299 (2010).

The stickiness of contractual default terms entails several normative implications. For one, it highlights the importance of setting the initial default. Since the assumption that parties will simply opt out of the default regime when it does not fit their needs no longer holds, default rules could turn out to be much closer to mandatory rules. This suggests that the law could achieve its goals through default rules, without being circumvented by the parties. As we have seen, a regulator who wishes to encourage people to buy more or less insurance (on grounds of efficiency, distribution, or fairness) can achieve this goal through the design of default rules.[80] This claim, however, has its limits. When enough is at stake, sophisticated parties who control the content of the contract will use this power to bypass the default rule.[81] Such control may countervail and eliminate the distributive effect of default rules described above.[82] This phenomenon is most prevalent in the domain of consumer contracts, and will be further discussed in the following chapter.

Finally, when the source of the sticky default term is non-legal (as was the case with Israeli real-estate contracts), the law may want to consider the need to regulate this contracting norm. This raises difficult questions about the ability of the law to change contracting behavior that fails to adjust to changing circumstances. In the Israeli case, for example, mild regulation aimed at softly shifting the market away from dollar indexing proved unsuccessful.[83]

D. Contract Formation

Most promises and agreements people make are not legally binding—that is to say, their breach may give rise to social or economic sanctions, but not legal ones. One basic task of contract law is thus to draw the line between legally enforceable agreements and promises and non-legal ones. The criteria used to delineate this line vary to some extent between legal systems. Typically, in addition to communication between the parties (often described as *offer and acceptance*), the formation of a contract may require an intention to be legally bound (which may be deduced from the social and economic context in which the communication is made), sufficient specificity of the parties' rights and obligations under the contract, and requirements such as form (e.g., a written document in real-estate transactions), consideration (in common law systems), and causa (in some civil law systems).[84] While nineteenth-century contract law tended to rest on a subjective, meeting-of-minds notion of contract formation, modern legal systems tend to place greater emphasis on the external

80. *See supra* note 75, and accompanying text.

81. *See* Lauren E. Willis, *When Nudges Fail: Slippery Defaults*, 80 U. CHI. L. REV. 1157 (2013).

82. *See supra* note 74 and accompanying text. On the absence of correlation between the one-sidedness of most terms in standard-form contracts, and the contract price, see *infra* p. 302.

83. Teichman, *supra* note 79 at 322–24.

84. *See generally* Arthur T. von Mehren, *The Formation of Contracts, in* 7 INTERNATIONAL ENCYCLOPEDIA OF COMPARATIVE LAW, ch. 9 (Arthur T. von Mehren ed., 2008); Arthur T. von Mehren, *Formal Requirements, in* 7 INTERNATIONAL ENCYCLOPEDIA OF COMPARATIVE LAW, ch. 10 (Arthur T. von Mehren ed., 2008); KONARD ZWEIGERT & HEIN KÖTZ, INTRODUCTION TO COMPARATIVE LAW 356–79, 388–99 (Tony Weir Trans., 3d ed. 1998).

expression of the parties' will (although both subjective and objective elements play a role in all legal systems).[85] Throughout most of the twentieth century, the tendency in contract law and theory, especially in common law systems, was to blur the boundaries between contractual and pre- or non-contractual liability, thus concomitantly blurring the boundaries between contract law and other spheres of private law, especially torts and unjust enrichment.[86] In recent decades, especially in the United States, there has been a certain revival of neo-formalist attitudes to contract law, largely spearheaded by law-and-economics scholars.[87]

Given the relevance of the parties' psychological state of mind to contract-formation law, it is not surprising that legal scholarship often casually alludes to the interaction between contracting practices and people's state of mind. Thus, in his classic article, "Consideration and Form," Lon Fuller argued that formalities such as the use of a seal or writing have a cautionary function, as they induce "the circumspective frame of mind appropriate in one pledging his future."[88] Along these lines, it has been argued that the doctrine of consideration and the exchange it requires may fulfill this function as well.[89]

Recently, scholars have started to examine empirically how people actually perceive the act of contracting. Since the studies were conducted in the United Sates, they naturally paid considerable attention to the requirement of consideration.[90] As conventionally understood, one major role of consideration (serving as a substitute for legal formalities, such as writing), is cautionary. The assumption is that the exchange of things of value will draw people to understand that they are entering the domain of contracts. Some jurisdictions hold that, to fulfill this cautionary role, mere statements by the parties that consideration has changed hands (e.g., "for good and valuable consideration hereby exchanged") are sufficient.[91] To examine this assumption, participants in a web-based experiment were asked to divide a sum of money between two charities.[92] After making their initial allocation, they were randomly assigned to one of several experimental conditions. The first condition included a recital of consideration, along with an actual additional payment that they received to solidify the commitment to the initial allocation between the charities. The second included a recital of consideration ("You also acknowledge that you did this in exchange

85. *See, e.g.*, Melvin Aron Eisenberg, *Expression Rules in Contact Law and Problems of Offer and Acceptance*, 82 Cal. L. Rev. 1127, 1130–35 (1994).

86. *See, e.g.*, Lon L. Fuller & William R. Perdue, *The Reliance Interest in Contract Damages*, 46 Yale L.J. 52, 373 (two parts), at 54 (1936–37); Grant Gilmore, The Death of Contract (1974); Patrick S. Atiyah, Promises, Morals, and Law (1981); Israel Gilead, *Non-consensual Liability of a Contracting Party—Contract, Negligence, Both, or In-Between?*, *in* Classification of Private Law: Bases of Liability and Remedies 35 (Celia Wasserstein Fassberg & Israel Gilead eds., 2003).

87. *See, e.g., Symposium, Formalism Revisited: Formalism in Commercial Law,* 66 U. Chi. L. Rev. 710–857 (1999).

88. Lon L. Fuller, *Consideration and Form*, 41 Colum. L. Rev. 799, 800 (1941).

89. *Id.* at 814–24.

90. On this requirement, see generally Restatement (Second) of Contracts §§ 71–94 (Am. Law Inst. 1981); 1 E. Allan Farnsworth, Farnsworth on Contracts 75–198 (3d ed. 2004).

91. *See* David A. Hoffman & Zev J. Eigen, *Contract Consideration and Behavior*, 85 Geo. Wash. L. Rev. 351 (2017).

92. *Id.* at 368–83.

for good and valid consideration") without actual consideration. The third condition, functioning as a control, included none of the above.[93] After the experimental treatment, all subjects were given an opportunity to back out of their initial allocation of money to the charities, and to apportion all or some of it to themselves.

The key result of the study was that backing-out rates did not differ significantly between the recital-of-consideration and the control group. Neither was there a difference between the control group and the condition in which the recital was accompanied by a nominal consideration of $0.05 (all participants were paid $1.00 for their participation in the experiment). Only a recital accompanied by an actual consideration, ranging from $0.25 to $1.00 (in addition to the participation fee of $1.00) managed to bolster the power of the initial commitment, and statistically significantly reduce the rate of backing out. Although the absence of a difference between the recital (and nominal consideration) and control group may be attributed to the experimental design, the fact that there was a difference between the actual-consideration and control groups suggests that the experiment did capture certain elements of the subjects' choices in a meaningful way.

While it would be far-fetched to draw firm theoretical or policy conclusions for U.S. contract law and theory (let alone for the law of other nations) from a single experimental study, these findings are intriguing. If corroborated by further experimental and observational studies, they may indicate that in modern Western societies, mere recitals do not fulfill a cautionary role. A sense of commitment requires (either legal formalities or) real consideration, and nominal consideration is insufficient.[94] This result possibly echoes the findings of experimental game theory that attest to an entrenched norm of reciprocity.[95] In contract theory, it arguably lends support to theories that emphasize restitution (and reliance, which has not been tested in this study), rather than the parties' will or promises, as the foundation of contractual liability.[96]

Another study dealing with contract formation compared prevailing perceptions regarding the point at which a contract is formed, with existing doctrine.[97] The results suggest that these perceptions rest on heuristics that do not necessarily reflect the legal rules. People tend to identify contract formation with salient moments, such as signing a document or

93. A fourth condition included an explicit contract disclaimer statement that the initial allocation was not binding.

94. Another study tested the effectiveness of the requirement of consideration through variations of the dictator game. It was found that promises given in exchange for counter-promises (which, under the common law, are considered a sufficient consideration) were not kept more than promises given without counter-promises. *See* Christoph Engel & André Schmelzer, *Committing the English and the Continental Way: An Experiment* (working paper, June 2017, *available at*: https://ssrn.com/abstract=3024525).

95. *See supra* pp. 107, 109–10.

96. *See, e.g.*, ATIYAH, *supra* note 86, at 177–215. These results may also echo ancient traditions, such as Jewish law's requirement of an act of acquisition (*Ma'aseh Kinyan*) to finalize a legal bargain. *See, e.g.* Ron S. Kleinman, *Delivery of Keys (Traditio Clavium) as a Mode of Acquisition: Between Jewish and Roman Law*, 16 JEWISH L. ASS'N STUD. 123 (2007).

97. Tess Wilkinson-Ryan & David H. Hoffman, *The Common Sense of Contract Formation*, 67 STAN. L. REV. 1269 (2015).

making a payment. Contrary to prevailing legal rules, most subjects did not view the communication of acceptance as the decisive moment. In line with previous theoretical and observational studies, the findings suggest that people's commitment to a deal is continuous (i.e., contingent upon the degree of assent), rather than dichotomous (contingent only on the existence of a contract).[98] When parties faced a dilemma whether to make use of a liberal return policy in a contract for the purchase of a used car, their decision was influenced by the extent to which they had moved forward into the deal. Whereas 80.8 percent were willing to cancel the contract when they only made a written offer to purchase the car, once that offer was accepted the figure dropped to 60.8 percent, and only 42.8 percent were willing to cancel after they had actually paid for the car.[99]

Arguably, these findings carry normative implications—for example, for situations in which customers gain access to the contract terms only after performing acts that they perceive as creating a legally binding contract. Such arrangements—sometimes labeled PNTL ("pay now, terms later")—are common, for example, in transactions made over the phone, where the customer gets the written terms of the contract along with the goods, and in online purchase of software, when the terms are only accessible when the software is downloaded or installed on one's computer ("clickwrap" or "shrink-wrap" agreements). Sophisticated parties might defer the provision of the contract terms till after the other party clicks "I Agree" or signs a document, knowing that such an act will be viewed as the closing of a deal and will reduce the influence of any following terms—as well as the chance that they would ever be read.[100] The current findings thus weigh against the rulings in *ProCD Inc. v. Zeidenberg*,[101] and *Hill v. Gateway*,[102] according to which the customer's right to withdraw from the transaction once she receives the contract terms is sufficient to make those terms enforceable.[103]

Finally, it is worth noting that the concept of signing on the dotted line may be increasingly foreign to younger people, who are accustomed to online contracting and the digital means of indicating consent. In fact, initial findings suggest that younger people are more likely to view contracts formed online as binding, and less likely to view oral contracts as such.[104] As this strand of literature is still in its infancy, we prefer not to speculate too heavily on this front, and are merely flagging this issue as an important area for future research.

98. *Cf.* Macaulay, *supra* note 66, at 56–60 (empirical evidence indicating that businesspeople are least concerned about the legal enforceability of their transactions and about remedies for breach).

99. Wilkinson-Ryan & Hoffman, *supra* note 97, at 1290–93.

100. On the no-reading problem, see generally *infra* pp. 301–04.

101. 86 F.3d 1447 (7th Cir 1996) (enforcing shrink-wrap terms in a license).

102. 105 F3d 1147 (7th Cir 1997) (enforcing terms that were revealed to the buyer in a transaction conducted over the phone only upon delivery).

103. For a critique of these rulings, see also Roger C. Bern, *"Terms Later" Contracting: Bad Economics, Bad Morals, and a Bad Idea for a Uniform Law, Judge Easterbrook Notwithstanding*, 12 J.L. & Pol'y 641 (2004); Nancy S. Kim, Wrap Contracts: Foundations and Ramifications (2013); Joseph M. Perillo, Calamari and Perillo on Contracts 64–65 (6th ed. 2009).

104. David H. Hoffman, *From Promise to Form: How Contracting Online Changes Consumers*, 91 N.Y.U. L. Rev. 1595 (2016).

E. Interpretation and Supplementation

Given the costs of negotiation, the limits of human imagination, and the inevitable ambiguities of language, contracts never fully and unequivocally address every question that might arise regarding their performance or nonperformance. Consequently, a significant percentage of contract disputes involve interpretative questions.[105] The process of contract interpretation and supplementation is conventionally described as comprising several stages. It starts with the express wording of the contract; moves on to interpreting the contractual terms and filling gaps therein, in light of external sources (such as the course of performance of the contract, previous dealings between the parties, and usages of trade); is then followed by the application of legal default rules; and ends with employing general standards of reasonableness and good faith.[106] The process is hierarchical in the sense that once the adjudicator finds an answer to the question in one of those sources, he or she is supposed to look no further. It is believed to fall in line with both respect for the parties' autonomy and promotion of social welfare, as both liberal and economic theories of contract law maintain that the law should, first and foremost, effectuate the parties' will. A competing account emphasizes the primacy of standards of reasonableness and good faith, legal default rules, and trade usages. It has been argued that an inverted model of this sort better captures the courts' practice, more accurately realizes the parties' actual expectations, and more effectively advances the multiple goals of contract law.[107] A huge body of literature discusses these and related doctrinal and normative issues. The debate involves normative, pragmatic, and institutional issues: what should be the goals of contract interpretation and supplementation; how are those goals best achieved; and how competent are the courts in pursuing these goals.[108] Here we focus on the contribution of behavioral studies to the debate.

At the very general level, there is a correlation between one's assumptions about the cognitive abilities and motivations of contracting parties, and one's position about the appropriate role of the court in determining the content of the contract. Scholars who assume that the contracting parties—or, at least, commercial ones—are rational maximizers of their utility tend to advocate a formalist approach, whereby courts should take a passive stance in determining the content of contracts. This means that the courts should not read implied terms into contracts, attempt to identify and apply trade usages, or introduce standards of

105. Alan Schwartz & Robert E. Scott, *Contract Interpretation Redux*, 119 YALE L.J. 926, 928 n.3 (2010). For a review of different sources of contractual uncertainty, see 2 E. ALLAN FARNSWORTH, FARNSWORTH ON CONTRACTS 269–74 (3d ed. 2004).

106. Zamir, *supra* note 1, at 1715–19.

107. Zamir, *supra* note 1.

108. *See, e.g.*, Lisa Bernstein, *Merchant Law in a Merchant Court: Rethinking the Code's Search for Immanent Business Norms*, 144 U. PA. L. REV. 1765 (1996); Zamir, *supra* note 1; Eric A. Posner, *Parol Evidence Rule, the Plain Meaning Rule, and the Principles of Contractual Interpretation*, 146 U. PA. L. REV. 533 (1998); Schwartz & Scott, *supra* note 6; Schwartz & Scott, *supra* note 105; Kent Greenawalt, *A Pluralist Approach to Interpretation: Wills and Contracts*, 42 SAN DIEGO L. REV. 533 (2005).

reasonableness and good faith into the contractual relations.[109] In contrast, commentators who realize that contracting parties do not necessarily behave as rational maximizers—both because of their bounded cognitive abilities and because they have other motives besides their self-interest—tend to legitimize a greater role for the court, in which it more explicitly applies values of fairness and reasonableness in contract interpretation and supplementation.[110] If deviations from default rules and trade usages do not reflect the parties' idiosyncratic preferences (but rather cognitive biases such as overly optimistic risk assessments and inattention to non-salient aspects of the transaction), then the inverted model of contract interpretation and supplementation may arguably serve as a moderate means of mitigating the ramifications of these biases.

Another behavioral contribution pertains to the thought processes of the arbiter in charge of determining the content of the contract. Scholars have long observed that courts routinely interpret contracts with a view to achieving (what they view as) just, fair, and reasonable results.[111] Very often, judges explain that their interpretation of the contract is at once consistent with the plain meaning of the contract text; fulfilling the parties' actual intentions (indeed, sometimes stating that *no other meaning* could sensibly be attributed to the parties); consistent with the established norms in the relevant trade; and mandated by considerations of efficiency, fairness, and equivalence of exchange. Even when judges differ over the correct interpretation of a contract, they each usually authoritatively state that their interpretation is the only one that coherently comports with the contract wording, surrounding circumstances, parties' reasonable expectations, general usage, and norms of fair dealing and good faith. The cognitive processes behind the creation of such internally coherent pictures have been extensively studied in the judicial context under the headings of the *story model* and *coherence-based reasoning* (discussed later in the book),[112] and are closely linked to the general phenomena of motivated reasoning and the confirmation bias (discussed earlier).[113]

Those processes shed light on what appears to be a disparity between formalistic judicial rhetoric and activist practice. Even when judges rely, for example, on the *plain meaning rule* (where the language of a contract is plain and unambiguous, either there is no room for judicial interpretation whatsoever, or the contract's meaning should be determined without reference to extrinsic facts), they often aim at the fairest and most reasonable interpretation of the contract.[114] The same is true of the common adage that the court will not make a new contract for the parties, which often appears to disguise an activist judicial

109. *See, e.g.*, Bernstein, *supra* note 108; Schwartz & Scott, *supra* note 6; Schwartz & Scott, *supra* note 105.

110. *See, e.g.*, Zamir, *supra* note 1, at 1793–800.

111. *See, e.g.*, LAWRENCE M. FRIEDMAN, CONTRACT LAW IN AMERICA: A SOCIAL AND ECONOMIC CASE STUDY 105–07 (1965); P.S. Atiyah, *Contract and Fair Exchange*, *in* ESSAYS ON CONTRACT 329, 337–41 (1990).

112. *See infra* pp. 528–32.

113. *See supra* pp. 58–61.

114. *See* Zamir, *supra* note 1, at 1728–31.

interpretation.[115] In those cases—contrary to appearances—judges may sincerely believe that they are interpreting the contract according to its plain meaning rather than drawing up a new contract for the parties.

Finally, behavioral studies also shed light on more specific rules of contract interpretation, such as the long-standing rule of interpretation *contra proferentem* (against the drafter). According to this rule, ambiguous terms are interpreted against the interest of the party who drafted them. Although this rule governs all types of contracts, it is mostly applied in the context of standard-form contracts.[116] It is justified, inter alia, on grounds of fault (the drafting party is to blame for the ambiguity), efficiency (incentivizing the drafter to use clearer terms), and distributive justice (leveling the playing ground).[117] In addition, the behavioral findings regarding the performance of obligations included in standard-form contracts[118] suggest that the *contra proferentem* doctrine is aligned with people's moral intuitions and with their actions. People view contractual obligations that are dictated by the other party as possessing weaker moral value—and are consequently more inclined to interpret them in a self-serving manner. Such congruity between people's moral intuitions and legal doctrine may indicate that judges share these intuitions and therefore incorporate them into their decisions (leaving the question of the desirability of the doctrine unanswered). This congruity may also arise from judges' deliberate effort to align the legal doctrine with people's expectations (suggesting that the doctrine is at least potentially efficient for this reason as well).[119]

F. Performance

Once a contract is entered into, the parties face various decisions regarding the performance of their obligations and the exercise of their rights. This section focuses on cases where the contract does not unequivocally delineate the scope and content of the parties' rights and obligations.

While some contractual clauses leave little or no discretion to the parties, others allow for varying degrees of flexibility. This is clearly the case when contracts deliberately use phrases such as "material change of circumstances," "best effort," or "within a reasonable time." Considerable leeway may also result from inadvertent ambiguities. For example, a famous U.S. case discussed the question of whether a chicken that is only suitable for stewing and not for broiling or frying constitutes a "chicken" under a particular sales contract.[120] In all those cases, a party needs to decide in real time whether and how to perform

115. *See, e.g.*, Clarence D. Ashley, *Should There Be Freedom of Contract*, 4 COLUM. L. REV. 423, 424 (1904).

116. *See* FARNSWORTH, *supra* note 105, at 302–03.

117. *See* Zamir, *supra* note 1, at 1724–25.

118. *See supra* pp. 243–45.

119. On aligning the law with people's moral intuitions, see *supra* pp. 161–62.

120. *Frigaliment Importing Co. v. B.N.S. Int'l Sales Corp.*, 190 F. Supp. 116 (S.D.N.Y. 1960).

her contractual obligations or exercise her rights, and courts may have to decide in retrospect whether the parties' behavior accorded with their rights and obligations. Note that while the behavior of a contracting party ordinarily influences the interests of both parties, some aspects of a person's behavior may be unobservable, and even if the other party can observe them, they may still be unverifiable if litigation ensues. Moreover, even when a contracting party's behavior is observable and verifiable, very often there is no real threat of legal sanctions, due to the disproportionate costs of legal measures. Non-legal sanctions may still be relevant in those cases, however.

A common theme in studies of contract performance is the role of the contract as a reference point. Drawing on previous behavioral studies of altruism, reciprocity, and retaliation, Oliver Hart and John Moore constructed a model of parties' behavior with regard to contract performance.[121] Their model distinguishes between "performance within the letter of the contract and performance within the spirit of the contract," and assumes that only the former can be judicially enforced. It also states that when a party's contractual expectations are fulfilled, he is happy to reciprocate with cooperative behavior along both dimensions of performance. However, when a party's expectations are frustrated, he *shades*—that is, complies with the letter of the contract, but not with its spirit—which reduces the contract surplus. One implication of this model is that there is a trade-off in choosing between rigid and flexible contract clauses. Rigid contracts precisely define expectations, thereby limiting the incidence of shading—but at a cost of limiting the parties' ability to reap the full potential benefits of their relationships when unforeseen contingencies occur. Flexible contracts enable the parties to adjust their conduct to changing circumstances, but at the cost of inducing shading when people's expectations are frustrated.

These predictions were subsequently corroborated empirically in an experiment that allowed buyers to exercise bargaining power over sellers in a way that enabled them to extract the contractual surplus.[122] It turned out that when this power was used *before* the contract was formed, sellers were willing to accept the low profits that the contract entailed and did not retaliate against buyers. However, when this power was used *after* the contract has been made, as part of an adjustment mechanism included in the contract, sellers were less receptive of this outcome and exhibited a tendency to punish buyers who used their bargaining power. In other words, once a contract is formed and expectations are set, the parties judge outcomes in light of those expectations. These findings point to a significant difference between parties' expectations and decision-making before and after formation of the contract.

Another study of post-contracting behavior examined the degree of effort put in by workers at a pear-packing factory.[123] The researchers exploited the fact that workers in the

121. *See* Oliver Hart & John Moore, *Contracts as Reference Points*, 123 Q.J. Econ 1, 5–13 (2008).

122. Ernst Fehr, Oliver Hart & Christian Zehnder, *Contracts as Reference Points—Experimental Evidence*, 101 Am. Econ. Rev. 493 (2011).

123. *See* Tom Chang & Tal Gross, *How Many Pears Would a Pear Packer Pack if a Pear Packer Could Pack Pears at Quasi-exogenously Varying Piece Rates?*, 99 J. Econ. Behav. & Org. 1 (2013).

factory were routinely (i.e., every fifteen minutes) rotated between working stations, in which their effective wage varied substantially. Specifically, at some stations workers were required to pack small pears, while at others they were required to pack large ones. Since the size of the boxes in question was constant, filling a box with large pears required much less effort. Workers' compensation, however, was equal at the different stations—that is, they were paid a flat per-box rate.

According to the rational choice model, workers should exert more effort when packing large pears, to maximize their payoffs—since the per-pear wage then is highest. However, the study documented the opposite: when working at the low-payoff stations workers actually increased their pace. The researchers interpreted this finding to mean that workers set certain hourly targets and then adjust their effort to avoid outputs that are below the target and might be viewed as a loss. These findings and their interpretation accord with previous studies of non-contractual behavior.[124]

Empirical findings suggest that decisions made by disinterested third parties also echo the role of reference points. When subjects were asked to judge what is meant by a "reasonable effort," the framing of the payoff environment influenced their judgment.[125] The experiment centered on a series of twenty vowel-counting tasks, which varied in difficulty in terms of the number of words in the sentence, but all offering the same payoff. Effort was measured by the minimal number of hard tasks that subjects expected others to do in order to adhere to the "reasonable effort" requirement and to avoid a sanction. The results show that when payoffs were framed as losses (money deducted for errors) rather than as gains (monetary rewards for correct answers), the minimal threshold went down. More specifically, while subjects in the gain frame set the minimum threshold for reasonable effort at 8.4 (out of 20) hard tasks, in the loss frame they set this threshold at only 5.75.

These results highlight two points about ambiguous contract terms. First, prevailing views reflect a somewhat moderate perspective—one that rejects purely selfish behavior, while not expecting complete altruism. Participants did not view the rational option of opting to do no hard tasks whatsoever as legitimate, but neither did they expect subjects to ignore their self-interest entirely and complete ten hard tasks to oblige the other party. Rather, the line was drawn somewhere between these two extremes. Second, and perhaps more interestingly, where this line is drawn is systematically governed by the decision-making environment, and independently from the interpreted text. Specifically, subjects adopted a more demanding interpretation of the "reasonable effort" requirement when the additional effort entailed less profit than when it involved greater losses.

124. *See, e.g.*, Colin Camerer et al., *Labor Supply of New York Cabdrivers: One Day at a Time*, 112 Q.J. ECON 407 (1997). For another study of the role of expectations as a reference point that affects levels of effort, see Johannes Abeler et al., *Reference Points and Effort Provision*, 101 AM. ECON. REV. 470 (2011). For the implications of the insight that expectations may serve as a reference point for the design of remedies for breach of contract, see *infra* pp. 265–66.

125. *See* Yuval Feldman, Amos Schurr & Doron Teichman, *Reference Points and Contractual Choices: An Experimental Examination*, 10 J. EMPIRICAL LEGAL STUD. 512, 530–32 (2013).

The findings described earlier about people's perceptions of contracts as involving a moral duty to fulfill promises, as well as people's trust and trustworthiness,[126] bear upon contract performance. Tess Wilkinson-Ryan and David Hoffman have argued that the norms of promise-keeping and trust can lead to the adversarial attitudes of caution and suspicion that characterize negotiations to be substituted by a cooperative attitude at the performance stage.[127] A party who no longer views her obligations through the prism of cost-benefit analysis might assume that the other party shares this perspective. Motivational factors might further bolster people's tendency to adopt a cooperative attitude toward their contract partners once formation is complete. Cognitive dissonance, coupled with the confirmation bias, may drive people to rationalize their choice of contracting partner.[128] People may exhibit great vigilance at the pre-contractual stage and search for the best possible option—but once in the contract, they view their decision as a "done deal." They may selectively recall evidence that suggests that the contract is beneficial, and avoid looking for evidence to the contrary. The result is contractual inertia—parties who do not monitor each other or evaluate the quality of performance.

The link between formation and trust suggests that once parties enter a contract, they will tend to lower their guard, and apply fewer precautions toward their counterparts. For example, it was found that parties to a sales contract were substantially less likely to purchase a supplemental warranty immediately after the transaction is completed, than those who are offered the same warranty before completion.[129] Similarly, parties were less likely to search for alternative contracting parties once they were in a contractual relationship that included a cancelation option than when they were not yet bound by contract.[130] Apparently, when the performance stage kicks in, the ethics of promise-keeping starts to influence people's decisions.

These findings may bear upon the question of whether, and to what extent, the law should impose a duty of good faith in contract performance. Such a duty is widely recognized in civil law systems.[131] Even under U.S. contract law, in which the good faith doctrine is relatively underdeveloped, it is commonly accepted that "[e]very contract imposes upon each party a duty of good faith and fair dealing in its performance and its enforcement."[132] It is famously difficult to pin down the precise scope and meaning of the good faith requirement. Often, descriptions of the concept of good faith use terms that are as vague as the concept

126. *See supra* pp. 239–45.

127. Hoffman & Wilkinson-Ryan, *Precautions*, *supra* note 54, at 423–24.

128. *Id.* at 425–26. On the confirmation bias, see generally *supra* pp. 58–61.

129. *Id.* at 412–15.

130. *Id.* at 416–18.

131. *See, e.g.*, Martijn W. Hesselink, *The Concept of Good Faith*, *in* TOWARDS A EUROPEAN CIVIL CODE 619 (Arthur S. Hartkamp et al. eds., 4th ed. 2010).

132. RESTATEMENT (SECOND) OF CONTRACTS § 205 (1981). *See also* U.C.C. § 1-304 (AM. LAW INST. & UNIF. LAW COMM'N, 2001).

being described. For example, it is often stated that the requirement of good faith implies a duty to comply with "community standards of decency, fairness or reasonableness."[133]

Beyond the doctrinal details, the behavioral findings appear to support the imposition of a legal duty to perform contracts in good faith. This duty can be viewed, at least in part, as a regulator of the norms of commitment and trust that govern contractual conduct. While behavioral research suggests that these norms have been internalized by many, there will always be individuals who deviate from them, and try to abuse the trust generated by the norm to further their own payoffs at the expense of others. The doctrine of good faith prevents such behavior, and prohibits attempts to exercise contractual rights in an antisocial manner.[134]

As is often the case when moving from a positive to a normative analysis, some commentators do not share this conclusion. Instead, they posit that the existence of social and moral norms of trust and cooperation actually militates against the imposition of a legal duty of good faith. They advocate a division of labor between contract law on the one hand, and non-legal (economic, social, and moral) norm systems on the other. They argue that contract law should be formalistic, leaving the advancement of trust and cooperation to other social systems.[135]

G. Legal Remedies for Breach of Contract

1. Analytical and Doctrinal Background

For many decades, the analysis of contract remedies has been dominated by Lon Fuller and William Perdue's classification of the "interests" protected by remedies for breach of contract: expectation, reliance, and restitution.[136] As ordinarily conceived, the *expectation interest* focuses on the injured party, and is forward-looking in the sense that it aims at putting her in the same position that she would have been in had the contract been fully performed. The *reliance interest* also focuses on the injured party, but is backward-looking, in the sense that it strives to put her in the position that she would have been in had she not entered the contract in the first place. It does so by reimbursing her for the loss caused by her reliance on the contract. The *restitution interest*, on the other hand, focuses on the breaching party. It is backward-looking in that it aims to put the breaching party in a position similar to the one he would have been in had no contract been made. Forcing the breaching party to return the benefits he obtained from the injured party achieves this goal.

133. *See* RESTATEMENT (SECOND) OF CONTRACTS § 205 cmt. a (AM. LAW INST. 1981). For reviews see Robert S. Summers, *The General Duty of Good Faith—Its Recognition and Conceptualization*, 67 CORNELL L. REV. 810 (1982); Simon Whittaker & Reinhard Zimmermann, *Good Faith in European Contract Law: Surveying the Legal Landscape*, *in* GOOD FAITH IN EUROPEAN CONTRACT LAW (Reinhard Zimmermann & Simon Whittaker eds., 2000).

134. Wilkinson-Ryan & Hoffman, *Precautions*, *supra* note 54, at 429–33.

135. *See, e.g.*, Kidwell, *A Caveat*, 1985 WIS. L. REV. 615; Bernstein, *supra* note 108; Robert E. Scott, *The Death of Contract Law*, 54 U. TORONTO L.J. 369 (2004).

136. Fuller & Perdue, *supra* note 86. *See also* RESTATEMENT (SECOND) OF CONTRACTS § 344 (AM. LAW INST. 1981); 24 SAMUEL WILLISTON, A TREATISE ON THE LAW OF CONTRACTS 20–44 (Richard A. Lord ed., Thomas West 4th ed. 2002).

This classification is analytically incomplete, since it disregards the possibility of remedies that are designed to put the breaching party in the position he would have been in had he performed the contract. This goal can typically be achieved by disgorging the breaching party of any benefit he gained by breaching the contract, even if that benefit was not derived from anything he received from the injured party. It is therefore conventionally known as the *disgorgement interest.*

The prevailing convention in contract law and theory is that the law primarily protects the injured party's expectation interest.[137] This is sometimes done by awarding specific performance, but more often through damages.[138] The reliance measure of damages is sometimes used instrumentally as a minimal approximation of the injured party's expectation interest when the latter is unverifiable. Under some circumstances, the injured party may opt for remedies that protect her restitution interest.[139] In contrast, disgorgement remedies are not ordinarily available for breach of contract.[140]

At the normative level, there is an ongoing debate as to which interests are most worthy of legal protection. The central controversy is between those who argue that contract remedies should primarily, or even exclusively, protect the promisee's expectation interest,[141] and those who assert that the law should (and does) content itself with protecting reliance and restitution.[142] Interestingly, none of the major theories of contract law—such as the will theory, economic efficiency, and corrective justice—unequivocally supports any of the above four types of interest. Instead, conflicting arguments for and against protecting any one of them are made *within* almost any theoretical framework.[143]

This section examines the contribution of behavioral insights to these controversies. It first discusses the structuring of the doctrine and the normative debate around the interests described above, and then focuses on two ongoing debates: the choice between expectation damages and specific performance as the default remedy for breach, and the appropriate scope of disgorgement remedies. The legal treatment of agreed remedies—liquidated damages, in particular—will be discussed in a separate section.

137. 3 E. ALLAN FARNSWORTH, FARNSWORTH ON CONTRACTS, 149–50, 190 (3d ed. 2004); WILLISTON, *supra* note 136, at 20–30; G.H. TREITEL, REMEDIES FOR BREACH OF CONTRACT: A COMPARATIVE ACCOUNT 82–83 (1988); SOLÈNE ROWAN, REMEDIES FOR BREACH OF CONTRACT 17, 109 (2012).

138. *See infra* pp. 266–69.

139. FARNSWORTH, *supra* note 137, at 323–38; 3 DAN B. DOBBS, DOBBS LAW OF REMEDIES 159–70, 178–89 (1993); Eyal Zamir, *The Missing Interest: Restoration of the Contractual Equivalence,* 93 VA. L. REV. 59, 79–85 (2007).

140. *See infra* p. 270.

141. *See, e.g.,* FRIED, *supra* note 3, at 17–27 (2015) (grounding this claim on a theory of contract-as-promise); Steven Shavell, *Damages Measures for Breach of Contract,* 11 BELL J. ECON. 466 (1980) (favoring expectation damages from an efficiency perspective).

142. *See, e.g.,* Fuller & Perdue, *supra* note 86, at 53–66; ATIYAH, *supra* note 86.

143. Richard Craswell, *Against Fuller and Perdue,* 67 U. CHI. L. REV. 99, 106–36 (2000). *See also* EYAL ZAMIR & BARAK MEDINA, LAW, ECONOMICS, AND MORALITY 294–301, 305–10 (2010).

2. The Four Interests as Reference Points

In a thought-provoking article,[144] Richard Craswell has powerfully argued that Fuller and Perdue's tripartite classification (and, by extension, the quadripartite classification described above), should be abandoned. Whether one's perspective on contract remedies is instrumental (such as the economic approach), or non-instrumental (such as the liberal theory of contract as promise), "there is no reason to think that the remedy that best serves the chosen substantive goal will necessarily coincide with one of Fuller and Perdue's three 'interests.'"[145] In fact, Craswell argues, both instrumental and non-instrumental theories may endorse a measure of damages that can lie anywhere on the real number axis.[146] He goes on to maintain that the common classification is not even helpful as a descriptive framework. In some instances, courts award remedies that do not fit neatly into any of the recognized interests,[147] and judgments that purportedly aim to protect the same interest often award the injured party such markedly dissimilar remedies, that grouping them under the same category is almost meaningless.[148]

While Craswell's analysis has been contested,[149] his arguments are well taken. Nonetheless, courts, scholars, and legal educators continue to refer to the three (or four) interests as useful organizing principles of contract remedies. As Craswell concedes, legal reasoning cannot function without some points of reference. Neither drawing up a very long list of all conceivable remedies with no organizing principle, nor authorizing the courts to choose the most appropriate measure of damages in each and every case based on all pertinent policy considerations, is a viable option for the law.[150] Meaningful reference points are essential to people's perceptions and decisions,[151] and legal decisions are no exception. Craswell may be right in arguing that, from an efficiency standpoint or some other normative perspective, the optimal measure of damages, all things considered, may be, say, "63% of expectation interest."[152] However, from a psychological standpoint, at least, he is wrong in arguing that aiming at 100 percent of the expectation (or any other) measure "is no less arbitrary" than aiming at the 63 percent of expectation measure of damages. Unlike

144. Craswell, *supra* note 143.

145. *Id.* at 107.

146. *Id.* at 110, 114, 116.

147. *Id.* at 136–54. *See also* Zamir, *supra* note 139 (identifying restoration of the contractual equivalence as a fifth goal of contract remedies).

148. Craswell, *supra* note 143, at 136–54.

149. For counterarguments, see, e.g., DORI KIMEL, FROM PROMISE TO CONTRACT: TOWARDS A LIBERAL THEORY OF CONTRACT 89–100 (2003); Daniel Markovits, *Contract and Collaboration*, 113 YALE L.J. 1417, 1491–514 (2004).

150. Craswell, *supra* note 143, at 155.

151. *See generally supra* pp. 42–57, 76–86.

152. Craswell, *supra* note 143, at 111, 117.

63 percent of whatever interest, 100 percent is a natural focal point.[153] Thus, it is much more likely to serve as a reference point.

In Chapter 5, we argued that while the law sometimes protects people's expectations to obtain a gain, much more often, and more powerfully, it protects people from incurring losses.[154] What is, or what should be, the pertinent reference point when designing contract remedies? Fuller and Perdue assumed that the benchmark is the parties' position prior to entering into the contract—and hence that the justification for protecting the reliance and restitution interest has a "self-evident quality."[155] Corrective justice requires protecting those interests, while protecting the expectation interest goes beyond corrective justice. An award of expectation damages gives the injured party something she never had. It is a form of distributive justice, and as such considerably less justified.[156]

However, from both a psychological and normative standpoint, Fuller and Perdue's assumption is far from self-evident. Amos Tversky and Daniel Kahneman postulated that "the reference state usually corresponds to the decision-maker's current position," but "it can be influenced by aspirations, expectations, norms, and social comparisons."[157] More recently, Botond Köszegi and Matthew Rabin introduced a formal model of reference points that are derived from people's expectations.[158] According to this model, the reference point is determined by people's rational expectations, based on the recent past. This allows them to explain the behavior of parties when their expectations differ from the status quo. In the context of contracting, this means that the formation of a contract can alter the parties' reference point, causing them to view their expected profits as the benchmark against which outcomes are evaluated.[159] For example, when a seller delivers defective goods, or does not deliver the goods on time, the reference point may well be the buyer's position had she received conforming goods, and in a timely fashion. Fuller and Perdue actually recognized this point when they asserted that there is a " 'psychological' " explanation for why the law protects expectation interest: "Whether or not he has actually changed his position because of the promise, the promisee has formed an attitude of expectancy such that a breach of the

153. The notion of focal points was introduced in Thomas C. Schelling, The Strategy of Conflict (1960). While Schelling's primary concern was coordination without communication, he also discussed the role of focal points in explicit bargaining (*id.* at 67–74). For a brief summary of game theory studies of focal points, see Maarten C.W. Janssen, *Focal Points, in* 2 The New Palgrave Dictionary of Economics and the Law 150 (Peter Newman ed., 1998).

154. *See supra* pp. 189–92.

155. Fuller & Perdue, *supra* note 86, at 56–57.

156. The same assumption characterizes Cohen and Knetsch's more recent analysis: David Cohen & Jack L. Knetsch, *Judicial Choice and Disparities between Measures of Economic Values,* 30 Osgoode Hall L.J. 737, 755–56 (1992).

157. Amos Tversky & Daniel Kahneman, *Loss Aversion in Riskless Choice: A Reference-Dependent Model,* 106 Q.J. Econ. 1039, 1046–47 (1991).

158. Botond Köszegi & Matthew Rabin, *A Model of Reference-Dependent Preferences,* 121 Q.J. Econ. 1133 (2006). *See also* Botond Köszegi & Matthew Rabin, *Reference-Dependent Risk Attitude,* 97 Am. Econ. Rev. 1047 (2007); Johannes Abeler et al., *Reference Points and Effort Provision,* 101 Am. Econ. Rev. 470 (2011).

159. *See, e.g.,* Craswell, *supra* note 143, at 125–27; Zamir, *supra* note 139, at 108–10.

promise causes him to feel that he has been 'deprived' of something that was 'his.'" They further characterized "this sentiment" as "a relatively uniform one."[160]

It follows that, just as Fuller and Perdue relied on corrective justice to justify the reliance measure of damages, corrective justice can justify the protection of the expectation interest.[161] To be sure, neither the (basically structural) concept of corrective justice, nor the prevailing perceptions of the reference point, resolve the normative question of which interests the law of contract should protect. The lessons to be learned from behavioral studies are therefore modest, yet important. They include the recognition that (1) meaningful reference points are essential for a workable system of remedies for breach of contract, and that (2) both the parties' positions prior to contracting, and their positions had the contract been fully performed, are conceivable reference points. A related point is that the legal remedies not only reflect the prevailing perceptions of the reference point, but—as shown below—may shape those perceptions, as well.[162]

3. Expectation Damages versus Specific Performance

In addition to the general observations presented above, behavioral insights shed light on more specific controversies in remedy rules, such as the choice between expectation damages and specific performance. Under the common law, damages are the ordinary remedy for breach of contract, and specific performance is the exception. Conversely, in civil law systems, such as German law, enforced performance is the standard remedy for breach, and only in exceptional cases is the injured party limited to monetary compensation. In reality, terminological differences across legal systems, the existence of important exceptions to the rules (with considerable correspondence between the incidence of the rule in one system and the incidence of exceptions in the other), the interplay between substantive and procedural rules, and disparities between legal rhetoric and judicial practice—all result in much smaller differences between the legal systems than is often assumed to exist.[163] Concomitantly, there is an ongoing, spirited debate regarding the desirable remedy.[164]

160. Fuller & Perdue, *supra* note 86, at 57.

161. *See, e.g.*, Peter Benson, *The Unity of Contract Law*, *in* THE THEORY OF CONTRACT LAW: NEW ESSAYS 118, 127–38 (Peter Benson ed., 2001); Daniel Friedmann, *The Efficient Breach Fallacy*, 18 J. LEGAL STUD. 1, 13–18 (1989); Ernst J. Weinrib, *Punishment and Disgorgement as Contract Remedies*, 78 CHI.-KENT L. REV. 55, 62–70 (2003).

162. *See infra* p. 169.

163. *See, e.g.*, Louis J. Romero, *Specific Performance of Contracts in Comparative Law: Some Preliminary Observations*, 27 LES CAHIERS DE DROIT 785 (1986); Henrik Lando & Caspar Rose, *On the Enforcement of Specific Performance in Civil Law Countries*, 24 INT'L REV. L. & ECON. 473 (2004). *But see* ROWAN, *supra* note 137, at 18–69 (arguing that the differences between French and English law in this regard are significant in both theory and practice). Section 1221 of the French Civil Code was amended in 2016. The injured party's right to specific performance was curtailed, and it is no longer available when "there is a manifest disproportion between its cost to the debtor and its interest for the creditor"—thus further narrowing the gap between civil law and common law systems. *See* Yves-Marie Laithier, *Exécution Forcée en Nature*, *in* THE CODE NAPOLÉON REWRITTEN: FRENCH CONTRACT LAW AFTER THE 2016 REFORMS 257 (John Cartwright & Simon Whittaker eds., 2017).

164. For an excellent review of the extensive literature, see Gregory Klass, *Efficient Breach*, *in* PHILOSOPHICAL FOUNDATIONS OF CONTRACT LAW 362 (Gregory Klass, George Letsas & Prince Saprai eds., 2014).

The basic theory of *efficient breach*—the most celebrated (and contested) economic theory of contract remedies—points to the advantages of expectation damages over specific performance. From an economic perspective, the role of remedies is to create optimal incentives for performance and breach, which would maximize the contractual surplus.[165] According to the efficient breach hypothesis, when the promisor's benefit from breach is greater than the loss to the promisee, performance becomes inefficient—meaning that the promisor *ought* to breach. If a buyer purchases a custom-made fountain for his or her backyard with the expectation of deriving a benefit of $1,000 from it, and the cost of producing the fountain rises to $2,000 due to a shortage in Italian marble, then the production of the fountain becomes undesirable. The same is true if a third person offers the promisor $2,000 for the same fountain, and for some reason the promisor cannot produce two fountains. In such cases, breaching the contract enhances the contractual surplus, as the buyer can be fully compensated for his or her losses by payment of expectation damages, while the seller can avoid the high costs (including opportunity costs) associated with the contract's performance. Moreover, since in the contractual setting ex-post behavior is priced ex ante, the benefits associated with granting the promisor an option to breach are incorporated into the contract price—thus benefitting both parties. Conversely, if the default remedy were specific performance, the seller would be compelled to produce a good of negative social value. This waste, in turn, would diminish the welfare of both parties.

From this perspective, contractual relationships represent an option either to perform or to pay expectation damages.[166] However, this conclusion is subject to a host of critiques, from economic and non-economic perspectives alike. From an economic perspective, the simple version of the efficient breach theory is flawed, because it unrealistically assumes that expectation damages put the injured party in the same position he or she would have occupied had the contract been fully performed. In reality, unverifiable losses, losses that exceed the foreseeability requirement, the requirement of mitigation of damages, and litigation costs very often render expectation damages infra-compensatory[167]—thus creating insufficient incentive for efficient performance. Furthermore, the availability of specific performance need not prevent efficient nonperformance. In the paradigmatic case of a seller who can sell the object to a third party who values it more than the promisee, even if the third party is unlikely to approach the buyer, the seller may still negotiate a discharge of the original contract with the buyer, thus facilitating its efficient nonperformance. Granted, such negotiation may be costly due to the bilateral monopoly situation[168]—but the cost of resolving a dispute resulting from a breach of contract, and of judicially determining the

165. *See* Kaplow & Shavell, *supra* note 2 at 189; Richard A. Posner, Economic Analysis of Law 130 (9th ed. 2014).

166. *See* Richard A. Posner, *Let Us Never Blame a Contract Breaker*, 107 Mich. L. Rev. 1349, 1349–61 (2009).

167. *See, e.g.*, Treitel, *supra* note 137, at 143–207 (1988); William S. Dodge, *The Case for Punitive Damages in Contracts*, 48 Duke L.J. 629, 664–65 (1999); Melvin A. Eisenberg, *Actual and Virtual Specific Performance, the Theory of Efficient Breach, and the Indifference Principle in Contract Law*, 93 Cal. L. Rev. 975, 989–97 (2005).

168. *Id.* at 744–45.

damages for the breach, is likely to be higher.[169] Additional factors—such as the parties' attitude to risk,[170] the difficulty in ascertaining and quantifying the injured party's expectation interest when the contract pertains to unique objects (such as real property), and the impact of the legal remedy on the extent of the promisee's reliance on the contract[171]—all call for a much more nuanced economic analysis of remedies for breach of contract.[172] In fact, nowadays virtually no one defends the simple theory of efficient breach.[173]

Notwithstanding all these disagreements, one point on which there is a consensus among legal economists is that there is nothing inherently immoral in efficiently breaching a contract. Rather, economists tend to view contracts as an option to perform or pay damages, and a breach as an exercise of this option.[174] However, this notion seems to be at odds with basic intuitions regarding contracts. Somehow, the scene of two parties shaking hands to strike a sales deal, followed by the seller stating "I'm off to look for a higher paying buyer, but have no worry—if I find one, your expectation-damages check is in the mail" sounds absurd to most of us. It surely sounds troubling to theoreticians who base contract law on the deontological moral duty to keep one's promise.[175]

The mismatch between the efficient breach hypothesis and most people's perception of contracts is not founded on a hypothetical thought experiment. Field studies of the actual behavior of contracting parties have repeatedly shown that breach-and-compensate is not considered an acceptable behavior. In his seminal study of contractual behavior in the manufacturing industry, Stewart Macaulay documented a widely accepted norm that "commitments are to be honored in almost all situations."[176] Similarly, Lisa Bernstein quoted one transactor in the cotton industry, who bluntly stated: "You do not just breach and pay. This is not done."[177]

Experimental studies have confirmed these observations in a more refined setting. Daphna Lewinsohn-Zamir has shown that when faced with a choice between specific performance and fully compensatory expectation damages, the vast majority of subjects opted

169. Alan Schwartz, *The Case for Specific Performance*, 89 YALE L.J. 271, 284–91 (1979); Friedmann, *supra* note 161, at 6–7.

170. A. Mitchell Polinsky, *Risk Sharing through Breach of Contract Remedies*, 12 J. LEGAL STUD. 427 (1983) (attitudes toward risk).

171. Robert Cooter, *Unity in Tort, Contract and Property: The Model of Precaution*, 73 CAL. L. REV. 1, 11–19 (1985).

172. *See, e.g.*, Richard Craswell, *Instrumental Theories of Compensation: A Survey*, 40 SAN DIEGO L. REV. 1135 (2003).

173. *See* Posner, *supra* note 4, at 834–39, 880; Klass, *supra* note 164, at 362.

174. *See, e.g.*, Steven Shavell, *Is Breach of Contract Immoral?*, 56 EMORY L.J. 439 (2006); POSNER, *supra* note 165, at 152–53; Daniel Markovits & Alan Schwartz, *The Expectation Remedy and the Promissory Basis of Contract*, 45 SUFFOLK U. L. REV. 799, 808–12 (2012).

175. *See, e.g.*, Seana Valentine Shiffrin, *Must I Mean What You Think I* Should *Have Said?*, 98 VA. L. REV. 159 (2012). *See also* Gregory Klass, *To Perform or Pay Damages*, 98 VA. L. REV. 143 (2012).

176. Macaulay, *supra* note 66, at 63.

177. Lisa Bernstein, *Private Commercial Law in the Cotton Industry: Creating Cooperation through Rules, Norms, and Institutions*, 99 MICH. L. REV. 1724, 1755 (2001).

for specific performance.[178] While this finding on its own might be unsurprising—since specific performance offers the promisee an opportunity to extract value from the promisor ex post—subjects also exhibited a reluctance to choose the damages option in return for a price discount. A large group of subjects flatly refused to agree to a contract term that reflected the breach-and-compensate norm, and many of those who did agree required extraordinarily large discounts that amount to a de facto refusal. Similar results were obtained when the sample population consisted of experienced business people.[179]

The normative conclusions arising from this line of studies are that, inasmuch as the law strives to reflect people's actual preferences with regard to remedies, the domain of specific performance in contract law should be expanded.[180] In this respect, Anglo-American law might take a page from civil law systems that award specific performance more generously. Alternatively, and perhaps more realistically—given the myriad of principled, practical, and institutional considerations against a sweeping expansion of the right to specific performance[181]—this body of work suggests that to truly compensate an injured party for breach of contract, the sum of damages awarded should be increased.[182] If people have an independent preference for actual performance—even when contracts pertain to fungible goods—this alone bolsters the case for elevated damages.

In addition—as though things were not complicated enough—one should acknowledge the possibility that the law might be endogenous to people's views on this point. That is to say, once the law offers stronger protection of performance, this in itself may induce people to value it more highly.[183] This suggests that there is a lower chance for bargaining for a release from specific performance, due to the sense of entitlement generated by the strong remedy. To the extent that one views the creation of such preferences as counterproductive, this would count against the use of specific performance as the default remedy in contract law.

178. Daphna Lewinsohn-Zamir, *Can't Buy Me Love: Monetary versus In-Kind Remedies*, 2013 U. Ill. L. Rev. 151, 159–63.

179. *See also* Christoph Engel & Lars Freund, *Behaviorally Efficient Remedies—An Experiment* (working paper, Sep. 2017, *available at*: https://ssrn.com/abstract=2988653) (participants in a stylized experiment were more willing to contribute money to a certain goal when they could purchase "an insurance" that the money would reach its destination, than when they could only purchase an entitlement to a monetary protection of their expectation or reliance interests).

180. Lewinsohn-Zamir, *supra* note 178, at 182.

181. These include the breaching party's autonomy (*see, e.g.*, Kimel, *supra* note 149, at 95–109) and the hardship that specific performance may entail for her, as well as the fact that specific performance is often much more costly to administer than a monetary remedy.

182. Lewinsohn-Zamir, *supra* note 178, at 182–83.

183. For experimental findings along these lines, see Ben Depoorter & Stephan Tontrup, *How Law Frames Moral Intuitions: The Expressive Effect of Specific Performance*, 54 Ariz. L. Rev. 673 (2012). On the more general claim that protecting entitlements through *property rules* (such as specific performance), rather than *liability rules* (such as damages), increases the endowment effect, see *supra* pp. 232–34.

4. Disgorgement

Expectation damages and specific performance share the basic goal of placing the injured party in the position he or she would have been in had the contract been performed. Another issue that has attracted considerable attention in recent years is the question of whether the law should (and to what extent it already does) protect the disgorgement interest—namely, strive to put the *breacher* in the position she would have been in had she performed the contract.[184] A disgorgement remedy entitles the injured party to strip away from the promisor the benefits that she reaped from breach. As a matter of fact, the availability and use of disgorgement as a remedy for breach of contract are quite limited in virtually all legal systems.[185] Even in Israel—where the injured party is, in principle, entitled to recover all profits gained by the breaching party as a result of the breach[186]—disgorgement remedies are rarely sought or awarded.[187]

From an economic viewpoint, a disgorgement remedy would arguably eliminate the incentive for an efficient breach, and is thus inefficient.[188] But much like the case of specific performance,[189] the economic case against disgorgement is inconclusive. For one thing, the promisor may negotiate a release from her contractual obligations, which may be less costly than a unilateral breach. Entitling the injured party to disgorgement remedies need not preclude an efficient breach, for another reason. As Richard Brooks has pointed out, one way to incentivize the promisor to efficiently perform or breach is by providing *the promisee* a choice between performance and disgorgement. That is, once the seller encounters an opportunity for efficient breach, she would have to pay the promisee a sum equal to the additional gain from breach even if she does not breach the original contract.[190]

Deontological moral theories are all the more likely to endorse disgorgement, to expressively and practically strengthen the notion that a promisor must keep her promises.[191]

184. *See, e.g.*, E. Allan Farnsworth, *Your Loss or My Gain? The Dilemma of the Disgorgement Principle in Breach of Contract*, 94 YALE L.J. 1339 (1985); COOTER & ULEN, *supra* note 17, at 319–20; JAMES EDELMAN, GAIN-BASED DAMAGES: CONTRACT, TORT, EQUITY AND INTELLECTUAL PROPERTY 149–89 (2002); Melvin A. Eisenberg, *The Disgorgement Interest in Contract Law*, 105 MICH. L. REV. 559 (2006).

185. FARNSWORTH, *supra* note 137, at 338–83; Dobbs, *supra* note 139, at 1170–78; EDELMAN, *supra* note 184; KATY BARNETT, ACCOUNTING FOR PROFIT FOR BREACH OF CONTACT: THEORY AND PRACTICE 8–9 (2012). *See also* RESTATEMENT (THIRD) OF RESTITUTION AND UNJUST ENRICHMENT § 39 (AM. LAW INST. 2011) (recognizing the availability of disgorgement as a remedy for opportunistic breach); Eisenberg, *supra* note 184, at 565–66, 578–98 (arguing that the disgorgement interest is actually more protected than is usually realized).

186. *See* F.H. 20/82 Adras Ltd. v. Harlow & Jones GmbH, 42(1) P.D. 221 (1988), *translated in* 3 RESTITUTION L. REV. 235 (1995).

187. Eyal Zamir, *Loss Aversion and the Marginality of the Disgorgement Interest*, *in* SHLOMO LEVIN BOOK 323, 329–37 (Asher Grunis, Eliezer Rivlin & Michael Karayanni eds., 2013, in Hebrew).

188. Sidney W. DeLong, *The Efficiency of Disgorgement as a Remedy for Breach of Contract*, 22 IND. L. REV. 737, 742–45 (1989).

189. *See supra* pp. 267–68.

190. Richard R.W. Brooks, *The Efficient Performance Hypothesis*, 116 YALE L.J. 568 (2006).

191. Adras (trans.), *supra* note 186, at 241 (S. Levin J. explaining that the perception of contract breach as wrongdoing in Israeli law is incompatible with an economic analysis of law), 272 (rejecting the notion of efficient breach, Barak J. proclaims: "Promise-keeping is the basis of our life, as a society and a nation"); Daniel Friedmann,

However, this claim, too, may be challenged. If (and, as indicated in the previous subsection, this is a big if) contracting parties typically prefer, under such circumstances, for the seller to be free to breach the contract subject to the payment of expectation damages, then even deontological theories need not object to a default rule that denies the buyer's entitlement to disgorgement.[192] Other considerations pertain to the practical difficulties of enforcing disgorgement remedies, compared with remedies that protect other interests.[193]

This brief synopsis of the debate suffices to demonstrate that the explanations and justifications that have been proposed to date for the marginality of disgorgement remedies are contestable. Melvin Eisenberg, who has advocated broader recognition of disgorgement remedies, considered several explanations for the rarity of cases in which such remedies are actually sought and awarded.[194] One is that the injured party's loss is often greater than the breacher's gain, and hence expectation damages are more attractive. In other instances, the injured party is entitled to specific performance, thus preventing the promisor from making a gain by breaching. However, these arguments do not fully explain extant law. Breaches in which the breacher's observable and verifiable gains are greater than the injured party's verifiable losses are likely much more common than reflected in case law. Similarly, specific performance is often unobtainable—and even when it is available, disgorgement remedies may be superior. This would be the case, for example, where the opportunity to make the extra profit is only available to the promisor, and the costs of renegotiation are high.

Refocusing this debate around the notion of loss aversion and reference points provides a crucial insight into existing legal norms and practices. If, as is very plausibly the case, promisees do not ordinarily view promisors' profits from the breach as something that they have lost, then not getting these profits is considerably less painful than not getting back what they gave the breaching party (restitution) and the costs they incurred in performing the contract (reliance). Furthermore, not getting the promisor's profits is also less painful than not getting the profits they anticipated to earn from the contract due to the breach (expectation). When people's expectations differ from the status quo, those expectations are likely to become the reference point.[195] As we have seen, contracts can alter expectations and change the reference point.[196] Thus, promisees are likely to view unattained profits as a painful loss, rather than as a missed gain. Consequently, disgorgement remedies are relatively less likely to be sought, and legal decision-makers are less likely to award

Restitution of Benefits Obtained through the Appropriation of Property or the Commission of a Wrong, 80 Colum. L. Rev. 504, 515 (1980); Eisenberg, *supra* note 184, at 578–80. *See also* Seana Valentine Shiffrin, *The Divergence of Contract and Promise,* 120 Harv. L. Rev. 708 (2007).

192. For a deontological objection to disgorgement as a standard remedy for breach, see, e.g., Weinrib, *supra* note 161, at 70–84. *See also* Hanoch Dagan, *Restitutionary Damages for Breach of Contract: An Exercise in Private Law Theory,* 1 Theoretical Inq. L. 115, 118–25 (2000) (arguing that the inherent value of promise-keeping is neutral to the desirability of disgorgement remedies).

193. *See* Eyal Zamir, Law, Psychology, and Morality: The Role of Loss Aversion 131 (2015).

194. Eisenberg, *supra* note 184, at 597–99.

195. *See* Köszegi & Rabin, *supra* note 158.

196. *See* Hart & Moore, *supra* note 121.

them. This conjecture is in line with the general theory about the correspondence between legal doctrine and loss aversion and its possible causes, as discussed in Chapter 5.[197]

5. Intentions and Motivations

While intent reigns supreme in the realm of criminal law,[198] under Anglo-American contract law the intentionality of breach and the fault of the breaching party are generally deemed irrelevant.[199] Several justifications have been offered for the norm of strict liability in contract law, although the analysis is far from conclusive.[200] In any event, in line with current doctrine, the above discussion of remedies for breach skirted around the issue of the breaching party's fault. The discussion took into account the empirical and experimental findings indicating that people view breach as a type of moral wrong, akin to breaking a promise,[201] but did not discuss the breacher's intentions and motivations.

Some studies indicate that in this respect there is a gap between commonsense morality and the common law. When asked to evaluate two cases of identical pecuniary harm—one caused by an intentional breach of contract and the other by an unintentional tort—people judged the intentional breach to be significantly more immoral and were willing to award significantly greater damages to the injured party.[202] Similar results have also been documented in an experiment that compared an intentional breach of contract with an accidental breach.[203]

197. *See supra* pp. 187–97. The losses/gains distinction may help in explaining why disgorgement remedies—which are not ordinarily available for breach of contract—are available against a trustee who has breached her fiduciary duty (RESTATEMENT (THIRD) OF TRUSTS § 100(b) (AM. LAW INST. 2012); J.C. SHEPHERD, THE LAW OF FIDUCIARIES 116–19 (1981); Tamar Frankel, *Fiduciary Law*, 71 CAL. L. REV. 795, 829 (1983). Since the trust property is legally and conventionally perceived as something the beneficiary already has, if only in equity—rather than as something he is entitled to receive from the trustee—both beneficiaries and legal decision-makers are more likely to view the illicit profits made by the trustee as belonging to the domain of the beneficiary's losses, rather than to the realm of his unobtained gains.

198. *See* PAUL H. ROBINSON, CRIMINAL LAW: CASE STUDIES AND CONTROVERSIES 131 (rev. ed. 2005).

199. Omri Ben Shahar & Ariel Porat, *Forward: Fault in American Contract Law*, 107 MICH. L. REV. 1341, 1341 (2009); Seana Shiffrin, *Enhancing Moral Relationships through Strict Liability*, 66 U. TORONTO L.J. 353 (2016). This is, of course, an oversimplification. *See, e.g.*, George M. Cohen, *The Fault Lines in Contract Damages*, 80 VA. L. REV. 1225 (1994); FAULT IN AMERICAN CONTRACT LAW (Omri Ben Shahar & Ariel Porat eds., 2010). The situation is all the more complex in other legal systems, such as the French, where fact patterns that are governed by tort law in the Anglo-American tradition (such as professional liability) are governed by contract law and are subject to fault-based liability. *See, e.g.*, Solène Rowan, *Fault and Breach of Contract in France and England: Some Comparisons*, 22 EUR. BUS. L. REV. 467 (2011).

200. *See, e.g.*, Shiffrin, *supra* note 199. The economic analysis of strict versus fault-based liability mostly revolves around torts, but insofar as it refers to situations in which there are contractual relationships between the parties, it is applicable to contractual liability as well. *See, e.g.*, STEVEN SHAVELL, ECONOMIC ANALYSIS OF ACCIDENT LAW 51–64 (1987).

201. *See* Wilkinson-Ryan, *supra* note 24.

202. Tess Wilkinson-Ryan & Jonathan Baron, *Moral Judgment and Moral Heuristics in Breach of Contract*, 6 J. EMPIRICAL LEGAL STUD. 405, 417–20 (2009).

203. Wilkinson-Ryan & Hoffman, *Breach*, *supra* note 54, at 1030–32.

The motivation for breach has also been shown to affect how people judge breach decisions. A promisor might breach a contract either to avoid losses due to increased cost of performance, or to generate greater profits because of a change in the object's market price. From an economic perspective, there is no difference between losses and forgone gains, or between gains and forgone losses. Prospect theory, however, posits otherwise.[204] In fact, an experimental study of judgments of breach decisions has demonstrated that people treat a breach that is committed to cut losses as more acceptable than one designed to enhance the promisor's gain.[205] Subjects in that study were asked to evaluate a breach by a contractor who was hired to renovate a kitchen. Half of the subjects were told that the motivation for breach was that "the price of cabinets and countertop has skyrocketed"; the other half were told that the motivation arose from alternative, more lucrative, projects. The results show that subjects judged the gain-motivated breach as meriting a tougher legal response, in the form of significantly higher damages.[206]

To the extent that these intuitions are shared by jurors and judges, they may possibly seep through to their decisions. Even if the variables highlighted by this literature are not a formal part of contract doctrine, they may influence how judicial discretion is applied. For example, the decision as to what losses were "foreseeable," and whether the injured party could have reasonably mitigated her losses, may be swayed by the motivation behind the breach. Whether this is a good thing is a separate question. People's moral intuitions may not accord with the normatively correct decision. This might occur, for example, when people do not fully understand the ex-ante ramifications of their ex-post judgments. In all the experiments described in this subsection, pricing was not part of the experimental setup. To the extent that focusing on the promisor's motivation reduces the contractual surplus, it is unclear whether it ought to play a role in contract law.

H. Agreed Remedies: Liquidated Damages

1. A Puzzling Doctrine

So far, we have discussed the legally prescribed remedies for breach of contract. To some extent, parties can contract around ordinary remedy rules. They can, for example, stipulate the damages for breach, and determine the outcomes of breaching certain obligations by defining them as "express terms" under U.S. law,[207] or (under Israeli law) by defining certain breaches as "fundamental."[208] Such contract clauses, however, are subject to judicial

204. *See generally supra* pp. 42–57.

205. *See* Wilkinson-Ryan & Baron, *supra* note 202, at 413–14.

206. *See also* Maria Bigoni et al., *Unbundling Efficient Breach: An Experiment*, 14 J. Empirical Legal Stud. 527 (2017).

207. Restatement (Second) of Contracts § 203 (Am. Law. Inst. 1981).

208. *See* sections 6 and 7 of the Israeli Contracts (Remedies for Breach of Contract) Law, 1970. When a breach is fundamental, the breaching party is not entitled to an extension of time for performance as a precondition to rescission, and rescission is not subject to an objection for being "unjust." Section 6 provides that "a sweeping

scrutiny. Freedom of contract is more restricted in the domain of remedies than in other aspects of contract content and performance.[209]

For example, while both civil law and Anglo-American systems allow the parties to stipulate the amount of damages to be paid in case of breach, they limit this freedom. Under U.S. law, liquidated damages that exceed "an amount that is reasonable in the light of the anticipated or actual loss caused by the breach and the difficulties of proof of loss" are considered an invalid "penalty."[210] Civil law jurisdictions adopt a relatively more permissive attitude in this regard: instead of a dichotomous choice between fully enforcing such clauses and invalidating them, they allow the court to reduce the stipulated sum under certain circumstances.[211]

At first sight, these restrictions make economic sense, because supra-compensatory liquidated damages might hinder efficient nonperformance of the contract.[212] On closer inspection, however, they are puzzling. From an economic perspective, there is no difference in principle between the content of the contract and remedies for its breach. Both aim to allocate risks and prospects and to create optimal incentives for the parties' behavior. Hence, just as the parties are free to set the content of their obligations, they should be free to set the remedies for breach. Absent a defect in the contracting process, such as deception or duress, rational parties would not set supra- or infra-compensatory damages, because such stipulation would create inefficient incentives—thereby decreasing the contractual surplus. Neither the promisor nor the promisee would benefit from such clauses ex ante. When liquidated damages appear to be supra- or infra-compensatory in relation to the legal rules of damages, it must be because the rules do not adequately capture the promisee's true expected losses from the breach. The subjective value of performance might, for example, be higher than its market value, which is the common yardstick for legal damages. It follows that restrictions on liquidated damages and other deviations from legal remedy rules should be abolished.[213]

Yet another puzzle is the dissimilar legal treatment of liquidated damages and bonuses. Assume that a contractor undertakes to complete a project by a certain date X, at price

stipulation in a contract making breaches fundamental without differentiating between them is invalid unless it was reasonable at the time the contract was made."

209. *See, e.g.*, DAN B. DOBBS, DOBBS LAW OF REMEDIES 245–73 (1993); FARNSWORTH, *supra* note 137, at 300 (maintaining that the parties' "power to bargain over their remedial rights is surprisingly limited").

210. RESTATEMENT (SECOND) OF CONTRACTS § 356 (AM. LAW. INST. 1981). *See generally* Larry A. DiMatteo, *A Theory of Efficient Penalty: Eliminating the Law of Liquidated Damages*, 38 AM. BUS. L.J. 633, 668–75 (2001).

211. For a comparative review, see Ugo Mattei, *The Comparative Law and Economics of Penalty Clauses in Contracts*, 43 AM. J. COMP. L. 427, 434–38 (1995).

212. *See also* Philippe Aghion & Benjamin Hermalin, *Legal Restrictions on Private Contracts Can Enhance Efficiency*, 6 J.L. ECON. & ORG. 381 (1990) (discussing the role of legal restrictions on contract terms as a means to avoid the distorting signaling effect of such terms); Eric L. Talley, *Contract Renegotiation, Mechanism Design, and the Liquidated Damages Rule*, 46 STAN. L. REV. 1195 (1995) (arguing that the invalidation of penalty clauses discourages strategic behavior by the parties).

213. *See, e.g.*, Alan Schwartz, *The Myth That Promisees Prefer Supracompensatory Remedies: An Analysis of Contracting for Damage Measures*, 100 YALE L.J. 369 (1990).

P. The contract provides that for every day of delayed completion, the client is entitled to $1,000 in liquidated damages. Now assume a similar contract, where the agreed date of completion is X+100 and the price is P–$100,000. In the latter contract there is a liquidated damages clause of $1,000 for every day of delay, but also a clause entitling the contractor to a $1,000 bonus for every day of earlier completion, to a maximum of 100 days.

Presumably, the parties' payoffs, and hence their incentives, are identical under the two contracts. However, the legal treatment of the two contracts is very different. Assume, for example, that the project was completed on date X+50. Under the first contract, the contractor has breached her obligation to complete the contract by date X. The liquidated damages clause does not necessarily deprive the client of alternative or additional remedies for this breach.[214] Even if the contract purports to exclude such remedies, this exclusion will be scrutinized.[215] At the same time, if the court views the liquidated damages as disproportionately high, it would void the clause in Anglo-American systems, or reduce the liquidated damages to an acceptable level in others.[216] Finally, if delay is due to unexpected and unavoidable circumstances that make completion on time impossible or impracticable, the contractor may not have to pay any damages at all, because under those circumstances the delay is not considered a breach.[217]

In contrast, under the second contract, completion on date X+50 does not constitute a breach, but rather an expedited performance. Therefore, the client is not entitled to any remedy for breach of contract. Moreover, it is very unlikely that he or she could challenge the validity of the bonus clause on the grounds that it is excessive, or that the contractor could challenge the bonus for being too low. Finally, the client could not avoid paying the bonus by claiming that the earlier completion was made possible thanks to unexpectedly favorable circumstances for the contractor. Since the difference between penalties and bonuses seems to be merely "semantic," so it has been argued, their radically different legal status is unjustifiable.[218] In fact, the law of liquidated damages seems futile, because it can be easily circumvented by a simple contracting maneuver.[219] Inasmuch as the rules applying to liquidated damages and penalties are justified, courts should arguably expand them and regulate bonuses, just as they regulate penalties.[220]

214. TREITEL, *supra* note 137, at 212–13, 214–19; PRINCIPLES OF EUROPEAN CONTRACT LAW, PARTS I AND II, COMBINED AND REVISED 453–56 (Ole Lando & Hugh Beale eds., 2000); U.C.C. § 2–719 (AM. LAW INST. & UNIF. LAW COMM'N. 2002).

215. TREITEL, *supra* note 137, at 216–17; CODE CIVIL [Civil Code] art. 1152 para. 2 (Fr.); U.C.C. § 2–718, Comment 3 (as amended in 2003) ("A liquidated damages term that provided for damages that are unreasonably small is likewise unenforceable"). *See also* U.C.C. § 2–719 (AM. LAW INST. & UNIF. LAW COMM'N. 2002).

216. TREITEL, *supra* note 137, at 219–33.

217. *See, e.g.*, U.C.C. § 2–615 (AM. LAW INST. & UNIF. LAW COMM'N. 2002).

218. *See, e.g.*, Larry A. DiMatteo, *Penalties as Rational Response to Bargaining Irrationality*, 2006 MICH. ST. L. REV. 883, 908 (2006).

219. *See* COOTER & ULEN, *supra* note 17, at 322–23.

220. James P. George, *Reimposable Discounts and Medieval Contract Remedies*, 20 LOY. CONSUMER L. REV. 50, 68–79 (2007).

These puzzles have attracted the attention of scholars who have offered various ways of resolving them, from different normative perspectives.[221] Without necessarily detracting from those arguments, it seems that the behavioral perspective is particularly fruitful in this context, as detailed below.

2. Behavioral Insights

One powerful justification for the reluctance to enforce supra-compensatory liquidated-damages clauses is that such clauses—more than others—may be the product of cognitive biases, and hence are inefficient and unfair.[222] At least two cognitive forces might drive contracting parties to agree upon liquidated damages in a biased fashion.[223] First, since contracts are generally performed rather than breached, people might err in their estimation of the objective probability of a breach occurring. As is often the case with low-probability events, contracting parties may conclude from a small sample of recent transactions that the probability of breach is nil. As a result, they may agree to excessive compensation, assuming that breach is exceedingly unlikely.[224] In fact, empirical studies have shown that at the contracting stage, commercial parties pay much more attention to their primary obligations than to all sorts of contingencies that might affect performance, or to the outcomes of breach.[225]

Even if people pay attention to possible breaches and correctly gauge their objective probability, it is doubtful they will be able to properly estimate the probability of breach in their own individual case. Rather, over optimism might kick in and lead them to underestimate the probability of breach. At the time of contracting, people are likely to assume that even if there is a positive probability of breach, their particular characteristics will prevent them from breaching. After all, they are excellent at what they do, which is why they were chosen for the job. Overly optimistic predictions regarding the anticipated time and costs of completing projects have been repeatedly noted in various industries, and have been specifically studied by psychologists under the heading of *the planning fallacy*.[226] Much like people who are about to get married, contracting parties may underestimate the probability of "divorce" and overly trust the other party's kindness and considerateness.[227] Consequently, promisors are prone to agree to harsh and inefficient liquidated damages clauses.

221. *See, e.g.* Seana Shiffrin, *Remedial Clauses: The Overprivatization of Private Law*, 67 HASTINGS L.J. 407 (2016); Nathan B. Oman, *Consent to Retaliation: A Civil Recourse Theory of Contractual Liability*, 96 IOWA L. REV. 529, 553–57 (2011).

222. Comparable analysis may be applied to other clauses concerning the outcomes of nonperformance and other contingencies, such as the Anglo-American distinction between "express conditions" and other contractual terms. *See* Melvin Aron Eisenberg, *The Limits of Cognition and the Limits of Contract*, 47 STAN. L. REV. 211, 236–40 (1995).

223. *See id.* at 225–27.

224. On common errors in probability assessments, see generally *supra* pp. 28–42.

225. Macaulay, *supra* note 66, at 56–60.

226. On this phenomenon, see generally *supra* pp. 69–71. On overoptimism and related phenomena more generally, see *supra* pp. 58–76.

227. Lynn A. Baker & Robert E. Emery, *When Every Relationship Is above Average: Perceptions and Expectations of Divorce at the Time of Marriage*, 17 LAW & HUM. BEHAV. 439 (1993).

The possibility of biased contracting with regard to liquidated damages suggests that regulation may be justified.[228] In the small subset of cases in which liquidated damages provisions come into play, courts may take a "second look" at these provisions ex post. To the extent that this second look suggests that excessive liquidated damages resulted from cognitive biases at the contracting stage, judicial oversight might steer the parties toward achieving their true underlying goals. Of course, judicial oversight carries its own perils—including the concern that in assessing the reasonableness of liquidated-damages clauses, judges might exhibit the hindsight bias.[229]

The behavioral perspective may also illuminate the legal hostility to infra-compensatory liquidated damages.[230] For one thing, some of the biases that cause *promisors* to pay insufficient attention to supra-compensatory liquidated damages—such as underestimating the probability of breach, or excessive trust in the other party—may cause *promisees* to pay insufficient attention to infra-compensatory liquidated damages. In addition, both the hostility to infra-compensatory liquidated damages and the dissimilar treatment of penalties and bonuses likely reflect the parties' and the courts' moral sentiments toward the meaning of contractual obligations. As previously noted, the common perception is that a contract is not a choice between performance and paying damages. Infra-compensatory liquidated damages and similar provisions may be seen as undermining the moral underpinnings of contracts and contract law. Similarly, the normative implications of damages for breach (an infringement of the moral prohibition on breaking a promise) are fundamentally different from those of bonuses.[231]

An alternative, behaviorally-inspired reading of the penalty-bonus distinction has been offered by Yuval Feldman, Amos Schurr, and Doron Teichman,[232] who suggest that the liquidated damages doctrine should not be perceived as a mandatory rule, but as a default rule. From this standpoint, the differential treatment of bonuses and penalties enables the parties to opt out of the regulation of remedies and design a payoff structure that best fits their interests. The doctrine encourages parties who wish to opt out of its remedial regime to do so by means of bonuses, rather than penalties. This framing is conducive to greater cooperation between the parties, because, as previously noted, when contracting parties are uncertain about the content of their contractual obligations, they tend to adopt a more self-serving interpretation when their payoffs are framed as losses than as gains.[233] Moreover, even if there is no uncertainty about the content of the obligation, the framing of a payment as a bonus implies that it belongs to the domain of gains—and forgone gains are less likely

228. Eisenberg, *supra* note 222, at 234–35. *Cf.* Hillman, *supra* note 72; Jeffrey J. Rachlinski, *New Law and Psychology: A Reply to Critics, Skeptics, and Cautious Supporters*, 85 Cornell L. Rev. 739 (1999).

229. *See generally supra* pp. 38–39; *infra* pp. 535–36.

230. *See supra* note 215 and accompanying text.

231. *See also* Zamir & Medina, *supra* note 143, at 301–03.

232. Feldman, Schurr & Teichman, *supra* note 125, at 536–37.

233. *See supra* note 125 and accompanying text.

than losses to trigger litigation.[234] The downside of such framing is, however, that the prospect of not obtaining extra gains likely produces a weaker incentive than the fear of loss.[235]

3. Liquidated Damages and the Decision to Breach

Aside from the normative question associated with the legal status of liquidated damages terms, behavioral insights may also shed light on the positive question of how liquidated damages influence breach decisions. As noted, despite the view among legal economists that contracts are an option to breach and pay damages, the predominant perception among most people is that contracts represent a promise to perform. The insertion of a liquidated damages clause into the contract, however, may alter this perception. Inasmuch as liquidated damages are perceived as an agreed price tag for breach, they may increase the likelihood of breach. Accordingly, promisors might take a more "rational" view toward perform-or-breach dilemmas that they may encounter, and analyze them through the prism of cost-benefit analysis.

In essence, the claim is that this is another manifestation of the *crowding out effect.* A large body of literature has pointed out that formal regulation and market institutions may undermine alternative social mechanisms and altruistic motivations.[236] In the context of blood donations, for example, the introduction of monetary incentives may crowd out intrinsic motivations to help others. Thus, such incentives might actually *lower* the total level of donations.[237] In a context closer to remedies for breach, it was shown that the introduction of a payment for late pickups from day-care centers in Israel led to an *increase* of such occurrences, rather than a reduction.[238] These findings run counter to rational-choice analysis, which predicts that added monetary incentives can only raise motivation. Apparently, when explicit, ex ante, pricing mechanisms are introduced, implicit non-legal mechanisms (such as guilt and shame) are crowded out.

Building on these finding, Tess Wilkinson-Ryan examined the association between liquidated damages provisions and performance incentives.[239] In a series of experiments, she asked subjects to assume the role of a promisor faced with a breach dilemma following the arrival of a third party willing to pay a higher price. While half the subjects approached this dilemma with a liquidated damages clause stating that they need to pay $1,000 to the

234. *See supra* pp. 192–93.

235. *See* Richard R. Brooks, Alexander Stremitzer & Stephan Tontrup, *Framing Contracts: Why Loss Framing Increases Effort*, 168 J. INST. & THEO. ECON. 62 (2012); Tanjim Hoassain & John A. List, *The Behavioralist Factory: Increasing Productivity Using Simple Framing Manipulations*, 58 MGMT. SCI. 2151 (2012). On the comparable incentives created by bonuses and penalties more generally, see *supra* 131–32.

236. *See, e.g.*, RICHARD M. TITMUSS, THE GIFT OF RELATIONSHIP: FROM HUMAN BLOOD TO SOCIAL POLICY (1971). *See also* Axel Ostman, *External Control May Destroy the Commons*, 10 RATIONALITY & SOC'Y 103 (1998).

237. For an experimental study partially confirming this hypothesis, see Carl Mellström & Magnus Johannesson, *Crowding Out in Blood Donation: Was Titmuss Right?*, 6 J. EURO. ECON. ASS. 845 (2008).

238. *See* Uri Gneezy & Aldo Rustichini, *A Fine Is a Price*, 29 J. LEGAL STUD. 1 (2000).

239. Tess Wilkinson-Ryan, *Do Liquidated Damages Encourage Efficient Breach? A Psychological Experiment*, 108 MICH. L. REV. 633, 655–64 (2010).

promisee in the case of breach, the other half were informed that "the law of contracts will require that you pay them $1,000 as compensation." Despite the identical payoff structure, the minimal payment by the third party needed to induce breach was significantly lower in the liquidated damages condition.[240] Thus, some parties may be aware of the moral perceptions driving breach decisions, and use liquidated damages provisions to facilitate efficient nonperformance by eliminating the negative moral implication of breach.[241] At the same time, parties who wish to maintain this implication might stipulate that the duty to pay liquidated damages is "without prejudice to other remedies" that the promisee might have (or words to that effect). Future research should examine the possible effect of various formulations. More generally, it has been demonstrated that when the law prices harm-generating activities with ex-ante payments (e.g., fees), people may perceive such payments as the price for engaging in these activities. Conversely, when the law makes use of ex-post payments (such as fines), people may perceive such payments as a form of punishment that implies a moral judgment as well. Thus, when the law wishes to encourage decision-making based on cost-benefit analysis—such as when the activity creates both positive and negative externalities—clear and simple ex-ante payments may be preferable.[242]

I. Conclusion

The overall picture emerging from the behavioral analysis of contracting and contract law is that life is complicated. Contracting parties clearly care about maximizing their payoffs from the contract, but they also care about other things, such as keeping their promises and not betraying the trust bestowed on them by others. The same is true of legal policy- and decision-makers, who care not only about helping the parties to maximize their payoffs, but other values as well. Mapping out how these forces interact, and reaching generalizations as to how they do so in different domains of contracts, appears to be the main challenge that the field now faces. Of particular interest are consumer contracts, which is the topic of the next chapter.

240. However, since liquidated damages clauses may induce contracting parties to behave like rational maximizers of their own utility, they may adversely affect the emergence of mutual trust. *See* Ben Depoorter, Sven Hoeppner & Lars Freund, *The Moral-Hazard Effect of Liquidated Damages: An Experiment on Contract Remedies*, 173 J. Inst. & Theoretical Econ. 84 (2017).

241. Wilkinson-Ryan, *supra* note 239 at 665–67.

242. Yuval Feldman & Doron Teichman, *Are All Legal Dollars Created Equal?*, 102 Nw. U. L. Rev. 223 (2008).

8

Consumer Contracts

A. Introduction

Contracts are conventionally classified into three major categories. Schematically, firms contract with each other in *commercial contracts*, as part of their business or professional activities; individuals enter into *private contracts* with one another, outside of their professional activity; and *consumer contracts* are made between firms that make the contract in the course of their business activity and individuals who purchase goods and services, including financial services, for their personal, family, or household needs.[1] Of these, consumer contracts are the most common contracts that most people make. Whenever people ride a bus, buy gasoline for their family car, buy food, download an application to their smartphone, go to the movies, go on holiday, subscribe to internet services, open a bank account, or purchase life insurance—they are entering into a consumer contract. While daily consumer contracts often involve low stakes, some—such as buying a new apartment and taking a loan for that purpose—are complex and entail high stakes.

When consumer contracts are made in writing, contracting is almost invariably done through pre-formulated, standard forms, which consumers hardly ever read.[2] Indeed, some of these standard forms are not even accessible to consumers when they make the purchase decision.[3] Consumer contracts are therefore very different from the paradigm

1. This conventional trichotomy is not exclusive. An intriguing recent development is the rise of the "sharing economy," in which individuals contract with one another through internet platforms and applications, thus creating three-party relationships, which combine private- and consumer-contracts elements and pose new challenges for the law and for behavioral legal analysis. *See, e.g.*, Cait Lamberton, *Consumer Sharing: Collaborative Consumption, from Theoretical Roots to New Opportunities*, *in* The Cambridge Handbook of Consumer Psychology 693 (Michael I. Norton, Derek D. Rucker & Cait Lamberton eds., 2015).

2. *See infra* pp. 301–04.

3. On PNTLs ("Pay Now, Terms Later"), see, e.g., Robert A. Hillman, *Rolling Contracts*, 71 Fordham L. Rev. 743 (2002); Roger C. Bern, *Terms Later Contracting: Bad Economics, Bad Morals, and a Bad Idea for a Uniform Law, Judge Easterbrook Notwithstanding*, 12 J. L. & Pol'y 641 (2003); Stewart Macaulay, *Freedom of Contract: Solutions in Search for a Problem?*, 2004 Wis. L. Rev. 777, 802–19; Florencia Marotta-Wurgler, *Are "Pay Now, Terms Later"*

Behavioral Law and Economics. Eyal Zamir and Doron Teichman.

of an individually negotiated contract between two identified people or organizations, as envisioned by classical and much of modern contract law.

To be sure, the great majority of commercial contracts and some private contracts are not individually negotiated either, since nowadays in most commercial and some private transactions the parties use standard forms, as well (individuals may, for example, use templates they download from the internet). However, consumer contracts are typically different from commercial and private ones in that they are characterized by large asymmetries in the parties' power, sophistication, knowledge, and the ability of the single consumer to influence the content of the agreement (or even know what it says). Therefore, there is a common sentiment that governmental intervention is necessary to mitigate the unfairness and inefficiency that may result from these asymmetries.

From the perspective of standard economic analysis, which assumes that consumers are rational maximizers, only traditional market failures, such as monopolies, information problems, and externalities, may warrant legal intervention to enhance social welfare. However, once the rationality assumption is relaxed, and behavioral insights are taken into account, this position is called into question. The behavioral findings indicate that even when the objective attributes of a competitive market (such as many sellers and buyers, full information, and no externalities) exist, consumers' cognitive limitations and biases, and their exploitation by firms, may bring about inefficient (and unfair) outcomes—and, of course, cognitive biases may exacerbate the adverse effects of traditional market failures. For example, if due to their shortsightedness, overoptimism, and poor financial literacy, borrowers are tempted to take out large loans at an initially low interest rate that subsequently increases (either automatically, or according to variables under the lender's control), they may well find themselves unable to repay those loans—leading to personal, and in extreme cases even to societal or global, crises.[4] Behavioral economics thus calls for expansion of the notion of market failure to include *behavioral market failures* as well.[5]

Importantly, recognizing that consumers' decisions often reflect cognitive biases, and that suppliers systematically exploit these biases to maximize their profits, does not, in and of itself, yield any normative or policy conclusions. While a better understanding of the reality of consumer markets is essential to policymaking, policy decisions inevitably involve weighing up conflicting normative arguments.

This chapter does not provide a comprehensive survey of the vast literature on consumer psychology, as this would be excessively long, and in any event is unnecessary for

Contracts Worse for Buyers? Evidence from Software License Agreements, 38 J. LEGAL STUD. 309 (2009); *supra* p. 255.

4. Parenthetically, since such a crisis is expected to have an extreme adverse impact on both borrowers and lenders (as happened in the subprime mortgage crisis of 2007–2009 in the United States), it may well be the product of cognitive biases on both sides of the transaction.

5. OREN BAR-GILL, SEDUCTION BY CONTRACT: LAW, ECONOMICS, AND PSYCHOLOGY IN CONSUMER MARKETS 2 (2012).

our purposes.[6] Instead, it focuses on the aspects of consumers' judgment and decision-making that make them particularly vulnerable to suppliers' exploitation and may thus warrant legal attention.[7] The chapter first demonstrates the importance of behavioral insights to the understanding of consumer transactions, including marketing techniques (Section B), pricing (Section C), the design of non-price contract clauses (Section D), and post-contracting behavior (Section E). While some policy implications of the behavioral insights are mentioned along the way, a more comprehensive and systematic discussion of these implications is provided in Sections F and G. Section F describes the role of market forces, including competition and reputation, in mitigating the ramifications of consumers' bounded rationality. Section G then reflects on some of the measures the law might use to enhance the fairness and efficiency of consumer transactions, such as the imposition of disclosure duties and regulating the content of the contract. This reflection draws on the general discussion of the normative implications of behavioral findings set out in Chapter 4.[8]

Notably, some of the issues discussed in this chapter—such as the use of certain marketing and pricing techniques and the phenomenon of customers not reading standard-form contracts—are not unique to consumer transactions. The same marketing techniques may be used when customers are commercial entities; and in their routine transactions, businesspeople are just as unlikely as consumers to read standard-from contracts.[9] Much of the discussion in this chapter is therefore relevant to non-consumer contracts as well.

B. Marketing Techniques

1. General

In our daily lives, we often try to persuade other people to do, or refrain from doing, certain things (and are frequently the target of such attempts by others). In doing so, we do not necessarily appeal to people's reflective and deliberative capabilities. Rather, we often consciously or unconsciously use various cognitive and emotional tactics in an intuitive and amateurish way. As Eldar Shafir has put it, "being manipulated is an integral part of the human condition."[10] Professional marketers make their living by influencing other people's decisions. Hence, they can experiment with different tactics and learn from their experience (and the experience of others) as to what tactics work under what circumstances.

6. For critical surveys of the broad terrain of consumer psychology—including the cognitive, affective, and behavioral responses to products and services—see The Cambridge Handbook of Consumer Psychology, *supra* note 1; Handbook of Consumer Psychology (Curtis P. Haugtvedt, Paul M. Herr & Frank R. Kardes eds., 2008).

7. Even within this narrower context, our discussion is rather general, excluding specific issues, such as suppliers' exploitation of consumers' reluctance to engage in price comparison and price negotiation when purchasing goods and services that symbolize love (e.g., funeral services). On this issue, see A. Peter McGraw et al., *The Price of Not Putting a Price on Love*, 11 Judgment & Decision Making 40 (2016).

8. *See supra* pp. 171–85.

9. Stewart Macaulay, *Non-contractual Relations in Business: A Preliminary Study*, 28 Am. Soc. Rev. 55, 57–58 (1963).

10. Eldar Shafir, *Manipulated as a Way of Life*, 1 J. Marketing Behav. 245, 245 (2015).

Using effective marketing techniques is crucial to a firm's survival in a competitive market, and is essential for profit maximization in noncompetitive markets as well. Firms therefore allocate considerable resources to marketing, and the multi-disciplinary academic study of marketing, including from a behavioral perspective, is thriving.[11]

Due to space limitations, this section does not offer a comprehensive survey of the behavioral aspects of marketing, but rather focuses on a few topics that may be relevant to legal policymaking. It does not discuss important (and sometimes controversial) issues such as priming and subliminal advertising,[12] reciprocation (giving something for free to create a sense of indebtedness),[13] the use of sensory (visual, auditory, olfactory) or other nonverbal stimuli,[14] or emotional branding.[15] Rather, to keep the discussion manageable, this section focuses on information presentation, limited availability, the *low-ball* and *bait-and-switch* techniques, and lenient return policies. While pricing is part of marketing, it deserves special attention, and will therefore be discussed separately in the next section.

2. Information Presentation

Many consumer products and services, and the contracts under which they are provided, are quite complex; and consumers typically lack the knowledge necessary to accurately assess their benefits, costs, and risks. Therefore, the importance of providing consumers with truthful information prior to making their purchase decisions—for example, in advertisements—has been a cornerstone of consumer protection policies from early on. Since, under standard economic analysis, reasonably full and accurate information is key to the proper functioning of a competitive market, no behavioral studies were necessary to recognize that. However, behavioral studies have made a significant contribution in this regard as well. They have done so by casting doubt on the assumption, underpinning standard economic analysis of market information, that consumers draw logical inferences from sellers' failure to disclose information (i.e., that they infer silence to signal low quality), and the ensuing conclusion that sellers have sufficient incentives to disclose information.[16] It

11. *See, e.g.*, HANDBOOK OF MARKETING (Barton Weitz & Robin Wensley eds., 2002). The psychology of marketing is part of the broader sphere of attitude change and persuasion. *See generally* Zakary L. Tormala & Pablo Briñol, *Attitude Change and Persuasion, in* THE CAMBRIDGE HANDBOOK OF CONSUMER PSYCHOLOGY, *supra* note 1, at 29.

12. *See, e.g.*, Patrick T. Vargas, *Implicit Consumer Cognition, in* HANDBOOK OF CONSUMER PSYCHOLOGY, *supra* note 6, at 477.

13. *See, e.g.*, ROBERT B. CIALDINI, INFLUENCE: SCIENCE AND PRACTICE 18–50 (5th ed. 2009).

14. *See, e.g.*, Shmuel I. Becher & Yuval Feldman, *Manipulating, Fast and Slow: The Law of Non-verbal Market Manipulations*, 38 CARDOZO L. REV. 459 (2016); Jonathan E. Schroeder, VISUAL CONSUMPTION (2002); Joann Peck & Terry L. Childres, *Effects of Sensory Factors on Consumer Behavior: If It Tastes, Smells, Sounds, and Feels Like a Duck, Then It Must Be . . . , in* HANDBOOK OF CONSUMER PSYCHOLOGY, *supra* note 6, at 193.

15. *See, e.g.*, MARC GOBÉ, EMOTIONAL BRANDING (rev. ed. 2009); Jill Avery & Anat Keinan, *Consuming Brands, in* THE CAMBRIDGE HANDBOOK OF CONSUMER PSYCHOLOGY, *supra* note 1, at 180; Chris T. Allen, Susan Fournier & Felicia Miller, *Brands and Their Meaning Makers, in* HANDBOOK OF CONSUMER PSYCHOLOGY, *supra* note 6, at 781.

16. For classic contributions, see Sanford J. Grossman, *The Informational Role of Warranties and Private Disclosure of Product Quality*, 24 J.L. & ECON. 461 (1981); Paul R. Milgrom, *Good News and Bad News: Representation*

appears that people's general tendency to make decisions based on the immediately available information, while neglecting missing information,[17] characterizes their decisions as consumers, as well.[18] Moreover, even when the non-disclosure of crucial information is made salient, people may be insufficiently skeptical about the non-disclosed information (thus reducing the incentive to disclose information).[19] Beyond these important insights, the key contribution of behavioral studies lies in showing that merely making the necessary information available to consumers is not enough. These studies reveal that the amount of information, the timing in which it is disclosed, and the manner of its disclosure, are just as important—and marketers are all too well aware of that.

Thus, a direct corollary of people's cognitive limitations is *information overload*, which, among other things, implies that in any given unit of time, there is a limit to the amount of information people can perceive and process, and once this limit is surpassed, the quality of decisions tends to deteriorate.[20] The common human response to information overload is to focus on a few salient aspects of a decision, and ignore the others. Thus, by increasing or decreasing the saliency of particular information, marketers may affect the aspects of a product or a transaction that consumers take into account. Greater saliency of some pieces of information not only increases their impact on decision-making, but concomitantly decreases the impact of other pieces of information, due to people's inability to consider many aspects at the same time.[21] The highlighted information need not even be truly important or useful. By making normatively irrelevant or insignificant attributes salient, marketers both draw attention to those attributes and divert attention from more important ones.[22]

Another common feature of human perception and decision-making is *reference-dependence*. People's perceptions and assessments are strongly affected by context, and are

Theorems and Applications, 12 Bell J. Econ. 380 (1981). For a literature review, see David Dranove & Ginger Zhe Jin, *Quality Disclosure and Certification: Theory and Practice*, 48 J. Econ. Lit. 935 (2010).

17. *See generally supra* pp. 24, 135, 172; *infra* pp. 470, 475.

18. For a survey of the literature and new empirical evidence, see Nikolos Gurney & George Loewenstein, *Filling in the Blanks: What Customers Assume about Potentially Valuable but Missing Information* (working paper, Oct. 2017, *available at*: https://ssrn.com/abstract=3050641).

19. Ginger Zhe Jin, Michael Luca & Daniel Martin, *Is No News (Perceived as) Bad News? An Experimental Investigation of Information Disclosure* (working paper, Aug. 2016, *available at*: https://ssrn.com/abstract=2591450).

20. *See, e.g.*, Jacob Jacoby, Donald E. Speller & Carol Kohn Berning, *Brand Choice Behavior as a Function of Information Load: Replication and Extension*, 1 J. Consumer Res. 33 (1974); Kevin Lane Keller & Richard Staelin, *Effects of Quality and Quantity of Information on Decision Effectiveness*, 14 J. Consumer Res. 200 (1987); Ellen Peters et al., *Less Is More in Presenting Quality Information to Consumers*, 64 Med. Care Res. & Rev. 169 (2007); Russell Korobkin, *Bounded Rationality, Standard Form Contracts, and Unconscionability*, 70 U. Chi. L. Rev. 1203, 1222–25 (2003); Lauren E. Willis, *Decisionmaking and the Limits of Disclosure: The Problem of Predatory Lending: Price*, 65 Md. L. Rev. 707, 767–68 (2006).

21. Richard Craswell, *Taking Information Seriously: Misrepresentation and Nondisclosure in Contract Law and Elsewhere*, 92 Va. L. Rev. 565, 583–86 (2006) (discussing the issue in the context of disclosure duties).

22. On various effects of irrelevant information on consumer decision-making, see generally Barbara Loken, *Consumer Psychology: Categorization, Inferences, Affect, and Persuasion*, 57 Ann. Rev. Psychol. 453, 461 (2006).

typically comparative in nature, rather than context-independent or reflecting absolute measures.[23] Knowing that, firms sometimes influence consumer decisions by presenting information in comparative terms. For example, a cigarette manufacturer whose cigarettes contain comparatively less tar, or a mayonnaise manufacturer whose product contains less fat, would likely emphasize these facts, rather than the absolute amount of tar or fat in their products—which may still be rather high.[24] Moreover, when a firm presents a favorable comparison between a particular product of theirs and that of a competitor, consumers may draw false halo implications about the relative superiority of the firm's other products, as well.[25]

Different *framings* of the same information may produce different reactions by consumers.[26] For example, in several experiments, Irwin Levin and his coauthors presented subjects with positive and negative framings of the same information. They found that describing a product's attributes in a positive light (e.g., labeling ground beef as "75% lean") increased the likelihood of its purchase compared to describing it in negative terms ("25% fat")—although the two descriptions were substantively identical.[27] Interestingly, the positive framing not only increased the likelihood of purchase, but also (albeit to a lesser extent) the ex-post rating of the product's quality when it was actually consumed.[28]

To take another example, the statement that a car's fuel consumption is 8 kilometers per liter (KPL) is equivalent to the statement that its consumption is 12.5 liters per 100 kilometers. However, the two framings may lead to different choices. Compare the following two choice tasks. In the first, a consumer can choose between two very similar cars—the only difference being that the fuel consumption of the more expensive car is 12 KPL, while that of the cheaper one is 8 KPL. In the second task, the only difference is that the fuel consumption of the expensive car is 40 KPL, while that of the cheaper is 20 KPL. Which difference is larger, and should thus have a greater impact on the purchase decision? The intuitive—but wrong—answer is that the difference is larger in the second choice task. The correct answer is that it is larger in the first one. While opting for the cheaper car in the first choice task means saving the cost of more than four liters of gasoline per each 100 KM of driving one's car (12.5 minus 8.33), the saving in the second choice is only 2.5 liters per 100 KM (5 minus 2.5). The source of the error is that people tend to treat both measures—KPL

23. *See generally supra* pp. 42–57, 76–86.

24. *Cf.* Craswell, *supra* note 21, at 588–89.

25. Cornelia Penchmann, *Do Consumers Overgeneralize One-Sided Comparative Price Claims, and Are More Stringent Regulations Needed?*, 33 J. MARKETING RES. 150 (1996).

26. Here we focus on the framing of non-price information. On price framing, see *infra* pp. 294–96. On framing effects in general, see *supra* pp. 46–48.

27. Irwin P. Levin et al., *Framing Effects in Judgment Tasks with Varying Amounts of Information*, 36 ORG. BEHAV. & HUM. DECISION PROCESSES 362 (1985).

28. Irwin P. Levin & Gary J. Gaeth, *How Consumers are Affected by the Framing of Attribute Information Before and After Consuming the Product*, 15 J. CONSUMER RES. 374 (1988). *See also* Irwin P. Levin, Sandra L. Schneider & Gary J. Gaeth, *All Frames Are Not Created Equal: A Typology and Critical Analysis of Framing Effects*, 76 ORG. BEHAV. & HUM. DECISION PROCESSES 149, 158–67 (1998) (reviewing the literature on attribute framing).

and liters per 100 KM—as linearly related to fuel consumption, whereas the relationship between KPL and fuel consumption is actually curvilinear.[29] Requiring car manufacturers to indicate fuel consumption in liters per 100 KM, rather than KPL, may therefore improve consumer decision-making.

Finally, the *timing* of receiving the various pieces of information may also affect consumer decision-making. Generally speaking, the earlier a piece of information is conveyed to a consumer, the more it is likely to affect her choices. As the decision process progresses, consumers tend to narrow the scope of options they consider (using the *elimination-by-aspect* method as a simplifying technique);[30] hence they are likely to disregard information relating to options that they have already rejected. By the same token, as the inclination toward a particular option strengthens, consumers tend to pay more attention to information in support of that option, and to dismiss, or pay less attention to, information that militates against it. The confirmation bias, escalation of commitment, and the desire to avoid cognitive dissonance—all reinforce this phenomenon.[31]

All these findings are as crucial to policymakers as they are to marketers. However, while firms have always had a strong incentive to take the behavioral insights into account to maximize their profits, regulators have been much slower in internalizing them. Some disclosure duties—more so in the past, but to a considerable extent at present too—require suppliers to provide customers with a huge amount of information without ensuring that the information is provided in a comprehensible, concise, easy-to-compare, and timely fashion. In recent years, behavioral insights play a growing role in the design of disclosure duties—yet many remain skeptical about their effectiveness, relative to other regulatory means.[32]

3. Limited Availability

A common feature of sale promotions is that they are limited to a certain (often rather short) period, to a certain number of items, "while stocks last," etc.[33] Thus, one study reported that over 99 percent of coupons have an expiration date.[34] These limitations serve

29. T.M. Schouten, J. W. Bolderdijk & L. Steg, *Framing Car Fuel Efficiency: Linearity Heuristic for Fuel Consumption and Fuel-Efficiency Ratings*, 7 ENERGY EFFICIENCY 891 (2014).

30. *See supra* pp. 246–47.

31. On these phenomena, see generally *supra* pp. 58–61 and 56–58. On other marketing techniques that exploit these phenomena, see *infra* pp. 290–92, 304.

32. *See supra* pp. 171–77; *infra* pp. 314–18.

33. For a broader economic and behavioral analysis of sales promotions, see Scott A. Neslin, *Sales Promotion, in* HANDBOOK OF MARKETING, *supra* note 11, at 310.

34. J. Jeffrey Inman & Leigh McAlister, *Do Coupon Expiration Dates Affect Human Behavior?* 31 J. MARKETING RES. 423, 423 (1994). *See also* Daniel J. Howard, Suzanne B. Shu & Roger A. Kerin, *Reference Price and Scarcity Appeals and the Use of Multiple Influence Strategies in Retail Newspaper Advertising*, 2 SOC. INFLUENCE 18 (2007). Sale promotions may phrase such limitations and other aspects of the offer with greater or lesser precision, and may explicitly or implicitly subject them to the seller's discretion. On the impact of different formulations on customers' perceptions, see Soo-Jiuan Tan & Seow Hwang Chua, *"While Stocks Last!" Impact of Framing on Consumers' Perception of Sales Promotions*, 21 J. CONSUMER MARKETING 343 (2004).

various purposes, such as limiting the seller's financial liability, allowing for stock planning, and facilitating price discrimination (selling products to price-sensitive customers during sales periods, and charging other customers higher prices at other times).

Other explanations for these limitations are rooted in consumer psychology. One type of explanations concerns the broader phenomenon of scarcity or unavailability, and its effect on the desirability of objects. These explanations view time and quantity limitations of sale promotions as similar to other means of enhancing the subjective value of objects by increasing their scarcity—such as limits on the amount produced ("limited edition"), delays in provision, prestige pricing, and restricted maximum order size.[35] Some of the scarcity-related explanations—such as the perceived correlation between unavailability and quality or prestige[36]—are not necessarily relevant to sale promotions. Others, such as the physiological arousal resulting from the difficulty of attaining something, are relevant in some instances.[37]

Another explanation for time and quantity limitations in sale promotions is loss aversion: while customers plausibly view price reduction as a gain, missing the opportunity to attain this gain is likely perceived as a loss.[38] A consumer—who might not have bought the goods or services in question otherwise—might decide to buy them, or buy them in a larger quantity, both because the discount makes them more attractive and because she is afraid to miss out on the special offer. Such a missed opportunity is expected to cause regret.[39]

Accordingly, a large-scale study of newspaper retail advertisements found that cues of limited availability were used more frequently than reference pricing, and were strongly associated with the use of reference pricing.[40] In the same vein, an experimental study found that time-limited promotions were more effective than time-independent promotions in dissuading subjects from continuing to search for a better deal, as well as enhancing their willingness to buy, and making them view the deal more favorably.[41] Another experimental study found that scarcity signals significantly enhance the impact of price discounts and quality praises on the likelihood of purchase.[42] It has also been demonstrated empirically

35. *See generally* Michael Lynn, *Scarcity Effects on Value: A Quantitative Review of the Commodity Theory Literature,* 8 PSYCHOL. & MARKETING 45 (1991); Michael Lynn, *The Psychology of Unavailability: Explaining Scarcity and Cost Effects on Value,* 13 BASIC & APPLIED SOC. PSYCHOL. 3 (1992) [hereinafter Lynn, *Unavailability*]; Heribert Gierl, Michael Plantsch & Janine Schweidler, *Scarcity Effects on Sales Volume in Retail,* 18 INT'L REV. RETAIL, DISTRIBUTION & CONSUMER RES. 45 (2008); CIALDINI, *supra* note 13, at 198–226.

36. Michael Lynn, *Scarcity's Enhancement of Desirability: The Role of Naive Economic Theories,* 13 BASIC & APPLIED SOC. PSYCHOL. 67 (1992).

37. Jack W. Brehm & Rex A. Wright, *Perceived Difficulty, Energization, and the Magnitude of Goal Valence,* 19 J. EXPERIMENTAL SOC. PSYCHOL. 21 (1983); Lynn, *Unavailability, supra* note 35, at 4.

38. Howard, Shu & Kerin, *supra* note 34.

39. Inman & McAlister, *supra* note 34. On regret, see also *infra* pp. 505–07.

40. Howard, Shu & Kerin, *supra* note 34.

41. Praveen Aggarwal & Rajiv Vaidyanathan, *Use It or Lose It: Purchase Acceleration Effects of Time-Limited Promotions,* 2 J. CONSUMER BEHAV. 393, 397–99 (2003).

42. Gierl, Plantsch & Schweidler, *supra* note 35, at 57–58.

that, unlike time-independent promotions, time-limited promotions hasten purchase decisions.[43] The importance of the concern over losing an opportunity has also been established in an empirical study of the time patterns of coupon redemption. While in the absence of an expiration date, redemption rates drop steadily over time,[44] when coupons do have an expiration date, redemption rates rise considerably just before the expiration date.[45]

Limited availability is also a common marketing strategy in the fashion industry. Some fashion companies—who sell only their own private label in their own stores—purposely limit product availability by using a very short renewal cycle and limited supply, with a view to having their stock totally sold out within a couple of weeks.[46] Once an item is sold out, it cannot be purchased anywhere else or at any other time. Knowing this, shoppers make quick buying decisions. They also tend to take possession of items and carry them around while shopping, even if they are unsure as to whether they will eventually buy them—a phenomenon known as "in-store hoarding."[47] A field study has found that the primary motivation for such in-store hoarding is the perceived scarcity of the merchandise.[48] Once shoppers take possession of an item, the likelihood of their buying it increases—not only because of their concern about losing the opportunity of buying it in the future, but also because of the endowment effect.[49]

Limited availability may be the byproduct of ordinary marketing, but may also be strategically manipulated. To trigger loss aversion and expected regret in consumers, suppliers often create the false impression that if a certain item is not purchased soon, it will no longer be available, or will not be available on equally favorable terms,[50] or that they are about to shut down. Some of the aforementioned marketing techniques, such as very short renewal cycles, may seem legitimate in a market economy, and even create value for consumers, for example by fulfilling their desire for uniqueness.[51] Other techniques, however—especially those involving misinformation—are less legitimate. Accordingly, the EU Directive on Unfair Commercial Practices characterizes as unfair and misleading the practice of "[f]alsely stating that a product will only be available for a very limited time, or

43. Aggarwal & Vaidyanathan, *supra* note 41, at 394–97.

44. Ronald Ward & James Davis, *Coupon Redemption*, 18(4) J. Advertising Res. 51 (1978).

45. Inman & McAlister, *supra* note 34.

46. Sang-Eun Byun & Brenda Sternquist, *Here Today, Gone Tomorrow: Consumer Reactions to Perceived Limited Availability*, 20 J. Marketing Theory & Practice 223 (2012).

47. Sang-Eun Byun & Brenda Sternquist, *The Antecedents of In-Store Hoarding: Measurement and Application in the Fast Fashion Retail Environment*, 18 Int'l Rev. Retail, Distribution & Consumer Res. 133, 133 (2008).

48. *Id.* at 140–44.

49. Byun & Sternquist, *supra* note 46. On the endowment effect, see *supra* pp. 50–56, 209–13.

50. Cialdini, *supra* note 13, at 198–204; *see also* Donald C. Langevoort, *Selling Hope, Selling Risk: Some Lessons for Law from Behavioral Economics about Stockbrokers and Sophisticated Customers*, 84 Cal. L. Rev. 627, 652–53 (1996) (discussing investment broker techniques).

51. C.R. Snyder, *Product Scarcity by Need for Uniqueness Interaction: A Consumer Catch-22 Carousel?*, 13 Basic & Applied Soc. Psychol. 9 (1992).

that it will only be available on particular terms for a very limited time, in order to elicit an immediate decision and deprive consumers of sufficient opportunity or time to make an informed choice."[52]

4. *Low-Ball* and *Bait-and-Switch* Techniques

Contrary to expected utility theory, which posits that when choosing between different courses of action, only future costs and benefits should be taken into account, a host of studies have demonstrated that very often, people do not disregard *sunk costs* in their decisions. On the contrary—they tend to persist in endeavors the more resources, time, or efforts they have already invested in them.[53] A well-known marketing practice that exploits this phenomenon is the so-called *low-ball technique*. To persuade a customer to buy something, the salesperson initially understates the price. Once the customer agrees to the deal, the true, higher price is revealed. This may be done, for example, by explaining that the original price did not include certain elements of the transaction, or by "failing" to obtain a supervisor's approval of the special price.[54] A related marketing tactic is *bait-and-switch*: attracting customers by advertising an especially tempting offer on a certain product, and then persuading them to purchase another, more expensive product instead.[55] These techniques deliberately manipulate consumer decision-making and often involve false representations. Hence they call for regulatory attention. For example, both the U.S. Code of Federal Regulation and the EU Directive on Unfair Commercial Practices proscribe the bait-and-switch technique.[56]

5. Lenient Return Policies

Consumers often lack information about the product they purchase, the contract terms, and even their own needs. One seemingly attractive solution for this information problem (and for other difficulties—such as that of proving that the purchased object does not conform with verbal presentations made by a salesperson), is a *trial* or *cooling-off period*—a period in which consumers may retract the transaction and get their money back, or at least a store credit, without having to establish a flaw in the contracting process or a breach by the supplier. In many countries, including the United States, such lenient return policies

52. Item 7 of Annex I of Directive 2005/29/EC on Unfair Business-to-Consumer Commercial Practices in the Internal Market (2005). *See also* Item 15 of the same Annex, pertaining to the trader's false claim that it is about to close down, when it is not.

53. *See generally supra* pp. 56–57.

54. Robert B. Cialdini et al., *Low-Ball Procedure for Producing Compliance: Commitment then Cost*, 36 J. PERSONALITY & SOC. PSYCHOL. 463 (1978); Shmuel I. Becher, *Behavioral Science and Consumer Standard Form Contracts*, 68 LA. L. REV. 117, 133–35 (2007).

55. Edward P. Lazear, *Bait and Switch*, 103 J. POL. ECON. 813 (1995); William L. Wilkie, Carl F. Mela & Gregory T. Gundlach, *Does "Bait and Switch" Really Benefit Consumers?*, 17 MARKETING SCI. 273 (1998).

56. 16 C.F.R. § 238 (2016); Item 6 of Annex I of the European Directive on Unfair Commercial Practices, *supra* note 52.

are standard commercial practice.[57] A cooling-off period allows consumers an opportunity to carefully read the contract and calmly consider the desirability of the transaction. They can gain firsthand experience with the product, and learn whether it functions as expected and fits their needs. They may even examine alternative offers. A cooling-off period allows consumers to cancel the transaction when subsequent events (such as receiving a similar object as a gift from someone else) render it unnecessary or undesirable. Knowing that one can change one's mind makes the buying decision less stressful. A voluntary cooling-off period also signals that the seller is confident about the quality of her products.[58] In light of these advantages, many legal systems have established mandatory cooling-off periods for certain consumer transactions, or at least set them as the default rule unless an alternative return policy is clearly presented by the vendor.[59]

Lenient return policies have a considerable downside, however—namely, the gap between how customers perceive them ex ante, and the extent to which they make use of such policies ex post. At the contracting stage, the right to return the product and get a refund makes the buying decision considerably easier, as it appears to eliminate any potential regret. A liberal return policy may thus tip the scales in favor of buying a product that otherwise might not have been bought. It may even be perceived as rendering current decision-making unnecessary, as it postpones it to the point in time when the customer decides whether to keep the product or return it.

Once the transaction is made, however, and the consumer gets ownership and possession of the product, the likelihood that she would return the product decreases dramatically. One reason for this is practical. Sometimes, exercising the right proves to be more onerous than expected, due to requirements such as keeping the receipt and original packaging, and shipping the product back to the store (requirements that are usually specified in a standard-form contract that customers hardly ever read).[60]

Other important reasons for not exercising the right to return the product include the status quo and omission biases, and particularly the endowment effect.[61] Prior to the transaction, the endowment effect is irrelevant, as there is no endowment effect with regard to money or to goods held for exchange (such as commercial stock).[62] Once a consumer buys goods for her own use, an endowment effect may well ensue, resulting in the item being valued more highly by the consumer, and its return being framed as a loss.[63] In fact,

57. Omri Ben-Shahar & Eric Posner, *The Right to Withdraw in Contract Law,* 40 J. Legal Stud. 115, 120–21 (2011); Shmuel Becher & Tal Z. Zarsky, *Open Doors, Trap Doors and the Law*, 74 Law & Contemp. Probs. 63, 73 (2011).

58. Becher & Zarsky, *supra* note 57, at 65–70.

59. *Id.* at 70–73.

60. *See also infra* pp. 301–04.

61. On these phenomena, see generally *supra* pp. 48–56.

62. *See supra* p. 52.

63. Richard H. Thaler, *Toward a Positive Theory of Consumer Choice,* 1 J. Econ. Behav. & Org. 39, 45, 46 (1980); Smith & Nagel, *supra* note 87, at 101; Jon D. Hanson & Douglas A. Kysar, *Taking Behavioralism Seriously: The Problem of Market Manipulation*, 74 N.Y.U. L. Rev. 630, 733–34 (1999); Becher & Zarsky, *supra* note 57, at 77–80.

getting the item into the hands of the customer is a basic marketing technique. The endowment effect drastically reduces the likelihood of the object being returned—even if the costs of doing so are trivial. Similarly, once the consumer has bought a product, and she hesitates whether to return or keep it, she is likely to perceive the return of the product as actively changing the status quo, and keeping the product as a passive decision—or even as avoiding a decision altogether. Crucially, before they acquire an item, people underestimate how much they will value it once they do, and how powerful the omission bias may be.[64] Vendors can therefore offer free trials, money-back-guarantees, and similar arrangements to promote sales, in the full knowledge that, in practice, the return option will only rarely be exercised. This is plausibly the case in transactions involving services, as well—such as hotel reservations. As Shmuel Becher and Tal Zarsky point out, lenient return and cancelation policies that look like open doors may actually be trapdoors.[65]

These observations raise doubts about the desirability of lenient return policies and (mandatory or default) legal cooling-off periods. However, the normative implications of these observations are far from clear. On the one hand, knowing that the consumer might cancel the transaction may deter sellers from using inappropriate marketing techniques. On the other hand, when consumers know that they will be able to reconsider their purchase decision, while underestimating the power of inertia and their omission bias, they may be less circumspect at the time of purchase, and then keep the product despite being dissatisfied with it.[66] At the very least, contract terms that unreasonably raise the costs of exercising the return option appear to warrant regulation.[67]

C. Pricing

1. General

One of the issues, often *the* issue, which is of interest to consumers—and hence to consumer psychologists and behavioral economists—is price. In line with standard economic analysis, prices are highly affected by market competition.[68] According to rational choice theory, consumers make decisions based on the actual price they pay. However, numerous studies have shown that the perceived price upon which consumers base their decisions depends on a variety of variables apart from the actual price. The perceived price is affected

64. George Loewenstein & Daniel Adler, *A Bias in the Prediction of Tastes*, 105 ECON. J. 929 (1995).

65. Becher & Zarsky, *supra* note 57. As further described below (*infra* p. 305), rebates raise somewhat similar concerns.

66. A mandatory cooling-off period may appear to be desirable as it eliminates the (possibly misleading) signal by the voluntary cooling-off period that the seller is confident about the quality of the product (*see supra* note 58 and accompanying text). However, sellers may still create such a signal by offering an even more lenient return policy than the one mandated by law.

67. *See also* Jeff Sovern, *Toward a New Model of Consumer Protection: The Problem of Inflated Transaction Costs*, 47 WM. & MARY L. REV. 1635 (2006).

68. *See, e.g.*, Florencia Marotta-Wurgler, *Competition and the Quality of Standard Form Contracts: A Test Using Software License Agreements*, 5 J. EMPIRICAL LEGAL STUD. 447, 473 (2008).

by marketing techniques, including the framing of discounts and multiple discounts,[69] use of coupons and rebates, payment by a combination of currencies (such as cash and bonus points or Air Miles), temporal wording of prices (e.g., "only 60 cents a day"), mode of payment (cash or credit card), bundling of goods, the multiplicity and complexity of price attributes, and timing of payment. Price perceptions affect not only the decision whether to purchase a given product or service, but the subsequent use of the purchase as well (e.g., the moderating effect of bundling of goods on the sunk costs effect), and future purchase decisions.[70]

Sometimes, the decision to buy a product depends not only on the anticipated enjoyment from it (its *acquisition value*), but also on the satisfaction derived from having made a good bargain, or the dissatisfaction from an unprofitable one (the *transaction value*).[71] The transaction value depends, in part, on the perceived fairness of the price, which in turn depends, inter alia, on the seller's profit from the transaction (inasmuch as it is known to the buyer).[72]

Another discrepancy between standard economic analysis and behavioral findings pertains to the effect of prices on purchase decisions. This discrepancy stems from the fact that people sometimes use the heuristic of a positive correlation between a product's price and its quality—which, like other heuristics, is usually, but not invariably, sensible. Wealthier and less knowledgeable consumers tend to rely on this heuristic more than poorer and more knowledgeable ones. As a result, for the former group, price acceptability is not monotonically decreasing as prices go up, but rather bears an inverted U-shape. That is, prices are unacceptable when they are either higher than a certain (high) threshold or lower than a certain (low) threshold.[73]

More generally, while it is clear that psychological variables affect price perceptions and the attendant purchase decisions, the precise effects are far from being simple or straightforward. Experimental studies have sometimes produced conflicting results, and even widely used strategies—such as odd pricing (e.g., $9.99) and low introductory prices for new products—have varying short- and long-term effects on customers' decisions, depending on various factors.[74]

69. *See, e.g.*, Sunil Gupta & Lee G. Cooper, *The Discounting of Discounts and Promotion Thresholds*, 19 J. Consumer Res. 401 (1992).

70. For an overview, see Maggie Wenjing Liu & Dilip Soman, *Behavioral Pricing*, *in* Handbook of Consumer Psychology, *supra* note 6, at 659. On rebates, see also *infra* p. 305.

71. Dhruv Grewal, Kent B. Monroe & R. Krishnan, *The Effects of Price-Comparison Advertising on Buyers' Perceptions of Acquisition Value, Transaction Value, and Behavioral Intentions*, 62 J. Marketing 46 (1998).

72. Richard H. Thaler, *Mental Accounting and Consumer Choice*, 4 Marketing Sci. 199, 205–07 (1985).

73. For an overview, see Chezy Ofir & Russell S. Winer, *Pricing: Economic and Behavioral Models*, *in* Handbook of Marketing, *supra* note 11, at 267, 268–70. The heuristic that prices and quality are correlated also implies that sales promotions can either increase or decrease brand preferences, depending on the nature of the sales promotion and the promoted product. *See* Devon DelVecchio, David H. Henard & Traci H. Freling, *The Effect of Sales Promotion on Post-promotion Brand Preference: A Meta-analysis*, 82 J. Retailing 203, 203 (2006).

74. *See generally* Kent B. Monroe, Pricing: Making Profitable Decisions 101–251 (3d ed. 2003). On odd pricing, see *infra* pp. 299–301. On introductory prices, see Anthony Doob et al., *Effect of Initial Selling Price*

This section does not systematically survey this rich body of research. Rather, the following subsections focus on several pricing tactics that may be of particular interest from a legal perspective: price framing, multidimensional pricing, odd pricing, and deferred payments.

2. Price Framing

Standard economic analysis assumes that people determine the amount of money they are willing to pay (WTP) for a given good based on the utility they expect to derive from it, and that their valuation is at least relatively fixed and reference-independent. Experimental findings, however, suggest otherwise. In a series of experiments drawing on previous studies of the *anchoring effect*,[75] Dan Ariely, George Lowenstein, and Drazen Prelec have demonstrated that subjects' valuations of various goods were strongly influenced by arbitrary anchors.[76] In one experiment, subjects were first asked whether they would be willing to buy several products (e.g., a bottle of wine and a cordless keyboard) for a dollar figure equal to the last two digits of their social security number, and then to set their WTP for the product (being informed that, with some probability, a transaction would be carried out accordingly). It turned out that subjects in the top quintile of social security numbers were willing to pay more than twice, and sometimes more than three times, the amount that subjects in the bottom quintile were willing to pay.[77]

While the anchors in these experiments were evidently arbitrary, in real life consumers rely on more meaningful reference points in assessing prices and determining their WTP. Often, there is more than one possible reference point. Consumers usually have a general idea of what the ordinary price of a product or a category of products is (an *internal reference price*), but they are also influenced by stimuli such as the prices of comparable products displayed in the store, the manufacturer's suggested retail price (MSRP, or list price), and the proclaimed "regular price" in sales promotions. Empirical studies have found that both types of reference points—internal and external—affect purchase decisions.[78] Marketers can therefore influence consumer decisions by providing (accurate or inaccurate) information about the regular price. This tactic is especially effective when a consumer's ability to assess the true quality of a product is limited, so she is likely to use the high, "regular" price as an indication of its high quality.[79] Relatedly, marketers can influence purchase decisions

on Subsequent Sales, 11 J. PERSONALITY & SOC. PSYCHOL. 345 (1969) (describing field experiments showing that low introductory prices dramatically reduce sales when the promotion ends, and adversely affect sales in the long run).

75. *See generally supra* pp. 79–82.

76. Dan Ariely, George Loewenstein & Drazen Prelec, *"Coherent Arbitrariness": Stable Demand Curves without Stable Preferences,* 118 Q.J. ECON. 73 (2003).

77. *Id.* at 75–77.

78. Glenn E. Mayhew & Russell S. Winer, *An Empirical Analysis of Internal and External Reference Prices Using Scanner Data,* 19 J. CONSUMER RES. 62 (1992).

79. Tibor Scitovszky, *Some Consequences of the Habit of Judging Quality by Price,* 12 REV. ECON. STUD. 100 (1944).

by offering additional cheaper and costlier products in order to trigger the compromise and attraction effects.[80]

A meta-analysis of dozens of studies found that by advertising a reference price, marketers can enhance consumers' estimates of the ordinary price, increase their inclination to buy the product, and decrease their tendency to continue searching for another deal.[81] According to another large-scale meta-analysis, all else being equal, the more plausible a deal, the greater its effect on consumers' decisions.[82] However, the latter meta-analysis has found that "very large deal amounts, even if implausible, may still have a higher impact on perceived savings than lower deal amounts. For example, if the deal offers an implausible 80% savings through an exaggerated regular price, then perceived savings are higher versus a plausible 20% savings with a believable regular price."[83] In fact, the former meta-analysis found no relationship between the level of the advertised regular price and its believability,[84] making the possibility of deception about the regular price all the more tempting. In response to these concerns, the U.S. Code of Federal Regulation has established guidelines against deceptive advertising of price comparisons, as do regulations and guidelines of good practice in other countries.[85] However, the U.S. guidelines are rather vague, and have not been enforced by the Federal Trade Commission for decades.[86]

Suppliers' pricing practices exploit other behavioral insights as well. Besides the phenomenon that people perceive prices in relative, rather than absolute, terms, prospect theory suggests that consumers treat discounts and surcharges differently. While the two framings are economically equivalent, giving a cash discount seems more attractive than adding a surcharge for credit, since the former frames credit as entailing a forgone gain, rather than a loss.[87] For this reason, the difference between cash and credit prices is commonly presented as a cash discount rather than a credit surcharge.[88] The same is true of the framing of lunch versus dinner prices and "Happy Hour" prices that are common in restaurants and bars. By framing dinner and non-Happy-Hour prices as the reference point, restaurants and bars lead customers to think of themselves as either gainers (if they have lunch or buy drinks

80. *Id.*; Liu & Soman, *supra* note 70, at 670–72. On the compromise and attraction effects, see generally *supra* pp. 83–85.

81. Larry D. Compeau & Dhruv Grewal, *Comparative Price Advertising: An Integrative Review*, 17 J. PUB. POL'Y & MARKETING 257 (1998).

82. Aradhna Krishna et al., *A Meta-analysis of the Impact of Price Presentation on Perceived Savings*, 78 J. RETAILING 101 (2002).

83. *Id.* at 114.

84. Compeau & Grewal, *supra* note 81, at 263.

85. *See* 16 C.F.R. § 233 (2016) (United States); Competition Act, 1985 § 74.1(3) (Canada).

86. David Adam Friedman, *Reconsidering Fictitious Prices*, 100 MINN. L. REV. 921 (2016).

87. Thaler, *supra* note 63, at 45; ROBIN HOGARTH, JUDGEMENT AND CHOICE 104 (2d ed. 1987); Gerald E. Smith & Thomas T. Nagle, *Frames of Reference and Buyers' Perceptions of Price and Value*, 38 CAL. MGMT. REV. 98, 99–101 (1995).

88. Thaler, *supra* note 63, at 45.

during Happy Hour) or no-gainers (if they have dinner or buy drinks during other hours of the day)—but never as losers.

Small price reductions (such as 5 percent) do not significantly affect consumer buying decisions.[89] This finding is consistent with the diminishing sensitivity to increases in absolute payoffs.[90] Rather than giving larger discounts, some sellers offer buyers gifts: for example, instead of giving a 1 percent discount on an apartment, the seller may offer purchasers an expensive TV set whose market price is equivalent to such a discount. The superiority of gifts over small discounts plausibly stems from their different framing: since a gift is valued separately, receiving it is compared with not receiving it, rather than as a tiny decrease of a large loss. This may also be one of the underlying rationales of rebates: since they are paid to customers some time after the purchase, they are more likely to be framed separately, rather than merely as a small price reduction.[91] More generally, while expected utility theory suggests that only the dollar amount should affect a deal's attractiveness, empirical studies show that deal percentage has a greater impact on the perceived savings than absolute sums.[92]

Things get more complicated once one realizes that buying different items in different shops is often impracticable—hence a crucial decision is where to do one's shopping. Most consumers do not engage in comprehensive price comparisons between shops, but rather use simpler heuristics. Several studies compared two possible pricing tactics: frequent but shallow discounts (e.g., 20 percent discount on half of the items in the store, or on all items half of the time) versus deep but infrequent ones (e.g. 50 percent discount for one-fifth of the items or on all items for one-fifth of the time). Without going into detail, it appears that frequency is more influential when comparisons are more difficult to draw, due to the complexity of the pertinent information, whereas depth of discount is more influential when the information is simpler.[93] Either way, such heuristics may lead consumers to make suboptimal decisions.

The general picture emerging from this body of work represents rather bad news for traditional welfare economics. As Ariely, Lowenstein, and Prelec note, if consumers' WTP is highly manipulable or even arbitrary, then "market institutions that maximize consumer sovereignty need not maximize consumer welfare."[94] However, as further discussed below, designing a legal response to such challenges is a thorny task.[95]

89. *See, e.g.*, Albert J. Della Bitta & Kent B. Monroe, *A Multivariate Analysis of the Perception of Value from Retail Price Advertisements*, *in* 8 Advances in Consumer Res. 161–65 (Kent B. Monroe ed., 1980); Sunil Gupta & Lee G. Cooper, *The Discounting of Discounts and Promotion Thresholds*, 19 J. Consumer Res. 401 (1992).

90. *See generally supra* pp. 85–86.

91. Richard Thaler, *Mental Accounting Matters*, 12 J. Behav. Decision Making 183, 187 (1999). On rebates, see also *infra* p. 305. Diminishing sensitivity to increases in absolute payoffs also explains why—contrary to standard economic analysis—a consumer would make a certain effort to buy a product for $20 instead of $40 (thus saving $20), but not make a similar effort to buy a product for $2910 instead of $2940 (thereby saving $30).

92. Krishna et al., *supra* note 82, at 106–09.

93. *See, e.g.*, Joseph W. Alba et al., *The Effect of Discount Frequency and Depth on Consumer Price Judgments*, 26 J. Consumer Res. 99 (1999).

94. *See* Ariely, Loewenstein & Prelec, *supra* note 76, at 102.

95. *See infra* pp. 313–23.

3. Multidimensional and Complex Pricing

Many products, services, and contracts are inevitably complex: understanding them requires professional expertise, or at least substantial time and effort—both of which consumers generally lack. The resulting information problem may call for governmental intervention, for example by requiring suppliers to provide consumers with key information in a clear, concise, and easy-to-compare form, or by imposing minimal standards of quality and safety. We shall discuss these issues below.[96] In this section, we focus on instances where complexity is not inherent and inevitable, but rather avoidable, at least to some extent—and yet, suppliers choose to introduce more complexity than necessary, in order to exploit consumers' cognitive limitations and biases (of course, the line between inevitable and manipulated complexity may be blurred). Such exploitation is epitomized by multidimensional and complex price formulas, but may also pertain to other aspects of the transaction, such as the design of financial products[97] and legalistic contract clauses.[98] The following discussion thus applies, *mutatis mutandis*, to other types of complexity.

Oren Bar-Gill has examined the prevailing pricing schemes in three common and socially important types of contracts in the United States: credit cards, mortgages, and cellular phones.[99] He found that these schemes are extremely complex, comprising numerous fees, charges, and penalties—some of which are calculated by means of intricate formulas. For example, one component of the pricing in mortgage loans and credit cards (out of many) is the Adjustable Interest Rate, whereby the interest rate may change due to various triggers—some external, others fully or partly controlled by the lender. To calculate the expected cost of the credit, the borrower/cardholder should estimate the probability and magnitude of those changes, along with all other fees, charges, and penalties. However, accurate calculation requires computation skills that most people lack. "The imperfectly rational borrower deals with complexity by ignoring it. He simplifies his decision problem by overlooking nonsalient price dimensions. And he approximates, rather than calculates, the impact of the salient dimensions that cannot be ignored."[100] Consequently, borrowers and other consumers are often unable to come up with a single, total expected price that would enable them to compare between financial and other products available on the market,

96. *See infra* pp. 313–23.

97. *See, e.g.*, Claire Célérier & Boris Vallée, *Catering to Investors through Security Design: Headline Rate and Complexity*, 132 Q.J. ECON. 1469 (2017) (discussing complex securities issued to retail investors—products whose ex-post performance is lower but produce more profits for the issuing bank).

98. *See, e.g.*, Florencia Marotta-Wurgler & Robert Taylor, *Set in Stone: Change and Innovation in Consumer Standard-Form Contracts*, 88 N.Y.U. L. REV. 240, 253 (2013). This large-scale, empirical study of EULAs has found that from 2003 to 2010, their average length increased by 27 percent on average, and that according to a common measure of text difficulty, their readability was akin to that of articles in scientific journals.

99. BAR-GILL, *supra* note 5. For a critique of Bar-Gill's analysis of the credit-card market, see Joshua D. Wright, *Behavioral Law and Economics, Paternalism, and Consumer Contracts: An Empirical Perspective*, 2 N.Y.U. J.L. & LIBERTY 470 (2007). For a survey of comparable studies, see Michael D. Grubb, *Failing to Choose the Best Price: Theory, Evidence, and Policy*, 47 REV. INDUS. ORG. 303 (2015).

100. Oren Bar-Gill, *Consumer Transactions, in* THE OXFORD HANDBOOK OF BEHAVIORAL ECONOMICS AND THE LAW 465, 472 (Eyal Zamir & Doron Teichman eds., 2014). *See also* BAR-GILL, *supra* note 5, at 18–21.

and make a rational choice.[101] Aware of this difficulties, consumers often do not even try to search for the best price.[102]

To these observations, one may add that in estimating the effective cost of a loan, borrowers are vulnerable to cognitive biases, such as overoptimism (regarding their ability to repay the loan on time), and excessive trust in the lender.[103] Moreover, whereas consumers gain experience and expertise regarding transactions that they make on a regular basis, they are unlikely to gain such experience regarding infrequent, large-scale transactions, such as buying a house or purchasing life insurance. Finally, decisions about some transactions, such as payday loans, are taken under stressful conditions, or adversely affected by the customer's poverty and scarcity—factors that make accurate calculation of the transaction's cost all the more unlikely.[104]

Up to a point, multidimensional and adjustable prices are efficient, because they enable suppliers to tailor the initial transaction to the particular needs, abilities, and risks of each customer, and to adjust it to new, post-contracting information. Such tailoring reduces cross-subsidization between customers. Nonetheless, these considerations do not appear to fully explain "the staggering complexity" that consumers face.[105] Price complexity serves the supplier's interests because it hides the true cost of the transaction from the customer. Unsurprisingly, regulators around the world have reacted to this behavioral market failure by imposing (sometimes behaviorally informed) disclosure duties, requiring suppliers to simplify their pricing schemes, or banning certain pricing schemes altogether.[106]

For example, until 2008, in Israel banks used to collect hundreds of different fees for their services, many of which were practically hidden. Then, in a comprehensive reform, the Israeli Supervisor of Banks instructed the banks to drastically reduce the number of fees by unifying many of them and abolishing dozens. The reform applied to services provided to households and small businesses. An empirical study has found that as a result of this reform, the total fees for basic current account services declined at a nominal rate of 10 percent on average (and at a real rate of about 15 percent).[107]

101. *See, e.g.*, Ronald J. Mann & Jim Hawkins, *Just until Payday*, 54 UCLA L. REV. 855, 881–83 (2007) (discussing payday loans and other sources of consumer credit).

102. Grubb, *supra* note 99, at 305–08.

103. On these phenomena, see *supra* pp. 61–64, 276. Overoptimism about one's ability to repay one's loans on time, and its adverse social ramifications, characterize simpler loan contracts as well. *See* Paige Marta Skiba, *Regulation of Payday Loans: Misguided?*, 69 WASH. & LEE L. REV. 1023 (2012).

104. On the demographics of payday-loan customers, see Edward C. Lawrence & Gregory Elliehausen, *A Comparative Analysis of Payday Loan Customers,* 26 CONTEMP. ECON. POL'Y 299 (2008). On the effect of scarcity on decision-making, see generally *infra* pp. 483–85.

105. Bar-Gill, *supra* note 100, at 472.

106. *See also infra* pp. 315, 320–21.

107. AMIR BACHAR, BANK SERVICES CONTRACTS—REGULATION OF INFORMATION AND CONTENT 91–119, 222–32 (unpublished doctoral dissertation, Hebrew University of Jerusalem, 2012, in Hebrew). *See also* RUTH PLATO-SHINAR, BANKING REGULATION IN ISRAEL: PRUDENTIAL REGULATION VERSUS CONSUMER PROTECTION 143–46 (2016).

4. Deferred and Contingent Payments

Another common marketing technique, which aims at reducing the *perceived* price and is often used in conjunction with complex pricing, is deferred and contingent charges. One common example involves capital products (such as printers and cars) that are used with consumable products (such as ink cartridges), or may require periodic repairs and the use of replacement parts (as in the case of cars). To the extent that manufacturers of a capital product can technologically and legally compel buyers to buy the consumables or replacements from them (which is *not* always the case, due to the existence of competitors and anti-tying rules), they can enhance their profits by selling the capital product at or below its production cost, and overcharging for consumable and replacement products.[108] Further examples can be found in credit-card contracts (e.g., late-payment fees and foreign transaction fees) and airline contracts (e.g., cancelation fees).

To estimate the total cost of the transaction in such cases, the consumer must aggregate the immediate, certain payment and the expected cost of the contingent and deferred ones. However, while people accurately perceive immediate and certain costs, they tend to underestimate deferred and contingent ones. Deferred and contingent payments are considerably less salient, and their estimation is often biased by myopia (the hyperbolic discount of future costs) and overoptimism (with regard to the likelihood of events that trigger the deferred payments, such as a car breakdown and late payment).[109]

As in the case of complexity—which characterizes both the price and other aspects of the transaction—deferred and contingent costs may pertain not only to payments, but also to other aspects. For example, jurisdiction clauses may become operative only if the contract is breached and the parties resort to legal action—a contingency that the consumer may underestimate or disregard altogether.[110] Hence such clauses raise similar concerns.

5. Odd Pricing

Kenneth Manning and David Sprott conducted an experiment in which participants were presented with two pens, one somewhat better than the other, and were asked to choose which one to buy.[111] The participants were randomly allocated to one of four conditions, in which the prices of the two pens were as follows: A. $2.00 versus $2.99; B. $1.99 versus $3.00; C. $1.99 versus $2.99; and D. $2.00 versus $3.00.[112] Note, that the price differences in all conditions are almost identical, ranging from $0.99 to $1.01. However, if one focuses on the leftmost digit, the differences are large, ranging from no difference at all (in condition A) to three times higher (in condition B). As expected, the proportion of participants

108. *See also infra* pp. 381–83.

109. Bar-Gill, *supra* note 5, at 21–23, 81–91, 156–58. On myopia and overoptimism, see generally *supra* pp. 88–93 and 61–64, respectively.

110. *See also infra* p. 304.

111. Kenneth C. Manning & David E. Sprott, *Price Endings, Left-Digit Effects, and Choice,* 36 J. Consumer Res. 328 (2009).

112. In keeping with prevailing practice, the cents in the prices were indicated in superscript, as shown.

choosing the lower-priced pen was the smallest in condition A (56 percent) and largest in condition B (82 percent), with no statistically significant difference between conditions C and D (70 percent and 69 percent, respectively).

These results dramatically demonstrate the effectiveness of setting prices just below a round number, such as $199 or €9.98.[113] Other controlled experiments, including field experiments, have shown that such pricing does indeed increase sales.[114] Marketers have not waited for such demonstrations: they have been using this marketing technique—somewhat oddly known as *odd pricing*—since the nineteenth century.[115] Thus, according to a sample survey conducted in New Zealand, about 61 percent of advertised prices ended with the digit 9, 29 percent ended with 5, and 8 percent with 0—the remaining seven digits accounting for about 3 percent.[116]

While the prevalence of electronic registers and credit cards reduce the administrative costs of odd pricing, setting prices in whole numbers was certainly simpler and cheaper in the past—and still is when consumers pay in cash. Sellers' willingness to bear these costs means that odd pricing does convey a marketing advantage. It has been suggested that when people assess the meaning of numbers, they spontaneously map them onto an internal magnitude scale. Given the logic of the decimal numerical system, the processing is done from left to right, and people sensibly pay more attention to the leftmost digit. Hence, the *perceived* difference between 99 and 100 is larger than between, say, 98 and 99, as the latter two numbers share the same left digit.[117]

Sometimes, marketers set prices that end with units of payment that are no longer in use, or never have been. For example, in gasoline stations in the United States, the price per gallon usually ends with $^{9}/_{10}$ cent, despite the fact that whole cents are the smallest denomination. In Israel, until recently suppliers used to set prices with nine *agorot* (the New Shekel is divided into 100 *agorot*), despite the fact that the production of the 1- and 5-*agorot* coins was stopped years ago—hence the smallest coin in use is of 10 *agorot*. This meant that when buyers paid cash, prices were routinely rounded (upward, in the case of four or fewer items).

113. For a survey of the rich literature on odd pricing, see, e.g., E.S. Asamoah & M. Chovancová, *The Influence of Price Endings on Consumer Behavior: An Application of the Psychology of Perception*, 39 ACTA UNIVERSITATIS AGRICULTURAE ET SILVICULTURAE MENDELIANAE BRUNENSIS 29 (2011).

114. *See, e.g.*, Robert M. Schindler & Thomas M. Kibarian, *Increased Consumer Sales Response Though Use of 99-Ending Prices*, 72 J. RETAILING 187 (1996); Eric Anderson & Duncan Simester, *Effects of $9 Price Endings on Retail Sales: Evidence from Field Experiments*, 1 QUANTITATIVE MARKETING & ECON. 93.

115. *See, e.g.*, Robert M. Schindler & Alan R. Wiman, *Effects of Odd Pricing on Price Recall*, 19 J. BUS. RES. 165, 165 (1989).

116. Judith Holdershaw, Philip Gendall & Ron Garland, *The Widespread Use of Odd Pricing in the Retail Sector*, 8 MARKETING BULL. 53 (1997). For comparable findings elsewhere, see MONROE, *supra* note 74, at 106–07.

117. Manoj Thomas & Vicki Morwitz, *Penny Wise and Pound Foolish: The Left-Digit Effect in Price Cognition*, 32 J. CONSUMER RES. 55 (2005). For additional explanations, see, e.g., Robert M. Schindler & Patrick N. Kirby, *Patterns of Rightmost Digits Used in Advertised Prices: Implications for Nine-Ending Effects*. 24 J. CONSUMER RES. 192 (1997).

To the extent that odd pricing induces increased consumption, it arguably works against consumers' long-term interests, because it decreases savings.[118] Nevertheless, banning this marketing practice raises difficult policy issues, and at any rate, does not appear to be politically feasible due to strong expected opposition from suppliers. Banning the use of prices denominated in units that are not in use, with regard to consumer goods—without banning odd pricing altogether—may be less justifiable, but perhaps more politically feasible.[119] However, such legislation is unlikely to eliminate odd pricing entirely, but only prompt the use of odd pricing with the smallest units in circulation.[120]

D. Non-salient Contract Clauses

While marketing techniques, including pricing, have drawn considerable attention from legal scholars in recent years, jurists have long paid much more attention to another aspect of consumer contracts, namely the content and validity of the "fine print" or "invisible terms" in standard-form contracts.[121] Legal norms ordinarily come into play when a dispute arises and the parties fail to resolve it amicably. When that happens, the parties rely on their legal rights. Specifically, suppliers often rely on the one-sided terms they have unilaterally included in their standard-form contracts. A central task of the legal system is to determine the meaning and enforceability of those terms.

The ongoing debate about the validity of the fine-print clauses in standard-form contracts—that is, most clauses in the great majority of written contracts made nowadays—relates to facts, goals, and means. One of the basic factual disagreements has revolved around whether consumers (and other customers) read standard forms. While nobody has argued that all or most customers read standard-form contracts, one influential legal-economic theory has relied on the assumption that there is an *informed minority* of customers who do. According to the informed minority theory—which used to be a cornerstone of economic analysis of standard-form contracts—even if most customers do not read the fine print, it is enough that a minority of them do for sellers to provide all customers with terms that efficiently reflect the true preferences of both sellers and buyers.[122] Insofar as suppliers cannot

118. On the problem of insufficient saving for old age, see *supra* pp. 92–93, 180, 182–84; *infra* pp. 490–92.

119. Such a ban was introduced in Israel in 2013. For a critique, see Shmuel Becher, *We Demand the Penny by Hook or by Crook: Penny Wise, Dollar Foolish and Consumer Protection Legislation*, ONLINE ISR. J. LEGIS. (2015, in Hebrew).

120. For an empirical assessment of the effect of the abovementioned regulation on pricing practices in Israel, see Avichai Snir, Daniel Levy & Haipeng (Allan) Chen, *End of 9-Endings, Price Recall, and Price Perceptions*, 155 ECON. LETTERS 157 (2017).

121. Notable contributions to this immense literature include Friedrich Kessler, *Contracts of Adhesion—Some Thoughts about Freedom of Contract*, 43 COLUM. L. REV. 629 (1943); W. David Slawson, *Standard Form Contracts and Democratic Control of Lawmaking Power*, 84 HARV. L. REV. 529 (1971); Alan Schwartz & Louis L. Wilde, *Intervening in Markets on the Basis of Imperfect Information: A Legal and Economic Analysis*, 127 U. PA. L. REV. 630 (1979); Todd D. Rakoff, *Contracts of Adhesion: An Essay in Reconstruction*, 96 HARV. L. REV. 1174 (1983); MARGARET JANE RADIN, BOILERPLATE: THE FINE PRINT, VANISHING RIGHTS, AND THE RULE OF LAW (2013).

122. Schwartz & Wilde, *supra* note 121.

distinguish readers from nonreaders, catering to the preferences of the former benefits the latter—thus the minority creates a positive externality.

However, in line with most people's anecdotal impression, several recent empirical studies have demonstrated—first indirectly, then directly—that virtually no one reads standard-form contracts, even when it is particularly easy to do so (that is, when making a purchase online, in the comfort of one's home or office). One indirect piece of evidence has come from a large-scale empirical study of end-user licensing agreements (EULAs). It was found that while the EULAs varied considerably in terms of their pro-seller one-sidedness, there was no correlation between the one-sidedness and the product price (as one would expect in a competitive market, if buyers' willingness to pay were affected by the content of the contract).[123] Furthermore no correlation was found between the EULAs' one-sidedness and their pre-purchase accessibility: EULAs that customers could read prior to placing their order were as pro-seller as EULAs that were not accessible (suggesting that there is no informed minority in either case).[124] Finally, direct evidence has been provided by the analysis of a huge dataset that tracked the visits of tens of thousands of households to the websites of dozens of software retailers over a period of one month. Yannis Bakos, Florencia Marotta-Wurgler, and David Trossen found that fewer than two out of every thousand shoppers (0.2 percent) accessed the EULA page; and if one aggregates all visits of an individual user during the month in question, only about six out of every thousand (0.6 percent) did.[125] The very few shoppers who accessed the EULA page visited it for an average of about one minute, with a median of 32 seconds—meaning that they could not have read more than a very small portion of the agreement.[126] The current wisdom, therefore, even among legal economists, appears to be that customers do not read the fine print.[127]

Some of the reasons for not reading standard-form contracts are perfectly rational. There is no point in reading the fine print if all contracts look alike, no supplier is willing to open the pre-formulated terms for negotiation, and the content of the contract is unlikely to affect one's purchase decision anyway (for example, because the stakes are too low, or because the customer knows that regardless of what the contract might say, the

123. Florencia Marotta-Wurgler, *What's in a Standard Form Contract? An Empirical Analysis of Software License Agreements*, 4 J. EMPIRICAL LEGAL STUD. 677, 708, 711–12 (2007).

124. Marotta-Wurgler, *supra* note 3.

125. Yannis Bakos, Florencia Marotta-Wurgler & David R. Trossen, *Does Anyone Read the Fine Print? Consumer Attention to Standard-Form Contracts*, 43 J. LEGAL STUD. 1, 3, 16–17, 19–22 (2014). *See also* Victoria C. Plaut & Robert P. Bartlett, III, *Blind Consent? A Social Psychological Investigation of Non-readership of Click-through Agreements*, 36 LAW & HUM. BEHAV. 293, 295–298 (2012) (describing the self-reported habits of predominantly white college students with regard to the reading of online standard-form contracts).

126. For a critical review of these and comparable studies, see Eyal Zamir & Yuval Farkash, *Standard Form Contracts: Empirical Studies, Normative Implications, and the Fragmentation of Legal Scholarship*, 12 JERUSALEM REV. LEGAL STUD. 137, 138–55 (2015).

127. *See, e.g.*, OMRI BEN-SHAHAR & CARL E. SCHNEIDER, MORE THAN YOU WANTED TO KNOW: THE FAILURE OF MANDATED DISCLOSURE (2014); Ian Ayres & Alan Schwartz, *The No-Reading Problem in Consumer Contract Law*, 66 STAN. L. REV. 545 (2014).

supplier will treat her well).[128] These are all factual assumptions, whose validity may vary from one market to another. We do not know how true they are, as the empirical data about these issues is fairly limited.[129] A rational consumer who lacks reliable information about contracts' diversity, negotiability, or significance would weigh the costs (time and effort) of gathering this information against its benefits (the possibility that it might affect her contracting decision). Very often, the sensible conclusion is that the cost of acquiring reliable information exceeds its expected benefit—hence the rational thing to do is to proceed with the transaction under conditions of rational ignorance.[130] The longer and more complex the standard form, and the more it requires legal or other expertise to understand, the higher the costs of trying to decipher its meaning, and the more rational the decision to ignore it altogether.[131]

There are, however, additional, less rational, explanations for the no-reading phenomenon. If, due to their limited cognitive abilities, consumers use a selective, lexical, and non-compensatory decision strategy, such as *elimination by aspect*,[132] they are likely to focus on attributes such as the product's key characteristics, the manufacturer's reputation, and the price, while disregarding issues such as remedies for breach of contract or arbitration clauses. If the terms of the contract are unlikely to affect one's decision—why bother reading them, whatever the cost of reading?[133] When learning from experience, people tend to underweight rare events simply because they are rare. If not reading standard-form contracts had no adverse consequences on previous occasions, they would not read the next standard form even if it would be rational to do so given the *expected costs* of exploitative terms.[134] Additional reasons for not reading standard-form contracts are impatience and tediousness. Impatience plays a role, for example, when a customer downloads an application to her smartphone for immediate use, and reading the license agreement would delay using it.[135] Tediousness refers to the common trade-off between interest and importance: people

128. Plaut & Bartlett, *supra* note 125, at 295–99 (describing students' self-reported explanations for not reading online agreements).

129. Marotta-Wurgler's study has shown that in the end-user-software market, while there is considerable similarity between contracts in some respects, they vary much more than many commentators have assumed. *See* Marotta-Wurgler, *supra* note 123, at 702–03.

130. Robert A. Prentice, *Contract-Based Defenses in Securities Fraud Litigation: A Behavioral Analysis,* 2003 U. Ill. L. Rev. 337, 358–62.

131. This is yet another manifestation of how complexity serves suppliers' interests. *See supra* pp. 297–98 (specifically, *see supra* note 98 and accompanying text).

132. *See supra* pp. 246–47.

133. Korobkin, *supra* note 20, at 1233–34.

134. Yefim Roth, Michaela Wänke & Ido Erev, *Click or Skip: The Role of Experience in Easy-Click Checking Decisions,* 43 J. Consumer Res. 583 (2016).

135. *See generally* Stephen J. Hoch & George F. Loewenstein, *Time-Inconsistent Preferences and Consumer Self-Control,* 17 J. Consumer Res. 492 (1991).

may recommend others to read boring but important information, yet are less likely to follow this advice themselves.[136]

Moreover, suppliers usually present their standard-form contracts only at the end of the shopping process. By that time, the consumer may have already spent considerable time and energy in finding and selecting the product. According to rational choice theory, the consumer should disregard those sunk costs and decide whether to complete the transaction based on all pertinent factors, including the contract terms. However, a loss-averse consumer would hate to see the time and effort she has already spent as wasted, and might therefore avoid reading the contract, lest she finds it unacceptable.[137] Due to the confirmation bias, people tend to seek information that supports their decision and avoid information that might counter it, including disquieting contract terms.[138] Finally, when a consumer sees that all other consumers sign standard-form contracts without reading them, the conformity bias and herd effect reinforce her inclination to do the same.[139] Indeed, empirical evidence supports the conjecture that consumers are unlikely to pay much attention to information they receive at the final stage of contracting, or to be influenced by it if they do.[140]

Moreover, even if consumers somehow become aware of the content of unfavorable terms in the standard-form contract, this awareness is unlikely to affect their decisions.[141] Many of the "invisible" terms in standard-form contracts deal with uncertain contingencies, such as supervening circumstances, remedies for breach of contract, and dispute resolution. As in the case of deferred and uncertain payments, consumers are likely to underestimate chronologically remote and low-probability risks, due to overoptimism and myopia.[142] Moreover, even if, in reality, the probability of an untoward turn of events is fairly high, consumers may erroneously assume that it is low if they have never encountered it personally, due to the availability heuristic.[143]

As previously noted, there is an ongoing, heated debate over the appropriate legal treatment of one-sided clauses in standard-form contracts, and legal systems around the world do differ in this regard. We return to this issue in Section G below.

136. Rachel Barkan, Shai Danziger & Yaniv Shani, *Do as I Say, Not as I Do: Choice-Advice Differences in Decisions to Learn Information,* 125 J. ECON. BEHAV. & ORG. 57 (2016).

137. Becher, *supra* note 54, at 125–31; Doron Teichman, *Too Little, Too Much, Not Just Right: Behavioral Analysis and the Desirable Regulation of Consumer Contracts,* 9 JERUSALEM REV. LEGAL STUD. 52, 54–57 (2014). On escalation of commitment, see generally *supra* pp. 56–57.

138. Teichman, *supra* note 137, at 55. On the confirmation bias, see generally *supra* pp. 58–61.

139. *See also* Becher, *supra* note 54, at 132–33; Abhijit V. Banerjee, *A Simple Model of Herd Behavior*, 107 Q.J. ECON. 797 (1992); Yi-Fen Chen, *Herd Behavior in Purchasing Books Online*, 24 COMPUTERS HUM. BEHAV. 1977 (2008); *supra* pp. 68–69.

140. Jeff Sovern, *Preventing Future Economic Crises through Consumer Protection Law or How the Truth in Lending Act Failed the Subprime Borrowers*, 71 OHIO STATE L.J. 761, 779–86 (2010).

141. Korobkin, *supra* note 20, at 1234.

142. Becher, *supra* note 54, at 147–150. *See also supra* pp. 61–64, 88–93, 299.

143. Becher, *supra* note 54, at 144–47; Korobkin, *supra* note 20, at 1232–33. On availability, see generally *supra* pp. 34–36. For a list of further behavioral explanations of why people do not read standard-form contracts (and do not pay much attention to their content even if they do), see Prentice, *supra* note 130, at 362–78.

E. Post-contracting Behavior

The exploitation of consumers' cognitive biases by suppliers does not end at the contracting stage. Once a contract has been concluded—even more so once the consumer has received the purchased item or has started to receive the contracted services—the status quo and omission biases, as well as other cognitive phenomena, may kick in and powerfully affect consumer behavior.

One example of possible exploitation of consumers' omission bias and procrastination is rebates.[144] Rather than simply get a price reduction, rebates usually require customers to fill out a form, attach proof of purchase, and send them to the manufacturer. The combination of framing the rebate as a potential gain (rather than framing not-receiving-it as a loss), the omission bias, and people's tendency to procrastinate, results in a low percentage of rebate applications (although estimated rates vary markedly).[145] To reduce this percentage even further, some manufacturers purposefully make the process more onerous.[146] As in the case of lenient return policies, the gap between the ex-ante evaluation of the rebate and the limited exercise of this entitlement ex post—along with consumers' initial underappreciation of this gap—allows sellers to increase their profit at a relatively low cost by exploiting consumer biases.

Another example is the use of renewal clauses in periodic subscriptions and long-term service agreements, whereby the contract is automatically renewed unless the customer notifies the supplier that she is not interested in its renewal. Due to the powerful omission bias, such arrangements allow suppliers to greatly increase the rate of contract renewals, compared with opt-in arrangements. Often, suppliers strengthen the default effect by purposely raising the costs of opting out of the default. This may be done by setting burdensome formal and timing requirements for doing so. In response, some regulators have banned automatic renewal of long-term contracts, requiring instead a positive consent of the consumer for the contract's continuation.[147]

Finally, many long-term contracts authorize suppliers unilaterally to change the transaction terms, such as raising prices or changing cable-TV channel packages. Setting aside the question of why consumers agree to such terms in the first place,[148] one wonders why, when the supplier does introduce a detrimental change of the contract terms, consumers tend not to terminate the contract and switch to another supplier, even when they are free to do so. Sometimes the answer is that the costs of such a switch are higher than its benefits.

144. On the omission bias and procrastination, see generally *supra* pp. 48–50 and 87–88, respectively. While we discuss rebates in the context of post-contracting behavior, they are also a marketing technique and a pricing method—issues discussed in *supra* 283–92 and 292–301, respectively.

145. Sovern, *supra* note 67, at 1638.

146. *Id.* at 1640–41.

147. *See, e.g.*, Sec. 13A of the Israeli Consumer Protection Law, 1981 (as added in 2008). For a more lenient regulation of automatic renewals, see item (h) in the Annex to the European Directive 93/13/EEC on Unfair Terms in Consumer Contracts (1993).

148. On this question, see *supra* 301–04.

In some instances, however, the direct costs are rather low, and it is quite clear that the consumer would not have made the contract under the new terms. Plausibly, one key reason why consumers fail to switch to another supplier under such circumstances is their status quo and omission biases.[149] This tactic is akin to the low-ball technique discussed earlier. The general difficulties that characterize invisible terms in standard-form contracts and the specific effects of consumer status quo and omission bias, as well as numerous other phenomena (such as shortsightedness and possibly excessive trust in suppliers' decency), may warrant a legal response. This might include ex-ante regulation of unilateral-modification clauses,[150] and ex-post supervision of the actual use of those clauses through general doctrines, such as the duty to perform contracts in good faith, or specific ones.[151]

F. Market Solutions

1. General

The very existence of market failures—be they traditional (such as information problems and externalities) or behavioral (such as susceptibility to framing effects and the confirmation bias)—does not warrant legal intervention. Governmental regulation raises principled objections, and its benefits should always be weighed against its costs, including the costs of designing and implementing the regulation, policymakers' errors, and the perils of regulatory capture. The need for regulation should therefore be assessed in relation to alternative solutions, especially of the market-based variety.

Thus, for example, when considering how to deal with information problems, one must recall that in recent years, the internet—especially websites and blogs that provide expert and customer ratings and reviews of products and suppliers' practices—has emerged as a primary source of information.[152] The internet "facilitates the construction of communities in which users can both seek out knowledge and provide responses, while minimizing time and attention constraints. It also allows the quick retrieval of information previously conveyed within these circles."[153] A recent meta-analysis of twenty-six empirical studies examined the relative importance of several variables in this regard. It found that online product reviews have a significantly greater influence on sales elasticities when they are written by experts (compared to consumers) and when they appear on a non-seller website; and that the content of the reviews (positive or negative) has a greater

149. *See also* Becher, *supra* note 54, at 138–40. Here too, suppliers can exacerbate the problem by raising the costs of terminating the relationships.

150. *See, e.g.*, Sec. 308(4) of the German Civil Code; Sec. 4(4) of the Israeli Standard Contracts Law, 1982.

151. *See* Oren Bar-Gill & Kevin Davis, *Empty Promises*, 84 S. CAL. L. REV. 1 (2010).

152. Adam Thierer et al., *How the Internet, the Sharing Economy, and Reputational Feedback Mechanisms Solve the "Lemons Problem"*, 70 U. MIAMI L. REV. 830 (2016).

153. Shmuel I. Becher & Tal Z. Zarsky, *E-contract Doctrine 2.0: Standard Form Contracting in the Age of Online User Participation*, 14 MICH. TELECOM & TECH. L. REV. 303, 320, 327 (2008). *See also* Omri Ben-Shahar, *The Myth of the "Opportunity to Read" in Contract Law*, 5 EUR. REV. CONT. LAW 1, 33 (2009).

influence then their volume (although there is evidence that sometimes the volume is more influential).[154]

However, online reviews are no panacea. They provide valuable information about products' quality and suppliers' treatment of their customers, but do not necessarily solve other problems, such as consumers' failure to read standard-form contracts (which arguably eliminates suppliers' incentive to cater to consumers' preferences when drafting their standard forms). In theory, it is possible that even if consumers do not read standard-form contracts, they obtain information about the contract terms from other sources. But a theoretical possibility is not enough. In this regard, potential difficulties include: insufficient motivation to write reviews; too much information being presented in a non-user-friendly manner—resulting in information overload; contamination of consumer blogs by interested parties; and customers not visiting such sites or not skillfully using the information they provide. For example, Bakos, Marotta-Wurgler, and Trossen examined websites with information about software products, and found that very few purchasers visit them.[155] Another study has empirically examined the correlation between online product ratings in two websites (Epinions and Amazon), and contract one-sidedness.[156] While there was no statistically significant correlation between Epinions ratings and the one-sidedness of contracts, a statistically significant, *negative* correlation was found between Amazon's ratings and the contracts' bias: products with a more pro-seller contract tended to attract higher product ratings. It appears, therefore, that customers' product ratings do not convey useful information about contracts.

In addition to the existing market-based mechanisms, scholars have proposed new ones to overcome consumer market failures. One proposal, aimed at tackling the problem of unilateral modifications of contracts by suppliers, is to add so-called *Change Approval Boards* as parties to consumer contracts. Those CABs would supervise unilateral modifications in accordance with a predetermined policy, which the contracting parties would choose in advance.[157] Such proposals appeal to anyone opposing governmental interventions in the market. However, their feasibility and efficacy are questionable. The very fact that they do not yet exist may indicate that there is too little demand for them, or that the inherent difficulties of designing and operating them are not easily solvable.

Be that as it may, in this section we focus on more general and basic mechanisms that arguably obviate the need for a legal response to consumers' bounded rationality: market competition, and specifically, the power of reputation.

154. Kristopher Floyd et al., *How Online Product Reviews Affect Retail Sales: A Meta-analysis*, 90 J. Retailing 217 (2014).

155. Bakos, Marotta-Wurgler & Trossen, *supra* note 125, at 21–22 (finding that "out of the 131,729 sessions with at least two pages accessed, only three shoppers accessed pages with EULA information in consumer review sites," and that at the monthly level of aggregation, 16.8 percent "of visits accessed at least one of the 25 consumer sites, but not a single aspect of that activity was related to EULAs").

156. Nishanth V. Chari, *Disciplining Standard Form Contract Terms through Online Information Flows: An Empirical Study*, 85 N.Y.U. L. Rev. 1618 (2010).

157. Bar-Gill & Davis, *supra* note 151, at 36–41.

2. Competition

Several commentators have made the argument that even if people are vulnerable to widespread and systematic cognitive biases, there is no need for regulation, because in a functioning market, competition crowds out irrational behavior.[158] The basic argument goes like this: cognitive biases may lead consumers to either under- or overvalue products. In the first case, suppliers have a strong incentive to correct consumers' error, lest their products be driven out of the market. Even if such a correction may benefit competitors who sell comparable goods, firms can often overcome this difficulty by individuating their products; and knowledgeable consumers are likely to spread the word to their friends. In any event, such errors should not lead to exploitation of consumers by suppliers, but rather to a shutdown of the market in those products. An *overassessment* of a product's value due to cognitive biases will also not lead to an equilibrium in which suppliers exploit consumers. This is because (1) a Darwinian process of "survival of the fittest" will force people to learn from their mistakes; (2) knowledgeable consumers will share their information with other consumers; (3) competitors will draw consumers' attention to the fact that they overvalue their competitor's products; and (4) since consumers vary in their susceptibility to cognitive biases—and hence in their willingness to overpay for any given product—competition will push the price down to the competitive equilibrium (even if some consumers would have been willing to pay more for those products).

Indeed, the real challenge is posed by consumers' systematic overassessment of the value of products, rather than their underassessment. When we focus on the former, however, none of the aforementioned arguments appears to be compelling. As for the evolutionary argument, unlike firms—whose mistakes may drive them out of the market—boundedly rational consumers are unlikely to disappear (and the very long evolutionary process that has produced human heuristics and biases is unlikely to be undone in the short run).

The reliance on knowledgeable consumers is similarly doubtful. To date, empirical data does not support the assumption that there is an informed minority, at least not regarding some aspects of transactions.[159] If there is, it may be too small, or its members may lack sufficient incentive to share their knowledge reliably with others. Moreover, even if there is an informed and fully rational *majority* concerning certain aspects of a transaction, marketers may either target the *uninformed, cognitively bounded minority* (whom they would identify, for example, by means of demographic variables), or alternatively target the general population through low-cost marketing mechanisms, such as spam email, or transact with those who fall prey to cognitive biases.[160]

158. *See, e.g.*, Richard A. Epstein, *Behavioral Economics: Human Errors and Market Corrections*, 73 U. CHI. L. REV. 111, 118–32 (2006); Fred S. McChesney, *Behavioral Economics: Old Wine in Irrelevant New Bottles?*, 21 S. CT. ECON. REV. 43, 58, 61–66 (2013).

159. *See supra* pp. 301–04.

160. Jeffrey J. Rachlinski, *Cognitive Errors, Individual Differences, and Paternalism*, 73 U. CHI. L. REV. 207, 226–29 (2006).

By the same token, while firms occasionally expose the shortcomings of competitors' products, or the one-sidedness of their standard forms,[161] in most cases they do not. Tarnishing one's competitors, their products, or their contract terms may be overly risky, or even counterproductive. By drawing consumers' attention to products' flaws or risks that they had not previously paid attention to, such a strategy may also decrease the demand for the attacker's products.[162] Consumers may be suspicious of the critique, on the assumption that the competitor does not really care about their welfare but is merely trying to increase its own sales, and may even view such a practice as unfair.[163] Moreover, criticizing one's competitors may also trigger harmful retaliation by them.[164] Finally, criticizing one's competitors may be wasteful, inasmuch as consumers may not respond to the new information—and even if they do, the benefits of the critique are likely to be shared by other firms as well, thus creating a *free-rider* problem characteristic of positive externalities.[165]

Indeed, with regard to non-salient contract clauses, the available empirical data shows that—in the context of EULAs, at least—there is no correlation between the one-sidedness of contracts and product prices, or between contract one-sidedness and market competition.[166] More generally, notwithstanding the undeniable heterogeneity of consumers, as long as consumer errors lie mostly in the same direction, they are likely to yield a different equilibrium than the one expected in a fully competitive market with no cognitive biases.

Market competition is not only unlikely to reduce exploitation of consumer biases—in all likelihood it intensifies it. Fully rational consumers make their purchase decisions based on the expected benefit from a transaction and the expected price (both of which may be multidimensional). Under this assumption, competition induces suppliers to cater to consumer's preferences by offering the most attractive combinations of benefit and price. In contrast, boundedly rational consumers make their decisions based on the *perceived* expected benefit and the *perceived* expected price—which, according to the studies described in the preceding sections, may systematically differ from the actual ones. Under this assumption, rational suppliers are incentivized to offer the most attractive combinations of *perceived* benefits and prices—otherwise, they stand to lose business, revenue, and profits. When some firms successfully exploit consumer systematic biases, firms that would refrain

161. David Gilo & Ariel Porat, *Viewing Unconscionability through a Market Lens*, 52 Wm. & Mary L. Rev. 133, 163–67 (2010).

162. Xavier Gabaix & David Laibson, *Shrouded Attributes, Consumer Myopia, and Information Suppression in Competitive Markets*, 121 Q.J. Econ. 505 (2006) (analyzing the equilibrium in markets for products with hidden add-on prices); John Y. Campbell, *Household Finance*, 61 J. Fin. 1553, 1585–89 (2006) (discussing the issue in the context of retail financial markets); Gilo & Porat, *supra* note 161, at 170–72.

163. *See, e.g.*, Alina B. Sorescu & Betsy D. Gelb, *Negative Comparative Advertising: Evidence Favoring Fine-Tuning*, 29 J. Advertising 25 (2000).

164. Ming-Jer Chen & Danny Miller, *Competitive Attack, Retaliation, and Performance: An Expectancy-Valence Framework*, 15 Strategic Mgmt. J. 85 (1994) (theoretically and empirically examining several variables that affect the likelihood of retaliation).

165. Gilo & Porat, *supra* note 161, at 174.

166. Marotta-Wurgler, *supra* note 68.

from doing so would be driven out of the market.[167] Moreover, even if firms do not deliberately exploit consumers, but rather happen to use marketing and other techniques that increase their profitability due to consumer biases, competition is expected to induce all firms to use those techniques, lest they be driven out of the market.

Indeed, standard economic analysis recognizes that consumers sometimes make suboptimal decisions due to information problems. There are, however, two important differences between traditional and behavioral economic analyses. First, under the traditional model, information problems may result in both over- and underestimation of the net benefit of the transaction; and, second, consumers are aware that they have incomplete information and take this into account in their purchase decisions. Conversely, when cognitive biases drive decisions, their effects are often systematically and predictably in the same direction, and consumers are usually blissfully unaware of their biases, and thus unlikely to take measures to counter them.[168]

Ultimately, the best way to decide which of the conflicting analyses more accurately captures the reality of consumer markets is to observe how firms conduct themselves. According to the "optimistic" analysis, we would not expect firms to constantly engage in practices that take advantage of consumers' biases, because such biases are not sustainable in the long run, so it would be futile to try to exploit them. Conversely, the "pessimistic" analysis predicts that firms would extensively engage in such practices. The available empirical data clearly supports the pessimistic analysis.[169]

3. Reputation

Lucian Bebchuk and Richard Posner, among others, have argued that even if suppliers include one-sided, non-salient clauses in their standard-form contracts, this should not be a source of serious concern, because there is typically a gap between the paper transaction and the real transaction.[170] In a nutshell, the argument is that there is usually an asymmetry between suppliers and consumers. While suppliers are repeat players who care about their reputation, consumers are not constrained by reputation considerations (at least not as long as there is no mechanism by which their opportunistic behavior in any given transaction becomes known throughout the market). Given that contractual language is inevitably

167. Gabaix & Laibson, *supra* note 162; Campbell, *supra* note 162, at 1585–89; Paul Heidhues & Botond Kőszegi, *Exploiting Naïvete about Self-Control in the Credit Market,* 100 AM. ECON. REV. 2279 (2010); BAR-GILL, *supra* note 5, at 7–10; Jon D. Hanson & Douglas A. Kysar, *Taking Behavioralism Seriously: Some Evidence of Market Manipulation,* 112 HARV. L. REV. 1420, 1551–53 (1999); Korobkin, *supra* note 20, at 1234–44; Ran Spiegler, *Choice Complexity and Market Competition,* 8 ANN. REV. ECON. 1 (2016).

168. BAR-GILL, *supra* note 5, at 9.

169. *See, e.g., id.* at 51–115, 116–84, 185–247 (empirically examining firms' practices in the credit card, mortgage, and cellular phone markets, respectively); Hanson & Kysar, *supra* note 167 (discussing evidence of consumer manipulation by the tobacco industry). The same picture emerges from many of the studies discussed in the preceding sections of this chapter.

170. Lucian A. Bebchuk & Richard A. Posner, *One-Sided Contracts in Competitive Consumer Markets,* 104 MICH. L. REV. 827 (2006). *See also* Jason Scott Johnston, *The Return of Bargain: An Economic Theory of How Standard-Form Contracts Enable Cooperative Negotiation between Businesses and Consumers,* 104 MICH. L. REV. 857 (2006).

indeterminate, and that the parties' behavior is often unobservable or unverifiable, balanced clauses may allow opportunistic consumers to gain benefits they have not bargained for. Unbalanced clauses enable suppliers to fend off such opportunism. Conversely, suppliers wish to maintain their reputation, so they are expected to treat reasonable consumers fairly, even if contract terms allow them to do otherwise. Arguably, suppliers' concern for their reputation is greater than ever, due to the rapid flow of information through the Web—particularly sites and blogs that provide customer reviews and ratings of suppliers' products and practices.[171]

This important argument is essential to understanding how consumer markets function reasonably well, despite the prevalence of one-sided and exploitative standard forms. That said, there is reason to doubt that reputational forces alone obviate the need to regulate standard-form contracts, on several counts.[172] First, the flow of information in consumer markets, even in our information era, is far from perfect, and so, too, is the use of information by customers. For example, an insurer may set especially low premiums because it regularly denies meritorious insurance claims. Potential customers may pay more attention to the low premiums, which are clear and salient, than to the insurer's treatment of claims, because the information about the latter is less available and less unequivocal, because they are more interested in the immediate cost than in the future benefit (due to their myopia), and because they underestimate the likelihood that they would ever file an insurance claim (due to their overoptimism). The ability to properly assess reputational information may be further hampered in situations where the supplier's reputation concerns numerous dimensions of the product. An airline passenger, for example, cares about timely arrival, luggage handling, cancelation policies, the risk of overbooking, and many other factors. Suppliers operating in such settings can emphasize dimensions that they are good at, in an attempt to induce consumers to overvalue their product.

Reputation is not a panacea for additional, more principled reasons. One reason has to do with the role of legal norms. While for most people, most of the time, economic incentives, social norms, and moral convictions loom larger than the threat of legal sanctions,[173] it does not follow that the economic, social, and moral systems obviate the need for the law. Legal norms are essential in "pathological" cases where other systems fail to produce satisfactory outcomes. For example, even if suppliers handle most customers' complaints satisfactorily, thanks to reputational and other forces, and even if they do not routinely rely on, say, choice-of-forum clauses in their contracts, the law must still decide whether to enforce such clauses in the relatively rare instances in which suppliers do rely on them to the detriment of consumers. Moreover, economic, social, and moral norms are not entirely divorced from the legal system. Adequate background legal norms help to

171. On these means of sharing customer information and their limitations, see, e.g., Nishanth V. Chari, *Disciplining Standard Form Contract Terms through Online Information Flows: An Empirical Study,* 85 N.Y.U. L. Rev. 1618 (2010); Zamir & Farkash, *supra* note 126, at 159–60; *supra* pp. 306–07.

172. See Radin, *supra* note 121, at 190–92.

173. John Kidwell, *A Caveat,* 1985 Wis. L. Rev. 615.

instill trade practices and commercial norms that would then be self-imposed by virtue of reputational forces.

Another difficulty with excessive reliance on reputation is that it is much more likely to favor large, recurring, and sophisticated customers—whose goodwill is highly valued by suppliers—than weak, occasional, and unsophisticated customers, whose goodwill is less appreciated.[174] For anyone who cares about distributive justice in private law, this aspect of reputational forces is troubling.[175]

Finally, even if we ignore all these considerations and assume that firms invariably treat their customers fairly when one-sided clauses allow them to do otherwise, a problem still remains. A regime that grants suppliers unlimited license to treat customers as they please is harmful to customers' liberty. When customers are "nothing more than supplicants"[176] and suppliers honor customers' legitimate claims only at their discretion (rather than because they are legally bound to do so), the status of customers as autonomous and free subjects is compromised.[177] From a welfare perspective, receiving something as a matter of entitlement is more conducive to one's welfare, whether measured subjectively or objectively, than receiving the same thing as a favor.[178]

4. Conclusion

Sections B–E pointed to the prevalence and significance of various cognitive biases that lead to suboptimal decisions by consumers, which may bring about inefficient and unfair outcomes. However, identifying consumer cognitive biases, and suppliers' exploitation thereof, is only a first step in legal policymaking. As in the case of traditional market failures, the existence of a behavioral market failure does not, in and of itself, justify a legal response. There are possibly other factors that mitigate the adverse results of cognitive biases, and the net benefit of regulation, given its various shortcomings, may be smaller than that of other options, including doing nothing. With this in mind, this section examined whether market competition, including reputational forces, as well as other non-legal mechanisms, render legal responses to behavioral market failures unnecessary. While the emerging picture is complex, the bottom line is that one cannot rely on the market to rectify behavioral market failures. The next section briefly considers several courses of action in the light of this conclusion.

174. Margaret Jane Radin, *Boilerplate Today: The Rise of Modularity and the Waning of Consent,* 104 MICH. L. REV. 1223, 1228 (2006); Shmuel I. Becher, *Asymmetric Information in Consumer Contracts: The Challenge That Is Yet to Be Met,* 45 AM. BUS. L.J. 723, 747–48 (2008).

175. This concern is exacerbated by the fact that unsophisticated customers are more likely to assume, erroneously, that contract clauses are valid, when in fact they are not. *See infra* pp. 322–23.

176. Todd D. Rakoff, *The Law and Sociology of Boilerplate,* 104 MICH. L. REV. 1235, 1236 (2006).

177. *Cf.* ALON HAREL, WHY LAW MATTERS 147–90 (2014) (making a similar argument in the context of constitutional protection of moral and political rights).

178. *See* Daphna Lewinsohn-Zamir, *In Defense of Redistribution through Private Law,* 91 MINN. L. REV. 326, 358–60, 362–65 (2006).

G. Legal Solutions

1. General

The preceding sections described numerous ways in which suppliers exploit consumers' cognitive limitations and biases, and argued that the market itself cannot be expected to rectify this—if anything, it might make things worse. However, as emphasized in Chapter 4, it does not follow that the law should necessarily step in.[179] Not all forms of advantage-taking of cognitive limitations or biases are illegitimate, and not all forms of illegitimate advantage-taking merit a *legal* response. Drawing the lines is a difficult task, requiring close attention to factual details and to the relevant liberty, efficiency, redistribution, fairness, and institutional considerations.[180]

One measure that policymakers might use is to establish mandatory cooling-off periods that allow consumers to reconsider their initial decision to enter a contract and to examine the extent to which the purchased product conforms with the supplier's presentations and their own needs.[181] We discussed the pros and cons of cooling-off periods above.[182]

Another measure that is occasionally used to regulate consumer transactions is default rules. For example, under the U.S. Credit Card Accountability, Responsibility and Disclosure Act of 2009 (also known as the Credit CARD Act), cardholders cannot exceed the credit limit (that is, the issuer would decline charges that take the cardholder above her limit), unless the parties have agreed otherwise.[183] However, while default rules have proven a powerful regulatory means in other contexts—such as consenting to postmortem organ donation and increasing employee participation in retirement savings plans[184]—they are generally a poor means in the present context. Whenever the interests of the consumer and the supplier diverge, it is exceedingly easy for suppliers to contract around the default by inserting the necessary clause into their standard forms, which consumers virtually never read.[185] Moreover, even if consumers were required to positively and explicitly agree to such opt-outs, common cognitive biases, such as overoptimism and the limited ability to predict one's self-control problems, would almost certainly induce them to give their consent.

179. *See supra* pp. 163–65.

180. *See* Cass R. Sunstein, *Fifty Shades of Manipulation*, 1 J. Marketing Behav. 213 (2015) (discussing these issues in the context of market manipulations). The article is followed by seven commentaries and a response (*id.* at 245–361).

181. *See, e.g.*, Article 9 of the European Directive 2011/83/EU on Consumer Rights (2011) (setting a period of fourteen days to withdraw from a distance or off-premises contract); Sections 14–14G of the Israeli Consumer Protection Law, 1981, and the Consumer Regulations (Cancellation of Transaction), 2010 (laying down mandatory cooling-off periods in various types of consumer transactions, including ordinary ones conducted in brick-and-mortar stores).

182. *See supra* pp. 290–92.

183. §102, 123 Stat. 1738–40.

184. *See supra* pp. 179–82.

185. Lauren E. Willis, *When Nudges Fail: Slippery Defaults*, 80 U. Chi. L. Rev. 1155 (2013).

One possible variation of default rules is *safe harbors*. This notion refers to cases where the legislature sets a vague standard, and the regulator then defines a course of action that would presumptively satisfy the legislative standard. Opting out of that course of action triggers enhanced scrutiny, thereby turning the default rule into a quasi-mandatory one.[186] For example, the U.S. Consumer Financial Protection Bureau has issued guidelines for lenders, which, if followed, provides them with a presumption of compliance with the statutory requirement to make a reasonable, good faith determination of borrowers' ability to repay loans secured by a dwelling.[187]

Perhaps the most radical response to consumers' cognitive limitations and biases (which are often coupled with traditional market failures and other social and moral concerns) is to ban certain types of transactions altogether. For example, a European Directive prohibits pyramid promotional schemes—namely, schemes in which consumers give "consideration for the opportunity to receive compensation that is derived primarily from the introduction of other consumers into the scheme rather than from the sale or consumption of products."[188] Another example is the ban on payday loans enacted in a considerable number of U.S. states.[189] It should be noted that the boundary between banning certain transactions outright and regulating their content is sometimes blurred. For example, capping the interest rate on payday loans may be tantamount to prohibiting them if the cap renders these unsecured loans unprofitable.[190] In any event, banning a certain type of transaction altogether is a drastic measure that is inappropriate for run-of-the-mill consumer transactions.

For this reason, in this section we focus on two types of tools policymakers have at their disposal: disclosure duties, and mandatory regulation of contract content (and performance). We start with the former.

2. Disclosure

Disclosure duties are widely used in the sphere of consumer contracts.[191] Properly designed disclosures can highlight important attributes of the contract, and help consumers make informed choices that best serve their interests. Disclosure sidesteps many of the concerns associated with more intrusive regulation, as it does not limit the choice set faced by

186. *See* Bar-Gill, *supra* note 100, at 484. Numerous other legal doctrines tend to blur the line between default and mandatory rules. *See* Eyal Zamir, *The Inverted Hierarchy of Contract Interpretation and Supplementation*, 97 COLUM. L. REV. 1710, 1738–50 (1997).

187. Ability-to-Repay and Qualified Mortgage Standards Under the Truth in Lending Act (Regulation Z), 78 Fed. Reg. 6408 (2013).

188. Item 14 of Annex I of Directive 2005/29/EC on Unfair Business-to-Consumer Commercial Practices in the Internal Market (2005).

189. Some states prohibit this kind of consumer credit altogether, while others only ban repetitive payday loans, whose ramifications for lenders may be particularly damaging. On these prohibitions, their pros and cons, see, e.g., Mann & Hawkins, *supra* note 101; Skiba, *supra* note 103 (criticizing those bans).

190. John Y. Campbell et al., *Consumer Financial Protection*, 25 J. ECON. PERSP. 91, 102, 103 (2011).

191. For a general discussion of disclosure policies, see *supra* pp. 171–77. This section draws on the general discussion and merely highlights some of the unique issues associated with disclosures in the consumer arena.

consumers, and leaves the ultimate decision in their hands. Consequently, disclosure is often viewed as the only politically viable regulatory option,[192] although it should be stressed that this is not a principled argument in favor of disclosure, and that its validity hinges on the political landscape of the society in question.

Behavioral analysis of disclosure can guide policymakers along two dimensions. First, it can identify areas where consumers err, and pinpoint the information that might improve their choices. Both the bounded rationality and the bounded willpower of consumers might require certain issues to be underscored during the contracting process. Second, behavioral analysis can suggest how information should be presented to consumers to facilitate better decision-making. In this regard, behavioral analysis promotes the design of "smart" disclosures, by tackling questions such as where, when, and how information should be revealed to consumers in order to have a meaningful effect on their choices.

With regard to the first point, behavioral insights are important in determining the scope of information to be disclosed. Regarding the attributes of the product itself, attention should be drawn to non-salient features that consumers might not fully take into account when making their choices. For example, suppliers might be required to disclose in a salient manner the conditions of the product's warranty, or the circumstances under which the contract might be terminated or altered unilaterally. Similarly, disclosures might help alleviate the difficulties consumers face when they attempt to comprehend complex multidimensional pricing schemes. One option on this front is to require suppliers to present a standardized measure that encapsulates the different dimensions of the price. The APR (annual percentage rate), mandated in the United States by the Truth in Lending Act,[193] attempted to achieve this goal in the area of borrowing by providing consumers with a single figure that presented the effective cost of a loan, thereby facilitating comparisons between complex financial products.[194]

Disclosure duties need not be limited to attributes of the product—they can relate to the consumers as well.[195] Sophisticated suppliers are often better placed to assess consumers' future behavior than the consumers themselves. Thus, financial institutions may be better at predicting how consumers will conduct themselves throughout the contract than the boundedly rational consumers themselves (for example, with regard to late payments and refinancing); airlines may be more successful than passengers in assessing whether a change in the reservation is likely; and gyms may know better than their patrons how frequently said patrons will actually attend. To foster efficient contracting choices by consumers, disclosure duties should incorporate such information, when feasible.

192. Bar-Gill, *supra* note 5, at 32.

193. Truth in Lending Act, Pub. L. No. 90-321, § 107, 82 Stat. 146, 149 (1968) (codified as amended at 15 U.S.C. § 1606 (2012)) (defining APR).

194. To be sure, the APR did not achieve this goal perfectly, due to problems with the timing of the disclosure and the manner in which it is calculated. *See* Oren Bar Gill, *The Law, Economics, and Psychology of Subprime Mortgage Contracts*, 94 Cornell L. Rev. 1073, 1140–47 (2009).

195. Oren Bar-Gill & Oliver Board, *Product Use Information and the Limits of Voluntary Disclosure*, 14 Am. L. & Econ. Rev. 235 (2012).

With regard to the second point, smart disclosures aspire to be salient, simple, and timely.[196] Saliency in this context means the prominence of the disclosure in relation to other information that the consumer is exposed to. Disclosure is unlikely to matter much if it is printed on the bottom of the product's packaging. Simplicity means that disclosure should include only the necessary information, to minimize information overload and the numbing effect of complexity. At times, disclosures might be collapsed into a simple grading system that encompasses many aspects of the product.[197] Finally, in light of phenomena such as the sunk-cost effect and the confirmation bias, disclosures should be provided at an early stage, before the consumer makes his or her purchase decision. A disclosure presented late in the contracting process risks being viewed as a technical nuisance that should be ignored.[198]

As previously argued,[199] disclosures often do not influence choices in a meaningful way. This general insight is true for consumer contracts.[200] Many disclosure duties require highly detailed and complex information to be provided—with the result that almost nobody reads them.[201] Furthermore, the wide array of disclosures consumers face on a daily basis is likely to create a numbing effect. Even if consumers do read the disclosures they are bombarded with, they are unlikely to comprehend them and draw the appropriate conclusions, given their cognitive limitations. A clear, upfront disclosure, informing the consumer that she agrees to litigate all disputes with the supplier in arbitration, is unlikely to figure into the consumer's decision whether to consent to the contract, given the low probability of this issue coming into play (both objectively, and within the consumer's subjectively biased analysis), and the fact that many consumers might not even know what "arbitration" means. This is especially true for consumers who exhibit bounded willpower: simply improving the information provided to them is often not enough to steer them toward decisions that enhance their long-term welfare.[202]

In the area of consumer contracts there is yet another critical piece in the disclosure puzzle that might render such policies futile—namely, suppliers' attempts to strategically undermine mandated disclosures.[203] Suppliers might add complexity to their

196. *See e.g.*, Cass Sunstein, *Nudges.Gov: Behaviorally Informed Regulation*, *in* THE OXFORD HANDBOOK OF BEHAVIORAL ECONOMICS AND THE LAW, *supra* note 100, at 719, 727–33.

197. *See, e.g.*, Russell Korobkin, *Comparative Effectiveness Research as Choice Architecture: The Behavioral Law and Economics Solution to the Health Care Cost Crisis*, 112 MICH. L. REV. 523 (2014).

198. *See also supra* p. 287.

199. *See supra* pp. 173–77.

200. For a detailed review of the pitfalls of mandated disclosure, see BEN-SHAHAR & SCHNEIDER, *supra* note 127, at 59–118 (2014).

201. For example, according to Article 6(1) of the European Directive 2011/83/EU on Consumer Rights (2011), in any distance or off-premises sale, the seller must provide the consumer with clear information on twenty(!) different aspects of the product. Comparable obligations exist in many consumer laws throughout the world.

202. Ryan Bubb & Rischard Pildes, *How Behavioral Economics Trims Its Sails and Why*, 127 HARV. L. REV. 1593, 1649–52 (2014).

203. *Id.* at 1648–49; *supra* pp. 284–87.

products, resulting either in greater complexity of the disclosure (assuming it accounts for all dimensions), or limiting its relevance (if it does not account for all dimensions).[204] In addition, suppliers might postpone disclosures as much as possible, to ensure that consumers are heavily vested in the transaction before they are given the information. Finally, suppliers might employ agents to explain away disclosures and frame them as "red tape" or "paperwork."

Food labeling is a good example of the limitations associated with disclosure duties as a regulatory tool aimed at altering consumer choice. Traditional nutritional labels often contain a vast amount of information, presented in a complex way (e.g., what does 100 mg of sodium actually mean? How many "servings" of potato chips am I truly consuming?). Furthermore, this information is often displayed in a non-salient fashion (e.g., small print, side of the box). Consequently, it has been suggested that such labels have little influence on consumer behavior.[205] Behaviorally motivated labeling policies adopted in countries such as the United Kingdom and Australia attempted to simplify labels by limiting the amount of information and using intuitive color codes (red = bad; amber = medium; green = good), and making labels more salient by positioning them on the front of the packaging.[206] While this move certainly makes theoretical sense, empirical studies of such labels have yielded mixed results as to their impact on consumers' decisions in the field.[207] Apparently, forces such as product design, advertising, and promotions, coupled with the urge for immediate gratification, often outweigh the influence of cleverly designed disclosures.[208]

Regrettably, food labelling is not an isolated example. Similar effort has been put in recent years into developing smart disclosures that inform biased consumers of the long-term energy costs of household appliances to encourage them to overcome their tendency to buy cheap but inefficient products that end up costing more in the long run. For the most part, such disclosures have not managed to bring about the intended behavioral changes.[209]

204. This was the case, for example, with the APR, which became less relevant as lenders shifted costs to price dimensions that are not included in it. *See* Bar-Gill, *supra* note 194, at 1144.

205. Gerda I.J. Feunekes et al., *Front-of-Pack Nutrition Labelling: Testing Effectiveness of Different Nutrition Labelling Formats Front-of-Pack in Four European Countries*, 50 APPETITE 57, 58 (2008).

206. C.A. Roberto & N. Khandpur, *Improving the Design of Food Labels to Promote Healthier Food Choices and Reasonable Portion Sizes*, 38 INT'L J. OBESITY S25 (2014).

207. *See* Gary Sacks, Mike Rayner & Boyd Swinburn, *Impact of Front-of-Pack "Traffic-Light" Nutrition Labelling on Consumer Food Purchases in the UK*, 24 HEALTH PROMOTION INT'L 344 (2009) (before and after study of actual choices documenting no effect); Robert Hamlin & Lisa McNeill, *Does the Australasian "Health Star Rating" Front of Pack Nutritional Label System Work?*, 8 NUTRIENTS 327 (2016) (experimental study finding that labels did not influence product choices); Pauline Ducrot et al., *Impact of Different Front-of-Pack Nutrition Labels on Consumers Purchasing Intentions: A Randomized Control Trial*, 50 AM. J. PREVENTATIVE MED. 627 (2016) (labels influenced decisions in an online experimental setup); Lillian Sonnenberg et al., *A Traffic Light Food Labeling Intervention Increases Consumer Awareness of Health and Healthy Choices at the Point-of-Purchase*, 57 PREVENTIVE MED. 253 (2013) (controlled experiment in a cafeteria resulting in a change in choices for some consumers).

208. Hamlin & McNeill, *supra* note 207.

209. For recent empirical results on this front, along with a review of previous studies, see James Carroll, Eleanor Denny & Seán Lyons, *The Effects of Energy Cost Labelling on Appliance Purchasing Decisions: Trial Results from Ireland*, 39 J. CONSUMER POL'Y 23 (2016).

Of course, disclosure policies are not necessarily useless, nor are they inevitably doomed to fail. They are continually evolving, and should be rigorously examined with the best available methods, to improve their effectiveness.[210] Nonetheless, as things currently stand, the thought that smart disclosures can serve as the exclusive, or even primary, means of countering the cognitive limitations of consumers seems unrealistic. A more effective approach is to provide further nudges, combined with disclosures (e.g., making unhealthy options less accessible),[211] and more intrusive regulation that is not committed to sustaining existing consumer choice options (e.g., banning trans fats).[212] The next subsection examines this option in greater detail.

3. Mandatory Regulation

Given the limitations of disclosure duties and other liberty-preserving regulatory means (such as default rules), sometimes the most sensible response to behavioral (and other) market failures in consumer markets is compulsory regulation of the content of contracts and their performance. Some would describe such regulation as "hard paternalism,"[213] but others might argue that preventing the exploitation of one person (the consumer) by another (the supplier) is, at most, "impure paternalism," which may be justified on the grounds of the liberal "harm principle."[214] Moreover, it may be described as the least intrusive form of paternalism—namely refraining from actively helping others to harm themselves: "The nonenforcement of contractual terms that deviate from compulsory (or semicomplusory) rules is nothing but a refusal of the state to assist people in hurting themselves by enforcing their injurious agreements."[215]

From an efficiency perspective, since invalidation of contract terms deprives contracting parties of otherwise available options that might have been mutually beneficial to some of them, it entails social costs.[216] This argument calls for caution in using this measure, but does not constitute a principled objection, since any conceivable regulation entails both benefits and costs.[217]

210. For example, researchers have utilized eye tracking to examine how the effectiveness of labels might be improved. *See e.g.*, Gastón Ares et al., *Influence of Rational and Intuitive Thinking Styles on Food Choice: Preliminary Evidence from an Eye-Tracking Study with Yogurt Labels*, 31 FOOD, QUALITY & PREFERENCES 28 (2014).

211. *See* Paul Rosin et al., *Nudge to Nobesity I: Minor Changes in Accessibility Decrease Food Intake*, 6 JUDGMENT & DECISION MAKING 323 (2011).

212. *See* Shauna M. Downs, Anne Marie Thow & Stephen R. Leeder, *The Effectiveness of Policies for Reducing Dietary Trans Fat: A Systematic Review of the Evidence*, 91 BULL. WORLD HEALTH ORG. 262, 262–63 (2013) (reviewing trans-fat bans across the world).

213. *See, e.g.*, Bar-Gill, *supra* note 100, at 477–78.

214. *See, e.g.*, Gerald Dworkin, *Paternalism*, 56 THE MONIST 64, 67–68 (1972); JOEL FEINBERG, HARM TO SELF: THE MORAL LIMITS OF THE CRIMINAL LAW 9–10 (1986).

215. Zamir, *supra* note 186, at 1787–88.

216. For a simple model that takes into account those costs and an illustration of its application in the context of contract regulation, see Eyal Zamir, *The Efficiency of Paternalism*, 84 VA. L. REV. 229, 256–75 (1998).

217. *Id.* at 237–54.

Other concerns relate to the potential adverse effect of regulation on consumers' learning from their mistakes, but the weight of this argument varies from one context to another. It is particularly weak when it comes to cognitive errors that are difficult to debias,[218] when transactions are so complex that it is hardly likely that laypersons would ever acquire the necessary expertise to process all relevant information, or when the outcomes of error may be devastating or irreversible.[219] More cogent concerns pertain to the regulators' own information problems (especially given consumer heterogeneity), cognitive biases, and possible ulterior motives due to regulatory capture. Once again, these are real concerns that apply to any type of regulation, and therefore call for caution, use of expertise, and governmental checks and balances in the regulatory process.[220] In any event, the argument that every individual *necessarily* knows better than anyone else what is in her best interest is untenable, given the abundance of behavioral research pointing to people's systematic cognitive errors.

To address customers' limited expertise and information-processing abilities, and their vulnerability to cognitive biases, most legal systems set mandatory standards for the safety of cars, drugs, toys, and similar products, rather than requiring that the pertinent information be provided to customers for their consideration. As the subprime crisis has demonstrated, unsafe contracts can involve risks to individuals and society that are no less damaging than the risks of unsafe drugs and toys. While this consideration looms larger in some contexts than in others, it is relevant to many issues covered by standard-form contracts. Even when the risks involved and the complexity of the relevant issues are comparatively mild, cost-benefit analysis may point to the superiority of regulation of the contract's content over the provision of better information and other noncompulsory tools—and the curtailment of freedom involved in such regulation is also rather limited.[221]

In fact, the public discourse and policymakers' orientation with regard to compulsory regulation of market transactions vary considerably from one society to another. But even in countries where compulsory regulation of contract terms is particularly contentious, such as the United States, there is growing disillusion with the efficacy of disclosure duties;[222] and there have long been many instances of such regulation.[223]

One example of regulation that directly targets a behavioral market failure is found in a 2014 amendment to the Israeli Consumer Protection Law, 1981, which provides customers with an inalienable right to unilaterally cancel gym memberships, and sets out

218. *See generally supra* pp. 127–38.

219. Zamir, *supra* note 216, at 276–77.

220. *See generally id.* at 275, 281–82; *supra* p. 170; *infra* pp. 393–431.

221. Zamir, *supra* note 216, at 263; Eyal Zamir & Barak Medina, Law, Economics, and Morality 313–47 (2010) (proposing a cost-benefit analysis of legal paternalism, subject to a threshold deontological constraint against curtailing people's freedom).

222. *See, e.g.*, Ben-Shahar & Schneider, *supra* note 127.

223. *See, e.g.*, Korobkin, *supra* note 20, at 1247–52; Oren Bar-Gill & Ryan Bubb, *Credit Card Pricing: The CARD Act and Beyond*, 97 Cornell L. Rev. 967, 986–92 (2012) (describing direct regulation of some credit-card contract terms under the Credit CARD Act).

the conditions for, and outcomes of, such cancellation.[224] This rule recognizes that, at the time of contracting, people often exhibit overoptimism about their expected gym attendance, and then fail to meet their expectations due to self-control problems—a phenomenon that health clubs are well aware of.[225]

Many mandatory restrictions pertain to non-salient clauses in standard-form contacts that consumers are exceedingly unlikely to pay any attention to, since they refer to low-probability events or to obscure legal issues. Indeed, such sweeping invalidation imposes costs on parties for whom such clauses would be mutually beneficial. However, if in the great majority of cases consumers do not pay attention to those clauses—or could hardly understand them or assess their significance even if they did—such invalidation may be warranted. Thus, the German Civil Code renders ineffective clauses in standard-form contracts that deny the consumer's right to set off uncontested debts, condition a seller's liability for defects in a new product on prior court action taken against a third party, or modify the burden of proof to the disadvantage of the customer.[226] A less drastic measure, used by the German Code and other laws around the world, is to subject non-salient clauses in standard-form contracts to judicial scrutiny on a case-by-case basis, possibly against a backdrop of presumed invalidity.[227]

Turning to the financial market and focusing on housing loans, it has been estimated that "nearly a third of U.S. households could not afford their housing, and more than a tenth had severely unaffordable housing."[228] If this is true, the problem of over-borrowing cannot be dealt with by tinkering with the mortgage disclosure forms, and the only real solution may be mandatory rules that limit access to credit.[229] In Israel, for example, the maximum that consumers can borrow against their residential dwelling is 75 percent of its value.[230]

Similarly, loans involving a low introductory rate coupled with a significantly higher long-term rate is welfare enhancing for a very small subset of consumers, such as second-year law students (and even they may be overly optimistic about their future earnings). More often, they exploit borrowers' shortsightedness and poor financial literacy[231]—which no disclosure is likely to fully cure. While such loans deprive a small subset of borrowers

224. Consumer Protection Law, 1981, Section 13A1 & Fourth Supplement (added in 2014).

225. *See, e.g.*, Jean-Denis Garona, Alix Massea & Pierre-Carl Michauda, *Health Club Attendance, Expectations and Self-Control*, 119 J. ECON. BEHAV. & ORG. 364 (2015). Paradoxically, reducing the price of gym membership to reflect the member's actual expected use of the gym might make things worse health-wise, since, due to the sunk-costs effect, the more members pay for their membership the more likely they are to use it.

226. Subsections 309(3), 309(8)(b)(aa), and 309(12) of the German Civil Code, respectively.

227. *See, e.g.*, Sec. 308 of the German Civil Code; The European Directive on Unfair Terms in Consumer Contracts, *supra* note 147; Secs. 3 and 4 of the Israeli Standard Contracts Law, 1982.

228. Sovern *supra* note 140, at 790.

229. *See* Samuel Issacharoff, *Disclosure, Agents, and Consumer Protection*, 167 J. INST. & THEO. ECON. 56, 69 (2011).

230. *See* Bank of Israel, Limitations on Credit for Housing (2012), *available at:* http://www.boi.org.il/he/BankingSupervision/SupervisorsDirectives/DocLib/329.pdf (in Hebrew).

231. On financial literacy, see, e.g., Annamaria Lusardi & Olivia S. Mitchelli, *Financial Literacy and Retirement Preparedness: Evidence and Implications for Financial Education*, 42 BUS. ECON. 35 (2007); Victor Stango &

of profitable opportunities, banning them altogether may well be the only effective means of protecting many people from entering into contracts that may result in devastating outcomes to them and to society at large.[232]

A considerably less controversial—but also considerably less effective—means is judicial scrutiny of non-salient clauses in standard-form contracts on the basis of general doctrines such as unconscionability,[233] good faith, and creative use of the *interpretation against the draftsman* rule (rather than specifically devised norms, such as a list of clauses that are presumed invalid in standard-form contracts, subject to judicial discretion, as is the case in Germany and Israel).[234]

As these examples demonstrate, an important choice is between ex-ante, legislative invalidation of certain clauses (whether by the primary legislature or by administrative agencies), and ex-post, judicial invalidation, based on more or less broad standards. While economic analysis of rules (ex-ante regulation) versus standards (ex-post regulation) assumes that people are rational maximizers,[235] behavioral analysis relaxes this assumption.[236] Among other things, self-serving biases are likely to distort the incentives created by legal norms: it is easier to convince oneself that one is complying with vague standards even when one is not, than it is when one violates bright-line rules (this is in contrast with the prediction that risk-aversion would yield over-compliance with standards).[237] Self-serving biases may also result in more litigation, due to the parties' overoptimism regarding the soundness of their position.[238] People whose legal rights are defined by a simple, bright-line rule are also likely to have a stronger sense of entitlement, and hence to value their rights more highly, due to the endowment effect.[239] Finally, inasmuch as people's behavior is influenced by social norms, by their educational effect, and by the conformity

Jonathan Zinman, *Exponential Growth Bias and Household Finance*, 64 J. Fin. 2807 (2009); Annamaria Lusardi, Olivia S. Mitchel & Vilsa Curto, *Financial Literacy among the Young*, 44 J. Consumer Aff. 358 (2010).

232. Again, Israel might serve as an example in this regard. In 2004, well before the subprime crisis and the lessons learned from it, the Bank of Israel banned the practice of short-term teaser rates in mortgages. For a complete description of this regulation and an empirical evaluation of its effectiveness, see Bachar, *supra* note 107, at 68–88, 208–18. For a consideration of milder forms of regulation (primarily because disallowing teaser rates appears to be politically infeasible in the United States), see Bar-Gill & Bubb, *supra* note 223, at 1005–10.

233. Korobkin, *supra* note 20, at 1255–90.

234. *See supra* note 227 and accompanying text.

235. *See, e.g.*, Louis Kaplow, *Rules versus Standards: An Economic Analysis*, 42 Duke L.J. 557 (1992).

236. *See, e.g.*, Russell B. Korobkin, *Behavioral Analysis and Legal Form: Rules vs. Standards Revisited*, 79 Or. L. Rev. 23 (2000).

237. Yuval Feldman & Alon Harel, *Social Norms, Self-Interest and Ambiguity of Legal Norms: An Experimental Analysis of the Rule vs. Standard Dilemma*, 4 Rev. L. & Econ. 81, 100–08 (2008) (finding that self-interest triggers noncompliance with legal norms to a greater extent when norms are formulated as standards). *See also* Laetitia B. Mulder, Jennifer Jordan & Floor Rink, *The Effect of Specific and General Rules on Ethical Decisions*, 126 Org. Behav. & Hum. Decision Processes 115 (2015) (demonstrating that "specifically-framed rules elicit[ed] ethical decisions more strongly than generally-framed rules" due to "reductions in people's moral rationalizations").

238. Korobkin, *supra* note 236, at 46–47.

239. *Id.* at 51–53.

effect—rather than by self-interest alone—it stands to reason that thanks to their clarity, simple rules are more likely than general standards to shape social norms, and hence affect behavior.[240]

These are not the only considerations that should influence the choice between rules and standards, be it in general or in the context of regulation of consumer contracts. Other concerns include the relative costs of the design and implementation of norms; the relative institutional competence of the legislature, administrative agencies, and courts; and the possible trade-off between predictability and flexibility. It does appear, however, that the behavioral perspective strengthens the case for ex-ante, legislative regulation, as opposed to regulation of the ex-post, judicial variety.[241] Suppliers' self-serving biases may result in greater exploitation of consumers and greater tendency to litigate under a regime of vague standards than under a regime of rules. Concomitantly, a lower sense of entitlement and the difficulty of knowing one's legal position are likely to diminish consumers' inclination to stand up for their rights. These concerns exacerbate other causes for the under-enforcement problem in consumer law—both rational (such as the typically small losses caused by suppliers' breach, compared to the high costs of litigation), and less rational (such as the omission bias).[242]

Importantly, the above analysis refers to the choice between vague standards and simple, bright-line rules. When the choice is between vague standards and elaborate systems of complex rules, the conclusions may well be different, because—contrary to appearances, perhaps—the effect of elaborate systems of complex rules on people's behavior and judicial decision-making is very different from that of simple, general rules.[243]

The behavioral perspective sheds light on another policy choice, namely whether to be content with rendering certain clauses unenforceable, or to prohibit their inclusion in consumer contracts in the first place (in addition to their invalidation). Such prohibition may be backed up by administrative or criminal sanctions, and may take the form of either defining the prohibited clauses, or positively dictating the content of consumer contracts. This choice may have considerable practical significance, since suppliers habitually use non-salient clauses that are known to be unenforceable.[244] The explanation for this practice is straightforward: suppliers believe that many consumers may wrongly assume that those clauses are valid and accordingly not assert their rights. Given consumers' information problems and bounded rationality, this belief appears to be reasonable. In fact, empirical

240. *Id.* at 53–56.

241. *See generally* Oren Bar-Gill & Elizabeth Warren, *Making Credit Safer*, 157 U. PA. L. REV. 1, 70–97 (2008) (discussing the pros and cons of ex-post, judicial intervention versus ex-ante regulation in the sphere of consumer credit).

242. *See generally* Samuel Issacharoff, *Group Litigation of Consumer Claims: Lessons from the U.S. Experience*, 34 TEX. INT'L L. J. 135 (1999).

243. *See infra* pp. 556–59.

244. *See, e.g.*, Bailey Kuklin, *On the Knowing Inclusion of Unenforceable Contract and Lease Terms*, 56 U. CIN. L. REV. 845 (1988); Charles A. Sullivan, *The Puzzling Persistence of Unenforceable Contract Terms*, 70 OHIO ST. L.J. 1127 (2009).

studies have demonstrated that many consumers (including relatively sophisticated ones, such as undergraduate students), erroneously believe unenforceable exemption clauses to be enforceable.[245] These findings lend support for the more drastic measure.

In fact, the European Directive on Unfair Terms in Consumer Contracts calls on member states to "ensure that, in the interests of consumers and of competitors, adequate and effective means exist to prevent the continued use of unfair terms in contracts concluded with consumers by sellers or suppliers."[246] Outside the European Union, prohibitions on knowingly including unenforceable clauses in consumer contracts, such as residential leases, are few and far between.[247]

H. Conclusion

Compared with other spheres of human activity, marketing techniques and consumer behavior have attracted particularly large attention from cognitive and social psychologists, including judgment-and-decision-making researchers. The rich findings provide a reasonably sound basis for legal policymaking in the sphere of consumer contracts. Of course, there is still much to be learned. For example, most of the research on consumer decision-making pertains to small-scale, daily transactions.[248] While these are important, legal policymakers are just as interested in large and infrequent transactions that may have far-reaching effects on consumers' welfare, such as buying a house, taking a loan for that purpose, or purchasing life insurance. Future research should strive to encompass such high-stakes consumer decision-making. In addition, the changing realities brought about to consumer markets by new technologies raise a host of challenges for policymakers. For instance, the rise of big data might enable producers to segregate consumers according to their psychological traits, and design products, pricing schemes, and marketing tactics that are geared toward exploiting each consumer's cognitive vulnerability.[249]

Notwithstanding their limitations, existing findings about consumer psychology are sufficiently robust to render this body of research an indispensable input to legal policymaking. Given what we already know about human psychology, legal policymaking that rests exclusively on the assumption that consumers are rational maximizers is no longer viable. In fact, even before rigorous behavioral studies became available, much (albeit certainly not all) of consumer law rejected the premises of rational choice theory,

245. *See, e.g.*, Warren Mueller, *Residential Tenants and Their Leases: An Empirical Study*, 69 Mich. L. Rev. 247, 272–74 (1970); Dennis P. Stolle & Andrew J. Slain, *Standard Form Contracts and Contracts Schemas: A Preliminary Investigation of the Effects of Exculpatory Clauses on Consumers' Propensity to Sue*, 15 Behav. Sci. & L. 83 (1997); Meirav Furth-Matzkin, *On the Unexpected Use of Unenforceable Contract Terms: Evidence from the Residential Rental Market*, 9 J. Legal. Analysis 1 (2017).

246. Sec. 7(1) of the European Directive on Unfair Terms in Consumer Contracts, *supra* note 147.

247. Kuklin, *supra* note 244, at 846 & n.4.

248. James R. Bettman, Mary Frances Luce & John W. Pane, *Consumer Decision Making: A Choice Goals Approach*, *in* Handbook of Consumer Psychology, *supra* note 6, at 589, 589–90, 601–02.

249. *See* Ryan Calo, *Digital Market Manipulation*, 82 Geo. Wash. L. Rev. 995 (2014).

relying instead on more realistic assumptions regarding consumer behavior (even if only in an intuitive and rudimentary way). This means that in many legal systems (though, again, not all) behavioral insights do not call for a revolution, but rather can inform the interpretation and application of extant norms,[250] and inspire necessary reforms.[251] However, in some spheres, and in certain legal systems, more profound changes are arguably called for.

250. *See, e.g.*, Anne-Lise Sibony, *Can EU Consumer Law Benefit from Behavioural Insights? An Analysis of the Unfair Practices Directive*, 22 EUR. REV. PRIVATE L. 901 (2014).

251. *See* Anne-Lise Sibony & Geneviève Helleringer, *EU Consumer Protection and Behavioural Sciences: Revolution or Reform?*, *in* NUDGES AND THE LAW: A EUROPEAN PERSPECTIVE 209 (Alberto Alemanno & Anne-Lise Sibony eds., 2015).

9

Tort Law

A. Introduction

Tort law is the body of private law that deals with the harms that agents inflict upon each other. The typical tort case involves the accidental infliction of harm on someone else—for example, when a driver carelessly injures a pedestrian with his car. Some tort cases, however, involve intentional harming—such as when a driver punches another driver in a dispute over a parking spot, which is the tort of *battery*. Although tort law deals with both accidental and intentional harms, in the interests of brevity, and since most of the behavioral contributions to tort law have hitherto revolved around accidents, this chapter discusses only accidental harms.[1]

According to some accounts, modern economic analysis of law began in the area of tort law. Two early seminal articles in the field—by Ronald Coase and Guido Calabresi, respectively—lay the groundwork for the intellectual project of applying economic insights to the entire body of law.[2] By the late 1980s, the topic had been rigorously studied, and several comprehensive books had outlined the main insights in the field.[3] While the economic analysis of torts continues to expand and flourish,[4] the key results from that early work continue to hold true.

Given its predominant role in economic analysis of law, it is not surprising that tort law was one of the first areas to be revisited by researchers seeking to wield a behavioral

1. Intentional harms are discussed in the context of criminal law. *See infra* pp. 433–63.

2. *See* Ronald Coase, *The Problem of Social Cost*, 3 J. L. & Econ. 1 (1960); Guido Calabresi, *Some Thoughts on Risk Distribution and the Law of Torts*, 70 Yale L.J. 499 (1961).

3. *See* Guido Calabresi, The Costs of Accidents: A Legal and Economic Analysis (1970); Steven Shavell, Economic Analysis of Accident Law (1987); William M. Landes & Richard A. Posner, The Economic Structure of Tort Law (1987).

4. For reviews, see Steven Shavell, Foundations of Economic Analysis of Law 175–287 (2004); Robert Cooter & Thomas Ulen, Law and Economics 187–275 (6th ed. 2012); Richard Posner, Economic Analysis of Law 191–251 (9th ed. 2014).

Behavioral Law and Economics. Eyal Zamir and Doron Teichman.

perspective.[5] Over the years, this body of work has grown, to the point where it now covers much of the tort landscape.[6] In this literature, the dominant theme is the impact of the bounded rationality of tortfeasors and of adjudicators, respectively (in each case, while assuming the other is perfectly rational) on the design of tort law.

This chapter is structured as follows: after this brief introduction, Section B presents an overview of the fundamentals of the economic analysis of tort law. Section C then incorporates behavioral insights into the analysis of tort liability regimes—with particular attention to the implications of bounded rationality of potential tortfeasors or of adjudicators for the design of tort law. Section D applies a similar framework to the analysis of tort damages. Section E focuses on a particular area of tort law that has drawn significant attention from legal economists—product liability. Finally, Section F offers some concluding remarks.

B. Economic Analysis of Tort Law: An Overview

From an economic perspective, most tort cases involve actions with negative externalities, in the shape of risk of harm. In addition, these cases entail high transaction costs, which prevent the parties involved from tackling such externalities on their own. A paradigmatic example of this is that of auto-pedestrian accidents: driving a car carries an inherent risk to the safety and well-being of pedestrians, who, every so often, tend to get run over by cars. In a world with no transaction costs, pedestrians and drivers might conceivably draw up a contract about the degree of safety that the parties should employ, which would clearly set out the behavior required of drivers (drive slowly near a school, turn on lights at night, etc.) and of pedestrians (walk on sidewalks, cross streets only at designated spots, etc.). However, given the high transaction costs involved, such contracts are not feasible. Consequently, the law provides drivers and pedestrians (or any other category of tortfeasors and victims) with a set of rules that distribute the risks of accidents between them.

The key normative point put forward by legal economists is that any hypothetical contract between tortfeasors and victims would aim not to eliminate accidents altogether, but to minimize the *overall* social costs of accidents.[7] These costs comprise two main elements. The first is the harm caused by accidents—a dent in the bumper, a broken limb, or, alas, death. The second are the costs of the precautions aimed at preventing such accidents from occurring. These precautions can take the form of monetary investments in prevention measures (such as ensuring one's brakes are in order), or intangible ones (such as driving more slowly). In addition, economic analysis has focused on the ancillary

5. *See* Christine Jolls, Cass R. Sunstein & Richard Thaler, *A Behavioral Approach to Law and Economics*, 50 STAN. L. REV. 1471, 1523–32 (1998); Russell B, Korobkin & Thomas S. Ulen, *Law and Behavioral Science: Removing the Rationality Assumption from Law and Economics*, 88 CAL. L. REV. 1051, 1095–100 (2000).

6. *See* Yoed Halbersberg & Ehud Guttel, *The Behavioral Economics of Tort Law*, *in* THE OXFORD HANDBOOK OF BEHAVIORAL ECONOMICS AND THE LAW 405 (Eyal Zamir & Doron Teichman eds., 2014); JENNIFER K. ROBBENNOLT & VALERIE P. HANS, THE PSYCHOLOGY OF TORT LAW (2016).

7. *See* CALABRESI, *supra* note 3, at 9–24.

costs associated with accidents—such as the costs of spreading the risk of accidents, given people's general aversion to risks, and the administrative costs incurred by society to sustain the tort system.[8]

The standard unilateral economic model of torts looks at the decisions that tortfeasors make regarding the precautions they take when engaging in a risky activity (i.e., *level of* care). In this model, each additional unit of care reduces the probability of harm occurring, but at a decreasing marginal rate—that is, each additional unit of precaution is less effective than the previous one. Thus, when viewed from an economic perspective, the optimal social outcome can never be infinite care, but rather the level of care obtained from striking a balance between the costs of care and its benefits. To reach optimality, this balance must be conducted *at the margin*—that is to say, by comparing the marginal benefit associated with each unit of care and the marginal cost of that unit. Social optimality is achieved when these two values are equal, and the total cost of accidents is minimized.

Table 1 presents a numerical example of the link between investment in precautions and the probability of an accident (which, for the sake of simplicity, is assumed to create a harm of 100). In this example, investing in 1 unit of care is efficient, since it costs 10 and generates a benefit of 17 in terms of reduced expected accident costs. Conversely, investing in 2 units of care is inefficient—since it costs an additional 15, but generates a benefit of only 12 (investing in three units of care or more entails an even greater social loss). From an economic perspective, therefore, this suggests that the law should strive to incentivize potential tortfeasors to invest in one unit of care.

With this framework in place, one can now examine how different liability regimes fare from an economic perspective. More specifically, there are three legal regimes to consider in this regard: (1) *no liability*, (2) *strict liability*, and (3) *negligence*. The no-liability regime is one where the tortfeasor is not held legally responsible for harms inflicted on the victim. For example, if a court rejects a tort claim because it finds that the defendant does not owe a "duty of care" to the defendant, this suggests that the governing rule in this relationship is a no-liability rule.[9] At the other extreme lies strict liability—whereby tortfeasors must compensate victims for the harm they have caused, irrespective of the level of care they have taken. This is the case, for example, in jurisdictions where drivers are held strictly

TABLE 1 **Numerical example of connection between investment in care and the probability of an accident (Harm = 100)**

Level of Care	Cost of Care	Probability of Accident	Expected Accident Losses	Total Cost of Accidents
0	0	42%	42	42
1	10	25%	25	35
2	25	13%	13	38
3	45	2%	2	47

8. *Id.*

9. *See* Caparo Industries Plc v. Dickman [1990] 1 All ER 568 (HL).

liable for any harm they inflict on pedestrians.[10] Finally, a negligence rule assigns liability to the tortfeasor (unlike the no-liability rule)—but only after examining his behavior, and determining that he had not taken adequate precautions (unlike the strict-liability rule). From an economic perspective, negligence is defined as behavior in which the level of care taken was less than the socially optimal level of care, and in that regard it incorporates cost-benefit analysis into the law.[11]

Using the figures in Table 1, the incentive structure generated by these three rules can now be easily assessed. In a no-liability regime, tortfeasors can engage in an activity that is profitable but risky at no cost to themselves. As a result, this rule will incentivize tortfeasors to take insufficient care. In concrete terms, potential tortfeasors in this case would focus exclusively on the *Cost-of-Care* column, and seek to minimize that cost by taking no care. In essence, this result is merely another manifestation of the economic analysis of negative externalities, which suggests that there will be excess behavior generating such externalities.

Conversely, under a strict liability regime a tortfeasor internalizes the cost of the risk that she imposes on victims, since she is required to compensate victims whenever they incur harm resulting from her actions. In addition, she internalizes all the costs of precautions, as she must pay these out of pocket. Thus, a strict-liability rule incentivizes tortfeasors to take optimal care, since their costs are the sum of the total costs of the accidents to themselves and to the potential victims. Notably, despite the "strict" nature of this regime, tortfeasors that are subject to it do not have an incentive to take excessive care—since such care would cost more than the benefit it yields in the form of reduced expected liability. In the above numerical example, a tortfeasor under this regime would not choose a care level of 2 (or above), since the total cost of doing so, for her (in terms of cost-of-care and expected tort compensation) would exceed the costs of choosing a care level of 1.

Finally, the negligence rule involves a unique discontinuous cost structure that also incentivizes potential tortfeasors to take optimal care. Under this rule, tortfeasors who take less-than-optimal care pay both for the care they have taken and for the harm they have caused—since their choice of care is deemed by the court to be negligent. When tortfeasors choose to take optimal care (or higher), they are deemed by the court to be non-negligent, and therefore not required to compensate the victim. This gives tortfeasors a strong incentive to be on the "right" side of the negligence line, as it grants them legal immunity for the harms they cause. In terms of the numerical example above, if the tortfeasor takes optimal care (i.e., 1) then the only cost she bears is the cost of precautions (i.e., 10), since she would not have to compensate the victims for their losses. If, however, the tortfeasor takes less-than-optimal care (i.e., 0), she is held liable and must bear the expected costs of accidents (i.e., 42).

10. As is the case in Israel, for example. *See* Auto Accident Compensation Act § 2 (1975).

11. *See United States v. Carroll Towing Co.* 159 F.2d 169 (2d Cir. 1947) in which the court introduced the Learned Hand formula as the tool used to examine negligence claims. According to the court, "if the probability be called P; the injury, L; and the burden, B; liability depends upon whether B is less than L multiplied by P: i.e., whether B > PL." *Id.* at 173.

In conclusion, this very basic analysis suggests that both the strict-liability and the negligence rules incentivize potential tortfeasors to take optimal care, while a no-liability regime fails to do so. More complex economic models of tort law have reached more nuanced results. Two main issues in this regard are *bilateral care* and *activity levels*. Bilateral-care cases are instances where efficiency requires both the tortfeasor and the victim to take certain precautions, to minimize the total costs of care and harm. Economic analysis has shown that negligence regimes fare better in such settings, as they incentivize both parties to take optimal care.[12] This picture, however, becomes considerably more complex under modern negligence regimes, which allow for liability to be proportionally divided between the two parties.[13] Activity level denotes the scope of risky activities that someone engages in. In the context of driving, for example, activity decisions relate to *how much* people drive (as distinct from care decisions, which are about to *how cautiously* they drive). Incorporating this dimension into the analysis highlights a relative advantage of the strict liability rule, which incentivizes tortfeasors to adopt an efficient level of activity.[14] For the most part, these important results lie beyond the scope of this chapter, so we shall focus on the simple case of unilateral care.

C. Behavioral Analysis: Liability Regimes

Given that tort law deals with the regulation of risk-creating activities, the application of behavioral insights to this body of law is quite natural. If one wishes to model the choices that people make with respect to risky decisions ex ante, one should incorporate into this model the best available information regarding how people react to risks. Moreover, many cognitive phenomena affect how adjudicators apply tort rules—which suggests that behavioral analysis of tort litigation might also shed light on the choice between the different rules. This section tackles these two issues in order—first with regard to the agents, then to the adjudicators.

12. *See* Shavell, *supra* note 3, at 14–15. The key insight in this regard is that under a negligence regime tortfeasors are expected to behave non-negligently in order to avoid paying damages. Consequently, victims under this regime live in a de facto no-liability regime, since they are not compensated for any harms they incur. Thus, victims can be expected to behave in a non-negligent manner as well, since they wish to minimize the risk of uncompensated harm. Under a strict liability regime, on the other hand, victims always enjoy full compensation, and are therefore not incentivized to take optimal care.

13. *See, e.g.*, Oren Bar-Gill & Omri Ben-Shahar, *The Uneasy Case for Comparative Negligence*, 5 Am. L. & Econ. Rev. 433 (2003).

14. *See* Shavell, *supra* note 3, at 21–26. The key insight in this regard is that under a strict liability rule, tortfeasors must pay for all harms linked to their actions—even when these were carried out with optimal care. Under a negligence regime, on the other hand, they are not required to compensate victims when they have demonstrated optimal care. In the latter case, therefore, tortfeasors might be tempted to engage in an excessive amount of risky behavior, in the knowledge that, by taking optimal care, they can externalize the residual risk created by their actions.

1. Boundedly Rational Agents

Legal scholars who apply economic insights to the analysis of tort law have long since acknowledged that people's decision-making capabilities are relevant to the design of tort law. In their early study on the role of strict liability in tort law, for example, Calabresi and Hirschoof stressed that their model does not rest on theoretical assumptions about people's ability to optimize.[15] Rather, it is attuned to people's actual abilities, including the psychological impediments that might drive their choices.[16] Nonetheless, the reality of mainstream economic analysis of tort law is rational-choice analysis, and behavioral insights are at best delegated to the role of a caveat.[17]

However, a vast body of knowledge that has built up over the years in the area of risky choices suggests that potential tortfeasors do not behave like rational agents. Rather, when engaging in a host of risky activities—ranging from driving a car to performing heart surgery—people tend systematically to err in their decision-making. These errors, in turn, can alter some of the main policy conclusions derived from economic analysis of tort law.

One major factor of human cognition that can affect decisions in risky contexts is *overoptimism*.[18] A large body of literature has shown that people tend to underestimate the probability of adverse events. This phenomenon is widespread, and encompasses most of the population (approximately 80 percent, according to one recent estimate).[19] Researchers have attributed the prevalence of unrealistic optimism to the adaptive nature of this trait,[20] and have even mapped its neurological foundations.[21]

Within the literature documenting people's overoptimism, a significant number of studies have examined it in the context of decisions that people make in tortious situations. For example, many studies have shown that people tend to exhibit unrealistic optimism about the safety of their own driving[22]—in particular, the probability of their causing an auto accident. This, in turn, leads them to take inadequate precautions against accidents.[23]

15. *See* Guido Calabresi & Jon T. Hirschoff, *Toward a Test for Strict Liability in Torts*, 81 YALE L.J. 1055, 1059 (1972).

16. *Id.* at 1059, n.17.

17. *See, e.g.*, SHAVELL, *supra* note 3, at 292 (briefly discussing the decision-making capabilities of individuals).

18. *See supra* pp. 61–64.

19. Tali Sharot, *The Optimism Bias*, 21 CURRENT BIOLOGY R941 (2011).

20. Daniel Nettle, *Adaptive Illusions: Optimism, Control and Human Rationality*, *in* EMOTION, EVOLUTION AND RATIONALITY 193 (Dylan Evans & Pierre Cruse eds., 2004).

21. *See* Tali Sharot et al., *Neural Mechanisms Mediating Optimism Bias*, 450 NATURE 102 (2007); Tali Sharot, *How Dopamine Enhances an Optimism Bias in Humans*, 22 CURRENT BIOLOGY 1477 (2012).

22. *See, e.g.*, Ola Svenson, Baruch Fischhoff & Donald MacGregor, *Perceived Driving Safety and Seatbelt Usage*, 17 ACCIDENT ANALYSIS & PREVENTION 119 (1985); Iain A. McCormick, Frank H. Walkey & Dianne E. Green, *Comparative Perceptions of Driver Ability—A Confirmation and Expansion*, 18 ACCIDENT ANALYSIS & PREVENTION 205 (1986). For similar findings in the context of occupational safety, see Carlo Caponecchia, *It Won't Happen to Me: An Investigation of Optimism Bias in Occupational Health and Safety*, 40 J. APP. SOC. PSYCHOL. 601 (2010).

23. *See* R.F. Soames Job, Virginia Hamer & Michael Walker, *The Effects of Optimism Bias and Fear on Protective Behaviours*, *in* AUSTRALIA'S ADOLESCENTS: A HEALTH PSYCHOLOGY PERSPECTIVE 151, 151–56 (Dianna Kenny & R.F. Soames Job eds., 1995).

Based on these findings, behavioral researchers have argued that policies geared toward encouraging safe driving might prove futile, since most people believe that their driving does not need much improvement.[24] More generally, it has been argued that the optimism bias "may seriously hinder efforts to promote risk-reducing behaviors."[25]

A related but distinct phenomenon is the underweighting of rare events in decisions based on experience.[26] A large body of psychological research suggests that when people are asked to use their experience to gauge the probability of an outcome in a repeated task, they tend to do so based on a small sample of choices. However, while doing so might save time,[27] reduce memory load,[28] and help simplify a complex task,[29] it also leads to systematically suboptimal decisions. Specifically, it causes people to underestimate, or even ignore, low-probability events, and consequently to make choices that do not maximize expected payoffs.

Safety decisions often involve rare events. While failing to take adequate precautions is generally not, in and of itself, sufficient to cause harm to materialize, when coupled with external factors (such as the conduct of someone else, a mechanical problem, or adverse weather conditions), bad outcomes can occur. By way of illustration, readers might consider their own personal driving behavior: while (hopefully) most readers have not recently (or ever) been involved in a serious auto accident, their driving has undoubtedly involved a vast number of careless moments and close calls. Indeed, a survey conducted in the United States found that 21 percent of the population admitted to running a red light in the week preceding the survey, and 16 percent reported driving 10 mph over the speed limit in the same period.[30] These figures clearly underestimate the incidence of unsafe driving, as they are based on self-reporting, and therefore reflect a self-serving bias. Moreover, many safety decisions involve far more nuanced and arguably common aspects of driving—such as paying insufficient attention to the rearview mirror, or too much attention to billboards and cell phones.

24. *Id.*

25. Neil D. Weinstein, *Optimistic Biases about Personal Risks*, 246 Sci. 1232 (1989).

26. *See* Ralph Hertwig et al., *Decisions from Experience and the Effect of Rare Events in Risky Choice*, 15 Psychol. Sci. 534 (2004).

27. *See* Craig R. Fox & Liat Hadar, *"Decisions from Experience" = Sampling Error + Prospect Theory: Reconsidering Hertwig, Barron, Weber, & Erev (2004)*, 1 Judgment & Decision Making 159 (2006).

28. *See* Yaakov Kareev, *Seven (Indeed, Plus or Minus Two) and the Detection of Correlations*, 107 Psychol. Rev. 397 (2000).

29. Ralph Hertwig & Timothy J. Pleskac, *Decisions from Experience: Why Small Samples?*, 115 Cognition 225 (2010).

30. *See* U.S. Dep't of Transp., Nat'l Highway Traffic Safety Admin., National Survey of Speeding and Other Unsafe Driving Actions: Driver Attitudes and Behavior 119–35 (1998). *See also* Bryan E. Porter & Thomas D. Berry, *A Nationwide Survey of Self-Reported Red Light Running: Measuring Prevalence, Predictors, and Perceived Consequence*, 33 Accident Analysis & Prevention 735, 737 (2001) (presenting survey data that approximately 20 percent of the population report running a red light during one of their previous ten crossings at a signalized intersection).

Systematic data on workplace accidents offers a more rigorous demonstration of the rarity of harmful events in relation to risky behavior. For example, in a seminal early study of workplace accidents, Herbert William Heinrich estimated that given the human tendency to take inadequate precautions, the probability of an accident is 1:300.[31] Other studies have since expanded this finding, and have demonstrated how rare harmful events are. Based on a study of 1.7 million accidents at 297 companies, Frank Bird concluded that the ratio of fatal accidents to near-miss incidents is 1:600.[32] A later study conducted by the multinational oil-and-gas company ConcoPhillips Marine estimated that each fatal event is linked to some 300,000 incidents of at-risk behavior (i.e., behavior contrary to safety guidelines or to machinery operation training).[33] The overall picture from these studies is that people engaging in risky behavior can repeatedly make careless decisions with no adverse consequences.

Several models have attempted to incorporate overoptimism into the analysis of liability rules. Eric Posner, for example, analyzed overoptimism in conjunction with probability insensitivity.[34] The framework of his model is that overoptimism causes tortfeasors to overestimate the effectiveness of precautions—so that once the perceived probability of an accident falls below a certain threshold, tortfeasors assume that it is equal to zero. Under these assumptions, Posner demonstrates that bounded rationality can lead to a host of different outcomes, though he does not point to any clear difference with respect to care decisions between strict liability and negligence. According to his analysis, when people's overoptimism is low, it does not change their choices, and they continue to take optimal care, for fear of tort liability. Conversely, when their overoptimism is high, people may be driven to take too little care, as they underestimate the probability of an accident. Somewhat counterintuitively, however, when their optimism is moderate, Posner's model suggests that tortfeasors may be driven to take *excessive* care. The underlying intuition of this result is that the moderately optimistic tortfeasor may overestimate the effectiveness of marginal precautions, and wrongfully assume that such precautions completely eliminate the risk of accidents.

While this model is internally consistent, its logical underpinnings are problematic. For one, overoptimism in this model is tied to the *effectiveness of precautions*, rather than to the perceived probability of an accident. Although this premise is key to the results of the model, its empirical basis is unclear. Also uncertain is how the probability threshold in the model translates into reality: if the probability of an accident is sufficiently low, the nuanced analysis of various levels of overoptimism is not expected to come into play, since tortfeasors will routinely assume that "it will never happen to me."[35]

31. *See* HERBERT WILLIAM HEINRICH, INDUSTRIAL ACCIDENT PREVENTION: A SCIENTIFIC APPROACH 26–28 (1931).

32. *See* FRANK E. BIRD, JR. MANAGEMENT GUIDE TO LOSS CONTROL 17–18 (1974).

33. *See id.* (describing the results of ConcoPhillips Marine, *Safety Pyramid Based on a Study* (April 2003)).

34. Eric A. Posner, *Probability Errors: Some Positive and Normative Implications for Tort and Contract Law*, 11 SUP. COURT ECON. REV. 125 (2004).

35. For a similar critique of Posner's model, see Halbersberg & Guttel, *supra* note 6, at 414.

Subsequent models whose analysis incorporated overoptimism in conjunction with attitudes toward ambiguity reached somewhat more intuitive results.[36] As they demonstrate, overoptimism per se is associated with a clear decline in levels of care taken by tortfeasors. However, when overoptimism is coupled with ambiguity, a set of highly stylized and nuanced results emerges in comparisons between strict liability and negligence, depending on the parameters of the model. For example, when the harm caused by an accident is fixed, and only its probability is affected by the level of care, tortfeasors will always take too little care under a strict liability regime, while under a negligence rule they will take too little, or optimal, care (depending on the parameters of the model). Generally, however, these models suggest that the negligence rule offers better incentives to take optimal care, due to the discontinuous nature of the payoffs associated with taking due care.

In light of these complex predictions, the dearth of published empirical findings in this area is somewhat surprising. The key study in the area was authored by Lewis Kornhauser and Andrew Schotter.[37] In the experiments of their study, participants repeatedly faced the decision regarding the level of care they needed to take, under a strict liability or under a negligence rule. Their findings were at odds with the predictions of the traditional model that negligence and strict liability are equivalent: under the negligence rule, participants generally chose to take optimal care in their decisions throughout the experiment, while those operating under the strict-liability rule changed strategy over time. Specifically, they tended to take excessive care in the early rounds of the experiment, then relaxed their precautions and took insufficient care in the final rounds. Based on these results, Kornhauser and Schotter have argued that there is a bounded-rationality justification for the negligence rule.[38] According to their analysis, the negligence rule helps people with the complex task of choosing the appropriate level of care by highlighting a specific level in particular. Strict liability, in contrast, leaves this decision to the discretion of the potential tortfeasors—a decision that, it seems, is too onerous for some.

In general, therefore, it appears that behavioral analysis of tort liability rules lends more support to adopting the negligence rule. This conclusion, however, should be treated with caution. For one, it is derived from highly stylized models that are sensitive to their defining parameters. Second, it is founded on fairly limited empirical evidence. Finally, taking into account the cognitive limitations of adjudicators in the analysis can lead to the opposite conclusion.[39] In this respect, behavioral economic analysis does not differ much from mainstream economic analysis, which has also yet to offer a definitive answer to this question.[40]

36. *See* Joshua C. Teitelbaum, *A Unilateral Accident Model under Ambiguity*, 36 J. Legal Stud. 431 (2007); Surajeet Chakravarty & David Kelsey, *Ambiguity and Accident Law*, 19 J. Pub. Econ. Theory 97 (2017).

37. *See* Lewis Kornhauser & Andrew Schotter, *An Experimental Study of Single-Actor Accidents*, 19 J. Legal Stud. 203 (1990). *See also* Vera Angelova, *Relative Performance of Liability Rules: Experimental Evidence*, 77 Theory & Decision 531 (2014).

38. Kornhauser & Schotter, *supra* note 37, at 231–32.

39. *See infra* pp. 336–40.

40. *See supra* pp. 326–29.

However, there is a more radical normative conclusion to be drawn from behavioral analysis—namely, that in many instances tort law is not the proper legal means of regulating risk-creating activities. The major alternatives to tort law are risk-based legal regimes that assign liability to the *creators of risks*—irrespective of whether these risks result in actual harm. For example, if lighting fireworks close to a residential dwelling produces a 1:100 risk of $1,000,000 worth of damage, tort law kicks in only in the rare cases when harm has actually occurred—whereupon the tortfeasor is required to fully compensate the victim. A risk-based regime, on the other hand, would require anyone who creates such a risk to pay $10,000 for doing so—regardless of whether harm has occurred.

All else being equal, both a harm-based regime and a risk-based regime can create efficient incentives for tortfeasors.[41] From an ex-ante perspective, it does not matter whether an individual who is contemplating setting off dangerous fireworks faces a 1 percent chance of paying $1,000,000, or a 100 percent probability of paying $10,000. However, all else is *not* equal, and legal economists have devoted significant attention to highlighting the relative advantages of each regime.[42] Informational issues, for example, might point toward adopting one of the regimes.[43] Generally, when the parties possess superior information, a harm-based regime is best, whereas when the regulator is better informed, a risk-based regime might be preferable. Similarly, the magnitude of harm can also factor in the choice of regime.[44] When the harm is exceptionally small, or exceptionally large, a tort system may be problematic. With small harms, the high costs of litigation might eliminate the victims' incentive to file a lawsuit, thus negating the deterrence effect of the tort system. With large harms, defendants may lack the resources to compensate for them as they occur—once again, diluting the incentives to take care.

To some extent, the many considerations in this context have allowed legal economists to avoid taking an unequivocal position as to which legal regime is preferable. Recently, however, Steven Shavell has proposed that there is a "fundamental" enforcement advantage to harm-based regimes[45]—namely, that, unlike regulation (which must be enforced regardless of whether or not harm materializes), harm-based regimes trigger enforcement costs only in the small subset of cases where harm actually occurs. Consequently, under a harm-based regime, appropriate incentives can be generated at lower cost. For this reason, he argues that a harm-based regime may be "a cheaper, more efficient method of enforcing socially desired behavior than regulation."[46] Interestingly, even when Shavell acknowledges

41. *See* Samuel Issacharoff, *Preclusion, Due Process, and the Right to Opt Out of Class Actions*, 77 NOTRE DAME L. REV. 1057, 1076 (2002).

42. Donald Wittman, *Prior Regulation versus Post Liability: The Choice between Input and Output*, 26 J. LEGAL STUD. 145 (1977); Steven Shavell, *A Model of the Optimal Use of Liability and Safety Regulation*, 15 RAND J. ECON. 271 (1984), SHAVELL *supra* note 3, at 279–82.

43. SHAVELL, *supra* note 3, at 281.

44. *Id.* at 179–80.

45. *See* Steven Shavell, *A Fundamental Enforcement Cost Advantage of the Negligence Rule over Regulation*, 42 J. LEGAL STUD. 275 (2013).

46. *Id.* at 276.

factors outside the regulation-favoring model, his analysis continues to assume perfect rationality—so the only two issues he alludes to are the judgment-proof problem, and the difficulties associated with proving causation in court.[47]

This type of analysis, however, overlooks the fundamental behavioral argument in favor of safety regulation. Given people's tendency to disregard rare events, the very advantage at the heart of Shavell's model—the relative rarity of enforcement under a harm regime—turns out to be a disadvantage. If people routinely engage in risky behavior with no adverse consequences, they may, in time, no longer view this behavior as entailing any risk. As a result, in a harm-based regime individuals will tend to take excessive risks. Unfortunately, incentivizing imperfectly rational agents to take sufficient care is a costly endeavor, requiring frequent enforcement that continually reminds people that not taking care comes at a price.

Evidence in the field supports this view. Many private entities seeking to reduce risky behavior by their employees use behavioral insights—in particular, a form of soft regulation based on frequent acts of enforcement that carry relatively minor sanctions. For example, one hospital introduced a gentle reminder policy whereby employees were encouraged to remind their coworkers of the safety norm whenever they observed it being violated. This policy proved effective in increasing safe behavior:[48] compliance with the norm rose from 55 percent before the policy to around 90 percent after its introduction (a level that it remained at, for years to come). A similar intervention in eleven mid-sized (50–700 workers) factories raised compliance with safety norms from around 60 percent to approximately 90 percent (once again, for years after that).[49] Within the workplace safety literature, it is common knowledge that "risk management does not wait for an injury or damage to occur rather it encourages training, processes and systems to address possible risks that may present in the future."[50] To the extent that one can infer *ought* from *is*—as lawyer-economists tend to believe—these findings count as evidence against strong reliance on a harm-based regime.

Of course, risk regulation is no panacea. Since enforcement of risk regulation is still imperfect, overoptimism can cause people to underestimate the probability of legal liability. For example, people tend to systematically underestimate the chances that they will be ticketed for risky behavior, such as speeding or running a red light.[51] Nonetheless, the probability of legal liability in a risk-based regime is generally much higher than in a harm-based regime—which suggests that the problem would, at least, be smaller. Moreover, in a

47. *Id.* at 297–98.

48. *See* Ido Erev et al., *The Value of Gentle Enforcement on Safe Medical Procedures*, 19 Quality & Safety in Health Care 1 (2010).

49. *See* Amos Schurr, Dotan Rodensky & Ido Erev, *The Effect of Unpleasant Experiences on Evaluation and Behavior*, 106 J. Econ. Behav. & Org. 1 (2014).

50. *See* Susanne Bahn, *Workplace Hazard Identification and Management: The Case of an Underground Mining Operation*, 57 Safety Sci. 129, 129 (2013).

51. *See* Patricia Delhomme, Jean-François Verlhiac & Cécile Martha, *Are Drivers' Comparative Risk Judgments about Speeding Realistic?*, 40 J. Safety Res. 333 (2009).

risk-based regime the ability of policymakers to change the probability of legal liability is greater, since they can allocate additional resources for enforcement.

2. Boundedly Rational Adjudicators

In this subsection we turn to examining how adjudicators' cognitive biases and heuristics might influence the design of tort law.[52] We start by re-examining the comparison between negligence and strict liability regimes in light of the hindsight and outcome biases, then look at the more specific instances of tort regimes that divide responsibility between plaintiffs and defendants, and highlight the ramifications that the phenomenon of *anchoring* may have on the application of legal rules in this context.

(a) Negligence versus Strict Liability and the Hindsight Bias

The *hindsight bias* refers to peoples' tendency to overestimate the probability of an event, once they are aware that it has happened. In the wake of psychologists who documented this phenomenon in a broad range of settings,[53] legal researchers have demonstrated its effect on decisions in the realm of tort law.[54] In an influential article, Kim Kamin and Jeffrey Rachlinski showed that ex-ante evaluations of precautions differ significantly from ex-post ones.[55] Participants in their study were asked to evaluate a city's decision about the proper precautions to be taken with regard to the risk of floods. All subjects were given the same facts about the costs and effectiveness of the possible measures—however, they differed in the perspective they were provided from which to evaluate the precautions. Subjects in the Foresight group simulated an administrative hearing that was held to decide what precautions to take before any harm materialized, while subjects in the Hindsight group simulated a trial that was held in the aftermath of such harm. The results showed a significant difference between the two groups: participants in the Hindsight group were far more likely to determine that the precautions should have been taken. Similar results were documented in another study, involving precautions to be taken by a therapist against the risk of a patient behaving violently.[56] Other studies have examined this issue in the context of actual court decisions: one such study—that looked at 1,004 cases of alleged anesthesia-related negligence—found that in over 40 percent of them the court found the defendant physician liable, even though he or she had acted appropriately.[57]

52. For behavioral analysis of judicial decision-making, see generally *infra* pp. 525–65.

53. *See generally supra* pp. 38–39.

54. For a review of the hindsight bias in different legal contexts, see Doron Teichman, *The Hindsight Bias and the Law in Hindsight*, *in* THE OXFORD HANDBOOK OF BEHAVIORAL ECONOMICS AND THE LAW, *supra* note 6, at 354.

55. *See* Kim A. Kamin & Jeffrey J. Rachlinski, *Ex Post ≠ Ex Ante: Determining Liability in Hindsight*, 19 LAW & HUM. BEHAV. 89 (1995).

56. *See* Susan J. LaBine & Gary LaBine, *Determinations of Negligence and the Hindsight Bias*, 20 LAW & HUM. BEHAV. 501 (1996).

57. *See* Frederick W. Cheney, *Standard of Care and Anesthesia Liability*, 261 J. AM. MEDICAL ASS'N 1599 (1989). *See also* Mark I. Taragin et al., *The Influence of Standard of Care and Severity of Injury on the Resolution of Medical Malpractice Claims*, 117 ANNALS INTERNAL MED. 780 (1992) (showing that in 21 percent of the cases examined, the physicians in question were found liable for wholly defensible practices).

Another phenomenon related to the hindsight bias is the *outcome bias*, which denotes the influence of outcomes on peoples' judgments of the wisdom of decisions.[58] While the hindsight bias focuses on evaluators' ex-post assessments of probability, the outcome bias focuses on evaluators' assessments of the *quality* of decisions made by a decision-maker, given precisely the same information that the decision-maker had possessed ex ante (including explicit probabilities). This body of literature found a direct link between outcomes and judgments: simply put, people have a harsher view of decisions with bad outcomes. In one tort-related experiment, Johnathan Baron and John Hershey asked subjects to evaluate a surgeon's decision to conduct heart surgery that entailed an 8 percent risk of death, but also numerous potential benefits.[59] They found that peoples' evaluation of the decision to operate depended significantly on the outcome of the operation: when the outcome was death, they viewed the decision to operate as less reasonable, even though they had been informed of the specific risks involved.

Both the hindsight bias and the outcome bias suggest that adjudicators who retrospectively evaluate decisions that ultimately prove to be harmful tend to assign liability even if the tortfeasors took reasonable decisions ex ante. As the literature has shown, however, the normative conclusions to be derived from this point are somewhat elusive.[60] More specifically, the impact of these biases on the behavior of tortfeasors depends on the magnitude of their effect on judicial decisions: when the bias is relatively small, tortfeasors are incentivized to take excessive care that meets the standard set by biased adjudicators. By taking further, inefficient, precautions, tortfeasors can ensure that they will be found non-negligent, and therefore absolved of the costs of their risky activity.

This point can be illustrated by the numerical example presented earlier. Table 2 presents a modified version of that example, in which adjudicators overestimate the probability of an accident by 50 percent in tort cases. As a result, these adjudicators erroneously determine that the required level of care under a negligence regime is 2, rather than 1. This, in turn, prompts tortfeasors to adopt a care level of 2. To see why, note that the tortfeasors'

TABLE 2 **Numerical example of link between investment in care and the probability of accident when the probability of accident is judged in hindsight to be 50% higher (Harm = 100)**

Level of Care	Cost of Care	Probability of Accident	Biased Probability Assessment	Expected Accident Losses	Biased Expected Losses	Total Cost of Accidents	Biased Total Cost
0	0	42%	63%	42	63	42	63
1	10	25%	37.5%	25	37.5	35	47.5
2	25	13%	19.5%	13	19.5	38	44.5
3	45	2%	3%	14	3	47	48

58. *See* Jonathan Baron & John C. Hershey, *Outcome Bias in Decision Evaluation*, 54 J. PERSONALITY & SOC. PSYCHOL. 569 (1988).

59. *Id.* at 571–72.

60. *See* Jeffery J. Rachlinski, *A Positive Psychological Theory of Judging in Hindsight*, 65 U. CHI. L. REV. 571 (1998).

TABLE 3 **Numerical example of the link between investment in care and the probability of accident, when the probability of accident is judged in hindsight to be 100% higher (Harm = 100)**

Level of Care	Cost of Care	Probability of Accident	Biased Probability Assessment	Expected Accident Losses	Biased Expected Losses	Total Cost of Accidents	Biased Total Cost
0	0	42%	84%	42	84	42	84
1	10	25%	50%	25	50	35	60
2	25	13%	26%	13	26	48	51
3	45	2%	4%	14	24	47	49

expected cost of care at Level 1 is 47.5 (the cost of care coupled with the cost of accidents, since they will be found liable)—whereas their expected cost of taking care at a Level 2 is only 25 (since then they are found to be non-liable, and do not bear the costs of accidents).

However, when the bias is sufficiently large, negligence regime begins to mimic a de facto strict liability regime. In these cases, regardless of what the tortfeasors do, they are always held liable for the harms they cause, since any choice they make is deemed negligent in hindsight. As we have seen, a strict liability regime actually incentivizes tortfeasors to take optimal care, since it induces them to internalize the full costs of their activity. Table 3 demonstrates this by highlighting the change in the incentive structure if adjudicators in hindsight overestimate probabilities by 100 percent. In this example, this bias will cause adjudicators to erroneously determine that the required level of care is 3, rather than 1. In reality, however, tortfeasors will not take this high level of care, since doing so will cost them 45, while taking optimal care will only cost them 35.

While this analysis shows that the negligence rule does not always lead to inefficient outcomes, it does highlight potential systemic problems with its application. The possibility that judges will be able to craft rules that distinguish between cases based on their degree of bias seems extremely unlikely. Even more unlikely is that potential tortfeasors will be able to work out the different implications of biased judicial decisions in this context. Finally, efforts to debias decision-makers in these conditions have been proven to be mostly ineffective.[61] Consequently, the legal literature has mapped out numerous potential policies—both substantive and procedural—that might ameliorate the perverse incentives created by biased decisions in negligence cases.

At the substantive level, legal scholars have found a potential advantage to moving to liability rules that are based on standards that are formulated ex ante.[62] By shifting the analysis in this way, some of the problems created by the hindsight bias can be alleviated. The two main tools that come to mind in this regard are statutory regulations set by governmental agencies and backed up by criminal or administrative sanctions, and standard practices established by the relevant industry. Any rule that accepts compliance with such

61. *See* Teichman, *supra* note 54, at 364–66.

62. *See, e.g.*, Rachlinski, *supra* note 60, at 608–13.

standards as a complete defense against negligence liability would negate the problems associated with ex-post evaluation.

In practice, however, courts mostly refuse to adopt a deferential stance toward compliance with such regulations or standard practices. In the United States, the *Restatement of Torts* provides that compliance with "custom of the community" can be introduced as evidence of non-negligence, but does not offer a complete defense.[63] This legal policy may be reasonable in light of other considerations, such as the desire to keep legal precautions up to date and innovative,[64] or the concern that government agencies are captured by interest groups.[65] Ultimately, however, it means that potential tortfeasors cannot avoid the risks associated with hindsight judgments by relying on compliance with standard practices and regulations.

Despite the general rule of the *Restatement of Torts*, there are concrete contexts where the law does defer to standards that are set ex ante. Designated "safe harbors" enable tortfeasors who take the specified precautions to avoid liability. Certain pockets of tort law—ranging from parts of product liability law, to liability for the sale of alcohol to intoxicated individuals who are subsequently involved in an accident—are governed by such safe harbors for those who meet the statutory level of care.[66] In the area of medical malpractice, there are many calls for the creation of similar safe harbors, based on evidence-based standards.[67]

Another path that the law could take to deal with the pitfalls of biased decisions in negligence cases is procedural in nature: scholars have proposed bifurcating tort proceedings so that the negligence question is dealt with separately.[68] For example, Christine Jolls, Cass Sunstein, and Richard Thaler have proposed that in medical malpractice cases that involve striking a balance between two risky options (e.g., cesarean section versus vaginal birth), jurors will be presented with the facts as the physician knew them ex ante, but not told the outcome of the procedure.[69] If jurors are unaware of the outcome, so the argument goes, the problems of hindsight judgments can be eliminated.

While bifurcation might prove useful in cases that involve choosing between two risky strategies, it is far less useful in most tort cases. As Russell Korobkin and Thomas

63. *See* Restatement (Third) of Torts: Liability for Physical and Emotional Harm §13(a) (Am. Law Inst. 2009).

64. Gideon Parchomovsky & Alex Stein, *Torts and Innovation*, 107 Mich. L. Rev. 285 (2008).

65. *See generally* Ernesto Dal Bó, *Regulatory Capture: A Review*, 22 Oxford Rev. Econ. Pol'y. 203 (2006).

66. *See* Alexandra B. Klass, *Tort Experiments in the Laboratories of Democracy*, 50 Wm & Mary L. Rev. 1501 (2009) (product liability); Milton Augustus Turner, *Recent Developments in Indiana Tort Law*, 43 Ind. L. Rev. 1053 (2009) (dram shop).

67. *See* James F. Blumstein, *Medical Malpractice Standard-Setting: Developing Malpractice "Safe Harbors" as a New Role for QIOs*, 59 Vand. L. Rev. 1017 (2006).

68. *See* Norman G. Poythress, *Negligent Release Litigation: A Proposal for Procedural Reform*, 17 J. Psychiatry & L. 595 (1989); Jolls, Sunstein & Thaler, *supra* note 5, at 1528–29.

69. Jolls, Sunstein & Thaler, *supra* note 5.

Ulen have pointed out,[70] in the majority of such cases jurors are asked to examine whether the tortfeasor was required to take additional (costly) safety measures. In other words, the tortfeasor's choice is not between measure X and measure Y, but between adopting a level of care of X, or X+A. In this paradigm, there is no way to insulate fact-finders from knowing whether or not harm occurred, since the litigation itself is evidence that it did.

(b) Contributory Negligence versus Comparative Negligence and Anchoring

So far, we have focused on only one party—the tortfeasor. Often, however, tort law examines both the behavior of the tortfeasor and that of the victim. This might be done on grounds of efficiency (the need to incentivize potential victims to take due care),[71] or for non-instrumental reasons (such as the desire to reach a fair outcome toward both parties).[72]

Tort law has focused on victim behavior through doctrines such as *contributory negligence* and *comparative negligence*.[73] The former adopts an all-or-nothing approach, and denies compensation from victims who have behaved negligently, while the latter reduces compensation in proportion to the relative fault of both the plaintiff and the defendant. The clear trend in common law jurisdictions in recent decades has been toward comparative, rather than contributory, negligence.[74]

Given the continuous nature of the comparative negligence regime, decision-makers have significant discretion when called upon to divide liability. As a practical matter, the law offers limited guidance as to the ratio to be used in such cases (e.g., 20:80, 30:70, etc.)—even though this can have substantial implications.[75] Behavioral analysis, however, has shown that cognitive bias can affect how this rule is applied.

Specifically, judicial decision-makers charged with translating human behavior into a numerical liability scale might be influenced by a range of anchors.[76] These anchors might be introduced by the litigants themselves, in an effort to structure the discussion around a figure that serves their interests. Alternatively—and perhaps more interestingly—the law itself might introduce an anchor into the comparative negligence litigation. While many jurisdictions apply a pure comparative negligence regime that allows for any division of responsibility between the plaintiff and the defendant, others use a modified rule according

70. *See* Russell B. Korobkin & Thomas S. Ulen, *Law and Behavioral Science: Removing the Rationality Assumption from Law and Economics*, 88 CAL. L. REV. 1051, 1095–100 (2000).

71. *See, e.g.*, Bar-Gill & Ben-Shahar, *supra* note 13.

72. *See, e.g.*, Gary T. Schwartz, *Contributory and Comparative Negligence: A Reappraisal*, 87 YALE L.J. 697, 721–27 (1978).

73. *See generally* DAN B. DOBBS, PAUL T. HAYDEN & ELLEN M. BUBLICK, HORNBOOK ON TORTS 384–85 (2d ed., 2000).

74. *Id.*

75. *See, e.g.*, VICTOR E. SCHWARTZ & EVELYN F. ROWE, COMPARATIVE NEGLIGENCE 356 (4th ed. 2002).

76. On anchoring and adjustment, see generally *supra* pp. 79–82.

to which the doctrine kicks in only if the plaintiff's share of responsibility is below 50 percent.[77] If the plaintiff's share of fault is higher than 50 percent, his claim is dismissed, and he receives no compensation whatsoever (even though he is not fully to blame).

An experiment conducted with advanced-years law students at a leading American university confirmed the anchoring effect of the 50 percent rule.[78] Participants read a short vignette about a hypothetical tort case brought by a pedestrian who had been hit by a car. The case was designed to reflect a relatively low fault on the part of the plaintiff. After reading the facts of the case, subjects in the No-Anchor group were told that the jurisdiction applies a comparative negligence rule, and were asked to determine the degree of responsibility to assign to the victim. Subjects in the Anchor group were told that the jurisdiction in question went by a 50 percent rule, and asked the same question. The key difference between the groups was that subjects in the Anchor group were asked to rule on a motion made by the defendant's lawyer (with no supporting evidence or legal arguments) that the plaintiff's fault exceeded 50 percent, and therefore the case should be dismissed. Although subjects in that group were almost unanimous in the view that the motion should be denied (recall that by design, the plaintiff's fault was low), the motion did significantly influence their decisions: when they were presented with no anchor, the mean level of fault assigned to the plaintiff was 15.2 percent, but when presented with the 50 percent anchor, the mean level of fault assigned to the plaintiff rose to 26.25 percent. In other words, an entirely meritless legal claim that anchored the legal analysis on a salient high number managed to almost double the level of fault that the respondents attributed to the plaintiff. This finding can be added to the host of arguments raised against the 50 percent rule.[79]

D. Behavioral Analysis: Damages

This section examines the implications of behavioral analysis for the calculation of tort damages. It focuses on the aspects of damages that are unique to the area of tort law. Issues relating to damages beyond the realm of tort law (though very relevant to tort law) are discussed in Chapter 15 on judicial decision-making.[80] These issues include topics such as the role of heuristics and biases in the calculation of damages, the influence of group decision-making on the determination of damages, and differences between judges and jurors in this respect.

77. *See* Dobbs, Hayden & Bublick, *supra* note 73, at 385.

78. *See* Yuval Feldman, Amos Schurr & Doron Teichman, *Anchoring Legal Standards*, 13 J. Empirical Legal Stud. 298, 318–20 (2016).

79. *See, e.g.*, Eli K. Best & John J. Donohue, III, *Jury Nullification in Modified Comparative Negligence Regimes*, 79 U. Chi. L. Rev. 945 (2012).

80. *See infra* pp. 538–43.

1. Framing the Question

Tort law deals with injuries involving both monetary and non-monetary losses. While calculating the precise value of monetary losses can be complex, the debate surrounding such damages is relatively constrained. Although the task facing a decision-maker who is asked to calculate the present value of the lost earnings of a young accident victim may be challenging, the parameters of the task can be worked out within reason. With non-monetary damages, however, the calculation task becomes far more challenging: there is arguably no clear benchmark for determining the appropriate dollar amount to be attached to the pain and suffering associated with losing one's arm, eyesight, reproductive abilities, or a close relative. Consequently, in cases of this sort behavioral phenomena may play a significant part in the determinations made of such damages by judges and jurors.

The effect that cognitive forces can have on how people calculate damages for pain and suffering can be illustrated by the extent to which framing can influence damage decisions.[81] Tort damages can be framed in two distinct ways. One centers on the pre-accident perspective, by examining how much money people would demand in order to agree to incur the loss they incurred. This is the *willingness-to-accept* (WTA) criterion. The other frame is based on the post-accident perspective, and asks how much money needs to be paid to victims to make them whole again. This is the *willingness-to-pay* (WTP) criterion.[82]

While the difference between these two perspectives might seem semantic, empirical findings suggest that this framing has a significant effect on people's damage assessments. In an experimental study, Edward McCaffery, Daniel Kahneman, and Matthew Spitzer asked subjects to determine damages for pain and suffering for the same injury, while manipulating the instructions:[83] whereas some subjects were told to analyze the case from a WTA perspective, others were instructed to use the WTP perspective.[84] The mean damage award rendered by subjects who were asked to use the WTA perspective was approximately twice as much as the mean damage award from the WTP perspective.[85]

These findings echo the core insights of prospect theory.[86] When asked to assess damages in a WTA frame, the pre-accident state functions as the reference point, and subjects place a high price on changing it for the worse. In a WTP frame, on the other hand, the reference point is the post-accident state, so the decision pertains to the realm of gains.[87] However, the tort damages context is unique, and other forces might be at play. For example, while both the WTP and WTA involve *monetization* (assigning money value to objects), the WTA perspective is more closely related to *commodification* (allocating objects

81. *See* Edward J. McCaffery, Daniel J. Kahneman & Matthew L. Spitzer, *Framing the Jury: Cognitive Perspectives on Pain and Suffering Awards*, 81 VA. L. REV. 1341 (1995).

82. On these notions and on the WTA-WTP disparity, see *supra* pp. 16–17, 50–56.

83. *See* McCaffery, Kahneman & Spitzer, *supra* note 81, at 1354–73.

84. The experiment also included a control group that received no instructions. *Id.* at 1356.

85. *Id.* at 1359.

86. *Id.* at 1372–73. On prospect theory, see generally *supra* pp. 42–57.

87. *See also infra* pp. 503–04, 510–12, 593–95.

through the market)—something that most people strongly resent when it comes to health and body organs.[88]

At the positive level, these findings might help explain at least some of the volatility in pain and suffering awards. As we have seen, nuanced changes in instructions can produce dramatic differences in damage awards. In addition, these findings are clearly relevant to plaintiff lawyers who want to bolster the damages awarded to their clients. As one trial judge noted in a questionnaire administered by McCaffery, Kahneman, and Spitzer: "This approach [WTA] is always used by good and effective plaintiff trial lawyers [. . .] This tactic is particularly useful in cases where human injury is great, but economic loss may be small (e.g., facial scarring)."[89]

The normative conclusions to be drawn from this result with regard to the proper framing of damages are not straightforward. If one views loss aversion as a type of bias, the high damage assessments obtained in the WTA frame might arguably be viewed as irrationally excessive—so the law should strive to frame damage rulings in WTP terms. But, as previously noted, there is no inherent reason to view loss aversion or its attendant decisions as irrational.[90] That said, it is quite possible that in the unique context of tortious injuries, people tend to assign an excessive valuation to the pre-accident state of affairs. The next subsection will explore this point in greater detail.

2. Hedonic Damages

Hedonic damages aim to capture the *loss of enjoyment of life* resulting from a tortious act.[91] They aim to compensate the victim for limiting his "ability to participate in and derive pleasure from the normal activities of daily life," as well as for his "inability to pursue his talents, recreational interests, hobbies, or avocations"[92]—as distinct from *pain and suffering damages*, which focus on the discomfort caused directly by the injury itself.[93] Hedonic damages are compensable by law in many jurisdictions, although precisely how they are proven and calculated may differ.[94]

The development of hedonic damages by the courts has gone hand in hand with the growing acceptance of the view that disabilities are a tragedy that dramatically impairs people's ability to derive pleasure from life.[95] Court rulings on hedonic damages routinely

88. *Cf.* Russell Korobkin, *The Endowment Effect and Legal Analysis*, 97 NW. U. L. REV. 1227, 1288 (2003).

89. McCaffery, Kahneman & Spitzer, *supra* note 81, at 1377.

90. *See supra* pp. 196–97.

91. *See generally* Tina M. Tabacchi, *Hedonic Damages: A New Trend in Compensation?*, 52 OHIO ST. L.J. 331, 331–35 (1991).

92. *See* Boan v. Blackwell, 541 S.E.2d 242, 244 (S.C. 2001).

93. For a discussion of the nuanced distinction between these types of damages, see Cass R. Sunstein, *Illusory Losses*, 37:S2 J. LEGAL STUD. S157, S159–60 (2008).

94. *Id.*

95. For a review of the case law in the United States, see Samuel R. Bagenstos & Margo Schlanger, *Hedonic Damages, Hedonic Adaptation, and Disability*, 60 VAND. L. REV. 745, 755–60 (2009).

view disabled people as being unable to obtain any significant pleasure from life due to their physical impairment. According to this perspective, disabilities are seen as depriving people of their dignity and of their ability to lead a meaningful and joyful life—either intrinsically, or through the limitations that they impose on certain activities. This view is particularly prevalent in cases involving major injuries (e.g., quadriplegia), but is also true in cases of relatively minor injuries (such as amputation of fingers).

The approach of granting generous compensation for hedonic damages arguably overlooks the well-documented phenomenon of *hedonic adaptation*—namely, people's tendency to adjust to new situations, such that even dramatic changes in their lives ultimately result in relatively minor changes in their subjective well-being. While in the short run people's happiness might be impacted by positive or negative events, in the long term they tend to revert to their happiness "set-point"—even in the face of significant life events.[96] In an early classic study, Philip Brickman, Dan Coates, and Ronnie Janoff Bulman compared the happiness levels of three groups—lottery winners, accident victims (paraplegics or quadriplegics), and a control group. The three groups reported surprisingly similar happiness measures, and exhibited a tendency to converge toward their long-term well-being level.[97] Since that study, a large body of literature has documented the ability of people to cope with disabilities in various settings. Studies of specific disabilities have shown that people adjust to physical conditions such as paraplegia,[98] quadriplegia,[99] amputation,[100] and severe burns.[101] A longitudinal study of approximately 10,000 British individuals reached similar conclusions.[102] However, there is a caveat to this general picture: people suffering from disabilities involving constant chronic pain do tend to exhibit a long-term drop in their happiness level.[103] This may be due to the uncertainty associated with such conditions, and the attendant perpetual fear that the situation might deteriorate still further.[104]

96. For a review, see Sonja Lyubomirsky, *Hedonic Adaption to Positive and Negative Experiences*, *in* THE OXFORD HANDBOOK OF STRESS, HEALTH AND COPING 200 (Susan Folkman ed., 2011).

97. *See* Philip Brickman, Dan Coates & Ronnie Janoff Bulman, *Lottery Winners and Accident Victims: Is Happiness Relative?*, 36 J. PERSONALITY & SOC. PSYCHOL. 917, 918–21 (1978).

98. *See* Richard Schulz & Susan Decker, *Long-Term Adjustment to Physical Disability: The Role of Social Support, Perceived Control and Self-Blame,* 48 J. PERSONALITY & SOC. PSYCHOL. 1162 (1985).

99. *See* Camille B. Wortman & Roxane C. Silver, *Coping with Irrevocable Loss*, *in* CATACLYSMS, CRISES, AND CATASTROPHES: PSYCHOLOGY IN ACTION 185 (Gary R. VandenBos & Brenda K. Bryant eds., 1987).

100. *See* Olga Horgan & Malcolm MacLachlan, *Psychosocial Adjustment to Lower-Limb Amputation: A Review*, 26 DISABILITY & REHABILITATION 837 (2004).

101. *See* David R. Patterson et al., *Psychological Effects of Severe Burn Injuries*. 113 PSYCHOL. BULL. 362 (1993).

102. *See* Martin Binder & Alex Coad, *"I'm Afraid I Have Bad News for You . . ." Estimating the Impact of Different Health Impairments on Subjective Well-Being*, 87 SOC. SCI. & MED. 155 (2013).

103. For a review of the findings, see Edie Greene, Kristin A. Sturm & Andrew J. Evelo, *Affective Forecasting about Hedonic Loss and Adaptation: Implications for Damage Awards*, 40 LAW & HUM. BEHAV. 244, 246 (2016).

104. *See* Sunstein, *supra* note 93, at S167.

Hedonic adaption reflects the function of a "psychological immune system that detects and neutralizes events that challenge people's sense of well-being."[105] It achieves this goal through a variety of coping mechanisms that involve learning how to deal with the new situation, exploring its benefits, and readjusting expectations and aspirations to align them with the new reality.[106] Through this process of *hedonic transformation*, people learn to gain a new appreciation of their condition, and focus on new things that can bring them joy given their physical limitations, rather than dwell on activities that are no longer possible.

The legal situation as depicted above, whereby courts view disabilities as a tragedy that precludes any chance of happiness while ignoring hedonic adaptation, is linked to another behavioral phenomenon—*affective forecasting*, namely, people's inability to predict the emotional impact of life events. As a large body of literature shows, people are poor predictors of the intensity or the duration of their feelings.[107] One study in this line of research demonstrated that subjects residing in the Midwest and in California both thought that Californians enjoyed greater happiness, when in fact the actual self-reported measures of life satisfaction in the two groups of subjects were much the same.[108] (Readers contemplating a move to a warmer climate in the hope of becoming happier might learn from this that such a move is unlikely to bring about a significant long-term change in their well-being.) Other studies have focused specifically on the anticipated emotional impacts of disabilities, and found that people tend to underestimate their ability to cope and adapt,[109] and assume, instead, that disabilities bring about a permanent loss of happiness.[110]

Several theoretical explanations have been put forward for these empirical findings about affective forecasting. One is that when subjects are asked to think about a debilitating event, they tend to focus on the narrow consequences of that event, rather than the broader picture.[111] When one thinks of a mobility disability caused by the amputation of both legs, for example, one might easily forget about all the dimensions of one's life that are unaffected by it—such as spending time with loved ones, reading a book, watching a film, or enjoying a glass of red wine. A second explanation focuses on people's lack of experience:[112] extreme

105. *See* Timothy D. Wilson & Daniel T. Gilbert, *Affective Forecasting*, 35 Advances Experimental & Soc. Psychol. 345, 380 (2003).

106. For a review of the different mechanisms, see Bagenstos & Schlanger, *supra* note 95, at 762.

107. For reviews of the literature, see Wilson & Gilbert, *supra* note 105; George Loewenstein & David Schkade, *Wouldn't It Be Nice? Predicting Future Feelings*, *in* Well-Being: The Foundations of Hedonic Psychology 85 (Daniel Kahneman, Ed Diener & Norbert Schwarz eds., 1999).

108. *See* David A. Schkade & Daniel Kahneman, *Does Living in California Make People Happy?: A Focusing Illusion in Judgments of Life Satisfaction*, 9 Psychol. Sci. 340 (1998). *See also* George Loewenstein & Shane Frederick, *Predicting Reactions to Environmental Change*, *in* Environment, Ethics, and Behavior: The Psychology of Environmental Valuation and Degradation 52 (Max H. Bazerman et al. eds., 1997).

109. *See, e.g.*, Peter A. Ubel, George Loewenstein & Christopher Jepson, *Disability and Sunshine: Can Hedonic Predictions Be Improved by Drawing Attention to Focusing Illusions or Emotional Adaptation?*, 11 J. Experimental Psychol.: Applied 111, 120–22 (2005); Greene, Sturm & Evelo, *supra* note 103.

110. Bagenstos & Schlanger, *supra* note 95, at 771.

111. *See* Schkade & Kahneman, *supra* note 108.

112. *See* Greene, Sturm & Evelo, *supra* note 103, at 246.

events such as incurring a disability (or, conversely, winning the lottery) are, by their very nature, rare—so predicting one's emotional reaction to them is done without past knowledge of the consequences of such an event. Finally, *immune neglect* may be another factor behind the phenomenon.[113] The effectiveness of our psychological immune system stems largely from its unconscious function, which allows people to engage in self-deception and similar mechanisms. Thus, leg amputees seeking to cope with the loss of the ability to jog in the park might convince themselves that they never actually enjoyed this activity, but this can be done only after a subconscious process of recalibrating one's perceptions.

To sum up this positive analysis: tort victims learn to cope with many disabilities, and do not suffer a significant long-term decline in their happiness levels—but in their failure to recognize this human ability to adapt to changing circumstances, courts award significant hedonic damages.

On the face of it, the normative conclusion from this analysis is that hedonic damages are systematically inflated, and should therefore be curtailed, or even eliminated.[114] By its very nature, the judicial process focuses the attention of decision-makers on the tangible loss incurred by the plaintiff, so judges and jurors tend to overestimate the degree of long-term harm associated with disabilities. The literature has illustrated this point through cases involving loss of fingers and toes:[115] arguably, while these cases (and ones like them) may involve significant short-term pain (and in some cases substantial adjustment costs), the injuries in these cases probably did not alter the plaintiffs' long-term happiness to a significant degree.

Moreover, the process of adjudicating hedonic damages might undermine the function of the human coping system, and exacerbate the injuries of tort victims.[116] A lengthy trial that requires plaintiffs to repeatedly dwell upon their limitations might undermine their recovery and adaptation. There is a danger that the cognitive process in which plaintiffs become mentally vested in convincing themselves, and others, that they are miserable and deserve pity (along with monetary compensation) might become a self-fulfilling prophecy. Indeed, plaintiff lawyers are likely to intensify this process, to ensure that their clients present themselves in a suitably gloomy and despondent manner during trial or settlement negotiations. Some of our readers might recall the rage with which Jackie Chiles reacted

113. *See* Daniel T. Gilbert et al., *Immune Neglect: A Source of Durability Bias in Affective Forecasting*, 75 J. PERSONALITY & SOC. PSYCHOL. 617 (1998).

114. *See* Sunstein, *supra* note 93, at S173–75; Bagenstos & Schlanger, *supra* note 95, at 773–88. To be sure, the argument in favor of limiting hedonic damages is limited to cases involving injuries with no long-term hedonic consequences. In cases that do entail such consequences—as in the case of injuries that create chronic pain (*see supra* note 103 and accompanying text)—the behavioral evidence suggests that hedonic damages should be increased (*see* Sunstein, *supra* note 93, at S174–75).

115. *See* Sunstein, *supra* note 93, at S174 (critically reviewing the decision to award $1.5 million for the amputation of a finger in Thornton v. Amtrak, 802 So. 2d 816 (2001)); Bagenstos & Schlanger, *supra* note 95, at 758–59 (critically reviewing a jury verdict to award $17 million for the amputation of three toes in Schindler Elevator Corp. v. Anderson, 78 S.W.3d 392 (Tex. App. 2001), *vacated on settlement*, Docket No. 02-0426 (May 22, 2003)).

116. Bagenstos & Schlanger, *supra* note 95, at 785–87.

upon learning that his client, Cosmo Kramer, had treated a scalding wound that he had incurred from hot coffee with a balm that cured it, prior to settlement negotiations.[117]

However, incorporating hedonic adaptation and affective forecasting into the analysis of tort damages requires further scrutiny. As several scholars have noted, research findings on hedonic adaptation suggest that tort damages aimed at compensating for psychological or emotional harm (rather than for monetary expenses that are actually incurred) may fail to enhance the victim's welfare.[118] The hedonic adaptation literature has shown that isolated negative events—and *positive* ones, for that matter—have but a limited effect on happiness levels. As previously noted, in their original classic study of the topic, Brickman, Coates, and Bulman found that lottery winnings had a small impact on people's happiness over time.[119] Later studies found that positive life events—such as marriage, or a voluntary change of workplace—only brought about a temporary spike in happiness levels, and no long-term effect.[120] In fact, it has been suggested that hedonic adaptation to positive life events is both more rapid and more complete (i.e., resulting in no change in happiness) than in the case of negative events.[121] These findings suggest that monetary damages awarded by courts have a relatively small impact on victims' long-term hedonic state. Two diametrically opposite conclusions can be drawn from these findings: one is that tort awards for non-monetary damages are futile, and should be eliminated; the other is that the law may wish to counteract adaptation by prescribing even greater damages.[122]

Note, however, that this quandary is relevant only if the focus of tort law is on the victims, and on making them whole. If, on the other hand, the objective of tort law is to deter potential tortfeasors, then the fact that victims reap little hedonic benefit from damages is inconsequential. From this perspective, what is important is the perceived disutility that tort damages inflict on those who are required to pay them. Here, the behavioral phenomenon of affective forecasting is indeed relevant: since potential tortfeasors presume (however erroneously) that having to pay tort damages for non-monetary harms would significantly decrease their happiness, they are more likely to be deterred by that prospect.

More fundamentally, all the above claims and counterclaims implicitly assume that human welfare is determined by people's subjective mental states of happiness and pain. However, this hedonic theory of human well-being (which famously underpinned Jeremy Bentham's utilitarianism) has been seriously challenged, and is not accepted in

117. *Seinfeld: The Maestro* (NBC television broadcast Oct. 5, 1995).

118. *See* David E. Depianto, *Tort Damages and the (Misunderstood) Money-Happiness Connection*, 44 Ariz. St. L.J. 1385 (2013); Halbersberg & Guttel, *supra* note 6, at 423.

119. *See* Brickman, Coates & Janoff Bulman, *supra* note 97.

120. *See* Richard E. Lucas & Andrew E. Clark, *Do People Really Adapt to Marriage?*, 7 J. Happiness Stud. 405 (2006) (marriage); Wendy R. Boswell, John W. Boudreau & Jan Tichy, *The Relationship between Employee Job Change and Job Satisfaction: The Honeymoon-Hangover Effect*, 90 J. App. Psychol. 882 (2005) (employment).

121. *See* Lyubomirsky, *supra* note 96, at 203.

122. Halbersberg & Guttel, *supra* note 6, at 423.

standard economic analysis, including economic analysis of law.[123] Regardless of whether one espouses a *preference-satisfaction* theory of human welfare (as economic analysis usually does), or an *objective-list* theory (as many philosophers and legal theoreticians do), the argument that tort damages should be dramatically curtailed loses much of its cogency. If people's utility is measured by their preferences, and if people have strong preferences not to lose a limb (for which they would be willing to pay a great deal), then—notwithstanding the phenomenon of hedonic adaptation—awarding high damages may indeed be warranted. The same is true according to an objective-list theory of welfare, which attributes objective value to good health and bodily integrity.[124] Similarly, it may be argued that the process of adapting to serious injuries involves substantial adjustments of one's goals and ideals, which adversely affects the victim's self-identity.[125]

This is not to say that subjective feelings are not important—in either the preference-based or the objective-list theory of well-being. Most people prefer to be happy and free of pain, and subjective happiness is plausibly an important *item* on everybody's objective list. However, according to these theories, the implications of hedonic adaptation with regard to damages are much more limited and nuanced.

The psychological findings regarding hedonic adaptation are important for the preference-satisfaction theory of human welfare in another way, as well, in that they shed light on the discussion in the preceding subsection about the framing of damages in terms of either WTA or WTP.[126] Poor affective forecasting may account for people's high damage assessments in the WTA frame, since examining tort damages in that frame requires people to judge from an ex-ante perspective how an injury will affect their welfare, and people tend to overestimate their losses in this regard. Thus, the reluctance of the legal system to adopt this point of view may be justified. Of course, this argument is not conclusive, as the choice between the two chronological perspectives is not free of normative judgment, since it assumes that there are external criteria for prioritizing one actual preference over another.

E. Product Liability

Product liability law is the body of law dealing with the physical harms to consumers caused by defective products.[127] This area of law has gone through several significant transformations

123. *See generally supra* pp. 14–15, 158–60. *See also* Mark Kelman, *Hedonic Psychology and the Ambiguities of "Welfare,"* 33 PHIL. & PUB. AFF. 391 (2005).

124. *See also* Peter A. Ubel & George Loewenstein, *Pain and Suffering Awards: They Shouldn't Be (Just) about Pain and Suffering,* 37 J. LEGAL STUD. S195 (2008); Lucy Wang, *Non-illusory Losses: Why Pain and Suffering Damages Should (Just) Be about Pain and Suffering* (Yale Law School, Student Prize Papers, 2008, *available at:* http://digitalcommons.law.yale.edu/ylsspps_papers/37).

125. Sean Hannon Williams, *Self-Altering Injury: The Hidden Harms of Hedonic Adaptation,* 96 CORNELL L. REV. 535 (2011).

126. *See* McCaffery, Kahneman & Spitzer, *supra* note 81, at 1391; Sunstein, *supra* note 93, at S162.

127. For overviews, see DAVID G. OWEN & MARY J. DAVIS, PRODUCT LIABILITY (4th ed. 2014); MARSHALL S. SHAPO, SHAPO ON THE LAW OF PRODUCT LIABILITY (7th ed. 2017).

during the twentieth century, resulting in consumers being able to sue producers of defective goods—even when there was no contract between them.[128] In addition, these transformations have changed the governing liability regime, by introducing strict liability into some parts of this body of law.[129] The debate surrounding the desirable scope of product liability law is still ongoing, and proposals to reform it are frequently debated by academics and policymakers.[130]

In the United States, the law distinguishes between three types of product defects.[131] One is a manufacturing defect in the particular item purchased by the consumer, which fails to meet the producer's own standards (e.g., a car that explodes because it was not assembled properly). A second type is a flaw in the manufacturer's design of the product (e.g., a car that explodes because its gas tank tends to rupture). A third type is a product that fails to provide consumers with the necessary information on how to use it safely (e.g., a car that explodes if fueled with diesel as opposed to gasoline, without its owner being properly warned about this danger). In the remainder of this section, we focus on the last two of these categories, in light of the relevance of behavioral analysis to the legal questions that they raise.

1. Defective Design

The legal analysis of design defects is conducted under a *reasonableness* standard. In the United States, for example, a product is deemed defective if "the foreseeable risks of harm posed by the product could have been reduced or avoided by the adoption of a reasonable alternative design [. . .] and the omission of the alternative design renders the product not reasonably safe."[132] As we have already seen in the context of liability regimes, using a reasonableness test as the basis for accident law entails some type of cost-benefit analysis. In the context of design defects, courts are required to conduct a *risk-utility test*, which balances the risks associated with the product against the utility that consumers can derive from it.[133] In cases of this sort, the courts are expected to compare the product with alternative designs, and decide whether the manufacturer's chosen design was reasonable.[134]

128. *See* Marshall S. Shapo, Product Liability and the Search for Justice 19–22 (1993).

129. *See id.* at 22–24.

130. For a brief overview of reforms at the U.S. state and federal level, see Joanna M. Shepherd, *Products Liability and Economic Activity: An Empirical Analysis of Tort's Reform Impact on Businesses, Employment, and Production*, 66 Vand. L. Rev. 257, 267–78 (2013).

131. Restatement of the Law, Third, Torts: Products Liability § 2 (Am. Law Inst. 1998). Other legal systems use different legal frameworks, but in essence deal mostly with similar situations. For a comparative overview, see Product Liability in a Comparative Perspective (Duncan Fairgrieve ed., 2005).

132. Restatement (Third) of Torts: Products Liability § 2(b) (Am. Law Inst. 1998).

133. *See* Shapo, *supra* note 128, at 118–20.

134. *Id.* at 124–26.

Behavioral findings teach us that any producers who explicitly use risk-utility analysis do so at their peril. People tend to view human lives and health as a type of protected value, which must not be explicitly traded like any other commodity.[135] While people routinely make implicit trade-offs between safety and other considerations in their daily lives (e.g., when deciding whether or not to fly, or when choosing a car model), they find the notion of putting an actual price tag on a human life to be morally repugnant. Since moral outrage is a primary predictive variable of punitive damages,[136] this means that companies can be punished for doing precisely what economic reasoning (and the law) require them to do—namely, careful cost-benefit analysis of their products.

The most famous example of what happens to a company that engages in explicit cost-benefit analysis in the context of product safety is probably *Grimshaw v. Ford Motor Co.*,[137] which involved an exploding Ford Pinto. Evidence in this case revealed that Ford engineers had conducted a comprehensive cost-benefit analysis that led them to conclude that the cost of fixing the relevant problem in the design of the car's gas tank ($137.5 million) exceeded the potential costs associated with it ($49.6 million), and was therefore not worthwhile.[138] The public outcry in response to this revelation was huge, and the document detailing the cost-benefit analysis dubbed "possibly the most remarkable document ever produced in an American lawsuit . . ."[139] The trial eventually ended with the jury awarding the plaintiff $2.5 million in compensatory damages, and $125 million in punitive damages.[140]

More rigorous experimental studies corroborate this finding. A large-scale survey conducted by Kip Viscusi found that the mere fact that firms engage in cost-benefit analysis of safety measures raises the ire of juries, leading them to increase punitive damages.[141] The overall results of the study were that corporations that conducted cost-benefit analysis were assessed damages with a geometric mean value of $4.59 million (and a median of $10 million)—compared with only $2.91 million (and a median of $1 million) when no such analysis was conducted.[142] Professional judges were less likely to adopt such a zero-risk attitude that permits no cost/safety trade-offs whatsoever, and less likely to award punitive damages, when firms engaged in such cost-benefit analysis. Nonetheless—and contrary to the mandates of economic efficiency—many of them did award such damages, especially when the risks involved human lives.[143]

135. On protected values and taboo trade-offs, see generally *supra* pp. 97–98. *See also infra* pp. 595–98.

136. *See* Daniel Kahneman, David Schkade & Cass R. Sunstein, *Shared Outrage and Erratic Awards: The Psychology of Punitive Damages*, 16 J. RISK & UNCERTAINTY 49, 55–62 (1998); *infra* pp. 538–40.

137. 119 Cal. App. 3d 757 (1981).

138. *See* Gary T. Schwartz, *The Myth of the Ford Pinto Case*, 43 RUTGERS L. REV. 1013, 1020 (1991).

139. STUART M. SPEISER, LAWSUIT 357 (1980).

140. Grimshaw, *supra* note 137, at 771. The punitive damages in this case were later reduced to $3.5 million by the trial judge, and this reduction was approved by the court of appeals. *See id.* at 823–24.

141. W. Kip Viscusi, *Corporate Risk Analysis: A Reckless Act?*, 52 STAN. L. REV. 547 (2000).

142. *Id.* at 557.

143. W. Kip Viscusi, *Jurors, Judges, and the Mistreatment of Risk by the Courts*, 30 J. LEGAL STUD. 107 (2001).

2. Warnings

A second strand of product liability law where behavioral analysis can offer significant insights concerns defective warnings. In the United States, a product is deemed to be defective "when the foreseeable risks of harm posed by the product could have been reduced or avoided by the provision of reasonable instructions or warnings . . . and the omission of the instructions or warnings renders the product not reasonably safe."[144] This framework presumably helps consumers make informed choices about the products they buy, and encourages them to take simple precautions that can significantly lower the risks associated with many products.[145]

Elsewhere in this book we have elaborated on the pitfalls of policies that focus on the disclosure of information to decision-makers.[146] In essence, we argued that disclosures often fail to exert any meaningful influence on people's choices, due to people's cognitive limitations. This general argument is true for product warnings, as well, so we will only give a brief outline of our concerns in this context.[147]

For a product warning to be effective, it must: (1) be noticed and read, (2) understood, and (3) induce consumers to take the necessary precautions.[148] In reality, these conditions are often not fulfilled, and as a result the warning is rendered useless. With regard to the first condition, given the vast amount of information directed at consumers on a daily basis, their ability to notice and read individual warnings is significantly curtailed. Even seeking out warnings and reading them is a significant upfront cost for the consumer in terms of time and effort, and the potential payoff associated with this effort is extremely remote. Accordingly, rational consumers—to say nothing of myopic ones—will often not bother with deciphering the 6-pt.-single-spaced text warning located somewhere inside the package of the over-the-counter medicine they have just purchased (especially if they have a headache). Moreover, even if consumers do notice and read warnings, their ability to understand them accurately is limited. Issues such as illiteracy and innumeracy might hamper people's understanding of warnings, overoptimism may induce people to underestimate the risks involved, and confirmation bias might cause them to ignore the warning altogether, since they have already decided to purchase the product. Studies of the impact of warnings on cigarette packs on consumers' understanding of the risks involved with smoking have shown that a significant percentage of consumers misperceive these risks—even in an experimental setting where they are forced to focus on the warning.[149] Finally, even if people read and understand warnings, they frequently ignore them: overconfidence, and the illusion of control, can lead people to believe that they can successfully avoid any

144. Restatement (Third) of Torts: Products Liability § 2(c) (Am. Law Inst. 1998).

145. *See* Shapo, *supra* note 128, at 140.

146. *See supra* pp. 171–77, 314–18.

147. For a comprehensive analysis, see Howard Latin, *Good Warnings, Bad Products, and Cognitive Limitations*, 41 UCLA L. Rev. 1193 (1994).

148. *See* Robbennolt & Hans, *supra* note 6, at 173–81.

149. *See* Christine Jolls, *Product Warnings, Debiasing, and Free Speech: The Case of Tobacco Regulation*, 169 J. Institutional & Theo. Econ. 53, 61–68 (2013).

harm to themselves.[150] In addition, when the probability of harm is low, consumers who base their risk assessment on their own experience with the product tend to assume that the product poses no risk.[151]

Tort law appears to have incorporated the insights of behavioral analysis, and places less weight on warnings. In the past, manufacturers could significantly limit the scope of their liability by placing warnings on their products. The *Restatement (Second) of Torts* explicitly noted that "[w]here warning is given, the seller may reasonably assume that it will be read and heeded; and a product bearing such a warning, which is safe for use if it is followed, is not in defective condition, nor is it unreasonably dangerous."[152] In line with this reasoning, courts often dismissed cases based purely on the presence of warnings (even if these were buried on the back of a label, or inside a lengthy manual). For example, in *Skyhook Corp. v. Jasper*,[153] the decedent was killed when a crane that he operated touched a powerline. Evidence at trial showed that this risk could have been eliminated by the manufacturer by introducing a safety measure that cost as little as $300 (in 1968 dollars)—but the New Mexico Supreme Court found that a warning stipulating that "all equipment shall be so positioned, equipped or protected so that no part shall be capable of coming within ten feet of high voltage lines" was sufficient to exempt the seller from liability.[154] In its reasoning, it argued that the seller "could reasonably assume that the warning would be read and heeded."[155]

The *Restatement (Third) of Torts*, however, has adopted a different position on this issue, to reflect a more realistic vision of human decision-making. This places greater emphasis on the design of the product itself, given the inherent limitations of warnings. Thus, the Restatement now stipulates that—

> when a safer design can reasonably be implemented and risks can reasonably be designed out of a product, adoption of the safer design is required over a warning that leaves a significant residuum of such risks. For example, instructions and warnings may be ineffective because users of the product may not be adequately reached, may be likely to be inattentive, or may be insufficiently motivated to follow the instructions or heed the warnings.[156]

This attitude is echoed in case law, leading, inter alia, to the above *Skyhook* decision being overturned.[157]

150. *See* Latin, *supra* note 147, at 1243–44.

151. *See supra* notes 26–33 and accompanying text.

152. RESTATEMENT (SECOND) OF TORTS § 402A cmt. j (AM. LAW INST. 1965).

153. 560 P.2d 934 (N.M. 1977).

154. *Id.* at 938.

155. *Id.*

156. RESTATEMENT (THIRD) OF TORTS: PRODUCTS LIABILITY § 2 cmt. i (AM. LAW INST. 1998).

157. Klopp v. Wackenhut Corp., 824 P.2d 293 (1992).

The big remaining question is what constitutes a "reasonable warning." While we are reluctant to offer a definitive answer to this question, a few behavioral insights may be instructive.[158] First, warnings must be short and simple, and worded so as to be comprehensible to people with limited language skills.[159] Of course, given the complexity of many products, not all warnings can be phrased so simply. In those cases, the law should make use of other regulatory tools. Second, the warning should be salient, to ensure that consumers' attention is actually drawn to it—by means such as prominent placement on the product, its size, color, etc.[160] Both these points suggest that adding graphic images to the warning can help bolster its effectiveness, since these can enhance both comprehensibility and salience.[161] Third, warnings should highlight how and why they should be complied with—for example, the warning must not only state "DANGER," but specify the concrete risks posed by the product, and how these can be avoided.[162]

Behavioral analysis can also clarify what kind of decisions are likely to be guided by well-designed warnings. Generally, warnings are expected to be more effective in relation to decisions that stand alone. Decisions such as whether to buy a given product, or how to assemble or install it, and the like, are likely to invoke System-2 decision-making, and therefore more likely be influenced by further information. Conversely, with routine decisions regarding the day-to-day operation of a product, warnings are expected to have only limited impact, since these decisions are often repetitive, and given the small risks involved, consumers are likely to neglect to follow warnings, in light of their past uneventful experience with the product.

To illustrate these points, consider the warnings attached to an infant car seat: consumers are more likely to heed a warning about its installation than one about its day-to-day use. Given the repetitive nature of buckling the child into the seat—which usually has few implications, even if done improperly—over time users are likely to fail to follow to the letter instructions about this operation. Add to this the fact that children are often buckled into their seats while kicking and screaming, and the chances of failing to heed the warning only increase. As for the design of such warnings, they should be salient, graphic, and if possible placed on the installation latches themselves, to ensure that they are seen. Whenever possible, warnings should also clarify the implications of *not* adhering to them. Thus, for example, pointing out that installing an infant seat in the front passenger seat is dangerous because of the hazards of inflated airbags in the event of an accident is sufficiently

158. The psychological research on this point is voluminous. For a comprehensive review of many of the findings, see Michael S. Wogalter, Kenneth R. Laughery, Sr. & Christopher B. Mayhorn, *Warnings and Hazard Communications*, *in* HANDBOOK OF HUMAN FACTORS AND ERGONOMICS 868 (Gavriel Salvendy ed., 4th ed. 2012).

159. Michael S. Wogalter & Kenneth R. Laughery, *Warning! Sign and Label Effectiveness*, 5 CURRENT DIRECTIONS PSYCHOL. SCI. 33 (1996).

160. *Id.*

161. *See* Jolls, *supra* note 149 (presenting data on the effectiveness of images on cigarette warnings).

162. Valerie A. Taylor & Amanda B. Bower, *Improving Product Instruction Compliance: "If You Tell Me Why, I Might Comply"*, 21 PSYCHOL. & MARKETING 229 (2004).

specific to be achieved through clear and visible warnings. Conversely, finer points such as the proper tightening of the straps, or how these should be adjusted to accommodate the winter jacket that the baby may be wearing, cannot be resolved by warnings or lengthy instructions buried in the manual.

F. Conclusion

This chapter highlighted the main implications of behavioral analysis for the area of tort law. As we have seen, many of the existing conclusions of legal scholarship in this area are still valid, even when behavioral insights are taken into account. However, the bounded rationality of tortfeasors and adjudicators does raise concerns about certain key issues. In the case of tortfeasors, research has shown that incentivizing boundedly rational individuals to behave safely cannot rely exclusively on low-probability liability. With respect to adjudicators, case law analysis shows that the limitations of decision-makers in certain contexts (such as judging liability in hindsight, or determining damages for pain and suffering) may warrant the use of procedural and substantive tools that help to curb biased decisions.

10

Commercial Law: Corporate Law, Securities Regulation, and Antitrust

A. Introduction

This chapter focuses on the behavioral analysis of commercial law—specifically, the body of law regulating corporations, securities, and competition within markets. Since economic analysis has developed out of thinking about markets, and since in this area notions such as culpability, desert, and distributive justice have traditionally played a more limited role than in areas such as tort law and criminal law, economic analysis of law has had a particularly powerful impact on commercial law.[1] Given the magnitude of the literature on economic analysis of commercial law, the scope of the corresponding literature on the behavioral analysis of this field is vast, as well.[2] Consequently, this chapter will only highlight several key contributions within this body of work, and focus on a handful of applications that demonstrate the relevance of behavioral insights to the legal treatment of commercial markets. The chapter begins by examining the preliminary question of whether irrationality can persist in well-functioning, highly competitive markets. As the theoretical analysis and empirical evidence show, irrational behavior is present even in such settings. After establishing this general point, the chapter goes on to discuss the implications of behavioral analysis for corporate law, securities regulation, and antitrust law.

1. For notable contributions, see Henry G. Manne, Insider Trading and the Stock Market (1966); Frank H. Easterbrook & Daniel R. Fischel, The Economic Structure of Corporate Law (1996); Richard A. Posner, Antitrust Law (2d ed. 2001).

2. For recent reviews, see Donald C. Langevoort, *Behavioral Approaches to Corporate Law*, *in* Research Handbook on the Economics of Corporate Law 442 (Claire A. Hill & Brett H. McDonnell eds., 2012); Kent Greenfield, *The End of Contractarianism?*, *in* The Oxford Handbook of Behavioral Economics and the Law 518 (Eyal Zamir & Doron Teichman eds., 2014); Avishalom Tor, *The Market, The Firm, and Behavioral Antitrust*, *in* The Oxford Handbook of Behavioral Economics and the Law, *supra*, at 539.

B. Firms, Markets, and Rational Choice

1. The Efficient Market Hypothesis

A cornerstone of the economic analysis of commercial law is the *Efficient Market Hypothesis* (EMH). According to the EMH, prices in markets fully reflect all available information on listed companies.[3] In other words, any new piece of public information that is disseminated into the market is quickly incorporated into stock prices. As a result, stock exchange prices always reflect a firm's fundamental value, and it is impossible to buy undervalued or overvalued stock at any given moment in the market. The fundamental value of the firm within this framework is determined by two criteria: expected returns and non-diversifiable risk.

The EMH has had a profound influence on the law-and-economics literature. Generally, law-and-economics scholars have advocated for a laissez faire attitude toward stock markets, given their presumed efficiency,[4] on the grounds that if markets are efficient and prices accurately reflect company value, this has a disciplining effect on management via the market for control, compensation schemes, and other mechanisms that firms can install.[5] By the same token, there is little need to regulate the information that companies provide to investors, since market mechanisms provide sufficient incentives for companies to provide investors with accurate information.[6]

Note that the EMH does not assume perfect rationality among all market participants. While irrational decisions may persist at the individual level, economists assume that these decisions will cancel each other out, and the market will correspond with whatever is the rational choice.[7] While overly optimistic investors might push the price of a stock irrationally upward, their overly pessimistic counterpart will push it downward. Thus, on average, the market will behave as if all participants approximate rationality.

According to this view, even systematic deviations from rationality are not expected to influence pricing over time in well-functioning markets, because of the possibility of *arbitrage*—simultaneous buying and selling that takes advantage of price gaps for similar assets. To understand why this is so, imagine that the stock of supermarket chain X has risen irrationally simply because the company changed its name to X.COM. This did not occur because of a change in X.COM's business model (which remains the same), but simply due to herd behavior in the stock market.[8] A sophisticated investor who identifies this trend

3. Ronald J. Gilson & Reinier H. Kraakman, *The Mechanisms of Market Efficiency*, 70 VA. L. REV. 549, 554 (1984).

4. *See* EASTERBROOK & FISCHEL, *supra* note 1, at 35–39.

5. *See* Ralph K. Winter, Jr., *State Law, Shareholder Protection and the Theory of the Corporation*, 6 J. LEGAL STUD. 251, 255–57 (1977).

6. *See, e.g.*, Stephen J. Choi & Andrew T. Guzman, *Portable Reciprocity: Rethinking the International Reach of Securities Regulation*, 71 S. CAL. L. REV. 903 (1998); Adam C. Pritchard, *Markets as Monitors: A Proposal to Replace Class Actions with Exchanges as Securities Fraud Monitors*, 85 VA. L. REV. 925 (1999).

7. *See* RICHARD A. POSNER, FRONTIERS OF LEGAL THEORY 260–62 (2001).

8. It has been shown that such cosmetic name changes can in fact influence stock prices. *See* Michael J. Cooper, Orlin Dimitrov & P. Raghavendra Rau, *A Rose.com by Any Other Name*, 56 J. FIN. 2371 (2001); Michael J. Copper et al., *Managerial Actions in Response to a Market Downturn: Valuation Effects of Name Changes in the dot.com Decline*, 11 J. CORP. FIN. 319 (2005).

can profit from it by purchasing the stock of a similar company (call it supermarket chain Y), and short-selling X.COM stock. By assuming this position, the investor can isolate and exploit the irrational gap between the price of X.COM and the price of Y, and make a profit once this disparity disappears, as the price of X.COM reconverges with its fundamental economic value. In fact, the presence of a certain amount of noise in the market due to individual irrationality is important for the proper functioning of markets, since it adds liquidity and information to it, as rational traders interact with irrational ones.[9]

2. Behavioral Corporate Finance

Deviations from rationality cancel out only if the assumptions underpinning the EMH are correct. In reality, the growing field of behavioral corporate finance has documented systematic deviations from the EMH. These studies demonstrate that prices within well-functioning markets may deviate from the fundamental value of the firm.[10]

One assumption underlying the EMH that apparently does not hold up to scrutiny is the ability of market players to profit through arbitrage when assets are mispriced.[11] Liquidity constraints, along with transaction costs and the risk inherent in arbitrage, can limit the ability of sophisticated market actors to exploit mispricing. Once arbitrage is curtailed in this way, a host of cognitive phenomena that systematically influence a large proportion of market players—such as loss aversion and anchoring—can have a significant impact on asset pricing. This can explain a host of market phenomena that traditional rational choice theory has had difficulty accounting for. For example, prospect theory and ambiguity aversion have been used to explain the *equity premium puzzle*—the unreasonably high premium that investors require to invest in stocks, as opposed to government bonds.[12]

To the extent that company managers are sophisticated people, who can identify systematic deviations from efficient pricing in markets, they might attempt to design corporate policies that exploit such deviations. To name but a few of the issues studied through this prism: equity issuances may be timed to periods when management believes the stock is overvalued (and vice versa with respect to repurchases); earnings can be managed so that they exceed expectations; and dividends can be paid out to cater to investors' loss aversion or desire for tools that enable mental accounting.[13] If the EMH is indeed a flawed portrayal of market reality, then relying exclusively on market forces to achieve efficient outcomes

9. *See* Gregory La Blanc & Jeffrey J. Rachlinski, *In Praise of Investor Irrationality*, *in* THE LAW AND ECONOMICS OF IRRATIONAL BEHAVIOR 542 (Francesco Parisi & Vernon Smith eds., 2005).

10. For reviews, see Nicholas Barberis & Richard Thaler, *A Survey of Behavioral Finance*, *in* 1A HANDBOOK OF THE ECONOMICS OF FINANCE 1053 (George M. Constantinides, Milton Harris & René M. Stulz eds., 2003); Malcolm Baker & Jeffery Wurgler, *Behavioral Corporate Finance: An Updated Survey* (NBER Working Paper Series, Paper No. 17333, 2011, *available at:* http://www.nber.org/papers/w17333); David Hirshleifer, *Behavioral Finance*, 7 ANN. REV. FIN. ECON. 133 (2015).

11. *See* Baker & Wurgler, *supra* note 10, at 6–8; Andrei Shleifer & Robert Vishny, *The Limits of Arbitrage*, 52 J. FIN. 35 (1997).

12. *See* Barberis & Thaler, *supra* note 10, at 1078–83; *supra* pp. 43–44.

13. *See* Baker & Wurgler, *supra* note 10, at 22–49.

may be misplaced, and at least some legal intervention in the functioning of markets may be needed to enhance efficiency. The following sections of this chapter explore this possibility in detail.

C. Corporate Law

1. General

Corporate law is the body of law that defines and regulates the relationship between a corporation and its shareholders, managers, debtors, and other relevant constituencies. Corporate law establishes the boundaries of the firm, and delineates which assets belong to it and who has access to those assets. In addition, corporate law establishes the basic governance rules that allocate authority within the firm, and outlines the procedures associated with different contingencies for the duration of its existence.[14]

Economic analysis has had a tremendous impact on corporate law—indeed, in recent decades it has arguably become the main lens through which corporate questions are analyzed by jurists. Within this framework, the contractual paradigm—most notably advocated by Frank Easterbrook and Daniel Fischel—has come to dominate the corporate landscape.[15] According to Easterbrook and Fischel, corporate law sets the ground rules for the establishment of consensual business relationships surrounding the firm. Given the voluntary nature of these relationships, they argue, corporate law should function much like contract law, and establish non-binding default rules that fit the preferences of most parties, while allowing parties to freely contract around those rules if they so wish.

According to most modern accounts, at the heart of corporate law lies the *agency problem*—the conflict of interest between those who control the firm (i.e., management or controlling shareholders) and other constituencies (e.g., minority shareholders).[16] In the case of a corporation with dispersed ownership, in which the management effectively controls the firm, key issues in this regard are the entrenchment of management in its position, and generous compensation schemes. In the case of firms with controlling shareholders, the key concern is the tunneling of value from the firm to the controlling shareholders.

This section reviews some of the contributions made by behavioral analysis to corporate law. It begins with examining the implications of the susceptibility of adjudicators to the hindsight bias for the structure of corporate law. It then examines potential deviations from rationality among corporate officers, and highlights their legal ramifications.

14. For an overview of the field, see ROBERT CHARLES CLARK, CORPORATE LAW (1986); FRANKLIN GEVURTZ, CORPORATION LAW (2010).

15. *See generally* EASTERBROOK & FISCHEL, *supra* note 1.

16. *See* Michael C. Jensen & William H. Meckling, *Theory of the Firm: Managerial Behavior, Agency Costs and Ownership Structure*, 3 J. FIN. ECON. 305 (1976). For a discussion of the centrality of agency costs in legal analysis and the role of other theories, see Zohar Goshen & Richard Squire, *Principal Costs: A New Theory for Corporate Law and Corporate Governance*, 117 COLUM. L. REV. 767 (2017).

2. Hindsight Bias and the Business Judgment Rule

Judicial decisions are influenced by an array of cognitive phenomena.[17] In the context of corporate law, a key concern is that judges who examine business decisions in retrospect might wrongly view them as unreasonable due to hindsight bias (the propensity of people to overestimate the probability of an event once they know that the event has occurred).[18] The hindsight bias has been shown to influence judicial decisions in various legal settings.[19] In the specific context of corporate law, the main concern is that judges or jurors may overestimate the probability of adverse events if they are required to assess them in hindsight.

Merrie Jo Stallard and Debra Worthington demonstrated this point in a controlled experiment in which subjects were presented with materials based on the facts of a real case concerning the responsibility of board members for the failure of a corporation.[20] Participants in the hindsight group were informed of the outcome of the board's decision, and asked to evaluate it as part of an ex-post adjudicative process. Conversely, participants in the foresight group were not informed of the outcome, and asked to evaluate the board's decision as part of a review hearing. The results revealed a significant difference between the two groups: members of the hindsight group were more likely to determine that the board had acted negligently.

Judging managerial decisions in hindsight may have a chilling effect on managers, deterring them from taking efficient risks, for fear that if these decisions turn out badly, they will be held legally liable. As a result, risky projects such as developing a new drug or searching for a new gas field might not be undertaken, even if they have a positive present value. This chilling effect may harm shareholders (and society at large), since shareholders want managers to take efficient risks, even if these sometime turn out to be detrimental. Shareholders can usually hedge these risks through prudent diversification, and thus need not be overly concerned with risks related to specific firms.

The doctrinal implication of this point is the *Business Judgment Rule* (BJR).[21] The BJR is the standard of review that courts apply when examining the decisions made by corporate officers in cases of alleged negligent conduct (i.e., duty-of-care cases).[22] While there are

17. *See generally infra* pp. 525–65.

18. On the hindsight bias, see generally *supra* pp. 38–39.

19. *See* Doron Teichman, *The Hindsight Bias and the Law in Hindsight*, *in* The Oxford Handbook of Behavioral Economics and the Law, *supra* note 2, at 354, 356–59.

20. *See* Merrie Jo Stallard & Debra J. Worthington, *Reducing the Hindsight Bias Utilizing Attorney Closing Arguments*, 22 Law & Hum. Behav. 671 (1998).

21. *See* Jeffery Rachlinski, *A Positive Psychological Theory of Judging in Hindsight*, 65 U. Chi. L. Rev. 571, 619–23 (1998).

22. *See generally*, Arthur R. Pinto & Douglas M. Branson, Corporate Law 229–31 (4th ed. 2013). The terminology used in the text alludes to U.S. corporate jurisprudence. While the BJR is not a universal rule, numerous other legal systems adopted some versions of it. As is always the case with comparative law, careful attention should be given to the institutional setting that the substantive rule pertains to, to fully understand its effect. *See, e.g.*, Bruce E. Aronson, *Learning from Comparative Law in Teaching U.S. Corporate Law: Director's Liability in Japan and the U.S.*, 22 Penn St. Int'l L. Rev. 213, 236–38 (2003); Carlos Andrés Laguado Giraldo, *Factors*

jurisdictional nuances to the BJR, it represents nearly complete deference to the decisions of corporate officers and directors. In essence, it states that as long as a company officer made an informed decision and was not an interested party, he or she will not be held liable for that decision, even if it turns out to be profoundly unwise in retrospect.[23]

The BJR reflects the courts' understanding that any examination of corporate decisions in hindsight will inevitably be biased,[24] and that such biased decisions harm the people they aim to protect—shareholders.[25] While in a perfect world it may be beneficial to have a neutral entity examine the wisdom of decisions made by management, in a world with biased courts this is not the case. Thus, corporate law has evolved to offer managers a safe harbor with respect to a broad set of business decisions.

3. Behavioral Corporate Governance

The documentary film *The Corporation* depicts corporations as clinically diagnosed psychopaths.[26] Among other things, it portrays them as being incapable of feeling guilt or remorse, lacking concern for the feelings of others, and being willing to violate laws and social norms to further their ends, and to engage in deceitful practices. In other words, corporations are depicted as the poster boy of the rational choice model—a lean and mean profit-making machine. While behavioral research has not incorporated the definitions of mental disorders into its analysis, the findings of several studies suggest that shifting activity into corporations might alter decisions such that they come closer to the rational choice model.

Jennifer Arlen and Stephan Tontrup examined the interaction between the endowment effect and legal institutions such as the corporation.[27] They deployed a setup commonly used in endowment effect studies, and tested subjects' willingness to trade a lottery ticket for an alternative ticket of equal value after being incentivized to do so.[28] As Arlen and Tontrup show, while there is a pronounced endowment effect when subjects decide on their own whether or not to trade, the amount of trading increases significantly when trade decisions are made jointly by subjects and agents, or by several subjects through a vote. Furthermore, when given an option to delegate decision-making power to an agent or to a vote, subjects chose to do so. These results suggest that the corporation—which entails both

Governing the Application of the Business Judgment Rule: An Empirical Study of the US, UK, Australia and the EU, 111 VNIVERSITAS, 115, 125–46 (2006).

23. *See In re* Walt Disney Co. Derivative Litig., 906 Del. A.2d 27 (2006).

24. *See* Joy v. North, 692 F.2d 880, 886 (2d Cir. 1982).

25. *Id.*

26. THE CORPORATION (Big Picture Media 2003).

27. *See* Jennifer Arlen & Stephan Tontrup, *Does the Endowment Effect Justify Legal Intervention? The Debiasing Effect of Institutions*, 44 J. LEGAL STUD. 143 (2015). *See also* Jennifer Arlen, Matthew Spitzer & Eric Talley, *Endowment Effects within Corporate Agency Relationships*, 31 J. LEGAL STUD. 1 (2002).

28. *See* Maya Bar-Hillel & Efrat Neter, *Why Are People Reluctant to Exchange Lottery Tickets?*, 70 J. PERSONALITY & SOC. PSYCHOL. 17 (1996). On the endowment effect, see *supra* pp. 50–56.

an agency relationship and collective decision-making by voting—might serve as a tool to limit the endowment effect and foster trade.

Kent Greenfield and Peter Kostant studied the corresponding question relating to the motivational dimension of rationality—namely, the assumption that people care only about their self-interest.[29] To this end, they introduced an agency relationship into the *Ultimatum* game. Specifically, the first-move-proposers acted either for themselves, or for a third party, or for a third party with an instruction to use their judgment "to get the biggest actual return for the party for whom [they] are working."[30] This instruction—which captures the fiduciary relationship between board members and shareholders—altered the participants' behavior, and caused them to reduce the offers they made significantly. Greenfield and Kostant interpreted this result as suggesting that the fiduciary relationship between board members and shareholders may drive the former to behave more rationally when pursuing the interests of shareholders.[31]

While in many corporate and commercial settings behavior might be *closer* to the predictions of the rational choice model, this does not mean that corporations exhibit *perfect* rationality across all dimensions. As the findings reviewed below suggest, key corporate actors may exhibit systematic deviations from rationality that are likely to influence corporate decisions. The two main corporate governance institutions of interest in this regard are the company's management as led by the Chief Executive Officer (CEO), and the board of directors. While this focus sidesteps important constituencies in the corporate arena (such as controlling shareholders, minority block holders, and bond holders), it covers major policy questions currently discussed in the corporate governance literature.

It is worth noting at the outset that inserting behavioral insights into the analysis of corporate governance is not merely an intellectual exercise. The conclusions arising from the academic discussion over behavioral corporate governance have already worked their way into legislative debates and judicial decisions. In his comments on *In re Southern Peru Copper Corp. Shareholder Derivative Litigation*, Delaware vice chancellor Laster tied the court's ruling to the influence of cognitive biases such as anchoring, loss aversion, and groupthink on the board's decision.[32] As he notes, "good people are often blinded, wholly or in part, by cognitive biases. . . . in controller situations like *Southern Peru*, cognitive biases can result in liability—here, a $1.4 billion judgment."[33]

29. Kent Greenfield & Peter Kostant, *An Experimental Test of Fairness under Agency and Profit Constraints (With Notes on Implications for Corporate Governance)*, 71 Geo. Wash. L. Rev. 983 (2003).

30. *Id.* at 997–98.

31. Relatedly, studies in the area of behavioral ethics have shown that people's willingness to behave dishonestly increases when they act to further the interests of others along with their own (as opposed to furthering their personal self-interest only). *See, e.g.*, Scott S. Wiltermuth, *Cheating More When the Spoils Are Split*, 115 Org. Behav. & Hum. Decision Processes 157 (2011).

32. *See* Travis Laster, *Cognitive Bias in Director Decision-Making*, 20 Corp. Governance Advisor 1 (2012).

33. *Id.* at 8.

(a) Overconfident CEOs

The CEO is usually the most senior officer in the corporate hierarchy.[34] While the precise function of the CEO varies from one company to another, the CEO is generally responsible for the firm's operation and for setting policies and strategies. The power to appoint the CEO—and to terminate that person's employment, if necessary—lies in the hands of the board of directors.

CEOs typically ascend to their position through a highly competitive process, which produces a shortlist of highly qualified individuals, with extensive experience in the relevant industry. CEOs are routinely appointed based on their track record of successful business decisions. Given their record of success, it stands to reason that as a group, CEOs tend to make rational decisions that maximize corporate value over time.

However, an examination of the dynamics of the competitive process by which CEOs are chosen suggests that irrationality may persist even in this elite group. In particular, within a competitive setting, *lucky* individuals who exhibit overconfidence may outperform rational competitors.[35] Such individuals might choose projects that are inferior from a net-present-value perspective, but are successful in retrospect, due to sheer luck. Couple this good fortune with the *fundamental attribution error*,[36] and the result is overconfident individuals who are perceived to be exceptionally talented.[37]

Moreover, the decision-making environment that CEOs operate in does not always enable them to learn from their experience.[38] There is often a time lag between when the CEO's decision is made and its outcomes materialize, and given the complexity of the business environment, inferring causality can be tricky (objectively speaking—and even more so with motivational factors in play).[39] In addition, many business decisions are unique, and do not lend themselves to cross-sectional learning.[40] As a result, managers might make major mistakes in contexts such as a large merger or a significant increase in capacity, and the proper conclusions from these mistakes may never be drawn.

34. *See, e.g.*, Gevurtz, *supra* note 14 at 179–85.

35. *See* Anand M. Goel & Anjan V. Thakor, *Overconfidence, CEO Selection, and Corporate Governance*, 63 J. FIN. 2737 (2008).

36. *See supra* pp. 68–69.

37. While we focus on the role of overconfidence, other behavioral phenomena may also influence CEO decisions. *See, e.g.*, Malcom Baker, Xin Pan & Jeffrey Wurgler, *The Effect of Reference Point Prices on Mergers and Acquisitions*, 106 J. FIN. ECON. 49 (2012); Olivier Dessaint & Adrien Matray, *Do Managers Overreact to Salient Risks? Evidence from Hurricane Strikes*, 126 J. FIN. ECON. 97 (2017).

38. *See* Troy A. Paredes, *Too Much Pay, Too Much Deference: Behavioral Corporate Finance, CEOs, and Corporate Governance*, 32 FLA. ST. U. L. REV. 673, 693–94 (2005). For further discussion about learning from experience, see *supra* pp. 114–17.

39. *See* Edward J. Zajac & Max H. Bazerman, *Blind Spots in Industry and Competitor Analysis: Implications of Interfirm (Mis)Perceptions for Strategic Decisions*, 16 ACAD. MGMT. REV. 37, 41–42 (1991).

40. *Id.*

By this point, a large corpus of finance studies suggests that a significant portion of CEOs (40 percent by one account) exhibit overconfidence.[41] The main method used to identify overconfidence in this line of research has been to observe the decisions that CEOs make with respect to stock options that they receive as part of their compensation package.[42] This is based on the premise that CEOs who choose not to exercise vested stock options that are "in the money" exhibit overconfidence, since a rational investor in their place would exercise the option and diversify their investment portfolio. Subsequent studies have used text analysis to identify other proxies of overconfidence—such as the use of words suggesting overconfidence (e.g., "confident," "optimistic") or the opposite (e.g., "cautious," "conservative").[43] Finally, an important strand of papers has documented CEO overconfidence directly by using survey data.[44]

Studies have linked CEO overconfidence to the decisions made by firms, and have shown that it can lead to poor outcomes. In an early influential article, Ulrike Malmendier and Geoffrey Tate demonstrated that overconfidence is significantly associated with investment decisions made by firms.[45] Specifically, they found that overly confident managers tend to overinvest when the firm has an abundance of cash (since they overestimate the value of investment opportunities), and to underinvest when the firm is illiquid (since they overestimate the firm's value and are reluctant to raise external funds). Subsequent studies found associations between CEO overconfidence and other phenomena—such as the risk of a crash in the firm's stock price, merger decisions, and earnings management.[46] It should be noted, however, that all these studies reported only correlations between overconfidence and certain types of corporate decisions, and should therefore be read with caution. Recent work has attempted to use exogenous shocks to capital markets to examine this point more rigorously.[47]

To be sure, some degree of overconfidence may indeed maximize value for shareholders: moderate overconfidence can counter risk aversion, and induce CEOs to make better

41. For an overview of the findings, see Ulrike Malmendier & Geoffrey Tate, *Behavioral CEOs: The Role of Managerial Overconfidence*, 29 J. Econ. Persp. 37 (2015).

42. For the initial contribution to the development of this empirical strategy, see Ulrike Malmendier & Geoffrey Tate, *CEO Overconfidence and Corporate Investment*, 60 J. Fin. 2661 (2005).

43. *See, e.g.*, David Hirshleifer, Angie Low & Siew Hong Teoh, *Are Overconfident CEOs Better Innovators?*, 67 J. Fin. 1457 (2012) (textual analysis of press reports); Thomas J. Boulton & T. Colin Campbell, *Managerial Confidence and Initial Public Offerings*, 37 J. Corp. Fin. 375 (2016) (textual analysis of registration statement).

44. *See, e.g.*, Itzhak Ben-David, John R. Graham & Campbell R. Harvey, *Managerial Miscalibration*, 128 Q.J. Econ. 1547 (2013); John R. Graham, Campbell R. Harvey & Manju Puri, *Managerial Attitudes and Corporate Actions*, 109 J. Fin. Econ. 103 (2013).

45. *See* Malmendier & Tate, *supra* note 42.

46. *See* Ulrike Malmendier & Geoffrey Tate, *Who Makes Acquisition Decisions? CEO Overconfidence and the Market's Reaction*, 89 J. Fin. Econ. 20 (2008); Jeong-Bon Kim, Zheng Wang & Liandong Zhang, *CEO Overconfidence and Stock Price Crash Risk*, 33 Contemp. Acct. Res. 1720 (2016); Tien-Shih Hsieh & Jean C. Bedard, *CEO Overconfidence and Earnings Management during Shifting Regulatory Regimes*, 41 J. Bus. Fin. & Acct. 1243 (2014).

47. *See* Malmendier & Tate, *supra* note 41, at 53–55.

decisions from the perspective of risk-neutral shareholders.[48] It has been shown, for example, that CEO overconfidence can produce value in innovative industries.[49] Overconfidence can also be useful for the CEO from an internal managerial perspective.[50] Clear conviction in a chosen course of action can help rally the company's management around a common goal. An indecisive CEO, who constantly questions his or her own choices, might find it difficult to steer the corporation toward achieving its goals. In some settings, CEO overconfidence can have important competitive advantages[51]—for example, by helping the company enter a new market with fewer rivals.

(b) Passive Boards

The chief entity vested with the task of overseeing the management's decisions is the board of directors.[52] It has the authority to hire and fire the corporation's management (and to set its compensation), and is expected to vet its major decisions, on matters such as mergers. Board members have a fiduciary duty to the corporation and an obligation to act in its best interests. To achieve these goals, corporate boards are staffed with experienced businesspeople, who often hold senior positions in other firms as well.

An array of behavioral findings, however, suggests that board members may encounter significant obstacles that may hinder their ability to oversee the management effectively. One such concern is that they might exhibit deference to management, and fail to challenge the views put forward by the CEO.[53] A large body of psychological literature in the wake of Stanley Milgram's seminal early studies on the topic shows that humans tend to respect and obey authority figures.[54] Since the CEO is the main authority figure within the firm, controlling its administration and possessing more information about it than any other, board members may find it difficult to challenge him or her. In most cases, therefore, board members might prefer to exhibit loyalty toward the company's leadership and cooperate with it.

Other, more nuanced forces might influence board members as well. Management is often involved to some degree in the nomination process of board members. Board members are therefore likely to try to avoid the label of troublemakers, in order to sustain their position on the board. Even if they have no fears of being removed, they might still

48. *See* Goel & Thakor, *supra* note 35, at 2739.

49. *See* Hirshleifer, Low & Teoh, *supra* note 43.

50. *See* Paredes, *supra* note 38, at 698–700.

51. *Id.* at 701.

52. *See, e.g.*, Gevurtz, *supra* note 14, at 186–95.

53. Randall Morck, *Behavioral Finance in Corporate Governance: Economics and Ethics of the Devil's Advocate*, 12 J. MGMT. & GOVERNANCE 179 (2008).

54. *See* Stanley Milgram, *Behavioral Study of Obedience*, 67 J. ABNORMAL & SOC. PSYCHOL. 371 (1963). For later reviews, see Thomas Blass, *The Milgram Paradigm after 35 Years: Some Things We Now Know about Obedience to Authority*, 29 J. APP. SOC. PSYCHOL. 955 (1999); Dominic J. Packer, *Identifying Systematic Disobedience in Milgram's Obedience Experiments: A Meta-analytic Review*, 3 PERSP. PSYCHOL. SCI. 301 (2008).

avoid conflicts with the company's senior management, simply out of reciprocity.[55] Thus, board members tend to be lenient in their oversight of those involved in granting them their lucrative position. While the notion that board members—a group of usually senior and experienced individuals—are eager to please may seem surprising at first, it should be noted that the psychological forces at play are substantial. If the justices of the U.S. Supreme Court—who are senior, experienced, and enjoy life tenure—exhibit a "loyalty effect" to the president who appointed them, independent of their ideological stance,[56] it should not be surprising that board members might exhibit a similar loyalty to their CEO.

Another cognitive phenomenon that might hinder effective oversight of management by the board is the *status quo bias*.[57] Oversight implies challenging existing management and its policies, but—by design—management holds significantly more information than board members about the issues in question. At the individual level, this can cause board members to avoid speaking up, for fear that their informational disadvantage in the debate will result in loss of face when they are proven wrong. Moreover, monitoring often requires critical appraisal of past decisions (including the decision to appoint the CEO). Hence, the confirmation bias, coupled with the sunk cost effect and cognitive dissonance, may reinforce the tendency of board members to seek and interpret information in a manner that justifies the status quo, as well as their previous decisions.[58] Finally, the omission bias may also make board members inclined to inaction.[59] Barring a major crisis threatening the company's very operation, most board members might choose not to interfere with the policies set by management.

All of these factors at the individual level may be amplified at the group level. Social psychologists have long studied the phenomenon of *groupthink*.[60] Groupthink alludes to the tendency of groups to suppress opposition and alternative views, and to foster conformity and consent with the group's views and practices. As part of this process, group members emphasize building group cohesion and consensus, and deflect information that might bring about disagreements. In the corporate context, groupthink can result in a myopic board of directors that fails to adjust to changing circumstances.[61]

55. *See* Donald C. Langevoort, *The Human Nature of Corporate Boards: Law, Norms, and the Unintended Consequences of Independence and Accountability*, 89 Geo. L.J. 797, 811 (2001).

56. *See* Lee Epstein & Eric A. Posner, *Supreme Court Justices' Loyalty to the President*, 45 J. Legal Stud. 401 (2016).

57. *See* Donald C. Langevoort, *Resetting the Corporate Thermostat: Lessons from the Recent Financial Scandals about Self-Deception, Deceiving Others and the Design of Internal Controls*, 93 Geo. L.J. 285 (2004).

58. On these phenomena, see generally *supra* pp. 56–57, 58–61.

59. *See generally supra* pp. 48–50.

60. For early contribution to this body of work, see Irving L. Janis, Victims of Groupthink: A Psychological Study of Foreign-Policy Decisions and Fiascoes (1972). For later contributions, see James K. Esser, *Alive and Well after 25 Years: A Review of Groupthink Research*, 73 Org. Behav. & Hum. Decision Processes 116 (1998); Roland Benabou, *Groupthink: Collective Delusions in Organizations and Markets*, 80 Rev. Econ. Stud. 429 (2013). On group decision-making, see also *supra* pp. 120–24.

61. *See* Donald C. Langevoort, *Organized Illusions: A Behavioral Theory of Why Corporations Mislead Stock Market Investors (and Cause Other Social Harms)*, 146 U. Pa. L. Rev 101, 138–39 (1997).

The process of group conformity may be further strengthened by the *herd effect*. Faced with a complex situation while having limited information, people may view the behavior of others as an indication of appropriate behavior. A typical example is a new board member who is relatively unfamiliar with the firm's business and the norms governing the board. As she searches for cues on how she should behave, she observes how her fellow board members do not challenge the firm's management. Over time, this norm of board deference perpetuates itself.

Finally, membership in a group such as a board might itself trigger an in-group bias, causing board members to favor their fellow board colleagues over the interests of others (including those to whom they owe a fiduciary duty).[62] Aside from the psychological factors in play, social dynamics can also drive the board toward loyalty to the group.[63] Board members are frequently drawn from the same social group as senior management—based on ties of friendship (if the CEO nominates his or her friends to serve on the board), or on a more nuanced sense of community. Board members also often function as senior management in other firms. As friends or as members of the same corporate class, board members may be inclined to a cooperative attitude toward management, and refrain from unpleasant challenges.

(c) Legal Responses

The picture emerging from the body of work reviewed in the two preceding subsections is of powerful and overconfident CEOs who are monitored by passive boards that are unlikely to provide rigorous oversight. Moving from descriptive claims to normative arguments is always a tricky task, as it requires a careful balance between competing goals and a cautious analysis of all of the forces in play. This is certainly the case in the corporate arena as well. For one, while there is an interest in assuring that boards oversee management effectively, cooperation between the board and management is also valuable, since the board needs to advise management on strategic decisions. In addition, there is the institutional question: despite their imperfections, markets can incentivize firms to adopt efficient corporate governance structures. Thus, while the study of the imperfections of decision-making in firms is very important, the business community—rather than the legal one—may be best placed to draw the necessary conclusions. Accordingly, we limit our normative discussion to examining whether corporate law fulfills its intended policy goals—that is to say, we take it as given that company management should be overseen by its board of directors to promote desirable outcomes (as corporate law presupposes), and examine how this goal might be promoted.

One course of action that the law can take to encourage more active monitoring by boards is to strengthen ex-post scrutiny of board decisions. As previously noted, courts generally defer to corporate decisions (except in the narrow set of cases involving a clear

62. *See* James D. Cox & Harry L. Munsinger, *Bias in the Boardroom: Psychological Foundations and Legal Implications of Corporate Cohesion*, 48 L. & CONTEP. PROBS. 83 (1985); Kenneth B. Davis, Jr., *Structural Bias, Special Litigation Committees, and the Vagaries of Director Independence*, 90 IOWA L. REV. 1305 (2005).

63. *See* Claire A. Hill & Brett H. McDonnell, *Disney, Good Faith, and Structural Bias*, 32 J. CORP. L. 833 (2007).

conflict of interest).[64] In light of the structural mechanisms that encourage boards to defer to management, Claire Hill and Brett McDonnell have proposed creating an intermediate review standard between duty-of-care and duty-of-loyalty.[65] Under this proposal, in order to prevail, plaintiffs will need to demonstrate both the existence of a structural bias—that is, the presence of factors that suggest that the board's decisions are biased against the firm's best interests; and that, because of this bias, directors exhibited gross negligence in the case at hand. The limited scope of liability under this regime may alleviate many of the concerns associated with additional judicial scrutiny of corporate decisions, while spurring board members to adopt a more proactive role.

One concrete example of legal regulation of board decisions can be found in the context of the procedure for filing derivative lawsuits. Derivative lawsuits are suits filed by a shareholder of a corporation against a third party on behalf of the corporation, when the corporation refuses to do so. Such suits often involve legal claims against insiders (past or present), which the company's management refuses to pursue. There is an ongoing vigorous debate over whether such lawsuits are desirable,[66] but since the law clearly views them as an important tool in the effort to regulate agency problems in corporations, we too shall take it as a given that derivative lawsuits are desirable, and examine whether the legal framework surrounding them is founded on realistic assumptions.

Filing a derivative lawsuit entails its own agency costs as the single shareholder (or more realistically, an outside lawyer) gains control of a legal claim belonging to the corporation. Consequently, derivative lawsuits must go through a screening process to ascertain that the lawsuit can benefit the firm. U.S. corporate law assigns the board a pivotal role in reviewing the lawsuit and deciding whether to pursue it.[67] To this end, the board typically establishes a special litigation committee composed of disinterested and independent board members.[68]

The behavioral findings we reviewed above, however, suggest that in reality the members of this special litigation committee may lack sufficient independence to ensure an unbiased evaluation of the derivative lawsuit. Even if members of the special litigation committee are completely independent and disinterested, they may still find it difficult to approve a lawsuit against their friends and colleagues on the board.[69] The legal implication of this is that there should be more judicial involvement in the substance of derivative lawsuits.[70] In this regard, it has been suggested that courts should apply a more stringent

64. *See supra* pp. 359–60.

65. *See* Hill & McDonnell, *supra* note 63, at 855–56. *See also* Paredes, *supra* note 38, at 747–57.

66. For a review, see Quinn Curtis & Minor Myers, *Do the Merits Matter? Empirical Evidence on Shareholder Suits from Options Backdating Litigation*, 164 U. Pa. L. Rev. 291, 298–306 (2016).

67. *See* Clark, *supra* note 14, at 639–41.

68. *See id.* at 645–49.

69. *See* Cox & Munsinger, *supra* note 62, at 85–108.

70. To this end, the Delaware courts have adopted a two-step test that examines both the independence of the committee and the substance of its decision. *See* Zapata Corp. v. Maldonado, 430 A.2d 779 (Del. 1981).

review standard when examining the decisions made by the committee.[71] Alternatively, it has been proposed to scrap the entire board review process in such matters in favor of a different, court-based screening mechanism.[72] To be sure, while behavioral research has contributed immensely to the understanding of the decision-making process in corporate board assessments of derivative lawsuits, the final normative determination as to the appropriate legal treatment of such suits hinges on an overall evaluation of their efficacy.

Another set of legal policies aimed at strengthening the board oversight of senior management is structural in nature. These policies alter the institutions governing the firm in order to bolster the power of the board. Thus, Randall Morck has argued that to overcome board deference, the role of chair of the board must be separated from that of the CEO.[73] According to Morck, a senior chairperson could then challenge the CEO's authority, and foster a critical discussion in the boardroom. Of course, such proposals do not come without their own set of drawbacks. For the chairperson of the board to function as a true authority figure, she must be provided with effective tools that enable her to scrutinize the corporate management's operations.[74] Aside from the chair of the board, there are other figures in the firm who can help promote a critical discussion—corporate officials such as the Chief Risk Officer, Chief Ethics Officer, and Chief Compliance Officer, could function as internal "devil's advocates" whose job it is to offer an alternative viewpoint.[75]

Other proposals have focused on the method by which board members are selected, in a bid to sever the tie between management and appointments. In the past, the focus of examinations of board member independence was on the financial interest that board members might have in the firm (directly, or through a family member).[76] More recent regulation, however, has shifted scrutiny to the appointment process itself, and to minimizing the involvement of management in the selection of new board members. The NYSE listing rules, for example, clearly set out the process by which directors are appointed, which is controlled by independent board members.[77] In a corporation with a single controlling shareholder, severing the tie between the controller and the appointment of independent directors is a delicate task. In view of this, Lucian Bebchuk and Assaf Hamdani have

71. *See* Davis, *supra* note 61, at 1357–60; Hill & McDonnell, *supra* note 63, at 859.

72. *See* Cox & Munsinger, *supra* note 62, at 132.

73. *See* Morck, *supra* note 53, at 190.

74. *See* Langenvoort, *supra* note 2, at 446–48.

75. Along these lines, Troy Paredes has advocated for the appointment of a chief naysayer in corporations. *See* Paredes, *supra* note 38, at 740–47.

76. *See Developments in the Law—Corporations and Society*, 117 HARV. L. REV. 2169, 2187–91 (2004).

77. *See* NYSE, INC. LISTED COMPANY MANUAL. § 303A.04(a) (2017), http://wallstreet.cch.com/LCMTools/PlatformViewer.asp?selectednode=chp_1_4_3&manual=%2Flcm%2Fsections%2Flcm-sections%2F (noting that "listed companies must have a nominating/corporate governance committee composed entirely of independent directors").

proposed establishing "enhanced independence" directors who are accountable to the minority public investors.[78]

More radical proposals have highlighted an association between the demographics of modern boards and the quality of their decision-making. Hitherto, American boards have predominantly comprised wealthy white men who had attended a small set of elite schools.[79] This uniformity is liable to foster board deference, as it strengthens group identity.[80] Male domination of boards is of particular interest from a behavioral perspective, as well, given that a growing body of work has demonstrated that men are more likely than women to exhibit overconfidence in their investment decisions.[81] This observation has been linked to testosterone and other hormonal factors driving human behavior.[82]

Based on these findings, researchers have put forward the *Lehman Sisters Hypothesis*, which states that if more women had sat on the management boards of financial institutions, the 2008 financial meltdown might have been avoided.[83] Empirical backing for this hypothesis, however, has been elusive:[84] while some evidence supports the claim that gender diversity on boards of directors reduces the risk of financial fraud,[85] other evidence suggests that share prices drop when women are appointed to a company's board.[86] Given the relatively low level of female representation on boards and the non-random nature of board appointments, it is not surprising that unequivocal conclusions on this question are difficult to draw.

Even if one assumes that added diversity to boards is a step in the right direction, and that market reaction to the appointment of female board members reflects entrenched stereotypes rather than well-founded assessments of a firm's long-term prospects,[87] caution

78. *See* Lucian Bebchuk & Assaf Hamdani, *Independent Directors and Controlling Shareholders*, 165 U. Pa. L. Rev. 1271 (2017).

79. *See* Greenfield, *supra* note 2, at 528–33.

80. *See* Clark McCauley, *The Nature of Social Influence in Groupthink: Compliance and Internalization*, 57 J. Personality & Soc. Psychol. 250, 252 (1989) (highlighting the link between social homogeneity, cohesion, and groupthink).

81. *See, e.g.*, Jiekun Huang & Darren J. Kisgen. *Gender and Corporate Finance: Are Male Executives Overconfident Relative to Female Executives?*, 108 J. Fin. Econ. 822 (2013). For an overview of the findings, see Rachel Croson & Uri Gneezy, *Gender Differences in Preferences*, 47 J. Econ. Literature 448, 452–53 (2009).

82. *See, e.g.*, J. M. Coates & J. Herbert, *Endogenous Steroids and Financial Risk Taking on a London Trading Floor*, 16 Proc. Nat'l Acad. Sci. 6167 (2008).

83. *See* Irene van Staveren, *The Lehman Sisters Hypothesis*, 38 Cambridge J. Econ. 995 (2014).

84. *See* Vathunyoo Sila, Angelica Gonzalez & Jens Hagendorff, *Women on Board: Does Boardroom Gender Diversity Affect Firm Risk?*, 36 J. Corp. Fin. 26 (2016) (failing to detect a link between gender diversity and risk-taking).

85. *See, e.g.*, Douglas Cumming, Tak Yan Leung, & Oliver M. Rui, *Gender Diversity and Securities Fraud*, 58 Acad. Mgmt. J. 1459 (2015).

86. *See, e.g.*, Renée B. Adams & Daniel Ferreira, *Women in the Boardroom and Their Impact on Governance and Performance*, 94 J. Fin. Econ. 291 (2009); Kenneth R. Ahern & Amy K. Dittmar, *The Changing of the Boards: The Impact on Firm Valuation of Mandated Female Board Representation*, 127 Q. J. Econ. 137 (2012).

87. *See* Frank Dobbin & Jiwook Jung, *Corporate Board Gender Diversity and Stock Performance: The Competence Gap or Institutional Investor Bias?*, 89 N.C. L. Rev. 809 (2011).

should still be taken before adopting policies based on this body of work. For one, there are numerous unknowns about critical issues such the effects of interaction between men and women. In addition, women differ from men not only with respect to overconfidence, but also in relation to risk preferences, since they tend to be more risk averse.[88] In this regard, while a rigid legislative quota system might fail to offer corporations the requisite level of flexibility,[89] a regulatory nudge—in the shape of voluntary targets regarding board composition—can go a long way. In the United Kingdom, for example, the number of female directors in FTSE 100 boards doubled in five years after the creation of a voluntary target of 25 percent female representation on boards (a figure that has since risen to 33 percent).[90]

Regulating the structure of the core building blocks of a corporation—its management and its board of directors—is a delicate task. Corporate failures can have calamitous economic consequences that extend well beyond the shareholders of an individual firm. On the other hand, corporate risk-taking plays a key role in enhancing human welfare. Behavioral analysis does not dictate where corporate law should draw the precise regulatory line. Nonetheless, behavioral analysis does suggest that when regulation is enacted, it should be founded on sound empirical grounds. If courts and legislatures view the board of directors as a key element in serious oversight of managerial conduct, we should make sure it is fit for the job.

D. Securities Regulation

1. General

Securities regulation is the body of law aimed at protecting investors who purchase financial instruments in public trading markets.[91] The key goals of this legal field are to ensure that investors receive all significant information about the financial instruments they are investing in, and to safeguard the quality of corporations that sell their securities in public markets. Given the close link between securities regulation and the functioning of efficient capital markets, the need to apply behavioral insights in this area seems straightforward. If current regulation is based on the premise that capital markets function efficiently, the legal framework in this field may not fit market realities, nor achieve its goals.

88. *See* Croson & Gneezy, *supra* note 81, at 449–54. *But see* Renée B. Adams & Patricia Funk, *Beyond the Glass Ceiling: Does Gender Matter?*, 58 MGMT. SCI. 219 (2011) (survey data suggesting that female directors are more risk-loving than male directors).

89. *See* Mara Faccio, Maria-Teresa Marchica & Roberto Mura, *CEO Gender, Corporate Risk-Taking, and the Efficiency of Capital Allocation*, 39 J. CORP. FIN. 193 (2016).

90. *See* DEPARTMENT FOR BUS., INNOVATION & SKILLS, WOMEN ON BOARDS: FIVE-YEAR SUMMARY (2015), *available at*: https://www.gov.uk/government/publications/women-on-boards-5-year-summary-davies-review.

91. *See generally* THOMAS LEE HAZEN, THE LAW OF SECURITIES REGULATION (7th ed., 2016). For a comparative view of the topic, see Gerard Hertig, Reinier Kraakman & Edward Rock, *Issuers and Investor Protection*, *in* THE ANATOMY OF CORPORATE LAW: A COMPARATIVE AND FUNCTIONAL APPROACH 275 (Reinier Kraakman et al. eds., 2d ed. 2009).

This section reviews the implications of behavioral findings for two key areas within this extensive body of law.[92] It first examines the psychological underpinnings of managerial fraud, and highlights the legal implications of these findings. It then turns to investor behavior and explores the regulation of one of the key tools used by retail investors—mutual funds.

2. Securities Fraud

As previously noted, securities regulation aims to ensure that markets function on the basis of truthful information. The cornerstone of this legislative body is the prohibition of fraud. Within the U.S. legal framework, SEC Rule 10b-5 is the main tool through which the prohibition of fraud in relation to the sale or purchase of securities is enforced.[93] To prevail in a 10b-5 claim, a plaintiff must demonstrate (1) the defendant's manipulation of investors with regard to a material fact, (2) the plaintiff's reliance on that information, and (3) scienter on the part of the defendants.[94]

One key doctrine relating to the application of Rule 10b-5, which appears to rely heavily on the efficiency of capital markets, is the *fraud-on-the-market* doctrine. The reliance requirement embedded in Rule 10b-5 was liable to be an insurmountable obstacle for class actions, since individual issues would routinely arise. To overcome this problem, the U.S. Supreme Court, in *Basic Inc. v. Levinson*,[95] created a rebuttable presumption that "the market price of shares traded on well-developed markets reflects all publicly available information."[96] Consequently, according to the Court, one can assume that an investor relies on public misstatements whenever he or she "buys or sells stock at the price set by the market."[97]

The findings of studies in the behavioral finance literature that a firm's stock-market price can deviate from its fundamental value appear to call this judicial presumption into question. Even so, as Donald Langevoort has pointed out,[98] the documented mispricing exhibited in thick financial markets does not invalidate the judicial presumption of efficient pricing. Rather, one should view the presumption as creating an *entitlement* to rely on stock prices—even if investors realize that these prices might not reflect the firm's fundamental value, due to an array of behavioral factors. Creating such an entitlement facilitates reliance, and lowers the costs of capital formation.

92. For further discussion of the behavioral analysis of securities regulation, see Donald C. Langevoort, *Taming the Animal Spirits of the Stock Markets: A Behavioral Approach to Securities Regulation*, 97 Nw. U. L. Rev. 135 (2002).

93. The substantive legal rules in this regard are similar across numerous major jurisdictions, yet the procedural rules through which these norms are enforced differ significantly. *See* Hertig, Kraakman & Rock, *supra* note 91, at 295.

94. For a more detailed analysis of the elements of a 10b-5 claim, see 3 Thomas Lee Hazen, Treatise on the Law of Securities Regulation, 199–207 (5th ed. 2002).

95. 485 U.S. 224 (1988).

96. *Id.* at 246.

97. *Id.* at 247.

98. *See* Donald C. Langevoort, Basic *at Twenty: Rethinking Fraud on the Market,* 2009 Wis. L. Rev. 151.

A separate aspect of behavioral analysis of Rule 10b-5 litigation concerns the state of mind of the corporate actors involved in the alleged fraud. Many fraud cases involve situations where the company fails to disclose bad news in its official reports to the market regarding its business operations (such as loss of market share, or negative feedback about a major company product). Since market pricing relies at least to some degree on the flow of information from management, the concealment of bad news can cause mispricing.

From a rational choice perspective, this sort of behavior is somewhat puzzling, as managers have no clear incentive to misrepresent information to the market.[99] On the one hand, the penalties for misrepresentation are clear—criminal sanctions, civil liability, and termination of employment; on the other hand (apart from situations where the firm is on the verge of bankruptcy and its managers have little to lose) the benefits are unclear, since in many cases the concealed information is bound to emerge at some point. When the assumptions of rationality are relaxed, however, it is more readily apparent how fraud can slowly evolve within a corporation due to psychological and sociological forces.[100] The key point in this regard is that corporate fraud often does not spring from a deliberate decision to cheat investors, but rather from several features of the company's decision-making process. Once the company is set on a plotted business plan, cognitive forces such as the confirmation bias, escalation of commitment, and overconfidence may cause management to discount any looming negative information that suggests that the plan is misconceived. This individual behavior can be magnified in a group setting, when the silence of other group members in the face of bad information strengthens the perception that there is no cause for alarm.[101]

This analysis suggests that fraud lawsuits may face a serious challenge over the *scienter* requirement. Without our getting into the details of the legal doctrine, the essence of this requirement is that there must be a mental state of intent to deceive or manipulate investors.[102] As we have seen, however, corporate managers who mislead investors often do so without such devious intent. That said, one should not overstate this point: hindsight can cause adjudicators to overestimate the ability of managers to properly assess the facts, and the *fundamental attribution* error may cause adjudicators to assign personal responsibility even when it is unfounded.[103] Finally, even allowing that the psychological forces described above may have triggered the initial stages of fraud, at some point the reality is likely to become apparent to management, and a cover-up (which involves scienter) then ensues.

In any event, the normative conclusions arising from these findings hinge on one's assessment of the efficacy of fraud lawsuits. If one views such litigation as an important

99. *See* Jennifer H. Arlen & William J. Carney, *Vicarious Liability for Fraud on Securities Markets: Theory and Evidence,* 1992 U. ILL. L. REV. 691, 702.

100. *See* Langevoort, *supra* note 61, at 135–48. *See also supra* pp. 72–76; *infra* pp. 455–61.

101. *See supra* pp. 365–66.

102. For a review, see Allan Horwich, *An Inquiry into the Perception of Materiality as an Element of Scienter under SEC Rule 10b-5,* 67 BUS. LAWYER 1, 3–9 (2011).

103. On these phenomena, see generally *supra* pp. 38–39 and 68–69, respectively.

piece of the regulatory puzzle, then relaxing the scienter requirement may be justified.[104] Alternatively, given the unintentional dimension of fraud, regulators might focus their attention on enhancing the role of external auditors (although such actors come with their own set of agency problems and cognitive limitations).[105] At any rate, such interventions should account for the fact that while the process described above might adversely affect investors, curbing corporate overconfidence does not necessarily maximize value as far as shareholders are concerned.[106]

3. Retail Investors

Once the focal point of the analysis shifts to the demand side of capital markets—namely, retail investors—the application of behavioral insights is more straightforward. Retail investors are not subject to the competitive environment of the market, and are liable to make persistently irrational investment decisions,[107] due to an array of heuristics and cognitive biases, as well as poor financial literacy. Numerous studies have demonstrated that retail investors often fail to grasp issues such as compound interest, diversification, and fees—or even simple numeric concepts such as percentage.[108]

A vast behavioral finance literature has documented investor susceptibility to cognitive biases and heuristics. Studies have demonstrated how phenomena such as loss aversion, regret aversion, anchoring, and representativeness impel investors to make suboptimal decision.[109] Given the sheer volume of research on this topic, we shall focus on a small sample of issues related to a key investment tool that is used primarily by retail investors—mutual funds. As we shall see, the legal questions surrounding the regulation of such funds bring to the forefront the entire range of behaviorally informed policies—from choice-preserving tools such as disclosures and defaults, to clear legislated mandates.

Mutual funds are an investment tool that pools together financial assets (stocks, bonds, etc.). Investors purchase shares or units in these funds, which represent a pro rata ownership interest in the fund's assets. While some mutual funds actively manage the pool of assets they control in a bid to beat the market (so called "smart money"), other funds use passive investment strategies and merely track a market index such as the S&P 500 or the DAX. The services provided by mutual fund managers are obviously not free, and investors are charged a range of fees when they utilize this tool.

Ideally, when choosing a mutual fund, an investor should focus on the returns the fund will generate and the costs it will charge. In reality, however, investors are not good

104. *See* Langevoort, *supra* note 61 at 158.

105. *Id.* at 159.

106. *See supra* pp. 363–64.

107. For a similar argument in the context of consumer contracts, see *supra* p. 308.

108. For a review, see Justine S. Hastings, Brigitte C. Madrian & William L. Skimmyhorn, *Financial Literacy, Financial Education, and Economic Outcomes*, 5 Ann. Rev. Econ. 347 (2013).

109. *See, e.g.*, Sudhir Singh, *Investor Irrationality and Self-Defeating Behavior: Insights from Behavioral Finance*, 8 J. Global Bus. Mgmt. 116 (2012); Baker & Wurgler, *supra* note 10, at 5–50.

at conducting this cost-benefit analysis, and allow their decisions to be influenced by numerous behavioral phenomena.[110] One key mistake that investors seem to make in this regard is to infer future performance from past performance.[111] Generally, the finance literature suggests that over time, mutual funds that actively manage assets fail to achieve greater returns than the market index.[112] In fact, the data suggests that mutual funds with high management fees produce *lower* returns, even on a pre-fee basis.[113] Investors' mistaken focus on past performance is coupled with a lack of attention to fees. Overall, the finance literature suggests that fund costs are the best predictor of future returns, and that consumers should therefore channel their money toward low-cost funds.[114] However, issues such as the complexity of fees, coupled with the erroneous (but intuitive) assumption that expensive mutual funds are better than low-cost ones, cause consumers to opt for expensive products.[115] Some scholars have gone as far as to describe individual investors as "Dumb Money,"[116] noting that they "have a striking ability to do the wrong thing."[117]

Expert advice by financial intermediators does not appear to alleviate these problems, and may actually exacerbate them given the conflict of interest that these agents face.[118] In a carefully designed audit study that examined the actual advice given to trained, professional auditors who impersonated regular customers, Sendhil Mullainathan, Marcus Nöth, and Antoinette Schoar documented a tendency by investment agents to advise clients to opt for high-cost investments.[119] Based on their findings, the authors concluded that "advice by and large fails to de-bias clients and if anything may exaggerate existing biases or, in some cases,

110. *See* Warren Bailey, Alok Kumar & David Ng, *Behavioral Biases of Mutual Fund Investors*, 102 J. FIN. ECON. 1 (2011).

111. *See, e.g.*, Don A. Moore et al., *Positive Illusions and Forecasting Errors in Mutual Fund Investment Decisions*, 79 ORG. BEHAV. & HUM. DECISION PROCESSES 95, 105–07 (1999); Travis Sapp & Ashish Tiwari, *Does Stock Return Momentum Explain the "Smart Money" Effect?*, 59 J. FIN. 2605 (2004).

112. *See* Mark M. Carhart, *On Persistence in Mutual Fund Performance,* 52 J. FIN. 57 (1997); Nicolas P.B. Bollen & Jeffrey A. Busse, *Short-Term Persistence in Mutual Fund Performance,* 18 REV. FIN. STUD. 569 (2004).

113. *See* Javier Gil-Bazo & Pablo Ruiz-Verdú, *The Relation between Price and Performance in the Mutual Fund Industry*, 64 J. FIN. 2153 (2009).

114. For a summary of the findings, see Jill E. Fisch, *Rethinking the Regulation of Securities Intermediaries,* 158 U. PA. L. REV. 1961, 1993 (2010).

115. *See, e.g.*, Jill E. Fisch & Tess Wilkinson-Ryan, *Why Do Retail Investors Make Costly Mistakes? An Experiment on Mutual Fund Choice*, 162 U. PA. L. REV. 605, 621–22 (2014).

116. Andrea Frazzini & Owen A. Lamont, *Dumb Money: Mutual Fund Flows and the Cross-Section of Stock Returns*, 88 J. FIN. ECON. 299 (2008). Another indication of the folly of at least some of the money going into mutual funds can be found in the documented impact of meaningless name changes on the flow of money into funds. *See* Michael J. Cooper et al., *Changing Names with Style: Mutual Fund Name Changes and Their Effects on Fund Flows*, 60 J. FIN. 2825 (2005).

117. Frazzini & Lamont, *supra* note 116, at 319.

118. *See, e.g.*, Fisch, *supra* note 114, at 1998–2010.

119. *See* Sendhil Mullainathan, Marcus Nöth, & Antoinette Schoar, *The Market for Financial Advice: An Audit Study* (NBER Working Paper No. 17929, Mar. 2012, *available at:* http://www.nber.org/papers/w17929).

even makes the clients worse off."[120] Focusing on observational data, Diane Del Guercio and Jonathan Reuter exploit the fact that while some mutual funds are marketed to consumers through brokers, others are sold to consumers directly.[121] They found that active (i.e., costly) mutual funds marketed through brokers systematically underperform mutual funds that are sold directly to consumers.

The regulatory responses on this front are numerous and complex, and obviously vary across jurisdictions.[122] Notwithstanding these differences, one key aspect within the regulatory framework surrounding mutual funds is its reliance on disclosure.[123] As in other contexts, disclosure policies are popular with regulators, because they sustain individual choice and do not limit the products available on the market. Unfortunately, however—and once again, as in other contexts—disclosure may be an insufficient means of helping investors navigate the maze of complex investment tools available on the market, given their bounded rationality and limited cognitive skills.[124] There are numerous examples of investors misunderstanding their investment choices, despite the regulatory regime in place. For example, investors in target date mutual funds—funds that are supposed to progressively reduce their risk level as they approach the target date at which the investor plans to retire—were surprised (and probably disappointed) to learn that funds with a target date of 2010 had invested as much as 79 percent of their assets in equities when the 2008 financial crisis occurred.[125]

A more rigorous demonstration of the limited ability of disclosures to guide investors' decisions can be found in the context of past performance data. As previously noted, investors often base their decisions on the past performance of mutual funds, even though they would be better off not doing so. Being well aware of this tendency, suppliers highlight their past performance in their advertising. In the United States, the SEC addressed the concern that ads of this sort might drive consumers to make imprudent choices by requiring advertisements to include a disclaimer to prospective investors that past returns are not indicative of future performance.[126] In accordance with this rule, mutual funds now routinely accompany their advertisements that highlight past performance with disclaimers such as: "The performance data featured represents past performance, which is no guarantee of future results. Investment return and principal value of an investment will fluctuate;

120. *Id.* at 4.

121. *See* Diane Del Guercio & Jonathan Reuter, *Mutual Fund Performance and the Incentive to Generate Alpha*, 69 J. Fin. 1673 (2014).

122. Market conditions vary significantly in this regard, and consequently any analysis requires careful consideration of the specific legal and economic framework. *See* Ajay Khorana, Henri Servaes & Peter Tufano, *Mutual Fund Fees around the World*, 22 Rev. Fin. Stud. 1279 (2008) (documenting significant differences in pricing and regulation across the world).

123. James D. Cox & John W. Payne, *Mutual Fund Expense Disclosures: A Behavioral Perspective*, 83 Wash. U. L.Q. 907, 908 (2005).

124. On the limits of disclosure, see *supra* pp. 171–77, 314–18.

125. *See* Leslie Wayne, *Mutual Funds with Targets, and Misfires*, N.Y. TIMES, June 25, 2009, at B1.

126. *See* 17 C.F.R. § 230.482 (b)(3)(i) (2017).

therefore, you may have a gain or loss when you sell your shares. Current performance may be higher or lower than the performance data quoted."[127]

Such disclaimers, however, have proven to be ineffective—as evident from the continued use of past performance data in mutual fund advertisements. This point has also been demonstrated experimentally in a study that randomized the content of ads that subjects were exposed to before making investment decisions.[128] The wording mandated by the SEC had no measurable effect on participants' decisions when compared with a control group that was not exposed to the disclaimer. Only a stronger disclaimer that explicitly warned subjects that future performance cannot be predicted by past returns had a significant impact on investment decisions.[129]

Even such strengthened disclaimers, however, are likely to be of limited effectiveness in the real world. For one, the subjects in the reported study were MBA students, law students, and undergraduate business students—a population far more sophisticated and financially literate than the average investor. In addition, people are significantly more likely to notice nuanced details such as the text of a disclaimer in an experimental setting, where they are exposed to a single ad, than when they are reading the morning newspaper. Finally, the general shortcomings of disclosure as a regulatory mechanism—such as the public's failure to read disclosed information, or to understand it, and its desensitization in the face of recurring boring text—are just as relevant in the present context as in others.[130] Consequently, if regulators wish to rely on disclosure in this context, they must make the wording and form of disclaimers significantly more prominent. More fundamentally, they must also address the question as to why mutual funds are allowed to continue to highlight in their ads information that is known to induce suboptimal investment.[131]

As noted, the most important aspect that investors should focus on when choosing a mutual fund are its management fees. Properly assessing those fees, however, is often very difficult, as mutual-fund fees are notoriously complex. In the United States, investors are charged a management fee along with additional fees such as 12b-1 fees (that cover, among other things, the advertising of the fund), and load fees or redemption fees that are charged only once—when the investment is made or realized. Publication of the *Total Expense Ratio*—namely, the percentage of fees in relation to the managed assets—may certainly allow for more informed price comparisons, but still leaves much complexity in place. For

127. This is the disclaimer used by Fidelity, one of the leading managers of mutual funds in the United States, on its website. *See* https://fundresearch.fidelity.com/mutual-funds/performance-and-risk/315911701.

128. *See* Molly Mercer, Alan R. Palmiter & Ahmed E. Taha, *Worthless Warnings? Testing the Effectiveness of Disclaimers in Mutual Fund Advertisements*, 7 J. EMPIRICAL LEGAL STUD. 429, 459 (2010).

129. The wording used was "Do not expect the fund's quoted past performance to continue in the future. Studies show that mutual funds that have outperformed their peers in the past generally do not outperform them in the future. Strong past performance is often a matter of chance." *Id.* at 445.

130. *See supra* pp. 171–77, 314–18.

131. Limiting the ability of advertisers to include truthful information in ads raises a host of questions regarding commercial free speech, which exceed the scope of our discussion.

example, if load fees are involved, the effective fee may vary significantly with the duration of the investment, since they diminish the longer the investment is held.

To date, the main regulatory response to the issue of fees has been on the disclosure front. The SEC has attempted to simplify the information investors receive by creating a brief disclosure, known as the *Summary Prospectus*.[132] A study of this form of disclosure suggests that its main achievement has been to reduce the time spent by investors when choosing investments (as well as a significant reduction in paper consumption).[133] However, the Summary Prospectus has not led to any measurable change in the decisions of investors. One clear culprit in this regard were load and redemption fees. Apparently, due to their complexity or their variation with the duration of the investment, investors tend to miscalculate or ignore them.

Behaviorally motivated responses to the challenge posed by mutual-fund fees have been diverse. Jill Fisch has proposed to create "plain vanilla" mutual funds that would fit the preferences of most investors in several respects (including fees), coupled with a robust duty on the part of the mutual fund managers to "conform or explain."[134] According to this framework, providers of financial products that deviate from the plain vanilla option would be required to carefully explain to consumers the unique aspects of their products. In a later study, Fisch and Tess Wilkinson-Ryan highlighted the importance of disclosures with regard to the motivational—as opposed to the cognitive—aspect of investment decisions.[135] Specifically, their experimental findings demonstrate that even when fees are perfectly simple and transparent, investors lack the motivation to minimize them—perhaps due to failure to understand their long-term impact.[136] The authors further demonstrated that disclosures that explain the importance of fees to investors did influence their decisions, and steered them toward more cost-effective mutual funds (although, once again, the external validity of this conclusion may be debatable, given the differences between the laboratory and real-life circumstances).

Behaviorally informed regulation of excessive mutual fund fees is still in its infancy. Non-intrusive nudges such as the creation of "plain vanilla" defaults, coupled with smart disclosures, could certainly benefit investors. That said, their limitations should also be acknowledged. While participants in Fisch and Wilkinson-Ryan's experiment did improve their choices when informed about the importance of fees, they continued to make costly mistakes.[137] Tackling investors' bounded rationality may therefore require tools beyond the behavioral toolkit. For example, regulators might consider banning multidimensional

132. *See* Alan R. Palmiter & Ahmed E. Taha, *Mutual Fund Investors: Divergent Profiles*, 2008 Colum. Bus. L. Rev. 934, 961–64.

133. *See* John Beshears et al., *How Does Simplified Disclosure Affect Individuals' Mutual Funds Choices?*, *in* Explorations in the Economics of Aging 75 (David A. Wise ed., 2011).

134. *See* Fisch, *supra* note 114, at 2028–35.

135. *See* Fisch & Wilkinson-Ryan, *supra* note 115.

136. *Id.* at 643–44.

137. *Id.* at 641–42.

complex fees altogether, in favor of a single mandatory and uniform fee structure.[138] As with all mandates, banning certain financial instruments may also eliminate the efficiencies associated with them, so the enactment of such regulation requires careful cost-benefit analysis that may differ from one market to the other.

Another issue regarding mutual-funds fees concerns the practice of *low-balling* fees. Occasionally, mutual funds offer exceptionally low fees—or even a zero-fees policy. Naturally, these are offered for a limited period only, and are substituted by higher fees down the road. This practice is common in other retail domains as well—such as teaser rates in loans, free introductory periods for subscriptions, etc.[139] The underlying behavioral explanation for such seemingly irrational pricing schemes is that consumers' excessive optimism, omission bias, or myopia will induce them to continue using the product or service after the price increases. In addition, suppliers exploit the trust that customers place in them once the deal has been struck,[140] which in the case of mutual funds may cause investors to be less vigilant in monitoring subsequent unilateral changes to the deal. Finally, zero pricing (i.e., "free") has been shown to exert a particularly compelling allure to consumers.[141] The net outcome of all these forces may be investment decisions that are not optimal in the long run.

The Israeli Securities Authority (the local equivalent of the SEC) has expressed concerns over the practice of low-ball fees that are increased soon after. Its response was to extract a voluntary commitment by fund managers to limit fee changes to a single day in the year—January 1st.[142] While such a regime may prove helpful, as it reduces the need of consumers to monitor their portfolio constantly,[143] we are somewhat skeptical about its effectiveness. In fact, both of us like to think of ourselves as more informed than the average investor, and yet neither of us was aware of this program prior to researching this chapter. Perhaps for this very reason, all mutual fund managers volunteered to join this program shortly after it had been introduced.[144]

While the effectiveness of the regulatory reaction adopted by Israeli authorities may be questioned, caution should be taken before any more intrusive regulation is adopted on this front. Low prices are generally a good thing, and fierce competition that drives prices downward should be welcomed, not banned. Sophisticated, behaviorally motivated

138. As did the Supervisors of Banks in Israel, in the context of bank fees. *See supra* p. 298.

139. *See* Oren Bar-Gill, *Bundling and Consumer Misperception*, 73 U. CHI. L. REV. 33, 46–50 (2006).

140. *See supra* pp. 261–62.

141. *See* Kristina Shampanier, Nina Mazar & Dan Ariely, *Zero as a Special Price: The True Value of Free Products*, 26 MARKETING SCI. 742 (2007).

142. A full description of the policy is *available at*: http://www.isa.gov.il/%D7%92%D7%95%D7%A4%D7%99%D7%9D%20%D7%9E%D7%A4%D7%95%D7%A7%D7%97%D7%99%D7%9D/Mutual_Funds/Data%20on%20mutual%20funds/Pages/kranot.aspx.

143. However, given the fact that the month of December involves a disproportionally high incidence of investment decisions due to tax considerations, it is surprising that the uniform fee shifting date was not set for the beginning of that month.

144. *See supra* note 142.

solutions might turn to market forces and create mechanisms that will enable competing mutual funds to quickly draw investors when fees are elevated. That said—as in other contexts[145]—mandates that prohibit price schemes with little economic justification (such as zero-fee pricing) should not be taken off the regulatory table.

Finally, a unique issue regarding mutual funds that is of interest to U.S. investors in particular (but with general ramifications elsewhere, as well) concerns the selection of mutual funds included in individual retirement accounts, commonly known as 401(k) plans. These plans are a key channel through which many Americans save for retirement. They are offered to employees as part of their compensation package, allowing them to make their own decisions as to how their retirement investments are allocated. These decisions, however, are not without constraints: such allocations may be chosen from a predetermined "menu" of set options that the plan service provider offers. As it turns out, the structure of this menu has been found to greatly influence investment decisions.

A robust behavioral literature demonstrates that when investors make selections within a menu, they engage in *naïve diversification.*[146] That is, they tend to follow a rule of thumb of allocating 1/*n* of their investment to each of the various options on the menu. While early studies highlighted the impact of such investment menus on the proportion of the portfolio allocated by investors to stocks, subsequent experimental and observational studies found that naïve diversification can result in investors paying excessive fees.[147] Specifically, they found that investors who engage in naïve diversification tend to allocate part of their savings to *dominated funds*—that is, funds that are clearly inferior to at least one other item on the menu, since they offer approximately the same financial product for a higher price. The inclusion of such inferior items on the menu likely stems from revenue-sharing mechanisms, whereby plan service providers receive a share of the fees paid by participants in the program.[148]

The current regulatory framework governing 401(k) programs does not offer a robust solution to the problem of dominated funds. Rather, it favors procedure over substance, by granting employers and plan service providers a safe harbor from liability, as long as they offer employees a large menu with a variety of options—even if some of these options are completely unreasonable.[149] In light of these findings on naïve diversification, Ian Ayres and Quinn Curtis have suggested that courts look beyond the length of the menu, and examine

145. *See supra* pp. 320–21 (discussing mandates in the context of teaser rates in loans).

146. *See* Shlomo Benartzi & Richard H. Thaler, *Naive Diversification Strategies in Defined Contribution Saving Plans*, 91 Am. Econ. Rev. 79 (2001). This is one manifestation of a general phenomenon known as the *diversification heuristic. See* Daniel Read & George Loewenstein, *Diversification Bias: Explaining the Discrepancy in Variety Seeking between Combined and Separated Choices*, 1 J. Experimental Psychol.: Applied. 34 (1995).

147. *See* Fisch & Wilkinson-Ryan, *supra* note 115 (experimental data); Ian Ayres & Quinn Curtis, *Beyond Diversification: The Pervasive Problem of Excessive Fees and "Dominated Funds" in 401(k) Plans*, 124 Yale L.J. 1476 (2015) (observational data).

148. *See* Ayres & Curtis, *supra* note 147, at 1487.

149. Mercer Bullard, *The Social Costs of Choice, Free Market Ideology and the Empirical Consequences of the 401(k) Plan Large Menu Defense*, 20 Conn. Ins. L.J. 335, 340–50 (2014) (reviewing the case law).

whether it includes options that no prudent investor would ever choose.[150] In addition, Ayres and Curtis proposed that low-fee investment tools be set as defaults, and that surmountable barriers be erected to opting out of these defaults such that only sophisticated investors, based on informed decision, would opt for alternative, costly investment tools.[151]

This subsection has offered a glimpse into the world of investors' bounded rationality and the regulatory response to such behavior. Its analysis demonstrated how behavioral insights can guide policymakers in defining and achieving appropriate goals and means of regulation. There is significantly more work to be done on this front, and careful attention should be given to the unique characteristics of each financial market before tailoring the appropriate legal response. Further interesting questions lie on the horizon regarding new investment tools, including cryptocurrencies (such as Bitcoin) and crowdfunding.[152]

E. Antitrust Law

1. General

Antitrust law is the body of law dealing with the structure of markets.[153] Broadly put, it deals with regulating the behavior of monopolistic suppliers and the arrangements between market actors aimed at hindering competition. At its core, antitrust law aims to foster competitive market conditions that lead to the efficient pricing of goods and services. To this end, it has built upon a well-established body of economic theory, such as the theory of monopolistic and oligopolistic pricing. Consequently, traditional economic analysis—with its assumption of rationality—has dominated the legal discourse on antitrust[154] and the courts' jurisprudence on the matter.[155]

A growing body of literature under the rubric of behavioral antitrust, however, has demonstrated that in order to accurately model market behavior one must relax the assumption of rationality, and incorporate behavioral insights into the analysis.[156] Based on the findings of behavioral finance, this body of work suggests that decisions made by businesses with regard to competition policy can at times deviate from rationality. Furthermore, studies of behavioral industrial organization show that even when firms

150. Ayres & Curtis, *supra* note 147, at 1507–14.

151. *Id.* at 1524–31.

152. *See, e.g.*, David Groshoff, *Kickstarter My Heart: Extraordinary Popular Delusions and the Madness of Crowdfunding Constraints and Bitcoin Bubbles*, 5 WM. & MARY BUS. L. REV. 489 (2014).

153. For an introduction to this area, see HERBERT HOVENKAMP, FEDERAL ANTITRUST POLICY: THE LAW OF COMPETITION AND ITS PRACTICE (5th ed. 2016); MORITZ LORENZ, AN INTRODUCTION TO EU COMPETITION LAW (2013).

154. *See, e.g.*, ROBERT H. BORK, THE ANTITRUST PARADOX: A POLICY AT WAR WITH ITSELF (1978); ANTITRUST LAW AND ECONOMICS (Keith N. Hylton ed., 2010); POSNER, *supra* note 1.

155. *See* Amanda P. Reeves & Maurice E. Stucke, *Behavioral Antitrust*, 86 IND. L.J. 1527, 1545–53 (2011).

156. *See, e.g.*, Tor, *supra* note 2. For a European-centered review of the literature, see Andreas Heinemann, *Behavioral Antitrust—A "More Realistic Approach" to Competition Law*, *in* EUROPEAN PERSPECTIVES ON BEHAVIOURAL LAW AND ECONOMICS 211 (Klaus Mathis ed., 2015).

behave rationally, irrational consumers can cause firms to adopt policies that diverge from the predictions of traditional market models.[157] Both these lines of research suggest that legal policies should be re-examined in light of behavioral insights to better fit market realities. This section is devoted to this re-examination—starting with deviations from rationality on the demand side of the market, and then on the supply side.

2. Boundedly Rational Consumers

Behavioral antitrust has examined the implications of consumer deviations from rationality for competition policy. This body of work is largely an extension of the behavioral literature on consumer contracts.[158] It highlights the potential anticompetitive effects of the interaction between producers and consumers. Generally, these studies suggest that firms might take advantage of consumers' bounded rationality to reap supra-competitive profits.

Take, for example, the case of a firm that attempts to bolster its profits by exploiting its aftermarket power. A paradigmatic aftermarket case involves a supplier that requires its customers to purchase services (such as maintenance) or goods (such as ink cartridges) exclusively from it. Antitrust scholars have raised concerns that these practices may allow producers to limit competition and charge supra-competitive prices in the aftermarket.[159]

Traditional rational choice theory analysis suggests that producers cannot abuse consumers in the aftermarket,[160] because market forces in the primary market will keep such behavior in check. Thus, a producer of espresso machines that requires its customers to purchase coffee exclusively from it at exorbitant prices will find it difficult to sell those machines in the first place. Moreover, the prevalence of such practices may be explained by the numerous efficiencies that traditional analysis has found to be associated with contractual provisions that limit aftermarket choice. In the context of franchise contracts, for example, franchisors might want to dictate the supply chain to franchisees as a form of quality assurance.[161] More generally, aftermarket arrangements can serve as a tool to price-discriminate between low and high intensity users, such that the latter pay more in practice.[162] As a result, legal economists have exhibited a laissez faire attitude toward the issue, and urged for regulatory restraint.[163]

Behavioral analysis of aftermarkets does not offer a definitive answer to the ongoing policy debate on this matter, but does generally suggest that closer regulatory scrutiny

157. For an overview of behavioral industrial organization, see Ran Spiegler, Bounded Rationality and Industrial Organization (2011).

158. *See generally supra* pp. 281–324.

159. Joseph B. Bauer, *Antitrust Implications of Aftermarkets*, 52 Antitrust Bull. 31, 45 (2007). *See also supra* p. 299.

160. *See* Posner, *supra* note 1, at 197–200.

161. *See* Benjamin Klein & Lester F. Saft, *The Law and Economics of Franchise Tying Contracts*, 28 J.L. & Econ. 345 (1985).

162. *See* Ward S. Bowman, Jr., *Tying Arrangements and the Leverage Problem*, 67 Yale L.J. 19, 23 (1957).

163. *See* Posner, *supra* note 1, at 197–200.

is in order. As behavioral scholars have pointed out, boundedly rational purchasers may misperceive the long-term costs of ownership due to myopia and similar phenomena.[164] Rational producers might therefore strategically exploit this misperception to bolster their profits. By using a two-tiered pricing scheme based on low upfront costs and high long-term costs, producers might drive consumers to purchase goods and services that do not enhance their welfare. The precise magnitude of this effect will depend on the distribution of rational and irrational purchasers in the market.[165]

This analysis suggests that courts and regulators should carefully examine specific practices on a case-by-case basis. The U.S. Supreme Court adopted this line of thought in *Eastman Kodak Co. v. Image Technical Services, Inc.*,[166] which dealt with Kodak's attempt to dominate the market for servicing the photocopying machines it produced. In this case, the Court rejected the traditional rational-choice perspective resulting in summary judgment in favor of Kodak, and required a detailed factual examination of whether Kodak did in fact abuse its power.[167] European competition law has adopted a similar perspective on the matter, requiring case-specific evidence as well.[168]

Another context in which behavioral research has shed new light on competition policy is that of loyalty programs. Companies often encourage buyers to purchase their goods and services through loyalty rebate programs that reward their customers for reaching certain purchasing targets. Within a rational-choice framework, competitive concerns about such programs are mostly limited to cases where dominant incumbent suppliers use them to entrench their market dominance.[169] For example, given their existing large market share, a rebate scheme might lower the per-unit cost for the incumbent firm such that small competitors are driven out of the market. Under certain market conditions, therefore, loyalty programs may require legal scrutiny.[170]

Behavioral analysis, however, suggests that loyalty programs could be used to raise switching costs and reduce competition in a broader set of cases, since they might alter the psychology of buyers' choice. If suppliers manage to shift the reference point, such that not getting the rebate obtained via the loyalty program is framed as a loss (while the lesser costs of buying from competitors are framed as a gain), buyers may exhibit greater loyalty than their self-interest strictly justifies. Alexander Morell, Andreas Glöckner, and Emanuel Towfigh demonstrated this point in a nicely designed experiment.[171] Participants made a

164. *See* Bar-Gill, *supra* note 139, at 38–46. On myopia, see generally *supra* pp. 88–93.

165. *See* Tor, *supra* note 2, at 551–52.

166. 504 U.S. 451 (1992).

167. *Id.* at 486.

168. *See* Heinemann, *supra* note 156, at 222–23.

169. *See* Gianluca Faella, *The Antitrust Assessment of Loyalty Discounts and Rebates*, 4 J. COMP. L. & ECON. 375, 377–81 (2008).

170. The United States and the European Union differ in their legal policies on this point. *See id.* at 383–409.

171. Alexander Morell, Andreas Glöckner & Emanuel Towfigh, *Sticky Rebates: Loyalty Rebates Impede Rational Switching of Consumers—Experimental Evidence*, 11 J. COMP. L. & ECON. 431 (2015).

series of purchasing decisions and faced uncertainty as to whether they would manage to reach the required threshold for a loyalty rebate. The rewards of the experiment were structured such that once this uncertainty was resolved, it would become rational to switch from the rebate program to an alternative option. Yet even with this payoff structure, the loyalty rebate program proved to be sticky: subjects opted to remain with it, even when this involved greater risks and a lower expected payoff. This finding suggests that loyalty rebate programs may deserve greater scrutiny from regulators.[172]

3. Boundedly Rational Firms

While the specific details of the application of behavioral insights to the demand side of the market might generate disagreement as to the required policy conclusion (mainly over issues such as the ubiquity of irrationality, and the ability of consumers to learn), the analysis is similar to that of consumer contracts. As we have argued in that context, incorporating behavioral insights into legal analysis is necessary to achieve efficient and fair outcomes.[173] Applying behavioral insights to the *supply side* of the market has generated a much fiercer debate over whether antitrust policies should incorporate behavioral insights. The two topics that have drawn the greatest attention in this regard are predatory pricing and horizontal mergers. We examine these two topics in order, and highlight the contributions made by behavioral analysis, as well as its limitations.

Predatory pricing refers to a strategy used by dominant businesses of cutting prices to unsustainably low levels in order to drive new entrants out of the market, and then raising them to a supra-competitive level. Applying antitrust law to cases of alleged predatory pricing is highly controversial. On the face of it, outlawing low prices is at odds with the core goal of antitrust law—bolstering competition to drive prices down. As then-Judge Stephen Breyer famously put it, the existing price cut is a "beneficial bird in the hand," which the law should be careful not to sacrifice for the "speculative bird in the bush" of lower future prices.[174]

This approach has been supported by the claim that predatory pricing rarely occurs. Economists who espouse a rational choice framework have argued that predation is an irrational pricing strategy, given its high costs and long-term ineffectiveness.[175] Based on that premise, Frank Easterbrook famously argued that instances of predation are about as rare as confirmed sightings of dragons.[176] American case law followed this line of thought. The U.S. Supreme Court set significant barriers to claims of alleged predatory pricing, requiring plaintiffs to prove both that the defendant had engaged in below-cost pricing and that the

172. *See* Heinemann, *supra* note 156, at 225–26.

173. *See supra* pp. 281–324.

174. *See* Barry Wright Corp. v. ITT Grinnell Corp., 724 F.2d 227, 234 (1st Cir. 1983).

175. For a review, see Bruce Kobayashi, *The Law and Economics of Predatory Pricing*, *in* ANTITRUST LAW AND ECONOMICS, *supra* note 154, at 116, 118–19.

176. Frank Easterbrook, *Predatory Strategies and Counterstrategies*, 48 U. CHI. L. REV. 263, 264 (1981).

defendant could reasonably expect to recoup the losses that this entailed.[177] The de-facto consequence of this rule is that plaintiffs in predatory pricing cases rarely prevail.[178]

However, this traditional approach to predatory pricing has recently come under significant scrutiny. Theoretical work has shown that under fairly standard conditions (such as asymmetric information or asymmetric production costs), predation may indeed be rational.[179] Moreover, a large body of empirical literature has shown that predatory pricing is not, in fact, as rare as dragons, and has documented its occurrence in numerous settings.[180] For example, a study of airline pricing practices concluded that "predation not only occurs in airline markets, but has been a key tool to preserve market power held by the surviving legacy carriers."[181]

Behavioral analysis adds yet another dimension to this debate, by highlighting other reasons why predatory pricing exists. As Avishalom Tor has shown, in settings where an incumbent business faces competition from an emerging entrant, the two firms might view the situation differently.[182] While the entrant likely views its increase in market share as a gain, the incumbent is likely to perceive the situation as involving a loss. Consequently, the latter may choose a risk-seeking strategy with a negative present value.[183] Moreover, overconfident incumbents might err in their assessment of the potential benefits of predation.[184] To the extent that incumbents systematically overestimate their ability to endure the costs of predation (and underestimate their rival's ability to do so), they may embark on a predation campaign even if it is not expected to be profitable in the long run.

Furthermore, the very fact that cognitively biased incumbents might adopt predatory strategies suggests yet another avenue through which predation might function. Existing game theoretic models based on a rational-choice approach have shown that predation can also emerge from the reputation that predation generates.[185] This is doubly true when there are boundedly rational incumbents in the marketplace. If entrants cannot distinguish

177. *See* Brooke Group Ltd. v. Brown & Williamson Tobacco Corp., 509 U.S. 209 (1993).

178. *See* Derek W. Moore & Joshua D. Wright, *Conditional Discounts and the Law of Exclusive Dealing*, 22 GEORGE MASON L. REV. 1205, 1209 (2015). European jurisprudence on the matter is somewhat more open to claims of predation. *See* Eleanor M. Fox, *US and EU Competition Law: A Comparison*, *in* GLOBAL COMPETITION POLICY 339, 351–52 (Edward M. Graham & J. David Richardson eds., 1997).

179. *See* Aaron Edlin, *Predatory Pricing*, *in* RESEARCH HANDBOOK ON THE ECONOMICS OF ANTITRUST LAW 144, 147–53 (Einer Elhauge ed., 2012).

180. For a review, see Kobayashi, *supra* note 175, at 124–29.

181. Christopher Sagers, *"Rarely Tried, and . . . Rarely Successful": Theoretically Impossible Price Predation among the Airlines*, 74 J. AIR L. & COM. 919, 919 (2009).

182. Avishalom Tor, *Illustrating a Behaviorally Informed Approach to Antitrust Law: The Case of Predatory Pricing*, 18 ANTITRUST 52, 55–56 (2003).

183. On attitude to risk in the realms of gains and losses, see generally *supra* pp. 42–44.

184. Christopher R. Leslie, *Rationality Analysis in Antitrust*, 158 U. PA. L. REV. 261, 307 (2010).

185. *See* Paul Milgrom & John Roberts, *Predation, Reputation, and Entry Deterrence*, 27 J. ECON. THEORY 280 (1982).

between rational and irrational incumbents, a reputation of irrationality may be a worthwhile investment for incumbents seeking to deter entry by new players.[186]

This analysis suggests that the U.S. jurisprudence of predatory pricing may be over-restrictive. Current doctrine leads to the dismissal of most cases at the summary judgment stage, even in the face of strong evidence of predatory practices.[187] Behavioral analysis suggests that this stringent policy should be somewhat relaxed, and that courts should be more open to examining the possibility of predatory pricing.[188] To be sure, courts should not eliminate all the hurdles imposed on cases of alleged predatory pricing. While pricing below cost can occur, it is a fairly rare tactic given the high costs associated with it and the availability of alternative anticompetitive strategies that are often more effective. Moreover, relaxing restrictions on litigation entails significant costs itself—both in direct litigation costs and in terms of suppliers' reluctance to lower prices for fear of litigation. All that a behavioral perspective is proposing in this context is that courts take care not to create a rule that amounts to de-facto legalization of predatory pricing, based on unrealistic empirical assumptions.

Another area of interest that behavioral analysis has shed light on is horizontal mergers—that is, mergers between two competing firms. Antitrust law has long since debated how such mergers should be treated.[189] On the one hand, horizontal mergers can facilitate economies of scale and enhance efficiency; on the other hand, they might result in a merged firm that hinders competition by dominating the market. The legal policies put in place with respect to such mergers attempt to strike a delicate balance between these two conflicting considerations. Thus, while antitrust law allows competitors to merge, these mergers are often subject to some type of regulatory review.

Traditional law and economics has been associated with a relatively permissive attitude toward horizontal mergers, especially in markets where there are no significant barriers to entry.[190] Potential entry is a key consideration in antitrust analysis, since the mere possibility of entry of a new player can exert competitive pressure on incumbent firms. According to traditional economic theory, markets with little competition and supra-competitive profits tend to attract capital in the form of new firms. These, in turn, raise output and drive prices downward, pushing the market toward a competitive equilibrium. Hence, the significant risk to competitive pricing that might initially appear to be posed by a merger may not materialize if firms at the margin of the market can easily enter it.

From a rational-choice perspective, a prospective competitor will enter a market if, and only if, this yields a positive expected value. Behavioral findings, however, suggest that entry decisions may be swayed by cognitive biases. Specifically, overoptimism and the illusion of control might drive entrepreneurs to enter the market even if the net present value

186. *See* Leslie, *supra* note 184, at 295–305.

187. *See id.* at 319–24.

188. *Id.* at 344–48.

189. *See generally* Hovenkamp, *supra* note 153, at 496–557.

190. *See* Bork, *supra* note 154, at 217–24.

of this choice is negative.[191] This theoretical conjecture is supported by ample empirical evidence that new entrants exhibit both high attrition rates and insensitivity to basic predictors of future profitability, such as existing competition level and the presence of barriers to entry.[192] From an antitrust perspective, this irrational competitive pressure may justify a more permissive attitude toward horizontal mergers. However, careful analysis suggests that most new entrants exert only limited pressure on incumbent firms and detract little from their market share in the long run.[193]

Behavioral analysis can also shed light on the other dimension of merger analysis—the potential efficiencies created by the merger. There are numerous anecdotal examples of mergers that failed to produce the expected synergies and went terribly wrong. The AOL-Time Warner merger, which destroyed $200 billion in equity value, is a case in point.[194] Empirical findings on the average returns gained by acquirers from mergers are mixed, but generally they suggest that these returns are negative or close to nil.[195] Estimating the overall long-term effects of mergers on efficiency is more complicated, but the bulk of the evidence suggests that mergers fail to live up to expectations, and do not create value.[196]

These findings are in line with the *hubris hypothesis* of mergers put forward by Richard Roll in a seminal article on behavioral corporate finance.[197] According to Roll, bidders in mergers are overconfident and excessively optimistic in their valuation of the target firm, and consequently tend to overbid. Subsequent research on CEO overconfidence has corroborated this hypothesis, and suggested a positive association between CEO overconfidence and value-destroying mergers.[198] Overconfidence in valuations is further exacerbated by attribution error when managers are engaged in multiple mergers, as they tend to interpret successful deals as a sign of their talent, and discount unsuccessful deals as mere bad luck.[199]

191. Avishalom Tor, *The Fable of Entry: Bounded Rationality, Market Discipline, and Legal Policy*, 101 MICH. L. REV. 482, 514–20 (2002). On overoptimism and the illusion of control, see *supra* pp. 61–64 and 71–72, respectively.

192. For a review of the industrial organization literature on these points, *see id.* at 490–94.

193. *See* Tor, *supra* note 2, at 553–54.

194. *See* Matthew T. Bodie, *AOL Time Warner and the False God of Shareholder Primacy*, 31 J. CORP. L. 975, 975 (2006).

195. *See* Sara B. Moeller, Frederik P. Schlingemann & René M. Stulz, *Wealth Destruction on a Massive Scale? A Study of Acquiring-Firm Returns in the Recent Merger Wave*, 60 J. FIN. 60, 757 (2005); Ulrike Malmendier, Enrico Moretti & Florian S. Peters, *Winning by Losing: Evidence on the Long-Run Effects of Mergers* (Nat'l Bureau of Econ. Research, Working Paper No. 18024, 2012), *available at*: http://www.nber.org/papers/w18024.

196. For a review, see Marina Martynova & Luc Renneboog, *A Century of Corporate Takeovers: What Have We Learned and Where Do We Stand?*, 32 J. BANKING & FIN. 2148, 2164–68 (2008). As noted, the results on this front are complex, and researchers are attempting to identify factors that distinguish between value-creating and value-destroying mergers. *See e.g.*, Gayle DeLong, *Does Long-Term Performance of Mergers Match Market Expectations: Evidence from the US Banking Industry*, 32 FIN. MGMT. 5 (2003).

197. *See* Richard Roll, *The Hubris Hypothesis of Corporate Takeovers*, 59 J. BUS. 197 (1986).

198. *See* Malmendier & Tate, *supra* note 46.

199. *See* Matthew T. Billett & Yiming Qian, *Are Overconfident CEOs Born or Made? Evidence of Self-Attribution Bias from Frequent Acquirers*, 54 MGMT. SCI. 1037 (2008).

If we turn back from behavioral finance to antitrust law, we see the regulation of mergers aims to prevent mergers that create market power and harm consumers, while not preventing those that create synergies and enhance efficiency. Unsurprisingly, merging firms routinely argue that their merger entails significant efficiencies, and should therefore be cleared by regulators. In light of the findings on overconfidence, regulators should be somewhat skeptical of such efficiency arguments.[200] In the long run, antitrust and competition agencies may benefit from examining mergers in retrospect, to ascertain which types of efficiencies materialize over time, and which are mostly overconfident hype.[201]

Finally, behavioral analysis of consumer behavior is also relevant to analyzing the competitive outcomes of a merger. While traditional models focus on the economic barriers to entry, a new firm attempting to enter the market might also need to deal with consumer loyalty to incumbent firms that rests on purely psychological grounds.[202] Inasmuch as loyalty to such brands is significant, this may pose an additional obstacle to competition. Thus, a market that appears to have few barriers to entry might actually turn out to be one that is immune to competitive threats.

The overall picture emerging from this analysis is inconclusive. While some aspects of behavioral analysis suggest that a more permissive approach toward horizontal mergers is in order, others call for more caution in allowing them. Further theoretical and empirical work may enable policymakers to draw clearer conclusions.

4. Concluding Remarks and Reply to Critics

Critics of the application of behavioral analysis to antitrust law have raised concerns about this body of research. Their main point is the recurring argument relating to countervailing biases, namely the contradictory predictions that behavioral analysis may generate.[203] Often, behavioral arguments can be raised in antitrust contexts in a manner that leads to conflicting legal conclusions. This is clearly a valid point, as our analysis of horizontal mergers has just demonstrated. Another claim made by critics of behavioral analysis with regard to antitrust regulation is that it is a "disorganized amalgam of context-dependent biases that operate in varying directions and to varying degrees," and that it suffers from "fatal problems."[204] This conclusion, which echoes a general criticism of behavioral economics,[205] is hardly compelling.

200. *See* Reeves & Stucke, *supra* note 155, at 1560–63.

201. *See* Maurice E. Stucke, *How Can Competition Agencies Use Behavioral Economics?*, 59 ANTITRUST BULL. 695, 711–15 (2014).

202. On the psychology of brand loyalty, see Birger Wernerfell, *Brand Loyalty and User Skills*, 6 J. ECON. BEHAV. & ORG. 381 (1985); Thomas A Burnham, Judy K. Frels & Vijay Mahajan, *Consumer Switching Costs: A Typology, Antecedents, and Consequences*, 31 J. ACAD. MARKETING SCI. 109 (2003).

203. *See* Joshua D. Wright & Judd E. Stone II, *Misbehavioral Economics: The Case against Behavioral Antitrust*, 33 CARDOZO L. REV. 1517 (2012); Alan Devlin & Michael Jacobs, *The Empty Promise of Behavioral Antitrust*, 37 HARV. J.L. & PUB. POL'Y 1009 (2014).

204. Devlin & Jacobs, *supra* note 203, at 1041.

205. *See supra* pp. 152–54.

As in other contexts, concern over countervailing biases is real, but is not a fatal refutation of behavioral analysis. For one, in several contexts the concern raised is overstated. Alan Devlin and Michael Jacobs, for example, argue that the status quo bias lowers consumers' tendency to substitute products (a reasonable conclusion),[206] but also that it is negated by another bias—loss aversion—which in their view "may spur purchasers to make great efforts to avoid the costs incurred in continuing to buy from a price-increasing firm."[207] This, to our mind, is an unreasonable conclusion. Loss aversion and the status quo bias are not mutually countervailing phenomena. One cannot view current consumption choices as the status quo, and at the same time view the forgone benefits associated with changing such choices as a loss (rather, they are commonly viewed as unattained gains). Thus, loss aversion is highly unlikely to counteract the tendency of consumers to stick with their existing habits. The more general conclusion to be drawn from this example is that heuristics and biases exist within a general theoretical framework that presents systematic predictions, and therefore that rigorous behavioral analysis does constrain the legal discussion that is based on it.

Furthermore, the concern over predictive power is not always relevant in legal settings. Antitrust litigation is often backward-looking, and its key purpose is to understand the nature of the defendants' behavior, rather than to predict their future behavior.[208] In such settings, behavioral analysis may help shed light on past behavior, thus illuminating the legal discussion. Examining whether a given defendant engaged in predatory pricing does not require the court to predict future behavior.

Finally, and more fundamentally, the problem with the abovementioned argument is that it tends to prefer a simple but erroneous model over one that is complex and more accurate. As the breadth of the analysis in this book has demonstrated, careful behavioral analysis that is attuned to the contours of the decision-making environment can generate concrete predictions, given the systematic patterns of decision-making that it identifies. Admittedly, this model may require nuanced distinctions, and verifying these distinctions empirically may be challenging. While the literature on behavioral antitrust is undoubtedly at an early stage—as indeed many of its contributors have openly acknowledged—this only suggests that there is much more work to be done in this area.

F. Conclusion

This chapter presented an overview of the behavioral analysis of commercial law, which demonstrates that deviations from rationality can persist in highly competitive and thick markets, and influence their operation. Based on this insight, the chapter examined numerous legal questions in the areas of corporate law, securities regulation, and antitrust

206. Devlin & Jacobs, *supra* note 203, at 1027–28.

207. *Id.* at 1030.

208. *See* Christopher R. Leslie, *Can Antitrust Law Incorporate Insights from Behavioral Economics?*, 92 TEX. L. REV. SEE ALSO 53, 60–61 (2014).

law, and put forward several regulatory proposals. Before we conclude, it is important to note that care should be taken when implementing the suggested framework in any concrete legal environment. The legal and economic institutions discussed in this chapter vary significantly from one country to the next. Thus, the shift to policy setting requires careful analysis of legal questions, such as the precise definition of incorporation and the institutional competence of courts, and of economic questions such as the structure of capital markets and the size of the economy.

PART FOUR

Public Law

11

Administrative, Constitutional, and International Law

A. Introduction

In a comprehensive review of the impact of judgment-and-decision-making research on legal scholarship, published in 1998, Donald Langevoort surveyed eleven legal spheres—including contracts, torts, property, tax law, and corporate and securities law.[1] If we put aside judicial decision-making, the closest the review referred to public law was in describing the literature on "social risk analysis and policy formulation," and mentioning an article that asked whether the law of takings should take the endowment effect into account (and answering in the negative).[2] A similar picture emerges from *The Oxford Handbook of Behavioral Economics and the Law*, published in 2014.[3] While there have been some behavioral analyses of constitutional and administrative law issues, the impact of behavioral studies on public law—with the notable exception of regulation techniques—has been rather limited in comparison with other legal spheres.[4] This is all the more true of public international law.[5] Contrary to recent developments in other legal spheres, inasmuch as there is a behavioral analysis of administrative, constitutional, or international law, it is based hardly at all on empirical or experimental *legal* studies, but draws mostly on psychological effects demonstrated in other spheres. Similarly, while there have been significant

1. Donald C. Langevoort, *Behavioral Theories of Judgment and Decision Making in Legal Scholarship: A Literature Review*, 51 Vand. L. Rev. 1499 (1998).

2. *Id.* at 1519 and 1517, respectively.

3. The Oxford Handbook of Behavioral Economics and the Law (Eyal Zamir & Doron Teichman eds., 2014). Featuring twenty-nine chapters, this handbook contains one chapter on regulation, one on environmental law, and no chapters on constitutional, administrative, or international law.

4. One important exception has been the conference on *Getting Beyond Cynicism: New Theories of the Regulatory State*, 87 Cornell L. Rev. 267–696 (2002).

5. Anne van Aaken, *Behavioral International Law and Economics*, 55 Harv. Int'l L.J. 421, 421 (2014); Tomer Broude, *Behavioral International Law*, 163 U. Pa. L. Rev. 1099, 1100–03 (2015).

Behavioral Law and Economics. Eyal Zamir and Doron Teichman.

references to behavioral insights in the international relations literature, the impact of cognitive psychology in this sphere has generally been smaller than in other social sciences, such as finance and economics.

There may be several explanations for the relative dearth of behavioral analysis of administrative, constitutional, and international law. Historically, the expansion of heuristics-and-biases research outside the field of psychology has occurred largely in reaction to standard economic analysis. This is true of legal scholarship, too, where behavioral insights were initially introduced in response to standard economic analysis of law. Just as the impact of standard economic analysis has been more rapid and pronounced in private and commercial law (and in specific spheres such as litigation and settlement) than in public law, so, too, has been the behavioral response.

Substantively, judgment-and-decision-making research focuses on the decision-making of individuals. While it examines decisions by small groups, its research methodologies are largely unsuitable to studying decision-making by large groups or in institutional contexts, such as by parliament and administrative agencies.[6] Since public law is mostly about group and institutional decision-making, it is not surprising that the impact of behavioral studies in this area has been limited.

Nevertheless, behavioral analysis can provide—and has provided—important insights into some aspects of constitutional, administrative, and international law. This chapter surveys the existing literature, and highlights potential future developments in these spheres. Section B begins with a comparison between Public Choice Theory (PCT)—the application of rational choice theory to the governmental sphere—and the psychological perspective on governmental decision-making. It argues that the psychological model can provide not only an alternative or a complement to PCT, but a sounder foundation for many predictions of PCT as well. It goes on to discuss several issues concerning governmental institutions and policymaking, from a behavioral viewpoint. It compares the implications of PCT versus the psychological perspective with regard to the allocation of governmental powers in general. It then highlights the strengths and weaknesses of the legislature, the executive, and the judiciary with regard to rule-making. Finally, it focuses on a particular legislative technique: temporary legislation.

Section C shifts the focus from governmental institutions to citizens. It examines how citizens' heuristics and biases affect their voting behavior and impinge upon the political system, and how politicians and public officials can manipulate public opinion by exploiting people's cognitive biases. Section D discusses the contribution of the behavioral perspective to several human and civil rights' issues: restrictions on freedom of speech, the fight against terrorism, and affirmative action. Section E reviews the emerging field of behavioral analysis of public international law.

6. Samuel Issacharoff, *Behavioral Decision Theory in the Court of Public Law*, 87 CORNELL L. REV. 671, 671–73 (2001); William N. Eskridge, Jr., & John Ferejohn, *Structuring Lawmaking to Reduce Cognitive Bias: A Critical View*, 87 CORNELL L. REV. 616, 620–21 (2002).

B. Institutions

1. Public Choice Theory and Cognitive Psychology

(a) General

In a symposium titled *Getting Beyond Cynicism: New Theories of the Regulatory State,* Jeffrey Rachlinski and Cynthia Farina contrasted two conceptions of governmental failures: Public Choice Theory (PCT) and the psychological model.[7] PCT—a leading theory in political science—shares the premise underpinning standard economic analysis that all people are rational maximizers of their utility.[8] It posits that organized interest groups seek to persuade similarly self-interested government officials to enact and implement policies that advance the former's interests at the expense of the public good. Due to the collective action problem, relatively small and homogenous groups are much more effective than the public at large in lobbying for the advancement of their narrow interests. Elected officials, who often represent a particular geographical or political constituency and wish to maximize their chances of re-election, reallocate resources to their electoral constituency and benefit powerful interest groups that can help them be re-elected. Entrusting decisions with non-elected officials does not necessarily solve the problem, as their decisions might be affected by the prospect of future employment in the private sector. Even officials who do not represent particular constituencies, such as the U.S. president, may need the support of powerful groups to be re-elected, and therefore might serve their interests. Ultimately, the only effective way to overcome the ills of governmental failure may be to minimize the powers and roles of the government, to deregulate, and so forth.

There are, of course, various versions of PCT, and not all are as one-dimensional and simplistic as the above portrayal.[9] However, they do all tend to take a rather cynical view of government. In response, Rachlinski and Farina have argued that "self-interest is not the only, and perhaps not even the primary, reason" for governmental failures. Rather, "poor decisions are often the result of fallibility rather than culpability."[10] According to this theory, much of governmental failure is due not to the selfish motives of officials, but to their inability to make optimal decisions, due to cognitive limitations and biases—including

7. Jeffrey J. Rachlinski & Cynthia R. Farina, *Cognitive Psychology and Optimal Government Design,* 87 CORNELL L. REV. 549 (2002).

8. *See generally* DANIEL A. FARBER & PHILIP P. FRICKEY, LAW AND PUBLIC CHOICE: A CRITICAL INTRODUCTION (1991); DONALD P. GREEN & IAN SHAPIRO, PATHOLOGIES OF RATIONAL CHOICE THEORY: A CRITIQUE OF APPLICATIONS IN POLITICAL SCIENCE (1994); DENNIS C. MUELLER, PUBLIC CHOICE III (2003); RESEARCH HANDBOOK ON PUBLIC CHOICE AND PUBLIC LAW (Daniel A. Farber & Anne Joseph O'Connell eds., 2010); Daniel A. Farber, *Public Choice Theory and Legal Institutions, in* 1 THE OXFORD HANDBOOK OF LAW AND ECONOMICS 181 (Francesco Parisi ed., 2017).

9. For a more nuanced analysis, see, e.g., JERRY L. MASHAW, GREED, CHAOS, AND GOVERNANCE: USING PUBLIC CHOICE TO IMPROVE PUBLIC LAW (1997). For a critical overview, see Steven Croley, *Interest Groups and Public Choice, in* RESEARCH HANDBOOK ON PUBLIC CHOICE AND PUBLIC LAW, *supra* note 8, at 49. *See also* Jeremy A. Blumenthal, *Expert Paternalism,* 64 FLA. L. REV. 721, 730–32 (2012).

10. Rachlinski & Farina, *supra* note 7, at 554. *See also* Gary M. Lucas, Jr. & Slaviša Tasić, *Behavioral Public Choice and the Law,* 118 W. VA. L. REV. 199 (2015); Jan Schnellenbach & Christian Schubert, *Behavioral Political Economy: A Survey,* 40 EUR. J. POL. ECON. 395 (2015).

availability, the representativeness heuristic, and framing effects. As detailed below, PCT and the competing psychological model may lead to different conclusions when considering the comparative suitability of different branches of government to making various decisions and the possible cures to governmental failures.

In response to Rachlinski and Farina's proposal to shift the focus from the selfish motives of public officials to their cognitive limitations, Samuel Issacharoff has insisted that the "argument that 'poor [governmental] decisions are often the result of fallibility rather than culpability,' . . . does not refute the public choice claim that errors borne of capture exist in the administrative state."[11] In fact, Rachlinski and Farina had not argued otherwise.[12] Poor governmental decisions may be the result of ulterior motives, cognitive biases, or both. We will further explore the implications of these competing theories below.

More important—and contrary to the assumption held by both proponents and opponents of behavioral analysis of public law[13]—the psychological perspective is not necessarily antithetical to that of PCT. Behavioral studies can explain not only why well-intentioned officials make suboptimal decisions due to phenomena such as the availability heuristic or groupthink, but also the circumstances in which honest officials might make decisions that maximize their own utility and advance the interests of rent-seekers, rather than the overall good. Studies of self-serving biases, and of bounded ethicality more generally, point to situations in which "good people" are likely to violate moral and social norms.[14] For our purposes, these studies may reveal when and how officials violate the norm that governmental authorities should pursue the public good. These studies can lend support to the argument that public officials often advance their personal interests, without portraying them as cynical. Rather than (or, better yet, in addition to) championing behavioral economics as an alternative to PCT, one may utilize behavioral ethics—specifically, the studies of bounded ethicality—to provide a complementary empirical basis for the predictions PCT.[15] Unfortunately, many contributions of psychological insights to political science and public law are yet to be explored.

(b) Designing Governmental Institutions

This subsection sums up the main positive claims and policy implications of the heuristics-and-biases perspective in the design of governmental institutions, compared with those of PCT. Focusing on policymakers' motivations, PCT points to the importance of the size of the constituency of elected public officials: the smaller the constituency, the greater the risk that an official seeking re-election would make decisions that benefit her constituency

11. Issacharoff, *supra* note 6, at 674.

12. Rachlinski & Farina, *supra* note 7, at 554, 580–81.

13. *See also* John O. McGinnis & Charles W. Mulaney, *Judging Facts like Law*, 25 CONST. COMMENT. 69, 94–103 (2008) (juxtaposing PCT and behavioral explanations for the alleged unreliability of congressional fact-finding).

14. *See generally supra* pp. 73–75.

15. Eyal Zamir & Raanan Sulitzeanu-Kenan, *Explaining Self-Interested Behavior of Public-Spirited Policy Makers*, PUB. ADMIN. REV. (forthcoming 2018), *available at:* http://onlinelibrary.wiley.com/journal/10.1111/(ISSN)1540-6210/earlyview.

at the expense of the overall social good—and the more frequent the elections, the greater the risk. Thus, for example, in the U.S. federal government, members of Congress—each representing a particular state—are more likely to serve sectorial interests than the president, who is elected by the entire nation. Given the huge costs of re-election, the president may also be motivated to benefit the rich and powerful. However, the president's decisions are typically subject to greater scrutiny than those of individual legislators, so it is more difficult for him or her to advance the interests of small groups. Accordingly, all else being equal, these observations call for limiting the policymaking powers of the legislature, and expanding those of the president.[16]

While the staff of administrative agencies do not face re-election, the heads of those agencies are appointed by politicians, who also control the agencies' budgets and powers. Agencies may therefore strive to serve the interests of politicians and their constituencies. Agency officials also tend to develop close relationships with interest groups in their spheres of responsibility—relationships that may result in mutual benefitting, at the expense of the public at large. The greater the discretion that agencies have, the greater their risk of being captured by organized interest groups. It follows that the best way to serve the general interest is to curtail the powers and discretion possessed by agencies.

Finally, judges who are appointed for life, and who are not dependent on politicians for promotion (possibly because the prospects of promotion are slim), have no significant incentives to promote the interests of a particular constituency. Hence, from the PCT perspective, judicial review of policies designed by other branches of government appears to be a good idea.[17]

Unlike PCT's focus on the self-interest of officials, Rachlinski and Farina's model focuses on their competence, expertise, and likelihood of overcoming common cognitive illusions: "the policymaking process should be designed to exploit the distinctive strengths, and compensate for the distinctive weaknesses, of experts and laypersons."[18] When viewed this way, the president, legislators, and nonspecialist judges are more likely to display the cognitive biases and illusions of laypersons, because they typically lack professional expertise with regard to most of the decisions they make, compared with agency officials who, being professionally trained and experienced, are less vulnerable to such biases and illusions.[19] Arguably, it follows that more policymaking powers should be handed over to administrative agencies. It would certainly be a bad idea to concentrate more power in the hands of the U.S. president or other heads of state, who face a particularly daunting task of making complex decisions in diverse spheres within limited time frames.[20]

16. *See, e.g.*, Steven G. Calabresi, *Some Normative Arguments for the Unitary Executive*, 48 Ark. L. Rev. 23 (1995).

17. For a critique of this common claim, see, e.g., Einer R. Elhauge, *Does Interest Group Theory Justify More Intrusive Judicial Review?*, 101 Yale L.J. 31 (1991).

18. Rachlinski & Farina, *supra* note 7, at 593.

19. *See also supra* p. 170.

20. Cynthia R. Farina, *False Comfort & Impossible Promises: Uncertainty, Information Overload & the Unitary Executive*, 12 U. Pa. J. Const. L. 357 (2009).

In reality, however, the picture is more complicated. The U.S. Congress and other legislative bodies around the world usually delegate much of their work to committees and subcommittees. These committees are assisted by professionals, and their members—who are often re-elected—gain expertise over time. The U.S. president and other heads of state are similarly helped by a large apparatus of professional experts. Inasmuch as professional expertise improves decision-making, these observations appear to support greater decentralization: from the Congress to its committees and subcommittees, from the president to professional branches of government.

Moreover, professional expertise and experience are no panacea for cognitive limitations.[21] Since experts are more knowledgeable and experienced, and have more opportunities to deliberate on their decision processes, they are more likely to overcome certain cognitive biases, such as availability and representativeness. However, even experts do not always get meaningful feedback on the quality of their decisions (which is crucial to learning from experience), and they are particularly vulnerable to certain biases—such as *overconfidence*, *escalation of commitment*, and the *confirmation bias*.[22] Depending on their particular training, they are inclined to focus on certain factors and promote certain values (such as efficiency in the case of economists, or environmental protection in the case environmentalists), while ignoring or downplaying other goals. Decision-making by experts may, therefore, become narrow-minded and dogmatic.

To mitigate the risks of overconfidence and narrow-mindedness, mechanisms should be in place that compel decision-makers to look at issues from different perspectives. There should also be "practices that take problems that appear to be unique . . . and move them from the illusion-filled realm of intuition into the more disciplined regime of a broader class of problems approached through deductive reasoning."[23] Internal supervision and inspection procedures, external political oversight, and judicial review—all provide additional perspectives on any given issue, and can thereby correct at least some of the mistakes that are due to the cognitive biases of agency officials. The fact that most courts, including those that conduct judicial review of other branches of government on a regular basis, consist of generalists—who are experts in judicial procedure but not in the substance of the decisions they review—dictates the scope and nature of the judicial review. The judges should generally defer to the experts on matters requiring professional expertise, while ensuring that the decision procedures are adequate, and that due weight is given to broader concerns, such as human rights.

Another measure that some legal systems adopt in response to the concerns about the overconfidence and narrow-mindedness of agencies is *notice-and-comment procedures*.

21. *See generally supra* pp. 114–17. *See also* Lucas & Tasić, *supra* note 10, at 251–57. For a recent study showing that expertise (measured by years of study, work experience, and interest in the relevant issues) does not make one immune from framing effects in policymaking, see Colin R. Kuehnhanss, Bruno Heyndels & Katharina Hilken, *Choice in Politics: Equivalency Framing in Economic Policy Decisions and the Influence of Expertise*, 40 EUR. J. POL. ECON. 360 (2015).

22. *See supra* pp. 56–57, 58–61, 64–66, 115–17.

23. Rachlinski & Farina, *supra* note 7, at 581.

Under these procedures, proposed rules are publicized and the general public is called upon to comment on them, as part of the rule-making process. The efficacy of this measure may, however, be limited, due to cognitive biases. The notice-and-comment procedure usually takes place at a rather late stage of the rule-making process. By that time, the agency has already spent much time and effort in preparing the proposed rules, and has possibly also made public announcements in which it expressed its commitment to enact them. Due to phenomena such as the confirmation bias and escalation of commitment, in these circumstances the agency's consideration of the responses to its proposal is most likely suboptimal.[24]

On a more general and abstract level, the fallibility of human decision-making militates against the concentration of excessive power in the hands of a single body—let alone a single individual such as the president. Recognition of human cognitive limitations and biases supports governmental separation of powers, where complex mechanisms of checks and balances provide some protection from gross errors.[25] A more radical conclusion might be to considerably limit the role and powers of the government, and rely instead on the free market.[26] Alas, the behavioral analysis of contract, consumer, and commercial law casts serious doubt on this proposal.[27]

2. Rule-Making

(a) Judicial versus Legislative Rule-Making

The general considerations discussed above bear on a more specific issue that has attracted particular attention: judicial law-making. There is virtually a consensus nowadays that courts are engaged not only in resolving disputes. Much like the legislature and the executive, higher courts, especially (but not exclusively) in cases of first impression, establish new legal norms. This is certainly the case in common-law systems, and practically true for civil law systems, as well.[28] While no one disputes that the legislature should legislate, there is an ongoing debate about the pros and cons, and the desirable scope, of judicial law-making.[29]

24. Stephanie Stern, *Cognitive Consistency: Theory Maintenance and Administrative Rulemaking*, 63 U. Pitt. L. Rev. 589 (2002).

25. Eskridge & Ferejohn, *supra* note 6, at 638–45. *See also* Jeffrey J. Rachlinski, *Heuristics, Biases, and Governance*, *in* Blackwell Handbook of Judgment and Decision Making 567, 580–81 (Derek J. Koehler & Nigel Harvey eds., 2004). Another mechanism that may be understood as an antidote to the self-serving bias and motivated reasoning of officials is "subjecting the decisionmakers to uncertainty about the distribution of benefits and burdens that will result from a decision." *See* Adrian Vermeule, *Veil of Ignorance Rules in Constitutional Law*, 111 Yale L.J. 399, 399, 403 (2001).

26. *See, e.g.*, Lucas & Tasić, *supra* note 10, at 257–65.

27. *See supra* pp. 237–79, 281–324, and 355–89, respectively.

28. *See, e.g.*, Rudolf B. Schlesinger et al., Comparative Law 667–70, 690–694 (6th ed. 1998); Helga Dedek & Martin J. Schermaier, *German Law*, *in* Elgar Encyclopedia of Comparative Law 349, 362–63 (Jan M. Smits ed., 2d ed. 2012).

29. *See, e.g.*, Benjamin N. Cardozo, The Nature of the Judicial Process (1921); Karl N. Llewellyn, The Common Law Tradition: Deciding Appeals (1960); Jürgen Habermas, Between Facts and

From a behavioral viewpoint, the most salient characteristic of judicial legislation is that it is conducted in the context of resolving actual disputes. Courts gain a firsthand familiarity of the disputes between real people, but the rules they create apply to other situations as well. Presumably, in developing general legal norms, the judge should take into account the full range of circumstances in which the rule would apply. In principle, a judge is no different in this respect from a legislator, who also envisages various cases in which the proposed rule would apply. Specifically, the judge should consider to what extent the case at hand is representative of the relevant set of cases.[30] However, several heuristics and biases may influence judicial rule-making to a greater extent than statutory legislation. To begin with, a host of studies have shown that the mode of evaluation—that is, whether a given case is assessed on its own, or as part of a comparative assessment of a set of cases—yields different judgments.[31] In particular, these studies have demonstrated that isolated judgments are more likely to produce reversals of judgments and choices in multidimensional contexts involving fairness versus preference,[32] satisfaction versus choice,[33] and so on. The very fact that courts consider one case at a time may thus adversely affect their decisions.[34] Moreover, because of the availability heuristic, judges are likely to overestimate the incidence of cases that are similar to the one before them, whose features are concrete and vivid.[35] Even if judges realize that the specifics of the present case must be adjusted to capture more typical cases, those specifics may serve as an anchor and distort judges' assessment due to the anchoring effect.[36] The court's reasoning may also focus on the most salient features of the present case, even if considering the relevant issues in the abstract might have resulted in placing greater emphasis on other aspects.[37] The identifiability effect—the tendency to treat identified persons differently from unidentified ones, due primarily to the stronger emotional reactions that are aroused in the former case—is also likely to result in differences between precedents set by courts and abstract rules set by the

NORMS: CONTRIBUTIONS TO A DISCOURSE THEORY OF LAW AND DEMOCRACY (William H. Rehg trans., 1996) (1992); Aharon Barak, *Foreword: A Judge on Judging: The Role of a Supreme Court in a Democracy,* 116 HARV. L. REV. 19 (2002).

30. Frederick Schauer, *Do Cases Make Bad Law?,* 73 U. CHI. L. REV. 883, 894 (2006).

31. *See generally* Christopher K. Hsee et al., *Preference Reversals between Joint and Separate Evaluations of Options: A Review and Theoretical Analysis,* 125 PSYCHOL. BULL. 576 (1999).

32. *See, e.g.,* David M. Messick & Keith Sentis, *Fairness and Preference,* 15 J. EXPERIMENTAL SOC. PSYCHOL. 418 (1979); Max H. Bazerman, George F. Loewenstein & Sally Blount White, *Reversals of Preference in Allocation Decisions: Judging an Alternative versus Choosing among Alternatives,* 37 ADMIN. SCI. Q. 220 (1992).

33. Amos Tversky & Dale Griffin, *Endowment and Contrast in Judgments of Well-Being, in* SUBJECTIVE WELL-BEING: AN INTERDISCIPLINARY PERSPECTIVE 101, 113–15 (Fritz Strack et al. eds., 1991).

34. Jeffrey J. Rachlinski, *Rulemaking versus Adjudication: A Psychological Perspective,* 32 FLA. ST. U. L. REV. 529, 539–41 (2005). While Rachlinski compares adjudication and legislation as two modes of lawmaking by administrative agencies, his analysis equally applies to the comparison between the legislature and the judiciary.

35. Schauer, *supra* note 30, at 894–96. On availability, see generally *supra* pp. 34–36.

36. Schauer, *supra* note 30, at 896–97. On the anchoring effect, see generally *supra* pp. 79–82.

37. Rachlinski, *supra* note 34, at 541–42; Schauer, *supra* note 30, at 897–98.

legislature.[38] Finally, judicial rule-making may also be adversely affected by the *hindsight bias*.[39] Admittedly, similar concerns may be raised whenever the legislature or an administrative agency establishes general rules in response to a specific, salient event, as they sometimes do.[40] However, since judge-made law is *invariably* the product of deliberation in the context of a particular case, those concerns loom larger in the judicial sphere.

That said, it should be noted that judicial decision-making, even in the absence of any statutory law, is not conducted in a vacuum. Courts typically highlight parallels in similar cases, and generally follow precedents—thus broadening their perspective beyond the circumstances of the particular case.[41] In doing so, they employ the "remarkable human ability to categorize" and identify patterns.[42] Over time, professional judges may also recognize, from their experience, the perils of excessive focus on the individual case at the expense of broader considerations.[43] The appellate processes, and the deliberation of similar issues by different panels of judges facing a variety of factual scenarios, can also mitigate the impact of the aforementioned biases.[44] Judges' professional experience, and the fact that they must justify their decisions in accordance with the constraints of conventional judicial reasoning (and in writing), may also serve to counteract some cognitive biases.[45] Most significantly, the common law contains a built-in mechanism for correcting misguided or overinclusive rules—namely, the courts' ability to constantly reform and amend judge-made law.[46]

The courts' lawmaking competence must, of course, be compared with that of the legislature, which has its own challenges. Among other things, since courts often face the same issue repeatedly in various contexts, they have more opportunities to fine-tune

38. *See* Daphna Lewinsohn-Zamir, Ilana Ritov & Tehila Kogut, *Law and Identifiability*, 92 Ind. L.J. 505 (2017). For additional biases that may affect judicial rule-making, see Jeffrey J. Rachlinski, *Bottom-up versus Top-down Lawmaking*, 73 U. Chi. L. Rev. 933, 937–51 (2006); Rachlinski, *supra* note 34, at 542–46. Rachlinski discusses context dependence, emotional responses, the contrast effect, the fundamental attribution error (the tendency to put excessive emphasis on individual responsibility as opposed to situational factors), and more.

39. *See generally infra* pp. 535–56.

40. *See also infra* p. 403.

41. Emily L. Sherwin, *Judges as Rulemakers*, 73 U. Chi. L. Rev. 933 (2006).

42. Rachlinski, *supra* note 38, at 960–63.

43. *Id.* at 951.

44. *Id.* at 952–55. *See also* Ronald J. Krotoszynski, Jr., *The Unitary Executive and the Plural Judiciary: On the Potential Virtues of Decentralized Judicial Power*, 89 Notre Dame L. Rev. 1021, 1066–79 (2014) (pointing to the advantages of a decentralized court system as a corrective to groupthink).

45. On the impact of having to justify one's judgment on the susceptibility to various cognitive biases, see generally Jennifer S. Lerner & Philip E. Tetlock, *Accounting for the Effects of Accountability*, 125 Psychol. Bull. 255 (1999); *supra* pp. 132–34.

46. Schauer, *supra* note 30, at 906–08. However, this process may be impaired by the selection of cases for adjudication and appeal (*id.* at 908–11). One rather unorthodox suggestion for improving judicial decision-making has been to use a notice-and-comment procedure (*see supra* note 24 and accompanying text) whereby judges make their judgments available for public comment after they are drafted but before they are finalized. *See* Michael Abramowicz & Thomas Colby, *Notice-and-Comment Judicial Decisionmaking*, 76 U. Chi. L. Rev. 965 (2009).

the rules than the legislature, which typically tackles a given issue only infrequently.[47] In addition, some characteristics of legislation, which may at first appear to be advantageous, may actually be detrimental. Thus, while the emotional reactions of judges to situations might distort their judgment, they may also provide useful cues to making normative judgments—which abstract deliberation lacks.[48] Finally, the risks of overreacting to an exceptional event (such as a deadly terrorist attack or an environmental disaster) are considerably greater in the legislative context than in the judicial one—if only because the arsenal of regulatory means and legal remedies available to the legislature is much larger than that available to the courts.[49]

To be fair, it should be noted that the legislative process (as well as the process of rule-making by administrative agencies) is structured in ways that may lessen the adverse effects of cognitive biases. The very complexity of the process, the bicameral structure of parliaments in many legal systems, the veto power given to heads of state over legislative proposals in some systems, the federal structure of some countries, and the prospect of judicial review of legislation—all mitigate the adverse effects of cognitive biases on legislation.[50] The legislature can also enact temporary laws, thus enabling controversial issues to be reconsidered in a calmer atmosphere, and with the benefit of additional information.[51]

Ultimately, both judicial and legislative lawmaking are susceptible to behavioral and other imperfections, both have their advantages and disadvantages—and, of course, the behavioral perspective is only one aspect of the comparison between them.[52]

(b) Temporary Legislation

Temporary legislation is more prevalent than people tend to assume.[53] It can reduce legislation costs at the initial stage, because the stakes are lower (the law is expected to be in force only for a limited time), and possible errors can be corrected when the law comes up for renewal. Since the renewal of temporary legislation requires an additional legislative process, however, its total costs may equal or exceed those of permanent legislation. When laws broaden the powers of the executive branch, sunset clauses can result in greater legislative control over the executive, since the latter must, from time to time, persuade the legislature of the need to extend the temporary legislation.[54] Temporary legislation can also facilitate the gathering and processing of new information and stimulate public debate at the renewal

47. Rachlinski, *supra* note 34, at 546–47.

48. *Id.* at 549–50.

49. Rachlinski, *supra* note 38, at 956–60.

50. Eskridge & Ferehohn, *supra* note 6, at 638–47.

51. However, as discussed in the next subsection, temporary legislation raises other concerns.

52. Rachlinski, *supra* note 34; Rachlinski, *supra* note 38.

53. Jacob E. Gersen, *Temporary Legislation*, 74 U. CHI. L. REV. 247, 249–61 (2007); Rebecca M. Kysar, *Lasting Legislation*, 159 U. PA. L. REV. 1007, 1010 (2011).

54. Gersen, *supra* note 53, at 279.

stage, thereby possibly improving the legislative outcome.[55] It may be particularly appropriate for meeting short-term challenges, since with permanent legislation there is a concern that it will remain in force even when it is no longer necessary or justified.

When it comes to legislation enacted in response to emergency situations—such as antiterrorism laws—temporary legislation provides an opportunity to calmly reconsider what may have been an overreaction to threats, due to public panic and the policymakers' availability heuristic.[56] In that regard, temporary legislation can help counter cognitive biases.[57] More generally, it has been argued that temporary legislation can mitigate against policymakers' escalation of commitment and status quo bias.[58] Knowing that failing to act will result in the expiration of a statute whose wisdom and necessity are questionable (and may have been so all along), and feeling less committed to statutes enacted by past legislators, legislators are more likely to allow bad temporary laws to expire than actively repeal permanent laws.

This analysis assumes that temporary legislation inverts the default arrangement: while ordinary legislation remains in force unless subsequently repealed, temporary legislation expires unless it is subsequently extended.[59] This assumption is analytically correct, and many of the above characterizations of temporary legislation are sound. However, more often than not, temporary legislation appears to serve not as a means of improving the legislative process, solving information problems, or overcoming cognitive phenomena such as the status quo bias and escalation of commitment, but as a strategy of using cognitive biases to overcome objections to proposed legislation.

Since "temporary legislation is frequently extended and permanent legislation is often amended and sometimes repealed, there is no necessary correlation between a temporary or permanent default rule and the actual duration of legislation."[60] In fact, while some temporary legislation expires by default at the end of its initial period, or is not extended after public debate, commentators have long observed that most temporary legislation is either repeatedly renewed, or subsequently replaced by permanent legislation.[61]

55. *Id.* at 266–68, 271–72; John E. Finn, *Sunset Clauses and Democratic Deliberation: Assessing the Significance of Sunset Provisions in Antiterrorism Legislation,* 48 COLUM. J. TRANSNAT'L. L. 442, 456–59 (2010).

56. Finn, *supra* note 55, at 450–51. *See also infra* pp. 414–19.

57. Gersen, *supra* note 53, at 268–71.

58. Rachlinski & Farina, *supra* note 7, at 603–05. On escalation of commitment and the status-quo bias, see generally *supra* pp. 56–57 and 48–50, respectively.

59. Gersen, *supra* note 53, at 261; Rachlinski & Farina, *supra* note 7, at 605; Finn, *supra* note 55, at 449; Eric A. Posner & Adrian Vermeule, *Accommodating Emergencies*, 56 STAN. L. REV. 605, 617 (2003).

60. Gersen, *supra* note 53, at 281.

61. *See, e.g.,* GUIDO CALABRESI, A COMMON LAW FOR THE AGE OF STATUTES 62 (1982); Finn, *supra* note 55; Oren Gross, *Chaos and Rules: Should Responses to Violent Crises Always Be Constitutional?* 112 YALE L.J. 1011, 1073–75 (2003); Manoj Viswanathan, *Sunset Provisions in the Tax Code: A Critical Evaluation and Prescriptions for the Future*, 82 N.Y.U. L. REV. 656, 658 (2007); Emily Berman, *The Paradox of Counterterrorism Sunset Provisions,* 81 FORDHAM L. REV. 1777 (2013).

Setting an expiration date for laws is an effective way of overcoming political and public opposition to controversial legislative proposals. However, setting an expiration date is often nothing more than "a spoonful of sugar that helps controversial legislation go down."[62] At the time of legislation, opponents may be overly optimistic about the temporary nature of the circumstances triggering the legislation,[63] and underestimate the powerful framing effect of "temporary" laws[64]—because, once enacted, temporary laws change the reference point. Legal measures, such as emergency powers, that previously had been considered exceptional and extreme, gradually become the accepted norm.[65] This shift in reference point facilitates the renewal of temporary legislation, replacing it by permanent legislation, and the conversion of measures that were once considered extraordinary into other, permanent laws.[66] By the same token, people who enjoy tax exemptions or other benefits become accustomed to them and develop a sense of entitlement—an *endowment effect*—even if those benefits were provided under "temporary" legislation.[67] The combination of legislature inertia and the endowment effect created by the temporary law—including the endowment of governmental agencies with extended powers—often guarantees the extension of temporary legislation. Once extended, further extensions of temporary legislation are perceived all the more as the default.

It should be noted that this positive analysis does not entail that the use of temporary legislation as a means of overcoming opposition to a legal reform is necessarily undesirable. It may well be that a given reform is desirable, that the opposition to it (which may possibly result from the default effect) is unsound, and that—all things considered—the framing effect produced by the temporary legislation is a legitimate device for passing the reform.

3. Concluding Remarks

This section demonstrated the contribution of behavioral insights to positive and normative analysis of the institutional aspect of public law. It did so at the general level of comparing the psychological model of governmental decision-making with PCT, and in the more concrete contexts of judicial rule-making and temporary legislation. While the behavioral perspective is not meant to supplant PCT, it certainly complements it—and as suggested in Subsection C.1, may also provide a behavioral foundation for some of PCT's predictions.

62. Chris Mooney, *A Short History of Sunsets*, LEGAL AFF. (Feb. 2004), *available at*: http://www.legalaffairs.org/issues/January-February-2004/story_mooney_janfeb04.msp. *See also* Finn, *supra* note 55, at 485; Viswanathan, *supra* note 61, at 658, 682 (arguing that "sunset provisions used in tax legislation are . . . exploited as a means of enacting permanent legislation under the guise of an ostensible expiration date").

63. Berman, *supra* note 61, at 1777.

64. On the framing effect of legal norms, see generally *supra* pp. 179–82.

65. Finn, *supra* note 55, at 489–90. Similar concerns have been expressed with regard to court rulings in times of national security crises, especially when they curtail human rights in contexts unrelated to the war. *See* Lee Epstein et al., *The Supreme Court during Crisis: How War Affects Only Non-war Cases*, 80 N.Y.U. L. REV. 1, 94–98 (2005).

66. Finn, *supra* note 52.

67. Viswanathan, *supra* note 61, at 672–76. *See also* Kysar, *supra* note 53, at 1026–35 (describing alteration of the baseline in extensions of temporary fiscal legislation).

Regardless of PCT, since governmental decision-makers are human beings, a better understanding of human judgment and decision-making can certainly enrich public law.

This is the "glass-half-full" perspective. As the somewhat preliminary and sporadic nature of the claims made in this section have illustrated, the empty half of the glass is that there is much more to be learned about the psychology of decision-making by governmental officials.

C. Citizens

1. General

Citizens' judgment and decision-making are relevant to administrative and constitutional law in various ways—four of which are particularly important. First, inasmuch as the government's role is to maximize overall social welfare, and people's welfare is determined (or affected) by the extent to which their preferences are fulfilled, factors that shape people's preferences are relevant to governmental decision-making. A preference-fulfillment theory of human welfare may refer to people's actual preferences or to their ideal ones. Insofar as the gap between people's actual and ideal preferences is due to their bounded rationality and cognitive biases, these phenomena are an important consideration when choosing between competing theories of human welfare (actual or ideal) as the basis for policy analysis of governmental policies. Second, since the law sets out to affect human behavior, the choice of legal devices must take the psychology of those affected by the law into account. This is true of any legal norm, but especially of regulation, including paternalistic and libertarian-paternalistic regulation (so-called *nudges*). Third, people's judgments are relevant to public law because, in liberal democracies, people's voting behavior determines the identity of the elected leadership, and public opinion influences the decisions of government officials. Fourth, it follows from the last point that policymakers may try to influence citizens' judgments in order to gain public support for themselves and for their policies.

Since the first two issues (the relevance of behavioral insights to a theory of human welfare and to the design of regulatory means) are discussed elsewhere in this book,[68] this section addresses the latter two—namely the bidirectional influence of citizens' judgments on the identity of governmental decision-makers and their policies, and of the government on citizens' judgment.

2. Citizens' Judgments and Choices

Citizens' judgments with regard to public affairs are important for public law because they are likely to impinge on policymaking. As previously noted, there is an ongoing debate about the extent to which policymakers are susceptible to cognitive biases.[69] However, even if professional training, experience, use of sophisticated decision aids, and checks-and-balances mechanisms reduce or even eliminate the impact of policymakers' cognitive biases, they may still think it perfectly rational to adopt policies and take actions that

68. *See supra* pp. 158–61 and 162–85, respectively.

69. *See supra* pp. 170, 395–405.

reflect the heuristics and biases of their constituencies. By doing so, they can enhance their own popularity and increase the public support for their initiatives, which may be crucial for the successful implementation of those initiatives.[70] Thus, even perfectly rational policymakers might act as though they were susceptible to the status quo bias, shortsightedness, availability heuristic, base-rate neglect, psychic numbing, or any other cognitive bias characterizing their constituency.

One of the primary issues studied by political psychologists is the factors determining citizens' political judgments, attitudes, and voting behavior. When studying these matters, political psychology draws on theories and findings from several sub-disciplines—including social psychology, intergroup relations, personality psychology, neuroscience, and cognitive and affective psychology.[71] Contrary to rational choice theory, it has been shown that citizens' political judgments and choices are profoundly affected by the limitations on their ability to acquire, recall, and process information (especially given the relatively low priority of politics in most people's lives). Citizens' decisions are mostly determined by implicit attitudes and automatic reactions that they are not aware of, and by the interplay of affect and cognition. Very often, political deliberation is nothing more than a post-hoc rationalization of preconscious attitudes.[72]

A comprehensive description of the numerous insights provided by political psychology lies beyond the scope of our discussion. We therefore suffice with mentioning a number of studies attesting to the susceptibility of citizens to known heuristics and biases, which in turn affect legislative and administrative actions.

One area that has attracted considerable attention is the effect of availability on people's assessment of various risks. People tend to assess the frequency of events according to the ease with which they can recall instances of those events—hence they tend to overestimate the frequency and significance of risks whose materialization is more vivid, emotionally laden, and highly publicized, compared to dull and mundane ones.[73] Consequently, there is a greater public demand for regulation of risks of the former type compared to the latter,[74] which is then satisfied by a governmental regulation regime that does not stand up to rational scrutiny based on the costs and benefits of regulating each risk.[75] While much of the

70. *Cf.* Rachlinski, *supra* note 25, at 574; *infra* pp. 436, 438–40, 584.

71. *See generally* THE OXFORD HANDBOOK OF POLITICAL PSYCHOLOGY (Leonie Huddy, David O. Sears & Jack S. Levy eds., 2d ed. 2013); CITIZENS AND POLITICS: PERSPECTIVES FROM POLITICAL PSYCHOLOGY (James H. Kuklinski ed., 2008).

72. *See generally* MILTON LODGE & CHARLES S. TABER, THE RATIONALIZING VOTER (2013).

73. *See generally supra* pp. 34–36. Similarly, people tend to overestimate the frequency of recently materialized risks, compared with ones that materialized in the more distant past.

74. Paul Slovic, Baruch Fischhoff & Sarah Lichtenstein, *Facts versus Fears: Understanding Perceived Risk*, *in* JUDGMENT UNDER UNCERTAINTY: HEURISTICS AND BIASES 463 (Daniel Kahneman, Paul Slovic & Amos Tversky eds., 1982).

75. Timur Kuran & Cass R. Sunstein, *Availability Cascades and Risk Regulation*, 51 STAN. L. REV. 683 (1999); W. Kip Viscusi & Ted Gayer, *Behavioral Public Choice: The Behavioral Paradox of Government Policy*, 28 HARV. J.L. & PUB. POL'Y 973, 988–96 (2015).

discussion of the perils of availability has revolved around the regulation surrounding environmental protection and product safety,[76] it is equally relevant to other spheres, such as the largely unfounded concern about mega-awards of damages for pain and suffering and punitive damages in tort cases, whose frequency is overestimated due to their high publicity.[77]

Availability arising from a lively public discussion of events is self-reinforcing. Moreover, "availability entrepreneurs"—be they public-spirited or self-interested—may exacerbate the problem by deliberately drawing public attention to risks whose regulation they wish to promote.[78] Safeguards against the distortive effect of availability include greater use of long-run statistical information and other scientific data, mandatory use of cost-benefit analysis, and institutional mechanisms of checks and balances within and among governmental branches.[79]

Governmental policies are also affected by the citizenry's framing effect, the greater willingness to take risks in the domain of losses than in the domain of gains, and the greater aversion to losses, compared to unobtained gains. For instance, in one experiment, subjects were given reliable information about the expected outcomes of the economic policies of two presidential candidates and the economic outlook in comparable countries (which served as a natural reference point). When their own country was expected to do better than the other countries in the comparison, a clear majority of subjects supported the candidate whose policy was less risky, but when it was expected to do worse, half the subjects supported the candidate with the riskier policy.[80] In another experiment, subjects exhibited status quo bias: when candidates' policies involved expected improvement in one economic parameter and decline in another, their choice between the candidates depended on what was described as the status quo.[81] Loss aversion has also been offered as an additional explanation for the tendency of elected politicians to avoid cutting welfare benefits: as the loss experienced by those who would cease to get these benefits looms larger than the gains experienced by others, welfare state retrenchment is usually unpopular.[82] Finally, empirical analysis has demonstrated that support for U.S. military intervention abroad depends on how the rationale for the intervention is framed: to avert a loss of a geopolitical position, or to secure a foreign policy gain. Public support for the former is greater than for the latter, so framing the initiative as such is a necessary (albeit not sufficient) condition for Congress's support.[83]

76. *See, e.g.*, Cass R. Sunstein, *Cognition and Cost-Benefit Analysis*, 29 J. Legal Stud. 1059 (2000).

77. *See* Theodore Eisenberg, *Damage Awards in Perspective: Behind the Headline-Grabbing Awards in* Exxon Valdez *and* Engle, 36 Wake Forest L. Rev. 1129 (2001).

78. Kuran & Sunstein, *supra* note 75.

79. *Id.* at 746–60.

80. George A. Quattrone & Amos Tversky, *Contrasting Rational and Psychological Analyses of Political Choice*, 82 Am. Pol. Sci. Rev. 719, 721–24 (1988).

81. *Id.* at 724–26.

82. Paul Pierson, *The New Politics of the Welfare State*, 48 World Politics 143, 145–47 (1996). *See also infra* pp. 468–69.

83. Miroslav Nincic, *Loss Aversion and the Domestic Context of Military Intervention*, 50 Pol. Res. Q. 97 (1997).

It should be noted that using the public emotional reaction to disasters and people's susceptibility to other heuristics and biases to promote new legislation is not necessarily a bad thing. A case in point is the amendment to New York's Workers' Compensation Law, advocated by gay and lesbian activists, which equated the rights of surviving same-sex domestic partners for workers' compensation to those of married people. This amendment was unanimously approved by the New York State Assembly and Senate in response to the plight of individuals whose same-sex partners were killed in the terrorist attack on the World Trade Center in September 11, 2001.[84] Plausibly, the emotional reaction to the terrorist attack, as well as people's framing of the victims and surviving partners as American compatriots, rather than gays and lesbians, facilitated this legislation.

While the effect of availability, reference dependence, and other heuristics and biases on the judgments and choices made by citizens must not be disregarded, its actual significance is unclear. This is not because most or many citizens are able to overcome these biases when deliberating about political issues. Rather, it is because political judgments and choices are often not the product of conscious deliberation at all, but of preconscious attitudes, as some political psychologists argue.[85] Nonetheless, when it comes to people whose attitudes on certain issues are weak and unstable (and who occasionally have a decisive effect on public opinion as a whole), their opinions may possibly be affected to a greater extent by conscious deliberation, and such deliberation may be affected by cognitive heuristics and biases.[86]

3. Governmental Manipulation of Citizens' Heuristics and Biases

Political leaders and public officials are not only influenced by public perceptions and judgments: they plausibly strive to shape those perceptions and judgments as well, to gain support for themselves and for their policies. In that respect, governmental entities—and their political opponents—may not be fundamentally different from commercial firms seeking to increase their sales and profits.[87] Both commercial and political players are liable to abuse people's bounded rationality. For example, the government may take advantage of people's overreaction to a recent disaster to gain support for emergency legislation. In a similar fashion, regulators might use people's availability heuristic to justify the regulation of highly visible, but extremely improbable, risks that sometimes enrich special interest

84. John O. Enright, *The New York's Post-September 11, 2001 Recognition of Same-Sex Relationships: A Victory Suggestive of Future Change*, 72 FORDHAM L. REV. 2823 (2004). *See also* Yvette M. Barksdale, *Cynicism, Phenomenology, and the Problem of Paradox: Dilemmas of Public Law Discourse*, 87 CORNELL L. REV. 384, 390 (2002).

85. LODGE & TABER, *supra* note 72.

86. *Cf.* James N. Druckman & Thomas J. Leeper, *Is Public Opinion Stable? Resolving the Micro/Macro Disconnect in Studies of Public Opinion*, 141 DAEDALUS 50 (2012).

87. The government may, of course, exploit people's biases in other ways—for example, through the use of lottery programs that function as a highly regressive tax.

groups at the expense of the public at large.[88] Similarly, political leaders may frame international disputes as being about the protection of existing entitlements, rather than as an attempt to attain new ones, thus triggering people's loss aversion to gain public support for taking a firm stand in such disputes.[89] In election campaigns in particular, candidates make every effort to frame controversial issues in a way that is favorable to them, and to attract voters by exploiting phenomena such as availability, priming, and the confirmation bias.[90]

While it can hardly be denied that the government can, and sometimes does, make use of citizens' heuristics and biases, the actual significance and normative implications of this phenomenon are debatable. Under most conceivable circumstances, both instrumental and principled reasons appear to militate against attempts to legally prohibit the misuse of people's heuristics and biases by governmental officials (or others)—a prohibition that is unlikely to be effective anyway. Arguably, in an open, liberal democracy that cherishes freedom of speech, the most powerful antidote to governmental manipulation is a lively public debate. Political opponents, publicists, and others may expose suppressed information and hidden motives, contradict misinformation, and offer alternative framings of the relevant issues.[91]

Moreover, while in a perfect world any manipulation of public opinion would be undesirable, it has been argued that in the real world, the very fact that the government makes use of people's heuristics to gain support for policies that might not have been carried out otherwise is not necessarily a bad thing, all things considered. Exploiting public emotional reaction to a highly publicized airplane accident to advance regulation of aviation safety, or taking advantage of public alarm after a school massacre to promote gun-control regulation—initiatives that might otherwise be blocked by regulatory capture—are cases in point. At the end of the day, public discourse in liberal democracies does not necessarily epitomize the pursuit of truth and rational deliberation—but, as Winston Churchill once famously noted, "democracy is the worst form of government, except for all those other forms that have been tried from time to time."

D. Human Rights

In addition to the contribution of behavioral insights to the institutional aspects of public law and to the understanding of citizens' attitudes and choices, behavioral insights have also been used to illuminate substantive constitutional issues, such as human and civil rights.

88. Jonathan R. Macey, *Cynicism and Trust in Politics and Constitutional Theory*, 87 Cornell L. Rev. 280, 299–301 (2002).

89. *See supra* note 83 and accompanying text.

90. Molly J. Walker Wilson, *Behavioral Decision Theory and Implications for the Supreme Court's Campaign Finance Jurisprudence*, 31 Cardozo L. Rev. 679, 685–710 (2010).

91. *Cf.* Lawrence B. Solum, *Freedom of Communicative Action: A Theory of the First Amendment Freedom of Speech*, 83 Nw. U. L. Rev. 54, 91–93, 107–09, 114–15, 119–26 (1989) (discussing strategic, as opposed to communicative, action); Eyal Zamir & Barak Medina, Law, Economics, and Morality 203–04 (2010) (objecting to suppressing speech that strives to affect people's behavior in a manipulative way, on pragmatic and principled grounds).

In Chapter 5, we argued that reference-dependence and loss aversion may explain the fact that in many jurisdictions, the scope of constitutional protection afforded to social and economic human rights is far narrower than that given to civil and political human rights—if it exists at all.[92] Here we describe the contribution and limitations of behavioral insights to freedom of speech, antiterrorist measures, and affirmative action policies.

1. Freedom of Speech

(a) Theoretical and Doctrinal Background

Freedom of speech is considered a basic human right, often enjoying a special status. An abundance of scholarship discusses freedom of speech from doctrinal, comparative, philosophical, and economic perspectives.[93] Given the vast complexity of the subject, it is impossible to sum it up in a few paragraphs. The following is therefore nothing more than a cursory overview of the justifications for protecting free speech and some elements of the doctrine, which will serve as a background for the ensuing behavioral discussion.

There are instrumental and non-instrumental justifications for protecting freedom of speech. Instrumental justifications focus on the contribution of free speech to human flourishing and to the democratic process. According to the famous metaphor, freedom of speech ensures that in the "marketplace of ideas," truthful factual claims and sound normative arguments triumph over others in the competition between conflicting claims and arguments. Rather than suppressing harmful speech, the best cure for false and injurious information is more information, which facilitates rational deliberation. The social goods produced by free speech include the discovery of truth, social stability, exposure and deterrence of abuses of power, facilitation of liberal democracy, and promotion of tolerance.[94]

According to non-instrumental justifications for freedom of speech, respect for people's autonomy requires everyone—including the state—to refrain from silencing other people or preventing them from listening to others. Such respect underlies the liberal theory of the state. Expressions of ideas and feelings are essential to self-realization, and therefore their suppression is harmful to one's dignity. In the same way, treating people as autonomous human beings necessitates allowing them to shape their own lives, which in turn means free access to any information, view, or argument. Silencing some views rather than others also violates the requirement to treat people with *equal* respect.

92. *See supra* pp. 190–91.

93. *See, e.g.*, LAURENCE H. TRIBE, AMERICAN CONSTITUTIONAL LAW 785–1061 (2d ed. 1988) (U.S. doctrine); ERIC BARENDT, FREEDOM OF SPEECH (2d ed. 2005) (comparative perspective); Fredrick Schauer, *Freedom of Expression Adjudication in Europe and the United States: A Case Study in Comparative Constitutional Architecture*, *in* EUROPEAN AND US CONSTITUTIONALISM 49 (Georg Nolte ed., 2005) (same); FREDERICK SCHAUER, FREE SPEECH: A PHILOSOPHICAL ENQUIRY (1982) (philosophical outlook); LARRY ALEXANDER, IS THERE A RIGHT OF FREEDOM OF EXPRESSION? (2005) (same); FREEDOM OF SPEECH, VOL. 1: FOUNDATIONS; VOL. 2: DOCTRINE (Larry Alexander ed., 2000) (collection of essays); Richard A. Posner, *Pragmatism versus Purposivism in First Amendment Analysis*, 54 STAN. L. REV. 737 (2002) (standard economic analysis); ZAMIR & MEDINA, *supra* note 91, at 177–224 (economic analysis subject to deontological constraints).

94. Kent Greenawalt, *Free Speech Justifications*, 89 COLUM. L. REV. 119, 130–47 (1989).

However, since freedom of speech sometimes clashes with other liberties and values, no legal system accords absolute constitutional protection to this freedom. The two principal techniques used to delimit the constitutional protection of free speech are exclusion of some types of speech from the ambit of protection, and permitting the curtailment of free speech when necessary to protect compelling interests. Thus, for example, verbal communications involved in a criminal conspiracy are not constitutionally protected. Obscenity and the provocation of racial hatred are similarly unprotected in some legal systems. The latter technique is used when free speech is curtailed to protect competing interests, such as national security, privacy, and prevention of imminent violence. Often, different formulae for balancing the competing values are established for different categories of speech, such as political, commercial, and artistic. Sexually explicit material and commercial advertising often enjoy lesser protection than other categories of speech.

One basic distinction in the free speech doctrine is between *content-based* and *content-neutral* restrictions of speech. Content-based restrictions curtail certain expressions because their content is thought to be harmful, or because the very discussion of certain issues in public is considered dangerous. Content-based restrictions are subject to strict judicial scrutiny. Content-neutral restrictions typically regulate the place, timing, or manner of expression, due to its noncommunicative impacts (such as excessive noise in residential neighborhood and traffic congestion). These restrictions are subject to considerably more lenient scrutiny.

With regard to content-based restrictions, a distinction is commonly drawn between two ways in which speech may be thought to cause harm—namely, in one step or two. Revelation of secrets or intimate information are examples of *one-step harm*: the very expression causes the harm, even if it does not affect anyone's behavior. Often, however, the ultimate harm is brought about in two steps: the speaker incites, persuades, or provides useful information to people, who might then do harmful things. Calling for the overthrow of the government, or otherwise advocating illegal actions, are typical examples of this type.

Legal systems vary with regard to the positions they take toward content-based regulation of speech. These differences may be illuminated by the prohibitions imposed against incitement to violence or other unlawful conduct, and the suppression of hate speech. Many legal systems prohibit any advocacy of ethnic or religious hatred that incites to discrimination, violence, or hostility. According to this approach, there is no need to assess the specific consequences of suppressing such expressions in any particular case. In contrast, under U.S. law, determining the constitutionality of silencing incitements to violence or hatred requires a case-by-case assessment of the expected consequences of the government's action or inaction. The U.S. Supreme Court has ruled that proscribing "advocacy of the use of force or of law violation" is unconstitutional "except where such advocacy is directed to inciting or producing imminent lawless action and is likely to incite or produce such action."[95] The scope of free speech protection is hence considerably broader in the United States than in other liberal democracies.

95. Brandenburg v. Ohio, 395 U.S. 444, 447 (1969).

(b) Behavioral Analysis

Behavioral insights shed light on free speech in several ways. First, they are relevant to the very justification for the constitutional protection of free speech, which in turn determines the scope of protection. Specifically, behavioral findings may cast doubt on the instrumental justifications for free speech. These justifications assume that listeners are capable of rationally assessing the truthfulness, credibility, and soundness of information, and that more information is preferable to less. While doubts about these assumptions are not new, they have been empirically substantiated by behavioral studies.[96] If—due to information overload, the impact of irrelevant information on people's decisions, or other related phenomena—more information does not facilitate better choices, then the assumption that more speech is always preferable to less may be questioned.[97] Moreover, if citizens' judgments and choices in public affairs are primarily determined by implicit attitudes and automatic reactions—thus rendering political deliberation often to nothing more than a post-hoc rationalization of preconscious attitudes[98]—then the contribution of free speech to the democratic process is smaller than proponents of free speech commonly assume.

A similar critique has been leveled against the growing protection of commercial speech, such as advertisements, under U.S. law. Originally not protected, in recent decades commercial speech has been accorded constitutional protection, albeit to a lesser extent than political expression (for instance, the protection does not extend to misleading information).[99] According to this critique, an abundance of behavioral research has demonstrated that suppliers can and do manipulate customers' decision-making to increase profits, without providing information that is inaccurate *stricto sensu* (often without providing any real information about the product).[100] Hence, prohibiting the regulation of non-misleading commercial speech, on the assumption that customers are able to rationally consider any information, is arguably unwarranted.[101] It has also been argued that, while there are good behavioral reasons to entrust judges with decisions about the advocacy of illegal actions, professional agencies are better qualified to make decisions about restrictions on commercial speech.[102]

96. Paul Horwitz, *Free Speech as Risk Analysis: Heuristics, Biases, and Institutions in the First Amendment*, 76 TEMP. L. REV. 1 (2003); Derek E. Bambauer, *Shopping Badly: Cognitive Biases, Communications, and the Fallacy of the Marketplace of Ideas*, 77 U. COLO. L. REV. 649 (2006); Lyrissa Barnett Lidsky, *Nobody's Fools: The Rational Audience as First Amendment Ideal*, 2010 U. ILL. L. REV. 799.

97. Bambaur, *supra* note 96, at 696–98. *See also* Lidsky, *supra* note 96, at 816–19.

98. *See supra* pp. 405–08.

99. *See generally* Horwitz, *supra* note 96, at 50–53.

100. *See, e.g.*, OREN BAR-GILL, SEDUCTION BY CONTRACT: LAW, ECONOMICS, AND PSYCHOLOGY IN CONSUMER MARKETS 75-77, 79–81, 153–55, 158–60, 208–11, 227–29 (2012) (describing consumer contracts whose complexity renders them unintelligible). On marketing techniques that exploit customers' heuristics, for example by reframing prices and other products' attributes, see *supra* pp. 284–87, 294–96.

101. Horwitz, *supra* note 96, at 49–61.

102. *Id.* at 61, 62. Some concern about the first half of this assertion may be raised, however, based on the empirical finding that, due to in-group bias (or motivated reasoning), liberal justices tend to protect liberal speech, and

While the doubts concerning the rationality of *listeners* have been used to criticize free-speech doctrine, doubts over the rationality of *policymakers* have been the basis for praise for the current doctrine in the United States. The court's insistence on clear evidence for imminent lawless actions that would result from uncensored incitements has been justified as an appropriate antidote to the human tendency to overestimate low-probability risks—a tendency that is particularly strong when the pertinent risks (such as criminal or political violence) are emotionally highly salient, when similar risks have recently materialized, or when such overestimations serve the interests of law-enforcement authorities.[103]

While both critique and praise for current doctrine demonstrate the fruitful contribution of behavioral insights to the legal analysis of free speech, they also demonstrate its limitations. Empirical evidence informs the normative debate—but does not resolve it.[104] This is particularly true when the issues in question are complex and highly ideological, or when the controversy is largely about ends, rather than just about means. The aforementioned critique and praise are important for the instrumental justifications of free speech (namely, facilitating listeners' deliberation and preventing unlawful actions), which shape much of the debate. However, at the heart of the debate lie non-instrumental values. One might concede that listeners very often do not rationally consider the available information, but insist that people have a right to receive the information, and that the state should not paternalistically curtail the flow of information.[105] In the same vein, one may accept that policymakers are prone to overestimating the risk that racial incitement would result in unlawful behavior, while maintaining that such incitement should be prohibited regardless of its possible outcomes, because it disrespects the dignity of minority groups.

The observation that studies of bounded rationality and cognitive biases play—and plausibly would always play—a limited role in the freedom-of-speech debate is consistent with behavioral studies of moral judgment. Take, for example, the entrenched distinction between content-based and content-neutral restrictions of speech. As previously noted, the constitutional safeguards against governmental censoring of the content of speech are much stronger than those against regulation of expressive behaviors that curtail free speech as a mere side effect of attaining legitimate goals, such as preventing traffic congestion or excessive noise in residential neighborhoods. In his proposed economic analysis of free speech, Richard Posner intentionally disregarded the government's motivation for suppressing any particular speech.[106] This disregard is perfectly compatible with the consequentialist foundations of standard economic analysis, but it is utterly incompatible with the existing

conservative justices tend to protect conservative speech. *See* Lee Epstein, Christopher M. Parker & Jeffrey Segal, *Do Justices Defend the Speech They Hate? In-Group Bias, Opportunism, and the First Amendment* (working paper, Aug. 2013, *available at*: http://ssrn.com/abstract=2300572).

103. Horwitz, *supra* note 96, at 26–49; Jonathan S. Masur, *Probability Thresholds*, 92 Iowa L. Rev. 1293 (2006).

104. Horwitz, *supra* note 96, at 64–65; Lidsky, *supra* note 96.

105. Lidsky, *supra* note 96, at 835–49.

106. Richard A. Posner, Frontiers of Legal Theory 74–75 (2001). Posner subsequently conceded that the motivation behind a regulation may be instrumentally important when assessing its consequences. Posner, *supra* note 93, at 745.

legal doctrine,[107] which reflects the deontological distinction between intending harm and merely foreseeing it that is embedded in prevailing moral judgments.[108] Other features of free speech law similarly reflect deontological, rather than consequentialist, morality.[109] Inasmuch as studies of cognitive biases are mostly relevant to the instrumental justifications of free speech, their impact on the doctrine that rests to a large extent on non-instrumental rationales is thus limited.

2. The Fight against Terrorism

Terrorism poses a great challenge to liberal democracies. It presents policymakers with tough dilemmas, and requires the legal system to delimit the boundaries of legality in resolving those dilemmas. Arguably, effective measures against terrorism necessitate limitations on freedom of speech, privacy, and other human rights; the use of aggressive interrogation techniques, administrative detentions, and targeted killings; and even the harming of innocent people to save others. Following the events of September 11, 2001, and other terrorist attacks, many countries introduced legal reforms that broadened the powers of government at the expense of civil rights. A huge body of literature has discussed these challenges.

Schematically, this extensive literature is split between two camps. One—to which legal economists usually belong—calls for pragmatic balancing between the need for effective measures against terrorism and the protection of human rights.[110] The other camp warns against such ad-hoc balancing, arguing that compromising constitutional principles to meet the short-term demands of the fight against terrorism violates liberal values and threatens democracy's endurance in the long term.[111]

The behavioral perspective has contributed to this debate by highlighting the various psychological phenomena that may affect decision-making in this sphere. In general, it has been argued that "in times of crisis, when panic, fear, hatred, and similar emotions prevail . . . the general public and its leaders are unlikely to be able to assess accurately the risks facing the nation." Hence, any attempt at balancing competing needs and values "is going to be heavily biased, even when applied with the best of intentions."[112]

107. TRIBE, *supra* note 93, at 789–804; Elena Kagan, *Private Speech, Public Purpose: The Role of Governmental Motive in First Amendment Doctrine,* 63 U. CHI. L. REV. 413 (1996).

108. *See supra* pp. 94–101, 194.

109. ZAMIR & MEDINA, *supra* note 91, at 187–224.

110. *See, e.g.,* RICHARD A. POSNER, NOT A SUICIDE PACT: THE CONSTITUTION IN A TIME OF NATIONAL EMERGENCY (2006); ERIC A. POSNER & ADRIAN VERMEULE, TERROR IN THE BALANCE: SECURITY, LIBERTY, AND THE COURTS 24 (2007).

111. *See, e.g.,* JEREMY WALDRON, TORTURE, TERROR, AND TRADE-OFFS: PHILOSOPHY FOR THE WHITE HOUSE (2010); DAVID LUBAN, TORTURE, POWER, AND LAW (2014). *See also* Zamir & Medina, *supra* note 91, at 127–76. In the absence of a clear demarcation between emergency and normal conditions, seemingly temporary measures that curtail human rights are likely to have lingering adverse effects. *See* Gross, *supra* note 61, at 1022, 1069–96; *supra* pp. 402–04.

112. Gross, *supra* note 61, at 1038.

Intense emotions affect decision-making in direct and indirect ways.[113] They do so directly when, for example, anger sparks aggression. Emotions indirectly affect decisions when they influence the quality of information gathering and processing. For example, negative emotions tend to narrow attentional focus. While emotions characterized by a sense of certainty, such as anger, lead people to rely more on heuristics, emotions characterized by uncertainty, such as worry, lead people to scrutinize information more carefully.[114] Some behavioral analyses of decision-making in the fight against terrorism have referred to both the direct and indirect effects of emotions on decision-making,[115] but most have focused on the latter.

While these findings seem directly relevant to decisions made in the immediate aftermath of a terrorist attack, it is less clear how relevant they are to measures adopted later, during prolonged antiterrorist campaigns. In any event, other cognitive phenomena may affect decision-making throughout such campaigns.[116] Specifically, it has been claimed that the high emotional impact and saliency of major terrorist attacks lead decision-makers and the public at large to overestimate the likelihood of such risks due to the availability heuristic.[117] Obsessive public discussion of such risks—possibly fueled by governmental bodies seeking to expand their powers and resources—reinforces such overestimation. Moreover, according to prospect theory, the weight people assign to the outcomes of highly unlikely events in making choices is often excessive (although, in some cases, people disregard such events altogether). This phenomenon exacerbates the effect of overestimation of the probability of such rare events.[118] The cumulative effect of these phenomena likely skews the perceived risk of terrorist threats.

It has also been conjectured that decisions made in the wake of traumatic terrorist attacks are framed as belonging to the domain of losses, rather than gains.[119] Since people tend to be risk-seeking in the domain of losses,[120] responses to terrorist attacks may be

113. For an overview, see George Loewenstein & Jennifer S. Lerner, *The Role of Affect in Decision Making*, *in* Handbook of Affective Sciences 619, 626–30 (Richard J. Davidson, Klaus R. Scherer & H. Hill Goldsmith eds., 2003).

114. Larissa Z. Tiedens & Susan Linton, *Judgment under Emotional Certainty and Uncertainty: The Effects of Specific Emotions on Information Processing*, 81 J. Personality & Soc. Psychol. 973 (2001).

115. *See, e.g.*, Jonathan H. Marks, *9/11 + 3/11 + 7/7 =? What Counts in Counterterrorism*, 37 Colum. Hum. Rights L. Rev. 559, 566–71 (2006).

116. Berman, *supra* note 61, at 1801–07 (arguing that unlike other emergencies, terrorist threats do not tend to subside over time, and the cognitive biases affecting decision-making with regard to counterterrorism measures do not disappear).

117. Gross, *supra* note 61, at 1039–41; Christina E. Wells, *Questioning Deference*, 69 Mo. L. Rev. 903, 922–23, 928–29 (2004); Jules Lobel, *The Preventive Paradigm and the Perils of Ad Hoc Balancing*, 91 Minn. L. Rev. 1407, 1441–44 (2007).

118. Daniel Kahneman & Amos Tversky, *Prospect Theory: An Analysis of Decision under Risk*, 47 Econometrica 263, 281–83 (1979).

119. Peter Margulies, *Judging Myopia in Hindsight: Bivens Actions, National Security Decisions, and the Rule of Law*, 96 Iowa L. Rev. 195, 207 (2010).

120. *See supra* pp. 42–44.

overly adventurous. Relatedly, studies of bounded ethicality have shown that people are much more likely to break moral and legal norms to cut losses than to make extra gains.[121] This phenomenon may also raise concerns about the practices of law-enforcement and military officials following terrorist attacks.

In contrast to the very vivid and tangible outcomes of terrorist attacks, the adverse effects of emergency measures on people's liberties and on other democratic values are somewhat abstract and pallid. People are therefore prone to underestimating their significance. The adverse effects of extreme counterterrorism measures may also be perceived as a distant prospect, compared to the perceived immediate threat of terrorist violence. People's myopia can therefore further weaken the objection to harsh measures.[122] For these reasons, while the development of "libertarian panics," namely "episodes in which aroused publics become irrationally convinced that justified security measures represent unjustified attempts to curtail civil liberties,"[123] is logically possible, it is psychologically implausible.[124] Libertarian panic is also highly unlikely due to the phenomena of in-group bias, out-group negativity, and prejudice,[125] because most citizens and decision-makers assume that anti-terrorist measures primarily affect the liberties of members of other groups (foreigners and minorities) rather than their own.[126]

Other heuristics and biases that might distort decision-making in the present context include the confirmation bias (once decisions to take harsh measures against terrorism are made, decision-makers seek information that corroborates these decisions, and ignore or underestimate conflicting information),[127] overconfidence (characterizing professional decision-makers),[128] group polarization, and groupthink (where decisions are made by people of similar background and worldview).[129]

Finally, while people generally display *omission bias* when facing risky choices, studies have shown that an *action bias* occasionally plays a part as well. People usually prefer inaction to action because they predict that the regret experienced following an action that has resulted in worse outcomes than omission would be greater than the regret experienced following an omission that has resulted in worse outcomes than action. People are also seen as bearing a greater moral responsibility for harmful outcomes that they actively bring

121. EYAL ZAMIR, LAW, PSYCHOLOGY, AND MORALITY: THE ROLE OF LOSS AVERSION 31–33 (2015).

122. Margulies, *supra* note 119, at 205–06; Gross, *supra* note 61, at 1041.

123. Adrian Vermeule, *Libertarian Panics*, 36 RUTGERS L.J. 871, 871 (2005).

124. Marks, *supra* note 115, at 583–84.

125. On these phenomena, see generally Monica Biernat & Kelly Danaher, *Prejudice*, *in* HANDBOOK OF PSYCHOLOGY, VOL. 5: PERSONALITY AND SOCIAL PSYCHOLOGY 341 (Irving B. Weiner, Howard A. Tennen & Jerry M. Suls eds., 2d ed. 2012); John F. Dovidio et al., *Social Conflict, Harmony, and Integration*, *in* HANDBOOK OF PSYCHOLOGY, *id.* at 428.

126. Marks, *supra* note 115, at 585–88; Gross, *supra* note 61, at 1037.

127. Wells, *supra* note 117, at 923. On the confirmation bias, see generally *supra* pp. 58–61.

128. *Id.* at 923–24, 929. On overconfidence, see generally *supra* pp. 64–66.

129. *Id.* at 927–29. On group polarization and groupthink, see generally *supra* pp. 120–23, 365.

about than for those they passively let happen. These phenomena may be due to differences in counterfactual thinking: it is easier to imagine what would have happened if one had not acted, than if one did act.[130] However, things are different when people are expected to act—for example, due to their social role.[131] Given those expectations, imagining the outcome of an action is no more difficult than imagining the outcome of inaction, and the moral responsibility for harmful inaction is not necessarily any less than for action. Like goalkeepers—who almost invariably jump right or left, even though the optimal strategy is to stay in the goal's center[132]—governmental officials in charge of protecting national security are liable to display an action bias, thus overly reacting to terrorist threats.[133] Take, for example, a decision on whether to place a suspect terrorist under administrative detention. If the suspect is detained, it would be very difficult to know whether he might otherwise have committed unlawful acts, thus making regret (and external criticism of the decision) unlikely. In contrast, if he is not detained and then commits a terrorist attack, the cost of regret—and the public reproach for governmental inaction—are expected to be great.

This analysis is clearly relevant to the substantive and institutional debates about the legality of possible antiterrorist measures, the proper decision procedures within the executive branch, and the appropriate scope of judicial review of counterterrorism policies and actions. However, as each of these issues (particularly that of judicial review) involves an array of complex policy issues, we will not delve into them here. We will only mention one suggestion for improving the decision-making process within the executive and briefly comment on the issue of judicial review.

It has been suggested that the biases described above might be mitigated, and a more rational and dispassionate deliberation facilitated, through the use of *human rights impact assessments*.[134] The inspiration for such assessments comes from the requirement to prepare environmental impact assessments as a requisite step in the process of approving new policies or projects that are likely to have a significant effect on the environment. Human rights impact assessments may include the nature and intensity of counterterrorism measures' harm to human rights; the number of people whose rights are going to be curtailed; the extent to which the proposed measures discriminate between different groups in society; and the availability of alternative means for achieving similar results with fewer infringements of human rights. In considering harsh antiterrorist measures, their marginal benefit should be weighed against their marginal harm to human rights, compared with

130. On the omission bias and its causes, see generally *supra* pp. 48–50.

131. Carmen Tanner & Douglas L. Medin, *Protected Values: No Omission Bias and No Framing Effects*, 11 Psychonomic Bull. & Rev. 185, 189 (2004); Mark Seidenfeld, *Why Agencies Act: A Reassessment of the Ossification Critique of Judicial Review*, 70 Ohio St. L.J. 251, 294–97 (2009).

132. Michael Bar-Eli et al., *Action Bias among Elite Soccer Goalkeepers: The Case of Penalty Kicks*, 28 J. Econ. Psychol. 606 (2007).

133. Of course, action bias may distort governmental decision-making in other spheres as well. *See* Lucas & Tasić, *supra* note 10, at 231–32.

134. Marks, *supra* note 115, at 603–24.

more moderate means.[135] Such assessments may facilitate a calmer, more rational, and possibly more transparent deliberation about antiterrorist measures.

With regard to judicial review of administrative actions and legislation, courts usually tend to defer to the other branches on issues of national security in general, and on counterterrorism measures in particular.[136] While advocates of such judicial restraint point to the importance of flexibility, quick response, and professional expertise in handling crises, advocates of stricter judicial review rely, in part, on the psychological phenomena described above, which are likely to result in skewed decision-making and unnecessary curtailment of liberties.[137] Arguably, judicial review increases the executive's accountability, which may in turn help to overcome at least some cognitive biases.[138]

While the behavioral insights discussed above strengthen the case for judicial review in times of crisis, the picture is more complex even from a strictly behavioral perspective. First, while decision-making by law-enforcement bodies and by the legislature is susceptible to cognitive biases, so, too, is judicial decision-making.[139] For example, ex-post judicial remedies for flawed governmental handling of terrorist threats (in the form of either insufficient measures or excessive ones) may indeed increase the executive's accountability, which may in turn spur policymakers to improve their decision-making processes. However, such judicial supervision (as well as other forms of external, ex-post review of governmental actions) is susceptible to cognitive imperfections—in particular the hindsight bias.[140] Courts striving to strike an appropriate balance between judicial deference and judicial activism in this sphere are thus caught between Scylla and Charybdis.

Second, inasmuch as it is true that, in times of national crisis, courts around the globe tend to be more deferential to the other branches of government, this tendency likely has social-psychological and cognitive roots, such as in-group bias, out-group negativity, and judges' omission bias when the stakes appear to be particularly high.[141] These factors may exert greater influence on the courts than any rational argument in support of greater judicial activism in times of external threats to national security.

To sum up, while the cognitive biases affecting decision-making by those in charge of the fight against terrorism are clearly important, their ramifications are much less clear-cut. From both a positive and a normative perspective, the great complexity of the psychological,

135. *See also* ZAMIR & MEDINA, *supra* note 91, at 140–76.

136. *See, e.g.*, Wells, *supra* note 115; Gross, *supra* note 61, at 1034–35. *But see* Epstein, *supra* note 65 (arguing, based on empirical analysis of U.S. Supreme Court decisions, that in times of national security crisis, the greater curtailment of liberties affects only cases that are unrelated to the war).

137. *See, e.g.*, Wells, *supra* note 117.

138. On accountability, see generally *supra* pp. 129, 132–34.

139. *See generally infra* pp. 532–54, 561–63.

140. Margulies, *supra* note 119. On the hindsight bias, see generally *supra* pp. 38–39; on the manifestation of this bias in judicial decision-making, see *infra* pp. 336–40, 359–60, 535–36.

141. *See, e.g.*, Christina E. Wells, *Fear and Loathing in Constitutional Decision-Making*, 2005 WIS. L. REV. 115; Lauryn P. Gouldin, *When Difference Is Dangerous: The Judicial Role in Material-Witness Detentions*, 49 AM. CRIM. L. REV. 1333 (2012).

institutional, moral, and legal issues involved, and the incompleteness of our understanding of the behavioral mechanism behind decision-making in intricate institutional settings, call for caution.

3. Affirmative Action

Affirmative action refers to the adoption of positive steps to increase the representation of minorities and women in the workplace, in education, and in other areas from which they have historically been excluded.[142] It is adopted in many societies by public and semi-public entities (and sometimes by private ones, as well), to counteract ethnic and gender discrimination. Increasing the participation of some populations necessarily entails decreasing the participation of others whose credentials may be equivalent (or even superior). Affirmative action is, therefore, politically, morally, and legally controversial.[143] This controversy is reflected in the fact that legal systems around the world vary on a spectrum ranging from an absolute ban on affirmative action to mandatory quotas for women and minorities in certain spheres. The affirmative-action debate is part of a broader normative debate about antidiscrimination laws.[144]

Due to space limitations, neither the broader social, psychological, and legal background of racial and gender discrimination, nor the normative debate surrounding antidiscrimination laws, can be discussed here in any depth.[145] Instead, this subsection will highlight the contribution of behavioral insights by demonstrating how they can help in designing more acceptable and effective affirmative plans. Two key psychological phenomena in this regard are loss aversion and the identifiability effect.

Loss aversion manifests itself not only in self-regarding choices, but also in decisions affecting other people. It is closely related to the moral constraint against harming other

142. *See, e.g.*, Robert Fullinwider, *Affirmative Action*, *in* Stanford Encyclopedia of Philosophy (2011, rev. 2013), *available at:* http://plato.stanford.edu/entries/affirmative-action; Faye J. Crosby & Diana I. Cordova, *Words Worth of Wisdom: Toward an Understanding of Affirmative Action*, *in* Sex, Race, and Merit: Debating Affirmative Action in Education and Employment 13 (Faye J. Crosby & Cheryl VanDeVeer eds., 2000). For a general survey of U.S. affirmative-action law, see 2 Barbara T. Lindemann & Paul Grossman, Employment Discrimination Law 39-1–39-151 (5th ed. 2012).

143. *See generally* Sex, Race, and Merit, *supra* note 142; Jerry Kang & Mahzarin R. Banaji, *Fair Measures: A Behavioral Realist Revision of "Affirmative Action"*, 94 Calif. L. Rev. 1063 (2006); Randall Kennedy, *Persuasion and Distrust: A Comment on the Affirmative Action Debate*, 99 Harv. L. Rev. 1327 (1986); Jed Rubenfeld, *Affirmative Action*, 107 Yale L.J. 427 (1997); Peter H. Schuck, *Affirmative Action: Past, Present and Future*, 20 Yale L. & Pol'y Rev. 1 (2002).

144. *See generally* Zamir & Medina, *supra* note 91, at 225–56.

145. For an influential social-psychology analysis of the behavioral factors underlying discriminatory practices, see Linda Hamilton Krieger, *The Content of Our Categories: A Cognitive Bias Approach to Discrimination and Equal Employment Opportunity*, 47 Stan. L. Rev. 1161 (1995). In Chapter 15 we discuss the use of the Implicit Association Test (IAT) to examine unconscious prejudicial attitudes toward marginalized groups and their implications for the study of judicial decision-making. *See infra* pp. 550–54. It has been argued that the prevailing implicit racial bias found in IATs justifies affirmative action plans. *See, e.g.*, Christine Jolls & Cass R. Sunstein, *The Law of Implicit Bias*, 94 Cal. L. Rev. 969, 978–88 (2006); Kang & Banaji, *supra* note 143. This argument has been contested, however. *See, e.g.*, Gregory Mitchell & Philip E. Tetlock, *Antidiscrimination Law and the Perils of Mindreading*, 67 Ohio St. L.J. 1023 (2006).

people—which is much stricter than the moral duty to assist others.[146] One implication of loss aversion for affirmative action is that the resentment to affirmative-action plans is much greater when they deprive people of an entitlement they already have than when they cause people not to receive a new entitlement.[147] Not giving people something—such as the opportunity to study at a certain institution—is considerably less painful than taking away an existing entitlement. In fact, a common denominator of virtually all existing affirmative plans is that they refer to benefits that people do not yet have. When affirmative-action policies are implemented at a university or in the workplace, they mandate that a certain individual, rather than another, will gain admission or secure a job. Very rarely, if ever, do they dictate that an employee who already occupies a certain position, or a student who has already been admitted to an academic program, should give it up for someone else. This perception holds true regardless of whether removing the entitlement from those who already have it involves greater or lesser transaction costs or other losses (such as investment in job-specific skills),[148] and irrespective of the identifiability of those adversely affected (an issue we discuss below).[149] In one experiment, support for an affirmative-action plan significantly decreased when respondents were given descriptions that highlighted the loss incurred by the non-minority individuals, rather than the gain to the minority ones.[150] The perception that existing affirmative policies do not deprive people of entitlements they already have may also make the beneficiaries of these plans feel more comfortable with these policies.

Loss aversion assumes that outcomes are assessed in relation to some reference point—hence the importance of framing.[151] In the present context, it is not always clear whether an affirmative policy involves losses or merely relinquished gains. Thus, it has been experimentally demonstrated that giving some individuals a certain benefit that had been promised to others is less objectionable than taking it from people who had already received the benefit. However, giving someone a benefit that had been promised to others is considered far more objectionable than giving some people priority over others in allocating a benefit—plausibly because the promise changed the promisees' reference point.[152] Affirmative plans may also be perceived as involving losses—and thus as illegitimate or even illegal—when people develop reasonable expectations of receiving an entitlement, even if they have not received it yet.[153]

146. *See generally supra* pp. 94–101, 194–95.

147. For experimental support of this claim, see Fredrick E. Vars, *Attitudes toward Affirmative Action: Paradox or Paradigm?*, *in* RACE VERSUS CLASS: THE NEW AFFIRMATIVE ACTION DEBATE 73 (Carol M. Swain ed., 1996); ZAMIR, *supra* note 121, at 146–47 (describing a survey experiment).

148. Vars, *supra* note 147, at 92 (analyzing a survey that substantiates this claim).

149. ZAMIR, *supra* note 121, at 147.

150. *Id.*

151. *See supra* pp. 42–44, 46–48.

152. Vars, *supra* note 147, at 82–89.

153. ZAMIR, *supra* note 121, at 147–48.

The gains/losses distinction also plays a role with respect to remedial rules. When awarding remedies against discriminatory practices or noncompliance with affirmative-action plans, courts are far more reluctant to deprive non-minority individuals of a benefit (such as a job) that they received in good faith, than to prohibit such an inappropriate allocation in the first place.[154] While the former involves a taking, the latter merely entails not giving.

Finally, loss aversion and the framing effect can explain the different presentations of the issue in the public and legal discourse. Affirmative action policies are conventionally viewed as providing gains to minority individuals and losses to non-minority ones. However, since such plans aim to undo the outcomes of prior long-standing discriminatory practices, they may be—and are indeed sometimes—presented as remedying the losses incurred by members of minorities, and reducing the unjust enrichment of the majority from those practices.[155] To be sure, this claim is not an argument stopper, if only because the individuals who are denied the benefit under the affirmative plan are not necessarily those who benefited from the discrimination in the past. However, merely reframing affirmative action policies as denying illegitimate gains from non-minority people, rather than as imposing losses on innocent individuals, can render these policies less objectionable.

Another psychological phenomenon that impinges on the public and legal debate over affirmative action is identifiability—the tendency to treat identified individuals differently than unidentified ones.[156] In a series of experiments, Ilana Ritov and Eyal Zamir compared support for several hypothetical affirmative action procedures that were equivalent in terms of overall harm and benefit, but differed with respect to the identifiability of those who stood to lose from their implementation.[157] The results showed that the identifiability of those adversely affected significantly reduced support for affirmative action (and for similar procedures that involved a trade-off between the interests of different groups). Support for the affirmative program decreased even when the identifiable "victims" of the program were unaware that they might have been selected, were it not for the program, and even when the lost entitlement was nothing more than the chance of being selected.

In and outside the laboratory, it is difficult to disentangle identifiability from loss aversion in the context of affirmative action, as the two are often confounded. However, the evidence indicates that each phenomenon plays an independent role in this regard, and both affect the acceptability of affirmative action plans.

154. *See, e.g.*, Lindemann & Grossman, *supra* note 142, at 40-19–40-23.

155. *See, e.g.*, Fullilove v. Klutznick, 448 U.S. 448, 484–85 (1980) (Burger, C.J.) (plurality opinion) ("[I]t was within congressional power to act on the assumption that in the past some nonminority businesses may have reaped competitive benefit over the years from the virtual exclusion of minority firms from these contracting opportunities"); Ian Ayres & Fredrick E. Vars, *When Does Private Discrimination Justify Public Affirmative Action?*, 98 Colum. L. Rev. 1577, 1616–19 (1998) (discussing the "unjust enrichment principle").

156. *See generally supra* pp. 101, 400–01.

157. Ilana Ritov & Eyal Zamir, *Affirmative Action and Other Group Tradeoff Policies: Identifiability of the Adversely Affected*, 125 Org. Behav. & Hum. Decision Processes 50 (2014).

While the law does not explicitly refer to the issue of identifiability when determining the validity of affirmative action plans, that factor is reflected in some legal systems. Thus, current affirmative action plans in higher education in the United States—designed to meet the judicial standards set by the Supreme Court[158]—use an elaborate set of procedures and flexible criteria that make it practically impossible to pinpoint the non-minority candidates who would have been admitted but for the plan. Accordingly, when describing the University of Texas's selection procedure, the court in *Fisher v. University of Texas* noted that "it is difficult to evaluate which applicants have been positively or negatively affected by its consideration or which applicants were ultimately offered admission due to their race who would not have otherwise been offered admission."[159]

The unidentifiability of those adversely affected by affirmative action programs therefore contributes to the social acceptability of these programs. Arguably, the identifiability of the adversely affected individuals should not bear upon the programs' legality. However, even if it might seem unprincipled to classify plans according to the identifiability of their "victims," the visibility of the people who are affected by such policies appears to be a valid concern.[160]

4. Concluding Remarks

The legal and constitutional protection of human rights involves heated normative controversies. The conflicting normative positions usually rest, explicitly or implicitly, on certain factual assumptions, including those about human psychology and decision-making. These assumptions refer to human behavior in spheres governed by human rights laws, decision-making by officials whose policies affect those behaviors, and public perceptions of those policies. Inasmuch as those assumptions are unsound, so are the normative claims resting on them. In this sense, the importance of behavioral findings can hardly be disputed. The psychology of normative judgments (by both policymakers and the citizenry) is also important for positive, and possibly normative, analysis of the law. However, even if all the factual issues were to be resolved, the normative debate would persist, because much of the dispute is not about facts, but about moral issues.[161] For this reason, the importance of the behavioral insights in this sphere should not be overstated. Nonetheless, there is much room for conducting additional behavioral studies and for further application of existing behavioral findings to human rights issues.

158. *See, e.g.*, Grutter v. Bollinger, 539 U.S. 306 (2003) (holding that an admissions process that may favor members of minority groups, but also considers several other factors on an individual basis, is not unconstitutional).

159. Fisher v. Univ. of Texas, 631 F.3d 213, 230 (5th Cir. 2011).

160. Richard Primus, *The Future of Disparate Impact*, 108 MICH. L. REV. 1341, 1369–74 (2010).

161. Theories of coherence-based reasoning (discussed in *infra* pp. 528–32.) explain why people who hold opposite views on normative issues are also most likely to diverge on the factual ones. In the present context, this is nicely demonstrated, for example, in the debate surrounding IAT findings and their normative implications. *Compare, e.g.*, Kang & Banaji (*supra* note 145) *and* Mitchell & Tetlock (*supra* note 145).

E. International Law

1. Challenges

The expansion of standard economic analysis to public international law is a relatively recent development,[162] and the application of behavioral insights in this sphere is in its infancy.[163] This is somewhat surprising, given that behavioral insights have been used by international-relations scholars for quite some time.[164] For example, international-relations scholars have used prospect theory—including loss aversion and risk-seeking in the domain of losses—to explain the tendency of countries to take greater risks to avoid perceived losses,[165] and to "fight harder and hold out longer in trade disputes with preventive objectives than [. . .] in cases with promotive ones."[166] It has also been argued that several cognitive heuristics and biases, such as overconfidence, the fundamental attribution error, and loss aversion,[167] tend to produce more hawkish decisions in international conflict situations.[168] Scholars have also referred to sunk costs and escalation of commitment to explain the tendency of countries to keep fighting futile wars,[169] and studied the role of emotions, such as revenge, in foreign policy.[170] Another example is analyzing how biased gathering and processing of information (due to phenomena such as availability and the confirmation bias) have affected decision-making in international crises.[171] These analyses have focused mostly on international conflict situations, and ignored the role of law in international relations.[172]

162. *See generally* Eric A. Posner & Alan O. Sykes, Economic Foundations of International Law (2013); Economic Analysis of International law (Eugene Kontorovich & Francesco Parisi eds., 2016); Alan Sykes & Andrew Guzman, *Economics of International Law, in* 3 The Oxford Handbook of Law and Economics 439 (Francesco Parisi ed., 2017).

163. *See generally* van Aaken, *supra* note 5, at 439–49; Broude, *supra* note 5.

164. For overviews, see, e.g., Rose McDermott, Political Psychology and International Relations (2004); Jack S. Levy, *Psychology and Foreign Policy Decision-Making, in* The Oxford Handbook of Political Psychology, *supra* note 71, at 301. *See also* Janice Gross Stein, *Threat Perception in International Relations, in* The Oxford Handbook of Political Psychology, *supra* note 71, at 364; *Symposium, The Behavioral Revolution and International Relations*, 71 Int'l Org. S1–S277 (2017).

165. *See, e.g.*, Avoiding Losses / Taking Risks: Prospect Theory and International Conflict (Barbara Farnham ed., 1994); Rose McDermott, Risk-Taking in International Politics: Prospect Theory in American Foreign Policy (2001).

166. Jeffrey D. Berejikian & Bryan R. Early, *Loss Aversion and Foreign Policy Resolve*, 34 Pol. Psychol. 649, 649 (2013) (statistically analyzing 100 trade disputes initiated by U.S. officials). *See also* Deborah Kay Elms, *Large Costs, Small Benefits: Explaining Trade Dispute Outcomes,* 25 Pol. Psychol. 241 (2004) (using loss aversion to explain arguably irrational handling of a protracted trade dispute between the United States and Japan).

167. *See supra* pp. 64–66, 68–69, and 42–57, respectively.

168. Daniel Kahneman & Jonathan Renshon, *Hawkish Biases, in* American Foreign Policy and the Threat of Fear: Threat Inflation since 9/11 79 (A. Trevor Thrall & Jane K. Cramer eds., 2009).

169. *See, e.g.*, Robert Jervis, *Political Implications of Loss Aversion,* 13 Pol. Psychol. 187 (1992); Jack S. Levy, *Application of Prospect Theory to Political Science,* 135 Synthese 215, 227 (2003).

170. Oded Löwenheim & Gadi Heiman, *Revenge in International Politics,* 17 Security Stud. 685 (2008).

171. Chaim D. Kaufmann, *Out of the Lab and into the Archives: A Method for Testing Psychological Explanations of Political Decision Making,* 38 Int'l Stud. Q. 557 (1994). *See also* Gross, *supra* note 61, at 1038–42.

172. van Aaken, *supra* note 5, at 435–37.

The challenges facing behavioral analysis of public international law are basically similar to those facing behavioral analysis of public law at the national level. The greatest challenge stems from the fact that most players in the international arena—including states, international organizations, and nongovernmental organizations—comprise many (sometimes millions) people. It is therefore unclear how the psychology of individuals translates into decision-making by such entities.[173] Moreover, the distinction in this respect is not merely one of groups versus individuals: the players in the international arena also vary in their institutional design and decision-making processes, and often include heterogeneous subgroups with conflicting interests and perspectives. Thus, a new treaty might result in a net gain or loss to a negotiating country, but within that country, some factions might gain while others may lose from the treaty. Even if behavioral insights may explain the behavior of each faction separately, to understand and predict the behavior of state organs and their representatives one has to know much more about the interactions between those factions within the country, the country's constitutional design, the role played by nongovernmental entities (such as NGOs and the media), and so forth. Institutions can help overcome the cognitive biases of individuals, but they can also exacerbate their adverse effects.[174] Furthermore, even if institutional designs result in political leaders and public officials making perfectly rational decisions, insofar as they are responsive to public opinion, the rational course of action may be to follow the general public's heuristics and biases.[175] Thus, for example, if due to psychic numbing, the general public is indifferent to the plight of masses of people (as in cases of mass murder and genocide), political leaders may fail to provide an adequate response to such atrocities.[176]

While these difficulties must not be overlooked, it should be noted that they are not unique to the behavioral perspective. The question of whether to treat the sovereign state as a "black box," or to take into account the complexity of decision-making within states, is equally troubling for rational-choice analysis of international law and international relations. True, adding behavioral insights complicates the picture. There is an inevitable tradeoff between the parsimony and elegance of simple models and the greater accuracy and nuance of more complex analyses. While this challenge may explain why behavioral analysis of international law has developed more slowly than behavioral analyses in other legal spheres, it does not imply that behavioral international law is unfruitful.

A related difficulty behavioral analysis of international law faces is methodological. The effect of heuristics and biases on people's judgment and decision-making sometimes vary from one context to another, differ across cultures, and depends on decision-makers'

173. Broude, *supra* note 5, at 1121–30.

174. van Aaken, *supra* note 5, at 441–49.

175. *See supra* pp. 405–06.

176. David Fetherstonhaugh et al., *Insensitivity to the Value of Human Life: A Study of Psychophysical Numbing*, 14 J. RISK & UNCERTAINTY 283 (1997); Paul Slovic, *"If I Look at the Mass I Will Never Act": Psychic Numbing and Genocide*, 2 JUDGMENT & DECISION MAKING 79 (2007).

experience.[177] Hence, drawing on findings from other contexts and applying them to international law, or conducting experiments with laypersons in a single society, are suboptimal.[178] Conducting laboratory experiments with heads of state, judges on international tribunals, and other policymakers is not ordinarily feasible, and randomized field experiments do not seem practicable either. However, these methodological obstacles are not insurmountable. For instance, a recent experimental study, involving both students and experienced U.S. policymakers as subjects, examined how people's behavioral traits (patience and strategic reasoning) affected their preferences with regard to negotiating and joining international agreements.[179] The fact that similar patterns were found in both subject groups demonstrated that under some conditions, at least, student convenience samples can be a useful means of exploring decision-making by policymakers. In general, the challenges of empirical studies in international law are not unique to the behavioral perspective, and progress can be made using the best available empirical and theoretical methodologies.[180]

2. Prospects

Despite the relatively early stage of behavioral analysis of international law, several fruitful applications of behavioral insights have already been put forward in this sphere. Generally speaking, the greater the similarity between decision-making in the national and international arenas, the easier it is to apply behavioral insights developed in the former to the latter. Primary examples are negotiations, judicial decision-making, and the framing of dilemmas involving life and death. Behavioral studies help explain why negotiators behave as they do, why some negotiations are more likely to succeed than others, and what can be done to increase the prospects of negotiation's success.[181] Similarly, numerous studies have revealed the extent to which various heuristics and biases affect judicial decision-making,[182] and the effect that framing has on the choice between courses of action of varying levels of risk in military conflicts.[183] The insights provided by these studies are prime candidates for a behaviorally informed analysis of international law.[184] In applying these insights to

177. *See generally supra* pp. 114–17, 124–27, 152.

178. Broude, *supra* note 5, at 1132–33.

179. Emilie M. Hafner-Burton et al., *Decision Maker Preferences for International Legal Cooperation,* 68 Int'l Org. 845 (2014).

180. *See also* Broude, *supra* note 5, at 1130–35.

181. *See generally supra* pp. 245–52; *infra* pp. 497–507.

182. *See generally infra* pp. 525–65.

183. *See supra* pp. 414–19.

184. *See, e.g.,* van Aaken, *supra* note 5, at 457–59 (behaviorally analyzing treaty negotiations); Broude, *supra* note 5, at 1143–49 (judicial decision-making), 74–83 (the framing effect in targeted killing); Sergio Puig, *Blinding International Justice,* 56 Va. J. Int'l L. 647 (2016) (discussing the *affiliation bias* of international arbitrators and ways to counteract it); Yahli Shereshevsky & Tom Noah, *Does Exposure to Preparatory Work Affect Treaty Interpretation? An Experimental Study on International Law Students and Experts,* 28 Eur. J. Int'l L. 1287 (2017) (experimentally studying the ability of international-law experts to disregard preparatory work they are exposed to, when interpreting treaties).

international law issues, one must take into account possible differences between national and international contexts. For example, judges in international tribunals are often selected by, or at least identify with, particular countries—which may affect their decision-making (although such judges arguably bear some resemblance to some judges in national systems, whose decisions may be influenced by the identity of those who appointed them, as in the case of the U.S. Supreme Court).

Behavioral insights may also help explain one of the fundamental characteristics of international law compared to national legal systems—namely the absence of both a central legislative body and of strong enforcement mechanisms. One key source of international law is custom—commonly defined as a general and repeated practice of states followed out of a sense of legal obligation (*opinio juris sive necessitatis*).[185] The emergence of customary international norms, and the common—though far from perfect—compliance with these norms, are quite puzzling from the perspective of rational choice theory. As Jack Goldsmith and Eric Posner have ably explained, in a two-party game, habitual compliance with norms may emerge thanks to (1) *coincidence* of interest, (2) *coercion* by the stronger party, (3) a convergence of interests contingent upon *coordination* between them, and (4) *cooperation* due to the fear of retaliation in an infinitely repeated game of prisoner's dilemma.[186] However, standard game theory suggests that in the absence of a central enforcement mechanism, stable *cooperation* is unlikely to emerge in large groups, because no group member would find it worthwhile to bear the costs of punishing defectors (and even stable *coordination* faces considerable difficulties).[187]

Whether or not standard game theory inevitably leads to these skeptical conclusions,[188] it appears that behavioral insights based on experimental findings, mostly from public-goods games, cast doubt on the premise that people are purely selfish[189]—thus portraying a less pessimistic picture of customary international law.[190] Public goods experiments have demonstrated that even in the absence of verbal communication, convergence of behavior emerges, in which the mean of contributions in the previous round serves as an implicit norm.[191] People regard free-riding on this implicit norm as illegitimate, and co-operation is stabilized through decentralized punishment. The cumulative effect of legal

185. RESTATEMENT (THIRD) OF THE FOREIGN RELATIONS LAW OF THE UNITED STATES § 102(2) (AM. LAW INST. 1987).

186. JACK L. GOLDSMITH & ERIC A. POSNER, THE LIMITS OF INTERNATIONAL LAW 26–35 (2005).

187. *Id.* at 35–38.

188. For critiques of the skeptical view from within game theory, see, e.g., Mark A. Chinen, *Game Theory and Customary International Law: A Response to Professors Goldsmith and Posner*, 23 MICH. J. INT'L L. 143 (2001); Edward T. Swaine, *Rational Custom*, 52 DUKE L.J. 559 (2002).

189. *See generally* Simon Gächter, *Human ProSocial Motivation and the Maintenance of Social Order*, *in* THE OXFORD HANDBOOK OF BEHAVIORAL ECONOMICS AND THE LAW, *supra* note 3, at 28; *supra* pp. 106–10.

190. van Aaken, *supra* note 5, at 454–56.

191. Christoph Engel, *The Emergence of a New Rule of Customary Law: An Experimental Contribution*, 7 REV. L. & ECON. 767 (2011).

framing (the experimental analog of *opinio juris*), and decentralized sanctions increases cooperation.[192]

Another contribution of behavioral insights to international law concerns the considerable significance of the choice between opt-in and opt-out arrangements in multilateral treaties, due to the powerful default effect. Jean Galbraith has examined a dataset of over 300 multilateral treaties, in which ratifying countries could choose whether disputes arising from the treaty would be adjudicated by the International Court of Justice (ICJ).[193] The treaties vary in their framing of this choice. Some of them subject disputes to the jurisdiction of the ICJ, while implicitly allowing countries to make reservations to the pertinent provisions; others explicitly allow countries to opt out of the ICJ's jurisdiction; and still others require countries to explicitly opt in to the court's jurisdiction. It was found that in the implied-reservation framing, very few countries chose to opt out of ICJ jurisdiction, resulting in 95 percent implicitly submitting to its jurisdiction. Twenty percent opted out of ICJ's jurisdiction when the explicit-opt-out framing was adopted—meaning 80 percent accepted it by default. Finally, in the explicit-opt-in framing, only 5 percent of the countries chose ICJ's jurisdiction. From the perspective of rational choice theory, these findings may seem puzzling, but they fall neatly in line with the predictions one would make based on the default effect and salience.[194] The fact that very few countries opted into the ICJ jurisdiction in the opting-in framing, while relatively few opted out of it in the opt-out framing, is consistent with the findings about the default effect in individual decision-making. The fact that considerably more countries opted out of the jurisdiction when this option was made explicit is in line with comparable findings in other contexts.[195]

As Galbraith rightly emphasizes, however, correlation does not imply causation. Specifically, there is a real possibility that the drafters of the treaties tried to fit the default arrangement to the presumed preferences of the ratifying countries. Nonetheless, the magnitude of the effect, and qualitative evidence from the records of treaty negotiations themselves, lend support to the conjecture that cognitive factors played a part in this regard.[196]

That said, one should be wary of overstating the power of the default effect. In both domestic and international arenas, interested parties might opt out of the default for reasons

192. Christoph Engel & Michael Kurschilgen, *The Coevolution of Behavior and Normative Expectations: An Experiment*, 15 AM. L. & ECON. REV. 578 (2013).

193. Jean Galbraith, *Treaty Options: Towards a Behavioral Understanding of Treaty Design*, 53 VA. J. INT'L L. 309 (2013). *See also* van Aaken, *supra* note 5, at 463–68.

194. *See generally supra* pp. 48–50, 179–82, and 24, respectively.

195. *See, e.g.*, Baruch Fischhoff, Paul Slovic & Sarah Lichtenstein, *Fault Trees: Sensitivity of Estimated Failure Probabilities to Problem Presentation*, 4 J. EXPERIMENTAL PSYCHOL.: HUM. PERCEPTION & PERFORMANCE 330 (1978) (finding that subjects largely ignored what had been left outside of the possibilities presented to them). *Cf.* DANIEL KAHNEMAN, THINKING FAST AND SLOW 85–88 & passim (2011) (discussing the "what you see is all there is" (WYSIATI) phenomenon).

196. Galbraith, *supra* note 193, at 336–44 (finding support in negotiation history for delegates' recognition that choices of the form of opt-in and opt-out arrangements can have a practical effect, even if they are of no substantive legal importance).

of either rational cost-benefit analysis or cognitive heuristics. Thus, for example, attempts to harmonize international trade law might be thwarted by the reluctance of lawyers to apply unfamiliar norms to the contracts they draw up, prompting them to opt out of applicable conventions.[197]

Nonetheless, the policy implications of the behavioral findings are straightforward: if the representatives of countries negotiating a given treaty wish to increase the adoption of a certain arrangement, they should strive to make it the default, and make the possibility of opting out of the default less conspicuous. Since the officials involved in the drafting of treaties often differ in their professional skills, institutional affiliation, and ideological inclinations from those who decide on whether or not to ratify the treaty; and since the countries taking part in the drafting of a treaty need not be the same as those considering its ratification—these findings are of considerable practical significance.

Another example of the use of behavioral insights to better understand treaty negotiations is Jeffrey Rachlinski's analysis of the international community's (slow and largely inadequate) response to the threat of global climate change.[198] In addition to the familiar problems of collective action and the influence of powerful interest groups, Rachlinski points to several behavioral impediments to attaining international cooperation in this sphere. Among other things, because there is no full consensus among scientists (although such consensus has continued to grow since the publication of Rachlinski's article), the confirmation bias leads people—including those who doubt the scientific claims about the great hazards of climate change and its human causes—to collect and process new information in a way that confirms their prior beliefs.[199] From a different perspective, the consequences of global climate change and the measures necessary to prevent or mitigate them (such as drastically reducing the use of certain sources of energy) are commonly perceived as belonging to the domain of losses. While losses due to climate change are (or are perceived to be) uncertain, the losses due to the measures needed to combat climate change are certain. Since people tend to be risk-seeking in the domain of losses,[200] they may object to adopting the necessary measures. Moreover, the pertinent trade-off is between the *future* costs of climate change and the *immediate* costs of the steps needed to reduce it. People's myopia or hyperbolic discounting may therefore cause biased assessment of the different costs.[201] Other phenomena, such as the status quo bias, the omission bias, and the known obstacles involved in any negotiations involving losses, all stand in the way of effective and timely handling of global climate change.[202]

197. Lisa Spagnolo, *Green Eggs and Ham: The CISG, Path Dependence, and the Behavioural Economics of Lawyers' Choices of Law in International Sales Contracts*, 6 J. PRIVATE INT'L L. 417 (2010).

198. Jeffrey J. Rachlinski, *The Psychology of Global Climate Change*, 2000 U. ILL. L. REV. 299.

199. On the confirmation bias, see generally *supra* pp. 58–61.

200. *See generally supra* pp. 42–44.

201. On these biases, see generally *supra* pp. 88–93.

202. For further discussion of these and other difficulties, as well as possible, behaviorally informed solutions, see Rachlinski, *supra* note 198. For a behavioral analysis of environmental law more generally, see Adrian Kuenzler &

A more specific example of public international law that has been analyzed from a behavioral perspective is the manner in which countries treat refugees or asylum seekers who have already entered their territory, versus those who are still seeking entry. In recent years, most U.N. officials and scholars have held the view that the prohibition to expel or return ("*refouler*") refugees and asylum seekers when this would imperil their life or freedom, under the 1951 Refugee Convention, extends to asylum seekers who are seeking entry into a state's territory.[203] However, there is considerable evidence that this interpretation is neither generally reflected in countries' practice nor shared by national courts.[204] The distinction made between asylum seekers who have already entered a country's territory and those who have not seems at odds with the humanitarian goals of the Refugee Convention, and is puzzling given the incentive it creates for asylum seekers to illegally cross the border.

One of us has suggested that a partial explanation for this problematic distinction (and a tentative normative argument in its favor) may be rooted in loss aversion.[205] Once asylum seekers enter a territory, their reference point likely changes: they are no longer trying to gain entry, but to avoid being expelled. Since experiencing a loss is more harmful than not obtaining a gain, expulsion is seen as more detrimental to asylum seekers' welfare than denying them entry. State officials may feel more comfortable refusing entry to asylum seekers than to expel them once they have entered the country's territory. Complementarily, expelling an unwanted individual who is already in the country is likely perceived as the country's gain in relation to the status quo—while letting an unwanted person enter the country's territory is seen as the country's loss. Loss-averse policymakers may therefore be more reluctant to allow entry than to expel an asylum seeker.

Another behavioral explanation for the puzzling distinction between refugees or asylum seekers who have already entered a country's territory, and those who have not, is the *identifiability effect*—the different reaction to identified individuals and to unidentified ones.[206] Since identified individuals elicit stronger emotional reaction, emphatic emotions, such as compassion and distress at the plight of another, play a greater role when the individual is identified rather than anonymous or statistical. In the present context, when

Douglas A. Kysar, *Environmental Law, in* The Oxford Handbook of Behavioral Economics and the Law, *supra* note 3, at 748.

203. *See, e.g.*, UNHCR Advisory Opinion on the Extraterritorial Application of Non-Refoulement Obligations under the 1951 Convention relating to the Status of Refugees and its 1967 Protocol (2007), *available at:* http://www.unhcr.org/refworld/pdfid/45f17a1a4.pdf; James C. Hathaway, The Rights of Refugees under International Law 315–16 (2005).

204. *See, e.g.*, Patricia Hyndman, *Refugees under International Law with a Reference to the Concept of Asylum*, 60 Australian L.J. 148, 153(1986); Zamir, *supra* note 121, at 150. Some countries regularly interdict vessels suspected of carrying would-be asylum seekers and return them to their home countries (*see* Stephen H. Legomsky, *Refugees, Asylum and the Rule of Law in the USA, in* Refugees, Asylum Seekers and the Rule of Law: Comparative Perspectives 122, 144–47 (Susan Kneebone ed., 2009)). Many others screen passengers who wish to enter their territory in their country of origin, thus effectively preventing them from seeking asylum at their destination.

205. Zamir, *supra* note 121, at 152–53. On loss aversion, see generally *supra* pp. 42–57.

206. *See supra* pp. 101, 400–01, 421–22.

the authorities consider the deportation of a person who has already entered a state's territory, that person is invariably identified. In contrast, when a state erects a wall to prevent the entrance of refugees and asylum seekers, the individuals blocked by the wall are often unidentified. Indeed, some measures taken against refugees and asylum seekers who seek entrance (such as denying them visas at the country of origin) are directed at identified people—hence the identifiability effect is at most a partial, complementary explanation for the existing practice. In fact, it is clear that both the identifiablity effect and loss aversion are just two factors among many that must be taken into account in this context.

Other issues in international law that may benefit—or already benefit—from a behavioral analysis include the trade-off between ex-ante credibility of commitment and ex-post flexibility in treaty design;[207] the pros and cons of creating links between treaties dealing with different issues (such as human rights and trade);[208] the relative rarity of unilateral exits from multilateral treaties, despite the fact that such exits are often explicitly allowed;[209] the implications of social-psychology insights for the design and implementation of human rights law;[210] and the pros and cons of international fact-finding reports given people's confirmation bias and attitude polarization.[211]

In summary, despite the various challenges facing behavioral analysis of international law, there can be little doubt that such analysis may be useful in shedding new light on many issues, thus providing a complementary perspective to the one offered by standard economic analysis. Studies conducted by behavioral legal scholars in other legal fields, and by non-lawyers in the field of international relations, provide the infrastructure for behavioral analysis of international law. Given the importance of context in the study of human judgment and decision-making, the greatest remaining challenge is to provide experimental and empirical support for behavioral analysis in this field—however, even this challenge is not insurmountable.

F. Conclusion

This chapter provided an overview of existing behavioral analyses of administrative, constitutional, and international law; the significant contribution they have already made to positive and normative issues in these spheres; and their limitations. Compared with most other legal spheres, behavioral analysis of these spheres is still in its early stages, but the scope for its potential development is great.

A general characteristic of behavioral analyses of public and international law is that they usually draw on behavioral phenomena that are well documented in other contexts.

207. *See* van Aaken, *supra* note 5, at 459–63.

208. *Id.* at 548–49.

209. *Id.* at 557.

210. Andrew K. Woods, *A Behavioral Approach to Human Rights*, 51 HARV. J. INT'L L. 51 (2010).

211. Shiri Krebs, *The Legalization of Truth in International Fact-Finding*, 18 CHI. J. INT'L L. 83 (2017). On confirmation bias and attitude polarization, see *supra* pp. 58–61.

Relatively few studies have employed empirical methods to directly examine the effect of heuristics and biases on judgment and decision-making in those spheres. This limitation is likely due to the comparatively late expansion of behavioral legal studies into administrative, constitutional, and public law, and to the considerable methodological difficulties of empirically studying decision-making in complex institutional environments. As in other legal spheres, we expect such empirical studies to be carried out in the future.

12

Criminal Law and Enforcement

A. Introduction

The field of criminal law and enforcement has long been a focal point for economic analysis. In 1968, Gary Becker published his seminal article on the topic[1]—perhaps the first instance of the application of the modeling tools of modern economics to core legal questions in a non-market setting. Since the publication of this article, a significant body of theoretical literature has analyzed various aspects of legal policies aimed at controlling crime,[2] and a growing number of empirical studies have tested the predictions generated by this body of work.[3]

This chapter examines the relationship between the economic analysis of crime and punishment, and the findings of behavioral economics. We begin by introducing the basic insights of the economic analysis of crime control, and highlighting the main themes within this literature. We then turn to examining whether people's moral judgments are in line with the dictates of economic analysis in this sphere, and examine the associated normative implications. The bulk of the rest of the chapter will focus on the ramifications of behavioral analysis on deterrence theory.[4]

1. *See* Gary S. Becker, *Crime and Punishment: An Economic Approach*, 76 J. Pol. Econ. 169 (1968).

2. For a review, see Steven Shavell, Foundations of Economic Analysis of Law 473–530 (2004).

3. For reviews of the literature, see Steven D. Levitt & Thomas J. Miles, *Empirical Study of Criminal Punishment*, *in* 1 Handbook in Law And Economics 455 (A. Mitchell Polinsky & Steven Shavell eds., 2007); Isaac Ehrlich, *Economics of Criminal Law*, *in* 3 The Oxford Handbook of Law and Economics 295, 304–16 (Francesco Parisi ed., 2017).

4. For reviews of the literature, see Nuno Garoupa, *Behavioral Economic Analysis of Crime: A Critical Review*, 15 Euro. J. L. & Econ. 5 (2003); Christine Jolls, *On Law Enforcement with Boundedly Rational Actors*, *in* The Law and Economics of Irrational Behavior 268 (Francesco Parisi & Vernon L. Smith eds., 2005); Richard H. McAdams & Thomas S. Ulen, *Behavioral Criminal Law and Economics*, *in* Criminal Law and Economics 403 (Nuno Garoupa ed., 2009); Alon Harel, *Behavioral Analysis of Criminal Law: A Survey*, *in* The Oxford Handbook of Behavioral Economics and the Law (Eyal Zamir & Doron Teichman eds., 2014).

Behavioral Law and Economics. Eyal Zamir and Doron Teichman.

B. Efficient Crime Control

The three central goals of punishment analyzed from an economic perspective are *incapacitation, specific deterrence*, and *general deterrence*. Incapacitation focuses on the removal of dangerous individuals from society, primarily (although not exclusively) through incarceration. Specific deterrence alludes to dissuading the individual being punished from committing further crimes in the future by "teaching him a lesson." Finally, general deterrence refers to the process of discouraging the entire population from committing crimes, by presenting the punishment of a given criminal as the price for criminal behavior.

Of these three goals, legal economists have focused the bulk of their intellectual efforts on general deterrence. Incapacitation, while clearly a central issue in crime-control policy debates, has proven to be a rather simple economic question at the theoretical level. Generally, within an economic framework, dangerous individuals should be incapacitated if the expected harm they create exceeds the costs of incapacitation—and continue to be incapacitated as long as this condition holds true.[5] Specific deterrence is generally considered to be a nonexistent phenomenon within rational choice theory, unless one assumes that the application of the sanction causes people to adjust their perception of its magnitude, or the probability that it would be applied.[6] Thus, if John receives a ticket on Monday for parking his car illegally, this is not expected to influence his behavior if he faces a similar dilemma the following day. The ticket he received on Monday is a sunk cost, and on Tuesday (or any other day) John should focus his attention only on future costs and benefits. Therefore, much of this chapter, in line with the existing literature, focuses on general deterrence.

The assumption at the core of the positive economic analysis of criminal law and enforcement is that criminals are sensitive to the payoff structure created by the legal system. In other words, the sanctions attached by the legal system to various crimes function as prices and influence the decisions made by potential criminals on whether or not to commit those crimes. In general, criminals are assumed to behave rationally and weigh the costs and benefits associated with committing a crime. Thus, the theory predicts an inverse relationship between the magnitude of sanctions and the tendency of individuals to engage in wrongful behavior. Testing this prediction has proven to be extraordinarily difficult, given the endogeneity of crime rates and incarceration rates, and the fact that incarceration generates both deterrence and incapacitation.[7] As a result, while some hold the view that potential criminals are insensitive to changes in sanctions,[8] others present a more

5. Steven S. Shavell, *A Model of Optimal Incapacitation*, 77 AM. ECON. REV. (PAPERS AND PROCEEDINGS) 107 (1987).

6. SHAVELL, *supra* note 2, at 516–18.

7. For an analysis of these difficulties and others, see Steven N. Durlauf & Daniel S. Nagin, *The Deterrent Effect of Imprisonment*, *in* CONTROLLING CRIME: STRATEGIES AND TRADEOFFS 43, 50–58 (Philip Cook, Jens Ludwig & Justin McCrary eds., 2011).

8. *See, e.g.*, Anthony N. Doob & Cheryl Marry Webster, *Sentence Severity and Crime: Accepting the Null Hypothesis*, 30 CRIME & JUST. 143 (2003).

nuanced view that legal penalties do deter under certain conditions.[9] Furthermore, most of the studies on this issue focus on policies in the United States—a country with extraordinarily high penalties for crimes[10]—and while it is possible that the United States operates in a policy space in which the marginal utility of elevated sanctions is minor (or even nonexistent), other countries do not.

One important aspect of the economic analysis of criminal behavior is the recognition that criminal sanctions are applied probabilistically: due to a range of difficulties throughout the enforcement process, only a fraction of offenders are actually punished. As a result, the true price tag that the legal system applies to crimes is the *expected* sanction—the sanction applied ex post discounted by the probability that it will actually be applied. Thus, the attitudes of potential criminals' toward risk become a key point when analyzing their behavior. While the economic model can encompass all types of attitudes toward risk, the literature has routinely limited itself to acknowledging the various options and their implications, without attempting to present systematic predictions of criminals' risk preferences.[11]

The key normative proposition of the economic analysis of criminal law and enforcement is that policies should be tailored to minimize the total social costs of crime. According to this framework, policymakers should pay attention both to the direct costs that crimes impose on society (e.g., loss of life or property) and to the costs associated with preventing those crimes (e.g., police force and prisons). It is the aggregate of these costs that society should strive to minimize. This framework is very similar to the one used by economists in order to analyze tort law, with costly enforcement being the main distinguishing factor.[12]

The fact that the enforcement of criminal law is costly drives many of the conclusions of the economic analysis in the area. For example, one of the major policy recommendations repeatedly drawn by legal economists is that an efficient crime control policy is based on relatively low enforcement rates coupled with high sanctions. This insight is based on the observation that raising the probability of punishment is more costly than raising the penalty.[13] Thus, policymakers can maintain the same level of expected sanctions and save money if they reduce enforcement and raise sanctions. If, for example, the current regime with respect to parking laws entails a $100 fine that is enforced by two traffic officers that generate a 5 percent probability of sanctioning, then the policymaker can generate an identical amount of deterrence by using only one traffic officer and doubling the size of the fine to $200.

9. *See, e.g.*, Levitt & Miles, *supra* note 3.

10. *See* HARRY R. DAMMER & JAY S. ALBANESE, COMPARATIVE CRIMINAL JUSTICE SYSTEMS 213–38 (2013).

11. In his early work on the topic, Becker was careful to acknowledge the respective implications of various risk attitudes. *See* Becker, *supra* note 1, at 179. *See also* SHAVELL, *supra* note 2, at 502–08.

12. On the economic analysis of tort law, see *supra* pp. 326–29.

13. In the context of monetary sanctions, this assumption holds true, since raising sanctions is almost costless, as long as they do not exceed the offender's wealth (note that fines are a form of wealth transfer, and therefore do not entail an actual social cost). In the context of non-monetary sanctions, this assumption is less obvious, since locking up people in jail generates significant costs.

C. Do People Want Efficient Crime Control Policies?

One fundamental question that we address at the start of our behavioral analysis is whether people's views on criminal sanctions are in line with the dictates of economic theory. This point is not merely an interesting intellectual exercise, but has practical implications as well. Moral constraints aside, maintaining a fit between penal policies and people's views may be of importance within a consequentialist framework of punishment. A significant body of research suggests that if this link is severed and the criminal justice system is seen as not reflecting the core values of society, then the motivation of many people to obey the law may be undermined. The result might be a need to invest additional resources in enforcement, as voluntary compliance (which comes at no direct cost) is eroded.[14]

The short answer to the question posed in the title of this section is no: people's views on sanctions differ significantly from the dictates of consequentialist theories of punishment. Rather, they are often aligned with moral convictions that reflect principles of *just deserts*. While it is unclear whether these moral convictions are ingrained in all human beings through an evolutionary or social process,[15] their wide and uniform scope has been demonstrated in numerous studies, through a variety of methodological tools.[16]

The moral convictions underpinning penal decisions concentrate on two main factors: *wrongfulness* and *culpability*.[17] Wrongfulness pertains to the act in question and the degree to which it deviates from expected behavior. Thus, causing someone's death is worse than assaulting him, which in turn is worse than stealing his property, and so forth. Culpability, on the other hand, denotes the degree of blame one can attribute to the defendant's state of mind. Deliberately inflicting harm is worse than doing so recklessly, which in turn is worse than doing so negligently, and so on. We will first review some of the main findings, which suggest that people's views on penal policies are in keeping with a non-consequentialist approach,[18] and then analyze the policy implications of this body of work.

1. Punishment and the Probability of Detection

Economic and non-economic theories of punishment diverge on whether the probability of detection should affect sanctions. While from an economic perspective the probability

14. Within the legal literature, this thesis has been most clearly articulated by Paul Robinson and John Darley. *See, e.g.*, Paul H. Robinson & John M. Darley, *The Utility of Desert*, 91 NW. U. L. REV. 453 (1997) [hereinafter Robinson & Darley, *The Utility of Desert*]; Paul H. Robinson & John M. Darley, *The Role of Deterrence in the Formulation of Criminal Law Rules: At Its Worst When Doing Its Best*, 91 GEO. L.J. 949 (2003); Paul H. Robinson & John M. Darley, *Intuitions of Justice: Implications for Criminal Law and Justice Policy*, 81 S. CAL. L. REV. 1 (2007).

15. *See* John Mikhail, *Universal Moral Grammar: Theory, Evidence and the Future*, 11 TRENDS COGNITIVE SCI. 143 (2007).

16. *See, e.g.*, John M. Darley, *Citizens' Assignment of Punishments for Moral Transgressions: A Case Study in the Psychology of Punishment*, 8 OHIO ST. J. CRIM. L. 101 (2010).

17. *See* ANTONY R. DUFF, INTENTION, AGENCY AND CRIMINAL LIABILITY: PHILOSOPHY OF ACTION AND THE CRIMINAL LAW 103 (1990).

18. For further reviews, see Kevin M. Carlsmith & John M. Darley, *Psychological Aspects of Retributive Justice*, 40 ADVANCES EXP. SOC. PSYCHOL. 193 (2008); John M. Darley & Adam L. Alter, *Behavioral Issues of Punishment, Retribution, and Deterrence*, *in* THE BEHAVIORAL FOUNDATION OF PUBLIC POLICY (Eldar Shafir ed., 2013).

of detection is an important factor in the design of sanctions (possibly *the* most important factor), non-economic theories do not consider it very important, and focus instead on the wrongfulness of the act and the culpability of the offender. Empirical findings suggest that people's views in this matter are mostly non-economic, and they do not believe that sanctions should be raised when the probability of detection is low.

Cass Sunstein, David Schkade, and Daniel Kahneman examined whether people believed that sanctions for tax violations should be adjusted to tackle enforcement problems in one particular region of the United States (Utah, versus California).[19] Their key finding was that the study's subjects (law students at the University of Chicago) did not think that such an adjustment was desirable. The particular details of the vignette used in the study, however, were somewhat restrictive. First, the enforcement deficit in question was the result of "practical constraints" associated with hiring more agents in Utah,[20] rather than factors beyond the control of the enforcing agency—such as the nature of the crime (e.g., income earned abroad), or the offenders' efforts to conceal their tax evasion (e.g., intentional use of cash). Presumably, the study's subjects wanted to incentivize the IRS to resolve the constraints they faced, rather than endorse the easy option of raising sanctions. Second, the policy outcome that the subjects were asked to support (i.e., varying sanctions on U.S. citizens based on their state of residence) might have triggered unique policy concerns concerning federalism: allowing the federal government to discriminate between citizens based on their place of residence could be abused.

Other studies have replicated this result in more generalizable settings. Kevin Carlsmith, Paul Robinson, and John Darley asked subjects to judge various criminal scenarios, and manipulated the deterrence aspect of the case by simply describing it as either very difficult to detect, or very easily detectable.[21] Their results showed that while the study's subjects varied in their judgment of the wrongfulness of various aspects of the act, they were unaffected by the issue of detection. In addition, after reporting their intuitive judgment of the event, the participants were asked to re-evaluate it from a deterrence or moral wrongfulness perspective.[22] Interestingly, when asked explicitly to consider deterrence in their determination, the participants' judgments of appropriate punishment differed significantly from their initial judgment. Conversely, when asked to consider moral wrongfulness as their guiding principle of punishment, their judgments did not differ significantly from their initial judgment. Thus, one might argue that people's initial intuition with regard to punishment tends to be non-economic in nature.[23]

19. *See* Cass R. Sunstein, David Schkade & Daniel Kahneman, *Do People Want Optimal Deterrence?*, 29 J. Legal Stud. 237, 244–46 (2000).

20. *Id.* at 245.

21. Kevin M. Carlsmith, John M. Darley & Paul H. Robinson, *Why Do We Punish? Deterrence and Just Deserts as Motives for Punishment*, 83 J. Personality & Soc. Psychol. 284, 288–95 (2002).

22. *Id.* at 292.

23. Based on a series of nine experiments, Baron and Ritov also conclude that "[i]n general, subjects do not seem very sensitive to the probability of detection between cases." *See* Jonathan Baron & Ilana Ritov, *The Role*

2. Punishment and the Risk of Future Offending

Another distinction between just-deserts theories and economic theories is the offender's risk of recidivism. While locking up risky individuals for long periods of time may be justifiable from an economic perspective,[24] it is usually not part of a traditional just-deserts analysis.[25] Thus, examining how offenders' riskiness alters punishment perceptions may serve to measure the driving forces underlying people's attitudes toward sanctions.

To examine this point, Darley, Carlsmith, and Robinson used a similar experimental approach to the one described above.[26] The conditions in the study included various types of crimes and distinct levels of risk of future offending (created by providing information on offending history). The results of the study showed that people's initial intuitive judgments of punishment were in line with a just-deserts perspective rather than one focused on incapacitation. As the authors conclude, "there is a general consensus on just deserts as the appropriate punishment motive for a perpetrator who intentionally commits a known wrong."[27]

3. Punishment Judgments and Policy Design

As previously noted, legal scholars—most notably Paul Robinson and John Darley—have taken the normative step of moving from describing people's penal judgments to the argument that the criminal code should follow those judgments.[28] Notably, they did so on the utilitarian grounds that maintaining a penal regime that is perceived to be fair helps to bolster voluntary compliance. Thus, aligning the law with people's moral intuitions comes with the large (and seemingly costless) benefit of widespread respect for the dictates of the law.

Several studies support the argument that if people perceive the criminal justice system to be unjust, their willingness to obey the law is eroded.[29] Clearly, one should be wary of a mere correlation between people's perceptions of the fairness of the criminal justice system and their attitudes toward compliance, since this might be driven by unaccounted variables. For example, people who tend to criminal behavior might choose to view the criminal justice system as unfair to justify their decision to engage in crime. In recent years, however, researchers have overcome this methodological obstacle by using elegantly

of Probability of Detection in Judgments of Punishment, 1 J. LEGAL ANALYSIS 553, 581 (2009). For a later study examining this question in an incentive-compatible lab setting, see Aurélie Ouss & Alexander Peysakhovich, *When Punishment Doesn't Pay: Cold Glow and Decisions to Punish*, 58 J.L. & ECON 625, 639–45 (2015).

24. *See supra* note 5 and accompanying text.

25. *See* GEORGE P. FLETCHER, RETHINKING CRIMINAL LAW 459–69 (2000). For a nuanced view of this issue, see Andrew Von Hirsch, *Criminal Record Rides Again*, 10 CRIM. JUST. ETHICS 2 (1991).

26. *See* John M. Darley, Kevin M. Carlsmith & Paul H. Robinson, *Incapacitation and Just Deserts as Motives for Punishment*, 24 LAW & HUM. BEHAV. 659, 660–71 (2000).

27. *Id.* at 676.

28. *See* Robinson & Darley, *The Utility of Desert*, *supra* note 14.

29. For a review, see Darley & Alter, *supra* note 18, at 184–85. The focus of the analysis in this case is on the substantive content of criminal law—however a large body of work has also linked this point to the fairness of enforcement procedures. *See, e.g.*, TOM R. TYLER, WHY PEOPLE OBEY THE LAW (1990).

designed experiments.[30] In one such study, Janice Nadler first exposed participants to news stories that described either fair or unfair laws, and then asked them to evaluate those laws.[31] Participants were then requested to complete questionnaires in which they were asked to assess the probability that they would engage in a variety of illegal activities. The results suggest that participants who are first exposed to news stories about unfair legal rules were significantly more likely to violate the law.

Nonetheless, one should be careful not to overstate the scope of this argument by systematically favoring fairness judgments when designing penal policies—for several reasons. First, people might not have strong moral convictions about many of the issues governed by criminal law. Criminal law includes a vast body of prohibitions—ranging from core offenses concerning harm to other individuals or their property, to more peripheral ones regarding protection of the environment, market integrity, and more. While the public might hold strong views about the content of criminal law in core issues, it is less clear that it holds such unequivocal views about other parts of the criminal code—such as money laundering, mail fraud, etc. Insofar as there are large parts of the criminal code that the public has less clear-cut views about, policymakers can regulate such areas relatively free of this consideration.

Second, people may not even know what the position of criminal law is on many issues. Robinson and Darley emphasize this point in their claim that criminal law does not deter,[32] while overlooking that it may also undermine their argument that criminal law must be consistent with people's penal attitudes. If people do not know what the law's position on a given matter is, then the law cannot drive them to incompliance. Moreover, this point is far more detrimental to Robinson and Darley's theory than to deterrence theory. Robinson and Darley's theory focuses on the behavior of the general population (i.e., not professional criminals), so it is truly undermined by data about the legal knowledge possessed by the general population. Deterrence theory, on the other hand, can always pull back and focus on professional criminals—a sector that is likely to be more knowledgeable about how the criminal justice system operates.

Finally, the claim that unfair (yet efficient) laws may drive people to disobedience appears to take people's views as a given. While the concept of general deterrence is complicated and may not be intuitive to many, people may still understand the merits of the idea if it is explained properly. Once that explanation is provided, people's views on deterrence-centered sanctions may change. And indeed, Jonathan Baron and Ilana Ritov have shown that presenting subjects with a series of probing questions that highlight how general deterrence works increased their willingness to endorse sanctions that were based on the probability of detection.[33] That said, inasmuch as non-consequentialist judgments are deeply

30. *See, e.g.*, Janice Nadler, *Flouting the Law*, 83 Tex. L. Rev. 1399 (2005).

31. *Id.* at 1410–16.

32. *See* Paul H. Robinson & John M. Darley, *Does Criminal Law Deter? A Behavioural Science Investigation*, 24 Oxford J. Legal Stud. 173, 175–78 (2004).

33. *See* Baron & Ritov, *supra* note 23, at 566–69.

ingrained in the human mindset,[34] the difficulties associated with swaying such judgments may be significant.

In summary, adopting a Stalinistic crime-control regime with unjustly draconian punishments that are administered through unfair enforcement will likely have a detrimental effect on voluntary compliance. That said, this is not a particularly valuable point to make, since it has no bearing upon the actual dilemmas that policymakers face in modern liberal democracies (although it may well be relevant to readers in many countries, which shall remain unnamed). A more nuanced analysis should be sensitive to the magnitude of deviation from people's perceptions of fairness and the strength of their views. One may speculate that people's opinion with respect to core criminal offenses such as murder and rape are relatively clear. Furthermore, these offenses tend to capture the public's attention, and therefore deviations from those well-developed views may be problematic. With respect to much of criminal law, however, we suspect that many people simply do not have strong views as to what the appropriate penal regime should be. In those areas, policymakers could probably focus on the consequences of crime-control policies.

4. Case in Point: The Law of Criminal Attempts

The preceding discussion presented the general aspects associated with people's moral intuitions and the structure of penal policies. This subsection presents a concrete application of this framework in the context of attempted criminal activity. As the following analysis suggests, incorporating behavioral insights into this debate may help to clarify existing legal practices.

Most penal systems include an array of primary offenses, coupled with a general inchoate crime that criminalizes attempts to commit those offenses.[35] Such attempts may be divided into two categories: *incomplete* and *complete*.[36] The former refers to situations where the transgressor fell short of all the steps that constitute the crime.[37] The penalty for incomplete crimes therefore requires a definition of the minimum conduct that qualifies as an attempt. Legal systems distinguish between *acts of preparation*—which are viewed as legal (e.g., the defendant bought a knife)—and behaviors of a more advanced stage that qualify as a *criminal attempt* (e.g., the defendant approached the victim with a knife and was caught just before stabbing her).[38] The latter category (complete attempts) pertains to situations where the offender completed all the acts that constitute the crime, yet his plan did not succeed. Thus, incompletion may be due to the offender failing to bring about the consequences that define the crime (e.g., the defendant stabbed his victim, but failed to

34. *See generally supra* pp. 97–101.

35. *See* ANTHONY DUFF, CRIMINAL ATTEMPTS 1 (1996).

36. *See* ANDREW ASHWORTH, PRINCIPLES OF CRIMINAL LAW 445–47 (5th ed. 2006) (reviewing the two types of attempts).

37. *See, e.g.*, MODEL PENAL CODE § 5.01(1)(c) (1985) (criminalizing acts that constitute only a substantial step toward committing a crime).

38. For a review of Anglo-American case law on this point, see DUFF, *supra* note 35, at 33–61; Hamish Stewart, *The Centrality of the Act Requirement for Criminal Attempts*, 51 U. TORONTO L.J. 399, 402–11 (2001).

cause her death), or because one of the essential conditions for the crime's completion did not exist (e.g., the defendant stabbed the victim, but the latter was already dead).

The attempt doctrine can be justified on consequentialist or on non-consequentialist grounds. From a consequentialist perspective, criminalizing attempts enhances deterrence by punishing transgressors whether or not their plan succeeded, thereby raising the probability of punishment and the expected sanction.[39] Inasmuch as transgressors are not deterred, and choose to engage in illicit behavior, punishing attempts also helps to prevent harm. Such prevention is achieved either by virtue of police intervention before the criminal act is perpetrated, or through incapacitation of individuals with a demonstrable propensity to criminal activity.[40] From a non-consequentialist perspective, punishing those who attempted to commit a crime is justified, because the actions of such individuals are morally blameworthy, even if they fail to realize their criminal intent.[41]

While criminalizing attempts achieves important policy goals, it also raises a serious policy question: What is the appropriate punishment for those who are found guilty of attempting to commit a crime? The prevailing view on this matter among many jurists is that the punishment for attempts should equal the punishment of the completed crime. If the focal point of the penal theory is the moment when the offender decided to violate the law and acted accordingly, then the punishment must not be influenced by external events that were beyond the offender's control. A salient demonstration of this prevalent view is the U.S. Model Penal Code's provision on the matter, based on the *equal punishment* framework.[42] This consensus, however, appears to be at odds with prevailing legal policies. Most legal systems hold the view that attempted crimes should be punished less harshly than completed ones.[43] Moreover, even in legal systems that have adopted equal-punishment policies in their criminal codes, in practice uncompleted crimes appear to involve reduced penalties.[44]

Traditional economic analysis has offered two explanations for the practice of discounting sanctions for criminal attempts—however, both are problematic. The first explanation focuses on the greater possibility of wrongful conviction in attempt cases:[45] in the absence of an objective element of the crime in such cases, the chances of error are greater. For example, it is difficult to know in such cases whether the defendant truly had the resolve needed to carry out the criminal plan. To reflect this evidentiary uncertainty, so the

39. *See* Steven Shavell, *Deterrence and the Punishment of Attempts*, 19 J. Legal Stud. 435 (1990).

40. *See* Wayne R. LaFave, Criminal Law § 11.2(b) (5th ed. 2010) (analyzing criminal attempts from an early prevention perspective); Shavell, *id.* at 458 (analyzing criminal attempts from the perspective of incapacitation).

41. *See* Fletcher, *supra* note 25, at 131–97.

42. *See* Model Penal Code § 5.05(1) (Official Draft and Revised Comments 1985).

43. *See* Omri Ben-Shahar & Alon Harel, *The Economics of the Law of Criminal Attempts: A Victim-Centered Perspective*, 145 U. Pa. L. Rev. 299, 318–19 (1996).

44. *Id.* at 319 n.44.

45. *See* Richard A. Posner, *An Economic Theory of the Criminal Law*, 85 Colum. L. Rev. 1193, 1217–18 (1985); Shavell, *supra* note 39, at 452–55.

argument goes, the sanction for attempts should be discounted. This argument, however, implicitly assumes that reducing the severity of the sanctions will not influence the standard of proof that judges and jurors will employ, and there is empirical (albeit inconclusive) evidence to suggest that this is not the case: when sanctions are reduced, the effective standard of proof tends to drop as well.[46] Inasmuch as this is true, reducing the penalty for attempted crimes may actually increase error costs, since it will increase the number of unsubstantiated convictions.[47]

The second explanation for lesser sanctions for attempted crimes focuses on the notion of *marginal deterrence*.[48] According to this argument, if the law applies the same punishment to attempted crimes as to perpetrated ones, offenders who cross the preparation line would no longer be deterred from completing the crime, since taking additional steps toward the completion of the crime would not entail a greater sanction. This argument, however, overlooks the incentives offered by the *abandonment doctrine*, whereby those charged with attempted crimes are offered a complete defense from criminal liability if they voluntary repudiate their plan.[49] In addition, this argument does not account for the fact that the probability of detection tends to rise once the crime is completed, since the police are often unaware of criminal plans that have been abandoned.

Behavioral insights offer a far more straightforward explanation for existing penal practices. One key phenomenon in this regard is the *outcome bias*—the tendency of people to judge decisions based on their outcomes.[50] There are many contexts where individuals make risky decisions that might have varying outcomes that lie beyond their control. Thus, in some cases, a prudent decision to perform surgery might lead to terrible outcomes. As Jonathan Baron and John Hershey have demonstrated, even if the probabilities associated with the decision are clear and transparent, in the aftermath people tend to judge choices that led to unfavorable outcomes more harshly than those that led to favorable outcomes. This phenomenon has been documented in numerous settings, with laypersons and experts alike.[51]

46. *See, e.g.*, Rita James Simon & Linda Mahan, *Quantifying Burdens of Proof: A View from the Bench, the Jury, and the Classroom*, 5 LAW & SOC'Y REV. 319 (1971); Norbert L. Kerr, *Severity of Prescribed Penalty and Mock Juror's Verdicts*, 36 J. PERSONALITY & SOC. PSYCHOL. 1431 (1978). *But see* Angela M. Jones, Shayne Jones & Steven Penrod, *Examining Legal Authoritarianism in the Impact of Punishment Severity on Juror Decisions*, 21 PSYCHOL. CRIME & LAW 939 (2015); Eyal Zamir, Elisha Harlev & Ilana Ritov, *New Evidence about Circumstantial Evidence*, 41 LAW & PSYCHOL. REV. 107, 138–45 (2017).

47. *See* Ehud Guttel & Doron Teichman, *Criminal Sanctions in the Defense of the Innocent*, 110 MICH. L. REV. 597, 611–20 (2012).

48. *See* Posner, *supra* note 45, at 1217–18.

49. *See* MODEL PENAL CODE §5.01(4) (Official Draft and Revised Comments, 1985).

50. *See* Jonathan Baron & John C. Hershey, *Outcome Bias in Decision Evaluation*, 54 J. PERSONALITY & SOC. PSYCHOL. 569 (1988).

51. *See* Robert A. Caplan, Karen L. Posner & Frederick W. Cheney, *Effect of Outcome on Physician Judgments of Appropriateness of Care*, 265 JAMA: J. AM. MED. ASS. 1957 (1991); Francesca Gino, Lisa L. Shu & Max H. Bazerman, *Nameless + Harmless = Blameless: When Seemingly Irrelevant Factors Influence Judgment of (Un)ethical Behavior*, 111 ORG. BEHAV. & HUM. DECISION PROCESSES 93 (2010).

A second behavioral phenomenon that may also come into play in this regard is the *fundamental attribution error* (also known as the *correspondence bias*).[52] A large body of research has shown that when people are called upon to evaluate the behavior of another actor, they tend to attribute responsibility to the actor's choices rather than to the circumstances in which the actor operated. To put it another way, people tend to link bad outcomes to *someone* rather than *something*.[53]

The outcome bias and the fundamental attribution error appear to apply to people's judgments of attempted crimes. While, under the equal punishment theory, an assassin who shoots someone with the intention to kill but fails deserves the same punishment as an assassin who succeeds, in practice—due to the outcome bias—the successful assassin is judged more harshly than the failed one. Similarly, the fundamental attribution error might influence the judgment of attempted crimes that have failed or are incomplete.[54] The tendency to underestimate the importance of external forces that lie beyond the actor's control can cause people to interpret failure of a criminal plot as a mark of lesser blame.[55]

Robinson and Darley examined this point directly by comparing people's judgment of completed and uncompleted crimes.[56] Their findings show that people assign normative weight to outcomes, and impose more severe sanctions on individuals who succeed in inflicting the harm they intended. As in the case in our general discussion of the correspondence between penal intuitions and policymaking, we are reluctant to draw sweeping normative conclusions from this result. Nonetheless, the outcome bias, coupled with the fundamental attribution error, appear to offer a strong explanation for existing legal practices.

D. Deterrence Theory and Behavioral Analysis

Since deterrence theory focuses on how the risk of penalty alters behavior, incorporating people's attitudes toward risks and their perceptions of sanctions is crucial to generating accurate predictions and desirable policy recommendations. It is here that behavioral analysis can contribute to deterrence theory by offering a richer and more nuanced model of

52. *See supra* pp. 68–69.

53. *See* Neal Feigenson, Legal Blame: How Jurors Think and Talk about Accidents 59 (2000).

54. *See* Donald A. Dripps, *Fundamental Retribution Error: Criminal Justice and the Social Psychology of Blame*, 56 Vand. L. Rev. 1383, 1401–03 (2003).

55. The mirror image of this phenomenon concerns cases involving harms that are only remotely connected to the acts perpetrated by the accused. The law aims to somewhat limit criminal responsibility for bad outcomes through the doctrine of *proximate cause*—in a bid to exclude adverse outcomes that are not sufficiently linked to the accused's alleged actions. Given the tendency to attribute responsibility to people rather than to circumstances, causation is expected to be determined in a manner that tends to broaden the scope of criminal responsibility. *See id.* at 1405.

56. *See* Paul H. Robinson & John M. Darley, *Objectivist versus Subjectivist Views of Criminality: A Study in the Role of Social Science in Criminal Law Theory*, 18 Oxford J. Legal Stud. 409 (1998).

human choice. Nonetheless, as in the case in other areas, one should be cautious when shifting from abstract psychological findings to concrete legal applications.

1. Attitudes toward Risk

The level of risk generated by the criminal justice system is endogenous, and can be changed through different policy choices. This is true with respect to enforcement policies, as the riskiness of the regime may be reduced or increased by making appropriate changes to the probability of detection and the actual penalties imposed. It is also true with respect to the structure of the legal rules governing criminal law. For example, by limiting judicial discretion, policymakers might be able to reduce inter-judge variability and reduce the risk generated by the legal system. This subsection examines what is the desirable level of risk that the criminal justice system should adopt, given the risk preferences of crime perpetrators (assuming, for the time being, that the latter are capable of perfectly assessing the risks associated with committing crimes).[57]

Within a utilitarian framework, policymakers can use the risk preferences of the perpetrators of crimes to strengthen deterrence. By adopting a penal regime that is *the opposite* of those preferences, the deterrent power of sanctions is bolstered by the added disutility. Thus, with respect to risk-averse offenders, the high-sanction-low-probability regime envisioned by many legal economists is desirable, since the high risk it entails provides further deterrence (usually, at no cost). Conversely, with regard to risk-seeking offenders, deterrence may be enhanced by increasing the certainty of punishment (albeit, possibly at the cost of increased enforcement).

The minor question that remains to be addressed is what are the risk preferences of perpetrators of crimes? The somewhat disappointing answer we put forward at this point is that it depends, and that no single general prediction can be offered that applies to all criminals and all crimes. Criminal behavior is one of those instances where a prudent application of behavioral findings requires field data—that regretfully does not exist yet—to fully understand people's decisions. Nonetheless, numerous theories have been put forward in this area, and we now turn to examine them more closely.

Let's start with basics—prospect theory.[58] In order to apply the insights of prospect theory to criminal behavior, one must determine whether criminals are operating within the domain of gains, or of losses. Since we are dealing with the analysis of penalties, it seems reasonable to assume that decision-makers are situated within the domain of losses, and are therefore expected to be risk-seeking. Alon Harel and Uzi Segal have adopted this approach, and have linked sanctions with risk-seeking behavior.[59] Accordingly, they have argued that criminals prefer a sentencing lottery over a clear and uniform sentencing regime, and therefore to enhance deterrence, the law should aim to minimize the uncertainty associated with sanctions.

57. We relax this assumption further below. *See infra* pp. 446–51.

58. *See generally supra* pp. 42–57.

59. Alon Harel & Uzi Segal, *Criminal Law and Behavioral Law and Economics: Observations on the Neglected Role of Uncertainty in Deterring Crime*, 1 AM. L. & ECON. REV. 276 (1999).

While the Harel-Segal framework is plausible, it focuses on only one aspect of the decision to commit a crime—namely, the risk of incurring sanctions. In reality, however, the decision whether to commit a crime involves a further dimension—namely, the expected benefits (i.e., gains) that the crime is expected to yield. If criminals focus on the potential gains from crime when deciding whether to engage in illegal activities, one might expect them to exhibit risk aversion[60]—and indeed, a later study conducted by Tom Baker, Alon Harel, and Tamar Kugler found experimental evidence to suggest that this is the case.[61]

We refrain from committing ourselves to either side of this debate for two reasons. First, the amount of data collected on this question is inadequate. Without a critical mass of studies with numerous settings, it is difficult to draw clear conclusions as to the relevant reference point for decision-making by criminals. Second, it may be theoretically impossible to extrapolate this point across all crimes: while in some crimes the benefits of the crime might play a central role (e.g., crimes involving tangible and immediate gains such as larceny), in others the benefits might play a relatively minor role (e.g., crimes involving contingent or vague gains such as obstruction of justice). Indeed, it is quite possible that each type of crime involves a different frame, and thus generates distinct risk preferences—not to mention the likely differences between criminals and the particular circumstances of each case.

But things get even more complicated. The association of gains with risk-averse behavior, and of losses with risk-seeking behavior, only holds in the domain of moderate-to-high probabilities. In the domain of low probabilities, these preferences invert—resulting in risk-averse behavior with respect to losses, and risk-seeking behavior with respect to gains.[62] The realities of the criminal justice system mean that there is no way to reach a general conclusion as to which of these two probability domains pertains to criminal behavior. Crime data shows that the probability of punishment varies dramatically between offenses: while perpetrators of assault, burglary, larceny, or motor vehicle theft face a probability of approximately 1 percent, those engaged in rape or homicide face probabilities of 12 and 44.7 percent, respectively.[63] Thus, in order to predict how changes in uncertainty affect behavior, one must distinguish between different types of crime (and between jurisdictions—since the cited data is only true for the United States).

Notably, the problems we have highlighted—unclear reference points and murky domains of probabilities—cannot be addressed by fine-tuning the model's predictions. Rather, a mischaracterization of the reference point or of the domain of probabilities turns the predictions of the analysis on their head. If, for instance, criminals are actually risk-averse, this would imply that uncertainty enhances deterrence, and that policymakers should adopt precisely the opposite policies of those suggested by Harel and Segal.

60. James Cox, for example, adopted this framework in his analysis of white-collar crime. *See* James D. Cox, *Private Litigation and the Deterrence of Corporate Misconduct*, 60 LAW & CONTEMP. PROBS. 1 (1997).

61. *See* Tom Baker, Alon Harel & Tamar Kugler, *The Virtues of Uncertainty in Law: An Experimental Approach*, 89 IOWA L. REV. 443, 463 (2004).

62. *See supra* p. 43.

63. *See* Robinson & Darley, *The Utility of Desert*, *supra* note 14, at 459–60.

2. Perceptions of the Risk of Punishment

Thus far, we examined the attitude of offenders to the risk of punishment. A closely related issue is the accuracy of their risk assessment. In this regard the question to be asked is: Do the perpetrators of crime accurately assess the probability of getting caught (at least on average), or do they make systematic mistakes on this front? Numerous behavioral findings suggest that criminals' perception of risk is biased, and as we shall see, this potentially has normative implications. Since deterrence is built on perception, changes in the perceived risk of punishment may have greater impact on criminal behavior than changes in the actual probability of detection.

(a) Overoptimism

One behavioral phenomenon that might influence criminals' risk-assessment is overoptimism. As described in greater detail in Chapter 2,[64] this bias relates to people's tendency to overestimate their personal abilities and prospects. From a deterrence perspective, this tendency is bad news, as it suggests that criminals systematically perceive the probability of detection to be lower than it truly is. As a result, they will assume that the costs associated with crime are lower than they actually are, and will commit more crimes than rational criminals would. The policy implication to be drawn is that sanctions must be adjusted upward to compensate for the dilution of deterrence.[65]

Interestingly, while overoptimism undermines deterrence measures, it is unclear whether it impedes crime control at a more general level. As Nuno Garoupa points out, optimistic criminals are expected to take relatively fewer precautions when committing crimes, since they misperceive the risk of getting caught.[66] Thus, they will pay less attention to surveillance cameras, to witnesses, and to other factors that might raise their risk of detection. As a result, the effective probability of detection will rise, and more criminals will be incapacitated.[67] Whether this increase in incapacitation outweighs the decrease in deterrence is an empirical question that has yet to be answered.

(b) Availability

Another behavioral phenomenon that may influence probability assessment is availability. A large body of studies has demonstrated that when individuals need to make assessments about uncertain events, they tend to base these estimates on the ease with which similar events come to mind.[68] Thus, people tend to systematically overestimate the probability that salient and vivid events will occur. For example, they might exaggerate their estimate

64. *See supra* pp. 61–64.

65. *See* Christine Jolls, Cass R. Sunstein & Richard Thaler, *A Behavioral Approach to Law and Economics*, 50 STAN. L. REV. 1471, 1538 (1998).

66. *See* Garoupa, *supra* note 4, at 9.

67. *See also infra* pp. 598–99.

68. *See supra* pp. 34–36.

of the chance of an airplane crash, simply because such events are easily remembered—that is, they are "available."

Legal scholars have incorporated availability into the design of crime-control policies. With respect to enforcement, it has been argued that authorities should make their enforcement efforts highly visible, to boost offenders' perception of the probability of detection, thereby raising deterrence. For example, it has been suggested that authorities use large, brightly colored parking tickets rather than small, unnoticeable ones.[69] Similarly, with respect to the choice of sanctions, legal scholars have argued that vividly unique penalties might generate additional deterrence. For example, Cass Sunstein and Adrian Vermeule have contended that because "executions are highly salient and cognitively available," potential criminals might overestimate their incidence.[70]

While these ideas seem plausible, given our current understanding of how availability influences decisions, they should be treated with caution. Specifically, it is not entirely clear what are the conditions that generate availability. These may include group dynamics, individual predispositions, media, and social norms.[71] If "different cultural orientations play a large role in determining what turns out to be available,"[72] then the ability to make robust predictions is rather limited. Furthermore, inasmuch as the "impact of vivid information on risk perceptions is conditional on individuals' cultural worldviews,"[73] then the ability to draw conclusions from one jurisdiction to the other is limited.

Consider the examples mentioned above. All else being equal, changing the color of parking tickets from plain white to bright colors might raise the saliency of enforcement once the change is implemented. But what would be the effect of a wide-scale saliency-assault that bombards the public with more information on the prevalence of enforcement with regard to a range of crimes? Assuming that the public does not simply filter out all this new information as annoying background noise,[74] it is unclear what its precise effect will be. We do not know which enforcement effort would become a focal point for public attention, and which will go unnoticed. To the extent that criminals would shift their activity from salient-enforcement crimes to non-salient-enforcement ones, a saliency-centered crime control policy might produce erratic substitution effects. Thus, designing a crime-control plan based on utilizing the availability bias to tackle a broad array of criminal activities might prove impossible. Similarly, while an occasional execution might serve as a vivid reminder for potential criminals of the grave consequences of crime, it is not clear whether this effect will

69. *See* Jolls, Sunstein & Thaler, *supra* note 65, at 1538.

70. Cass R. Sunstein & Adrian Vermeule, *Is Capital Punishment Morally Required? Acts, Omissions, and Life-Life Tradeoffs*, 58 Stan. L. Rev. 703, 714 (2005).

71. Cass R. Sunstein, *What's Available? Social Influences and Behavioral Economics*, 97 Nw. U. L. Rev. 1295, 1305–11 (2003).

72. Sunstein, *supra* note 71, at 1311.

73. Dan M. Kahan, *Two Conceptions of Emotion in Risk Regulation*, 156 U. Pa. L. Rev. 741, 755–56 (2008).

74. This may be seen as a condition of information overload. *See generally* Martin J. Eppler & Jeanne Mengis, *The Concept of Information Overload: A Review of Literature from Organization Science, Accounting, Marketing, MIS, and Related Disciplines*, 20 Info. Soc'y 325 (2004). *See also supra* pp. 314–18.

last over time. When dealing with crime control, an occasional policy can quickly turn into a casual one—that is to say, over time the public might grow accustomed to a certain type of punishment, which will lose its impact. This is not to say that policymakers would not be able to add interesting twists to the penal regime in order to maintain the "vividness" of the punishment (say, by shifting from boiling thieves in oil to feeding them to hungry piranhas)—although we are not sure we would endorse such policies.

Furthermore, the availability analysis overlooks other behavioral phenomena that suggest that enforcement efforts should remain subtle. One such phenomenon is *ambiguity aversion*. While people are averse to risky situations, they are even more averse to ambiguous ones—which are defined as situations in which people are not informed of the underlying probabilities.[75] For example, people systematically prefer to participate in a lottery that has a 50 percent success rate than in one that has a success rate of between 0 percent and 100 percent with equal probabilities. This finding suggests that authorities should attempt to minimize the amount of information potential criminals have about the probability of apprehension. As Harel and Segal argue, "[a]n optimal legal system is [. . .] a system that disguises as much as possible the probability of sentencing."[76] Since salient enforcement efforts are expected to increase the amount of information that potential criminals have about the risks of punishment, adopting such policies requires a careful balance that takes into account their advantages and disadvantages.

Another body of behavioral studies that bear upon enforcement policies pertains to the effect of other people's compliance with the law on one's behavior. These studies suggest that people often follow a simple rule of thumb: if everyone else does it—so will I.[77] In their seminal study on student behavior, Daniel Katz and Floyd Allport demonstrated that students who believed that their fellow students were cheating on exams were far more likely to cheat on exams themselves.[78] More recently, Bruno Frey and Benno Torgler showed that the perceived level of tax evasion affects the willingness of people to comply with the tax code.[79] These findings again suggest that making incidents of incompliance more visible might be counterproductive, since it could create a norm of noncompliance.

(c) Prediction and Postdiction

Another behavioral phenomenon that is relevant to criminal enforcement is the distinction that people draw between uncertainty about past events (*postdiction*) and uncertainty about future events (*prediction*). Psychological studies suggest that people are much less willing to bet on past events than they are on future ones.[80] When faced with two equal bets

75. *See supra* pp. 39–42.

76. Harel & Segal, *supra* note 59, at 304.

77. On the conformity effect, see also *supra* pp. 68–69, 76, 183.

78. DANIEL KATZ & FLOYD H. ALLPORT, STUDENT ATTITUDES (1931).

79. Bruno S. Frey & Benno Torgler, *Tax Morale and Conditional Cooperation*, 35 J. COMP. ECON. 136 (2007).

80. For a review, see Ehud Guttel & Alon Harel, *Uncertainty Revisited: Legal Prediction and Legal Postdiction*, 107 MICH. L. REV. 467, 471–79 (2008).

that involve the tossing of an identical die that only differ with respect to the timing of the tossing of the die—before or after the bet is placed—people prefer to bet on the future toss.

Interestingly, the decision whether or not to commit a crime might be structured as a bet involving postdiction or prediction.[81] Take, for example, the decision that a taxpayer makes on whether or not to deceive in his annual tax-return form. The current regime in the United States is based on a prediction bet, since the taxpayer must bet at the time of filing whether his return will be chosen in the audit lottery to be conducted later. However, the audit lottery could be restructured such that it is held *prior* to the filing of the annual returns. Since people tend to dislike bets about past events, this simple move may enhance deterrence at little to no cost.[82]

(d) Probability Estimates and Repeat Behavior

Thus far our analysis has focused on situations where the potential offender's decision is presented as a one-off event—for example, someone who decides only once whether to park his car illegally to obtain the illicit benefit associated with that act, with an approximate knowledge of the probability of a fine and its size. The examination of such scenarios has been carried out within experimental studies where participants were faced with a particular lottery with a given set of payoffs, and were required to make choices.

The reality of criminal offenses, however, is often somewhat different. The hypothetical parking transgressor is not faced with a one-off lottery with well-defined probabilities and rewards. Rather, he faces a repeat decision on whether or not to park illegally each time he goes downtown. Furthermore, he is not informed about the probability of being fined for illegal parking (for the present purposes, we may assume that he is perfectly informed about the size of the fine), but only learns this through experience.

Within the world of decision-making, the distinction between a one-off parking offender and a repeat parking violator may be captured by the distinction between making decisions based on *description* as opposed to *experience*.[83] While the former alludes to situations where the decision-maker makes a choice after certain risky prospects are introduced to him, the latter denotes situations where he learns of the underlying payoff structure through active choices. In the latter case, decisions are made through a learning process, as the offender tries to decide his course of action based on his past choices.

In the paradigmatic experience experiment, participants are asked to choose between two unmarked keys, and after doing so are told what the payoff for each key is. They then choose again, and their choices over time can be documented. Importantly, while people are informed that each key reflects a distinct distribution of payoffs, they are not told what

81. *Id.* at 479–98.

82. *Id.* at 487–91. While we find the idea presented by Guttel and Harel to be intriguing, we also acknowledge the practical problems that it raises. The greatest concern, perhaps, is the difficulty of concealing the identity of those to be audited, and the potential for a corrupt market of insider information.

83. *See* Ralph Hertwig & Ido Erev, *The Description—Experience Gap in Risky Choice*, 13 Trends Cognitive Sci. 517 (2009).

this distribution actually is. Ido Erev and Ernan Haruvy, for example, presented this task to two groups of subjects.[84] Subjects in the first group were asked to choose between a key that maintained the status quo (expected value = 0) and a key that included a payoff structure of −10 with a probability of 10 percent and +1 with a probability of 90 percent (expected value = −0.1). Subjects in the second group, on the other hand, were asked to choose between a key that maintained the status quo (expected value = 0), and one that offered a payoff structure of +10 with a probability of 10 percent and −1 with a probability of 90 percent (expected value = +0.1). The results show that participants in both groups deviated from the value maximizing options, but did so while exhibiting inverted risk preferences. More specifically, participants in the first group tended to prefer the risky option, while participants in the second group tended to favor the assured status quo. The results of this and other experiments on experience-based decisions suggest that when people face low-probability events in a repeated setting, they tend to underestimate those events. As the foregoing example suggests, this is true irrespective of whether the risky prospect entails a gain or a loss. Generally, people simply are inclined to behave as if they believe that "it won't happen to them."[85]

The finding that people prefer negative expected value gambles with a frequent attractive outcome has significant implications for the design of optimal criminal sanctions. The enforcement of many crimes is a relatively infrequent event.[86] This suggests that tinkering with criminal sanctions will have little effect on behavior, as people tend to discount such sanctions to zero. A more effective way to deter crime is, therefore, based on a significant (yet costly) increase of the *probability* of punishment, coupled with a decrease in its severity. As penalties become more frequent, people's underestimation of their occurrence is expected to diminish. This conclusion is in line with the bulk of the criminological literature, which suggests that certainty of sanctions has a greater impact on behavior than their magnitude,[87] and is in tension with traditional economic analysis that often highlights the cost-saving advantages of a low-detection-high-sanction regime.[88]

Finally, the insights described shed light on the importance of the *timing* of enforcement. Compliance models suggest that multiple equilibria are common in rule enforcement problems, including tax compliance and corruption.[89] In one equilibrium, obeying the rules

84. *See* Ido Erev & Ernan Haruvy, *Learning and the Economics of Small Decisions*, *in* 2 THE HANDBOOK OF EXPERIMENTAL ECONOMICS 638 (John H. Kagel & Alvin E. Roth eds., 2016).

85. *Id.* at 689.

86. For example, it has been estimated that the probability of punishment in the case of drunk driving in the United States is less than one in a thousand incidents. *See* H. LAURENCE ROSS, CONFRONTING DRUNK DRIVING: SOCIAL POLICIES FOR SAVING LIVES 61–62 (1992).

87. *See, e.g.*, Durlauf & Nagin, *supra* note 7, at 43; Daniel S. Nagin, *Deterrence: A Review of the Evidence by a Criminologist for Economists*, 5 ANN. REV. ECON. 83, 101 (2013).

88. *See* SHAVELL, *supra* note 2, at 484.

89. *See* James Alm & Michael McKee, *Tax Compliance as a Coordination Game*, 54 J. ECON. BEHAV. & ORG. 297 (2004) (tax); Christopher J. Waller, Thierry Verdier & Roy Gardner, *Corruption: Top Down or Bottom Up?*, 40 ECON. INQ. 688 (2002) (corruption).

is the norm, and enforcers can easily detect and punish deviations if they occur. Thus, no one is motivated to start violating the rule in the first place. In another equilibrium, violation is the norm, and the enforcers are unable to cope with the frequent violations. The possibility of two extreme equilibria, coupled with the hypothesis that small decisions are made based on experience in similar situations, implies that the effectiveness of enforcement policies is likely to be sensitive to the initial actions taken to combat crime. More specifically, concentrated early enforcement efforts can lead to a convergence to the "good" equilibrium in which compliance is the norm. This insight has been corroborated in a field experiment concerning behavior in campus exams,[90] which found that raising the probability of detection during the first stage of the exam (by postponing the administrative tasks the proctors had to perform during the exam) significantly reduced the incidence of cheating perceived by the students who took the exam. Note that this was achieved without raising the overall intensity of enforcement (i.e., at no cost), but simply by restructuring its temporal distribution.

3. Perceptions of Sanctions

Another way in which behavioral findings can shed light on penal policies concerns how people experience punishment itself. Traditional legal theory presumes that as the legal sanction is made more punitive, so too does the actual sanction that the transgressor experiences. Behavioral findings, however, suggest that the picture is more complex. In this subsection we first review the literature dealing with hedonic adaptation and its relationship to theories of punishment, and then examine the potential interaction between formal sanctions and internal motivations.

(a) The Hedonic Dimensions of Punishment

The focus of deterrence theory and of many retributive theories is on the subjective displeasure that is inflicted on a criminal when he or she is punished.[91] The corresponding assumption, in deterrence theory and in retributive theories alike, is that "more is more"—that is, pain increases with the severity of sanctions, and accordingly so does their deterrent effect or retributive power. Of course, this does not mean that the relationship between severity of sanctions and the level of pain is necessarily linear. It may well be that, due to the discounting of future years, prison sentences exhibit diminishing marginal returns. But this premise does imply that any increase in sanctions will result in at least some increase in the suffering they cause, thus reflecting a greater punitive reaction.

90. *See* Ido Erev et al., *Continuous Punishment and the Potential of Gentle Rule Enforcement*, 84 Behav. Processes 366, 370 (2010).

91. Deterrence theory focuses on incentives, so the manner in which offenders experience penalties is an integral part of it. Retributive theories, in contrast, are far more complex in this regard. While some incorporate the subjective experience of punishment, others evaluate policies through an objective prism. *See, e.g.*, Adam Kolber, *The Subjective Experience of Punishment*, 109 Colum. L. Rev. 182 (2009); Dan Markel & Chad Flanders, *Bentham on Stilts: The Bare Relevance of Subjectivity to Retributive Justice*, 98 Cal. L. Rev. 97 (2010); Harel, *supra* note 4, at 591–94.

At a first glance, the assumption that increased sanctions generate greater discomfort seems completely realistic. Most people probably perceive a thousand dollar fine to be worse than a hundred dollar one, and would prefer to spend one year behind bars rather than two. Several bodies of behavioral research, however, suggest that the more-is-more premise requires closer scrutiny. Specifically, research findings of *hedonic adaptation*, *affective forecasting*, and *duration neglect* suggest, somewhat counterintuitively, that extended prison sentences do not cause more suffering than shorter sentences, and in retrospect may even be recalled as less harsh.[92]

Hedonic adaptation refers to people's tendency to adjust to new situations, such that even dramatic changes in their lives produce relatively minor changes in their subjective well-being.[93] While in the short run people's happiness might be influenced by positive and negative events alike, in the long run they tend to revert to their happiness "set-point," even in the face of significant life events.[94] In one classic study, researchers compared the happiness levels of three groups—lottery winners, accident victims (paraplegics or quadriplegics), and a control group. The three groups reported surprisingly similar happiness measures, reflecting a tendency to converge toward their long-term well-being level.[95]

Hedonic adaptation suggests that penalties may lack the bite that the law attributes to them.[96] If people's long-term happiness remains stable over time, the assumption that policymakers can increase the severity of sanctions by ratcheting up sentences is unrealistic. Moreover, even if one assumes that the collateral effects of imprisonment cause people's happiness set-point to reset downward (because, for example, prison causes their spousal relationship to collapse),[97] this poses a serious problem for most penal theories, since it suggests that punishment is not a well-behaved continuous variable. Rather, it is more likely that up to a certain threshold, increasing prison terms does not create long-term disutility, and beyond that threshold the drop in utility is sudden and one-off. From a deterrence perspective, this suggests that it is impossible to fine-tune the calibration of sanctions to account for different levels of detection and harm. As for subjective retributive theories of punishment, if all sentences beyond a certain threshold result in more or less the same decline in welfare, the criminal justice system cannot tailor sanctions in proportion to wrongfulness and culpability.

92. For an extended discussion of this point, including its implications for various theories of punishment, see John Bronsteen, Christopher Buccafusco & Jonathan Masur, *Happiness and Punishment*, 76 U. CHI. L. REV. 1037 (2009).

93. *See*, in greater detail, *supra* pp. 343–48.

94. *See* Sonja Lyubomirsky, *Hedonic Adaption to Positive and Negative Experiences*, *in* THE OXFORD HANDBOOK OF STRESS, HEALTH AND COPING 200 (Susan Folkman ed., 2010).

95. *See* Philip Brickman, Dan Coates & Ronnie Janoff-Bulman, *Lottery Winners and Accident Victims: Is Happiness Relative?*, 36 J. PERSONALITY & SOC. PSYCHOL. 917, 918–21 (1978).

96. *See* Robinson & Darley, *supra* note 32, at 188–89.

97. *See* Richard E. Lucas, *Time Does Not Heal All Wounds: A Longitudinal Study of Reaction and Adaptation to Divorce*, 16 PSYCHOL. SCI. 945 (2005) (reporting on a long-term decline in happiness level as a result of divorce).

As further elaborated in the discussion of hedonic damages, these observations lose much of their validity—from a retributive perspective, at least—if one adopts a preference-satisfaction or an objective-list theory of human well-being instead of a hedonic theory approach.[98] Moreover, these observations do not invalidate the basic relationship between incarceration and deterrence. The years spent behind bars are unpleasant, and more of those years undoubtedly entails more unpleasantness. Furthermore, as the studies on affective forecasting show, people are not very good at predicting their ability to adapt to changing circumstances.[99] Rather, they think that they will be happier if they win the lottery, and that their long-term welfare will drastically diminish if they are seriously injured. In the world of general deterrence, which is governed by the *perceptions* of sanctions, this means that people will continue to be deterred because they think (however erroneously) that greater sanctions will have graver consequences.[100]

While hedonic adaption challenges the "more is more" assumption, it does not suggest that more might be less. Research on patterns of memories of experiences, however, suggests that longer prison sentences might actually be perceived by criminals as less harsh than short sentences. The implicit assumption of penal theories is that people experience prison by aggregating the disutility that they experience there—but behavioral findings on duration neglect show that people recall unpleasant experiences in a distinct fashion. People judge experiences according to a *peak-end rule*—that is, they focus on the most intense point of the experience, and on its ending. Daniel Kahneman and his colleagues demonstrated this phenomenon in a neatly designed experiment that examined people's willingness to tolerate pain.[101] Participants in this study endured an unpleasant experience in the form of immersing their arms in cold water. The submerging took two forms (which were alternated): one consisted of submerging the arm in water at a temperature of 14° C for sixty seconds, while the other involved the same procedure plus an *additional* thirty seconds in which—unbeknown to participants—the water temperature was slightly raised (albeit still uncomfortably cold). After these two unpleasant experiences, the participants were asked which of the two they would prefer to endure again. Since the ninety-second experience included all of the discomfort associated with the sixty-second experience and then some, one might expect that participants who aim to minimize total displeasure would strictly prefer the sixty-second experience. In fact, however, the experiment found that most participants compared the two experiences based on their respective endings, which was less painful in the ninety-second experience—resulting in 69 percent of the subjects opting to reiterate the ninety-second experience.

98. *See supra* pp. 347–48.

99. *See* Timothy D. Wilson et al., *Focalism: A Source of Durability Bias in Affective Forecasting*, 78 J. Personality & Soc. Psychol. 821 (2000); Timothy D. Wilson & Daniel T. Gilbert, *Affective Forecasting*, *in* 35 Advances in Experimental Social Psychology 345 (Mark P. Zanna ed., 2003).

100. *See* McAdams & Ulen, *supra* note 4. And, of course, the findings of hedonic adaptation do not bear upon other goals of incarceration, such as incapacitation.

101. Daniel Kahneman et al., *When More Pain Is Preferred to Less: Adding a Better End*, 4 Psychol. Sci. 401 (1993).

Duration neglect poses a considerable challenge to the notion of punishment based on prolonged prison terms. Studies have shown that prison is experienced much like the ninety-second treatment in the above experiment. While all the time in prison is unpleasant, it is the initial stage of incarceration that is worst.[102] After the initial shock, inmates begin to adapt to their new environment as their coping mechanisms kick in. They develop new social contacts, become accustomed to the living conditions, and after a few years may even get to sleep in the coveted lower bunk. This implies that people might recall their time in prison based on the least painful part of it. As a result, extending prison sentences might actually undermine deterrence, since people will view prison in a better light. Again, however, one should note that this critique pertains to people who have actually experienced incarceration, rather than to the public at large, as it captures how people recall their own experiences. The general public who has not experienced prison is still expected to view longer prison terms as worse than shorter ones.

Finally, one should note that the analysis in this subsection takes existing incarceration practices as given. One could, of course, use the insights presented here to promote reforms in the system, which are geared toward intensifying the suffering induced by punishments. According to some scholars, the only way the criminal justice system can overcome the problem created by duration neglect is by employing "torture" as a form of punishment.[103] This may be an overkill: there are many incarceration regimes involving increasingly harsh conditions (e.g., food quality, visitation rights, etc.) that maintain unpleasant memories from one's time in prison, without resorting to torture. In addition, one can deny prisoners the chance of acclimatizing to their conditions and gaining social capital in prison by constantly shifting them between different facilities after relatively short periods of time. Thus, carefully crafted penal policies could increase the impact of incarceration, while respecting the human dignity of offenders and avoiding delving into the abyss of torture.

(b) Formal Sanctions and Internal Motivations

Wrongful behavior is often regulated both by law, with its formal sanctions, and by internal motivations. It is the combined impact of these external and internal forces that drives people's choices. Penal theories have long since incorporated this insight, and have examined how formal sanctions should be designed, given the existence of additional mechanisms that operate side by side with the law.[104]

The more-is-more premise regarding criminal penalties presupposes that changes in the legal sanctions do not alter other motivational forces. Research on the motivational *crowding out effect*, however, suggests that formal incentive mechanisms might undermine intrinsic motivations to behave in a prosocial manner.[105] For example, it has been

102. *See, e.g.*, Edward Zamble, *Behavior and Adaptation in Long-Term Prison Inmates: Descriptive Longitudinal Results*, 19 CRIM. JUST. & BEHAV. 409 (1992).

103. *See* Robinson & Darley, *supra* note 32, at 191.

104. *See, e.g.*, Doron Teichman, *Sex, Shame, and the Law: An Economic Perspective on Megan's Laws*, 42 HARV. J. ON LEGIS. 355, 357–78 (2005).

105. For a review, see Bruno S. Frey & Reto Jegen, *Motivation Crowding Out*, 15 J. ECON. SURV. 589 (2001).

hypothesized that paying people for their blood might reduce or even eliminate the altruistic motivation to donate.[106] Similarly, it is possible that formal punishments might crowd out intrinsic motivations.

A field experiment conducted by Uri Gneezy and Aldo Rustichini at a daycare center in Israel corroborated this hypothesis.[107] The experiment examined the effect of introducing a monetary fine for late arrivals on the tendency of parents to pick up their children on time.[108] After the introduction of the fine, the researchers observed a steady *increase* in the number of parents arriving late. This result runs counter to traditional deterrence models, which predict that increasing the cost of an activity decreases its incidence (the "more is more" principle). Apparently, the introduction of the fine changed the parents' perception of the social dynamic between themselves and the daycare center. To put it another way, the parents appear to view the fine as a price for arriving late—so as long as they paid the price for such behavior, they no longer felt guilty for doing so.

Admittedly, one should be careful not to overgeneralize this finding. Fines differ from the setup of the experiment designed by Gneezy and Rustichini in two respects. First, the imposition of the fine in the experiment was certain: all the parents knew that they would be fined, each time they arrived late. In most real-world situations, however, fines are imposed probabilistically. Second, the payment of the fine was made directly to the entity harmed by the transgression. Fines, on the other hand, are usually paid to the state, rather than to the victims. Together, these features arguably made the fine in this experiment look much like a contractual price.

Empirical evidence suggests that people have a nuanced view of legal tools that impose monetary costs, in a manner that is attuned to the above two aspects.[109] At one end of the spectrum of legal payment mechanisms are tools that are similar in structure to a paradigmatic price. These are payments made to another private party in advance. At the other end of the spectrum are legal payments that are similar in structure to the paradigmatic punishment. These are payments that are made to the state after the fact, and are imposed probabilistically. As legal payments shift from the price end of the spectrum to its punishment end, people begin to see the payment-triggering activity as less moral, and are less inclined to engage in it.

E. Behavioral Ethics—Predicting When Crime Is More Likely

In the previous section we examined how the insights of cognitive psychology can shed light on the design of penal policies aimed at deterrence and retribution. In this section we

106. *See* Richard M. Titmuss, The Gift Relationship (1971).

107. Uri Gneezy & Aldo Rustichini, *A Fine Is a Price*, 29 J. Legal Stud. 1 (2000).

108. *Id.* at 4–5.

109. Yuval Feldman & Doron Teichman, *Are All Legal Dollars Created Equal?*, 102 Nw. U. L. Rev. 223 (2008).

turn to examine the contribution of behavioral ethics to the discussion of crime control.[110] The gist of this line of research is that most people wish to view their behavior as moral and worthy, and do not utilize every opportunity they have to enhance their own welfare—that is, most people are "good" and not evil. As a result, people's tendency to engage in antisocial behavior increases when they feel that they can justify their (selfish) choice. As George Costanza eloquently put it in his explanation to Jerry Seinfeld how to defeat a lie-detector test: "Jerry, just remember [. . .] It's not a lie [. . .] if you believe it."[111]

Behavioral economists and psychologists have studied the conditions in which people are more likely to believe that their lies are not really lies—or, more generally, that their self-serving choices are justifiable. A key point in this regard is the degree of malleability of the situation. For people to interpret their actions in a self-serving manner, these actions must reflect at least some moral ambiguity that can be used to justify their behavior. While one might be able to rationalize to oneself the theft of office supplies from one's employer (e.g., "I was going to bring it back," "I use my private pen for work—so this is payback"), it is much more difficult justifying the theft of money from one's employer's cash register. By identifying these conditions, one can pinpoint situations where the probability of wrongdoing is greater.

Once the circumstances in which wrongful behavior is more likely to occur are identified, two policy avenues emerge to deal with them. The first addresses such situations by targeting deterrence efforts at them. For example, additional enforcement resources might be allocated to boost the chances of detecting offenders. Alternatively, policymakers might try to redesign the decision-making environment such that it reduces the ability of people to justify wrongful choices to themselves, or bolsters their motivations to act morally. For example, researchers have demonstrated that requiring people to recall the Ten Commandments reduced their tendency to cheat.[112] This effect was independent of the level of recall demonstrated—suggesting that it was driven by drawing people's attention to morality in general, rather than by activating religious beliefs. In the following subsections we examine more closely specific findings from the area of behavioral ethics, and highlight their potential implications with regard to crime control.

1. Factual Ambiguity

As noted above, situations that are somewhat ambiguous can allow people to interpret that ambiguity in a self-serving manner. This implies that minor changes in the decision-making environment might influence the level of crime. Once we are no longer in a paradigmatic criminal fact pattern (e.g., Dan steals Ariel's wallet), the psychological mechanism described above can kick in.

110. On behavioral ethics, see generally *supra* pp. 72–76.

111. *Seinfeld* (NBC television broadcast Feb. 9, 1995) (season 6, episode 16).

112. Nina Mazar, On Amir & Dan Ariely, *The Dishonesty of Honest People: A Theory of Self-Concept Maintenance*, 45 J. MARKETING RES. 633, 635–36 (2008).

Nina Mazar, On Amir, and Dan Ariely demonstrated this point in a simple stylized experiment.[113] Participants in this experiment were asked to complete a mathematical task and were paid according to their performance. The experiment was structured such that participants were randomly assigned to one of three groups: (1) a control group in which the experimenter examined their answers and paid them in cash; (2) a cash-cheating group in which participants self-reported their results and were immediately paid in cash; and (3) a token-cheating group that was identical to group (2) but for the fact that participants received from the experimenter tokens that seconds later were redeemed to cash. Introducing tokens into the experiment significantly increased people's willingness to overstate their achievements and cheat. As the authors note, tokens allowed participants to "interpret their dishonesty in a more self-serving manner, thus reducing the negative self-signal they otherwise would have received."[114]

Moving from the lab to the world of crime, this finding suggests that as crime becomes more detached from the clear immoral act of harming another person, people's willingness to engage in it might grow. Take, for example, white-collar crime. In recent years numerous financial scandals have caused tremendous harm to large numbers of people. In some instances, these scandals involved the funneling of billions of dollars from investors and homeowners to corrupt managers. It is quite possible that the abstract nature of modern financial markets and the securities sold within them lend themselves to a process of rationalizing within which stealing is deemed not stealing by people who truly believe it.[115]

2. Legal Ambiguity

At times the ambiguity of the situation stems from the law governing it. Law is inherently uncertain. This uncertainty may result from various sources, including the limitation of the language to capture every potential occurrence. For example, it might be unclear whether a law that forbids "vehicles" from entering into a park applies to bicycles, roller skates, or even toy automobiles.[116] Thus, bicycle drivers who need to decide whether to drive through the park face uncertainty as to the legal ramifications of their choice. Another source of uncertainty is the common use of legal standards that depend on an ex-post evaluation of the circumstances to determine legal liability, such as "negligence," "good faith," and "fair use." Hence, for example, a driver who decides whether to drive in a risky fashion often does not know whether his choice constitutes a violation of the governing legal standard.

Expected utility theory predicts that one's decision whether to violate a norm depends on the expected sanction, which in turn depends on the probability of being sanctioned. Behavioral ethics predicts that not only the sheer probability, but also the source of

113. *Id.* at 637–38.

114. *Id.* at 638.

115. Max H. Bazerman & Francesca Gino, *Behavioral Ethics: Toward a Deeper Understanding of Moral Judgment and Dishonesty*, 8 Ann. Rev. L. & Soc. Sci. 85, 95–6 (2012) (linking part of the Bernard Madoff's Ponzi scheme to behavioral ethics).

116. Alluding to Hart's famous example in H.L.A. Hart, *Positivism and the Separation of Law from Morals*, 71 Harv. L. Rev. 593, 607 (1958).

uncertainty about the sanction matters. Vague legal norms lend themselves to motivated reasoning.[117] Once the governing norm allows for some normative wiggle room, people might use this wiggle room in their favor. Yuval Feldman and Doron Teichman demonstrated this in a series of experiments that examined people's willingness to engage in harmful behavior.[118] These experiments held the expected sanction constant, yet manipulated the source of uncertainty. Whereas for some subjects it stemmed from uncertain enforcement, for others it stemmed from legal uncertainty. The results showed that participants in the groups involving legal uncertainty exhibited a greater willingness to engage in the harmful behavior, suggesting that ambiguous legal norms might be interpreted in a self-serving manner.

This finding has various normative implications.[119] For example, it sheds a behavioral light on the discussion over the trade-off between uncertain law and uncertain enforcement as policy tools aimed at enhancing compliance. This general question has drawn particular attention in the tax compliance literature.[120] The gist of the argument when framed in purely rational choice terms is that legal uncertainty is simply another probability lumped into the expected sanction, and does not influence behavior aside from discounting sanctions. As a result, under certain conditions elevating legal uncertainty might be useful from a deterrence perspective. Conversely, from a behavioral perspective, legal uncertainty alters people's decisions in a much more fundamental way, as it opens the door for a psychological process that licenses antisocial behavior. As a result, compliance might be undermined by legal uncertainty.[121]

3. Driving Forces

Thus far we have focused on the act of rationalizing, without paying attention to the motivating factors that drive people to use ambiguity to further their self-interest. Obviously, this is a complex question with numerous answers, all of which have yet to be mapped. Nonetheless, several mediating factors have been documented as influencing this process.

First, several studies have demonstrated the role of *loss aversion* in people's ethical decisions.[122] In one experiment, subjects had to complete an extremely difficult task—either to earn (in the gain frame), or to avoid losing (in the loss frame), a certain amount of money. While cheating was equally easy in both conditions, participants were much more prone to

117. *See generally supra* pp. 242, 321–22.

118. Yuval Feldman & Doron Teichman, *Are All Legal Probabilities Created Equal?*, 84 N.Y.U. L. REV. 980 (2009).

119. *Id.* at 1009–19.

120. The policy debate was formally framed in Suzanne Scotchmer & Joel Slemrod, *Randomness in Tax Enforcement*, 38 J. PUB. ECON. 17 (1989). For later economic treatment of the issue, see, e.g., James Alm, Betty Jackson & Michael McKee, *Institutional Uncertainty and Tax Payer Compliance*, 82 AM. ECON. REV. 1018 (1992); James Andreoni, Brian Erard & Jonathan Feinstein, *Tax Compliance*, 36 J. ECON. LITERATURE 818, 852–53 (1998).

121. Rational choice analysis has also underlined the adverse effects of legal uncertainty in settings where uncertainty is linked to the compliance decision (e.g., when enforcement is targeted at those who deviate more from the standard, or when greater sanctions are imposed upon them). *See* Scott Baker & Alex Raskolnikov, *Harmful, Harmless, and Beneficial Uncertainty in Law*, 46 J. LEGAL STUD. 281 (2017).

122. For an overview, see EYAL ZAMIR, LAW, PSYCHOLOGY, AND MORALITY 31–33 (2015).

cheating in the loss condition.[123] In an earlier experiment, conducted with experienced tax preparers, subjects were significantly more inclined to sign off on a tax return that exploited an ambiguity in tax legislation in order to keep an existing client (a loss framing) than to win a potential new client (a gain framing).[124] More generally, a host of empirical and experimental studies have shown that tax compliance is higher when, following over-withholding taxpayers expect a refund (a gain frame), than when, after under-withholding, they expect to pay additional sums (a loss frame).[125] It has also been shown that people with unmet goals (which serve as reference points) were more likely to engage in unethical behavior than those seeking to do their best.[126] In keeping with the literature on goal-setting,[127] the tendency to behave unethically was particularly strong when people fell just short of reaching their goals.

A second mediating factor that might play a role in the process of motivated reasoning is people's perception of their relative financial standing. People constantly measure their financial well-being based on objective measures such as their income, and subjective measures such as expectations. Within this process, social comparisons play a significant role. If people feel that their financial situation is inferior to that of their peers, they will experience financial deprivation. Furthermore, research on financial deprivation suggests that when this type of feeling is triggered, it alters people's choices. For example, people who feel financially deprived have been shown to increase their consumption of scarce goods that other consumers do not possess in order to avoid comparisons.[128]

More recently, researchers have shown that financial deprivation can affect people's inclination to behave unethically.[129] Subjects in these experiments were first randomly

123. Jessica S. Cameron & Dale T. Miller, *Ethical Standards in Gain versus Loss Frames*, *in* Psychological Perspectives on Ethical Behavior and Decision Making 91 (David De Cremer ed., 2009).

124. Kaye J. Newberry, Philip M.J. Reckers & Robert W. Wyndelts, *An Examination of Tax Practitioner Decisions: The Role of Preparer Sanctions and Framing Effects Associated with Client Condition*, 14 J. Econ. Psychol. 439 (1993).

125. *See, e.g.*, Paul Corcoro & Peter Adelsheim, *A Balance Due before Remittance: The Effect on Reporting Compliance*, *in* Recent Research on Tax Administration and Compliance: Selected Papers Given at the 2010 IRS Research Conference (2010), *available at:* http://www.irs.gov/pub/irs-soi/10rescon.pdf (empirical data); Dennis R. Schmidt, *The Prospects of Taxpayer Agreement with Aggressive Tax Advice*, 22 J. Econ. Psychol. 157 (2001) (experimental findings); Erich Kirchler & Boris Maciejovsky, *Tax Compliance within the Context of Gain and Loss Situations, Expected and Current Asset Position, and Profession*, 22 J. Econ. Psychol. 173 (2001) (same); Kathleen DeLaney Thomas, *Presumptive Collection: A Prospect Theory Approach to Increasing Small Business Tax Compliance*, 67 Tax L. Rev. 111 (2014) (an overview).

126. Maurice E. Schweitzer, Lisa Ordóñez & Bambi Douma, *Goal Setting as a Motivator of Unethical Behavior*, 47 Acad. Mgmt. J. 422 (2004).

127. *See, e.g.*, Chip Heath, Richard P. Larrick & George Wu, *Goals as Reference Points*, 38 Cognitive Psychol. 79 (1999).

128. *See* Eesha Sharma & Adam L. Alter, *Financial Deprivation Prompts Consumers to Seek Scarce Goods*, 39 J. Consumer Res. 545 (2012).

129. *See* Eesha Sharma et al., *Financial Deprivation Selectively Shifts Moral Standards and Compromises Moral Decisions*, 123 Org. Behav. & Hum. Decision Processes 90 (2014); Leslie K. John, George Loewenstein & Scott I. Rick, *Cheating More for Less: Upward Social Comparisons Motivate the Poorly Compensated to Cheat*, 123 Org. Behav. & Hum. Decision Processes 101 (2014).

assigned to different conditions, including a task that caused half of them to feel financially deprived. After this initial task, subjects were presented with a second task that included an opportunity to cheat in order to boost their payoff from the experiment. Subjects who were made to feel deprived in the first task were significantly more likely to cheat in the second task. Relatedly, Francesco Gino and Lamar Pierce have demonstrated that merely putting a pile of $7,000 in cash in the center of the room in which the experiment was conducted was sufficient to bring about a significant increase in the incidence of cheating.[130] As they note, the presence of wealth in the decision-making environment can "push individuals beyond an ethical tipping point, corrupting them into fraud."[131]

These findings have potential policy implications at both the micro and the macro level. At the micro level, they suggest that potential victims should be attuned to situations that might generate feelings of financial deprivation. For example, an employer who decides to cut the wages of her employees should realize that this cut might increase the risk of employee theft.[132] This effect might, in turn, be diminished by explaining to the employees the reasons leading to the pay cut in a sensitive manner[133] (unless, of course, the reason is greed—in which case increased investment in detection might be a superior option). At the macro level, these findings suggest a potential connection between growing inequality and crime. According to this line of thought, progressive taxation may prove to be an effective crime control tool.[134]

Another mediating factor that may spur unethical behavior is competition. In an elegantly designed experiment, Amos Schurr and Ilana Ritov asked subjects to report the result of a toss of two concealed dice that only the subjects could observe.[135] The reported result of the toss served as a measurement of subjects' ethicality, since overstating the result of the toss increased one's own payoff at the expense of another participant. Interestingly, participants who were victorious in a preliminary competitive task exhibited a tendency to overstate the result of the dice toss. While the losers' mean reported toss was 6.35, the winners' mean reported toss was 8.75—significantly higher than both the losers' mean and the expected mean (7). Schurr and Ritov explain this result by the sense of entitlement that victory in the competition can generate. In light of the central role that competition plays in the distribution of power in both markets (within and between firms) and politics, it is very possible that those in power are the most prone to exhibit unethical behavior.

130. *See* Francesca Gino & Lamar Pierce, *The Abundance Effect: Unethical Behavior in the Presence of Wealth*, 109 ORG. BEHAV. & HUM. DECISION PROCESSES 142 (2009).

131. *Id.* at 152.

132. Jerald Greenberg, *Employee Theft as a Reaction to Underpayment Inequity: The Hidden Cost of Pay Cuts*, 75 J. APP. PSYCHOL. 561 (1990).

133. *Id.*

134. *See* Sharma et al., *supra* note 129, at 99.

135. *See* Amos Schurr & Ilana Ritov, *Winning a Competition Predicts Dishonest Behavior*, 113 PROC. NAT'L ACAD. SCI. USA 1754 (2016).

Finally, aside from the foregoing psychological factors, an emerging body of research has started to draw a causal link between people's physiological condition and unethical behavior.[136] Generally, this body of work suggests that as people's physical resources are depleted, their ability to exert self-control diminishes. Consequently, people who are physically deprived (hungry, tired, etc.) have a greater tendency to act immorally. For example, it has been shown that dishonest behavior is more prevalent in the afternoon than in the morning.[137] While one can perhaps draw policy recommendations from this body of work (the behaviorally inclined police chief will probably consider adding patrols right before dinnertime), we are somewhat reluctant to go that far at this early stage.[138]

F. Punishing Recidivists

Having dealt with policies geared toward "good" people who do bad things under certain conditions, we turn to "bad" people who do many bad things—criminal recidivists. Dealing with repeat offenders properly is of great importance, as this small group of people is responsible for a disproportionate share of the crime pie. In Sweden, for example, researchers have found that 1 percent of the population is responsible for 63 percent of the violent crimes committed in the country.[139]

Given the importance of recidivism, it is not surprising that defendants' criminal history is a key factor in determining the severity of their punishment.[140] All else being equal, repeat offenders are subject to harsher penalties than people who committed an identical crime for the first time. Statutory enhancements of punishment for recidivists are widespread. Throughout the United States, for instance, all state sentencing guidelines adjust the grading of an offense upward in cases where the offender has a criminal record.[141] Moreover,

136. *See, e.g.*, Christopher M. Barnes et al., *Lack of Sleep and Unethical Conduct*, 115 Org. Behav. & Hum. Decision Processes 169 (2011) (sleep deprivation); Kai Chi Yam, Scott J. Reynolds & Jacob B. Hirsh, *The Hungry Thief: Physiological Deprivation and Its Effects on Unethical Behavior*, 125 Org. Behav. & Hum. Decision Processes 123 (2014) (food deprivation); Nicole L. Mead et al., *Too Tired to Tell the Truth: Self-Control Resource Depletion and Dishonesty*, 45 J. Exp. Soc. Psychol. 594 (2009) (exhausting additional task); Francesca Gino, *Unable to Resist Temptation: How Self-Control Depletion Promotes Unethical Behavior*, 115 Org. Behav. & Hum. Decision Processes 191 (2011) (same).

137. *See* Maryam Kouchaki & Isaac H. Smith, *The Morning Morality Effect: The Influence of Time of Day on Unethical Behavior*, 25 Psychol. Sci. 95 (2013).

138. At a broader level, research has linked poverty to rationality, suggesting that growing up in an impoverished environment might limit people's impulse control due to physiological changes to the brain. *See* Stephanie Plamondon Bair, *Dynamic Rationality*, Ohio St. L.J. (forthcoming, working paper, May 2017, *available at*: https://ssrn.com/abstract=2974416). However, given the complex causal relationships associated with these findings, we find it difficult to endorse specific policies based on them.

139. Örjan Fank et al., *The 1% of the Population Accountable for 63% of All Violent Crime Convictions*, 49 Soc. Psychiatry & Psychiatric Epidemiology 559 (2014).

140. *See* Julian V. Roberts, *The Role of Criminal Record in the Sentencing Process*, 22 Crime & Just. 303, 304 (1997); Bureau of Justice Assistance, National Assessment of Structured Sentencing 67 (1996).

141. Michael H. Tonry, The Future of Imprisonment 97 (2004).

several states have adopted specific statutes that prescribe mandatory enhanced penalties for habitual criminals.[142]

While this legal regime may seem intuitive, its justification is not completely clear. If the legal system focuses on efficient deterrence—which suggests focusing on social harm and on the probability of detection—there is no reason to view a repeat offense as worthy of greater punishment. In fact, a case can be made for the precise opposite claim: since the probability of detection is greater when the offender has a criminal record (since his DNA and fingerprints are in the system, and the police immediately check his whereabouts at the time of the crime, etc.), such an individual should arguably be subject to a *lesser* sanction when caught.[143] Retributivists have also struggled with this point, since—from a just-deserts perspective—"a person who robs another of $20 at gun point is no more blameworthy simply because she had five years earlier been convicted of burglary."[144]

Rational choice theory has nonetheless offered several explanations for the existing legal regime. One of these theories focuses on deterrence and the need to tailor sanctions, while taking into account the propensity of individual offenders to commit crimes.[145] According to this theory, individuals who are repeatedly convicted are likely to exhibit a greater propensity to offend. If John continues to possess commercial amounts of an illegal substance after being punished, one may assume that the punishment he had incurred was insufficient to deter him, given the utility he derives from the crime. By reserving severe sanctions only for such individuals, the criminal justice system can effectively price-discriminate and use expensive and grave sanctions only in a small subset of cases. Another theory is based on the adjudication process, and the potential for judicial errors.[146] According to this approach, the more convictions an offender incurs, the lesser the chance that this person might be wrongly convicted. If Mark repeatedly leaves the supermarket with unpaid goods in his shopping cart, then the third time this happens a sentencing judge may be relatively certain that this was not an honest mistake. Thus, while sanctions in early cases might be discounted due to the risk of a wrongful conviction, this discount should not be applied in the case of recidivists.

Behavioral analysis offers yet another justification for the existing regime. Ehud Guttel and Alon Harel have linked current penal policies toward recidivists with the phenomenon of *probability matching*—namely, the tendency to adopt a mixed strategy based on the distribution of payoffs, rather than a pure strategy focused on the utility maximizing option. In other words, when faced with a repeated gamble with consistent payoffs of 70 percent

142. These laws are often referred to as "three strike" laws. For a comparative description, see JOHN CLARCK ET AL., U.S. DEP'T OF JUSTICE, "THREE STRIKES AND YOU'RE OUT": A REVIEW OF STATE LEGISLATION 6 (1997).

143. David A. Dana, *Rethinking the Puzzle of Escalating Penalties for Repeat Offenders*, 110 YALE L.J. 733, 736 (2001).

144. *See* Markus Dirk Dubber, *Recidivist Statutes as Arational Punishment*, 43 BUFF. L. REV. 689, 705 (1995).

145. *See* A. Mitchell Polinsky & Daniel L. Rubinfeld, *A Model of Optimal Fines for Repeat Offenders*, 46 J. PUB. ECON. 291 (1991).

146. *See* Ariel Rubinstein, *An Optimal Conviction Policy for Offenses That May Have Been Committed by Accident*, *in* APPLIED GAME THEORY 406 (S.J. Brams, A. Schotter & G. Schwodiauer eds., 1979).

Red and 30 percent Blue, people do not choose Red every time, even though this is the utility maximizing strategy. Rather, every so often they choose Blue, to match the underlying distribution of payoffs. As Guttel and Harel's analysis shows, offenders who repeatedly decide whether to commit a crime might not be deterred by optimally designed sanctions that are expected to bring about complete compliance. Unlike one-shot offenders who will analyze the situation rationally and refrain from committing the crime (i.e., always bet Red), repeat offenders might adopt a mixed strategy based on probability matching that involves committing the crime sporadically (i.e., betting Blue once in a while). Once the law identifies such individuals, the effective route is to increase their penalties, in order to deter them as well.

The above analysis looked exclusively at the behavior of offenders. As previously noted,[147] however, studies focused on commonly perceived notions of justice have suggested that people are reluctant to increase the punishment of an individual defendant based on his perceived danger to society. This divergence may serve as an illustration of the complex nature of the behavioral analysis of criminal law and enforcement.

G. Conclusion

Behavioral analysis has covered significant ground in the area of criminal law and enforcement. It has broadened our understanding of the interaction between expected sanctions and the population of potential criminals, and of the interface between criminal law and commonly held perceptions of justice. Ultimately, behavioral analysis appears to demonstrate the shortcomings of traditional models of deterrence that assume perfect rationality. That said, one must also acknowledge that behavioral analysis does not provide a clear alternative model to guide policymakers engaged in structuring the criminal justice system. This is not to say that behavioral analysis has failed in this regard: crime is a complex human phenomenon, driven by numerous psychological, sociological, economic, and physiological forces. This complexity, in turn, suggests that it is unrealistic to expect any single model to offer policymakers anywhere in the world, in any given period (or even a single policymaker at a specific point in time) answers to all their questions. The most that behavioral analysis can aspire to is to enrich existing policy debates and to highlight potential paths that the criminal justice system might consider pursuing.

147. *See supra* p. 438.

13

Tax Law and Redistribution

A. Introduction

Taxes are used to finance governmental expenditures. Concomitantly, they influence economic growth and the distribution of burdens and benefits among different segments of society. They create incentives and disincentives for a great many activities, including acquiring knowledge and skills, joining the workforce, consumption, designing transactions and investments, saving for old age, conserving energy, smoking, and even marriage and childbearing. The popular demand for governmental services, coupled with the common dislike of paying taxes, make tax policies a highly controversial political issue in any society.

Economists, lawyers, and legal economists have studied the tax system for a long time. In 1994, Edward McCaffery called attention to the various ways in which behavioral insights can contribute to positive and normative analyses of the tax system, and set an agenda for empirical and normative study of this field.[1] Since then, experimental studies have specifically studied how various heuristics and biases affect people's judgments and decisions about tax and tax-related matters. These studies have found that people's judgments and decisions about tax exhibit framing effects,[2] and display an isolation (or disaggregation) effect.[3] People prefer "hidden" taxes,[4] and underreact to non-salient ones.[5] People's judgments depend on the metric used to present the data (percentage versus absolute

1. Edward J. McCaffery, *Cognitive Theory and Tax*, 41 UCLA L. Rev.1861 (1994).

2. Edward J. McCaffery & Jonathan Baron, *Framing and Taxation: Evaluation of Tax Policies Involving Household Composition*, 25 J. Econ. Psychol. 679 (2004).

3. Edward J. McCaffery & Jonathan Baron, *The Humpty-Dumpty Blues: Disaggregation Bias in the Evaluation of Tax Systems*, 91 Org. Behav. & Hum. Decision Processes 230 (2003).

4. Edward J. McCaffery & Jonathan Baron, *Isolation Effects and the Neglect of Indirect Effects of Fiscal Policies*, 19 J. Behav. Decision Making, 289 (2006).

5. Raj Chetty, Adam Looney & Kory Kroft, *Salience and Taxation: Theory and Evidence*, 99 Am. Econ. Rev. 1145 (2009).

sums),[6] and confuse between marginal and average tax rates.[7] The very use of the label "tax" produces negative reactions;[8] and consumers prefer to avoid tax-related costs more than equal-sized (or larger) non-tax monetary costs.[9] Concurrently, a lively debate has sprung up concerning the normative and policy implications of the empirical findings.[10]

These and comparable findings are highly relevant to several aspects of the tax system, including (1) tax design; (2) the impact of taxes on people's economic decision-making; (3) tax compliance; and (4) the inclination of taxpayers to challenge tax liability. With regard to tax design, policymakers who display cognitive biases may produce an inconsistent, inefficient, and unfair tax system. Moreover, even policymakers who are not vulnerable to, or overcome, such biases may instrumentally cater to the biased judgments of the public at large in a bid to gain political support for their proposals and for themselves. Of course, policymakers may also take advantage of common heuristics and biases to gain support for desirable reforms.

The remaining three aspects pertain not to the behavior of policymakers, but to that of taxpayers. Thus, the second aspect is the effect of taxes on people's economic decisions, such as choosing jobs, buying goods, and saving for retirement. In this context too, heuristics and biases have both dark and bright sides. The dark side is that people's biases may result in suboptimal decisions. For example, people may overconsume goods if they make their purchase decisions based on the pretax price, rather than on the goods' full cost, including tax. The bright side has to do with the fact that taxes often discourage otherwise socially beneficial transactions and other activities, thus creating a *deadweight loss*.[11] Hiding the tax outcomes of a transaction or an activity in such cases may possibly enhance social welfare.[12]

The third aspect is tax compliance. Psychological insights are crucial to understanding why people pay taxes (even when the expected legal sanctions for not doing so are very

6. McCaffery & Baron, *supra* note 3; McCaffery & Baron, *supra* note 2, at 686, 696, 699.

7. David Gamage & Darien Shanske, *Three Essays on Tax Salience: Market Salience and Political Salience,* 65 TAX L. REV. 19, 31–33 (2011).

8. Catherine C. Eckel, Philip Grossman & Rachel M. Johnston, *An Experimental Test of the Crowding Out Hypothesis*, J. PUB. ECON. 1543 (2005) (subjects were willing to contribute to a charity when the contribution was unlabeled, but not when it was labeled "tax"); David J. Hardisty, Eric J. Johnson & Elke U. Weber, *A Dirty Word or a Dirty World?: Attribute Framing, Political Affiliation, and Query Theory,* 21 PSYCHOL. SCI. 86 (2009) (finding that Americans who identify as Republicans or Independent—but not as Democrats—were more likely to purchase a more expensive product when an added fee was labeled "carbon offset," rather than "carbon tax"); Edward J. McCaffery & Jonathan Baron, *Thinking about Tax*, 12 PSYCHOL. PUB. POL'Y & L. 106, 117–19 (2006).

9. Abigail B. Sussman & Christopher Y. Olivola, *Axe the Tax: Taxes Are Disliked More than Equivalent Costs*, 48 J. MARKETING RES. S91 (2011).

10. For overviews of the literature, see Edward J. McCaffery, *Behavioral Economics and the Law: Tax, in* THE OXFORD HANDBOOK OF BEHAVIORAL ECONOMICS AND THE LAW 599 (Eyal Zamir & Doron Teichman eds., 2014); WILLIAM J. CONGDON, JEFFREY R. KLING & SENDHIL MULLAINATHAN, POLICY AND CHOICE: PUBLIC FINANCE THROUGH THE LENS OF BEHAVIORAL ECONOMICS 173–200 (2011). For a useful collection of studies, see BEHAVIORAL PUBLIC FINANCE (Edward J. McCaffery & Joel Slemrod eds., 2006).

11. *See generally* N. GREGORY MANKIW, ESSENTIALS OF ECONOMICS 155–68 (7th ed. 2014).

12. *But see infra* pp. 478–80.

small), and under what circumstances tax evasion is more likely. Psychological insights may thus be used to increase tax compliance. Finally, cognitive factors, especially tax salience, also affect taxpayers' inclination to use administrative and judicial procedures to challenge tax liability.

Distinguishing between the different aspects of the tax system to which the psychological phenomena are relevant is important, because the same phenomenon may have dissimilar effects and policy implications in different contexts. Thus, Deborah Schenk, as well as David Gamage and Darien Shanske, have highlighted the distinction between *political salience* (the effect of tax visibility on tax design, the first aspect mentioned above), and *economic* or *market salience* (the effect of tax visibility on economic decision-making, the second aspect).[13] For example, including value added tax (VAT) in the price tag enhances its economic salience, as buyers are more likely to consider the total cost of the good when making their purchase decisions. At the same time, such inclusion reduces the political salience of VAT, because customers are not constantly reminded of the existence of the tax.

Beside the contribution of behavioral findings to the four aspects of the tax system mentioned above—examined in Sections B and C below—this chapter discusses two further issues. One is redistribution, which is undeniably a central (and controversial) goal of any modern tax system.[14] In recent years, behavioral studies have enriched the positive and normative analyses of redistribution by shedding new light on how people form judgments about tax progressivity, the cognitive ramifications of poverty, the correlation between wealth and subjective well-being, and the choice between various methods and objects of redistribution. Section D surveys these findings and their implications. Finally, Section E comments on the use of taxes as a means of modifying human behavior—in particular, discouraging self-injurious behavior resulting from cognitive biases.

B. Tax Design

1. General

Tax design is a special case of governmental policy- and decision-making, generally discussed in Chapter 11 of this book. As such, it raises the issues of public officials' motivation and their susceptibility to cognitive biases, the effect of citizens' heuristics and biases on their voting behavior and support for governmental policies, and governmental manipulation of public opinion by exploiting the public's cognitive biases.[15] Against this backdrop, the present section highlights several manifestations of these issues in the context of tax design. Citizens' attitudes to taxes will only be discussed here inasmuch as they affect tax design. The effects of these attitudes on people's economic decision-making, tax compliance,

13. Deborah H. Schenk, *Exploiting the Salience Bias in Designing Taxes*, 28 Yale J. on Reg. 253, 272–75 (2011); Gamage & Shanske, *supra* note 7.

14. *See, e.g.*, Louis Kaplow, The Theory of Taxation and Public Economics (2008); Reuven S. Avi-Yonah, *The Three Goals of Taxation*, 60 Tax L. Rev. 1 (2006).

15. *See supra* pp. 395–99, 405–08, 408–09, respectively.

and the inclination to challenge tax liability will be discussed separately, as will the issue of tax progressivity.[16]

2. Budget Balance

Economists, politicians, and citizens hold conflicting views about the optimal size of government, and relatedly about the optimal levels of the national annual deficit and overall debt. But even if consensus could somehow be reached on these issues (including on the scope and method of governmental redistributive policies) in the abstract, there would remain a concern about the prospect of implementing it. While individuals like to receive governmental services and dislike paying taxes, they do realize that the two are interlinked. Fully rational people, who see the entire picture (rather than exhibiting an isolation effect), and whose preferences are time-consistent (rather than myopic) and reference-independent (rather than displaying the status-quo bias, the endowment effect, and the like) would support the measures necessary to achieve (what they believe to be) optimal levels of deficit and debt. Real people might not. In keeping with the confirmation bias,[17] both sides of the political divide tend to describe their opponents' judgments as irrational. As nicely encapsulated by Jonathan Baron and Edward McCaffery, "[s]mall-government partisans fear that citizens will want [programs such as Medicare and Social Security] now, neglecting their long-term costs, and then will be reluctant to cut these programs later. Big-government partisans—who assume that such programs are desirable . . .—fear that citizens will support tax cuts now, ignoring the long-term effects of any resulting deficit (or diminished surplus) on the ability of the government to do its job in the future."[18]

In a web-based survey experiment, Baron and McCaffery first presented subjects with the basic options about tax, spending, and debt, in general, abstract terms; and then asked them to make a policy choice. They found that subjects did not support tax cuts without spending cuts. Rather, when subjects were told that the total taxes currently constitute 20 percent of a typical household's income, and that U.S. debt is about three times the size of the annual federal budget "so there is plenty of room to reduce it," they supported a smaller government and the maintaining of a small budgetary surplus.[19] However, when a similar question was asked, but subjects had to indicate the specific spending category or categories to be cut (such as healthcare, social security, or the armed forces), they were unwilling to cut spending at all.[20] Baron and McCaffery dubbed this inconsistency the *identified-victim bias*.[21]

16. *See infra* pp. 474–76, 476–78, 478, and 481–83, respectively.

17. *See supra* pp. 58–61.

18. Jonathan Baron & Edward J. McCaffery, *Starving the Beast: The Political Psychology of Budget Deficits*, *in* FISCAL CHALLENGES: AN INTERDISCIPLINARY APPROACH TO BUDGET POLICY 221, 223 (Elizabeth Garrett, Elizabeth A. Graddy & Howell E. Jackson eds., 2008).

19. *Id.* at 227–30.

20. *Id.* at 230–33. In both experiments, subjects also exhibited an anchoring effect, being highly influenced by the figures presented in the questionnaire. On anchoring and adjustment, see generally *supra* pp. 79–82. No evidence of myopia was found, but this may have to do with the experimental design.

21. On the identifiability effect, see also *supra* pp. 101, 400–01, 421–22, 429–30.

Based on these and additional experiments, Baron and McCaffery concluded that, while people are not fully rational, some of the biases cancel each other out. Ultimately, citizens are reluctant to cut benefits that people already have—a reluctance associated with the status-quo bias, the endowment effect, and loss aversion. This position is likely to obstruct spending cuts, even if previous tax cuts increased the budgetary deficit. Thus, one possible way to reduce budgetary deficit and national debt may include self-imposed, perhaps constitutional, restrictions on deficit and debt, which would be adopted on a general and abstract level and set limits on subsequent, concrete decisions. Another technique might be to condition any new spending on the availability of new resources.

Closely related to the issue of budget balance—particularly with regard to enlisting public support for new taxes (or for increasing existing ones)—is the common practice of earmarking tax revenues for specific expenditures. For example, fuel taxes are often designated for highway improvements, and cigarette taxes are frequently channeled to cancer research. From a traditional economic perspective, this practice is puzzling and potentially troubling—puzzling given the fungible nature of money, and troubling to the extent that it creates a rigidity in governmental budgets, and perpetuates spending on inefficient projects as circumstances change.

According to public choice theory, the prevalence of earmarking taxes may stem from the political dynamics associated with enacting them. When the incidence of the tax is broad and the group of beneficiaries from the added earmarked revenue is small, that group is likely to more effectively support the new tax than the public at large is to oppose it.[22] More generally, it has been argued that linking taxes to popular governmental projects may bolster voluntary payment of taxes.[23]

However, none of these theories can account for a distinctive feature of earmarked taxes—namely, the typical alignment of the taxed activity and the expected use of the revenue. Often, the activity being taxed and the use made with the tax revenues are closely related. For instance, revenues raised from taxing pollutants are frequently used for environmental purposes, and not for other popular projects such as education. Experimental and observational studies have shown that such alignment does indeed increase public support for taxes.[24] As it turns out, when taxes are misaligned with spending (e.g., when a restaurant tax funds highways, or a fuel tax funds restaurant inspections) their popularity is not only lower than when they are aligned, but even lower than when the generated revenue is not earmarked at all.[25] This result suggests that the popularity of earmarked taxes stems not only from the inherent popularity of the intended expenditure, but also from the connection they create between payment and use.

22. Susannah Camic Tahk, *Public Choice Theory and Earmarked Taxes*, 68 Tax L. Rev. 755 (2015).

23. Alice Rivlin, *The Continuing Search for a Popular Tax*, 79 Am. Econ. Rev. 113 (1989); Yair Listokin & David M. Schizer, *I Like to Pay Taxes: Taxpayer Support for Government Spending and the Efficiency of the Tax System*, 66 Tax L. Rev. 179 (2014).

24. Daniel Hemel & Ethan Porter, *Aligning Taxes and Spending: Theory and Experimental Evidence* (working paper, July 2016, *available at*: http://ssrn.com/abstract=2807969).

25. *Id.* at 13–15.

Possibly, this judgment echoes the prevailing intuition—as confirmed in psychological research—that positive and negative reciprocation should be done with resources of the same kind.[26] Satisfaction from reciprocity is significantly diminished when repayment is made with resources of a different kind—such as when love is traded for money.[27] This finding carries implications for an array of legal contexts. In the area of civil remedies, subjects have been shown to prefer in-kind remedies (such as reciprocal land use) to monetary payments.[28] Similarly, in the area of state enforcement, it has been shown that subjects prefer sanctions that are tailored to alleviating the specific type of harm caused by the transgressor.[29]

3. The Political Salience of Taxes

In making judgments and decisions, people often do not take into account all pertinent variables, but rather tend to focus on the information that is immediately available to them and ignore less salient information.[30] In the context of tax design, this means that people react more strongly to conspicuous taxes than to non-conspicuous ones. Policymakers who are aware of the public's stronger opposition to salient taxes (and possibly share this sentiment themselves) tend to prefer less salient taxes to more salient ones. Political salience may explain, for example, the attraction of the corporate income tax. Since individuals do not directly pay the tax, popular opposition to it is likely to be limited, even though much of the costs of this tax (depending on the elasticities of supply and demand) may be passed on to the corporations' customers (of course, opposition to the corporate tax from organized interest groups may countervail the absence of popular opposition).[31] Studies have found that, even when people were prompted to think about the indirect effects of such taxes, their preference for them was reduced, but not eliminated.[32]

In the same vein, tax-inclusive price tags render VAT less politically salient, because people pay less attention to the fact that part of the price they pay for products and services is actually a tax.[33] Even taxes that are directly calculated based on employees' income may be rendered less politically salient by imposing part of the payroll tax on the employer,[34]

26. *See* Uriel G. Foa, *Interpersonal and Economic Resources*, 171 SCI. 345 (1971); Edna B. Foa et al., *Response Generalization in Aggression*, 25 HUM. REL. 337 (1972).

27. *See* Meir Teichman & Uriel Foa, *Effect of Resources Similarity on Satisfaction with Exchange*, 3 SOC. BEHAV. & PERSONALITY 213 (1975).

28. Daphna Lewinsohn-Zamir, *Can't Buy Me Love: Monetary versus In Kind Remedies*, 2013 U. ILL. L. REV. 151. *See also supra* pp. 218–19, 268–69.

29. *See* Jane Beattie & Jonathan Baron, *In-Kind and Out-of-Kind Penalties: Preference and Valuation*, 1 J. EXPERIMENTAL PSYCHOL.: APPLIED 136 (1995).

30. On the *isolation effect* and WYSIATI ("what you see is all there is"), see generally *supra* p. 24.

31. McCaffery, *supra* note 1, at 1883–86.

32. McCaffery & Baron, *supra* note 4.

33. *Id.* at 1875.

34. *Id.* at 1883–86.

deducting the tax at the source (tax withholding),[35] and labeling social security payments as "contributions" rather than as taxes (as is the case in the United States).[36] Political salience also explains the higher rates of the same tax (e.g., property tax) when its collection is carried out in a less visible manner.[37] Thus, it has been found that implementing electronic toll-collection systems on toll roads reduced drivers' awareness of the toll rates, facilitated an increase of rates by 20 to 40 percent, and rendered toll-setting behavior less sensitive to the local election calendar.[38]

One way in which governments can minimize the perceived burden of taxes is to follow marketers' practice of *odd pricing*,[39] namely to set tax rates that are slightly below a whole or a round number, such as 19.9 percent.[40] Interestingly, however, tax legislation sometimes sets top tax rates that are round numbers (e.g., 50 percent as the marginal tax rate for the highest earners). It has been suggested that this practice serves politicians' wish to maximize the burden of taxes paid by the richest taxpayers as perceived by the typical voter (who might then view her own marginal tax as comparatively low).[41]

The main arguments for and against the use of less visible (or "hidden") taxes revolve around the impact of those taxes on taxpayers' behavior, including economic decision-making and tax compliance, that is, around *market salience*. Accordingly, they are discussed below.[42] However, there are also powerful arguments for and against the exploitation of the low *political salience* of certain taxes to increase the overall tax burden. As in the debate about the use of nudges by the government,[43] this debate raises issues of government transparency, voters' autonomy, democratic values, social welfare maximization, and expediency.[44] Unsurprisingly, advocates of small government detest the use of low political salience as a means of increasing taxes (while possibly approving of the use of low political salience to carry out cuts in government expenditure and taxes).[45]

35. *See infra* pp. 476–77.

36. McCaffery, *supra* note 1, at 1876–83.

37. Marika Cabral & Caroline Hoxby, *The Hated Property Tax: Salience, Tax Rates, and Tax Revolts* (NBER Working Paper No. 18514, 2012, *available at*: http://www.nber.org/papers/w18514). *See also infra* note 78 and accompanying text.

38. Amy Finkelstein, *EZ-Tax: Tax Salience and Tax Rates*, 124 Q.J. Econ. 969 (2009).

39. *See supra* pp. 299–301.

40. Asmus Leth Olsen, *The Politics of Digits: Evidence of Odd Taxation*, 154 Pub. Choice 59 (2013).

41. Aradhna Krishna & Joel Slemrod, *Behavioral Public Finance: Tax Design as Price Presentation*, 10 Int'l Tax & Pub. Fin. 189, 197 (2003).

42. *See infra* pp. 474–80.

43. *See supra* pp. 177–85.

44. For a comprehensive discussion, see Schenk, *supra* note 13 (arguing that exploiting the low political salience of certain taxes may well be justified).

45. *See, e.g.*, Milton Friedman & Rose D. Friedman, Two Lucky People 123 (1998) (economist Milton Friedman regretting his role in creating the system of withholding for federal income taxes, which facilitated the expansion of U.S. government; on tax withholding, see also *infra* pp. 476–77); McCaffery, *supra* note 10, at 616 (describing a tacit agreement between Democrats and Republicans, during the 2013 "fiscal cliff" crisis, to let the

Of course, the fact that a certain legal measure is more or less politically salient does not make it more or less desirable per se. There appears to be no clear yardstick for assessing the optimal level of political salience of any tax. If, for example, there are compelling substantive reasons to increase the overall tax burden, then arguably the main problem is that the income tax is overly salient—not that VAT is insufficiently so.[46] At any rate, unlike the issue of market salience, which is unique to tax policy, the issue of the political salience of taxes raises similar questions to those presented by the political salience of any other policy—be it choosing between different (combinations of) taxes, different ways of allocating governmental benefits, or different regimes of tort liability.

In the next subsection, we illustrate the above observations by taking a closer look at the choice between tax exemptions and governmental spending—an issue that has attracted considerable attention in the United States and elsewhere, and in which an active attempt to reframe the decision-making process has been made with a view to overcoming political salience and other biases.

4. Tax Exemptions versus Spending

Governments collect taxes to finance their activities, including the allocation of benefits to individuals, organizations, and firms. Such allocations may aim at redistributing resources to the needy, supporting charitable organizations, encouraging industrial enterprises, and so forth. Basically, there are two methods of making such allocations: direct spending and tax exemptions. Examples of the former include providing or subsidizing loans for higher education or for particular economic enterprises. The latter method includes measures such as real-estate tax exemptions for the disabled and senior citizens, and tax credits for charitable contributions and for installing and operating renewable energy systems.

Each of the two methods has advantages and disadvantages. The broader the tax base, the more neutral it is between different economic activities. Since tax exemptions narrow the tax base, they are likely to introduce inefficient distortions of economic decision-making. However, this argument also applies to direct spending.[47] More importantly, the choice between the two methods entails an institutional choice: while tax credits and deductions are handled by tax authorities, direct spending is administered by the particular branches of government in charge of education, housing, healthcare, etc.[48] Presumably, the latter are more competent to design and implement accurate criteria for the allocation of benefits.

Another argument against tax credits, deductions, and exemptions is that they complicate the tax system. However, this complexity does not disappear when tax exemptions are replaced by direct spending programs. Rather, the latter become more complicated. It is

"payroll tax holiday," which was enacted two years earlier and saved many taxpayers considerable sums of money, quietly expire).

46. Gamage & Shanske, *supra* note 7, at 78–98.

47. Stanley S. Surrey, *Tax Incentives as a Device for Implementing Government Policy: A Comparison with Direct Government,* 83 HARV. L. REV. 705, 725 (1970).

48. David A. Weisbach & Jacob Nussim, *The Integration of Tax and Spending Programs,* 113 YALE L.J. 955 (2004).

also argued that tax deductions may benefit the wealthy more than the poor, because they have less impact on people with a low marginal tax rate or who pay no tax at all.[49] Unlike tax exemptions, direct spending can be used to provide in-kind benefits, rather than merely monetary ones. While monetary benefits impose fewer restrictions on the recipients' liberty, in-kind benefits can have a greater impact on their welfare.[50] Finally, tax exemptions are particularly apt as a means of encouraging "volunteering" activities without transforming them into overtly paid activities and thereby crowding out potential "volunteers" (people who would not engage in those activities were they framed as paid work).[51]

This brief survey of the arguments pertaining to the choice between tax exemptions and spending shows that neither method is invariably superior to the other. However, tax exemptions appear to be used far more than may be justified based exclusively on their relative merits.[52] Two interrelated psychological explanations for this phenomenon are loss aversion and low political salience.[53] From the government's perspective, collecting less tax is plausibly perceived as not obtaining a gain, while allocating benefits is seen as giving or losing. From the perspective of those who do not get the tax exemptions, not receiving them may be framed as not-gaining, rather than losing. Finally, from the perspective of the beneficiaries, not paying taxes (that is, not losing) is possibly more pleasing than paying taxes (losing), and then receiving comparable benefits (gaining). Insofar as losses loom larger than gains, tax exemptions are therefore likely to encounter less resistance and to be scrutinized less stringently.[54] Due in part to these framing, channeling benefits through the tax system makes them less politically visible than direct spending. When the true costs of tax exemptions are non-salient, parliamentary supervision on the government is less effective.[55]

Exposing the various pitfalls of treating tax exemptions differently from direct governmental spending, Stanley Surrey has successfully advocated the promulgation of "tax expenditure budgets" in the United States.[56] A primary goal of the tax expenditure budget was to increase the salience of tax exemptions and reframe them as akin to direct spending. However, this attempt at reframing tax exemptions as expenditures has, on the whole, failed: there has been no decrease in the use of tax credits, deductions, and exemptions

49. Surrey, *supra* note 47, at 720–25; Stanley S. Surrey & Paul R. McDaniel, Tax Expenditures 71–82 (1985).

50. *See infra* pp. 488–89.

51. Edward A. Zelinsky, *Do Tax Expenditures Create Framing Effects? Volunteer Firefighters, Property Tax Exemptions, and the Paradox of Tax Expenditures Analysis*, 24 Va. Tax Rev. 797 (2005).

52. Edward D. Kleinbard, *Tax Expenditure Framework Legislation*, 63 Nat'l Tax J. 353 (2010); Zelinsky, *supra* note 51.

53. On loss aversion, see generally *supra* pp. 42–57.

54. *See also* Zelinsky, *supra* note 51, at 814–20 (experimentally examining the framing effect of outright payments and tax exemptions).

55. Surrey, *supra* note 47, at 728–30; Kleinbard, *supra* note 52.

56. *See, e.g.*, Surrey, *supra* note 47; *see also* Surrey & McDaniel, *supra* note 49.

since the introduction of the tax expenditure budgets.[57] The conventional framing, so it seems, has proven more resilient than some might have expected.[58]

C. Taxpayers' Behavior

Behavioral studies elucidate not only tax design, but taxpayers' behavior as well. This section discusses the contribution of psychological insights to the understanding of taxpayers' behavior in economic decision-making, in tax compliance, and in challenging tax liabilities. It then comments on the normative implications of the relevant findings.

1. Economic Decision-Making

Taxes impose additional costs on transactions and other activities, thus reducing the net benefit for the parties involved (while subsidies increase the net benefit). Rational people are expected to take account of the added cost (or benefit) when deciding whether and under what terms to make a transaction or engage in an activity, such as taking on a job or buying a good. However, studies have shown that sometimes, at least some people do not take full account of the tax in making those decisions. A major factor that determines the extent to which people consider the tax outcomes of their activity is the tax's visibility or salience.

Raj Chetty, Adam Looney, and Kory Kroft famously conducted a field experiment and an observational study to examine the effect of taxes on purchasing behavior.[59] The experiment was executed at a supermarket over three weeks. As in most retail stores in the United States, the prices posted on the shelf did not include the sales tax of 7.375 percent, which was added at the register. The treatment—which was applied to all products in three categories (cosmetics, haircare, and deodorants), but not to other products in the store—included posting tags showing the tax-inclusive price along with the pretax price tags. Using a *difference-in-differences* technique,[60] the researchers found that the quantity sold and total revenue in the treated group of products fell by about 8 percent during the intervention period, compared with other products in the same aisle and to products in other stores.

To rule out the possibility that this drop was caused by the exceptional nature of the treated price tags, in the observational study the researchers examined the effect of state-level changes in the rates of two taxes on the consumption of beer between 1970 and 2003. One was an excise tax that is included in the posted price, and the other was a sales tax that

57. Victor Thuronyi, *Tax Expenditures: A Reassessment*, 1988 DUKE L.J. 1155, 1170–81; Kleinbard, *supra* note 52; Zelinsky, *supra* note 51, at 801–04.

58. Zelinsky, *supra* note 51, at 826. On framing, see generally *supra* pp. 46–48.

59. Chetty, Looney & Kroft, *supra* note 5.

60. Difference in differences (DID) is a technique whereby the effect of a treatment is calculated by comparing the average change over time in the outcomes for the treatment group, compared with the average change over time for the control group.

is added at the register. They found that increases in the excise tax reduced beer consumption by an order of magnitude more than similar increases in the sales tax.

Finally, the researchers conducted a survey among store shoppers, which revealed that the latter were quite well informed about the sales tax. Thus, it was not lack of information about the tax, but its non-salience when not included in the price tag, that appears to have driven those results.[61] In a clear demonstration of the isolation effect or WYSIATI (what you see is all there is), shoppers who were generally aware of the existence of the sales tax behaved differently when the full price of a product was presented prior to making the purchase decision than when the tax was added to the pretax price shortly afterward, at the register.

Other studies provide further evidence for the impact of tax salience on people's consumption decisions. Thus, the study of toll roads mentioned above found that the adoption of electronic toll collection, which decreased drivers' awareness of toll rates (compared with manual collection), reduced the elasticity of demand for using the toll road.[62]

Saliency may also affect reactions to tax *benefits*. For example, policymakers can incentivize consumers to purchase environmentally friendly cars by using a sales tax waiver or an income tax credit. Arguably, the sales tax waiver is more salient than the income tax credit, as it is a clear saving that is made directly during the purchasing of the car, and not conditional saving that will materialize in the future only if the purchasers will properly file their tax returns. Indeed, an empirical study estimated that a one thousand dollar tax waiver is associated with a 45 percent increase in hybrid vehicle sales, while an equivalent income tax credit is associated with only a 3 percent increase in hybrid vehicle sales.[63] Furthermore, customer-based incentives such as a sales tax waiver might create an independent welfare surplus, since consumers value the very fact that a transaction is labeled tax free, thus increasing the *market salience* of the benefit beyond its objective value.[64]

Interestingly, tax salience is not solely determined by governmental design of taxes and the means of collecting them. Third parties may also play a role in this respect. A case in point is tax deductions for charitable contributions. Charitable organizations are highly motivated to inform potential donors that donations are tax-deductible, but have no interest in drawing donors' attention to the limitations of the deductions, which render them unavailable to many donors or diminish their magnitude. The same is true of deductions for home mortgage interest. Since the non-salience of limitations on tax deductions and tax credits affects economic decision-making in the same way as the non-salience of taxes,

61. On the distinction between tax salience and tax knowledge, see David A. Weisbach, *Is Knowledge of the Tax Law Socially Desirable?*, 15 Am. L. & Econ. Rev. 187 (2013).

62. Finkelstein, *supra* note 38, at 986–90. For surveys of additional empirical and experimental studies of tax salience, see Schenk, *supra* note 13, at 264–70; Gamage & Shanske, *supra* note 7, at 27–31.

63. *See* Kelly Sims Gallagher & Erich Muehlegger, *Giving Green to Get Green: Incentives and Consumer Adoption of Hybrid Vehicle Technology*, 61 J. Envtl. Econ. & Mgmt. 1, 9–11 (2011).

64. *See* Hayes R. Holderness, *The Unexpected Role of Tax Salience in State Competition for Businesses*, 84 U. Chi. L. Rev. 1091 (2017). It has further been argued that customer-based incentives are more likely than traditional in centives to mitigate deadweight loss and increase consumer surplus. *Id.* at 1138–41.

the involvement of third parties likely magnifies the significance of this phenomenon.[65] In fact, a survey study found widespread misconceptions about taxpayers' eligibility to tax subsidies and their magnitude, in both directions.[66]

While the accumulated evidence clearly suggests that tax salience affects taxpayers' economic decision-making, the normative and policy implications of these findings are still debated. We return to this issue below.[67]

2. Tax Compliance

Tax evasion carries various undesirable effects. It inefficiently induces people to engage in activities where it is easier to evade taxes, and increases the consumption of the products of those activities (as their cost is lower when taxes are not paid). Tax evasion also unfairly increases the tax burden on those who pay their taxes more faithfully. Unsurprisingly, tax compliance has attracted the attention of tax authorities and scholars alike.

The main puzzle with regard to tax compliance is not that people sometimes violate the law, but that they appear to comply with the law more than might be expected, based on a cost-benefit analysis of the benefits of tax evasion versus the costs of legal sanctions for noncompliance, multiplied by the probability of incurring them.[68] This is not to say that legal sanctions are unimportant. Evidently, there are much higher rates of noncompliance in spheres where legal enforcement is particularly weak, such as with regard to self-employed individuals.[69] Yet, it is quite clear that tax compliance cannot be fully explained by the premise that taxpayers are rational maximizers of their utility, measured in monetary terms. Indeed, the past decades have witnessed a slew of behavioral studies—theoretical, empirical, and experimental—on the issue of tax compliance.[70] These studies have found that tax compliance depends on, or at least correlates with, people's perception of the rate of compliance by other people (so-called *conditional cooperation*); their attitude to risk, including overweighting of very low probabilities; their perceptions of the fairness of the allocation of tax burdens and the procedural fairness of the tax-collection system; the degree to which they trust the government and support the ends to which it uses the collected

65. Lilian V. Faulhaber, *The Hidden Limits of the Charitable Deduction: An Introduction to Hypersalience*, 92 B.U. L. REV. 1307 (2012).

66. Jacob Golding & Yair Listokin, *Tax Expenditure Salience*, 16 AM. L. & ECON. REV. 144 (2014).

67. *See infra* pp. 478–80.

68. The cornerstone of theoretical economic analysis of tax compliance is Michael G. Allingham & Agnar Sandmo, *Income Tax Evasion: A Theoretical Analysis*, 1 J. PUB. ECON. 323 (1972).

69. Joel Slemrod, *Cheating Ourselves: The Economics of Tax Evasion*, 21 J. ECON. PERSP. 25, 26–30 (2007).

70. *See, e.g.*, James Alm, Garry H. McClelland & William D. Schulze, *Why Do People Pay Taxes?*, 48 J. PUB. ECON. 21 (1992); Bruno S. Frey & Benno Torgler, *Tax Morale and Conditional Cooperation*, 35 J. COMP. ECON. 136 (2007); Kai A. Konrad & Salmai Qari, *The Last Refuge of a Scoundrel? Patriotism and Tax Compliance*, 79 ECONOMICA 516 (2012). For a collection of studies, see DEVELOPING ALTERNATIVE FRAMEWORKS FOR EXPLAINING TAX COMPLIANCE (James Alm, Jorge Martinez-Vazquez & Benno Torgler eds., 2010). For surveys of the literature, see ERICH KIRCHLER, THE ECONOMIC PSYCHOLOGY OF TAX BEHAVIOUR (2007); Michael Pickhardt & Aloys Prinz, *Behavioral Dynamics of Tax Evasion—A Survey*, 40 J. ECON. PSYCHOL. 1 (2014); Christopher Y. Olivola & Abigail B. Sussman, *Taxes and Consumer Behavior*, *in* THE CAMBRIDGE HANDBOOK OF CONSUMER PSYCHOLOGY 564, 565–68 (Michael I. Norton, Derek D. Rucker & Cait Lamberton eds., 2015).

tax revenue; a sense of patriotism (especially, but not only, in war times); and various situational factors that affect people's ethical behavior.[71] We will not review those studies here, because their findings do not fundamentally differ from those dealing with compliance in other legal spheres—an issue discussed in Chapter 12, with reference to studies of tax compliance.[72]

The observation that people comply with their tax (and other legal) duties more than predicted by standard cost-benefit analysis does not detract from the importance of behavioral insights in encouraging tax compliance, given the undesirable effects of tax evasion. Employing such insights may be preferable to more aggressive tax enforcement, which may also be politically unpopular. The relevance of behavioral insights to tax compliance may best be demonstrated by what appears to be the single most effective means of tax enforcement: *tax withholding*.

Tax authorities around the world use tax withholding (also known as *deduction at source*) as an effective means of collecting taxes. Under this common arrangement, the payer of a taxable sum of money deducts the tax from the payment and forwards the deducted sum to the government. Tax withholding often applies to salaries, investors' interest and dividends, royalties, and payments to foreign entities. Withholding requirements decrease the costs of tax collection and reduce tax evasion. Once an employee (or another payee) knows that the payer has already reported the payment to the tax authorities, there is little point in omitting it in their own annual report.[73]

In addition to its other advantages, the great popularity of tax withholding appears to be due to the fact that it makes tax payment less salient and hence less painful. A taxpayer who receives a taxable income and subsequently pays the tax will likely experience that payment as a loss. In contrast, when the tax is deducted at the source, the taxpayer is much more likely to regard her net payment as the reference point, thus framing the deducted tax as an unobtained gain.[74] This framing effect influences the propensity for tax evasion. Since people tend to behave less ethically and take more risks in the domain of losses,[75] tax withholding increases tax compliance by reframing the deducted tax as an unobtained gain. This claim has been substantiated by a host of empirical and experimental studies that compared the behavior of taxpayers when they are in a balance-due position (in the absence of withholding or due to under-withholding), versus when they are in a refund position (due, for example, to over-withholding).[76]

71. In addition to the studies and surveys cited in *supra* note 70, see *supra* pp. 109–10 (on social cooperation), 34 (overweighting of low probabilities), 101–06 (judgments of substantive and procedural fairness), and 72–76 (behavioral ethics).

72. *See supra* pp. 433–63.

73. *See generally* Piroska Soos, *Self-Employed Evasion and Tax Withholding: A Comparative Study and Analysis of the Issues*, 24 U.C. DAVIS L. REV. 107 (1990).

74. McCaffery, *supra* note 1, at 1875.

75. *See supra* pp. 42–44, 458–59.

76. *See, e.g.*, Paul Corcoro & Peter Adelsheim, *A Balance Due before Remittance: The Effect on Reporting Compliance*, *in* RECENT RESEARCH ON TAX ADMINISTRATION AND COMPLIANCE: SELECTED PAPERS GIVEN AT THE

3. Challenging Taxes

Thus far, we have discussed behavioral aspects of tax design, the impact of taxes on people's economic decision-making, and tax compliance. Closely related to the latter two, it has been pointed out that cognitive phenomena—specifically, tax salience—also affect the inclination of taxpayers to take legal measures to challenge their tax liability. A large-scale empirical study took advantage of the fact that there are two ways of paying property tax in New York City.[77] Some owners receive a bill and pay the tax directly to the municipality; others pay the tax through an escrow account as part of their monthly mortgage payments. In the latter case, the tax is part of the owners' monthly payment that also includes mortgage principal, interest, and insurance. Consequently, the tax is less salient for the latter group of taxpayers.[78] By comparing the rate of appeals on property assessments by the same owners of the same properties in two different years, one in which it had an escrow and one in which it did not (rather than comparing across different owners and properties), the study controlled for other variables that could, and plausibly did, affect the decision to appeal tax assessments.[79]

It was found that the use of mortgage escrow had a large and statistically significant negative effect on the probability that a taxpayer would appeal her property assessment.[80] This means that owners who pay through escrow accounts, and who are less likely to appeal, pay higher taxes than those who pay directly to the municipality. Moreover, compared with properties without escrow, properties with escrow are more likely to be owned by ethnic minorities and immigrants. Consequently, the reduced saliency of the property tax, which results in paying higher taxes, produces troubling distributive effects.[81]

4. The Normative Debate

The upshot of the behavioral studies described above is that people's reaction to taxes—including their economic decision-making, tax compliance, and propensity to appeal tax liability—depends not only on the net monetary effect of the tax, but also on its framing,

2010 IRS RESEARCH CONFERENCE (2010), *available at:* http://www.irs.gov/pub/irs-soi/10rescon.pdf; Henry S.J. Robben et al., *Decision Frame and Opportunity as Determinants of Tax Cheating: An International Experimental Study,* 11 J. ECON. PSYCHOL. 341 (1990); Albert Schepanski & Teri Shearer, *A Prospect Theory Account of the Income Tax Withholding Phenomenon*, 63 ORG. BEHAV. & HUM. DECISION PROCESSES 174 (1995); Erich Kirchler & Boris Maciejovsky, *Tax Compliance within the Context of Gain and Loss Situations, Expected and Current Asset Position, and Profession*, 22 J. ECON. PSYCHOL. 173 (2001); Kathleen DeLaney Thomas, *Presumptive Collection: A Prospect Theory Approach to Increasing Small Business Tax Compliance,* 67 TAX L. REV. 111 (2013).

77. Andrew T. Hayashi, *The Legal Salience of Taxation,* 81 U. CHI. L. REV. 1443 (2014).

78. This conjecture is supported by the findings of another large-scale empirical study concerning the political salience of property tax (Cabral & Hoxby, *supra* note 37). The latter study took advantage of the fact that the prevalence of payment of property tax through escrow varies in different parts of the United States—hence making it less salient in some areas than in others. It was found that higher rates of collection through escrows (implying lower political saliency of the tax) are strongly and positively correlated with higher property tax rates.

79. Hayashi, *supra* note 77, at 1474–75.

80. *Id.* at 1484–85.

81. *Id.* at 1480.

salience, perceived fairness, perceived behavior of other people, and so forth. Most important, the behavioral studies point to the strong effect of tax salience on people's behavior. The precise magnitude, incidence, and interrelationships of these phenomena are not entirely clear as yet (if they could ever be), but they are robust enough to warrant consideration of their policy implications.

The basic argument in favor of low-market-salience taxes rests on the economic insight that taxes may reduce aggregate social welfare.[82] Taxes increase the effective price of products and services, including labor. Consequently, goods and services that would have been purchased absent the tax might not be purchased once it is imposed, despite the fact that their production costs are lower than their utility to purchasers. Such forgone transactions create a deadweight loss, unabated by comparable gain to the government, because no taxes are collected on the forgone transactions. Taxes also adversely affect efficiency because they induce people to substitute their most favored goods (which are subject to the tax) with untaxed ones or with goods for which the tax is lower (assuming that not all possible substitutes are equally taxed), thus reducing their net benefit. Finally, in addition to the deadweight loss and *substitution effect*, taxes also produce an *income effect*—that is, they leave taxpayers with fewer resources. While the deadweight loss and substitution effect clearly reduce efficiency, this is not necessarily true of the income effect, as the resources that are taken from the taxpayer are not lost, but rather move to the government.

Now, if taxes are fully or partially invisible, they have a lesser effect on people's behavior. Transactions that would have not been carried out under full consideration of the tax are executed despite the tax, thus reducing the deadweight loss and substitution effects. In these respects, decreasing taxes' salience appears to be desirable.[83] At first glance, since the income effect does not necessarily impinge on efficiency, the impact of taxes' invisibility on the income effect may be ignored from an efficiency perspective. However, such a conclusion would be too hasty. To the extent that ignoring a tax leads people to miscalculate their expenses, such that they spend too much on luxuries and are left with too little money for basic necessities, invisible taxes may decrease the overall social welfare.[84]

This basic analysis lends support for the use of non-salient taxes, but not unequivocally. Other considerations make the picture considerably more complex. Even if low-market-salience is desirable for the reasons described thus far, there are limits to tax invisibility. To use the example of the sales tax studied by Chetty and his colleagues,[85] had the

82. Taxes do not *necessarily* reduce overall social welfare, as they may also enhance it, for example, by moving resources from people whose marginal utility is low to people whose marginal utility is high (because they are poorer). Our analysis focuses on the downsides of taxes, and specifically on the question of whether using fewer salient taxes may mitigate these downsides.

83. This conclusion is akin to the standard claim that, all else being equal, it is preferable to levy taxes on goods and services for which the demand is inelastic. *See also* Chetty, Looney & Kroft, *supra* note 5, at 1166–76; Jacob Nussim, *To Confuse and Protect: Taxes and Consumer Protection*, 1 Colum. J. Tax L. 218 (2010).

84. For a lucid presentation of these and additional considerations, see Brian Galle, *Hidden Taxes*, 87 Wash. U. L. Rev. 59, 65–72, 77–81 (2009). *See also* Gamage & Shanske, *supra* note 7, at 61–65.

85. *See supra* pp. 474–75.

rate of the tax been 50 percent, it stands to reason that shoppers would not have disregarded it to the same extent that they disregard a 7.375 percent tax. Rather, they would have quickly learned of the tax's large impact. More generally, the usefulness of low-salience taxes may diminish due to learning from experience and the possible use of debiasing techniques.[86] More importantly, taxpayers likely vary in their tendency to disregard low-salience taxes. Inasmuch as people of lower socioeconomic status are more likely to disregard such taxes, the negative income effects of those taxes may be harsher for the poor.[87] The poor may also be less inclined to challenge less conspicuous taxes, and consequently pay relatively higher taxes.[88] Moreover, even if non-salient taxes equally induce all consumers to overconsume, such overconsumption adversely affects consumers' long-term welfare, because it means that they save too little for the future.[89]

Finally, while market salience and political salience are distinct phenomena (and a certain tax may be salient in one sense and not in the other), in all-things-considered policy decisions, both types of saliency must be taken into account. As shown in the discussion of political salience, these issues are closely related to the fundamental debate about small versus big government.[90] People who hold strong views against big government or in favor of governmental transparency, as well as those who resent the manipulation of consumers' decisions to promote aggregate efficiency, may attribute limited weight to the advantages of low-salient taxes. Ultimately, while the behavioral findings certainly enrich the analysis, they do not resolve the normative debate.

D. Behavioral Insights and Redistribution

1. General

A central objective of tax systems throughout the world is to redistribute wealth and other benefits among different segments of society. Distributive justice in general, and the legitimacy and efficacy of governmental redistributive means in particular, have long been debated by philosophers, political scientists, economists, and jurists. On the one hand, it is argued that the rights to adequate nutrition, clothing, housing, and medical treatment are fundamental human rights; that redistributive policies would be adopted by anyone beyond a veil of ignorance (that is, when no one knows what his or her actual position and holdings in society might be); that the existing distribution of wealth and other social resources is often a product of unjust and exploitive practices; that due to the diminishing marginal

86. Galle, *supra* note 84, at 85–93.

87. *Id.* at 100–04.

88. *See supra* note 81 and accompanying text. On these and additional concerns, see Gamage & Shanske, *supra* note 7, at 65–79. Gamage and Shanske conclude that the drawbacks of low market salience have been overstated in the literature, that some of them may be overcome, and hence that it is generally desirable to decrease the market salience of taxes.

89. McCaffery, *supra* note 1, at 613. Based on this and other considerations, McCaffery firmly objects to non-salient taxes (*id.* at 610–15).

90. *See supra* pp. 467–74.

utility of resources, transferring resources from the rich to the poor is likely to increase overall social utility; and that extreme inequality may result in social instability and high crime rates. On the other hand, it is argued that compulsory taking of resources from the rich to give to the poor violates the former's fundamental rights and is akin to theft; that redistribution adversely affects the incentives to engage in productive activities for both the rich (who no longer reap the full fruits of their efforts) and the poor (because they are guaranteed minimal existence even if they do not work)—hence it is likely to decrease overall social utility; and so forth.

An exploration of these controversies, which directly inform the political and legal debate about governmental redistribution, lies beyond the scope of the present discussion. Instead, we would like to make a general observation and then focus on several contributions of behavioral studies to this ongoing debate. The general observation is that, contrary to standard economic analysis, behavioral studies have shown that people often care not only about their own welfare but about the welfare of others as well, and that they tend to assess their own position in comparison to the position of others, rather than in absolute terms.[91] While none of these findings carry conclusive implications for redistribution policies, they provide prima facie arguments in favor of narrowing socioeconomic gaps in society. The first finding implies that people might have a preference for greater equality and fairness, and the second that reducing inequalities may enhance aggregate social utility not only due to the decreasing marginal utility of resources, but also due to the disutility experienced by the underprivileged *because* others are privileged.[92]

Beyond this general observation, this section highlights four major contributions of behavioral studies to the ongoing debate about governmental redistributive policies: the malleability of normative judgments of progressivity, the effect of scarcity on decision-making, the effect of wealth on happiness, and the behavioral aspects of the choice between different methods of redistribution.[93]

2. Judgments of Progressivity

The behavioral aspects of tax design in general were discussed earlier in this chapter.[94] Here we focus on a particular aspect of tax design, namely the redistributive effects of the tax system. Specifically, several studies have examined people's normative judgments of progressive taxes—that is, taxes where the marginal tax rate increases as the taxable amount increases. Prevailing normative judgments do not resolve the normative debate, as they may be morally wrong. However, to the extent that the legal system should reflect those judgments, for democratic or instrumental reasons, such judgments are nonetheless important. They are also important inasmuch as they can explain the existing legal regime, which was designed by people who may share the prevailing convictions.

91. *See generally supra* pp. 45–46, 101–10.

92. Congdon, Kling & Mullainathan, *supra* note 10, at 145–49.

93. Behavioral findings are important for the design of governmental redistribution programs as well. *See id.* at 155–72.

94. *See supra* pp. 467–74.

Suppose that couples with an annual income of $30,000 are allowed to deduct $1,500 from their gross income per child (because child rearing is costly)—thereby reducing their taxable income accordingly. Should the deductible per child for couples whose annual income is $180,000 be the same, lower, or higher? The prevailing intuition is that it certainly *should not be higher*. Now, assume that the benchmark is not a childless couple, but rather a couple with two children. Assume further that, since child rearing is costly, there is a tax increase imposed on couples with only one child, or no child at all. This increase may be achieved by canceling some other deductions or exemptions that the couple might otherwise have enjoyed, or by adding "virtual income" to their actual one. Should the additional tax imposed on childless couples be the same for all such couples, regardless of their income? The prevailing intuition is that it *should be higher* for the rich than for the poor. Since these are two framings of the same question, only with different benchmarks, these prevailing intuitions are inconsistent. Originally proposed by Thomas Schelling as a thought experiment,[95] this inconsistency was confirmed experimentally by McCaffery and Baron.[96] The experiments also showed that people believe that deductibles (bonuses) for having children are fairer than surcharges (penalties) for not having children. Reference dependence, loss aversion, and framing effects thus characterize people's judgments about progressive taxation.[97]

Another well-known phenomenon, the *status-quo bias*, was evident in judgments about tax progressivity as well. In comparing between two possible tax regimes, subjects tended to favor the one that was presented as the existing one, whichever it was.[98]

McCaffery and Baron also found a *neutrality bias*. Income tax systems define the taxpayer unit: an individual, a couple, a family, etc. However, it is impossible to reconcile tax progressivity with two other, intuitively appealing goals: *marriage neutrality* and *couples neutrality*. Marriage neutrality means that the taxes of a couple are unaffected by whether they marry or not. Couple neutrality means that couples with the same total income pay the same total tax.

To use McCaffery and Baron's numerical example, imagine a tax system with a tax rate of zero for people earning up to $10,000 per person per year, and 20 percent above that amount.[99] If the zero rate threshold is doubled for married couples ($20,000), then married couples where one partner earns $20,000 and the other $0 effectively enjoy a "marriage bonus," as their taxes fall from $2,000 (that the earning partner would have paid) to nil. If, on the other hand, the $10,000 threshold applies to single individuals as well as couples, then a couple in which each partner earns $10,000 would pay taxes of $2,000 instead of the zero taxes each partner would have paid separately (a "marriage penalty"). If, to avoid these violations of the marriage-neutrality principle, each partner is taxed separately, then couple

95. Thomas C. Schelling, *Economic Reasoning and the Ethics of Policy*, 63 PUB. INTEREST 37, 53–56 (1981).

96. McCaffery & Baron, *supra* note 2, at 688–91.

97. On these phenomena, see generally *supra* pp. 42–57.

98. McCaffery & Baron, *supra* note 2, at 691–95. On the status-quo bias, see generally *supra* pp. 48–50.

99. *Id.* at 684.

neutrality is violated, because two couples who both earn a total income of $20,000 would pay different taxes: $2,000 where there is only one earner, and zero where there are two.

Here again, McCaffery and Baron found that subjects' preferences between the two possible filing systems depended on how the same dilemma was presented to them. They preferred separate filing when the presentation emphasized the effect of marriage, but joint filing when the emphasis was on the number of earners.[100]

In another series of experiments concerning people's judgments of tax progressivity, McCaffery and Baron asked participants either to design a single, global tax system, or to vary one component of a tax system with the other component held constant. In a typical manifestation of the *isolation effect*, the participants focused on the component they were asked to manipulate, and did not take full account of changes in the other component.[101] Finally, subjects demonstrated a dramatic *metric effect*. They were considerably more inclined toward progressive taxes when the options were presented in percentage terms rather than in absolute monetary amounts.[102]

Two general lessons may be learned from these and comparable experimental studies.[103] First—at least among the participants in these studies—there is broad support for progressivity in taxes. Second, people's judgments in this sphere, as with other complex issues, are not absolute or unwavering. Rather, they depend on the framing of the dilemmas, and exhibit a host of other heuristics and biases. The prospects of debiasing those biases, and the possibility of coping with them institutionally, are no different from the prospects and possibilities in other spheres of governmental policymaking.[104]

3. Scarcity

An important contribution of behavioral research to the issue of redistribution comes from recent studies that uncovered previously unnoticed ramifications of poverty, thus augmenting the call for redistributive policies. Clearly, the inability to pay for adequate medical treatment and housing adversely affects one's health and housing conditions. The essence of money is the ability to purchase goods and services—hence a lack of money means a lack of basic goods and services. Poverty leads to famine in some parts of the world, and to dangerous levels of obesity in others.[105] Less obviously, poverty is associated with poor

100. *Id.* at 694–95.

101. McCaffery & Baron, *supra* note 3.

102. *Id.*; McCaffery & Baron, *supra* note 2, at 686, 696, 699.

103. *For additional studies, see* McCaffery & Baron, *supra* note 8; Jonathan Baron & Edward J. McCaffery, *Masking Redistribution (or Its Absence), in* BEHAVIORAL PUBLIC FINANCE, *supra* note 10, at 85.

104. *See generally supra* pp. 127–38 (on debiasing techniques) and 393–431 (on governmental decision-making). *See also* Edward J. McCaffery & Jonathan Baron, *The Political Psychology of Redistribution*, 52 UCLA L. Rev. 1745, 1784–90 (2005). On the unsuccessful attempt to deal with the non-salience of tax expenditures, see *supra* pp. 472–74.

105. Adam Drewnowski & S.E. Specter, *Poverty and Obesity: The Role of Energy Density and Energy Costs*, 79 AM. J. CLINICAL NUTRITION 6 (2004).

sleep quality;[106] economic insecurity increases physical pain and reduces pain tolerance;[107] financially stressed smokers are more likely to want to quit but less likely to try and succeed in doing so;[108] and child maltreatment is affected by parental economic circumstances.[109]

Focusing on judgment and decision-making, recent studies—including studies conducted by Sendhil Mullainathan, Eldar Shafir, and their colleagues—have shown how poverty (and other types of scarcity, such as time pressure and dieting) adversely affects people's cognitive performance and self-control.[110] When people are preoccupied by scarcity, their minds continually return to it, and they have less mental capacity for other aspects of life. For example, in one experiment, U.S. participants were presented with hypothetical scenarios that described a financial problem they might encounter (such as having to fix their car), when the costs of doing so were either low ($150) or high ($1,500). While thinking about how they would handle the problem, the participants performed nonverbal tasks that measured their ability to solve problems and their cognitive control. It was found that when presented with the easy financial problem, the performance of poor participants was as good as that of the well-off. In contrast, when presented with the more challenging financial problem, the cognitive performance of the poor—but not of the well-off—was reduced.[111] Another study examined the cognitive performance of sugar-cane farmers in India, over the planting cycle. It was found that the cognitive performance of the same farmers was diminished before harvest, when poor, as compared with after harvest, when flush with the proceeds of its sale.[112]

Scarcity thus adversely affects people's mental capacity—what Mullainathan and Shafir dub *bandwidth*. It hinders people ability to process information, solve problems, and make decisions. It decreases cognitive control, thereby hindering the selection and successful monitoring of behaviors that facilitate the attainment of one's goals. Shortage of money (like other scarcities) therefore results in poor decision-making. To this one might add that, for the poor, the margins of error are often much narrower than for the affluent, meaning that the same imprudent decision may have far worse outcomes.[113] Contrary to

106. Nirav P. Patel et al., *"Sleep Disparity" in the Population: Poor Sleep Quality Is Strongly Associated with Poverty and Ethnicity*, 10 BMC PUB. HEALTH 475 (2010).

107. Eileen Y. Chou, Bidhan L. Parmar & Adam D. Galinsky, *Economic Insecurity Increases Physical Pain*, 27 PSYCHOL. SCI. 443 (2016).

108. Mohammad Siahpush et al., *Smokers with Financial Stress Are More Likely to Want to Quit but Less Likely to Try or Succeed: Findings from the International Tobacco Control (ITC) Four Country Survey*, 104 ADDICTION 1382 (2009).

109. Christina Paxson & Jane Weldfogel, *Work, Welfare, and Child Maltreatment*, 20 J. LABOR ECON. 435 (2002).

110. *See generally* SENDHIL MULLAINATHAN & ELDAR SHAFIR, SCARCITY: WHY HAVING TOO LITTLE MEANS SO MUCH (2013).

111. Anandi Mani et al., *Poverty Impedes Cognitive Ability*, 341 SCI. 976, 977–78 (2013).

112. *Id.* at 979–80. *See also* Anuj K. Shah, Sendhil Mullainathan & Eldar Shafir, *Some Consequences of Having Too Little*, 338 SCI. 682 (2012) (experimentally examining borrowing decisions by "rich" and "poor" participants).

113. Marianne Bertrand, Sendhil Mullainathan & Eldar Shafir, *A Behavioral-Economics View of Poverty*, 94 AM. ECON. REV. 419–23 (2004).

some perceptions, being poor is not (or at least not only, or even primarily) a product of bad decisions; to a large extent, being poor leads to bad decisions—resulting in a vicious circle of poverty. This phenomenon accounts for the observations that, compared with the affluent, the poor do not take their medicines as regularly, do not send their children to school, do not save enough, and borrow too much.

These findings carry policy implications. For example, if poor decision-making by the poor is a product of tunnel vision, then imposing additional tasks on them in the form of financial education and other skill-development programs may actually make things worse, as it taxes their mental capacity even further (and the more exacting such programs are, the less successful they might be).[114] These findings also enrich the normative and policy analysis of redistributive policies, providing new arguments in their favor. Translating the behavioral findings into a concrete tax and other redistributive policies may, however, be extremely challenging.[115]

4. Wealth and Subjective Well-Being

Another important behavioral contribution to the issue of wealth redistribution comes from a large body of research into the correlation between wealth and happiness.[116] As indicated by the studies cited in the previous subsection and in a host of other studies, wealth is correlated with many aspects of life, including greater longevity, better physical and mental health, greater interpersonal trust, and lower risk of being a victim of violent crime.[117] According to objective goods theories of well-being, wealth is thus instrumental to attaining things that are intrinsically good. The picture is more nuanced from a hedonistic perspective, that is, according to a theory that defines human welfare in terms of having positive mental states, such as happiness and pleasure, and avoiding negative ones, such as pain and suffering.[118]

In the psychological literature, the hedonistic theory of human welfare is reflected in the notion of *subjective well-being* (SWB).[119] A large body of research has examined the correlation between wealth and SWB. The emerging picture is quite complex. The correlation between wealth and SWB depends, among other things, on the measure of SWB used, such as life satisfaction, pleasant affect, or lack of unpleasant affect, with considerable variations

114. Mullainathan & Shafir, *supra* note 110, at 173–76.

115. *See also infra* note 135 and accompanying text.

116. Happiness studies have other implications for the law as well. *See generally Conference on Legal Implications of the New Research on Happiness*, 37 J. Legal Stud. S1–S353 (2008); Happiness and the Law (John Bronsteen, Christopher Buccafusco & Jonathan S. Masur eds., 2015). *See also supra* pp. 343–48, 451–54.

117. Ed Diener & Robert Biswas-Diener, *Will Money Increase Subjective Well-Being? A Literature Review and Guide to Needed Research*, 57 Soc. Indicators Res. 119, 121 (2002).

118. On theories of human welfare, see generally Shelly Kagan, Normative Ethics 29–41 (1998); *supra* 14–15, 158–60.

119. On SWB and other conceptions of human welfare in the psychological literature, see Richard M. Ryan & Edward L. Deci, *On Happiness and Human Potentials: A Review of Research on Hedonic and Eudaimonic Well-Being*, 52 Ann. Rev. Psychol. 141 (2001).

across societies and contexts.[120] It has also been found that while the correlation between wealth and SWB remains significant even when controlling for variables such as education, gender, and marital status, these variables do affect the strength of the correlation. For example, income has a greater effect on the SWB of men than of women.[121] Unsurprisingly, an important moderator between income and global SWB is financial satisfaction—that is, the degree to which one is subjectively satisfied with one's financial situation.[122]

Two findings are particularly relevant to the present discussion. First, while there are statistically significant correlations between income and SWB within countries, these correlations are more pronounced in poor countries, such as India, and are quite small in wealthier countries, such as the United States and Germany.[123] In other words, the risk of unhappiness is much higher for poor people in poor societies. Second—and in keeping with the previous finding—income has a diminishing effect on SWB at the upper levels of income. Like the economic notion of decreasing marginal utility of money (resting on a preference-satisfaction notion of human well-being), income has a curvilinear effect on SWB.[124]

Relatedly, some longitudinal and experimental studies have examined the effect of *changes* in people's financial condition on their SWB. The evidence here is mixed. Not only does an increase in one's income not necessarily improve SWB, it may actually decrease it.[125] In a seminal study, Philip Brickman and his colleagues examined the effect of winning a lottery on people's happiness.[126] They tested the hypothesis that the contrast with the peak experience of winning a lottery would lessen the impact of ordinary pleasures, and that habituation would reduce the effect of new pleasures made possible by the winning—thus making winners not as happier as one might expect them to be. Indeed, lottery winners were not happier than people in the control group.[127] Moving from the individual to the national level, studies show that in countries that have experienced dramatic economic growth and huge increase in people's income over the years, such as the United States and Japan, the parallel increase in SWB has been hardly noticeable.[128]

120. Diener & Biswas-Diener, *supra* note 117, at 127.

121. For a review, see Diener & Biswas-Diener, *supra* note 117, at 128–30.

122. *Id.* at 130. *See also* MISHNA, *Pirkei Avot* (Ethics of our Fathers) 4:1 ("Who is rich? He who is satisfied with his lot").

123. *Id.* at 122–27, 129.

124. *Id.* at 129–30.

125. *Id.* at 131–34.

126. Philip Brickman, Dan Coates & Ronnie Janoff-Bulman, *Lottery Winners and Accident Victims: Is Happiness Relative?*, 36 J. PERSONALITY & SOC. PSYCHOL. 917 (1978).

127. Another study, however, found that medium-size lottery wins do reduce mental strain a year after the winning, compared with small-size and no wins. *See* Jonathan Gardner & Andrew J. Oswald, *Money and Mental Wellbeing: A Longitudinal Study of Medium-Sized Lottery Wins*, 26 J. HEALTH ECON. 49 (2007).

128. Diener & Biswas-Diener, *supra* note 117, at 139–42.

The finding that for middle- and upper-income people in developed countries, more income is unlikely to enhance subjective happiness considerably, if at all, should affect people's decisions how to lead their lives. It is also important in designing governmental redistributive policies, because it implies that taking money from the rich may have a very small impact on their subjective happiness, if any. Happiness studies thus provide a strong justification for progressive taxation.[129] Indeed, a study of national levels of SWB and tax progressivity across fifty-four countries found a positive correlation between the two (but no correlation between level of SWB and overall tax rate or government spending).[130]

Drawing concrete policy conclusions from the studies described above is not an easy task, however. For one thing, it is not self-evident that subjective well-being is an appropriate measure of human well-being for legal policymaking purposes.[131] For another, SWB studies typically rely on reported happiness and life satisfaction. Arguably, if people with very high levels of happiness tend to report lower happiness scores, then the concavity of the SWB function might reflect the reported SWB, rather than the actual one.[132] However, the concavity result has been found robust to extreme distortions of reported SWB.[133] Moreover, a large-scale comparison between reported SWB across U.S. states and objective measures of quality of life in those states found a strong correlation between the two, thus lending support for the validity of reported SWB.[134]

Assuming that subjective happiness is important for legal policymaking and that we can overcome the reported versus actual SWB difficulty, translating the findings of happiness studies into tax policy still remains a daunting task. The interactions between variables that have been found to affect SWB, such as absolute and relative income, marital status, and disability—and between them and the redistributive and incentive effects of taxation—are complex; and the data about people's SWB does not easily fit into the economic models of optimal taxation.[135] That said, the standard economic models of optimal taxation do not rest on sounder empirical evidence, so taking into account crude psychological evidence appears to be advisable nevertheless.

129. Thomas D. Griffith, *Progressive Taxation and Happiness,* 45 B.C. L. Rev. 1363 (2004).

130. Shigehiro Oishi, Ulrich Schimmack & Ed Diener, *Progressive Taxation and the Subjective Well-Being of Nations,* 23 Psychol. Sci. 86 (2012). The correlation between progressivity and SWB was mediated by citizens' satisfaction with public goods, such as education and public transportation.

131. *See supra* note 118 and accompanying text. For the claim that SWB is at least as good a measure of human welfare as preferences-satisfaction, and superior to income, for the purpose of public policy, see Paul Dolan & Tessa Peasgood, *Measuring Well-Being for Public Policy: Preferences or Experiences?,* 37 J. Legal Studies S5 (2008).

132. David A. Weisbach, *What Does Happiness Research Tell Us about Taxation?,* 37 J. Legal Stud. S293, S308–09 (2008). For additional concerns about reported SWB as a measure of welfare for the purposes of tax policymaking, see Diane M. Ring, *Why Happiness?: A Commentary on Griffith's Progressive Taxation and Happiness,* 45 B.C. L. Rev. 1413, 1415–16 (2004).

133. Maarten C.M. Vendrik & Geert B. Woltjer, *Happiness and Loss Aversion: Is Utility Concave or Convex in Relative Income?,* 91 J. Pub. Econ. 1423 (2007).

134. Andrew J. Oswald & Stephen Wu, *Objective Confirmation of Subjective Measures of Human Well-Being: Evidence from the U.S.A.,* 327 Sci. 576 (2010).

135. Weisbach, *supra* note 132; Ring, *supra* note 132, at 1417–22.

5. Methods and Objects of Redistribution

Even people who agree that advancing a certain pattern of distributive justice is a worthy goal, and that attaining this goal is a legitimate (or even vital) role of the state, may disagree about the appropriate means of doing so. Specifically, while some believe that redistribution should be implemented through tax-and-transfer means—including progressive taxation, subsidies, unemployment benefits, and the like—others argue that redistribution could and should be achieved through private-law rules as well, such as passing minimum wage legislation, setting minimal standards of habitability in residential leases, and interpreting insurance policies according to the reasonable expectations of the insured. A key argument against the use of private-law rules as a means of redistribution is that they result in a "double distortion."[136] In addition to the adverse effect on productivity—which is common to all modes of redistribution—redistributive legal rules also distort the market and obstruct otherwise mutually beneficial transactions. For example, minimum wage legislation arguably increases the rate of unemployment because some people, who would have been hired for a lower wage, would not be hired at all due to this legislation.[137] Inasmuch as this is the case, redistributive legal rules may actually yield a perverse outcome, making some of the underprivileged worse off. Once again, we cannot discuss this and comparable arguments in the ongoing debate about the legitimacy and efficacy of different means of redistribution, specifically private-law rules.[138] Instead, we shall focus on some behavioral contributions to this debate.

To begin with, the assumption that private-law rules have the same adverse effect on the incentive to work as taxes is questionable, once overoptimism, the certainty effect, and mental accounting are taken into account.[139] Suppose, for example, that tort liability is expanded for redistributive purposes in a context where the typical tortfeasor is richer than the typical tort victim. While a rational maximizer would treat the expected cost of the expanded liability as akin to a tax on her income, actual people might not. This is because overly optimistic people are likely to underestimate the chances that they will commit a tort, and because people do not treat certain outcomes (such as paying a tax) in the same way as they treat uncertain ones (being liable in tort).[140] As for mental accounting, since income tax is calculated according to one's earnings, it is likely to be perceived as a direct charge

136. Louis Kaplow & Steven Shavell, *Why the Legal System Is Less Efficient than the Income Tax in Redistributing Income*, 23 J. LEGAL STUD. 667 (1994).

137. *See* David Neumark & William Wascher, *Minimum Wages and Low-Wage Workers: How Well Does Reality Match the Rhetoric*, 92 MINN. L. REV. 1296 1309–11 (2008) (reviewing the literature and concluding that minimum wages tend to raise unemployment). For an opposing view, see DAVID CARD & ALAN B. KRUEGER, MYTH AND MEASUREMENT: THE NEW ECONOMICS OF THE MINIMUM WAGE (1995).

138. Notable contributions to this debate include Anthony T. Kronman, *Contract Law and Distributive Justice*, 89 YALE L.J. 472, 498–510 (1980); Richard Craswell, *Passing on the Costs of Legal Rules: Efficiency and Distribution in Buyer-Seller Relationships*, 43 STAN. L. REV. 361 (1991); Chris William Sanchirico, *Taxes versus Legal Rules as Instruments for Equity: A More Equitable View*, 29 J. LEGAL STUD. 797 (2000).

139. Christine Jolls, *Behavioral Economics Analysis of Redistributive Legal Rules*, 51 VAND. L. REV. 1653 (1998).

140. On overoptimism and the certainty effect, see generally *supra* pp. 61–64 and 34, respectively.

against income, while tort liability might not.[141] To be sure, the generality and empirical basis of these arguments are not self-evident; hence a more nuanced examination is called for. But those insights cannot be disregarded.

Moreover, thus far we have implicitly assumed that the appropriate object of redistribution is money. This premise is consistent with the preferences-fulfillment theory of human welfare underpinning standard economic analysis,[142] since money can be used in various ways, as one sees fit. Behavioral insights complicate the picture, however. First, if recipients are likely to use welfare payments in a suboptimal fashion due, among other things, to their cognitive biases and the adverse effects of poverty on decision-making, giving in-kind benefits may enhance recipients' welfare more than money.[143] For example, the government may use the money collected through taxes to provide the underprivileged with subsidized education and medical treatment, rather than with money. In the same vein, private-law rules ordinarily provide in-kind benefits when they set, for example, minimal standards of products' safety and apartments' habitability. Unlike tax-and-transfer mechanisms, private-law rules may also convey non-monetary benefits, such as fair and respectful treatment by one's employer, landlord, supplier, and insurer. Such treatment is directly conducive to one's welfare, and (unlike taxes) is unlikely to have any effect on one's incentives to engage in productive activity.

Behavioral studies have also shown that the value attributed to an object depends on its source and the process by which it has been obtained. For example, subjects who were led to believe that they have received something as a reward for doing well in a task valued it more highly than those who were led to believe that they received it because they did poorly at the same task.[144] A sense of entitlement increases the valuation of an object. Alas, tax-and-transfer payments are more likely to be perceived as handouts than entitlements.[145] The fact that people value things that they feel they are getting as a matter of right more highly than things that are associated with failure and charity means that private-law rules have an important advantage as a redistributive means.

A similar dynamic exists on the part of the givers. Suppliers, employers, and landlords who pay high taxes to finance transfer payments to the poor may resent this much more than if they are required to treat buyers, employees, and tenants according to fair "rules of the game." Private-law redistributive rules thus enjoy an advantage in terms of their effect on the givers and their political acceptability, as well.

141. On mental accounting, see *supra* note 152 and accompanying text.

142. *See supra* p. 14–15.

143. Daphna Lewinsohn-Zamir, *In Defense of Redistribution through Private Law*, 91 Minn. L. Rev. 326 (2006). On the adverse effects of poverty on decision-making, see *supra* pp. 483–85. On legal paternalism, see also *supra* pp. 165–71.

144. George Loewenstein & Samuel Issacharoff, *Source Dependence in the Valuation of Objects*, 7 J. Behav. Decision Making 157 (1994). For comparable studies, see Lewinsohn-Zamir, *supra* note 143, at 362–66.

145. Lewinsohn-Zamir, *supra* note 143, at 367–68.

E. Modifying Behavior through Taxes

Taking measures to prevent or deter people from harming other people—whether because the negative externalities of one's behavior are likely to detract from the overall social utility, or because such harming violates the deontological constraint against harming other people—is relatively uncontroversial. Along with other legal measures (such as tort law), taxes have long been recognized and are actually used as a possible means of causing people to internalize the costs of their harmful behavior (and the benefits of their beneficial behavior). Named after the economist Arthur Pigou, such Pigovian taxes (and Pigovian subsidies for positive externalities) raise all sorts of measurement and other difficulties, which lie beyond the scope of our discussion.

At any rate, the levying of Pigovian taxes assumes that people are rational maximizers who do not care about the welfare of other people per se, but react to the incentives and disincentives created by taxes. More controversially, governments throughout the world use the tax system to deter self-injurious behaviors and encourage self-benefitting ones, as well. Common examples include sin taxes on alcohol and tobacco products, and tax subsidies for long-term savings. In that sense, taxes are yet another means, along with compulsory duties and soft nudges, that the state can use to assist people in overcoming common cognitive limitations, such as motivated reasoning, myopia, and bounded willpower. Of course, the very distinction between harming others and harming oneself is sometimes blurred. For example, becoming an alcoholic adversely affects both the alcoholic and his or her environment.

Using the tax system in that way raises the general issue of legal paternalism, which we discussed elsewhere in the book.[146] Of the various paternalistic measures in states' arsenals, taxes are a relatively mild measure, as people remain free to engage in the discouraged activity (for a higher price) and to refrain from engaging in the beneficial (and financially encouraged) one. The relative merits and demerits of various paternalistic measures—specifically, the choice between taxes/subsidies and other means—vary from one context to another, and involve contentious normative and policy issues.[147]

The behavioral perspective can directly contribute to this debate in two primary ways. First, behavioral studies help in identifying, and understanding the causes of, self- (and other-) harming behavior, which may possibly justify legal treatment. Second, behavioral insights may be taken into account in designing taxes (and tax benefits) that aim to modify people's behavior. For instance, consistent with the notion of loss aversion, it has been found that a five-cent shopping-bag tax reduced the use of disposable bags by over forty percentage points, whereas an equivalent five-cent bonus for using reusable bags had no effect.[148] Generally, inasmuch as the primary purpose of sin taxes is to discourage injurious

146. *See supra* pp. 165–71.

147. Brian D. Galle, *Tax, Command . . . or Nudge? Evaluating the New Regulation*, 92 TEX. L. REV. 837 (2014).

148. Tatiana Homonoff, *Can Small Incentives Have Large Effects? The Impact of Taxes versus Bonuses on Disposable Bag Use*, AM. ECON. J.: ECON. POL'Y (forthcoming, working paper, June 2015, *available at:* https://

behavior rather than to maximize revenues for the state, such taxes should presumably be made as salient as possible, rather than concealed (although the picture becomes considerably more complex once people's heterogeneity, taxes' substitution and income effects, and the distinction between taxes and tax benefits are taken into account).[149]

Theoretically, paternalistic sin taxes can produce Pareto improvements: people with self-control problems would benefit from consuming less unhealthy products, and people without such problems would benefit from the proceeds of the tax.[150] Arguably, since such sin taxes have a greater impact on the poor, because their consumption of unhealthy products is more price-sensitive, the poor benefit from those taxes more than the affluent. Not only are such taxes less regressive than is commonly assumed, they may even have progressive effects.[151]

These arguments, however, raise several concerns. For one thing, the standard measure of Pareto improvements is the satisfaction of people's actual preferences, and sin taxes obviously do not meet this criteria. But even if one uses an objective measure of human welfare, people's heterogeneity makes the design of a sin tax that would indeed benefit everyone practically impossible. Moreover, inasmuch as the consumption of unhealthy products, such as tobacco and alcohol, is addictive, the effect of the tax on consumption may be limited, while its regressive effect—assuming that such addictions are more common among the poor—may be quite large.

Another example of using the tax system as a means of modifying behavior draws on the finding that people do not necessarily treat money as fungible. Rather, they use a set of processes—*mental accounting*—to manage their financial activities. People assign activities to specific accounts, group expenditures into categories, and constrain their spending by implicit or explicit budgets. Accounts can be defined narrowly or broadly, and may be balanced once a week, a month, and so forth.[152] It follows, for example, that receiving a tax rebate as a lump sum at the end of the fiscal year may be more conducive to saving than fully incorporating a tax cut or a tax credit in the monthly withholding, as people are more likely to save an extraordinary bonus than a portion of their regular income.[153]

In general, people's heterogeneity, the multiplicity of cognitive biases, and the concern that profit-seeking firms might induce individuals to act in self-harming ways—all pose

wagner.nyu.edu/files/faculty/publications/Homonoff%20-%20Can%20Small%20Incentives%20Have%20Large%20Effects_0.pdf).

149. Brian D. Galle, *Carrots, Sticks, and Salience,* 67 Tax L. Rev. 53 (2013).

150. Ted O'Donoghue & Matthew Rabin, *Optimal Sin Taxes,* 90 J. Pub. Econ. 1825 (2006).

151. Jonathan Gruber & Bottond Köszegi, *Tax Incidence when Individuals Are Time-Inconsistent: The Case of Cigarette Excise Taxes,* 88 J. Pub. Econ. 1959 (2004). *But see supra* note 108 and accompanying text. On the behavioral economics of redistribution, see generally *supra* pp. 480–89.

152. On mental accounting, see generally Richard H. Thaler, *Mental Accounting and Consumer Choice,* 4 Marketing Sci. 199 (1985); Richard H. Thaler, *Mental Accounting Matters,* 12 J. Behav. Decision Making 183 (1999).

153. Hersh M. Shefrin & Richard H. Thaler, *The Behavioral Life-Cycle Hypothesis,* 26 Econ. Inquiry 609, 636 (1988).

great challenges to any attempt to modify people's behavior through taxes.[154] In that respect, the tax system is no different from other means of modifying people's behavior.[155]

F. Conclusion

This chapter surveyed the behavioral findings pertaining to tax law (including the design of the tax system, economic decision-making by taxpayers, tax compliance, and people's normative judgments with regard to taxes in general and tax progressivity in particular), redistribution (including the cognitive ramifications of poverty, the correlation between wealth and subjective well-being, and the choice of methods and objects of redistribution), and the use of taxes as a means of modifying human behavior. The introduction of behavioral insights into tax law and policy is a relatively new development. Nevertheless, the fact that much of the literature builds on experimental and empirical studies that were specifically designed to examine judgments and decision-making on taxes and tax-related matters (rather than on general psychological studies) makes the behavioral contribution particularly apt and insightful in this sphere. Additional progress may possibly be made by more closely distinguishing between various taxes and various factual contexts. For example, even after we break down the notion of tax salience into political salience and market salience, each of these two categories may be overly broad. It is possible that people's judgments and decisions are context-dependent to an extent that makes any generalization about reactions to market salience, for example, somewhat problematic. Ultimately, while the debates about tax policy have not become less intense as a result of the new empirical and experimental findings, these findings have surely placed the debate on sounder empirical and behavioral footings.

154. *See, e.g.*, Edward J. McCaffery, *Behavioral Economics and Fundamental Tax Reform, in* FUNDAMENTAL TAX REFORM: ISSUE, CHOICES, AND IMPLICATIONS 455 (John W. Diamond & George R. Zodrow eds., 2008); Faulhaber, *supra* note 65; Galle, *supra* note 149; Ryan Bubb, Patrick Corrigan & Patrick L. Warren, *A Behavioral Contract Theory Perspective on Retirement Savings*, 47 CONN. L. REV. 1317 (2015).

155. *See supra* pp. 171–85.

PART FIVE

The Legal Process

14

Litigants' Behavior

A. Introduction

Litigation and settlement behavior has attracted the attention of legal economists and behavioral researchers from early on. The bargaining, or bargaining-like, structure of litigation suggested that economic insights that had been developed in other contexts of bargaining could be applied to it, and that the behavioral findings regarding negotiation behavior could be applied to litigants. In addition to the litigation and settlement literature, which pertains to civil litigation, this chapter broadens the discussion to include several aspects of client-attorney relationships and plea bargains in criminal proceedings.[1]

The chapter opens with a brief overview of the standard economic analysis of litigation and settlement (Section B). It then analyzes a series of behavioral impediments to settlement—including biases in the gathering and interpretation of information, litigants' overoptimism, "irrational" concerns about fairness and retribution, biases stemming from the adversarial nature of litigation, reference dependence in the assessment of settlement proposals, and defendants' risk seeking (Section C). Despite the multitude of strategic and behavioral obstacles to settlement, the majority of legal disputes do settle. Section D points to two behavioral phenomena—regret avoidance and loss aversion—that strongly encourage settlements. Section E looks at behavioral explanations for the relatively limited use of alternative dispute resolution mechanisms, and Section F takes a closer look at the role of lawyers and client-lawyer relationships. Finally, Section G highlights the behavioral contribution to the understanding of plea bargaining in criminal proceedings.[2]

1. On the overall effect of litigants' behavior on the evolution of the law, see *supra* pp. 192–93.

2. For a comprehensive survey of the behavioral study of litigation and settlement, see Jennifer K. Robbennolt, *Litigation and Settlement, in* The Oxford Handbook of Behavioral Economics and the Law 623 (Eyal Zamir & Doron Teichman eds., 2014).

B. Standard Economic Analysis of Litigation and Settlement

A vast number of studies have analyzed litigants' behavior from an economic perspective.[3] Broadly speaking, a potential plaintiff will sue when the expected gross return from litigation exceeds its expected costs. The expected gross return depends on the underlying facts of the case and the applicable legal rules, as well as the amount of resources the plaintiff puts into the case. The outcomes of litigation (and the plaintiff's optimal investment in the case) also depend on the scope of the defendant's investment in her defense. Pursuing a case all the way to trial is usually very costly for both parties. For both litigants, the costs of litigation include not only the direct, monetary expenses of court and lawyer fees, but also the effort, time, and unpleasantness of judicial confrontation, and possible reputational and other indirect costs. It is therefore not surprising that most lawsuits are settled before trial, and some are resolved through various alternative dispute resolution (ADR) mechanisms.[4]

A rational plaintiff who considers whether to settle or litigate a case would first calculate the expected return of the case, based on the expected judicial award (or the monetary equivalent of other judicial reliefs), and the probability of attaining it. She would then subtract her expected costs of litigation from the gross expected return, to determine the minimal amount for which she might settle the case—that is, her *reservation value*. The defendant's reservation value—the maximum amount he might agree to pay to settle the case out of court—would be the expected judicial award plus his litigation costs. Under conditions of full information, accurate assessments of the expected award, and positive litigation costs, a settlement would be Pareto superior to litigation. As long as litigation costs are sufficiently high, even asymmetric information and divergent assessments of the expected judicial outcome do not obstruct settlement.

While settlement is almost always mutually beneficial, economic analysis does not predict that all cases would be settled. One major obstacle to settlement may be asymmetric information. If, due to lack of information or misinformation, the plaintiff's reservation value is higher than the defendant's, there is no scope for potential mutually beneficial agreements. Moreover, even under full information, the bargaining over settlement is carried out under conditions of bilateral monopoly: the plaintiff can only settle with the defendant, and the defendant can only settle with the plaintiff. Each party may rationally reject a settlement offer within the range of possible agreements, in an attempt to extract a larger share of the settlement surplus. Tough bargaining may yield a better bargain, but may also result in a bargaining impasse.

A party's inclination to settle depends, among other things, on her bargaining power. The more costly any delay in payment is for the plaintiff, the more quickly she will settle the case; the more profitable such delay is for the defendant, the slower he will be to settle.

3. For an overview of the literature, see Kathryn E. Spier, *Litigation, in* 1 HANDBOOK OF LAW AND ECONOMICS 259 (A. Mitchell Polinsky & Steven Shavell eds., 2007). *See also* Robert G. Bone, *Economics of Civil Procedure, in* 3 THE OXFORD HANDBOOK OF LAW AND ECONOMICS (Francesco Parisi ed., 2017).

4. RICHARD A. POSNER, ECONOMIC ANALYSIS OF LAW 779–80 (9th ed. 2014).

Differences in the cost of continued negotiations may result from the fee arrangement between each litigant and his or her lawyer, the expenses involved at different stages of the trial preparation, and the parties' opportunity costs. The prospect and timing of settlement also hinge on the parties' attitude to risk: the less risk-averse a party, the more likely he or she is to reject settlement offers within the range of mutually beneficial settlements.

This brief description does not do justice to the richness and sophistication of economic analysis of litigation and settlement. Among other things, it disregards cases in which the object of litigation is indivisible; neglects the possible effects of various civil procedure rules (such as rules about pretrial discovery and the allocation of litigation costs); and ignores the role of attorneys (whose interests often diverge from those of the clients, depending on the agreed fee arrangement). It is nevertheless sufficient for the limited purpose of providing a background for the ensuing discussion.

C. Behavioral Impediments to Settlement

1. General

Several empirical studies have shown that litigants sometimes reject settlement offers that in retrospect turn out to be more favorable than the court judgment.[5] Of course, the fact that the ultimate judgment turns out to be less favorable than the rejected settlement offer does not necessarily imply that the initial decision was irrational or imprudent. Decisions over settlement offers are made under conditions of uncertainty, and may be based on incomplete information. Litigants may also rationally dismiss settlement offers for various strategic and other reasons (such as a desire for publicity, or an interest in establishing a precedent), even if they do not expect to do better financially at trial. Nevertheless, there is ample evidence that failures to settle cases are due in part to behavioral biases, which are described below. Moreover, even when cases are eventually settled, they are often settled too late—to the detriment of both the parties and the court system. Such delays may also be due to behavioral causes.[6]

2. Information, Self-Serving Bias, and Overoptimism

Settlement decisions crucially depend on litigants' estimation of trial outcomes in the absence of settlement. Divergent predictions regarding trial outcomes are therefore a major cause of impasses in settlement negotiations. Both overestimation and underestimation of trial outcomes are likely to yield suboptimal settlement decisions. We focus on

5. Samuel Gross & Kent Syverud, *Getting to No: A Study of Settlement Negotiations and the Selection of Cases for Trial*, 90 MICH. L. REV. 319 (1991); Samuel Gross & Kent Syverud, *Don't Try: Civil Jury Verdicts in a System Geared to Settlement*, 44 UCLA L. REV. 51 (1996); Jeffrey Rachlinski, *Gains, Losses, and the Psychology of Litigation*, 70 S. CALIF. L. REV. 113, 149–67 (1996); Randall L. Kiser, Martin A. Asher & Blakeley B. McShane, *Let's Not Make a Deal: An Empirical Study of Decision-Making in Unsuccessful Settlement Negotiations*, 5 J. EMPIRICAL LEGAL STUD. 551 (2008).

6. Andrew J. Wistrich & Jeffrey J. Rachlinski, *How Lawyers' Intuitions Prolong Litigation*, 86 S. CAL. L. REV. 571 (2013).

overestimation, however, because it is more prevalent, and because underestimation likely results in a stronger willingness to settle—hence it is not an impediment to settlement.

One obvious cause of unrealistic predictions about trial outcomes is incomplete information. However, in addition to the objective scarcity of information, litigants' information gathering may be skewed due to the *confirmation bias*—namely, the tendency to seek out information that meshes with one's beliefs and prior decisions.[7] In the present context, plaintiffs may be more attentive to new information that corroborates their initial decision to file suit, and defendants to information that aligns with their decision to defend the suit.

Furthermore, when information is not readily available, the very search for it affects the way it is used once it is obtained.[8] Initially, litigants may postpone the decision on whether to settle a case until additional information becomes available—following the heuristic that "more information is better than less."[9] Once litigants get the information, the very fact that they had to wait for it, or to actively search for it, increases its salience and perceived importance. Consequently, their decision may be different from the one they would have made had the information been available all along. When the newly obtained information strengthens a litigant's position, it may thus hinder a settlement. This may occur even if the same settlement offer would have been accepted (1) had the information been available all along, or (2) had the litigant made the settlement decision without waiting for the missing information.[10]

Impediments to settlement may result not only from biased information gathering (due to the confirmation bias) and the increased perceived importance of sought-after information, but also from well-known biases in the recollection and interpretation of information. People tend to recall selectively, and to interpret information in a self-serving manner.[11] Thus, even if both litigants are exposed to the same new evidence, when the evidence is open to conflicting interpretations, each party is likely to interpret it in her own favor.[12] This *attitude polarization* broadens, rather than narrows, the gap between the parties' predictions. Due to the adversarial nature of litigation, and in keeping with

7. *See generally supra* pp. 58–61.

8. Maia J. Young et al., *The Pursuit of Missing Information in Negotiation,* 117 ORG. BEHAV. & HUM. DECISION PROCESSES 88 (2012).

9. Another heuristic that may possibly delay a settlement decision is "keeping doors open." *See generally* Jiwoong Shin & Dan Ariely, *Keeping Doors Open: The Effect of Unavailability on Incentives to Keep Options Viable,* 50 MGMT. SCI. 575 (2004).

10. *See also* Amos Tversky & Eldar Shafir, *The Disjunction Effect in Choice under Uncertainty,* 3 PSYCHOL. SCI. 305 (1992); Anthony Bastardi & Eldar Shafir, *Nonconsequential Reasoning and Its Consequences,* 9 CURRENT DIRECTIONS PSYCHOL. SCI. 216 (2000); Donald A. Redelmeier, Eldar Shafir & Prince S. Aujla, *The Beguiling Pursuit of More Information,* 21 MED. DECISION MAKING 374 (2001); Wistrich & Rachlinski, *supra* note 6, at 604–12.

11. On self-serving biases, see *supra* pp. 58–76.

12. Charles G. Lord, Lee Ross & Mark R. Lepper, *Biased Assimilation and Attitude Polarization: The Effects of Prior Theories on Subsequently Considered Evidence,* 37 J. PERSONALITY & SOC. PSYCHOL. 2098 (1979); George Loewenstein & Don A. Moore, *When Ignorance Is Bliss: Information Exchange and Inefficiency in Bargaining,* 33 J. LEGAL STUD. 37 (2004).

the biases accompanying such relationships,[13] litigants may be particularly suspicious of evidence that is provided by the other party. The self-serving bias may produce not only divergent interpretation of the facts and conflicting assessment of the evidence, but also divergent interpretation of the legal norms and conflicting assessment of what would constitute a fair resolution of the dispute.[14]

All these biases in gathering and interpreting information lead to overoptimism about each party's prospects in court.[15] People tend to assume that their perceptions and judgments are unbiased (the so-called *naïve realism*),[16] while those of their adversaries are biased. They therefore tend to believe that an unbiased arbiter—the court—will side with them. Experimental studies have demonstrated that these psychological biases play a role in settlement negotiations, and that the more the parties manifest them, the less likely they are to settle the case successfully.[17]

People's predictions are not only overoptimistic—they are often overconfident about the accuracy of those predictions, as well.[18] In one study, all subjects received the same background information about a legal dispute. In addition, some of the subjects received the plaintiff's arguments, some the defendant's arguments, and some both sets of arguments. Although it was clear to the subjects of the first two groups that they were seeing only one-sided arguments, their predictions were nevertheless tilted in favor of the party whose arguments they received. Compared with the subjects who had received both sets of arguments, members of the first two groups were generally less accurate, but more confident, in their predictions.[19] Inasmuch as these findings accurately reflect litigants' perceptions, the combined effect of overoptimism and overconfidence may obstruct mutually beneficial settlements.

The involvement of attorneys in settlement negotiations may help to overcome these behavioral hurdles to settlement. However, as discussed below, attorneys are not immune

13. *See infra* pp. 501–02.

14. Linda Babcock & George Loewenstein, *Explaining Bargaining Impasse: The Role of Self-Serving Biases*, 11 J. ECON. PERSP. 109 (1997). On the importance of perceived fairness, see also *infra* 101–06.

15. On overoptimism, see generally *supra* pp. 61–64.

16. Lee Ross & Andrew Ward, *Naive Realism in Everyday Life: Implications for Social Conflict and Misunderstanding*, *in* VALUES AND KNOWLEDGE 103 (Edward S. Reed, Elliot Turiel & Terrance Brown eds., 1996); Emily Pronin, Carolyn Puccio & Lee Ross, *Understanding Misunderstanding: Social Psychological Perspectives*, *in* HEURISTICS AND BIASES: THE PSYCHOLOGY OF INTUITIVE JUDGMENT 636, 641–53 (Thomas Gilovich, Dale Griffin & Daniel Kahneman eds., 2002).

17. *See, e.g.*, George Loewenstein et al., *Self-Serving Assessments of Fairness and Pretrial Bargaining*, 22 J. LEGAL STUD. 135 (1993).

18. On overconfidence, see generally Don A. Moore & Paul J. Healy, *The Trouble with Overconfidence*, 115 PSYCHOL. REV. 502 (2008). Of the three meanings of overconfidence discussed in that article—overestimation of one's performance, over-ranking of one's performance relative to others, and excessive certainty about the accuracy of one's beliefs—we refer here to the last. *See also supra* pp. 64–66.

19. Lyle A. Brenner, Derek J. Koehler & Amos Tversky, *On the Evaluation of One-Sided Evidence*, 9 J. BEHAV. DECISION MAKING 59 (1996).

to these cognitive biases,[20] so their involvement in settlement negotiations may not remove these hurdles.

3. "Irrational" Motives

While standard economic analysis conventionally measures utility by people's willingness to pay for things, it does not assume that people care only about money. Thus, for example, litigants may rationally prefer litigation to settlement in order to gain more publicity, or to exert indirect pressure on policymakers. If litigants are repeat players, they may prefer a court judgment in order to establish a favorable precedent, even if the expected monetary award is lower than the settlement offer in the current case. However, as discussed in Chapter 2, contrary to the assumption that people are rational maximizers of their own utility, people also have other-regarding preferences and moral commitments.[21] Such preferences and commitments may stand in the way of settlements.

Thus, while people strive to maximize their own utility, they also care about substantive fairness—even when this is contrary to their own self-interest.[22] The concern about substantive fairness may affect the prospect of settlement either way. A litigant may agree to a settlement that is possibly worse than what she expects to get in court, if she believes the proposed settlement is fair. By the same token, she may reject a settlement offer that is possibly better than the expected court ruling, if she views the offer to be unfair.[23] Unfortunately, given that litigants' judgments of substantive fairness are often self-biased,[24] litigants' concern about fairness is more likely to impede settlements than to encourage them.

Retribution and vengeance motivations may also preclude settlements.[25] Thus, in an experiment conducted by Russell Korobkin and Chris Guthrie, subjects were more inclined to accept a settlement offer when the other party's behavior was deemed less offensive and more excusable.[26] Plaintiffs may prefer litigation when they seek judicial recognition of their suffering and condemnation of the defendant's wrongdoing. Sometimes, litigants

20. *See infra* pp. 512–16.

21. *See supra* pp. 94–110.

22. *See supra* pp. 102–04.

23. *See, e.g.*, Robert Mnookin & Lee Ross, *Introduction, in* BARRIERS TO CONFLICT RESOLUTION 2, 11 (Kenneth Arrow et al. eds., 1995).

24. *See, e.g.*, Loewenstein et al., *supra* note 17; Babcock & Loewenstein, *supra* note 14.

25. On the psychology of retribution, see generally Linda J. Skitka & Daniel C. Wisneski, *Justice Theory and Research: A Social Functionalist Perspective, in* HANDBOOK OF PSYCHOLOGY, VOL. 5: PERSONALITY AND SOCIAL PSYCHOLOGY 406, 415–16 (Irving B. Weiner, Howard A. Tennen & Jerry M. Suls eds., 2d ed. 2012); John T. Jost & Aaron C. Kay, *Social Justice: History, Theory, and Research, in* 2 HANDBOOK OF SOCIAL PSYCHOLOGY 1122, 1144–45 (Susan T. Fiske, Daniel T. Gilbert & Gardner Lindzey eds., 5th ed. 2010).

26. Russell Korobkin & Chris Guthrie, *Psychological Barriers to Litigation Settlement: An Experimental Approach*, 93 MICH. L. REV. 107, 142–47 (1994).

prefer litigation to settlement even if they expect smaller material gains from the former, because they believe that litigation will inflict greater damage on their opponent.[27]

Another concern has to do with procedural justice. People care not only about their self-interest, substantive fairness, and retribution, but also about procedural fairness.[28] Specifically, litigants may prefer a trial or a court-annexed arbitration over settlement because they wish to tell their side of the story.[29] For similar reasons, however, the prospects of reaching an agreement, and litigants' satisfaction with its content, are enhanced to the extent that the settlement negotiations are perceived as procedurally fair.[30]

Finally, behavioral studies have shed light on the effect of apologies—or lack thereof—on the prospect of settlement. As summarized by Jennifer Robbennolt, these studies have generally found that "apologies influence claimants' perceptions, judgments, and decisions in ways that are likely to make settlement more likely—for example, altering perceptions of the dispute and the disputants, decreasing negative emotion, improving expectations about the future conduct and relationship of the parties, changing negotiation aspirations and fairness judgments, and increasing willingness to accept an offer of settlement."[31]

4. Biases Stemming from the Adversarial Nature of Litigation

Perfectly rational litigants might miss opportunities for mutually beneficial settlements due to strategic conduct, such as withholding information or using delay tactics. However, in addition to such strategic reasons, settlement negotiations may fail due to biases associated with the adversarial nature of litigation. People's tendency to ignore or underestimate their own self-serving biases in perceptions and judgments[32] may lead them to view the positions of the other party as biased, unreasonable, or even cynical. Attributing bias to the other party may prompt one to bargain less cooperatively—which may, in turn, cause the other party to view her as more biased and thus react in a more belligerent manner, and so forth. The outcome of such process may well be escalation, rather than resolution, of the conflict.[33]

27. Jean R. Sternlight, *Lawyers' Representation of Clients in Mediation: Using Economics and Psychology to Structure Advocacy in a Nonadversarial Setting*, 14 OHIO ST. J. ON DISP. RESOL. 269, 306 (1999).

28. *See generally supra* pp. 104–06.

29. Robert J. MacCoun, *Voice, Control, and Belonging: The Double-Edged Sword of Procedural Fairness*, 1 ANN. REV. L. & SOC. SCI. 171, 172, 189 (2005); Sternlight, *supra* note 27, at 304–05.

30. Rebecca Hollander-Blumoff & Tom R. Tyler, *Procedural Justice in Negotiation: Procedural Fairness, Outcome Acceptance, and Integrative Potential*, 33 LAW & SOC. INQ. 473 (2008).

31. Jennifer K. Robbennolt, *Attorneys, Apologies, and Settlement Negotiation*, 13 HARV. NEGOTIATION L. REV. 349, 350 (2008) [hereinafter Robbennolt, *Attorneys and Apologies*]. *See also* Korobkin & Guthrie, *supra* note 26, at 147–50; Jennifer K. Robbennolt, *Apologies and Legal Settlement: An Empirical Examination*, 102 MICH. L. REV. 460 (2003); Jennifer K. Robbennolt, *Apologies and Settlement Levers*, 3 J. EMPIRICAL LEGAL STUD. 333 (2006).

32. *See supra* note 16 and accompanying text; *supra* pp. 66–68.

33. *Cf.* Kathleen A. Kennedy & Emily Pronin, *When Disagreement Gets Ugly: Perceptions of Bias and the Escalation of Conflict*, 34 PERSONALITY & SOC. PSYCHOL. BULL. 833 (2008).

In principle, the greater flexibility of a settlement agreement (compared with a court ruling) facilitates integrative bargaining, rather than a purely distributive one. Such bargaining may produce creative solutions that better serve the parties' interests. However, the adversarial posture of litigation may lead litigants to assume that they are in a win-lose situation, whereby any benefit to one party is necessarily to the other's detriment. This *fixed-pie bias* may result in a bargaining impasse.[34]

Finally, another phenomenon related to the adversarial nature of settlement negotiations is *reactive devaluation.* Several studies have shown that people tend to devalue a proposal made by one's opponent rather than by a neutral party or an ally.[35] Involvement of a third party, such as a mediator, may help to overcome this difficulty.[36]

5. Reference-Dependence in Assessing Settlement Offers

Depending on the particular circumstances of the negotiation, otherwise beneficial settlement offers may be rejected because they are worse than some perceived benchmark.[37] For instance, plaintiffs may compare the sum of damages offered to them in settlement to damages awards reported in the media. Since media reports typically focus on outlier awards and overrepresent successes by plaintiffs, and since even the benchmarks proposed by litigants' attorneys may be unrepresentative due to the availability heuristic, such comparisons may lead to unwise rejections of settlement offers.[38]

In the same vein, if a party makes a settlement offer, then reneges on it and makes an inferior offer, the other party may dismiss the new offer because it seems less attractive than the initial offer—even if she might have accepted it had the initial offer never been made. Since the initial offer is no longer available, dismissing the subsequent offer seems irrational if it is greater than the expected net return from litigation.[39] Another scenario was studied experimentally by Korobkin and Guthrie. In a between-subject design, subjects were asked to imagine themselves as plaintiffs. They were then told that they had received, and rejected, an initial settlement offer of either \$2,000 or \$10,000, and were asked to consider a final offer of \$12,000. Since the initial offer served as a reference point, subjects were significantly

34. Max H. Bazerman & Margaret A. Neale, *Heuristics in Negotiation: Limitations to Effective Dispute Resolution*, *in* NEGOTIATING IN ORGANIZATIONS 51, 62–63 (Max H. Bazerman & Roy J. Lewicki eds., 1983). *See also* Leigh Thompson & Reid Hastie, *Social Perception in Negotiation*, 47 ORG. BEHAV. & HUM. DECISION PROCESSES 98 (1990).

35. Constance Stillinger et al., *The Reactive Devaluation Barrier to Conflict Resolution* (unpublished manuscript, 1990, *described in* Lee Ross & Constance Stillinger, *Barriers to Conflict Resolution*, 7 NEGOT. J. 389, 394 (1991)); Ifat Maoz et al., *Reactive Devaluation of an "Israeli" vs. "Palestinian" Peace Proposal*, 46 J. CONFLICT RES. 515 (2002). *See also* Korobkin & Guthrie, *supra* note 26, at 150–60.

36. On mediation and other alternative dispute resolution mechanisms, see *infra* pp. 507–09.

37. On reference dependence, see generally *supra* pp. 42–57, 76–86.

38. Jennifer K. Robbennolt & Christina A. Studebaker, *News Media Reporting on Civil Litigation and Its Influence on Civil Justice Decision Making*, 27 LAW & HUM. BEHAV. 5 (2003).

39. *Cf.* Robbennolt, *supra* note 2, at 630.

more willing to accept the final offer when it followed an initial one of $2,000 than when it followed an offer of $10,000.[40]

These and other phenomena of reference-dependence, such as the compromise and contrast effects,[41] may obstruct successful settlements.[42]

6. Framing Litigation Outcomes and Risk Attitude

The claim that the behavior of negotiators depends on how they frame the outcomes of negotiation—in particular, whether they perceive the outcomes as belonging to the domains of gains or losses—was established experimentally by Margaret Neal and Max Bazerman in 1985.[43] Neale and Bazerman found that positive (gains) framing leads to more concessionary behavior and greater success in negotiation than negative (losses) framing. They explained these results as stemming from the negotiators' different attitude to risk: since people are more risk-averse in the domain of gains, they are willing to make more concessions to avoid the risk of impasse.[44] It was then hypothesized that plaintiffs would be more risk-averse than defendants when negotiating a settlement, because plaintiffs likely frame the bargaining as pertaining to potential gains (the judicial award they might get), while defendants likely frame it as potential losses (the award they might have to pay).[45] In the mid-1990s, Linda Babcock and her coauthors and Jeffery Rachlinski provided experimental and empirical support for the conjecture that settlement negotiations may fail due to the defendants' risk-seeking behavior.[46] According to the natural framing of settlement negotiations, plaintiffs face a choice between accepting a sure gain by settling the case, and an uncertain outcome through continued negotiations or litigation. Defendants, on the other hand, choose between accepting a sure loss and the uncertain outcome of continued negotiations or litigation. Since—contrary to the axioms of expected utility theory—people tend to be risk-averse in the domain of gains and risk-seeking in the domain of losses, plaintiffs tend to set themselves a reservation value that is lower than their expected net recovery, while defendants' reservation value is more favorable to them than the expected outcome of litigation. These results were obtained in experiments using students (in both studies) and trial attorneys (in the study by Babcock et al.) as subjects. A subsequent study found a similar effect when federal magistrate judges were asked to assess settlement offers

40. Korobkin & Guthrie, *supra* note 26, at 139–42.

41. *See supra* pp. 77–79, 83–85.

42. *See generally* Robbennolt, *supra* note 2, at 627, 633–34. On the contrast effect and settlements, see also Mark Kelman, Yuval Rottenstreich & Amos Tversky, *Context-Dependence in Legal Decision Making*, 25 J. Legal Stud. 287 (1996).

43. Margaret A. Neale & Max H. Bazerman, *The Effects of Framing and Negotiator Overconfidence on Bargaining Behavior*, 28 Acad. Mgmt. J. 34 (1985).

44. On people's different risk attitudes in the domains of gains and losses, see generally *supra* 42–44.

45. Robin Hogarth, Judgement and Choice 105 & n.20 (2d ed. 1987).

46. Linda Babcock et al., *Forming Beliefs about Adjudicated Outcomes: Perceptions of Risk and Reservation Values*, 15 Int'l Rev. L. & Econ. 289 (1995); Rachlinski, *supra* note 5.

from the perspectives of plaintiffs and defendants.[47] Examination of databases of settlement offers and trial outcomes has found strong empirical support for the experimental findings.[48]

Framing litigation as entailing gains for plaintiffs assumes that the pertinent reference point for them is their current position. This assumption—which is consistent with the documented phenomenon of hedonic adaptation to injuries[49]—has been supported by several studies.[50] However, this framing is not universal, and some studies have been able to experimentally manipulate the framing of settlement and litigation outcomes for plaintiffs as either gains or losses.[51] In addition to the plaintiff's position prior to the event that had triggered the lawsuit (e.g., an accident), another possible reference point is the litigant's level of aspiration. As in other bargaining contexts, the litigant's expectations and aspirations may determine whether a certain settlement offer is viewed as entailing a loss or a gain, thus inducing different risk attitudes.[52]

While prospect theory posits that people are generally risk-averse with regard to gains and risk-seeking in the domain of losses, it also posits that these attitudes to risk are reversed for low-probability gains and losses.[53] It follows that plaintiffs in high-stakes, low-probability claims are likely to be risk-seeking, and therefore reject settlement offers that exceed the expected value of the claim. Chris Guthrie has provided some experimental support for this conjecture, and discussed regulatory measures aimed at deterring plaintiffs from filing frivolous suits—or, failing that, encouraging them to settle.[54]

Some studies indicate that certain litigants, such as insurance professionals, are less susceptible to framing effects.[55] It has also been claimed that attorneys are less prone to framing effects, and may therefore play a constructive role in attaining settlements[56]—but the evidence in this regard is inconclusive.[57]

47. Chris Guthrie, Jeffrey J. Rachlinski & Andrew J. Wistrich, *Inside the Judicial Mind*, 86 CORNELL L. REV. 777, 794–99 (2001).

48. Rachlinski, *supra* note 5, at 150–60; Kiser, Asher & McShane, *supra* note 5, at 566–67.

49. John Bronsteen, Christopher Buccafusco & Jonathan S. Masur, *Hedonic Adaptation and the Settlement of Civil Lawsuits*, 108 COLUM. L. REV. 1516 (2008).

50. *See, e.g.*, Rachlinski, *supra* note 5, at 128–30; Babcock et al., *supra* note 46; Eyal Zamir & Ilana Ritov, *Revisiting the Debate over Attorneys' Contingent Fees: A Behavioral Analysis*, 39 J. LEGAL STUD. 245, 268–69 (2010).

51. Korobkin & Guthrie, *supra* note 26, at 120–38; Zamir & Ritov, *supra* note 50, at 262–64. *See also infra* pp. 510–12, 593–94.

52. Russell Korobkin, *Aspirations and Settlement*, 88 CORNELL L. REV. 1 (2002).

53. Amos Tversky & Daniel Kahneman, *Advances in Prospect Theory: Cumulative Representation of Uncertainty*, 5 J. RISK & UNCERTAINTY 297 (1992); *supra* p. 43.

54. Chris Guthrie, *Framing Frivolous Litigation: A Psychological Theory*, 67 U. CHI. L. REV. 163 (2000).

55. Chris Guthrie & Jeffrey J. Rachlinski, *Insurers, Illusions of Judgment & Litigation*, 59 VAND. L. REV. 2017, 2033–42 (2006).

56. Russell Korobkin & Chris Guthrie, *Psychology, Economics, and Settlement: A New Look at the Role of the Lawyer*, 76 TEX. L. REV. 77 (1997).

57. *See infra* p. 515.

7. Conclusion

This section reviewed a host of psychological biases in perception, processing information, judgment, and choice that might impede mutually beneficial settlements. These include deviations from the assumptions of cognitive rationality (such as availability and reference dependence) and motivational rationality (such as concerns about substantive fairness and vengeance). These phenomena may account for the empirical finding that many settlement offers that in retrospect should have been accepted, are nevertheless rejected.

D. Behavioral Factors Encouraging Settlement: Anticipated Regret and Loss Aversion

The studies described above explain how people's heuristics and biases may hinder beneficial settlements. Conversely, the combination of regret and loss aversion may explain why the majority of cases do settle.[58]

People experience the unpleasant feeling of regret when they realize that they could have obtained a better outcome had they made a different decision.[59] Regret entails self-recrimination,[60] and threatens one's self-image.[61] The anticipation of possible ex-post regret affects people's decisions ex ante.[62] All else being equal, people prefer the option that minimizes or eliminates their exposure to an ex-post feeling of regret.

When a decision-maker faces a choice between two (or more) options, the anticipation of regret primarily depends on what she expects to know ex post. She may know the outcomes of neither the chosen option nor the unchosen one (no knowledge); she may know the outcome of both options (full knowledge); or she may know the outcome of the chosen option, but not of the forgone one (partial knowledge).[63] In the full-knowledge condition, the outcome of the forgone option is a salient reference point: if it turns out to be better than the outcome of the chosen option, one is likely to feel regret. Regret is also possible in the partial-knowledge condition, as the decision-maker may imagine what the

58. Theodore Eisenberg & Charlotte Lanvers, *What Is the Settlement Rate and Why Should We Care?*, 6 J. EMPIRICAL LEGAL STUD. 111 (2009).

59. Marcel Zeelenberg & Rik Pieters, *A Theory of Regret Regulation 1.0*, 17 J. CONSUMER PSYCHOL. 3 (2007).

60. Robert Sugden, *Regret, Recrimination, and Rationality*, 19 THEORY & DECISION 77 (1985).

61. Richard P. Larrick, *Motivational Factors in Decision Theories: The Role of Self-Protection*, 113 PSYCHOL. BULL. 440 (1993).

62. David Bell, *Regret in Decision Making under Uncertainty*, 30 OPERATIONS RES. 961 (1982); Graham Loomes & Robert Sugden, *Regret Theory: An Alternative Theory of Rational Choice under Uncertainty*, 92 ECON. J. 805 (1982); Graham Loomes, *Further Evidence of the Impact of Regret and Disappointment in Choice under Uncertainty*, 55 ECONOMICA 47 (1988); Richard P. Larrick & Terry L. Boles, *Avoiding Regret in Decisions with Feedback: A Negotiation Example*, 63 ORG. BEHAV. & HUM. DECISION PROCESSES 87 (1995). For an overview, see Zeelenberg & Pieters, *supra* note 59.

63. David E. Bell, *Risk Premiums for Decision Regret*, 29 MGMT. SCI. 1156 (1983); Ilana Ritov & Jonathan Baron, *Outcome Knowledge, Regret, and Omission Bias*, 64 ORG. BEHAV. & HUM. DECISION PROCESSES 119 (1995).

outcomes of the unchosen alternative might have been—but it is clearly less likely in that case.[64]

In and of themselves, neither the earlier regret theories,[65] nor the more recent *decision affect theory*,[66] hinge on the decision-maker's loss aversion. However, loss aversion intensifies the effect of anticipated regret. Whenever the forgone option may turn out better or worse than the chosen one, the chooser may anticipate either ex-post regret or ex-post delight. Loss aversion implies that the potential regret would loom larger than the delight.[67] Anticipated delight is therefore unlikely to offset anticipated regret.

Often, the options a person faces do not differ in terms of the ex-post resolution of the uncertainties they involve. When an investor faces a choice between buying stock A and stock B, she will eventually know which stock did better. Similarly, when following a choice between two gambles, only the chosen gamble is resolved; the subject anticipates partial knowledge whatever she chooses. However, sometimes the available options differ from one another, with one resulting in full knowledge, and the other resulting in only partial knowledge. All else being equal, under such circumstances a loss- and regret-averse person would likely view the partial-knowledge option as considerably more attractive than the full-knowledge one, because not knowing the outcome of the forgone option shields one from anticipated regret. Such asymmetry is characteristic of choices between a certain outcome and a gamble whose outcomes are not resolved if not chosen.

This is precisely the typical situation in settlement negotiations. The litigant either accepts a settlement offer—a certain result—or goes to trial, whose results would never be known if the parties settle the case. Regret- and loss-aversions thus explain why so many litigants (plaintiffs and defendants alike) prefer to settle their cases despite the prevalence of asymmetric information, strategic considerations, and a host of psychological barriers to settlement. Chris Guthrie has provided some experimental and anecdotal support for this claim, as well as advice to lawyers whose clients or adversaries are regret- and loss-averse.[68]

Initially, lawyers should assess how regret-averse their clients and their opponents are. For example, Guthrie conjectures that large, institutional litigants would display less

64. Barbara Mellers and her coauthors did not find support for the imagined outcomes hypothesis. Barbara Mellers, Alan Schwartz & Ilana Ritov, *Emotion-Based Choice*, 128 J. EXPERIMENTAL PSYCHOL.: GENERAL 332, 339–40, 342 (1999). Additional factors that were found to impinge on the anticipated regret are the probability that the forgone option would indeed yield a better outcome (surprising events tend to yield greater regret); the difference between the two outcomes (the larger the difference, the greater the anticipated regret); the decision-maker's personal traits (people with low self-esteem are more prone to experience regret); and the question of whether the outcome would result from an action or inaction. *See* Ilana Ritov, *Probability of Regret: Anticipation of Uncertainty Resolution in Choice*, 66 ORG. BEHAV. & HUM. DECISION PROCESSES 228 (1997); Mellers, Schwartz & Ritov, *supra*; Robert A. Josephs et al., *Protecting the Self from the Negative Consequences of Risky Decisions*, 62 J. PERSONALITY & SOC. PSYCHOL. 26 (1992); Larrick, *supra* note 61.

65. Bell, *supra* note 62; Bell, *supra* note 63; Loomes & Sugden, *supra* note 62.

66. Barbara Mellers et al., *Decision Affect Theory: Emotional Reactions to the Outcomes of Risky Options*, 8 PSYCHOL. SCI. 423 (1997); Mellers, Schwartz & Ritov, *supra* note 64.

67. Larrick & Boles, *supra* note 62, at 89; Mellers, Schwartz & Ritov, *supra* note 64, at 338, 339.

68. Chris Guthrie, *Better Settle than Sorry: The Regret Aversion Theory of Litigation Behavior*, 1999 U. ILL. L. REV. 43, 73–81, 81–88.

regret-aversion than one-shot, individual litigants, and that regret-aversion may loom larger on the eve of trial.[69] Lawyers might also take into account the evidence that suggests that people with low self-esteem are more prone to experience regret.[70] Once it is apparent that one's client is regret-averse, this should be factored into the decision of whether to accept a settlement offer. However, as subsequent studies have shown, people are remarkably good at avoiding self-blame, so the experienced, ex-post regret is usually much smaller than anticipated. This means that people "who pay to avoid future regrets may be buying emotional insurance that they do not actually need,"[71] and lawyers would do well to advise their clients accordingly. By the same token, lawyers may wish to take advantage of their opponents' regret- and loss-aversion in settlement negotiations.

E. Alternative Dispute Resolution

As an alternative to adjudication or a negotiated settlement without the help of a neutral third party, disputants may resort to alternative dispute resolution (ADR) mechanisms—primarily arbitration and mediation. Often, parties opt for ADR because they are compelled to do so under the contract that forged their relationship, or pursuant to a court order mandating the use of court-annexed dispute-resolution procedures. Here we only discuss the voluntary use of ADR when disputants are free to choose between litigation and ADR.

ADR has several advantages over litigation.[72] In arbitration, the parties may choose an arbitrator who is an expert in the subject matter of the dispute rather than a generalist. This expertise saves the disputants the need to provide the arbitrator with background information, and presumably improves the quality of her decision. Arbitration may thus be less costly, and result in a decision based on a more accurate understanding of the pertinent issues. The arbitrator's expertise, and the less formal nature of the arbitration procedure, are also likely to facilitate a speedier resolution. The resolution of the dispute is faster also because an arbitrator's schedule may be more flexible than that of a court, and because her decision usually cannot be appealed. While there are also downsides to these characteristics, the parties' ability to tailor the process to their needs should enable them to overcome at least some of these drawbacks.

Mediation, too, is usually quicker and considerably cheaper than adjudication. Like private arbitration, it provides the disputants with confidentiality. Unlike arbitration, since the mediator cannot impose any solution, mediation leaves the parties with far more control over the outcomes of the process. The fact that a successful mediation results in an agreed solution enhances the prospects of compliance, and may facilitate future cooperation

69. *Id.* at 82–84.

70. Josephs et al., *supra* note 64; Larrick, *supra* note 61.

71. Daniel Gilbert et al., *Looking Forward to Looking Backward: The Misprediction of Regret*, 15 Psychol. Sci. 346 (2004). *See also* Deborah A. Kermer et al., *Loss Aversion Is an Affective Forecasting Error*, 17 Psychol. Sci. 649 (2006).

72. *See, e.g.*, Robert H. Mnookin, *Alternative Dispute Resolution*, *in* The New Palgrave Dictionary of Economics and the Law (Peter Newman ed., 2002).

between the parties. The scope of solutions available through mediation is broader than in litigation or arbitration. A mediator can help the parties find a creative arrangement that would more effectively serve their interests than a court order or an arbitration award.

There is not much empirical data about the extent to which private, voluntary ADR mechanisms are in fact superior to ordinary litigation. Numerous experimental and empirical studies have examined the ex-ante preferences for, and ex-post satisfaction with, various nonjudicial dispute-resolution mechanisms. These studies mostly compare arbitration to mediation or court-annexed ADR to ordinary litigation, rather than private, voluntary ADR to litigation.[73] However, some studies do provide a fairly clear picture of people's attitudes to ADR compared with litigation. For example, a large qualitative and quantitative survey established that most lawyers (both outside and inside counsels) and business executives have positive opinions of mediation and of ADR more generally.[74] It is therefore puzzling why so few disputants voluntarily opt for ADR. "Voluntary ex post arbitration and mediation seem to occur, but in negligible proportions of the number of disputes in which a neutral third party intervenes."[75]

Various explanations have been offered for this puzzle, including unfamiliarity with ADR and the interests of lawyers who prefer litigation. Here we focus on behavioral ones. Many of the behavioral obstacles to settlement discussed above—such as overoptimism and overconfidence, "irrational" concerns about retribution and vengeance, reactive devaluation, and risk-seeking in the domain of losses—may also hinder an agreement to transfer a dispute to ADR.[76]

In addition, it has been suggested that litigants may be reluctant to opt for ADR due to their *ambiguity aversion*.[77] People usually prefer gambles in which the probabilities of the possible outcomes are known (risks) to gambles in which the probabilities are unknown (uncertainty). Therefore, to the extent that people know—or believe that they know—more about litigation and unaided negotiation (for settlement) than about mediation or arbitration, they may prefer the former.[78]

Yet another explanation for the infrequent use of ADR is the *default effect*, or *status-quo bias*.[79] For most people, the default is litigation (including settlement negotiations in the shadow of litigation). As commonly described and perceived, alternative dispute resolution mechanisms are merely an alternative. Faced with a suggestion to give up litigation and opt

73. For an overview, see Donna Shestowsky, *Disputants' Preferences for Court-Connected Dispute Resolution Procedures: Why We Should Care and Why We Know So Little*, 23 OHIO STATE J. ON DISP. RESUL. 549 (2008).

74. John Lande, *Getting the Faith: Why Business Lawyers and Executives Believe in Mediation*, 5 HARV. NEGOT. L. REV. 137 (2000).

75. Maurits Barendrecht & Berend R. de Vries, *Fitting the Forum to the Fuss with Sticky Defaults: Failure in the Market for Dispute Resolution Services?*, 7 CARDOZO J. CONFLICT RESOL. 83, 90 (2005).

76. *See supra* pp. 497–500, 500–01, 502–03, and 503–04, respectively; Barendrecht & de Vries, *supra* note 75, at 96–105.

77. *See generally supra* pp. 39–42.

78. Barendrecht & de Vries, *supra* note 75, at 102–03.

79. *See generally supra* pp. 48–50.

for ADR, a disputant would likely view accepting this suggestion as an action, and sticking with litigation as an omission. Since opting for ADR usually involves both prospects and risks, loss-averse people may be reluctant to part with their entitlement to have their dispute adjudicated in the court. The status quo and omission biases would therefore result in a reluctance to use ADR mechanisms.

Adjudication and ADR are ordinarily symmetrical, in the sense that both result in partial knowledge: only the outcome of the chosen option will be known ex post. Unlike a settlement, opting for ADR does not shield one from ex-post regret more than sticking with the default of litigation.[80] Since mediation often implies mutual concessions, it may be more attractive to plaintiffs (who frame the outcome as a possible gain) than to defendants (who frame it as a possible loss), due to the different risk attitudes in the realms of gains and losses. However, once a mediation has begun, an agreement is just as attractive as an unaided settlement, since it protects the parties from ex-post regret. Also, the more time and effort the parties invest in mediation, the more reluctant they might be to abandon it and opt for litigation, due to their *sunk costs*.[81]

F. Attorneys and Clients

1. General

In line with its ordinary assumptions, standard economic analysis posits that lawyers and their clients are rational maximizers of their respective interests. The interests of attorneys and clients diverge not only because each one strives to maximize her net returns, but also because they often have additional personal concerns, such as publicity and enhanced reputation (in the case of the lawyer), and vindication of rights and recognition of wrongdoing (in the case of the client). Thus, for example, plaintiffs and their attorneys typically react differently to defendants' apologies: while laypersons show greater willingness to settle a dispute after an apology, attorneys may set higher aspirations and take a tougher position in negotiations when an apology is offered.[82] Generally, attorneys may seek primarily to maximize expected financial outcomes, while clients may be more concerned about equity.[83]

The inherent agency problem in the lawyer-client relationships is exacerbated by the fact that the quality and quantity of the lawyer's services are largely unobservable and unverifiable. Standard economic analysis thus focuses on contractual and other means to align the lawyer's interests with those of the client—mainly through the incentive effects of fee arrangements.[84]

80. *See supra* pp. 505–07. Expected regret is likely to affect the decision as to whether to accept a settlement offer made by a mediator or adjudicate the case in court, but it is unclear how it would affect the initial decision as to whether to opt for mediation.

81. *See supra* pp. 56–57.

82. Robbennolt, *Attorneys and Apologies*, supra note 31.

83. Korobkin & Guthrie, *supra* note 56, at 108–12.

84. *See, e.g.*, Kevin M. Clermont & John D. Currivan, *Improving on the Contingent Fee*, 63 CORNELL. L. REV. 529 (1978); Rudy Santore & Alan D. Viard, *Legal Fee Restrictions, Moral Hazard, and Attorney Rents*, 44 J. L. & ECON.

To date, the main contribution of behavioral studies to the understanding of attorney-client relationships and their effect on litigation and settlement has been twofold. First, the "irrational" cognitive biases of clients and attorneys—such as loss aversion, the default effect, and fairness constraints—help explain otherwise puzzling aspects of legal fee arrangements. Second, many studies have examined the effect of agency (making decisions for others rather than for oneself) and professional expertise on judgment and decision-making, including in the specific context of attorneys' decisions on litigation and settlement. Accordingly, Subsection 2 will describe behavioral factors affecting the design of fee arrangements, and Subsection 3 will discuss the questions of whether, and to what extent, the involvement of attorneys affects decision-making with regard to litigation and settlement. Finally, Subsection 4 will point to empirical and experimental findings that call into question the assumption that lawyers are rational maximizers of their own utility.

2. Fee Arrangements

Lawyers representing clients in legal disputes are usually paid on one of three bases, or some combination thereof: a fixed fee, an hourly fee, or a contingent fee (CF)—with or without reimbursement for specific costs. Schematically, a fixed fee assures the client that he would not have to pay more than the agreed sum, but provides the weakest incentive for the lawyer to invest time and effort in handling the case, because her remuneration does not depend on the outcomes of her efforts. An hourly fee assures a reasonable proportion between the scope of the lawyer's work and her fee, and is particularly appropriate when it is difficult to foresee how much work the case will require. However, it incentivizes the lawyer to spend excessive time and effort on the case, and to delay or obstruct settlements in order to maximize her fee. Under the CF arrangement, the attorney's fee is contingent on the success of the claim, calculated as a certain percentage of the amount recovered, and paid upon recovery. CFs enable plaintiffs of limited financial means to secure otherwise unaffordable legal services. CFs induce attorneys not to take cases whose expected value is too small, thus saving their clients the costs involved in pursuing such claims. They also incentivize the attorney to win the case or attain a favorable settlement, while avoiding investing too much time in handling it. However, CFs do not achieve perfect alignment of interests. Since the attorney reaps only a portion of the fruits of her efforts, she is incentivized to put too little effort into the case and to settle too early.[85] While under a CF the plaintiff does not have to pay any fee if his claim fails, he might have to pay a very high fee for very little work. In the United States, CF arrangements are the standard method of financing civil litigation in several types of suits, including personal injuries. Interestingly, the CF rate is rather uniform: the conventional flat CF rate is one-third of the recovery.

549 (2001); A. Mitchell Polinsky & Daniel L. Rubinfeld, *Aligning the Interests of Lawyers and Clients,* 5 AM. L. & ECON. REV. 165 (2003); Albert Choi, *Allocating Settlement Authority under a Contingent-Fee Arrangement,* 32 J. LEGAL STUD. 585 (2003); Winand Emons, *Playing It Safe with Low Conditional Fees versus Being Insured by High Contingent Fees,* 8 AM. LAW & ECON. REV. 20 (2006).

85. *See also* Eric Helland & Alexander Tabarrok, *Contingency Fees, Settlement Delay and Low-Quality Litigation: Empirical Evidence from Two Datasets,* 19 J.L. ECON. & ORG. 517 (2003). CFs also induce attorneys to prefer monetary awards over alternative relief.

Many aspects of fee arrangements—specifically CFs—have been fiercely debated among economists, jurists, and sociologists.[86] Among other things, it has been claimed that the standard fee rate in the United States is not a competitive zero-profit rate, either due to various market failures[87] or because it pays out to provide the attorney with a stronger monetary incentive to win a high recovery (the higher the lawyer's share of the recovery through the CF, the more her interest converges with that of the client).[88] Others have claimed that, all things considered, the prevailing rate is quite reasonable.[89]

Behavioral insights may help explain several features of the legal services market. First, a series of controlled experiments have demonstrated that the attractiveness of CF for plaintiffs is due largely to loss aversion.[90] Since the outcomes of the lawyer's work are uncertain, the plaintiffs likely perceive their choice between a contingent and non-contingent fee as a choice between two gambles. Non-contingent fees expose the plaintiff to the risk of losing her case and still having to pay the attorney's fee. It is therefore a *mixed gamble,* in which the plaintiff may either win some gain or incur a loss. In contrast, while a CF may yield a smaller gain in the case of success, it eliminates the risk of loss, because no fee is paid to the lawyer if the case is lost. It is therefore perceived as a *pure positive gamble,* in which the plaintiff may either gain or break even. Loss-averse people strongly prefer pure positive gambles over mixed ones, as the former preclude the possibility of losing.[91] Some of the experiments supporting this argument were conducted with experienced tort lawyers as subjects (making decisions as though they were clients), and involving relatively small sums—suggesting that information problems and the decreasing marginal utility of money play only a modest role in plaintiffs' choices in this context. Moreover, the subjects' preferences did not significantly change when the incentive effects of the fees were neutralized—indicating that loss aversion plausibly plays a greater role than incentives in plaintiffs' choice of fee arrangement.

Another puzzle is that despite their logical possibility, economic sensibility, and practical feasibility, CFs are very popular with plaintiffs but quite rare with defendants. One behavioral explanation for this rarity is based on people's risk attitude in the domain of losses. Unlike plaintiffs, defendants plausibly frame both a judgment compelling them to pay damages, and the attorney's fee, as pure losses. Hence, the unique appeal of CF for

86. For brief overviews and numerous references, see Zamir & Ritov, *supra* note 50, at 250–52; Eyal Zamir, Barak Medina & Uzi Segal, *Who Benefits from the Uniformity of Contingent Fee Rates?,* 9 Rev. L. & Econ. 357, 358–59, 361–62 (2013); Winand Emons, *Legal Fees and Lawyers' Compensation, in* 3 The Oxford Handbook of Law and Economics, *supra* note 3, at 247.

87. *See, e.g.*, Lester Brickman, *The Market for Contingent Fee-Financed Tort Litigation: Is It Price Competitive?*, 25 Cardozo L. Rev. 68 (2003).

88. Santore & Viard, *supra* note 84.

89. Herbert M. Kritzer, Risks, Reputations, and Rewards: Contingency Fee Legal Practice in the United States 180–218 (2004).

90. Zamir & Ritov, *supra* note 50. On loss aversion, see generally *supra* pp. 42–57.

91. This claim assumes that plaintiffs typically take their position prior to hiring the lawyer as the pertinent reference point. This assumption has been supported by several studies. *See* Zamir & Ritov, *supra* note 50, at 268–69; *supra* note 50 and accompanying text.

plaintiffs—turning a mixed gamble into a pure positive one—does not exist for defendants, who face a choice between two pure negative gambles. Moreover, people are typically risk-seeking in the domain of losses.[92] Hence, while CF narrows the range of potential losses, this risk reduction is not something defendants are ordinarily willing to pay for.[93] This explanation has been borne out experimentally.[94]

Finally, it has been argued that the uniformity of CF rates in the United States (one-third of the recovery) attests to anticompetitive price-fixing, which results in clients paying supra-competitive fees.[95] In response, it has been pointed out that inasmuch as there is a "positive assortative matching" of cases and attorneys, such that the best attorneys handle the most lucrative cases, the second-best attorneys handle the second-most lucrative cases, and so forth, uniform CF rates result in fees that are effectively correlated to the quality of legal services provided.[96] Several behavioral phenomena support the stability of this market. First, while it may be mutually beneficial for the attorney and her client to agree on a very high CF rate— especially when the case is expected to require a lot of work while the expected recovery is small—such rates are plausibly rare because they are perceived as being unfair. Experimental studies have demonstrated that people tend to view CF arrangements as raising an issue of *division fairness* (the fairness of the division of the recovery between the client and her attorney), as opposed to *fairness of exchange* (the equivalence between the attorney's work and her remuneration). Consequently, attorneys who care about fairness or about their reputation avoid very high CF rates.[97] Within these fairness constraints, the great popularity of a CF rate of one-third is likely due to the fact that this is a fraction with a small denominator—that is, a natural *focal point*.[98] Finally, the very existence of a standard CF rate leads people to believe that it is fair.[99] It serves as a benchmark for judging fairness in particular cases, and creates a default effect, that is, a tendency not to opt out of this default arrangement.[100]

3. Lawyers' Decision-Making

Once a lawyer is hired, her involvement in the litigation and settlement processes may improve decision-making for several reasons. First, thanks to their training and experience, lawyers are better informed about the pertinent risks and prospects. Second, the analytical skills of lawyers are often superior to those of their clients. Third, since they are usually less

92. *See generally supra* pp. 42–44.

93. On defendant's greater risk seeking, see also *supra* pp. 503–04.

94. Zamir & Ritov, *supra* note 50, at 275–79.

95. *See, e.g.*, Brickman, *supra* note 87.

96. Zamir, Medina & Segal, *supra* note 86.

97. Eyal Zamir & Ilana Ritov, *Notions of Fairness and Contingent Fees*, 74 LAW & CONTEMP. PROBS. 1 (2011). *See also supra* pp. 102–04.

98. Zamir, Medina & Segal, *supra* note 86, at 369.

99. *Cf. supra* p. 106.

100. *See also* Zamir, Medina & Segal, *supra* note 86, at 369–71. On the default effect, see generally *supra* pp. 179–82.

emotionally involved in the dispute, attorneys are more likely to calmly consider the pros and cons of the available options. However, as previously noted, lawyers' financial and other interests may not coincide with those of their clients—in which case their advice may not serve the latter's best financial and other interests.

Beyond these general observations, attorneys may also be less susceptible to cognitive biases than their clients for two reasons. First, lawyers' training and experience may teach them to overcome those biases. Second, it is possible that people who advise others or make decisions on their behalf are less susceptible to cognitive biases than people who decide for themselves.

Both conjectures have been explored in relation to various professional agents, including attorneys. With regard to professional expertise, although the findings are somewhat ambiguous, it appears that judgments can reflect true expertise if they are reached within a decision-making environment that (1) is regular and predictable, and (2) offers people an opportunity to learn those regularities.[101] Litigation and settlement provide imperfect opportunities for learning from experience. As for the first condition, the difficulty lies in the fact that cases differ from one another in various respects, including the characteristics of the client, the opponent, and the judge; the events giving rise to the claim; and the legal environment (due, for example, to new precedents). Regarding the second condition, the difficulty is that when making decisions about litigation and settlement, more often than not one does not know what would have happened had one made a different decision.[102]

A considerable body of research has directly examined attorneys' susceptibility to various cognitive biases. Some of the studies have dealt with attorneys' predictions of case outcomes, which are crucial to litigation and settlement decisions. In one study, involving both civil and criminal cases, attorneys were asked to describe the minimum goal for the outcome of a case they were actually handling, and to state the degree of certainty, in percentage terms, that they would meet that goal.[103] Employing the *consider-the-opposite* debiasing technique,[104] about half of the participants were asked to generate reasons why they might fail to achieve their minimum goal before describing it. The other half were asked to generate such reasons only after setting the minimum goal.

It turned out that in 32 percent of all cases, the final outcome matched the goal set by the lawyer; in 24 percent of the cases the final outcome exceeded the minimum goal; and in 44 percent the minimum goal was not achieved. Overall, lawyers were overoptimistic and overconfident in their predictions. Interestingly, the more overoptimistic lawyers were in setting their minimum goals, the more overconfident they were about their predictions.

101. Daniel Kahneman & Gary Klein, *Conditions for Intuitive Expertise: A Failure to Disagree*, 64 Am. Psychologist 515 (2009).

102. *See supra* pp. 505–07.

103. Jane Goodman-Delahunty et al., *Insightful or Wishful: Lawyers' Ability to Predict Case Outcomes*, 16 Psychol. Pub. Pol'y & L. 133 (2010).

104. *See generally supra* pp. 135–36.

Accuracy of prediction did not increase with years of legal experience. Female lawyers were slightly less overoptimistic and less overconfident than males. Although 44 percent of the lawyers failed to attain their stated minimum goal, only 18 percent expressed disappointment with the case outcome in retrospect, and some indicated that they had met their goal when in fact they had not. Generating possible reasons for failing to achieve the minimum goal did not enhance the accuracy of lawyer's predictions.

These findings do not offer much optimism about lawyers' immunity to the overoptimism and overconfidence biases, their ability to learn from experience, or the effectiveness of simple debiasing techniques in this regard. In fact, professional experience may teach lawyers that moderate overoptimism and overconfidence are instrumental in attracting clients, assuring clients that they will represent them zealously, attaining favorable settlements,[105] and winning cases in court.[106] However, people's role-induced, biased predictions of litigation outcomes have been shown to exist even when subjects have ceased to act in their assigned role, and even when they had monetary incentives to make accurate predictions.[107]

Lawyers' and law students' overconfidence has also been demonstrated in an experimental study of predictions of verdicts. Pairs of law students and of experienced trial attorneys estimated actual jury verdicts. When participants were given access to a partner's estimate, lawyers improved their predictions, especially when their initial prediction had been far off the mark. However, participants failed to make full use of the "second opinion," because they underweighted their partners' estimates relative to their own. Indeed, experienced attorneys gave less weight to their partners' opinions than did law students.[108]

Predicting litigation outcomes may also be affected by how possible outcomes are described. It has been shown that people's probability assessments of uncertain events depend on the events' description. While the judged probabilities of complementary events add up to 1, the judged probabilities of more than two exclusive and exhaustive events often add up to more than 1 (a phenomenon dubbed *subadditivity*), and the judged probability of an event generally increases when it is described as a disjunction of specific possibilities.[109]

Imagine that a judge may either accept or dismiss a breach-of-contract claim; and that dismissal of the case may rest on the ruling that no contract has been made in the first place, that the contract has been lawfully rescinded by the defendant, or that the contract

105. Oren Bar-Gill, *The Evolution and Persistence of Optimism in Litigation*, 22 J. LAW, ECON. & ORG. 490 (2006).

106. *See also* Elizabeth F. Loftus & Willem A. Wagenaar, *Lawyers' Predictions of Success*, 28 JURIMETRICS 437, 450 (1988). Babcock and her colleagues found that lawyers with considerable experience in representing plaintiffs, but little experience in representing defendants, displayed overoptimism when answering questions in the former role, but not in the latter. Babcock et al., *supra* note 46, at 294.

107. Christoph Engel & Andreas Glöckner, *Role-Induced Bias in Court: An Experimental Analysis*, 26 J. BEHAV. DECISION MAKING 272 (2013). *See also* Don A. Moore, Lloyd Tanlu & Max H. Bazerman, *Conflict of Interest and the Intrusion of Bias*, 5 JUDGMENT & DECISION MAKING 37 (2010).

108. Jonas Jacobson et al., *Predicting Civil Jury Verdicts: How Attorneys Use (and Misuse) a Second Opinion*, 8 J. EMPIRICAL LEGAL STUD. 99 (Supp. 2011). *See also supra* pp. 123–24.

109. *See supra* pp. 37–38.

did not call for performance under the specific circumstances. When people are called to assess either the probability of acceptance or the probability of dismissal, the sum of their judged probabilities will ordinarily add up to 1. However, the sum of separately judged probabilities of acceptance, dismissal for lack of contract, dismissal for rescission, and dismissal for absence of contractual duty will likely exceed 1. It is also predicted that when people are asked to assess the probability of dismissal without further details, the judged probability will be lower than when they are asked to assess the probability of dismissal, and they are told the possible reasons for it. A series of studies conducted with experienced attorneys showed that their predictions of trial outcomes (including on issues squarely within their sphere of experience) were indeed affected by the description of the possible outcomes, in the predicted way.[110] These included an experiment in which participants were asked to imagine themselves as senior attorneys advising a junior colleague on whether to accept a settlement proposed by the defendant. When the various difficulties facing the claim (which were identically described to all participants) were grouped under a single heading, participants were much less likely to recommend accepting the settlement than when they were mentioned separately.

With regard to other heuristics and biases, the picture emerging from studies of the decision-making by attorneys and by other professionals' is mixed. For example, most studies have found that professionals are just as susceptible as laypersons to framing effects—displaying risk aversion when outcomes were framed as gains, and risk-seeking when the same outcomes were framed as losses.[111] In one study, lawyers displayed greater risk aversion when asked to consider a settlement proposal as the plaintiff's attorney (a gain frame) than when considering it from the defendant attorney's point of view (a loss frame).[112] However, in a subsequent experiment, Korobkin and Guthrie found that unlike laypersons, lawyers' risk attitude in settlement decisions was not affected by framing manipulations.[113] Korobkin and Guthrie also found some indication that lawyers are less susceptible than laypersons to anchoring effects, but the differences were not statistically significant.[114]

Finally, based on a series of experiments, Andrew Wistrich and Jeffrey Rachlinski have argued that settlements may be delayed and litigation unnecessarily prolonged due to attorneys' cognitive illusions that induce them to postpone settlement negotiations and reject settlement proposals. These include excessive reliance on intuitions, framing effects, the confirmation bias, the sunk-cost fallacy, and unwarranted searches for additional information (and overrating its importance once obtained).[115]

110. Craig R. Fox & Richard Birke, *Forecasting Trial Outcomes: Lawyers Assign Higher Probability to Possibilities That Are Described in Greater Detail*, 26 Law & Hum. Behav. 159 (2002).

111. For a brief overview and various references, see Eyal Zamir, Law, Psychology, and Morality: The Role of Loss Aversion 34–35 (2014). On risk attitudes in the realms of gains and losses, see generally *supra* pp. 42–44.

112. Babcock et al., *supra* note 46.

113. Korobkin & Guthrie, *supra* note 56, at 95–101.

114. *Id.* at 101–07. On anchoring, see *supra* pp. 79–82.

115. Wistrich & Rachlinski, *supra* note 6.

Besides their professional expertise, attorneys may possibly be less susceptible to cognitive biases because they are advising others, rather than making decisions for themselves. Differences between these two modes of decision-making have indeed been observed and associated with factors such as the decision-makers' degree of information-seeking, omission bias, and power.[116] For example, while the findings are not unequivocal, it appears that when making decisions for others, or advising others how to decide, people are less susceptible to the endowment effect than when deciding for themselves.[117] At the same time, experienced lawyers did show different risk attitudes in the realm of gains (when asked to negotiate on behalf of a plaintiff) and in the realm of losses (when representing the defendant).[118] More generally, the findings described above show that attorneys do display biases when representing or advising other people. Clearly, this and other aspects of attorneys' decision-making call for further empirical research.

4. Lawyers' Motivation

The preceding subsections discussed two aspects of attorney-client's relationships that have attracted substantial attention from a behavioral perspective: fee arrangements, and differences in decision-making due to lawyers' professional experience and agency role. Considerably less attention has been given to an equally important, third aspect of these relationships: the economic assumption that lawyers ultimately care only about their self-interest. This assumption does not imply that lawyers would cynically disregard clients' interests and behave opportunistically, since cynicism and opportunism are likely to adversely affect the client's cooperation with the lawyer, decrease the likelihood that the client would hire the same lawyer again, and harm the lawyer's reputation. This assumption does, however, suggest that subject to such instrumental considerations, lawyers care only about themselves. It follows that the incentive effects of fee arrangements are extremely important.

Contrary to this assumption, behavioral studies have shown that people often care about the welfare of others and about fairness and desert.[119] Particularly (but not exclusively) in bilateral relationships, people are willing to reciprocate fair behavior even if they expect no present or future material reward in return. These findings are in line with *social exchange theory* (or, more precisely, *theories*), as developed by sociologists and social psychologists to explain social interactions.[120] Social exchange theories start from micro-level processes of exchange, and go on to trace the social structures that emerge from such

116. *See supra* pp. 117–20.

117. James D. Marshall, Jack L. Knetsch, & J.A. Sinden, *Agents' Evaluations and the Disparity in Measures of Economic Loss*, 7 J. ECON. BEHAV. & ORG. 115 (1986); *supra* p. 118. In Korobkin & Guthrie's study (*supra* note 56, at 95–101), lawyers—unlike litigants—showed no loss aversion.

118. Babcock et al., *supra* note 46.

119. *See generally* Simon Gächter, *Human Prosocial Motivation and the Maintenance of Social Order, in* THE OXFORD HANDBOOK ON BEHAVIORAL ECONOMICS AND THE LAW, *supra* note 2, at 28; *supra* pp. 93–110.

120. For an overview, see Karen S. Cook et al., *Social Exchange Theory, in* HANDBOOK OF SOCIAL PSYCHOLOGY 61 (John DeLamater & Amanda Ward eds., 2d ed. 2013).

processes. While there is considerable variation between social exchange theories, they all share a broader perspective of human behavior and motivation than that of rational choice theory. Therefore, along with negotiated exchanges, they point to the existence of interactions that emerge from reciprocal acts of contingent giving. They emphasize the role of intangible rewards and costs, along with tangible ones. Some of them incorporate notions of power and status along with costs and benefits. They posit that people care not only about maximizing their self-interest, but also about fairness, feelings of obligation, and interpersonal commitments.[121] In recent years there is also a growing body of research on the role of emotions in exchanges.[122]

Indirect evidence of the limited ability of standard economic models to explain and predict attorney's actual behavior may be found in an empirical study of the amount of time lawyers spend on cases taken on different fee bases, which revealed a much more nuanced picture than what abstract economic models predict based exclusively on the incentive effect of each fee arrangement.[123] Additional evidence may be found more generally in studies of principal-agent relationships. Contrary to standard economic models, social exchange theory predicts that "agents who perceive a fixed wage as a benefit guaranteed by the principal will feel an obligation to repay the debt . . . and will provide a high effort to discharge the obligation. A cycle of obligations incurred and repaid will over time deepen trust and affection between the principal and the agent. This should facilitate future mutually beneficial exchanges."[124]

Thus, in one experimental study, subjects were asked to make a series of choices. In the "investment condition," the choice was presented in the abstract, stating probabilities, payoffs, and possible levels of investment. In the "exchange condition," the description was modified to include cues of social context, where the fixed return was depicted as a flat wage, the variable return as a performance bonus, and the possible investments as possible levels of effort.[125] The framing of the choice as being one of investment or one of exchange was found to influence the participants' behavior: significantly more subjects chose the low-investment option (as opposed to avoiding the investment altogether, or choosing the high investment) in the investment framing than in the exchange framing. When low investment produced the highest expected payoff for the decision-maker, most subjects chose this option in the investment framing, while in the exchange framing, most subjects preferred either to avoid the exchange or the high-effort option.[126]

121. For an overview, see *id.* at 68–72.

122. For an overview, see *id.* at 72.

123. Herbert M. Kritzer, The Justice Broker: Lawyers and Ordinary Litigation 111–34 (1990). On the incentive effects of different fee arrangements, see *supra* pp. 510–12. On the role of reputation, see also Herbert M. Kritzer, Risks, Reputations, and Rewards: Contingency Fee Legal Practice in the United States 219–52 (2004).

124. William P. Bottom et al., *Building a Pathway to Cooperation: Negotiation and Social Exchange between Principal and Agent*, 51 Admin. Sci. Q. 29, 32–33 (2006).

125. *Id.* at 34–37.

126. *Id.* at 37–41.

In another experiment, pairs of subjects (a principal and an agent) negotiated a reward scheme for a project in which the agent's subsequent decision as to how much effort to put into the project would be unobservable. In line with rational choice theory, monetary incentives were found to be very effective at inducing a high level of effort by the agent. However, most pairs (57 percent) agreed on a reward scheme that included a substantial fixed payment, under which a low level of effort by the agent would have maximized her expected payoff. Nonetheless, nineteen out of thirty-one agents in this group chose the high level of effort. Within this group, the chosen level of effort was not correlated with the payoff structure, but rather with the agent's perception of the principal's benevolence.[127]

More generally, studies of professionals' conduct point to the existence of several types of constraints on opportunistic behavior. These include the professionals' view of their work as a calling, rather than merely as a way of earning a living—a view that promotes self-control, trust, and altruism.[128] Even if principals are unable to judge the quality of services they receive or to impose reputational costs on misbehaving professionals, reputational and formal sanctions may be inflicted by the professional community and its organizations, such as the bar.[129] The very dichotomy between the client's and the lawyer's interests may be blurred in long-term relationships that create a collective identity, possibly vis-à-vis other groups. Sometimes, monetary incentives and active supervision may not only be superfluous, but even counterproductive, as they "crowd out the very qualities in a relationship that make social efficiency possible."[130]

In contrast to these encouraging behavioral findings, studies of behavioral ethics indicate that even well-intentioned people are susceptible to automatic and mostly unconscious psychological mechanisms that lead them to make self-serving decisions that violate ethical norms.[131] Indeed, it has been argued that several factors, including the ubiquity of conflicts of interest, the adversarial nature of litigation, the lawyer's expertise in argumentation and rationalization, the professional emphasis on legal rules rather than moral values, the typical time-pressure and high cognitive load, and the possibility of justifying unethical conduct as meant to help another person (the client)—all make lawyers particularly liable to such behavior.[132] The result may be akin to the behavior predicted by rational choice theory.

Sympathy, commitment, and possibly group identity may therefore counteract attorneys' self-interest—at least to some extent. The import of these factors likely varies from

127. *Id.* at 41–54.

128. Anurag Sharma, *Professional as Agent: Knowledge Asymmetry in Agency Exchange*, 22 ACAD. MGMT. REV. 758, 777–78 (1997).

129. *Id.* at 778–81. It should be noted that, while this and comparable factors reduce the importance of fee arrangements, they are not incompatible with standard economic analysis.

130. Gary J. Miller & Andrew B. Whitford, *Trust and Incentives in Principal-Agent Negotiations: The "Insurance/Incentive Trade-Off,"* 14 J. THEORETICAL POL. 231, 231 (2002). *See also* Sharma, *supra* note 128, at 776 ("emphasis on self-interest encourages deployment of counterproductive surveillance and monitoring devices").

131. *See generally supra* pp. 72–75.

132. Jennifer K. Robbennolt, *Behavioral Ethics Meets Legal Ethics,* 11 ANN. REV. L. & SOC. SCI. 75 (2015).

one context to another.[133] In any event, if one wishes to understand the complex realities of attorney-client relationships, one must take into account not only calculated self-interest and unconscious self-serving biases, but non-selfish motivations and commitments as well. While there is every reason to believe that attorneys' motivations (like those of other human beings) are more complex than rational choice theory posits, this claim awaits further direct empirical examination.

G. A Note on Plea Bargains

This chapter has focused on civil litigation and settlement, but it would be useful to highlight the main contributions of behavioral studies to analogous issues in the sphere of criminal litigation.[134]

In most common law systems, the vast majority of criminal cases are resolved through plea bargaining.[135] While disputants' preferences and choices play a decisive role in the resolution of civil disputes, the criminal justice system aims at broader social goals, such as specific and general deterrence, retribution, and rehabilitation. Plea bargains raise more complex issues than civil dispute settlements also because the prosecution handles numerous cases (and is expected to treat similar cases alike), and because of the parties' typical unequal bargaining power; the low socioeconomic status of most defendants; the presence of crime victims who are not ordinarily involved in the negotiations; the prosecution's budgetary constraints; and the alleged use of high-pressure bargaining techniques by prosecutors. Unsurprisingly, the plea bargaining system is highly controversial.[136]

This controversy notwithstanding, the standard economic analysis of plea bargaining is not fundamentally different from the economic analysis of litigation and settlement. Given the high costs of trial for the parties and the court system, plea bargains not only benefit the prosecution and the defendant, but—within certain limits—also enhance overall

133. Sometimes, other-regarding commitments go hand in hand with self-interest. Compare, for example, long-term client-attorney relationships with the one-time relationships between a court-appointed attorney and a poor defendant. Both other-regarding and selfish motivations are likely to result in the attorney putting more effort and giving more weight to the client's interests in the former case than in the latter. *See also infra* note 155 and accompanying text.

134. This section draws on ZAMIR, *supra* note 111, at 92–96. For behavioral studies of other aspects of the criminal process, see, e.g., DAN SIMON, IN DOUBT: THE PSYCHOLOGY OF THE CRIMINAL JUSTICE PROCESS 17–143 (2012) (analyzing the effect of behavioral biases throughout the police investigation and interrogation processes); Andrew J. Wistrich, Chris Guthrie & Jeffrey J. Rachlinski, *Can Judges Ignore Inadmissible Information? The Difficulty of Deliberately Disregarding*, 153 U. PA. L. REV. 1251 (2005) (discussing judges' decisions regarding the legality of police searches); *infra* Chapters 15, 16.

135. Oren Gazal-Ayal & Limor Riza, *Plea-Bargaining and Prosecution*, *in* CRIMINAL LAW AND ECONOMICS 145 (Nuno Garoupa ed., 2009).

136. *See, e.g.*, Stephanos Bibas, *Plea Bargaining outside the Shadow of Trial*, 117 HARV. L. REV. 2463 (2004); Rebecca Hollander-Blumoff, *Social Psychology, Information Processing, and Plea Bargaining*, 91 MARQ. L. REV. 163 (2007); Michael O'Hear, *Plea Bargaining and Procedural Justice*, 42 GA. L. REV. 407 (2008); H. Mitchell Caldwell, *Coercive Plea Bargaining: The Unrecognized Scourge of the Justice System*, 61 CATH. U. L. REV. 63 (2011).

social welfare.[137] Bargaining in the shadow of the expected trial outcome (namely, the expected sentence multiplied by the probability of conviction), the parties can strike a bargain that would leave both of them better off by sharing the saved costs of trial. Although it means relinquishing the prospect of complete acquittal, the defendant often benefits from the elimination of some of the charges, a more lenient punishment, and avoidance of the monetary and nonmonetary costs of trial. From the prosecution's perspective, a plea bargain eliminates the risk of acquittal and facilitates the allocation of more resources to cases where they can be used more effectively—thereby enhancing overall deterrence and advancing other goals of the criminal justice system. Plea bargains also save judicial resources. However, as in civil litigation, plea bargaining may fail, or fail to serve the interests of one of the parties, due to asymmetric information, agency problems on both sides, and negotiators' strategic behavior.

Relaxing the assumption of economic rationality, several studies have employed insights of cognitive psychology to better understand the plea bargaining process and assess its outcomes. These studies bear close resemblance to the behavioral studies of litigation and settlement in the civil sphere. Since plea bargains result in conviction and punishment, defendants presumably frame their outcomes as sure losses. Given people's tendency to be risk-seeking in the domain of losses, one might be concerned that too many defendants would refuse to accept favorable plea bargains, and prefer instead to take the risks of trial. Inasmuch as criminal defendants are on average more risk-seeking than the general population, this concern is even more pronounced.[138] Negotiations for a plea bargain may also fail due to self-serving bias, overoptimism, overconfidence, and illusion of control.[139] Signing a plea bargain may also hasten the application of punishment, while going to trial often postpones it. Excessive discounting of future costs (such as imprisonment), compared with present ones, may thus create another psychological barrier to a plea bargain.[140] Finally, plea bargaining may fail because defendants care not only about their expected utility, but also about substantive fairness.[141] There is empirical evidence that defendants who perceive themselves as innocent usually reject plea offers, even if the expected outcome of trial is less favorable.[142] This concern is amplified to the extent that defendants find it difficult to take responsibility for their wrongful deeds, since feelings of guilt are painful.[143]

137. For an overview of the literature, see Gazal-Ayal & Riza, *supra* note 135. *See also* POSNER, *supra* note 4, at 792–97.

138. Bibas, *supra* note 136, at 2507–12. *Cf.* Richard Birke, *Reconciling Loss Aversion and Guilty Pleas,* 1999 UTAH L. REV. 205, 245–46.

139. Bibas, *supra* note 136, at 2498–502; Russell Covey, *Behavioral Economics and Plea Bargaining, in* THE OXFORD HANDBOOK ON BEHAVIORAL ECONOMICS AND THE LAW, *supra* note 2, at 643, 646–47; *supra* pp. 497–500.

140. Bibas, *supra* note 136, at 2504–07.

141. *See also supra* pp. 102–04, 500–01.

142. Oren Gazal-Ayal & Avishalom Tor, *The Innocence Effect,* 62 DUKE L.J. 339 (2011).

143. Bibas, *supra* note 136, at 2502–04.

In reality, however, the failure of some plea bargaining has never been a major concern. Both the empirical fact that the lion's share of criminal cases are resolved through plea bargaining, and the normative judgment that pleading guilty to an offense one has not committed is much worse than unwisely failing to accept a plea bargain, have led commentators to focus on the complementary puzzle: given people's tendency to take risks in the domain of losses, why do so many defendants enter into plea bargains with the prosecution?

Richard Birke thoroughly considered four possible explanations for this phenomenon: (1) that from the defendants' perspective, the terms of plea bargains are so much better than the expected outcomes of trial that they outweigh any risk-taking tendency; (2) that, unlike the general population, criminal defendants are risk-averse in the domain of losses; (3) that defendants tend to frame plea bargaining as pertaining to gains rather than losses; and (4) that defense lawyers have strong institutional, financial, and reputational incentives to persuade their clients to accept plea bargains, and therefore misinform their clients as to their options.[144] Birke found the first two of these answers to be unpersuasive, and concluded that the fourth—defendants' misinformation—is the most compelling. Accordingly, he discussed various means of providing defendants with better information.[145]

While sharing Birke's point of departure, Russell Covey offered a competing interpretation of the data.[146] Covey demonstrated that plea bargains provide defendants with very large punishment discounts (which are even larger when one considers the anguish associated with a trial). More relevant to the present discussion, he questioned the assumption that defendants frame their options as a certain loss (plea bargain) versus uncertainty (trial). First, the defendants' access to the prosecution's evidence and sentencing guidelines (where applicable) significantly reduce the uncertainties associated with trial. The less uncertainty is involved, the less risk-loving plays a role in the choice between a plea bargain and a trial.[147] Second, pretrial detention likely changes the defendants' reference point: when the defendant is already behind bars, continued incarceration becomes the status quo. Therefore, the longer the expected period of pretrial detention (and the shorter the expected period of subsequent incarceration), the less a plea bargain is likely to be perceived as a loss.[148]

Finally, Covey pointed to the role loss aversion plays in inducing defendants to accept a plea bargain when prosecutors make an "exploding offer." This tactic—often used

144. Birke, *supra* note 138, at 219–32, 245–46, 244–45, and 232–44, respectively.

145. *Id.* at 247–50.

146. Russell Covey, *Reconsidering the Relationship between Cognitive Psychology and Plea Bargaining*, 91 Marq. L. Rev. 213 (2007). *See also* Covey, *supra* note 139.

147. Covey, *supra* note 146, at 233–39. *But see* Uzi Segal & Alex Stein, *Ambiguity Aversion and the Criminal Process*, 81 Notre Dame L. Rev. 1495 (2006) (arguing that unlike the prosecution, defendants display ambiguity aversion, which may be exploited by the prosecution to force defendants into harsh plea bargains; on ambiguity aversion, see generally *supra* pp. 39–42).

148. Covey, *supra* note 146, at 239–42.

by suppliers in consumer markets[149]—can induce a reframing of the options. Rather than viewing accepting a plea bargain as entailing a loss, the defendant may perceive the rejection of a soon-to-be-expired offer as losing a one-time opportunity.[150]

A related argument is that a plea bargain and a trial differ from one another in terms of the ability of the defendant and her attorney to compare between the various outcomes of the defendant's decision. While opting for a trial results in full knowledge (one may compare the outcome of the trial to the terms of the rejected plea bargain), accepting a plea bargain yields partial knowledge (the outcomes of the forgone trial will never be known). Loss- and regret-averse defendants and their counsels are therefore likely to find the latter considerably more attractive.[151]

One commentator has questioned the applicability of the findings of behavioral studies to plea bargaining, given the atypical personality traits, cultural background, and education of criminal defendants and the uniqueness of the situation.[152] However, while people differ in the extent to which they use heuristics in decision-making, it is unclear why one should expect criminal defendants to differ significantly from the general population with regard to such basic and general phenomena as loss aversion.

Another question involves the prosecutors' and defense attorneys' ability to overcome cognitive biases and help defendants make utility-maximizing decisions. As we have seen,[153] the evidence in this regard is mixed. On the one hand, the fact that attorneys are professional, repeat players, who can assess the various options in a more detached manner, may enable them to overcome at least some biases, under some circumstances.[154] In this respect, it has been pointed out that in the criminal context, due to their limited education and low social status, most defendants are less able to direct their attorneys to take an adversarial approach in negotiations. The fact that many defense attorneys are not paid by the defendant (and do not expect repeated interactions with him) further weakens the defendant's level of control over their attorneys.[155]

On the other hand, numerous studies—including studies of lawyers—have shown that experienced professionals usually exhibit similar biases and use the same heuristics as laypersons.[156] Indeed, in some respects, attorneys may actually magnify the role of psychological heuristics in decisions regarding plea bargains. Studies of people's motivation to acquire information and process it systematically ("epistemic motivation") have shown

149. *See supra* pp. 287–90.

150. Covey, *supra* note 146, at 242–43.

151. Albert W. Alschuler, *The Defense Attorney's Role in Plea Bargaining,* 84 YALE L.J. 1179, 1205–06 (1975); Birke, *supra* note 138, at 242; *supra* pp. 505–07.

152. Chad M. Oldfather, *Heuristics, Biases, and Criminal Defendants,* 91 MARQ. L. REV. 249 (2007).

153. *See supra* pp. 512–16.

154. Bibas, *supra* note 136, at 2519–27; Covey, *supra* note 146, at 236; *cf.* Korobkin & Guthrie, *supra* note 56.

155. Andrea Kupfer Schneider, *Cooperating or Caving In: Are Defense Attorneys Shrewd or Exploited in Plea Bargaining Negotiations?*, 91 MARQ. L. REV. 145, 159–60 (2007).

156. *See supra* pp. 114–17, 512–16.

that this motivation diminishes significantly when people bargain under time-pressure—as is often the case in plea bargaining between prosecutors and defense counsels. In these circumstances, the people's resort to heuristics is enhanced.[157] In addition, social psychology studies have demonstrated that group identification plays a major role in how people process information. The strong institutional group identity of prosecutors and of defense attorneys may thus strengthen cognitive biases.[158]

H. Conclusion

The consensual nature of settlements and plea bargains has attracted the attention of legal economists from early on. In the past two decades, the gradual recognition of the limitations of analyses based exclusi-vely on rational choice theory has resulted in a growing body of behavioral studies in these spheres. As described above, the self-serving and confirmation biases, risk-seeking in the domain of losses, the combined effect of regret- and loss-aversion, the status-quo bias, the endowment effect, and sunk costs—as well as a host of other heuristics and biases—loom large in litigation, settlement, plea bargaining, and ADR. Specific phenomena, such as reactive devaluation and attitude polarization, which have been identified in psychological studies of social conflicts and negotiations, are also directly relevant to litigation and settlement.

There are, however, considerable gaps in what we know about the behavioral economics of litigation, settlement, plea bargaining, and ADR. In general, there is much room for qualitative research of the actual behavior of litigants and their attorneys in settlement negotiations, plea bargaining, and ADR—along with controlled surveys and laboratory experiments (and statistical analyses of databases). Such research would shed light on the external validity of the laboratory findings. More specifically, not much is known about attorneys' non-selfish motivations and about ADR processes.

157. Hollander-Blumoff, *supra* note 136, at 174–77.

158. *Id.* at 177–81. *Cf.* Alafair S. Burke, *Improving Prosecutorial Decision Making: Some Lessons of Cognitive Science*, 47 Wm. & Mary L. Rev. 1587 (2006).

15

Judicial Decision-Making

A. Introduction

Drawing on psychological insights to explain judicial decision-making goes back more than eighty-five years.[1] However, most of the progress in the application of insights and methodologies of judgment-and-decision-making research to judicial decision-making has been made in the past two decades. At the outset, the behavioral approach to judicial decision-making should be differentiated from other interfaces between psychology and the judicial system. In particular, it should be distinguished from forensic psychology—that is, the contribution of psychologists to the operation of the court system through the provision of expert testimonies in legal proceedings.[2] Judicial decision-making is also to be distinguished from judges' verbal and nonverbal communicative behavior in court.[3]

Similarly, the behavioral analysis of judicial decision-making should be differentiated from the empirical study of the relationships between judges' decisions, their ideological inclinations, and law as a system of norms and an institution. This latter body of research, connected in part to rational choice theory, is primarily the province of political scientists. It focuses on higher court decisions on public and constitutional issues.[4] It does not ordinarily

1. Jerome Frank, Law and the Modern Mind (1930).

2. *See generally* Handbook of Psychology, Vol. 11: Forensic Psychology (Irving B. Weiner & Randy K. Otto eds., 2d ed. 2012).

3. Peter David Blanck et al., *The Measure of the Judge: An Empirically-Based Framework for Exploring Trial Judges' Behavior*, 75 Iowa L. Rev. 653 (1990).

4. Within this literature, the *attitudinal model* posits that, rather than legal norms, judges' decisions are primarily determined by their attitude to the facts of the case. *Rational choice models* add strategic considerations of judges who wish their attitudes to be accepted and implemented. Finally, the *neo-institutionalist model* supplements the above factors with institutional variables, including the law—which is defined as the dynamic mindset of legal actors. *See* Keren Weinshall-Margel, *Attitudinal and Neo-institutional Models of Supreme Court Decision Making: An Empirical and Comparative Perspective from Israel*, 8 J. Empirical Legal Stud. 556, 569 (2011). *See also* Jeffrey A. Segal & Harold J. Spaeth, The Supreme Court and the Attitudinal Model Revisited (2002); Lee Epstein & Jack Knight, The Choices Justices Make (1998); Michael A. Bailey & Forrest Maltzman, The Constrained Court: Law, Politics, and the Decisions Justices Make (2011).

Behavioral Law and Economics. Eyal Zamir and Doron Teichman.

take into account insights from cognitive and social psychology,[5] and is less relevant to the great majority of run-of-the-mill judicial decisions made by lower courts. Some scholars—notably Dan Kahan and his coauthors—do, however, use empirically-based, behavioral insights to elucidate the relationships between group commitments, courts' decisions in ideologically charged issues, and the public perception of those decisions.[6]

Since judges are generally insulated from market incentives, and since their decisions in particular cases do not directly affect their own well-being, standard economic analysis—which assumes that people are rational maximizers of their own utility—is not very helpful in explaining judicial behavior. In an attempt to meet this challenge, Richard Posner suggested drawing an analogy between judges' decisions and those made by managers of nonprofit enterprises (whose income does not depend on the profits of their enterprise); people who vote in political elections (despite the infinitesimal probability that their vote would affect election outcomes); and theater spectators (who identify with the characters and form an opinion on their entitlements).[7] Contrary to the attitudinal and rational choice models offered by social scientists,[8] Posner portrays judges as being driven by a multitude of motives beyond making good legal policy, such as a preference for expending less effort, a desire for prestige and popularity, an aversion to being reversed by higher courts, and the desire to move the docket.[9] Though insightful, Posner's more complex depiction of judicial decision-making still disregards the behavioral perspective. It does not overcome the basic difficulty facing economic analysis, as it largely assumes that judges derive utility from "playing by the rules" of judicial decision-making, advancing the public interest, and so forth.[10] While this analysis may explain why judges do not decide randomly, or why they exert effort in the absence of direct monetary incentives, it sheds little light on how judges make decisions.[11]

5. Lawrence Baum, *Motivation and Judicial Behavior: Expanding the Scope of Inquiry*, *in* THE PSYCHOLOGY OF JUDICIAL DECISION MAKING 3, 8 (David Klein & Gregory Mitchell eds., 2010); Wendy L. Martinek, *Judges as Members of Small Groups*, *in* THE PSYCHOLOGY OF JUDICIAL DECISION MAKING, *id.* at 73, 73–76; Jeffrey A. Segal, Benjamin Woodson & Joshua Johnson, *The Behavioral Economics Alternative: The Legal-Model Fiction in Epstein, Landes, and Posner's The Behavior of Federal Judges*, 97 JUDICATURE 75 (2013) (book review).

6. *See, e.g.*, Dan M. Kahan, *Foreword: Neutral Principles, Motivated Cognition, and Some Problems for Constitutional Law*, 125 HARV. L. REV. 1 (2011); Dan M. Kahan et al., *"Ideology" or "Situation Sense"? An Experimental Investigation of Motivated Reasoning and Professional Judgment*, 164 U. PA. L. REV. 349 (2016).

7. Richard A. Posner, *What Do Judges and Justices Maximize? (The Same Thing Everybody Else Does)*, 3 SUP. CT. ECON. REV. 1 (1993).

8. *See supra* note 4 and accompanying text.

9. *See also* LEE EPSTEIN, WILLIAM M. LANDES & RICHARD A. POSNER, THE BEHAVIOR OF FEDERAL JUDGES: A THEORETICAL AND EMPIRICAL STUDY OF RATIONAL CHOICE (2013).

10. *See also* Christoph Engel & Lilia Zhurakhovska, *You Are In Charge—Experimentally Testing the Motivating Power of Holding a Judicial Office*, 46 J. LEGAL STUD. 1 (2017) (surveying the economic literature on judges' motivation, and experimentally demonstrating that even when other incentives are neutralized, subjects are motivated by the desire to fulfill the expectations that come with being assigned the role of "a judge," including enforcing norms and furthering the common good).

11. Neil S. Siegel, *Sen and the Hart of Jurisprudence: A Critique of the Economic Analysis of Judicial Behavior*, 87 CALIF. L. REV. 1581 (1999).

Hence, unlike other spheres, where behavioral law and economics has largely evolved as a reaction to standard economic analysis, in the absence of established economic analysis of judicial decision-making, the behavioral studies in this sphere do not relate to the economic perspective. Nonetheless, in keeping with the general spirit of this book, we focus on those aspects of the behavioral research that are more closely connected to the main themes of behavioral law and economics. It would therefore be useful to describe the contribution of behavioral studies of judicial decision-making by referring to the three primary contrasts between the economic and the behavioral perspectives described in Chapter 2. These are the deviations from the assumption of cognitive rationality (the heuristics-and-biases literature), from the assumption of motivational rationality (other-regarding preferences), and from consequentialist morality.[12]

Most behavioral studies of judicial decision-making belong to the heuristics-and-biases school of research. Accordingly, they constitute the lion's share of this chapter. The chapter also touches upon the contributions of social psychology to the understanding of decision-making in small groups, such as juries. Since judicial decisions are inevitably normative, behavioral studies of moral judgments are important in this sphere as well. Conversely, since almost no one argues that judges and juries make their decisions with a view to directly maximizing their own utility, the behavioral studies of human motivation are less relevant here.

Several issues pertaining to judicial decision-making are discussed elsewhere in the book, and so will be omitted here. Thus, to fully understand judges' and juries' decision-making, one must pay heed to the psychology of other key figures in the adjudication process: litigants, attorneys, and witnesses—but these issues will not be discussed here, since the conduct of litigants and attorneys is discussed in Chapter 14, and evidence law in Chapter 16. Chapter 16 will also analyze certain aspects of judicial decision-making that are closely connected to the law of evidence, such as the import and meaning of burden of proof, and the puzzling reluctance to impose liability based on certain types of evidence.[13]

While the discussion will occasionally touch upon decisions made by legislators and administrative agencies, general issues regarding the division of labor among and comparative competence of, different branches of government are discussed in Chapter 11, which deals with administrative and constitutional law. At the same time, many of the findings discussed in the present chapter may be relevant to quasi-judicial functions performed by other bodies—a rather under-researched topic.[14] Finally, to keep the discussion manageable, we shall not delve into the behavioral aspects of judicial decision-making in specific types of adjudication, such as mass tort actions.[15]

12. *See supra* pp. 28–86, 101–10, and 94–101, respectively.

13. *See infra* pp. 593–98 and 576–85, respectively.

14. For an exception, see, e.g., Omer Dekel & Amos Schurr, *Cognitive Biases in Government Procurement—An Experimental Study,* 10 REV. L. & ECON. 169 (2014).

15. *See, e.g.,* William N. Eskridge, Jr. & John Ferejohn, *Structuring Lawmaking to Reduce Cognitive Bias: A Critical View,* 87 CORNELL L. REV. 616, 634–38 (2002).

The remainder of this chapter is divided into nine sections. Section B presents general theories of the cognitive process of judicial decision-making. Section C examines how various cognitive phenomena are reflected in judicial decision-making—such as the compromise and contrast effects, the hindsight bias, the omission bias and related phenomena, and the anchoring effect. Section D provides an overview of the extensive literature on the limited ability of fact-finders to disregard inadmissible evidence and other irrelevant information (such as media reports), and of attempts to mitigate this problem. Section E presents the contribution of behavioral studies to understanding the interactions between race and judicial decision-making. Section F briefly illustrates how non-consequentialist moral judgments are reflected in judicial decision-making. Section G describes studies of quintessentially judicial decisions: the application of legal norms to facts—specifically the impact of the choice between rules and standards on the predictability of judgments. Sections H and I discuss two fundamental questions in the behavioral analysis of judicial decision-making: group decision-making, and decision-making by judges as opposed to laypersons. Finally, Section J offers a general assessment of the behavioral research of judicial decision-making.

B. The Story Model and Coherence-Based Reasoning

This section briefly presents general theories of the cognitive mechanisms by which judicial decision-makers process complex information and reach their decisions. These theories set the framework for examining cognitive phenomena such as the reluctance to base liability on statistical evidence, and the application of legal standards to specific circumstances.[16]

Primary contributions to this body of research include the work of Nancy Pennington and Reid Hastie on the story model,[17] and the studies of Keith Holyoak, Stephen Read, and Dan Simon on constraint satisfaction and coherence-based reasoning.[18] While the story model focuses on fact-finding, studies of coherence-based reasoning pertain to decisions on legal issues as well.[19]

The story model contests other theories of fact-finding, such as Bayesian probability theory, algebraic models that attribute differential weights to pieces of evidence, and stochastic process models.[20] Developed on the basis of interviews and experimental

16. *See infra* 577–79 and 556–59, respectively.

17. *See* Nancy Pennington & Reid Hastie, *A Cognitive Theory of Juror Decision Making: The Story Model,* 13 Cardozo L. Rev. 519 (1991).

18. *See* Dan Simon, *A Psychological Model of Judicial Decision Making,* 30 Rutgers L.J. 1 (1998); Dan Simon, *A Third View of the Black Box: Cognitive Coherence in Legal Decision Making,* 71 U. Chi. L. Rev. 511 (2004) [hereinafter Simon, *Third View*].

19. These studies rest on connectionist models of mental representations. For an overview, see Simon, *Third View, supra* note 18; Stephen J. Read & Dan Simon, *Parallel Constraint Satisfaction as a Mechanism for Cognitive Consistency, in* Cognitive Consistency: A Fundamental Principle in Social Cognition 77 (Bertram Gawronsky & Fritz Strack eds., 2012).

20. Reid Hastie, *Introduction, in* Inside the Juror: The Psychology of Juror Decision Making 3, 10–22 (Reid Hastie ed., 1993).

studies,[21] the story model appears to better describe the actual psychological process of fact-finding in adjudication. According to the model, story construction—that is, the creation of a narrative that explains the various items of evidence that have been deemed reliable and relevant—is the core cognitive process by which the facts in adjudication are determined. Interviews and experiments have indicated that the mental representation of the evidence is structured not according to factors such as the order of its presentation in court, the pertinent legal issues, or whether the evidence supports or undermines the plaintiff's version of the events. Rather, fact-finders structure the evidence to create a story. The story is constructed from three types of knowledge: the evidence presented at trial, knowledge about events similar to the one in dispute, and general notions of what constitutes a complete story. Story construction is an active process, resulting in one or more interpretations of the evidence. When faced with different interpretations, fact-finders adopt the one that best explains the evidence, that is, the story that is most coherent and provides the broadest coverage of the evidence. Coherence requires the story to contain no internal contradictions or missing elements, and that it conforms to the fact-finders' beliefs about the physical world and people's motivations and behavior. Since fact-finders' beliefs about the physical and social world are influenced by their group commitments and ideological inclinations, the latter indirectly affect the constructed story.[22]

Complex stories often comprise several episodes. They include motivations, actions, and consequences, linked by physical and intentional causality. Some of the events—or their elements—may not be supported by any direct evidence and require the drawing of inferences. Hence, the same set of evidence might give rise to more than one story—with different fact-finders finding different stories more or less compelling. Pennington and Hastie found that the more complete and coherent a given story is, and the more it covers the available evidence, the more confident the fact-finders are about its accuracy. Fact-finders' confidence about a story's veracity is further enhanced by its uniqueness, that is, by the lack of plausible alternative stories that could account for the same evidence.

It has also been found that when the evidence in support of a possible conclusion was presented in a chronological and causal story order, and the evidence supporting a rival conclusion was presented in a non-story order (e.g., according to the order of the testimonies), subjects tended to adopt the former conclusion.[23] Even more intriguingly, when, after

21. *See* Nancy Pennington & Reid Hastie, *Evidence Evaluation in Complex Decision Making*, 51 J. Personality & Soc. Psychol. 242 (1986); Nancy Pennington & Reid Hastie, *Explanation-Based Decision Making: Effects of Memory Structure on Judgment*, 14 J. Experimental Psychol.: Learning, Memory & Cognition 521 (1988) [hereinafter Pennington & Hastie, *Explanation-Based Decision Making*]; Nancy Pennington & Reid Hastie, *Explaining the Evidence: Tests of the Story Model for Juror Decision Making*, 62 J. Personality & Soc. Psychol. 189 (1992) [hereinafter Pennington & Hastie, *Explaining the Evidence*].

22. *See, e.g.*, Dan M. Kahan, David A. Hoffman & Donald Braman, *Whose Eyes Are You Going to Believe?* Scott v. Harris *and the Perils of Cognitive Illiberalism*, 122 Harv. L. Rev. 837 (2009); Dan M. Kahan, *Culture, Cognition, and Consent: Who Perceives What, and Why, in Acquaintance-Rape Cases*, 158 U. Pa. L. Rev. 729 (2010); Dan M. Kahan et al., *"They Saw a Protest": Cognitive Illiberalism and the Speech-Conduct Distinction*, 64 Stan. L. Rev. 851 (2012).

23. Pennington & Hastie, *Explanation-Based Decision Making*, *supra* note 21, at 528–30.

hearing the evidence, subjects were presented with sentences allegedly describing the evidence, including lure sentences referring to facts that had not been included in the evidence, they were almost twice as likely to recognize lure statements in support of their adopted story than those corroborating the alternative one.[24] Fact-finders thus use various techniques to fill in gaps and to strengthen their story.

The idea that fact-finding involves a choice between possible narratives is supported by an experimental study that found that evidence judged to offer only meager support for one side's version boosted the fact-finders' confidence in the veracity of the opposite version.[25] Coherence-based theories of decision-making are also supported by the finding that decision time depends on the coherence of the available information, rather than its amount: higher coherence facilitates quicker decisions even if it involves more information.[26]

According to the story model and coherence-based theories, the chosen story and legal conclusions may change in the course of the trial and even following the jury instructions. The coherent story and its legal implications are not a post-hoc justification of the decision, but rather created during the trial and the decision-making process.[27] This observation is closely connected to a central tenet of coherence-based theories of judicial decision-making, namely that the decision process is bidirectional. The strength of evidence and arguments does not only determine the story that the decision-maker adopts and the decision she makes. The adopted story and decision concomitantly determine the assessment of the relevance, reliability, and importance of various pieces of evidence, and the power of competing legal arguments. Subjects tend to attribute greater weight to evidence items and legal arguments that support their decision, and lesser weight to evidence and arguments that contradict it.[28] As a corollary, a given piece of evidence or argument can indirectly influence the assessed reliability or persuasiveness of other pieces of evidence and legal arguments, even in the absence of any plausible relationship between the two.

Even if the evidence and legal arguments are initially confusing and incoherent, this bidirectional process tends to yield a conclusion that decision-makers sincerely believe to be clear and conclusive. Decision-makers are typically unaware of this *coherence shift*, as they do not accurately recall their original assessment of the evidence and legal argumentation.[29] Thus, when participants in an experiment were presented with a new piece of evidence that

24. *Id.* at 523–28.

25. Craig R.M. McKenzie, Susanna M. Lee & Karen K. Chen, *When Negative Evidence Increases Confidence: Change in Belief after Hearing Two Sides of a Dispute,* 15 J. BEHAV. DECISION MAKING 1 (2002).

26. Andreas Glöckner & Tilmann Betsch, *Decisions beyond Boundaries: When More Information Is Processed Faster than Less,* 139 ACTA PSYCHOLOGICA 532 (2012).

27. Pennington & Hastie, *supra* note 17, at 523, 531; Keith Holyoak & Dan Simon, *Bidirectional Reasoning in Decision Making by Constraint Satisfaction,* 128 J. EXPERIMENTAL PSYCHOL.: GENERAL 3 (1999); Dan Simon et al., *The Emergence of Coherence over the Course of Decision Making,* 27 J. EXPERIMENTAL PSYCHOL.: LEARNING, MEMORY & COGNITION 1250 (2001).

28. Pennington & Hastie, *Explanation-Based Decision Making, supra* note 21; Holyoak & Simon, *supra* note 27; Dan Simon, Chadwick J. Snow & Stephen J. Read, *The Redux of Cognitive Consistency Theories: Evidence Judgments by Constraint Satisfaction,* 86 J. PERSONALITY & SOC. PSYCHOL. 814 (2004).

29. Holyoak & Simon, *supra* note 27, at 10–18; Simon, *Third View, supra* note 18, at 533.

was sufficiently compelling to cause some of them to change their initial verdict, the final verdict was accompanied by a corresponding (second) coherence shift; and switchers were no less confident in their final verdict than were those who had not changed their verdict.[30]

Without necessarily doubting the empirical basis of the story model and coherence-based theories, or their normative implications as described above, recent studies have questioned the alleged incompatibility between these theories and Bayesian reasoning,[31] and there are even attempts to integrate these two with argumentative approaches—the approaches most akin to traditional legal reasoning.[32] It is argued that even if untrained people are unable to make the complex mathematical calculations required by formal Bayesian networks, their reasoning does follow the qualitative prescriptions of such networks.[33] These findings enrich and complement the story model and coherence-based theories by offering an explanation of the mechanisms by which fact-finders determine how well the evidence supports the various stories and assess the strength, credibility, and reliability of the evidence.[34]

The story model and coherence-based theories of judicial decision-making arguably have normative implications. Simon, for instance, argued that to enhance the accuracy of juries' fact-finding, instructions about substantive law should be given prior to the evidence hearings, because subsequent instructions are unlikely to alter a coherent story that was formed on the basis of inaccurate assumptions about the law.[35] Another possible implication pertains to the admissibility of prejudicial evidence. Given that a sufficiently strong piece of evidence can affect the entire mental model of a case by indirectly influencing other variables, the admission of prejudicial evidence may be more detrimental than assumed, for example, by a Bayesian theory of fact-finding, because it affects the assessed reliability and relevance of pieces of evidence regarding substantively unrelated issues.[36] It has also been suggested that juries should be warned "against not only premature decisions but also

30. Simon, Snow & Read, *supra* note 28, at 824–27.

31. *See, e.g.*, David Lagnado, *Thinking about Evidence*, 171 PROC. BRIT. ACAD. 183, 196–220 (2011); David Lagnado, Norman Fenton & Martin Neil, *Legal Idioms: A Framework for Evidential Reasoning*, 4 ARGUMENT & COMPUTATION 46 (2012).

32. Bart Verheij et al., *Arguments, Scenarios and Probabilities: Connections between Three Normative Frameworks for Evidential Reasoning*, 15 LAW, PROBABILITY & RISK 35 (2016).

33. Lagnado, *supra* note 31, at 196–220. For experimental findings suggesting that people are relatively good Bayesian reasoners, in the context of considering expert testimony, see Adam J.L. Harris & Ulrike Hahn, *The Appeal to Expert Opinion: Quantitative Support for a Bayesian Network Approach*, 40 COGNITIVE SCI. 1496 (2016).

34. A separate issue is whether, and how, judicial fact-finders should explicitly use Bayesian networks in their reasoning, and how experts should effectively and reliably present them in court. *See, e.g.*, Norman E. Fenton & Martin Neil, *Avoiding Probabilistic Reasoning Fallacies in Legal Practice Using Bayesian Networks*, 36 AUSTRAL. J. LEGAL PHIL. 114 (2011); Norman Fenton, Martin Neil & David Lagnado, *A General Structure for Legal Arguments about Evidence Using Bayesian Networks*, 37 COGNITIVE SCI. 1 (2012); *see also infra* pp. 585–87.

35. Simon, *Third View*, *supra* note 18, at 550–59. On additional advantages of pretrial instructions, see Vicki L. Smith, *Impact of Pretrial Instruction on Jurors' Information Processing and Decision Making*, 76 J. APP. PSYCHOL. 220 (1991). *But see infra* p. 591 (conflicting experimental findings regarding the effect of giving jury instructions about burden of proof before the presentation of evidence).

36. Simon, *Third View*, *supra* note 18, at 559–69.

any tentative judgments, lest such opinions influence jurors' evaluations of subsequent evidence."[37] However, one may doubt the effectiveness of such direct warnings.[38]

After this introduction to general theories of judicial decision-making, we turn to a discussion of specific cognitive phenomena.

C. Judicial Decision-Makers' Heuristics and Biases

The extent to which judges can and should implement legal norms in a mechanistic way, unaffected by their personal values and normative inclinations, has long been debated. However, even those who believe that judges have (and should have) considerable discretion in interpreting, applying, and developing legal norms agree that judges must not employ their discretion arbitrarily, and should not be influenced by obviously irrelevant factors. Thus, mocking American Legal Realism as positing that judicial decisions depend on what the judge had for breakfast has never been fair. However, while this caricature of judicial decision-making has never been corroborated, a recent study showed that *who* judges have breakfast with might actually influence their rulings. Mark Lemley and Shawn Miller found that appeal judges are less inclined to reverse decisions by lower-court judges after the latter have been sitting for a few days as visiting judges in the appellate court (compared to decisions by other lower-court judges and decisions of the same judges before visiting the appellate court).[39] Controlling for other variables (including, inasmuch as possible, the non-random selection of visiting judges), the authors conclude that the most likely explanation is that personal acquaintance increases the trust of appeal-court judges in the discretion of lower-court judges.

Be that as it may, the remainder of this section focuses on the role of more conventional heuristics and biases. It examines whether heuristics and biases identified in other contexts manifest themselves in legal decision-making. Due to space limitations, the examination is far from being exhaustive.

1. Context Dependence

Contrary to the assumptions of rational choice theory, people's judgments and decisions are affected by context, and are typically comparative in nature, rather than reference- or context-independent.[40] Three specific manifestations of this general feature of human thinking have been studied in the context of judicial decision-making: the *order effect*, the *compromise effect*, and the *contrast effect*.[41]

37. Kurt A. Carlson & J. Edward Russo, *Biased Interpretation of Evidence by Mock Jurors*, 7 J. EXPERIMENTAL PSYCHOL.: APPLIED 91, 91 (2001).

38. *See also infra* pp. 548–50.

39. Mark A. Lemley & Shawn P. Miller, *If You Can't Beat 'Em, Join 'Em? How Sitting by Designation Affects Judicial Behavior*, 94 TEX. L. REV. 451 (2016).

40. *See generally supra* pp. 42–57, 76–86.

41. On these and other context effects, see generally R. Scott Tindale et al., *Procedural Mechanisms and Jury Behavior*, *in* BLACKWELL HANDBOOK OF SOCIAL PSYCHOLOGY: GROUP PROCESSES 574, 591–94 (Michael A. Hogg & R. Scott Tindale eds., 2001).

The *order effect* refers to the impact of the order in which information is presented to a decision-maker on his or her judgment. Depending on several variables, basic and applied studies have demonstrated either *primacy* or *recency* effects—that is, instances in which either earlier or later information exerts greater influence on the final decision.[42] In adjudication, ordinarily the plaintiff (in civil cases) or the prosecutor (in criminal ones) presents her evidence first, and then the defendant presents his evidence. Each litigant controls the order of presentation of his or her evidence and arguments. When judges and juries hear the evidence of the prosecutor or plaintiff, they expect to hear conflicting evidence and arguments from the defendant—an expectation that is usually fulfilled. While the underlying psychological mechanisms are not wholly clear, studies in the judicial context consistently point to a recency effect: it is advantageous to be the second presenter, and for each party it is generally preferable to present his or her strongest evidence and arguments last.[43]

This finding may have ramifications for the procedure of judicial decision-making. Thus, in a large-scale experimental study, Irwin Horowitz and Kenneth Bordens compared a *separated-trial* procedure (in which juries were asked to make consecutive decisions about various issues, such as causality, liability, damages, etc., based on the information relevant to each one of them) and a *unitary-trial* procedure, in which they made a decision on all issues after being presented with all of the information.[44] Consistent with the story model and coherence-based reasoning, it was found that in the unitary-trial procedure, information that was presumably relevant for later judgments in the sequence tended to influence earlier judgments. It was also found that the order of evidence presentation (e.g., whether evidence on causation or on liability was presented first) affected the average damages awarded by juries that found the defendant liable.

The *compromise effect* alludes to people's tendency to choose intermediate rather than extreme options. Thus, the relative ranking of two options may well be influenced by the sheer availability of additional ones.[45] Mark Kelman and his colleagues demonstrated that the compromise effect can influence judicial decisions.[46] Their experiment focused on conviction decisions with respect to different types of homicide offenses: manslaughter, murder, and murder with aggravating circumstances. The results showed that the introduction of an additional, more severe offense pulled fact-finders toward the intermediate

42. *See generally supra* pp. 82–83.

43. *See* Laurens Walker, John Thibaut & Virginia Andreoli, *Order of Presentation at Trial*, 82 Yale L.J. 216 (1972); Adrian Furnham, *The Robustness of the Recency Effect: Studies Using Legal Evidence*, 113 J. General Psychol. 351 (1986); José H. Kerstholt & Janet L. Jackson, *Judicial Decision Making: Order of Evidence Presentation and Availability of Background Information*, 12 Applied Cognitive Psychol. 445 (1998); Steve D. Charman et al., *Evidence Evaluation and Evidence Integration in Legal Decision-Making: Order of Evidence Presentation as a Moderator of Context Effects*, 30 App. Cognitive Psychol. 214 (2016). *But see* Donald C. Pennington, *Witnesses and Their Testimony: Effects of Ordering on Juror Verdicts*, 12 J. Applied Soc. Psychol. 318 (1982).

44. Irwin A. Horowitz & Kenneth S. Bordens, *An Experimental Investigation of Procedural Issues in Complex Tort Trials*, 14 Law & Hum. Behav. 269 (1990).

45. *See generally supra* pp. 83–85.

46. Mark Kelman, Yuval Rottenstreich & Amos Tversky, *Context-Dependence in Legal Decision Making*, 25 J. Legal Stud. 287 (1996).

option. Faced with a choice between manslaughter and murder, 47 percent of the subjects chose manslaughter while 53 percent chose murder. When the third option was added, only 19 percent of the subjects chose the manslaughter option, whereas 39 percent chose murder, and 42 percent chose murder with aggravating circumstances.[47]

Another type of context dependence is the *contrast effect*. Adding an option that highlights the attributes of one of the items being evaluated can cause people to choose that item, even if the added option itself is strictly inferior and therefore irrelevant to the decision.[48] Kelman and his colleagues showed that the contrast effect can influence legal choices. Participants in their study were asked to choose the sanction suitable for a criminal. When deliberating between jail and probation, the introduction of an inferior sanctioning option that highlighted the advantages of the probation option caused more people to choose it.[49]

Context dependence is not necessarily undesirable. As further described below, one of the critiques of jury decision-making—for example, in setting damages for non-pecuniary harms—is that jurors lack information about conventional awards, so the amounts they award are sometimes unpredictable and influenced by irrelevant information.[50] Decisions by judges, who are familiar with customary awards, are therefore more consistent and predictable. However, judges' familiarity with other cases is a cause of concern when different judges are exposed to different sets of cases. In a cleverly designed empirical study of sentencing decisions, Adi Leibovitch took advantage of the fact that in Pennsylvania, criminal cases are assigned to judges at random.[51] While random assignment ensures that in the long run judges see a similar composition of cases, in the short run—including during the first period following their appointment to the bench—the average severity of cases allocated to each judge may vary considerably. Leibovitch constructed a matched sample of judges randomly located on different ends of the caseloads distribution during the first period after their appointment. She found that, with regard to similar cases, judges who had initially been exposed to higher levels of criminal gravity tended to impose shorter sentences and were less likely to use aggravated sentencing guidelines range than judges who had been exposed to lower levels of criminal gravity. These findings have important policy implications, for example in the context of establishing courts of limited jurisdiction, such as juvenile courts. Paradoxically, courts who specialize in relatively less serious crimes are likely to treat mild offenses on their docket more harshly than generalist courts.[52]

47. *Id.* at 290–92.

48. *See generally supra* pp. 77–79.

49. Kelman, Rottenstreich & Tversky, *supra* note 46, at 295–97. Similar results were reported with respect to years of sentencing. *See* Jeffrey J. Rachlinski & Forest Jourden, *The Cognitive Components of Punishment*, 88 CORNELL L. REV. 457 (2003).

50. *See infra* pp. 538–43.

51. Adi Leibovitch, *Relative Judgments*, 45 J. LEGAL STUD. 281 (2017).

52. On this and other concerns, and possible responses to them, see Adi Leibovitch, *Punishing on a Curve*, 111 NW. U. L. REV. 1205 (2017).

More work remains to be done to improve our understanding of how context dependence influences judicial decision-making. To date, with a few exceptions,[53] most studies have focused on decisions by laypersons. Possibly, decision-makers more familiar with the legal decision environment will be less prone to influences by irrelevant factors. Furthermore, the existing studies do not account for the many nuances associated with different legal questions. For example, while Jeffrey Rachlinski and Forest Jourden identified a contrast effect with respect to years of imprisonment, they found no such effect with respect to the death penalty.[54]

2. Hindsight Bias

Courts are frequently called upon to evaluate a decision in retrospect, after the decision's outcomes are known. In negligence cases, for example, the reasonableness of the precautions taken by the defendant are examined after the risk associated with a harm has materialized. The law often requires judicial decision-makers to ignore the outcome information revealed ex post and evaluate the issues from a purely ex-ante perspective.[55] Behavioral findings suggest, however, that decision-makers find it difficult to ignore such information.

As described in Chapter 2, a large body of work has documented the existence of a *hindsight bias*[56]—namely, people's tendency to overestimate the probability of an event once they are aware that it has occurred. Those studies have also provided cognitive and motivational explanations for this phenomenon.

Hindsight bias has been examined in several legal contexts. In tort law, negligence cases involve situations where a plaintiff asserts that she was harmed due to the defendant's failure to exercise reasonable care. In principle, the court should examine the defendant's decision about precautions at the time when it was made.[57] However, Kim Kamin and Jeffrey Rachlinski demonstrated that ex-ante evaluation of precautions differ significantly from ex-post ones.[58] Similar results have been documented in the context of the precautions needed to be taken by a therapist in light of a risk of a patient behaving violently.[59] Other

53. These include Jeffrey J. Rachlinski, Andrew J. Wistrich & Chris Guthrie, *Altering Attention in Adjudication*, 60 UCLA L. Rev. 1586, 1597–604 (2013); Leibovitch, *supra* note 51.

54. Rachlinski & Jourden, *supra* note 49.

55. Whether this is desirable in light of the potential probative value of outcome information is a separate question. For a comprehensive discussion of the normative question, see Maggie Wittlin, *Hindsight Evidence*, 116 Colum. L. Rev. 1323 (2016).

56. *See supra* pp. 38–39.

57. *See, e.g.*, Restatement (Third) of Torts: Liability for Physical and Emotional Harm § 3 (Am. Law Inst. 2010).

58. Kim A. Kamin & Jeffrey J. Rachlinski, *Ex post ≠ ex ante: Determining Liability in Hindsight*, 19 Law & Hum. Behav. 89 (1995). For a description of the study and its results, see *supra* p. 336. For more experimental studies in this context, see Reid Hastie & W. Kip Viscusi, *What Juries Can't Do Well: The Jury's Performance as a Risk Manager*, 40 Ariz. L. Rev. 901 (1998); W. Kip Viscusi, *How Do Judges Think about Risk?*, 1 Am. L. & Econ Rev. 26, 46–56, 59 (1999).

59. Susan J. LaBine & Gary LaBine, *Determinations of Negligence and the Hindsight Bias*, 20 Law & Hum. Behav. 501 (1996). Comparable results were obtained in an experiment in which participants were asked to assess the

studies have examined the issue in the context of actual court decisions. One such study, which examined 1,004 cases, contended that in over 40 percent of them the court had imposed liability for anesthesia-related negligence, even though the physician had acted appropriately.[60]

The hindsight bias may affect decisions outside the context of assigning liability for harms, as well. For example, in U.S. patent law the validity of a patent requires the relevant invention to be "non-obvious."[61] When required to assess obviousness in retrospect, however, decision-makers influenced by the hindsight bias are expected to systematically view non-obvious inventions as obvious—a hypothesis that was indeed confirmed in controlled experiments.[62]

Another context in which the hindsight bias has been tested is police searches. In this context, courts are often required to determine whether the officers who conducted the search had probable cause to do so. This determination might arise in both foresight and hindsight situations. Foresight situations involve police officers seeking a warrant prior to conducting the search; hindsight situations involve evidentiary rulings about the admissibility of evidence obtained in a search. The hindsight bias suggests that judges are more inclined to find probable cause in the latter category of cases, because in those cases incriminating evidence was actually found in the search (otherwise the question would not arise). This hypothesis was tested extensively in a series of experiments involving several hundred judges in the United States.[63] The picture arising from this wide body of research is that, unlike laypersons, judges did not differ significantly in their decisions between the foresight and the hindsight conditions.

The general picture is that the hindsight bias influences legal decisions to a significant degree. When adjudication requires an ex-post evaluation of behavior, courts might fail to ignore outcome information. However, while judges are not immune from the bias, research suggests that its effect on their behavior is significantly smaller than on untrained individuals, such as jurors.

reasonableness of decisions made by a corporate board. *See* Merrie Jo Stallard & Debra L. Worthington, *Reducing the Hindsight Bias Utilizing Attorney Closing Arguments,* 22 LAW & HUM. BEHAV. 671 (1998).

60. Frederick W. Cheney, *Standard of Care and Anesthesia Liability,* 261 J. AM. MED. ASS'N 1599 (1989). *See also* Mark I. Taragin et al, *The Influence of Standard of Care and Severity of Injury on the Resolution of Medical Malpractice Claims,* 117 ANNALS INTERNAL MED. 780 (1992) (showing that in 21 percent of the cases examined, physicians were found liable for practices that were, in fact, entirely defensible).

61. 35 U.S.C. §§ 101–03 (2012).

62. Gregory N. Mandel, *Patently Non-obvious: Empirical Demonstration That the Hindsight Bias Renders Patent Decisions Irrational,* 67 OHIO STATE L.J. 1391 (2006). *See also infra* pp. 228–29.

63. Andrew J. Wistrich, Chris Guthrie & Jeffrey J. Rachlinski, *Can Judges Ignore Inadmissible Information? The Difficulty of Deliberately Disregarding,* 153 U. PA. L. REV. 1251 (2005) [hereinafter Wistrich, Guthrie & Rachlinski, *Inadmissible Information*]; Chris Guthrie, Jeffrey J. Rachlinski & Andrew J. Wistrich, *Blinking on the Bench: How Judges Decide Cases,* 93 CORNELL L. REV. 1 (2007) [hereinafter Guthrie, Rachlinski & Wistrich, *Blinking on the Bench*]; Jeffrey J. Rachlinski, Chris Guthrie & Andrew J. Wistrich, *Probable Cause, Probability, and Hindsight,* 8 J. EMPIRICAL LEGAL STUD. 72 (2011) [hereinafter Rachlinski, Guthrie & Wistrich, *Probable Cause*].

3. Omission Bias and Related Phenomena

Omission bias is the tendency to prefer inaction to action when facing risky alternatives. People are considered to bear greater moral responsibility for harmful outcomes that they actively caused, than for those they brought about passively. People anticipate experiencing greater regret if their action resulted in a worse outcome than inaction, compared with the regret they expect to feel if they refrain from action and subsequently learn that action would have produced a better outcome. Harmful omissions might therefore be preferred to less harmful commissions.[64]

Presumably, a judge called upon to decide a case cannot refrain from delivering a judgment; hence omission bias may seem irrelevant to judicial decision-making. However, there is experimental support for the claim that laypersons perceive accepting a claim as more active than dismissing it.[65] If this perception is shared by judges, omission bias may help explain why they are reluctant to accept claims even when the plaintiff's version of the facts is slightly more persuasive than that of the defendant. The general standard of proof in civil litigation in common-law systems is preponderance of evidence: to prevail, plaintiffs must establish their case as more probable than not. Notwithstanding this formal rule, in a series of experiments conducted with advanced-years law students and experienced lawyers, Eyal Zamir and Ilana Ritov found that the actual standard of proof is considerably higher. To accept a claim, the decision-maker should rate the persuasiveness of the plaintiff's version around 70 or higher on a scale of 0 to 100 (where 0 denotes that there is no doubt that the plaintiff's version is incorrect and 100 signifies that there is no doubt that it is correct).[66] These experiments provide prima facie evidence that judges exhibit an omission bias. Direct support for this claim has subsequently been provided by Mark Schweizer, who found that Swiss judges and judicial clerks who exhibit greater loss aversion employ a higher decision threshold in civil cases.[67] It has also been suggested that omission bias can explain the strong tendency of appellate courts to dismiss appeals.[68]

Psychologists have also identified the closely related phenomenon of *status-quo bias*. Other things being equal, people tend to stick to the state of affairs they perceive to be the status quo than to opt for an alternative. Ordinarily, changing the status quo requires some action, whereas retaining the status quo involves mere omission. Hence, the status quo bias is usually confounded with the omission bias although they can exist separately and can pull in opposite directions.[69]

64. *See generally supra* pp. 48–50.

65. Eyal Zamir & Ilana Ritov, *Loss Aversion, Omission Bias, and the Burden of Proof in Civil Litigation*, 41 J. LEGAL STUD. 165, 180–82 (2012).

66. *Id.* at 174–80, 186–87. *See also infra* pp. 594–95.

67. Mark Schweizer, *Loss Aversion, Omission Bias, and the Civil Standard of Proof*, in EUROPEAN PERSPECTIVES ON BEHAVIOURAL LAW AND ECONOMICS 125 (Klaus Mathis ed., 2015).

68. Chris Guthrie & Tracey E. George, *The Futility of Appeal: Disciplinary Insights into the "Affirmance Effect" on the United States Courts of Appeals*, 32 FLA ST. U. L. REV. 357, 379–80 (2005).

69. *See generally supra* pp. 48–49.

Status-quo bias has been cited as a possible explanation for court reluctance to issue preliminary injunctions that disrupt the status quo,[70] as well as for appellate courts' aversion to reverse the decisions of lower courts.[71] It has also been proposed as a possible explanation for court adherence to the doctrine of stare decisis (the binding force of precedents);[72] to lower courts' resistance to legal change;[73] and more generally to the great influence exerted by the past on current law.[74] Nonetheless, when Zamir and Ritov presented their subjects with a scenario in which dismissing a claim for a declaratory judgment would alter the status quo, while accepting it would maintain it, the omission bias appears to have had a greater impact on their decision than the status-quo bias.[75]

Another related phenomenon is escalation of commitment. Expected utility theory posits that when choosing between different courses of action, only future costs and benefits should be taken into account, because the past cannot be changed. This implies that unrecoverable, incurred costs that do not affect future costs or benefits should not influence current decisions. However, numerous empirical studies have established that people very often do consider sunk costs when making decisions. As a result, the more resources, time, or efforts people have already invested in a given endeavor, the more they are inclined to pursue it.[76]

It has been suggested that the rich literature on escalation of commitment and its psychological, social, and institutional determinants can fruitfully contribute to a better understanding of the application of the concept of stare decisis, which is a cornerstone of the common law.[77] Indeed, there is much scope for future research of judicial decision-making and the sunk costs effect. For example, under the *mootness doctrine*, a court should halt adjudication and dismiss the case once the dispute has become academic because, for example, the defendant agency has abandoned the policy challenged by the petitioner. It would be interesting to examine whether court receptiveness to mootness claims might depend on the amount of judicial resources already spent on the case.

4. Converting Qualitative into Quantitative Judgments and the Anchoring Effect

Numerical judicial decisions are sometimes problematic due to people's limited proficiency with numbers, especially among lay jurors.[78] Judicial decision-makers face a particularly

70. EYAL ZAMIR, LAW, PSYCHOLOGY, AND MORALITY: THE ROLE OF LOSS AVERSION 162–64 (2015).

71. Guthrie & George, *supra* note 68, at 377–79.

72. Robert A. Prentice & Jonathan J. Koehler, *A Normality Bias in Legal Decision Making*, 88 CORNELL L. REV. 583, 638 (2003); Goutam U. Jois, *Stare Decisis Is Cognitive Error*, 75 BROOK. L. REV. 63 (2009).

73. Matthew Tokson, *Judicial Resistance and Legal Change*, 82 U. CHI. L. REV. 901 (2015).

74. Andrew J. Wistrich, *The Evolving Temporality of Lawmaking*, 44 CONN. L. REV. 737, 740 (2012).

75. Zamir & Ritov, *supra* note 65, at 177–80.

76. *See generally supra* pp. 56–57.

77. Rafael Gely, *Of Sinking and Escalating: A (Somewhat) New Look at* Stare Decisis, 60 U. PITT. L. REV. 89 (1998).

78. Valerie P. Hans & Valerie F. Reyna, *To Dollars from Sense: Qualitative to Quantitative Translation in Jury Damage Awards*, 8 J. EMPIRICAL LEGAL STUD. 120 (2011).

challenging task when they are required to convert from one scale to another, as in the award of damages for non-pecuniary harms and the imposition of criminal sanctions. Much of the behavioral research of judicial decision-making centers on this particular difficulty.

While conversion from one scale to another inherently poses a challenge, the scope of this challenge varies with the respective legal norms and decision-maker expertise. At one extreme we find cases where the law allows largely unfettered discretion—for example, when setting "reasonable" damages for pain and suffering. Such unfettered discretion is particularly troublesome when decision-makers such as lay jurors lack the relevant experience and meaningful reference points.[79] This situation persists in many jurisdictions in the United States.[80] At the other end of the spectrum we find no room for discretion—as when the law lays down precise sanctions or remedies. Between these two extremes, more or less specific guidelines for quantification may be established, as some legal systems have done with regard to criminal sentencing.

When legal decision-makers convert qualitative judgments into quantitative ones, their decisions should serve the law's goals—such as just desert and deterrence—and ideally be consistent, predictable, and justifiable. Empirical and experimental studies reveal a remarkable degree of similarity and predictability in the qualitative judgments made by judges and jurors on matters such as the severity of the plaintiff's injury, the outrageousness of a defendant's behavior, and the appropriate severity of punishment.[81] At the same time, considerable variability is evident when decision-makers—judges and jurors alike—are asked to convert these qualitative, ordinal judgments into quantitative monetary awards.[82] For instance, in a large-scale experiment involving more than 1,000 jury-eligible participants who viewed a videotape of a product liability trial, the standard deviation of the damages awarded was 138 percent of the mean for economic damages, and 313 percent of the mean for pain and suffering damages. When analyzing trimmed values (where values above the 97th percentile were treated as though the jurors favored the award determined by jurors at the 97th percentile), the standard deviation was 75 percent for economic damages, and 154 percent for pain and suffering damages.[83]

79. On the crucial role of knowledge and reference points in determining evaluability, especially in contexts where people lack an innate reference system, see Christopher K. Hsee & Jiao Zhang, *General Evaluability Theory,* 5 PERSP. PSYCHOL. SCI. 343 (2010).

80. Oscar G. Chase, *Helping Jurors Determine Pain and Suffering Awards,* 23 HOFSTRA L. REV. 763 (1995); EDIE GREENE & BRIAN H. BORNSTEIN, DETERMINING DAMAGES: THE PSYCHOLOGY OF JURY AWARDS 175–76 (2003).

81. Roselle L. Wissler, Allen J. Hart & Michael J. Saks, *Decisionmaking about General Damages: A Comparison of Jurors, Judges, and Lawyers,* 98 MICH. L. REV. 751, 773–82 (1999); Daniel Kahneman, David Schkade & Cass R. Sunstein, *Shared Outrage and Erratic Awards: The Psychology of Punitive Damages,* 16 J. RISK & UNCERTAINTY 49, 55–62 (1998).

82. Michael J. Saks et al., *Reducing Variability in Civil Jury Awards,* 21 LAW & HUM. BEHAV. 243 (1997); Shari Seidman Diamond, Michael J. Saks & Stephan Landsman, *Juror Judgments about Liability and Damages: Sources of Variability and Ways to Increase Consistency,* 48 DEPAUL L. REV. 301 (1998); Kahneman, Schkade & Sunstein, *supra* note 81, at 62–78; Wissler, Hart & Saks, *supra* note 81, at 782–96.

83. Diamond, Saks & Landsman, *supra* note 82, at 313–14.

The scope of this variability, and whether it should be a cause of serious concern outside the laboratory are, however, a matter of debate. Commentators claim that damage awards, for example, are largely predictable and sensible, when one takes into account the subtle differences in the characteristics of seemingly similar cases.[84] The power of judges to review jury awards, the appellate courts' oversight of awards made by trial judges, and the fact that most claims are settled through negotiations that are managed by experienced attorneys—all significantly reduce the actual impact of the distorting factors observed in the laboratory.[85] Moreover, it may be argued that some apparently irrelevant anchors (such as the effect of economic damages on punitive damages) are not normatively irrelevant.[86] Nonetheless, the overall picture that emerges from experimental and empirical research, and is echoed in the common sentiment expressed in the legal community, is that monetary awards by jury, especially for non-economic and punitive damages, are unjustifiably variable and irregular.

Several models have been proposed to describe the cognitive process of deriving numerical values from qualitative assessments. Daniel Kahneman, David Schkade, and Cass Sunstein proposed a descriptive model of the process by which individual jurors set punitive damages, dubbed the "outrage model."[87] According to the model, outrage results from evaluation of the defendant's behavior. Coupled with the ensuing harm, outrage stimulates the intent to punish. Once the intent to punish is formed, jurors express this attitude by transforming intent into a dollar scale. Since there is no obvious way to make such a conversion, the process is susceptible to strong influences by various anchors (see below). Reid Hastie has proposed a more general, four-stage model—the "intention + anchor model"—that applies to the determination of other numerical verdicts, as well.[88] These models leave open the question of the order of damage determination: Do decision-makers first calculate damages for each category or subcategory of harms and losses separately, and then add up the numbers—or do they first determine a global award, and then—if required to do so—break down the total into the different categories? The available data appears to indicate that both mechanisms come into play.[89]

Both the experimental findings and the explanatory theories behind them point to the key role played by anchors. When people are presented with a salient number before they make a numerical judgment, they tend to make their judgment through adjustments from the initial number, which serves as an anchor. These adjustments, however, are often insufficient, resulting in the judgment being biased toward the anchor. The anchor also biases

84. GREENE & BORNSTEIN, *supra* note 80, at 200–01; NEIL VIDMAR & VALERIE P. HANS, AMERICAN JURIES: THE VERDICT 299–302 (2007).

85. *See generally* Theodore Eisenberg, Jeffrey J. Rachlinski, & Martin T. Wells, *Reconciling Experimental Incoherence with Real-World Coherence in Punitive Awards*, 54 STAN. L. REV. 1239 (2002).

86. *Id.* at 1264. *See also infra* pp. 541–42.

87. Kahneman, Schkade & Sunstein, *supra* note 81, at 51–53.

88. Reid Hastie, *The Challenge to Produce Useful "Legal Numbers,"* 8 J. EMPIRICAL LEGAL STUD. 6 (2011).

89. Greene & Bornstein, *supra* note 80, at 159–61.

information sampling. It draws people's attention to information that is consistent with the initial anchor and away from information that would lead to greater adjustment. Moreover, the closer a factor is to the initial anchor, the more the decision-maker is likely to focus on the similarity between the two; and the further away a factor is from the initial anchor, the more the decision-maker is likely to focus on the dissimilarity, thereby downplaying its relevance. Numbers can serve as anchors even if they provide no meaningful information about the issue at hand, and even if decision-makers are fully aware of their meaninglessness.[90] Anchoring influences both laypersons and experts, including judges and experienced international arbitrators.[91]

Experimental and empirical studies have highlighted the role of several anchors in the context of quantitative judicial decision-making. One common anchor is the *amount of economic damage.* Strong correlations have been found between economic and non-economic damages, and between compensatory and punitive damages.[92] These correlations may indicate that the former serve as an anchor when determining the latter. Since the severity of the harm is a relevant factor when determining economic, non-economic, and punitive damages, this correlation may seem perfectly sensible; and even a direct inference from economic to non-economic and punitive damages is not necessarily groundless. At the same time, there is evidence that the amount of economic damages affects the amount of non-economic damages more strongly among jurors than among judges.[93] This finding arguably indicates that laypersons are overly influenced by the plaintiff's economic loss when determining non-economic and punitive damages.

A more troubling anchor is the *amount of damages claimed by the plaintiff.*[94] In one experiment, even though plaintiffs who asked for exorbitant compensation were perceived less favorably by the subjects, the amount requested served as an anchor affecting the damages awarded.[95] The effect was linear even for extreme amounts. The manner in which the figures are presented to the jury also influences the award.[96] An empirical study of actual

90. *See generally supra* pp. 79–82.

91. Chris Guthrie, Jeffrey J. Rachlinski & Andrew Wistrich, *Inside the Judicial Mind,* 86 CORNELL L. REV. 777, 787–94 (2001) [hereinafter Guthrie, Rachlinski & Wistrich, *Judicial Mind*]; Birte Englich, Thomas Mussweiler & Fritz Strack, *Playing Dice with Criminal Sentences: The Influence of Irrelevant Anchors on Experts' Judicial Decision Making,* 32 PERSONALITY & SOC. PSYCHOL. BULL. 188 (2006); Susan D. Franck et al., *Inside the Arbitrator's Mind,* 66 EMORY L.J. 1115, 1140–51 (2017).

92. Theodore Eisenberg et al., *Predictability of Punitive Damages,* 26 J. LEGAL STUD. 623 (1997); Theodore Eisenberg et al., *Juries, Judges, and Punitive Damages: Empirical Analyses Using the Civil Justice Survey of State Courts 1992, 1996, and 2001 Data,* 3 J. EMPIRICAL LEGAL STUD. 263 (2006).

93. Hans & Reyna, *supra* note 78, at 141–42.

94. Gretchen B. Chapman & Brian H. Bornstein, *The More You Ask for the More You Get: Anchoring in Personal Injury Verdicts,* 10 APPLIED COGNITIVE PSYCHOL. 519 (1996); Reid Hastie, David A. Schkade & John W. Payne, *Juror Judgments in Civil Cases: Effects of Plaintiff's Requests and Plaintiff's Identity on Punitive Damage Awards,* 23 LAW & HUM. BEHAV. 445 (1999); W. Kip Viscusi, *The Challenge of Punitive Damages Mathematics,* 30 J. LEGAL STUD. 313 (2001).

95. Chapman & Bornstein, *supra* note 94, at 523–28.

96. Dradley B. McAuliff & Brian H. Bornstein, *All Anchors Are Not Created Equal: The Effects of Per Diem versus Lump Sum Requests on Pain and Suffering Awards,* 34 LAW & HUM. BEHAV. 164 (2010).

trials and jury deliberations revealed a more nuanced picture, in which very high claims by the plaintiffs—especially for non-monetary harms—was sometimes perceived not only as irrelevant, but also as outrageous and hence counterproductive.[97] Some experimental studies have also noted the existence of a boomerang effect.[98]

While it may be argued that the compensation requested is an indication of the scope of harm suffered by the plaintiff, inasmuch as it serves as an anchor, its obvious manipulability is a cause for concern. This is particularly true if the linear effect of the damages claimed manifests itself even when the decision-makers do not believe that the damages requested are a true reflection of the level of the plaintiff's suffering or medical expenses, as demonstrated in a study by Gretchen Chapman and Brian Bornstein.[99]

Another study appears to demonstrate the anchoring effect of an additional irrelevant factor: a meritless motion to dismiss a tort case because it did not meet the minimum threshold of damages required for jurisdiction.[100] The meritless jurisdictional motion induced a significant decline in the damages awarded by the judges who were exposed to it.

A particularly intriguing anchoring effect has been observed in experiments that studied the impact of *caps* on damages. One study found that caps dramatically increased the median total award in a case referring to the death of two children.[101] Another study examined the influence of caps on damages for pain and suffering.[102] As regards a highly severe injury, when subjects were informed about the cap, it dramatically reduced both the mean and the variability of the awards. Regarding a medium-severity injury, the introduction of the cap slightly increased the mean and decreased the variability of the awards, but none of these effects was statistically significant. For a low-severity injury, however, the cap greatly increased both the mean and the variability of the awards. Caps are thus able to prevent mega-awards for pain and suffering, but to the extent that they are meant to increase the predictability of non-economic damages, they likely produce the opposite outcome due to their anchoring effect in cases of low-severity injuries.[103] Not informing the jury about the existence of a cap (with the judge imposing it after the jury has set the damages) may ameliorate this concern, as well as the concern that the jury might evade the

97. Shari Seidman Diamond et al., *Damage Anchors on Real Juries,* 8 J. EMPIRICAL LEGAL STUD. 148 (2011).

98. Mollei W. Marti & Roselle Wissler, *Be Careful What You Ask for: The Effect of Anchors on Personal Injury Damages Awards,* 6 J. EXPERIMENTAL PSYCHOL.: APPLIED 91 (2000); GREENE & BORNSTEIN, *supra* note 80, at 153.

99. Chapman & Bornstein, *supra* note 94, at 527. Even more surprisingly, the amount requested also affected the judgment of causality: the higher the amount, the higher the assessed probability that the defendant caused the plaintiff's injury (*id.* at 525–26).

100. Guthrie, Rachlinski & Wistrich, *supra* note 91, at 787–94.

101. Verlin B. Hinsz & Kristin E. Indhal, *Assimilation to Anchors for Damage Awards in a Mock Civil Trial,* 25 J. APPLIED SOC. PSYCHOL. 991 (1995).

102. Saks et al., *supra* note 82.

103. Moreover, inasmuch as there is a problem of under-compensation for high-severity injuries and overcompensation for low-severity injuries, caps exacerbate this problem (Saks et al., *supra* note 82, at 253–54). Comparable results were obtained in an experimental study of caps on punitive damages. *See* Jennifer K. Robbennolt, *Anchoring in the Courtroom: The Effects of Caps on Punitive Damages,* 23 LAW & HUM. BEHAV. 353 (1999).

cap by increasing the damages for uncapped counts.[104] However, the likelihood that such caps can remain secret in the long run does not seem very high.

In summary, the translation of qualitative judgments into quantitative decisions reduces the predictability of decisions, increases their variability, and involves considerable differences between judges and juries.[105] These differences most probably result from jurors' limited information about the customary awards and punishments and from the vagueness of the instructions they receive. In the absence of any reliable point of reference, juries are forced to rely on questionable data, such as the amount of damages claimed by the plaintiff, or the defendant's profits.

One way to tackle the special difficulties that jurors face in this respect is not to entrust such decisions to juries, but to judges, who are presumably familiar with customary awards and sentences. This route has been adopted by most legal systems around the world. Another way to circumvent the problem is to provide juries with clearer instructions, such as sentencing guidelines, the average and range of customary awards, and examples of verdicts handed down in similar cases.[106] The lack of clear jury instructions regarding quantitative decisions in many U.S. jurisdictions is rather puzzling, and the calls for reforms are quite compelling.[107]

5. Conclusion

The picture emerging from this survey is that heuristics and biases that characterize human decision-making in other contexts—such as the compromise and contrast effects, the hindsight bias, the omission bias and related phenomena, and the anchoring effect—generally, but not uniformly, characterize judicial decision-making as well. Similar findings have been reported with regard to other heuristics and biases, such as *framing effects*,[108] the *conjunction fallacy*,[109] the *inverse fallacy*,[110] and the *better-than-average effect*.[111] Finally, in several

104. On the latter concern, see, e.g., Edith Greene, David Coon & Brian H. Bornstein, *The Effects of Limiting Punitive Damage Awards*, 25 LAW & HUM. BEHAV. 217 (2001); Catherine M. Sharkey, *Unintended Consequences of Medical Malpractice Damages Caps*, 80 N.Y.U. L. REV. 391 (2005).

105. Wissler, Hart & Saks, *supra* note 81, at 804–10.

106. Oscar G. Chase, *Helping Jurors Determine Pain and Suffering Awards*, 23 HOFSTRA L. REV. 763 (1995); Saks et al., *supra* note 82; Wissler, Hart & Saks, *supra* note 81, at 812–17.

107. *See, e.g.*, GREENE & BORNSTEIN, *supra* note 80, at 202–03.

108. Guthrie, Rachlinski & Wistrich, *Judicial Mind*, *supra* note 91, at 794–99. Similar results were obtained with elite commercial arbitrators (Rebecca Helm, Andrew J. Wistrich & Jeffrey J. Rachlinski, *Are Arbitrators Human?*, 13 J. EMPIRICAL LEGAL STUD. 666, 677–81 (2016)) and experienced international arbitrators (Franck et al., *supra* note 91, at 1151–59). On framing effects, see generally *supra* pp. 46–48.

109. Chris Guthrie, Jeffrey J. Rachlinski & Andrew J. Wistrich, *The "Hidden Judiciary": An Empirical Examination of Executive Branch Justice*, 58 DUKE L.J. 1477, 1509–12 (2009) [hereinafter Guthrie, Rachlinski & Wistrich, *Hidden Judiciary*]. *See also* Helm, Wistrich & Rachlinski, *supra* note 108, at 647–77. On the conjunction fallacy, see generally *supra* pp. 28–29.

110. *See, e.g.*, Guthrie, Rachlinski & Wistrich, *Blinking on the Bench*, *supra* note 63, at 22–24. On the inverse fallacy, see generally *supra* p. 32.

111. Guthrie, Rachlinski & Wistrich, *Judicial Mind*, *supra* note 91, at 811–16; Guthrie, Rachlinski & Wistrich, *Hidden Judiciary*, *supra* note 109, at 1518–20. The same is true of international arbitrators. *See* Franck et al., *supra* note 91, at 1163–66. On the better-than-average effect, see generally *supra* pp. 61–64.

studies, Dan Kahan and his colleagues have shown that fact-finders may be influenced by their group commitments and ideological inclinations. The underlying mechanisms in those cases are *motivated reasoning* and related phenomena, including *naïve realism, identity-protection cognition,* and *cultural cognition.*[112]

Beyond particular remedies to specific heuristics and biases, policymakers should consider broader responses to judicial decision-makers' susceptibility to cognitive biases. At least some of these biases are the product of System 1, intuitive thinking.[113] As further indicated in Section I below, legal training and experience do help professional judges to overcome some of these biases. However, as in other decision environments, improved decision-making thanks to expertise and experience requires rapid and continual feedback about the accuracy of one's decisions[114]—which, more often than not, is unavailable to judges.[115] Allowing judges and juries more time for deliberation may increase their use of System 2 thinking, thereby reducing their susceptibility to cognitive biases (although not invariably so). However, this solution directly depends on the resources available to the court system, which are often limited due to other demands on governmental budgets.[116] Requiring judges to write reasoned opinions may also induce more deliberate thinking, but once again, it entails the allocation of more resources, since writing an opinion is time-consuming.[117] Increasing the awareness of judges to their own heuristics and biases—possibly as part of continued education programs—may have a beneficial effect, although the efficacy of this debiasing technique varies from one context to another, and is generally not great.[118] Based on studies of debiasing in other contexts, additional measures that should be considered include the use of scripts and checklists, reducing decision-makers' exposure to biasing cues (such as anchors), and so forth.[119] Finally, it has been suggested that offering judges more meal breaks and rest time may counteract mental depletion and lead to more reasoned decision-making.[120] The available data, however, is insufficient to support the causal claim underlying this recommendation.[121]

112. *See, e.g.,* Kahan, Hoffman & Braman, *supra* note 22; Kahan, *supra* note 22; Kahan et al., *supra* note 22. On motivated reasoning, see generally *supra* pp. 58–61. On cultural cognition, see also Kahan, *supra* note 6.

113. *See generally supra* pp. 21–23.

114. *See generally supra* pp. 114–15.

115. Guthrie, Rachlinski & Wistrich, *Blinking on the Bench, supra* note 63, at 33–35.

116. *Id.* at 35–36.

117. *Id.* at 36–38.

118. *Id.* at 38–40. *See also supra* p. 135.

119. Guthrie, Rachlinski & Wistrich, *Blinking on the Bench, supra* note 63, at 40–43. On debiasing in general, see *supra* pp. 127–38.

120. In an influential study Shai Danziger, Jonathan Levav, and Liora Avnaim-Pesso examined the decisions of parole boards in Israel, which are chaired by experienced judges. Those boards make dozens of decisions in one day, during which they take two meal breaks. It was found that the percentage of decisions to accept parole requests drops gradually from about 65 percent to nearly zero within each decision session and returns abruptly to about 65 percent after each meal break. *See* Shai Danziger, Jonathan Levav & Liora Avnaim-Pesso, *Extraneous Factors in Judicial Decisions*, 108 PROC. NAT'L ACAD. SCI. USA 6889 (2011).

121. *See* Keren Weinshall-Margel & John Shapard, *Overlooked Factors in the Analysis of Parole Decisions,* 108 PROC. NAT'L ACAD. SCI. USA E833 (2011) (showing that contrary to the assumption of Danziger, Levav, and

D. Inadmissible Evidence and Other Irrelevant Information

1. The Challenge

The courtroom provides a unique decision-making environment. While the human mind is trained to incorporate all available information so as to render the best decision, this is not always the case in court. At times, both the rules of evidence and substantive legal rules dictate that certain facts be excluded from the information made available to the decision-maker. Some exclusionary rules are based on the premise that the prejudicial effects of certain types of evidence outweigh their probative value. For example, information about the defendant's past convictions may be relevant to a determination of liability in a given case, but may also skew decisions toward a finding of guilt. Other types of evidence, such as hearsay testimony, can be excluded due to their limited probative value. Finally, some exclusionary rules stem from policy considerations that are unrelated to the probative weight of the evidence. For example, evidence obtained through illegal police practices might be deemed inadmissible, in order to incentivize the police to behave appropriately in future cases and to protect the fairness of the judicial process.[122]

During adjudication, however, fact-finders are often exposed to evidence that is subsequently determined to be inadmissible. This can happen when a witness inadvertently exposes the inadmissible evidence in the courtroom. Attorneys and witnesses might also deliberately introduce legally irrelevant information in order to influence decisions. Inadmissibility can also characterize information coming from external sources, such as the media—both prior to and during an extended trial.

Unsurprisingly, the question of whether fact-finders actually manage to ignore inadmissible information has long troubled legal scholars and courts. In the past few decades scholars have turned to examining this question empirically. This subsection examines the degree to which such information affects judicial decision-makers, and the next subsection discusses possible measures for counteracting this effect.

A case in point is the impact of information about the defendant's past convictions. Taking an experimental approach, Edith Greene and Mary Dodge exposed one group of mock jurors to the defendant's past convictions, while another group was not exposed to such information. The mock jurors who were informed about the past convictions were significantly more likely to reach a guilty verdict.[123] More recently, Theodore Eisenberg and

Avnaim-Pesso—the order of cases in Israeli parole hearings is not random and not exogenous to the timing of meal breaks). *See also* Shai Danziger, Jonathan Levav & Liora Avnaim-Pesso, *Reply to Weinshall-Margel and Shapard: Extraneous Factors in Judicial Decisions Persist,* 108 PROC. NAT'L ACAD. SCI. USA E834 (2011); Andreas Glöckner, *The Irrational Hungry Judge Effect Revisited: Simulations Reveal that the Magnitude of the Effect Is Overestimated,* 11 JUDGMENT & DECISION MAKING 601 (2016).

122. On various grounds for rendering evidence inadmissible, see generally 1 MCCORMICK ON EVIDENCE 897–991, 1013–87 (Kenneth S. Broun et al. eds., 7th ed. 2013); 2 MCCORMICK ON EVIDENCE 175–257.

123. Edith Greene & Mary Dodge, *The Influence of Prior Record Evidence on Juror Decision-Making,* 19 LAW & HUM. BEHAV. 67 (1995). *See also* Roselle L. Wissler & Michael J. Saks, *On the Inefficacy of Limiting Instructions: When Jurors Use Prior Conviction Evidence to Decide on Guilt,* 9 LAW & HUM. BEHAV. 37 (1985); Sarah Tanford & Michele

Valerie Hans took an observational approach to the topic.[124] As part of their study, they assembled a unique data set documenting the behavior of defendants in criminal trials. Criminal records are often introduced into evidence when the defendant takes the stand. When introduced at that stage of the trial, such records induced a significant rise in conviction rates in close cases, that is, in cases where the evidence presented by the prosecution is not overwhelmingly strong. Notably, this increase was not driven by the effect of previous convictions on the defendant's credibility (which is the reason usually cited for admitting such information), but rather by the effect that it had on the jury's decision threshold.

Numerous studies have documented the effects of inadmissible evidence in other legal domains, such as hearsay evidence,[125] pretrial media reports,[126] and illegally obtained evidence.[127] While the vast majority of these studies deal with incriminating evidence in criminal cases, there is support for the claim that inadmissible evidence affects judicial decision-making in civil settings as well, irrespective of which party the evidence favors.[128] A large-scale meta-analysis concluded that "[i]nadmissible evidence produced a significant impact on guilty verdicts."[129] While this impact is relatively small, it is statistically significant.

Researchers have also documented similar behavior among professional judges. In a study of inadmissible evidence in relation to remedial measures in a product liability case, Stephan Landsman and Richard Rakos found that judges and mock jurors were similarly unable to disregard the facts that they were required to disregard.[130] In a subsequent series of experiments, Andrew Wistrich, Chris Guthrie, and Jeffrey Rachlinski reported somewhat more nuanced results.[131] They found that judges were unable to ignore inadmissible

Cox, *The Effects of Impeachment Evidence and Limiting Instructions on Individual and Group Decision Making*, 12 LAW & HUM. BEHAV. 477 (1988).

124. Theodore Eisenberg & Valerie P. Hans, *Taking a Stand on Taking the Stand: The Effect of a Prior Criminal Record on the Decision to Testify and on Trial Outcomes*, 94 CORNELL L. REV. 1353 (2009).

125. *See, e.g.*, Regina A. Schuller, *Expert Evidence and Hearsay: The Influence of "Secondhand" Information on Jurors' Decisions*, 19 LAW & HUM. BEHAV. 345 (1995).

126. *See, e.g.*, Steven Fein, Allison L. McCloskey & Thomas M. Tomlinson, *Can the Jury Disregard That Information? The Use of Suspicion to Reduce the Prejudicial Effects of Pretrial Publicity and Inadmissible Testimony*, 23 PERSONALITY & SOC. PSYCHOL. BULL. 1215 (1997). For a meta-analysis of forty-four pretrial publicity studies, documenting the negative effect of pretrial publicity, see Nancy Mehrkens Steblay et al., *The Effects of Pretrial Publicity on Juror Verdicts: A Meta-analytic Review*, 23 LAW & HUM. BEHAV. 219 (1999). For an overview, see Joel D. Lieberman, Jamie Arndt & Matthew Vess, *Inadmissible Evidence and Pretrial Publicity: The Effects (and Ineffectiveness) of Admonitions to Disregard*, in PSYCHOLOGY IN THE COURTROOM: SOCIAL ASPECTS OF TRIAL PROCESSES, Vol. 1: JURY PSYCHOLOGY 67, 69–71 (Joel D. Lieberman & Daniel A. Krauss eds., 2009).

127. *See, e.g.*, Jeffrey Kerwin & David R. Shaffer, *Mock Jurors versus Mock Juries: The Role of Deliberations in Reactions to Inadmissible Testimony*, 20 PERSONALITY & SOC. PSYCHOL. BULL. 153 (1994).

128. Nancy Steblay et al., *The Impact on Juror Verdicts of Judicial Instruction to Disregard Inadmissible Evidence: A Meta-analysis*, 30 LAW & HUM. BEHAV. 469, 476 (2006).

129. *Id.* at 477.

130. Stephan Landsman & Richard Rakos, *A Preliminary Inquiry into the Effect of Potentially Biasing Information on Judges and Jurors in Civil Litigation*, 12 BEHAV. SCI. & LAW 113 (1994).

131. Wistrich, Guthrie & Rachlinski, *Inadmissible Information*, *supra* note 63.

evidence with regard to settlement offers, privileged information, prior sexual history of a rape victim, prior criminal records of a plaintiff, or information that the government had agreed not to use in trial. However, they were able to ignore a confession that had been obtained in violation of a defendant's right to counsel, and the outcome of a search that had been conducted without probable cause. In another context, it was found that, unlike law students, legal experts were able to disregard preparatory work they were exposed to, when the rules of treaties' interpretation required them to do so.[132] Wistrich, Guthrie, and Rachlinski acknowledge that the pattern of results they observed "defies easy explanation" and requires more data.[133] We agree with this assessment.[134]

Finally, admissible information that is irrelevant from a legal perspective might also influence judicial decisions. Take, for example, the decision adjudicators need to make whether to admit a piece of evidence obtained in a search conducted by the police. Generally, under U.S. law this ruling requires careful analysis of the police's behavior.[135] Importantly, when making this decision courts are required not to take into account the egregiousness of the defendant's conduct.[136] However, decision-makers subject to motivated reasoning might construe the facts of the case in a selective manner to reach the desired outcome from their perspective.[137]

Avani Mehta Sood corroborated this hypothesis in an experiment conducted with laypersons.[138] Subjects in this experiment were required to decide whether to admit evidence obtained in an illegal car search. Their decision hinged on an exception to the exclusionary rule that allows for the admission of evidence that would have been discovered by the police inevitably (without using the illegal means).[139] The experimental manipulation altered the seriousness of the crime involved. Whereas half of the subjects examined the case of a heroin dealer selling drugs to high-school students, the other half examined the case of a marijuana dealer selling drugs to terminally ill cancer patients. The results of the

132. Yahli Shereshevsky & Tom Noah, *Does Exposure to Preparatory Work Affect Treaty Interpretation? An Experimental Study on International Law Students and Experts,* 28 Eur. J. Int'l L. 1287 (2017).

133. Wistrich, Guthrie & Rachlinski, *Inadmissible Information, supra* note 63, at 1324.

134. While the inability (or limited ability) to disregard information challenges the effectiveness of exclusionary rules, it may actually justify such rules. Ehud Guttel has argued that unreliable evidence—namely, evidence that is likely to be refuted by the other party, such as hearsay—should be excluded altogether, because it is highly likely to be refuted subsequently. Such refutation may distort factfinders' decisions due to the cognitive phenomenon known as *overcorrection*—the tendency to overcorrect when a certain piece of information is added and then subtracted, compared to the starting point. *See* Ehud Guttel, *Overcorrection,* 93 Geo. L.J. 241 (2004).

135. *See, e.g.,* David Gray, *A Spectacular Non Sequitur: The Supreme Court's Contemporary Fourth Amendment Exclusionary Rule Jurisprudence,* 50 Am. Crim. L. Rev. 1 (2013).

136. Yale Kamisar, *"Comparative Reprehensibility" and the Fourth Amendment Exclusionary Rule,* 86 Mich. L. Rev. 1, 9–10 (1987).

137. On motivated reasoning, see *supra* pp. 58–61.

138. Avani Mehta Sood, *Cognitive Cleansing: Experimental Psychology and the Exclusionary Rule,* 103 Geo. L.J. 1543 (2015).

139. Nix v.Williams, 467 U.S. 431 (1984).

experiment show that the defendant's conduct significantly influenced the way in which subjects applied the law to the facts of the case. While approximately 60 percent of the subjects in the heroin condition admitted the evidence obtained in the illegal search, only 15 percent did so in the marijuana condition. This result was replicated in an experimental study conducted with presiding judges and corroborated by observational data.[140]

2. Jury Instructions and Other Remedies

When prospective jurors are exposed to prejudicial information prior to a trial, it may be possible to exclude them from the jury during the initial selection process (voir dire). However, this is not a complete solution to the problem, because when it comes to highly publicized events, there may be very few people who were not exposed to media reports, and because jurors may be exposed to inadmissible evidence during the trial itself. Moreover, the screening process relies on the would-be jurors' self-reported susceptibility to influence by pretrial publicity, which is not a reliable predictor of their actual susceptibility. Moreover, the screening process itself may enhance the damaging effect of the publicity.[141]

Another possible response to pretrial publicity is to postpone the trial for some time. However, one study found that the effect of such postponement depends on the nature of pretrial publicity—specifically, whether it is factual or emotionally oriented. The former may refer to incriminating evidence, while the latter arouses negative feelings toward the defendant. It was found that even when delaying the trial for several days proves to be an effective remedy for factual publicity, it does not reduce the effect of emotional publicity.[142]

At the trial itself, the defendant in criminal cases may refrain from testifying, thus avoiding the risk that the prosecution would present her criminal record in an attempt to impeach her credibility as a witness (as allowed, for example, under U.S. law). However, a recent study has demonstrated that, just as juries might be inappropriately influenced by the defendant's criminal record, they tend to inappropriately hold the fact that the defendant chose not to testify against her, and to infer guilt from silence.[143]

A straightforward response to jurors' exposure to inadmissible evidence and irrelevant information is to instruct jurors to disregard it. Since jurors are laypersons, they are guided by the court regarding the substantive rules and rules of evidence (e.g., burden of proof and inadmissible evidence) by which they should make their decisions. Due to space limitations, we will not survey the voluminous psychological literature on jury instructions

140. *See* Andrew J. Wistrich, Jeffrey J. Rachlinski & Chris Guthrie, *Heart versus Head: Do Judges Follow the Law or Follow Their Feelings?*, 93 TEX. L. REV. 855, 890–93 (2015).

141. Lieberman, Arndt & Vess, *supra* note 126, at 69, 72–73.

142. Geoffrey P. Kramer, Norbert L. Kerr & John S. Carroll, *Pretrial Publicity, Judicial Remedies, and Jury Bias*, 14 LAW & HUM. BEHAV. 409 (1990). *But see* Jeffrey R. Wilson & Brian H. Bornstein, *Methodological Considerations in Pretrial Publicity Research. Is the Medium the Message?*, 22 LAW & HUM. BEHAV. 585 (1998) (finding no difference between factual and emotional pretrial publicity).

143. Jeffrey Bellin, *The Silence Penalty*, 103 IOWA L. REV. 395 (2018).

in general,[144] but rather focus on studies pertaining to inadmissible evidence and irrelevant information. In this regard, since the "human mind cannot simply forget information on command," there is room for skepticism as to the effectiveness of such jury instructions.[145] And indeed, a meta-analysis conducted by Nancy Steblay and her colleagues suggests that "judicial instruction did not return verdicts to the level generated by jurors never exposed to the inadmissible evidence."[146]

Aside from this general finding, other findings related to admonitions merit closer attention. First, in some instances admonitions may draw greater attention to inadmissible evidence, thus producing a boomerang effect.[147] For example, it has been reported that mock jurors who had been exposed to a detailed admonition showed a greater tendency to convict compared with mock jurors who had only been told about the inadmissibility of the evidence.[148] Furthermore, instructions that require juries to differentiate between firsthand and hearsay portions of testimony are likely to backfire, due to their complexity and the cognitive effort involved in following them, because the more cognitive activity allocated to a given piece of information, the more readily available it is in one's working memory.[149] Finally, jurors are sensitive to the substance of an admonition. When they are instructed to disregard a certain piece of evidence on a technicality, they are relatively reluctant to do so—but when they are asked to disregard evidence because of its limited probative weight, they show a greater willingness to comply.[150]

These findings are consistent with various explanations for the ineffectiveness of instructions to disregard inadmissible evidence, including *belief perseverance* (or *confirmation bias*); the *hindsight bias* (in the case of illegally obtained evidence); jurors' resistance to having restrictions placed on their freedom to use reliable and relevant information (known as *reactance theory*); and the effort involved in mental control (which ironically makes the

144. On jury instructions in general, see, e.g., Theodore Eisenberg & Martin T. Wells, *Deadly Confusion: Juror Instructions in Capital Cases,* 79 Cornell L. Rev. 1 (1993); Joel D. Lieberman & Bruce D. Sales, *What Social Science Teaches Us about the Jury Instruction Process,* 3 Psychol.Pub. Pol'y & L. 589 (1997); Joel D. Lieberman, *The Psychology of the Jury Instruction Process, in* Psychology in the Courtroom, *supra* note 126, at 129; Vidmar & Hans, *supra* note 84, at 158–68, 175–76, 236–40, 260–62.

145. Tarika Daftary-Kapur, Rafaele Dumas & Steven D. Penrod, *Jury Decision-Making Biases and Methods to Counter Them,* 15 Legal & Criminological Psychol. 133, 138 (2010).

146. Steblay et al., *supra* note 128, at 478. *See also* Michael J. Saks & Barbara A. Spellman, The Psychological Foundations of Evidence Law 85–108 (2016); Lieberman, Arndt & Vess, *supra* note 126, at 73, 77–79.

147. Lieberman, Arndt & Vess, *supra* note 126, at 73, 79–80.

148. Kerri L. Pickel, *Inducing Jurors to Disregard Inadmissible Evidence: A Legal Explanation Does Not Help,* 19 Law & Hum. Behav. 407 (1995). *See also* Michele Cox & Sarah Tanford, *Effects of Evidence and Instructions in Civil Trials: An Experimental Investigation of Rules of Admissibility,* 4 Soc. Behav. 31 (1989); Dae Ho Lee, Daniel A. Krauss & Joel Lieberman, *The Effects of Judicial Admonitions on Hearsay Evidence,* 28 Int'l J.L. & Psychiatry 589 (2005).

149. Angela Paglia & Regina A. Schuller, *Jurors' Use of Hearsay Evidence: The Effects of Type and Timing of Instructions,* 22 Law & Hum. Behav. 501, 504 (1998).

150. Steblay et al., *supra* note 128, at 487.

inadmissible evidence more accessible).[151] The multiplicity of effects and corresponding explanations make it difficult to come up with comprehensive policy recommendations in this regard.

E. Priming and Prejudice

Priming refers to "the incidental activation of knowledge structures, such as trait concepts and stereotypes, by the current situational context," leading to a particular cognitive or affective response.[152] By definition, priming occurs in implicit memory, which is accessible only indirectly.[153] Retention of prior experiences within a knowledge structure can be revealed by measuring the difference in the performance of certain tasks after exposure to a prime (the stimulus) and in the absence of such exposure. For example, in a classic study, John Bargh and his colleagues primed half of their subjects with stereotypical traits of elderly people (by asking them to construct sentences with words such as *old*, *gray*, *forgetful*, and *wrinkle*), while the other half of their subjects were primed differently (asked to construct sentences with neutral words such as *clean* and *private*).[154] The study's dependent variable was the time that it took participants to walk down a hall once they had completed writing their first set of sentences. Participants exposed to the stereotypical prime walked more slowly than those who had received the neutral treatment. While the findings of this study have been challenged (and the challenge in turn sparked a fierce debate),[155] the very phenomenon of priming is well-established.[156]

Priming can have various implications for judicial decision-making, ranging from lawyers' litigation tactics and their ability to prime jurors and judges,[157] to the influence of religious and national symbols incorporated in the interior design of courtrooms.[158] This section does not discuss these implications, but rather focuses on the use of priming as an effective experimental procedure to determine whether subjects possess implicit racial biases—an issue of the utmost theoretical and normative importance. This issue obviously

151. Lieberman, Arndt & Vess, *supra* note 126, at 80–87.

152. John A. Bargh, Mark Chen & Lara Burrows, *Automaticity of Social Behavior: Direct Effects of Trait Construct and Stereotype Activation on Action*, 71 J. PERSONALITY & SOC. PSYCHOL. 230, 230 (1996).

153. John A. Bargh & Tanya L. Chamrand, *The Mind in the Middle: A Practical Guide to Priming and Automaticity Research*, *in* HANDBOOK OF RESEARCH METHODS IN SOCIAL AND PERSONALITY PSYCHOLOGY 253 (Harry T. Reis & Charles M. Judd eds., 2000).

154. Bargh, Chen & Burrows, *supra* note 152.

155. *See, e.g.*, Stéphane Doyen et al., *Behavioral Priming: It's All in the Mind, but Whose Mind?*, 27 PLoS ONE, 7, E29081 (2012); M. Lynne Cooper, *Editorial*, 110 J. PERSONALITY & SOC. PSYCHOL. 431 (2016).

156. For a general overview of the phenomenon, see GORDON B. MOSKOWITZ, SOCIAL COGNITION: UNDERSTANDING SELF AND OTHERS (2005).

157. Kathryn Stanchi, *The Power of Priming in Legal Advocacy: Using the Science of First Impressions to Persuade the Reader*, 89 OR. L. REV. 305 (2010).

158. Ran R. Hassin et al., *Subliminal Exposure to National Flags Affects Political Thought and Behavior*, 104 PROC. NAT'L ACAD. SCI. USA 19757 (2007).

exceeds the context of judicial decision-making, since racial and other biases may affect the behavior of other dramatis personae in litigation,[159] other governmental decision-makers,[160] participants in the political discourse,[161] employers,[162] and anybody else—issues that we will not discuss due to space limitations.

Researchers have demonstrated that racially charged primes (such as rap versus pop music) can cause people to judge the behavior of blacks as more hostile than that of other groups.[163] More generally, scholars have employed the Implicit Association Test (IAT) to examine attitudes toward marginalized groups such as blacks, Asians, and homosexuals. The IAT documents peoples' implicit associations by measuring their response time in a computerized task.[164] These studies have demonstrated that people hold many implicit biases toward different social groups, and that these biases often predict behavior better than explicit biases.[165]

Implicit bias research has been slowly trickling into legal analysis, including judicial decision-making.[166] In the interests of brevity, we shall focus our discussion exclusively on the issue of race and the adverse effects of implicit bias on black litigants in the United States.

Jennifer Eberhardt and her colleagues documented an implicit bidirectional association between blacks and criminality.[167] When subliminally primed with black male faces,

159. *See, e.g.*, Robert J. Smith & Justin D. Levinson, *The Impact of Implicit Racial Bias on the Exercise of Prosecutorial Discretion*, 35 Seattle U. L. Rev. 795 (2012); Justin Murray, *Re-imagining Criminal Prosecution: Toward a Color-Conscious Professional Ethic for Prosecutors*, 49 Am. Crim. L. Rev. 1 (2012); L. Song Richardson & Phillip Atiba Goff, *Implicit Racial Bias in Public Defender Triage*, 122 Yale L.J. 100 (2013).

160. *See, e.g.*, Reshnia M. Saujani, *"The Implicit Association Test": A Measure of Unconscious Racism in Legislative Decision-Making*, 8 Mich. J. Race & L. 395 (2003); Sanford F. Schram et al., *Deciding to Discipline: Race, Choice, and Punishment at the Frontlines of Welfare Reform*, 74 Am. Soc. Rev. 398 (2009).

161. *See, e.g.*, David Domke, *Racial Cues and Political Ideology: An Examination of Associative Priming*, 28 Comm. Res. 772 (2001); Gregory S. Parks & Jeffrey J. Rachlinski, *Implicit Bias, Election '08, and the Myth of a Post-racial America*, 37 Fla. St. U. L. Rev. 659 (2010).

162. *See, e.g.*, Linda Hamilton Krieger, *The Content of Our Categories: A Cognitive Bias Approach to Discrimination and Equal Employment Opportunity*, 47 Stan. L. Rev. 1161 (1995); Anthony G. Greenwald & Linda Hamilton Krieger, *Implicit Bias: Scientific Foundations*, 94 Calif. L. Rev. 945 (2006); Parks & Rachlinski, *supra* note 161.

163. Laurie A. Rudman & Matthew R. Lee., *Implicit and Explicit Consequences of Exposure to Violent and Misogynous Rap Music*, 5 Group Processes & Intergroup Rel. 133 (2002).

164. For a detailed description of the methodology and a meta-analysis, see Anthony G. Greenwald et al., *Understanding and Using the Implicit Association Test: III. Meta-analysis of Predictive Validity*, 97 J. Personality & Soc. Psychol. 17 (2009).

165. *Id.* The use of the IAT to measure implicit bias is not a matter of consensus. For a discussion, see Hal R. Arkes & Philip E. Tetlock, *Attributions of Implicit Prejudice, or "Would Jesse Jackson 'Fail' the Implicit Association Test?"*, 15 Psychol. Inquiry 257 (2004); Mahzarin R. Banaji, Brian A. Nosek & Anthony G. Greenwald, *No Place for Nostalgia in Science: A Response to Arkes and Tetlock*, 15 Psychol. Inquiry 279 (2004); Gregory Mitchell & Philip E. Tetlock, *Antidiscrimination Law and the Perils of Mindreading*, 67 Ohio St. L.J. 1023 (2006). Moreover, the very assumption that "unconscious biases" are truly unconscious has been challenged. *See* Ralph Richard Banks & Richard Thompson Ford, *(How) Does Unconscious Bias Matter?: Law, Politics, and Racial Inequality*, 58 Emory L.J. 1053 (2009).

166. For a collection of studies, see Implicit Racial Bias across the Law (Justin D. Levinson & Robert J. Smith eds., 2012).

167. Jennifer Eberhardt et al., *Seeing Black: Race, Crime, and Visual Processing*, 87 J. Personality & Soc. Psychol. 876 (2004).

subjects were quicker to recognize blurred images of items associated with crime (e.g., guns). Perhaps more surprisingly, when subliminally primed with images of items associated with crime, participants were more attendant to black male faces. Thus, as the authors note, "Not only are Blacks thought of as criminal, but also crime is thought of as Black."[168] Related findings demonstrating an implicit association between black males and guns have been reported in numerous studies that examined people's tendency to shoot in a video simulation involving armed and unarmed whites and blacks.[169] However, while all these findings suggest that people tend to draw a link between race and crime—a connection that might well carry into the courtroom—they were not conducted in the concrete context of judicial decision-making.

Several other studies have more directly examined the role of implicit racial bias in judicial contexts. Sandra Graham and Brian Lowery asked a sample of police officers and juvenile probation officers to analyze vignettes of a crime-related scenario.[170] Unbeknownst to the participants, half were subliminally primed with words associated with blacks, while the other half were primed with words without a common theme. Immediately afterward, the officers read two ambiguous criminal scenarios, and were asked to rate the hypothetical offender on several traits (e.g., hostility and maturity) and to assess the culpability, expected recidivism, and deserved punishment of offenders whose race remained unspecified. Finally, the officers completed a general attitudes and beliefs questionnaire about race. The results suggest that an implicit bias rather than explicit attitudes channeled participants' decisions. Participants in the race-primed group viewed the offender more negatively and were willing to punish him more harshly.

Justin Levinson, Huajian Cai, and Danielle Young have introduced a new IAT that measured the association between whites/blacks and guilty/not guilty judgments.[171] They discovered an implicit association between black and guilty. Moreover, this association was indicative of how their subjects analyzed the evidence in ambiguous cases.[172] More recently, Justin Levinson, Robert Smith, and Danielle Young presented several troubling findings in the context of the death penalty.[173] They showed that when examining the willingness of prospective jury members to impose the death penalty during the screening of capital juries, the process stacks those juries with people who exhibit a relatively strong implicit

168. *Id.* at 883.

169. Joshua Correll, *The Police Officer's Dilemma: Using Ethnicity to Disambiguate Potentially Threatening Individuals*, 83 J. PERSONALITY & SOC. PSYCHOL. 1314 (2002); E. Ashby Plant & B. Michelle Peruche, *The Consequences of Race for Police Officers' Responses to Criminal Suspects*, 16 PSYCHOL. SCI. 180 (2005).

170. Sandra Graham & Brian S. Lowery, *Priming Unconscious Racial Stereotypes about Adolescent Offenders*, 28 LAW & HUM. BEHAV. 483 (2004).

171. Justin D. Levinson, Huajian Cai & Danielle Young, *Guilty by Implicit Racial Bias: The Guilty / Not Guilty Implicit Association Test*, 8 OHIO ST. J. CRIM. L. 187 (2010).

172. *See also* Justin D. Levinson, *Forgotten Racial Equality: Implicit Bias, Decisionmaking, and Misremembering*, 57 DUKE L.J. 345 (2007).

173. Justin D. Levinson, Robert J. Smith & Danielle Young, *Devaluing Death: An Empirical Study of Implicit Racial Bias on Jury-Eligible Citizens in Six Death Penalty States*, 89 N.Y.U. L. REV. 513 (2014).

racial bias. They also found a connection between people's IAT score and their willingness to impose the death penalty. That is, people who exhibited a greater implicit bias were more willing to convict a black defendant than a white defendant.

A more nuanced analysis of this point has been offered by Rachlinski and his colleagues.[174] Their study, which involved presiding judges, employed a two-stage design. In the first stage, judges performed a standard IAT to determine their racial preferences. The results showed the existence of a white preference among white judges, but no racial preference among black judges. In the second stage, judges were asked to evaluate three vignettes of ambiguous criminal cases. Prior to the first two vignettes, where the culprits' race remained obscured, half the judges were subliminally subjected to racial priming. In the third vignette, the race of the defendant was overtly manipulated (African-American or Caucasian). In contrast to Graham and Lowery,[175] Rachlinski and his colleagues did not identify a main effect associated with the racial priming. The evaluations of judges who were primed did not differ significantly from the evaluations of judges who were not primed. However, the researchers did identify a marginally significant effect of judges' IAT scores on their sentencing decisions: judges with a white preference on the IAT gave harsher sentences to defendants when primed with black-associated words as opposed to neutral words. Conversely, judges with a black preference on the IAT gave lower sentences when primed with black-associated words as opposed to neutral words. With respect to the third vignette in which race was explicitly operationalized, the authors could not identify any effect when analyzing the group of judges as a whole. However, further analysis did reveal a three-way interaction between IAT scores, the judge's race, and the defendant's race. Specifically, IAT scores were unrelated to the outcomes reached by white judges, whereas black judges with a black preference tended to acquit more often. While it is difficult to generalize these results, one conclusion does seem to stand out: the explicitness of race matters. As the authors note, "when judges are aware of a need to monitor their own responses for the influence of implicit racial biases, and are motivated to suppress that bias, they appear able to do so."[176] Arguably, decisions in the courtroom more closely resemble the scenario depicted in the third vignette; hence, the extent to which implicit biases actually influence real-world decisions remains unclear.

Implicit bias is an emerging field in the judicial decision-making context, and much work needs to be done before we fully understand the phenomenon's impact. Further research should explore precisely how implicit bias operates (if at all) in actual courtrooms, where people are more likely to attempt to overcome their predispositions. As Jerry Kang and colleagues acknowledge, "because of the incredible difficulties in research design, we do not have studies that evaluate implicit bias in real criminal trials."[177] Moreover, we currently

174. Jeffrey J. Rachlinski et al., *Does Unconscious Racial Bias Affect Trial Judges?*, 84 NOTRE DAME L. REV. 1195 (2009).

175. Graham & Lowery, *supra* note 170.

176. Rachlinski et al., *supra* note 174, at 1221.

177. Jerry Kang et al., *Implicit Bias in the Courtroom*, 59 UCLA L. REV. 1124, 1146 (2012).

have very little information on how racial bias functions in the domain of civil litigation. After thoroughly examining implicit bias in this context, Kang and his colleagues did "concede that [their] claims about implicit bias influencing jury decision-making in civil cases are somewhat speculative and not well quantified."[178]

Finally, identification of effective interventions capable of mitigating the effects of the bias is probably the ultimate goal of this research project, and should be addressed. Elevating the accountability of judges (by, for example, requiring written opinions and limiting the amount of quick decisions made from the bench) might help promote deliberative rather than intuitive rulings.[179] Similarly, employing checklists that will assure that judges consider all of the relevant factors for their decisions may help deal with the bias.[180] Obviously, however, promoting well-reasoned decisions could be in tension with other goals of the judicial system, such as the quick delivery of justice, and the implementation of actual policies requires a careful balancing.[181]

F. Judicial Decision-Making: Moral Judgments

The previous sections argued that judicial decision-making may deviate from the assumptions of cognitive rationality (reflecting, instead, various heuristics and biases), and impartiality (possibly reflecting subconscious prejudicial attitudes). This section highlights examples of deviations of judicial decision-making from the consequentialist morality underpinning standard economic analysis.

As described in Chapter 2, while standard economic analysis is founded on consequentialist morality, prevailing moral convictions reflect moderate deontology.[182] Most people believe that it is important to promote overall good outcomes, but that such promotion is subject to agent-relative moral constraints, and that people have moral options to (sometimes) prioritize their own welfare over the overall good.

Very often, the implications of consequentialist reasoning are similar to those of nonconsequentialist, commonsense morality. Thus, in a claim for damages for breach of contract, the injured party is not compensated for losses that she could have reasonably avoided or mitigated. At the same time, she is entitled to reimbursement for the reasonable costs she

178. *Id.* at 1168. On the implications of implicit bias in other spheres, see, e.g., Christine Jolls & Cass R. Sunstein, *The Law of Implicit Bias*, 94 CAL. L. REV. 969 (2006); Jerry Kang & Mahzarin R. Banaji, *Fair Measures: A Behavioral Realist Revision of "Affirmative Action"*, 94 CALIF. L. REV. 1063 (2006); Samuel R. Bagenstos, *Implicit Bias, "Science," and Antidiscrimination Law*, 1 HARV. L. & POL'Y REV. 477 (2007).

179. *See* Andrew J. Wistrich & Jeffrey J. Rachlinski, *Implicit Bias in Judicial Decision Making: How It Affects Judgment and What Judges Can Do about It*, *in* ENHANCING JUSTICE: REDUCING BIAS 87, 117–18 (Sarah E. Redfield ed., 2017).

180. *See id.* at 119.

181. On additional measures, see Anna Roberts, *(Re)forming the Jury: Detection and Disinfection of Implicit Juror Bias*, 44 CONN. L. REV. 827 (2012); Pamela A. Wilkins, *Confronting the Invisible Witness: The Use of Narrative to Neutralize Capital Jurors' Implicit Racial Biases*, 115 W. VA. L. REV. 305 (2012).

182. *See supra* pp. 13–14, 94–101.

incurred in attempting to prevent losses, even if these attempts ultimately proved to be unsuccessful. These rules provide efficient incentives to injured parties ex ante, and at the same time are consistent with non-consequentialist notions of blame and corrective justice. More interesting for the present purpose, however, are cases in which economic efficiency and non-efficiency moral values diverge. Some such cases have been examined experimentally.

Thus, according to standard economic analysis—which focuses on optimal deterrence—criminal sanctions and punitive damages should be inversely related to the probability of detection and conviction (in criminal proceedings), or of imposing liability and recovering damages (in civil cases).[183] In contrast, the retributivist tradition holds that the actual (rather than expected) punishment should correspond to the wrongfulness of the act and the actor's culpability.[184] In several experimental studies, subjects did not award higher punitive damages or impose more severe criminal sanctions when the probability of detection was lower.[185] Some of these studies found no difference in this regard between laypersons and professional judges.[186] Even when probability of detection was made salient by juxtaposing two similar cases that differed from one another only with respect to the probability of detection, only a minority of respondents increased the penalty in the low-detection cases.[187]

Even more telling are the findings of a survey conducted to elicit people's attitude to risk analysis. Tort law imposes liability for negligently harming other people. From an efficiency perspective, the goal is to incentivize suppliers of products and services to take efficient precautions against risks. Since greater precautions ordinarily increase the costs of production, and since customers' willingness to pay for safer products is not unlimited, efficient investment in safety measures is in the interest of suppliers, customers, and society at large. Just as governmental regulation of environmental risks should ideally rest on evidence-based, sound cost-benefit analysis, so should manufacturers' choice of safety measures be founded on sound cost-benefit analysis.[188] However, both anecdotal evidence and a large-scale survey conducted by Kip Viscusi indicate that the very fact that firms engage in cost-benefit analysis of safety measures is resented by juries, leading them to impose higher punitive damages.[189] Not only does sound cost-benefit analysis of safety measures not reduce the likelihood of awarding punitive damages—the higher the value attached to

183. *See, e.g.*, Gary S. Becker, *Crime and Punishment: An Economic Approach*, 76 J. Pol. Econ. 169 (1968); A. Mitchell Polinsky & Steven Shavell, *Punitive Damages: An Economic Analysis*, 111 Harv. L. Rev. 869 (1998); *supra* pp. 434–35 and 326–29, respectively.

184. *See supra* p. 436.

185. *See, e.g.*, Cass Sunstein, David Schkade & Daniel Kahneman, *Do People Want Optimal Deterrence?*, 29 J. Legal Stud. 237 (2000); Jonathan Baron & Ilana Ritov, *The Role of Probability of Detection in Judgments of Punishment*, 1 J. Legal Analysis 553 (2009).

186. Baron & Ritov, *supra* note 185; *see also* Jonathan Baron & Ilana Ritov, *Intuitions about Penalties and Compensation in the Context of Tort Law*, 7 J. Risk & Uncertainty 17 (1993).

187. Baron & Ritov, *supra* note 185. For further discussion of these findings and their policy implications, see *supra* pp. 436–40.

188. *See supra* pp. 326–29.

189. W. Kip Viscusi, *Corporate Risk Analysis: A Reckless Act?*, 52 Stan. L. Rev. 547 (2000). *See also* pp. 349–50.

human life in such analysis, the greater the punitive award. Professional judges were less likely to follow a zero-risk attitude that does not permit cost/safety trade-offs, and less likely to award punitive damages when firms engage in such cost-benefit analysis. Nonetheless, many of them did award such damages, especially when the risks involved human lives, contrary to the mandates of economic efficiency.[190]

Beyond these specific experimental findings, many legal doctrines discussed in Chapter 5 and elsewhere in the book are more in line with deontological morality than with consequentialism or welfare economics.[191]

G. Rules versus Standards: Certainty and Predictability

Thus far, this chapter has dealt mostly with specific behavioral phenomena, and the ensuing sections will discuss general issues, such as decision-making by groups versus individuals, and by judges versus laypersons. But before turning to those general issues, however, this section discusses decision tasks that are particularly important in the legal sphere—specifically, the use of rules and standards to decide particular cases.

Legal norms are conventionally classified into *rules* and *standards*. Rules typically make legal outcomes contingent upon the existence of a limited number of easily ascertainable facts. Examples of paradigmatic rules include establishing legal capacity solely by age, and penalizing drivers who exceed a certain speed limit with a fixed fine. Standards, in contrast, embody substantive objectives and values, such as reasonableness, good faith, and unconscionability. Judgments based on standards require consideration of the entire set of circumstances of the case, and assessing these in light of the values that the standard embodies.

For centuries, it has been recognized that the primary advantage of rules over standards is their ability to limit people's discretion and enhance the law's certainty and predictability. This common wisdom was challenged by the American legal realists and Critical Legal Studies scholars, who doubted that general legal norms, however detailed, can dictate the judicial outcome in any particular case.[192] One reason for this skepticism was that even a system of detailed rules allows the court to choose which rule applies in any given set of facts. Paradoxically, the more elaborate the system of rules, the broader the judge's discretion in determining which rule to apply in a given case.[193]

It took more than fifty years before experimental and empirical findings were brought to bear on this debate. Experiments conducted with law students and recent law

190. Viscusi, *supra* note 58; W. Kip Viscusi, *Jurors, Judges, and the Mistreatment of Risk by the Courts*, 30 J. LEGAL STUD. 107 (2001) [hereinafter Viscusi, *Mistreatment of Risk*].

191. *See, e.g.*, *supra* pp. 189–92, 262–73, 410–14, 436–43.

192. *See, e.g.*, Karl N. Llewellyn, *On Reading and Using the Newer Jurisprudence*, 40 COLUM. L. REV. 581 (1940); Joseph W. Singer, *Legal Realism Now*, 76 CALIF. L. REV. 465, 469–70 (1988).

193. *See also* Pierre Schlag, *Rules and Standards*, 33 UCLA L. REV. 379, 405–18 (1985).

school graduates demonstrated that a simple, bright-line rule requiring a certain action to be performed within a specific time-limit constrains the discretion of decision-makers more than a vague standard of "reasonable time."[194] Social norms of noncompliance, as well as self-interest, reduce compliance with legal norms to a greater extent when the latter are formulated as standards, rather than as rules.[195] These findings have important ramifications for the design of, for example, consumer law.[196] Similarly, it has been empirically demonstrated that rules constrain lower courts decisions more effectively than standards.[197] Interestingly, legal argumentation has been found to have a greater impact on decisions that were made according to a rule rather than according to a standard. When decisions are made based on a vague standard, decision-makers can opt for the outcome they prefer, with or without legal arguments. Legal arguments help decision-makers reach their desired outcome when this outcome is in tension with the straightforward meaning of the rule.[198] Various behavioral phenomena—including motivated reasoning and other cognitive biases, differences in background knowledge and personal attitudes, and situational factors—have been invoked to explain why decisions under standards are likely to be less predictable and certain.[199]

While the above experimental studies compared judicial decisions (and human behavior more generally) according to a standard to decisions made according to a single, simple rule, very often the real choice is between a vague standard and an elaborate system of rules with myriad distinctions, provisos, and exceptions. Two experimental studies examined the predictability of judgments that were made according to a set of detailed rules versus those made based on a few general standards. Specifically, in a series of large-scale experiments conducted with advanced-years law students, Ellinghaus, Wright, and Karras compared different models of legal norms: detailed rules, slightly less detailed rules, and very general, vague standards. Subjects read a description of a legal dispute, and made a decision according to one of the models of legal norms.[200] The certainty and predictability of the legal norms were measured by the degree of consensus among the separate verdicts—namely, the broader the consensus, the more certain and predictable the legal norms.

194. *See* Brian Sheppard, *Judging under Pressure: A Behavioral Examination of the Relationship between Legal Decisionmaking and Time*, 39 FLA. ST. U. L. REV. 931 (2012); Brian Sheppard & Andrew Moshirnia, *For the Sake of Argument: A Behavioral Analysis of Whether and How Legal Argument Matters in Decisionmaking*, 40 FLA. ST. U. L. REV. 537 (2013).

195. Yuval Feldman & Alon Harel, *Social Norms, Self-Interest and Ambiguity of Legal Norms: An Experimental Analysis of the Rule vs. Standard Dilemma*, 4 REV. L. & ECON. 81 (2008). *See also* Laetitia B. Mulder, Jennifer Jordan & Floor Rink, *The Effect of Specific and General Rules on Ethical Decisions*, 126 ORG. BEHAV. & HUM. DECISION PROCESSES 115 (2015).

196. *See supra* pp. 321–22.

197. Joseph L. Smith & James A. Todd, *Rules, Standards, and Lower Court Decisions*, 3 J.L. & COURTS 257 (2015).

198. Sheppard & Moshirnia, *supra* note 194.

199. Jeremy W. Bock, *Behavioral Claim Construction*, 102 MINN. L. REV. 1273 (2018).

200. M.P. ELLINGHAUS, E.W. WRIGHT & M. KARRAS, MODELS OF CONTRACT LAW: AN EMPIRICAL EVALUATION OF THEIR UTILITY (2005).

The main finding of these experiments was that systems of elaborate legal rules do not yield more certain and predictable outcomes than do systems of vague standards. Moreover, while standards produced more predictable outcomes in easy cases, the application of rules to relatively easy cases did not increase predictability.[201]

In another experiment, Ellinghaus and his coauthors asked responders to rate the fairness of the outcome and the extent to which the judgment took the important facts of the case into account. They found that in easy cases that were decided according to standards, a positive correlation was found between the rated fairness of the judgment and the extent to which the responders believed that the judgment had considered all pertinent circumstances. No such correlation was found with regard to judgments based on detailed rules.[202] Thus, standards appeared to be superior to rules in drawing decision-makers' attention to the more important aspects of a case.

In a follow-up study, the researchers examined how the scope of data considered by the judge affected the judgment's certainty and predictability.[203] In addition to making a judicial decision, the subjects in this experiment were asked to assess the importance of fifteen factual circumstances that, in the experimenters' judgment, fell under one of three categories in terms of their importance. The participants were asked to make this assessment four times during the experiment: after reading the factual description; after reading the description of the applicable legal norms; after writing the arguments in support of each side's position; and after writing their reasoned judgment. In this experiment the predictability and certainty of the legal norms were similarly determined by the degree of consensus regarding the decision.

The participants generally shared the experimenters' judgment as to the relative importance of the different circumstances. As they progressed along the decision process, they ranked the important facts as more important and the unimportant facts as less important. However, unlike the participants who reached their decisions based on standards (who attributed increasing importance to the circumstances in the middle category), those who made their decisions according to specific rules attributed decreasing importance to intermediate circumstances. This finding supports the contention that the greater predictability and certainty of decisions under a regime of standards is due to the decision-makers' increased attention to a broader set of circumstances. Wright and his colleagues also constructed a connectionist model of mental representations of the data presented to their subjects—the type of model underlying the coherence-based theories of legal decision-makers discussed in Section B. They showed that the phenomenon of coherence shift neatly explains their findings.

Considerably more experimental work is required to determine the generality of these findings. Strong support for the results can be found in a large comparative, empirical study

201. *Id.* at 38–41.

202. *Id.* at 72–74.

203. E.W. Wright et al., *The Effect of Rule Determinacy on Deciding Contract Disputes: Experimental Data and Network Simulation* (working paper, July 2011, *available at:* http://ssrn.com/abstract=1884195).

that examined the certainty and consistency of enforcement mechanisms under either legal rules or standards, in the context of nursing-home regulation.[204] The study found much greater consistency among assessments made by supervisors under a system of standards compared with those based on a very detailed, intricate set of rules. The multiplicity of technical rules appears to have given supervisors greater discretion in employing them and in choosing how much emphasis to place on each one.

Finally, the design of legal norms as rules, standards, or any combination thereof is only one factor influencing the certainty and predictability of judicial decision-making. Therefore, understanding how the formulation of norms affects decision-making does not yield direct and conclusive recommendations about the design of legal norms. Further investigation of the interactions between the pertinent factors may be required first.

H. Group Decision-Making

Thus far we have focused mainly on judicial decision-making at the individual level. However, many judicial decisions are reached by a group—either a panel of judges, or a jury. This section examines how group dynamics influence the outcomes of the judicial process.

As detailed in Chapter 2, the transition from individual to group decision-making can elicit a wide variety of outcomes.[205] Group dynamics may mitigate cognitive heuristics and biases, intensify them, or have no effect whatsoever—depending on the group characteristics, the decision procedure, and the object of decision. The effect of group deliberation also depends on the nature of the relevant heuristic. When the issue is complex or involves a value judgment, and there is no demonstrably correct answer—as is often the case with judicial decision-making—the deliberation process can drive the group toward extreme outcomes that do not reflect members' predeliberation preferences. This phenomenon, known as *group polarization*, stems from social comparison (members who strive to perceive themselves and be perceived favorably by others adopt a position that accords with the dominant view within the group but somewhat more extreme), and informational influences (being exposed to more and better arguments in support of the majority position).

Researchers have documented how group polarization affects judicial decision-making. Studies show that the phenomenon can lead to contrasting outcomes, depending on the specific context. With respect to a jury's decision to convict or acquit, a meta-analysis of existing studies has pointed to a so-called *bias toward leniency*:[206] when there is no clear majority within the jury, the deliberation process becomes skewed toward acquittal.

204. John Braithwaite & Valerie Braithwaite, *The Politics of Legalism: Rules versus Standards in Nursing-Home Regulation*, 4 Soc. & Legal Stud. 307 (1995).

205. *Supra* pp. 120–24; Norbert L. Kerr, Robert J. MacCoun, and Geoffrey P. Kramer, *Bias in Judgment: Comparing Individuals and Groups*, 103 Psychol. Rev. 687 (1996).

206. Robert J. MacCoun & Norbert L. Kerr, *Asymmetric Influence in Mock Jury Deliberation: Jurors' Bias for Leniency*, 54 J. Personality & Soc. Psychol. 21 (1988).

Another experiment has suggested that this result may stem from the unique standard of proof applied in this decision-setting—namely, beyond a reasonable doubt.[207] To the extent that this standard reflects a well-entrenched social and legal norm, jury members advocating acquittal may have an asymmetric advantage during deliberations, which helps them swing the other members toward their view.

However, group polarization does not only mitigate legal outcomes. There is conflicting evidence as to whether group deliberation increases the coherence and predictability of judicial quantitative decisions.[208] Thus, in one study, Shari Diamond, Michael Saks, and Stephan Landsman found that the standard deviation of total individual awards, prior to deliberation, was over $7,000,000. However, after deliberation in groups of six, the standard deviation of total jury awards dropped dramatically to under $1,000,000. This dramatic decrease in variability was exhibited in economic and non-economic damages alike.[209] Conversely, in a very large experimental study involving over 3,000 subjects, Schkade, Sunstein, and Kahneman found that jury deliberation actually reduced predictability—at least in the context of punitive damages.[210] Due to group polarization, jury dollar verdicts were systematically higher than median predeliberation judgments.[211] Since this tendency was more pronounced when the median of jurors' predeliberation judgments was high, the overall variability of the awards increased. Among juries that awarded punitive damages, 27 percent awarded sums that were as high as, or higher than, the highest predeliberation judgment of their individual members.

Inasmuch as Schkade and his colleagues' findings accurately reflect actual judicial decisions, they raise a clear concern. They show that group deliberation that spurs the group toward more extreme outcomes also significantly increases the uncertainty of its outcomes. Based on this result, the authors conclude that "deliberation is a significantly poorer way of aggregating opinions than is statistical pooling at least if the goal is to decrease the arbitrary unpredictability of awards."[212]

As previously noted, the outcomes of group deliberation depend on the background norms governing the group. Accordingly, Schkade and his colleagues acknowledge that their findings cannot be automatically generalized. For example, in all their studies the defendant was a corporation, and it is unclear whether similar attitudes would have been evident with respect to individual defendants.[213] Furthermore, societies differ from one

207. *Id.* at 26–30. *See also infra* pp. 595–98.

208. On such decisions, see generally *supra* pp. 538–43.

209. Diamond, Saks & Landsman, *supra* note 82, at 313–17.

210. David Schkade, Cass R. Sunstein & Daniel Kahneman, *Deliberating about Dollars: The Severity Shift*, 100 COLUM. L. REV. 1139 (2000).

211. *See also* Shari Seidman Diamond & Jonathan D. Casper, *Blindfolding the Jury to Verdict Consequences: Damages, Experts, and the Civil Jury*, 26 LAW & SOC'Y. REV. 513, 553–57 (1992).

212. Schkade, Sunstein & Kahneman, *supra* note 210, at 1160.

213. *Id.* at 1162–63.

another in their attitudes toward legal issues such as punishment.[214] While some societies may be inclined toward leniency, others might favor the punitive approach. In addition, these findings should be treated with caution when norms change over time. For example, a more recent study has demonstrated a severity rather than leniency effect among jurors.[215] As the authors noted, this finding may reflect an attitudinal shift since the 1970s, when most of the pioneering work in this area was conducted. Apparently, the subtleties attached to group decision-making provide endless room for further research.[216]

I. Judges versus Laypersons

A general question regarding cognitive biases pertains to the extent to which expertise diminishes the effect of those biases on decision-making. In the context of adjudication, the question is whether professional judges make the same mistakes that people lacking legal training are likely to make. To address this issue, in this section we review some of the main findings on the susceptibility of judges to cognitive biases, with particular focus on controlled experiments that have sought to isolate this issue.[217]

The psychological research on expertise is somewhat ambiguous. In general, judgments can reflect true expertise if they are reached within a decision-making environment that (1) is regular and predictable, and (2) offers people an opportunity to learn these regularities.[218] It is therefore important that decision-makers receive feedback on the quality of their choices in a timely fashion. Empirical studies have shown that while some experts exhibit resilience to various biases,[219] others do not.[220]

214. Pat Mayhew & John van Kesteren, *Cross-National Attitudes to Punishment*, *in* Changing Attitudes to Punishment 63 (J.V. Roberts & M. Hough eds., 2002).

215. Dennis J. Devine et al., *Explaining Jury Verdicts: Is Leniency Bias for Real?*, 34 J. Applied Soc. Psychol. 2069 (2004).

216. On jury group decision-making, see also Saks & Spellman, *supra* note 146, at 46–49.

217. Some empirical studies have found considerable differences between juries and judges, for example, in the granting of mega-awards of punitive damages. *See, e.g.*, Joni Hersch & W. Kip Viscusi, *Punitive Damages: How Judges and Juries Perform*, 33 J. Legal Stud. 1 (2004). However, since the routing of cases between judges and juries is not random, it is difficult to draw clear conclusions from these findings. *See* Eisenberg et al., *supra* note 92. On other aspects of judges' versus juries' decision-making, see Saks & Spellman, *supra* note 146, at 50–55.

218. Daniel Kahneman & Gary Klein, *Conditions for Intuitive Expertise: A Failure to Disagree*, 64 Am. Psychologist 515 (2009). On expertise and susceptibility to cognitive biases, see generally *supra* pp. 114–17.

219. *See, e.g.*, Russell Korobkin & Chris Guthrie, *Psychology, Economics, and Settlement: A New Look at the Role of the Lawyer*, 76 Texas L. Rev. 77 (1997) (experimentally demonstrating that lawyers can facilitate a higher rate of settlement than litigants negotiating on their own); Chris Guthrie, *Panacea or Pandora's Box? The Costs of Options in Negotiation*, 88 Iowa L. Rev. 601 (2003) (arguing that lawyer-negotiators, acting on behalf of clients, are more likely than non-lawyer-negotiators, acting on their own behalf, to overcome certain psychological hurdles in negotiation).

220. *See, e.g.*, John C. Anderson, D. Jordan Lowe & Philip M.J. Reckers, *Evaluation of Auditor Decisions: Hindsight Bias Effects and the Expectation Gap*, 14 J. Econ. Psychol. 711 (1993) (demonstrating that judges exhibit a hindsight bias); Gregory B. Northcraft & Margaret A. Neale, *Experts, Amateurs, and Real Estate: An Anchoring-and-Adjustment Perspective on Property Pricing Decisions*, 39 Org. Behav. & Hum. Decision Processes 84 (1987) (empirically showing that real-estate agents are susceptible to the anchoring effect).

The broadest body of work on the cognitive aspects of professional judges' decisions has been presented by Chris Guthrie, Jeffrey Rachlinski, and Andrew Wistrich (GRW).[221] Throughout this chapter, we have cited many of their findings. At this point we would like to briefly highlight the "big picture" emerging from their studies of judicial behavior. According to GRW, judges are "generally susceptible to the heuristics and biases that tend to induce intuitive and impressionistic judgments".[222] Like most people, judges exhibit a tendency to base decisions on quick intuitions rather than more complex deliberation. Judges' results in the Cognitive Reflection Test—which measures people's disposition to reflect on a question (System 2), rather than giving an intuitive and spontaneous (System 1) answer—mirrored those of other well-educated individuals.[223] In numerous studies conducted with different groups of judges, GRW demonstrated that anchoring, hindsight, framing, and other documented biases influence the way in which judges analyze legal vignettes.[224] These results were replicated with generalist judges and those specializing in a specific area of law.[225] Studies involving commercial and international arbitrators yielded comparable results.[226]

GRW did, however, document the aptitude of judges to overcome some of the pitfalls of human decision-making. For example, while judges usually found it difficult to ignore inadmissible evidence, they did succeed in doing so at times.[227] Specifically, a substantial body of work has demonstrated that judges can successfully deal with the challenge of ignoring inadmissible evidence in the context of determining probable cause. As described in Subsection C.2,[228] judges in the United States examine whether probable cause for a search exists either in foresight (for search warrant purposes) or in hindsight, when the outcome of the search is already known (for evidentiary purposes). In a study involving

221. Major contributions in this literature include Guthrie, Rachlinski & Wistrich, *supra* note 91; Wistrich, Guthrie & Rachlinski, *Inadmissible Information, supra* note 63; Jeffrey J. Rachlinski, Chris Guthrie & Andrew J. Wistrich, *Heuristics and Biases in Bankruptcy Judges,* 163 J. INSTITUTIONAL & THEORETICAL ECON. 167 (2007) [hereinafter Rachlinski, Guthrie & Wistrich, *Bankruptcy Judges*]; Guthrie, Rachlinski & Wistrich, *Blinking on the Bench, supra* note 63; Guthrie, Rachlinski & Wistrich, *Hidden Judiciary, supra* note 109; Rachlinski, Guthrie & Wistrich, *Probable Cause, supra* note 63.

222. Guthrie, Rachlinski & Wistrich, *Hidden Judiciary, supra* note 109, at 1521.

223. *Id.* at 1495–500. On CRT and dual-process theories of thinking, see generally *supra* pp. 21–23.

224. *See, e.g.,* Guthrie, Rachlinski & Wistrich, *supra* note 91.

225. Rachlinski, Guthrie & Wistrich, *Bankruptcy Judges, supra* note 221; Guthrie, Rachlinski & Wistrich, *Hidden Judiciary, supra* note 109.

226. Helm, Wistrich & Rachlinski, *supra* note 108; Franck et al., *supra* note 108.

227. Wistrich, Guthrie & Rachlinski, *Inadmissible Information, supra* note 63 (finding that judges were unable to disregard demands disclosed during a settlement conference, conversation protected by attorney-client privilege, and a plaintiff's prior criminal convictions. In contrast, they were able to ignore inadmissible information obtained in violation of a criminal defendant's right to counsel and—as further described below—the outcome of a search, when determining whether probable cause existed). *See also* Shereshevski & Noah, *supra* note 132 (finding that, unlike law students, legal experts were able to disregard preparatory work they were not allowed to use in interpreting treaties).

228. *See supra* p. 536. *See also supra* pp. 546–47.

900 state and federal judges, GRW showed that their subjects made similar rulings in both contexts.[229]

Although GRW clearly show that judges are influenced by cognitive biases, their findings do not clarify how judges fare in this regard compared with jurors. Several studies have attempted to examine this question directly by using the same survey instruments with judges and mock jurors. Reid Hastie and Kip Viscusi, for example, compared the extent to which the hindsight bias influenced the decisions of 95 judges and 277 mock-jurors.[230] They found that while mock jurors exhibited a clear hindsight bias, judges exhibited only an inclination toward this bias (that was mostly statistically insignificant). In another study, Viscusi compared judges and jurors along numerous dimensions of tort litigation, and again found "fewer biases by judges in their treatment of risk."[231] Judges were more open to conducting unbiased cost-benefit analyses of precautions, and tended to perceive risk more accurately. In contrast, jurors more strongly exhibited a "zero-risk mentality" that does not permit cost/safety trade-offs, and were more willing to spend unlimited amounts of money to eliminate small risks.

Inasmuch as there are differences between judges and laypersons, it is an intriguing question whether these are due to the judges' legal training or to their practical experience. Some light on this question has been shed by a study conducted by Stephan Dickert and his colleagues.[232] The study used case descriptions based on actual judgments of the German Federal Court, and compared them with decisions made by advanced-years law students, official lay judges, and students of other disciplines. The law students' decisions were more congruent with those of the Federal Court than those of lay judges, and those of lay judges showed lower congruency even in comparison to those of non-law students. Subjects without legal training showed stronger emotional reactions to the legal cases when more information was given to them, whereas law students did not. Plausibly, this was due to the fact that legally trained participants constructed their mental representation using abstract legal concepts, while the student controls and lay judges relied more on comparisons with similar cases that they had heard about, or on their personal experience. Finally, legal training and experience both corresponded with higher confidence.

J. A General Assessment of Behavioral Research of Judicial Decision-Making

The behavioral study of judicial decision-making faces unique challenges. Judges are, of course, human beings. But they are also trained jurists and professional adjudicators.

229. Rachlinski, Guthrie & Wistrich, *Probable Cause, supra* note 63; *see also* Wistrich, Guthrie & Rachlinski, *Inadmissible Information, supra* note 63.

230. Hastie & Viscusi, *supra* note 58. *See also* John C. Anderson et al., *The Effect of Using Diagnostic Decision Aids for Analytical Procedures on Judges' Liability Judgments,* 14 J. ACCT. & PUB. POL'Y 33 (1995); Viscusi, *supra* note 58 at 50–55.

231. Viscusi, *Mistreatment of Risk, supra* note 190, at 110.

232. Stephan Dickert et al., *The More the Better? Effects of Training, Experience and Information Amount in Legal Judgments*, 26 APPLIED COGNITIVE PSYCHOL. 223 (2012).

A fundamental task of behavioral research is to examine to what extent, if any, legal training and judicial experience affect how judges make decisions. Drawing conclusions about judicial decision-making based on the findings of experiments conducted with laypersons is intrinsically problematic.

In this context, Frederick Schauer has claimed that a distinction should be drawn between tasks that both judges and other people (including lay jurors) perform—such as fact-finding and verdict-rendering—and tasks that lie within judges' exclusive province, such as selecting, interpreting, applying, and developing legal norms.[233] Even if judges' decision-making is not fundamentally different from that of others when performing nonexclusive tasks, there is special interest in examining how judges perform their uniquely designated tasks. Possibly, judges' legal training and experience, their self-selection to become judges, and the institutional environment in which they operate all make a difference in this regard. In fact, Schauer argues, if there is no significant difference between "thinking as a lawyer" or "reasoning as a judge," and thinking and reasoning as a layperson, then there is no reason to investigate judicial decision-making any more than there is to investigate that of, say, mechanics or dentists.[234] Schauer further claims that current behavioral research of judicial decision-making leaves much to be desired.

While behavioral research of judicial decision-making is indeed in a relatively early stage of its development, Shauer's critique appears to be overstated, for several reasons. First, as detailed in Section I, a considerable number of studies have used professional judges as subjects. There have also been a number of experimental studies of the "exclusive" judicial tasks of applying rules and standards to given sets of facts, and of treaties' interpretation.[235] At the same time, one should concede that even laboratory experiments using professional judges as subjects differ strikingly from the real-world performance of judges; hence any inference drawn from the former to the latter must be treated with caution.[236] Conducting randomized field experiments and reporting natural experiments is particularly challenging in the context of adjudication, for practical and ethical reasons—however, it is conceivable.[237]

With regard to judicial functions carried out by juries, a huge body of empirical and experimental research has dwelt on jury decision-making, using jury-eligible people as subjects and observing actual jury deliberations.[238] Moreover, inasmuch as the hypothesized difference between judges and laypersons is founded on the former's legal training,

233. Frederick Schauer, *Is There a Psychology of Judging?*, *in* THE PSYCHOLOGY OF JUDICIAL DECISION MAKING, *supra* note 5, at 103. *See also* Barbara Spellman & Frederick Schauer, *Legal Reasoning*, *in* THE OXFORD HANDBOOK OF THINKING AND REASONING 719 (Keith J. Holyoak & Robert G. Morrison eds., 2d ed. 2012).

234. *Id.* at 105–06.

235. *See supra* pp. 556–69; *supra* note 132 and accompanying text.

236. Neil Vidmar, *The Psychology of Trial Judges*, 20 CURRENT DIRECTIONS IN PSYCHOL. SCI. 58 (2011).

237. *See, e.g.*, Leibovitch, *supra* note 51.

238. For an overview, see VIDMAR & HANS, *supra* note 84; *see also* GREENE & BORENSTEIN, *supra* note 80; CIVIL JURIES AND CIVIL JUSTICE: PSYCHOLOGICAL AND LEGAL PERSPECTIVES (Brian H. Bornstein et al. eds., 2008).

experiments conducted with advanced-year law students and experienced advocates provide further relevant insights.[239]

A considerable number of studies have also compared judges and laypersons directly. As discussed in Section I, some of these studies found certain differences between professional judges and the general population,[240] while others found no divergence.[241] Even if there are no significant differences between judges' decision-making and that of other people, there is much to be gained from examining how general psychological phenomena interact with the unique procedural and institutional characteristics of judicial decision-making.[242] Such an examination could lead to reforms in institutional design, court procedures, and even substantive legal rules. Just as the huge corpus of behavioral research on decision-making by physicians informs the operation of health systems, there is a need for similar research in the judicial sphere, irrespective of whether judges differ from other decision-makers.

Finally, there is often further support for the external validity of laboratory experiments of judicial decision-making. This includes studies conducted with experienced professionals in other domains, judges' self-reported descriptions of judging, and analyses of actual judgments.[243]

At the end of the day, one should concede that further research is necessary to establish the validity and generality of behavioral claims about judicial decision-making. This is particularly true with regard to judges' unique tasks of interpreting, developing, and applying legal norms. There is also scope for qualitative research of judges' actual behavior in court, to ascertain the external validity of some laboratory findings.[244] At the same time, much has already been achieved in this sphere. Furthermore, behaviorally informed theories and policy recommendations that are based on imperfect experimental and empirical data are generally preferable to theories and recommendations that rest on no such data.[245]

239. *See, e.g.*, ELLINGHAUS, WRIGHT & KARRAS, *supra* note 200; Zamir & Ritov, *supra* note 65; Eyal Zamir, Ilana Ritov & Doron Teichman, *Seeing Is Believing: The Anti-inference Bias*, 89 IND. L.J. 195 (2014).

240. *See, e.g.*, Wistrich, Guthrie & Rachlinski, *Inadmissible Information*, *supra* note 63.

241. *See, e.g.*, Landsman & Rakos, *supra* note 130.

242. Emily Sherwin, *Features of Judicial Reasoning*, *in* THE PSYCHOLOGY OF JUDICIAL DECISION MAKING, *supra* note 5, at 121.

243. Dan Simon, *In Praise of Pedantic Eclecticism: Pitfalls and Opportunities in the Psychology of Judges*, *in* THE PSYCHOLOGY OF JUDICIAL DECISION MAKING, *supra* note 5, at 131, 136–38.

244. Vidmar, *supra* note 236, at 61.

245. *See also supra* p. 150.

16

Evidence Law

A. Introduction

The law of evidence deals with the proof of facts in legal proceedings. It determines the admissibility and weight given to various pieces of evidence, as well as the amount and quality of proof necessary to prevail. Among other goals, the law of evidence strives to enhance the accuracy of fact-finding, to allocate the risks of error between the litigants according to the pertinent normative considerations, and to strike a balance between minimizing judicial errors and minimizing the costs of avoiding them. Rules of admissibility and weight may serve additional goals—such as deterring unlawful police investigation techniques, or promoting marital harmony. Trial outcomes (and indirectly, the content of settlements and plea bargains, as well) depend to a large extent on the perceptions, recollection, and motivations of witnesses; the decisions and actions of those who prepare the evidence for trial (including police investigators, litigants, and attorneys); and judicial fact-finders' decision-making. Studies of the mental processes of witnesses, litigants, investigators, and fact-finders are therefore crucial to the law of evidence. In fact, even prior to the emergence of behavioral law and economics, a large body of research applied psychological insights to legal issues, such as eyewitness identification and the formation of beliefs about facts—some of which are discussed in this chapter.[1]

There is partial overlap between the behavioral study of evidence law and that of judicial decision-making. In particular, behavioral analysis of evidence law must take into account (1) general theories of the cognitive process of judicial fact-finding—specifically, the story model and coherence-based reasoning; (2) the difficulty that fact-finders have in ignoring inadmissible evidence and other information they have been exposed to; and (3) the difficulties involved in jury instructions. These issues were discussed in Chapter 15,[2] and the present chapter draws on that discussion.

1. For recent surveys of the behavioral analysis of evidence law, see Michael J. Saks & Barbara A. Spellman, The Psychological Foundations of Evidence Law (2016); Fredrick E. Vars, *Evidence Law*, *in* The Oxford Handbook of Behavioral Economics and the Law 703 (Eyal Zamir & Doron Teichman eds., 2014).

2. *See supra* pp. 528–32, 545–48, and 548–50, respectively.

Behavioral Law and Economics. Eyal Zamir and Doron Teichman.

This chapter consists of three sections. Section B discusses the effect of various cognitive limitations, heuristics, and biases on the actual and perceived credibility of different types of evidence, including eyewitness testimonies, probabilistic data, and circumstantial evidence. It further examines the extent to which the use of expert testimonies can overcome such heuristics and biases. Section C analyzes behavioral aspects of burden-of-proof rules, including the justification for placing the burden on the plaintiff, and the actual meaning of the standard of proof in civil and criminal proceedings. Finally, Section D argues that people's bounded rationality not only creates obstacles for judicial truth finding, but also makes it much harder for interested parties, litigants and witnesses, to hide the truth—thus facilitating accurate fact-finding.

B. Types of Evidence and Cognitive Biases

People's heuristics and biases affect the way they assess evidence, and their willingness to assign liability based on it. Fact-finders treat different types of evidence—eyewitness testimonies, probabilistic and circumstantial evidence, and expert opinions—differently, even when there is arguably no rational basis for doing so. Behavioral studies have also demonstrated that the difficulties stemming from fact-finders' heuristics and biases are heightened by the witnesses' own psychological limitations—particularly in the case of eyewitnesses. This section discusses these findings and their normative implications.

1. Eyewitnesses

Notwithstanding the increased use of scientific and forensic evidence, such as fingerprints and DNA profiling, eyewitness testimonies continue to play a key role in civil and criminal trials. In the past few decades, a huge body of empirical research has examined the ability of eyewitnesses to identify perpetrators and accurately describe the events giving rise to litigation, as well as the ability of judicial fact-finders to assess the reliability and trustworthiness of testimonies.[3] The picture emerging from this body of research is rather troubling.

Since it would be impossible to summarize the immense literature on this subject in any systematic fashion, this section merely highlights some of the main contributions made by behavioral research to the study of eyewitness testimony and its assessment by courts.[4]

(a) Eyewitness Testimony

Eyewitness testimony is considerably less accurate than people tend to assume. Of the more than 350 convicted persons exonerated of their crimes based on DNA testing as part of the Innocence Project in the United States, 70 percent had been convicted based on eyewitness

3. *See, e.g.*, BRIAN L. CUTLER & STEVEN D. PENROD, MISTAKEN IDENTIFICATION: THE EYEWITNESS, PSYCHOLOGY, AND THE LAW (1995); DAN SIMON, IN DOUBT: THE PSYCHOLOGY OF THE CRIMINAL JUSTICE PROCESS (2012).

4. For a comprehensive survey of the vast literature in the area, see THE HANDBOOK OF EYEWITNESS PSYCHOLOGY, VOL. I: MEMORY FOR EVENTS (Michael P. Toglia et al. eds., 2006); THE HANDBOOK OF EYEWITNESS PSYCHOLOGY, VOL. II: MEMORY FOR PEOPLE (R.C.L. Lindsay et al. eds., 2007).

misidentification—in some instances, by more than one witness.[5] Numerous field and laboratory studies of eyewitness identification have examined the ability of eyewitnesses to pick out a suspect from a group of people. Overall, fewer than half the witnesses (about 45 percent) identified the suspect when he was present in the lineup; between a quarter and one-fifth picked an innocent foil, and the rest—around one-third—declined to make a choice.[6] This means that approximately one-third of identifications, excluding no-identification choices, are wrong. Even more strikingly, ninety-four laboratory experiments compared lineup identifications in which the suspect was not included in the lineup (which may well be the case in actual police investigations) to lineups where the suspect was present. Forty-eight percent of the participants in the former condition picked out someone in the lineup, who by definition was not the perpetrator.[7]

Reliable identification requires accurate encoding, retention, and retrieval of information—but all three processes are imperfect. People are usually not very good in encoding strangers' faces, and their ability to do so diminishes as the distance between the witness and the other person increases, the illumination in the scene decreases, the duration of exposure to the target is shorter, and the witness's level of stress is higher.[8] People are particularly bad at identifying members of other races or ethnicities.[9]

As for the retention phase, memories fade over time. Memories may also be contaminated, for example, by being exposed to the suspect's image in the media.[10]

Finally, the retrieval phase is often problematic as well. In criminal investigations, identification is often done by means of lineups. As previously noted, numerous studies have demonstrated that witnesses are over-inclined to choose someone in a lineup—particularly when they assume that the perpetrator is present in it, or when the suspect is singled out in some fashion. Consequently, sequential lineups—in which the witness is shown one person (or one photo) at a time, and asked whether this is the perpetrator (and possibly how certain she is about her reply), before seeing the next person—reduce the rate of false identifications.[11] Various other factors have been shown to affect the reliability of lineups.

5. The Innocence Project is a U.S. litigation and public policy organization dedicated to exonerating wrongfully convicted people through DNA testing. *See* http://www.innocenceproject.org/dna-exonerations-in-the-united-states (last visited Dec. 31, 2017).

6. *See, e.g.*, Tim Valentine, Alan Pickering & Stephen Darling, *Characteristics of Eyewitness Identification That Predict the Outcome of Real Lineups*, 17 Applied Cognitive Psychol. 969 (2003) (a large-scale field study); Steven E. Clark, Ryan T. Howell & Sherrie L. Davey, *Regularities in Eyewitness Identification*, 32 Law & Hum. Behav. 187 (2008) (a meta-analysis of ninety-four experiments).

7. Clark, Howell & Davey, *supra* note 6, at 192.

8. Simon, *supra* note 3, at 58–63; Kathy Pezdek, *Fallible Eyewitness Memory and Identification*, *in* Conviction of the Innocent: Lessons from Psychological Research 105, 113–15, 117–18 (Brian L. Cutler ed., 2012).

9. *See, e.g.*, Christian A. Meissner & John C. Brigham, *Thirty Years of Investigating the Own-Race Bias in Memory for Faces: A Meta-analytic Review*, 7 Psychol. Pub. Pol'y & L. 3 (2001) (a meta-analysis of thirty-nine research articles).

10. Simon, *supra* note 3, at 64–69.

11. Nancy K. Steblay, Jennifer E. Dysart & Gary L. Wells, *Seventy-Two Tests of the Sequential Lineup Superiority Effect: A Meta-analysis and Policy Discussion*, 17 Psychol. Pub. Pol'y & L. 99 (2011).

Thus, the reliability of identification increases when the foil's appearance is neither very different nor overly similar to that of the suspect; when the witness is told that the actual perpetrator may be absent from the lineup; and when the administrator gives no verbal or nonverbal clues about the identity of the suspect (which makes double-blind lineups—in which the administrator does not know the identity of the suspect—more credible).[12] Administrators' reactions may also boost the confidence of the witness in her identification, which, as we shall see below, may increase the danger of false convictions by fact-finders who are overly impressed by the witness's confidence.[13] In fact, some studies have found a negligible correlation between witnesses' identification accuracy and their confidence.[14]

Eyewitnesses face difficulties not only in identifying the perpetrator, but in accurately describing the incident they saw, as well. Studies of event memory, in contexts akin to criminal investigations, found that people's reports were between 65 to 95 percent accurate.[15] Here too, errors may be caused by problems in the perception, retention, and retrieval of the information. At the perception stage, due to their limited attention capacity, people are much better at encoding the gist of an event than its peripheral details (which may be crucial for assigning criminal and civil liability).[16] People are not very good at estimating distances between objects, the duration of events, the speed of objects, and other people's features, such as height, weight, and age.[17]

Importantly, remembering is an active process of constructing an account of an event—a process whereby one's perceptions are integrated with additional information, including one's prior beliefs and expectations about the world. Psychological studies have demonstrated that people sometimes confuse the sources of fragments of memories, thus mistakenly inserting elements from one event into another. In several studies, subjects reported recalling things that could not have happened, such as watching a television report that never existed. False memories may also result from external influences, such as exposure to other people's accounts of the event. Simple manipulations, such as misleading questions, lead people to remember things that never happened.[18] From the time of the event until they testify in court, eyewitnesses' description of the occurrence is edited and synthesized in their minds, as they interact with investigators, other witnesses, and attorneys, and through their exposure to other sources of information.

12. Simon, *supra* note 3, at 71–74;Nancy K. Steblay & Elizabeth F. Loftus, *Eyewitness Identification and the Legal System, in* The Behavioral Foundations of Public Policy 145 (Eldar Shafir ed., 2013).

13. Simon, *supra* note 3, at 71–74; *infra* p. 572.

14. *See, e.g.,* R.C.L. Lindsay, Gary L. Wells & Carolyn M. Rumpel, *Can People Detect Eyewitness-Identification Accuracy within and across Situations?* 66 J. Applied Psychol. 79 (1981).

15. Günter Köhnken et al., *The Cognitive Interview: A Meta-analysis,* 5 Psychol. Crime & L. 3 (1999); Simon, *supra* note 3, at 92–93.

16. Simon, *supra* note 3, at 97–99.

17. *Id.* at 99.

18. *Id.* at 95–111.

These phenomena imply that witnesses' accounts of events may be intentionally or unintentionally distorted by police interviews and interrogations—a common occurrence according to several field studies.[19] Faulty interrogation techniques even result in false confessions.[20]

Indeed, the fallibility of eyewitness identification and event description is exacerbated by the pitfalls of police investigations—the primary source of evidence used by the prosecution in criminal proceedings. Police investigators are usually highly motivated to solve crimes. They have to come up with hypotheses and obtain evidence that verifies or refutes them. Given the external and internal pressure to solve cases and the police's limited resources, it is usually impossible to pursue many hypotheses at the same time. Against this backdrop, several well-known psychological phenomena may result in erroneous conclusions, and eventually to miscarriage of justice.

One such phenomenon is the *confirmation bias*. People tend to retain their extant beliefs. Accordingly, they tend to overestimate the relevance and import of new evidence that comports with their favored hypothesis, and to downplay the reliability and weight of evidence to the contrary.[21] In extreme cases, this *coherence shift*[22] may result in a so-called *tunnel vision*—excessive focus on a particular line of investigation at the expense of alternative possibilities, and dismissing evidence that does not tally with one's hypothesis.[23] Tunnel vision is due, in part, to the fact that most arrests are made early on in the investigation, thus singling out the arrestee as the focus of interest. Tunnel vision reinforces, and is reinforced by, other biases. For example, an early misidentification of a suspect by an eyewitness may prompt investigators to put all their efforts into producing incriminating evidence against that suspect, and this seemingly supportive evidence may in turn boost the eyewitness's confidence in the accuracy of her initial identification.

Apart from the confirmation bias, other psychological phenomena that may lead investigations astray are emotional involvement in the case, group membership, and escalation of commitment. Investigators who are exposed to heinous crimes or to victims' suffering may feel intense anger. This feeling may in turn adversely affect their discretion. It may increase the attribution of blame for negative outcomes, yield a desire to retaliate, and result in superficial information processing.[24] As part of the police force, investigators usually share both a common commitment to fight crime and hostility toward criminal offenders. Thus, group membership may facilitate consensus, increase aggressiveness, and reduce inhibitions.[25] Finally, the more time and effort have been invested in a particular

19. *Id.* at 111–16.

20. *Id.* at 120–43.

21. *Id.* at 22–25. On the confirmation bias, see generally *supra* 58–61.

22. On coherence-based reasoning, see also *supra* pp. 528–32.

23. Keith A. Findley, *Tunnel Vision, in* CONVICTION OF THE INNOCENT, *supra* note 8, at 303.

24. SIMON, *supra* note 3, at 27–28.

25. *Id.* at 28–29.

avenue of investigation, the less likely investigators are to admit that it is wrong, due to escalation of commitment.[26]

(b) Fact-Finders' Assessment of Eyewitness Testimonies

Along with the extensive psychological research of eyewitness testimonies, a large body of research has examined the ability of fact-finders to gauge the accuracy and reliability of such testimonies. Here too, the emerging picture is not very encouraging. In general, people are not very good at detecting lies.[27] In the legal context, people overtrust the ability of others to accurately identify the perpetrator, and are insensitive to factors that compromise that ability.[28] Instead, they tend to place considerable emphasis on the witness's confidence in his or her identification. Unfortunately, many studies have shown that eyewitnesses are often overly confident (due, in part, to post-identification events, such as positive feedback from investigators), and that the correlation between their accuracy and confidence is not very high.[29] However, it has recently been suggested that the reported low correlation was not a result of an inherent shortcoming of eyewitness testimonies, but rather of procedural defects in eliciting them, and when the process is pristine, high confidence may indeed be correlated with accuracy.[30]

Fact-finders' assessments of eyewitness testimonies pertain both to the witness's sincerity and to his or her ability to accurately recall the event. Assessing a witness's sincerity is no less crucial than gauging the accuracy of his or her recall, because very often witnesses are not disinterested third parties, but associated in some way to one of the litigants, or have some other interest in the outcome of the proceedings. Obviously, when the litigants themselves testify, they too have high stakes in the proceedings.[31]

Fact-finders may judge the sincerity of a witness by her demeanor and the content of her testimony. Bella DePaulo and her colleagues conducted a meta-analysis of 158 potential deception cues, based on published studies of thirty-six independent samples.[32] They found that the effect sizes for many classic demeanor cues—such as gaze aversion, fidgeting, blinking, shrugging, face touching, and smiling—are fairly minor and often not statistically significant. It turns out that some people are perceived as trustworthy and others as

26. *Id.* at 29–31. On escalation of commitment, see generally *supra* pp. 56–57.

27. ALDERT VRIJ, DETECTING LIES AND DECEIT 1–7, 141–88 (2d ed. 2008); Charles F. Bond, Jr. & Bella M. DePaulo, *Accuracy of Deception Judgments*, 10 PERSONALITY & SOC. PSYCHOL. REV. 214 (2006) (a large-scale meta-analysis).

28. SIMON, *supra* note 3, at 150–53; CUTLER & PENROD, *supra* note 3, at 171–80, 197–209.

29. CUTLER & PENROD, *supra* note 3, at 181–96; SIMON, *supra* note 3, at 153–54; Amy Bradfield Douglass & Afton Pavletic, *Eyewitness Confidence Malleability, in* CONVICTION OF THE INNOCENT, *supra* note 8, at 149.

30. John T. Wixted & Gary L. Wells, *The Relationship between Eyewitness Confidence and Identification Accuracy: A New Synthesis*, 18 PSYCHOL. SCI. PUB. INTEREST 10 (2017).

31. *See* Chris William Sanchirico, *Evidence, Procedure, and the Upside of Cognitive Error*, 57 STAN. L. REV. 291, 302–06 (2004).

32. Bella M. DePaulo et al., *Cues to Deception*, 129 PSYCHOL. BULL. 74 (2003).

untrustworthy, regardless of whether they are truthful or not.[33] At the same time, people are generally overconfident about their ability to detect lies (and there is virtually no correlation between their confidence and actual ability).[34] Large-effect demeanor cues—such as speaking with higher-pitched voice—consisted mainly of cues related to stress and arousal. However, testifying in court can be stressful even for truth tellers, so the conclusions to be drawn from such cues are arguably limited. In that respect, laboratory experiments, where the baseline level of stress is much lower than in courts, may be lacking external validity.[35] Another reason to doubt judicial fact-finders' ability to detect lies based on witnesses' demeanor is that, while in most laboratory studies speakers either lie or tell the truth, witnesses can and do testify in ways that conceal the whole truth, but do not constitute outright lies. Such misleading testimonies may be harder to detect, because the witness does not feel that she is lying, or feels so to a lesser extent.[36]

While these differences between the experimental findings and judicial fact-finding may lead to strong skepticism about fact-finders' ability to detect lies based on witnesses' demeanor, other differences give rise to more optimism. Most psychological studies pertain to small, pedestrian, mundane lies,[37] rather than serious ones, as in the case of a false testimony in court. If deception cues become more conspicuous when the lies are more consequential, then directly extrapolating from experimental findings to judicial fact-finding, and concluding that witnesses' demeanor is unhelpful, may be too hasty.[38] In the same vein, DePaulo and her colleagues found considerable differences between motivated and unmotivated lies: "Cues to deception were more pronounced when people were motivated to succeed."[39] This finding too means that lying cues may be more conspicuous in court—where witnesses very often have a strong interest in the outcomes of adjudication—than in many reported experiments. Furthermore, DePaulo and her colleagues analyzed the effect size and statistical significance of each cue separately. As they note, the effect size and significance may be higher when fact-finders take several factors into account, as they are likely

33. Timothy R. Levine et al., *Sender Demeanor: Individual Differences in Sender Believability Have a Powerful Impact on Deception Detection Judgments*, 37 HUM. COMM. RES. 377 (2011). *See also* Charles F. Bond, Timothy R. Levine & Maria Hartwig, *New Findings in Non-verbal Lie Detection*, *in* DETECTING DECEPTION: CURRENT CHALLENGES AND COGNITIVE APPROACHES 37, 47–50 (Pär Anders Granhag, Aldert Vrij & Bruno Verschuere eds., 2015).

34. Bella M. DePaulo et al., *The Accuracy-Confidence Correlation in the Detection of Deception*, 1 PERSONALITY & SOC. PSYCHOL. REV. 346 (1997) (a meta-analysis of eighteen independent samples); VRIJ, *supra* note 27, at 164–66.

35. Sanchrico, *supra* note 31, at 312; DePaulo et al., *supra* note 32, at 105. On the problematic relationship between stress and demeanor, see also Olin Guy Wellburn III, *Demeanor*, 76 CORNELL L. REV. 1075, 1080, 1084–86 (1991).

36. DePaulo et al., *supra* note 32, at 106. *See also supra* p. 456.

37. *Id.* at 77.

38. Examples of legal scholars' tendency to dismiss outright the usefulness of demeanor as an indicator of witnesses' dishonesty include: Wellburn, *supra* note 35; Sanchrico, *supra* note 31, at 310–12; SIMON, *supra* note 3, at 123–24, 165–68.

39. DePaulo et al., *supra* note 32, at 74, 79, 97–98, 103.

to do.[40] In fact, studies have shown that when a combination of several cues is taken into account, the rate of success in distinguishing truth tellers from liars rises considerably.[41]

Be that as it may, demeanor is rarely the sole or even primary basis for detecting lies, whether in daily life[42] or in the courtroom.[43] Content-based analysis is usually far more important in this regard. Two primary features of testimonies content that may serve as cues to their truthfulness are their consistency—both internal consistency and compatibility with other evidence available to the court—and the level of detail. While neither of these are decisive indicators of truth-telling (or insincerity), and some inconsistency may result from differences in how questions are put to the witness,[44] these indicators do appear to be considerably more telling than demeanor.[45] Judicial fact-finders (and others) may do a particularly good job when they have information about a given event from different sources—especially when the witness does not know what information they possess.[46] Determining the truthfulness of a statement based on the characteristics of the content of a testimony alone (such as how vivid and detailed it is, or whether the description is chronological or not), is considerably less reliable—even when conducted by professional investigators in accordance with structured protocols.[47]

(c) Policy Implications

The above survey of the literature on eyewitness reliability and fact-finders' ability to determine the accuracy of testimonies is rather skeletal. Nonetheless, it suffices to demonstrate the complexity of the pertinent issues. Trying to come up with policy recommendations is even more complex, because reducing errors in judicial fact-finding often conflicts with other goals of adjudication, such as ensuring the public legitimacy of the court system, and finalizing disputes. To the extent that reducing judicial errors requires the allocation of more resources, such allocation must be weighed against other demands on public resources. Finally, even if one prioritizes factual accuracy over other objectives, two difficulties remain. First, in the face of conflicting findings, varying interpretations of the findings, and

40. *Id.* at 104.

41. VRIJ, *supra* note 27, at 66–67, 89.

42. Hee Sun Park et al., *How People Really Detect Lies*, 69 COMM. MONOGRAPHS 144 (2002).

43. Max Minzner, *Detecting Lies Using Demeanor, Bias, and Context*, 29 CARDOZO L. REV. 2557, 2568 (2008).

44. Julian A.E. Gilbert & Ronald P. Fisher, *The Effects of Varied Retrieval Cues on Reminiscence in Eyewitness Memory*, 20 APPLIED COGNITIVE PSYCHOL. 723 (2006); Neil Brewer et al., *Beliefs and Data on the Relationship between Consistency and Accuracy of Eyewitness Testimony*, 13 APPLIED COGNITIVE PSYCHOL. 297 (1999).

45. DePaulo et al., *supra* note 32, at 91–94, 96; Sanchrico, *supra* note 31, at 314–17; Minzner, *supra* note 43, at 2568–69.

46. Minzner, *supra* note 43, at 2571–72. *Cf.* Maria Hartwig et al., *Detecting Deception via Strategic Disclosure of Evidence*, 29 LAW & HUM. BEHAV. 469 (2005); Maria Hartwig et al., *Strategic Use of Evidence during Police Interviews: When Training to Detect Deception Works*, 30 LAW & HUM. BEHAV. 603 (2006).

47. For a recent overview of such techniques and their limited reliability, see Aldert Vrij, *Verbal Lie Detection Tools: Statement Validity Analysis, Reality Monitoring and Scientific Content Analysis*, *in* DETECTING DECEPTION, *supra* note 33, at 3.

possible interactions between different psychological phenomena, it is not always easy to predict how any reform of police practices or judicial procedures would affect the accuracy of fact-finding. This difficulty is associated with the general concerns about the generalizability and external validity of experimental findings that invariably arise with the use of behavioral findings in legal policymaking.[48] Second, while some measures are likely to reduce both false positives and false negatives, there is often a trade-off between these two goals: taking measures to reduce false convictions or false rulings in favor of the plaintiff may increase false acquittals and dismissals of sound claims.

This is not to say that nothing can or should be done, and in some legal systems some steps have actually been taken in response to the psychological findings described above.[49] With regard to lineups, the list of recommendations include, inter alia, conducting the lineup as early as possible; conducting sequential lineups rather than simultaneous ones; preventing administrator cues by conducting double-blind lineups; and advising the witness that the suspect may or may not be present in the lineup.[50]

To avoid memory contamination, witness interviews should be conducted as soon as possible, and witnesses should be questioned separately. Investigators should neither share information about the investigation with the witness nor give her feedback on her ability to recall.[51]

To overcome the confirmation bias and tunnel vision of police investigators, it has been suggested that the *consider-the-opposite* technique be used,[52] but its efficacy may be limited.[53] Similar doubts may be raised regarding the proposal to designate one member of the investigation team to offer competing hypotheses to the leading one.[54] A more promising measure is to ensure that all witness interviews and suspect interrogations are fully recorded and preserved. An audiovisual recording would make it possible, for example, to examine the witness's initial level of confidence in her identification, and ensure that a lineup was conducted in accordance with appropriate standards.[55]

48. *See* Gregory Mitchell, *Mapping Evidence Law,* 2003 MICH. ST. L. REV. 1065; *supra* pp. 25–26, 150–56.

49. *See, e.g.,* Steblay & Loftus, *supra* note 12 (describing lineup reforms in the United States); NATIONAL CENTRE FOR POLICE EXCELLENCE, POLICE ADVICE ON CORE INVESTIGATIVE DOCTRINE 62 (2005), *available at:* http://www.caerphilly.gov.uk/pdf/Health_SocialCare/POVA/Core_Investigation_Doctrine_Interactive.pdf (instructing police investigators to adopt the *ABC approach*: "Assume nothing; Believe nothing; Challenge everything," because "experience shows that even those sources of material which at first appear to be of unquestionable reliability can be wrong, and that material that appears to indicate one thing can later be found to support a totally different interpretation").

50. David M. Zimmerman, Jacqueline L. Austin & Margaret Bull Kovera, *Suggestive Eyewitness Identification Procedures, in* CONVICTION OF THE INNOCENT, *supra* note 8, at 125; Steblay & Loftus, *supra* note 12; SIMON, *supra* note 3, at 80–86.

51. SIMON, *supra* note 3, at 117–19.

52. POLICE ADVICE, *supra* note 49, at 62; SIMON, *supra* note 3, at 45.

53. SIMON, *supra* note 3, at 45; *supra* pp. 135–36.

54. SIMON, *supra* note 3, at 45–47.

55. *Id.* at 47–49.

As regards judicial fact-finding, it has been recommended, for example, that eyewitness identification arising from inappropriate lineups be excluded, and that stronger measures be taken to prevent jurors' exposure to extra-evidential information.[56] Dan Simon has also recommended abolishing jury instructions that advise jurors to take into account witnesses' demeanor when assessing their credibility.[57] For each of these recommendations, one might come up with counterarguments, but further elaboration on these issues would exceed the scope of the present discussion.[58]

2. Probabilistic Evidence

One alternative to eyewitness testimony is probabilistic evidence. However, it has long been shown that, while people tend to overvalue eyewitness testimonies, they tend to undervalue probabilistic information.[59] Decision-makers often refuse, or hesitate, to rely on probabilistic evidence, and sometimes err in its use. In the legal context, researchers have shown that people can easily be manipulated into undervaluing the probative power of scientific evidence that links someone to a given act. For example, because within a population of one million people, ten thousand people share a trait that is attributed to 1 percent of the population, many people tend to think that this trait has no legal relevance. It has thus been argued that people underuse associative evidence.[60] Notably, while the reluctance to rely on probabilistic evidence often results in refusal to impose legal liability, ignoring such evidence may also lead to unwarranted imposition of liability. This section discusses three interrelated phenomena in this area: the *Wells effect*, *base-rate neglect*, and the *inverse fallacy*.[61]

56. *Id.* at 177–79. *See also supra* pp. 545–50.

57. *Id.*

58. Another possible reaction to the difficulties of eyewitness testimonies (and to other behavioral phenomena that adversely affect judicial fact-finding) is expert testimonies that would draw fact-finders' attention to the existence and significance of these difficulties. *See infra* pp. 585–87.

59. Amos Tversky & Daniel Kahneman, *Judgment under Uncertainty: Heuristics and Biases*, 185 SCI. 1124 (1974).

60. William C. Thompson & Edward L. Schumann, *Interpretation of Statistical Evidence in Criminal Trials: The Prosecutor's Fallacy and the Defense Attorney's Fallacy*, 11 LAW & HUM. BEHAV. 167 (1987); *see also* Jane Goodman, *Jurors' Comprehension and Assessment of Probabilistic Evidence*, 16 AM. J. TRIAL ADVOC. 361 (1992); Norman E. Fenton & Martin Neil, *Avoiding Probabilistic Reasoning Fallacies in Legal Practice Using Bayesian Networks*, 36 AUSTRAL. J. LEGAL PHIL. 114 (2011). The issue of statistical evidence is often discussed in the specific context of DNA evidence. *See, e.g.*, Dale A. Nance & Scott B. Morris, *Juror Understanding of DNA Evidence: An Empirical Assessment of Presentation Formats for Trace Evidence with a Relatively Small Random-Match Probability*, 34 J. LEGAL STUD. 395 (2005); Nicholas Scurich & Richard S. John, *Trawling Genetic Databases: When a DNA Match Is Just a Naked Statistic*, 8 J. EMPIRICAL LEGAL STUD. 49, 58–59 (supp. 2011). To keep our discussion manageable, we will not delve into the DNA controversy.

61. For other uses of probabilistic reasoning by legal decision-makers, and the difficulties they face, see, e.g., Andreas Mokros et al., *Assessment of Risk for Violent Recidivism through Multivariate Bayesian Classification*, 16 PSYCHOL. PUB. POL'Y & L. 418 (2010) (analyzing the use of Bayesian reasoning for assessing recidivism risk); Deborah M. Weiss, *The Impossibility of Agnostic Discrimination Law*, 2011 UTAH L. REV. 1677 (criticizing the reluctance to use social framework analysis in alleged discrimination cases); Charles J. Snyder, *Moneyball Lawyering*, 65 ARK. L. REV. 837 (2012) (discussing the use of statistical data, primarily base rates, by attorneys in litigation and settlement decision-making). *See also* Ward Edwards & Detlof von Winterfeldt, *Cognitive Illusions and Their*

(a) The Wells Effect

Sometimes, the only information available to judicial fact-finders is statistical, with no eyewitness or other direct evidence about the incident in question. As Gary Wells demonstrated in a seminal study, people are reluctant to assign liability based on *naked statistical evidence*.[62] For example, if the only available information about a hit-and-run accident is that it was caused by a bus; that there are only two bus companies in town; and that one of them operates 80 percent of the buses—most people would not find that company liable to pay damages for the accident.

Wells hypothesized that "in order for evidence to have a significant impact on people's verdict preferences, one's hypothetical belief about the ultimate fact must affect one's belief about the evidence."[63] For instance, the fact that 80 percent of the buses in a given town belong to the Blue Bus Company and 20 percent to the Grey Bus Company is insufficient grounds to find the former liable for an accident caused by an unidentified bus, because the determination of liability would not change one's belief about the accuracy of the statistical data. The statistical data remains true, regardless of whether or not a blue bus was involved in the accident. In contrast, when a weigh-station attendant testifies that according to his records, a blue bus weighed in at the nearby station just before the accident—thus linking that bus company to the accident—the determination of liability would more likely bear on the reliability of that testimony, even if the defendant had already established that those records were wrong 20 percent of the time. In this case, determining which bus was involved in the accident does bear on the accuracy of the weigh-station's records and the reliability of the attendant's testimony. Wells found that fact-finders are much more likely to assign liability in the second scenario. Importantly, subjects in both conditions accurately assessed the probability that the accident had been caused by a blue bus—thus challenging the hypothesis that the reluctance to assign liability based on probabilistic evidence stems from people's difficulty in dealing with such evidence or from disparities between objective probability and subjective probability estimates.[64]

Wells's hypothesis has been challenged by subsequent studies that offered competing hypotheses and explanations for the "Wells effect." One such explanation was inspired by Daniel Kahneman and Amos Tversky's *simulation heuristic*.[65] Kahneman and Tversky argued that the ease with which different scenarios can be simulated is used to judge the probability of specific events, to assess the causal connection between two events, and so

Implications for the Law, 59 S. Cal. L. Rev. 227–51 (1985) (a survey of cognitive biases in probability assessments, their relevance to the law, and attempts to overcome them).

62. Gary L. Wells, *Naked Statistical Evidence of Liability: Is Subjective Probability Enough?*, 62 J. Personality & Soc. Psychol. 739 (1992).

63. *Id.* at 746.

64. On this hypothesis, see Laurence H. Tribe, *Trial by Mathematics: Precision and Ritual in the Legal Process*, 84 Harv. L. Rev. 1329, 1344–50 (1971). *See also* Thompson & Schumann, *supra* note 60 (experimentally demonstrating subjects' errors when using probabilistic information).

65. Daniel Kahneman & Amos Tversky, *The Simulation Heuristic*, *in* Judgment under Uncertainty: Heuristics and Biases 201 (Daniel Kahneman, Paul Slovic & Amos Tversky eds., 1982).

forth. In the present context, Keith Niedermeier, Norbert Kerr, and Lawrence Messé have argued that the willingness to ground liability on statistical evidence depends on how easily one can imagine an alternative scenario that is equally consistent with the evidence.[66] In their experiments, subjects read various vignettes of a lawsuit concerning an accident similar to the one that Wells had analyzed. Keeping the probability constant, they used vignettes that differed with regard to the ease with which one might imagine a counterfactual scenario in which the defendant was not the culprit. The results showed that while the assessed probability was similar under the different conditions, willingness to accept the claim declined considerably under conditions conducive to imagining an alternative scenario.

In the same vein, Deanna Sykes and Joel Johnson have argued that, since comprehension of a witness's assertion entails an initial belief in that assertion, undoing the mental representation created by the testimony and imagining an alternative scenario requires cognitive effort. Such an effort is not required when decision-makers are presented with probabilistic evidence that does not include a concrete assertion that needs to be undone.[67]

Both Wells's hypothesis and the ease-of-simulation explanation have since been called into question. Based on a series of experiments, Hal Arkes, Brittany Shoot-Reinhard, and Ryan Mayes argued that the decision to assign liability is based not only on the probability of the defendant being liable, but also on other factors that may affect liability without affecting assessed probability, such as the existence of another witness whose testimony is non-diagnostic.[68]

As is often the case with behavioral analyses of law, not only the psychological mechanisms underlying the phenomenon in question (in this case, the Wells effect) are disputed, but its normative implications, as well. Some commentators argue that there is simply no compelling epistemic or normative reason not to assign liability based on naked statistical evidence.[69] In fact, so the argument goes, *all* evidence—including seemingly case-specific evidence—is ultimately statistical.[70] Others insist that the reluctance to impose such liability is normatively justified. One key justification draws on the distinction between the probability that an alleged fact is true, and the weight or resiliency of the evidence supporting that claim. Decision-makers may sensibly reject a claim, even if the probability that the plaintiff's version is correct meets the controlling standard of proof, if assessment of this probability rests on too little information, or on general, non-case-specific evidence.[71]

66. Keith E. Niedermeier, Norbert L. Kerr & Lawrence A. Messé, *Jurors' Use of Naked Statistical Evidence: Exploring Bases and Implications of the Wells Effect*, 76 J. PERSONALITY & SOC. PSYCHOL. 533 (1999).

67. Deanna L. Sykes & Joel T. Johnson, *Probabilistic Evidence versus the Representation of an Event: The Curious Case of Mrs. Prob's Dog*, 21 BASIC & APPLIED SOC. PSYCHOL. 199 (1999).

68. Hal R. Arkes, Brittany Shoots-Reihard & Ryan S. Mayers, *Disjunction between Probability and Verdict in Juror Decision Making*, 25 J. BEHAV. DEC. MAKING 276 (2012).

69. Amit Pundik, *What Is Wrong with Statistical Evidence? The Attempts to Establish an Epistemic Deficiency*, 4 CIV. JUST. Q. 461 (2008).

70. Michael J. Saks & Robert F. Kidd, *Human Information Processing and Adjudication: Trial by Heuristics*, 15 LAW & SOC'Y REV. 123, 151–54 (1980).

71. For detailed discussions of this claim, see L. JONATHAN COHEN, THE PROBABLE AND THE PROVABLE 36–39 (1977); ALEX STEIN, FOUNDATIONS OF EVIDENCE LAW 40–56, 80–106 (2005); DALE A. NANCE, THE BURDENS OF

For example, the fact that there are a thousand spectators in a rodeo, but only 400 tickets have been sold, means that for any spectator chosen at random, there is a 60 percent probability that he or she is a gatecrasher. The fact-finder may nonetheless dismiss a claim based exclusively on this evidence as resting on too thin an evidentiary basis.[72] Whenever case-specific evidence is available, refusing to impose liability based on mere statistical evidence incentivizes the production of concrete evidence. Opponents might respond that this argument presupposes that case-specific evidence is superior to statistical evidence, when in fact it is not.

Last, it should be noted that the reluctance to base judicial decisions on naked statistical evidence is not universal. An analysis of appellate court decisions in the United States revealed that courts are willing to decide on the basis of such evidence in several types of cases, when individuating evidence cannot be produced. Courts rely on naked statistical evidence when they reject motions for summary judgments, when calculating damages for lost income, and when imposing market share liability for mass torts.[73]

Jonathan Koehler has argued that the willingness of courts to use naked statistical evidence in these cases is in line with psychological studies of base-rate neglect.[74] As further described below, these studies have shown that when people are provided with both statistical and individuating information about an event, they tend to underweight or even neglect the former; but when they get only statistical information, they make accurate probability assessments based on this information. However, these findings may be largely beside the point. As the studies described above have demonstrated, what underlies the Wells effect is not a misassessment of probability, but rather people's reluctance to assign liability based on naked statistical evidence, notwithstanding their accurate assessments of probabilities and the absence of individuating information. Hence, other normative considerations must play a role in cases such as calculating damages for lost income or assigning liability for mass torts.

(b) Base-Rate Neglect

Thus far we have focused on the reluctance of judicial decision-makers to base liability on statistical evidence. However, other aspects of human decision-making might cause people to assign liability when such assignment is unwarranted. Special attention in this regard has been given to the phenomenon of base-rate neglect. Base-rate neglect refers to people's tendency to discount information about the frequency with which a given event occurs, and

Proof: Discriminatory Power, Weight of Evidence, and Tenacity of Belief 1-14, 103-83, 251-94 (2016); L. Jonathan Cohen, *The Role of Evidential Weight in Criminal Proof*, 66 B.U. L. Rev. 635 (1986); David Kaye, *Apples and Oranges: Confidence Coefficient and the Burden of Persuasion*, 73 Cornell L. Rev. 54 (1987); Pundik, *supra* note 69, at 474–87.

72. Cohen, *supra* note 71, at 74–76; L. Jonathan Cohen, *Subjective Probability and the Paradox of the Gatecrasher*, 1981 Ariz. St. L.J. 627.

73. Jonathan J. Koehler, *When Do Courts Think Base Rate Statistics Are Relevant?* 42 Jurimetrics 373, 395–400 (2002).

74. *Id.* at 400.

focus instead on available individuating information.[75] Thus, unlike the Wells effect, which occurs when fact-finders are provided with statistical evidence only, base-rate neglect refers to situations where fact-finders are presented with both statistical and concrete evidence.

In an early study of decisions across a wide range of fields, Maya Bar-Hillel demonstrated that base-rate neglect can cause errors in judicial contexts.[76] Subjects in her study were informed that a hit-and-run accident involving a cab occurred at night, with 85 percent of the city's cabs being blue, and the remaining 15 percent being green. In court, an eyewitness testified that the cab involved in the accident was green. The court examined the witness's capabilities and concluded that he was correct 80 percent of the time (and wrong 20 percent of the time). Subjects were then asked to assess the probability that a green cab was in fact involved in the accident. The results showed that the subjects focused solely on the witness's credibility rate: their mode and median estimates of the probability that a green cab was the culprit were 80 percent. Calculating the actual probability, however, requires taking into account the underlying probability that the cab is green, and is thus only 41 percent. Only around 10 percent of the participants approximated that answer.[77]

A subsequent experimental study also found base-rate neglect in a legal context.[78] Moreover, the subjects in the latter study were reluctant to use explanations presented to them by a statistician when deciding whether to convict a defendant. While subjects with mathematical background demonstrated a better understanding of the statistician's Bayesian presentation, they were just as likely as the others to disregard it when making their decisions.

As noted in Chapter 2, at least in the legal context, some commentators object to the characterization of base-rate neglect as an irrational bias, arguing that base rates *should* be ignored, or at least given very low weight.[79] At the very least, base-rate information must be considered very carefully, because any given event may be described as part of various reference classes, the homogeneity of any class in relevant respects may be low, and so forth.[80]

In fact, courts do tend to take base-rate evidence into account when it is offered in response to defendants' claims that certain things (such as a suspicious death) occurred by chance.[81] In line with general psychological studies of base-rate neglect, courts are more likely to use base-rate evidence the more specific the class is, that is to say, the more its defining features resemble the disputed event.[82]

75. *See generally supra* pp. 30–31.

76. Maya Bar-Hillel, *The Base-Rate Fallacy in Probability Judgments,* 44 ACTA PSYCHOLOGICA 211 (1980).

77. *Id.* at 211–12, 219–20.

78. David. L. Faigman & A.J. Baglioni, Jr., *Bayes' Theorem in the Trial Process,* 12 LAW & HUM. BEHAV. 1 (1988).

79. *See supra* p. 31; Koehler, *supra* note 73, at 377–79, 380–85 (critically discussing the scholarly and judicial arguments against the use of base-rate evidence in judicial decision-making).

80. Ronald J. Allen & Michael S. Pardo, *The Problematic Value of Mathematical Models of Evidence,* 36 J. LEGAL STUD. 107 (2007).

81. Koehler, *supra* note 73, at 388–90.

82. *Id.* at 390–95.

(c) Inverse Fallacy

The inverse fallacy is the erroneous tendency to assume—contrary to Bayes' theorem—that the probability of A given B is about the same as the probability of B given A.[83] This error has been demonstrated in an experiment conducted with acting judges, using a tort case in which a warehouse barrel inadvertently harmed a passerby.[84] The legal question was whether the accident was caused by the warehouse workers' negligence, or by some other factor. Participants in the study were informed that "(1) when barrels are negligently secured, there is a 90% chance that they will break loose; (2) when barrels are safely secured, they break loose only 1% of the time; (3) workers negligently secure barrels only 1 in 1,000 times."[85] Based on this information, participants were asked to estimate the probability of negligence, from four probability ranges: 0–25 percent, 26–50 percent, 51–75 percent, and 76–100 percent. While the precise answer is 8.3 percent, most participants did not choose the lowest option. However, 40 percent of them did choose this option, which is a better result than that achieved by other populations in comparable studies.[86]

The inverse fallacy was arguably enshrined in the Restatement (Second) of Torts. In describing the res ipsa loquitur doctrine, it stated that a fact-finder may infer that an event that caused injury to a plaintiff resulted from the defendant's negligence when "the event is of a kind which ordinarily does not occur in the absence of negligence."[87] This formulation has since been replaced in the Restatement (Third) of Torts, which states that negligence may be inferred "when the accident causing the plaintiff's harm is a type of accident that ordinarily happens as a result of the negligence of a class of actors of which the defendant is the relevant member."[88] Thus, while the previous formulation incorrectly referred to the probability of the accident given the defendant's negligence, the present formulation rightly refers to the likelihood of negligence given the occurrence of the accident. As the scenario used in the above experiment demonstrates, the previous formulation could lead to erroneous determination of liability, because it disregarded the base rate of negligent behavior and committed the inverse fallacy.[89]

83. *See generally supra* p. 32.

84. Chris Guthrie, Jeffrey J. Rachlinski & Andrew J. Wistrich, *Inside the Judicial Mind,* 86 CORNELL L. REV. 777 (2001).

85. *Id.* at 808.

86. Chris Guthrie, Jeffrey J. Rachlinski & Andrew J. Wistrich, *Blinking on the Bench: How Judges Decide Cases,* 93 CORNELL L. REV. 1, 22–24 (2007).

87. RESTATEMENT (SECOND) OF TORTS § 328D(1)(a) (AM. LAW INST. 1965).

88. RESTATEMENT (THIRD) OF TORTS: LIABILITY FOR PHYSICAL AND EMOTIONAL HARM § 17 (AM. LAW INST. 2010).

89. For a critique of the previous formulation, see David Kaye, *Probability Theory Meets Res Ipsa Loquitur,* 77 MICH. L. REV. 1456 (1979). *See also* Jeffrey J. Rachlinski, *Heuristics and Biases in the Courts: Ignorance or Adaptation?,* 79 OR. L. REV. 61, 90–93 (2000).

3. Circumstantial Evidence: The Anti-inference Bias

Probabilistic evidence of the type discussed in the previous subsection is conventionally regarded as circumstantial evidence. Besides the findings about fact-finders' treatment of probabilistic evidence, there is considerable support for the more general phenomenon that judicial fact-finders tend to treat circumstantial evidence differently from direct evidence,[90] and are more reluctant to impose liability based on circumstantial evidence alone.[91] When exhibiting this reluctance, fact-finders sometimes follow legal norms that caution against relying on circumstantial evidence, but much more often disregard legal norms that deny the relevance of this distinction.[92] Scholars largely agree that this tendency is indefensible.[93] In fact, it is sometimes noted that due to the difficulties with eyewitness testimonies, circumstantial evidence is *more* reliable than direct evidence, and therefore discounting its probative value is a "paradox."[94]

Several explanations have been offered for the tendency not to impose liability based solely on circumstantial evidence. Some of these explanations pertain only to probabilistic evidence, as discussed in the previous subsection, so here we focus on explanations that are applicable to non-probabilistic circumstantial evidence, as well. One such explanation is that unlike direct evidence, inferences are based on generalizations "which by definition are accurate less than 100% of the time."[95] Even reliable circumstantial evidence may be compatible with numerous competing inferences.[96] Another explanation does not assume that circumstantial evidence is objectively less conclusive than direct evidence, yet argues that it may be subjectively perceived as such. Fact-finders may believe that the reliability and probative weight of circumstantial evidence is considerably lower than it actually is, and therefore may be reluctant to rely on it.[97]

A third explanation focuses on the typical features of eyewitness testimony, which are often not typical of circumstantial evidence. Inter alia, eyewitness testimonies provide "a verbal representation of the crime itself," whereas indirect evidence is often abstract.[98]

90. While the distinction between direct and circumstantial evidence is contested analytically, the conventional understanding is that direct evidence proves a material fact without the mediation of a deductive process, whereas circumstantial evidence requires an additional mental step of inference, to determine that the material fact existed. 1 CHARLES T. MCCORMICK, MCCORMICK ON EVIDENCE 308 (Kenneth S. Broun et al. eds., 6th, one-vol. ed. 2006).

91. Kevin Jon Heller, *The Cognitive Psychology of Circumstantial Evidence*, 105 MICH. L. REV. 241, 247–55 (2006).

92. *See* Richard K. Greenstein, *Determining Facts: The Myth of Direct Evidence.* 45 HOUS. L. REV. 1801, 1802–04 (2009); Eyal Zamir, Ilana Ritov & Doron Teichman, *Seeing Is Believing: The Anti-inference Bias,* 89 IND. L.J. 195, 199–200 (2014).

93. 1A JOHN HENRY WIGMORE, EVIDENCE IN TRIALS AT COMMON LAW 957–64 (revised by Peter Tillers, 1983); Greenstein, *supra* note 92, at 1804.

94. Heller, *supra* note 91, at 244; *see also* Greenstein, *supra* note 92, at 1803.

95. Paul Bergman, *A Bunch of Circumstantial Evidence,* 30 U.S.F. L. REV. 985, 988 (1996).

96. *See also* ALBERT J. MOORE, PAUL BERGMAN & DAVID A. BINDER, TRIAL ADVOCACY: INFERENCES, ARGUMENTS, AND TECHNIQUES 4–7 (1996).

97. *See supra* note 64 and accompanying text.

98. Heller, *supra* note 91, at 265.

Direct evidence is a story-like narrative, while arguments based on circumstantial evidence often resemble deductive reasoning. The former is often vivid, concrete, and stirring, while the latter is pallid, general, and unexciting.[99] These characteristics make it easier for fact-finders to form a coherent story of the events from direct evidence.[100]

Yet another possibility is that from the fact-finders' perspective, decisions based on direct testimonies involve a lesser degree of responsibility. If it transpires that a testimony was inaccurate or deceptive, the fact-finder can rationalize that the witness is to blame for the erroneous verdict. Conversely, if liability is found to have been erroneously imposed due to faulty inference from circumstantial evidence, the responsibility arguably lies with the fact-finder.[101] To avoid such feelings of regret, a fact-finder would therefore be less inclined to rely on circumstantial evidence.[102]

The last explanation draws on the simulation heuristic (discussed above in the context of probabilistic evidence), and posits that the willingness to base liability on circumstantial evidence depends on how easily one can imagine an alternative scenario that is consistent with the evidence.[103] Arguably, it is easier to imagine such a scenario when the only evidence is circumstantial, since by its very nature, such evidence does not prove the material fact itself.[104]

In a study conducted with Ilana Ritov, we found a general disinclination to base liability on circumstantial evidence that goes beyond differences in objective probabilities or subjective probability assessments, the case-specificity of the evidence, the imaginability of an alternative scenario compatible with the evidence, and the nature of evidence (eyewitness, statistical, or forensic). We dubbed it the *anti-inference bias*.[105] In our experiments, subjects analyzed situations where the probability of wrongdoing was held constant, but the type of evidence was randomized between direct and circumstantial. For instance, people were more willing to assign liability for a speeding violation when it had been detected by a single speed camera than when it was detected by a system of two cameras placed at two points on a toll road, which documented the precise time that the driver drove between them, but not the actual speed. Similarly, when it was undisputed that a given loss could have been caused by two people only—the defendant and/or another individual—subjects were much more inclined to find the defendant liable when a laboratory test implicated him and exonerated the other individual, than when it was only possible to examine the involvement of the other person and the examination exonerated him—even though the

99. *Id.* at 265–80.

100. On the story model of judicial decision-making, see generally *supra* pp. 528–32.

101. Heller, *supra* note 91, at 287.

102. On anticipated regret and its effect on people's decisions, see generally *supra* pp. 505–07.

103. *See supra* notes 65–67 and accompanying text.

104. Heller, *supra* note 91, at 258–64.

105. Zamir, Ritov & Teichman, *supra* note 92.

objective reliability of the conclusions was identical.[106] These differences were not mediated by differences in subjective probability assessments.

A follow-up study revealed that the anti-inference bias is significantly reduced when legal decision-makers are conferring benefits, rather than imposing liability.[107] In fact, the dissimilar treatment of direct and circumstantial evidence was found to be only marginally statistically significant in the domain of gains—thus demonstrating yet another facet of loss aversion.[108]

Like other biases and heuristics, the anti-inference heuristic very often yields accurate decisions. Ordinarily, when we see something with our own eyes, or when someone tells us that she saw something herself, that event actually happened; whereas this is not necessarily true of conclusions drawn from circumstantial evidence. However, as with other biases and heuristics, the anti-inference heuristic also gives rise to systematic error when the objective and subjective probabilities of the pertinent occurrence are the same according to circumstantial and direct evidence.

Inasmuch as the laboratory findings accurately reflect judicial fact-finding, the anti-inference bias may possibly drive judicial decision-making astray. Apparently, it follows that the law should react with debiasing measures. However, the effectiveness—and very desirability—of such debiasing techniques are not self-evident. In terms of effectiveness, guiding participants by asking them what can logically be inferred from the proven facts, and/or by emphasizing the positive, direct findings that give rise to the inference in the inference condition, was found not to eliminate or even statistically significantly mitigate the anti-inference bias.[109] Instructing fact-finders to attribute equal weight to direct and circumstantial evidence may be equally ineffective, since studies of jury instructions have cast doubt on their efficacy.[110] While educating judges and juries about the anti-inference bias and a host of other biases may be beneficial, it may also be rather costly in the case of juries, and its effectiveness may be limited.[111] Finally, if the anti-inference bias reflects deeply held epistemological and moral intuitions, circumventing it might adversely affect the desirable correspondence between peoples' prevailing perceptions and the outcomes of adjudication.[112]

Alternatively, policymakers might overcome the anti-inference bias by introducing legal presumptions, or by broadening the scope of legal liability. For example, in the context of the law of criminal attempts, legislators could address the reluctance of fact-finders to deduce liability in cases of incomplete attempts by criminalizing the preparatory acts. Once

106. A follow-up study replicated these results where the available evidence consisted of a single laboratory test in both the direct- and circumstantial-evidence conditions. *See* Eyal Zamir, Elisha Harlev & Ilana Ritov, *New Evidence about Circumstantial Evidence,* 41 LAW & PSYCHOL. REV. 107, 116–20 (2017).

107. *Id.* at 120–38.

108. On loss aversion, see generally *supra* pp. 42–57.

109. Zamir, Harlev & Ritov, *supra* note 106, at 145–48.

110. *See supra* pp. 548–50.

111. On this debiasing technique, see generally *supra* p. 135.

112. *See generally supra* pp. 438–40.

such acts are criminalized, fact-finders are no longer asked to infer whether an attempt was made to commit the greater crime, and the anti-inference bias no longer plays a role.[113]

4. Expert Testimonies

Ostensibly, one straightforward antidote to the cognitive biases of witnesses, juries, and judges is expert testimony.[114] Experts can expose the biases affecting the provision and use of evidence, and provide scientific information that is free of such biases. Unfortunately, the use of experts is no panacea, for several reasons. First, numerous studies of expert decision-making and reasoning have shown that experts of all kinds use heuristics and display cognitive biases.[115] To share our own experience as authors of legal expert testimonies, we have often experienced coherence shifts in our reasoning.[116] When we are asked to write an expert opinion on a complex question, the factual data and applicable legal norms often seem rather unclear and ambiguous at first. By the time the opinion is complete, however, all the factual and legal pieces of the puzzle appear to fit together perfectly, to form a coherent picture with decisive legal conclusions. Indeed, studies have shown that experts are particularly susceptible to certain biases, such as overconfidence.[117] In an adversarial system, where each party hires her own expert, further biases may arise, as the experts, consciously and unconsciously, seek to serve the interests of the party that hired them—another phenomenon that we can attest to from our personal experience as legal experts.[118] However, court-appointed experts may be immune to the last bias.

Not only are experts subject to cognitive biases that may adversely affect the reliability of their testimony—sophisticated experts can actually manipulate judges' and juries' cognitive biases. For example, knowing that people are inclined to overestimate anecdotal, concrete examples, experts may deliberately use the former even if their probative value is smaller than that of the latter (in fact, we employed this technique in the previous paragraph, when describing our experience as legal experts).[119]

One particular type of evidence that merits attention in this regard is forensic evidence. Despite its seemingly objective nature, forensic evidence often hinges on subjective judgments and personal interpretation. Finding a match between sets of fingerprints, bite marks, or even DNA samples sometimes requires an individual assessment of the facts. As a

113. Zamir, Ritov & Teichman, *supra* note 92, at 224–27.

114. Saks & Kidd, *supra* note 70, at 134. *See also* EXPERT TESTIMONY ON THE PSYCHOLOGY OF EYEWITNESS IDENTIFICATION (Brian L. Cutler ed., 2009). On the psychology of scientific and other expert evidence, see generally SAKS & SPELLMAN, *supra* note 1, at 202–31.

115. *See, e.g.*, David Faust & Jay Ziskin, *The Expert Witness in Psychology and Psychiatry*, 241 SCI. (New Series) 31, 33–34 (1988) (describing common judgment errors in clinicians' expert testimonies); William Meadow & Cass R. Sunstein, *Statistics, Not Experts*, 51 DUKE L.J. 629 (2001) (demonstrating that physicians display overoptimism in assessing common medical practices). *See also supra* pp. 114–17.

116. On coherence shifts, see generally *supra* pp. 528–32; *infra* pp. 589–91.

117. *See supra* p. 115.

118. On motivated reasoning, see generally *supra* pp. 58–61.

119. Saks & Kidd, *supra* note 70, at 138.

result, forensic analysis can be susceptible to cognitive biases. In particular, a growing body of work has documented a *forensic confirmation bias.*[120] That is, preexisting beliefs and expectations might influence how experts interpret the evidence they are presented with. For example, fingerprint experts might be swayed in their analysis of fingerprints when exposed to contextual information that suggests guilt or innocence.[121]

Several proposals have been made regarding the processing and presentation of forensic evidence in court, to minimize its contamination by the confirmation bias.[122] One is that the forensic team be prevented from viewing any information that is not relevant to their narrow task. Thus, a forensic scientist charged with analyzing a fingerprint should not be informed that it belongs to a suspect who has confessed or has been identified by an eyewitness. For their part, courts should attempt to enforce proper procedures whenever possible—much as they do with regard to eyewitness lineups. Moreover, courts should not treat forensic evidence as independent from other pieces of evidence in the case, given the risk of confirmation bias.

In principle, any biases of a cognitive or other nature that experts may have, as well as the manipulation of legal decision-makers by sophisticated experts, may be counteracted by cross-examination in adversarial systems, by offering contrary expert opinions, and by expert opinions about human decision-making and its abuse by experts.[123] However, none of these measures is perfect. The costs of producing expert evidence about expert testimonies are often prohibitive for the parties and for the court system. Moreover, at the end of the day it is the judicial fact-finder—who almost always lacks expertise in the relevant scientific or technological sphere—who must determine the relevance and persuasiveness of the expert testimony. While this is not impossible, telling good science from bad science and resolving controversies between experts may be difficult.[124] A more drastic measure that has been proposed in the United States is to create a governmental agency in charge of licensing forensic scientists and establishing and enforcing standards within the forensic science community.[125] While such regulatory measures might weed out incompetent and dishonest experts, it is unlikely to overcome the run-of-the-mill challenges facing judicial decision-makers when dealing with expert testimonies.

120. *See generally* Saul M. Kassin, Itiel E. Dror & Jeff Kukucka, *The Forensic Confirmation Bias: Problems, Perspectives, and Proposed Solutions*, 2 J. APPLIED RES. MEMORY & COGNITION 42, 45–48 (2013).

121. *See e.g.*, Itiel E. Dror, David Charlton & Alisa E. Péron, *Contextual Information Renders Experts Vulnerable to Making Erroneous Identifications*, 156 FORENSIC SCI. INT'L 74 (2006); Itiel E. Dror et al., *Cognitive Issues in Fingerprint Analysis: Inter- and Intra-Expert Consistency and the Effect of a "Target" Comparison*, 208 FORENSIC SCI. INT'L 10 (2011).

122. Kassin, Dror & Kukucka, *supra* note 120, at 48–50.

123. For a proposal to appoint independent experts and science panels that would assist the court in differentiating between sound and unsound scientific arguments, see Debra L. Worthington et al., *Hindsight Bias,* Daubert, *and the Silicone Breast Implant Litigation,* 8 PSYCHOL. PUB. POL'Y & L. 154 (2002).

124. *Cf.* Thomas D. Lyon & Jonathan J. Koehler, *The Relevance Ratio: Evaluating the Probative Value of Expert Testimony in Child Sexual Abuse Cases,* 82 CORNELL L. REV. 43 (1996); Erica Beecher-Monas, *The Heuristics of Intellectual Due Process: A Primer for Triers of Science,* 75 N.Y.U. L. REV. 1563 (2000).

125. NATIONAL ACADEMY OF SCIENCES, STRENGTHENING FORENSIC SCIENCE IN THE UNITED STATES: A PATH FORWARD (2009).

Extending the use of experts—including experts on decision-making—also raises a more fundamental issue of popular acceptance and legitimacy. As in other spheres of human activity, such as healthcare, there is widespread reluctance to replace human, holistic decision-making and expertise with "evidence-based," or statistics-based decision-making.[126] Even if this reluctance is unjustified,[127] the law cannot ignore it, if only for instrumental reasons, as the efficacy of the legal system depends, in part, on its perceived fairness and popular legitimacy.[128]

As Fredrick Vars has noted, when it comes to expert testimonies, as in other spheres, identifying biases in decision-making is much easier than "crafting a solution that fixes more problems than it creates."[129]

5. Conclusion

This section looked at numerous psychological phenomena that bear upon the reliability of several types of evidence, as well as on how fact-finders assess their reliability. It also discussed the weight and relevance that fact-finders attribute to different types of evidence when resolving factual disputes and assigning legal liability. It has shown that fact-finders generally tend to overweight direct, eyewitness testimonies, and to underweight circumstantial (especially probabilistic) evidence. There is considerable evidence that when performing these tasks, fact-finders use certain heuristics and exhibit biases in predictable and systematic ways. We considered existing and proposed methods to overcome these difficulties, both within the law of evidence (for example, by using expert testimonies) and outside it (e.g., by changing substantive law, or entrusting decisions to better-trained decision-makers). In light of the complexity of the psychological findings and the fact that the psychological perspective is but one facet of multifaceted issues, we conceded that there are no simple solutions to the pertinent difficulties, and some solutions create new difficulties.[130]

C. Burden of Proof

1. Normative and Doctrinal Background

The term *burden of proof* refers to two burdens: the *burden of producing evidence*, which in an adversarial system may shift from one party to the other in the course of the trial, and the *burden of persuasion*, which determines which party prevails when all the evidence has been

126. Such reluctance has famously been expressed with regard to the related issue of the courts' use of statistical tools. *See* Tribe, *supra* note 64. On comparable sentiments regarding evidence-based medicine, see, e.g., Geoffrey R. Norman, *Examining the Assumptions of Evidence-Based Medicine,* 5 J. Evaluation Clinical Practice 139 (1999).

127. *Cf.* Meadow & Sunstein, *supra* note 115 (calling to prefer statistical data over experts' description of common practices, wherever such statistics is available).

128. *See also supra* pp. 438–40, 584.

129. Vars, *supra* note 1, at 708.

130. The same holds true for the closely related phenomenon of the limited ability of fact-finders to disregard inadmissible and normatively irrelevant information, and the limited success of measures designed to overcome this problem. *See supra* pp. 545–50.

introduced and the trier of fact is left in doubt. In this section, we discuss the latter. The rules concerning burden of persuasion also set the *standard of proof*—namely, the level of confidence required to decide a contested issue one way or the other.[131]

From an economic perspective, a primary consideration in allocating the burden of proof and establishing the standard of proof is the utility of trial outcomes. The standard should be set so as to maximize the sum of the utilities of true positive (correct finding for the plaintiff) and true negative (correct finding for the defendant), minus the disutilities of false positive (erroneously finding for the plaintiff) and false negative (erroneously finding for the defendant).[132] Additional factors are the incentives created by the standard of proof for people's primary activity (such as the level of care taken to avoid accidents),[133] the standard's effect on the costs of litigation, and its effect on the legitimacy of court rulings.[134] Other considerations pertain to the possibility of setting different—or even continuous—standards of proof for different issues, and the suggestion that the rules of standard of proof be replaced with a probability-based recovery regime that splits the stakes according to the probabilities in favor of each party's case.[135] Non-efficiency considerations, such as the inherent value of the pursuit of truth, render the normative picture considerably more complex.

Doctrinally, civil law systems do not differentiate between civil and criminal proceedings: in either case, the standard of proof is *intime conviction*—that is, the (full) conviction of the judge, or a reasoned or reasonable conviction.[136] In contrast, common law systems set three different standards of proof. In criminal proceedings, conviction requires the elements of the offense to be established beyond reasonable doubt. The ordinary standard of proof in civil cases is *preponderance of the evidence* (also known as the *balance of probabilities*). In certain specific contexts, such as allegations of fraud, the law sets a higher standard of persuasion in civil cases: *clear and convincing evidence*.[137] More specific rules complicate the picture further by imposing the burden of proof for affirmative defenses on the defendant, by introducing legal presumptions that place the burden of persuasion regarding particular issues on the defendant, or by setting specific standards of persuasion for particular facts.[138]

Against this normative and doctrinal background, this section highlights four contributions of behavioral studies to the understanding of burden of proof: the implications

131. *See generally* McCormick, *supra* note 90, at 562–94; Phipson on Evidence 160–200 (Hodge M. Malek & Jonathan Auburn eds., 18th ed. 2013).

132. John Kaplan, *Decision Theory and the Fact-finding Process*, 20 Stan. L. Rev. 1065 (1968); Fredrick E. Vars, *Toward a General Theory of Standards of Proof*, 60 Cath. U. L. Rev. 1 (2010).

133. *See, e.g.*, Louis Kaplow, *Burden of Proof*, 121 Yale L.J. 738 (2012).

134. Christoph Engel, *Preponderance of the Evidence versus* Intime *Conviction: A Behavioral Perspective on a Conflict between American and Continental European Law*, 33 Vt. L. Rev. 435, 442–48 (2009).

135. *See, e.g.*, Neil Orloff & Jery Stedinger, *A Framework for Evaluating the Preponderance-of-the-Evidence Standard*, 131 U. Pa. L. Rev. 1159 (1983); Stein, *supra* note 71, at 144–53, 219–21.

136. Mark Schweizer, *The Civil Standard of Proof—What Is It, Actually?*, 20 Int'l J. Evidence & Proof 217, 218–20 (2016).

137. Engel, *supra* note 134.

138. 2 McCormick on Evidence, *supra* note 90, at 675–732.

of the story model of judicial fact-finding; the default effect created by the burden of proof; the relationships between loss aversion, omission bias, and the burden of proof in civil litigation; and the possibility that the "beyond a reasonable doubt" standard in criminal cases has become a "protected value," whereby any trade-off between it and other concerns is resented by many people.

2. Burden of Proof and the Story Model

Christoph Engel has suggested that the divergence between civil law and common law as described above may be understood through the lens of the distinction between intuitive and deliberative thinking.[139] According to the *story model*, people do not mathematically integrate the different pieces of evidence, but rather create a narrative that best explains the evidence.[140] The chosen story is created during the trial, in an unconscious and bidirectional process: the strength of evidence determines which story the decision-maker adopts, and the adopted story, in turn, determines the assessment made of the relevance, reliability, and weight of the various pieces of evidence. Even if the evidence is initially confusing, this bidirectional process of *coherence shift* tends to produce a conclusion that decision-makers sincerely believe to be clear and conclusive. The notion of *intime conviction* may thus be understood as reflecting skepticism about the feasibility of controlling fact-finding by objective legal standards. In contrast, in view of the limitations of intuitive thinking, the common law strives to impose as much rationality as possible on this process. But what are the prospects of this endeavor?

The story model arguably calls into question both the conventional understanding of the burden of persuasion and its effectiveness. One of the model's implications is that the conventional portrayal of burden- and standard-of-proof rules as coming into play only after all evidence has been presented is inaccurate. Given the gradual process of making sense of the evidence, insofar as the standard of proof affects fact-finding, it must play a role throughout the trial. More fundamentally, the story model arguably casts doubt on the effectiveness of standard-of-proof rules. It suggests that fact-finders may react to stricter standards of proof by experiencing greater coherence shifts. Facing a stricter standard of proof, a fact-finder who is inclined to assign liability may come to believe that the evidence in support of such assignment is all the more persuasive, or that the opposing evidence is even less relevant and credible. Experiments in which subjects who had convicted defendants in criminal cases were found to exhibit greater coherence shifts than acquitters may be interpreted as corroborating this conjecture.[141]

This concern is heightened by the finding that the verbal formulations of the different standards of proof convey no specific probability threshold for the imposition of liability. Even professional judges have been shown to hold widely divergent perceptions of the

139. Engel, *supra* note 134. On the distinction between System 1 and System 2, see *supra* pp. 21–23.

140. On the story model, see *supra* pp. 528–32.

141. Andreas Glöckner & Christoph Engel, *Can We Trust Intuitive Jurors? Standards of Proof and the Probative Value of Evidence in Coherence-Based Reasoning*, 10 J. EMPIRICAL LEGAL STUD. 230, 239–40 (2013). However, the

probabilistic meaning of the different standards of proof.[142] There is also some support for the assertion that, formal rules notwithstanding, fact-finders employ varying evidentiary thresholds for conviction, depending on the severity of the applicable sanction: the higher the sanction, the stricter the standard of proof actually applied.[143] Fact-finders may also adapt their actual threshold to the preferred outcome.[144] In fact, one study found that, unlike quantified definitions of standard of proof, varying the verbal formulation of the standard—preponderance of the evidence, clear and convincing evidence, or beyond a reasonable doubt—had no significant effect on conviction rate.[145]

All this might suggest that standards of proof are meaningless in practice. However, such a conclusion would be too hasty, as other studies have shown that the choice of burden-of-proof rule, and even different definitions of the same rule, do affect decision-making. In an early study, Norbert Kerr and his colleagues instructed participants to decide whether to convict the accused according to one of three decision rules.[146] Under the *stringent* criterion of guilt, participants were informed that essentially any doubt about the defendant's guilt qualifies as a reasonable one. Under the *lax* criterion, a reasonable doubt must be substantial. Finally, under the *undefined* criterion, no definition of reasonable doubt was provided. The decision rules had a highly significant effect on the rate of conviction. The conviction rate was lowest under the stringent criterion, and highest under the lax criterion. Significantly more participants gave a no-opinion response under the undefined criterion than under the stringent and lax criteria.[147]

In a more recent study, Andreas Glöckner and Christoph Engel compared decision-making under the preponderance-of-the-evidence and beyond-a-reasonable-doubt rules, using U.S.-style jury instructions that do not include explicit probability information about the threshold for conviction.[148] They found that the conviction rate under the preponderance-of-the-evidence rule was much higher than under the beyond-a-reasonable-doubt rule. While the decision process was marked by coherence shifts, those were not more pronounced under the more stringent standard. It appears, therefore, that people are

fact that convictors showed larger coherence shifts may have a more benign interpretation. Under the beyond-a-reasonable-doubt standard, acquitters can acquit for lack of sufficient evidence, and are therefore not induced to devalue conflicting evidence. *See* Engel, *supra* note 134, at 461.

142. Rita James Simon & Linda Mahan, *Quantifying Burdens of Proof: A View from the Bench, the Jury and the Classroom,* 5 LAW & SOC'Y REV. 319 (1971).

143. Ehud Guttel & Doron Teichman, *Criminal Sanctions in the Defense of the Innocent,* 110 MICH. L. REV. 597, 601–07 (2012). *But see* Angela M. Jones, Shayne Jones & Steven Penrod, *Examining Legal Authoritarianism in the Impact of Punishment Severity on Juror Decisions,* 21 PSYCHOL. CRIME & LAW 939 (2015); Zamir, Harlev & Ritov, *supra* note 106, at 138–41.

144. Glöckner & Engel, *supra* note 141, at 232.

145. Dorothy K. Kagehiro, *Defining the Standard of Proof in Jury Instructions,* 1 PSYCHOL. SCI. 194 (1990).

146. Norbert L. Kerr et al., *Guilt beyond a Reasonable Doubt: Effects of Concept Definition and Assigned Decision Rule on the Judgments of Mock Jurors,* 34 J. PERSONALITY & SOC. PSYCHOL. 282 (1976).

147. *Id.* at 287.

148. Glöckner & Engel, *supra* note 141.

able to evaluate the resulting coherence levels against different evidentiary thresholds. To use the terms of coherence-based reasoning, under a stricter standard of proof decision-makers insist on a stricter standard of coverage, coherence, and uniqueness.[149] Glöckner and Engel's findings thus fall into line with previous studies that found that automatic-intuitive processes are partially controlled by deliberate processes.[150]

Some of the pieces of evidence described in Glöckner and Engel's vignettes included explicit probabilities—such as the self-reported confidence level of an eyewitness (ranging from 80 percent to 99 percent), and the relative prevalence in the region of the type of car seen at the site of crime and driven by the defendant (ranging from 6 percent to 0.01 percent). They found that changes in such explicitly stated probabilities did not affect conviction rates.[151] This finding provides further support for the claim that judicial fact-finders do not mathematically integrate the different pieces of evidence, as required by Bayesian probability theory.

Thus, the story model and coherence-based reasoning do not render rules of burden of proof futile: stricter standards of proof yield fewer assignments of liability. Beyond this reassuring conclusion, the normative implications of the story model and coherence-based reasoning for the burden of proof rules are unclear. For example, according to the story model, one would expect that jury instructions about the heightened evidentiary standard of beyond a reasonable doubt would be more effective if given before the presentation of evidence by the litigants, than after. However, while one experimental study provided clear support for this hypothesis,[152] subsequent studies failed to replicate this result, possibly because most people are familiar with the beyond-a-reasonable-doubt standard, and apply it in criminal cases anyway.[153]

3. Burden of Proof: A Tiebreaker or a Reference Point?

Experimental studies have established that the perceived reference point—which determines whether changes are viewed as gains or losses—is sometimes unfixed and even manipulable.[154] Specifically, it has been demonstrated that legal norms can establish the relevant baseline for people who are subject to such norms, thereby affecting their behavior by producing a default effect.[155] The relationship between people's perceptions and the law

149. Engel, *supra* note 134, at 461. On these aspects, see *supra* p. 529.

150. *See supra* pp. 21–23.

151. Glöckner & Engel, *supra* note 141, at 235–38. *See also* Eyal Zamir & Ilana Ritov, *Loss Aversion, Omission Bias, and the Burden of Proof in Civil Litigation,* 41 J. Legal Stud. 165, 174–75, 198–201 (2012) (finding that comparable slight differences in vignettes produced no differences in liability assignment).

152. Saul M. Kassin & Lawrence S. Wrightsman, *On the Requirements of Proof: The Timing of Judicial Instruction and Mock Juror Verdicts,* 37 J. Personality & Soc. Psychol. 1877 (1979).

153. Vicki L. Smith, *Impact of Pretrial Instruction on Jurors' Information Processing and Decision Making,* 76 J. Applied Psychol. 220, 225 (1991); Dan Simon, *A Third View of the Black Box: Cognitive Coherence in Legal Decision Making,* 71 U. Chi. L. Rev. 511, 557 & n.146 (2004). On jury instructions, see generally *supra* pp. 548–50.

154. *See supra* pp. 46–48.

155. *See supra* pp. 179–82.

is thus bidirectional: the law not only reflects people's perceptions, but also shapes them, to some extent. It stands to reason, therefore, that legal norms affect judicial decisions not only through their direct and explicit content, but also through their more subtle effect on how judges and juries frame the pertinent issues. This proposition bears upon the very notion and the actual impact of burden of proof.

According to common wisdom, the only function that burden of proof plays in civil cases is to resolve ties.[156] If this were true, the burden of proof would only be significant in cases of insufficient evidence, where the incomplete evidentiary basis or lack of any evidence thwarts any factual determination. Whenever the parties present a sufficient amount of evidence, the burden of persuasion would play a role "only when the evidence is in perfect equipoise, in other words (since perfect equipoise is chimerical), virtually never."[157] Why, then, does burden of proof attract so much doctrinal and theoretical interest, and why do legislators and courts devote time and energy to promulgating various rules placing and shifting the burden of proof from one party to another?

One answer is that the burden of persuasion is often associated with the burden of producing evidence, and the latter does significantly affect outcomes whenever neither party has access to good evidence.[158] A more direct and at least equally important answer is that evidentiary presumptions and the burden of persuasion are not mere tiebreakers. They affect fact-finding even when there is sufficient evidence by establishing a reference point. As Karl Llewellyn insightfully observed some eighty years ago, "burden of proof is more than burden of proof; it also indicates base-lines for judging proof, when offered."[159] Unless the burden is discharged, the legal default assumption is that the alleged fact does not exist. The party bearing the burden of proof must therefore overcome the default effect created by the rule.

This behaviorally inspired understanding of the burden of proof is consistent with the analysis in the previous subsection, which showed that burdens and standards of proof significantly affect verdicts, irrespective of the burden of producing evidence. It is also in line with the findings described in the next subsection, which show that to meet the preponderance-of-the-evidence standard, plaintiffs must persuade fact-finders that their version of the facts is considerably—rather than only slightly—more persuasive than not.

156. *See, e.g.*, Ralph K. Winter, Jr., *The Jury and the Risk of Nonpersuasion*, 5 LAW & SOC'Y REV. 335, 339 (1971); Thomas R. Lee, *Pleading and Proof: The Economics of Legal Burdens*, 1997 BRIGHAM YOUNG U. L. REV. 1, 11, 16; Alex Stein, *An Essay on Uncertainty and Fact-Finding in Civil Litigation, with Special Reference to Contract Cases*, 48 U. TORONTO L.J. 299, 319 (1998); Steve R. Johnson, *The Dangers of Symbolic Legislation: Perceptions and Realities of the New Burden-of-Proof Rules*, 84 IOWA L. REV. 413, 438–39, 444–46 (1999).

157. Johnson, *supra* note 156, at 438.

158. Ronald J. Allen, *How Presumptions Should Be Allocated: Burdens of Proof, Uncertainty, and Ambiguity in Modern Legal Discourse*, 17 HARV. J.L. & PUB. POL'Y 627, 639–40 (1994).

159. Karl N. Llewellyn, *On Warranty of Quality, and Society: II*, 37 COLUM. L. REV. 341, 385 n.114 (1937).

4. Loss Aversion, Omission Bias, and the Burden of Proof in Civil Litigation

Another contribution of behavioral studies to the study of the burden of proof concerns the justification for, and the actual meaning of, the preponderance-of-the-evidence rule. We address both these issues in turn.

(a) Who Should Bear the Burden?

Why is it that, when the plaintiff's explanation of the evidence is as plausible as alternative explanations, the claim is dismissed? Various grounds have been offered for this allocation of risk—including the elimination of enforcement costs,[160] the discouragement of unmeritorious and frivolous lawsuits,[161] the principle of civility,[162] the equality principle,[163] and the diminishing marginal utility of wealth.[164] Eyal Zamir and Ilana Ritov have argued that some of these justifications are weak, and none of them is sufficient.[165] Thus, they offered litigants' loss aversion as a possible justification for the rule.[166]

As previously noted, there is ample experimental evidence that litigants ordinarily view the status quo prior to litigation as the relevant point of reference.[167] Consequently, plaintiffs are much more likely to view judicially awarded damages and other relief as belonging to the domain of gains, and defendants are likely to view a judgment that compels them to pay damages, transfer property, or the like, as a loss. Dismissing the claim in instances of an evidentiary tie is therefore consistent with the notion that losses (to the defendant) loom larger than unobtained gains (to the plaintiff). Unlike diminishing marginal utility, this explanation does not depend on the relative affluence of the parties concerned. While this justification is consistent with other bases for the preponderance of the evidence rule, it runs counter to the common assumption that the disutility of an erroneous judgment is typically similar for defendants and plaintiffs.[168]

160. RICHARD A. POSNER, ECONOMIC ANALYSIS OF LAW 844 (9th ed. 2014); Lee, *supra* note 156, at 12–13.

161. Winter, *supra* note 156, at 337.

162. Dale A. Nance, *Civility and the Burden of Proof*, 17 HARV. J.L. & PUB. POL'Y 647 (1994). According to this argument, whenever a litigant asserts that her opponent has violated a serious norm, the assumption that people comply with such norms requires placing the burden of proof on the litigant making those allegations.

163. STEIN, *supra* note 71, at 216. Stein has argued that the Kantian requirement to treat plaintiffs and defendants with equal respect mandates that the risk of error be equally divided between the parties. Hence, each party bears the risk of error with regard to establishing the facts that benefit him or her.

164. RICHARD A. POSNER, ECONOMIC ANALYSIS OF LAW 827 (8th ed. 2011) Assuming that the plaintiffs' and defendants' level of wealth are similar on average, the principle of diminishing marginal utility implies that the loss to the deserving plaintiff who loses her case is slightly smaller than the loss to the deserving defendant who loses. This argument has been omitted in the ninth edition of Posner's book (POSNER, *supra* note 160).

165. Zamir & Ritov, *supra* note 151, at 187–89, 196 n.22.

166. On loss aversion, see generally *supra* pp. 42–57.

167. *See supra* pp. 503–04, 510–12.

168. *See, e.g.*, MICHAEL FINKELSTEIN, QUANTITATIVE METHODS IN LAW: STUDIES IN THE APPLICATION OF MATHEMATICAL PROBABILITY AND STATISTICS TO LEGAL PROBLEMS 67 (1978); STEIN, *supra* note 71, at 148; POSNER, *supra* note 160, at 845.

To be sure, minimizing the overall expected costs of judicial error is only one of many considerations to be taken into account. Were minimizing the cost of judicial error the only concern, then arguably *all* claims—rather than only claims that do not meet the burden of proof—should be dismissed, because the defendant's losses typically loom larger than the plaintiff's gains. However, this would mean that no substantive legal entitlements would ever be judicially enforced, which would adversely affect or eliminate the deterrent effect of legal norms. Other considerations may call for shifting the burden of proof from one litigant to the other, and setting different standards of proof for different issues.[169]

It should also be emphasized that, while litigants' loss aversion may provide a normative basis for placing the burden of proof on the plaintiff, it does not follow that this normative justification actually explains the dismissal of claims by courts in cases of an evidentiary tie. In their experimental study, Zamir and Ritov found that the tendency to dismiss claims that do not meet a rather high standard of persuasion in civil cases was apparent even when the plaintiff had sought a declaratory judgment that would validate the status quo, and dismissing the claim would open the door to changing the status quo in favor of the defendant.[170] This experiment did not lend support to the hypothesis that judges tend to require a fairly high standard of proof to minimize the cost of judicial error in light of the litigants' loss aversion, as in this scenario dismissing the claim was plausibly framed as inflicting a loss on the plaintiff, while awarding the declaratory judgment maintained the status quo. A follow-up experiment provided support for an alternative explanation for this tendency—namely the fact-finders' own omission bias. Apparently, people tend to view the acceptance of a claim as an action, and its dismissal as an omission. Loss-averse judges, who plausibly view making a correct decision as a gain and a wrong decision as a loss, therefore exhibit an omission bias by dismissing the claim whenever the evidence does not clearly support the plaintiff's case.[171] Direct support for this claim has subsequently been provided by Mark Schweizer.[172]

(b) What Is the Actual Standard of Proof?

Inasmuch as litigants' loss aversion and judicial decision-makers' omission bias affect verdicts in civil cases, these psychological phenomena may explain not only the placing of the burden of proof on the plaintiff, but also the adoption of a considerably higher standard of proof than the balance of probabilities or preponderance of the evidence. If losses typically loom larger than do gains—often by a factor of 2.25 or so—then to minimize the total costs of judicial errors, the standard of proof should be considerably higher than 0.5. This increase is necessary because the total cost of errors is a product of multiplying

169. *See generally* Zamir & Ritov, *supra* note 151, at 193–97.

170. *Id.* at 177–80.

171. *Id.* at 180–82, 192–93. *See also supra* pp. 537–38.

172. Mark Schweizer, *Loss Aversion, Omission Bias, and the Civil Standard of Proof*, *in* EUROPEAN PERSPECTIVES ON BEHAVIOURAL LAW AND ECONOMICS 125 (Klaus Mathis ed., 2015).

the number of errors by the average disutility that they generate.[173] Similarly, if judicial decision-makers are omission-biased, and if dismissing a claim is perceived as an omission while accepting it as a commission, then to overcome this bias, decision-makers must be *clearly* persuaded by the plaintiffs' evidence.

In fact, Zamir and Ritov's experiments (in which participants were law students and lawyers) support the conclusion that the standard of proof in civil litigation is considerably higher than 0.5—ranging from 60 to 75 on a scale of 0 to 100, where 0 indicates that there is no doubt that the plaintiff's version of the facts is incorrect and 100 indicates that there is no doubt that it is correct.[174] Similarly, in their experiments, using actual U.S. jury instructions about standard of proof, Glöckner and Engel found that the mean explicated standard for assigning liability under the preponderance-of-the-evidence standard was 76 percent—much higher than the formal rule and jury instructions. At the same time, the explicated standard under the beyond-a-reasonable-doubt rule was only 85 percent—considerably lower than the conventional understanding of this standard.[175]

In line with the results of other studies,[176] these findings indicate that the actual gap between civil law systems, which employ a single standard of *intime conviction*, and common law systems, employing presumably very different standards of proof in civil and criminal proceedings, is considerably smaller (if it exists at all) than the formal legal regimes imply.

5. Protected Values, Taboo Trade-Offs, and the Burden of Proof in Criminal Litigation

Just as it sheds light on the meaning of burden of proof in civil litigation, behavioral analysis sheds light on the operation of the criminal justice system on this front. The elevated standard of proof used by common-law systems in criminal trials—beyond a reasonable doubt—is often viewed as a rigid external constraint. One early American case described this standard as a "divine precept."[177] More recently, the leading U.S. Supreme Court case on the topic referred to the standard as a "bedrock 'axiomatic and elementary' principle whose 'enforcement lies at the foundation of the administration of our criminal law.' "[178] As Daniel Epps notes, many commentators regard the standard as a type of "self-evident truth."[179]

Furthermore, while by definition the beyond-a-reasonable-doubt standard entails some risk of convicting the innocent, courts have stubbornly refused to quantify this risk

173. The standard of persuasion (S) that would minimize the total costs of errors equals $\lambda/(\lambda+1)$, where λ is the factor by which losses to the defendant loom larger than no-gains for the plaintiff. For instance, if $\lambda=2.25$ then $S=0.69$.

174. Zamir & Ritov, *supra* note 151, at 176, 177, 180, 186–87.

175. Glöckner & Engel, *supra* note 141, at 241–43, 246.

176. Simon & Mahan, *supra* note 142; Schweizer, *supra* note 136.

177. State v. Baldwin, 1813 WL, *8 (S.C. Const. Ct. App. 1813).

178. *In Re* Winship, 397 U.S. 358, 363 (1970).

179. Daniel Epps, *The Consequences of Error in Criminal Justice*, 128 Harv. L. Rev. 1065, 1081 (2015).

explicitly.[180] Survey data also suggests that judges are opposed to quantifying the burden of proof. Rita James Simon and Linda Mahan report that over 90 percent of judges who took part in their study favored existing practices over practices that would require explicit quantification of proof.[181] Surprisingly, this reluctance persists even in the face of empirical evidence that quantifying the burden could be useful.[182]

The common perception of the burden of proof in criminal trials as a non-quantifiable and absolute principle that requires no reasoned justification suggests that it might reflect a *protected* (or *sacred*) *value* that resist trade-offs with other values (*taboo trade-offs*).[183] As the psychological literature has shown, people tend to reject cost-benefit analysis with respect to protected values, and many deny that there are any costs entailed with adhering to them.[184] While this type of reasoning may be fine when dealing with hypothetical moral dilemmas, it may be quite problematic when dealing with actual policy decisions where hard trade-offs are inevitable.

The literature on the burden of proof in criminal trials has mapped the significant costs associated with an elevated decision threshold. Focusing on incapacitation, Larry Laudan has argued that the available empirical data suggests that each false acquittal entails the cost of enabling more than thirty-six crimes (seven of which are violent).[185] Accordingly, he advocated a relaxed burden of proof in criminal trials.[186] From a consequentialist perspective, one should be particularly concerned about the ex-ante incentives created by the burden of proof. As Louis Kaplow has shown, when viewed from this perspective, the decision threshold should be set to balance the benefits associated with deterring harmful behavior against the risks associated with chilling benign behavior.[187] Kaplow's nuanced analysis is sensitive to the relative costs and benefits that could differ across policy domains. Based on that analysis, he concludes that, given the parameters of social welfare, the decision threshold should be modified in some contexts.[188]

180. *See, e.g.*, Peter Tillers & Jonathan Gottfried, *Case Comment—*United States v. Copeland, *369 F. Supp. 2d 275 (E.D.N.Y. 2005): A Collateral Attack on the Legal Maxim That Proof beyond a Reasonable Doubt Is Unquantifiable?*, 5 LAW PROBABILITY & RISK 135, 135–38 (2006).

181. Simon & Mahan, *supra* note 142, at 329.

182. *Id.* at 329–30; Dorothy K. Kagehiro, *Defining the Standard of Proof in Jury Instructions*, 1 PSYCHOL. SCI. 194, 196 (1990).

183. On these notions, see *supra* pp. 97–98.

184. Jonathan Baron & Mark Spranca, *Protected Values*, 70 ORG. BEHAV. & HUM. DECISION PROCESSES 1, 5 (1997).

185. *See* Larry Laudan, *The Rules of Trial, Political Morality, and the Costs of Error: Or, Is Proof beyond a Reasonable Doubt Doing More Harm than Good?*, *in* 1 OXFORD STUDIES IN PHILOSOPHY OF LAW 195, 202 (Leslie Green & Brian Leiter eds., 2011).

186. *Id.* at 206. For a careful examination of Lauden's analysis, explaining why it might over- or undervalue the costs of wrongful acquittals, see Epps, *supra* note 179, at 1090–91. Epps nonetheless concludes that Lauden's analysis is a useful tool when considering the costs of false acquittals.

187. Kaplow, *supra* note 133, at 752–72.

188. *Id.* at 748.

The retributivist literature has also weighed in on this issue. Given the richness of this body of work, one cannot pinpoint a single conclusion as to the desirable burden of proof in criminal trials.[189] That said, retributivists who argue that there is a *duty* to punish the guilty have expressed permissive views with regard to relaxing the burden of proof. Michael Moore, for example, has recognized that the preponderance of the evidence could serve as the decision threshold in criminal cases, depending on the weight given to the injustice associated with punishing the innocent, as opposed to the injustice associated with not punishing the guilty.[190]

As we have seen, the academic discussion over the desirable error rate in criminal trials has not extended to a policy debate in the courts or legislatures. Upon closer examination, however, one can see that the law has found ways to relax the burden of proof in criminal trials in subtle and non-explicit manners. One way to achieve this is by criminalizing behaviors that correlate with blameworthy behavior.[191] By defining crimes that encompass behaviors that correlate with offenses that were committed in the past (e.g., money laundering), or will be committed in the future (e.g., being in possession of burglary tools), the legislature can effectively alter the error rate of criminal trials in favor of more convictions of the innocent. Similarly, lowering the required mental state of a crime to negligence (or even imposing strict liability) serves to secure more convictions in cases where proving the defendant's state of mind beyond a reasonable doubt would be difficult.

Adjusting the error rate in criminal trials through the substantive norms of criminal law allows society to sidestep the difficult question of how many innocent people it is willing to punish in order to further the goals of the criminal justice system? While all criminals under this regime are punished if, and only if, their guilt has been proven beyond a reasonable doubt, by relaxing the substantive demands for a conviction, a different balance is struck between errors of Type 1 and Type 2. The rhetoric surrounding this regime allows society to continue to believe that a uniformly high threshold for convictions is enforced in all criminal cases. This legal tactic is consistent with the psychological literature that showed that the public discourse surrounding protected values tends to use rhetorical obfuscation, to obscure or overlook transgressions.[192]

To be sure, while categorizing the beyond-a-reasonable-doubt standard as a protected value might help clarify the unique path that the law took to sidestep it, it does little to resolve the related normative questions. On one hand, protected values and the rhetorical

189. In fact, retributivists often sidestep the issue. *See e.g.*, Jeffrey Reiman & Ernest van den Haag, *On the Common Saying That It Is Better That Ten Guilty Persons Escape than That One Innocent Suffer: Pro and Con*, 7 Soc. Phil. & Pol'y 226, 242–43 (1990).

190. *See* Michael S. Moore, Placing Blame: A Theory of Criminal Law 156–57 (1997).

191. *See* Doron Teichman, *Convicting with Reasonable Doubt: An Evidentiary Theory of Criminal Law*, 93 Notre Dame L. Rev. 757 (2017).

192. Michael R. Waldmann et al., *Moral Judgments*, *in* The Oxford Handbook of Thinking and Reasoning 364, 383 (Keith J. Holyoak & Robert G. Morrison eds., 2012); Baron & Spranca, *supra* note 184, at 13. *Cf.* Guido Calabresi & Philip Bobbit, Tragic Choices (1978); Guido Calabresi, The Future of Law and Economics 21 (2016) (discussing similar issues from an economic perspective).

maneuvers used to circumvent them might be viewed as a type of bias that stands in the way of a reasoned analysis of difficult policy questions.[193] On the other hand, they might be seen as a subtle means of helping to prevent the subversion of meaningful cultural institutions.[194]

D. The Upside of Bounded Rationality

Much of the discussion in this chapter revolved around how people's bounded rationality and cognitive biases obstruct accurate fact-finding. However, as Chris Sanchirico has pointed out, to a large extent people's bounded rationality is actually conducive to judicial truth-finding.[195]

Litigants and many (if not most) witnesses are not indifferent to the outcomes of litigation. Similarly, the police and the criminal prosecution service, while serving the public interest, are usually highly motivated to attain convictions.[196] There is therefore a material risk that witnesses, including expert witnesses, would do their best to persuade fact-finders to adopt their version of the facts, even at the expense of the truth. Consequently, if all players involved in the litigation were perfect "rational maximizers," it would be much harder for courts to uncover the truth.

Rather than complying with legal norms, rational maximizers would focus on precluding or erasing evidence of noncompliance. Perfectly rational crime perpetrators, tortfeasors, and contract breachers would conduct themselves in ways that would frustrate the imposition of liability. They would leave no written evidence of their illicit plans, thereby leaving no paper trail, or comprehensively obliterate such traces. They would be able to fabricate an airtight alibi. Anticipating the evidence available to the other party, they would construct perfect lies. Even when presented with unanticipated questions in cross-examination, the rational maximizer would immediately answer in a manner consistent with both her own prior statements and other available evidence.

In reality, however, most people are unable to conduct their primary activity, to prepare for trial, or to testify as perfectly rational maximizers. People leave evidence of their wrongdoing, and litigants, other witnesses, and attorneys fail to fully predict what evidence the other party will present and what questions will be asked in cross-examination. As a result, false testimonies are often inconsistent and self-contradictory. Cautious witnesses hesitate and pause before answering questions that might expose inconsistencies within their testimony or between their testimony and other reliable evidence. Insincere witnesses find it particularly difficult to provide testimony that is consistent and detailed at the same

193. *See* Jonathan Baron, *Moral Judgement*, *in* THE OXFORD HANDBOOK OF BEHAVIORAL ECONOMICS AND THE LAW, 61, 70 (Eyal Zamir & Doron Teichman eds., 2014).

194. *See* Alan Page Fiske & Philip E. Tetlock, *Taboo Trade-Offs: Reactions to Transactions That Transgress the Spheres of Justice*, 18 POL. PSYCHOL. 255, 291–94 (1997); *supra* pp. 97–98.

195. Sanchirico, *supra* note 31.

196. *See supra* pp. 571–72.

time.[197] Even if they do manage to avoid inconsistencies, it may come at the price of providing fewer details about the pertinent events, which may in turn detract from credibility. Over long hours of testimony and depositions people become tired and fail to remember the details of untruthful answers they gave to similar questions several hours before. Rehearsals are unhelpful when it comes to unanticipated questions.

The contribution of litigants' and witnesses' bounded rationality to truth-finding stems not only from their limited cognitive abilities, but also from their moral convictions. People often feel uncomfortable telling lies, which makes their lies more detectable.

Furthermore, the contribution of bounded rationality to accurate fact-finding is enhanced by legal rules that make it more difficult for the insincere witness to hide the truth. Since "lying can be more mentally taxing than telling the truth," increasing the cognitive load experienced by a witness likely produces cues that make lie detection easier.[198] The procedure of cross-examination, which allows for surprising questions and may last for many hours; the requirement to testify from memory rather than using notes; disclosure rights with regard to materials used solely in preparation by expert witnesses for the other party; and preventing witnesses from hearing each other's testimony are examples of legal rules that may be understood as aiming to make it more difficult for boundedly rational witnesses to deceive the court.[199]

E. Conclusion

Even before the emergence of behavioral legal studies, psychologists extensively studied how people perceive, remember, and report events; how they gauge the reliability and sincerity of other people's statements; and how they judge other sources of information. While people routinely do these things in their daily lives, psychologists have found the controlled setting of a trial particularly apt for studying these phenomena—thus providing important insights into judicial fact-finding, and offering policy implications for the judicial process (including evidence law and the parts of civil and criminal procedure dealing with the fact-finding process). These findings—most of which were discussed in this chapter, and some in the previous one—highlight serious pitfalls in the judicial fact-finding process, and the limited efficacy of measures used to overcome them (such as exclusion rules and jury instructions). The studies also expose possible disparities between formal rules of evidence

197. VRIJ, *supra* note 27, at 39–41, 45, 101–14. It should be noted, though, that even theory-based, expert-designed techniques for distinguishing lies from truth-telling based on statements' content are not very reliable. Moreover, the external validity of laboratory studies in this sphere may be questioned, and when it comes to field studies, it is often impossible to know for sure what the truth was. *See* Vrij, *supra* note 47.

198. Aldert Vrij, *A Cognitive Approach to Lie Detecting, in* DETECTING DECEPTION, *supra* note 33, at 205, 205.

199. *See* Sanchirico, *supra* note 31, at 332–41 (surprising questions), 343–44, 351–52 (fatigue), 323–25 (testifying from memory), 325–27 (disclosure rights), 331–32 (separate testimonies). On the efficacy of asking unanticipated questions as a lie-detecting means, see Aldert Vrij et al., *Outsmarting the Liars: The Benefit of Asking Unanticipated Questions,* 33 LAW & HUM. BEHAV. 159 (2009); Gary Lancaster et al., *Sorting the Liars from the Truth Tellers: The Benefits of Asking Unanticipated Questions,* 27 APPLIED COGNITIVE PSYCHOL. 107 (2012).

(such as those concerning the burden of proof) and their actual employment by judicial fact-finders.

While these findings paint a troubling picture, they are immensely important for understanding and improving judicial fact-finding, including the design of evidence law. In fact, there are few legal contexts where the contribution of behavioral studies is so direct and so compelling. Nonetheless, as demonstrated throughout this chapter, there is still much to be learned in this sphere.

Index

Behavioral Law and Economics. Eyal Zamir and Doron Teichman.

www.ingramcontent.com/pod-product-compliance
Ingram Content Group UK Ltd.
Pitfield, Milton Keynes, MK11 3LW, UK
UKHW051048150926
475595UK00005B/169

9 780190 901349